# Fundamentals of Advanced Accounting

# Fundamentals of Advanced Accounting

**Joe B. Hoyle**
*Associate Professor of Accounting*
*Robins School of Business*
*University of Richmond*

**Thomas F. Schaefer**
*KPMG Professor of Accounting*
*Mendoza College of Business*
*University of Notre Dame*

**Timothy S. Doupnik**
*Professor of Accounting*
*The Darla Moore School of Business*
*University of South Carolina*

Boston  Burr Ridge, IL  Dubuque, IA  Madison, WI  New York  San Francisco  St. Louis
Bangkok  Bogotá  Caracas  Kuala Lumpur  Lisbon  London  Madrid  Mexico City
Milan  Montreal  New Delhi  Santiago  Seoul  Singapore  Sydney  Taipei  Toronto

FUNDAMENTALS OF ADVANCED ACCOUNTING

Published by McGraw-Hill/Irwin, a business unit of The McGraw-Hill Companies, Inc., 1221 Avenue of the Americas, New York, NY, 10020. Copyright © 2004, by The McGraw-Hill Companies, Inc. All rights reserved. No part of this publication may be reproduced or distributed in any form or by any means, or stored in a database or retrieval system, without the prior written consent of The McGraw-Hill Companies, Inc., including, but not limited to, in any network or other electronic storage or transmission, or broadcast for distance learning.

Some ancillaries, including electronic and print components, may not be available to customers outside the United States.

This book is printed on acid-free paper.

domestic    1 2 3 4 5 6 7 8 9 0 VNH/VNH 0 9 8 7 6 5 4 3
international  1 2 3 4 5 6 7 8 9 0 VNH/VNH 0 9 8 7 6 5 4 3

ISBN 0-07-287117-2

Editorial director: *Brent Gordon*
Publisher: *Stewart Mattson*
Developmental editor I: *Kelly Odom*
Senior marketing manager: *Richard Kolasa*
Senior producer, Media technology: *Ed Przyzycki*
Senior project manager: *Christine A. Vaughan*
Production supervisor: *Debra R. Sylvester*
Designer: *Adam Rooke*
Supplement producer: *Matthew Perry*
Senior digital content specialist: *Brian Nacik*
Cover image: *© Philip Rostron/Masterfile*
Typeface: *10/12 Times Roman*
Compositor: *GAC Indianapolis*
Printer: *Von Hoffmann Corporation*

**Library of Congress Cataloging-in-Publication Data**

Hoyle, Joe Ben.
   Fundamentals of advanced accounting / Joe B. Hoyle, Thomas F. Schaefer,
Timothy S. Doupnik.
    p. cm.
   A short version of the authors' Advanced accounting. 7th ed. c2004.
   Includes index.
   ISBN 0-07-287117-2 (alk. paper)
   1. Accounting.  I. Schaefer, Thomas F.  II. Doupnik, Timothy S.  III. Hoyle, Joe
Ben. Advanced accounting. IV. Title.
HF5635.H865 2004
657'.046—dc21
                                               2003054120

www.mhhe.com

To our families

The real purpose of books is to trap the mind into doing its own thinking.
        Christopher Morley

# About the Authors

### Joe B. Hoyle
*University of Richmond*

Joe B. Hoyle is Associate Professor of Accounting at the Robins School of Business at the University of Richmond, where he has been named a Distinguished Educator five times. He has been named Professor of the Year on two occasions and teaches Intermediate Accounting I and II and Advanced Accounting. He is also author of *Fast Track CPA Examination Review* and coauthor of *The Lakeside Company Case Studies in Auditing*. He is president of HoyleCPA Success, which sells review material worldwide.

### Thomas F. Schaefer
*University of Notre Dame*

Thomas F. Schaefer is the KPMG Professor of Accounting at the University of Notre Dame. He has written a number of articles in scholarly journals such as *The Accounting Review, Journal of Accounting Research, Journal of Accounting & Economics, Accounting Horizons,* and others. His primary teaching and research interests are in financial accounting and reporting. Tom served as President during the 2003–2004 term for the American Accounting Association's Accounting Programs Leadership Group and served as a member on the Board of Directors for the Federation of Schools of Accounting.

### Timothy S. Doupnik
*University of South Carolina*

Timothy S. Doupnik is Professor of Accounting at the University of South Carolina, where his primary teaching and research interest is in international accounting. Tim has been a visiting professor at several universities wordwide and worked as a visiting research professor at the Universidade de São Paulo, Brazil. He has published extensively in this area in journals such as the *International Journal of Accounting* and the *Journal of International Business Studies*. He has also written two research monographs on foreign currency translation published by the FASB. Tim is active in the American Accounting Association and recently completed a term as chair of the International Accounting Section.

# Fundamentals Solves the Puzzle

*Fundamentals of Advanced Accounting* pulls together the 12 most-commonly taught chapters in advanced accounting. Hoyle, Schaefer, and Doupnik use the same approach in *Fundamentals* as in their full *Advanced Accounting* text, which gets students thinking critically about accounting, just as they will do as they prepare for the CPA exam. Read on to understand how students will succeed as accounting majors and as future CPAs by using *Fundamentals of Advanced Accounting*.

## Thinking Critically

With this text, students gain a well-balanced appreciation of the accounting profession. As Hoyle *Fundamentals* introduces them to the field's many aspects, it will often focus on past and present issues. The development of financial reporting is shown as a result of a history of considered debate that continues today and into the future.

## Readability

The writing style of the full *Advanced Accounting* text has been highly praised, and the same style is used in *Fundamentals*. **Students easily comprehend** chapter concepts because of the conversational tone. The authors have made every effort to ensure that the writing style remains engaging, lively, and consistent.

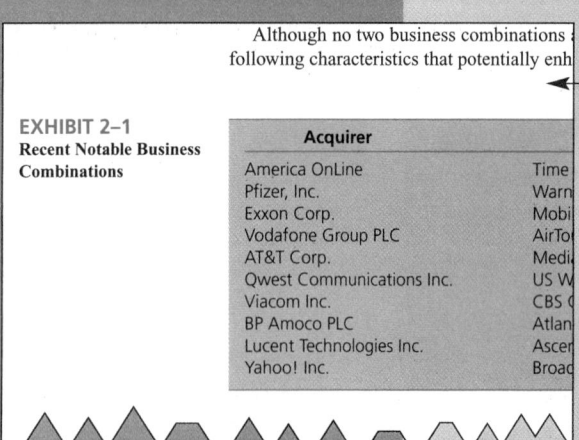

## Real-World Examples

**Students better relate** what they learn to what they will encounter in the business world after reading these frequent examples. Quotations and articles from *Forbes, The Wall Street Journal, Time,* and *Business Week* are incorporated throughout the text. Data have been pulled from business and government financial statements as well as official pronouncements.

## Discussion Questions

This feature **facilitates student understanding** of the underlying accounting principles at work in particular business events. Similar to mini-cases, these questions help explain the issues at hand in practical terms. Many times, these cases are designed to demonstrate to students why a problem is a problem and worth considering.

# for Your Students

## CPA Exam Prep

In response to the new CPA exam, the authors have developed an end-of-chapter feature to **better prepare students** for the CPA exam. "Develop Your Skills" asks questions that address the four skills students will need to master in order to pass the exam: Research, Analysis, Excel, and Communication. An icon appears to indicate when these skills are tested.

**FARS RESEARCH CASE—*SFAS 141* "BUSINESS COME**

*CPA skills*

Acello Company has agreed to merge with BlairCo usir the agreement include the following:

- BlairCo, the larger firm, will issue additional shares change for their shares after which the corporate en will survive as the continuing firm.
- The former owners of Acello will hold 65 percent of change ratios reflected a premium paid by Acello's o
- BlairCo's former chief executive office (CEO) and c roles in the combined firm for at least two years.
- The former chairman of the board of directors of Ace of directors of the combined firm. Within two month

## End-of-Chapter Materials

As in *Advanced Accounting* by Hoyle, et al., the homework material remains a strength of *Fundamentals*. The sheer quantity of questions, problems, and Internet assignments will test, and therefore **expand the student's knowledge** of chapter concepts. Excel Spreadsheet Assignments extend specific problems and are located on the text's Online Learning Center at www.mhhe.com/hoylefundamentals. An Excel icon appears next to those problems that have corresponding spreadsheet assignments.

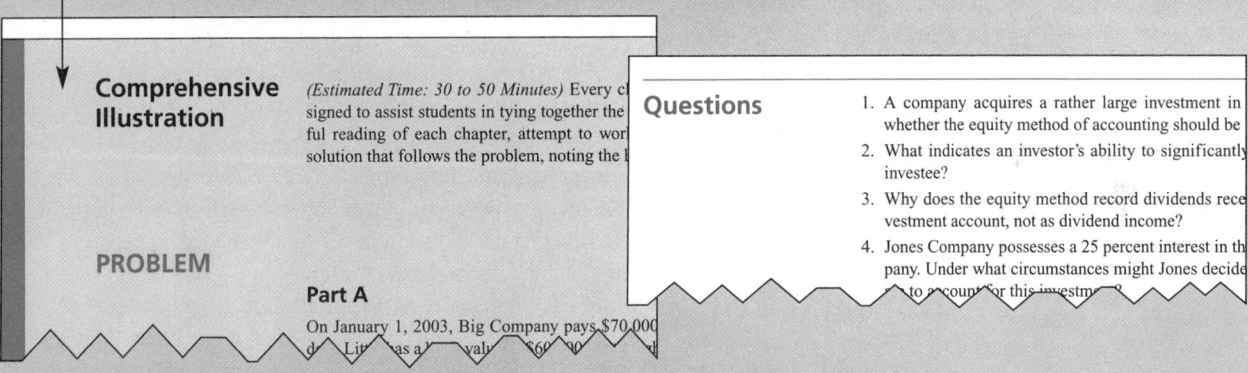

**Comprehensive Illustration**

*(Estimated Time: 30 to 50 Minutes)* Every c signed to assist students in tying together the ful reading of each chapter, attempt to wor solution that follows the problem, noting the l

**PROBLEM**

**Part A**

On January 1, 2003, Big Company pays $70,000

**Questions**

1. A company acquires a rather large investment in whether the equity method of accounting should be
2. What indicates an investor's ability to significantly investee?
3. Why does the equity method record dividends rece vestment account, not as dividend income?
4. Jones Company possesses a 25 percent interest in th pany. Under what circumstances might Jones decide to account for this investment

**Develop Your Skills**

**EXCEL CASE 1**

*CPA skills*

On January 1, 2004, Acme Co. is considering a privately held enterprise, for $700,000. PH 10 percent annual increase in profits in each dividend of $30,000 for the foreseeable futur valued by $375,000, Acme realizes that it wi year over the next 10 years—the patent's esti have book values that approximate market values

**Problems**

1. When an investor uses the equity method to accoun dends received by the investor from the investee sho
   a. A deduction from the investor's share of the inve
   b. Dividend income.
   c. A deduction from the stockholders' equity accou
   d. A deduction from the investment account.
   (AICPA adapted)
2. Which of the following is not an indication that an i

# Supplements

Instructor's Resource CD
(ISBN 0072871180)
This includes electronic files for all of the Instructor Supplements:

## For the Instructor

- **Instructor's Resource and Solutions Manual,** by the text authors, includes the solutions to all discussion questions, end-of-chapter questions, and problems. Chapter outlines are provided to assist instructors in preparing for class.
- **Test Bank,** by John Hamer, University of Massachusetts at Lowell, and Lynn Clements, Florida Southern College, was developed in accordance with the new CPA exam. Each chapter offers a large pool of material to choose from when creating a test.
- **Brownstone Computerized Test Bank** is delivered in the latest version of Diploma, from Brownstone. It can be used to make different versions of the same test, change the answer order, edit and add questions, and conduct online testing. Technical support for this software is available at (800) 331-5094.
- **PowerPoint Presentations,** revised by Richard Rand of Tennessee Technological University, a complete set of slides covers many of the key concepts presented in each chapter.
- **Excel Template Problems** and **Solutions,** revised by Jack Terry of ComSource Associates, Inc, allow students to develop important spreadsheet skills by using Excel templates to solve selected assignments.

## For the Student

**Study Guide/Working Papers** (ISBN 0072871199). By Richard Rand, this combination study guide and working papers reinforces the key concepts of the book by providing students with chapter outlines, multiple-choice questions, and problems for each chapter in the text. In addition, this paperback contains all the forms necessary for completing the end-of-chapter material.

**Excel Template Problems** (mhhe.com/hoylefundamentals) are available on the Student Center of the text's Online Learning Center. The software includes innovatively designed templates that may be used with Excel '97 and 2000 to solve many complicated problems found in the book. These problems are identified by a logo in the margin.

**PowerPoint Presentations** (mhhe.com/hoylefundamentals) are available on the Student Center of the text's Online Learning Center. These presentations accompany each chapter of the text and contain the same slides that are available to the instructor.

# Technology

## Online Learning Center

www.mhhe.com/hoylefundamentals
For instructors, the book's website contains the Instructor's Resource and Solutions Manual, PowerPoint slides, Excel templates and solutions, Interactive Activities, Text and Supplement Updates, and links to professional resources.

The student section of the site features online chapter quizzing activities, including a multiple choice quiz and a key term flashcard quiz to accompany each chapter of the text. Students are able to download a sample Study Guide chapter in PDF format. PowerPoint presentations and Check Figures are also available to download and the chapter Excel template exercises are located here, as well. The authors have listed several CPA-related links and other important links relating to text and professional material.

In addition, students and instructors alike will appreciate the OLC's links to many of McGraw-Hill's most popular online technologies, including PowerWeb, PageOut, and ALEKS.

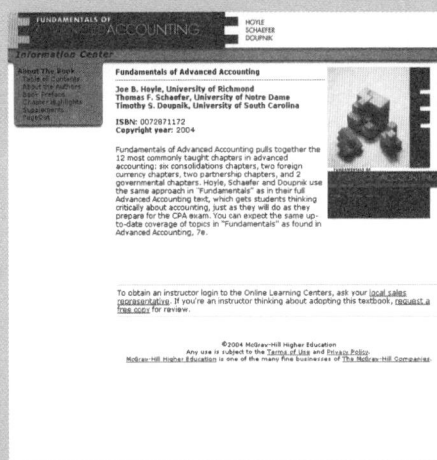

## HoyleCPA Success

Joe B. Hoyle has taught his own CPA Exam Review program since 1980. Nearly a decade ago, he formed HoyleCPA Success with three other partners to help accountants inside and outside the United States conquer this challenging exam. From the beginning, they had very specific goals: to produce the best possible review products on the market; to provide these products at reasonable prices; to treat each customer like a friend; and to help as many people as possible pass the CPA Exam. To date, Joe Hoyle is very pleased with their achievements. Messages arrive almost daily from customers around the world telling them just how much their products have helped. To see what is available to the prospective CPA, visit www.hoylecpa.com.

## ALEKS® for Financial Accounting

ALEKS (Assessment and LEarning in Knowledge Spaces) delivers precise, qualitative diagnostic assessments of students' knowledge, guides them in the selection of appropriate new study material, and records their progress toward mastery of curricular goals in a robust classroom management system.

ALEKS interacts with the student much as a skilled human tutor would, moving between explanation and practice as needed, correcting and analyzing errors, defining terms and changing topics on request. By sophisticated modeling of a student's knowledge state for a given subject, ALEKS can focus clearly on what the student is most ready to learn next. When students focus on exactly what they are ready to learn, they build confidence and a learning momentum that fuels success.

## PowerWeb

PowerWeb: The Dynamic Accounting Profession takes you beyond Enron and looks at issues currently impacting the accounting profession. It offers timely articles and links culled by a real-world expert in advanced accounting. PowerWeb users can also take advantage of self-grading quizzes, interactive glossaries and exercises, and study tips.

Visit the PowerWeb site at www.dushkin.com/powerweb to see firsthand what PowerWeb can mean to your course.

# Stay Current in the Accounting Field

- Text and supplement authors have gone to great lengths to create their material in accordance with the **new CPA exam.**
- In the wake of corporate scandals, the new **Sarbanes-Oxley Act** material has been incorporated into *Fundamentals*.
- The text and supplements reflect the most current **FASB** and **GASB** standards.

## Chapter highlights include:

**1**
Expanded discussion of decision making involving equity method investments and criticisms of the equity method

Introduction of the use of the equity method in the presence of substantive minority participation rights.

Two Excel Cases, two FARS Research Cases, and an Analysis Case.

**2**
Introduction of Variable Interest Entities in the discussion of controlling financial interests.

Discussions of the Sears–Lands' End and Chevron–Texaco acquisitions.

Expanded coverage of purchased in-process research and development acquired in business combinations in the text and end-of-chapter material.

Excel cases and FARS research cases in the end-of-chapter material.

**3**
Expanded coverage of goodwill, reporting units, and goodwill impairment in both the text and end-of-chapter material.

FARS research cases and Excel cases in the end-of-chapter material.

A revised and updated computer project in the end-of-chapter material.

**4**
Coverage of the consolidation of Variable Interest Entities (FIN 46).

Updated references to current FASB activity on the Economic Unit concept of reporting non-controlling interests.

Updated references to current FASB activity on the financial statement placements for reporting non-controlling interests.

FARS research cases and Excel cases in the end-of-chapter material.

**5**
Discussion Question on Enron's earning management through its special purpose entities.

FARS research cases and Excel cases in the end-of-chapter material.

Analysis and Research Case on intercompany transactions.

Alternative accounting adjustment presentations for downstream intercompany inventory profit.

**6**
Coverage of FIN 46.

Updated references to the FASB Project on Liabilities and Equity.

Excel Case in the end-of-chapter material.

**7**
Section on Hedging Foreign Exchange Risk.

Detailed information on the accounting for derivatives in general, and foreign currency derivatives in particular in accordance with SFAS 133 and SFAS 138.

Detailed description of conditions under which hedge accounting is allowed.

Description of differences in accounting for cash flow hedge and fair value hedge.

Examples with journal entries for the following hedging combinations:

- Forward contract fair value hedge of foreign currency denominated asset.
- Forward contract cash flow hedge of foreign currency denominated asset.
- Option cash flow hedge of foreign currency denominated asset.
- Option fair value hedge of foreign currency denominated asset.
- Forward contract fair value hedge of foreign currency firm commitment.

# with Hoyle Fundamentals...

- Option fair value hedge of foreign currency firm commitment.
- Forward contract cash flow hedge of forecasted foreign currency denominated transaction.
- Option cash flow hedge of forecasted foreign currency denominated transaction.

**8** Excerpts from annual reports.
End-of-chapter material designed around the new CPA Exam.

**9** Described some of the new types of legal formats being devised to limit the liability of ownership.
End-of-chapter material designed around the new CPA Exam.

**10** Discussed the possible protection afforded Arthur Andersen partners by being structured as an LLP, a limited liability partnership.
End-of-chapter material designed around the new CPA Exam.

**11** Heightened the coverage of the changes in governmental accounting that are occurring as cities, counties, and the like begin to adopt GASB Statement Number 34.
End-of-chapter material designed around the new CPA Exam.

**12** Used the financial statements of the City of Sacramento, California to illustrate the practical process of applying the provisions of GASB Statement Number 34. Sacramento was one of the first major cities to apply this new pronouncement so that its statements can serve as a model of the new reporting system.
End-of-chapter material designed around the new CPA Exam.

# Acknowledgments

We could not produce a textbook of the quality and scope of *Fundamentals of Advanced Accounting* without the help of a great number of people. We extend a special thank you to: Richard Rand at Tennessee Technological University for preparing the Study Guide, Online Quizzes, and PowerPoint presentations; John Hamer at the University of Massachusetts-Lowell and Lynn Clements at Florida Southern College for preparing the Test Bank; Jack Terry of ComSource Associates for creating Excel template exercises for students to use as they work through selected end-of-chapter material; Kim Temme at Maryville University and Beth Woods, CPA, for checking the text for accuracy; and Alice Sineath at Forsyth Technical Community College for checking the test bank for accuracy.

We acknowledge that FASB Exposure Draft, *Business Combinations and Intangible Assets,* is copyrighted by the Financial Accounting Standards Board, 401 Merritt 7, P.O. Box 5116, Norwalk, Connecticut 06856-5116, U.S.A. Portions are reprinted with permission. Complete copies of this document are available from the FASB. GASB Statement No. 33, Accounting and Financial Reporting for Nonexchange Transactions, is copyrighted by the Governmental Accounting Standards Board, 401 Merritt 7, P.O. Box 5116, Norwalk, Connecticut 06856-5116, U.S.A. Portions are reprinted with permission. Complete copies of this document are available from the GASB.

We also want to thank the many people who participated in phone surveys, completed questionnaires, and reviewed the manuscript. Our sincerest thanks to them all:

Myrtle Clark
*University of Kentucky*

Lynn Clements
*Florida Southern College*

Paul Copley
*University of Georgia*

Richard Cross
*Bentley College*

James De Simpelare
*University of Michigan*

Kevin Den Adel
*Purdue University*

Bill Dent
*University of Texas–Dallas*

Dave Eichelberger
*Austin Peay State University*

Jim Emig
*Villanova University*

Chuck Fazzi
*Robert Morris College*

David Fetyko
*Kent State University*

Marry Harris
*Syracuse University*

Cynthia Jeffrey
*Iowa State University*

David Mautz
*North Carolina A&T University*

Edward McTague
*CUNY–Brooklyn College*

Perry Moore
*Lipscomb University*

Gary Olsen
*Carroll College*

Frank Page
*University of Missouri–St. Louis*

Tina Quinn
*Arkansas State University*

Richard S. Rand, Jr.
*Tennessee Technological University*

Jack Reagan
*KPMG*

Reg Rezac
*Texas Woman's University*

Linda Schain
*Hofstra University*

Bunney Schmidt
*Utah Valley State College–Orem*

Richard Scott
*University of Virginia*

Abba Spero
*Cleveland State University*

Margaret M. Tanner
*University of Northern Iowa*

Mark Trombley
*University of Arizona*

Howard Turetsky
*St. Mary's College of California*

Marcia Veit
*University of Central Florida*

David R. Vruwink
*Kansas State University*

Zhemin Wang
*University of Wisconsin–Parkside*

Hannah Wong
*Rutgers University*

Roger A. Woods
*Northwest Missouri State University*

Jian Zhou
*Binghamton University*

We also pass along a word of thanks to all the people at McGraw-Hill/Irwin who participated in the creation of this edition. In particular, Christine Vaughan, Senior Project Manager; Debra Sylvester, Production Supervisor; Adam Rooke, Designer; Kelly Odom, Developmental Editor; Stewart Mattson, Publisher; Ed Przyzycki, New Media Producer; Rich Kolasa, Senior Marketing Manager; and Brent Gordon, Editorial Director, all contributed significantly to the project and we appreciate their efforts.

# Brief Contents

1. The Equity Method of Accounting for Investments 1
2. Consolidation of Financial Information 36
3. Consolidations—Subsequent to the Date of Acquisition 90
4. Consolidated Financial Statements and Outside Ownership 149
5. Consolidated Financial Statements—Intercompany Asset Transactions 204
6. Variable Interest Entities, Intercompany Debt, Consolidated Statement of Cash Flows, and Other Issues 255
7. Foreign Currency Transactions and Hedging Foreign Exchange Risk 312
8. Translation of Foreign Currency Financial Statements 372
9. Partnerships: Formation and Operation 427
10. Partnerships: Termination and Liquidation 466
11. Accounting for State and Local Governments (Part 1) 502
12. Accounting for State and Local Governments (Part 2) 553

# Contents

## Chapter 1
### The Equity Method of Accounting for Investments 1

Reporting Investments in Corporate Equity Securities 1
Applying the Equity Method 3
   *Criteria for Utilizing the Equity Method 4*
   *Accounting for an Investment—The Equity Method 5*
Accounting Procedures Used in Applying the Equity Method 7
**Discussion Question:** Does the Equity Method Really Apply Here? 9
   *Reporting Investee Income from Sources Other than Continuing Operations 10*
   *Reporting Investee Losses 11*
   *Reporting the Sale of an Equity Investment 12*
Excess of Investment Cost Over Book Value Acquired 13
   *The Amortization Process 14*
Elimination of Unrealized Gains in Inventory 17
   *Downstream Sales of Inventory 18*
   *Upstream Sales of Inventory 18*
**Discussion Question:** Is This Really Only Significant Influence? 19
   *Decision Making and Criticisms of the Equity Method 20*
   *Criticisms of the Equity Method 21*
Summary 22

## Chapter 2
### Consolidation of Financial Information 36

Expansion through Corporate Takeovers 37
   *Why Do Firms Combine? 37*
   *Sears, Roebuck & Company and Land's End 38*
   *Pfizer and Warner-Lambert 39*
   *Chevron and Texaco 39*
The Consolidation Process 39
   *Business Combinations—Creating a Single Economic Entity 40*
   *Control—An Elusive Quality from ARB 51 to FIN 46 41*
   *Consolidation of Financial Information 42*
Financial Reporting for Business Combinations—*SFAS 141* 43
   *The Purchase Method: Change in Ownership 43*
Procedures for Consolidating Financial Information 44
   *Purchase Method When Dissolution Takes Place 44*
   *Purchase Method When Separate Incorporation Is Maintained 50*
Purchase Price Allocations—Additional Issues—*SFAS 141* 53
   *Intangibles 53*
   *Purchased In-Process Research and Development 54*
Unconsolidated Subsidiaries 57
The Pooling of Interests Method of Accounting for Business Combinations 58
   *Continuity of Ownership 58*
   *Pooling of Interests When Dissolution Takes Place 59*
   *Pooling of Interests When Separate Incorporation Is Maintained 62*
**Discussion Question:** How Does a Purchase Differ from a Pooling of Interests? 63
Pooling of Interests—The Controversy 65
   *FASB Position 67*
Summary 67
**Appendix**
*APB No. 16* Criteria for a Pooling of Interests 72

## Chapter 3
### Consolidations—Subsequent to the Date of Acquisition 90

Consolidation—The Effects Created by the Passage of Time 90
*SFAS 142*—Goodwill and Intangible Assets 91
   *Investment Accounting by the Acquiring Company 91*
   *Subsequent Consolidation—Investment Recorded by the Equity Method 92*
   *Acquisition Made during the Current Year 92*
   *Determining Consolidated Totals 94*
   *Consolidation Worksheet 96*
   *Consolidation Subsequent to Year of Acquisition—Equity Method 99*
Subsequent Consolidations—Investment Recorded on Other than the Equity Method 103
   *Acquisition Made during the Current Year 103*
   *Consolidation Subsequent to Year of Acquisition—Other than the Equity Method 107*
**Discussion Question:** How Does a Company Really Decide Which Investment Method to Apply? 112
Intangibles Acquired in Business Combinations and Related Amortizations 112
*SFAS 142*—Goodwill Impairment 114
   *Testing Goodwill for Impairment 114*
   *Assigning Values to Reporting Units 115*
Purchase Price—Contingent Consideration 117
**Discussion Question:** Is This Income? 118
Push-Down Accounting 119
   *External Reporting 119*
   *Push-Down Accounting—Internal Reporting 120*
Subsequent Consolidations—Pooling of Interests 121
Summary 123

# Chapter 4
## Consolidated Financial Statements and Outside Ownership   149

Consolidations Involving a Noncontrolling Interest   150
**Discussion Question:** How Do We Report This Other Owner?   151
   *The Economic Unit Concept   152*
   *The Proportionate Consolidation Concept   153*
   *The Parent Company Concept   154*
**Discussion Question:** What Decision Should the FASB Make?   157
   *Valuation Theories—Overview   158*
Consolidations Involving a Noncontrolling Interest—Subsequent to Acquisition   158
   *Effects Created by Alternative Investment Methods   167*
Step Acquisitions   167
   *Step Acquisitions—Parent Company Concept   168*
   *Worksheet Consolidation for a Step Acquisition   169*
   *Retroactive Treatment Created by Step Acquisition   170*
   *Step Acquisitions—Economic Unit Concept   171*
Preacquisition Income   174
   *Closing the Subsidiary Books at Acquisition Date   175*
Sales of Subsidiary Stock   175
   *Establishment of Investment Book Value   176*
   *Cost-Flow Assumptions   177*
   *Accounting for Shares that Remain   178*
Summary   178

# Chapter 5
## Consolidated Financial Statements—Intercompany Asset Transactions   204

Intercompany Inventory Transactions   205
   *The Sales and Purchases Accounts   205*
   *Unrealized Gains—Year of Transfer (Year 1)   206*
**Discussion Question:** Earnings Management   207
   *Unrealized Gains—Year Following Transfer (Year 2)   208*
   *Unrealized Gains—Effect on Noncontrolling Interest Valuation   209*
   *Intercompany Inventory Transfers Summarized   211*
   *Intercompany Inventory Transfers Illustrated   212*
**Discussion Question:** What Price Should We Charge Ourselves?   220
   *Effects on Consolidation of Alternative Investment Methods   220*
Intercompany Land Transfers   226
   *Accounting for Land Transactions   226*
   *Eliminating Unrealized Gains—Land Transfers   226*
   *Effect on Noncontrolling Interest Valuation—Land Transfers   228*
Intercompany Transfer of Depreciable Assets   228
   *The Deferral of Unrealized Gains   228*
   *Depreciable Asset Transfers Illustrated   229*
   *Depreciable Intercompany Asset Transfers—Downstream Transfers When the Parent Uses the Equity Method   231*
   *Effect on Noncontrolling Interest Valuation—Depreciable Asset Transfers   232*
Summary   232
**Appendix**
**Transfers—Alternative Approaches   237**

# Chapter 6
## Variable Interest Entities, Intercompany Debt, Consolidated Statement of Cash Flows, and Other Issues   255

FIN 46—Consolidation of Variable Interest Entities   255
   *What is an SPE?   256*
   *Consolidation of SPEs as Variable Interest Entities   258*
   *Procedures to Consolidate Variable Interest Entities   261*
   *Other FIN 46 Disclosure Requirements   263*
Intercompany Debt Transactions   263
   *Acquisition of Affiliate's Debt from an Outside Party   264*
   *Accounting for Intercompany Debt Transactions—Individual Financial Records   264*
   *Effects on Consolidation Process   267*
   *Assignment of Retirement Gain or Loss   267*
**Discussion Question:** Who Lost This $300,000?   268
   *Intercompany Debt Transactions—Subsequent to Year of Acquisition   269*
Subsidiary Preferred Stock   271
   *Preferred Stock Viewed as a Debt Instrument   271*
   *Preferred Stock Viewed as an Equity Interest   275*
Consolidated Statement of Cash Flows   277
Consolidated Earnings per Share   282
Subsidiary Stock Transactions   284
   *Changes in Subsidiary Book Value—Stock Transactions   284*
   *Subsidiary Stock Transactions—Illustrated   287*
Summary   290

# Chapter 7
## Foreign Currency Transactions and Hedging Foreign Exchange Risk   312

Foreign Exchange Markets   312
   *Exchange Rate Mechanisms   313*
   *Foreign Exchange Rates   313*
   *Spot and Forward Rates   315*
   *Option Contracts   315*
Foreign Currency Transactions   316
   *Accounting Issue   317*
   *Accounting Alternatives   317*
   *Balance Sheet Date before Date of Payment   318*
Hedging Foreign Exchange Risk   320
Accounting for Derivatives   321
   *Fundamental Requirement of Derivatives Accounting   321*
   *Determining the Fair Value of Derivatives   321*

*Accounting for Changes in the Fair Value of Derivatives* 322
Hedge Accounting 322
  *Nature of the Hedged Risk* 322
  *Hedge Effectiveness* 323
  *Hedge Documentation* 323
Hedges of Foreign Currency Denominated Assets and Liabilities 323
  *Cash Flow Hedge* 323
  *Fair Value Hedge* 324
Forward Contract Used to Hedge a Foreign Currency Denominated Asset 324
  *Forward Contract Designated as Cash Flow Hedge* 326
  *Forward Contract Designated as Fair Value Hedge* 328
**Discussion Question:** Do We Have a Gain or What? 330
Foreign Currency Option Used to Hedge a Foreign Currency Denominated Asset 331
  *Option Designated as Cash Flow Hedge* 332
  *Option Designated as Fair Value Hedge* 334
  *Spot Rate Exceeds Strike Price* 335
Hedges of Unrecognized Foreign Currency Firm Commitments 336
  *Forward Contract Used as Fair Value Hedge of Firm Commitment* 336
  *Option Used as Fair Value Hedge of Firm Commitment* 338
Hedge of Forecasted Foreign Currency Denominated Transaction 340
  *Forward Contract Cash Flow Hedge of a Forecasted Transaction* 341
  *Option Designated as Cash Flow Hedge of a Forecasted Transaction* 342
Use of Hedging Instruments 344
  *The Euro* 345
Foreign Currency Borrowing 345
  *Foreign Currency Loan* 346
Summary 346

## Chapter 8
## Translation of Foreign Currency Financial Statements 372

Exchange Rates Used in Translation 373
**Discussion Question:** How Do We Report This? 374
  *Translation Adjustments* 375
  *Balance Sheet Exposure* 375
Translation Methods 376
  *Current Rate Method* 376
  *Temporal Method* 376
  *Translation of Retained Earnings* 378
Complicating Aspects of the Temporal Method 379
  *Calculation of Cost of Goods Sold (COGS)* 379
  *Application of the Lower-of-Cost-or-Market Rule* 379
  *Fixed Assets, Depreciation, Accumulated Depreciation* 379
  *Gain or Loss on the Sale of an Asset* 380
Disposition of Translation Adjustment 380
U.S. Rules 381
  *SFAS 52* 381
  *Highly Inflationary Economies* 383
The Process Illustrated 384
Translation of Financial Statements—Current Rate Method 385
  *Translation of the Balance Sheet* 385
  *Translation of the Statement of Cash Flows* 388
Remeasurement of Financial Statements—Temporal Method 389
  *Remeasurement of the Income Statement* 390
  *Remeasurement of the Statement of Cash Flows* 392
  *Nonlocal Currency Balances* 392
Comparison of the Results from Applying the Two Different Methods 392
  *Underlying Valuation Method* 394
  *Underlying Relationships* 394
Hedging Balance Sheet Exposure 394
Disclosures Related to Translation 395
Consolidation of a Foreign Subsidiary 397
  *Translation of Foreign Subsidiary Trial Balance* 398
  *Determination of Balance in Investment Account—Equity Method* 399
  *Consolidation Worksheet* 399
Summary 401

## Chapter 9
## Partnerships: Formation and Operation 427

Partnerships—Advantages and Disadvantages 428
Alternative Legal Forms 430
Partnership Accounting—Capital Accounts 431
  *Articles of Partnership* 432
  *Accounting for Capital Contributions* 433
**Discussion Question:** What Kind of Business Is This? 434
  *Additional Capital Contributions and Withdrawals* 436
  *Allocation of Income* 437
**Discussion Question:** How Will the Profits Be Split? 438
Accounting for Partnership Dissolution 441
  *Dissolution—Admission of a New Partner* 442
  *Dissolution—Withdrawal of a Partner* 447
Summary 449

## Chapter 10
## Partnerships: Termination and Liquidation 466

Termination and Liquidation—Protecting the Interests of All Parties 467
  *Termination and Liquidation Procedures Illustrated* 468
  *Schedule of Liquidation* 470

*Deficit Capital Balance—Contribution Made by Partner* 471
*Deficit Capital Balance—Loss to Remaining Partners* 472
*Marshaling of Assets* 474
**Discussion Question:** What Happens if a Partner Becomes Insolvent? 479
*Preliminary Distribution of Partnership Assets* 480
*Predistribution Plan* 483
Summary 486

## Chapter 11
## Accounting for State and Local Governments (Part 1) 502

Introduction to the Accounting for State and Local Governments 503
*Governmental Accounting—User Needs* 504
*Financial Accountability* 505
*Control of Public Funds* 506
*Reporting Diverse Governmental Activities—Fund Accounting* 507
*Fund Accounting Classifications* 508
Overview of State and Local Government Financial Statements 512
Accounting for Governmental Funds 514
*The Importance of Budgets and the Recording of Budgetary Entries* 514
*Encumbrances* 518
*Recognition of Expenditures for Operations and Capital Additions* 520
**Discussion Question:** Is It an Asset or a Liability? 522
*Recognition of Revenues—Overview* 523
*Derived Tax Revenues Such as Income Taxes and Sales Taxes* 525
*Imposed Nonexchange Revenues Such as Property Taxes and Fines* 525
*Government-Mandated Nonexchange Transactions and Voluntary Nonexchange Transactions* 526
*Issuance of Bonds* 527
*Special Assessments* 530
*Interfund Transactions* 532
Summary 535

## Chapter 12
## Accounting for State and Local Governments (Part 2) 553

Capital Leases 554
*Government-Wide Financial Statements* 554
*Fund-Based Financial Statements* 555
Solid Waste Landfill 557
*Government-Wide Financial Statements* 557
*Fund-Based Financial Statements* 558
Compensated Absences 558
Works of Art and Historical Treasures 559
Infrastructure Assets and Depreciation 561
Management's Discussion and Analysis 563
The Primary Government and Component Units 565
*Component Units* 567
**Discussion Question:** Is It Part of the County? 568
General Purpose External Financial Statements 569
*Statement of Net Assets—Government-Wide Financial Statements* 569
*Statement of Activities—Government-Wide Financial Statements* 571
*Balance Sheet—Governmental Funds—Fund-Based Statements* 574
*Statement of Revenues, Expenditures, and Changes in Fund Balances—Government Funds—Fund-Based Statements* 576
*Statement of Net Assets—Proprietary Funds* 576
*Statement of Revenues, Expenses, and Changes in Fund Net Assets—Proprietary Funds* 580
*Statement of Cash Flows—Proprietary Funds* 580
*Financial Statements—Fiduciary Funds* 581
*Reporting Public Colleges and Universities* 586
Summary 589

**Index** 607

# Chapter One

# The Equity Method of Accounting for Investments

The first seven chapters of this text present the accounting and reporting for investment activities of businesses. The focus is on investments where one firm possesses either significant influence or control over another through ownership of voting shares. When one firm owns enough voting shares to be able to affect the decisions of another, accounting for the investment becomes challenging and often complex. The source of such complexities typically stems from the fact that transactions among the firms affiliated through ownership cannot be considered independent, arm's-length transactions. As in all matters relating to financial reporting, we look to transactions with *outside parties* to provide a basis for accounting valuation. When firms are affiliated through a common set of owners, objectivity in accounting calls for measurements that recognize the relationships among the firms.

### Questions to Consider

- Why do corporations invest in ownership shares of other corporations?
- One corporation buys equity shares of another company. What methods are available to account for this investment and the income it generates? When is each method appropriate?
- What factors affect the way income is recognized (cash basis, accrual basis, or market value changes) from investments in other corporations? What factors affect how the investment asset account is reported (at cost, at equity, or at market value)?
- In recognizing income from investments on the accrual basis, how is the cost of the investment matched against the revenue from the investment?
- At what point should profits be recognized on inventory that is transferred between related parties?
- What financial reporting incentives could exist for managers to maintain a firm's equity investments at 50 percent of an investee's voting stock or less?

## REPORTING INVESTMENTS IN CORPORATE EQUITY SECURITIES

In a recent annual report, JB Hunt Transport Services describes the creation of Transplace, Inc. (TPC), an Internet-based global transportation logistics company. JB Hunt contributed all of its logistics segment business and all related intangible assets plus $5 million of cash in exchange for an approximate 27 percent initial membership interest in TPC. The company accounts for its interest in TPC utilizing the equity method of accounting and stated, "The financial results of TPC are included on a one-line, nonoperating item included on the Consolidated Statements of Earnings entitled 'equity in earnings of associated companies.'"

Such information is hardly unusual in the business world; corporate as well as individual investors frequently acquire ownership shares of both domestic and foreign businesses. These investments can range from the purchase of a few shares to the acquisition of 100 percent control. Although purchases of corporate equity securities (such as the one made by JB Hunt) are not uncommon, they pose a considerable number of problems for the accountant because a close relationship has been established without the investor gaining actual control. These issues are currently addressed by the **equity method.** This chapter deals with the procedures utilized in accounting for stock investments that fall under the application of this method.

At present, accounting standards recognize three different approaches to the financial reporting of investments in corporate equity securities:

The fair-value method.

The consolidation of financial statements.

The equity method.

These three approaches are not interchangeable; a specific method is required by any given situation. The reporting of a particular investment depends on the degree of influence that the investor (stockholder) has over the investee, a factor best indicated by the relative size of ownership.

### *Fair-Value Method*

In many instances, an investor possesses only a small percentage of an investee company's outstanding stock, perhaps only a few shares. Because of the limited level of ownership, the investor cannot expect to have a significant impact on the investee's operations or decision making. These shares are bought in anticipation of cash dividends or in appreciation of stock market values. Such investments are recorded at cost and periodically adjusted to fair value according to the Financial Accounting Standards Board (FASB) in its *Statement of Financial Accounting Standards No. 115 (SFAS 115),* "Accounting for Certain Investments in Debt and Equity Securities," May 1993.

Since a full coverage of *SFAS 115* is presented in intermediate accounting textbooks, only the following basic principles are noted here.

- Initial investments in equity securities are recorded at cost and subsequently adjusted to fair value if fair value is readily determinable; otherwise, the investment remains at cost.
- Equity securities held for the purpose of selling them in the short term are classified as *trading securities* and reported at fair value, with unrealized gains and losses included in earnings.
- Equity securities not classified as trading securities are classified as *available-for-sale securities* and reported at fair value, with unrealized gains and losses excluded from earnings and reported in a separate component of shareholders' equity as part of *other comprehensive income.*
- Dividends received are recognized as income for both trading and available-for-sale securities.

These procedures are required for equity security investments when neither significant influence nor control is present. The recognition of unrealized gains and losses for *SFAS 115* investments represents a departure from past procedures that prevented the anticipation of income. As will be shown, the procedures for significant influence investments in equity securities, while somewhat complex, adhere more closely to traditional accrual accounting.

### *Consolidation of Financial Statements*

Although many investments involve only a small percentage of stock, an investor can acquire enough shares to gain actual control over an investee's operation. In financial accounting, such control is recognized whenever a stockholder accumulates more than 50 percent of an organization's outstanding voting stock. At that point, rather than simply influencing the decisions of the investee, the investor clearly can direct the entire decision-making process. A review of the financial statements of America's largest organizations indicates that legal control of one or more subsidiary companies is an almost universal practice. PepsiCo, Inc., as just one example, holds a majority interest in the voting stock of literally hundreds of corporations.

A level of ownership large enough to enable an investor to control an investee presents an economic situation not adequately addressed by *SFAS 115*. Normally, when a majority of voting stock is held, the investor-investee relationship has become so closely connected that the two corporations are viewed as a single entity for reporting purposes. Hence, an entirely different set of accounting procedures is applicable. According to *Accounting Research Bulletin No. 51 (ARB No. 51)*, "Consolidated Financial Statements," August 1959, control generally requires the consolidation of the accounting information produced by the individual companies. Thus, a single set of financial statements is created for external reporting purposes with all assets, liabilities, revenues, and expenses being brought together.[1] The various procedures applied within this consolidation process are examined in subsequent chapters of the textbook.

### *Equity Method*

Finally, another investment relationship is appropriately accounted for using the equity method. JB Hunt's ownership of 27 percent of the voting stock of TPC is less than enough to control the voting stock. Yet, despite the lack of voting control, JB Hunt maintains a large interest in this investee company. Through its ownership, JB Hunt can undoubtedly affect the decisions and operations of TPC.

Especially important is the investor's ability to influence the timing of dividend distributions. Because of this influence, the receipt of a dividend from an investee does not qualify as an objective basis for recording income to the investor firm. Because managerial compensation contracts often are based on net income, incentives exist for managers to use whatever discretion they have available in reporting net income. *Thus, to provide an objective basis for reporting investment income, the equity method requires that income be recognized by the investor as it is earned by the investee, not when dividends are received.*

In today's business world, many corporations such as JB Hunt hold significant ownership interests in other companies without having actual control. Sears, Roebuck & Company alone holds between 20 and 50 percent ownership in dozens of separate corporations. Many other large investments are created through joint ventures whereby two or more companies form a new enterprise to carry out a specified operating purpose. For example, Microsoft and NBC formed a joint venture to operate MSNBC, a cable channel and online site to go with NBC's broadcast network. Each partner owns 50 percent of the joint venture.

For each of these investments, the investors do not possess absolute control because they hold less than a majority of the voting stock. Thus, the preparation of consolidated financial statements is inappropriate. However, the large percentage of ownership indicates that each investor possesses some ability to affect the decision-making process of the investee. To reflect this relationship, such investments are accounted for by the equity method as officially established by *Opinion 18*, "The Equity Method of Accounting for Investments in Common Stock," issued by the Accounting Principles Board (APB) in March of 1971, and as amended in 2001 by *SFAS 142*, "Goodwill and Other Intangible Assets."

## APPLYING THE EQUITY METHOD

An understanding of the equity method is best gained by initially examining the APB's treatment of two questions:

1. What parameters identify the area of ownership for which the equity method is applicable?
2. How should the investor report this investment and the income generated by it to reflect the relationship between the two companies?

---

[1] As is discussed in the next chapter, owning a majority of the voting shares of an investee does not always lead to consolidated financial statements. Also, FASB Interpretation No. 46 "Consolidation of Variable Interest Entities," describes when control is present without majority ownership (see Chapters 2 and 6).

## Criteria for Utilizing the Equity Method

In sanctioning application of the equity method, the APB reasoned that an investor begins to gain the ability to influence the decision-making process of an investee as the level of ownership rises. According to *APB Opinion 18* (par. 17), achieving this "ability to exercise significant influence over operating and financial policies of an investee even though the investor holds 50 percent or less of the voting stock" is the sole criterion for requiring application of the equity method.

Clearly, a term such as *the ability to exercise significant influence* is nebulous and subject to a variety of judgments and interpretations in practice. At what point does the acquisition of one additional share of stock give an owner the ability to exercise significant influence? This decision becomes even more difficult in that only the *ability* to exercise significant influence need be present: The pronouncement does not specify that any actual influence must have ever been applied.

*APB Opinion 18* provides guidance to the accountant by listing several conditions that indicate the presence of this degree of influence:

- Investor representation on the board of directors of the investee.
- Investor participation in the policy-making process of the investee.
- Material intercompany transactions.
- Interchange of managerial personnel.
- Technological dependency.
- Extent of ownership by the investor in relation to the size and concentration of other ownership interests in the investee.

No single one of these guides should be used exclusively in assessing the applicability of the equity method. Instead, all are evaluated together to determine the presence or absence of the sole criterion: the ability to exercise significant influence over the investee.

These guidelines alone do not eliminate the leeway available to each investor when deciding whether use of the equity method is appropriate. To provide a degree of consistency in applying this standard, the APB established a general ownership test. *If an investor holds between 20 and 50 percent of the voting stock of the investee, significant influence is normally assumed and the equity method applied.*

> The Board recognizes that determining the ability of an investor to exercise such influence is not always clear and applying judgment is necessary to assess the status of each investment. In order to achieve a reasonable degree of uniformity in application, the Board concludes that an investment (direct or indirect) of 20 percent or more of the voting stock of an investee should lead to a presumption that in the absence of evidence to the contrary an investor has the ability to exercise significant influence over an investee. Conversely, an investment of less than 20 percent of the voting stock of an investee should lead to a presumption that an investor does not have the ability to exercise significant influence unless such ability can be demonstrated.[2]

At first, the 20 percent rule appears to be an arbitrarily chosen boundary established merely to provide accountants with a consistent method of reporting all investments. However, the essential criterion is still the ability to significantly influence the investee, rather than 20 percent ownership.[3] If the absence of this ability is proven, the equity method should not be applied regardless of the percentage of shares held. Conversely, whenever this ability can be demonstrated, the equity method is appropriate without concern for the degree of ownership.

As an example, in a recent annual report, International Paper Company disclosed that it accounts for its investment in Scitex Corporation using the equity method despite holding only a 13 percent interest. International Paper cited its ability to exercise significant influence

---

[2] *APB Opinion 18*, para. 17.

[3] Not everyone agrees with the wisdom of this rule. Two members of the APB, George R. Catlett and Charles T. Horngren, voted for *Opinion 18* but argued in an attached statement that "they do not agree with the arbitrary criterion of 20 percent combined with a variable test of 'significant influence' in paragraph 17, because such an approach is not convincing in concept and will be very difficult to apply in practice."

"because the Company is party to a shareowners' agreement with two other entities which together with the Company own just over 39% of Scitex."

Further guidance on the precise applicability of the equity method was provided in May 1981 when the FASB issued its *Interpretation 35,* "Criteria for Applying the Equity Method of Accounting for Investments in Common Stock." This pronouncement dealt specifically with using the equity method for investments in which the owner holds more than 20 percent of the outstanding shares. It is important because companies had tended to apply the equity method to all investments in the 20 to 50 percent range with little regard for the degree of influence actually present.

According to *Interpretation 35* (par. 3), above the 20 percent level of ownership, "the presumption that the investor has the ability to exercise significant influence over the investee's operating and financial policies stands until overcome by predominant evidence to the contrary." However, the pronouncement then went on to offer clarification by listing examples of occurrences that would provide evidence to nullify this presumption. *Interpretation 35* specifically states that the equity method is not appropriate for investments that demonstrate any of the following characteristics regardless of the investor's degree of ownership:

- An agreement exists between investor and investee whereby the investor surrenders significant rights as a shareholder.
- A concentration of ownership operates the investee without regard for the views of the investor.
- The investor attempts but fails to obtain representation on the investee's board of directors.

Finally, although a controlling financial interest is the usual condition for consolidating an investee company, conditions can exist so that the equity method is appropriate despite a majority voting interest. As discussed in the FASB's Emerging Issues Task Force (EITF) *Issue 96-16,* in some instances the powers of the majority shareholder can be restricted by approval or veto rights granted to the minority shareholder. If the minority rights are so restrictive as to call into question whether control rests with the majority owner, the equity method is employed for appropriate financial reporting rather than consolidation. As noted in *EITF 96-16,* substantive minority participation rights can affect the hiring, termination, and compensation of management. Other important minority rights can include establishing operating and capital decisions of the investee. In these cases, minority rights can overcome the presumption that an investor with a majority voting interest should consolidate its investee. For example, in its 2001 annual report, SBC Communications stated that "we account for our 60 percent economic investment in Cingular under the equity method of accounting because we share control equally with our 40 percent partner."

To summarize, the following table indicates the method of accounting that is typically applicable to various stock investments:

| Criterion | Normal Ownership Level | Applicable Accounting Method |
|---|---|---|
| Lack of ability to significantly influence | Less than 20% | Fair value *(SFAS 115)* or cost |
| Presence of ability to significantly influence | 20%–50% | Equity method *(APB Opinion 18* and *SFAS 142)* |
| Control | More than 50% | Consolidated financial statements *(ARB No. 51,* and *SFAS 141* and *142)* |

## Accounting for an Investment—The Equity Method

Now that the criteria leading to the application of the equity method have been identified, a review of its reporting procedures is appropriate. Knowledge of this accounting process is especially important to users of the investor's financial statements because the equity method affects both the timing of income recognition as well as the carrying value of the investment account.

*In applying the equity method, the accounting objective is to report the investor's investment and investment income reflecting the close relationship between the companies.* After recording the cost of the acquisition, two equity method entries periodically record the investment's impact:

- The investor's investment account is *increased as the investee earns and reports income.* Also, investment income is recognized by the investor using the accrual method—that is, in the same time period as it is earned by the investee. If an investee reports income of $100,000, a 30 percent owner should immediately increase its own income by $30,000. This earnings accrual reflects the essence of the equity method by emphasizing the connection between the two companies; as the owners' equity of the investee increases through the earnings process, so the investment account also increases. Although the acquisition is initially recorded by the investor at cost, upward adjustments in the asset balance are recorded as soon as the investee makes a profit. A reduction is necessary if a loss is reported.

- The investor's investment account is *decreased whenever a dividend is collected.* Since distribution of cash dividends reduces the book value of the investee company, the investor mirrors this change by recording the receipt as a decrease in the carrying value of the investment rather than as revenue. Once again, a parallel is established between the investment account and the underlying activities of the investee: The reduction in owners' equity of the investee creates a decrease in the investment. Furthermore, since income is recognized immediately by the investor when it is earned by the investee, double counting would occur if subsequent dividend collections also were recorded by the investor as revenue. Importantly, because of the investor's significant influence over the investee, the collection of a cash dividend is not an appropriate point for income recognition. Because the investor can influence the timing of investee dividend distributions, the receipt of a dividend is not an objective measure of the income generated from the investment.

| Application of Equity Method | |
|---|---|
| **Investee Event** | **Investor Accounting** |
| Income is earned. | Proportionate share of income is recognized. |
| Dividends are distributed. | Dividends received are recorded as a reduction in investment. |

Application of the equity method causes the investment account on the investor's balance sheet to fluctuate in direct relation to changes occurring in the equity of the investee company. As an illustration, assume that an investor acquires a 40 percent interest in a business enterprise. If the investor has the ability to significantly influence the investee, the equity method must be utilized. If the investee subsequently reports net income of $50,000, the investor increases the investment account (and its own net income) by $20,000 in recognition of a 40 percent share of these earnings. Conversely, a $20,000 dividend collected from the investee necessitates a reduction of $8,000 in this same asset account (40 percent of the total payout).

In contrast, the fair-value method reports investments at market value if readily determinable. Also, income is recognized only on receipt of dividends. Consequently, financial reports can vary depending on whether the equity method or fair-value method is appropriate for reporting purposes.

To illustrate, assume that Big Company owns a 20 percent interest in Little Company purchased on January 1, 2004, for $200,000. Little then reports net income of $200,000, $300,000, and $400,000 in the next three years while paying dividends of $50,000, $100,000, and $200,000. The fair values of Big's investment in Little, as determined by market prices, were $235,000, $255,000, and $320,000 at the end of 2004, 2005, and 2006, respectively.

Exhibit 1–1 compares the accounting for Big's investment in Little across the two methods. The fair-value method carries the investment at its market values, presumed to be readily avail-

**EXHIBIT 1–1** Comparison of Fair-Value Method and Equity Method

| | | | Accounting by Big Company When Influence Is Not Significant (available-for-sale security) | | | Accounting by Big Company When Influence Is Significant (equity method) | |
|---|---|---|---|---|---|---|---|
| Year | Income of Little Company | Dividends Paid by Little Company | Dividend Income | Carrying Value of Investment | Fair-Value Adjustment to Stockholders' Equity | Equity in Investee Income | Carrying Value of Investment |
| 2004 | $200,000 | $ 50,000 | $10,000 | $235,000 | $ 35,000 | $ 40,000* | $230,000† |
| 2005 | 300,000 | 100,000 | 20,000 | 255,000 | 55,000 | 60,000* | 270,000† |
| 2006 | 400,000 | 200,000 | 40,000 | 320,000 | 120,000 | 80,000* | 310,000† |
| Total income recognized | | | $70,000 | | | $180,000 | |

*Equity in investee income is 20 percent of the current year income reported by Little Company.
†The carrying value of an investment under the equity method is the original cost plus income recognized less dividends received. For 2004, as an example, the $230,000 reported balance is the $200,000 cost plus $40,000 equity income less $10,000 in dividends received.

able in this example. Because the investment is classified as an *available-for-sale security*, the excess of market value over cost is reported as a separate component of stockholders' equity.[4] Income is recognized as dividends are received.

In contrast, under the equity method, Big recognizes income as it is earned by Little. As shown in Exhibit 1–1, Big recognizes $180,000 in income over the three years, and the carrying value of the investment is adjusted upward to $310,000. Dividends received are not considered an appropriate measure of income because of the assumed significant influence when the equity method is applied. Big's ability to influence the decisions of Little applies to the timing of dividend distributions. Therefore, dividends received do not represent an objective measure of Big's income from its investment in Little. However, as Little earns income, under the equity method Big recognizes its share (20%) of the income and increases the investment account. The equity method reflects the accrual model: Income is recognized as it is earned, not when cash (dividend) is received.

Exhibit 1–1 shows that the carrying value of the investment fluctuates each year under the equity method. This recording parallels the changes occurring in the net asset figures reported by the investee. If the owner's equity of the investee rises through income, an increase is made in the investment account; decreases such as losses and dividends cause reductions to be recorded. Thus, the equity method conveys information that describes the relationship created by the investor's ability to significantly influence the investee.

## ACCOUNTING PROCEDURES USED IN APPLYING THE EQUITY METHOD

Once guidelines for the application of the equity method have been established, the mechanical process necessary for recording basic transactions is quite straightforward. The investor accrues its percentage of the earnings reported by the investee each period. Dividend declarations reduce the investment balance to reflect the decrease in the investee's book value.

Referring again to the information presented in Exhibit 1–1, Little Company reported a net income of $200,000 during 2004 and paid cash dividends of $50,000. These figures indicate that Little's net assets have increased by $150,000 during the year. Therefore, in the financial records of Big Company, the following journal entries are made in applying the equity method:

---

[4] Fluctuations in the market values of *trading securities* are recognized in income in the period in which they occur.

| | | |
|---|---:|---:|
| Investment in Little Company | 40,000 | |
|     Equity in Investee Income | | 40,000 |
| To accrue earnings of a 20 percent owned investee ($200,000 × 20%). | | |
| Cash | 10,000 | |
|     Investment in Little Company | | 10,000 |
| To record receipt of cash dividend from Little Company ($50,000 × 20%). | | |

In the first entry, Big accrues income based on the reported earnings of the investee even though this amount greatly exceeds the cash dividend. The second entry reflects the actual receipt of the dividend and the related reduction in Little's net assets. The $30,000 net increment recorded here in Big's investment account ($40,000 − $10,000) represents 20 percent of the $150,000 increase in Little's book value that occurred during the year.

Although these two entries illustrate the basic reporting process used in applying the equity method, several other issues must be explored for a full understanding of this approach. More specifically, special procedures are required in accounting for each of the following:

1. Reporting a change to the equity method.
2. Reporting investee income from sources other than continuing operations.
3. Reporting investee losses.
4. Reporting the sale of an equity investment.

## Reporting a Change to the Equity Method

In many instances, an investor's ability to significantly influence an investee will not be gained through a single stock acquisition. The investor could possess only a minor ownership for some years before purchasing enough additional shares to require conversion to the equity method. Before the investor achieves significant influence, any investment should be reported by the fair-value method. After the investment reaches the point at which the equity method becomes applicable, a technical question arises about the appropriate means of changing from one method to the other.[5]

*APB Opinion 18* (par. 19) answers this concern by stating that "the investment, results of operations (current and prior periods presented), and retained earnings of the investor should be adjusted retroactively." *Thus, all accounts are restated so that the investor's financial statements appear as if the equity method had been applied from the date of the first acquisition. By mandating retroactive treatment, the APB is attempting to ensure comparability from year to year in the financial reporting of the investor company.*[6]

To illustrate this restatement procedure, assume that Giant Company acquires a 10 percent ownership in Small Company on January 1, 2004. Officials of Giant do not believe that their company has gained the ability to exert significant influence over Small. The investment is properly recorded through the use of the fair-value method as an available-for-sale security. Subsequently, on January 1, 2006, Giant purchases an additional 30 percent of the outstanding voting stock of Small, thereby achieving the ability to significantly influence the investee's decision making. From 2004 through 2006, Small reports net income, pays cash dividends, and has fair values at January 1 of each year as follows:

| Year | Net Income | Cash Dividends | Fair Value at January 1 |
|---|---|---|---|
| 2004 | $ 70,000 | $20,000 | $800,000 |
| 2005 | 110,000 | 40,000 | 840,000 |
| 2006 | 130,000 | 50,000 | 930,000 |

In Giant's 2004 and 2005 financial statements, as originally reported, dividend revenue of $2,000 and $4,000, respectively, would be recognized based on receiving 10 percent of these distributions. The investment account is maintained at fair value since it is readily deter-

# Discussion Question

**DOES THE EQUITY METHOD REALLY APPLY HERE?**

Abraham, Inc., a New Jersey corporation, operates 57 bakeries throughout the northeastern section of the United States. In the past, the company's outstanding common stock has been owned entirely by its founder, James Abraham. However, during the early part of this year, the corporation suffered a severe cash flow problem brought on by rapid expansion. To avoid bankruptcy, Abraham sought additional investment capital from a friend, Dennis Bostitch, who owned Highland Laboratories. Subsequently Highland paid $700,000 cash to Abraham, Inc., to acquire enough newly issued shares of common stock for a one-third ownership interest.

At the end of this year, the accountants for Highland Laboratories are discussing the proper method of reporting this investment. One argues for maintaining the asset at its original cost: "This purchase is no more than a loan to bail out the bakeries. Mr. Abraham will continue to run the organization with little or no attention paid to us. After all, what does anyone in our company know about baking bread? I would not be surprised if these shares are not reacquired by Abraham as soon as the bakery business is profitable again."

One of the other accountants disagrees, stating that the equity method is appropriate. "I realize that our company is not capable of running a bakery. However, the official rules state that we must have only the *ability* to exert significant influence. With one-third of the common stock in our possession, we certainly have that ability. Whether we use it or not, this ability means that we are required to apply the equity method."

How should Highland Laboratories account for its investment in Abraham, Inc.?

---

minable. Also, the change in the fair value of the investment results in a credit to an unrealized cumulative holding gain of $4,000 in 2004 and an additional credit of $9,000 in 2005 for a cumulative amount of $13,000 reported in Giant's 2005 stockholders' equity section. However, after changing to the equity method on January 1, 2006, Giant must restate these prior years to present the investment *as if the equity method had always been applied*. Subsequently, in comparative statements showing columns for previous periods, the 2004 statements should indicate equity income of $7,000 with $11,000 being disclosed for 2005 based on a 10 percent accrual of Small's income for each of these years.

The income restatement for these earlier years can be computed as follows:

| Year | Equity in Investee Income (10%) | Income Reported from Dividends | Retroactive Adjustment |
|---|---|---|---|
| 2004 | $ 7,000 | $ 2,000 | $ 5,000 |
| 2005 | 11,000 | 4,000 | 7,000 |
| Total adjustment to Retained Earnings | | | $12,000 |

Giant's reported earnings for 2004 will be increased by $5,000 with a $7,000 increment needed for 2005. To bring about this retroactive change to the equity method, Giant prepares the following journal entry on January 1, 2006:

---

[5] A switch to the equity method also can be required if the investee purchases a portion of its own shares as treasury stock. This transaction can increase the investor's percentage of outstanding stock.

[6] One member of the APB voted against issuance of *Opinion 18* based in part on this retroactive approach. In his dissent, Newman T. Halvorson contended that "at the time an investment qualifies for use of the equity method, a new reporting entity is created, and the accounts of the investor for periods prior to that time should not be adjusted retroactively to reflect an entity that did not exist."

| | | |
|---|---:|---:|
| Investment in Small Company | 12,000 | |
|     Retained Earnings—Prior Period Adjustment— Equity in Investee Income | | 12,000 |
| To adjust 2004 and 2005 records so that investment is accounted for using the equity method in a consistent manner. | | |
| Unrealized Holding Gain—Shareholders' Equity | 13,000 | |
|     Fair Value Adjustment (Available-for-Sale) | | 13,000 |
| To remove the investor's percentage of the increase in fair value (10% × $130,000) from stockholders' equity and the available-for-sale portfolio valuation account. | | |

The $13,000 adjustment removes the accounts required by *SFAS No. 115* that pertain to the investment prior to the obtaining of significant influence. Because the investment is no longer part of the available-for-sale portfolio, it is carried under the equity method rather than at fair value. Accordingly, the fair-value adjustment accounts are reduced as part of the reclassification.

Continuing with this example, Giant will make two other journal entries at the end of 2006, but they relate solely to the operations and distributions of that period.

| | | |
|---|---:|---:|
| Investment in Small Company | 52,000 | |
|     Equity in Investee Income | | 52,000 |
| To accrue 40 percent of the year 2006 income reported by the Small Company ($130,000 × 40%). | | |
| Cash | 20,000 | |
|     Investment in Small Company | | 20,000 |
| To record receipt of year 2006 cash dividend from Small Company ($50,000 × 40%). | | |

## Reporting Investee Income from Sources Other than Continuing Operations

Traditionally, certain elements of income are presented separately within a set of financial statements. Examples include extraordinary items (see *APB Opinion 30*, "Reporting the Results of Operations," June 1973) and prior period adjustments (see FASB *SFAS 16*, "Prior Period Adjustments," June 1977). A concern that arises in applying the equity method is whether items appearing separately in the investee's income statement require similar treatment by the investor.

To examine this issue, assume that Large Company owns 40 percent of the voting stock of Tiny Company and accounts for this investment by means of the equity method. In 2004, Tiny reports net income of $200,000, a figure composed of $250,000 in income from continuing operations and a $50,000 extraordinary loss. Large Company accrues earnings of $80,000 based on 40 percent of the $200,000 net figure. However, for proper disclosure, the extraordinary loss incurred by the investee must also be reported separately on the financial statements of the investor. This handling is intended, once again, to mirror the close relationship between the two companies.

Based on the level of ownership, Large recognizes $100,000 as a component of operating income (40 percent of Tiny Company's $250,000 income from continuing operations) along with a $20,000 extraordinary loss (40 percent of $50,000). The overall effect is still an $80,000 net increment in Large's earnings, but this amount has been appropriately allocated between income from continuing operations and extraordinary items.

The journal entry to record Large's equity interest in the income of Tiny would be as follows:

| | | |
|---|---|---|
| Investment in Tiny Company | 80,000 | |
| Extraordinary Loss of Investee | 20,000 | |
|     Equity in Investee Income | | 100,000 |
| To accrue operating income and extraordinary loss from equity investment. | | |

One additional aspect of this accounting should be noted. Even though this loss has already been judged as extraordinary by the investee, Large does not report its $20,000 share as a separate item unless that figure is considered to be material with respect to the investor's own operations.

## Reporting Investee Losses

Although most of the previous illustrations are based on the recording of profits, accounting for losses incurred by the investee is handled in a similar manner. The investor recognizes the appropriate percentage of each loss and reduces the carrying value of the investment account. Even though these procedures are consistent with the concept of the equity method, they fail to take into account all possible loss situations.

### *Permanent Losses in Value*

*APB Opinion 18* recognizes that investments can suffer permanent losses in market value that are not properly reflected through the equity method. Such declines can be caused by the loss of major customers, changes in economic conditions, loss of a significant patent or other legal right, damage to the company's reputation, and the like. Permanent reductions in market value resulting from such adverse events might not be reported immediately by the investor through the normal equity entries discussed previously. Thus, *APB Opinion 18* (par. 19) established the following guideline:

> A loss in value of an investment which is other than a temporary decline should be recognized the same as a loss in value of other long-term assets. Evidence of a loss in value might include, but would not necessarily be limited to, absence of an ability to recover the carrying amount of the investment or inability of the investee to sustain an earnings capacity which would justify the carrying amount of the investment.

Thus, when a permanent decline in an equity method investment's value occurs, the investor must reduce the asset to fair-market value. However, *APB Opinion 18* stresses that this loss must be permanent before such recognition becomes necessary. Under the equity method, a temporary drop in the market value of an investment is simply ignored.

### *Investment Reduced to Zero*

Through the recognition of reported losses as well as any permanent drops in market value, the investment account can eventually be reduced to a zero balance. This condition is most likely to occur if extreme losses have been suffered by the investee or if the original purchase was made at a low, bargain price. Regardless of the reason, the carrying value of the investment account could conceivably be eliminated in total.

At the point at which an investment account is reduced to zero, the investor should discontinue using the equity method rather than establish a negative balance. The investment retains a zero balance until subsequent investee profits eliminate all unrealized losses. Once the original cost of the investment has been eliminated, no additional losses can accrue to the investor (since the entire cost has been written off) *unless* some further commitment has been made on behalf of the investee.

Noise Cancellation Technologies, Inc., for example, in recent financial statements explains the discontinued use of the equity method when the investment account has been reduced to zero:

When the Company's share of cumulative losses equals its investment and the Company has no obligation or intention to fund such additional losses, the Company suspends applying the equity method. . . . The Company will not be able to record any equity in income with respect to an entity until its share of future profits is sufficient to recover any cumulative losses that have not previously been recorded.

### Reporting the Sale of an Equity Investment

At any time, the investor can choose to sell part or all of its holdings in the investee company. If a sale occurs, the equity method continues to be applied until the transaction date, thus establishing an appropriate carrying value for the investment. The investor then reduces this balance by the percentage of shares being sold.

As an example, assume that Top Company owns 40 percent of the 100,000 outstanding shares of Bottom Company, an investment accounted for by the equity method. Although these 40,000 shares were acquired some years ago for $200,000, application of the equity method has increased the asset balance to $320,000 as of January 1, 2004. On July 1, 2004, Top elects to sell 10,000 of these shares (one-fourth of its investment) for $110,000 in cash, thereby reducing ownership in Bottom from 40 percent to 30 percent. Bottom Company reports income of $70,000 during the first six months of 2004 and distributes cash dividends of $30,000.

Top, as the investor, initially makes the following journal entries on July 1, 2004, to accrue the proper income and establish the correct investment balance:

| | | |
|---|---:|---:|
| Investment in Bottom Company | 28,000 | |
|     Equity in Investee Income | | 28,000 |
| To accrue equity income for first six months of 2004 ($70,000 × 40%). | | |
| Cash | 12,000 | |
|     Investment in Bottom Company | | 12,000 |
| To record receipt of cash dividends from January through June 2004 ($30,000 × 40%). | | |

These two entries increase the carrying value of Top's investment by $16,000, creating a balance of $336,000 as of July 1, 2004. The sale of one-fourth of these shares can then be recorded as follows:

| | | |
|---|---:|---:|
| Cash | 110,000 | |
|     Investment in Bottom Company | | 84,000 |
|     Gain on Sale of Investment | | 26,000 |
| To record sale of one-fourth of investment in Bottom Company (¼ × $336,000 = $84,000). | | |

After the sale has been consummated, Top continues to apply the equity method to this investment based on 30 percent ownership rather than 40 percent. However, if the sale had been of sufficient magnitude to cause Top to lose its ability to exercise significant influence over Bottom, the equity method ceases to be applicable. For example, if Top Company's holdings were reduced from 40 percent to 15 percent, the equity method might no longer be appropriate after the sale. The shares still being held are reported according to the fair-value method with the remaining book value becoming the new *cost* figure for the investment rather than the amount originally paid.

If an investor is required to change from the equity method to the fair-value method, no retroactive adjustment is made. Although, as previously demonstrated, a change to the equity method mandates a restatement of prior periods, the treatment is not the same when the investor's change is to the fair-value method.

# EXCESS OF INVESTMENT COST OVER BOOK VALUE ACQUIRED

After the basic concepts and procedures of the equity method are mastered, more complex accounting issues can be introduced. Surely one of the most common problems encountered in applying the equity method concerns investment costs that exceed the proportionate book value of the investee company.[7]

Unless the investor acquires its ownership at the time of the investee's conception, paying an amount equal to book value is rare. Dell Computer Corporation, as just one example, reported a book value of approximately $1.74 per share on February 1, 2002, but on that date, the company's common stock closed at $26.80 per share on the NASDAQ Exchange. To obtain Dell Computer shares as well as the stock of many other businesses, payment of a significant premium over book value is required.

A number of possible reasons exist for such a marked difference in the book value of a company and the price of its stock. A company's value at any time is based on a multitude of factors such as company profitability, the introduction of a new product, expected dividend payments, projected operating results, and general economic conditions. Furthermore, stock prices are based, at least partially, on the perceived worth of a company's net assets, amounts that often vary dramatically from underlying book values. Asset and liability accounts shown on a balance sheet tend to measure historical costs rather than current value. In addition, these reported figures are affected by the specific accounting methods adopted by a company. Inventory costing methods such as LIFO and FIFO, for example, obviously lead to different book values as do each of the acceptable depreciation methods.

If an investment is acquired at a price in excess of book value, logical reasons should explain the additional cost incurred by the investor. The source of the excess of cost over book value is important. Income recognition requires matching the income generated from the investment with its cost. Excess costs allocated to fixed assets will likely be expensed over longer periods than costs allocated to inventory. In applying the equity method, the cause of such an excess payment can be divided into two general categories:

1. Specific investee assets and liabilities can have market values that differ from their present book values. The excess payment can be identified directly with individual accounts such as inventory, equipment, franchise rights, etc.

2. The investor could be willing to pay an extra amount because future benefits are expected to accrue from the investment. Such benefits could be anticipated as the result of factors such as the estimated profitability of the investee or the relationship being established between the two companies. In this case, the additional payment is attributed to an intangible future value generally referred to as *goodwill* rather than to any specific investee asset or liability. For example, in a recent annual report, Ameritech Corporation disclosed that its long-term investment in Tele Danmark, accounted for under the equity method, includes goodwill of approximately $1.4 billion.

As an illustration, assume that Big Company is negotiating the acquisition of 30 percent of the outstanding shares of Little Company. Little's balance sheet reports assets of $500,000 and liabilities of $300,000 for a net book value of $200,000. After investigation, Big determines that Little's equipment is undervalued in the company's financial records by $60,000. One of its patents is also undervalued, but only by $40,000. By adding these valuation adjustments to Little's book value, Big arrives at an estimated worth for the company's net assets of $300,000. Based on this computation, Big offers $90,000 for a 30 percent share of the investee's outstanding stock.

---

[7] Although encountered less frequently, investments can be purchased at a cost that is less than the underlying book value of the investee. Accounting for this possibility is explored in later chapters.

| | |
|---|---:|
| Book value of Little Company (assets minus liabilities [or stockholders' equity]) | $200,000 |
| Undervaluation of equipment | 60,000 |
| Undervaluation of patent | 40,000 |
| Value of net assets | $300,000 |
| Portion being acquired | 30% |
| Acquisition price | $ 90,000 |

Although Big's purchase price is in excess of the proportionate share of Little's book value, this additional amount can be attributed to two specific accounts: Equipment and Patents. No part of the extra payment is traceable to any other projected future benefit. Thus, the cost of Big's investment is allocated as follows:

| | | |
|---|---:|---:|
| Payment by investor | | $90,000 |
| Percentage of book value acquired ($200,000 × 30%) | | 60,000 |
| Payment in excess of book value | | 30,000 |
| Excess payment identified with specific assets: | | |
|    Equipment ($60,000 undervaluation × 30%) | $18,000 | |
|    Patent ($40,000 undervaluation × 30%) | 12,000 | 30,000 |
| Excess payment not identified with specific assets—goodwill | | –0– |

Of the $30,000 excess payment made by the investor, $18,000 is assigned to the equipment whereas $12,000 is traced to a patent and its undervaluation. No amount of the purchase price is allocated to goodwill.

To take this example one step further, assume that the owners of Little reject the $90,000 price proposed by Big. They believe that the value of the company as a going concern is greater than the market value of its net assets. Since the management of Big believes that valuable synergies will be created through this purchase, the bid price is raised to $125,000 and accepted. This new acquisition price is allocated as follows:

| | | |
|---|---:|---:|
| Payment by investor | | $125,000 |
| Percentage of book value acquired ($200,000 × 30%) | | 60,000 |
| Payment in excess of book value | | 65,000 |
| Excess payment identified with specific assets: | | |
|    Equipment ($60,000 undervaluation × 30%) | $18,000 | |
|    Patent ($40,000 undervaluation × 30%) | 12,000 | 30,000 |
| Excess payment not identified with specific assets—goodwill | | $ 35,000 |

As can be seen from this example, *any extra payment that cannot be attributed to a specific asset or liability is assigned to the intangible asset goodwill.* Although the actual purchase price can be computed by a number of different techniques or simply result from negotiations, goodwill is always the excess amount not allocated to identifiable asset or liability accounts.

Under the equity method, the investor enters total cost in a single investment account, regardless of the allocation of any excess purchase price. If Big's bid of $125,000 is accepted by all parties, the acquisition is initially recorded at that amount despite the internal assignments made to equipment, patents, and goodwill. The entire $125,000 was paid to acquire this investment, and it is recorded as such.

### The Amortization Process

The preceding extra payments were made in connection with specific assets (equipment, patents, and goodwill). Even though the actual dollar amounts are recorded within the investment account, a definite historical cost can be attributed to these assets. With a cost to the investor as well as a specified life, the payment relating to each asset should be amortized over an appropriate time period.

Historically, goodwill implicit in equity method investments had been amortized over periods less than or equal to 40 years. However, in June 2001, the FASB approved a major and fundamental change in accounting for goodwill. *SFAS No. 142*, "Goodwill and Other Intangible Assets," states that for fiscal periods beginning December 15, 2001, and after, the useful life for goodwill is considered indefinite. Therefore, no goodwill amortization expense will be allowed in future periods. The change was accounted for prospectively with no retroactive adjustments permitted. Firms continued to amortize existing goodwill for the 2001 fiscal year (prior to the *SFAS 142* effective date) and then discontinued the practice. The unamortized portion of implicit goodwill is carried forward without adjustment until the investment is sold or a permanent decline in value occurs.

In arriving at its decision, the FASB noted that goodwill can maintain its value and can even increase over time. The notion of an indefinite life for goodwill recognizes the argument that amortization of goodwill over an arbitrary period fails to reflect economic reality and therefore could not provide useful information. A primary reason for the presumption of an indefinite life for goodwill relates to the accounting for business combinations (covered in Chapters 2 through 6). The FASB reasoned that goodwill associated with equity method investments should be accounted for in the same manner as goodwill arising from a business combination. One difference, however, is that goodwill arising from a business combination will be subject to annual impairment reviews, whereas goodwill implicit in equity investments will not. Equity method investments will continue to be tested for permanent declines in value.

Assume, for illustration purposes, that the equipment has a 10-year remaining life, the patent a 5-year life, and the goodwill an indefinite life. If the straight-line method is used with no salvage value, *the investor's cost* should be amortized initially as follows:[8]

| Account | Cost Assigned | Useful Life | Annual Amortization |
|---|---|---|---|
| Equipment | $18,000 | 10 years | $1,800 |
| Patent | 12,000 | 5 years | 2,400 |
| Goodwill | 35,000 | Indefinite | –0– |
| Annual expense (for five years until patent cost is completely amortized) | | | $4,200 |

In recording this annual expense, Big is reducing a portion of the investment balance in the same way it would amortize the cost of any other asset that had a limited life. Therefore, at the end of the first year, the investor records the following journal entry under the equity method:

| | | |
|---|---|---|
| Equity in Investee Income .................................... | 4,200 | |
|     Investment in Little Company .......................... | | 4,200 |
| To record amortization of excess payment allocated to equipment and patent. | | |

Because this amortization relates to investee assets, the investor does not establish a specific expense account. Instead, as shown in the previous entry, the expense is recognized through a decrease in the equity income accruing from the investee company.

To illustrate this entire process, assume that Tall Company purchases 20 percent of Short Company for $200,000. Tall can exercise significant influence over the investee; thus, the equity method is appropriately applied. The acquisition is made on January 1, 2004, when Short holds net assets with a book value of $700,000. Tall believes that the investee's building (10-year life) is undervalued within the financial records by $80,000 and equipment with a 5-year

---

[8] Unless otherwise stated, all amortization computations are based on the straight-line method with no salvage value.

life is undervalued by $120,000. Any goodwill established by this purchase is considered to have an indefinite life. During 2004, Short reports a net income of $150,000 and pays a cash dividend at year's end of $60,000.

Tall's three basic journal entries for 2004 pose little problem:

*January 1, 2004*

| | | |
|---|---|---|
| Investment in Short Company | 200,000 | |
|     Cash | | 200,000 |
| To record acquisition of 20 percent of the outstanding shares of Short Company. | | |

*December 31, 2004*

| | | |
|---|---|---|
| Investment in Short Company | 30,000 | |
|     Equity in Investee Income | | 30,000 |
| To accrue 20 percent of the 2004 reported earnings of investee ($150,000 × 20%). | | |
| Cash | 12,000 | |
|     Investment in Short Company | | 12,000 |
| To record receipt of 2004 cash dividend ($60,000 × 20%). | | |

An allocation must be made of Tall's $200,000 purchase price to determine whether an additional adjusting entry is necessary to recognize annual amortization associated with the extra payment:

| | | |
|---|---:|---:|
| Payment by investor | | $200,000 |
| Percentage of 1/1/04 book value ($700,000 × 20%) | | 140,000 |
| Payment in excess of book value | | 60,000 |
| Excess payment identified with specific assets: | | |
|     Building ($80,000 × 20%) | $16,000 | |
|     Equipment ($120,000 × 20%) | 24,000 | 40,000 |
| Excess payment not identified with specific assets—goodwill | | $ 20,000 |

As can be seen, $16,000 of the purchase price is assigned to a building, $24,000 to equipment, with the remaining $20,000 attributed to goodwill. For each asset with a definite useful life, periodic amortization is required.

| Asset | Attributed Cost | Useful Life | Annual Amortization |
|---|---|---|---|
| Building | $16,000 | 10 years | $1,600 |
| Equipment | 24,000 | 5 years | 4,800 |
| Goodwill | 20,000 | Indefinite | –0– |
| Total for 2004 | | | $6,400 |

At the end of 2004, Tall must also record the following adjustment in connection with these cost allocations:

| | | |
|---|---|---|
| Equity in Investee Income | 6,400 | |
|     Investment in Short Company | | 6,400 |
| To record 2004 amortization of extra cost of building ($1,600) and equipment ($4,800). | | |

Although these entries are shown separately here for better explanation, Tall would probably net the income accrual for the year ($30,000) and the amortization ($6,400) to create a single entry increasing the investment and recognizing equity income of $23,600. Thus, the first year return on Tall Company's beginning investment balance (defined as equity earnings/beginning investment balance) is equal to 11.80 percent ($23,600/$200,000).

## ELIMINATION OF UNREALIZED GAINS IN INVENTORY[9]

Many equity acquisitions establish ties between companies to facilitate the direct purchase and sale of inventory items. Such intercompany transactions can occur either on a regular basis or only sporadically. For example, The Coca-Cola Company recently disclosed that syrup and concentrate sales of $3.9 billion were made to its 38 percent-owned investee Coca-Cola Enterprises Inc.

Regardless of their frequency, inventory sales between investor and investee necessitate special accounting procedures to ensure proper timing of revenue recognition. An underlying principle of accounting is that "revenues are not recognized until earned . . . and revenues are considered to have been earned when the entity has substantially accomplished what it must do to be entitled to the benefits represented by the revenues."[10] In the sale of inventory to an unrelated party, recognition of revenue is normally not in question; substantial accomplishment is achieved when the exchange takes place unless special terms are included in the contract.

Unfortunately, the earning process is not so clearly delineated in sales made between related parties. *Because of the relationship between investor and investee, the seller of the goods is said to retain a partial stake in the inventory for as long as it is held by the buyer.* Thus, the earning process is not considered complete at the time of the original sale. For proper accounting, revenue recognition must be deferred until substantial accomplishment is proven. Consequently, when the investor applies the equity method, reporting of the related profit on intercompany transfers is delayed until the ultimate disposition of the goods by the buyer. When the inventory is eventually consumed within operations or resold to an unrelated party, the original sale is culminated and the gross profit is fully recognized.

In accounting, transactions between related companies are identified as either *downstream* or *upstream*. Downstream transfers refer to the sale of an item by the investor to the investee. Conversely, an upstream sale describes one made to the investor by the investee (see Exhibit 1–2). *Although this distinction is not significant for carrying out the procedures of the equity method, it has definite consequences in the consolidation of financial statements, as discussed in Chapter 5.* Therefore, these two types of intercompany sales are examined separately even at this introductory stage.

**EXHIBIT 1–2**

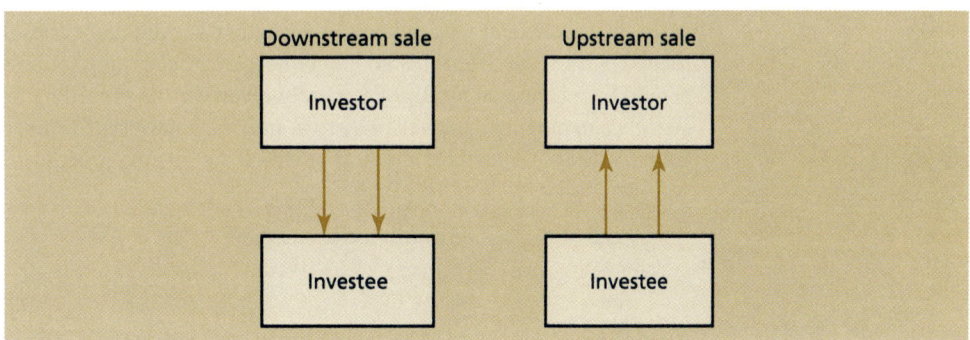

---

[9] Unrealized gains can involve the sale of items other than inventory. The intercompany transfer of depreciable fixed assets and land are discussed in a later chapter.

[10] FASB, *Statement of Financial Accounting Concepts No. 6*, "Recognition and Measurement in Financial Statements of Business Enterprises" (Stamford, Conn.: December 1984), para. 83.

### Downstream Sales of Inventory

Assume that Big Company owns a 40 percent share of Little Company and accounts for this investment through the equity method. In 2004, Big sells inventory to Little at a price of $50,000. This figure includes a markup of 30 percent, or $15,000. By the end of 2004, Little has sold $40,000 of these goods to outside parties while retaining $10,000 in inventory for sale during the subsequent year.

Downstream sales have been made by the investor to the investee. In applying the equity method, recognition of the related profit must be delayed until these goods are disposed of by the buyer. Although total intercompany transfers amounted to $50,000 in 2004, $40,000 of this merchandise has already been resold to outsiders, thereby justifying the normal reporting of profits. For the $10,000 still in the investee's inventory, the earning process is not finished. In computing equity income, this portion of the intercompany gain must be deferred until the goods are disposed of by Little.

The markup on the original sale was 30 percent of the transfer price; therefore, Big's profit associated with these remaining items is $3,000 ($10,000 × 30%). *However, because only 40 percent of the investee's stock is being held, just $1,200 ($3,000 × 40%) of this gain is unearned.* Big's ownership percentage reflects the intercompany portion of the gain. The total $3,000 gross profit within the ending inventory balance is not the amount deferred. Rather, 40 percent of that gain is viewed as the currently unrealized figure.

| Remaining Ending Inventory | Gross Profit Percentage | Gain in Ending Inventory | Investor Ownership Percentage | Unrealized Intercompany Gain |
|---|---|---|---|---|
| $10,000 | 30% | $3,000 | 40% | $1,200 |

After calculating the appropriate deferral, the investor decreases current equity income by $1,200 to reflect the unearned portion of the intercompany gain. This procedure temporarily removes this portion of the profit from the books of the investor in 2004 until the inventory is disposed of by the investee in 2005. Big accomplishes the actual deferral through the following year-end journal entry:

**Deferral of Unrealized Gain**
| | | |
|---|---|---|
| Equity in Investee Income | 1,200 | |
|     Investment in Little Company | | 1,200 |
| To defer unrealized gain on sale of inventory to Little Company. | | |

In the subsequent year, when this inventory is eventually consumed by Little or sold to unrelated parties, the deferral is no longer needed. The earning process is complete and the $1,200 should be recognized by Big. By merely reversing the preceding deferral entry, the accountant succeeds in moving the investor's profit into the appropriate time period. Recognition is shifted from the year of transfer to the year in which the earning process is substantially accomplished.

**Subsequent Realization of Intercompany Gain**
| | | |
|---|---|---|
| Investment in Little Company | 1,200 | |
|     Equity in Investee Income | | 1,200 |
| To recognize income on intercompany sale that has now been earned through sales to outsiders. | | |

### Upstream Sales of Inventory

Unlike consolidated financial statements (see Chapter 5), the equity method reports upstream sales of inventory in the same manner as downstream sales. Hence, unrealized gains remaining

# Discussion Question

**IS THIS REALLY ONLY SIGNIFICANT INFLUENCE?**

The Coca-Cola Company accounts for its ownership of Coca-Cola Enterprises (CCE) by use of the equity method as described in this chapter. In 2001, Coca-Cola held approximately 38 percent of the outstanding stock of CCE. According to the financial statements of CCE, the products of The Coca-Cola Company account for approximately 90 percent of total CCE revenues. Moreover, four directors of CCE are executive officers or former executive officers of The Coca-Cola Company. CCE conducts its business primarily under agreements with The Coca-Cola Company. These agreements give the Company the exclusive right to market, distribute, and produce beverage products of The Coca-Cola Company in authorized containers in specified territories. These agreements provide The Coca-Cola Company with the ability, in its sole discretion, to establish prices, terms of payment, and other terms and conditions for the purchase of concentrates and syrups from The Coca-Cola Company.

If Coca-Cola acquires approximately 12 percent more of CCE, a majority of the stock will be held so that consolidation becomes a requirement. However, given the size of the present ownership and the dependence that CCE has on Coca-Cola for products and marketing, does Coca-Cola truly have no more than "the ability to exercise significant influence over the operating and financial policies" of CCE? Does the equity method fairly represent the relationship that exists? Or does Coca-Cola actually control CCE despite the level of ownership, and should consolidation be required? Currently, the FASB is reexamining the boundary between the application of the equity method and consolidation. Should the rules be rewritten so that Coca-Cola must consolidate CCE rather than use the equity method? If so, at what level of ownership would the equity method no longer be appropriate?

---

in ending inventory are deferred until the items are used or sold to unrelated parties. To illustrate, assume that Big Company once again owns 40 percent of Little Company. During the current year, Little sells merchandise costing $40,000 to Big for $60,000. At the end of the fiscal period, Big still retains $15,000 of these goods. Little reports net income of $120,000 for the year.

To reflect the basic accrual of the investee's earnings, Big records the following journal entry at the end of this year:

**Income Accrual**
| | | |
|---|---|---|
| Investment in Little Company | 48,000 | |
|     Equity in Investee Income | | 48,000 |
| To accrue income from 40 percent owned investee ($120,000 × 40%). | | |

The amount of the gain remaining unrealized at year-end is computed using the markup of 33⅓ percent of the sales price ($20,000/$60,000):

| Remaining Ending Inventory | Gross Profit Percentage | Gain in Ending Inventory | Investor Ownership Percentage | Unrealized Intercompany Gain |
|---|---|---|---|---|
| $15,000 | 33⅓% | $5,000 | 40% | $2,000 |

Based on this calculation, a second entry is required of the investor at year-end. Once again, a deferral of the unrealized gain created by the intercompany transfer is necessary for proper timing of income recognition. *Under the equity method, the direction of the sale has no influence on either the amount or the method of reporting.*

| Deferral of Unrealized Gain | | |
|---|---|---|
| Equity in Investee Income . . . . . . . . . . . . . . . . . . . . . . . . . . . . . . . . . . . . . . . . . . | 2,000 | |
|     Investment in Little Company . . . . . . . . . . . . . . . . . . . . . . . . . . . . . . . . | | 2,000 |
| To defer recognition of intercompany unrealized gain until inventory is used or sold to unrelated parties. | | |

After the adjustment, Big, the investor, reports earnings from this equity investment of $46,000 ($48,000 − $2,000). The income accrual is reduced because a portion of the intercompany gross profit is considered unrealized. When the $15,000 in merchandise is eventually consumed or sold by the investor, the preceding journal entry is reversed. In this way, the effects of the gain are reported in the proper accounting period when the gain is earned by sales to an outside party.

In an upstream sale, the investor's own inventory account contains the unrealized gain. The previous entry, though, defers recognition of this profit by decreasing Big's investment account rather than the inventory balance. *APB Accounting Interpretation No. 1 of APB Opinion 18,* "Intercompany Profit Eliminations under Equity Method," November 1971, permits the direct reduction of the investor's inventory balance as a means of accounting for this unrealized gain. Although this alternative is acceptable, decreasing the investment remains the traditional approach for deferring unrealized gains, even for upstream sales.

Whether upstream or downstream, the investor's sales and purchases are still reported as if the transactions were carried out with outside parties. Only the unrealized gain is deferred and that amount is adjusted solely through the equity income account. Furthermore, since the companies are not consolidated, the investee's reported balances are not altered at all to reflect the nature of these sales/purchases. Obviously, readers of the financial statements need to be made aware of the inclusion of these amounts in the income statement. Thus, the FASB issued *Statement No. 57,* "Related Party Disclosures," in March 1982; it required reporting companies to disclose certain information about related-party transactions. These disclosures include the nature of the relationship, a description of the transactions, the dollar amounts of the transactions, and amounts due to or from any related parties at year-end.

## Decision Making and the Equity Method

It is important to realize that business decisions, including equity investments, typically involve the assessment of a wide range of consequences. For example, managers frequently are very interested in how the effects of their decisions are reported in financial statements. This attention to financial reporting effects of business decisions arises because measurements of financial performance often affect the following:

- The firm's ability to raise capital.
- Managerial compensation.
- The ability to meet debt covenants and future interest rates.
- Managers' reputations.

Managers are also keenly aware that measures of earnings per share can strongly affect investors' perceptions of the underlying value of their firms' publicly traded stock. Consequently, prior to making investment decisions, firms will study and assess the prospective effects of applying the equity method on the income reported in financial statements. Additionally, such analyses of prospective reported income effects can influence firms regarding the degree of influence they wish to have or even on the decision of whether to invest. For example, managers could have a required projected rate of return on an initial investment. In such cases, an analysis of projected income will be made to assist in setting an offer price.

For example, Investmor Co. is examining a potential 25 percent equity investment in Marco that will provide a significant level of influence. Marco projects an annual income of $300,000 for the near future. Marco's book value is $450,000 and has an unrecorded newly developed technology appraised at $200,000 with an estimated useful life of 10 years. In considering offer prices for the 25 percent investment in Marco, Investmor projects equity earnings as follows:

| | |
|---|---:|
| Projected income (25% × $300,000) | $75,000 |
| Excess patent amortization ([25% × 200,000]/10 years) | (5,000) |
| Annual expected equity in Marco earnings | 70,000 |

Investmor's required first year rate of return (before tax) on these types of investments is 20 percent. Therefore, to meet the first year rate of return requirement indicates a maximum price of $350,000 ($70,000/20% = $350,000). If the shares are publicly traded (leaving the firm a "price taker"), such income projections can assist in making a recommendation to wait for share prices to move to make the investment attractive.

## Criticisms of the Equity Method

In the past several decades since *APB Opinion 18*, thousands of business firms have accounted for their investments using the equity method. Recently, however, the equity method has come under criticism for the following:

- Emphasizing the 20–50 percent of voting stock in determining significant influence vs. control.
- Allowing off-balance sheet financing.
- Potentially biasing performance ratios.

The guidelines for the equity method suggest that a 20–50 percent ownership of voting shares indicates significant influence that falls short of control. But can one firm exert "control" over another firm absent a greater than 50 percent interest? Clearly, if one firm controls another, consolidation is the appropriate financial reporting technique. However, over the years, firms have learned ways to control other firms despite owning less than 50 percent of voting shares. For example, contracts across companies can limit one firm's ability to act without permission of the other. Such contractual control can be seen in debt arrangements, long-term sales and purchase agreements, and agreements concerning board membership. As a result, control is exerted through a variety of contractual arrangements. For financial reporting purposes, however, if ownership is 50 percent or less, a firm can argue that technically control does not exist.

In contrast to consolidated financial reports, when applying the equity method, the investee's assets and liabilities are not combined with the investor's amounts. Instead, the investor's balance sheet reports a single amount for the investment and the income statement reports a single amount for its equity in the earnings of the investee. If consolidated, the assets, liabilities, revenues, and expenses of the investee are combined and reported in the body of the investor's financial statements.

Thus, for those companies wishing to actively manage their reported balance sheet numbers, the equity method provides an effective means. By keeping its ownership of voting shares below 50 percent, a company can technically meet the rules for applying the equity method for its investments and at the same time report investee assets and liabilities "off balance sheet." As a result, relative to consolidation, a firm employing the equity method will report smaller values for assets and liabilities. Consequently, higher rates of return for its assets and sales, as well as lower debt-to-equity ratios could result. For example, *Accounting Horizons* recently discussed Coca-Cola's application of the equity method as follows:

> Even today, if Coca-Cola consolidates its equity method investments in which it owns more than 40 percent of the outstanding voting stock, Coke's total liabilities increase by almost 300 percent, substantially raising its debt-to-equity ratio from 1.24 to 4.79. Media reports indicate that the debt-rating agencies actually calculate Coke's ratios on a pro forma basis assuming consolidation.[11]

---

[11] Hartgraves, A., and G. Benston, "The Evolving Accounting Standards for Special Purpose Entities and Consolidations," *Accounting Horizons*, September 2002.

On the surface it appears that firms can avoid balance sheet disclosure of debts by maintaining investments at less that 50 percent ownership. However, *APB 18* requires "summarized information as to assets, liabilities, and results of operations of the investees to be presented in the notes or in separate statements, either individually or in groups, as appropriate." Therefore, supplementary information could be available under the equity method that would not be separately identified in consolidation. Nonetheless, some companies have contractual provisions (e.g., debt covenants, managerial compensation agreements) based on ratios in the main body of the financial statements. Meeting the provisions of such contracts could provide managers strong incentives to maintain technical eligibility to use the equity method rather than full consolidation.

## Summary

1. The equity method of accounting for an investment reflects the close relationship that could exist between an investor and an investee. More specifically, this approach is applied whenever the owner achieves the ability to apply significant influence to the investee's operating and financial decisions. Significant influence is presumed to exist at the 20 to 50 percent ownership level. However, the accountant must evaluate each situation, regardless of the percentage of ownership, to determine whether this ability is actually present.

2. To mirror the relationship between the companies, the equity method requires the investor to accrue income when earned by the investee. In recording this profit or loss, the investor separately reports items such as extraordinary gains and losses as well as prior period adjustments to highlight their nonrecurring nature. Dividend payments decrease the owners' equity of the investee company; therefore, the investor reduces the investment account when collected.

3. When acquiring capital stock, an investor often pays an amount that exceeds the underlying book value of the investee company. For accounting purposes, such excess payments must be identified with either specific assets and liabilities (such as land or buildings) or allocated to an intangible asset referred to as *goodwill*. Each assigned cost (except for any amount attributed to land or goodwill after 2001) is then amortized by the investor over the expected useful lives of the assets and liabilities. This amortization reduces the amount of equity income being reported.

4. If the entire investment or any portion is sold, the equity method is applied consistently until the date of disposal. A gain or loss is computed based on the adjusted book value at that time. Remaining shares are accounted for by means of either the equity method or the fair-value method, depending on the investor's subsequent ability to significantly influence the investee.

5. Inventory (or other assets) can be transferred between investor and investee. Because of the relationship between the two companies, the equity income accrual should be reduced to defer the intercompany portion of any markup included on these transfers until the items are either sold to outsiders or consumed. Thus, the amount of intercompany gain in ending inventory decreases the amount of equity income being recognized in the current period although this effect is subsequently reversed.

## Comprehensive Illustration

*(Estimated Time: 30 to 50 Minutes)* Every chapter in this textbook concludes with an illustration designed to assist students in tying together the essential elements of the material presented. After a careful reading of each chapter, attempt to work through the comprehensive problem. Then review the solution that follows the problem, noting the handling of each significant accounting issue.

## PROBLEM

### Part A

On January 1, 2003, Big Company pays $70,000 for a 10 percent interest in Little Company. On that date, Little has a book value of $600,000, although equipment, which has a five-year life, is undervalued by $100,000 on its books. Little Company's stock is closely held by a few investors and is traded only infrequently. Because fair values are not readily available on a continuing basis, the investment account is appropriately maintained at cost.

On January 1, 2004, Big acquires an additional 30 percent of Little Company for $264,000. This second purchase provides Big with the ability to exert significant influence over Little. At the time of this transaction, Little's equipment with a four-year life was undervalued by only $80,000.

During these two years, Little reported the following operational results:

| Year | Net Income | Cash Dividends Paid |
|------|------------|---------------------|
| 2003 | $210,000   | $110,000            |
| 2004 | 250,000    | 100,000             |

## Additional Information

- Cash dividends are always paid on July 1 of each year.
- Any goodwill is considered to have an indefinite life.

## Required:

a. What income did Big originally report for 2003 in connection with this investment?

b. On comparative financial statements for 2003 and 2004, what figures should Big report in connection with this investment?

## Part B (This problem is a continuation of Part A)

In 2005, Little Company reports $400,000 in income from continuing operations plus a $60,000 extraordinary gain. The company pays a $120,000 cash dividend. During this fiscal year, Big sells inventory costing $80,000 to Little for $100,000. Little continues to hold 30 percent of this merchandise at the end of 2005. Big maintains 40 percent ownership of Little throughout the period.

## Required:

Prepare all necessary journal entries for Big for the year of 2005.

# SOLUTION

## Part A

a. Big Company accounts for its investment in Little Company at cost during 2003. Since only 10 percent of the outstanding shares were held, significant influence was apparently not present. Because the stock is not actively traded, fair values are not available and the investment remains at cost. Therefore, only the $11,000 ($110,000 × 10%) received as dividends is recorded by the investor as income in the original financial reporting for that year.

b. To make comparative reports consistent, a change to the equity method is recorded retroactively. Therefore, when the ability to exert significant influence over the operations of Little is established on January 1, 2004, both Big's 2003 and 2004 financial statements must reflect the equity method.

Big first evaluates the initial purchase of Little's stock to determine whether either goodwill or incremental asset values need be reflected within the equity method procedures.

### Purchase of 10 Percent of Voting Stock on January 1, 2003

| | |
|---|---:|
| Payment by investor | $70,000 |
| Percentage of book value acquired ($600,000 × 10%) | 60,000 |
| Payment in excess of book value | 10,000 |
| Excess payment identified with specific assets: | |
|     Equipment ($100,000 × 10%) | 10,000 |
| Excess payment not identified with specific assets—goodwill | –0– |

As shown here, the $10,000 excess payment was made in recognition of the undervaluation of Little's equipment. This asset had a useful life at that time of five years; thus, the investor records amortization expense of $2,000 each year.

A similar calculation must be carried out for Big's second stock purchase:

### Purchase of 30 Percent of Voting Stock on January 1, 2004

| | |
|---|---:|
| Payment by investor | $264,000 |
| Percentage of book value* acquired ($700,000 × 30%) | 210,000 |
| Payment in excess of book value | 54,000 |
| Excess payment identified with specific assets: | |
|    Equipment ($80,000 × 30%) | 24,000 |
| Excess payment not identified with specific assets—goodwill | $ 30,000 |

*Little's book value on January 1, 2004, is computed by adding the 2003 net income of $210,000 less dividends paid of $110,000 to the previous book value of $600,000.

In this second acquisition, $24,000 of the payment is attributable to the undervalued equipment with $30,000 assigned to goodwill. Since the equipment now has only a four-year remaining life, annual amortization of $6,000 is appropriate ($24,000/4).

After the additional shares are acquired on January 1, 2004, Big's financial records for 2003 must be retroactively restated as if the equity method had been applied from the date of the initial investment.

### Financial Reporting—2003

| | |
|---|---:|
| Equity in Investee Income (income statement) | |
|   Income reported by Little | $210,000 |
|   Big's ownership | 10% |
|     Accrual for 2003 | $ 21,000 |
|   Less: Equipment amortization (first purchase) | (2,000) |
| Equity in investee income—2003 | $ 19,000 |
| | |
| Investment in Little (Balance Sheet) | |
|   Cost of first acquisition | $ 70,000 |
|   2003 Equity in investee income (above) | 19,000 |
|   Less: Dividends received ($110,000 × 10%) | (11,000) |
| Investment in Little—12/31/03 | $ 78,000 |

### Financial Reporting—2004

| | |
|---|---:|
| Equity in Investee Income (income statement) | |
|   Income reported by Little | $250,000 |
|   Big's ownership | 40% |
|     Big's share of Little's reported income | $100,000 |
| Less amortization expense: | |
|   Equipment (first purchase) | (2,000) |
|   Equipment (second purchase) | (6,000) |
| Equity in investee income—2004 | $ 92,000 |
| | |
| Investment in Little (balance sheet) | |
|   Book value—12/31/03 (above) | $ 78,000 |
|   Cost of 2004 acquisition | 264,000 |
|   Equity in investee income (above) | 92,000 |
|   Less: Dividends received ($100,000 × 40%) | (40,000) |
| Investment in Little—12/31/04 | $394,000 |

## Part B

On July 1, 2005, Big receives a $48,000 cash dividend from Little (40% × $120,000). According to the equity method, receipt of this dividend reduces the carrying value of the investment account:

| | | |
|---|---:|---:|
| Cash | 48,000 | |
|     Investment in Little Company | | 48,000 |
| To record receipt of 2005 dividend from investee. | | |

Big records no other journal entries in connection with this investment until the end of 2005. At that time, the annual accrual of income is made as well as the adjustment to record amortization (see Part A for computation of expense). The investee's continuing income is reported separately from the extraordinary item.

| | | |
|---|---:|---:|
| Investment in Little Company | 184,000 | |
|     Equity in Investee Income | | 160,000 |
|     Extraordinary Gain of Investee | | 24,000 |
| To recognize reported income of investee based on a 40 percent ownership level of $400,000 operating income and $60,000 extraordinary gain. | | |
| Equity in Investee Income | 8,000 | |
|     Investment in Little Company | | 8,000 |
| To record annual amortization on excess payment made in relation to equipment ($2,000 from first purchase and $6,000 from second). | | |

Big needs to make only one other equity entry during 2005. Intercompany sales have occurred and a portion of the inventory continues to be held by Little. Therefore, an unrealized gain exists that must be deferred. The markup on the sales price was 20 percent ($20,000/$100,000). Since $30,000 of this merchandise is still in the possession of the investee, the related gain is $6,000 ($30,000 × 20%). However, Big owns only 40 percent of the outstanding stock of Little; thus, the unrealized intercompany gain at year's end is $2,400 ($6,000 × 40%). That amount must be deferred until the inventory is consumed by Little or sold to unrelated parties in subsequent years.

| | | |
|---|---:|---:|
| Equity in Investee Company | 2,400 | |
|     Investment in Little Company | | 2,400 |
| To defer unrealized gain on intercompany sale. | | |

## Questions

1. A company acquires a rather large investment in another corporation. What criteria determine whether the equity method of accounting should be applied by the investor to this investment?
2. What indicates an investor's ability to significantly influence the decision-making process of an investee?
3. Why does the equity method record dividends received from an investee as a reduction in the investment account, not as dividend income?
4. Jones Company possesses a 25 percent interest in the outstanding voting shares of Sandridge Company. Under what circumstances might Jones decide that the equity method would not be appropriate to account for this investment?
5. Smith, Inc., has maintained an ownership interest in Watts Corporation for a number of years. This investment has been accounted for by means of the equity method. What transactions or events create changes in the Investment in Watts Corporation account being recorded by Smith?
6. Although the equity method is a generally accepted accounting principle (GAAP), recognition of equity income has been criticized. What theoretical problems can be brought up by opponents of the equity method? What managerial incentives exist that could influence a firm's percentage ownership interest in another firm?

7. Because of the acquisition of additional investee shares, an investor can be forced to change from the fair-value method to the equity method. Which procedures are applied to effect this accounting change?

8. Riggins Company accounts for its investment in Bostic Company by means of the equity method. During the past fiscal year, Bostic reported an extraordinary gain on its income statement. How would this extraordinary item affect the financial records of the investor?

9. During the current year, the common stock of the Davis Company suffers a permanent drop in market value. In the past, Davis has made a significant portion of its sales to one customer. This buyer recently announced its decision to make no further purchases from the Davis Company, an action that led to the loss of market value. Hawkins, Inc., owns 35 percent of the outstanding shares of Davis, an investment that is recorded according to the equity method. How would the loss in value affect the financial reporting of this investor?

10. Wilson Company acquired 40 percent of Andrews Company at a bargain price because of losses expected to result from Andrews' failure in marketing several new products. The price paid by Wilson was only $100,000, although Andrews' corresponding book value was much higher. In the first year after acquisition, Andrews lost $300,000. In applying the equity method, how should Wilson account for this loss?

11. In a stock acquisition accounted for by the equity method, a portion of the purchase price often is attributed to goodwill or to specific assets or liabilities. How are these amounts determined at the time of acquisition? How are these amounts accounted for in subsequent periods?

12. Princeton Company holds a 40 percent interest in the outstanding voting stock of Yale Company. On June 19 of the current year, Princeton sells part of this investment. What accounting should Princeton make on June 19? What accounting will Princeton make for the remainder of the current year?

13. What is the difference between downstream and upstream sales? How does this difference impact application of the equity method?

14. How is the unrealized gain on intercompany sales calculated? What effect does an unrealized gain have on the recording of an investment if the equity method is applied?

15. How are intercompany transfers reported in the separate financial statements of an investee if the investor is using the equity method?

## Problems

1. When an investor uses the equity method to account for investments in common stock, cash dividends received by the investor from the investee should be recorded as
   a. A deduction from the investor's share of the investee's profits.
   b. Dividend income.
   c. A deduction from the stockholders' equity account, dividends to stockholders.
   d. A deduction from the investment account.
   (AICPA adapted)

2. Which of the following is not an indication that an investor company has the ability to significantly influence an investee?
   a. Material intercompany transactions.
   b. The company owns 30 percent of the company but another owner holds the remaining 70 percent.
   c. Interchange of personnel.
   d. Technological dependency.

3. Sisk Company has owned 10 percent of Maust, Inc., for the past several years. This ownership did not allow Sisk to have significant influence over Maust. Recently, Sisk acquires an additional 30 percent of Maust and now has this ability. How will this change be reported by the investor?
   a. A cumulative effect of an accounting change is shown in the current income statement.
   b. No change is recorded; the equity method is used from the date of the new acquisition.
   c. A retroactive adjustment is made to restate all prior years to the equity method.
   d. Sisk has the option of choosing the method to be used to show this change.

4. On January 1, Puckett Company paid $1.6 million for 50,000 shares of Harrison's voting common stock, which represents a 40 percent investment. No allocation to goodwill or other specific account was made. Significant influence over Harrison is achieved by this acquisition. Harrison distributed a dividend of $2 per share during the year and reported net income of $560,000. What is the balance in the Investment in Harrison account found in the financial records of Puckett as of December 31?

a. $1,724,000.
b. $1,784,000.
c. $1,844,000.
d. $1,884,000.

5. In January 2004, Wilkinson, Inc., acquired 20 percent of the outstanding common stock of Bremm, Inc., for $700,000. This investment gave Wilkinson the ability to exercise significant influence over Bremm. Bremm's assets on that date were recorded at $3,900,000 with liabilities of $900,000. Any excess of cost over book value of the investment was attributed to a patent having a remaining useful life of 10 years.

    In 2004, Bremm reported net income of $170,000. In 2005, Bremm reported net income of $210,000. Dividends of $70,000 were paid in each of these two years. What is the reported balance of Wilkinson's Investment in Bremm at December 31, 2005?

    a. $728,000.
    b. $748,000.
    c. $756,000.
    d. $776,000.

6. Ace purchases 40 percent of Baskett Company on January 1 for $500,000. Although not used, this acquisition gave Ace the ability to apply significant influence to the operating and financing policies of Baskett. Baskett reports assets on that date of $1,400,000 with liabilities of $500,000. One building with a seven-year life is undervalued on Baskett's books by $140,000. Also, Baskett's book value for equipment (10-year life) is undervalued by $210,000. During the year, Baskett reports net income of $90,000 while paying dividends of $30,000. What is the Investment in Baskett balance in Ace's financial records as of December 31?

    a. $504,000.
    b. $507,600.
    c. $513,900.
    d. $516,000.

7. Goldman Company reports net income of $140,000 each year and pays an annual cash dividend of $50,000. The company holds net assets of $1,200,000 on January 1, 2003. On that date, Wallace purchases 40 percent of the outstanding stock for $600,000, which gives Wallace the ability to significantly influence Goldman. At the purchase date, the excess of Wallace's cost over its proportionate share of Goldman's book value was assigned to goodwill. On December 31, 2005, what is the Investment in Goldman balance in Wallace's financial records?

    a. $600,000.
    b. $660,000.
    c. $690,000.
    d. $708,000.

8. Perez, Inc., owns 25 percent of Senior, Inc. During 2004, Perez sold goods with a 40 percent gross profit to Senior. Senior sold all of these goods in 2004. How should Perez report the effect of the intercompany sale on its 2004 income statement?

    a. Sales and cost of goods sold should be reduced by the intercompany sales.
    b. Sales and cost of goods sold should be reduced by 25 percent of the intercompany sales.
    c. Investment income should be reduced by 25 percent of the gross profit on intercompany sales.
    d. No adjustment is necessary.

9. Panner, Inc., owns 30 percent of Watkins and applies the equity method. During the current year, Panner buys inventory costing $54,000 and then sells it to Watkins for $90,000. At the end of the year, only $20,000 of merchandise is still being held by Watkins. What amount of unrealized gain must be deferred by Panner in reporting this investment on the equity method?

    a. $2,400.
    b. $4,800.
    c. $8,000.
    d. $10,800.

10. Alex, Inc., buys 40 percent of Steinbart Company on January 1, 2004, for $530,000. The equity method of accounting is to be used. The net assets of Steinbart on that date were $1.2 million. Any excess of cost over book value is attributable to a trade name with a 20-year remaining life. Steinbart immediately begins supplying inventory to Alex as follows:

| Year | Cost to Steinbart | Transfer Price | Amount Held by Alex at Year-End (at Transfer Price) |
|------|-------------------|----------------|-----------------------------------------------------|
| 2004 | $70,000 | $100,000 | $25,000 |
| 2005 | 96,000 | 150,000 | 45,000 |

Inventory held at the end of one year by Alex is sold at the beginning of the next.

Steinbart reports net income of $80,000 in 2004 and $110,000 in 2005 while paying $30,000 in dividends each year. What is the equity income in Steinbart to be reported by Alex in 2005?

a. $34,050.
b. $38,020.
c. $46,230.
d. $51,450.

11. On January 3, 2004, Haskins Corporation acquired 40 percent of the outstanding common stock of Clem Company for $990,000. This acquisition gave Haskins the ability to exercise significant influence over the investee. The book value of the acquired shares was $790,000. Any excess cost over the underlying book value was assigned to a patent that was undervalued on Clem's balance sheet. This patent has a remaining useful life of 10 years. For the year ended December 31, 2004, Clem reported net income of $260,000 and paid cash dividends of $80,000. At December 31, 2004, what should Haskins report as its investment in Clem?

12. On January 1, 2004, Alison, Inc., paid $60,000 for a 40 percent interest in Holister Corporation. This investee had assets with a book value of $200,000 and liabilities of $75,000. A patent held by Holister having a $5,000 book value was actually worth $20,000. This patent had a six-year remaining life. Any further excess cost associated with this acquisition was attributed to goodwill. During 2004, Holister earned income of $30,000 and paid dividends of $10,000. In 2005, income was $50,000 and dividends $15,000.

Assuming that Alison has the ability to significantly influence the operations of Holister, what balance should appear in the Investment in Holister account as of December 31, 2005?

13. On January 1, 2004, Ruark Corporation acquired a 40 percent interest in Batson, Inc., for $210,000. On that date, Batson's balance sheet disclosed net assets of $360,000. During 2004, Batson reported net income of $80,000 and paid cash dividends of $25,000. Ruark sold inventory costing $30,000 to Batson during 2004 for $40,000. Batson used all of this merchandise in its operations during 2004. Make all of Ruark's journal entries for 2004 to apply the equity method to this investment.

14. Waters, Inc., acquires 10 percent of Denton Corporation on January 1, 2004, for $210,000 although the book value of Denton on that date was $1,700,000. Denton held land that was undervalued on its accounting records by $100,000. During 2004, Denton earned a net income of $240,000 while paying cash dividends of $90,000. On January 1, 2005, Waters purchased an additional 30 percent of Denton for $600,000. Denton's land is still undervalued on that date but now by $120,000. Any additional excess cost was attributable to a trademark with a 10-year life for the first purchase and a 9-year life for the second. The initial 10 percent investment had been maintained at cost because fair values were not readily available. The equity method will now be applied. During 2005, Denton reported income of $300,000 and distributed dividends of $110,000. Prepare all of the 2005 journal entries for Waters.

15. Tiberand Inc. sold $150,000 in inventory to Schilling Company during 2004 for $225,000. Schilling resold $105,000 of this merchandise in 2004 with the remainder to be disposed of during 2005. Assuming Tiberand owns 25 percent of Schilling and applies the equity method, what journal entry is recorded at the end of 2005 to defer the unrealized gain?

16. Hager holds 30 percent of the outstanding shares of Jenkins and appropriately applies the equity method of accounting. Excess cost amortization (related to a patent) associated with this investment amounts to $9,000 per year. For 2004, Jenkins reports earnings of $80,000 and pays cash dividends of $30,000. During that year, Jenkins acquired inventory for $50,000, which was then sold to Hager for $80,000. At the end of 2004, Hager continues to hold merchandise with a transfer price of $40,000.

a. What Equity in Investee Income should Hager report for 2004?
b. How will the intercompany transfer affect Hager's reporting in 2005?
c. If the inventory had been sold by Hager to Jenkins, how would the above answers have changed?

17. On January 1, 2003, Monroe, Inc., purchased 10,000 shares of Brown Company for $250,000, giving Monroe 10 percent ownership of Brown. On January 1, 2004, Monroe purchased an additional 20,000 shares (20 percent) for $590,000. This latest purchase gave Monroe the ability to apply significant influence over Brown. Assume that no goodwill is involved in either acquisition and the original 10 percent investment was categorized as an available-for-sale security.

    Brown reports net income and dividends as follows. These amounts are assumed to have occurred evenly throughout these years.

    |      | Net Income | Cash Dividends (paid quarterly) |
    |------|-----------|-------------------------------|
    | 2003 | $350,000  | $100,000                      |
    | 2004 | 480,000   | 110,000                       |
    | 2005 | 500,000   | 120,000                       |

    On July 1, 2005, Monroe sells 2,000 shares of this investment for $46 per share, thus reducing its interest from 30 to 28 percent. However, the company retains the ability to significantly influence Brown. What amounts appear in Monroe's 2005 income statement?

18. Collins, Inc., purchases 10 percent of Merton Corporation on January 1, 2004, for $345,000 and classified the investment as an available-for-sale security. Collins acquires an additional 15 percent of Merton on January 1, 2005, for $580,000. The equity method of accounting has now become appropriate for this investment. No intercompany sales have occurred.

    a. How does Collins initially determine the income to be reported in 2004 in connection with its ownership of Merton?
    b. What factors should have influenced Collins in its decision to apply the equity method in 2005?
    c. What factors could have prevented Collins from adopting the equity method after this second purchase?
    d. What is the objective of the equity method of accounting?
    e. What criticisms have been leveled at the equity method?
    f. In comparative statements for 2004 and 2005, how would Collins determine the income to be reported in 2004 in connection with its ownership of Merton? Why is this accounting appropriate?
    g. How is the allocation of Collins' acquisition payments made?
    h. If Merton pays a cash dividend, what impact does it have on the financial records of Collins under the equity method? Why is this accounting appropriate?
    i. On financial statements for 2005, what amounts are included in Collins' Investment in Merton account? What amounts are included in Collins' Equity in Income of Merton account?

19. Parrot Corporation holds a 42 percent ownership of Sunrise, Inc. The equity method is being applied. No goodwill or other allocation occurred in the purchase of this investment. During 2004, intercompany inventory transfers were made between the two companies. A portion of this merchandise was not resold until 2005. During 2005, additional transfers were made.

    a. What is the difference in upstream transfers and downstream transfers?
    b. How does the direction of an intercompany transfer (upstream versus downstream) affect the application of the equity method?
    c. How is the intercompany unrealized gain computed in applying the equity method?
    d. How should Parrot compute the amount of equity income to be recognized in 2004? What entry is made to record this income?
    e. How should Parrot compute the amount of equity income to be recognized in 2005?
    f. If none of the transferred inventory had remained at the end of 2004, how would application of the equity method have been affected by these transfers?
    g. How do these intercompany transfers affect the financial reporting of Sunrise?

20. Several years ago, Einstein, Inc., bought 40 percent of the outstanding voting stock of Brooks Company. The equity method is appropriately applied. On August 1 of the current year, Einstein sold a portion of these shares.

    a. How does Einstein compute the book value of this investment on August 1 to determine its gain or loss on the sale?
    b. How should Einstein account for this investment after August 1?

c. If Einstein retains only a 2 percent interest in Brooks so that virtually no influence is held, what figures appear in the investor's income statement for the current year?

d. If Einstein retains only a 2 percent interest in Brooks so that virtually no influence is held, does the investor have to retroactively adjust any previously reported figures?

21. Russell owns 30 percent of the outstanding stock of Thacker and has the ability to significantly influence the investee's operations and decision making. On January 1, 2004, the balance in the Investment in Thacker account is $335,000. Amortization associated with this acquisition is $9,000 per year. In 2004, Thacker earns an income of $90,000 and pays cash dividends of $30,000. Previously, in 2003, Thacker had sold inventory costing $24,000 to Russell for $40,000. All but 25 percent of this merchandise was consumed by Russell during 2003. The remainder was used during the first few weeks of 2004. Additional sales were made to Russell in 2004; inventory costing $28,000 was transferred at a price of $50,000. Of this total, 40 percent was not consumed until 2005.

    a. What amount of income would Russell recognize in 2004 from its ownership interest in Thacker?
    b. What is the balance in the Investment in Thacker account at the end of 2004?

22. On January 1, 2004, Ace acquires 15 percent of Zach's outstanding common stock for $52,000 and classifies the investment as an available-for-sale security. On January 1, 2005, Ace buys an additional 10 percent of Zach for $43,800. This second purchase gives Ace the ability to influence Zach's decision making significantly.

    During 2004 and 2005, Zach reports the following:

    |      | Income    | Dividends | Market Value |
    |------|-----------|-----------|--------------|
    | 2004 | $ 80,000  | $30,000   | $ 60,000     |
    | 2005 | 100,000   | 40,000    | 117,000      |

    In each purchase, Ace attributes any excess of cost over book value to Zach's franchise agreements that had a remaining life of 10 years at January 1, 2004. As of December 31, 2005, Zach reports a net book value of $390,000.

    a. On Ace's December 31, 2005, balance sheet, what amount is reported for the Investment in Zach account?
    b. What amount of equity income should Ace report for 2005?
    c. Prepare the January 1, 2005, journal entries to retroactively adjust the Investment in Zach account to the equity method.

23. Anderson acquires 10 percent of the outstanding voting shares of Barringer on January 1, 2003, for $92,000 and categorizes the investment as an available-for-sale security. An additional 20 percent of the stock is purchased on January 1, 2004, for $210,000, which gives Anderson the ability to significantly influence Barringer. Barringer has a book value of $800,000 at January 1, 2003, and records net income of $180,000 for the following year. Dividends of $80,000 were paid by Barringer during 2003. The book values of Barringer's asset and liability accounts are considered as equal to fair market values except for a copyright whose value accounted for Anderson's excess cost in each purchase. The copyright had a remaining life of 16 years at January 1, 2003.

    Barringer reports $210,000 of net income during 2004 and $230,000 in 2005. Dividends of $100,000 are paid in each of these years.

    a. On comparative income statements issued in 2005 by Anderson for 2003 and 2004, what amounts of income would be reported in connection with the company's investment in Barringer?
    b. If Anderson sells its entire investment in Barringer on January 1, 2006, for $400,000 cash, what is the impact on Anderson's income?
    c. Assume that Anderson sells inventory to Barringer during 2004 and 2005 as follows:

    | Year | Cost to Anderson | Price to Barringer | Year-End Balance (at Transfer Price) |
    |------|------------------|--------------------|--------------------------------------|
    | 2004 | $35,000          | $50,000            | $20,000 (sold in following year)     |
    |      | 33,000           | 60,000             | 40,000 (sold in following year)      |

    What amount of equity income should be recognized by Anderson for the year 2005?

24. Smith purchases 5 percent of Barker's outstanding stock on October 1, 2003, for $7,475. An additional 10 percent of Barker is acquired for $14,900 on July 1, 2004. Both of these purchases were accounted for as available-for-sale investments. A final 20 percent is purchased on December 31, 2005, for $34,200. With this final acquisition, Smith achieves the ability to significantly influence the decision-making process of Barker.

    Barker has a book value of $100,000 as of January 1, 2003. Information follows concerning the operations of this company for the 2003–05 period. Assume all income was earned uniformly in each year. Assume one-fourth of the total annual dividends are paid at the end of each calendar quarter.

    | Year | Reported Income | Dividends |
    |------|-----------------|-----------|
    | 2003 | $20,000 | $ 8,000 |
    | 2004 | 30,000 | 16,000 |
    | 2005 | 24,000 | 9,000 |

    On Barker's financial records, the book values of all assets and liabilities are the same as their fair market values. Any excess cost from either purchase relates to identifiable intangible assets. For each purchase, the excess cost is amortized over 15 years. Amortization for a portion of a year should be based on months.

    a. On comparative income statements issued in 2006 for the years of 2003, 2004, and 2005, what would Smith report as its income derived from this investment in Barker?
    b. On a balance sheet as of December 31, 2005, what should Smith report as investment in Barker?

25. Hobson acquires 40 percent of the outstanding voting stock of Stokes Company on January 1, 2004, for $210,000 in cash. The book value of Stokes's net assets on that date was $400,000, although one of the company's buildings, with a $60,000 carrying value, was actually worth $100,000. This building had a 10-year remaining life. A royalty agreement owned by Stokes with a 20-year remaining life was undervalued by $85,000.

    Stokes sells inventory to Hobson during 2004 with an original cost of $60,000. This merchandise was sold to Hobson at a price of $90,000. Hobson still holds $15,000 (transfer price) of this amount in inventory as of December 31, 2004. These goods are to be sold to outside parties during 2005.

    Stokes reports a loss of $60,000 for 2004, $40,000 from continuing operations, and $20,000 from an extraordinary loss. The company still manages to pay a $10,000 cash dividend during the year.

    During 2005, Stokes reports a $40,000 net income and distributes a cash dividend of $12,000. Additional inventory sales of $80,000 are made to Hobson during the period. The original cost of the merchandise was $50,000. All but 30 percent of this inventory has been resold to outside parties by the end of the 2005 fiscal year.

    Prepare all journal entries for Hobson for 2004 and 2005 in connection with this investment. Assume that the equity method is applied.

26. Penston Company owns 40 percent (40,000 shares) of Scranton, Inc., which was purchased several years ago for $182,000. Since the date of acquisition, the equity method has been properly applied, and the book value of the investment account as of January 1, 2004, is $248,000. Excess patent cost amortization of $12,000 is still being recognized each year. During 2004, Scranton reports net income of $200,000, $320,000 in operating income earned evenly throughout the year, and a $120,000 extraordinary loss incurred on October 1. No dividends were paid during the year. Penston sells 8,000 shares of Scranton on August 1, 2004, for $94,000 in cash. However, Penston does retain the ability to significantly influence the investee.

    During the last quarter of 2003, Penston sold $50,000 in inventory (which had originally cost Penston only $30,000) to Scranton. At the end of that fiscal year, Scranton's inventory retained $9,000 (at sales price) of this merchandise, which was subsequently sold in the first quarter of 2004.

    On Penston's financial statements for the year ended December 31, 2004, what income effects would be reported from its ownership in Scranton?

27. On July 1, 2003, Abernethy Company acquires 65,000 of the outstanding shares of the Chapman Company for $13 per share. This acquisition gave Abernethy a 25 percent ownership of Chapman and allowed Abernethy to significantly influence the decisions of the investee.

    As of July 1, 2003, the investee had assets with a book value of $2 million and liabilities of $400,000. At the time, Chapman held equipment appraised at $120,000 above book value. Company land was valued at $160,000 above book value. The equipment was considered to have an eight-year life with no salvage value. Remaining excess cost is attributable to a copyright with a 15-year remaining life. Depreciation and amortization are computed using the straight-line method.

Chapman follows a policy of paying 50 cents per share as a cash dividend every April 1 and October 1. Chapman's income, earned evenly throughout each year, was 2003—$280,000; 2004—$360,000; and 2005—$380,000.

In addition, Abernethy sold inventory costing $90,000 to Chapman for $150,000 during 2004. Chapman resold $90,000 of this inventory during 2004 and the remaining $60,000 during 2005.

    *a.* Prepare a schedule computing the equity income to be recognized by Abernethy during each of these years.

    *b.* Compute Abernethy's investment balance as of December 31, 2005.

28. On January 1, 2003, Plano Company acquired 8 percent (16,000 shares) of the outstanding voting shares of the Sumter Company for $192,000, an amount equal to the underlying book and fair value of Sumter. Sumter pays a cash dividend to its stockholders each year of $100,000 on September 15. Sumter reports net income of $300,000 in 2003, $360,000 in 2004, $400,000 in 2005, and $380,000 in 2006. Each income figure can be assumed to have been earned evenly throughout its respective year. In addition, the market value of these 16,000 shares was indeterminate and therefore the investment account remained at cost.

    On January 1, 2005, Plano purchased an additional 32 percent (64,000 shares) of Sumter for $965,750 in cash. This price represented a $50,550 payment in excess of the book value of Sumter's underlying net assets. Plano was willing to make this extra payment because of a recently developed patent held by Sumter with a 15-year remaining life. All other assets were considered appropriately valued on Sumter's books.

    On July 1, 2006, Plano sold 10 percent (20,000 shares) of the outstanding shares of Sumter for $425,000 in cash. Although this interest was sold, Plano maintained the ability to significantly influence the decision-making process of Sumter. Assume that a weighted average costing system is used by Plano.

    Prepare the journal entries for Plano for the years of 2003 through 2006.

29. On January 1, 2004, Lake Company acquired 40 percent of the outstanding voting shares of Slide Company for $600,000. On that date, Slide reports assets and liabilities with book values of $1.8 million and $600,000, respectively. A building owned by Slide had an appraised value of $250,000, although it had a book value of only $100,000. This building had a 12-year remaining life and no salvage value. It was being depreciated on the straight-line method.

    Slide generated net income of $250,000 in 2004 and a loss of $100,000 in 2005. In each of these two years, Slide paid a cash dividend of $60,000 to its stockholders.

    During 2004, Slide sold inventory to Lake that had an original cost of $50,000. The merchandise was sold to Lake for $80,000. Of this balance, $60,000 was resold to outsiders during 2004 and the remainder was sold during 2005. In 2005, Slide sold inventory to Lake for $150,000. This inventory had cost only $90,000. Lake resold $100,000 of the inventory during 2005 and the rest during 2006.

    For 2004 and then for 2005, compute the equity income to be reported by Lake for external reporting purposes.

# Develop Your Skills

## EXCEL CASE 1

On January 1, 2004, Acme Co. is considering purchasing a 40 percent ownership interest in PHC Co., a privately held enterprise, for $700,000. PHC predicts its profit will be $185,000 in 2004, projects a 10 percent annual increase in profits in each of the next four years, and expects to pay a steady annual dividend of $30,000 for the foreseeable future. Because PHC has a patent on its books that is undervalued by $375,000, Acme realizes that it will have an additional amortization expense of $15,000 per year over the next 10 years—the patent's estimated useful life. All of PHC's other assets and liabilities have book values that approximate market values.

### Required:

1. Using an Excel spreadsheet, set the following values in cells:

- Acme's cost of investment in PHC.
- Percentage acquired.
- First year PHC reported income.
- Projected growth rate in income.
- PHC annual dividends.
- Annual excess patent amortization.

2. Referring to the values in (1), prepare the following schedules using columns for the years 2004 thru 2008.
    - Acme's equity in PHC earnings with rows showing these:
        - Acme's share of PHC reported income.
        - Amortization expense.
        - Acme's Equity in PHC Earnings.
    - Acme's Investment in PHC balance with rows showing the following:
        - Beginning balance.
        - Equity earnings.
        - Dividends.
        - Ending balance.
    - Return on beginning investment balance = Equity earnings/Beginning investment balance in each year

3. Given the preceding values, compute the average of the projected returns on beginning investment balances for the first five years of Acme's investment in PHC. What is the maximum Acme can pay for PHC if it wishes to earn at least a 10 percent average return on beginning investment balance? (*Hint:* Under Excel's Tools heading, use the Solver or Goal Seek capability to produce a 10 percent average return on beginning investment balance by changing the cell that contains Acme's cost of investment in PHC. Excel's Solver should produce an exact answer while Goal Seek should produce a close approximation. You may need to first add-in the Solver capability under Excel's Tools heading.)

# EXCEL CASE 2

On January 1, Intergen, Inc., invests $200,000 for a 40 percent interest in Ryan, a new joint venture with two other partners each investing $150,000 for 30 percent interests. Intergen plans to sell all of its production to Ryan, which will resell the inventory to retail outlets. The equity partners agree that Ryan will buy inventory only from Intergen.

During the year, Intergen expects to incur costs of $850,000 to produce goods with a final retail market value of $1,200,000. Ryan projects that, during this year, it will resell three-fourths of these goods for $900,000. It should sell the remainder in the following year.

The equity partners plan a meeting to set the price Intergen will charge Ryan for its production. One partner suggests a transfer price of $1,025,000 but is unsure whether it will result in an equitable return across the equity holders. Importantly, Intergen agrees that its total rate of return (including its own operations and its investment in Ryan) should be equal to that of the other investors' return on their investments in Ryan. All agree that Intergen's value including its investment in Ryan is $1,000,000.

### Required:

1. Create an Excel spreadsheet analysis showing the following:
    - Projected income statements for Intergen and Ryan. Formulate the statements to do the following:
        - Link Ryan's cost of goods sold to Intergen's sales (use a starting value of $1,025,000 for Intergen's sales).
        - Link Intergen's equity in Ryan's earnings to Ryan's net income (adjusted for Intergen's gross profit rate × Ryan's ending inventory × 40 percent ownership percentage).
        - Be able to change Intergen's sales and see the effects throughout the income statements of Ryan and Intergen. Note the Cost of Goods Sold for Intergen is fixed.
    - The rate of return for the two 30 percent equity partners on their investment in Ryan.
    - The total rate of return for Intergen based on its $1,000,000 value.

2. What transfer price will provide an equal rate of return for each of the investors in the first year of operation? (*Hint:* Under Excel's Tools heading, use the Goal Seek or Solver capability to produce a zero difference in rates of return across the equity partners by changing the cell that contains Intergen's sales.)

## ANALYSIS CASE

Refer to the websites www.cokecce.com and www.coca-cola.com.

### Required:

Address the following:

1. How does Coca-Cola account for its investment in Coca-Cola Enterprises (CCE)? What are the accounting implications of the method Coca-Cola uses?
2. What criterion does Coca-Cola use to choose the method of accounting for its investment in CCE?
3. Describe the relationship between Coca-Cola and CCE.
4. Calculate the debt-to-equity ratios in the most recent two years for both Coca-Cola and CCE. Does Coca-Cola have the ability to influence the debt levels of CCE?
5. How are Coca-Cola's financials affected by its relationship with CCE? In general, how would Coca-Cola's financials change if it consolidated CCE?

## RESEARCH AND COMMUNICATION CASE

BellCo, your client, is interested in making an investment in the equity shares of CellCo. and asks your guidance about financial reporting for equity investments. BellCo has frequent and substantial intercompany transactions with CellCo and hopes to be able to significantly influence CellCo's operating and financing decisions through the ownership of its voting shares. BellCo states that because it does not wish to use the equity method, it intends to make sure it purchases less than 20 percent of the outstanding voting shares of CellCo to comply with the technical provisions of *APB No. 18,* "The Equity Method of Accounting for Investments in Common Stock."

### Required:

Prepare a memo to BellCo's management that responds to its request for your guidance. Be sure your memo

- Cites appropriate references from *APB No. 18.*
- Identifies the relevant decision parameters for determining the appropriate accounting for an equity investment.
- Comments on BellCo's plan to avoid the equity method by owning less than a 20 percent voting interest.

## RESEARCH CASE

FASB *Statement No. 94* states that consolidation is appropriate when one entity has a controlling financial interest in another entity and that the usual condition for a controlling financial interest is ownership of a majority voting interest. But *FASB 94* also notes that in some circumstances control does not rest with the majority owner—especially when minority owners are contractually provided with approval or veto rights that can restrict the actions of the majority owner. In these cases, the majority owner employs the equity method rather than consolidation. The FASB's Emerging Issues Task Force (EITF) 96-16 addresses these issues.

### Required:

Address the following by searching *EITF 96-16*.

1. How does EITF 96-16 define protective minority rights?
2. How does EITF 96-16 define participating minority rights?
3. What minority rights overcome the presumption that all majority-owned investees should be consolidated?
4. Zee Company buys 60 percent of the voting stock of Bee Company with the remaining 40 percent minority interest held by the former owners of Bee who negotiated the following minority rights:
   - Any new debt above $1,000,000 must be approved by the 40 percent minority shareholders.
   - Any dividends or other cash distributions to owners in excess of customary historical amounts must be approved by the 40 percent minority shareholders.

According to EITF 96-16, what are the issues in determining whether Zee should consolidate Bee or report its investment in Bee under the equity method?

# Chapter Two

# Consolidation of Financial Information

## Questions to Consider

- Why do firms engage in business combinations?

- When one company gains control over another company, how should the relationship between the two parties be presented for external reporting purposes?

- In assessing the relationship between two companies how is control determined?

- The assets and liabilities of some subsidiary organizations are added directly to the records of the parent company. In other cases, the parent chooses to let the new subsidiary remain in operation as a separate legal entity. How is the accounting process affected by this decision?

- Business combinations historically have been accounted for as either a purchase or a pooling of interests. Why were two methods available? How do they differ? Why did the FASB prohibit the pooling of interests method?

- How do firms account for the ongoing research and development activities of an acquired business? How do firms account for the wide range of intangible assets that frequently comprise a large proportion of the value in many business combinations?

- What are the recent changes in financial reporting for business combinations? Will these reporting changes affect the number of mergers and acquisitions?

Financial statements, published and distributed to owners, creditors, and other interested parties, appear to report the operations and financial position of a single company. In reality, these statements frequently represent a number of separate organizations tied together through common control (a *business combination*). Whenever financial statements represent more than one corporation, we refer to them as *consolidated financial statements*.

Consolidated financial statements are typical in today's business world. Most major organizations, and many smaller ones, hold control over an array of organizations. For example, between 1993 and 2002, Cisco Systems, Inc., reported more than 40 business acquisitions that now are consolidated in its financial reports. PepsiCo, Inc., as another example, annually consolidates data from a multitude of companies into a single set of financial statements. By gaining control over these companies (often known as *subsidiaries*)—which include among others Pepsi-Cola Company, Tropicana Products, and Frito-Lay—a single business combination and single reporting entity is formed by PepsiCo (the *parent*).

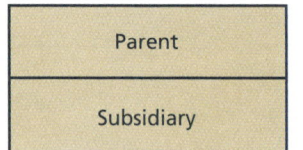

The consolidation of financial information as exemplified by Cisco Systems and PepsiCo is one of the most complex procedures in all of accounting. To comprehend this process completely, the theoretical logic that underlies the creation of a business combination must be understood. Furthermore, a variety of procedural steps must be mastered to ensure that proper accounting is achieved for this single reporting entity. The following coverage introduces both of these aspects of the consolidation process.

Importantly, major changes have recently been introduced in financial reporting for business combinations. These changes are documented in the 2001 FASB pronouncements *SFAS 141*, "Business Combinations," and *SFAS 142*, "Goodwill and Other Intangible Assets." One of the most important of these changes is the FASB requirement that all business combinations be accounted for using the purchase method, thus effectively eliminating the pooling of interests method.

*FASB Interpretation No. 46* "Consolidation of Variable Interest Entities," an interpretation of ARB No. 51 (FIN 46), represents further recent changes in accounting for business combinations. FIN 46 addresses the consolidation of an entity whose control is established not through voting interests, but through other arrangements such as governance agreements and contracts among the various parties with financial interests in the entity. In this chapter we introduce such entities in our discussion of controlling financial interests. Later, in Chapter 6 we include more comprehensive coverage of FIN 46.

In this chapter, we next provide coverage of expansion through corporate takeovers and an overview of the consolidation process. Then we present the purchase method of accounting for business combinations with specific references to *SFAS 141*. Finally, coverage of pooling of interests is provided in a separate section.

# EXPANSION THROUGH CORPORATE TAKEOVERS

## Why Do Firms Combine?

A common economic phenomenon is the combining of two or more businesses into a single entity under common management and owner control. During recent decades, the United States and the rest of the world have seen an enormous number of corporate mergers and takeovers, transactions in which one company gains control over another. According to *Mergerstat* (March 2003), the number of business combinations in 2002 totaled 7,441 with a total market value of $441 billion. As indicated by Exhibit 2–1, the magnitude of recent combinations continues to be large.

As with any other economic activity, business combinations can be part of an overall managerial strategy to maximize shareholder value. Shareholders—the owners of the firm—hire managers to direct resources so that the value of the firm grows over time. In this way, owners receive a return on their investment. Successful firms receive substantial benefits through enhanced share value. Importantly, the managers of successful firms also receive substantial benefits in salaries, especially if their compensation contracts are partly based on stock market performance of the firm's shares.

If the goal of business activity is to maximize the value of the firm, in what ways do business combinations help achieve that goal? Clearly, the business community is moving rapidly toward business combinations as a strategy for growth and competitiveness. Size and scale are obviously becoming critical as firms compete in today's markets. If larger firms can be more efficient in delivering goods and services, then they gain a competitive advantage and become more profitable for the owners. Increases in scale can produce larger profits from enhanced sales volume despite smaller (more competitive) profit margins. For example, if a combination can integrate successive stages of production and distribution of products, substantial savings can result in coordinating raw material purchases, manufacturing, and delivery. For example, when Ford Motor Co. acquired Hertz Rental (one of its largest customers), it not only enabled Ford to ensure demand for its cars but also allowed Ford to closely coordinate production with the need for new rental cars. Other cost savings resulting from elimination of duplicate efforts, such as data processing and marketing, can make a single entity more profitable than the separate parent and subsidiary had been in the past.

Although no two business combinations are exactly alike, many share one or more of the following characteristics that potentially enhance profitability:

**EXHIBIT 2–1**
**Recent Notable Business Combinations**

| Acquirer | Target | Cost (in billions) |
|---|---|---|
| America OnLine | Time Warner | $180.0 |
| Pfizer, Inc. | Warner-Lambert, Inc. | 80.0 |
| Exxon Corp. | Mobil Corp. | 80.0 |
| Vodafone Group PLC | AirTouch Communications Inc. | 62.8 |
| AT&T Corp. | MediaOne Group Inc. | 55.8 |
| Qwest Communications Inc. | US West, Inc. | 34.7 |
| Viacom Inc. | CBS Corp. | 34.5 |
| BP Amoco PLC | Atlantic Richfield Inc. | 26.6 |
| Lucent Technologies Inc. | Ascend Communications Inc. | 24.1 |
| Yahoo! Inc. | Broadcast.com | 4.3 |

- Vertical integration of one firm's output and another firm's distribution or further processing.
- Cost savings through elimination of duplicate facilities and staff.
- Quick entry for new and existing products into domestic and foreign markets.
- Economies of scale allowing greater efficiency and negotiating power.
- The ability to access financing at more attractive rates. As firms grow in size, negotiating power with financial institutions can grow also.
- Diversification of business risk.

Business combinations also result because many firms seek the continuous expansion of their organizations, often into diversified areas. Acquiring control over a vast network of different businesses has been a strategy utilized by a number of companies (sometimes known as *conglomerates*) for decades. Entry into new industries is immediately available to the parent without having to construct facilities, develop products, train management, or create market recognition. Many corporations have successfully utilized this strategy to produce huge, highly profitable organizations. Unfortunately, others have discovered that the task of managing a widely diverse group of businesses can prove to be a costly learning experience. Even combinations that purportedly take advantage of operating synergies and cost savings often fail if the integration is not managed carefully.[1]

Overall, the primary motivations for many business combinations can be traced to an increasingly competitive environment. Three recent examples of large business combinations provide interesting examples of some distinct motivations to combine: Sears' acquisition of Lands' End, Pfizer's acquisition of Warner-Lambert, and Chevron's merger with Texaco Corporation. Each is discussed briefly in turn.

### Sears, Roebuck & Co. and Lands' End[2]

In May 2002, **Sears, Roebuck & Co.,** in its largest acquisition in decades, announced an agreement to purchase the nation's largest mail-order and Internet specialty apparel retailer, **Lands' End,** Inc., for $1.86 billion in cash. The deal was widely described as a uniting of "bricks and clicks." Sears is a large national retailer that offers a wide variety of apparel, home, and automotive products through approximately 870 full-line stores with recent annual revenues exceeding $41 billion. Lands' End has embraced the use of specialty catalogs and Internet strategies to generate recent annual revenues of approximately $1.6 billion. The deal signals an acknowledgement that to compete effectively in the large national and international markets, retailers need a strong presence in multiple ordering and distribution channels. The acquisition provides several potential revenue synergies for both firms and saves Lands' End from developing and constructing its own set of retail outlets.

The Lands' End acquisition will give Sears an immediate stake in the Internet sales arena. In 2001, Lands' End generated $299 million in Internet sales. Importantly, in recent years, the Internet was Lands' End's fastest growing retail operation. Moreover, Sears will combine its remaining catalog and Internet operations with those of Lands' End, perhaps in an effort to take advantage of the Lands' End reputation for high service standards. Notably, to maintain the individual brand recognition power of the Lands' End name, there are reportedly no plans to mention the Sears name in Lands' End catalogs or Internet websites.

For Lands' End, whose sales have relied almost exclusively on shipping by mail, the Sears deal provides access to a vast nationwide distribution network through traditional bricks-and-mortar retail outlets. By merging with a major retail chain, Lands' End could find an additional source of growth without having to undertake construction and operation of its own series of stores that has challenged other clothing retailers such as Abercrombie & Fitch. In fact, Lands' End had sought out friendly buyers whose traditional retail presence would complement its highly successful direct marketing operation. Another sign that the acquisition was

---

[1] Mark Sirower, "What Acquiring Minds Need to Know," *Wall Street Journal—Manager's Journal,* February 22, 1999.

[2] "Sears Agrees to Buy Land's End in Deal Uniting Bricks, Clicks," *The Wall Street Journal Online*, May 14, 2002.

friendly is the fact that the management of Lands' End will remain intact and continue operations from its Dodgeville, Wisconsin, headquarters.

### Pfizer and Warner-Lambert

On February 7, 2000, Pfizer, Inc., announced an agreement to acquire all of the outstanding shares of Warner-Lambert Company by issuing stock valued at $90 billion. A Pfizer press release declared that the "merger of the two fastest-growing pharmaceutical companies will create the strongest, most dynamic pharmaceutical company in the world."

Pfizer's efforts to acquire Warner-Lambert represented the largest hostile takeover attempt to date.[3] At the time of Pfizer's bid, Warner-Lambert had already agreed to merge with American Home Products. Further complicating the merger was Pfizer's ongoing partnership with Warner-Lambert to produce and market Lipitor, a highly profitable cholesterol-reducing drug. The merger agreement between Warner-Lambert and American Home Products could have threatened the Lipitor alliance and thus prompted Pfizer to make its own merger bid for Warner-Lambert. The Pfizer and Warner-Lambert merger, however, can be attributable primarily to the need for economies of scale in the pharmaceutical industry.

Competition in the pharmaceutical industry increasingly rewards those firms that are able to quickly develop and market new drug therapies. In this environment, the ability to assemble and manage a large scientific infrastructure is essential for success and leads to a strategy of rapid growth. Because increases in research capacity can take years to develop, pharmaceutical firms such as Pfizer look to acquisition strategies as growth opportunities. Warner-Lambert, for example, has a modern lab in Ann Arbor, Michigan, and a scientific staff that would significantly add to Pfizer's ability to develop new products. The combined research and development expenditures of the combined Pfizer–Warner-Lambert will approximate $4 billion annually, the largest in the pharmaceutical industry.

### Chevron and Texaco

When Chevron and Texaco merged in October 2001, the combined firm became the second largest U.S.-based energy company with approximately $110 million in annual revenues, massive oil reserves and refining capacity, more than 25,000 retail gasoline stations, and operations in 180 countries. In contrast to Sears and Lands' End, Chevron and Texaco expect their merger to produce primarily cost-savings and efficiency synergies. As noted in *Business Week,*

> The combined company should be able to realize significant cost savings, as well as economies of scale from a broader base of assets, skills, and technology. . . . A broader portfolio will result in advanced technologies, e-business ventures and alternative energy, such as fuel cells and gas-to-liquid conversion. . . . The newly minted giant should achieve cost savings of at least $1.2 billion per year, within six to nine months of the merger. Most savings (approximately $700 million) will come from more efficient exploration and production activities, but some $300 million will come from the consolidation of corporate functions and $200 million from other operations.[4]

Clearly, in the energy business, particularly oil, the ChevronTexaco combination reflects a trend toward growth and competitiveness through mergers and acquisitions. Recent combination actions by competitors in the industry include British Petroleum-Amoco and Exxon Mobil—each achieving "super major" status in the oil business.

# THE CONSOLIDATION PROCESS

*The consolidation of financial information into a single set of statements becomes necessary whenever a single economic entity is created by the business combination of two or more companies.* As stated in *Accounting Research Bulletin No. 51* (abbreviated *ARB 51*), "Consolidated Financial Statements," August 1959 (par. 2): "There is a presumption that consolidated statements are more meaningful than separate statements and that they are usually necessary

---

[3] *Wall Street Journal,* "In Biggest Hostile Bid, Pfizer Offers $80 Billion for Warner-Lambert," November 5, 1999, p. 1.

[4] "Combination Gives ChevronTexaco an Energy Boost," *Business Week Online,* October 22, 2001.

for a fair presentation when one of the companies in the group directly or indirectly has a controlling financial interest in the other companies."

This sentiment was reiterated nearly 30 years later in *Financial Accounting Standards Board Statement No. 94,* "Consolidation of All Majority-Owned Subsidiaries," October 1987 (par. 30): "Consolidated financial statements became common once it was recognized that boundaries between separate corporate entities must be ignored to report the business carried on by a group of affiliated corporations as the economic and financial whole that it actually is."

Thus, in producing financial statements for external distribution, the reporting entity transcends the boundaries of incorporation to encompass all companies where control is present. Even though the various companies may retain their legal identities as separate corporations, the resulting information is more meaningful to outside parties when consolidated into a single set of financial statements.

To explain the process of preparing consolidated financial statements for a business combination, we address three questions:

- How is a business combination formed?
- What constitutes a controlling financial interest?
- How is the consolidation process carried out?

## Business Combinations—Creating a Single Economic Entity

A business combination refers to any set of conditions in which two or more organizations are joined together through common control. *SFAS 141* defines a business combination as follows:

> A *business combination* occurs when an enterprise acquires net assets that constitute a business or equity interests of one or more other enterprises and obtains control over that enterprise or enterprises.

Business combinations are formed by a wide variety of transactions with various formats. For example, each of the following is identified as a business combination although differing widely in legal form. In every case, two or more enterprises are being united into a single economic entity so that consolidated financial statements are required.

1. One company obtains the assets, and often the liabilities, of another company in exchange for cash, other assets, liabilities, stock, or a combination of these. The second organization normally dissolves itself as a legal corporation. Thus, only the acquiring company remains in existence, having absorbed the acquired net assets directly into its own operations. Any business combination in which only one of the original companies continues to exist is referred to in legal terms as a *statutory merger.*

2. One company obtains the capital stock of another in exchange for cash, other assets, liabilities, stock, or a combination of these. After gaining control, the acquiring company can decide to transfer all assets and liabilities to its own financial records with the second company being dissolved as a separate corporation.[5] The business combination is, once again, a statutory merger because only one of the companies maintains legal existence. This statutory merger, however, is achieved by obtaining equity securities rather than by buying the target company's assets. Because stock is purchased, the acquiring company must gain 100 percent control of all shares before legally dissolving the subsidiary.

3. Two or more companies transfer either their assets or their capital stock to a newly formed corporation. The original companies both are dissolved, leaving only the new organization in existence. A business combination effected in this manner is a *statutory consolidation.* The use here of the term *consolidation* should not be confused with the accounting meaning of that same word. In accounting, consolidation refers to the mechanical process of bringing together the financial records of two or more organizations to form a single set of statements. A statutory consolidation denotes a specific type of business combination in which two or more existing companies are united under the ownership of a newly created company.

---

[5] Although the acquired company has been legally dissolved, it frequently continues to operate as a separate division within the surviving company's organization.

The business combination of NCNB Corporation and C&S/Sovran Corporation illustrates the formation of a statutory consolidation. The stockholders of these two organizations created a single entity by transferring their ownership interests to a newly established corporation known as NationsBank Corporation. Because only this new company remained in existence as a legal entity, the business combination is a statutory consolidation.

4. One company achieves legal control over another by the acquisition of a majority of voting stock. *Although control is present, no dissolution takes place; each company remains in existence as an incorporated operation.* The National Broadcasting Company (NBC), as an example, continued to retain its legal status as a corporation after being acquired by General Electric Company. Separate incorporation is frequently preferred to take full advantage of any intangible benefits accruing to the acquired company as a going concern. Better utilization of such factors as trade names, employee loyalty, and the company's reputation can be possible when the subsidiary maintains its own legal identity.

One important aspect of this final type of business combination should be noted. Because the asset and liability account balances are not physically combined as in statutory mergers and consolidations, each company continues to maintain an independent accounting system. To reflect the creation of the combination, the acquiring company enters the financial impact of the takeover transaction into its own records by establishing a single investment asset account. However, the newly acquired subsidiary omits any recording of this event; the stock being obtained by the parent comes from the subsidiary's shareholders. Thus, the financial records of the subsidiary are not directly affected by a takeover.

As can be seen, business combinations are created in many distinct forms. Since the specific format is a critical factor in the subsequent consolidation of financial information, Exhibit 2–2 provides an overview of the various combinations.

## Control—An Elusive Quality from ARB 51 to FIN 46
*Control Exercised through Voting Interests*

*ARB 51,* as quoted previously, states that consolidated financial statements are usually necessary when one company has a controlling financial interest over another. However, nowhere in the official accounting pronouncements is a "controlling financial interest" actually defined.

**EXHIBIT 2–2**
**Business Combinations**

| Type of Combination | Action of Acquiring Company | Action of Acquired Company |
|---|---|---|
| Statutory merger through asset acquisition. | Acquires assets and often liabilities. | Dissolves and goes out of business. |
| Statutory merger through capital stock acquisition. | Acquires all stock and then transfers assets and liabilities to its own books. | Dissolves as a separate corporation, often remaining as a division of the acquiring company. |
| Statutory consolidation through capital stock or asset acquisition. | Newly created to receive assets or capital stock of original companies. | Original companies may dissolve while remaining as separate divisions of newly created company. |
| Acquisition of more than 50 percent of the voting stock. | Acquires stock that is recorded as an investment; controls decision making of acquired company. | Remains in existence as legal corporation, although now a subsidiary of the acquiring company. |
| Control through ownership of variable interests (see Chapter 4). Risks and rewards often flow to a sponsoring firm rather than the equity holders. | A sponsoring firm creates an entity—often referred to as an SPE—to engage in a specific activity. | Remains in existence as a separate legal entity—often a trust or partnership. |

Traditionally, in the United States, control is considered to exist if one company holds more than 50 percent of another company's voting stock. Thus, control has been tied directly to ownership. Control through ownership of a majority of voting shares continues to define the vast majority of "controlling financial interests." However, in the decades since *ARB 51* was issued, the complexity of business combinations has grown significantly so that control is not always that easy to define.

### *Control Exercised through Variable Interests*

The difficulty in defining control is exemplified in FASB *Interpretation 46* "Consolidation of Variable Interest Entities," January 2003 (*FIN 46*). One popular type of variable interest entities have become widely known as special purpose entities (SPEs). SPEs typically take the form of a trust, partnership, joint venture, or corporation. In most cases a sponsoring firm creates these entities to engage in a limited and well-defined set of business activities. For example, a business may create an SPE to finance the acquisition of a large asset. The SPE purchases the asset using debt and equity financing, and then leases the asset back to the sponsoring firm. If their activities are strictly limited and the asset is pledged as collateral, SPEs are often viewed by lenders as less risky than their sponsoring firms. As a result, such arrangements can allow financing at lower interest rates than would otherwise be available to the sponsor.

Control of SPEs, by design, often does not rest with its equity holders. Instead, control is exercised through contractual arrangements with the sponsoring firm who becomes the "primary beneficiary" of the entity. These contracts can take the form of leases, participation rights, guarantees, or other residual interests. Through contracting, the primary beneficiary bears a majority of the risks and receives a majority of the rewards of the entity, often without owning any voting shares. Consequently, an exclusive examination of voting interests can fail to identify the firm with the controlling financial interest in an SPE or similar entity.

Throughout the 1990s and early 2000s, SPEs and other variable interest entities became very popular. The increasing use of SPEs was criticized, in part because these structures allowed off-balance-sheet financing for the sponsoring firm. Other critics observed that sponsors recorded questionable profits on sales to their SPEs. Many SPEs were often characterized simply as vehicles to hide debt and manipulate earnings. Prior to FIN 46, many sponsoring entities of SPEs did not technically meet the definition of a controlling financial interest and thus did not consolidate their SPEs.

To prevent future financial reporting abuses, FIN 46 expanded the definition of control beyond simply holding a majority of another entity's voting shares. An entity (e.g., an SPE) whose control rests a primary beneficiary is referred to as a *variable interest entity*. The following characteristics indicate a controlling financial interest in a variable interest entity.

- The direct or indirect ability to make decisions about the entity's activities
- The obligation to absorb the expected losses of the entity if they occur, or
- The right to receive the expected residual returns of the entity if they occur

The primary beneficiary bears the risks and receives the rewards of a variable interest entity and is considered to have a controlling financial interest. The fact that the primary beneficiary may own no voting shares whatsoever becomes inconsequential because such shares do not effectively allow the equity holders to exercise control. FIN 46 reasons that if a "business enterprise has a controlling financial interest in a variable interest entity, assets, liabilities, and results of the activities of the variable interest entity should be included with those of the business enterprise."

In this text, we first examine control relationships established through voting interests. Owning a majority of voting interests continues to be the primary mechanism through which one firm controls another. In Chapter 6, however, we expand our coverage to include the consolidation of firms where control is exercised through variable interests.

## Consolidation of Financial Information

Whenever one company gains control over another, a business combination is established. Financial data gathered from the individual companies is then brought together to form a single set of consolidated statements. Although this process can be complicated, the objectives of a consolidation are straightforward. The asset, liability, equity, revenue, and expense accounts of the companies simply are combined. As a part of this process, reciprocal accounts and intercompany transactions must be adjusted or eliminated to ensure that all reported balances truly represent the single entity.

Applicable consolidation procedures vary significantly depending on the legal format employed in creating a business combination. *For a statutory merger or a statutory consolidation, when the acquired company (or companies) is legally dissolved, only one accounting consolidation ever occurs.* On the date of the combination, the surviving company simply records the various account balances from each of the dissolving companies. Because all accounts are brought together permanently in this manner, no further consolidation procedures are necessary. After all of the balances are transferred to the survivor, the financial records of the acquired companies are closed out as part of the dissolution.

Conversely, in a combination when all companies retain incorporation, a different set of consolidation procedures is appropriate. Because the companies preserve their legal identities, each continues to maintain its own independent accounting records. *Thus, no permanent consolidation of the account balances is ever made. Rather, the consolidation process must be carried out anew each time that the reporting entity prepares financial statements for external reporting purposes.*

When separate record-keeping is maintained, the accountant faces a unique problem: The financial information must be brought together periodically without disturbing the accounting systems of the individual companies. Since these consolidations are produced outside the financial records, worksheets traditionally are used to expedite the process. Worksheets are neither part of either company's accounting records nor the resulting financial statements. Instead, they are an efficient structure for organizing and adjusting the information used in the preparation of externally reported consolidated statements.

Consequently, the legal characteristics of a business combination have a significant impact on the approach taken to the consolidation process:

What is to be consolidated?

- If dissolution takes place, all account balances are physically consolidated in the financial records of the surviving company.
- If separate incorporation is maintained, only the financial statement information is consolidated and not the actual records.

When does the consolidation take place?

- If dissolution takes place, a permanent consolidation occurs at the date of the combination.
- If separate incorporation is maintained, the consolidation process is carried out at regular intervals whenever financial statements are to be prepared.

How are the accounting records affected?

- If dissolution takes place, the surviving company's accounts are adjusted to include all balances of the dissolved company. The dissolved company's records are closed out.
- If separate incorporation is maintained, each company continues to retain its own records. Using worksheets facilitates the periodic consolidation process without disturbing the individual accounting systems.

# FINANCIAL REPORTING FOR BUSINESS COMBINATIONS—*SFAS 141*

## The Purchase Method: Change in Ownership

The fundamental characteristic of any purchase—whether a single asset or a multibillion dollar corporation—is a change in ownership. In any exchange transaction, a basic accounting principle is the recording of the cost to the new owners. Thus, in a business combination accounted for as a purchase, the acquisition cost to the new owners provides the valuation basis

**EXHIBIT 2–3**
Business Combination—
Purchase

for the net assets acquired. For example, as shown in Exhibit 2–3, MGM Grand, Inc. recently purchased Mirage Resorts, Inc. for approximately $6.4 billion. This purchase price then served as the basis for valuing Mirage Resorts' assets and liabilities in the preparation of MGM Grand's consolidated financial statements.

When a single asset is purchased, application of the cost principle is straightforward. In a business combination, however, the application of the cost principle is complicated because of the literally hundreds of assets and liabilities that often are acquired. *As a result, the purchase method not only establishes cost as the appropriate valuation basis for these items but also must allocate the total acquisition cost among the various assets and liabilities received in the bargained exchange.* The cost allocation procedure employed by the purchase method is based on the fair market values of the acquired assets and liabilities at the date of acquisition. Moreover, because income can accrue to owners only after the purchase of an asset (or an entire company), only revenues and expenses generated by these assets and liabilities after the acquisition date are attributed to the business combination.

## PROCEDURES FOR CONSOLIDATING FINANCIAL INFORMATION

Legal as well as accounting distinctions divide business combinations into at least four separate categories. To facilitate the introduction of consolidation accounting, we present the various procedures utilized in this process according to the following sequence:

1. Purchase method when dissolution takes place.
2. Purchase method when separate incorporation is maintained.

As a basis for this coverage, assume that Smallport Company owns computers, telecommunications equipment, and software that allow its customers to implement billing and ordering systems through the Internet/World Wide Web. Although the computers and equipment have a book value of $400,000, they have a current value of $600,000. The software developed by Smallport has only a $100,000 value on its books; the costs of developing the software were primarily expensed as incurred. The observable fair market value of the software, however, is $1,600,000. Smallport also has a note payable of $200,000 incurred to help finance the software development. Because interest rates are currently low, this liability (incurred at a higher rate of interest) has a present value of $250,000.

BigNet Company owns Internet communications equipment and other business software applications that complement those of Smallport. BigNet wants to expand its operations and plans to acquire Smallport on December 31. The accounts reported by both BigNet and Smallport on that date are listed in Exhibit 2–4. In addition, the estimated fair market value of Smallport's assets and liabilities is included.

Smallport's net assets (assets less liabilities) have a book value of $600,000 but a fair market value of $2,250,000. Only the assets and liabilities have been appraised here; the capital stock, retained earnings, dividend, revenue, and expense accounts represent historical measurements rather than any type of future values. Although these equity and income accounts can give some indication of the overall worth of the organization, they are not property and thus not transferred in the combination.

### Purchase Method When Dissolution Takes Place

The purchase method employs the cost principle in recording a business combination—the total value assigned to the net assets received equals the total cost of the acquisition. The major accounting challenge, however, is the allocation of that cost among the various assets and liabilities obtained in the acquisition. These allocations depend on the relation between total cost

## EXHIBIT 2–4  Basic Consolidation Information

|  | BigNet Company Book Value December 31 | Smallport Company Book Value December 31 | Smallport Company Fair Market Value December 31 |
|---|---|---|---|
| Current assets | $ 400,000 | $300,000 | $ 300,000 |
| Computers and equipment (net) | 2,000,000 | 400,000 | 600,000 |
| Capitalized software (net) | 500,000 | 100,000 | 1,600,000 |
| Notes payable | (300,000) | (200,000) | (250,000) |
| **Net assets** | **$2,600,000** | **$600,000** | **$2,250,000** |
| Common stock—$5 par value | $1,600,000 | | |
| Common stock—$10 par value | | $ 100,000 | |
| Additional paid-in capital | 40,000 | 20,000 | |
| Retained earnings, 1/1 | 870,000 | 370,000 | |
| Dividends paid | (110,000) | (10,000) | |
| Revenues | 1,000,000 | 500,000 | |
| Expenses | (800,000) | (380,000) | |
| **Owners' equity 12/31** | **$2,600,000** | **$600,000** | |
| Retained earnings, 12/31 | 960,000* | 480,000* | |

*Retained earnings balance after closing out revenues, expenses, and dividends paid.

and the fair market values of the acquired firm's assets and liabilities. Therefore, we demonstrate the consolidation procedures in this initial section using four examples, each with a different price relative to fair market value.

### Purchase Price Equals Fair Market Value

Assume that after negotiations with the owners of Smallport, BigNet agrees to pay $2,250,000 for all of Smallport's assets and liabilities: cash of $250,000 and 20,000 unissued shares of its $5 par value common stock that is currently selling for $100 per share. Smallport will then dissolve itself as a legal entity.

As with any acquisition, the price established here is based on the value of the consideration paid.

| | |
|---|---|
| Cash | $ 250,000 |
| Common stock issued (20,000 shares at a $100 per share fair market value) | 2,000,000 |
| Purchase price | $2,250,000 |

Therefore, BigNet's cost is exactly equal to the $2,250,000 fair market value of the individual assets and liabilities acquired.

The purchase method is appropriate for consolidating the financial information of these two companies; all of the essential characteristics are present. A bargained exchange occurred between BigNet, the acquiring company, and the owners of Smallport. This transaction indicates a $2,250,000 purchase price will form the basis for the consolidated figures in the financial statements of the resulting single economic entity.

*At the date of acquisition, the purchase method consolidates all subsidiary asset and liability accounts based on their fair market values.* The acquired assets and liabilities are recorded as if the parent had simply obtained them by paying market value. Because the negotiated price here equals this total value, the parent records each of these accounts as though purchased individually. As we subsequently demonstrate, variations from this rule exist if the parent pays less than market value.

Because Smallport Company will be dissolved, BigNet (the surviving company) directly records a consolidation entry in its financial records. As a purchase, BigNet consolidates Smallport's assets and liabilities at market value; original book values are ignored. Revenue, expense, dividend, and equity accounts cannot be transferred to a parent and are omitted in recording the business combination as a purchase.

### Purchase Method—Parent Pays Market Value—Subsidiary Dissolved

| BigNet Company's Financial Records—December 31 | | |
|---|---:|---:|
| Current Assets | 300,000 | |
| Computers and Equipment | 600,000 | |
| Capitalized Software | 1,600,000 | |
|     Notes Payable | | 250,000 |
|     Cash (paid by BigNet) | | 250,000 |
|     Common Stock (20,000 shares issued by BigNet at $5 par value) | | 100,000 |
|     Additional Paid-In Capital (value of shares issued by BigNet in excess of par value) | | 1,900,000 |
| To record purchase of net assets of Smallport Company for $2,250,000. Subsidiary accounts are recorded at market value which total (net) to the same $2,250,000. | | |

BigNet's financial records now show $2,600,000 in the Computers and Equipment account ($2,000,000 former balance + $600,000 acquired), $2,100,000 in Capitalized Software ($500,000 + $1,600,000), and so forth. These items have been added into BigNet's balances (see Exhibit 2–4) at their fair market values. Conversely, BigNet's revenue balance continues to report the company's own $1,000,000 with expenses remaining at $800,000 and dividends of $110,000. *In a purchase, only the subsidiary's revenues, expenses, dividends, and equity transactions that occur subsequent to the takeover affect the business combination.*

### Purchase Price Exceeds Fair Market Value

The negotiated price in this second illustration is assumed to be $3,000,000 in exchange for all of Smallport's assets and liabilities. The mode of payment by BigNet will be $1,000,000 in cash plus 20,000 shares of common stock with a market value of $100 per share. The resulting purchase price is $750,000 more than the $2,250,000 fair market value of Smallport's net assets. In purchase combinations, such excess payments are not unusual. For example, when Amazon.com acquired Junglee, a provider of Web-based virtual database technology, substantially the entire $180 million purchase price was allocated to goodwill and other intangibles.

The $2,250,000 market value of Smallport's net assets certainly can influence any takeover offer. However, any number of other factors can affect BigNet's $3,000,000 acquisition offer, such as Smallport's history of profitability, the company's reputation, the quality of its personnel, or the economic condition of the industry in which it operates. If Smallport, for example, demonstrates the ability to generate especially high profits, BigNet could be willing to pay an extra amount for this company. One additional factor frequently affects an acquisition price: the presence of competitive buyers. If BigNet must outbid other companies to acquire Smallport, the purchase price could simply represent the bidding war.

*Whenever the price paid in a purchase exceeds total fair market value, all of the subsidiary's assets and liabilities are consolidated at fair market value with the additional payment allocated to the intangible asset goodwill.* This excess amount could actually reflect the profitability often inherent in a going concern, the creative ability of a research group, market conditions that surrounded the acquisition, or myriad other possible factors. Because the conditions that can influence a purchase price are virtually unlimited, any amount paid in excess of the fair market value assigned to identifiable assets (both tangible and intangible) is simply assigned to goodwill.[6]

Alternative account titles such as Unamortized Cost in Excess of Market Value or some variation have also been widely used in recent years to identify this general allocation of any

---

[6] As discussed in Chapter 3, the assets and liabilities (including goodwill) acquired in a business combination are assigned to identified *reporting units* of the combined entity. A reporting unit is simply a level of business in which an acquired asset or liability will be employed. Overall, the objective of the assignment of acquired assets and liabilities to reporting units is to facilitate periodic impairment testing.

excess purchase price. Unisys, for example, recently reported a $1.0 billion asset as a "cost in excess of net assets acquired" on its balance sheet. Traditionally, the term *goodwill* refers to a computationally derived excess payment based on the estimated future profits of a going concern. Because the extra amount paid in the purchase of another company may result from many factors, a more descriptive label such as the one reported by Unisys might be preferable. However, goodwill is specifically used in the FASB documents and professional literature and is, therefore, incorporated throughout this textbook.

Returning to BigNet's $3,000,000 purchase, $750,000 of this price was in excess of the fair market value of Smallport's net assets. Thus, goodwill of that amount is entered into BigNet's accounting system along with the fair market value of each individual account. The actual journal entry made by BigNet at the date of acquisition follows:

*Purchase Method—Parent Pays More Than Market Value—Subsidiary Dissolved*

| BigNet Company's Financial Records—December 31 | | |
|---|---|---|
| Current Assets | 300,000 | |
| Computers and Equipment | 600,000 | |
| Capitalized Software | 1,600,000 | |
| Goodwill | 750,000 | |
| Notes Payable | | 250,000 |
| Cash (paid by BigNet) | | 1,000,000 |
| Common Stock (20,000 shares issued by BigNet at $5 par value) | | 100,000 |
| Additional Paid-In Capital (value of shares issued by BigNet in excess of par value) | | 1,900,000 |
| To record purchase of net assets of Smallport Company for $3,000,000. Subsidiary accounts are recorded at market value with $750,000 excess payment attributed to goodwill. | | |

Once again, BigNet's financial records now show $2,600,000 in the Computers and Equipment account ($2,000,000 former balance + $600,000 acquired), $2,100,000 in Capitalized Software ($500,000 + $1,600,000), and so forth. As the only change, a Goodwill balance of $750,000 is established to account for the excess purchase price paid by BigNet.

### Purchase Price Less Than Fair Market Value

For this third example, the price paid to the owners of Smallport is assumed to be $2,000,000. BigNet conveys no cash and issues 20,000 shares of common stock having a $100 per share fair market value. To add a new element to this illustration, BigNet elects to pay $30,000 in accountants' and lawyers' fees directly associated with the combination as well as $10,000 for registering and issuing the shares of common stock.

In this combination, the parent's cost comprises more than one component. According to current reporting standards, any direct costs of establishing a purchase combination is regarded as part of the total acquisition price. Expenditures such as payments to lawyers and accountants as well as finders' fees are necessary to carry out a purchase and are thus capitalized. Such combination costs can be significant. In describing the takeover battle for RJR Nabisco, *Time* magazine estimated that the "hundreds of lawyers and investment bankers involved in the bidding stand to earn a total of as much as $1 billion for their expertise."

The accountants' and lawyers' fees of $30,000 are thus included by BigNet in computing a purchase price of $2,030,000, the total cost of acquiring Smallport's assets and liabilities ($2,000,000 to the owners of Smallport and $30,000 for these direct costs). However, the remaining $10,000 was paid to register and issue the common stock. This amount is considered a cost associated with these securities rather than a cost of the purchase. As such, the $10,000 is assumed to be a reduction in the additional paid-in capital recorded for the newly issued shares.

BigNet's total purchase price of $2,030,000 is $220,000 less than the fair market value of Smallport's net assets. Allocation of full market values to each asset and liability is simply not possible; some reduction must be made. A cost of $2,030,000 cannot be assigned to accounts having a fair market value of $2,250,000 without an adjustment. To address this problem, the values otherwise assignable to noncurrent assets acquired should be reduced by a proportionate part of the excess to determine the assigned values.[7] *Therefore, when a purchase price is less than total fair market value of the net assets, noncurrent accounts, such as Computers and Equipment and Capitalized Software, are consolidated at reduced balances. All remaining assets and liabilities continue to be recorded at their fair market values.*

Because BigNet paid $220,000 less than fair market value ($2,250,000 − $2,030,000), the balances of any noncurrent assets being acquired (other than long-term investments in marketable securities) must be decreased by that amount. As indicated in Exhibit 2–4, the two applicable accounts in this example have a total fair market value of $2,200,000:

| Noncurrent Asset Accounts | Fair Market Values | |
|---|---|---|
| Computers and Equipment | $ 600,000 | 27.27% |
| Capitalized Software | 1,600,000 | 72.73 |
| Total | $2,200,000 | 100.00% |

Because of BigNet's payment, these two accounts must be reduced in consolidation by a total of $220,000 (from $2,200,000 to $1,980,000). The balance reported for Computers and Equipment is lowered by $60,000 ($220,000 × 27.27%). The remaining $160,000 ($220,000 × 72.73%) is assigned as a decrease to the Capitalized Software account. Therefore, for consolidation purposes, BigNet records Smallport's Computers and Equipment at $540,000 ($60,000 less than its $600,000 fair market value). The Capitalized Software account is entered at $1,440,000 ($1,600,000 − $160,000). All other assets and liabilities are consolidated at their fair market values.

### *Purchase Method—Parent Pays Less Than Market Value—Subsidiary Dissolved*

| BigNet Company's Financial Records—December 31 | | |
|---|---|---|
| Current Assets | 300,000 | |
| Computers and Equipment | 540,000 | |
| Capitalized Software | 1,440,000 | |
| Notes Payable | | 250,000 |
| Common Stock (20,000 shares issued by BigNet at $5 par value) | | 100,000 |
| Additional Paid-In Capital (value of shares issued by BigNet in excess of par value) | | 1,900,000 |
| Cash (direct acquisition costs) | | 30,000 |
| Additional Paid-In Capital (stock costs) | 10,000 | |
| Cash | | 10,000 |
| To record purchase of net assets of Smallport. Payment includes $30,000 direct acquisition costs and the $10,000 cost of registering and issuing common stock. Total purchase price of $2,030,000 is $220,000 less than market value of the net assets, an amount assigned to noncurrent assets. | | |

### *Purchase Price Substantially Less Than Fair Market Value*

In this final illustration, the exchange price for Smallport's net assets is assumed to be $40,000 with payment made entirely in cash. Obviously, expending this amount for net assets valued at $2,250,000 is an extreme case that indicates an unusual circumstance such as imminent bankruptcy, large contingent liabilities, or an urgent need by the present owners for immediate liquidation. A company, for example, that has its entire business centered on marketing one

---

[7] Excluded from the proportionate reduction are financial assets other than equity method investments, assets to be disposed of by sale, deferred tax assets, and prepaid assets relating to pension or other postretirement benefit plans. According to *SFAS 141*, these assets should be recorded at assessed fair values.

patent could see the price of its stock drop to nearly zero if the legality of that patent were seriously threatened.

With a purchase price of only $40,000, Smallport's assets and liabilities must be consolidated at $2,210,000—substantially less than their total fair market value of $2,250,000. As was indicated in the previous example, this decrease initially is made in recording the noncurrent assets. However, these two assets (computers and equipment and capitalized software) have a total worth of only $2,200,000. Even decreasing their balances to zero will not fully account for the $2,210,000 difference between the purchase price and total fair market value. A further reduction of $10,000 must be assigned within the consolidation process.

*Whenever a purchase price is less than fair market value so that the acquired applicable noncurrent asset balances are eliminated entirely, an additional reduction is needed. According to* SFAS 141, *the additional reduction is reported as an extraordinary gain.*[8] All other assets and liabilities are still brought into the combination at fair market value. The extraordinary gain results from a bargain purchase but comes into existence only after the applicable noncurrent assets are first decreased to zero. Thus, either the price has to be extremely low or the acquired noncurrent assets must be of a relatively small value.

The FASB decision that an unallocated excess fair value over cost should be reported as an extraordinary gain was not without its critics. Some argued that to record a gain upon a purchase transaction is conceptually unsound. However, the FASB reasoned that the extraordinary gain treatment appropriately highlights the fact that an excess exists and that such occurrences are both infrequent and unusual in nature. The Board also observed that regardless of whether an extraordinary gain or a deferred credit results, income ultimately increases—either immediately or in future periods.

Because the $40,000 price in this illustration is $2,210,000 less than fair market value, BigNet's journal entry to record its purchase of Smallport's assets and liabilities would do the following:

1. Recognize no balances for the two noncurrent asset accounts.
2. Allocate the remaining $10,000 reduction to an extraordinary gain.
3. Report all remaining asset and liability accounts at fair market value.

### Purchase Method—Parent Pays Substantially Less Than Market Value—Subsidiary Dissolved

| BigNet Company's Financial Records—December 31 | |
|---|---:|
| Current Assets | 300,000 |
| Computers and Equipment | –0– |
| Capitalized Software | –0– |
| Notes Payable | 250,000 |
| Extraordinary Gain—Excess of Market Value over Cost of Acquisition | 10,000 |
| Cash (paid by BigNet) | 40,000 |
| To record acquisition of Smallport's net assets for $40,000, an amount $2,210,000 below market value. | |

### Summary of the Purchase Method

In a purchase, acquired assets and liabilities are normally consolidated at their fair market values. However, the relationship between purchase price and total market value can necessitate some alterations to this rule. An excess payment, for example, leads to the creation of a Goodwill account. A low purchase price forces a reduction in the recorded balance of applicable noncurrent assets and possibly the recognition of an extraordinary gain. Exhibit 2–5 summarizes the possible allocation scenarios.

---

[8] Prior to *SFAS 141*, such additional reductions were reported in a deferred credit account and systematically amortized to income.

**EXHIBIT 2–5**
Consolidation Values—
The Purchase Method

| | |
|---|---|
| Purchase price equals the fair market value of net assets. | Acquired assets and liabilities are assigned their fair market values. |
| Purchase price is more than the fair market value of the net assets. | Acquired assets and liabilities are assigned their fair market values. The excess payment is attributed to goodwill. |
| Purchase price is less than the fair market value of the net assets. | Current assets, liabilities, financial assets, deferred taxes, assets to be held for sale, and prepaid pension assets are assigned their fair market values. The values of other noncurrent assets are reduced proportionally. If necessary, an extraordinary gain is recognized. |

## Purchase Method When Separate Incorporation Is Maintained

When each company retains separate incorporation in a purchase combination, many aspects of the consolidation process are identical to those demonstrated in the previous section. Fair market value, for example, remains as the basis for initially consolidating the subsidiary's asset and liability accounts.

Several significant differences exist in purchase combinations in which each company remains a legally incorporated entity. Most noticeably, the consolidation of the financial information is only simulated rather than having the acquiring company physically record the acquired assets and liabilities. Because dissolution does not occur, each company maintains independent record-keeping. To facilitate the preparation of consolidated financial statements, a worksheet and consolidation entries are employed using the data gathered from these separate companies.

A worksheet provides the structure for generating information to be reported by the single economic entity. An integral part of this process is the inclusion of consolidation worksheet entries. *These adjustments and eliminations are entered on the worksheet and represent alterations that would be required if the financial records were to be physically united.* Because no actual union occurs, consolidation entries are never formally recorded in the journals of either company. Instead, they are produced solely for use on the worksheet to assist in deriving consolidated account balances of the two separate companies. The resulting consolidated balances then form the basis for the financial reports of the consolidated entity.

To illustrate using the previous information, assume that BigNet acquires Smallport Company on December 31, by issuing 26,000 shares of $5 par value common stock valued at $100 per share (or $2,600,000 in total). Direct acquisition costs of $40,000 also are paid by BigNet, resulting in a total purchase price of $2,640,000.

For business reasons, BigNet decides to allow Smallport to continue as a separate corporation. Therefore, whenever financial statements for this combination are prepared, a worksheet is utilized in simulating the consolidation of these two companies. Although the assets and liabilities are not transferred, BigNet must still record the payment made to Smallport's owners. When the subsidiary remains separate, the parent establishes an investment account that initially reflects the purchase price.

*Purchase Method—Subsidiary Is Not Dissolved*

| BigNet Company's Financial Records—December 31 | | |
|---|---|---|
| Investment in Smallport Company (purchase price) | 2,640,000 | |
| Cash (paid for direct acquisition costs) | | 40,000 |
| Common Stock (26,000 shares issued by BigNet at $5 par value) | | 130,000 |

| | | |
|---|---|---|
| Additional Paid-In Capital (value of shares issued by BigNet in excess of par value) . . . . . . . . . . . . . . . . . . . . . . . . . . . . . . . . . . . . . . . | | 2,470,000 |
| To record purchase of Smallport Company, which will maintain its separate legal identity. | | |

As demonstrated in Exhibit 2–6, a worksheet can be prepared on the date of acquisition to arrive at consolidated totals for this combination. The entire process consists of seven steps:

### Step 1

Whenever a worksheet is constructed, a formal allocation of the purchase price should be made as was done for the equity method in Chapter 1.[9] Thus, the following schedule is appropriate for BigNet's purchase of Smallport:

| | | |
|---|---:|---:|
| Purchase price paid by BigNet . . . . . . . . . . . . . . . . . . . . . . . . . . . . . . | | $2,640,000 |
| Book value of Smallport (see Exhibit 2–4) . . . . . . . . . . . . . . . . . . . . | | 600,000 |
| Excess of cost over book value . . . . . . . . . . . . . . . . . . . . . . . . . . . . | | $2,040,000 |
| Allocations made to specific accounts based on difference in fair market values and book values: | | |
| Computers and Equipment ($600,000 − $400,000) . . . . . . . . . . . . | $ 200,000 | |
| Capitalized Software ($1,600,000 − $100,000) . . . . . . . . . . . . . . . | 1,500,000 | |
| Notes Payable ($250,000 − $200,000) . . . . . . . . . . . . . . . . . . . . . | (50,000) | 1,650,000 |
| Excess cost not identified with specific accounts—goodwill . . . . . | | $ 390,000 |

No part of the $2,040,000 excess payment is attributed to the current assets because the book value and market value are identical. The Notes Payable shows a negative allocation; because this debt's present value is more than book value, the company's net assets are actually worth *less*.

### Step 2

The financial figures from the separate companies as of the date of acquisition (see Exhibit 2–4) are shown in the first two columns of the worksheet (see Exhibit 2–6). BigNet's accounts have been adjusted for the investment entry recorded earlier. As another preliminary step, Smallport's revenue, expense, and dividend accounts have been closed into its Retained Earnings account. In a purchase, the operations of the subsidiary prior to the December 31st takeover have no direct bearing on the business combination. These activities occurred before Smallport was acquired; thus, the resulting data should not be reported as income earned by the new owners in the consolidated statements.

### Step 3

Smallport's stockholders' equity accounts are eliminated through consolidation Entry **S** (**S** is a reference to beginning subsidiary **S**tockholders' equity). These balances (Common Stock, Additional Paid-In Capital, and Retained Earnings) are historical measurements of subsidiary transactions that occurred prior to the combination. By removing these accounts, only Smallport's assets and liabilities remain to be combined with the parent company figures.

### Step 4

Also in worksheet Entry **S,** the $600,000 component of the Investment in Smallport Company account that equates to the book value of the subsidiary's net assets is removed. For external reporting purposes, the combination should report each individual account rather than a single

---

[9] This allocation procedure is helpful but not critical if dissolution occurs. Unless the purchase price is less than total market value, the asset and liability accounts are simply added directly into the parent's books at their assessed worth with any excess assigned to goodwill.

## EXHIBIT 2–6  Purchase Method—Date of Acquisition

**BIGNET COMPANY AND SMALLPORT COMPANY**
Consolidation Worksheet
For Period Ending December 31

| Accounts | BigNet | Smallport | Consolidation Entries Debits | Consolidation Entries Credits | Consolidated Totals |
|---|---|---|---|---|---|
| **Income Statement** | | | | | |
| Revenues | (1,000,000) | | | | (1,000,000) |
| Expenses | 800,000 | | | | 800,000 |
| Net income | (200,000) | | | | (200,000) |
| **Statement of Retained Earnings** | | | | | |
| Retained earnings, 1/1 | (870,000) | | | | (870,000) |
| Net income (above) | (200,000) | | | | (200,000) |
| Dividends paid | 110,000 | | | | 110,000 |
| Retained earnings, 12/31 | (960,000) | | | | (960,000) |
| **Balance Sheet** | | | | | |
| Current assets | 360,000* | 300,000 | | | 660,000 |
| Investment in Smallport Company | 2,640,000* | –0– | | (S) 600,000 | –0– |
| | | | | (A) 2,040,000 | |
| Computers and equipment | 2,000,000 | 400,000 | (A) 200,000 | | 2,600,000 |
| Capitalized software | 500,000 | 100,000 | (A) 1,500,000 | | 2,100,000 |
| Goodwill | –0– | –0– | (A) 390,000 | | 390,000 |
| Total assets | 5,500,000 | 800,000 | | | 5,750,000 |
| Notes payable | (300,000) | (200,000) | | (A) 50,000 | (550,000) |
| Common stock | (1,730,000)* | (100,000) | (S) 100,000 | | (1,730,000) |
| Additional paid-in capital | (2,510,000)* | (20,000) | (S) 20,000 | | (2,510,000) |
| Retained earnings, 12/31 (above) | (960,000) | (480,000) | (S) 480,000 | | (960,000) |
| Total liabilities and equities | (5,500,000) | (800,000) | | | (5,750,000) |

Note: Parentheses indicate a credit balance.
*Balances have been adjusted for issuance of stock and payment of consolidation costs.

investment balance. In effect, this portion of the Investment in Smallport Company account is deleted and replaced by the specific assets and liabilities that it represents.

### Step 5

In Entry **A,** the $2,040,000 excess payment in the Investment in Smallport Company is removed and assigned to the specific accounts indicated by the purchase price allocation. Consequently, Computers and Equipment is increased by $200,000 to agree with Smallport's market value; $1,500,000 is attributed to Capitalized Software and $50,000 to Notes Payable. The unexplained excess of $390,000 is recorded as goodwill. This entry is labeled Entry **A** to indicate that it represents the **A**llocations made in connection with the parent's purchase price. It also completes the elimination of the entire Investment in Smallport account.

### Step 6

All accounts are extended into the Consolidated Totals column. For accounts such as Current Assets, this process is no more than the addition of Smallport's book value to that of BigNet. However, when applicable, this extension also includes any allocations to establish the fair market value of Smallport's asset and liability accounts. Computers and Equipment, as an example, is increased by $200,000. By raising the subsidiary's book value to market value, the reported balances are the same as in the previous examples when dissolution occurred. The use of a worksheet does not alter the consolidated figures but only the method of deriving those numbers.

*Step 7*

Consolidated expenses are subtracted from revenues to arrive at a net income of $200,000. Note that because this is a date of acquisition worksheet, no amounts for Smallport's revenues and expenses are included in the Smallport Company column. BigNet has just purchased Smallport and therefore Smallport has not yet earned any income for the owners of BigNet. Consolidated revenues, expenses, and net income are identical to BigNet's balances. In years subsequent to acquisition, of course, Smallport's income accounts will be consolidated with BigNet's.

In general, totals (such as net income and ending retained earnings) are not directly consolidated on the worksheet. Rather, the components (such as revenues and expenses) are extended across and then combined to derive the appropriate figure. Net income is then carried down on the worksheet to the Statement of Retained Earnings and used (along with beginning retained earnings and dividends paid) to compute this December 31 equity balance. In the same manner, ending Retained Earnings of $960,000 is entered into the balance sheet to arrive at total liabilities and equities of $5,750,000, a number that reconciles with the total of consolidated assets.

The balances in the final column of Exhibit 2–6 are used to prepare consolidated financial statements for the business combination of BigNet Company and Smallport Company. The worksheet entries serve as a catalyst to bring together the two independent sets of financial information. Thus, the actual accounting records of both BigNet and Smallport remain unaltered by this consolidation process.

## PURCHASE PRICE ALLOCATIONS—ADDITIONAL ISSUES—*SFAS 141*

### Intangibles

An important accounting element of business combinations is the proper allocation of the purchase price to the underlying assets and liabilities acquired. In particular, the advent of the information age brings new challenges for a host of intangible assets that provide value in generating future cash flows. Often, intangible assets comprise the largest proportion of the purchase price of an acquired firm. For example, when AT&T acquired AT&T Broadband (formerly TCI), AT&T allocated approximately $19 billion of the $52 billion purchase price to franchise costs. Franchise costs are an intangible asset representing the value attributed to agreements with local authorities that allow access to homes. In addressing the importance of proper asset recognition, the FASB in *SFAS 141* observes that intangible assets include both current and noncurrent assets (not including financial instruments) that lack physical substance. Further, in determining whether to recognize an intangible asset in a business combination, *SFAS 141* relies on two essential attributes. First, does the intangible asset arise from contractual or other legal rights? Second, is the asset capable of being sold or otherwise separated from the acquired enterprise? As stated in *SFAS 141,*

> An intangible asset shall be recognized as an asset apart from goodwill if it arises from contractual or other legal rights (regardless of whether those rights are transferable or separable from the acquired entity or from other rights and obligations). If an intangible asset does not arise from contractual or other legal rights, it shall be recognized as an asset apart from goodwill only if it is separable, that is, it is capable of being separated or divided from the acquired entity and sold, transferred, licensed, rented, or exchanged (regardless of whether there is an intent to do so). For purposes of this Statement, however, an intangible asset that cannot be sold, transferred, licensed, rented, or exchanged individually is considered separable if it can be sold, transferred, licensed, rented, or exchanged with a related contract, asset, or liability. For purposes of this statement, an assembled workforce shall not be recognized as an intangible asset apart from goodwill.

Exhibit 2–7 provides a listing of intangible assets with indications of whether they typically meet the legal/contractual or separability criteria.

**EXHIBIT 2–7**  Illustrative Examples of Intangible Assets That Meet the Criteria for Recognition Separately from Goodwill (*SFAS 141*)

> The following are examples of intangible assets that meet the criteria for recognition as an asset apart from goodwill. The following illustrative list is not intended to be all-inclusive; thus, an acquired intangible asset might meet the recognition criteria of this Statement but not be included on that list. Assets designated by the symbol (c) are those that would generally be recognized separately from goodwill because they meet the contractual-legal criterion. Assets designated by the symbol (s) do not arise from contractual or other legal rights, but should nonetheless be recognized separately from goodwill because they meet the separability criterion. The determination of whether a specific acquired intangible asset meets the criteria in this Statement for recognition apart from goodwill should be based on the facts and circumstances of each individual business combination.*
>
> **Marketing-related intangible assets:**
> 1. Trademarks, tradenames.[c]
> 2. Service marks, collective marks, certification marks.[c]
> 3. Trade dress (unique color, shape, or package design).[c]
> 4. Newspaper mastheads.[c]
> 5. Internet domain names.[c]
> 6. Noncompetition agreements.[c]
>
> **Customer-related intangible assets:**
> 1. Customer lists.[s]
> 2. Order or production backlog.[c]
> 3. Customer contracts and related customer relationships.[c]
> 4. Noncontractual customer relationships.[s]
>
> **Artistic-related intangible assets:**
> 1. Plays, operas, and ballets.[c]
> 2. Books, magazines, newspapers, and other literary works.[c]
> 3. Musical works such as compositions, song lyrics, advertising jingles.[c]
> 4. Pictures and photographs.[c]
> 5. Video and audiovisual material, including motion pictures, music videos, and television programs.[c]
>
> **Contract-based intangible assets:**
> 1. Licensing, royalty, standstill agreements.[c]
> 2. Advertising, construction, management, service, or supply contracts.[c]
> 3. Lease agreements.[c]
> 4. Construction permits.[c]
> 5. Franchise agreements.[c]
> 6. Operating and broadcast rights.[c]
> 7. Use rights such as landing, drilling, water, air, mineral, timber cutting, and route authorities.[c]
> 8. Servicing contracts such as mortgage servicing contracts.[c]
> 9. Employment contracts.[c]
>
> **Technology-based intangible assets:**
> 1. Patented technology.[c]
> 2. Computer software and mask works.[c]
> 3. Unpatented technology.[s]
> 4. Databases, including title plants.[s]
> 5. Trade secrets, including secret formulas, processes, recipes.[c]
>
> *The intangible assets designated by the symbol (c) also could meet the separability criterion. However, separability is not a necessary condition for an asset to meet the contractual-legal criterion.

The FASB recognized the inherent difficulties in estimating the separate fair values of many intangibles and stated that

> Difficulties may arise in assigning the acquisition cost to individual intangible assets acquired in a basket purchase such as a business combination. Measuring some of those assets is less difficult than measuring other assets, particularly if they are exchangeable and traded regularly in the marketplace. . . . Nonetheless, even those assets that cannot be measured on that basis may have more cash flow streams directly or indirectly associated with them than can be used as the basis for measuring them. While the resulting measures may lack the precision of other measures, they provide information that is more representationally faithful than would be the case if those assets were simply subsumed into goodwill on the grounds of measurement difficulties. (FASB Exposure Draft, *Business Combinations and Intangible Assets*, para. 271)

Undoubtedly, as our knowledge economy continues its rapid growth, asset allocations to items such as those identified in Exhibit 2–7 are expected to be frequent.

## Purchased In-Process Research and Development

As discussed in this chapter, the accounting for a purchase business combination begins with the identification of the tangible and intangible assets acquired and liabilities assumed by the acquirer. The fair values of the individual assets and liabilities then provide the basis for purchase price allocations and financial statement valuations.

Recently, many firms—especially those in high-tech industries—have allocated significant portions of the purchase cost of acquired businesses to in-process research and development (IPR&D). A unique characteristic of IPR&D assets is that they must be written off immediately unless those assets have an alternative future use. FASB Interpretation No. 4, "Applicability of FASB Statement No. 2 to Business Combinations Accounted for by the Purchase Method," requires the identification and separation of assets resulting from research and development activities (for example, core technology) and assets to be used in research and development activities. The latter group of assets is considered to be "in-process research and development" and thus is expensed as part of the business combination. A common criterion employed in determining whether to expense or capitalize research and development costs is whether the resulting assets have reached technological feasibility. If the decision is made to capitalize the costs, estimates of the fair value of the resulting assets must be made. Important in estimating the fair value of research and development costs are factors such as stage of completion, technological uncertainties, and projected costs to complete the project.

The accounting for the immediate write-off of IPR&D acquired in a business combination is fairly straightforward. For example, assume that ProKey Company acquires 100 percent of the voting stock of SysLock for $900,000. SysLock is a startup company with $50,000 in equipment (fair value = $110,000) and research and development in process for a computer file locking system (fair value = $790,000). Although the locking system software is not technologically feasible yet, ProKey is confident that it will be developed sufficiently over the next several years. Therefore, ProKey allocates its purchase price of SysLock as follows:

| | | |
|---|---:|---:|
| Purchase price (cash) | | $900,000 |
| Book value acquired | | |
|     Common stock-SysLock | $ 50,000 | |
|     Retained earnings-SysLock | –0– | 50,000 |
| Excess of cost over book value | | $850,000 |
| Write-up equipment (110,000 − 50,000) | 60,000 | |
| Write-off IPR&D | 790,000 | 850,000 |
| | | –0– |

ProKey makes the following entries on its books on acquisition of SysLock:

| | | |
|---|---:|---:|
| Investment in SysLock | 900,000 | |
|     Cash | | 900,000 |
| To record the purchase of SysLock for $900,000 cash | | |

At acquisition, ProKey now has two options to accomplish the write-off of the acquired IPR&D. Under the first option, ProKey can simply leave the Investment in SysLock at $900,000 and rely on subsequent consolidated worksheet adjustments to accomplish the IPR&D allocation to expense.

Alternatively, ProKey can make the following entry on its books:

| | | |
|---|---:|---:|
| Research and development expense | 790,000 | |
|     Investment in SysLock | | 790,000 |
| To immediately write off to expense the $790,000 allocated to purchased in-process research and development. | | |

Under this second option, because the IPR&D has been expensed on ProKey's financial records, no other adjustments to IPR&D are required in consolidated worksheets. The Investment in SysLock simply carries forward a $110,000 balance. Whether ProKey chooses to rely

**EXHIBIT 2–8**
Recent Notable In-Process Research and Development Write-Offs

| | |
|---|---|
| Worldcom | $3,300 million |
| Compaq Computer | 3,200 million |
| Dupont | 1,441 million |
| Cadence Systems Design | 339 million* |

*Restated to $194 million in response to discussions with SEC.

on subsequent consolidated worksheet adjustments to accomplish the IPR&D write-off or immediately adjusts its own financial records, the reporting effect is the same. Current year income will be reduced by the $790,000 research and development expense.

Another example of an IPR&D expense is seen in the Yahoo! purchase of Log-Me-On.com. As noted in a recent Yahoo! 10-Q SEC filing, Log-Me-On's efforts were focused solely on developing an Internet browser technology that at the time was approximately 30 percent complete. This IPR&D was considered not to have reached technological feasibility and had no alternative future use as of the acquisition date. Of the $9.9 million purchase price for Log-Me-On.com, $9.8 million was allocated to IPR&D and immediately expensed.

The immediate expensing of IPR&D, although recently popular (see Exhibit 2–8), can be criticized as resulting in understated assets and distorted financial ratio results for many firms involved in purchase acquisitions. IPR&D in most cases clearly possesses value: One party pays another for the right to future cash flows resulting from the ongoing activity. However, the relevant FASB pronouncements not only allow immediate expensing but require it when technological feasibility and alternative future uses are not present in a research and development activity. Moreover, many firms prefer the immediate expensing of IPR&D. Although a one-time reduction of reported earnings takes place in the period of an acquisition involving IPR&D, subsequent reported earnings are free from such expenses and result in enhanced measures of return on equity, return on assets, and earnings per share.

The current application of the rules for expensing IPR&D has generated a great deal of controversy drawing the attention of the SEC and the FASB. In 1998 and 1999, the SEC cited several firms for overstating the allocated portion of IPR&D in business combinations. In the September 9, 1998, letter to the AICPA, Lynn Turner, the chief accountant for the SEC, notes that

> Although there was no change in the relevant accounting literature, IPR&D write-offs increased significantly in the 1990s. More intense merger activity in the technology sector may explain some of the increases, but abuses in the valuation of IPR&D are also suspected. This trend of larger write-offs could undermine public confidence in financial statements and presents significant challenges for the accounting profession.

The SEC cited several problems in the way firms allocated acquisition costs to IPR&D. In some cases, acquired firms with significant IPR&D reported no research and development expenditures in previous financial statements. In other cases, development work to update versions of existing products had been only partially completed at the time of acquisition. However, the vast majority of the purchase price was allocated to IPR&D, leaving little to support the value of the ongoing product. In several cases, firms were required to restate their IPR&D write-offs in response to SEC concerns. For example, in reporting on Digi International's fiscal third-quarter financial results on July 22, 1999, PR Newswire noted:

> In response to comments by the SEC regarding Digi's acquisition of ITK International, Inc., and Central Data Corporation, and the related purchase price allocation, the Company has elected to restate its previously issued financial statements to reduce the aggregate amount originally allocated to in-process research and development from $39.2 million to $16.1 million and, correspondingly, has increased the amount allocated to intangible assets and goodwill by $23.1 million.

The FASB is also struggling with the IPR&D controversy. On February 24, 1999, the FASB voted unanimously to revise the accounting rules for purchased IPR&D, calling for its capitalization and subsequent amortization to income. Nonetheless, the revision was short lived when the FASB later reversed itself, allowing the continued immediate expensing of IPR&D.

In *SFAS 141,* "Business Combinations," the FASB reaffirmed the expensing of acquired IPR&D until the matter is addressed comprehensively with all research and development activities, not just those involving business combinations. Then, in its recent project entitled, "Business Combinations: Purchase Method Procedures," (February 2003 update), the FASB is again revisiting the IPR&D issue. In this latest reconsideration, the preliminary recommendation is that certain IPR&D assets acquired in a business combination should be treated as assets subject to periodic impairment reviews. Given the value placed on research ideas and process development in today's economy, the problem of how to report the uncertain benefits associated with IPR&D will likely receive continued attention from regulators.

## UNCONSOLIDATED SUBSIDIARIES

Over the years, accountants have attempted to identify situations in which consolidated financial statements might not be appropriate for every subsidiary. Currently, however, only one exception is allowed where a majority-owned firm should not be consolidated. That exception is provided in FASB *Statement 94,* "Consolidation of All Majority-Owned Subsidiaries" as follows:

> An investment where control does not actually rest with the majority owners. Without control, the concept of a single economic entity is not applicable. In legal reorganizations and bankruptcies, for example, operational authority over the subsidiary is held by parties other than the parent company. Severe restrictions imposed by foreign governments also limit or remove the power held by the owners. For example, the financial statements of Unocal Corporation once reported "the consolidated financial statements of the company include the accounts of subsidiaries more than 50 percent owned, except for certain Brazilian subsidiaries which are accounted for by the cost method due to currency restrictions imposed by the Brazilian government." (FASB Statement 94)

This exception to the consolidation principle is predicated on the tentative quality of the control held by the parent. The relationship does not indicate the existence of a single economic entity.

A second exception to the consolidation of all majority-owned allowed by *Statement 94* was superceded in 2001 by FASB Statement 144, "Accounting for the Impairment or Disposal of Long-Lived Assets." Prior to Statement 144 if control was deemed to be temporary, such as when a business group of a consolidated entity was being held for sale, that business group's financial statements were not consolidated. However, Statement 144 concluded that "for any disposal group, information about the nature of both the assets and the liabilities of an asset group classified as held for sale is useful to users. Separately presenting those items in the statement of financial position provides information that is relevant and faithfully reports an entity's assets and its liabilities." Thus, even when control is temporary, a disposal group should be consolidated with separate presentation in the asset and liability sections of the statement of financial position.

Prior to the issuance of *Statement 94,* another important exception to consolidation was allowed. At that time, business combinations were permitted to omit subsidiaries from consolidation because of nonhomogeneity. *ARB 51* had suggested that a subsidiary should remain unconsolidated if the nature of its operations differed so significantly from that of the parent that the combined companies could not be viewed as a single entity. Despite ownership of a majority of voting stock, these companies had to be reported by use of the equity method so that only an investment asset and an equity income balance appeared in the consolidated statements.

Because of the complex nature of the activities in most modern businesses, application of the nonhomogeneity rule was subject to individual judgment. Traditionally, companies gave a broad interpretation to the concept of a single economic entity, so that virtually all subsidiaries were consolidated despite apparent differences in the nature of their operations. But, as *ARB 51* noted, "separate statements . . . may be preferable for a finance company where the parent and the other subsidiaries are engaged in manufacturing operations." Thus, prior to *Statement 94,* for example, General Motors did not consolidate its finance subsidiary, General Motors Acceptance Corporation (GMAC).

The practice of omitting such subsidiaries from consolidation has been criticized vigorously over the years as an excuse for removing large amounts of debt from the entity's balance sheet. Since the individual accounts of an unconsolidated subsidiary are not included in consolidated statements, finance operations could incur significant obligations that would not appear as liabilities of the business combination.

# THE POOLING OF INTERESTS METHOD OF ACCOUNTING FOR BUSINESS COMBINATIONS

In *SFAS 141,* "Business Combinations," the FASB states that "all business combinations should be accounted for using the purchase method," thereby eliminating the pooling method. However, the application of the purchase method will be applied prospectively, leaving intact long-lasting financial statement effects from past poolings. For example, the Pfizer–Warner-Lambert combination highlighted at the beginning of this chapter was accounted for as a pooling. Moreover, because differences between the purchase and pooling methods relate to fundamental issues of asset valuation and income recognition, the financial ratios resulting from past poolings will be affected for years to come. Therefore, to appreciate fully the financial reporting for business combinations, a solid familiarity with the pooling of interests accounting method remains necessary.

## Continuity of Ownership

Historically, many transactions did not involve a clean break in ownership. Often, former owners of separate firms would agree to combine for their mutual benefit and continue as owners of a combined firm. It was asserted that the assets and liabilities of the former firms were never really bought or sold; former owners merely exchanged ownership shares to become joint owners of the combined firm.

Combinations characterized by exchange of voting shares and continuation of previous ownership became known as *pooling of interests.* Rather than a purchase and sale transaction with one ownership group replacing another, a pooling of interests was characterized by a continuity of ownership interests before and after the business combination.

Because the basic characteristics of a purchase consolidation did not always appear in every business combination, the idea soon spread that two distinct types of combinations existed. Gradually, alternative consolidation procedures began to emerge based on pooling of interests concepts. Over the decades, this method was applied to a significant number of business combinations.

For example, the Goodyear Tire & Rubber Company exchanged nearly 25 million shares of its common stock for all of the outstanding common stock of Celeron Corporation to create a combination accounted for as a pooling of interests. As noted in Exhibit 2–9, Goodyear actually issued its stock in exchange for the shares held by the owners of Celeron. Consequently, the combined assets of these two companies were controlled by both the Goodyear shareholders and the previous Celeron owners (who now held Goodyear stock). Regardless of the number of shares exchanged, this same joint control has always been found in a pooling of interests.

Thus, a pooling of interests was characterized as a continuation of ownership in which neither a parent nor subsidiary could be easily identified. The combination was created by an exchange of voting stock and was not viewed as a bargained transaction with a precise acquisition price. To reflect these qualities, two important steps were required in accounting for a combination created as a pooling of interests:

1. The book values of the assets and liabilities of both companies became the book values reported by the combined entity. Because of the continuity of ownership, no new basis of accountability arose.
2. The revenue and expense accounts were combined retroactively as well as prospectively. Again, continuity of ownership allowed for the recognition of income accruing to the owners both before and after the combination.

**EXHIBIT 2–9**

**Business Combination—Pooling of Interests***

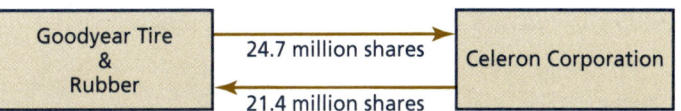

*This diagram is intended merely to represent the relationship created by a pooling of interests. The shares delivered by Celeron actually came from its owners who in turn received the 24.7 million shares of Goodyear Tire & Rubber directly from the company.

Therefore, in a pooling, reported income is typically higher than under purchase accounting. Under pooling, not only do the firms retroactively combine incomes but the smaller asset bases also result in smaller depreciation and amortization expenses. Because net income reported in financial statements often is used in a variety of contracts, including managerial compensation, the pooling method was considered an attractive alternative to purchase accounting.

The APB, in *Opinion 16,* allowed both the purchase and pooling of interest methods to account for business combinations. However, the Board placed tight restrictions on the pooling method to prevent managers from engaging in purchase transactions and reporting them as poolings of interest. *Opinion 16* established 12 criteria that had to be present in a business combination to justify adoption of the pooling method. By setting strict guidelines, the Board hoped to ensure that only combinations clearly outside the essence of a purchase would fall under the pooling of interests classification. *Business combinations that failed to meet even 1 of these 12 criteria had to be accounted for by the purchase method.*

These criteria, which are presented in the appendix at the end of this chapter, had two overriding objectives: First, they defined a pooling of interests as a single transaction (or series of transactions occurring over a limited time) in which two independent companies are united solely through the exchange of voting common stock. To ensure the complete fusion of the two organizations, one company had to obtain substantially all (90 percent or more) of the voting stock of the other.

The second general objective of these criteria was to prevent purchase combinations from being disguised as poolings. Past experience had shown the APB that combination transactions were frequently manipulated so that they would qualify for pooling of interests treatment (usually to increase reported earnings). However, subsequent events, often involving cash being paid or received by the parties, revealed the true nature of the combination: One company was purchasing the other in a bargained exchange. The APB designed a number of the 12 criteria to stop this practice.

For example, to be considered a pooling of interests, no agreement could exist to reacquire any of the shares issued in creating the combination. This rule prevented the parties from eventually receiving cash or other assets as part of the transaction. For the same reason, significant assets of the combined companies could not be sold for two years unless duplication existed. These restrictions helped to ensure that only combinations meeting the essence of a pooling were given that treatment—a continuation of the companies and a continuation of the ownership.

### Pooling of Interests When Dissolution Takes Place

To demonstrate the formation of a pooling of interests, assume that BigNet Company and Smallport Company decide to join operations on December 31 (see Exhibit 2–4).[10] This combination is created when BigNet issues 23,000 new shares of its common stock, with a $5 par value and a $100 market value per share, to the owners of Smallport in exchange for all of the company's outstanding common shares. Smallport transfers its assets and liabilities to BigNet and dissolves itself as a separate corporation. Stock registration fees of $5,000 are paid by BigNet as well as $3,000 in other costs directly associated with the combination. In creating this business combination, the companies followed all 12 criteria established by *APB Opinion 16* for a pooling of interests (see the appendix at the end of the chapter).

---

[10] We assume the initiation date for the combination occurs on or prior to June 30, 2001—the deadline for pooling accounting as stated in *SFAS 141,* "Business Combinations."

### Pooling of Interests Method—Subsidiary Dissolved

| BigNet Company's Financial Records—December 31 | | |
|---|---:|---:|
| Current Assets | 300,000 | |
| Computers and Equipment | 400,000 | |
| Capitalized Software | 100,000 | |
| Dividends Paid | 10,000 | |
| Expenses | 380,000 | |
|     Notes Payable | | 200,000 |
|     Revenues | | 500,000 |
|     Common Stock (23,000 shares issued by BigNet at $5 par value) | | 115,000 |
|     Additional Paid-In Capital (to equate contributed capital with $120,000 amount reported by Smallport) | | 5,000 |
|     Retained Earnings, 1/1 (to record amount equal to book value of Smallport) | | 370,000 |
| Expenses (combination costs) | 8,000 | |
|     Cash | | 8,000 |
| To record book value of Smallport's account obtained through a pooling of interests. Direct combination costs are expensed. | | |

As stated earlier, a pooling of interests consolidates all accounts at their historical book values. Therefore, the reported value of each of Smallport's accounts (assets, liabilities, revenues, expenses, and dividends paid) simply can be transferred into BigNet's financial records through a journal entry. To ensure that adequate disclosure is provided, *APB Opinion 16* does require that the details of the separate operations be presented in a note to the consolidated statements.

In contrast to the purchase method, no part of the $8,000 in combination costs is capitalized; the entire amount is recorded here as an expense. According to *APB Opinion 16* (par. 58), "The pooling of interests method records neither the acquiring of assets nor the obtaining of capital. Therefore, costs incurred to effect a combination accounted for by that method and to integrate the continuing operations are expenses of the combined corporation rather than additions to assets or direct reductions of stockholders' equity." To maintain book value, the cost of uniting the organizations is not viewed as a change in either asset or contributed capital accounts; thus, an expense is recorded by the combined entity.

Entering the book values of Smallport's assets, liabilities, revenues, expenses, and dividends into the records of BigNet poses little trouble.[11] Likewise, the $8,000 in direct combination costs is simply assigned directly to expense. However, the recording of the 23,000 shares of stock being issued by BigNet should be noted. According to Exhibit 2–4, Smallport is reporting contributed capital (the Common Stock and Additional Paid-In Capital accounts) of $120,000 and retained earnings of $370,000.[12] Because poolings retain book value, BigNet uses these same figures in recording the issuance of its own stock. In that way, Smallport's equity balances are included within the combined totals.

Regardless of the amounts reported by Smallport, BigNet's Common Stock account must be increased by $115,000 to reflect the $5 par value of these 23,000 shares. To arrive at the $120,000 figure that corresponds with Smallport's total contributed capital, BigNet also records $5,000 as Additional Paid-In Capital. The entry is then completed with a $370,000 credit to Retained Earnings. Smallport's contributed capital total and Retained Earnings both have been added into the business combination at book value.

---

[11] As is discussed in Chapter 3, dividends paid between the related companies after a combination is created are intercompany transfers that have to be eliminated. In a pooling of interests, though, any amounts distributed to previous owners before the combination was created continue to be reported as Dividends Paid.

[12] Although the date of the pooling was December 31, Smallport's Retained Earnings balance as of the first day of the year is recorded by the combination with the company's current revenues, expenses, and dividends being reported separately.

After recording these accounts, BigNet's financial records show $692,000 in Current Assets ($400,000 + $300,000 − 8,000), $2,400,000 in Computers and Equipment ($2,000,000 + $400,000), and so on. The Revenues account now holds $1,500,000 ($1,000,000 + $500,000) while expenses are recorded at $1,188,000 ($800,000 + $380,000 + $8,000 in combination costs). *Because book values are retained, the various asset, liability, revenue, expense, and dividend balances are not affected by the number of shares issued by BigNet.* If 2,300 shares or 230,000 shares had been exchanged rather than 23,000, the same consolidated figures still would have been appropriate for these accounts.

By comparing this consolidation to previous illustrations, several areas of distinct contrast can be seen between the purchase method and the pooling of interests method:

|  | Consolidation | |
| --- | --- | --- |
|  | **Purchase Method** | **Pooling of Interests Method** |
| Assets and liabilities of subsidiary | Recorded at fair value.* | Recorded at book value. |
| Goodwill | Excess of purchase price over fair value of subsidiary net assets. | Not recognized. |
| Revenues and expenses of subsidiary | Accrued only after date of acquisition. | Recognized retroactively. |
| Shares issued to create business combination | Recorded at fair value if any shares are issued. | Based on book value of subsidiary's contributed capital and retained earnings at beginning of year. |
| Combination costs | Included as part of purchase price unless incurred in connection with issuance of stock, a cost that reduces paid-in capital. | Expensed immediately. |

*If purchase price is less than fair market value, noncurrent assets (except for any long-term investments in marketable securities) are recorded at reduced amounts.

When reviewing the recording of a past pooling of interests, one potential variation to the previous entry can be encountered. Although poolings are based on retaining book values, the recording of contributed capital can cause a problem. Because issued shares are always credited for par value, BigNet's common stock had to be recorded as $115,000, although Smallport's balance for this same account was $100,000. As indicated, BigNet increased its additional paid-in capital by $5,000 so that total contributed capital equaled Smallport's $120,000 balance (see Exhibit 2–10).

If BigNet had originally issued only 18,000 shares, its Common Stock account would be credited for $90,000 with an accompanying $30,000 added to Additional Paid-In Capital. Once again, the $120,000 total book value of Smallport's contributed capital is replicated by the entry. Conversely, as shown in Exhibit 2–10, if 26,000 shares with a par value of $130,000 were exchanged by BigNet to create this pooling, a $10,000 *reduction* to Additional Paid-In Capital is necessary to arrive at the appropriate $120,000 total. In each case, the book value of Smallport's total contributed capital is retained by the combination.

A slightly different problem arises in recording total contributed capital for a pooling when the number of issued shares is relatively large. Assume, as an example, that 35,000 shares of common stock are exchanged by BigNet to establish this pooling of interests with Smallport. The $175,000 par value of the stock necessitates a $55,000 reduction in BigNet's Additional Paid-In Capital to equal the $120,000 contributed capital reported by Smallport.

However, Exhibit 2–4 indicates that BigNet's Additional Paid-In Capital account holds only a $40,000 balance. Because a negative contributed capital balance is not possible, BigNet's additional paid-in capital is first dropped to zero with the remaining $15,000 decrease being made in Retained Earnings. Exhibit 2–10 shows that only $355,000 in retained earnings

**EXHIBIT 2–10** Recording of Shares Issued in a Pooling of Interests

|  | Smallport's Book Values | BigNet Company Issues ||||
|---|---|---|---|---|---|
| (Exhibit 2–4) | | 18,000 Shares | 23,000 Shares | 26,000 Shares | 35,000 Shares |
| Common stock | $100,000 | $90,000 | $115,000 | $130,000 | $175,000 |
| Additional paid-in capital | 20,000 | 30,000 | 5,000 | (10,000) | (40,000)* |
| Total contributed capital | 120,000 | 120,000 | 120,000 | 120,000 | 135,000 |
| Retained earnings | 370,000 | 370,000 | 370,000 | 370,000 | 355,000† |

*BigNet's Additional Paid-In Capital account is reduced from $40,000 to zero.

†Because the contributed capital of issued shares is $55,000 greater than that reported by Smallport, BigNet's APIC is first reduced to zero ($40,000 reduction) and the amount recorded for Retained Earnings ($355,000) reflects the remaining $15,000 reduction.

(rather than Smallport's $370,000 balance) is recorded by the business combination when 35,000 shares are issued. *Thus, if BigNet's issued shares have a total par value more than Smallport's total contributed capital, a reduction must be made. BigNet initially decreases its own Additional Paid-In Capital account. However, if that amount proves to be insufficient, the Retained Earnings balance also must be reduced.*

### Pooling of Interests When Separate Incorporation Is Maintained

The combination of BigNet Company and Smallport Company is presented again to demonstrate a pooling of interests, one in which both companies retain their separate legal identities. For this illustration, the same financial information is used as in the purchase consolidation shown in Exhibit 2–6. As in the purchase situation, BigNet issues 26,000 shares of common stock on December 31 for all of Smallport's outstanding shares. Also, direct combination costs of $40,000 are incurred. Smallport's accounts are not transferred to BigNet's financial records; both companies continue as separate corporations and maintain independent accounting systems. However, the assumption is made here that the combination has met all 12 requirements for a pooling of interests.

BigNet must first record the issuance of 26,000 shares of common stock to create this business combination. Because Smallport is not being dissolved, BigNet establishes an investment balance rather than recording Smallport's individual accounts. Because the combination is a pooling, this figure is based on Smallport's $490,000 book value as of the beginning of the year. Using the January 1 total allows the current revenues, expenses, and dividends to be included as separate items in recording the business combination.

The issued shares are recorded by BigNet at their par value of $130,000. BigNet's Additional Paid-In Capital account is reduced by $10,000 to arrive at total contributed capital of $120,000, the same book value as Smallport's contributed capital. Retained earnings at January 1 also are included in this entry because operating activities are retroactively consolidated in a pooling of interests. The direct combination costs are expensed immediately.

*Pooling of Interests Method—Subsidiary Not Dissolved*

| BigNet's Financial Records—December 31 | | |
|---|---|---|
| Investment in Smallport Company (1/1 book value) | 490,000 | |
| Additional Paid-In Capital (to align contributed capital with that of Smallport) | 10,000 | |
|     Common Stock (26,000 shares at $5 par value) | | 130,000 |
|     Retained Earnings, 1/1 (to record balance equal to book value of Smallport) | | 370,000 |
| Expenses (direct combination costs) | 40,000 | |
|     Cash | | 40,000 |
| To record issuance of 26,000 shares of stock in exchange for all of the outstanding shares of Smallport in a combination accounted for as a pooling of interests. Direct combination costs are properly expensed. | | |

# Discussion Question

## HOW DOES A PURCHASE DIFFER FROM A POOLING OF INTERESTS?

On December 31, 2000, Acme Taxicab Company agreed to form a business combination with Wilbury's Cabs. Acme exchanged 600 shares of its previously unissued, $20 par value stock with Roy Wilbury for all of the outstanding shares of Wilbury's Cabs. Acme's common stock had a fair market value on that date of $100 per share.

The only assets owned by Wilbury's Cabs were eight used taxicabs having a fair market value of $5,000 each. Because of accelerated depreciation, the average book value of these assets was $2,000. Acme has 15 automobiles of its own with a total book value of $60,000 but a fair market value of $74,000.

During 2000, the two companies separately reported the following revenues and expenses:

|  | Acme | Wilbury |
|---|---|---|
| Revenues | $220,000 | $95,000 |
| Expenses | 150,000 | 60,000 |

Based on the information presented here, no determination is possible as to whether a pooling of interests or a purchase has been created.

On a consolidated balance sheet, how will the reported asset balances differ, depending on the type of method that is appropriate?

If a business combination is created as a purchase, one set of assets and liabilities is adjusted to fair market value whereas the other is left at book value. Why are both sets of assets and liabilities not revalued?

On a consolidated income statement, how will the balances differ, depending on the method considered appropriate?

Are external decision makers properly served by allowing such widely varying numbers to be reported depending on whether a purchase or a pooling of interests has taken place?

Based on the facts presented in the case, which set of financial statements best mirrors the economic reality of the business combination that has occurred?

---

When the common stock shares are exchanged, the combination is formed, and consolidated financial statements can be prepared using the worksheet produced in Exhibit 2–11. This pooling of interests is carried out through the following series of steps:

### Step 1

Prior to creating this worksheet, BigNet's balances are adjusted to show (1) the effect of its issuance of stock and (2) the direct combination costs. The updated accounts are then entered into the appropriate columns on the worksheet (see Exhibit 2–4 for original book values).

### Step 2

The Investment in Smallport Company account is eliminated as part of the basic consolidation Entry **S**. In the same manner as the purchase method, the Investment account is not consolidated; rather, the specific accounts that it represents should be reported by the business combination. Therefore, the $490,000 investment is removed on the worksheet so that it can be replaced by the individual balances of Smallport Company.

### Step 3

Smallport's stockholders' equity balances also are eliminated by this same Entry **S**. In a purchase, these figures are removed because only assets and liabilities can actually be transferred to the parent. Conversely, for a pooling when a fusion of ownership interests is said to occur,

## EXHIBIT 2–11  Pooling of Interests—Date of Acquisition

**BIGNET COMPANY AND SMALLPORT COMPANY**
Consolidation Worksheet
For Period Ending December 31

| Accounts | BigNet Company | Smallport Company | Consolidation Entries Debits | Consolidation Entries Credits | Consolidated Totals |
|---|---|---|---|---|---|
| **Income Statement** | | | | | |
| Revenues | (1,000,000) | (500,000) | | | (1,500,000) |
| Expenses | 840,000 | 380,000 | | | 1,220,000 |
| Net income | (160,000) | (120,000) | | | (280,000) |
| **Statement of Retained Earnings** | | | | | |
| Retained earnings, 1/1 | (1,240,000)* | (370,000) | (S) 370,000 | | (1,240,000) |
| Net income (above) | (160,000) | (120,000) | | | (280,000) |
| Dividends paid | 110,000 | 10,000 | | | 120,000 |
| Retained earnings, 12/31 | (1,290,000) | (480,000) | | | (1,400,000) |
| **Balance Sheet** | | | | | |
| Current assets | 360,000* | 300,000 | | | 660,000 |
| Investment in Smallport Company | 490,000* | –0– | | (S) 490,000 | –0– |
| Computers and equipment | 2,000,000 | 400,000 | | | 2,400,000 |
| Capitalized software | 500,000 | 100,000 | | | 600,000 |
| Total assets | 3,350,000 | 800,000 | | | 3,660,000 |
| Notes payable | (300,000) | (200,000) | | | (500,000) |
| Common stock | (1,730,000)* | (100,000) | (S) 100,000 | | (1,730,000) |
| Additional paid-in capital | (30,000)* | (20,000) | (S)  20,000 | | (30,000) |
| Retained earnings, 12/31 (above) | (1,290,000) | (480,000) | | | (1,400,000) |
| Total liabilities and equities | (3,350,000) | (800,000) | | | (3,660,000) |

Note: Parentheses indicate a credit balance.
*Balances have been adjusted for issuance of stock and payment of consolidation costs.

the equity figures for both companies must be included. However, Smallport's equity accounts have already been brought into the consolidated totals through the recording of BigNet's 26,000 shares of issued stock.

The initial investment entry has already added these equity balances to BigNet's records prior to consolidating the financial statements. Thus, Smallport's Common Stock, Additional Paid-In Capital, and Retained Earnings must be eliminated on the worksheet to prevent their inclusion in the final figures a second time. The beginning-of-year balance for Smallport's Retained Earnings is being removed to allow the current year's revenues, expenses, and dividends to be reported by the business combination.

### Step 4

For a pooling of interests, the consolidation process is carried out by adding together the book values of each account. For example, BigNet's revenue of $1,000,000 and Smallport's revenue of $500,000 are extended for a consolidated total of $1,500,000. When a consolidation entry affects an account (such as the elimination of Smallport's equity accounts), the impact of that adjustment also must be reflected in this extension process. However, because a purchase price is not determined in a pooling, no goodwill is recognized and no valuation adjustments are made to any asset or liability.

*Step 5*

For each of the financial statements on the worksheet, a total is calculated. The income statement ends with a net income balance, the statement of retained earnings computes ending Retained Earnings, and the balance sheet arrives at Total Assets as well as Total Liabilities and Equities. As discussed previously, these final figures are not derived by consolidating the respective balances of the separate companies. Instead, the components in each statement are extended and then used to compute the ending balance.

On the income statement demonstrated here, revenues and expenses are added to produce totals of $1,500,000 and $1,220,000, respectively, indicating consolidated net income of $280,000. This figure is moved to the corresponding line within the statement of retained earnings. Each of the other elements constituting this second statement are extended to produce ending retained earnings of $1,400,000. This total is then included within the stockholders' equity section of the consolidated balance sheet, enabling it to properly balance.

*Step 6*

After all accounts have been consolidated, the final balances on the worksheet are used to prepare financial statements for the business combination of BigNet Company and Smallport Company. Exhibit 2–12 provides a comparison of the figures developed for the purchase consolidation shown previously in Exhibit 2–6 and the pooling of interests in Exhibit 2–11. Note the more favorable portrayal of two popular financial performance ratios for pooling versus purchase despite the combination of identical firms.

## POOLING OF INTERESTS—THE CONTROVERSY

Over the years, the legitimacy of the pooling of interests method has frequently been questioned. One major theoretical problem associated with the pooling method is that it ignores cost figures indicated by the transaction that created the combination. The number of shares exchanged has no impact on consolidated asset and liability balances. What is normally a significant event for both companies is simply omitted from any accounting consideration. *All book values are retained as if nothing has happened. APB Opinion 16* (par. 39) itself admits

> The most serious defect attributed to pooling of interests accounting by those who oppose it is that it does not accurately reflect the economic substance of the business combination transaction. They believe that the method ignores the bargaining which results in the combination by accounting only for the amounts previously shown in accounts of the combining companies.

As a further argument against pooling of interests, many accountants believe that only one accounting approach should be applicable for all business combinations. They hold that all combinations are essentially the same. Even though a variety of formats does exist, critics contend that a parent and an acquisition price can be determined in virtually every case. In addition, conveying freely traded stock is held to be the same as conveying cash. According to this argument, the availability of two radically different accounting methods is simply not warranted. Interestingly, the pooling of interests method has been primarily found in the United States. "Of all the major industrialized countries, only Great Britain allows anything resembling pooling, and its rule makers are modifying the rules to prevent most poolings."[13]

The depth of controversy sparked by the pooling of interests method is clearly demonstrated in *Accounting Research Study No. 5 (ARS 5)* where Arthur Wyatt stated that "no basis exists in principle for a continuation of what is presently known as 'pooling-of-interests' accounting *if* the business combination involves an exchange of assets and/or equities between independent parties."[14]

---

[13] Michael Davis, "APB 16: Time to Reconsider," *Journal of Accountancy,* October 1991, p. 99.
[14] Arthur Wyatt, "A Critical Study of Accounting for Business Combinations," *Accounting Research Study No. 5* (New York: AICPA, 1963), p. 105.

## EXHIBIT 2–12
**Comparison of Purchase Method and Pooling of Interests Method**

General Information: 26,000 shares of BigNet Company (par value of $5 per share but a market value of $100 per share) issued for all outstanding shares of Smallport Company on December 31. Cash of $40,000 paid for direct consolidation costs.

|  | Purchase Method (Exhibit 2–6) | Pooling of Interests Method (Exhibit 2–11) |
|---|---:|---:|
| Revenues | $1,000,000 | $1,500,000 |
| Expenses | (800,000) | (1,220,000) |
| Net income | $ 200,000 | $ 280,000 |
|  |  |  |
| Beginning retained earnings | $ 870,000 | $1,240,000 |
| Net income (above) | 200,000 | 280,000 |
| Dividends paid | (110,000) | (120,000) |
| Ending retained earnings | $ 960,000 | $1,400,000 |
|  |  |  |
| Current assets | $ 660,000 | $ 660,000 |
| Computers and equipment | 2,600,000 | 2,400,000 |
| Capitalized software | 2,100,000 | 600,000 |
| Goodwill | 390,000 | –0– |
| Total assets | $5,750,000 | $3,660,000 |
|  |  |  |
| Notes payable | $ 550,000 | $ 500,000 |
| Common stock | 1,730,000 | 1,730,000 |
| Additional paid-in capital | 2,510,000 | 30,000 |
| Retained earnings (above) | 960,000 | 1,400,000 |
| Total liabilities and equities | $5,750,000 | $3,660,000 |
|  |  |  |
| **Financial Performance Ratios** |  |  |
| Net income/Total assets | 3.48% | 7.65% |
| Net income/Total equity | 3.85% | 8.86% |

Additionally, in a dissent to *APB Opinion 16,* Sidney Davidson, Charles Horngren, and J. S. Seidman asserted that

> The real abuse is pooling itself. On that, the only answer is to eliminate pooling. . . . Elimination of pooling will remove the confusion that comes from the coexistence of pooling and purchase accounting. Above all, the elimination of pooling would remove an aberration in historical cost accounting that permits an acquisition to be accounted for on the basis of the seller's cost rather than the buyer's cost of the assets obtained in a bargained exchange.

The acceptability of the pooling of interests method could, indeed, have been eliminated years ago except for its popularity in the business world. Preference for the pooling method has been based largely on the desirable impact that it usually produces on reported net income. The most obvious effect is the inclusion of the subsidiary's net income as if that company had always been part of the consolidated entity. This retroactive treatment can lead to immediate improvement in the profitability picture being reported. To the extent that managerial compensation contracts are based on accounting measures of profitability, a further motivation to employ the pooling of interests method to accounting for a business combination was provided.

Another income effect helped to further account for the popularity enjoyed by the pooling of interests method. In a purchase combination, the subsidiary's assets and liabilities are adjusted to fair market value with goodwill often recognized. Such allocations are viewed as cost figures of the business combination, costs that have only limited useful lives (except when relating to land). Thus, these amounts (which can be extremely large) required amortization over future accounting periods. The resulting expense, encountered only in the purchase method, served to reduce consolidated net income year after year.

Conversely, a pooling of interests consolidated all accounts at their book values so that no additional amortization expense was ever recognized. Therefore, in most past business combinations, the income reported for each succeeding year was higher using the pooling method than would have been the case if consolidated by the purchase method.[15]

Given these reporting advantages, the desire by businesses to create combinations that would qualify as poolings is not surprising. Historically, the accounting profession attempted to define the characteristics of a pooling of interests in such a way as to restrict its use to combinations that were clearly fusions of two independent companies. Over the years, however, the identification of attributes considered to be essential to a pooling of interests proved to be a difficult task.

## FASB Position

In an article supporting their unanimous decision to eliminate the pooling of interests method of accounting for business combinations, the FASB cited the following reasons for their action:

- The pooling method provides investors with less information—and less relevant information—than that provided by the purchase method.
- The pooling method ignores the values exchanged in a business combination while the purchase method reflects them.
- Under the pooling method, financial statement readers cannot tell how much was invested in the transaction, nor can they track the subsequent performance of the investment.
- Having two methods of accounting makes it difficult for investors to compare companies when they have used different methods to account for their business combinations.
- Because future cash flows are the same whether the pooling or purchase method is used, the boost in earnings under the pooling method reflects artificial accounting differences rather than real economic differences.
- Business combinations are acquisitions and should be accounted for as such, based on the value of what is given up in exchange, regardless of whether it is cash, other assets, debt, or equity shares.[16]

## Summary

1. Consolidation of financial information is required for external reporting purposes whenever one organization gains control of another, thus forming a single economic entity. In many combinations, all but one of the companies is dissolved as a separate legal corporation. Therefore, the consolidation process is carried out only at the date of acquisition to bring together all accounts into a single set of financial records. In other combinations, the companies retain their identities as separate enterprises and continue to maintain their own individual accounting systems. For these cases, consolidation is a periodic process necessary whenever financial statements are to be produced. This periodic procedure is frequently accomplished through the use of a worksheet and consolidation entries.

2. A purchase occurs when one entity acquires control over another. The acquisition price is based on the exchange transaction and includes all direct consolidation costs unless expended in the issuance of stock. The assets and liabilities of the acquired company are consolidated based on their fair market values at the date of purchase. If the price paid exceeds the total fair market value of the net assets, the residual amount is recorded in the consolidated financial statements as goodwill, an intangible asset.

3. For a purchase, if the acquisition price is less than total fair market value, a reduction in the consolidated balances is necessary. The acquired company's assets and liabilities are recorded at fair market value except for noncurrent assets (however, financial assets other than equity method investments, assets to be disposed of by sale, deferred tax assets, and prepaid pension assets still are recorded at fair market values). Because of the bargain purchase, these noncurrent assets are consolidated at amounts less than their fair values. The reduction is the difference between the parent's purchase price and the total fair market value of the subsidiary's assets and liabilities. This figure is prorated based on the fair market values of the various noncurrent assets. An extraordinary gain is reported if the reduction exceeds the total value of the applicable noncurrent assets.

---

[15] For example, see "Anatomy of a Pooling: The AT&T/NCR Merger," by Andrew Fioriti and Thomas Brady, *Ohio CPA Journal*, October 1994, p. 20.

[16] "Why Eliminate the Pooling Method," August 31, *1999 Financial Accounting Series Status Report No. 316* (Financial Accounting Foundation/FASB).

4. *SFAS 141* pays particular attention to the recognition of intangible assets in business combinations. It specifically identifies many categories of intangibles. An intangible asset must be recognized in an acquiring firm's financial statement if the intangible arises from a legal or contractual right (e.g., trademarks, copyrights, artistic materials, royalty agreements). If the intangible asset does not represent a legal or contractual right, the intangible will still be recognized if it is capable of being separated from the firm (e.g., customer lists, noncontractual customer relationships, unpatented technology). Acquired assets identified as in-process research and development will continue to be expensed at the acquisition date if the research has not reached technological feasibility and the assets associated with the research have no alternative future uses.

5. Past policy allowed a business combination to be accounted for as either a purchase or a pooling of interests. To differentiate the applicable use of these methods, 12 criteria were established by the APB. If all 12 were satisfied, the combination was to be viewed as a pooling of interests. Otherwise, the purchase method was appropriate. The two methods were not interchangeable; a specific approach was required based on these criteria. However, the FASB has mandated elimination of the pooling method, thus requiring all combinations to be accounted for as purchases.

6. Past pooling of interests were formed by uniting the ownership of two companies through the exchange of securities. This method accounts for the new combination by consolidating all accounts at book value. Neither goodwill nor any other account valuation adjustment is recognized because no acquisition price is established. Without a purchase price, direct consolidation costs cannot be capitalized; they must be expensed immediately. For a pooling of interests, all revenues, expenses, and other operational accounts are consolidated on a retroactive basis.

7. The pooling of interests method was criticized often because it relied on book values only and, therefore, ignored the exchange transaction that formed the economic entity. Poolings also were questioned because of the retroactive treatment of operating results. Consequently, companies were able to increase reported earnings by pooling with another company rather than by improving operating efficiency.

## Comprehensive Illustration

### PROBLEM

*(Estimated Time: 45 to 65 Minutes)* Following are the account balances of Marston Company and Richmond Company as of December 31. The appraised values of Richmond Company assets and liabilities have also been included.

|  | Marston Company Book Value 12/31/03 | Richmond Company Book Value 12/31/03 | Richmond Company Appraised Value 12/31/03 |
|---|---|---|---|
| Cash | $ 600,000 | $ 200,000 | $ 200,000 |
| Receivables | 900,000 | 300,000 | 290,000 |
| Inventory | 1,100,000 | 600,000 | 820,000 |
| Buildings (net) | 3,000,000 | 800,000 | 900,000 |
| Equipment (net) | 6,000,000 | 500,000 | 500,000 |
| In-process research and development | –0– | –0– | 100,000 |
| Accounts payable | (400,000) | (200,000) | (200,000) |
| Notes payable | (3,400,000) | (1,100,000) | (1,100,000) |
| Totals | $ 7,800,000 | $1,100,000 | $1,510,000 |
| Common stock—$20 par value | $(2,000,000) | | |
| Common stock—$5 par value | | $ (720,000) | |
| Additional paid-in capital | (900,000) | (100,000) | |
| Retained earnings, 1/1/03 | (2,300,000) | (130,000) | |
| Revenues | (6,000,000) | (900,000) | |
| Expenses | 3,400,000 | 750,000 | |

Note: Parentheses indicate a credit balance.

Also assume that Marston relies on consolidated worksheet adjustments to reflect any appropriate write-off to expense of acquired in-process research and development.

## Additional Information (not recorded in the preceding figures)

- On December 31, 2003, Marston issues 50,000 shares of its $20 par value common stock for all of the outstanding shares of Richmond Company.

- In creating this combination, Marston pays $10,000 in stock issuance costs and $20,000 in other direct combination costs.

## Required:

a. Assume that Marston's stock has a fair market value of $32.00 per share. Prepare the necessary journal entries if Richmond is to dissolve itself as a separate legal entity.

b. Assume that Marston's stock has a fair market value of $28.52 per share. Richmond will retain separate legal incorporation and maintain its own accounting systems. Prepare a worksheet to consolidate the accounts of the two companies.

# SOLUTION

a. In a business combination, the accountant should first determine the parent company's acquisition price. Since Marston's stock is valued at $32 per share, the 50,000 issued shares are worth $1,600,000 in total. The $10,000 stock issuance cost is reported as a reduction to Additional Paid-In Capital. The other $20,000 direct combination costs must be added to the value of the issued shares to arrive at a purchase price of $1,620,000. This total is compared to the $1,510,000 market value of Richmond's assets and liabilities (including the value of IPR&D). Since Marston has paid $110,000 more than fair market value ($1,620,000 − $1,510,000), that figure would be recognized as goodwill.

Because dissolution is to occur, Richmond's asset and liability accounts are transferred to Marston and entered at fair market value with the excess recorded as goodwill. The payment of the stock issuance costs is journalized separately to avoid confusion.

**Marston Company's Financial Records—December 31, 2003**

| | | |
|---|---:|---:|
| Cash | 200,000 | |
| Receivables | 290,000 | |
| Inventory | 820,000 | |
| Buildings | 900,000 | |
| Equipment | 500,000 | |
| Research and Development Expense | 100,000 | |
| Goodwill | 110,000 | |
|     Accounts Payable | | 200,000 |
|     Notes Payable | | 1,100,000 |
|     Common Stock (Marston) (par value) | | 1,000,000 |
|     Additional Paid-In Capital (market value in excess of par value) | | 600,000 |
|     Cash (paid for combination costs) | | 20,000 |
| To record purchase of Richmond Company. | | |
| Additional Paid-In Capital | 10,000 | |
|     Cash (stock issuance costs) | | 10,000 |
| To record payment of stock issuance costs. | | |

b. Under this scenario, because a different value is attributed to the issued shares, a new purchase price must be calculated:

|   |   |   |
|---|---:|---:|
| 50,000 shares of stock at $28.52 each | | $1,426,000 |
| Other direct combination costs | | 20,000 |
| Purchase price | | $1,446,000 |

Because the subsidiary is maintaining separate incorporation, Marston establishes an investment account to reflect the $1,446,000 purchase price:

**Marston's Financial Records—December 31, 2003**

|   |   |   |
|---|---:|---:|
| Investment in Richmond Company | 1,446,000 | |
|     Common Stock (Marston) (par value) | | 1,000,000 |
|     Additional Paid-In Capital (market value in excess of par value) | | 426,000 |
|     Cash (paid for combination costs) | | 20,000 |
| To record purchase of Richmond Company. | | |
| Additional Paid-In Capital | 10,000 | |
|     Cash (paid for stock issuance costs) | | 10,000 |
| To record payment of stock issuance costs. | | |

Separate incorporation is being maintained; thus, a worksheet must be developed for consolidation purposes. The parent needs to analyze the purchase price to determine the allocations required to the individual accounts:

|   |   |   |
|---|---:|---:|
| Purchase price paid by Marston | | $1,446,000 |
| Book value of Richmond | | 1,100,000 |
|     Excess of cost over book value | | $346,000 |

Allocations made to specific accounts based on differences in fair market values and book values:

|   |   |   |
|---|---:|---:|
| Receivables ($290,000 − $300,000) | $(10,000) | |
| Inventory ($820,000 − $600,000) | 220,000 | |
| Buildings ($900,000 − $800,000) | 100,000 | |
| In-process research and development | 100,000 | 410,000 |
|     Bargain purchase | | $ (64,000) |

Marston's $1,446,000 purchase price is $64,000 less than the $1,510,000 fair market value of Richmond's individual accounts. This reduction must be assigned to the subsidiary's applicable noncurrent assets (including IPR&D) based on their relative fair market values:

|   | Fair Market Value | Percentage of Fair Market Value | Reduction | Allocation to Individual Assets |
|---|---:|---:|---:|---:|
| Buildings | 900,000 | 60.00% | 64,000 | 38,400 |
| Equipment | 500,000 | 33.33% | 64,000 | 21,333 |
| IPR&D | 100,000 | 6.67% | 64,000 | 4,267 |
| Totals | 1,500,000 | 100.00% | | 64,000 |

Thus, within the consolidation worksheet, the subsidiary's buildings are assigned a reduced value of $861,600 ($900,000 − $38,400). The equipment is adjusted to $478,667 ($500,000 − $21,333), and the in-process research and development is expensed at $95,733 ($100,000 − $4,267).

Exhibit 2–13 can now be developed using the following steps to arrive at totals for the consolidated financial statements:

**EXHIBIT 2–13** Comprehensive Illustration—Solution—Purchase Method

**MARSTON COMPANY AND RICHMOND COMPANY**
Consolidation Worksheet
For Period Ending December 31, 2003

| Accounts | Marston Company | Richmond Company | Consolidation Entries Debit | Consolidation Entries Credit | Consolidated Totals |
|---|---|---|---|---|---|
| **Income Statement** | | | | | |
| Revenues | (6,000,000) | | | | (6,000,000) |
| Expenses | 3,400,000 | | (A) 95,733 | | 3,495,733 |
| Net income | (2,600,000) | | | | (2,504,267) |
| **Statement of Retained Earnings** | | | | | |
| Retained earnings, 1/1/03 | (2,300,000) | | | | (2,300,000) |
| Net income (above) | (2,600,000) | | | | (2,504,267) |
| Retained earnings, 12/31/03 | (4,900,000) | | | | (4,804,267) |
| **Balance Sheet** | | | | | |
| Cash | 570,000* | 200,000 | | | 770,000 |
| Receivables | 900,000 | 300,000 | | (A) 10,000 | 1,190,000 |
| Inventory | 1,100,000 | 600,000 | (A) 220,000 | | 1,920,000 |
| Investment in Richmond Company | 1,446,000* | –0– | | (S) 1,100,000 | –0– |
| | | | | (A) 346,000 | |
| Buildings (net) | 3,000,000 | 800,000 | (A) 61,600 | | 3,861,600 |
| Equipment (net) | 6,000,000 | 500,000 | | (A) 21,333 | 6,478,667 |
| Total assets | 13,016,000 | 2,400,000 | | | 14,220,267 |
| Accounts payable | (400,000) | (200,000) | | | (600,000) |
| Notes payable | (3,400,000) | (1,100,000) | | | (4,500,000) |
| Common stock | (3,000,000)* | (720,000) | (S) 720,000 | | (3,000,000) |
| Additional paid-in capital | (1,316,000)* | (100,000) | (S) 100,000 | | (1,316,000) |
| Retained earnings, 12/31/03 (above) | (4,900,000) | (280,000)† | (S) 280,000 | | (4,804,267) |
| Total liabilities and equities | (13,016,000) | (2,400,000) | | | (14,220,267) |

Note: Parentheses indicate a credit balance.
*Balances have been adjusted for issuance of stock and payment of combination costs.
†Beginning Retained Earnings plus revenues minus expenses.

- Marston's balances have been updated on this worksheet to include the effect of both the newly issued shares of stock and the combination costs.
- Richmond's revenue and expense accounts have been closed out to Retained Earnings since this combination is a purchase.
- Entry **S** on the worksheet eliminates the $1,100,000 book value component of the Investment in Richmond Company account along with the subsidiary's stockholders' equity accounts.
- Entry **A** adjusts all of Richmond's assets and liabilities to fair market value based on the allocations determined earlier. However, the values attributed to the Buildings account, the Equipment account, and the Expenses account (for IPR&D) have been reduced by a total of $64,000 to reflect the bargain purchase made.

# Appendix

## *APB No. 16* Criteria for a Pooling of Interests

1. Attributes of combining companies.
   a. Each of the combining companies is autonomous and has not been a subsidiary or division of another corporation within two years before the plan of combination is initiated.
   b. Each of the combining companies is independent of the other combining companies.
2. Characteristics of the combination.
   a. The combination is effected in a single transaction or is completed in accordance with a specific plan within one year after the plan is initiated.
   b. A corporation offers and issues only common stock with rights identical to those of the majority of its outstanding voting common stock in exchange for substantially all of the voting common stock interest of another company at the date the plan of combination is consummated. Substantially all of the voting common stock means 90 percent or more for this condition.
   c. None of the combining companies changes the equity interest of the voting common stock in contemplation of effecting the combination either within two years before the plan of combination is initiated or between the dates the combination is initiated and consummated; changes in contemplation of effecting the combination may include distributions to stockholders and additional issuances, exchanges, and retirements of securities.
   d. Each of the combining companies reacquires shares of voting common stock only for purposes other than business combinations, and no company reacquires more than a normal number of shares between the dates the plan of combination is initiated and consummated.
   e. The ratio of the interest of an individual common stockholder to those of other common stockholders in a combining company remains the same as a result of the exchange of stock to effect the combination.
   f. The voting rights to which the common stock ownership interests in the resulting combined corporation are entitled are exercisable by the stockholders; the stockholders are neither deprived of nor restricted in exercising those rights for a period.
   g. The combination is resolved at the date the plan is consummated and no provisions of the plan relating to the issue of securities or other consideration are pending.
3. Absence of planned transaction.
   a. The combined corporation does not agree directly or indirectly to retire or reacquire all or part of the common stock issued to effect the combination.
   b. The combined corporation does not enter into other financial arrangements for the benefit of the former stockholders of a combining company, such as a guaranty of loans secured by stock issued in the combination, which in effect negates the exchange of equity securities.
   c. The combined corporation does not intend or plan to dispose of a significant part of the assets of the combining companies within two years after the combination other than disposals in the ordinary course of business of the formerly separate companies and to eliminate duplicate facilities or excess capacity.

## Questions

1. What is a business combination?
2. Describe the different types of legal arrangements that can take place to create a business combination.
3. What is meant by consolidated financial statements?
4. Within the consolidation process, what is the purpose of a worksheet?
5. Jones Company obtains all of the common stock of Hudson, Inc., by issuing 50,000 shares of its own stock. Under these circumstances, why might the determination of an acquisition price be difficult?
6. What is the accounting basis for consolidating assets and liabilities in a business combination recorded as a purchase? What was the accounting basis for consolidating assets and liabilities in a business combination recorded as a pooling of interests?
7. How are a subsidiary's revenues and expenses consolidated?
8. Morgan Company purchases all of the outstanding shares of Jennings, Inc., for cash. Morgan pays more than the fair market value of the company's net assets. How should the payment in excess of fair market value be accounted for in the consolidation process?

9. Catron Corporation is having liquidity problems, and as a result, all of its outstanding shares are sold to Lambert, Inc., for cash. Because of Catron's problems, Lambert is able to acquire this stock at less than the fair market value of the company's net assets. How is this reduction in price accounted for within the consolidation process?

10. Sloane, Inc., issues 25,000 shares of its own common stock in exchange for all of the outstanding shares of Benjamin Company. Benjamin will remain a separately incorporated operation. How does Sloane record the issuance of these shares in a purchase combination?

11. To obtain all of the stock of Molly, Inc., Harrison Corporation issued its own common stock. Harrison had to pay $98,000 to lawyers, accountants, and a stock brokerage firm in connection with services rendered during the creation of this business combination. In addition, Harrison paid $56,000 in costs associated with the stock issuance. In a purchase combination, how will these two costs be recorded?

## Problems

Note: Problems 1 through 28 relate to the purchase method of accounting for business combinations. Problems 29 through 41 relate to the pooling of interests method.

### Purchase Method

1. Which of the following is the best theoretical justification for consolidated financial statements?
   a. In form the companies are one entity; in substance they are separate.
   b. In form the companies are separate; in substance they are one entity.
   c. In form and substance the companies are one entity.
   d. In form and substance the companies are separate.
   (AICPA)

2. What is a statutory merger?
   a. A merger approved by the Securities and Exchange Commission.
   b. An acquisition involving both the purchase of stock and assets.
   c. A takeover completed within one year of the initial tender offer.
   d. A business combination in which only one company continues to exist as a legal entity.

3. What is the appropriate accounting treatment for the value assigned to in-process research and development acquired in a business combination?
   a. Always expense upon acquisition.
   b. Always capitalize as an asset with future economic benefit.
   c. Expense if there is no alternative use for the assets used in the research and development and technological feasibility has yet to be reached.
   d. Expense until future economic benefits become certain and then capitalize as an asset.

4. Principles for allocating the cost of a business acquisition are provided in *SFAS 141*, "Business Combinations." When the current fair value of the net assets acquired exceeds the total cost of the acquisition, which of the following assets may be assigned an amount less than its fair value?
   a. Deferred tax assets.
   b. Assets to be disposed of by sale.
   c. Prepaid assets related to a pension plan.
   d. Investments accounted for by the equity method.

5. Principles for allocating the cost of a business combination are provided in *SFAS 141*, "Business Combinations." When the fair value of the net assets acquired exceeds the total cost of the investment, the difference should be
   a. Applied pro rata to reduce, but not below zero, the amounts initially assigned to specific non-current assets of the acquired firm.
   b. Treated as negative goodwill to be amortized over the period benefited, not to exceed 40 years.
   c. Treated as goodwill and tested for impairment on an annual basis.
   d. Allocated on a pro rata basis to the assets of the acquired firm.

6. An acquired entity has a long-term operating lease for an office building used for central management. The terms of the lease are very favorable relative to current market rates. However, the lease prohibits subleasing or any other transfer of rights. In its financial statements, the acquiring firm should report the value assigned to the lease contract as

a. An intangible asset under the contractual-legal criterion.
b. A part of goodwill.
c. An intangible asset under the separability criterion.
d. A building.

7. Williams Company obtains all of the outstanding stock of Jaminson, Inc., in a purchase transaction. In a consolidation prepared immediately after the takeover, at what value will the inventory owned by Jaminson be consolidated?

    a. Jaminson's historical cost.
    b. A percentage of the acquisition cost paid by Williams.
    c. The inventory will be omitted in the consolidation.
    d. At the fair market value on the date of the purchase.

8. When is an extraordinary gain recognized in consolidating financial information?

    a. When any bargain purchase is created.
    b. In a combination created in the middle of a fiscal year.
    c. In a purchase, when the value of all assets and liabilities cannot be determined.
    d. When the amount of a bargain purchase exceeds the value of the applicable noncurrent assets (other than certain exceptions) held by the acquired company.

9. On June 1, 2004, Cline Co. paid $800,000 cash for all the issued and outstanding common stock of Renn Corp. The carrying values for Renn's assets and liabilities on June 1, 2004, follow:

| | |
|---|---|
| Cash | $150,000 |
| Accounts receivable | 180,000 |
| Capitalized software costs | 320,000 |
| Goodwill (net of accumulated amortization of $80,000) | 100,000 |
| Liabilities | (130,000) |
| Net assets | $620,000 |

On June 1, 2004, Renn's accounts receivable had a fair value of $140,000. Additionally, Renn's in-process research and development was estimated to have a fair value of $200,000. All other items were stated at their fair values. On Cline's June 1, 2004, consolidated balance sheet, how much is reported for goodwill?

    a. $320,000
    b. $120,000
    c. $80,000
    d. $20,000

10. Which of the following is not an appropriate reason for leaving a subsidiary unconsolidated?

    a. The subsidiary is in bankruptcy.
    b. The subsidiary is to be sold in the near future.
    c. A foreign government threatens to take over the assets of the subsidiary.
    d. The subsidiary is in an industry that is significantly different than that of the parent.

11. Prior to being united in a business combination, Atkins, Inc., and Waterson Corporation had the following stockholders' equity figures:

| | Atkins | Waterson |
|---|---|---|
| Common stock ($1 par value) | $180,000 | $ 45,000 |
| Additional paid-in capital | 90,000 | 20,000 |
| Retained earnings | 300,000 | 110,000 |

Atkins issues 51,000 new shares of its common stock valued at $3 per share for all of the outstanding stock of Waterson. Assume that Atkins acquired Waterson through a purchase. Immediately afterward, what are consolidated Additional Paid-In Capital and Retained Earnings, respectively?

    a. $104,000 and $300,000.
    b. $110,000 and $410,000.
    c. $192,000 and $300,000.
    d. $212,000 and $410,000.

Problems 12 and 13 are based on the following information: Hampstead, Inc., has only three assets:

|  | Book Value | Fair Market Value |
|---|---|---|
| Inventory | $110,000 | $150,000 |
| Land | 700,000 | 600,000 |
| Buildings | 700,000 | 900,000 |

Miller Corporation purchases Hampstead by issuing 100,000 shares of its $10 par value common stock.

12. If Miller's stock is worth $20 per share, at what value will the inventory, land, and buildings be consolidated, respectively?

    a. $110,000, $600,000, $900,000.
    b. $110,000, $700,000, $700,000.
    c. $150,000, $600,000, $900,000.
    d. $150,000, $700,000, $900,000.

13. If Miller's stock is worth $15 per share, at what value will the inventory, land, and buildings be consolidated, respectively?

    a. $110,000, $695,000, $695,000.
    b. $150,000, $525,000, $825,000.
    c. $150,000, $540,000, $810,000.
    d. $136,363, $545,455, $818,182.

Problems 14 through 17 are based on the following information: Allen, Inc., obtains control over Tucker, Inc., on July 1, 2004. The book value and fair market value of Tucker's accounts on that date (prior to creating the combination) follow, along with the book value of Allen's accounts:

|  | Allen Book Value | Tucker Book Value | Tucker Market Value |
|---|---|---|---|
| Revenues | $250,000 | $130,000 |  |
| Expenses | 170,000 | 80,000 |  |
| Retained earnings, 1/1/04 | 130,000 | 150,000 |  |
| Cash and receivables | 140,000 | 60,000 | $ 60,000 |
| Inventory | 190,000 | 145,000 | 175,000 |
| Land | 230,000 | 180,000 | 200,000 |
| Buildings (net) | 400,000 | 200,000 | 225,000 |
| Equipment (net) | 100,000 | 75,000 | 75,000 |
| Liabilities | 540,000 | 360,000 | 350,000 |
| Common stock | 300,000 | 70,000 |  |
| Additional paid-in capital | 10,000 | 30,000 |  |

14. Assume that Allen issues 10,000 shares of common stock with a $5 par value and a $40 fair market value to obtain all of Tucker's outstanding stock. How much goodwill should be recognized?

    a. –0–
    b. $15,000
    c. $35,000
    d. $100,000

15. For the fiscal year ending December 31, 2004, how will consolidated net income of this business combination be determined if Allen acquires all of Tucker's stock in a purchase?

    a. Allen's income for the past year plus Tucker's income for the past six months.
    b. Allen's income for the past year plus Tucker's income for the past year.
    c. Allen's income for the past six months plus Tucker's income for the past six months.
    d. Allen's income for the past six months plus Tucker's income for the past year.

16. Assume that Allen issues preferred stock with a par value of $200,000 and a fair market value of $335,000 for all shares of Tucker. What will be the balance in the consolidated Inventory, Land, and beginning Retained Earnings accounts?

    a. $365,000, $410,000, and $130,000.
    b. $365,000, $430,000, and $130,000.
    c. $352,500, $417,500, and $280,000.
    d. $335,000, $430,000, and $280,000.

17. Assume that Allen pays a total of $370,000 in cash for all of the shares of Tucker. In addition, Allen pays $30,000 to a group of attorneys for their work in arranging the acquisition. What will be the balance in consolidated goodwill and retained earnings?

    a. 0 and $90,000.
    b. 0 and $280,000.
    c. $15,000 and $280,000.
    d. $15,000 and $130,000.
    (AICPA adapted)

18. Prycal Co. merges with InterBuy, Inc., and acquires several different categories of intangible assets including trademarks, a customer list, copyrights on artistic materials, agreements to receive royalties on leased intellectual property, and unpatented technology.

    a. Describe the criteria put forth in *SFAS No. 141* for determining whether an intangible asset acquired in a business combination should be separately recognized apart from goodwill.
    b. For each of the acquired intangibles listed, identify which recognition criteria (separability and legal/contractual) may or may not apply in recognizing the intangible on the acquiring firm's financial statements.

19. Bakel Corporation has the following account balances:

    | | |
    |---|---|
    | Receivables | $ 80,000 |
    | Inventory | 200,000 |
    | Land | 600,000 |
    | Building | 500,000 |
    | Liabilities | 400,000 |
    | Common stock | 100,000 |
    | Additional paid-in capital | 100,000 |
    | Retained earnings, 1/1/04 | 700,000 |
    | Revenues | 300,000 |
    | Expenses | 220,000 |

    Several of Bakel's accounts have market values that differ from book value: land—$400,000; building—$600,000; inventory—$280,000; and liabilities—$330,000. Homewood, Inc., obtains all of the outstanding shares of Bakel by issuing 20,000 shares of common stock having a $5 par value but a $55 fair market value. Stock issuance costs amount to $10,000. The transaction is to be accounted for as a purchase.

    a. What is the purchase price in this combination?
    b. What is the book value of Bakel's net assets on the date of the takeover?
    c. How are the stock issuance costs handled?
    d. How does the issuance of these shares affect the stockholders' equity accounts of Homewood, the parent?
    e. What allocations are made of Homewood's purchase price to specific accounts and to goodwill?
    f. If Bakel had in-process research and development assets (with no alternative future uses) valued at $60,000, how would the allocations in part (*e*) change? Where is acquired in-process research and development typically reported on consolidated financial statements?
    g. How do Bakel's revenues and expenses affect consolidated totals? Why?
    h. How do Bakel's common stock and additional paid-in capital balances affect consolidated totals?
    i. In financial statements prepared immediately following the takeover, what impact will this acquisition have on the various consolidated totals?
    j. If Homewood's stock had been worth only $40 per share rather than $55, how would the consolidation of Bakel's assets and liabilities have been affected?

20. Winston has the following account balances as of February 1, 2004.

| | |
|---|---:|
| Inventory | $ 600,000 |
| Land | 500,000 |
| Buildings (net) (valued at $1,000,000) | 900,000 |
| Common stock ($10 par value) | 800,000 |
| Retained earnings (1/1/04) | 1,100,000 |
| Revenues | 600,000 |
| Expenses | 500,000 |

Arlington pays $1.4 million cash and issues 10,000 shares of its $30 par value common stock (valued at $80 per share) for all of Winston's outstanding stock. Stock issuance costs amount to $30,000. Prior to recording these newly issued shares, Arlington reports a Common Stock account of $900,000 and Additional Paid-In Capital of $500,000. For each of the following accounts, determine what balance would be included in a February 1, 2004, consolidation.

- a. Goodwill.
- b. Expenses.
- c. Retained Earnings, 1/1/04.
- d. Buildings.

21. Use the same information as presented in question (20) but assume that Arlington pays cash of $2.3 million. No stock is issued. An additional $40,000 is paid in direct combination costs. For each of the following accounts, determine what balance would be included in a February 1, 2004, consolidation.

    - a. Goodwill.
    - b. Expenses.
    - c. Retained Earnings, 1/1/04.
    - d. Buildings.

22. Use the same information as presented in question (20) but assume that Arlington pays $2,020,000 in cash. An additional $20,000 is paid in direct combination costs. For each of the following accounts, determine what balance will be included in a February 1, 2004, consolidation.

    - a. Inventory.
    - b. Goodwill.
    - c. Expenses.
    - d. Buildings.
    - e. Land.

23. On December 31, 2004, Bingham Company and Laredo Company have the following account balances:

| | Bingham | Laredo |
|---|---:|---:|
| Revenues | $100,000 | $ 80,000 |
| Expenses | 60,000 | 50,000 |
| Net income | $ 40,000 | $ 30,000 |
| Retained earnings, 1/1/04 | $210,000 | $ 70,000 |
| Net income | 40,000 | 30,000 |
| Dividends | 30,000 | –0– |
| Retained earnings, 12/31/04 | $220,000 | $100,000 |
| Cash | $ 80,000 | $ 20,000 |
| Receivables | 60,000 | 60,000 |
| Inventory | 100,000 | 70,000 |
| Buildings and equipment (net) | 200,000 | 100,000 |
| Total assets | $440,000 | $250,000 |
| Current liabilities | $ 20,000 | $ 10,000 |
| Long-term liabilities | 70,000 | 50,000 |
| Common stock | 110,000 | 90,000 |
| Additional paid-in capital | 20,000 | –0– |
| Retained earnings, 12/31/04 | 220,000 | 100,000 |
| Total liabilities and equities | $440,000 | $250,000 |

After these figures were prepared, Bingham issued 10,000 shares of its $10 par value stock for all of the outstanding shares of Laredo. Bingham's stock had a $30 per share fair market value. Bingham also paid $10,000 in direct combination costs and $20,000 in stock issuance costs.

In determining its purchase offer for Laredo, Bingham noted the following pertaining to Laredo:
- It holds a building that is worth $40,000 more than its book value.
- It has developed a customer list appraised at $15,000, although is it not recorded in its financial records.
- It has several research and development activities in process that have a total appraised value of $30,000. However, none of the activities has reached technological feasibility, and the assets used in the projects have no alternative future uses.

Determine consolidated balances for this combination as of December 31, 2004.

24. Following are the financial balances for Parrot Company and Sun Company as of December 31, 2004. Also included are fair market values for Sun Company accounts.

|  | Parrot Company Book Value 12/31/04 | Sun Company Book Value 12/31/04 | Sun Company Market Value 12/31/04 |
|---|---|---|---|
| Cash | $ 290,000 | $ 120,000 | $ 120,000 |
| Receivables | 220,000 | 300,000 | 300,000 |
| Inventory | 410,000 | 210,000 | 260,000 |
| Land | 600,000 | 130,000 | 110,000 |
| Buildings (net) | 600,000 | 270,000 | 330,000 |
| Equipment (net) | 220,000 | 190,000 | 220,000 |
| Accounts payable | (190,000) | (120,000) | (120,000) |
| Accrued expenses | (90,000) | (30,000) | (30,000) |
| Long-term liabilities | (900,000) | (510,000) | (510,000) |
| Common stock—$20 par value | (660,000) | | |
| Common stock—$5 par value | | (210,000) | |
| Additional paid-in capital | (70,000) | (90,000) | |
| Retained earnings, 1/1/04 | (390,000) | (240,000) | |
| Revenues | (960,000) | (330,000) | |
| Expenses | 920,000 | 310,000 | |

Note: Parentheses indicate a credit balance.

In the following situations, determine the value that would be shown in consolidated financial statements for each of the accounts listed. Each problem should be viewed as an independent occurrence. These transactions all take place on December 31, 2004.

| Accounts | |
|---|---|
| Inventory | Revenues |
| Land | Additional Paid-In Capital |
| Buildings | Expenses |
| Goodwill | Retained Earnings, 1/1/04 |

a. Parrot acquires the outstanding stock of Sun by issuing $760,000 in long-term liabilities.
b. Parrot acquires the outstanding stock of Sun by paying $160,000 in cash and issuing 10,000 shares of its own common stock with a value of $40 per share. Direct combination costs of $20,000 are paid by Parrot as well as $5,000 in stock issuance costs.

25. The financial statements for Willeslye, Inc., and Barrett Company for the year ending December 31, 2005, follow:

|  | Willeslye | Barrett |
|---|---|---|
| Revenues | $ 900,000 | $ 300,000 |
| Expenses | 660,000 | 200,000 |
| Net income | $ 240,000 | $ 100,000 |
| Retained earnings, 1/1/05 | $ 800,000 | $ 200,000 |
| Net income | 240,000 | 100,000 |
| Dividends paid | 90,000 | –0– |
| Retained earnings, 12/31/05 | $ 950,000 | $ 300,000 |
| Cash | $ 80,000 | $ 110,000 |
| Receivables and inventory | 400,000 | 170,000 |
| Patented technology (net) | 900,000 | 300,000 |
| Equipment (net) | 700,000 | 600,000 |
| Total assets | $2,080,000 | $1,180,000 |
| Liabilities | $ 500,000 | $ 410,000 |
| Common stock | 360,000 | 200,000 |
| Additional paid-in capital | 270,000 | 270,000 |
| Retained earnings | 950,000 | 300,000 |
| Total liabilities and equities | $2,080,000 | $1,180,000 |

On December 31, 2005, Willeslye issues $300,000 in debt and 15,000 new shares of its $10 par value stock to the owners of Barrett to purchase all of the outstanding shares of that company. Willeslye shares had a fair market value of $40 per share.

Willeslye also paid $30,000 to a broker for arranging the transaction. In addition, Willeslye paid $40,000 in stock issuance costs. Barrett's equipment was actually worth $700,000 but its patented technology was valued at only $280,000.

What are the consolidated balances for the following accounts?

a. Net Income.
b. Retained Earnings, 1/1/05.
c. Patented technology.
d. Goodwill.
e. Liabilities.
f. Common Stock.
g. Additional Paid-In Capital.

26. Merrill acquires 100 percent of the outstanding voting shares of Harriss Company on January 1, 2004. To obtain these shares, Merrill pays $200,000 in cash and issues 10,000 shares of its own $10 par value common stock. On this date, Merrill's stock has a fair market value of $18 per share. Merrill also pays $10,000 to a local investment company for arranging the acquisition. Merrill paid an additional $6,000 in stock issuance costs.

The book values for both Merrill and Harriss as of January 1, 2004, follow. The fair market value of each of Harriss's accounts is also included. In addition, Harriss holds a fully amortized patent that still retains a $30,000 value.

|  | Merrill, Inc. Book Value | Harriss Company Book Value | Harriss Company Fair Market Value |
|---|---|---|---|
| Cash | $300,000 | $ 40,000 | $ 40,000 |
| Receivables | 160,000 | 90,000 | 80,000 |
| Inventory | 220,000 | 130,000 | 130,000 |
| Land | 100,000 | 60,000 | 60,000 |
| Buildings (net) | 400,000 | 110,000 | 140,000 |
| Equipment (net) | 120,000 | 50,000 | 50,000 |

|  | Merrill, Inc. Book Value | Harriss Company Book Value | Harriss Company Fair Market Value |
|---|---|---|---|
| Accounts payable | 160,000 | 30,000 | 30,000 |
| Long-term liabilities | 380,000 | 170,000 | 150,000 |
| Common stock | 400,000 | 40,000 |  |
| Retained earnings | 360,000 | 240,000 |  |

a. Assume that this combination is a statutory merger so that Harriss's accounts are to be transferred to the records of Merrill with Harriss subsequently being dissolved as a legal corporation. Prepare the journal entries for Merrill that are required to record this merger.

b. Assume that no dissolution is to take place in connection with this combination. Rather, both companies retain their separate legal identities. Prepare a worksheet to consolidate the two companies as of January 1, 2004.

27. On January 1, 2004, Lee Company purchased 100 percent of the outstanding common stock of Grant Company. To acquire these shares, Lee issued $200,000 in long-term liabilities and 20,000 shares of common stock having a par value of $1 per share but a fair market value of $10 per share. Lee paid $30,000 to accountants, lawyers, and brokers for assistance in bringing about this purchase. Another $12,000 was paid in connection with stock issuance costs.

Prior to these transactions, the balance sheets for the two companies were as follows:

|  | Lee Company Book Value | Grant Company Book Value |
|---|---|---|
| Cash | $ 60,000 | $ 20,000 |
| Receivables | 270,000 | 90,000 |
| Inventory | 360,000 | 140,000 |
| Land | 200,000 | 180,000 |
| Buildings (net) | 420,000 | 220,000 |
| Equipment (net) | 160,000 | 50,000 |
| Accounts payable | (150,000) | (40,000) |
| Long-term liabilities | (430,000) | (200,000) |
| Common stock—$1 par value | (110,000) |  |
| Common stock—$20 par value |  | (120,000) |
| Additional paid-in capital | (360,000) | –0– |
| Retained earnings, 1/1/04 | (420,000) | (340,000) |

Note: Parentheses indicate a credit balance.

In Lee's appraisal of Grant, three accounts were deemed to be undervalued on the subsidiary's books: Inventory by $5,000, Land by $20,000, and Buildings by $30,000.

a. Determine the consolidated balance for each of these accounts.
b. To verify the answers found in part (a), prepare a worksheet to consolidate the balance sheets of these two companies as of January 1, 2004.

28. Pratt Company purchased all of the outstanding shares of Spider, Inc., on December 31, 2004, for $495,000 cash. Although many of Spider's book values approximate fair values, several of its accounts have market values that differ from book values. In addition, Spider has internally developed assets that remain unrecorded on its books. In deriving a purchase price, Pratt made assessments of Spider's fair and book value differences as follows:

|  | Book Value | Fair Value |
|---|---|---|
| Computer software | $20,000 | $70,000 |
| Equipment | 40,000 | 30,000 |
| Client contracts | –0– | 100,000 |
| In-process research and development* | –0– | 40,000 |
| Notes payable | 60,000 | 65,000 |

*Technological feasibility has not yet been achieved. No future alternative uses are available for IPR&D assets employed in these projects.

At December 31, 2004, the following financial information is available for consolidation:

| | Pratt | Spider |
|---|---|---|
| Revenues | $ (200,000) | |
| Expenses | 125,000 | |
| Net income | (75,000) | |
| Retained earnings 1/1 | (707,000) | |
| Net income | (75,000) | |
| Dividends | 30,000 | |
| Retained Earnings 12/31 | $ (752,000) | |
| Cash | 36,000 | $ 18,000 |
| Receivables | 116,000 | 52,000 |
| Inventory | 140,000 | 90,000 |
| Investment in Spider (cost) | 495,000 | -0- |
| Computer software | 210,000 | 20,000 |
| Buildings (net) | 595,000 | 130,000 |
| Equipment (net) | 308,000 | 40,000 |
| Client contracts | -0- | -0- |
| Goodwill | -0- | -0- |
| Total assets | $ 1,900,000 | $ 350,000 |
| Accounts payable | (88,000) | (25,000) |
| Notes payable | (510,000) | (60,000) |
| Common stock | (380,000) | (100,000) |
| Additional paid-in capital | (170,000) | (25,000) |
| Retained earnings | (752,000) | (140,000) |
| Total liabilities and equities | $(1,900,000) | $(350,000) |

Prepare a consolidated balance sheet for Pratt and Spider as of December 31, 2004.

## Pooling Method

29. How would equipment obtained in a business combination been recorded under each of the following methods?

| | Pooling of Interests | Purchase |
|---|---|---|
| a. | Recorded value | Recorded value |
| b. | Recorded value | Fair value |
| c. | Fair value | Fair value |
| d. | Fair value | Recorded value |

(AICPA adapted)

30. Prior to being united in a business combination, Atkins, Inc., and Waterson Corporation had the following stockholders' equity figures:

| | Atkins | Waterson |
|---|---|---|
| Common stock ($1 par value) | $180,000 | $ 45,000 |
| Additional paid-in capital | 90,000 | 20,000 |
| Retained earnings | 300,000 | 110,000 |

Atkins issues 51,000 new shares of its common stock valued at $3 per share for all of the outstanding stock of Waterson. Assume that Atkins and Waterson were joined in a pooling of interests. Immediately afterward, what were the amounts in consolidated Additional Paid-In Capital and Retained Earnings, respectively?

a. $104,000 and $300,000.
b. $104,000 and $410,000.
c. $110,000 and $300,000.
d. $110,000 and $410,000.

Problems 31 through 34 are based on the following information: Allen, Inc., obtains control over Tucker, Inc., on July 1, 2000. The book value and fair market value of Tucker's accounts on that date (prior to creating the combination) follow, along with the book value of Allen's accounts:

|  | Allen Book Value | Tucker Book Value | Tucker Market Value |
|---|---|---|---|
| Revenues | $250,000 | $130,000 |  |
| Expenses | 170,000 | 80,000 |  |
| Retained earnings, 1/1/00 | 130,000 | 150,000 |  |
| Cash and receivables | 140,000 | 60,000 | $ 60,000 |
| Inventory | 190,000 | 145,000 | 175,000 |
| Land | 230,000 | 180,000 | 200,000 |
| Buildings (net) | 400,000 | 200,000 | 225,000 |
| Equipment (net) | 100,000 | 75,000 | 75,000 |
| Liabilities | 540,000 | 360,000 | 350,000 |
| Common stock | 300,000 | 70,000 |  |
| Additional paid-in capital | 10,000 | 30,000 |  |

31. Assume that Allen issued 10,000 shares of common stock with a $5 par value and a $40 fair market value for all of the outstanding stock of Tucker. What was the consolidated land balance if this transaction was a pooling of interests?

    a. $380,000
    b. $410,000
    c. $420,000
    d. $430,000

32. For the fiscal year ending December 31, 2000, how was consolidated net income of this business combination determined if Allen acquired all of Tucker's stock in a pooling of interests?

    a. Allen's income for the past year plus Tucker's income for the past six months.
    b. Allen's income for the past year plus Tucker's income for the past year.
    c. Allen's income for the past six months plus Tucker's income for the past six months.
    d. Allen's income for the past six months plus Tucker's income for the past year.

33. Assume that Allen issued 16,000 shares of common stock with a $5 per share par value and a $40 fair market value in exchange for all of the outstanding shares of Tucker. What was the consolidated Additional Paid-In Capital and Retained Earnings (January 1, 2000, balance) if this combination was recorded as a pooling of interests?

    a. $10,000 and $130,000.
    b. $30,000 and $280,000.
    c. $30,000 and $130,000.
    d. $40,000 and $280,000.

34. Assume that Allen issued 16,000 shares of common stock with a $10 per share par value and a $40 fair market value in exchange for all of the outstanding shares of Tucker. What was the consolidated Additional Paid-In Capital and Retained Earnings (January 1, 2000, balance) if this combination was recorded as a pooling of interests?

    a. $10,000 and $130,000.
    b. 0 and $230,000.
    c. 0 and $80,000.
    d. $40,000 and $280,000.

35. Flaherty Company entered into a business combination with Steeley Company during 2000. The combination was accounted for as a pooling of interests. Registration fees were incurred in issuing common stock in this combination. Other costs, such as legal and accounting fees, were also paid.

a. In the business combination accounted for as a pooling of interests, how should the assets and liabilities of the two companies be included within consolidated statements? What was the rationale for accounting for a business combination as a pooling of interests?
b. In the business combination accounted for as a pooling of interests, how were the registration fees and the other direct costs recorded?
c. In the business combination accounted for as a pooling of interests, how were the results of the operations for 2000 reported?
(AICPA adapted)

36. Harcourt Company has the following account balances:

| | |
|---|---:|
| Receivables | $ 90,000 |
| Inventory | 500,000 |
| Land | 700,000 |
| Buildings | 200,000 |
| Liabilities | 800,000 |
| Common stock | 100,000 |
| Additional paid-in capital | 90,000 |
| Retained earnings, 1/1/00 | 440,000 |
| Revenues | 400,000 |
| Expenses | 340,000 |

Several of Harcourt's accounts have market values that differ from book value: land—$900,000; building—$400,000; inventory—$470,000; and liabilities—$840,000. Lee Corporation obtains all of the outstanding shares of Harcourt by issuing 20,000 shares of common stock having a $10 par value but a $62 fair market value. Stock issuance costs amount to $10,000. The transaction is to be accounted for as a pooling of interests. Before recording the issuance of these new shares, Lee has a Common Stock account of $2 million and Additional Paid-In Capital of $1.3 million.

a. What is the book value of Harcourt's net assets on the date of the takeover?
b. How are the stock issuance costs handled?
c. Assume that both companies will retain their identities as separate corporations. What journal entry would Lee record for the issuance of its stock?
d. How would the answer to part (c) have changed if Lee's stock had a $1 per share par value rather than $10 per share?
e. How would the answer to part (c) have changed if Lee's stock had a $10 per share par value but Lee issued 30,000 shares rather than 20,000?
f. How do Harcourt's revenues and expenses affect consolidated totals? Why?
g. In financial statements prepared immediately following the takeover, what impact would Harcourt's accounts have on the various consolidated totals?

37. Winston has the following account balances as of February 1, 2000:

| | |
|---|---:|
| Inventory | $ 600,000 |
| Land | 500,000 |
| Buildings (net) (valued at $1,000,000) | 900,000 |
| Common stock ($10 par value) | 800,000 |
| Retained earnings (1/1/00) | 1,100,000 |
| Revenues | 600,000 |
| Expenses | 500,000 |

Assume that Arlington issues 30,000 shares of common stock ($30 par value but a fair market value of $80 per share) for all of Winston's outstanding stock in a transaction that has qualified as a pooling of interests. Stock issuance costs of $35,000 are paid along with $24,000 of other direct combination costs. For each of the following accounts, determine what balance will be included in a February 1, 2000, consolidation.

a. Buildings.
b. Goodwill.
c. Expenses.
d. Retained Earnings, 1/1/00.

38. Following are the financial balances for Parrot Company and Sun Company as of December 31, 2000. Also included are fair market values for the Sun Company accounts.

|  | Parrot Company Book Value 12/31/00 | Sun Company Book Value 12/31/00 | Sun Company Market Value 12/31/00 |
|---|---|---|---|
| Cash | $290,000 | $120,000 | $120,000 |
| Receivables | 220,000 | 300,000 | 300,000 |
| Inventory | 410,000 | 210,000 | 260,000 |
| Land | 600,000 | 130,000 | 110,000 |
| Buildings (net) | 600,000 | 270,000 | 330,000 |
| Equipment (net) | 220,000 | 190,000 | 220,000 |
| Accounts payable | (190,000) | (120,000) | (120,000) |
| Accrued expenses | (90,000) | (30,000) | (30,000) |
| Long-term liabilities | (900,000) | (510,000) | (510,000) |
| Common stock—$20 par value | (660,000) | | |
| Common stock—$5 par value | | (210,000) | |
| Additional paid-in capital | (70,000) | (90,000) | |
| Retained earnings, 1/1/00 | (390,000) | (240,000) | |
| Revenues | (960,000) | (330,000) | |
| Expenses | 920,000 | 310,000 | |

Note: Parentheses indicate a credit balance.

In the following situations, determine the value that would be shown in consolidated financial statements for each of the accounts listed. Each problem should be viewed as an independent occurrence. These transactions all took place on December 31, 2000.

| Accounts | |
|---|---|
| Inventory | Revenues |
| Land | Additional Paid-In Capital |
| Buildings | Expenses |
| Goodwill | Retained Earnings, 1/1/00 |

a. Parrot obtains the outstanding stock of Sun by issuing 12,000 shares of common stock with a value of $40 per share. This transaction was accounted for as a pooling of interests.

b. Parrot obtains the outstanding stock of Sun by issuing 16,000 shares of common stock with a value of $40 per share. This transaction was accounted for as a pooling of interests. Stock issuance costs of $8,000 were paid.

c. Parrot obtains the outstanding stock of Sun by issuing 19,000 shares of its common stock with a value of $40 per share. This transaction was accounted for as a pooling of interests. Direct combination costs of $9,000 were paid by Parrot.

39. The financial statements for Hope, Inc., and Kaisley Corporation for the year ending December 31, 2000, follow. Kaisley's buildings were undervalued on its financial records by $50,000.

|  | Hope | Kaisley |
|---|---|---|
| Revenues | $ 400,000 | $ 400,000 |
| Expenses | 240,000 | 240,000 |
| Net income | $ 160,000 | $ 160,000 |
| Retained earnings, 1/1/00 | $ 600,000 | $ 400,000 |
| Net income | 160,000 | 160,000 |
| Dividends paid | 90,000 | 90,000 |
| Retained earnings, 12/31/00 | $ 670,000 | $ 470,000 |
| Cash | $ 130,000 | $ 100,000 |
| Receivables and inventory | 200,000 | 200,000 |
| Buildings (net) | 600,000 | 300,000 |
| Equipment (net) | 600,000 | 500,000 |
| Total assets | $1,530,000 | $1,100,000 |

|  | Hope | Kaisley |
|---|---|---|
| Liabilities | $ 200,000 | $ 200,000 |
| Common stock | 630,000 | 360,000 |
| Additional paid-in capital | 30,000 | 70,000 |
| Retained earnings | 670,000 | 470,000 |
| Total liabilities and equities | $1,530,000 | $1,100,000 |

On December 31, 2000, Hope issued 45,000 new shares of its $10 par value stock to the owners of Kaisley in exchange for all of the outstanding shares of that company. Hope's shares had a fair market value on that date of $30 per share. Hope paid $30,000 to a bank for assisting in the arrangements. Hope also paid $20,000 in stock issuance costs. This combination was accounted for as a pooling of interests. What were the appropriate consolidated balances?

40. Lincoln Company obtained all of the outstanding shares of Swathmore, Inc., on December 31, 2000, in exchange for 7,000 shares of common stock. The combination was accounted for as a pooling of interests. Each of Lincoln's shares had a $10 par value and a $40 fair market value. Several of Swathmore's accounts had market values that differed from their book values on that date:

|  | Book Value | Fair Market Value |
|---|---|---|
| Inventory | $70,000 | $100,000 |
| Land | 30,000 | 30,000 |
| Equipment | 50,000 | 60,000 |
| Notes payable | 50,000 | 45,000 |

Financial statements for 2000 for the two companies were as follows:

|  | Lincoln | Swathmore |
|---|---|---|
| Revenues | $ 990,000 | $ 540,000 |
| Expenses | (640,000) | (330,000) |
| Net income | $ 350,000 | $ 210,000 |
| Retained earnings, 1/1/00 | $ 830,000 | $ 110,000 |
| Net income | 350,000 | 210,000 |
| Dividends paid | (220,000) | (130,000) |
| Retained earnings, 12/31/00 | $ 960,000 | $ 190,000 |
| Cash | $60,000 | $29,000 |
| Receivables | 150,000 | 65,000 |
| Inventory | 190,000 | 120,000 |
| Land | 310,000 | 30,000 |
| Buildings (net) | 840,000 | 60,000 |
| Equipment (net) | 320,000 | 50,000 |
| Totals | $1,870,000 | $ 354,000 |
| Accounts payable | $ 110,000 | $34,000 |
| Notes payable | 370,000 | 50,000 |
| Common stock | 400,000 | 50,000 |
| Additional paid-in capital | 30,000 | 30,000 |
| Retained earnings | 960,000 | 190,000 |
| Totals | $1,870,000 | $ 354,000 |

a. Determine the consolidated balance for each of these accounts.
b. To verify the answers found in part (a), prepare a worksheet to consolidate the financial statements of these two companies.

41. On December 31, 2000, Sherman Company exchanged 17,000 shares of its common stock with a market value of $57 per share for 100 percent of the outstanding shares of Atlanta Company. This transaction was accounted for as a pooling of interests. Prior to the exchange, the trial balances of both companies for the year 2000 were as follows:

|  | Sherman Company Book Value | Atlanta Company Book Value |
|---|---|---|
| **Debits** | | |
| Cash | $110,000 | $ 20,000 |
| Receivables (net) | 300,000 | 290,000 |
| Inventory | 440,000 | 260,000 |
| Land | 280,000 | 80,000 |
| Buildings (net) | 270,000 | 290,000 |
| Equipment (net) | 810,000 | 320,000 |
| Expenses | 540,000 | 210,000 |
| Dividends | 30,000 | –0– |
| **Credits** | | |
| Accounts payable | 120,000 | 60,000 |
| Long-term liabilities | 960,000 | 330,000 |
| Common stock—$20 par value | 520,000 | |
| Common stock—$25 par value | | 300,000 |
| Additional paid-in capital | 110,000 | 100,000 |
| Retained earnings, 1/1/00 | 470,000 | 200,000 |
| Revenues | 600,000 | 480,000 |

Additional Information:

- After the preparation of these trial balances, Sherman paid $20,000 in cash for costs incurred relating to this exchange. These expenditures covered the fees charged by lawyers and accountants involved with creating the business combination.
- Atlanta possesses land that has greatly appreciated in value since it was acquired. The book value of this land is estimated to be $60,000 less than fair market value.

a. Prepare a worksheet to consolidate the financial information of these two companies for the year ending December 31, 2000.

b. Prepare a worksheet to consolidate the financial information of these two companies for the year ending December 31, 2000, assuming that this combination was actually a purchase.

# Develop Your Skills

## EXCEL CASE

Alhambra, Inc., is considering acquiring all of the assets of Grenada Co. after which Granada would be formally dissolved. Granada has no liabilities. The fair market value of the sum of its individual assets totals $600,000. In addition, Alhambra estimates the value of Granada's assets as follows:

| Accounts receivable | $ 60,000 |
|---|---|
| Equipment | 360,000 |
| In-process research and development | 180,000 |

The in-process research and development has not yet reached technological feasibility, but Alhambra is confident that the research will produce a product that will eventually justify the initial value assigned.

In considering the acquisition, Alhambra wishes to assess the sensitivity of the acquired long-term asset valuation to the purchase price.

### Required:

Prepare an Excel spreadsheet analysis that automatically recomputes amounts allocated to the acquired accounts receivable, equipment, in-process research and development, and goodwill as the purchase price changes. Assume a purchase price range of $500,000 to $900,000. Calculate the asset allocations for the following purchase prices

(1) $500,000
(2) $550,000
(3) $600,000
(4) $900,000

## FARS RESEARCH CASE—*SFAS 141* "BUSINESS COMBINATIONS"

Acello Company has agreed to merge with BlairCo using an exchange of equity interests. The terms of the agreement include the following:

- BlairCo, the larger firm, will issue additional shares of common stock to the owners of Acello in exchange for their shares after which the corporate entity Acello will be formally dissolved. BlairCo will survive as the continuing firm.
- The former owners of Acello will hold 65 percent of the voting shares of the combined firm. The exchange ratios reflected a premium paid by Acello's owners over the market value of BlairCo's stock.
- BlairCo's former chief executive office (CEO) and chief financial officer (CFO) will continue their roles in the combined firm for at least two years.
- The former chairman of the board of directors of Acello will be the initial new chairman of the board of directors of the combined firm. Within two months after the merger, shareholders will elect a new board of directors.

### Required:

*SFAS 141* requires the identification of the acquiring firm in a business combination. Which of the firms, Acello or BlairCo, should be considered as the acquiring firm?

## RESEARCH AND ANALYSIS CASE 1—PEPSICO–QUAKER OATS MERGER

At the Pepsico.com website, obtain references to various SEC filings, press releases, and financial statements surrounding PepsiCo's merger with Quaker Oats to address the following items. In particular, the 2001 Quaker S-4/A Filing and SEC Form 8-K (both at Pepsico.com) should be useful in addressing these questions.

### Required:

1. How was the merger between PepsiCo and Quaker Oats structured? Which firm is the survivor? Who holds what stock after the merger?
2. What accounting method was used to account for the merger of PepsiCo and Quaker Oats? What are the reporting implications of the chosen accounting method?
3. What were the approximate amounts for the
   a. Recorded value of the acquisition of the surviving firm's books?
   b. Market value of the acquisition?
4. What items of value did Quaker Oats bring to the merger that will not be recorded in the acquisition? How will these items affect future reported income for the combined firm?
5. Using the criteria stated in the Summary to *SFAS 141* (first four pages of the document), evaluate the financial reporting for the PepsiCo acquisition of Quaker Oats.

## RESEARCH AND ANALYSIS CASE 2

Access the most recent financial statements for one of the following firms:

- Yahoo!
- Cisco Systems

- Cadence Designs
- Pennzoil–Quaker State
- Apple Computer
- Amazon.com
- America OnLine

**Required:**

Write a brief report that describes the firm's merger and acquisition activity for the past several years. Be sure to identify the accounting methods employed, cost allocations for purchase acquisitions, and motivations cited for the merger activities.

## RESEARCH AND ANALYSIS CASE 3

Find the annual 10-K reports for any firms involved in recent merger and acquisition activity and identify several of their recent successful takeovers. Then determine the market value of the target firm two months prior to the takeover announcement.

**Required:**

Write a brief report that

- Compares the price paid in the acquisition with the previous market value.
- Discusses possible motivations for any difference.
- Identifies the websites used in your search.

## RESEARCH AND ANALYSIS CASE 4

Search the Internet for financial reports containing references to purchased in-process research and development. Identify three firms that report purchased in-process research and development expenses in connection with merger and acquisition activities.

**Required:**

1. Discuss how they determined the proper amount for the write-off of the purchased in-process research and development.
2. Identify the percentage of the purchase price allocated to in-process research and development and other assets.

## COMMUNICATION CASE 1

Read the following as well as any other published information concerning the pooling of interests method:

"The Financial Statement Effects of Eliminating the Pooling-of-Interests Method of Acquisition Accounting," *Accounting Horizons,* March 2000.

"Why Eliminate the Pooling Method?" August 31, 1999, *Financial Accounting Series Status Report No. 316* (Financial Accounting Foundation/FASB).

"Special Report: The Battle Over Pooling of Interests," *Journal of Accountancy,* November 1999.

"FASB Plan Would Provide False Accounts," *Wall Street Journal,* January 31, 2000, Manager's Journal, page C1.

"Valuing the New Economy—How New Accounting Standards Will Inhibit Economically Sound Mergers and Hinder the Efficiency and Innovation of U.S. Business," *Merrill Lynch Forum White Paper*, June 1999.

**Required:**

Write a report discussing whether you agree with the FASB decision to eliminate the pooling of interests method as a generally accepted accounting principle.

## COMMUNICATION CASE 2

From the SEC's website (www.sec.gov), locate and read a speech given by Lynn Turner, then Chief Accountant at the SEC, on February 10, 1999 entitled "Making Financial Statements Real: Recent Problems In the Accounting for Purchased In-Process Research and Development."

**Required:**

Write a brief report that discusses the issues surrounding the current accounting treatment for in-process research and development costs. Provide three annual report examples of footnote disclosure and discussion for IPR&D costs related to business combinations.

# Chapter Three

# Consolidations—Subsequent to the Date of Acquisition

## Questions to Consider

- How does a parent company account for a subsidiary organization in the years that follow the creation of a business combination?

- What impact does the parent's method of accounting for a subsidiary have on subsequent consolidations?

- Why do intercompany balances exist within the financial records of the separate companies? How are these reciprocals eliminated on a consolidation worksheet?

- Why did the FASB decide that goodwill amortization should not be allowed and that instead goodwill should be periodically tested for impairment? How do firms determine when and if goodwill is impaired? How are goodwill impairment losses recognized in consolidated financial statements?

- How is amortization of other purchase price allocations recognized within consolidated financial statements?

- If the exact purchase price of a subsidiary is based on a future event, what effect does this contingency have on the consolidation process?

- Should a subsidiary company report on its financial statements the purchase price allocations and later amortization that can result from the purchase price paid by the parent?

In the mid-1980s, the General Electric Co. (GE) acquired the National Broadcasting Company (NBC) as part of its $6.4 billion cash purchase of RCA Corporation. Although this transaction involved well-known companies, it was not unique; mergers and acquisitions have long been common in the business world.

The current financial statements of GE indicate that NBC is still a component of this economic entity. However, NBC continues to be a separately incorporated concern long after its purchase. As discussed in Chapter 2, a parent often chooses to let a subsidiary retain its identity as a legal corporation to better utilize the value inherent in a going concern.

For external reporting purposes, maintenance of incorporation creates an ongoing challenge for the accountant. In each subsequent period, consolidation must be simulated anew through the use of a worksheet and consolidation entries. Thus, for almost 20 years, the financial data for GE and NBC have been brought together periodically to provide figures for the financial statements that represent this business combination.

## CONSOLIDATION—THE EFFECTS CREATED BY THE PASSAGE OF TIME

In the previous chapter, consolidation accounting is analyzed at the date that a combination is created. The present chapter carries this process one step further by examining the consolidation procedures that must be followed in subsequent periods whenever separate incorporation of the subsidiary is maintained.

Despite complexities created by the passage of time, the basic objective of all consolidations remains the same: to combine asset, liability, revenue, expense, and equity accounts of a parent and its subsidiaries. From a mechanical perspective, a worksheet and consolidation entries continue to provide structure for the production of a single set of financial statements for the combined business entity.

The time factor introduces additional complications into the consolidation process. For internal record-keeping purposes, the parent must select and apply an accounting method to monitor the relationship between the two companies. The investment balance recorded by the parent varies over time as a result of the method chosen, as does the income subsequently recognized. These differences affect the periodic consolidation process but not the figures to be reported by the combined entity. Regardless of the amount, the parent's Investment account is eliminated on the worksheet so that the subsidiary's actual assets and liabilities can be consolidated. Likewise, the income figure accrued by the parent is removed each period so that the subsidiary's revenues and expenses can be included when creating an income statement for the combined business entity.

## *SFAS 142*—GOODWILL AND INTANGIBLE ASSETS

In *SFAS 142,* "Goodwill and Other Intangible Assets," July 2001, the FASB approved significant changes in the way income is determined for combined business entities. The most prominent of these changes relates to the treatment of goodwill in periods subsequent to acquisition. For fiscal periods beginning after December 15, 2001, goodwill is no longer amortized systematically over time.[1] Instead, goodwill is now subject to an annual test for impairment. This nonamortization approach is applied to both previously recognized and newly acquired goodwill. Consequently, goodwill that arose from pre–*SFAS 142* combinations is simply carried forward at unamortized cost as of the beginning of annual reporting periods in 2002.

For consolidations of parent and subsidiary companies, goodwill amortization expense no longer appears on the combined income statement. The consolidated balance sheet frequently carries acquisition-related goodwill at its original cost. Only upon the recognition of an impairment loss (or partial sale of a subsidiary) will goodwill decline from one period to the next. In the next several sections of this chapter, the relation of the parent's investment accounting to the adjustments required for consolidation will be presented along with specific procedures for amortizing the cost of a business combination and testing for impairment as appropriate.

## INVESTMENT ACCOUNTING BY THE ACQUIRING COMPANY

For external reporting, consolidation of a subsidiary becomes necessary whenever control exists. For internal record-keeping, though, the parent has the choice of three alternatives for monitoring the activities of its subsidiaries: the cost method, the equity method, or the partial equity method. *Because both the resulting investment balance and the related income are eliminated as part of every recurring consolidation, the selection of a particular method does not affect the totals ultimately reported for the combined companies.* Rather, this decision dictates the specific procedures subsequently utilized in consolidating the financial information of the separate organizations.

The actual choice of a method is often based on the internal reporting philosophy of the acquiring company. The *cost method* might be selected because it is easy to apply. The investment balance remains permanently on the parent's balance sheet at original cost. The cost method uses the cash basis for income recognition. Therefore, only the dividends subsequently received from the subsidiary are recognized as income. No other adjustments are recorded. Thus, this method requires little effort while providing an accurate measure of the cash flows between the two companies.

In contrast, under the *equity method,* the acquiring company accrues income when earned by the subsidiary. To match acquisition costs against income, amortization expense stemming from the original acquisition is recognized through periodic adjusting entries. Unrealized gains on intercompany transactions are deferred; dividends paid by the subsidiary serve to reduce the investment balance. As discussed in Chapter 1, the equity method is designed to create a parallel between the parent's investment accounts and changes in the underlying equity of the acquired company.[2]

---

[1] Additionally, goodwill was not amortized for new business combinations occurring subsequent to June 30, 2001.

[2] In Chapter 1, the equity method was introduced in connection with the external reporting of investments in which the owner held the ability to apply significant influence over the investee (usually by possessing 20 to 50 percent of the company's voting stock). Here, the equity method is utilized for the *internal* reporting of the parent for investments in which control is maintained. Although the accounting procedures are identical, the reason for using the equity method is different.

## EXHIBIT 3–1   Internal Reporting of Investment Accounts by Acquiring Company

| Method | Investment Account | Income Account | Advantages |
| --- | --- | --- | --- |
| Equity | Continually adjusted to reflect ownership of acquired company. | Income is accrued as earned; amortization and other adjustments are recognized. | Acquiring company totals give a true representation of consolidation figures. |
| Cost | Remains at initially recorded cost. | Cash received is recorded as Dividend Income. | Easy to apply; measures cash flows. |
| Partial equity | Adjusted only for accrued income and dividends received from acquired company. | Income is accrued as earned; no other adjustments are recognized. | Usually gives balances approximating consolidation figures, but is easier to apply than equity method. |

Under the equity method, the parent's accounts reflect the income of the entire combined business entity. Consequently, the equity method often is referred to in accounting as a *single-line consolidation*. The equity method is especially popular in companies where management wants to get a picture of overall profitability by looking at the periodic (such as monthly) figures developed by the parent.

A third method available to the acquiring company is a *partial application of the equity method*. Under this approach, income accruing from the subsidiary is recognized immediately by the parent. Dividends that are collected reduce the investment balance. However, no other equity adjustments (amortization or deferral of unrealized gains) are recorded. Thus, in many cases, earnings figures on the parent's books approximate consolidated totals but without the effort associated with a full application of the equity method.

Each acquiring company must decide for itself the appropriate approach in recording the operations of its subsidiaries. For example, Alliant Food Service, Inc., applies the equity method. According to Joe Tomczak, vice president and controller of Alliant Food Service, Inc., "We maintain the parent holding company books on an equity basis. This approach provides the best method of providing information for our operational decisions."[3]

In contrast, Reynolds Metals Corporation has chosen to utilize the partial equity method approach. Allen Earehart, director of corporate accounting for Reynolds, states "we do adjust the carrying value of our investments annually to reflect the earnings of each subsidiary. We want to be able to evaluate the parent company on a stand-alone basis and a regular equity accrual is, therefore, necessary. However, we do separate certain adjustments such as the elimination of intercompany gains and losses and record them solely within the development of consolidated financial statements."[4]

Exhibit 3–1 provides a summary of these three reporting techniques. The method adopted affects only the acquiring company's separate financial records. No changes are created in either the subsidiary's accounts or the consolidated totals.

Because specific worksheet procedures differ based on the investment method being utilized by the parent, the consolidation process subsequent to the date of combination will be introduced twice. Initially, consolidations in which the acquiring company uses the equity method are reviewed. All procedures are then redeveloped when the investment is recorded by one of the alternative methods.

# SUBSEQUENT CONSOLIDATION—INVESTMENT RECORDED BY THE EQUITY METHOD

## Acquisition Made during the Current Year

As a basis for this illustration, assume that Parrot Company obtains all of the outstanding common stock of Sun Company on January 1, 2004. Parrot acquires this stock for $760,000 in cash but pays an additional $40,000 in direct combination costs.

---

[3] Telephone conversation with Joe Tomczak.
[4] Telephone conversation with Allen Earehart.

The book values as well as the appraised values of Sun's accounts are as follows:

|  | Book Value 1/1/04 | Fair Market Value 1/1/04 | Difference |
|---|---|---|---|
| Current assets | $ 320,000 | $ 320,000 | –0– |
| Land | 200,000 | 220,000 | + 20,000 |
| Buildings (10-year life) | 320,000 | 450,000 | +130,000 |
| Equipment (5-year life) | 180,000 | 150,000 | (30,000) |
| Liabilities | (420,000) | (420,000) | –0– |
| Net book value | $ 600,000 | $ 720,000 | $120,000 |
| Common stock—$40 par value | $(200,000) | | |
| Additional paid-in capital | (20,000) | | |
| Retained earnings, 1/1/04 | (380,000) | | |

For this combination, the assumption is being made that any amortization relating to purchase price allocations is calculated using the straight-line method with no estimated salvage value.[5]

With the inclusion of the $40,000 direct consolidation costs, a total of $800,000 has been paid by Parrot in this purchase of Sun Company. As shown in Exhibit 3–2, individual allocations are used to adjust Sun's accounts from their book values on January 1, 2004, to fair market values. Since the total value of these assets and liabilities was only $720,000, goodwill of $80,000 must be recognized for consolidation purposes.

Each of these allocated amounts (other than the $20,000 attributed to land and the $80,000 for goodwill) represents a cost incurred by Parrot that is associated with an account having a definite life. As discussed in Chapter 1, Parrot must amortize each of these cost figures over their expected lives. The expense recognition necessitated by this purchase price allocation is calculated in Exhibit 3–3.

One aspect of this amortization schedule warrants explanation. The fair market value of Sun's Equipment account was $30,000 *less* than book value. Therefore, instead of attributing an additional cost to this asset, the $30,000 allocation actually reflects a cost reduction. As such, the amortization shown in Exhibit 3–3 relating to Equipment is not an additional expense but rather an expense reduction.

Having determined the allocation of the purchase price in the previous example as well as the associated amortization, the parent's separate record-keeping for 2004 can be constructed. Assume that Sun earns income of $100,000 during the year and pays a $40,000 cash dividend on August 1, 2004.

**EXHIBIT 3–2**

**PARROT COMPANY**
**Allocation of Purchase Price**
**January 1, 2004**

| | | |
|---|---|---|
| Purchase price by Parrot Company | | $ 800,000 |
| Book value of Sun Company | | (600,000) |
| Excess of cost over book value | | 200,000 |
| Allocation to specific accounts based on fair market values: | | |
| Land | $ 20,000 | |
| Buildings | 130,000 | |
| Equipment (overvalued) | (30,000) | 120,000 |
| Excess cost not identified with specific accounts—goodwill | | $ 80,000 |

[5] Unless otherwise stated, all amortization expense computations in this textbook are based on the straight-line method with no salvage value.

**EXHIBIT 3–3**
**Annual Excess Amortization**

### PARROT COMPANY
### Excess Amortization Schedule—Allocation of Purchase Price

| Account | Allocation | Useful Life | Annual Excess Amortizations |
|---|---|---|---|
| Land | $ 20,000 | Indefinite | –0– |
| Buildings | 130,000 | 10 years | $13,000 |
| Equipment | (30,000) | 5 years | (6,000) |
| Goodwill | 80,000 | Indefinite | –0– |
| | | | $ 7,000* |

*Total excess amortizations will be $7,000 annually for five years until the equipment allocation is fully removed. At the end of each asset's life, future amortizations will change.

In this initial illustration, Parrot has adopted the equity method. Apparently, this company believes that the information derived from using the equity method is useful in its evaluation of Sun.

*Application of the Equity Method*

| | **Parrot's Financial Records** | | |
|---|---|---|---|
| 1/1/04 | Investment in Sun Company .................... | 800,000 | |
| | Cash ......................................... | | 800,000 |
| | To record purchase of Sun Company including direct combination costs. | | |
| 8/I/04 | Cash ......................................... | 40,000 | |
| | Investment in Sun Company ................ | | 40,000 |
| | To record receipt of cash dividend from subsidiary, an investment that is being accounted for by means of the equity method. | | |
| 12/31/04 | Investment in Sun Company .................... | 100,000 | |
| | Equity in Subsidiary Earnings ................ | | 100,000 |
| | To accrue income earned by 100 percent owned subsidiary. | | |
| 12/31/04 | Equity in Subsidiary Earnings ................ | 7,000 | |
| | Investment in Sun Company ................ | | 7,000 |
| | To recognize amortizations on allocations made in purchase of subsidiary (see Exhibit 3–3). | | |

Parrot's application of the equity method, as shown in this series of entries, causes the Investment in Sun Company account balance to rise from $800,000 to $853,000 ($800,000 − $40,000 + $100,000 − $7,000). During the same period, a $93,000 equity income figure (the $100,000 earnings accrual less the $7,000 excess amortization expenses) is recognized by the parent.

The consolidation procedures for Parrot and Sun one year after the date of acquisition are illustrated next. For this purpose, Exhibit 3–4 presents the separate 2004 financial statements for these two companies. Both investment-related accounts (the $853,000 asset balance and the $93,000 income accrual) have been recorded by Parrot based on applying the equity method.

## Determining Consolidated Totals

Before becoming immersed in the mechanical aspects of a consolidation, the objective of this process should be understood. As indicated in Chapter 2, the revenue, expense, asset, and

**EXHIBIT 3–4**
Separate Records—
Equity Method Applied

### PARROT COMPANY AND SUN COMPANY
#### Financial Statements
#### For Year Ending December 31, 2004

|  | Parrot Company | Sun Company |
|---|---:|---:|
| **Income Statement** | | |
| Revenues | $(1,500,000) | $ (400,000) |
| Cost of goods sold | 700,000 | 250,000 |
| Depreciation expense | 200,000 | 50,000 |
| Equity in subsidiary earnings | (93,000) | –0– |
| Net income | $ (693,000) | $ (100,000) |
| **Statement of Retained Earnings** | | |
| Retained earnings, 1/1/04 | $ (840,000) | $ (380,000) |
| Net income (above) | (693,000) | (100,000) |
| Dividends paid | 120,000 | 40,000 |
| Retained earnings, 12/31/04 | $(1,413,000) | $ (440,000) |
| **Balance Sheet** | | |
| Current assets | $ 1,040,000 | $ 400,000 |
| Investment in Sun Company (at equity) | 853,000 | –0– |
| Land | 600,000 | 200,000 |
| Buildings (net) | 370,000 | 288,000 |
| Equipment (net) | 250,000 | 220,000 |
| Total assets | $ 3,113,000 | $ 1,108,000 |
| Liabilities | $ (980,000) | $ (448,000) |
| Common stock | (600,000) | (200,000) |
| Additional paid-in capital | (120,000) | (20,000) |
| Retained earnings, 12/31/04 (above) | (1,413,000) | (440,000) |
| Total liabilities and equity | $(3,113,000) | $(1,108,000) |

Note: Parentheses indicate a credit balance.

liability accounts of the subsidiary are added to the parent company balances. Within this procedure, several important guidelines must be followed:

- Sun's assets and liabilities are adjusted to reflect any allocations originating from the purchase price.
- Because of the passage of time, the income effects (e.g., amortizations) of these allocations must also be recorded within the consolidation process.
- Any reciprocal or intercompany accounts have to be offset. If, for example, one of the companies owes money to the other, the receivable and the payable balances have no connection with an outside party. Both should be eliminated for external reporting purposes. When the companies are viewed as a single entity, the receivable and the payable are intercompany balances to be removed.

A consolidation of the two sets of financial information in Exhibit 3–4 is a relatively uncomplicated task and can even be carried out without the use of a worksheet. Understanding the origin of each reported figure is the first step in gaining a knowledge of this process.

- *Revenues* = $1,900,000. The revenues of the parent and the subsidiary are added together.
- *Cost of goods sold* = $950,000. The cost of goods sold of the parent and subsidiary are added together.

- *Depreciation expense* = $257,000. The depreciation expenses of the parent and subsidiary are added together along with the $13,000 additional building depreciation and the $6,000 reduction in equipment depreciation, as indicated in Exhibit 3–3.
- *Equity in subsidiary earnings* = –0–. The investment income recorded by the parent is eliminated so that the subsidiary's revenues and expenses can be included in the consolidated totals.
- *Net income* = $693,000. Consolidated revenues less consolidated expenses.
- *Retained earnings, 1/1/04* = $840,000. The parent figure only because the subsidiary was not owned prior to that date.
- *Dividends paid* = $120,000. The parent company balance only because the subsidiary's dividends were paid intercompany to the parent, not to an outside party.
- *Retained earnings, 12/31/04* = $1,413,000. Consolidated retained earnings as of the beginning of the year plus consolidated net income less consolidated dividends paid.
- *Current assets* = $1,440,000. The parent's book value plus the subsidiary's book value.
- *Investment in Sun Company* = –0–. The asset recorded by the parent is eliminated so that the subsidiary's assets and liabilities can be included in the consolidated totals.
- *Land* = $820,000. The parent's book value plus the subsidiary's book value plus the $20,000 allocation within the purchase price.
- *Buildings* = $775,000. The parent's book value plus the subsidiary's book value plus the $130,000 allocation within the purchase price less 2004 amortization of $13,000.
- *Equipment* = $446,000. The parent's book value plus the subsidiary's book value less the $30,000 cost reduction allocation plus the 2004 expense reduction of $6,000.
- *Goodwill* = $80,000. The residual allocation shown in Exhibit 3–2. Note that goodwill is not amortized.
- *Total assets* = $3,561,000. Summation of consolidated assets.
- *Liabilities* = $1,428,000. The parent's book value plus the subsidiary's book value.
- *Common stock* = $600,000. The parent's book value since this combination was a purchase.
- *Additional paid-in capital* = $120,000. The parent's book value since this combination was a purchase.
- *Retained earnings, 12/31/04* = $1,413,000. Computed above.
- *Total liabilities and equities* = $3,561,000. Summation of consolidated liabilities and equities.

## Consolidation Worksheet

Although the consolidated figures to be reported can be computed as just shown, accountants normally prefer to use a worksheet. A worksheet provides an organized structure for this process, a benefit that becomes especially important in consolidating complex combinations.

For Parrot and Sun, only five consolidation entries are needed to arrive at the same figures previously derived for this business combination. As discussed in Chapter 2, *worksheet entries are the catalyst for developing totals to be reported by the entity but are not physically recorded in the individual account balances of either company.*

### Consolidation Entry S

| | | |
|---|---:|---:|
| Common Stock (Sun Company) | 200,000 | |
| Additional Paid-In Capital (Sun Company) | 20,000 | |
| Retained Earnings, 1/1/04 (Sun Company) | 380,000 | |
|     Investment in Sun Company | | 600,000 |

As shown in Exhibit 3–2, Parrot's $800,000 purchase price reflects two components: (1) a $600,000 amount equal to Sun's book value and (2) a $200,000 figure attributed to the difference, at January 1, 2004, between the book value and market value of Sun's assets and liabilities (with a residual allocation made to goodwill). Entry **S** removes the $600,000 component of the Investment in Sun Company account so that the *book value* of each subsidiary asset and liability can be included in the consolidated figures. A second worksheet entry (Entry **A**) eliminates the remaining $200,000 portion of the purchase price, allowing the specific allocations to be recorded along with any goodwill.

Entry **S** also removes Sun's stockholders' equity accounts as of the beginning of the year. As a purchase, subsidiary equity balances generated prior to the acquisition are not relevant to the business combination and should be deleted. The elimination is made through this entry because the equity accounts and the $600,000 component of the investment account represent reciprocal balances: Both provide a measure of Sun's book value as of January 1, 2004.

Before moving to the next consolidation entry, a clarification point should be made. In actual practice, worksheet entries are usually identified numerically. However as in the previous chapter, the label "Entry **S**" used in this example refers to the elimination of Sun's beginning Stockholders' Equity. As a reminder of the purpose being served, all worksheet entries are identified in a similar fashion. Thus, throughout this textbook, "Entry **S**" always refers to the removal of the subsidiary's beginning stockholders' equity balances for the year against the book value portion of the investment account.

### Consolidation Entry A

| | | |
|---|---:|---:|
| Land | 20,000 | |
| Buildings | 130,000 | |
| Goodwill | 80,000 | |
|     Equipment | | 30,000 |
|     Investment in Sun Company | | 200,000 |

As indicated previously, the second worksheet entry removes the $200,000 component of the purchase price, replacing it with the specific allocations from the original purchase price (see Exhibit 3–2). In this manner, the individual assets and liabilities of the consolidated entity now reflect the cost incurred by Parrot in making this purchase. Sun's accounts are adjusted based on the $200,000 paid at the time of acquisition that was in excess of Sun's book value. No basis exists for continually revaluing the accounts to newly determined market values at the date of each subsequent consolidation.

This entry is labeled "Entry **A**" to indicate that it represents the **A**llocations made in connection with the parent's purchase price.

### Consolidation Entry I

| | | |
|---|---:|---:|
| Equity in Subsidiary Earnings | 93,000 | |
|     Investment in Sun Company | | 93,000 |

"Entry **I**" (for **I**ncome) removes the subsidiary income recognized by Parrot during the year so that the underlying revenue and expense accounts of Sun (and the current amortization expense) can be brought into the consolidated totals. The $93,000 figure eliminated here represents the $100,000 income accrual recognized by Parrot, reduced by the $7,000 in excess amortizations. For consolidation purposes, the one-line amount appearing in the parent's records is not appropriate and is removed so that the individual balances can be included. The entry originally recorded by the parent is simply reversed on the worksheet to remove its impact.

*Consolidation Entry D*

| | | |
|---|---|---|
| Investment in Sun Company | 40,000 | |
|     Dividends Paid | | 40,000 |

The dividends distributed by the subsidiary during 2004 also must be eliminated from the consolidated totals. The entire $40,000 payment was made to the parent so that, from the viewpoint of the consolidated entity, it is simply an intercompany transfer of cash. The distribution did not affect any outside party. Therefore, "Entry **D**" (for **D**ividends) is designed to offset the impact of this transaction by removing the subsidiary's Dividends Paid account. Because the equity method has been applied, receipt of this money by Parrot was recorded originally as a decrease in the Investment in Sun Company account. To eliminate the impact of this reduction, the Investment account is increased here.

*Consolidation Entry E*

| | | |
|---|---|---|
| Depreciation Expense | 7,000 | |
| Equipment | 6,000 | |
|     Buildings | | 13,000 |

This final worksheet entry records the current year's excess amortization expenses relating to Parrot's purchase price. Because the equity method amortization was eliminated within Entry I, "Entry **E**" (for **E**xpense) now records the 2004 expense attributed to each of the specific account allocations (see Exhibit 3–3).

Thus, the worksheet entries necessary for consolidation when the parent has applied the equity method are as follows:

*Entry S*—Eliminates the subsidiary's stockholders' equity accounts as of the beginning of the current year along with the equivalent book value component within the parent's purchase price in the investment account.

*Entry A*—Recognizes the unamortized allocations as of the beginning of the current year, costs that were associated with the original purchase price.

*Entry I*—Eliminates the impact of intercompany income accrued by the parent.

*Entry D*—Eliminates the impact of intercompany dividend payments made by the subsidiary.

*Entry E*—Recognizes excess amortization expenses for the current period on the allocations within the original purchase price.

Exhibit 3–5 provides a complete presentation of the December 31, 2004, consolidation worksheet developed for Parrot Company and Sun Company. The series of entries just described successfully brings together the separate financial statements of these two organizations. Note that the consolidated totals are the same as those computed previously for this combination.

One aspect of this worksheet should be explained. Parrot is separately reporting net income of $693,000 as well as ending retained earnings of $1,413,000, figures that are identical to the totals generated for the consolidated entity. However, in a purchase combination, subsidiary income earned after the date of acquisition is to be *added* to that of the parent. Thus, a question arises in this example as to why the parent company figures alone equal the consolidated balances of both operations.

In reality, Sun's income for this period is contained in both Parrot's reported balances and the consolidated totals. Through the application of the equity method, the 2004 earnings of the subsidiary have already been accrued by Parrot along with the appropriate amortization expense. *The parent's Equity in Subsidiary Earnings account is, therefore, an accurate representation of Sun's effect on consolidated net income.* If the equity method is employed properly, the worksheet process simply replaces this single $93,000 balance with the specific

## EXHIBIT 3–5

**PARROT COMPANY AND SUN COMPANY**
**Consolidated Worksheet**
**For Year Ending December 31, 2004**

*Consolidation: Purchase Method*
*Investment: Equity Method*

| Accounts | Parrot Company | Sun Company | Consolidation Entries Debit | Consolidation Entries Credit | Consolidated Totals |
|---|---|---|---|---|---|
| **Income Statement** | | | | | |
| Revenues | (1,500,000) | (400,000) | | | (1,900,000) |
| Cost of goods sold | 700,000 | 250,000 | | | 950,000 |
| Depreciation expense | 200,000 | 50,000 | (E) 7,000 | | 257,000 |
| Equity in subsidiary earnings | (93,000) | –0– | (I) 93,000 | | –0– |
| Net income | (693,000) | (100,000) | | | (693,000) |
| **Statement of Retained Earnings** | | | | | |
| Retained earnings, 1/1/04 | (840,000) | (380,000) | (S) 380,000 | | (840,000) |
| Net income (above) | (693,000) | (100,000) | | | (693,000) |
| Dividends paid | 120,000 | 40,000 | | (D) 40,000 | 120,000 |
| Retained earnings, 12/31/04 | (1,413,000) | (440,000) | | | (1,413,000) |
| **Balance Sheet** | | | | | |
| Current assets | 1,040,000 | 400,000 | | | 1,440,000 |
| Investment in Sun Company | 853,000 | –0– | (D) 40,000 | (S) 600,000 | –0– |
| | | | | (A) 200,000 | |
| | | | | (I) 93,000 | |
| Land | 600,000 | 200,000 | (A) 20,000 | | 820,000 |
| Buildings (net) | 370,000 | 288,000 | (A) 130,000 | (E) 13,000 | 775,000 |
| Equipment (net) | 250,000 | 220,000 | (E) 6,000 | (A) 30,000 | 446,000 |
| Goodwill | –0– | –0– | (A) 80,000 | | 80,000 |
| Total assets | 3,113,000 | 1,108,000 | | | 3,561,000 |
| Liabilities | (980,000) | (448,000) | | | (1,428,000) |
| Common stock | (600,000) | (200,000) | (S) 200,000 | | (600,000) |
| Additional paid-in capital | (120,000) | (20,000) | (S) 20,000 | | (120,000) |
| Retained earnings, 12/31/04 (above) | (1,413,000) | (440,000) | | | (1,413,000) |
| Total liabilities and equities | (3,113,000) | (1,108,000) | | | (3,561,000) |

Note: Parentheses indicate a credit balance.
Consolidation entries:
(S) Elimination of Sun's stockholders' equity accounts as of January 1, 2004, and book value portion of purchase price.
(A) Allocation of Parrot's cost in excess of Sun's book value.
(I) Elimination of intercompany equity income.
(D) Elimination of intercompany dividends.
(E) Recognition of excess amortization expenses on purchase price allocations.

---

revenue and expense accounts that it represents. *Consequently, the parent's net income and retained earnings mirror consolidated totals.*

## Consolidation Subsequent to Year of Acquisition—Equity Method

In many ways, every consolidation of Parrot and Sun prepared after the date of acquisition incorporates the same basic procedures outlined in the previous section. However, the continual financial evolution undergone by the companies prohibits an exact repetition of the consolidation entries demonstrated in Exhibit 3–5.

As a basis for analyzing the procedural changes necessitated by the passage of time, assume that Parrot Company continues to hold its ownership of Sun Company as of December 31, 2007. This date was selected at random; any date subsequent to 2004 would serve equally well to illustrate this process. As an additional factor, assume that Sun now has a $40,000 liability that is payable to Parrot.

For this consolidation, assume that the January 1, 2007, Retained Earnings balance of Sun Company has risen to $600,000. Since that account had a reported total of only $380,000 on January 1, 2004, Sun's book value apparently has increased by $220,000 during the 2004–2006 period. Although knowledge of individual operating figures in the past is not required, Sun's reported totals help to clarify the consolidation procedures.

| Year | Sun Company Net Income | Dividends Paid | Increase in Book Value | Ending Retained Earnings |
|---|---|---|---|---|
| 2004 | $100,000 | $ 40,000 | $ 60,000 | $440,000 |
| 2005 | 140,000 | 50,000 | 90,000 | 530,000 |
| 2006 | 90,000 | 20,000 | 70,000 | 600,000 |
|  | $330,000 | $110,000 | $220,000 |  |

For 2007, the current year, the assumption will be made that Sun reports net income of $160,000 and pays cash dividends of $70,000. Because it applies the equity method, earnings of $160,000 are recognized by Parrot. Furthermore, as shown in Exhibit 3–3, amortization expense of $7,000 is applicable to 2007 and must also be recorded by the parent. Consequently, Parrot reports an Equity in Subsidiary Earnings balance for the year of $153,000 ($160,000 − $7,000).

Although this income figure can be reconstructed with little difficulty, the current balance in the Investment in Sun Company account is more complicated. Over the years, the initial $800,000 purchase price has been subjected to adjustments for:

1. The annual accrual of Sun's income.
2. The receipt of dividends from Sun.
3. The recognition of annual excess amortization expenses.

However, by analyzing these changes, Exhibit 3–6 can be developed to show the components of the balance in the Investment in Sun Company account as of December 31, 2007.

Following the construction of the Investment in Sun Company account, the consolidation worksheet developed in Exhibit 3–7 should be easier to understand. Current figures for both companies are presented in the first two columns. The parent's investment balance and equity income accrual as well as Sun's income and stockholders' equity accounts correspond to the information given previously. Worksheet entries (lettered to agree with the previous illustration) are then utilized to consolidate all balances.

Several steps are necessary to arrive at these reported totals. The subsidiary's assets, liabilities, revenues, and expenses are added to those same accounts of the parent. The unamortized portion of the original purchase price allocations are included along with current excess amortization expenses. The investment and equity income balances are both eliminated as are the subsidiary's stockholders' equity accounts. Intercompany dividends are removed with the same treatment required for the debt existing between the two companies.

***Consolidation Entry S*** Once again, this first consolidation entry offsets reciprocal amounts representing the subsidiary's book value as of the beginning of the current year. Sun's January 1, 2007, stockholders' equity accounts are eliminated against the book value portion of the parent's investment account. Here, though, the amount eliminated is $820,000 rather than the $600,000 shown in Exhibit 3–5 for 2004. Both balances have changed during the 2004–2006 period. Sun's operations caused a $220,000 increase in retained earnings. Parrot's application of the equity method created a parallel effect on its Investment in Sun Company account (the income accrual of $330,000 less dividends collected of $110,000).

Although Sun's Retained Earnings balance is removed in this entry, the income earned by this company since the date of purchase is still included in the consolidated figures. Parrot accrues these profits annually through application of the equity method. Thus, elimination of the subsidiary's entire Retained Earnings is necessary; a portion was earned prior to the purchase and the remainder has already been recorded by the parent.

**EXHIBIT 3-6**

### PARROT COMPANY
### Investment in Sun Company Account
### As of December 31, 2007
### Equity Method Applied

| | | |
|---|---:|---:|
| Purchase price | | $ 800,000 |
| Entries recorded in prior years: | | |
|   Accrual of Sun Company's income | | |
|     2004 | $100,000 | |
|     2005 | 140,000 | |
|     2006 | 90,000 | 330,000 |
|   Sun Company—Dividends paid | | |
|     2004 | $ 40,000 | |
|     2005 | 50,000 | |
|     2006 | 20,000 | (110,000) |
|   Excess amortization expenses | | |
|     2004 | $ 7,000 | |
|     2005 | 7,000 | |
|     2006 | 7,000 | (21,000) |
| Entries recorded in current year—2007: | | |
|   Accrual of Sun Company's income | $160,000 | |
|   Sun Company—Dividends paid | (70,000) | |
|   Excess amortization expenses | (7,000) | 83,000 |
| Investment in Sun Company, 12/31/07 | | $1,082,000 |

Entry **S** removes these balances as of the first day of 2007 rather than at the end of the year. The consolidation process is made a bit simpler by segregating the effect of preceding operations from the transactions of the current year. Thus, *all worksheet entries relate specifically to either the previous years (S and A) or the current period (I, D, E, and P)*.

***Consolidation Entry A*** In the initial consolidation (2004), cost allocations amounting to $200,000 were recorded, but these balances have now undergone three years of amortization. As computed in Exhibit 3–8, expenses for these prior years totaled $21,000, leaving a balance of $179,000. Allocation of this amount to the individual accounts is also determined in Exhibit 3–8 and reflected in worksheet Entry **A**. As with Entry **S**, these balances are calculated as of January 1, 2007, so that the current year expenses can be recorded separately (in Entry **E**).

***Consolidation Entry I*** As before, this entry eliminates the equity income recorded currently by Parrot ($153,000) in connection with its ownership of Sun. The subsidiary's revenue and expense accounts are left intact so they can be included in the consolidated figures.

***Consolidation Entry D*** This worksheet entry offsets the $70,000 intercompany dividend payment made by Sun to Parrot during the current period.

***Consolidation Entry E*** Excess amortization expenses relating to Parrot's purchase price are individually recorded for 2007.

Before progressing to the final worksheet entry, note the close similarity of these entries with the five incorporated in the 2004 consolidation (Exhibit 3–5). Except for the numerical changes created by the passage of time, the entries are identical.

***Consolidation Entry P*** This last entry (labeled "Entry **P**" because it eliminates an intercompany **P**ayable) introduces a new element to the consolidation process. As noted earlier, intercompany debt transactions do not relate to outside parties. Therefore, Sun's $40,000 payable

## EXHIBIT 3–7

**PARROT COMPANY AND SUN COMPANY**
**Consolidated Worksheet**
**For Year Ending December 31, 2007**

*Consolidation: Purchase Method*
*Investment: Equity Method*

| Accounts | Parrot Company | Sun Company | Consolidation Entries Debit | Consolidation Entries Credit | Consolidated Totals |
|---|---|---|---|---|---|
| **Income Statement** | | | | | |
| Revenues | (2,100,000) | (600,000) | | | (2,700,000) |
| Cost of goods sold | 1,000,000 | 380,000 | | | 1,380,000 |
| Depreciation expense | 300,000 | 60,000 | (E) 7,000 | | 367,000 |
| Equity in subsidiary earnings | (153,000) | –0– | (I) 153,000 | | –0– |
| Net income | (953,000) | (160,000) | | | (953,000) |
| **Statement of Retained Earnings** | | | | | |
| Retained earnings, 1/1/07 | (2,044,000) | (600,000) | (S) 600,000 | | (2,044,000) |
| Net income (above) | (953,000) | (160,000) | | | (953,000) |
| Dividends paid | 420,000 | 70,000 | | (D) 70,000 | 420,000 |
| Retained earnings, 12/31/07 | (2,577,000) | (690,000) | | | (2,577,000) |
| **Balance Sheet** | | | | | |
| Current assets | 1,705,000 | 500,000 | | (P) 40,000 | 2,165,000 |
| Investment in Sun Company | 1,082,000 | –0– | (D) 70,000 | (S) 820,000 | –0– |
| | | | | (A) 179,000 | |
| | | | | (I) 153,000 | |
| Land | 600,000 | 240,000 | (A) 20,000 | | 860,000 |
| Buildings (net) | 540,000 | 420,000 | (A) 91,000 | (E) 13,000 | 1,038,000 |
| Equipment (net) | 420,000 | 210,000 | (E) 6,000 | (A) 12,000 | 624,000 |
| Goodwill | –0– | –0– | (A) 80,000 | | 80,000 |
| Total assets | 4,347,000 | 1,370,000 | | | 4,767,000 |
| Liabilities | (1,050,000) | (460,000) | (P) 40,000 | | (1,470,000) |
| Common stock | (600,000) | (200,000) | (S) 200,000 | | (600,000) |
| Additional paid-in capital | (120,000) | (20,000) | (S) 20,000 | | (120,000) |
| Retained earnings, 12/31/07 (above) | (2,577,000) | (690,000) | | | (2,577,000) |
| Total liabilities and equities | (4,347,000) | (1,370,000) | | | (4,767,000) |

Note: Parentheses indicate a credit balance.
Consolidation entries:
  (S) Elimination of Sun's stockholders' equity accounts as of January 1, 2007, and book value portion of Investment account.
  (A) Allocation of Parrot's cost in excess of Sun's book value, unamortized values as of January 1, 2007.
  (I) Elimination of intercompany income.
  (D) Elimination of intercompany dividends.
  (E) Recognition of excess amortization expenses on purchase price allocations.
  (P) Elimination of intercompany receivable/payable balances.

and Parrot's $40,000 receivable are reciprocals that must be removed on the worksheet because the companies are being reported as a single entity.

In reviewing Exhibit 3–7, note several aspects of the consolidation process:

- The stockholders' equity accounts of the subsidiary are removed.
- The Investment in Sun Company and the Equity in Subsidiary Earnings are both removed.
- The parent's Retained Earnings balance is not adjusted. Since the equity method has been applied, this account should be correct.

**EXHIBIT 3–8**
Excess Amortizations Relating to Individual Accounts as of January 1, 2007

| Accounts | Original Allocation | Annual Excess Amortizations | | | Balance 1/1/07 |
|---|---|---|---|---|---|
| | | 2004 | 2005 | 2006 | |
| Land | $ 20,000 | –0– | –0– | –0– | $ 20,000 |
| Buildings | 130,000 | $13,000 | $13,000 | $13,000 | 91,000 |
| Equipment | (30,000) | (6,000) | (6,000) | (6,000) | (12,000) |
| Goodwill | 80,000 | –0– | –0– | –0– | 80,000 |
| | $200,000 | $ 7,000 | $ 7,000 | $ 7,000 | $179,000 |

$21,000

- The original allocations created by the purchase price are recognized but only after adjustment for annual excess amortization expenses.
- Intercompany transactions such as dividend payments and the receivable/payable are offset.

# SUBSEQUENT CONSOLIDATIONS—INVESTMENT RECORDED ON OTHER THAN THE EQUITY METHOD

## Acquisition Made during the Current Year

As discussed at the beginning of this chapter, the parent company may opt to use the cost method or the partial equity method for internal record-keeping rather than the equity method. Application of either alternative changes the balances recorded by the parent over time and, thus, the procedures followed in creating consolidations. However, *choosing one of these other approaches does not affect any of the final consolidated figures to be reported.*

When the equity method is utilized, all reciprocal accounts are eliminated, unamortized cost allocations are assigned to specific accounts, and amortization expense is recorded for the current year. Application of either the cost method or the partial equity method has no effect on this basic process. For this reason, a number of the consolidation entries remain the same regardless of the accounting method being applied by the parent.

In reality, just three of the parent's accounts actually vary because of the method applied:

- The investment account.
- The income recognized from the subsidiary.
- The parent's retained earnings (in periods after the initial year of the combination).

Only the differences found in these balances affect the consolidation process when another method is applied. Thus, any time after the date of purchase, accounting for these three accounts is of special importance.

To illustrate the modifications required by the adoption of an alternative accounting method, the consolidation of Parrot and Sun as of December 31, 2004, is reconstructed. Only one differing factor is introduced: the method by which Parrot accounts for its investment. Exhibit 3–9 presents the 2004 consolidation based on Parrot's use of the cost method. Exhibit 3–10 demonstrates this same process assuming that the partial equity method was applied by the parent. Each entry on these worksheets is labeled to correspond with the 2004 consolidation in which the parent used the equity method (Exhibit 3–5). Furthermore, differences with the equity method (both on the parent company records and with the consolidation entries) are highlighted on each of the worksheets.

### *Cost Method Applied—2004 Consolidation*

Although the cost method theoretically stands in marked contrast to the equity method, just a narrow range of reporting differences actually result. In the year of acquisition, Parrot's income and investment accounts relating to the subsidiary are the only accounts altered.

# EXHIBIT 3–9

**Consolidation: Purchase Method**
**Investment: Cost Method**

**PARROT COMPANY AND SUN COMPANY**
**Consolidated Worksheet**
**For Year Ending December 31, 2004**

| Accounts | Parrot Company | Sun Company | Consolidation Entries Debit | Consolidation Entries Credit | Consolidated Totals |
|---|---|---|---|---|---|
| **Income Statement** | | | | | |
| Revenues | (1,500,000) | (400,000) | | | (1,900,000) |
| Cost of goods sold | 700,000 | 250,000 | | | 950,000 |
| Depreciation expense | 200,000 | 50,000 | (E) 7,000 | | 257,000 |
| Dividend income | (40,000) * | –0– | (I) 40,000 * | | –0– |
| Net income | (640,000) | (100,000) | | | (693,000) |
| **Statement of Retained Earnings** | | | | | |
| Retained earnings, 1/1/04 | (840,000) | (380,000) | (S) 380,000 | | (840,000) |
| Net income (above) | (640,000) | (100,000) | | | (693,000) |
| Dividends paid | 120,000 | 40,000 | | (I) 40,000 * | 120,000 |
| Retained earnings, 12/31/04 | (1,360,000) | (440,000) | | | (1,413,000) |
| **Balance Sheet** | | | | | |
| Current assets | 1,040,000 | 400,000 | | | 1,440,000 |
| Investment in Sun Company | 800,000 * | –0– | | (S) 600,000 | –0– |
| | | | | (A) 200,000 | |
| Land | 600,000 | 200,000 | (A) 20,000 | | 820,000 |
| Buildings (net) | 370,000 | 288,000 | (A) 130,000 | (E) 13,000 | 775,000 |
| Equipment (net) | 250,000 | 220,000 | (E) 6,000 | (A) 30,000 | 446,000 |
| Goodwill | –0– | –0– | (A) 80,000 | | 80,000 |
| Total assets | 3,060,000 | 1,108,000 | | | 3,561,000 |
| Liabilities | (980,000) | (448,000) | | | (1,428,000) |
| Common stock | (600,000) | (200,000) | (S) 200,000 | | (600,000) |
| Additional paid-in capital | (120,000) | (20,000) | (S) 20,000 | | (120,000) |
| Retained earnings, 12/31/04 (above) | (1,360,000) | (440,000) | | | (1,413,000) |
| Total liabilities and equities | (3,060,000) | (1,108,000) | | | (3,561,000) |

Note: Parentheses indicate a credit balance.
*Boxed items highlight differences with consolidation in Exhibit 3–5.
Consolidation entries:
 (S) Elimination of Sun's stockholders' equity accounts as of January 1, 2004, and book value portion of purchase price.
 (A) Allocation of Parrot's cost in excess of Sun's book value.
 (I) Elimination of intercompany dividends recognized by parent as income.
 (D) Entry is not needed when cost method is applied because Entry I eliminates intercompany dividends.
 (E) Recognition of excess amortization expenses on purchase price allocations.

Under the cost method, income recognition in 2004 is limited to the $40,000 dividend received by the parent; no equity income accrual is made. At the same time, the investment account retains its $800,000 cost. Unlike the equity method, no adjustments are recorded within this asset in connection with the current year operations, the dividends paid by the subsidiary, or amortization of any purchase price allocations.

After the composition of these two accounts has been established, worksheet entries can be used to produce the consolidated figures found in Exhibit 3–9 as of December 31, 2004.

***Consolidation Entry S*** As with the previous Entry **S** in Exhibit 3–5, the $600,000 component of the investment account is eliminated against the beginning stockholders' equity account of the subsidiary. Both are equivalent to Sun's net assets at January 1, 2004, and are,

## EXHIBIT 3–10

**Consolidation: Purchase Method**
**Investment: Partial Equity Method**

**PARROT COMPANY AND SUN COMPANY**
**Consolidated Worksheet**
**For Year Ending December 31, 2004**

| Accounts | Parrot Company | Sun Company | Consolidation Entries Debit | Consolidation Entries Credit | Consolidated Totals |
|---|---|---|---|---|---|
| **Income Statement** | | | | | |
| Revenues | (1,500,000) | (400,000) | | | (1,900,000) |
| Cost of goods sold | 700,000 | 250,000 | | | 950,000 |
| Depreciation expense | 200,000 | 50,000 | (E) 7,000 | | 257,000 |
| Equity in subsidiary earnings | (100,000) * | –0– | (I) 100,000 * | | –0– |
| Net income | (700,000) | (100,000) | | | (693,000) |
| **Statement of Retained Earnings** | | | | | |
| Retained earnings, 1/1/04 | (840,000) | (380,000) | (S) 380,000 | | (840,000) |
| Net income (above) | (700,000) | (100,000) | | | (693,000) |
| Dividends paid | 120,000 | 40,000 | | (D) 40,000 | 120,000 |
| Retained earnings, 12/31/04 | (1,420,000) | (440,000) | | | (1,413,000) |
| **Balance Sheet** | | | | | |
| Current assets | 1,040,000 | 400,000 | | | 1,440,000 |
| Investment in Sun Company | 860,000 * | –0– | (D) 40,000 | (S) 600,000 | –0– |
| | | | | (A) 200,000 | |
| | | | | (I) 100,000 * | |
| Land | 600,000 | 200,000 | (A) 20,000 | | 820,000 |
| Buildings (net) | 370,000 | 288,000 | (A) 130,000 | (E) 13,000 | 775,000 |
| Equipment (net) | 250,000 | 220,000 | (E) 6,000 | (A) 30,000 | 446,000 |
| Goodwill | –0– | –0– | (A) 80,000 | | 80,000 |
| Total assets | 3,120,000 | 1,108,000 | | | 3,561,000 |
| Liabilities | (980,000) | (448,000) | | | (1,428,000) |
| Common stock | (600,000) | (200,000) | (S) 200,000 | | (600,000) |
| Additional paid-in capital | (120,000) | (20,000) | (S) 20,000 | | (120,000) |
| Retained earnings, 12/31/04 (above) | (1,420,000) | (440,000) | | | (1,413,000) |
| Total liabilities and equities | (3,120,000) | (1,108,000) | | | (3,561,000) |

Note: Parentheses indicate a credit balance.
*Boxed items highlight differences with consolidation in Exhibit 3–5.
Consolidation entries:
  (S) Elimination of Sun's stockholders' equity accounts as of January 1, 2004, and book value portion of purchase price.
  (A) Allocation of Parrot's cost in excess of Sun's book value.
  (I) Elimination of parent's equity income accrual.
  (D) Elimination of intercompany dividend payment.
  (E) Recognition of excess amortization expenses on purchase price allocations.

therefore, reciprocal balances that must be offset. This entry is not affected by the accounting method in use.

***Consolidation Entry A*** Parrot's $200,000 excess payment is allocated to Sun's assets and liabilities based on the fair market values at the date of acquisition. The $80,000 residual is attributed to goodwill. This procedure is also identical to the corresponding entry in Exhibit 3–5 in which the equity method was applied.

***Consolidation Entry I*** Under the cost method, the parent records dividend collections as income. Entry **I** removes this Dividend Income account along with Sun's Dividends Paid. From a consolidated perspective, these two $40,000 balances represent an intercompany transfer of cash that had no financial impact outside of the entity. In contrast to the equity method, subsidiary income has not been accrued by Parrot, nor has amortization been recorded; thus, no further income elimination is needed.

| | | |
|---|---|---|
| Dividend Income | 40,000 | |
|     Dividends Paid | | 40,000 |
| To eliminate intercompany income. | | |

***Consolidation Entry D*** When the cost method is applied, intercompany dividends are recorded by the parent as income. Because these distributions were already removed from the consolidated totals by Entry **I**, no separate Entry **D** is required.

***Consolidation Entry E*** Regardless of the parent's method of accounting, the reporting entity must recognize excess amortizations for the current year in connection with the original purchase price allocations. Thus, Entry **E** serves to bring the 2004 expenses into the consolidated financial statements.

Consequently, using the cost method rather than the equity method changes only Entries **I** and **D** in the year of acquisition. Despite the change in methods, reported figures are still derived by (1) eliminating all reciprocals, (2) allocating the excess portion of the purchase price, and (3) recording amortizations on these allocations. As indicated previously, the consolidated totals appearing in Exhibit 3–9 are identical to the figures produced previously in Exhibit 3–5. Although the income and the investment accounts on the parent company's separate statements vary, the consolidated balances are not affected.

One significant difference between the cost method and equity method does exist: The parent's separate statements do not reflect consolidated income totals when the cost method is used. Because equity adjustments (such as excess amortizations) are ignored, neither Parrot's reported net income of $640,000 nor its retained earnings of $1,360,000 provides an accurate portrayal of consolidated figures.

### Partial Equity Method Applied—2004 Consolidation

Exhibit 3–10 presents a worksheet to consolidate these two companies for 2004 (the year of acquisition) based on the assumption that Parrot applied the partial equity method. Again, the only changes from previous examples are found in (1) the parent's separate records for this investment and its related income and (2) worksheet Entries **I** and **D.**

As discussed earlier, under the partial equity approach, the parent's record-keeping is limited to two periodic journal entries: the annual accrual of subsidiary income and the receipt of dividends. Hence, within the parent's records, only a few differences exist when the partial equity method is applied rather than the cost method. The entries recorded by Parrot in connection with Sun's 2004 operations illustrate both of these approaches.

| Parrot Company Cost Method 2004 | | | Parrot Company Partial Equity Method 2004 | | |
|---|---|---|---|---|---|
| Cash | 40,000 | | Cash | 40,000 | |
|     Dividend Income | | 40,000 |     Investment in Sun Company | | 40,000 |
| Dividends collected from subsidiary. | | | Dividends collected from subsidiary. | | |
| | | | Investment in Sun Company | 100,000 | |
| | | |     Equity in Subsidiary Earnings | | 100,000 |
| | | | Accrual of subsidiary income. | | |

Therefore, by applying the partial equity method, the Investment account on the parent's balance sheet rises to $860,000 by the end of 2004. This total is composed of the original $800,000 purchase price adjusted for the $100,000 income recognition and the $40,000 cash dividend payment. The same $100,000 equity income figure appears within the parent's income statement. These two balances are appropriately found in Parrot's records in Exhibit 3–10.

Because of the handling of income recognition and dividend payments, Entries **I** and **D** again differ on the worksheet. For the partial equity method, the $100,000 equity income is eliminated (Entry **I**) by reversing the parent's entry. Removing this accrual allows the individual revenue and expense accounts of the subsidiary to be reported without double-counting. The $40,000 intercompany dividend payment must also be removed (Entry **D**). The Dividend Paid account is simply deleted. However, elimination of the dividend from the Investment in Sun Company actually causes an increase because receipt was recorded by Parrot as a reduction in that account. All other consolidation entries (Entries **S, A,** and **E**) are the same for all three methods.

## Consolidation Subsequent to Year of Acquisition—Other than the Equity Method

By again incorporating the December 31, 2007, financial data for Parrot and Sun (presented in Exhibit 3–7), consolidation procedures for the cost method and the partial equity method can be examined for years subsequent to the date of acquisition. *In both cases, establishment of an appropriate beginning retained earnings figure becomes a significant goal of the consolidation.*

This concern was not faced previously when the equity method was adopted. Under that approach, the parent's Retained Earnings balance mirrors the consolidated total so that no adjustment is necessary. In the earlier illustration, the $330,000 income accrual for the 2004–2006 period as well as the $21,000 amortization expense were recognized by the parent based on employment of the equity method (see Exhibit 3–6). Having been recorded in this manner, these two balances form a permanent part of Parrot's retained earnings and are included automatically in the consolidated total. Consequently, if the equity method is applied, the process is simplified; no worksheet entries are needed to adjust the parent's Retained Earnings to record subsidiary operations or amortization for past years.

Conversely, if a method other than the equity method is used, a worksheet change must be made to the parent's beginning Retained Earnings (in every subsequent year) to equate this balance with the consolidated total. To quantify this adjustment, the parent's recognized income for these past three years under each method is first determined (Exhibit 3–11). For consolidation purposes, beginning Retained Earnings must then be increased or decreased to create the same effect as the equity method.

### Cost Method Applied—Subsequent Consolidation

As shown in Exhibit 3–11, if the cost method is applied by Parrot during the 2004–2006 period, $199,000 less income is recognized than under the equity method ($309,000 − $110,000). This difference has two causes. First, the $220,000 increase in the subsidiary's book value in the period prior to the current year has not been accrued by Parrot. Although the

**EXHIBIT 3–11**

| PARROT COMPANY AND SUN COMPANY Previous Years—2004–2006 | | | |
|---|---|---|---|
| | Equity Method | Cost Method | Partial Equity Method |
| Equity accrual | $330,000 | –0– | $330,000 |
| Dividend income | –0– | $110,000 | –0– |
| Excess amortization expenses | (21,000) | –0– | –0– |
| Increase in parent's retained earnings | $309,000 | $110,000 | $330,000 |

$110,000 in dividends were recorded as income, the remainder of the $330,000 earned by the subsidiary was never recognized by the parent.[6] Second, no accounting has been made of the $21,000 excess amortization expenses. Thus, the parent's beginning Retained Earnings is $199,000 ($220,000 − $21,000) below the appropriate consolidated total and must be adjusted.[7]

To simulate the equity method so that the parent's beginning Retained Earnings agree with that of the combination, this $199,000 increase is recorded through a worksheet entry. The cost method figures reported by the parent are effectively being converted into equity method balances.

### Consolidation Entry *C

| | | |
|---|---:|---:|
| Investment in Sun Company | 199,000 | |
|     Retained Earnings, 1/1/07 (Parrot Company) | | 199,000 |
| To convert parent's beginning retained earnings from cost method to equity method. | | |

This adjustment has been labeled Entry *C. The C refers to the conversion being made to equity method totals. The asterisk indicates that this equity simulation relates solely to transactions of prior periods. Thus, *Entry *C should be recorded before the other worksheet entries to align the beginning balances for the year.*

Exhibit 3–12 provides a complete presentation of the consolidation of Parrot and Sun as of December 31, 2007, based on the parent's application of the cost method. After Entry *C has been recorded on the worksheet, the remainder of this consolidation follows the same pattern as previous examples. Sun's stockholders' equity accounts are eliminated (Entry S) while the allocations stemming from the $800,000 purchase price are recorded (Entry A) at their unamortized balances as of January 1, 2007 (see Exhibit 3–8). Intercompany dividend income is removed (Entry I) and current year excess amortization expenses are recognized (Entry E). To complete this process, the intercompany debt of $40,000 is offset (Entry P).

In retrospect, the only new element introduced here is the adjustment of the parent's beginning Retained Earnings. For a consolidation produced after the initial year of acquisition, an Entry *C is required if the equity method has not been applied by the parent.

### Partial Equity Method Applied—Subsequent Consolidation

Exhibit 3–13 demonstrates the worksheet consolidation of Parrot and Sun as of December 31, 2007, when the investment accounts have been recorded by the parent using the partial equity method. This approach accrues subsidiary income each year but records no other equity adjustments. Therefore, as of December 31, 2007, Parrot's Investment in Sun Company account has a balance of $1,110,000:

| | | |
|---|---:|---:|
| Purchase price | | $800,000 |
| Sun Company's 2004–2006 increase in book value: | | |
|     Accrual of Sun Company's Income | $330,000 | |
|     Collection of Sun Company's Dividends | (110,000) | 220,000 |

---

[6] Two different methods are indicated here for determining the $220,000 in nonrecorded income for prior years: (1) subsidiary income less dividends paid and (2) the change in the subsidiary's book value as of the first day of the current year. The second method works only if the subsidiary has had no other equity transactions such as the issuance of new stock or the purchase of treasury shares. Unless otherwise stated, the assumption is made that no such transactions have occurred.

[7] Since neither the income in excess of dividends nor excess amortization is recorded by the parent under the cost method, its beginning Retained Earnings is $199,000 less than the $2,044,000 reported under the equity method (Exhibit 3–7). Thus, a $1,845,000 balance is shown in Exhibit 3–12 ($2,044,000 − this $199,000). Conversely, if the partial equity method had been applied, Parrot's failure to record amortization would cause Retained Earnings to be $21,000 higher than the figure derived by the equity method. For this reason, Exhibit 3–13 shows the parent with beginning Retained Earnings of $2,065,000 rather than $2,044,000.

# EXHIBIT 3–12

**PARROT COMPANY AND SUN COMPANY**
**Consolidated Worksheet**
**For Year Ending December 31, 2007**

*Consolidation: Purchase Method*
*Investment: Cost Method*

| Accounts | Parrot Company | Sun Company | Consolidation Entries Debit | Consolidation Entries Credit | Consolidated Totals |
|---|---|---|---|---|---|
| **Income Statement** | | | | | |
| Revenues | (2,100,000) | (600,000) | | | (2,700,000) |
| Cost of goods sold | 1,000,000 | 380,000 | | | 1,380,000 |
| Depreciation expense | 300,000 | 60,000 | (E) 7,000 | | 367,000 |
| Dividend income | (70,000)* | –0– | (I) 70,000 * | | –0– |
| Net income | (870,000) | (160,000) | | | (953,000) |
| **Statement of Retained Earnings** | | | | | |
| Retained earnings, 1/1/07: | | | | | |
| Parrot Company | (1,845,000)†* | | | (*C) 199,000 * | (2,044,000) |
| Sun Company | | (600,000) | (S) 600,000 | | –0– |
| Net income (above) | (870,000) | (160,000) | | | (953,000) |
| Dividends paid | 420,000 | 70,000 | | (I) 70,000 * | 420,000 |
| Retained earnings, 12/31/07 | (2,295,000) | (690,000) | | | (2,577,000) |
| **Balance Sheet** | | | | | |
| Current assets | 1,705,000 | 500,000 | | (P) 40,000 | 2,165,000 |
| Investment in Sun Company | 800,000 * | –0– | (*C) 199,000 | (S) 820,000 | –0– |
| | | | | (A) 179,000 | |
| Land | 600,000 | 240,000 | (A) 20,000 | | 860,000 |
| Buildings (net) | 540,000 | 420,000 | (A) 91,000 | (E) 13,000 | 1,038,000 |
| Equipment (net) | 420,000 | 210,000 | (E) 6,000 | (A) 12,000 | 624,000 |
| Goodwill | –0– | –0– | (A) 80,000 | | 80,000 |
| Total assets | 4,065,000 | 1,370,000 | | | 4,767,000 |
| Liabilities | (1,050,000) | (460,000) | (P) 40,000 | | (1,470,000) |
| Common stock | (600,000) | (200,000) | (S) 200,000 | | (600,000) |
| Additional paid-in capital | (120,000) | (20,000) | (S) 20,000 | | (120,000) |
| Retained earnings, 12/31/07 (above) | (2,295,000) | (690,000) | | | (2,577,000) |
| Total liabilities and equities | (4,065,000) | (1,370,000) | | | (4,767,000) |

Note: Parentheses indicate a credit balance.
*Boxed items highlight differences with consolidation in Exhibit 3–7.
†See footnote 7.

Consolidation entries:
- (*C) To recognize additional earnings and amortization relating to ownership of subsidiary for years prior to 2007.
- (S) Elimination of Sun's stockholders' equity accounts as of January 1, 2007, and book value portion of Investment account.
- (A) Allocation of Parrot's cost in excess of Sun's book value, unamortized values as of January 1, 2007.
- (I) Elimination of intercompany dividends recognized by parent as income.
- (D) Entry is not needed when cost method is applied because Entry I eliminates intercompany dividend income.
- (E) Recognition of excess amortization expenses on purchase price allocations.
- (P) Elimination of intercompany receivable/payable balances.

Sun Company's 2007 operations:
- Accrual of Sun Company's income .................... $160,000
- Collection of Sun Company's dividends ............... (70,000)   90,000
- Investment in Sun Company, 12/31/07 (Partial equity method) ..... $1,110,000

## EXHIBIT 3–13

**PARROT COMPANY AND SUN COMPANY**
**Consolidated Worksheet**
**For Year Ending December 31, 2007**

*Consolidation: Purchase Method*
*Investment: Partial Equity Method*

| Accounts | Parrot Company | Sun Company | Consolidation Entries Debit | Consolidation Entries Credit | Consolidated Totals |
|---|---|---|---|---|---|
| **Income Statement** | | | | | |
| Revenues | (2,100,000) | (600,000) | | | (2,700,000) |
| Cost of goods sold | 1,000,000 | 380,000 | | | 1,380,000 |
| Depreciation expense | 300,000 | 60,000 | (E) 7,000 | | 367,000 |
| Equity in subsidiary earnings | (160,000)* | –0– | (I) 160,000 * | | –0– |
| Net income | (960,000) | (160,000) | | | (953,000) |
| **Statement of Retained Earnings** | | | | | |
| Retained earnings, 1/1/07: | | | | | |
| Parrot Company | (2,065,000)†* | | (*C) 21,000 * | | (2,044,000) |
| Sun Company | | (600,000) | (S) 600,000 | | –0– |
| Net income (above) | (960,000) | (160,000) | | | (953,000) |
| Dividends paid | 420,000 | 70,000 | | (D) 70,000 | 420,000 |
| Retained earnings, 12/31/07 | (2,605,000) | (690,000) | | | (2,577,000) |
| **Balance Sheet** | | | | | |
| Current assets | 1,705,000 | 500,000 | | (P) 40,000 | 2,165,000 |
| Investment in Sun Company | 1,110,000 * | –0– | (D) 70,000 | (*C) 21,000 * | –0– |
| | | | | (S) 820,000 | |
| | | | | (A) 179,000 | |
| | | | | (I) 160,000 * | |
| Land | 600,000 | 240,000 | (A) 20,000 | | 860,000 |
| Buildings (net) | 540,000 | 420,000 | (A) 91,000 | (E) 13,000 | 1,038,000 |
| Equipment (net) | 420,000 | 210,000 | (E) 6,000 | (A) 12,000 | 624,000 |
| Goodwill | –0– | –0– | (A) 80,000 | | 80,000 |
| Total assets | 4,375,000 | 1,370,000 | | | 4,767,000 |
| Liabilities | (1,050,000) | (460,000) | (P) 40,000 | | (1,470,000) |
| Common stock | (600,000) | (200,000) | (S) 200,000 | | (600,000) |
| Additional paid-in capital | (120,000) | (20,000) | (S) 20,000 | | (120,000) |
| Retained earnings, 12/31/07 (above) | (2,605,000) | (690,000) | | | (2,577,000) |
| Total liabilities and equities | (4,375,000) | (1,370,000) | | | (4,767,000) |

Note: Parentheses indicate a credit balance.
*Boxed items highlight differences with consolidation in Exhibit 3–7.
†See footnote 7.

Consolidation entries:
- (*C) To record amortization of acquisition price allocations for years prior to 2007.
- (S) Elimination of Sun's stockholders' equity accounts as of January 1, 2007, and book value portion of investment account.
- (A) Allocation of Parrot's cost in excess of Sun's book value, unamortized values as of January 1, 2007.
- (I) Elimination of parent's equity income accrual.
- (D) Elimination of intercompany dividend payment.
- (E) Recognition of excess amortization expenses on purchase price allocations.
- (P) Elimination of intercompany receivable/payable balances.

As indicated here and in Exhibit 3–11, the yearly equity income accrual has been properly recognized by Parrot, but amortization has not. Consequently, if the partial equity method is in use, the parent's beginning Retained Earnings must be adjusted to include this expense. The

$21,000 amortization is recorded through Entry **C** to simulate the equity method and, hence, consolidated totals.

### Consolidation Entry *C

| | | |
|---|---|---|
| Retained Earnings, 1/1/07 (Parrot Company) .......................... | 21,000 | |
|     Investment in Sun Company ................................... | | 21,000 |
| To convert parent's beginning Retained Earnings from partial equity method to equity method by including excess amortizations. | | |

By recording Entry **C** on the worksheet, all of the subsidiary's operational results for the 2004–2006 period are included in the consolidation. As shown in Exhibit 3–13, the remainder of the worksheet entries follow the same basic pattern as that illustrated previously for the year of acquisition (Exhibit 3–10).

### Summary of Investment Methods

Having three investment methods available to the parent means that three sets of entries must be understood to arrive at reported figures appropriate for a business combination. The process can initially seem to be a confusing overlap of procedures. However, at this point in the coverage, only three worksheet entries actually are affected by the choice of either the equity method, partial equity method, or cost method: Entries **C, I,** and **D.** Furthermore, accountants should never get so involved with a worksheet and its entries that they lose sight of the balances that this process is designed to calculate. These figures are never impacted by the parent's choice of an accounting method.

**Consolidated Totals Subsequent to Acquisition—Purchase Method***

| | |
|---|---|
| Current revenues | Parent revenues are included. |
| | Subsidiary revenues are included but only for the period since the acquisition. |
| Current expenses | Parent expenses are included. |
| | Subsidiary expenses are included but only for the period since the acquisition. |
| | Excess amortization expenses on the purchase price allocations are included by recognition on the worksheet. |
| Investment (or dividend) income | Income recognized by parent is eliminated on the worksheet so that the balance is not included in consolidated figures. |
| Retained earnings, beginning balance | Parent balance is included. |
| | Subsidiary balance since the acquisition is included either as a regular accrual by the parent or through a worksheet entry to increase parent balance. |
| | Past excess amortization expenses on the purchase price allocations are included either as a part of parent balance or through a worksheet entry. |
| Assets and liabilities | Parent balances are included. |
| | Subsidiary balances are included. |
| | Remaining undepreciated purchase price allocations are included. |
| | Intercompany receivable/payable balances are eliminated. |
| Goodwill | Original purchase price allocation is included. |
| Investment in subsidiary | Asset account recorded by parent is eliminated on the worksheet so that the balance is not included in consolidated figures. |
| Capital stock and additional paid-in capital | Parent balances only are included although they will have been adjusted at date of purchase if stock was issued. |

*The next few chapters discuss the necessity of altering some of these balances for consolidation purposes. Thus, this table is not definitive but included only to provide a basic overview of the consolidation process as it has been described to this point.

# Discussion Question

## HOW DOES A COMPANY REALLY DECIDE WHICH INVESTMENT METHOD TO APPLY?

During the early stages of 2004, Pilgrim Products, Inc., buys a controlling interest in the common stock of Crestwood Corporation. Shortly after the acquisition, a meeting of Pilgrim's accounting department is convened to discuss the internal reporting procedures required by the ownership of this subsidiary. Each member of the staff has a definite opinion as to whether the equity method, cost method, or partial equity method should be adopted. To resolve this issue, Pilgrim's chief financial officer outlines several of her concerns about the decision.

"I already understand how each method works. I know the general advantages and disadvantages of all three. I realize, for example, that the equity method provides more detailed information whereas the cost method is much easier to apply. What I need to know are the factors specific to our situation that should be considered in deciding which method to adopt. I must make a recommendation to the president on this matter, and he will want firm reasons for my favoring a particular approach. I don't want us to select a method and then find out in six months that the information is not adequate for our needs or that the cost of adapting our system to monitor Crestwood outweighs the benefits derived from the data."

What are the factors that Pilgrim's officials should evaluate when making this decision?

---

Once the appropriate balance for each account is understood, worksheet entries assist the accountant in deriving these figures. To help clarify the consolidation process required under each of the three accounting methods, Exhibit 3–14 describes the purpose of each worksheet entry: first during the year of acquisition and second for any period following the year of acquisition.

## INTANGIBLES ACQUIRED IN BUSINESS COMBINATIONS AND RELATED AMORTIZATIONS

As discussed in Chapter 2, *SFAS 141,* "Business Combinations," does not alter significantly the purchase price allocation procedures required in a business acquisition. *SFAS 141* does, however, suggest several categories of purchased intangible assets for possible recognition in a business combination. Examples include noncompetition agreements, customer lists, patents, subscriber databases, trademarks, lease agreements, and licenses.

If fair values can be measured reliably for the identified intangibles in a business combination, they are separately recognized and subsequently amortized if appropriate. If a separate fair value estimation is unavailable or unreliable for a particular intangible, then any remaining unallocated purchase price is simply recognized as goodwill.

*SFAS 142,* "Goodwill and Other Intangible Assets," requires that all identified intangible assets be amortized over their economic useful life unless such life is considered *indefinite.* The term *indefinite life* is defined as a life that extends beyond the foreseeable future. A recognized intangible asset with an indefinite life should not be amortized unless and until its life is determined to be finite. Importantly, indefinite does not mean infinite. Also, the useful life of an intangible asset should not be considered indefinite because a precise finite life is not known.

For those intangible assets with finite lives, the method of amortization should reflect the pattern of decline in the economic usefulness of the asset. If no such pattern is apparent, the straight-line method of amortization should be used. The amount to be amortized should be the value assigned to the intangible asset less any residual value. In most cases the residual value is presumed to be zero. However, that presumption can be overcome if the acquiring enterprise has a commitment from a third party to purchase the intangible at the end of its useful life, or an observable market exists for the intangible asset that provides a basis for estimating a terminal value.

## EXHIBIT 3–14  Consolidation Worksheet Entries—Purchase Method

| Equity Method Applied | | Cost Method Applied | Partial Equity Method Applied |
|---|---|---|---|
| **Any time during year of acquisition:** | | | |
| Entry S | Beginning stockholders' equity of subsidiary is eliminated against book value portion of investment account. | Same as equity method. | Same as equity method. |
| Entry A | Excess purchase price is allocated to assets and liabilities based on difference in book values and fair market values; residual is assigned to goodwill. | Same as equity method. | Same as equity method. |
| Entry I | Equity income accrual (including amortization expense) is eliminated. | Dividend income is eliminated. | Equity income accrual is eliminated. |
| Entry D | Intercompany dividends paid by subsidiary are eliminated. | No entry—intercompany dividends are eliminated in Entry I. | Same as equity method. |
| Entry E | Current year excess amortization expenses of cost allocations are recorded. | Same as equity method. | Same as equity method. |
| Entry P | Intercompany payable/receivable balances are offset. | Same as equity method. | Same as equity method. |
| **Any time following year of acquisition:** | | | |
| Entry *C | No entry—equity income for prior years has already been recognized along with amortization expenses. | Increase in subsidiary's book value during prior years as well as excess amortization expenses are recognized (conversion is made to equity method). | Excess amortization expenses for prior years are recognized (conversion is made to equity method). |
| Entry S | Same as initial year. | Same as initial year. | Same as initial year. |
| Entry A | Unamortized cost at beginning of year is allocated to specific accounts and to goodwill. | Same as equity method. | Same as equity method. |
| Entry I | Same as initial year. | Same as initial year. | Same as initial year. |
| Entry D | Same as initial year. | Same as initial year. | Same as initial year. |
| Entry E | Same as initial year. | Same as initial year. | Same as initial year. |
| Entry P | Same as initial year. | Same as initial year. | Same as initial year. |

The length of the amortization period for identifiable intangibles (i.e., those not included in goodwill) depends primarily on the assumed economic life of the asset. Factors that should be considered in determining the useful life of an intangible asset include:

- Legal, regulatory, or contractual provisions.
- The effects of obsolescence, demand, competition, industry stability, rate of technological change, and expected changes in distribution channels.
- The expected use of the intangible asset by the enterprise.
- The level of maintenance expenditure required to obtain the asset's expected future benefits.

Any recognized intangible assets considered to possess indefinite lives are not amortized but instead are tested for impairment on an annual basis.[8] To test for impairment, the carrying amount of the intangible asset is compared to its fair value. If the fair value is less than the carrying amount, then the intangible asset is considered impaired and an impairment loss is recognized. The asset's carrying value is reduced accordingly.

---

[8] Impairment tests should also be conducted on an interim basis if an event or circumstance occurs between annual tests indicating that an intangible asset could be impaired.

# SFAS 142—GOODWILL IMPAIRMENT

A major change in accounting for goodwill is the *SFAS 142* requirement of an annual test for impairment. The FASB reasoned that while goodwill can decrease over time, it does not do so in the "rational and systematic" manner that periodic amortization suggests.[9] Thus, amortization was not viewed as representationally faithful of the pattern of goodwill decline. Moreover, because *SFAS 141* provides more guidelines for recognizing identifiable intangibles, it was argued that future amounts included in goodwill were more likely to be nonwasting. Ultimately, the FASB decided to record a decline in the value of goodwill only when

- It is apparent that goodwill becomes impaired—that is, when the carrying amount of goodwill exceeds its implied fair value, an impairment loss is recognized equal to that excess, or
- The operating unit where goodwill resides is partially or completely sold.

Importantly, goodwill impairment testing is performed at the *reporting unit* level. As discussed below, all goodwill acquired in a business combination must be assigned across reporting units within a consolidated enterprise. For example, AOL TimeWarner recently reported that its goodwill had been allocated to AOL, Cable, and Music reporting units, among others. The goodwill residing in each reporting unit is then separately subjected to periodic impairment testing. Recent evidence shows that goodwill impairment losses can be substantial. Exhibit 3-15 provides examples of goodwill impairment losses recognized under SFAS 142 reporting rules.

## Testing Goodwill for Impairment

The notion of an indefinite life for goodwill allows firms to report over time the original amount of goodwill acquired in a business combination at its assigned purchase value. However, such goodwill can, at some point in time, become impaired, requiring loss recognition and a reduction in the amount reported in the consolidated balance sheet. Unlike amortization, which periodically reduces goodwill, impairment must first be revealed before a write-down is justified. To detect when impairment has occurred, a two-step testing procedure is utilized.

*Step 1—Goodwill Impairment Test: Is the Fair Value of a Reporting Unit Less Than Its Carrying Value?*

In the first step of impairment testing, fair values of the consolidated entity's reporting units with allocated goodwill are compared with their carrying values *(including goodwill)*. If an individual reporting unit's total fair value exceeds its carrying value, its goodwill is not considered impaired, and the second step in testing is not performed. Goodwill remains at the amount assigned at the date of the business combination. However, if the fair value of a reporting unit has fallen below its carrying value, then a potential for goodwill impairment exists. In this case, a second step must be performed to determine if goodwill has been impaired.

*Step 2—Goodwill Impairment Test: Is Goodwill's Implied Value Less Than Its Carrying Value?*

*If Step 1 indicates a potential goodwill impairment for a reporting unit, goodwill's implied and carrying values are compared for that reporting unit.* If the fair value of a reporting unit falls below its carrying value, a second step in testing is performed. The second test requires a determination of the fair value of the related goodwill. Then if goodwill's fair value has declined below its carrying value, an impairment loss is recognized for the excess carrying value over fair value. However, determining fair values for reporting units and goodwill can be complex, making implementation of the necessary comparisons costly. These complexities are described in terms of three key attributes that govern the process of testing goodwill for impairment:

1. The assignment of acquisition values to reporting units.
2. The periodic determination of the fair values of reporting units.
3. The determination of goodwill implied fair value.

---

[9] L. Todd Johnson and Kimberly R. Petrone, *FASB Viewpoints*, "Why Did the Board Change Its Mind on Goodwill Amortization?" December 2000.

**EXHIBIT 3–15**
Goodwill Impairment Examples (in billions) 2002—First Year of *SFAS 142* Implementation

| | |
|---|---|
| AOL Time Warner | $99.7 billion |
| Boeing | 2.4 |
| Blockbuster | 1.8 |
| SBC Communications | 1.8 |
| General Electric | 1.0 |
| Coca-Cola | 926 million |
| AT&T | 856 |
| Safeway | 700 |
| Verizon Communications | 500 |

## Assigning Values to Reporting Units

In deciding to forgo amortization in favor of impairment testing for goodwill, the FASB noted that goodwill is primarily associated with individual *reporting units* within the consolidated entity. Such goodwill is often considered "synergistic" because it arises from the interaction of the assets of the acquired company with those of the acquirer in specific ways. To better assess potential declines in value for goodwill (in place of amortization), the most specific business level at which goodwill is evident was chosen as the appropriate level for impairment testing. This specific business level is referred to as the *reporting unit*. The FASB also noted that, in practice, goodwill is often assigned to reporting units either at the level of a reporting segment—as described in *SFAS 131,* "Disclosures about Segments of an Enterprise and Related Information"—or at a lower level within a segment of a combined enterprise. Consequently, the reporting unit became the designated enterprise component for tests of goodwill impairment. Reporting units may thus include the following:

- A component of an operating segment at a level below the operating segment. Segment management should review and assess performance at this level. Also, the component should be a business in which discrete financial information is available and should differ economically from other components of the operating segment.
- The segments of an enterprise.
- The entire enterprise.

For example, Intel Corporation reports four product-line operating segments in its recent annual report: the Intel Architecture Business, the Wireless Communications and Computing Group, the Intel Communications Group, and the New Business Group. In its report, Intel disclosed the following:

> The consolidated financial statements include the operating results of acquired businesses from the dates of acquisition. The operating results of all of the significant companies acquired have been included in the Intel Communications Group operating segment, except for the results of DSP Communications, which have been included in the Wireless Communications and Computing Group operating segment.

The Intel annual report also notes the following:

> Beginning in the first quarter of fiscal 2002, the company will no longer amortize goodwill, but will perform impairment tests annually or earlier if indicators of potential impairment exist. All other intangible assets continue to be amortized over their estimated useful lives. In conjunction with the implementation of *SFAS 142,* the company has completed a goodwill impairment review as of the beginning of fiscal 2002 using a fair-value–based approach in accordance with provisions of that standard and found no impairment.

In implementing impairment tests, it is essential first to identify the reporting units resulting from the acquisition. The assets and liabilities (including goodwill) acquired in a business combination are then assigned to these identified reporting units. The assignment should consider where the acquired assets and liabilities will be employed and whether they will be included in determining the reporting unit's fair value. The goodwill should be assigned to those reporting units that are expected to benefit from the synergies of the combination. Overall, the objective of the assignment of acquired assets and liabilities to reporting units is to facilitate the required fair value/carrying value comparisons for periodic impairment testing.

### *Periodic Determination of the Fair Values of Reporting Units*

The necessary comparisons to determine whether goodwill is impaired depend first on the fair-value computation of the reporting unit and then, if necessary, the fair-value computation for goodwill. But how are such values computed? How can fair values be known if the subsidiary is wholly owned and thus not traded publicly?

Several alternative methods exist for determining the fair values of the reporting units that comprise a consolidated entity. First, any quoted market prices that exist can provide a basis for assessing fair value—particularly for subsidiaries with actively traded noncontrolling interests. Second, comparable businesses could exist that can help indicate market values. Third, there is a variety of present value techniques for assessing the fair value of an identifiable set of future cash flow streams, or profit projections discounted for the riskiness of the future flows. Clearly, portions of consolidated entities are frequently bought and sold. In these transactions, parties do derive fair values. However, the required periodic assessment of fair value represents a new valuation exercise for many firms. These annual determinations of fair values will likely be a costly impact from implementing the provisions of *SFAS 141* and *SFAS 142*.

However, once a detailed determination of the fair value of a reporting unit is made, that fair value may be used in subsequent periods if *all* of the following criteria are met (*SFAS 142*):

- The assets and liabilities that compose the reporting unit have not changed significantly since the most recent fair-value determination. (A recent acquisition or a reorganization of an entity's segment reporting structure are examples of events that might significantly change the composition of a reporting unit.)
- The most recent fair-value determination resulted in an amount that exceeded the carrying amount of the reporting unit by a substantial margin.
- Based on an analysis of events that have occurred and circumstances that have changed since the most recent fair-value determination, it is remote that a current fair-value determination would be less than the current carrying amount of the reporting unit.

If any of these criteria is not met, an updated determination of the reporting unit's fair value is required.

### *Determination of Goodwill Implied Fair Value*

If the fair value of a reporting unit, once determined, falls below its carrying value, the second step of the impairment test focuses in on the possibility that goodwill could be impaired. Just as in the initial test of the reporting unit, now the fair value of goodwill must be determined in order to make the relevant comparison to its carrying value. Because, by definition, goodwill is not separable from other assets, it is not possible to directly observe its market value. Therefore, an *implied* value for goodwill is calculated in a similar manner to the determination of goodwill in a business combination. The fair value of the reporting unit is treated as the "purchase price" as if the reporting unit were being acquired in a business combination. Then this "purchase price" is allocated to all of the reporting unit's identifiable assets and liabilities with any remaining excess considered as the fair value of goodwill. This procedure is used only for assessing the fair value of goodwill. None of the other values allocated to assets and liabilities in the testing comparison are used to adjust their reported amounts.

***Example—Accounting and Reporting for a Goodwill Impairment Loss*** To illustrate the procedure for recognizing goodwill impairment, assume that on January 1, 2004, Newcall Corporation was formed to consolidate the telecommunications operations of DSM, Inc., Rocketel Company, and Visiontalk Company in a deal valued at $2.9 billion. Each of the three former firms is considered an operating segment, and each will be maintained as a subsidiary of Newcall. Additionally, DSM is composed of two divisions—DSM Wired and DSM Wireless—that along with Rocketel and Visiontalk are treated as independent reporting units for internal performance evaluation and management reviews. Following *SFAS 141,* "Business Combinations," Newcall allocated $221 million value to goodwill at the merger date to its reporting units. That information and each unit's purchase price were as follows:

| Newcall's Reporting Units | Goodwill | Purchase Price January 1, 2004 |
| --- | --- | --- |
| DSM Wired | $ 22,000,000 | $950,000,000 |
| DSM Wireless | 155,000,000 | 748,000,000 |
| Rocketel | 38,000,000 | 492,000,000 |
| Visiontalk | 6,000,000 | 710,000,000 |

In December 2004, Newcall tested each of its four reporting units for goodwill impairment. Accordingly, Newcall compared the fair market value of its reporting units to its carrying value. The comparisons revealed that the fair market value of each reporting unit exceeded its carrying value except for DSM Wireless, whose market value had fallen to $600 million, well below its current carrying value. The decline in value was attributed to a failure to realize expected cost-saving synergies with Rocketel.

As indicated by *SFAS 142,* Newcall then compared the implied fair value of the DSM Wireless goodwill to its carrying value. Newcall derived the implied fair value of goodwill through the following allocation of the fair value of DSM Wireless:

| | | |
| --- | --- | --- |
| DSM Wireless Dec. 31, 2004, fair market value | | $600,000,000 |
| Fair values of DSM Wireless net assets at Dec. 31, 2004: | | |
| Current assets | $ 50,000,000 | |
| Property | 125,000,000 | |
| Equipment | 265,000,000 | |
| Subscriber list | 140,000,000 | |
| Patented technology | 185,000,000 | |
| Current liabilities | (44,000,000) | |
| Long-term debt | (125,000,000) | |
| Value assigned to identifiable net assets | | 596,000,000 |
| Value assigned to goodwill | | 4,000,000 |
| Carrying value before impairment | | 155,000,000 |
| Impairment loss | | $151,000,000 |

Thus, $151,000,000 is reported as a separate line item in the operating section of Newcall's consolidated income statement as a goodwill impairment loss. Additional disclosures are required describing (1) the facts and circumstances leading to the impairment and (2) the method of determining the fair value of the associated reporting unit (e.g., market prices, comparable business, present value technique).

Although the amount reported for goodwill is changed, the amounts for the other assets and liabilities of DSM Wireless are not changed. The reported values for all of DSM Wireless's remaining assets and liabilities continue to be based on amounts assigned at the business combination date.

## PURCHASE PRICE—CONTINGENT CONSIDERATION

In its annual financial report, Computer Horizons Corporation noted the following contingency:

> The company acquired the assets of Enterprise Solutions Group, LLC (ESG), a Cincinnati, Ohio–based technology organization that provides training and educational services as well as consulting services for Fortune 500 companies. The acquisition was accounted for as a purchase.

# Discussion Question

**IS THIS INCOME?**

Artilio Corporation pays $1 million for all of the outstanding stock of Zepthan, Inc. Because of an urgent need for cash, the owners of Zepthan are forced to accept this price although the company's net assets have a value of $1.6 million.

Based on the guidelines for a bargain purchase previously demonstrated in Chapter 2, the $600,000 reduction is assigned to the subsidiary's noncurrent assets (other than certain specific exceptions). Consequently, assume that the consolidated value of Zepthan's land is reduced by $50,000 with its buildings and equipment decreased by a total of $550,000. If the buildings and equipment have a life of 10 years, these negative allocations reduce depreciation expense by $55,000 per year and, hence, increase income by that amount. Consolidated net income for the combination is projected to be approximately $250,000 per year for the foreseeable future. Thus, 22 percent is attributable to the bargain purchase ($55,000/$250,000). Despite the positive impact on income, depreciation of bargain purchase figures is required.

Because of the annual decrease from depreciation, a bargain purchase creates a consolidated entity that reports more income than the sum of the two component companies. As in the case of Artilio and Zepthan, the amount can be very significant.

Should a business combination be allowed to increase reported earnings based on paying a bargain price to acquire a new subsidiary? Does this practice distort earnings? Does a reasonable alternative exist?

---

The total purchase price was approximately $7,333,000 in cash and common stock. The purchase price may be adjusted based on the actual earnings of the company for the twelve months ended December 31, 1998, up to a maximum purchase price of $11,000,000. The remaining purchase price is to be paid out in three payments starting December 1998 and ending December 2000.

A business combination has been formed here but, as this footnote describes, a portion of the purchase price being paid by the parent was not finalized for several years after the date of acquisition.

When a subsequent payment, such as that described by Computer Horizon's statements, is based solely on future earnings, the contingency has no initial impact on the purchase price or the consolidated figures. The potential disbursement should be disclosed only in a note to the financial statements similar to the one just presented. When the contingency is ultimately resolved, any further payment made by the parent is simply added to the purchase price.

Thus, if goodwill was recognized at the date of acquisition, any later disbursement is assigned to this same intangible asset. Should another $100,000 be paid, for example, reported goodwill is increased by this amount. Conversely, if the original price was below fair market value so that the balances assigned to specific noncurrent assets were reduced, a subsequent payment serves to decrease the amount of these reductions. In either case, an increase in the initial purchase price resulting from a contingency of this type is not accounted for in a retroactive manner. Any resulting amortization expense is recorded only over the *remaining* life of the appropriate account.

A contingency can also result from the acquisition of a subsidiary if the price is based on the future value of the stock issued. Such arrangements are designed to ensure that the previous owners receive compensation that retains a minimum value for a specified period. For example, in discussing an earlier acquisition, financial statements of Munsingwear, Inc., once stated that "the Company is obligated to issue additional shares of common stock . . . in the event of a decline in the market value of the common stock." From an accounting perspective, this second type of extra payment is not viewed as an increase in the parent's purchase price. Rather, the possible distribution is a guarantee of the value of the consideration conveyed in the original transaction. Thus, no change is made in goodwill or any other allocations.

If additional shares of the parent's stock must be issued because of a subsequent drop in price, the parent records the new shares at fair market value. At the same time, the total attributed to the shares originally issued at the date of purchase is reduced by a corresponding amount to reflect the decrease in value. The net effect is that the parent's stock account is increased by the par value of the new shares issued with additional paid-in capital reduced by the same amount. The purchase price does not change.

To illustrate, assume that Large issues 10,000 shares of its $10 par value stock to acquire Small. This stock had a value on that date of $25 per share ($250,000 in total). In recording this transaction, Large increases:

- Its Common Stock account by the $100,000 par value of these shares.
- Additional Paid-In Capital by $150,000 to reflect the value in excess of par ($25 − $10).

Subsequently, the market value of this stock drops to $20 per share. Assume that the purchase agreement specified that the market value of the shares issued could not be reduced for a given period. To maintain the total value at $250,000, 2,500 more shares are issued to Small's previous owners. At $20 per share, the new total of 12,500 shares has the appropriate value of $250,000. The new shares are recorded at par value ($25,000, or 2,500 shares at $10 per share) with an accompanying reduction in Additional Paid-In Capital. Therefore, total contributed capital from this purchase remains at $250,000.

| Large's Financial Records—Subsequent Issuance of Shares | | |
|---|---|---|
| Additional Paid-In Capital | 25,000 | |
|     Common Stock (par value) | | 25,000 |
| To record issuance of 2,500 new shares of stock in connection with previous acquisition of Small. Additional shares were required because of drop in market value of shares originally issued. | | |

# PUSH-DOWN ACCOUNTING

## External Reporting

In the analysis of business combinations to this point, discussion has focused on (1) the recording by the parent company and (2) required consolidation procedures. Unfortunately, official accounting pronouncements give virtually no guidance as to the impact of a purchase on the separate financial statements of the subsidiary.

This issue has become especially significant in recent years because of a rash of management-led buyouts as well as corporate reorganizations. An organization, for example, might acquire a company and subsequently offer the shares back to the public in hopes of making a large profit. What should be reported in the subsidiary's financial statements being distributed with this offering? Such deals have reheated a long-standing debate over the merits of *push-down accounting,* the direct recording of purchase price allocations and subsequent amortization by a subsidiary.

For this reason, the FASB continues to explore various methods of reporting by a company that has been acquired or reorganized. To illustrate, assume that Yarrow Company owns one asset: a building with a book value of $200,000 but a fair market value of $900,000. Mannen Corporation pays exactly $900,000 in cash to acquire Yarrow. Consolidation offers no real problem here: The building will be reported by the business combination at $900,000.

However, if Yarrow continues to issue separate financial statements (for example, to its creditors or potential stockholders), should the building be reported at $200,000 or $900,000? If adjusted, should the $700,000 increase be reported as a gain by the subsidiary or as an addition to contributed capital? Should depreciation be based on $200,000 or $900,000? If the subsidiary is to be viewed as a new entity with a new basis for its assets and liabilities, should Retained Earnings be returned to zero? If the parent acquires only 51 percent of Yarrow, does that change the answers to the previous questions? These questions represent just a few of the difficult issues currently being explored.

Proponents of push-down accounting argue that a change in ownership creates a new basis for subsidiary assets and liabilities. An unadjusted balance ($200,000 in the preceding illustration) is a cost figure applicable to previous stockholders. That total is no longer relevant information. Rather, according to this argument, it is the historical cost *paid by the current owner* that is important, a figure that is best reflected by the expenditure made in acquiring the subsidiary. Balance sheet accounts should be reported at the cost incurred by the present stockholders ($900,000 in the illustration) rather than the cost incurred by the company.

Currently, primary guidance concerning push-down accounting for external reporting purposes is provided by the Securities and Exchange Commission (SEC). Through Staff Accounting Bulletin No. 54 *(Application of "Push Down" Basis of Accounting in Financial Statements of Subsidiaries Acquired by Purchase)* and Staff Accounting Bulletin No. 73 *("Push Down" Basis of Accounting for Parent Company Debt Related to Subsidiary Acquisitions),* the SEC has indicated that

> push down accounting should be used in the separate financial statements of a "substantially wholly owned" subsidiary. . . . That view is based on the notion that when the form of ownership is within the control of the parent company, the accounting basis should be the same whether the entity continues to exist or is merged into the parent's operations. If a purchase of a "substantially wholly owned" subsidiary is financed by debt of the parent, that debt generally must be pushed down to the subsidiary. . . . As a general rule, the SEC requires push down accounting when the ownership change is greater than 95 percent and objects to push down accounting when the ownership change is less than 80 percent. However, if the acquired subsidiary has outstanding public debt or preferred stock, push down accounting is encouraged by the SEC but not required.[10]

Thus, the SEC requires the use of push-down accounting for the separate financial statements of any subsidiary where no substantial outside ownership exists of the company's common stock, preferred stock, and publicly held debt. Apparently, the SEC believes that a change in ownership of that degree justifies a new basis of reporting for the subsidiary's assets and liabilities. Until the FASB takes action, though, application is only required when the subsidiary desires to issue securities (stock or debt) to the public as regulated by the SEC.

## Push-Down Accounting—Internal Reporting

Although the use of push-down accounting for external reporting is limited, this approach has gained significant popularity in recent years for internal reporting purposes.

> Subsidiaries owned by the Chesapeake Corporation are recorded using push-down accounting. Under this theory, the subsidiary adjusts its assets and liabilities to current value at the time of the acquisition while also recording the necessary goodwill. The subsidiary's net assets, as adjusted, would equal the amount recorded by the parent as the investment in subsidiary.[11]

> At the time of acquisition of each subsidiary, purchase method accounting is applied by James River Corporation on a push-down basis. The parent's investment equals the net book value of the subsidiary through an allocation of the purchase price to the net assets of the subsidiary on a fair market value basis.[12]

Push-down accounting has several advantages for internal reporting. For example, it simplifies the consolidation process. Because the allocations and amortization are already entered into the records of the subsidiary, worksheet Entries **A** (to recognize the allocations originating from the purchase price) and **E** (amortization expense) are not needed. Therefore, except for eliminating the effects of intercompany transactions, the assets, liabilities, revenues, and expenses of the subsidiary can be added directly to those of the parent to derive consolidated totals.

---

[10] FASB Discussion Memorandum, *An Analysis of Issues Related to New Basis Accounting,* December 18, 1991, p. 54.

[11] Letter from Timothy M. Harhan, senior corporate accountant with Chesapeake Corporation.

[12] Letter from Catherine M. Freeman, manager—financial projects with James River Corporation.

More importantly, push-down accounting provides better information for internal evaluation. Since the subsidiary's separate figures include amortization expense, the net income reported by the company is a good representation of the impact that the acquisition has on the earnings of the business combination. As an example, assume that Ace Corporation owns 100 percent of Waxworth, Inc. Waxworth uses push-down accounting and reports net income of $500,000: $600,000 from operations less $100,000 in amortization expense resulting from purchase price allocations. Thus, officials of Ace Corporation know that this acquisition has added $500,000 to the consolidated net income of the business combination. They can then evaluate whether these earnings provide a sufficient return for the parent's investment.

However, the recording of amortization expense by the subsidiary can lead to dissension. Members of the subsidiary's management could argue that they are being forced to record a large expense over which they have no control or responsibility. This amortization comes directly from the purchase price paid by the parent but is not a result of any action taken by the subsidiary. Chesapeake Corporation has considered this problem and resolved it in the following manner: "For internal reporting of income statement activity, earnings from operations are identified separately from amortization. This allows management to analyze the subsidiary's results without the effect of amortization."[13]

## SUBSEQUENT CONSOLIDATIONS—POOLING OF INTERESTS

Although the FASB prohibits the pooling of interests method of accounting for business combinations initiated after June 30, 2001, this restriction is for prospective application only. Given the popularity of poolings in the last century, the financial statement effects of this method of accounting will likely be encountered for decades to come. Therefore, familiarity with the effects of poolings in consolidations subsequent to acquisition will continue to be an important part of understanding financial reporting for business combinations.

For consolidations prepared after the date of combination, the pooling of interests method requires a slightly less complex set of procedures than does the purchase method. By reflecting on the fundamental concepts of a pooling, the essential differences between the subsequent consolidation entries employed by these two methods can be understood.

Pooling of interests combinations were assumed to be formed by a union of two companies. Because a takeover had not occurred, no acquisition price was ever calculated for a pooling. All assets and liabilities were simply consolidated at their book values. No allocations based on fair market value were computed, nor was any goodwill recognized. Hence, amortization that could have been associated with such cost factors was not encountered in a pooling of interests.

In mechanical terms, the absence of a purchase price means that worksheet entries relating to cost allocations (Entry **A**) and subsequent amortization expense (Entry **E**) are never found in a pooling. Obviously, as with push-down accounting, alleviating the necessity of working with these entries simplifies the entire consolidation process.

The company that issued its stock to consummate a pooling of interests recorded these shares along with the resulting investment. This company must then have adopted a method to account for this investment. One possibility is to apply the equity method to accrue income as it is earned by the other company and to adjust for intercompany transactions (as discussed in Chapter 5). The partial equity method also might be selected so that recording is limited to the periodic accrual of income.

Any reference to a cost method of interests would be a misnomer in a pooling because no acquisition cost is ever established. Thus, for internal reporting purposes, the cost method is replaced by a *book value method* that has the same essential characteristics: The investment account permanently retains its initial balance (the book value of the other company), with any dividends received being recognized as income.

---

[13] Letter from Timothy H. Harhan.

To illustrate the consolidation techniques employed in a pooling of interests, assume that Brother Company obtains 100 percent of the outstanding voting shares of Sister Company on January 1, 2001. To create this combination, Brother issued 10,000 shares of its own common stock in an exchange that met all 12 requirements for a pooling of interests. On that date, Sister reported a total book value of $700,000 although market value was $950,000. For reporting purposes, the additional $250,000 is unimportant; only book value is relevant in accounting for a pooling of interests. Consequently, $700,000 is recorded by Brother as an investment. The book value method is applied by Brother; thus, this balance remains unchanged over the years.

For this example, consolidated financial statements are prepared as of December 31, 2004. Sister's book value has risen by $610,000 to $1,310,000 as of the first day of 2004. Assume also that Sister owes $90,000 to Brother at the end of this year. Exhibit 3–16 presents the

## EXHIBIT 3–16

*Consolidation: Pooling of Interests Method*
*Investment: Book Value Method*

**BROTHER COMPANY AND SISTER COMPANY**
**Consolidated Worksheet**
**For Year Ending December 31, 2004**

| Accounts | Brother Company | Sister Company | Consolidation Entries Debit | Consolidation Entries Credit | Consolidated Totals |
|---|---|---|---|---|---|
| **Income Statement** | | | | | |
| Revenues | (1,600,000) | (550,000) | | | (2,150,000) |
| Expenses | 1,220,000 | 440,000 | | | 1,660,000 |
| Dividend income | (40,000) | –0– | (I) 40,000 | | –0– |
| Net income | (420,000) | (110,000) | | | (490,000) |
| **Statement of Retained Earnings** | | | | | |
| Retained earnings, 1/1/04 | (2,260,000) | (910,000) | (S) 910,000 | (*C) 610,000 | (2,870,000) |
| Net income (above) | (420,000) | (110,000) | | | (490,000) |
| Dividends paid | 60,000 | 40,000 | | (I) 40,000 | 60,000 |
| Retained earnings, 12/31/04 | (2,620,000) | (980,000) | | | (3,300,000) |
| **Balance Sheet** | | | | | |
| Cash and receivables | 590,000 | 140,000 | | (P) 90,000 | 640,000 |
| Inventory | 940,000 | 480,000 | | | 1,420,000 |
| Investment in Sister Company | 700,000 | –0– | (*C) 610,000 | (S) 1,310,000 | –0– |
| Land | 600,000 | 340,000 | | | 940,000 |
| Buildings (net) | 970,000 | 270,000 | | | 1,240,000 |
| Equipment (net) | 730,000 | 520,000 | | | 1,250,000 |
| Total assets | 4,530,000 | 1,750,000 | | | 5,490,000 |
| Liabilities | (810,000) | (370,000) | (P) 90,000 | | (1,090,000) |
| Common stock | (800,000) | (300,000) | (S) 300,000 | | (800,000) |
| Additional paid-in capital | (300,000) | (100,000) | (S) 100,000 | | (300,000) |
| Retained earnings, 12/31/04 (above) | (2,620,000) | (980,000) | | | (3,300,000) |
| Total liabilities and equities | (4,530,000) | (1,750,000) | | | (5,490,000) |

Note: Parentheses indicate a credit balance.
Consolidation entries:
  (*C) To recognize increase in book value of affiliate company during years prior to 2004.
  (S) Elimination of Sister's stockholders' equity accounts as of January 1, 2004, and book value portion of Investment account.
  (I) Elimination of intercompany dividends recognized by Brother as income.
  (P) Elimination of intercompany receivable/payable balances.

worksheet for the 2004 consolidation of these two companies under the pooling of interests concept. Once again, the entries have been labeled to parallel the earlier consolidation examples, although neither Entry **A** nor Entry **E** is applicable to a pooling.

Because Brother applies the book value method, no recognition has been made of the increase in Sister's book value since the date of combination. Consequently, Brother's retained earnings at January 1, 2004, do not reflect a consolidated total; the $610,000 increment is not included. An Entry ***C** must be recorded on the worksheet to accrue this income that has been earned by Sister in excess of dividends distributed (the increase in net book value). After Brother's beginning Retained Earnings have been properly adjusted in this manner, the remaining consolidation entries eliminate Sister's stockholders' equity (Entry **S**), the intercompany dividend income (Entry **I**), and the intercompany debt (Entry **P**).

## Summary

1. The procedures used to consolidate financial information generated by the separate companies in a business combination are affected by both the passage of time and the method applied by the parent in accounting for the subsidiary. Thus, no single consolidation process can be described that is applicable to all business combinations.

2. The parent might elect to utilize the equity method to account for a subsidiary. As discussed in Chapter 1, income is accrued by the parent when earned by the subsidiary and dividend receipts are recorded as reductions in the Investment account. The effects of excess amortizations or any intercompany transactions also are reflected within the parent's financial records. The equity method provides the parent with accurate information concerning the subsidiary's impact on consolidated totals; however, it is usually somewhat complicated to apply.

3. The cost method and the partial equity method are two alternatives to the equity method. The cost method recognizes only the subsidiary's dividends as income while the asset balance remains at cost. This approach is simple and provides a measure of cash flows between the two companies. Under the partial equity method, the parent accrues the subsidiary's income as earned but does not record adjustments that might be required by excess amortizations or intercompany transfers. The partial equity method is easier to apply than the equity method, and, in many cases, the parent's income is a reasonable approximation of the consolidated total.

4. For a consolidation in any subsequent period, all reciprocal balances have to be eliminated. Thus, the subsidiary's equity accounts, the parent's investment balance, and intercompany income, dividends, and liabilities are removed. In addition, the remaining unamortized portions of the purchase price allocations are recognized along with excess amortization expenses for the period. If the equity method has not been applied, the beginning Retained Earnings of the parent also must be adjusted for any previous income or excess amortizations that have not yet been recorded.

5. For each purchase of a subsidiary, the parent must assign the acquired assets and liabilities (including goodwill) to individual reporting units of its combined operations. The reporting units should be at the level of operating segment or lower and must provide the basis for future assessments of fair value. Any value assigned to goodwill is not amortized but instead is tested annually for impairment. This test consists of two steps. First, if the fair values of any of the consolidated entity's reporting units fall below their carrying values, then the implied value of the associated goodwill must be recomputed. Second, the recomputed implied value of goodwill is compared to its carrying value. An impairment loss must then be recognized if the carrying value of goodwill exceeds its implied value.

6. Push-down accounting is the adjustment of the subsidiary's account balances to recognize allocations and goodwill stemming from the parent's purchase price. Subsequent amortization of these cost figures also is recorded by the subsidiary as an expense. At this time, push-down accounting is required by the SEC for the separate statements of the subsidiary only when no substantial outside ownership exists. The FASB is currently studying push-down accounting and may issue more specific rules on its application. However, for internal reporting purposes, push-down accounting is gaining popularity because it aids company officials in evaluating the impact that the subsidiary has on the business combination.

7. The purchase price of a subsidiary can be based, at least in part, on future income levels or stock prices. If a subsequent payment is made because a specified amount of income is earned, consolidated goodwill is increased. However, if additional shares are issued because of a drop in the price of the parent's stock, the Common Stock and Additional Paid-In Capital accounts are realigned to agree with the new price.

## Comprehensive Illustration PROBLEM

(*Estimated Time: 40 to 65 Minutes*) On January 1, 2004, Top Company acquired all of the outstanding common stock of Bottom Company for $800,000 in cash. As of that date, one of Bottom's buildings with a five-year remaining life was undervalued on its financial records by $30,000. Equipment with a 10-year life was undervalued but only by $10,000. The book values of all of Bottom's other assets and liabilities were equal to their fair market values at that time, except for an unrecorded licensing agreement with an assessed value of $40,000 and a 20-year remaining useful life. Bottom's book value at January 1, 2004, was $720,000.

During 2004, Bottom reported net income of $100,000 and paid $30,000 in dividends. Earnings were $120,000 in 2005 with $20,000 in dividends distributed by the subsidiary. As of December 31, 2006, the companies reported the following selected balances:

|  | Top Company December 31, 2006 | | Bottom Company December 31, 2006 | |
|---|---|---|---|---|
|  | Debit | Credit | Debit | Credit |
| Buildings | $1,540,000 |  | $460,000 |  |
| Cash and receivables | 50,000 |  | 90,000 |  |
| Common stock |  | $ 900,000 |  | $400,000 |
| Dividends paid | 70,000 |  | 10,000 |  |
| Equipment | 280,000 |  | 200,000 |  |
| Cost of goods sold | 500,000 |  | 120,000 |  |
| Depreciation expense | 100,000 |  | 60,000 |  |
| Inventory | 280,000 |  | 260,000 |  |
| Land | 330,000 |  | 250,000 |  |
| Liabilities |  | 480,000 |  | 260,000 |
| Retained earnings, 1/1/06 |  | 1,360,000 |  | 490,000 |
| Revenues |  | 900,000 |  | 300,000 |

### Required:

a. If the equity method is applied by Top, what is its investment account balance as of December 31, 2006?
b. If the cost method is applied by Top, what is its investment account balance as of December 31, 2006?
c. Regardless of the accounting method in use by Top, what are the consolidated totals as of December 31, 2006, for each of the following accounts:

    Buildings                      Revenues
    Equipment               Net Income
    Land                           Investment in Bottom
    Depreciation Expense    Dividends Paid
    Amortization Expense    Cost of Goods Sold

d. If this combination had been initiated prior to June 30, 2001, and was recorded as a pooling of interests, what would be the consolidated totals as of December 31, 2006, for the accounts listed in requirement (*c*)?
e. Prepare the worksheet entries required on December 31, 2006, to consolidate the financial records of these two companies. Assume that Top applied the equity method to its investment accounts and that the combination is a purchase.
f. How would the worksheet entries in requirement (*e*) be altered if Top has used the cost method?

### SOLUTION

a. To determine the investment balances under the equity method, four items must be known: the original cost, the income accrual, dividend payments, and amortization of excess cost. Although the first three are indicated in the problem, amortizations must be calculated separately.

    An allocation of Top's purchase prices as well as the related amortization expense follows.

| Purchase price paid by Top Company | $ 800,000 |
|---|---|
| Book value of Bottom Company, 1/1/04 | (720,000) |
| Excess cost over book value | 80,000 |

Excess cost allocated to specific accounts based on fair market values:

|  |  | Life (years) | Annual Amortization |
|---|---:|:---:|---:|
| Buildings | 30,000 | 5 | $6,000 |
| Equipment | 10,000 | 10 | 1,000 |
| Licensing agreement | 40,000 | 20 | 2,000 |
| Total annual expense | $80,000 |  | $9,000 |

Thus, if Top adopts the equity method to account for this subsidiary, the Investment in Bottom account holds a December 31, 2006, balance of $1,053,000, computed as follows:

| | | |
|---|---:|---:|
| Purchase price | | $ 800,000 |
| Bottom Company's 2004–05 increase in book value (income less dividends) | | 170,000 |
| Excess amortizations for 2004–2005 ($9,000 per year for two years) | | (18,000) |
| Current year recognition (2006): | | |
|   Equity income accrual (Bottom's revenues less its expenses) | $120,000 | |
|   Excess amortization expenses | (9,000) | |
|   Dividend from Bottom | (10,000) | 101,000 |
| Investment in Bottom Company, 12/31/06 | | $1,053,000 |

The $120,000 income accrual for 2006 and the $9,000 excess amortization expenses indicate that an Equity in Subsidiary Earnings balance of $111,000 appears in Top's income statement for the current period.

b. If Top Company applies the cost method, the Investment in Bottom Company account permanently retains its original $800,000 balance and only the intercompany dividend of $10,000 is recognized by the parent as income in 2006.

c. 
- The consolidated Buildings account as of December 31, 2006, holds a balance of $2,012,000. Although the two book value figures total only $2 million, a $30,000 purchase price allocation was made to this account based on fair market value at date of acquisition. Because this amount is being depreciated at the rate of $6,000 per year, the original allocation will have been reduced by $18,000 by the end of 2006, leaving only a $12,000 increase.
- On December 31, 2006, the consolidated Equipment account amounts to $487,000. The book values found in the financial records of Top and Bottom provide a total of $480,000. Once again, the allocation ($10,000) established by the purchase price must be included in the consolidated balance after being adjusted for three years of depreciation ($1,000 × 3 years or $3,000).
- Land has a consolidated total of $580,000. Since the book value and fair market value of Bottom's land were in agreement at the date of acquisition, no allocation of the purchase price was made to this account. Thus, the book values are simply added together to derive a consolidated figure.
- Cost of goods sold = $620,000. The cost of goods sold of the parent and subsidiary are added together.
- Depreciation expense = $167,000. The depreciation expenses of the parent and subsidiary are added together along with the $6,000 additional building depreciation and the $1,000 additional equipment depreciation as presented in the purchase price allocation schedule.
- Amortization expense = $2,000. An additional expense of $2,000 is recognized from the amortization of the licensing agreement acquired in the business combination.
- The Revenues account appears as $1.2 million in the consolidated income statement. None of the worksheet entries in this example affects the individual balances of either company. Consolidation results merely from the addition of the two book values.
- Net income for this business combination is $411,000: consolidated expenses of $789,000 subtracted from revenues of $1.2 million.
- The parent's Investment in Bottom account is removed entirely on the worksheet so that no balance is reported. For consolidation purposes, this account is always eliminated so that the individual assets and liabilities of the subsidiary can be included.
- Dividends paid by the combination should be reported as $70,000, the amount distributed by Top. Because Bottom's dividend payments are entirely intercompany, they are deleted in arriving at consolidated figures.

d. The consolidation of companies under the pooling of interests method is based primarily on the addition of book values. Therefore, consolidated totals for the first five accounts in this question can be determined merely by summing the separate balances:
- Buildings = $2,000,000 ($1,540,000 + $460,000)
- Equipment = $480,000 ($280,000 + $200,000)
- Land = $580,000 ($330,000 + $250,000)
- Cost of Goods Sold = $620,000 ($500,000 + $120,000)
- Depreciation Expense = $160,000 ($100,000 + $60,000)
- Amortization Expense = 0
- Revenues = $1,200,000 ($900,000 + $300,000)
- Consolidated net income is calculated by subtracting the $780,000 in expenses (just computed) from revenues of $1.2 million for a reported total of $420,000.
- As in a purchase, the Investment in Bottom account is eliminated so that the subsidiary's individual balances can be included.
- Only the parent's dividend ($70,000) is reported in the consolidated statements since Bottom's payment is an intercompany cash transfer.

e. Consolidation Entries Assuming Equity Method Used by Parent

**Entry S**

| | | |
|---|---:|---:|
| Common Stock (Bottom Company) | 400,000 | |
| Retained Earnings, 1/1/06 (Bottom Company) | 490,000 | |
|     Investment in Bottom Company | | 890,000 |

Elimination of subsidiary's beginning stockholders' equity accounts against book value portion of investment account.

**Entry A**

| | | |
|---|---:|---:|
| Buildings | 18,000 | |
| Equipment | 8,000 | |
| Licensing Agreement | 36,000 | |
|     Investment in Bottom Company | | 62,000 |

To recognize allocation of parent's unamortized cost in excess of subsidiary's book value. Balances represent original allocations less two years of amortization for the 2004–05 period.

**Entry I**

| | | |
|---|---:|---:|
| Equity in Subsidiary Earnings | 111,000 | |
|     Investment in Bottom Company | | 111,000 |

To eliminate parent's equity income accrual, balance is computed in requirement (a).

**Entry D**

| | | |
|---|---:|---:|
| Investment in Bottom | 10,000 | |
|     Dividends Paid | | 10,000 |

To eliminate intercompany dividend payment made by subsidiary to the parent (and recorded as a reduction in the investment account since the equity method is in use).

### Entry E

| | | |
|---|---:|---:|
| Depreciation expense | 7,000 | |
| Amortization expense | 2,000 | |
|     Equipment | | 1,000 |
|     Buildings | | 6,000 |
|     Licensing Agreement | | 2,000 |

To recognize excess cost depreciation and amortization for 2006.

f. If the cost method rather than the equity method is utilized by Top, three changes are required in the development of consolidation entries:

(1) An Entry *C is required to update the beginning Retained Earnings of the parent as if the equity method had been applied. Both an income accrual as well as excess amortizations for the prior two years must be recognized since these balances were not recorded by the parent.

### Entry *C

| | | |
|---|---:|---:|
| Investment in Bottom Company | 152,000 | |
|     Retained Earnings, 1/1/06 (Top Company) | | 152,000 |

To convert cost figures to the equity method by accruing the net effect of the subsidiary's operations (income less dividends) for the prior two years ($170,000) along with excess amortization expenses ($18,000) for this same period.

(2) An alteration is needed in Entry I since, under the cost method, only dividend payments are recorded by the parent as income.

### Entry I

| | | |
|---|---:|---:|
| Dividend Income | 10,000 | |
|     Dividends Paid | | 10,000 |

To eliminate intercompany dividend payments recorded by parent as income.

(3) Finally, because the intercompany dividends have been eliminated in Entry I, no separate Entry D is needed.

## Questions

1. CCES Corporation acquires a controlling interest in Schmaling, Inc., in a purchase transaction. CCES may utilize any one of three methods to account for this investment. Describe each of these methods, indicating their advantages and disadvantages.
2. Maguire Company obtains 100 percent control over Williams Company. Several years after the takeover, consolidated financial statements are being produced. For each of the following accounts, indicate the values that should be included in consolidated totals. Assume that Maguire acquired Williams in a transaction that must be viewed as a purchase.
    a. Equipment.
    b. Investment in Williams Company.
    c. Dividends paid.
    d. Goodwill.
    e. Revenues.
    f. Expenses.

g. Common stock.
h. Net income.

3. Using the information presented in question 2, determine each of the consolidated totals if the combination was accounted for as a pooling of interests.
4. When a parent company uses the equity method to account for an investment in a subsidiary, why do both the parent's Net Income and Retained Earnings balances agree with the consolidated totals?
5. When a parent company uses the equity method to account for a purchased investment, the amortization expense entry recorded during the year is eliminated on a consolidation worksheet as a component of Entry **I**. What is the necessity of removing this amortization?
6. When a parent company is applying the cost method or the partial equity method to an investment, an adjustment must be made to the parent's beginning Retained Earnings (Entry *****C**) in every period after the year of acquisition. What is the necessity for this entry? Why is no similar entry found when the equity method is utilized by the parent?
7. Several years ago, Jenkins Company acquired a controlling interest in Lambert Company. Lambert recently borrowed $100,000 from Jenkins. In consolidating the financial records of these two companies, how will this debt be handled?
8. Benns Company acquires Waters Company in a combination accounted for as a purchase. Benns adopts the equity method. At the end of six years, Benns reports an investment in Waters of $920,000. What figures constitute this balance?
9. One company is acquired by another in a purchase transaction in which $100,000 of the acquisition price is assigned to goodwill. Several years later a worksheet is being produced to consolidate these two companies. How is the reported value of the goodwill determined at this date?
10. Remo Company purchases Albane Corporation on January 1, 2005. As part of the purchase agreement, the parent states that an additional $100,000 payment to the former owners of Albane could be required in 2006, depending on the outcome of specified conditions. If this payment is subsequently made, how will Remo account for the extra cost?
11. When is the use of push-down accounting required, and what is the rationale for its application?
12. How are the individual financial records of both the parent and the subsidiary affected in cases when push-down accounting is being applied?
13. Why has push-down accounting gained popularity for internal reporting purposes?
14. The consolidation process applicable to a pooling of interests often is viewed as easier than that used for a purchase. What creates this perception?
15. When should a parent consider recognizing an impairment loss for goodwill associated with a purchased subsidiary? How should the loss be reported in the financial statements?

## Problems

1. A company acquires a subsidiary on January 1, 2004, and will prepare consolidated financial statements for the year ending December 31, 2004. For internal reporting purposes, the company has decided to apply the cost method. Why might the company have made this decision?
   a. It is a relatively easy method to apply.
   b. Operating results appearing on the parent's financial records reflect consolidated totals.
   c. The FASB now requires the use of this particular method for internal reporting purposes.
   d. Consolidation is not required when the cost method is used by the parent.
2. A company acquires a subsidiary on January 1, 2004, and will prepare consolidated financial statements for the year ending December 31, 2004. For internal reporting purposes, the company has decided to apply the equity method. Why might the company have made this decision?
   a. It is a relatively easy method to apply.
   b. Operating results appearing on the parent's financial records reflect consolidated totals.
   c. The FASB now requires the use of this particular method for internal reporting purposes.
   d. Consolidation is not required when the equity method is used by the parent.
3. When should a consolidated entity recognize a goodwill impairment loss?
   a. If both the market value of a reporting unit and its associated implied goodwill fall below their respective carrying values.
   b. Whenever the market value of the entity declines significantly.
   c. If the market value of a reporting unit falls below its original acquisition price.
   d. Annually on a systematic and rational basis.
4. Willkom Corporation buys 100 percent of Szabo, Inc., on January 1, 2002, at a price in excess of the subsidiary's fair market value. On that date, Willkom's equipment (10-year life) has a book value of $300,000 but a fair market value of $400,000. Szabo has equipment (10-year life) with a book value of $200,000 but a fair market value of $300,000. Willkom uses the partial equity method to record

its investment in Szabo. On December 31, 2004, Willkom has equipment with a book value of $210,000 but a fair market value of $330,000. Szabo has equipment with a book value of $140,000 but a fair market value of $270,000. What is the consolidated balance for the Equipment account as of December 31, 2004?
   a. $600,000
   b. $490,000
   c. $480,000
   d. $420,000
5. How would the answer to problem 4 have been affected if the parent had applied the cost method rather than the partial equity method?
   a. No effect: The method used by the parent is for internal reporting purposes only and has no impact on consolidated totals.
   b. The consolidated Equipment account would have a higher reported balance.
   c. The consolidated Equipment account would have a lower reported balance.
   d. The balance in the consolidated Equipment account cannot be determined for the cost method using the information given.
6. According to *SFAS 142,* "Goodwill and Other Intangible Assets," purchased goodwill must be allocated among a firm's identified reporting units. If the fair value of a particular reporting unit with recognized goodwill falls below its carrying amount, which of the following is true?
   a. No goodwill impairment loss is recognized unless the implied value for goodwill exceeds its carrying amount.
   b. A goodwill impairment loss is recognized if the carrying amount for goodwill exceeds its implied value.
   c. A goodwill impairment loss is recognized for the difference between the reporting unit's fair value and carrying amount.
   d. The reporting unit reduces the values assigned to its long-term assets (including any unrecognized intangibles) to reflect its fair value.
7. According to the *SFAS 142,* "Goodwill and Other Intangible Assets," if no legal, regulatory, contractual, competitive, economic, or other factors limit the life of an intangible asset, the asset's cost is allocated to expense over which of the following?
   a. 20 years.
   b. 20 years with an annual impairment review.
   c. infinitely.
   d. indefinitely (no amortization) with an annual impairment review until its life becomes finite.
8. Dosmann, Incorporated buys all of the outstanding shares of Lizzi Corporation on January 1, 2003, for $700,000 in cash. This price resulted in a $35,000 allocation to equipment and goodwill of $88,000. Because the subsidiary subsequently earned especially high profits, Dosmann was required to pay the previous owners of Lizzi an additional $110,000 on January 1, 2005. How should this extra amount be reported?
   a. The additional $110,000 payment is a reduction in consolidated Retained Earnings.
   b. A retroactive adjustment is made to record the $110,000 as an additional expense for the year ending December 31, 2003.
   c. Consolidated goodwill as of January 1, 2005, is increased by $110,000.
   d. The $110,000 is recorded as an expense in 2005.
9. Lauren Corporation purchases Sarah, Inc., on January 1, 2003, by issuing 13,000 shares of common stock with a $10 per share par value and a $23 fair market value. This transaction results in the recording of $62,000 of goodwill. Subsequently, on January 1, 2005, Lauren is required to issue an additional 3,000 shares of stock to Sarah's previous owners because of a drop in the market value of the initial 13,000 shares. How is this additional issuance of stock recorded?
   a. The fair market value of the newly issued shares increases the Goodwill account balance.
   b. The Investment in Sarah balance is not affected, but the parent's Additional Paid-In Capital is reduced by the par value of the newly issued shares.
   c. All of the subsidiary's asset and liability accounts must be revalued for consolidation purposes based on their fair market values as of January 1, 2005.
   d. The additional shares are assumed to have been issued on January 1, 2003, so that a retroactive adjustment is required.
10. What is push-down accounting?
    a. A requirement that a subsidiary must use the same accounting principles as a parent company.
    b. Inventory transfers made from a parent company to a subsidiary.
    c. A subsidiary's recording of the market value allocations found within the purchase price paid by a parent as well as subsequent amortization.

d. The adjustments required for consolidation when a parent has applied the cost method of accounting for internal reporting purposes.

11. Treadway Corporation purchases Hooker, Inc., on January 1, 2004. The parent pays more for it than the fair market value of the subsidiary's net assets. On that date, Treadway has equipment with a book value of $420,000 and a fair market value of $530,000. Hooker has equipment with a book value of $330,000 and a fair market value of $390,000. Hooker is going to use push-down accounting. Immediately after the acquisition, what amounts in the Equipment account appear on Hooker's separate balance sheet and on the consolidated balance sheet?
    a. $330,000 and $750,000
    b. $330,000 and $860,000
    c. $390,000 and $810,000
    d. $390,000 and $920,000

12. Herbert, Inc., buys all of the outstanding stock of Rambis Company on January 1, 2003, for $574,000. Annual excess amortization of $12,000 results from this purchase transaction. On the date of the takeover, Herbert reported retained earnings of $400,000 while Rambis reported a $200,000 balance. Herbert reported internal income of $40,000 in 2003 and $50,000 in 2004 and paid $10,000 in dividends each year. Rambis reported net income of $20,000 in 2003 and $30,000 in 2004 and paid $5,000 in dividends each year.
    a. Assume that Herbert's internal income does not include any income derived from the subsidiary.
       - If the parent uses the equity method, what is the amount of consolidated Retained Earnings on December 31, 2004?
       - If the parent uses the partial equity method, what is the amount of consolidated Retained Earnings on December 31, 2004?
       - If the parent uses the cost method, what is the amount of consolidated Retained Earnings on December 31, 2004?
    b. Under each of the following situations, what is the Investment in Rambis account balance on Herbert's books on January 1, 2004?
       - The parent uses the equity method.
       - The parent uses the partial equity method.
       - The parent uses the cost method.
    c. Under each of the following situations, what is Entry *C on a 2004 consolidation worksheet?
       - The parent uses the equity method.
       - The parent uses the partial equity method.
       - The parent uses the cost method.

13. Haynes, Inc., obtains 100 percent of Turner Company's common stock on January 1, 2002, by issuing 9,000 shares of $10 par value common stock. Haynes's shares had a $15 per share fair market value. On that date, Turner reported a net book value of $100,000. However, its equipment (with a five-year remaining life) was undervalued by $5,000 in the company's accounting records. Also, Turner had developed a customer list with an assessed value of $30,000, although no value had been recorded on Turner's books. The customer list had an estimated remaining useful life of 10 years.

    The following figures come from the individual accounting records of these two companies as of December 31, 2002:

    |  | Haynes | Turner |
    | --- | --- | --- |
    | Revenues | $600,000 | $230,000 |
    | Expenses | 440,000 | 120,000 |
    | Investment income | not given | –0– |
    | Dividends paid | 80,000 | 50,000 |

    The following figures come from the individual accounting records of these two companies as of December 31, 2003:

    |  | Haynes | Turner |
    | --- | --- | --- |
    | Revenues | $700,000 | $280,000 |
    | Expenses | 460,000 | 150,000 |
    | Investment income | not given | –0– |
    | Dividends paid | 90,000 | 40,000 |
    | Equipment | 500,000 | 300,000 |

a. What balance does Haynes's Investment in Turner account show on December 31, 2003, when the equity method is applied?
b. What is the consolidated net income for the year ending December 31, 2003?
c. What is the consolidated Equipment balance as of December 31, 2003? How would this answer be affected by the investment method applied by the parent?
d. If Haynes has applied the cost method to account for its investment, what adjustment is needed to beginning Retained Earnings on a December 31, 2003, consolidation worksheet? How would this answer change if the partial equity method had been in use? How would this answer change if the equity method had been in use?

14. Acme Co., a consolidated enterprise, conducted an impairment review for each of its reporting units. One particular reporting unit, Martel, emerged as a candidate for possible goodwill impairment. Martel has recognized net assets of $780, including goodwill of $500. Martel's fair value is assessed at $650 and includes two internally developed unrecognized intangible assets (a patent and a customer list with fair values of $150 and $50, respectively). The following table summarizes current financial information for the Martel reporting unit:

|  | Carrying Amount | Fair Value |
|---|---|---|
| Tangible assets, net | $ 80 | $110 |
| Recognized intangible assets, net | 200 | 230 |
| Goodwill | 500 | ?? |
| Unrecognized intangible assets | NA | 200 |
| Total | $780 | $650 |

a. Show the two steps to determine the amount of any goodwill impairment for Acme's Martel reporting unit.
b. After recognition of any goodwill impairment loss, what are the reported book values for the following assets of Acme's reporting unit Martel?
   - Tangible assets, net
   - Goodwill
   - Customer list
   - Patent

15. Destin Company recently purchased several businesses and recognized goodwill in each acquisition. In accordance with *SFAS 142*, Destin has allocated its purchased goodwill to three reporting units as follows:

| Reporting Units | Goodwill |
|---|---|
| Sand Dollar | $120,000 |
| Salty Dog | 150,000 |
| Baytowne | 90,000 |

In its 2004 annual review for goodwill impairment, Destin further provides the following individual asset and liability values for each reporting unit:

|  | Carrying Value | Fair Value |
|---|---|---|
| **Sand Dollar** |  |  |
| Tangible assets | $180,000 | $190,000 |
| Trademark | 170,000 | 150,000 |
| Customer list | 90,000 | 100,000 |
| Liabilities | 30,000 | 30,000 |
| **Salty Dog** |  |  |
| Tangible assets | $200,000 | $200,000 |
| Unpatented technology | 170,000 | 125,000 |
| Licenses | 90,000 | 100,000 |

*(continued)*

|  | Carrying Value | Fair Value |
|---|---|---|
| **Baytowne** | | |
| Tangible assets | $140,000 | $150,000 |
| Unpatented technology | –0– | 100,000 |
| Copyrights | 50,000 | 80,000 |

The overall valuations for the entire reporting units (including goodwill) are $510,000 for Sand Dollar, $580,000 for Salty Dog, and $560,000 for Baytowne. To date, Destin has reported no goodwill impairments.

a. Which of Destin's reporting units require both steps to test for goodwill impairment?
b. How much goodwill impairment should Destin report for 2004?
c. What changes to the valuations of Destin's tangible assets and identified intangible assets should be reported based on the goodwill impairment tests?

16. Texas, Inc., obtains all of the outstanding stock of Chainsaw Corporation on January 1, 2002. At that date, Chainsaw owns only three assets and has no liabilities:

|  | Book Value | Fair Market Value |
|---|---|---|
| Inventory | $ 30,000 | $ 40,000 |
| Equipment (5-year life) | 70,000 | 50,000 |
| Building (10-year life) | 100,000 | 150,000 |

a. If Texas pays $250,000 in cash for Chainsaw, what allocation should be assigned to the subsidiary's Building account and its Equipment account in a December 31, 2004, consolidation?
b. If Texas pays $220,000 in cash for Chainsaw, what allocation should be assigned to the subsidiary's Building account and its Equipment account in a December 31, 2004, consolidation?
c. If Texas pays $180,000 in cash for Chainsaw, what allocation should be assigned to the subsidiary's Building account and its Equipment account in a December 31, 2004, consolidation?
d. If Texas issued common stock valued at $180,000 (rather than paying cash) for Chainsaw in a pooling of interests on June 30, 2001, what allocation should be assigned to the subsidiary's Building account and its Equipment account in a December 31, 2004, consolidation?

**Problems 17 through 20 should be viewed as independent situations. They are based on the following data:**

Chapman Company obtains 100 percent of the stock of Abernethy Company on January 1, 2004. As of that date, Abernethy has the following trial balance:

|  | Debit | Credit |
|---|---|---|
| Accounts payable | | $ 50,000 |
| Accounts receivable | $ 40,000 | |
| Additional paid-in capital | | 50,000 |
| Buildings (net) (4-year life) | 120,000 | |
| Cash and short-term investments | 60,000 | |
| Common stock | | 250,000 |
| Equipment (net) (5-year life) | 200,000 | |
| Inventory | 90,000 | |
| Land | 80,000 | |
| Long-term liabilities (mature 12/31/07) | | 150,000 |
| Retained earnings, 1/1/04 | | 100,000 |
| Supplies | 10,000 | |
| Totals | $600,000 | $600,000 |

During 2004, Abernethy reported income of $80,000 while paying dividends of $10,000. During 2005, Abernethy reported income of $110,000 while paying dividends of $30,000.

17. Assume that Chapman Company acquired the common stock of Abernethy for $490,000 in cash. As of January 1, 2004, Abernethy's land had a fair market value of $90,000, its buildings were valued at $160,000, and its equipment was appraised at $180,000. Chapman uses the equity method for this investment. Prepare consolidation worksheet entries for December 31, 2004, and December 31, 2005.

18. Assume that Chapman Company acquired the common stock of Abernethy for $500,000 in cash. Assume that the equipment and long-term liabilities had fair market values of $220,000 and $120,000, respectively, on that date. Chapman uses the cost method to account for its investment. Prepare consolidation worksheet entries for December 31, 2004, and December 31, 2005.

19. Assume that Chapman Company acquires the common stock of Abernethy by issuing 10,000 shares of its $30 par value common stock. The stock has a $42 per share fair market value on January 1, 2004. On January 1, 2004, Abernethy's inventory had a fair market value of $150,000. All of this inventory is assumed to have been sold during 2004. Chapman applies the equity method to account for this investment. Prepare the consolidation worksheet entries for December 31, 2004, and December 31, 2005.

20. Assume that Chapman Company acquired the common stock of Abernethy by paying $520,000 in cash. All accounts of Abernethy are estimated to have a value approximately equal to present book values. Chapman uses the partial equity method to account for its investment. Prepare the consolidation worksheet entries for December 31, 2004, and December 31, 2005.

21. Jefferson, Inc., purchases Hamilton Corporation on January 1, 2004. Immediately after the acquisition, the two companies have the following account balances. Hamilton's equipment (with a five-year life) is actually worth $450,000. Any goodwill is considered to have an indefinite life.

|  | Jefferson | Hamilton |
| --- | --- | --- |
| Current assets | $300,000 | $210,000 |
| Investment in Hamilton | 510,000 |  |
| Equipment | 600,000 | 400,000 |
| Liabilities | 200,000 | 160,000 |
| Common stock | 350,000 | 150,000 |
| Retained earnings | 860,000 | 300,000 |

In 2004, Hamilton earns a net income of $55,000 and pays a $5,000 cash dividend. At the end of 2005, selected account balances for the two companies are as follows:

|  | Jefferson | Hamilton |
| --- | --- | --- |
| Revenues | $400,000 | $240,000 |
| Expenses | 290,000 | 180,000 |
| Investment income | not given |  |
| Retained earnings, 1/1/05 | not given | 350,000 |
| Common stock | 350,000 | 150,000 |
| Current assets | 360,000 | 140,000 |
| Investment in Hamilton | not given |  |
| Equipment | 520,000 | 420,000 |
| Liabilities | 170,000 | 190,000 |

a. What will be the December 31, 2005, balance in the Investment Income account and the Investment in Hamilton account under each of the three methods described in this chapter?

b. How is the consolidated Expense account affected by the accounting method used by the parent to record ownership of this subsidiary?

c. How is the consolidated Equipment account affected by the accounting method used by the parent to record ownership of this subsidiary?

d. What is Jefferson's Retained Earnings balance as of January 1, 2005, under each of the three methods described in this chapter?

e. What is Entry *C on a consolidation worksheet for 2005 under each of the three methods described in this chapter?

f. What is Entry S on a consolidation worksheet for 2005 under each of the three methods described in this chapter?

g. What is consolidated net income for 2005?

22. Following are selected account balances from Profitt Company and Simon Corporation as of December 31, 2004:

|  | Profitt | Simon |
|---|---|---|
| Revenues | $700,000 | $400,000 |
| Cost of goods sold | 250,000 | 100,000 |
| Depreciation expense | 150,000 | 200,000 |
| Investment income | not given |  |
| Dividends paid | 80,000 | 60,000 |
| Retained earnings, 1/1/04 | 600,000 | 200,000 |
| Current assets | 400,000 | 500,000 |
| Buildings (net) | 900,000 | 400,000 |
| Equipment (net) | 600,000 | 1,000,000 |
| Investment in Simon | not given |  |
| Liabilities | 500,000 | 1,380,000 |
| Common stock | 600,000 ($20 par) | 200,000 ($10 par) |
| Additional paid-in capital | 150,000 | 80,000 |

On January 1, 2004, Profitt purchased all of the outstanding stock of Simon for $660,000 in cash and common stock. Profitt also paid $20,000 in lawyers' fees and other combination costs as well as $10,000 in stock issuance costs. At the date of acquisition, Simon's buildings (with a six-year remaining life) have a $440,000 book value but a fair market value of $560,000.

a. As of December 31, 2004, what is the consolidated Buildings balance?
b. For the year ending December 31, 2004, what is consolidated Net Income?
c. As of December 31, 2004, what is the consolidated Retained Earnings balance?
d. As of December 31, 2004, what is the consolidated balance to be reported for goodwill?

23. Foxx Corporation purchases all of the outstanding stock of Greenburg Company on January 1, 2002, for $600,000. Greenburg had net assets on that date of $470,000, although equipment with a 10-year life was undervalued on the records by $90,000. Any recognized goodwill is considered to have an indefinite life.

Greenburg reports net income in 2002 of $90,000 and $100,000 in 2003. Dividends of $20,000 are paid by the subsidiary in each of these two years.

Financial figures for the year ending December 31, 2004, follow:

|  | Foxx | Greenburg |
|---|---|---|
| Revenues | $ 800,000 | $ 600,000 |
| Cost of goods sold | (100,000) | (150,000) |
| Depreciation expense | (300,000) | (350,000) |
| Investment income | 20,000 | –0– |
| Net income | $ 420,000 | $ 100,000 |
| Retained earnings, 1/1/04 | $1,100,000 | $ 320,000 |
| Net income | 420,000 | 100,000 |
| Dividends paid | (120,000) | (20,000) |
| Retained earnings, 12/31/04 | $1,400,000 | $ 400,000 |
| Current assets | $ 300,000 | $ 100,000 |
| Investment in subsidiary | 600,000 | –0– |
| Equipment (net) | 900,000 | 600,000 |
| Buildings (net) | 800,000 | 400,000 |
| Land | 600,000 | 100,000 |
| Total assets | $3,200,000 | $1,200,000 |
| Liabilities | $ 900,000 | $ 500,000 |
| Common stock | 900,000 | 300,000 |
| Retained earnings | 1,400,000 | 400,000 |
| Total liabilities and equity | $3,200,000 | $1,200,000 |

a. Determine the December 31, 2004 consolidated balance for each of the following accounts:

  Depreciation Expense    Buildings
  Dividends Paid          Goodwill
  Revenues                Common Stock
  Equipment

b. How does the parent's choice of an accounting method for its investment affect the balances computed in requirement (a)?
c. Which method of accounting for this subsidiary is the parent actually using for internal reporting purposes?
d. If a different method of accounting for this investment had been used by the parent company, how could that method have been identified?
e. What would be Foxx's balance for retained earnings as of January 1, 2004, if each of the following methods had been in use?

  Cost method
  Partial equity method
  Equity method

24. Big Corporation purchased Little Company on January 1, 2004, for $400,000 in cash. Little reported net assets at that time of $320,000. However, several of Little's accounts had fair market values that differed from book values:

|  | Book Value | Fair Market Value |
|---|---|---|
| Land | $ 60,000 | $ 50,000 |
| Buildings (10-year life) | 100,000 | 120,000 |
| Equipment (6-year life) | 60,000 | 90,000 |

Any goodwill is considered to have an indefinite life.

Following are financial statements for these two companies for the year ending December 31, 2004. Credit balances are indicated by parentheses.

|  | Big | Little |
|---|---|---|
| Revenues | $ (600,000) | $(300,000) |
| Cost of goods sold | 300,000 | 110,000 |
| Depreciation expense | 100,000 | 70,000 |
| Income of Little | (113,000) | –0– |
| Net income | $ (313,000) | $(120,000) |
| Retained earnings, 1/1/04 | $ (700,000) | $(220,000) |
| Net income (above) | (313,000) | (120,000) |
| Dividends paid | 142,000 | 80,000 |
| Retained earnings, 12/31/04 | $ (871,000) | $(260,000) |
| Cash | $ 176,000 | $ 80,000 |
| Receivables | 210,000 | 90,000 |
| Inventory | 190,000 | 130,000 |
| Investment in Little | 433,000 | –0– |
| Land | 350,000 | 60,000 |
| Buildings (net) | 343,000 | 90,000 |
| Equipment (net) | 190,000 | 50,000 |
| Goodwill | –0– | –0– |
| Total assets | $ 1,892,000 | $ 500,000 |
| Liabilities | $ (621,000) | $(140,000) |
| Common stock | (400,000) | (100,000) |
| Retained earnings (above) | (871,000) | (260,000) |
| Total liabilities and equity | $(1,892,000) | $(500,000) |

a. How was the $113,000 Income of Little balance computed?
b. Without preparing a worksheet or consolidation entries, determine the totals to be reported for this business combination for the year ending December 31, 2004.
c. Verify the totals determined in part (b) by producing a consolidation worksheet for Big and Little for the year ending December 31, 2004.

25. Following are separate financial statements for Mitchell Company and Andrews Company as of December 31, 2004. Credit balances are indicated by parentheses. Mitchell acquired all of the outstanding stock of Andrews on January 1, 2000, by issuing 9,000 shares of its own common stock. This stock was valued at $50 per share while having a par value of $30 per share. In addition, Mitchell paid $20,000 to lawyers, accountants, and other parties for costs incurred in creating the combination. The combination is accounted for as a purchase.

|  | Mitchell Company 12/31/04 | Andrews Company 12/31/04 |
|---|---|---|
| Revenues | $ (610,000) | $ (370,000) |
| Cost of goods sold | 270,000 | 140,000 |
| Depreciation expense | 115,000 | 80,000 |
| Dividend income | (5,000) | -0- |
| Net income | $ (230,000) | $ (150,000) |
| Retained earnings, 1/1/04 | $ (880,000) | $ (490,000) |
| Net income (above) | (230,000) | (150,000) |
| Dividends paid | 90,000 | 5,000 |
| Retained earnings, 12/31/04 | $(1,020,000) | $ (635,000) |
| Cash | $ 110,000 | $ 15,000 |
| Receivables | 380,000 | 220,000 |
| Inventory | 560,000 | 280,000 |
| Investment in Andrews Company | 470,000 | -0- |
| Land | 460,000 | 340,000 |
| Buildings and equipment (net) | 920,000 | 380,000 |
| Total assets | $ 2,900,000 | $ 1,235,000 |
| Liabilities | $ (780,000) | $ (470,000) |
| Preferred stock | (300,000) | -0- |
| Common stock | (500,000) | (100,000) |
| Additional paid-in capital | (300,000) | (30,000) |
| Retained earnings, 12/31/04 | (1,020,000) | (635,000) |
| Total liabilities and equity | $(2,900,000) | $(1,235,000) |

On the date of purchase, Andrews reported retained earnings of $230,000 and a total book value of $360,000. At that time its buildings and equipment were undervalued by $60,000. This property was assumed to have a six-year life with no salvage value. Additionally, Andrews owned a trademark with a fair value of $50,000 and a 10-year remaining life that was not reflected on its books.

a. Using the preceding information, prepare a consolidation worksheet for these two companies as of December 31, 2004.
b. Assuming that Mitchell applied the equity method to this investment, what account balances would be altered on the parent's individual financial statements?
c. Assuming that Mitchell applied the equity method to this investment, what changes would be necessary in the consolidation entries found on a December 31, 2004, worksheet?
d. Assuming that Mitchell applied the equity method to this investment, what changes would be created in the consolidated figures to be reported by this combination?

26. Giant purchased all of the common stock of Small on January 1, 2002. Over the next few years, Giant applied the equity method to the recording of this investment. At the date of the original purchase, $90,000 of the price was attributed to undervalued land, while $50,000 was assigned to equipment having a 10-year life. The remaining $60,000 unallocated portion of the purchase price was viewed as goodwill.

Following are individual financial statements for the year ending December 31, 2006. On that date, Small owes Giant $10,000. Credits are indicated by parentheses.

a. How was the $135,000 Equity in Income of Small balance computed?
b. Without preparing a worksheet or consolidation entries, determine the totals to be reported by this business combination for the year ending December 31, 2006.

|  | Giant | Small |
|---|---|---|
| Revenues | $(1,175,000) | $ (360,000) |
| Cost of goods sold | 550,000 | 90,000 |
| Depreciation expense | 172,000 | 130,000 |
| Equity in income of Small | (135,000) | -0- |
| Net income | $ (588,000) | $ (140,000) |
| Retained earnings, 1/1/06 | $(1,417,000) | $ (620,000) |
| Net income (above) | (588,000) | (140,000) |
| Dividends paid | 310,000 | 110,000 |
| Retained earnings, 12/31/06 | $(1,695,000) | $ (650,000) |
| Current assets | $ 398,000 | $ 318,000 |
| Investment in Small | 995,000 | -0- |
| Land | 440,000 | 165,000 |
| Buildings (net) | 304,000 | 419,000 |
| Equipment (net) | 648,000 | 286,000 |
| Goodwill | -0- | -0- |
| Total assets | $ 2,785,000 | $ 1,188,000 |
| Liabilities | $ (840,000) | $ (368,000) |
| Common stock | (250,000) | (170,000) |
| Retained earnings (above) | (1,695,000) | (650,000) |
| Total liabilities and equity | $(2,785,000) | $(1,188,000) |

c. Verify the figures determined in part (b) by producing a consolidation worksheet for Giant and Small for the year ending December 31, 2006.
d. If Giant determined that the entire amount of goodwill from its investment in Small was impaired in 2006, how would the accounts of the parent reflect the impairment loss? How would the worksheet process change? What impact does an impairment loss have on consolidated financial statements?

27. Following are selected accounts for Mergaronite Company and Hill, Inc., as of December 31, 2004. Several of Mergaronite's accounts have been omitted.

|  | Mergaronite | Hill |
|---|---|---|
| Revenues | $600,000 | $250,000 |
| Cost of goods sold | 280,000 | 100,000 |
| Depreciation expense | 120,000 | 50,000 |
| Investment income | not given | NA |
| Retained earnings, 1/1/04 | 900,000 | 600,000 |
| Dividends paid | 130,000 | 40,000 |
| Current assets | 200,000 | 690,000 |
| Land | 300,000 | 90,000 |
| Buildings (net) | 500,000 | 140,000 |
| Equipment (net) | 200,000 | 250,000 |
| Liabilities | 400,000 | 310,000 |
| Common stock | 300,000 | 40,000 |
| Additional paid-in capital | 50,000 | 160,000 |

Assume that Mergaronite took over Hill on January 1, 2000, in a purchase by issuing 7,000 shares of common stock having a par value of $10 per share but a fair market value of $100 each.

On January 1, 2000, Hill's land was undervalued by $20,000, its buildings were overvalued by $30,000, and equipment was undervalued by $60,000. The buildings had a 10-year life; the equipment had a 5-year life. A customer list with an appraised value of $100,000 was developed internally by Hill and was to be written off over a 20-year period.

a. What are the December 31, 2004, consolidated totals for the following accounts:

   Revenues
   Cost of Goods Sold
   Depreciation Expense
   Amortization Expense
   Buildings
   Equipment
   Customer List
   Common Stock
   Additional Paid-In Capital

b. In requirement (a), why can the consolidated totals be determined without knowing which method the parent has used to account for the subsidiary?

c. If the equity method is used by the parent, what consolidation entries would be used on a 2004 worksheet?

28. Alton Company acquired Zeidner, Inc., on January 1, 1997, in a business combination properly accounted for as a purchase. On that date, Zeidner held assets and liabilities with book values of $700,000 and $200,000, respectively. Alton paid a total of $670,000 to acquire all of the outstanding stock of Zeidner. At the date of this purchase, Zeidner possessed equipment (with a five-year life) that had a value $50,000 in excess of its book value. In addition, Zeidner had buildings worth $80,000 more than their book value. These buildings had a remaining life expectancy of 20 years.

Any goodwill that resulted from the acquisition was initially amortized over a 20-year period.

Following are the individual financial statements for these two companies for the year ending December 31, 2006. Alton owes Zeidner $30,000 at this point in time. Without preparing consolidation entries or setting up a worksheet, determine the consolidated totals for Alton Company and Zeidner, Inc.

|  | Alton Company | Zeidner, Inc. |
|---|---|---|
| **Income Statement** | | |
| Revenues | $ 600,000 | $ 500,000 |
| Cost of goods sold | (175,000) | (160,000) |
| Depreciation expense | (125,000) | (140,000) |
| Investment income from Zeidner | 200,000 | –0– |
| Net income | $ 500,000 | $ 200,000 |
| **Statement of Retained Earnings** | | |
| Retained earnings, 1/1/06 | $1,500,000 | $ 650,000 |
| Net income (above) | 500,000 | 200,000 |
| Dividends paid | (200,000) | (50,000) |
| Retained earnings, 12/31/06 | $1,800,000 | $ 800,000 |
| **Balance Sheet** | | |
| Current assets | $ 230,000 | $ 300,000 |
| Investment in Zeidner | 1,270,000 | –0– |
| Land | 100,000 | 200,000 |
| Buildings | 300,000 | 400,000 |
| Equipment | 600,000 | 300,000 |
| Goodwill | –0– | –0– |
| Total assets | $2,500,000 | $1,200,000 |
| Liabilities | $ 300,000 | $ 100,000 |
| Common stock | 400,000 | 300,000 |
| Retained earnings, 12/31/06 | 1,800,000 | 800,000 |
| Total liabilities and equity | $2,500,000 | $1,200,000 |

29. On January 1, 2002, Romeo, Incorporated, exchanged 10,000 shares of previously unissued common stock for all of the outstanding shares of Juliet Company. This was accounted for as a pooling of interests that was initiated prior to June 30, 2001. Romeo's common stock had a $20 par value but a fair market value of $48 per share. On the date of the exchange, Juliet reported $370,000 in stockholders' equity:

| | |
|---|---:|
| Common Stock | $200,000 |
| Additional Paid-In Capital | 50,000 |
| Retained Earnings | 120,000 |

Romeo originally offered only 8,000 shares for Juliet's stock but raised that bid based on favorable earnings projections. In addition, equipment held by the subsidiary (with a 10-year remaining life) was estimated to be undervalued on the accounting records by $70,000.

During 2002, Juliet reported net income of $80,000 and paid cash dividends of $60,000. In accounting for this investment, Romeo utilized the equity method.

Following are the December 31, 2003, trial balances for these two companies.

| | Romeo, Incorporated | Juliet Company |
|---|---:|---:|
| **Debits** | | |
| Accounts receivable | $ 140,000 | $ 40,000 |
| Buildings | 620,000 | 260,000 |
| Cash | 60,000 | 10,000 |
| Dividends paid | 130,000 | 60,000 |
| Equipment | 490,000 | 330,000 |
| Expenses | 390,000 | 110,000 |
| Inventory | 190,000 | 110,000 |
| Investment in Juliet Company | 420,000 | –0– |
| Land | 300,000 | 200,000 |
| Total debits | $2,740,000 | $1,120,000 |
| **Credits** | | |
| Additional paid-in capital | $ 190,000 | $ 50,000 |
| Common stock | 600,000 | 200,000 |
| Investment income from Juliet Company | 90,000 | –0– |
| Liabilities | 580,000 | 530,000 |
| Retained earnings, 1/1/03 | 680,000 | 140,000 |
| Revenues | 600,000 | 200,000 |
| Total credits | $2,740,000 | $1,120,000 |

Determine the December 31, 2003 consolidated balances that would be reported by this combination.

30. Broome paid $430,000 cash for all of the outstanding common stock of Charlotte, Inc., on January 1, 2004. The subsidiary had a book value of $340,000 on that date (common stock of $200,000 and retained earnings of $140,000), although equipment recorded at $40,000 (with a five-year remaining life) was assessed as having an actual worth of $70,000.

During the subsequent three years, Charlotte reported the following balances:

| | Net Income | Dividends Paid |
|---|---:|---:|
| 2002 | $65,000 | $25,000 |
| 2003 | 75,000 | 35,000 |
| 2004 | 80,000 | 40,000 |

On January 1, 2004, Broome paid an additional $20,000 to the previous owners of Charlotte, an amount that was due because the subsidiary's earnings for the first two years had exceeded $120,000.

a. Prepare consolidation worksheet entries as of December 31, 2004, assuming that Broome has applied the cost method.

b. Prepare consolidation worksheet entries as of December 31, 2004, assuming that Broome has applied the partial equity method.

31. Palm Company acquired 100 percent of the voting stock of Storm Company on January 1, 2000, by issuing 10,000 shares of its $10 par value common stock (having a fair market value of $13 per share). Palm also paid $10,000 in consolidation costs to lawyers and investment analysts. As of that date, Storm had stockholders' equity totaling $105,000. Land shown on Storm's accounting records was undervalued by $10,000. Equipment (with a five-year life) was undervalued by $5,000. A secret formula developed by Storm was appraised at $20,000 with an estimated life of 20 years.

Following are the separate financial statements for the two companies for the year ending December 31, 2004. The combination was accounted for as a purchase.

|  | Palm Company | Storm Company |
|---|---|---|
| Revenues | $ 485,000 | $190,000 |
| Cost of goods sold | (160,000) | (70,000) |
| Depreciation expense | (130,000) | (52,000) |
| Equity in subsidiary earnings | 66,000 | –0– |
| Net income | $ 261,000 | $ 68,000 |
| Retained earnings, 1/1/04 | $ 659,000 | $ 98,000 |
| Net income (above) | 261,000 | 68,000 |
| Dividends paid | (175,500) | (40,000) |
| Retained earnings, 12/31/04 | $ 744,500 | $126,000 |
| Current assets | $ 268,000 | $ 75,000 |
| Investment in Storm Company | 216,000 | –0– |
| Land | 427,500 | 58,000 |
| Buildings and equipment (net) | 713,000 | 161,000 |
| Total assets | $1,624,500 | $294,000 |
| Current liabilities | $ 110,000 | $ 19,000 |
| Long-term liabilities | 80,000 | 84,000 |
| Common stock | 600,000 | 60,000 |
| Additional paid-in capital | 90,000 | 5,000 |
| Retained earnings, 12/31/04 | 744,500 | 126,000 |
| Total liabilities and equity | $1,624,500 | $294,000 |

a. How was the $66,000 balance in the Equity in Subsidiary Earnings account derived?

b. Prepare a worksheet to consolidate the financial information for these two companies.

c. How would Storm's individual financial records differ if the push-down method of accounting had been applied?

32. The Tyler Company acquired all of the outstanding stock of Jasmine Company on January 1, 2002, for $206,000 in cash. Jasmine had a book value of only $140,000 on that date. However, equipment (having an eight-year life) was undervalued by $54,400 on Jasmine's financial records. A building with a 20-year life was overvalued by $10,000. Subsequent to the acquisition, Jasmine reported the following:

|  | Net Income | Dividends Paid |
|---|---|---|
| 2002 | $50,000 | $10,000 |
| 2003 | 60,000 | 40,000 |
| 2004 | 30,000 | 20,000 |

In accounting for this investment, Tyler has used the equity method. Selected accounts taken from the financial records of these two companies as of December 31, 2004, are as follows:

|  | Tyler Company | Jasmine Company |
|---|---|---|
| Revenues—operating | $310,000 | $104,000 |
| Expenses | 198,000 | 74,000 |
| Equipment (net) | 320,000 | 50,000 |
| Buildings (net) | 220,000 | 68,000 |
| Common stock | 290,000 | 50,000 |
| Retained earnings, 12/31/04 balance | 410,000 | 160,000 |

Determine the following account balances as of December 31, 2004:
a. Investment in Jasmine Company (on Tyler's individual financial records).
b. Equity in Subsidiary Earnings (on Tyler's individual financial records).
c. Consolidated Net Income.
d. Consolidated Equipment (net).
e. Consolidated Buildings (net).
f. Consolidated Goodwill (net).
g. Consolidated Common Stock.
h. Consolidated Retained Earnings, 12/31/04.

33. During 2001, Abbott Corporation issued shares of its common stock for all of the outstanding stock of Drexel, Inc., in a transaction accounted for as a pooling of interests. Drexel's book value was only $120,000 at the time, but Abbott issued 10,000 shares valued at $18 per share. Abbott was willing to convey these shares because it felt that buildings (10-year life) were undervalued on Drexel's records by $40,000 while equipment (5-year life) was undervalued by $20,000.

Following are the individual financial records for these two companies for the year ending December 31, 2004.

|  | Abbott | Drexel |
|---|---|---|
| Revenues | $ 310,000 | $ 90,000 |
| Operating expenses | (220,000) | (60,000) |
| Equity in subsidiary earnings | 30,000 | –0– |
| Net income | $ 120,000 | $ 30,000 |
| Retained earnings, 1/1/04 | $ 640,000 | $ 85,000 |
| Net income | 120,000 | 30,000 |
| Less: Dividends paid | (70,000) | (20,000) |
| Retained earnings, 12/31/04 | $ 690,000 | $ 95,000 |
| Current assets | $ 159,000 | $ 57,000 |
| Investment in Drexel | 155,000 | –0– |
| Buildings (net) | 472,000 | 71,000 |
| Equipment (net) | 404,000 | 107,000 |
| Total assets | $1,190,000 | $235,000 |
| Liabilities | $ 160,000 | $ 80,000 |
| Common stock | 300,000 | 60,000 |
| Additional paid-in capital | 40,000 | –0– |
| Retained earnings, 12/31/04 (above) | 690,000 | 95,000 |
| Total liabilities and equity | $1,190,000 | $235,000 |

a. Without making consolidation entries or setting up a worksheet, determine the consolidated totals for this business combination.
b. Verify the balances determined in part (a) by preparing a worksheet as of December 31, 2004.

34. On January 1, 2003, Picante Corporation purchased 100 percent of the outstanding voting stock of Salsa Corporation for $1,765,000 cash. On the purchase date, Salsa had the following balance sheet:

| | | | |
|---|---:|---|---:|
| Cash | $ 14,000 | Accounts payable | $ 120,000 |
| Accounts receivable | 100,000 | Long-term debt | 930,000 |
| Land | 700,000 | Common stock | 1,000,000 |
| Equipment (net) | 1,886,000 | Retained earnings | 650,000 |
| | $2,700,000 | | $2,700,000 |

At the purchase date, the following cost allocation was prepared:

| | | |
|---|---:|---:|
| Purchase price | | $1,765,000 |
| Book value acquired | | 1,650,000 |
| Excess cost | | 115,000 |
|   To in-process research and development | $44,000 | |
|   To equipment (8-yr. remaining life) | 56,000 | 100,000 |
|   To goodwill (indefinite life) | | $ 15,000 |

The in-process research and development projects had not yet reached technological feasibility, and the assets used in the projects had no alternative future uses.

On December 31, 2004, Picante and Salsa submitted the following trial balances for consolidation:

| | Picante | Salsa |
|---|---:|---:|
| Sales | $ (3,500,000) | $(1,000,000) |
| Cost of goods sold | 1,600,000 | 630,000 |
| Depreciation expense | 540,000 | 160,000 |
| Subsidiary income | (203,000) | –0– |
| Net income | $ (1,563,000) | $ (210,000) |
| Retained earnings 1/1/04 | $ (3,000,000) | $ (800,000) |
| Net income | (1,563,000) | (210,000) |
| Dividends paid | 200,000 | 25,000 |
| Retained earnings 12/31/04 | $ (4,363,000) | $ (985,000) |
| Cash | $ 228,000 | $ 50,000 |
| Accounts receivable | 840,000 | 155,000 |
| Inventory | 900,000 | 580,000 |
| Investment in Salsa | 2,042,000 | –0– |
| Land | 3,500,000 | 700,000 |
| Equipment (net) | 5,000,000 | 1,700,000 |
| Goodwill | 290,000 | –0– |
| Total assets | $ 12,800,000 | $ 3,185,000 |
| Accounts payable | $ (193,000) | $ (400,000) |
| Long-term debt | (3,094,000) | (800,000) |
| Common stock | (5,150,000) | (1,000,000) |
| Retained earnings 12/31/04 | (4,363,000) | (985,000) |
| Total liabilities and equities | $(12,800,000) | $(3,185,000) |

    *a.* Show how Picante derived its December 31, 2004, Investment in Salsa account balance.
    *b.* Prepare a consolidated worksheet for Picante and Salsa as of December 31, 2004.
    *c.* Assume instead that Picante had used the cost method for its Investment in Salsa account and that Picante relies on worksheet adjustments to account for purchased in-process research and development. Prepare the *C entry to convert Picante's January 1, 2004, Retained Earnings balance to a full accrual basis.

35. On January 1, 2004, Prine, Inc., purchased 100 percent of the common stock of Lydia Company for $120,000,000 in cash and stock. Lydia's assets and liabilities equaled their fair values except for its equipment, which was undervalued by $500,000 and had a 10-year remaining life.

Prine specializes in media distribution and viewed its acquisition of Lydia as a strategic move into content ownership and creation. Prine expected both cost and revenue synergies from controlling Lydia's artistic content (a large library of classic movies) and its sports programming specialty video operation. Accordingly, Prine allocated Lydia's assets and liabilities (including $50,000,000 of goodwill) to a newly formed operating segment appropriately designated as a reporting unit.

The market values of the segment's identifiable assets and liabilities through the first year of operations were as follows.

|  | Fair Values | |
|---|---|---|
| Account | 1/1/04 | 12/31/04 |
| Cash | $ 215,000 | $ 109,000 |
| Receivables (net) | 525,000 | 897,000 |
| Movie library (25-year life) | 40,000,000 | 60,000,000 |
| Broadcast licenses (indefinite life) | 15,000,000 | 20,000,000 |
| Equipment (10-year life) | 20,750,000 | 19,000,000 |
| Current liabilities | (490,000) | (650,000) |
| Long-term debt | (6,000,000) | (6,250,000) |

However, Lydia's assets have taken longer than anticipated to produce the expected synergies with Prine's operations. At year-end, Prine reduced its assessment of the Lydia reporting unit's fair value to $110,000,000.

At December 31, 2004, Prine and Lydia submitted the following balances for consolidation:

|  | Prine, Inc. | Lydia Co. |
|---|---|---|
| Revenues | $ (18,000,000) | $(12,000,000) |
| Operating expenses | 10,350,000 | 11,800,000 |
| Equity in Lydia earnings | (150,000) | NA |
| Dividends paid | 300,000 | 80,000 |
| Retained earnings, 1/1/04 | (52,000,000) | (2,000,000) |
| Cash | 260,000 | 109,000 |
| Receivables (net) | 210,000 | 897,000 |
| Investment in Lydia | 120,070,000 | NA |
| Broadcast licenses | 350,000 | 14,014,000 |
| Movie library | 365,000 | 45,000,000 |
| Equipment (net) | 136,000,000 | 17,500,000 |
| Current liabilities | (755,000) | (650,000) |
| Long-term debt | (22,000,000) | (7,250,000) |
| Common stock | (175,000,000) | (67,500,000) |

a. What is the relevant initial test to determine whether goodwill could be impaired?
b. At what amount should Prine record an impairment loss for its Lydia reporting unit for 2004?
c. What is consolidated net income for 2004?
d. What is the December 31, 2004, consolidated balance for goodwill?
e. What is the December 31, 2004, consolidated balance for broadcast licenses?
f. Prepare a consolidated worksheet for Prine and Lydia (Prine's trial balance should first be adjusted for any appropriate impairment loss).

# Develop Your Skills

## FARS RESEARCH CASE

Jonas Tech Corporation recently acquired Innovation+ Company. The combined firm consists of three related business units that will require reporting as operating segments. In connection with the acquisition, Jonas requests your help with the following asset valuation and allocation issues. Support your answers with references to FASB standards as appropriate.

Jonas recognizes several identifiable intangibles from its acquisition of Innovation+. It expresses the desire to have these intangible assets written down to zero in the acquisition period.

The price paid by Jonas for Innovation+ indicates that a large amount was paid for goodwill. However, Jonas worries that any future goodwill impairment may send the wrong signal to its investors about the wisdom of the Innovation+ acquisition. Jonas thus wishes to allocate all the goodwill to one account called *enterprise goodwill*. In this way, Jonas hopes to minimize the possibility of goodwill impairment because a decline in goodwill in one business unit could be offset by an increase in the value of goodwill in another business unit.

### Required:

a. Advise Jonas on the acceptability of its suggested immediate write-off of its identifiable intangibles.
b. Indicate the relevant factors to consider in allocating the cost of identifiable intangibles acquired in a business combination to expense over time.
c. Advise Jonas on the acceptability of its suggested treatment of goodwill.
d. Indicate the relevant factors to consider in allocating goodwill across an enterprise's business units.

## AOL TIME WARNER ANALYSIS CASE

In July 2001, the FASB issued *SFAS 142,* which changed the accounting for goodwill and intangible assets. Upon adoption of *SFAS 142,* many large publicly traded companies recognized large goodwill impairment losses. For example, in 2002 AOL Time Warner recorded a $99 billion reduction in the carrying value of its goodwill—one of the largest goodwill impairments under *SFAS 142*.

Please use the website www.aoltimewarner.com and *SFAS 142* to address the following issues and questions.

### Required:

a. How did AOL determine the initial amount of goodwill to recognize in its merger with Time Warner?
b. How did AOL determine the $99 billion 2002 impairment charge to its goodwill? What procedures will AOL follow in the future to assess the value of its goodwill?
c. What business areas has AOL designated as its reporting units? Why is it important to define the reporting units?
d. What effects does *SFAS 142* have on AOL's earnings performance both in the short term and in the long term?
e. What is the rationale behind the accounting treatment for goodwill (initial recognition and subsequent allocation to income) in *SFAS 142?*

## EXCEL CASE

On January 1, 2003, Q-Net.com purchased 100 percent of the common stock of EZport Co. for $670,000. The purchase price was allocated among EZport's net assets as follows:

| | | |
|---|---:|---:|
| Cost | | $670,000 |
| Book value of EZport | | |
|   Common stock and APIC | $130,000 | |
|   Retained earnings | 370,000 | 500,000 |
| Excess cost over book value | | 170,000 |
|   To land | $ 54,000 | |
|   To in-process R&D | 76,000 | |
|   To equipment (overvalued) | (20,000) | |
|   To customer base | 60,000 | 170,000 |
| | | –0– |

At the acquisition date, the equipment had 4 years of remaining life, and the customer base was estimated to have a 10-year life. The acquired in-process R&D was judged to have no alternative future uses. At December 31, 2004, EZport's Accounts Payable account includes a $30,000 amount owed to Q-Net.

The December 31, 2004, trial balances for the parent and subsidiary follow:

| | | |
|---|---:|---:|
| Revenues | $ (990,000) | $(210,000) |
| Cost of good sold | 500,000 | 90,000 |
| Depreciation expense | 100,000 | 5,000 |
| Amortization expense | 55,000 | –0– |
| Equity in subsidiary earnings | (114,000) | –0– |
| Net income | $ (449,000) | $(115,000) |
| | | |
| Retained earnings 1/1/04 | $(1,555,000) | $(450,000) |
| Net income | (449,000) | (115,000) |
| Dividends paid | 250,000 | 40,000 |
| Retained earnings 12/31/04 | $(1,754,000) | $(525,000) |
| | | |
| Current assets | $ 960,000 | $ 355,000 |
| Investment in EZport | 747,000 | –0– |
| Land | 714,000 | 200,000 |
| Equipment (net) | 763,000 | 270,000 |
| Customer base | –0– | –0– |
| Total assets | $3,184,000 | $ 825,000 |
| | | |
| Liabilities | $ (810,000) | $(170,000) |
| Common stock | (500,000) | (110,000) |
| Additional paid-in capital | (120,000) | (20,000) |
| Retained earnings 12/31/04 | (1,754,000) | (525,000) |
| Total liabilities and equity | $(3,184,000) | $(825,000) |

## Required:

a. Using Excel, prepare the calculations that show how Q-Net derived the $747,000 value for its investment in EZport.
b. Using Excel, compute Q-Net's and EZport's consolidated balances. Either use a worksheet approach or compute the balances directly.

---

## Computer Project

### Alternative Investment Methods, Goodwill Impairment, and Consolidated Financial Statements

In this project you are to provide an analysis of alternative accounting methods for controlling interest investments and subsequent effects on consolidated reporting. The project requires the use of a computer and a spreadsheet software package (Microsoft Excel®, Lotus 123®, etc.). The use of these tools allows assessment of the sensitivity of alternative accounting methods on consolidated financial reporting without the necessity of preparing several similar worksheets by hand. Also, by modeling a worksheet process, a better understanding of accounting for combined reporting entities can result.

#### Consolidated Worksheet Preparation

You will be creating and entering formulas to complete four worksheets. The first objective is to demonstrate the effect of different methods of accounting for the investments (equity, cost, and partial equity) on the parent company's trial balance and on the consolidated worksheet subsequent to acquisition. The second objective is to show the effect on consolidated balances and key financial ratios of recognizing a goodwill impairment loss.

The project requires preparation of the following four separate worksheets:

1. Consolidated information worksheet (provided below).
2. Equity method consolidation worksheet.
3. Cost method consolidation worksheet.
4. Partial equity method consolidation worksheet.

If your spreadsheet package has multiple worksheet capabilities (e.g., Excel), separate worksheets can be used; otherwise, each of the four worksheets can reside in a separate area of a single spreadsheet.

**In formulating your solution, each worksheet should link directly to the first worksheet.** Also, feel free to create supplemental schedules to enhance the capabilities of your worksheet.

### Project Scenario

Pecos Company acquired 100 percent of Suaro's outstanding stock for $1,450,000 cash on January 1, 2002, when Suaro had the following balance sheet:

| Assets | | Liabilities and Equity | |
|---|---|---|---|
| Cash | $ 37,000 | Liabilities | $(422,000) |
| Receivables | 82,000 | | |
| Inventory | 149,000 | Common stock | (350,000) |
| Land | 90,000 | Retained earnings | (126,000) |
| Equipment (net) | 225,000 | | |
| Software | 315,000 | | |
| Total assets | $898,000 | Total liabilities and equity | $(898,000) |

At the purchase date, the fair market values of each identifiable asset and liability that differed from book value were as follows:

| | | |
|---|---|---|
| Land | $ 80,000 | |
| Brand name | 60,000 | (indefinite life—unrecognized on Suaro's books) |
| Software | 415,000 | (2-year estimated useful life) |
| In-Process R&D | 300,000 | (no alternative use for these R&D assets) |

**Additional Information**

- Pecos expects future benefits from the purchased in-process research and development (R&D) of Suaro. However, if the benefits are not realized, there is no alternative use for any of the purchased R&D assets.
- During 2002, Suaro earns $75,000 and pays no dividends.
- Selected amounts from Pecos and Suaro's separate financial statements at December 31, 2003, are presented in the Consolidation Information Worksheet. All consolidated worksheets are to be prepared as of December 31, 2003, two years subsequent to acquisition.
- Pecos' January 1, 2003, Retained Earnings balance—before any effect from Suaro's 2002 income—is $(930,000) (credit balance).
- Pecos has 500,000 common shares outstanding for EPS calculations and reported $2,943,100 for consolidated assets at the beginning of the period.

Following is the consolidation information worksheet.

## Consolidations—Subsequent to the Date of Acquisition

|    | A                              | B              | C            | D    |
|----|--------------------------------|----------------|--------------|------|
| 1  | **December 31, 2003, trial balances** |         |              |      |
| 2  |                                |                |              |      |
| 3  |                                | **Pecos**      | **Suaro**    |      |
| 4  | Revenues                       | ($1,052,000)   | ($427,000)   |      |
| 5  | Operating expenses             | $ 821,000      | $262,000     |      |
| 6  | Goodwill impairment loss       | ?              |              |      |
| 7  | Income of Suaro                | ?              |              |      |
| 8  | Net income                     | ?              | ($165,000)   |      |
| 9  |                                |                |              |      |
| 10 | Retained earnings–Pecos 1/1/03 | ?              |              |      |
| 11 | Retained earnings–Suaro 1/1/03 |                | ($201,000)   |      |
| 12 | Net income (above)             | ?              | ($165,000)   |      |
| 13 | Dividends paid                 | $ 200,000      | $ 35,000     |      |
| 14 | Retained earnings 12/31/03     | ?              | ($331,000)   |      |
| 15 |                                |                |              |      |
| 16 | Cash                           | $ 195,000      | $ 95,000     |      |
| 17 | Receivables                    | $ 247,000      | $143,000     |      |
| 18 | Inventory                      | $ 415,000      | $197,000     |      |
| 19 | Investment in Suaro            | ?              |              |      |
| 20 |                                |                |              |      |
| 21 |                                |                |              |      |
| 22 |                                |                |              |      |
| 23 | Land                           | $ 341,000      | $ 85,000     |      |
| 24 | Equipment (net)                | $ 240,100      | $100,000     |      |
| 25 | Software                       |                | $312,000     |      |
| 26 | Other intangibles              | $ 145,000      |              |      |
| 27 | Goodwill                       |                |              |      |
| 28 | Total assets                   | ?              | $932,000     |      |
| 29 |                                |                |              |      |
| 30 | Liabilities                    | ($1,537,100)   | ($251,000)   |      |
| 31 | Common stock                   | ($ 500,000)    | ($350,000)   |      |
| 32 | Retained earnings (above)      | ?              | ($331,000)   |      |
| 33 | Total liabilities and equity   | ?              | ($932,000)   |      |
| 34 |                                |                |              |      |
| 35 | Cost Allocation Schedule       |                |              |      |
| 36 | Price Paid                     | $1,450,000     |              |      |
| 37 | Book Value                     | $ 476,000      |              |      |
| 38 | Excess Cost                    | $ 974,000      | Amortizations|      |
| 39 | to Land                        | ($ 10,000)     | 2002         | 2003 |
| 40 | to Brand Name                  | $ 60,000       | ?            | ?    |
| 41 | to Software                    | $ 100,000      | ?            | ?    |
| 42 | to IPR&D                       | $ 300,000      | ?            | ?    |
| 43 | to Goodwill                    | $ 524,000      | ?            | ?    |
| 44 |                                |                |              |      |
| 45 | Suaro's RE Changes             | Income         | Dividends    |      |
| 46 | 2002                           | $ 75,000       | $0           |      |
| 47 | 2003                           | $ 165,000      | $ 35,000     |      |

## Project Requirements

Complete the four worksheets as follows:
1. Input the **consolidated information worksheet** provided and complete the cost allocation schedule by computing the excess amortizations for 2002 and 2003.
2. Using separate worksheets, prepare Pecos' trial balances for each of the indicated accounting methods (equity, cost, and partial equity). **Use only formulas for the Investment in Suaro, the Income of Suaro, and Retained Earnings accounts.**
3. **Using references to other cells only (either from the consolidation information worksheet or from the separate method sheets),** prepare for each of the three consolidating worksheets:
   - Adjustments and eliminations
   - Consolidated balances
4. Calculate and present the effects of a 2003 total goodwill impairment loss on the following ratios for the consolidated entity:
   - Earnings per share (EPS)
   - Return on assets
   - Return on equity
   - Debt to equity

Your worksheets should have the capability to adjust immediately for the possibility that all acquisition goodwill can be considered impaired in 2003.

**Prepare a word-processed report that describes and discusses the following worksheet results:**
a. The effects of alternative investment accounting methods on the parent's trial balances and the final consolidation figures.
b. The relation between consolidated retained earnings and the parent's retained earnings under each of the three (equity, cost, partial equity) investment accounting methods.
c. The effect on EPS, return on assets, return on equity, and debt-to-equity ratios of the recognition that all acquisition-related goodwill is considered impaired in 2003.

# Chapter Four

# Consolidated Financial Statements and Outside Ownership

A note to recent financial statements of Merck & Co., Inc., contains the following information:

> The consolidated financial statements include the accounts of the Company and all of its subsidiaries in which a controlling interest is maintained. For those consolidated subsidiaries where Company ownership is less than 100%, the outside stockholders' interests are shown as Minority interests. Investments in affiliates over which the Company has significant influence but not a controlling interest are carried on the equity basis.

Merck includes *all of the financial figures* generated by both its wholly and majority-owned subsidiaries within consolidated financial statements. How does Merck account for the partial ownership interest of the noncontrolling owners of its subsidiaries?

A number of reasons exist for one company to hold less than 100 percent ownership of a subsidiary. The parent could not have had sufficient resources available to obtain all of the outstanding stock. As a second possibility, a few stockholders of the subsidiary could have elected to retain their ownership, perhaps in hopes of getting a better price at a later date.

Lack of total ownership is frequently encountered with foreign subsidiaries. The laws of some countries prohibit outsiders from maintaining complete control of domestic business enterprises. In other areas of the world, a parent can seek to establish better relations with a subsidiary's employees, customers, and local government by maintaining some percentage of native ownership.

### Questions to Consider

- Total ownership is not an absolute requirement for consolidation; a parent need only gain control of another company to create a business combination. If less than 100 percent of a subsidiary's voting stock is obtained, how is the presence of the other owners reflected in consolidated financial statements? What accounting is appropriate for a noncontrolling interest? How are these figures computed and where are they reported on the consolidated statements?

- If a parent holds less than complete ownership, are the subsidiary's assets and liabilities consolidated at 100 percent of their fair market values or should the reported figures be affected by the degree of the parent's ownership?

- If a parent acquires several blocks of a subsidiary's stock over a period of time prior to gaining control, how are the various purchases consolidated?

- How are a subsidiary's revenues and expenses reported on a consolidated income statement when the parent gains control within the current year?

- When a portion, or all, of a subsidiary's stock is sold, how is the resulting gain or loss calculated? By what accounting method are any shares that remain reported?

Regardless of the reason for owning less than 100 percent, the parent consolidates the financial data of every subsidiary where control is present. As discussed in Chapter 2, *complete ownership is not a prerequisite for consolidation.* A single economic entity is formed whenever one company is able to control the decision-making process of another.

Although most parent companies do possess 100 percent ownership of their subsidiaries, a significant number, such as Merck & Co., establish control with a lesser amount of stock. The remaining outside owners are collectively referred to as a *noncontrolling interest* or by the more traditional term *minority interest.* The presence of these other stockholders poses a number of reporting questions for the accountant. Whenever less than 100 percent of a subsidiary's voting stock is held, how should the subsidiary's accounts be valued within consolidated financial statements? How should the presence of these additional owners be acknowledged?

## CONSOLIDATIONS INVOLVING A NONCONTROLLING INTEREST

In any combination in which a noncontrolling interest[1] remains, an intriguing theoretical controversy is created as to (1) the appropriate consolidation values that should be assigned to the subsidiary's accounts and (2) the method of disclosing the presence of the other owners. This debate involves more than a reporting problem; it ultimately concerns the fundamental objectives of consolidated financial statements.

When total ownership exists, the subsidiary's assets and liabilities are always consolidated based on their fair market values at the date of acquisition with any excess cost assigned to goodwill.[2] Since no other owners would exist, disclosure of a noncontrolling interest is not relevant. In contrast, whenever less than 100 percent of a subsidiary is acquired, several different theoretical methods exist to calculate the consolidated values of the acquired accounts. Each of these approaches uses a different technique for reporting the presence of the noncontrolling interest.

As a basis for examining these alternative valuation theories, assume that Small Company possesses net assets as follows:

| | |
|---|---:|
| Book value of net assets | $110,000 |
| Fair market value of identifiable net assets | 130,000 |

In the current year, Big Company purchases 70 percent of the outstanding voting stock of Small for $140,000. Big's willingness to pay this price can be viewed as an indication that Small, taken as a whole, has an implied value of $200,000 ($140,000/70 percent). *The accounting controversy centers on whether the parent's $140,000 cost or the $200,000 implied value of the subsidiary should serve as the valuation basis for subsequently consolidated figures.*[3]

Incorporating the cost figure suggests that consolidated statements are primarily intended as a report of the parent company and the results of its $140,000 investment. Conversely, by utilizing the $200,000 implied value, the emphasis is focused on accounting for Big and Small as two individual components forming a single economic entity.

---

[1] The term *minority interest* has been used almost universally over the decades to identify the presence of other outside owners. However, in the FASB's October 27, 2000, Exposure Draft, *Accounting for Financial Instruments with Characteristics of Liabilities, Equity, or Both,* the term *noncontrolling interest* was applied. Because this term is more descriptive, it is used throughout this textbook.

[2] To avoid unnecessary complexities in analyzing this issue, bargain purchases are not illustrated. In addition, this controversy does not relate to a pooling of interests when accounts are always consolidated at their book values.

[3] In a 100 percent purchase, the implied value of the subsidiary is the parent's purchase price. Thus, only one valuation basis is present and, at least from a mechanical perspective, no problem exists.

# Discussion Question

**HOW DO WE REPORT THIS OTHER OWNER?**

The Hartstone Company was created 15 years ago and presently owns several large retail clothing stores in and around Lakeland, Minnesota. Hartstone's capital stock is held equally by its four founders: Scott Arnold, Janine Bostio, Garrison Cantleberry, and Ingrid Jorgesson.

Until recently, Thomas Warwick was the sole owner of a competing business in the nearby city of Kalshburg. Because Warwick was nearing retirement age, he opted to sell 90 percent of his company (which encompassed only one store) to Hartstone. Because the business had been in Warwick's family for several generations, he wanted to retain 10 percent ownership. Hartstone paid cash for this acquisition. Based on past profitability, the negotiated price for the shares was set to indicate a total value of $2 million, although the current book value of the store was only $1.4 million.

At the end of the current year, the owners of Hartstone must produce consolidated financial statements for the first time. Consequently, they are having a discussion with their accountant concerning the appropriate method of reporting Thomas Warwick's 10 percent interest in the Kalshburg store.

**Scott Arnold:** These statements are designed to represent the Hartstone Company and our assets, liabilities, revenues, and expenses. Warwick owns none of our stock. I see no reason to include any figure at all for him. Readers would naturally assume that he controls a portion of Hartstone; we would be misleading them. He has nothing to do with our company.

**Janine Bostio:** I think you are wrong. Warwick owns 10 percent of one of our stores. He is a partial owner of this asset, and since we are consolidating the entire Kalshburg store, we have to recognize that he has an equity interest. The price indicates a $2,000,000 value; so his ownership should be recognized at $200,000.

**Garrison Cantleberry:** I agree with Scott; the statements are designed to represent Hartstone Company, and Warwick is certainly not a stockholder of Hartstone. However, we do have a legal obligation to him. If we ever liquidate the Kalshburg store, he would be entitled to a portion of the residual. Even now, when the store pays a dividend, he must be paid 10 percent of each distribution. We have an obligation to him that can be properly disclosed only as a liability.

**Ingrid Jorgesson:** I have trouble with recording a liability. I understand that we eventually might have a debt to Warwick, but at this point in time we are under no obligation to him. To me, a possible future claim should not be recorded as an actual liability. However, Warwick has retained a $140,000 investment in one of our assets. That is his cost. Since this amount doesn't seem to be either debt or equity, why don't we record it separately between our liabilities and the stockholders' equity? Anyone reading the statements can add this figure to either balance if desired or simply ignore it entirely.

As the accountant, what recommendation would you make to your clients and why? Should Warwick's interest be recognized? If so, where should the figure be reported and what amount should be disclosed?

Unfortunately, virtually nothing in official accounting pronouncements has ever addressed the issue of valuation theory in combinations involving less than 100 percent ownership. Thus, the positions adopted at present are based on traditional approaches that have evolved over the years. However, this issue continues to be examined by the FASB.[4] This examination might

[4] See FASB, *Business Combinations: Purchase Method Procedures* Project Summary, April 1, 2003.

possibly lead to the issuance of an official standard that requires one theory to be used. However, until that time, companies are free to apply any one of several approaches in reporting the accounts of a subsidiary. The following section presents three of the theories outlined by the FASB.[5]

## The Economic Unit Concept

If the accounting emphasis in preparing consolidated statements is placed on the business combination being formed (rather than on the parent's investment), an approach referred to as the *economic unit concept*[6] (also known as the *entity theory*) is generally endorsed. This concept is founded on the proposition that the subsidiary and especially the subsidiary's individual accounts cannot be divided along ownership lines. A controlled company must always be consolidated as a whole regardless of the parent's level of ownership.

Proponents argue that this concept provides the most consistent perspective of the consolidation process. It also gives the best view of the assets and liabilities that have come under the control of the parent company. If, in the previous illustration, Small owns land with a book value of $8,000 but a fair market value of $10,000, the economic unit concept requires the $10,000 figure to be reported within consolidated statements whether the parent acquires 70 percent, 100 percent, or any other level of control. The owners of Big control all of the resources of both Big and Small despite holding only 70 percent of the subsidiary's voting stock.

Therefore, in accounting for Big's acquisition of Small, the economic unit concept bases consolidated totals on the $200,000 implied value of the subsidiary taken as a whole. All of the subsidiary's assets and liabilities are included at their fair market values with any excess assigned to goodwill. Because the individual market values total only $130,000 but the implied value of the company as a whole equals $200,000, the excess $70,000 is assigned to goodwill.

Because the total value of every asset and liability is attributed to the consolidated entity, the partial ownership held by outside parties must also be acknowledged. *Including 100 percent of the value of a subsidiary's accounts when only 70 percent of the stock is owned creates an imbalance that requires the recognition of a 30 percent noncontrolling interest.* Hence, $60,000 (30 percent of the total implied value being included in the consolidation) is attributed to the other owners of Small.

*Economic Unit Concept*

| | |
|---|---:|
| Implied value of Small ($140,000/70%) | $200,000 |
| Fair market value assigned to Small's accounts | 130,000 |
| Fair market value not assigned to identifiable accounts—goodwill | $ 70,000 |
| Noncontrolling interest (30% of the $200,000 implied value included in consolidated totals) | $ 60,000 |

Although Small's outside owners do not possess an equity interest in the parent company, the $60,000 balance is presented within the consolidated stockholders' equity section when the economic unit concept is in use. This placement is based on the assertion that the two companies should be viewed together as a single entity. The outside parties own a component part of the resulting business combination; thus, their interest is viewed as an equity (or ownership) balance to be reported within the consolidated balance sheet.

After the balance sheet valuations are established for the economic unit concept, a logical extension can be made to the construction of a consolidated income statement. Once again this

---

[5] Variations of each approach presented here do exist. To avoid unnecessary complication, only three of the basic theories are described.

[6] In its April 1, 2003 *Business Combinations: Purchase Method Procedures* Project Summary, the FASB recommends the adoption of the economic unit concept as discussed in this section.

approach recognizes 100 percent of the subsidiary's balances. Its entire income is included. By consolidating every account in total, the fundamental objective of reporting the subsidiary as an indivisible unit within the consolidated entity is being fulfilled. Furthermore, this approach effectively reports the income that is generated by the net assets under the control of the parent company.

Consequently, for Big's acquisition of Small, 100 percent of the subsidiary's revenues and expenses should be included in the consolidated figures. Because only 70 percent of Small is owned by the parent, a 30 percent claim to the subsidiary's earnings must be deducted separately in recognition of the noncontrolling interest. This portion of consolidated net income is viewed as an allocation to these other owners.

In computing the part of consolidated income to be assigned to the noncontrolling interest, a theoretical question arises concerning the impact of any excess amortization incurred in connection with the price paid by the parent. As shown in Chapter 3, expense recognition is necessitated by the allocations made to specific accounts as well as to goodwill. Within the business combination, are these expenses attributed to the parent or to the subsidiary?

A logical extension of the economic unit concept is that each purchase price allocation is perceived as a revaluation of a subsidiary asset or liability to fair market value. Subsequent amortization of these costs, therefore, relates to the subsidiary rather than the parent. Because the expense is viewed as an adjustment to the subsidiary's net income, it affects the computation of the noncontrolling interest's share of these earnings.

For example, what is the noncontrolling interest in the subsidiary's income in the following situation?

| | |
|---|---|
| Portion of subsidiary owned by parent | 90 percent |
| Subsidiary's reported net income | $300,000 |
| Amortization expenses on purchase price allocations | $40,000 |

The economic unit concept presumes that excess amortizations relate to the subsidiary's assets. Thus, the allocation of consolidated income made to the noncontrolling interest is $26,000 (or 10 percent of earnings less excess amortization expenses).

Under the economic unit theory, all consolidated totals (except for noncontrolling interest figures) are identical regardless of the degree of parent ownership. The parent controls the entire decision-making process of the subsidiary whenever control exists. Therefore, the economic unit concept views the subsidiary as an indivisible unit within the business combination. As such, fair market value serves as the basis for consolidating each asset and liability, even though the parent's interest could be significantly below 100 percent control. Any contrived division of the subsidiary accounts is, thus, avoided.

## The Proportionate Consolidation Concept

The *proportionate consolidation concept* presumes that the ultimate objective of consolidated financial statements is to serve as a report to the stockholders of the parent company. These owners are perceived as being primarily interested in an accounting of parent company resources. Returning to the previous illustration, the accounting emphasis is placed on Big's $140,000 investment to acquire a 70 percent interest in Small.

Under proportionate consolidation, the values utilized for consolidation reflect the parent's payment attributed to each asset and liability. Big is paying for these assets, not for the company. Because 70 percent ownership has been acquired, that percentage of every account's fair market value at the date of purchase forms the basis for consolidated figures. If, for example, Small owns land with a book value of $8,000 but a fair market value of $10,000, a $7,000 component of the price (70 percent of fair market value) is said to have been Big's cost incurred in connection with this asset.

Under proportionate consolidation, goodwill of $49,000 is recognized: the amount of the purchase price in excess of the appropriate portion of the net assets' fair market value.

### Proportionate Consolidation Concept

| | |
|---|---:|
| Purchase price | $140,000 |
| Fair market value assigned to Small's accounts ($130,000 × 70%) | 91,000 |
| Cost in excess of fair market value—goodwill | $ 49,000 |
| Noncontrolling interest | –0– |

Although goodwill is computed here as a residual cost element, a more consistent view of proportionate consolidation is that this figure represents 70 percent of the subsidiary's total goodwill. As shown in the previous section, a goodwill figure of $70,000 is appropriate for the subsidiary as a whole (the $200,000 implied value of the company less the $130,000 market value of its net assets). Thus, the portion of this goodwill that is applicable to Big's investment is $49,000 ($70,000 × 70%).

A unique feature of proportionate consolidation is the reporting of the noncontrolling interest; these outside owners are totally ignored in consolidated statements. Proponents of this theory hold that the presence of a noncontrolling interest is irrelevant to the stockholders of the parent company. An outside owner of a subsidiary has no capital invested in the parent company; furthermore, the parent has no legal obligation to this group. Thus, including any type of balance within consolidated financial statements to reflect a noncontrolling interest is viewed as serving no purpose.

Before leaving this discussion of proportionate consolidation, a quick extension of this concept can be made to income statement reporting. Not surprisingly, Big Company includes 70 percent of each of the subsidiary's revenue and expense accounts in the consolidated balances while showing no amount of the income total as associated with the noncontrolling interest. Within the framework of proportionate consolidation, this presentation is consistent. The parent's ownership entitles it to accrue only 70 percent of the subsidiary's income; the remaining 30 percent is applicable to outside owners. Any recording of this 30 percent share of Small's net income has no apparent relevance to the owners of Big Company.

In actual practice, little evidence exists to indicate significant usage of proportionate consolidation. Although omitting any mention of outside stockholders can be appealing, the division of each subsidiary account based on the ownership percentage is hard to justify. The parent has achieved control over all assets and liabilities, not just a 70 percent interest of each. However, this concept has recently gained some support for use in cases where control is present without majority ownership. As discussed in Chapter 2, a parent can effectively control a subsidiary although holding only 50 percent or even less of the outstanding voting stock. Proponents argue that proportionate consolidation would be a better reflection of the relationship between the two companies than the equity method that is currently required.

## The Parent Company Concept

The *parent company concept* is sometimes viewed as a hybrid method because it incorporates a mixture of the assumptions found in the economic unit concept and proportionate consolidation. Two fundamental assertions underlie this approach to consolidation valuation:

1. Holding control of a subsidiary provides the parent with an indivisible interest in that company. This statement is clearly derived from the economic unit concept.
2. Consolidated financial statements are produced primarily for the benefit of parent company stockholders. This idea is, of course, the basic argument used to substantiate proportionate consolidation.

Both of the assertions attributed to the parent company concept appear to have merit. However, as shown in the previous sections, they lead to radically differing sets of consolidated financial statements: one based on the implied value of the entire subsidiary and the other on the cost incurred in a partial acquisition. The parent company approach combines both of these ideas in valuing the consolidated enterprise. The subsidiary's book value and the purchase price paid by the parent are viewed as separate elements that can be accounted for individually within the consolidation process.

The book value of each subsidiary asset and liability is presumed to be indivisible and, therefore, not subject to an artificial allocation because of the specific level of ownership. Conversely, differences between the market value and underlying book value of these same accounts are recognized only because of the purchase price paid by the parent. Thus, if the parent acquires less than 100 percent of the subsidiary's voting stock, allocations attributed to individual accounts at the date of purchase should be based on the resulting ownership percentage. *The subsidiary's book value is consolidated in total along the lines of the economic unit concept whereas any cost in excess of book value is assumed to be a parent company expenditure appropriately allocated as indicated by the proportionate consolidation.*

Returning to Big's acquisition of Small, the appropriate consolidation values to be assigned under the parent company concept are computed as follows.

### Parent Company Concept

| | | |
|---|---:|---:|
| Purchase price | | $140,000 |
| Book value of Small (100%) | $110,000 | |
| Less: Recognition of noncontrolling interest (30%) | (33,000) | (77,000) |
| Cost in excess of underlying book value | | 63,000 |
| Allocation based on fair market value in excess of book value ($130,000 − $110,000) × 70% | | (14,000) |
| Goodwill | | $ 49,000 |

The parent company concept includes the entire book value of each of Small's accounts within the consolidated statements but only 70 percent of the difference between fair market value and book value. Proponents justify this approach by pointing out that the subsidiary's cost figures are not affected by the parent's purchase and, therefore, should be consolidated in total. In contrast, the various allocations result solely from the price paid by the parent in a transaction negotiated to acquire 70 percent ownership. Thus, the investment is assumed to reflect only 70 percent of the change in the value of individual accounts.

As a practical example, Small's land, with an $8,000 cost but a fair market value of $10,000, is consolidated at a $9,400 balance: the entire $8,000 book value plus 70 percent of the $2,000 increase in its worth ($10,000 − $8,000). The subsidiary originally expended $8,000 for this land and the parent has now paid an additional $1,400 within the purchase price as a reflection of this change in value. Thus, to the business combination, the land's cost totals $9,400.

In the valuation schedule presented earlier, a noncontrolling interest of $33,000 is computed on the basis of Small's $110,000 book value rather than on either the fair market value of the net assets or the implied worth of the company taken as a whole. Under the parent company concept, only the book value of the subsidiary's accounts is consolidated in total. Although Big holds just 70 percent ownership, 100 percent of each book value is brought into the consolidation. Consequently, the presence of a noncontrolling interest equivalent to 30 percent of that particular total must also be recognized. The payment made by Big in excess of book value, however, has no impact on the remaining outside owners and is not included in this calculation.

Some amount of disagreement exists among the users of the parent company concept as to the appropriate placement of the noncontrolling interest figure within the consolidated balance sheet. Arguments can be made for showing the balance as either a liability or an equity. However, proponents of this theory are most likely to isolate the noncontrolling interest between liabilities and stockholders' equity.

> The parent company concept views the consolidated financial statements as those of the parent—with the assets, liabilities, revenues, and expenses of the subsidiary merely substituting for the parent's investment on the balance sheet. . . . From that perspective, the noncontrolling (minority) interest is not a liability because the parent does not have a present obligation to pay cash or other assets. Nor does it appear to be owners' equity from a parent company perspective

because the noncontrolling investors in a subsidiary do not have an ownership interest in the subsidiary's parent. . . . Thus, the parent company concept generally reports noncontrolling interest below liabilities but above stockholders' equity in consolidated statements.[7]

Currently, in practice the appropriate placement of a noncontrolling interest balance remains an unresolved question. *Statement of Financial Accounting Concepts No. 6 (SFAC 6)*, "Elements of Financial Statements," issued by the FASB recommends inclusion within equity (par. 254):

> Minority interests in net assets of consolidated subsidiaries do not represent present obligations of the enterprise to pay cash or distribute other assets to minority stockholders. *Rather, those stockholders have ownership or residual interests in components of a consolidated enterprise.* The definitions in this Statement do not, of course, preclude showing minority interests separately from majority interests or preclude emphasizing the interests of majority stockholders for whom consolidated statements are primarily provided. Stock purchase warrants are also sometimes called liabilities but entirely lack the characteristics of liabilities. They also are part of equity [emphasis added].

Consistent with *SFAC 6* reasoning, in its 2000 Exposure Draft *Accounting for Financial Instruments with Characteristics of Liabilities, Equity, or Both,* the FASB recommends the following (par. 226):

> For an entity with one or more less-than-wholly owned subsidiaries, the Board concluded in the Statement that the noncontrolling interest in a consolidated subsidiary should be reported in the consolidated financial statements as equity.

Interestingly, *International Accounting Standard No. 27*, "Consolidated Financial Statements and Accounting for Investments in Subsidiaries," 1989 (par. 33), addresses this same issue as follows: "Minority interests should be presented in the consolidated balance sheet separately from liabilities and parent shareholders' equity." In contrast to *SFAC 6*, this statement rejects the classification of a noncontrolling interest as an equity figure. Placement between the liability and equity sections is recommended in the same manner as used by the parent company concept.

Obviously, disagreement continues to exist as to the appropriate location of this balance sheet item. Today, the placement of a noncontrolling interest continues to vary with the reporting entity. Many companies disclose this figure as a single balance appearing directly after noncurrent liabilities. No accumulated total is provided for liabilities or equities, so that the reader is forced to decide whether the noncontrolling interest should be included in either classification or viewed as an item separate from both. Although this placement is often encountered in practice, no consensus currently exists as to the appropriate classification of this balance. However, if the FASB eventually takes action on consolidation policies and procedures, a specific location for the noncontrolling interest could well be required in the future.

In constructing a consolidated income statement, the parent company theory again demonstrates characteristics applicable to both the economic unit concept and proportionate consolidation. As with the economic unit concept, the book values of the various subsidiary accounts are included in the total. Since these revenues and expenses are consolidated at 100 percent of their recorded balances, a 30 percent share of the subsidiary's net income is identified with the noncontrolling interest.

However, similar to proportionate consolidation, excess amortization is associated solely with the parent's investment because the allocations that create the expense result from the original payment. Consequently, such amortizations do not affect the calculation of noncontrolling interest. The additional cost is presumed to be that of the parent company and, thus, the expense is not directly related to the subsidiary's operations. For reporting purposes, the subsidiary's income is simply multiplied times the outside ownership percentage.

---

[7] FASB Discussion Memorandum, *An Analysis of Issues Related to Consolidation Policy and Procedures,* September 10, 1991, pars. 69 and 70.

# Discussion Question

## WHAT DECISION SHOULD THE FASB MAKE?

Whenever the FASB is studying an accounting issue, the Board always seems to get plenty of advice. In response to its discussion memorandum, "An Analysis of Issues Related to Consolidation Policy and Procedures," the FASB received more than 70 letters. A sampling of these letters includes the following recommendations.

**M. R. Schools, Jr., Virginia Power:** Virginia Power believes that accounting information prepared under the proportionate consolidation approach provides the most relevant accounting information because it includes the interests of only the parent company shareholders.

**David K. Owens, Edison Electric Institute:** We generally support the "Parent Company Concept" because it emphasizes the interests of the parent shareholders and is most consistent with current practice.

**Richard G. Rademacher, Sara Lee Corporation:** By purchasing a controlling interest in an entity, management obtains the control of 100 percent of all assets and liabilities. It does not control only a proportionate share of each asset (i.e., 70% of a building) and the value of an asset recorded in consolidation does not vary dependent upon the percentage of ownership obtained. Therefore, we strongly oppose the parent company and proportionate share concepts of consolidation.

**J. Michael Kelly, GTE Corporation:** GTE has consistently responded in support of the parent company concept. The thrust of our support stems from this concept's emphasis on the interests of the parent's shareholders.

**P. J. Lynch, Texaco Inc.:** It is Texaco's view that neither the economic unit nor the parent company concept can be applied exclusively to all the issues raised in the DM. Accordingly any future promulgation concerning consolidation policy should be a hybrid of the two concepts.

**Joseph J. Martin, IBM:** While we take a parent's view of deciding when to consolidate, we generally favor an economic unit theory approach on the mechanics of consolidation and financial statement presentation.

**John J. Mesloh, Pfizer Inc.:** You may note that we favor the Parent Company view (which is consistent with our view of current written GAAP) of consolidation, as identified by the FASB. In short, we do not have too many issues with the current state of consolidation accounting.

What should the FASB decide to do?

---

Under the parent company concept, the resulting noncontrolling interest figure has traditionally appeared as a reduction in arriving at consolidated net income. For example, following is the bottom portion of a typical income statement as reported by Sears, Roebuck and Co.:

**SEARS, ROEBUCK AND CO.**
Year Ended December 31, 2001
(in millions)

| | |
|---|---:|
| Income before income taxes and minority interests | $1,223 |
| Income taxes | 467 |
| Minority interests | 21 |
| Net income | $ 735 |

As mentioned earlier, the FASB is currently studying valuation theories with the possibility that one concept can be mandated. Until that time, companies are free to select any approach and are not even required to disclose their choice. Although evidence is not readily available, the parent company concept is generally considered to be most commonly used in current practice. Therefore, except when noted, that concept is used throughout the remainder of this textbook. Knowledge of the alternatives is important, though; companies do apply these other approaches and their use can be promoted or required by the FASB in the future.

## VALUATION THEORIES—OVERVIEW

To provide a complete illustration of these three concepts, assume that Anderson Company acquires 60 percent of the voting stock of Zebulon Company on January 1, 2004. Anderson purchases this interest for $360,000 in cash at a time when Zebulon's assets and liabilities have the following values:

|  | Book Value 1/1/04 | Fair Market Value 1/1/04 |
|---|---|---|
| Current assets less liabilities | $160,000 | $160,000 |
| Buildings and equipment (10-year life) | 240,000 | 360,000 |
|  | $400,000 | $520,000 |

Because Anderson's $360,000 payment was made to acquire 60 percent interest, Zebulon is apparently worth $600,000 when taken as a whole ($360,000/60 percent). In comparison to the $520,000 appraised value of the net assets, this implied value signifies *total* goodwill associated with Zebulon of $80,000.

Exhibit 4–1 presents alternative values that can be attributed to Zebulon's accounts on consolidated statements produced as of the date of acquisition. Quite obviously, differing figures are derived from each of the three valuation theories. The economic unit concept makes no division of any balance, whereas proportionate consolidation includes only 60 percent of subsidiary accounts because that portion represents the parent's ownership. The parent company concept adopts a compromise position: The book values of the subsidiary's assets and liabilities remain intact while all cost allocations (based on the difference in book values and fair market values) are computed using the parent's ownership percentage.

To carry this illustration to a natural conclusion, assume that Zebulon reports the following condensed income statement for the year of 2004:

| Revenues | $400,000 |
|---|---|
| Expenses | 300,000 |
| Net income | $100,000 |

These balances permit an examination of the totals to be included in the 2004 consolidated income statement. Exhibit 4–2 presents these figures, once again computed under each of the three theories described in this chapter. The economic unit concept consolidates all accounts and assumes that amortization expense relates to the subsidiary. Proportionate consolidation includes only 60 percent of each revenue and expense and discloses no balance for the noncontrolling interest. The parent company concept recognizes all of the subsidiary's income statement accounts but attributes amortization to the parent so that the noncontrolling interest is not affected.

## CONSOLIDATIONS INVOLVING A NONCONTROLLING INTEREST—SUBSEQUENT TO ACQUISITION

Having reviewed the basic philosophies of each of these three theories, this textbook now concentrates on the mechanical aspects of the consolidation process when an outside ownership is present. More specifically, consolidations for time periods subsequent to the date of acquisition are examined to analyze the full range of accounting complexities created by a noncontrolling interest. As indicated previously, this discussion centers on the parent company concept because it appears to be the most prevalent method in practice.

## EXHIBIT 4–1 Valuation Theories in Practice—Balance Sheet

**ANDERSON COMPANY AND ZEBULON COMPANY**
Subsidiary Consolidation Figures
Balance Sheet
January 1, 2004

|  | Economic Unit Concept | Proportionate Consolidation Concept | Parent Company Concept |
|---|---|---|---|
| Current assets and liabilities: |  |  |  |
| Book value | $160,000 (100%) | $ 96,000 (60%) | $160,000 (100%) |
| Allocation based on fair market value | –0– | –0– | –0– |
| Consolidated value | $160,000 | $ 96,000 | $160,000 |
| Buildings and equipment: |  |  |  |
| Book value | $240,000 (100%) | $144,000 (60%) | $240,000 (100%) |
| Allocation based on fair market value | 120,000 (100%) | 72,000 (60%) | 72,000 (60%) |
| Consolidated value | $360,000 | $216,000 | $312,000 |
| Goodwill* | $ 80,000 (100%) | $ 48,000 (60%) | $ 48,000 (60%) |
| Noncontrolling interest, 1/1/04 | $240,000 (40% of implied value)* | –0– | $160,000 (40% of book value) |
| Annual amortizations of allocations: |  |  |  |
| Buildings and equipment (10-year life) | $ 12,000 | $ 7,200 | $ 7,200 |
| Goodwill (indefinite life) | –0– | –0– | –0– |
| Annual expense | $ 12,000 | $ 7,200 | $ 7,200 |

*Implied value of company is $600,000 ($360,000/60%) with the value of net assets only $520,000. Total goodwill is $80,000 ($600,000 − $520,000).

## EXHIBIT 4–2 Valuation Theories in Practice—Income Statement

**ANDERSON COMPANY AND ZEBULON COMPANY**
Subsidiary Consolidation Figures
Income Statement
For Year Ending December 31, 2004

|  | Economic Unit Concept | Proportionate Consolidation Concept | Parent Company Concept |
|---|---|---|---|
| Revenues | $400,000 (100%) | $240,000 (60%) | $400,000 (100%) |
| Expenses | 300,000 (100%) | 180,000 (60%) | 300,000 (100%) |
| Excess amortization expenses (see Exhibit 4–1) | 12,000 | 7,200 | 7,200 |
| Noncontrolling interest in subsidiary's net income |  |  | 40,000 (40% of subsidiary income, no amortization) |
| Net effect on consolidated income | $ 88,000 | $ 52,800 | $ 52,800 |
| Allocation of income: |  |  |  |
| To controlling interest (60%) | $ 52,800 |  |  |
| To noncontrolling interest (40%) | $ 35,200 |  |  |

The presence of a noncontrolling interest does not dramatically alter the consolidation procedures demonstrated in Chapter 3. The unamortized balance of each purchase price allocation (as well as any goodwill or deferred credit) must still be computed and included within the consolidated totals. Excess amortization expenses are recognized each year on these allocations as appropriate. Reciprocal balances are eliminated.

Beyond these basic steps, the valuation and recognition of four noncontrolling interest balances add a new dimension to the process of consolidating financial information. The accountant must determine and then enter each of these figures when constructing a worksheet:

- Noncontrolling interest in the subsidiary as of the beginning of the current year.
- Noncontrolling interest in the subsidiary's current year income.
- Noncontrolling interest in the subsidiary's dividend payments.
- Noncontrolling interest as of the end of the year (found by combining the three balances above).

To illustrate, assume that King Company acquires 80 percent of the outstanding stock of Pawn Company on January 1, 2004, for $960,000 in cash. The combination is to be accounted for as a purchase. King makes an additional $20,000 payment to lawyers, accountants, and appraisers to cover the direct costs associated with this acquisition. Exhibit 4–3 presents the book value of Pawn's accounts as well as the fair market value of each asset and liability on the date of purchase.

Including direct consolidation costs, King's payment totals $980,000. This purchase price is attributed to Pawn's accounts as shown in Exhibit 4–4. Annual amortization relating to these allocations also is included in this schedule. Although expense figures are computed for only the initial years, some amount of amortization is recognized in each of the 20 years following the acquisition (since that life is assumed for the buildings).

Assume that consolidated financial statements are to be produced for the year ending December 31, 2005. This date was chosen arbitrarily. Any time period subsequent to 2004 could have served to demonstrate the applicable consolidation procedures. Having already calculated the purchase price allocations and related amortization, the consolidation of these two companies can be constructed along the lines demonstrated in Chapter 3. Only the presence of the 20 percent noncontrolling interest alters the previously explained process.

To complete the information needed for this combination, assume that Pawn Company reports the following changes in book value since King's acquisition.

| | |
|---|---:|
| Current year (2005) | |
| Net income | $ 90,000 |
| Less: Dividends paid | (50,000) |
| Increase in book value | $ 40,000 |
| Prior years (only 2004 in this illustration): | |
| Increase in book value | $ 70,000 |

**EXHIBIT 4–3**
Subsidiary Accounts—Date of Acquisition

**PAWN COMPANY**
**Account Balances**
**January 1, 2004**

| | Book Value | Fair Market Value | Differences |
|---|---:|---:|---:|
| Current assets | $ 440,000 | $ 440,000 | –0– |
| Land | 260,000 | 320,000 | +$ 60,000 |
| Buildings (20-year life) | 480,000 | 600,000 | + 120,000 |
| Equipment (10-year life) | 110,000 | 100,000 | (10,000) |
| Long-term liabilities (8-year maturity) | (550,000) | (510,000) | + 40,000 |
| Net assets | $ 740,000 | $ 950,000 | +$210,000 |
| Common stock | $(230,000) | | |
| Retained earnings, 1/1/04 | (510,000) | | |

Note: Parentheses indicate a credit balance.

Assuming that King Company has applied the equity method, the Investment in Pawn Company account as of December 31, 2005, can be constructed as shown in Exhibit 4–5.

Exhibit 4–6 presents the separate financial statements for these two companies as of December 31, 2005, and the year then ended based on the information provided.

### Consolidated Totals

Although the inclusion of a 20 percent outside ownership complicates the consolidation process, the 2005 totals to be reported by this business combination can still be determined without the use of a worksheet:

**EXHIBIT 4–4**

**KING COMPANY AND PAWN COMPANY**
Purchase Price Allocation and Amortization
January 1, 2004

|  | Allocation | Estimated Life (years) | Annual Excess Amortizations |
|---|---|---|---|
| Purchase price paid by King Company | $980,000 | | |
| 80% of subsidiary book value ($740,000) (King Company's ownership)* | 592,000 | | |
| Cost in excess of book value | 388,000 | | |
| Allocation to specific accounts based on difference between fair market value and book value: | | | |
| Land ($60,000 × 80%) | 48,000 | | |
| Buildings ($120,000 × 80%) | 96,000 | 20 | 4,800 |
| Equipment ($10,000 × 80%) | (8,000) | 10 | (800) |
| Long-term liabilities ($40,000 × 80%) | 32,000 | 8 | 4,000 |
| Goodwill | $220,000 | Indefinite | –0– |
| Annual amortizations (initial years) | | | $8,000 |

*The parent company concept consolidates 100 percent of all asset and liability book values but also records an offsetting noncontrolling interest of 20 percent. The net effect is equal to 80 percent of the subsidiary's book value.

**EXHIBIT 4–5**

**KING COMPANY**
Investment in Pawn Company
Equity Method
December 31, 2005

| | | |
|---|---|---|
| Purchase price | | $ 980,000 |
| Prior year (2004): | | |
|   Increase in book value (80% × $70,000) | $ 56,000 | |
|   Excess amortization expenses (Exhibit 4–4) | (8,000) | 48,000 |
| Current year (2005): | | |
|   Income accrual (80% × $90,000) | 72,000 | |
|   Excess amortization expense (Exhibit 4–4) | (8,000) | |
|   Equity in subsidiary earnings | 64,000* | |
|   Dividends received (80% × $50,000) | (40,000) | 24,000 |
| Balance, 12/31/05 | | $1,052,000 |

*This figure appears in King's 2005 income statement.

## EXHIBIT 4–6

**KING COMPANY AND PAWN COMPANY**
Separate Financial Statements
For December 31, 2005 and the Year Then Ended

|  | King | Pawn |
|---|---:|---:|
| Revenues | $ 910,000 | $ 430,000 |
| Cost of goods sold | (350,000) | (200,000) |
| Depreciation expense | (160,000) | (95,000) |
| Interest expense | (70,000) | (45,000) |
| Equity in subsidiary earnings (see Exhibit 4–5) | 64,000 | –0– |
| Net income | $ 394,000 | $ 90,000 |
| | | |
| Retained earnings, 1/1/05 | $ 881,600 | $ 580,000 |
| Net income (above) | 394,000 | 90,000 |
| Dividends paid | (60,000) | (50,000) |
| Retained earnings, 12/31/05 | $1,215,600 | $ 620,000 |
| | | |
| Current assets | $ 626,000 | $ 445,000 |
| Land | 298,000 | 295,000 |
| Buildings (net) | 880,000 | 540,000 |
| Equipment (net) | 290,000 | 160,000 |
| Investment in Pawn Company (see Exhibit 4–5) | 1,052,000 | –0– |
| Total assets | $3,146,000 | $1,440,000 |
| | | |
| Long-term liabilities | $1,080,400 | $ 590,000 |
| Common stock | 850,000 | 230,000 |
| Retained earnings, 12/31/05 | 1,215,600 | 620,000 |
| Total liabilities and equities | $3,146,000 | $1,440,000 |

- *Revenues* = $1,340,000. The revenues of the parent and the subsidiary are added together. Under the parent company concept, the subsidiary's book value is included in total although only 80 percent of the stock is owned by King.
- *Cost of Goods Sold* = $550,000. The cost of goods sold of the parent and subsidiary are added together.
- *Depreciation Expense* = $259,000. The depreciation expenses of the parent and subsidiary are added together along with the $4,800 additional building depreciation and the $800 reduction in equipment depreciation as indicated in Exhibit 4–4.
- *Interest Expense* = $119,000. The interest expenses of the parent and subsidiary are added along with an additional $4,000. As indicated in Exhibit 4–4, a reduction to market value of Pawn's long-term debt accounted for $32,000 of the excess purchase price. Because the maturity value remains constant, the $32,000 represents a discount that is amortized to interest expense over the remaining eight-year life of the debt.
- *Equity in Subsidiary Earnings* = –0–. The investment income recorded by the parent is eliminated so that the subsidiary's revenues and expenses can be included in the consolidated totals.
- *Noncontrolling Interest in Subsidiary's Income* = $18,000. The outside owners are assigned 20 percent of Pawn's reported income of $90,000. According to the parent company concept, that amount is shown as a reduction within the consolidated income statement.
- *Net Income* = $394,000. Both consolidated expenses and the amount allocated to the noncontrolling interest are subtracted from consolidated revenues.
- *Retained Earnings, 1/1/05* = $881,600. The parent company figure equals the consolidated total since the equity method was applied. If the cost method or the partial equity method

had been used, the parent's balance would require adjustment to include any omitted figures.

- *Dividends Paid* = $60,000. Only the parent company balance is reported. Part of the subsidiary's payments (80 percent) were intercompany to the parent and are eliminated. The remaining distribution was made to the outside owners and serves to reduce the balance attributed to them.
- *Retained Earnings, 12/31/05* = $1,215,600. Balance is found by adding consolidated net income to the beginning Retained Earnings balance and then subtracting the consolidated dividends paid. Because the equity method is utilized, the parent company figure reflects the total for the business combination.
- *Current Assets* = $1,071,000. The parent's book value is added to the subsidiary's book value.
- *Land* = $641,000. The parent's book value is added to the subsidiary's book value plus the $48,000 allocation within the purchase price (see Exhibit 4–4).
- *Buildings* = $1,506,400. The parent's book value is added to the subsidiary's book value plus the $96,000 allocation within the purchase price less 2004 and 2005 excess amortization of $4,800 per year (see Exhibit 4–4).
- *Equipment* = $443,600. The parent's book value is added to the subsidiary's book value less the $8,000 cost reduction allocation plus the 2004 and 2005 expense reduction of $800 per year (see Exhibit 4–4).
- *Investment in Pawn Company* = –0–. The balance reported by the parent is eliminated so that the subsidiary's assets and liabilities can be included in the consolidated totals.
- *Goodwill* = $220,000. The original allocation shown in Exhibit 4–4 is reported.
- *Total assets* = $3,882,000. This balance is a summation of the consolidated assets.
- *Long-Term Liabilities* = $1,646,400. The parent's book value is added to the subsidiary's book value less the $32,000 allocation within the purchase price plus 2004 and 2005 amortization of $4,000 per year (see Exhibit 4–4).
- *Noncontrolling Interest in Subsidiary* = $170,000. The outside ownership is 20 percent of the subsidiary's year-end book value (common stock plus ending retained earnings) of $850,000. This $170,000 total can also be calculated as follows:

| | |
|---|---:|
| Noncontrolling interest at 1/1/05 (20 percent of $810,000 beginning book value—common stock plus 1/1/05 retained earnings) | $162,000 |
| Noncontrolling interest in subsidiary's income (computed above) | 18,000 |
| Dividends paid to noncontrolling interest (20 percent of $50,000 total) | (10,000) |
| Noncontrolling interest at 12/31/05 | $170,000 |

- *Common Stock* = $850,000. Only the parent's book value is reported since this combination is a purchase.
- *Retained Earnings, 12/31/05* = $1,215,600. Computed above.
- *Total Liabilities and Equities* = $3,882,000. This total is a summation of consolidated liabilities, noncontrolling interest, and equities.

### Worksheet Process

The consolidated totals for King and Pawn also can be determined by means of a worksheet as shown in Exhibit 4–7. A comparison of the worksheet entries made in this example with the entries incorporated in Chapter 3 (Exhibit 3–7) indicates that the presence of a noncontrolling interest does not create a significant number of changes in the consolidation procedures.

The worksheet still includes elimination of the subsidiary's stockholders' equity accounts (Entry **S**) although, as explained next, this entry is expanded to record the beginning noncontrolling interest for the year. The second worksheet entry recognizes the purchase price allocations at January 1 after one year of amortization (Entry **A**). Intercompany income as well as dividend payments are removed also (Entries **I** and **D**), while current year excess amortization

**EXHIBIT 4–7** Noncontrolling Interest Illustrated

*Consolidation: Purchase Method*
*Investment: Equity Method*

### KING COMPANY AND PAWN COMPANY
### Consolidation Worksheet
### For Year Ending December 31, 2005

Ownership: 80%

| Accounts | King Company* | Pawn Company* | Consolidation Entries Debit | Consolidation Entries Credit | Noncontrolling Interest | Consolidated Totals |
|---|---|---|---|---|---|---|
| **Income Statement** | | | | | | |
| Revenues | (910,000) | (430,000) | | | | (1,340,000) |
| Cost of goods sold | 350,000 | 200,000 | | | | 550,000 |
| Depreciation expense | 160,000 | 95,000 | (E) 4,000 | | | 259,000 |
| Interest expense | 70,000 | 45,000 | (E) 4,000 | | | 119,000 |
| Equity in subsidiary earnings | (64,000) | –0– | (I) 64,000 | | | –0– |
| Noncontrolling interest in Pawn Company's income | –0– | –0– | | | (18,000) | 18,000 |
| Net income | (394,000) | (90,000) | | | | (394,000) |
| **Statement of Retained Earnings** | | | | | | |
| Retained earnings, 1/1/05: | | | | | | |
| King Company | (881,600) | | | | | (881,600) |
| Pawn Company | | (580,000) | (S) 580,000 | | | –0– |
| Net income (above) | (394,000) | (90,000) | | | | (394,000) |
| Dividends paid | 60,000 | 50,000 | | (D) 40,000 | 10,000 | 60,000 |
| Retained earnings, 12/31/05 | (1,215,600) | (620,000) | | | | (1,215,600) |

*continued from page 164*

**Balance Sheet**

| | | | | | |
|---|---:|---:|---:|---:|---:|
| Current assets | 626,000 | 445,000 | | | 1,071,000 |
| Land | 298,000 | 295,000 | (A) 48,000 | | 641,000 |
| Buildings (net) | 880,000 | 540,000 | (A) 91,200 | (E) 4,800 | 1,506,400 |
| Equipment (net) | 290,000 | 160,000 | (E) 800 | (A) 7,200 | 443,600 |
| Investment in Pawn Company | 1,052,000 | –0– | (D) 40,000 | (S) 648,000 | –0– |
| | | | | (A) 380,000 | |
| | | | | (I) 64,000 | |
| Goodwill | –0– | –0– | (A) 220,000 | | 220,000 |
| Total assets | 3,146,000 | 1,440,000 | | | 3,882,000 |
| Long-term liabilities | (1,080,400) | (590,000) | (A) 28,000 | (E) 4,000 | (1,646,400) |
| Noncontrolling interest in Pawn Company, 1/1/05 | –0– | –0– | | (S) 162,000 | |
| | | | | (162,000) | |
| Noncontrolling interest in Pawn Company, 12/31/05 | –0– | –0– | | | (170,000) |
| | | | | (170,000) | |
| Common stock | (850,000) | (230,000) | (S) 230,000 | | (850,000) |
| Retained earnings, 12/31/05 (above) | (1,215,600) | (620,000) | | | (1,215,600) |
| Total liabilities and equities | (3,146,000) | (1,440,000) | | | (3,882,000) |

*See Exhibit 4–6.
Note : Parentheses indicate a credit balance.
Consolidation entries:
(S) Elimination of subsidiary's stockholders' equity accounts along with recognition of January 1, 2005, noncontrolling interest.
(A) Allocation of parent's cost in excess of subsidiary's book value, unamortized balances as of January 1, 2005.
(I) Elimination of intercompany income (equity accrual less amortization expenses).
(D) Elimination of intercompany dividend payments.
(E) Recognition of amortization expenses on purchase price allocations.

expenses are recognized (Entry **E**). The differences that can be cited with illustrations in the previous chapter relate exclusively to the recognition of four noncontrolling interest balances. In addition, *a separate Noncontrolling Interest column is added to the worksheet to accumulate the components that form the year-end figure to be reported on the consolidated balance sheet.*

***Noncontrolling Interest—Beginning of Year*** As discussed previously, Pawn's stockholders' equity accounts (common stock and beginning Retained Earnings) indicate a January 1, 2005, book value of $810,000. Thus, the 20 percent outside ownership is valued at $162,000 ($810,000 × 20 percent) as of the first day of the current year. This balance is recognized on the worksheet by means of Entry **S**:

***Consolidation Entry S***

| | | |
|---|---:|---:|
| Common Stock (Pawn) | 230,000 | |
| Retained Earnings, 1/1/05 (Pawn) | 580,000 | |
|     Investment in Pawn Company (80%) | | 648,000 |
|     Noncontrolling Interest in Pawn Company, 1/1/05 (20%) | | 162,000 |
| To eliminate beginning stockholders' equity accounts of subsidiary along with book value portion of investment (equal to 80 percent ownership). Noncontrolling interest of 20 percent is also recognized. | | |

The $162,000 balance assigned here to the outside owners at the beginning of the year is extended on the worksheet into the Noncontrolling Interest column (see Exhibit 4–7).

***Noncontrolling Interest—Current Year Income*** Exhibit 4–2 indicates that the parent company concept calculates the noncontrolling interest's share of current year earnings based on the subsidiary's income without regard for amortization. Thus, Pawn's 2005 earnings of $90,000 necessitate an assignment of $18,000 (20 percent) to the outside owners. This figure is shown as a reduction in arriving at consolidated net income. In effect, 100 percent of each subsidiary revenue and expense account is consolidated with an accompanying 20 percent decrease to reflect the presence of the noncontrolling interest. The 80 percent net effect corresponds to King's ownership.

Because this $18,000 portion of consolidated income is viewed as accruing to the noncontrolling interest, an increase is necessary in the $162,000 beginning balance assigned (in Entry **S**) to these outside owners. The amount attributed to the noncontrolling interest is raised because the subsidiary generated a profit during the period.

Although this allocation could be recorded on the worksheet through an additional entry, the $18,000 is usually shown, as in Exhibit 4–7, by means of a columnar adjustment. The current year accrual is simultaneously entered in the consolidated Income Statement column as a *reduction* and in the Noncontrolling Interest column as an *increase.* This procedure indicates that a portion of the earnings included in the consolidated figures must be assigned to the outside owners rather than to the business combination.

***Noncontrolling Interest—Dividend Payments*** The $40,000 dividend that went to the parent company is eliminated routinely through Entry **D,** but the remainder of Pawn's dividend was paid to the noncontrolling interest. The impact of the dividend (20 percent of the subsidiary's total payment) distributed to the other owners must be acknowledged. As shown in Exhibit 4–7, this remaining $10,000 is extended directly into the Noncontrolling Interest column on the worksheet as a reduction. It represents the drop in the underlying book value of the outside ownership that resulted from the subsidiary's asset distribution.

***Noncontrolling Interest—End of Year*** The ending assignment for these other owners is calculated by a summation of:

1. The beginning balance for the year ($162,000).
2. Plus the appropriate share of the subsidiary's current income ($18,000).
3. Less the dividends paid to the outside owners ($10,000).

The Noncontrolling Interest column on the worksheet in Exhibit 4–7 accumulates these figures. The $170,000 total is then transferred to the balance sheet where it appears in the consolidated statements.

### Consolidated Financial Statements

Having successfully consolidated the information for King and Pawn, the resulting financial statements for these two companies is produced in Exhibit 4–8. These figures can be computed directly or can be taken from the consolidation worksheet.

## Effects Created by Alternative Investment Methods

One final aspect of the accounting for a noncontrolling interest needs to be explored. In the King and Pawn illustration, the equity method was utilized by the parent, with all worksheet entries based on that approach. As discussed in Chapter 3, had King incorporated either the cost method or the partial equity method, a few specific changes in the consolidation process would be required although the reported figures are not affected.

### Cost Method

As in Chapter 3, two balances are omitted by the parent if the cost method is applied. First, dividend income is recognized rather than an equity income accrual. Thus, the parent fails to accrue the percentage of the subsidiary's income earned in past years in excess of dividends (the increase in book value). Second, amortization expense is not recorded under the cost method and must also be included in the consolidation process if proper totals are to be achieved. Because neither of these figures is recognized in applying the cost method, an Entry *C is added to the worksheet to convert the previously recorded balances to the equity method. The parent's beginning Retained Earnings is affected by this adjustment as well as the Investment in Subsidiary account. The exact amount is computed as follows.

*Conversion to Equity Method from Cost Method (Entry *C)* Combine:

1. The increase (since acquisition) in the subsidiary's book value during past years (income less dividends) times the parent's ownership percentage.
2. Total amortization expense for these same past years.

One other procedural change is required when the cost method is in use. Since no equity income accrual is recognized, only dividends received from the subsidiary are recorded by the parent as income. Entry **I** is used on the worksheet to remove this intercompany income. Because the dividends are eliminated in this manner, no Entry **D** is required.

### Partial Equity Method

Again, an Entry *C is needed to convert the parent's retained earnings as of January 1 to the equity method. In this case, however, only the amortization expense for the prior years must be included. Under the partial equity method, the income accrual is appropriately recognized each period by the parent company so that no further adjustment is necessary.

# STEP ACQUISITIONS

Marriott International, Inc., reported in its recent annual financial statements that:

> we increased our ownership interest in The Ritz-Carlton Hotel Company LLC, a luxury hotel brand and management company, to 99 percent from 49 percent. We expect to acquire the remaining one percent of this company within the next several years.

**EXHIBIT 4–8**
Consolidated Statements with Noncontrolling Interest

**KING COMPANY AND PAWN COMPANY**
Consolidated Financial Statements
Income Statement for December 31, 2005 and the Year Then Ended

| | |
|---|---:|
| Revenues | $1,340,000 |
| Cost of goods sold | (550,000) |
| Depreciation expense | (259,000) |
| Interest expense | (119,000) |
| Noncontrolling interest in subsidiary income | (18,000) |
| Consolidated net income | $ 394,000 |
| **Statement of Retained Earnings** | |
| Retained earnings, January 1, 2005 | $ 881,600 |
| Consolidated net income | 394,000 |
| Less: Dividends paid | (60,000) |
| Retained earnings, December 31, 2005 | $1,215,600 |
| **Balance Sheet** | |
| *Assets* | |
| Current assets | $1,071,000 |
| Land | 641,000 |
| Buildings (net) | 1,506,400 |
| Equipment (net) | 443,600 |
| Goodwill | 220,000 |
| Total assets | $3,882,000 |
| *Liabilities and Equities* | |
| Long-term liabilities | $1,646,400 |
| Noncontrolling interest in subsidiary | 170,000 |
| Common stock—King Company | 850,000 |
| Retained earnings | 1,215,600 |
| Total liabilities and equities | $3,882,000 |

In all previous consolidation illustrations, control over a subsidiary was assumed to have been achieved through a single transaction. Obviously, Marriott International's takeover of Ritz-Carlton Hotel Co. shows that a combination also can be the result of a series of stock purchases. These step acquisitions further complicate the consolidation process. The financial information of the separate companies must still be brought together, but no single purchase price exists. How do the initial acquisitions affect this process?

> If a parent-subsidiary relationship is established in a step acquisition, a problem arises that does not exist if the parent-subsidiary relationship is established in a single transaction. *That problem is how to include in consolidated financial statements the portion of the parent's interest in the subsidiary that was purchased prior to the date the parent-subsidiary relationship is established* [emphasis added].[8]

For example, in consolidating the accounts of Ritz-Carlton Hotel, the values to be reported could vary significantly depending on Marriott's handling of the 49 percent ownership that it held prior to gaining control.

## Step Acquisitions—Parent Company Concept

Under the parent company concept, each investment is viewed as an individual purchase (sometimes referred to as a *layer*) with its own cost allocations and related amortization. To illustrate, assume that Art Company purchases 30 percent of Zip Company on January 1, 2003,

---

[8] FASB, *An Analysis of Issues Related to Consolidation Policy and Procedures*, par. 289. The FASB's Project Summary *Business Combinations: Purchase Method Procedures*, April 1, 2003 also addresses the issue of step acquisitions.

**EXHIBIT 4–9**
Allocation of First Purchase

**ART COMPANY AND ZIP COMPANY**
Purchase Price Allocation and Amortization
January 1, 2003

| | |
|---|---:|
| Purchase price | $164,000 |
| Book value equivalent of Art's ownership ($400,000 × 30%) | (120,000) |
| Customer base | $ 44,000 |
| Assumed life | 20 years |
| Annual amortization expense | $ 2,200 |

for $164,000 in cash. As of the date of this acquisition, Zip is reporting a net book value of $400,000.

Assuming that Art has gained the ability to significantly influence the decision-making process of Zip, this investment, for external reporting purposes, is accounted for by means of the equity method as discussed in Chapter 1. Thus, Art must determine any allocations and amortization associated with its purchase price (see Exhibit 4–9). A customer base with a 20-year life represented the initial excess payment.

As discussed previously, application of the equity method requires the immediate accrual of investee income by the parent while any dividends received are recorded as a decrease in the Investment account. Art must also reduce both the income and asset balances in recognition of the annual $2,200 amortization indicated in Exhibit 4–9. If, over the next two years, Zip reports a total of $140,000 in net income and pays dividends of $40,000, the subsidiary's book value rises from $400,000 to $500,000. At the same time, the parent's investment account grows to $189,600:

| | |
|---|---:|
| Purchase price—1/1/03 | $164,000 |
| Accrual of 2003–04 equity income ($140,000 × 30 percent) | 42,000 |
| Dividends received 2003–04 ($40,000 × 30%) | (12,000) |
| Amortization ($2,200 per year for 2 years) | (4,400) |
| Investment in Zip, 12/31/04 | $189,600 |

On January 1, 2005, Art's ownership is raised to 80 percent by the purchase of another 50 percent of the outstanding common stock of Zip Company for $350,000. Although the equity method can still be utilized for internal reporting, this second purchase necessitates the preparation of consolidated financial statements beginning in 2005. Art now controls Zip; the two companies should be viewed as a single economic entity for external reporting purposes.

Before computing any consolidated balances, Art must make a separate cost allocation for this second purchase (Exhibit 4–10). In this purchase, the excess is attributable to Zip's substantially expanded customer base. This schedule does not supersede the allocation made in Exhibit 4–9 but merely supplements it for the price paid in acquiring the 50 percent block of Zip's stock.

## Worksheet Consolidation for a Step Acquisition

To complete this example, assume that the subsidiary earns $100,000 in net income during 2005 and distributes $20,000 as a cash dividend. If the parent company continues applying the equity method to this investment, Art reports an Equity in Subsidiary Earnings balance of $72,800 for 2005 and an Investment in Zip Company of $596,400:

| | | |
|---|---:|---:|
| Investment in Zip, 12/31/04 (computed above) | | $189,600 |
| January 1, 2005—Second acquisition | | 350,000 |
| Dividends received—2005 ($20,000 × 80%) | | (16,000) |
| Equity income accrual—2005 ($100,000 × 80%) | $80,000 | |
| 2005 amortization: First purchase (Exhibit 4–9) | (2,200) | |
| Second purchase (Exhibit 4–10) | (5,000) | 72,800 |
| Investment in Zip, 12/31/05 | | $596,400 |

**EXHIBIT 4–10**
Allocation of Second Purchase

**ART COMPANY AND ZIP COMPANY**
Purchase Price Allocation and Amortization
January 1, 2005

| | |
|---|---:|
| Purchase price | $ 350,000 |
| Book value equivalent of Art's ownership ($500,000 × 50%) | (250,000) |
| Customer base | $ 100,000 |
| Assumed life | 20 years |
| Annual amortization expense | $ 5,000 |

Once both investment balances have been determined, the worksheet shown in Exhibit 4–11 can be developed. Although this step acquisition might appear to be more complex than a single purchase, the actual consolidation process is the same as in previous examples.

- No conversion to the equity method (Entry **\*C**) is required since that method has been applied by the parent. If a different approach were used, amortization expense for prior years would have to be recognized along with, possibly, the proportionate increase in the subsidiary's book value for this same period.
- The stockholders' equity accounts of Zip are removed through Entry **S**. This worksheet entry also establishes the $100,000 beginning balance for the 20 percent noncontrolling interest that still remains (20 percent multiplied by the $500,000 stockholders' equity as of January 1 of the current year).
- The unamortized purchase price allocations are brought into the consolidation through Entry **A**. The $44,000 balance resulting from the first transaction has already undergone two years of amortization. Thus, a cost of only $39,600 remains at the beginning of the current period. Since the second allocation ($100,000) was made on January 1 of the current year, no expense has been recorded in prior years.
- Entry **I** on the worksheet eliminates the $72,800 equity income accrual calculated above.
- Entry **D** removes the $16,000 current year intercompany dividend paid to the parent. The remaining 20 percent ($4,000) was paid to the outside owners. Thus, that amount is extended to the Noncontrolling Interest column on the worksheet as a reduction.
- The final consolidation entry (Entry **E**) recognizes total excess amortizations for the current period.
- The noncontrolling interest balances to be reported on the income statement and balance sheet must be computed before the worksheet can be completed. Since Art now holds 80 percent of Zip, the outside owner's share of the subsidiary's income is 20 percent of the $100,000 reported earnings (or $20,000). Once again, this assignment is recorded on the worksheet through a columnar entry: The Noncontrolling Interest column is increased by that amount with a parallel decrease to consolidated net income.

For the balance sheet, the ending amount applicable to these outside owners is determined within the Noncontrolling Interest column: Assigned income of $20,000 is added to the $100,000 beginning balance with dividends of $4,000 being subtracted. The $116,000 total then is reported on the balance sheet between the liabilities and stockholders' equity.

## Retroactive Treatment Created by Step Acquisition

Because the initial 30 percent acquisition gave Art the ability to maintain significant influence over Zip, the investment balances in 2003 and 2004 were recorded using the equity method. For external reporting, the subsidiary's operations as well as related amortization were accounted for in those years in a manner that parallels the consolidation process. Thus, financial statements prepared and distributed by Art in 2003 and 2004 are considered comparable with the consolidated statements produced for 2005. Consequently, no retroactive adjustment of the earlier figures is required by Art's change in the method of reporting its investment in Zip.

Conversely, if Art had originally secured only a small percentage of Zip's shares (achieving less than significant influence), the market-value method would have been applied during 2003 and 2004. Under this approach, except for amounts received in the form of dividends, subsidiary income is ignored by the owner as is the recording of any amortization. However, gaining control of Zip in 2005 necessitates a transformation to consolidated statements, a change that strains the comparability of the results reported in the earlier years. Thus, to establish a proper degree of consistency, both the investment and income accounts are restated by the parent as if the equity method had been utilized from the date of the first acquisition.

*ARB 51* (par. 9) does allow one exception to this restatement policy by indicating that "if small purchases are made over a period of time and then a purchase is made which results in control, the date of the latest purchase, as a matter of convenience, may be considered as the date of acquisition." Therefore, retroactive adjustment is not required when initial acquisition levels are relatively small. The ARB apparently felt that the difficulties encountered in restating such minor amounts outweighed the benefits derived from establishing comparability.

## Step Acquisitions—Economic Unit Concept

Although this textbook primarily uses the parent company concept for illustration purposes, comparison with the economic unit concept demonstrates significant differences. Because the FASB is studying the issue of consolidation policies, one method or the other might eventually be mandated or an entirely new approach could be required. The economic unit concept, in particular, has received much attention.

To illustrate a step acquisition using the economic unit concept, assume that on January 1, 2004, Amanda Co. purchases 70 percent of Zoe, Inc., for $350,000. Because Zoe's net assets have book values equal to their fair market values of $400,000, under the economic unit concept, goodwill of $100,000 is recognized as the difference between the implied value of $500,000 ($350,000/70%) and net asset market value of $400,000. On January 1, 2005, when Zoe's book value has grown to $420,000, Amanda buys another 20 percent of Zoe for $95,000, bringing its total ownership up to 90 percent.

Under the economic unit concept, the valuation basis for Zoe's net assets was established on January 1, 2004, the date Amanda obtained control. Subsequent transactions in the subsidiary's stock (purchases or sales) are now viewed as transactions in the economic unit's own stock. Therefore, no gains or losses are recognized, and differences between transaction prices and the underlying subsidiary book value are simply treated as adjustments to Additional Paid-In Capital. The difference between the $95,000 price and the underlying consolidated book value is computed as follows:

| | | |
|---|---:|---:|
| 1/1/05 Purchase price for 20 percent interest | | $ 95,000 |
| Noncontrolling interest (NCI) acquired: | | |
|     Book value (20%) 1/1/05 | $84,000 | |
|     Goodwill (20%) | 20,000 | |
| Noncontrolling interest book value 1/1/05 | | 104,000 |
| Additional paid-in capital from 20 percent NCI acquisition | | $ 9,000 |

By purchasing 20 percent of Zoe for $95,000, the consolidated entity's owners have acquired a portion of their own firm at a price $9,000 less than consolidated book value. From a worksheet perspective, the recognition of the additional $104,000 in consolidated net assets from the 20 percent purchase is offset by the $95,000 purchase price and a $9,000 credit to additional paid-in capital. Importantly, the $95,000 purchase price for the 20 percent interest in Zoe's net assets does not affect consolidated asset valuation. From the economic unit perspective, the basis for the reported values in the consolidated financial statements was established on the date control was obtained.

**EXHIBIT 4–11** Step Acquisition Illustrated

*Consolidation: Purchase Method*
*Investment: Equity Method*

### ART COMPANY AND ZIP COMPANY
### Consolidation Worksheet
### For Year Ending December 31, 2005

| Accounts | Art Company | Zip Company | Consolidation Entries Debit | Consolidation Entries Credit | Noncontrolling Interest | Consolidated Totals |
|---|---|---|---|---|---|---|
| **Income Statement** | | | | | | |
| Revenues | (600,000) | (260,000) | | | | (860,000) |
| Expenses | 425,000 | 160,000 | (E) 7,200 | | | 592,200 |
| Equity in subsidiary earnings | (72,800) | –0– | (I) 72,800 | | | –0– |
| Noncontrolling interest in Zip Company's income | –0– | –0– | | | (20,000) | 20,000 |
| Net income | (247,800) | (100,000) | | | | (247,800) |
| **Statement of Retained Earnings** | | | | | | |
| Retained earnings, 1/1/05: | | | | | | |
| Art Company | (757,800) | | | | | (757,800) |
| Zip Company | | (230,000) | (S) 230,000 | | | |
| Net income (above) | (247,800) | (100,000) | | | | (247,800) |
| Dividends paid | 126,400 | 20,000 | | (D) 16,000 | 4,000 | 126,400 |
| Retained earnings, 12/31/05 | (879,200) | (310,000) | | | | (879,200) |

*continued from page 172*

**Balance Sheet**

| | | | | | |
|---|---:|---:|---:|---:|---:|
| Current assets | 505,800 | 280,000 | | | 785,800 |
| Land | 205,000 | 90,000 | | | 295,000 |
| Buildings (net) | 646,000 | 310,000 | | | 956,000 |
| Investment in Zip Company | 596,400 | -0- | (D) 16,000 | (A) 139,600 | -0- |
| | | | | (S) 400,000 | |
| | | | | (I) 72,800 | |
| | | | | (E) 2,200 | |
| | | | | (E) 5,000 | |
| Customer base | -0- | -0- | (A) 39,600 | | 132,400 |
| | | | (A) 100,000 | | |
| Total assets | 1,953,200 | 680,000 | | | 2,169,200 |
| Liabilities | (459,000) | (100,000) | | | (559,000) |
| Noncontrolling interest in Zip Company, 1/1/05 | -0- | -0- | | (S) 100,000 | |
| | | | | (100,000) | |
| Noncontrolling interest in Zip Company, 12/31/05 | | | | | (116,000) |
| | | | | (116,000) | |
| Common stock | (355,000) | (200,000) | (S) 200,000 | | (355,000) |
| Additional paid-in capital | (260,000) | (70,000) | (S) 70,000 | | (260,000) |
| Retained earnings, 12/31/05 (above) | (879,200) | (310,000) | | | (879,200) |
| Total liabilities and equities | (1,953,200) | (680,000) | | | (2,169,200) |

Note: Parentheses indicate a credit balance.

Consolidation entries:

(S) Elimination of subsidiary's stockholders' equity accounts along with recognition of January 1, 2005, noncontrolling interest.
(A) Allocation of parent's cost in excess of subsidiary's book value for unamortized balances as of January 1, 2005. Two separate allocations are shown because two purchases were made.
(I) Elimination of intercompany income (equity accrual less amortization expense).
(D) Elimination of intercompany dividend payments.
(E) Recognition of amortization expense on customer base resulting from purchase price.

## PREACQUISITION INCOME

In virtually all of the previous examples in this textbook, the parent has gained control of the subsidiary on the first day of the fiscal year. How is the consolidation process affected if a purchase is made on April 1 or August 19 or some other day within the year?[9]

If control is gained at a different time, a few obvious changes occur. The subsidiary's book value as of that date has to be computed so that an appropriate comparison with the purchase price can be made to determine allocations and goodwill. Amortization expense as well as any equity accrual and dividend collections are recognized for a period shorter than a year. The real issue to be resolved, though, is in consolidating the subsidiary's revenues and expenses. Obviously, these balances can be included just for the months after the takeover. However, this approach gives totals that may not be comparable to the figures reported in the future when ownership is for a full year.

Paragraph 10 of *ARB 51* addresses this issue by stating:

> When a subsidiary is purchased during the year, there are alternative ways of dealing with the results of its operations in the consolidated income statement. One method, which usually is preferable, especially where there are several dates of acquisition of blocks of shares, is to include the subsidiary in the consolidation as though it had been acquired at the beginning of the year, and to deduct at the bottom of the consolidated income statement the preacquisition earnings applicable to each block of stock. This method presents results which are more indicative of the current status of the group, and facilitates future comparison with subsequent years.

Thus, when a purchase combination is created during the current year, this pronouncement recommends that the reporting emphasis be placed on promoting the statement user's ability to compare current and future periods. *To achieve this objective, the income statement accounts should be consolidated as if the parent had possessed its interest for the entire year.* Consequently, revenues and expenses are included in total within the consolidated figures. However, a single-line reduction (often referred to as *preacquisition income*) appears at the bottom of the income statement to remove the portion of these earnings that apply to the previous owners.

For example, Advanced Semiconductor Engineering, Inc. (ASE), reported the following in a recent annual report regarding its May 4, 1999, acquisition of ISE Labs:

> Under the consolidation method used by ASE to consolidate the statement of income of ISE Labs for the year ended December 31, 1999, ISE Labs' full year 1999 net revenues, cost of revenues, and operating expenses are included in the Corporation's consolidated statements of income. The pre-acquisition income of ISE Labs for the period (from January 1, 1999 to May 4, 1999) is then subtracted from the Corporation's net income for 1999.

Inclusion of this balance is a means of accounting for the prior group of stockholders in a manner similar to that accorded to any noncontrolling interest that remains. The only difference is that these previous owners ceased during the current year to be associated with the subsidiary. Thus, although an income allocation is reported for the period of their ownership, no end-of-year balance is recognized. Any dividends paid to the previous owners are likewise omitted from consolidation consideration.

To illustrate, assume that Berkeley Company purchases 90 percent of Waltins Company on October 1, 2004. The 2004 operations of this new subsidiary would impact the consolidated income statement as follows:

---

[9] In a pooling of interests, operating results are consolidated retroactively as if the companies had always been together. Therefore, the specific date on which a pooling is formed has no impact on the resulting income statement.

| Impact on Consolidated Income Statement—2004 | |
|---|---|
| *Berkeley owns 90 percent of Waltins for last three months* | |
| **Revenues** | 100% of subsidiary's revenues are included. |
| **Expenses** | 100% of subsidiary's expenses are included plus amortization expense for three months. |
| **Noncontrolling interest** | Reduction is 10% of subsidiary's income for the entire year. |
| **Preacquisition income** | Reduction is 90% of subsidiary's income for the first nine months of the year. |
| **Net impact on consolidated net income** | Increased by 90% of subsidiary's income for the last three months of the year, reduced by any amortization expense for this same period. |

The establishment of a Preacquisition Income account permits comparability between the figures reported for current and future years. The reader of the financial statements is able to measure the full impact of creating this combination through the inclusion of 100 percent of each subsidiary revenue and expense account. By reporting reductions for the noncontrolling interest (10 percent) and the previous owners (90 percent for nine months), consolidated net income successfully mirrors the parent's 90 percent ownership for the last three months of the year. Thus, the *ARB*'s suggested handling of this matter has no effect on the amount of consolidated net income. Rather, the pronouncement simply constructs the income statement in a manner that provides comparability with future periods.

Before leaving this illustration, one further comment should be made. The term *preacquisition income* has been incorporated here since it appears to be most prevalent in practice. As can be observed in much of accounting, financial statement terminology is not always particularly descriptive. This allocation could also be reported as *current year income accruing to previous owners prior to the date subsidiary was acquired.* This title is significantly more wordy but less subject to misinterpretation by the users of the financial data.

### Closing the Subsidiary Books at Acquisition Date

Reporting a *preacquisition income* amount in the year of an acquisition is a useful technique to account for subsidiary income earned prior to the purchase date. By combining the preacquisition revenues and expenses into the single *preacquisition income* figure, the parent establishes a total income cutoff process without the cost of closing its new subsidiary's books. However, as internal information systems become more sophisticated, closing the income accounts on the subsidiary books at the date of acquisition becomes less costly. Moreover, such a closing effectively separates preacquisition and postacquisition revenues and expenses. The consolidation process then simply combines the end-of-period (postacquisition) remaining balances of each revenue and expense account. Thus, when an acquisition is accompanied by a closing of the revenue and expense accounts on the subsidiary books, no *preacquisition income* account is needed. Instead, the postacquisition revenue and expenses are individually combined with the parent's full-year amounts.

## SALES OF SUBSIDIARY STOCK

Although this textbook has concentrated on the acquisition and ownership of large blocks of corporate securities, the eventual sale of these stocks is also encountered in the business world. For example, a note to the 2002 financial statements of Sara Lee Corporation states (dollar amounts in millions other than per share values):

> A tax-free gain of $967, or $1.13 of diluted earnings per share, was recognized on the disposition of the Coach business in 2001. This disposition took place in two steps. In October 2000, the corporation's Coach subsidiary completed an initial public offering of 19.5 percent (8,487,000 shares) of its common stock. Cash proceeds of $122 were received and a tax-free

gain of $105 was recognized upon completion of the offering. In April 2001, the second step of the disposition was completed when the corporation's remaining 80.5 percent (35,026,333 shares) ownership interest in Coach was exchanged with third parties for 41,402,285 shares of Sara Lee common stock. The market value of the Coach shares disposed of was $998, and an $862 gain was recognized on this tax-free transaction.

Under the parent company concept, accounting for the disposition of such shares parallels the sale of any corporate asset: The investment is adjusted to the appropriate book value as of the date of sale and then removed from the records of the parent company.[10] Any difference in the recorded balance and the consideration being received is recognized as a gain or loss.

## Establishment of Investment Book Value

Any needed adjustment to the investment account depends on the accounting method used by the parent for internal reporting purposes. If the equity method has been applied, little problem should exist in recording the transaction. The investment is correctly reported by the parent as of the beginning of the year so that only the normal equity method adjustments are needed to reflect operations and amortization for the current period.

However, if either the cost or the partial equity method has been utilized, the adjustment process is more complicated. As indicated previously, both of these alternatives offer a convenient means to monitor a subsidiary. Unfortunately, neither produces the accurate book value necessary for recording a sales transaction. Therefore, when either of these other methods has been applied, the parent's Investment in Subsidiary account must be updated as if the equity method had been applied since the date of acquisition.

To illustrate, assume that Giant Company owns 80 percent of Tiny Company. Initially, a 50 percent interest was acquired in 2000 for $600,000 with the additional 30 percent being purchased in 2002 for $440,000. If Giant elects to account for this subsidiary using the equity method, the Investment in Tiny account contains a $1,245,000 balance as of January 1, 2004, based on the following assumed figures:

|  | Cost | Income Accrual Since Acquisition | Dividends | Excess Amortization | Investment Balance 1/1/04 |
|---|---|---|---|---|---|
| 2000 purchase | $ 600,000 | $200,000 | $(15,000) | $(40,000) | $ 745,000 |
| 2002 purchase | 440,000 | 100,000 | (6,000) | (34,000) | 500,000 |
| Totals | $1,040,000 | $300,000 | $(21,000) | $(74,000) | $1,245,000 |

*Sale Made at Beginning of Year*

Appropriate application of the equity method signifies that the $1,245,000 is a correctly recorded balance. Assuming that Giant sells this entire interest on January 1, 2004, for $1,400,000, the transaction is recorded as follows:[11]

**Giant's Financial Records—January 1, 2004**
| | | |
|---|---|---|
| Cash (or other assets) | 1,400,000 | |
|    Investment in Tiny Company | | 1,245,000 |
|    Gain on Sale of Investment | | 155,000 |
| To record January 1, 2004, sale of subsidiary. | | |

---

[10] Unless control is surrendered, the economic unit concept views the sale of a subsidiary's stock as a treasury stock transaction so that no gain or loss is recognized.

[11] Under the guidelines of *APB Opinion 30*, Giant could have to report this sale as the disposal of a segment. Because this issue is covered in most intermediate accounting textbooks, it is not explored here.

Because the sale is made on the first day of the year, no adjustment is required to recognize the 2004 operations of the subsidiary.

In contrast, if one of the alternative methods has been utilized by Giant, a preliminary entry is needed to establish the appropriate $1,245,000 balance.

*Application of the cost method.* The $1,040,000 total of the two original payments continues to be reported by the parent for this investment so that a $205,000 increase is necessary (income in excess of dividends and amortization).

*Application of the partial equity method.* A book value of $1,319,000 (income and dividends are recognized by the parent but not the $74,000 amortization) is found. An adjustment must be made to record the amortization.

Hence, depending on the method in use, one of the following entries is required of the parent prior to recording the sales transaction:

**Giant's Financial Records—January 1, 2004**
**Cost Method Has Been Applied**

| | | |
|---|---:|---:|
| Investment in Tiny Company | 205,000 | |
|     Retained Earnings, 1/1/04 (Giant) | | 205,000 |

To establish correct equity balance by recognizing income accrual (in excess of dividends) for previous years as well as amortization.

**Partial Equity Method Has Been Applied**

| | | |
|---|---:|---:|
| Retained Earnings, 1/1/04 (Giant) | 74,000 | |
|     Investment in Tiny Company | | 74,000 |

To establish correct equity balance by recognizing amortization relating to previous years.

These adjustments are equivalent to the Entry **\*C** used in past consolidations to update the investment account when either the cost or partial equity method has been applied. However, for a sale, this entry must be recorded directly into the parent's books rather than as a part of the worksheet process. Following the adjustment to $1,245,000, the parent records the sales transaction using the same journal entry presented in connection with the equity method.

### *Sale Made during the Year*

If this sale had transpired *within* the fiscal year, Giant still adjusts the investment to $1,245,000 (if necessary) but then extends application of the equity method over the period that the stock is held during 2004. The resulting book value must be correct as of the date of sale. The income accruing to Giant during this portion of the year is reported as a single-line item in the 2004 income statement. In this manner, subsidiary earnings continue to be recognized throughout the period of ownership even though consolidation is no longer applicable.

## Cost-Flow Assumptions

If less than an entire investment is sold, the parent must select an appropriate cost-flow assumption whenever more than one purchase has been made. In the sale of securities, the use of specific identification based on serial numbers is acceptable, although averaging or FIFO assumptions often are applied. Use of the averaging method is especially appealing in that all shares are truly identical, creating little justification for identifying different cost figures with individual shares.

Returning to Giant's ownership of Tiny Company, assume that the parent sold only a 20 percent portion of the subsidiary on January 1, 2004 (thereby reducing its holdings from 80 to 60 percent). Averaging dictates the removal of $311,250 ([20 percent/80 percent] × $1,245,000) from the investment account. Conversely, adoption of FIFO requires that

$298,000 be written off based on the currently reported value of the initial 2000 acquisition ([20 percent/50 percent] × $745,000).

## Accounting for Shares That Remain

If only a portion of Giant's investment is sold, a determination also must be made as to the proper method of accounting for the shares that remain. Three possible scenarios can be envisioned:

1. Giant's interest could have been so drastically reduced that the parent no longer controls the subsidiary or even has the ability to significantly influence its decision making. For example, assume that Giant's ownership drops from 80 to 5 percent. In the current period prior to the sale, the 80 percent investment is reported by means of the equity method with the market-value method used for the 5 percent that remains thereafter. Consolidated financial statements are no longer applicable.

2. Giant could still be able to apply significant influence over the operations of Tiny, although control is no longer maintained. A drop in the level of ownership from 80 to 30 percent would normally meet this condition. In this case, the equity method is utilized by the parent for the entire year. Application is based on 80 percent until the time of sale and then on 30 percent for the remainder of the year. Again, consolidated statements cease to be appropriate because control has been lost.

3. The decrease in ownership could be relatively small so that the parent continues to maintain control over the subsidiary even after the sale. Giant's reduction of its ownership in Tiny from 80 to 60 percent is an example of this situation. After the disposal, consolidated financial statements are still required, but the process is based on the *end-of-year ownership percentage*. As with step acquisitions, the accounting emphasis is placed here on maintaining comparability with future years. However, since only the retained shares (60 percent in this case) are consolidated, separate recognition must be made of any current year income accruing to the parent from its terminated interest. Thus, earnings on this portion of the investment (a 20 percent interest in Tiny for the time during the year that it is held) are shown in the consolidated income statement as a single-line item computed by means of the equity method.

## Summary

1. A parent company need not acquire 100 percent of a subsidiary's stock to form a business combination. Only control over the decision-making process is necessary, a level that has historically been achieved by obtaining a majority of the voting shares. Ownership of any subsidiary stock that is retained by outside, unrelated parties is collectively referred to as a *noncontrolling interest*.

2. A purchase consolidation takes on an added degree of complexity when a noncontrolling interest is present. A decision must be made as to the theoretical approach by which subsidiary assets and liabilities are to be valued within the financial statements of the business combination. One alternative, the economic unit concept, presumes that the combination is composed of two identifiable companies and should be accounted for as such. Allocations associated with the subsidiary's assets and liabilities are determined using their total fair market value regardless of the degree of parent ownership. The calculation of any noncontrolling interest is based on this total and reported by the business combination as a component of stockholders' equity.

3. The proportionate consolidation concept focuses on the parent company by stressing the cost of buying a portion of the subsidiary. Under this approach, allocations are computed using the ownership percentage of each account's fair market value. No recognition of noncontrolling interest is reported in either the consolidated balance sheet or income statement.

4. In practice, the parent company concept appears to be most popular. According to this method, the book value of each subsidiary asset and liability is included in the total whereas the difference between fair market value and book value is consolidated based on the parent's ownership percentage. Any noncontrolling interest is measured using only the subsidiary's book value and reported between the liabilities and stockholders' equity.

5. Four noncontrolling interest figures actually appear in the annual consolidation process. Calculation of each is derived by multiplying the percentage of outside ownership by the subsidiary's book value. A balance as of the beginning of the year is brought into the worksheet first (through Entry **S**) followed by the noncontrolling interest's share of the subsidiary's income for the period (recorded by a columnar entry). A decrease is recognized because of any dividends paid to these unrelated owners

(with the amount appearing on the worksheet as the subsidiary's dividends that were not eliminated as intercompany). The final balance for the year is found as a summation of the Noncontrolling Interest column and is presented on the consolidated balance sheet, usually between the Liability and Stockholders' Equity sections. The income figure appears as a reduction within the income statement.

6. A parent can obtain control of a subsidiary by means of several separate purchases occurring over time, a process often referred to as a *step acquisition*. In such cases, each purchase is viewed as an individual investment with separate allocations and amortization.

7. When a purchase is made within a year, operating figures that are comparable with those of future years should be reported. Thus, revenues and expenses can be consolidated as if the acquisition had taken place on the first day of the year. A *preacquisition income* figure is then subtracted within the consolidated income statement to remove the effects of the subsidiary's operations relating to the time prior to the takeover.

8. A parent company also can sell all, or a portion, of a subsidiary. The appropriate book value for the investment must be established within the parent's separate records so that the gain or loss can be computed accurately. If the equity method has not been applied, the parent's investment balance should be restated to recognize any income and amortization previously omitted. The resulting balance is then compared to the amount received for the stock to arrive at the gain or loss. Any shares still being held will subsequently be reported by either consolidation, the equity method, or the market-value method, depending on the influence retained by the parent.

## Comprehensive Illustration
### PROBLEM

*(Estimated Time: 60 to 75 Minutes)* On January 1, 2000, Father Company purchased an 80 percent interest in Sun Company for $410,000. As of that date, Sun reported total stockholders' equity of $400,000: $100,000 in common stock and $300,000 in retained earnings. In setting the acquisition price, Father had appraised four accounts as having values different from the balances reported within Sun's financial records.

| | |
|---|---|
| Buildings (8-year life) | Undervalued by $20,000 |
| Land | Undervalued by $50,000 |
| Equipment (5-year life) | Undervalued by $12,500 |
| Royalty agreement (20-year life) | Not recorded, valued at $30,000 |

As of December 31, 2004, the trial balances of these two companies are as follows:

| | Father Company | Sun Company |
|---|---|---|
| **Debits** | | |
| Current assets | $ 620,000 | $ 280,000 |
| Investment in Sun Company | 410,000 | –0– |
| Land | 200,000 | 300,000 |
| Buildings (net) | 640,000 | 290,000 |
| Equipment (net) | 380,000 | 160,000 |
| Expenses | 550,000 | 190,000 |
| Dividends | 90,000 | 20,000 |
| Total debits | $2,890,000 | $1,240,000 |
| **Credits** | | |
| Liabilities | $ 910,000 | $ 300,000 |
| Common stock | 480,000 | 100,000 |
| Retained earnings, 1/1/04 | 704,000 | 480,000 |
| Revenues | 780,000 | 360,000 |
| Dividend income | 16,000 | –0– |
| Total credits | $2,890,000 | $1,240,000 |

Within these figures, Sun has a $20,000 debt to the parent company.

### Required:

a. Determine consolidated totals for Father Company and Sun Company for the year 2004. Assume that the parent company concept is to be applied.
b. Prepare worksheet entries to consolidate the trial balances of Father Company and Sun Company for the year 2004.
c. Assume that Father acquires an additional 5 percent of the outstanding shares of Sun Company on December 31, 2004. Discuss the effects of this transaction on the consolidated figures computed in requirement (*a*).
d. Assume that Father uses the economic unit concept rather than the parent company concept. Discuss the effects of this change on the consolidated figures computed in requirement (*a*).

## SOLUTION

a. The consolidation of Father Company and Sun Company should begin with the allocation of the purchase price as shown in Exhibit 4–12. This process is based on the parent company concept and the parent's $410,000 expenditure. Since this consolidation is taking place after several years, the unamortized balances for the various allocations at the start of the current year also should be determined (see Exhibit 4–13).

Next, the parent's method of accounting for its subsidiary should be ascertained. The continuing presence in the investment account of the original $410,000 acquisition price indicates that Father is applying the cost method. This same determination can be made from the Dividend Income account that equals 80 percent of the subsidiary's dividends. Thus, the increase in Sun's book value as well as the excess amortization expenses for the prior periods of ownership have been ignored in Father's accounting records. These amounts have to be added to the parent's January 1, 2004, Retained Earnings account to arrive at a properly consolidated balance.

During the 2000–2003 period of ownership, Sun's Retained Earnings account rose by $180,000 ($480,000 − $300,000). Father's 80 percent interest necessitates an accrual of $144,000 ($180,000 × 80 percent) for these years. In addition, the purchase price allocations require the recognition of $20,800 in excess amortization expenses for this same period ($5,200 × 4 years). Thus, a net increase of $123,200 ($144,000 − $20,800) is needed to correct the parent's beginning Retained Earnings balance for the year.

Once the adjustment from the cost method to the equity method has been determined, the consolidated figures for 2004 can be calculated:

*Current assets* = $880,000. The parent's book value is added to the subsidiary's book value. The $20,000 intercompany balance is eliminated.
*Investment in Sun Company* = –0–. The intercompany ownership is eliminated so that the subsidiary's specific assets and liabilities can be consolidated.
*Land* = $540,000. The parent's book value is added to the subsidiary's book value plus the purchase price allocation (see Exhibit 4–12).
*Buildings (net)* = $936,000. The parent's book value is added to the subsidiary's book value plus the related purchase price allocation (see Exhibit 4–13) after taking into account five years of amortization (2000 through 2004).
*Equipment (net)* = $540,000. The parent's book value is added to the subsidiary's book value. The purchase price allocation has been completely amortized after five years.
*Expenses* = $745,200. The parent's book value is added to the subsidiary's book value plus amortization expenses on the purchase price allocations for the year (see Exhibit 4–12).
*Dividends Paid* = $90,000. Only the parent company dividends are consolidated. The subsidiary's dividends that were paid to the parent are eliminated; the remainder serve as a reduction in the Noncontrolling Interest balance.
*Royalty Agreement* = $18,000. The original residual allocation from the purchase price is recognized after taking into account five years of amortization (see Exhibit 4–13).
*Noncontrolling Interest in Subsidiary's Income* = $34,000. The outside owners are assigned a 20 percent share of the subsidiary's income (revenues of $360,000 less expenses of $190,000, or $170,000).
*Total of Consolidated Debit Balances* = $3,783,200. This figure is a summation of the preceding balances.
*Liabilities* = $1,190,000. The parent's book value is added to the subsidiary's book value. The $20,000 intercompany balance is eliminated.

## EXHIBIT 4–12

**FATHER COMPANY AND SUN COMPANY**
Purchase Price Allocation and Amortization
January 1, 2000

| | Allocation | Estimated Life (years) | Annual Excess Amortization |
|---|---|---|---|
| Purchase price paid by Father Company | $ 410,000 | | |
| 80% of subsidiary's $400,000 book value (Father Company's ownership) | (320,000) | | |
| Cost in excess of book value | 90,000 | | |
| Allocation to specific accounts based on fair market value: | | | |
| Buildings ($20,000 × 80%) | 16,000 | 8 | $ 2,000 |
| Land ($50,000 × 80%) | 40,000 | | |
| Equipment ($12,500 × 80%) | 10,000 | 5 | 2,000 |
| Royalty agreement ($30,000 × 80%) | 24,000 | 20 | 1,200 |
| | –0– | | |
| Annual excess amortization and depreciation expense | | | $ 5,200 |
| 2000–2003 excess amortization and depreciation expense ($5,200 × 4) | | | $20,800 |

## EXHIBIT 4–13

**FATHER COMPANY AND SUN COMPANY**
Unamortized Cost Allocation
January 1, 2004, Balances

| Account | Excess Original Allocation | Excess Amortization 2000–2003 | Balance 1/1/04 |
|---|---|---|---|
| Buildings | $16,000 | $ 8,000 | $ 8,000 |
| Land | 40,000 | –0– | 40,000 |
| Equipment | 10,000 | 8,000 | 2,000 |
| Royalty | 24,000 | 4,800 | 19,200 |
| Total | $90,000 | $20,800 | $69,200 |

*Common Stock* = $480,000. The parent company balance only is reported.
*Retained Earnings, 1/1/04* = $827,200. The parent company balance only is reported after a $123,200 increase is made as explained earlier to convert the parent's use of the cost method to the equity method.
*Revenues* = $1,140,000. The parent's book value is added to the subsidiary's book value.
*Dividend Income* = –0–. The intercompany dividend receipts are eliminated.
*Noncontrolling Interest in Subsidiary, 12/31/04* = $146,000. The beginning balance is $116,000, 20 percent of the subsidiary's 1/1/04 book value ($580,000 as shown by the stockholders' equity accounts). This figure is increased by the noncontrolling interest's share of net income ($34,000 as computed above). The dividends paid to the outside owners (20 percent of $20,000, or $4,000) serve to decrease the balance. The consolidated total is then derived from these three balances.
*Total of Consolidated Credit Balances* = $3,783,200. This figure is a summation of the preceding balances.

b. Six worksheet entries are necessary to produce a consolidation worksheet for Father Company and Sun Company.

### Entry *C

| | | |
|---|---:|---:|
| Investment in Sun Company | 123,200 | |
|     Retained Earnings, 1/1/04 (parent) | | 123,200 |

As discussed earlier, this increment is required to adjust the parent's Retained Earnings from the cost method to the equity method. The amount is $144,000 (80 percent of the $180,000 increase in the subsidiary's book value during previous years) less $20,800 in excess amortization over this same four-year period ($5,200 × 4 years).

### Entry S

| | | |
|---|---:|---:|
| Common Stock (subsidiary) | 100,000 | |
| Retained Earnings, 1/1/04 (subsidiary) | 480,000 | |
|     Investment in Sun Company (80 percent) | | 464,000 |
|     Noncontrolling Interest in Sun Company (20 percent) | | 116,000 |

To eliminate beginning stockholders' equity accounts of the subsidiary and recognize the beginning balance attributed to the outside owners (20 percent).

### Entry A

| | | |
|---|---:|---:|
| Buildings | 8,000 | |
| Land | 40,000 | |
| Equipment | 2,000 | |
| Royalty Agreement | 19,200 | |
|     Investment in Sun Company | | 69,200 |

To recognize unamortized purchase price allocations as of the first day of the current year (see Exhibit 4–13).

### Entry I

| | | |
|---|---:|---:|
| Dividend Income | 16,000 | |
|     Dividends Paid | | 16,000 |

To eliminate intercompany dividend payments recorded by parent (using the cost method) as income.

### Entry E

| | | |
|---|---:|---:|
| Depreciation Expense | 4,000 | |
| Amortization Expense | 1,200 | |
|     Buildings | | 2,000 |
|     Equipment | | 2,000 |
|     Royalty Agreement | | 1,200 |

To record excess amortization expenses for the current year (see Exhibit 4–12).

### Entry P

| | | |
|---|---:|---:|
| Liabilities | $20,000 | |
|     Current Assets | | 20,000 |

To adjust for intercompany debt.

c. This question asks about the impact created by Father's purchase of an additional 5 percent of Sun on December 31, 2004. Three direct effects can be listed:
   1. All of the noncontrolling interest balances will be calculated as if only 15 percent of the subsidiary's shares had been held by outside parties during the entire year. This handling allows for production of financial statements that will be comparable with the results reported in future years.
   2. A Preacquisition Income account is established to reflect the portion of Sun's 2004 income (5 percent) accruing to the previous owners. This balance reduces consolidated net income for the current year. In addition, any dividends paid to former stockholders must be eliminated since this group no longer holds an equity interest in Sun.
   3. Any cost in excess of book value paid by Father in this latest purchase must be allocated to specific accounts and then recognized within the consolidated balance sheet. Because the acquisition occurs at the end of the fiscal year, no additional amortization expense is necessary for 2004.
d. Recall that under the economic unit concept not only is an implied value for 100 percent of the subsidiary used in allocating market values to subsidiary assets but adjustments also are made for 100 percent of the differences in market and book values. The following cost allocation schedule reflects the economic unit concept for Father's purchase of Sun on January 1, 2000:

|  | Allocation | Estimated Life (years) | Annual Excess Amortization |
|---|---|---|---|
| Implied value ($410,000/80%) | $512,500 | | |
| Sun book value (100%) | 400,000 | | |
| Excess implied value | 112,500 | | |
| Allocation to specific subsidiary accounts based on fair market value: | | | |
| Buildings | $ 20,000 | 8 | $2,500 |
| Land | 50,000 | | |
| Equipment | 12,500 | 5 | 2,500 |
| Royalty agreement | 30,000 | 20 | 1,500 |
| | –0– | | |
| Annual excess amortization expenses (economic unit concept) | | | $6,500 |

Father's consolidated statements would therefore reflect the total market values of the subsidiary at acquisition date less the above amortizations. To offset the increased asset values, a larger noncontrolling interest also is recognized.

The noncontrolling interest would be reported in the December 31, 2004, stockholders' equity section of Father's consolidated balance sheet at $162,500, computed as follows:

| | |
|---|---|
| NCI in Sun's 1/1/04 book value (20% × $580,000) | $116,000 |
| NCI in unamortized excess allocations (20% × $86,500) | 17,300 |
| January 1, 2004, NCI in Sun implied value | 133,300 |
| NCI in Sun's economic unit income 20% × ($360,000 − 196,500) | 32,700 |
| NCI dividend share 20% × $20,000 | (4,000) |
| Total noncontrolling interest December 31, 2004 | $162,000 |

Note that the $162,000 noncontrolling interest amount is the same as the $146,000 amount reported in part (a), plus 20 percent of the $80,000 unamortized excess allocations at December 31, 2004 ($112,500 − 5 years × $6,500).

The noncontrolling interest's share of the subsidiary's net income is not reported on the consolidated income statement but rather as a separate allocation. This amount is based on the subsidiary's net income after deducting amortization expense, which is attributed to the company's asset and liability accounts.

## Questions

1. What is meant by the term *noncontrolling interest?*
2. Atwater Company acquires 80 percent of the outstanding voting stock of Belwood Company. On that date, Belwood possesses a building with a $160,000 book value but a fair market value of $220,000. Assuming that a bargain purchase has not been made, at what value would this building be consolidated under each of the following?
   a. Economic unit concept.
   b. Proportionate consolidation concept.
   c. Parent company concept.
3. How does the parent company concept merge the ideas put forth under the economic unit concept and proportionate consolidation?
4. Where should the noncontrolling interest's claims be reported in a consolidated set of financial statements?
5. How is the noncontrolling interest in a subsidiary company calculated as of the end of the current year?
6. Consolidated financial statements are being prepared by Sandridge Company and its consolidated subsidiary. Preacquisition income of $55,000 is presented within these statements. What does this Preacquisition Income account represent? How was the amount computed?
7. Tree, Inc., has held a 10 percent interest in the stock of Limb Company for several years. Because of the level of ownership, this investment has been accounted for by means of the market-value method. At the beginning of the current year, Tree acquires an additional 70 percent interest, which provides the company with control over Limb. In preparing consolidated financial statements for this business combination, how is the previous 10 percent ownership interest accounted for by Tree?
8. Duke Corporation owns a 70 percent equity interest in UNCCH, a subsidiary corporation. During the current year, a portion of this stock is sold to an outside party. Before recording this transaction, Duke adjusts the book value of its investment account. What is the purpose of this adjustment?
9. In question 8, how would the parent record the sales transaction?
10. In question 8, how would the parent record the sales transaction if the economic unit concept is being used and control is retained?
11. In question 8, how would Duke account for the remainder of its investment subsequent to the sale of this partial interest?

## Problems

*Note: Unless otherwise stated, assume that the parent company concept is being used.*

1. Bailey, Inc., buys 60 percent of the outstanding stock of Luebs, Inc., in a purchase that resulted in the recognition of goodwill. Luebs owns a piece of land that cost $200,000 but was worth $500,000 at the date of purchase. For each of the three concepts described in this chapter, what value would be attributed to this land in a consolidated balance sheet at the date of takeover?

   |    | Economic Unit Concept | Proportionate Consolidation | Parent Company Concept |
   |----|----|----|----|
   | a. | $500,000 | $300,000 | $500,000 |
   | b. | $200,000 | $120,000 | $500,000 |
   | c. | $200,000 | $120,000 | $380,000 |
   | d. | $500,000 | $300,000 | $380,000 |

2. Jordan, Inc., holds 75 percent of the outstanding stock of Paxson Corporation. Paxson currently owes Jordan $400,000 for inventory acquired over the past few months. In preparing consolidated financial statements, what amount of this debt should be eliminated?
   a. $0
   b. $100,000
   c. $300,000
   d. $400,000

3. On January 1, 2004, Brendan, Inc., reports net assets of $760,000 although equipment (with a four-year life) having a book value of $440,000 is worth $500,000 and an unrecorded patent is valued at $45,000. Hope Corporation pays $692,000 on that date for an 80 percent ownership in Brendan. If the patent is to be written off over a 10-year period, at what amount should the patent be reported on consolidated statements at December 31, 2005?
   a. $20,800
   b. $28,800

c. $34,200
   d. $67,200
4. On January 1, 2003, Turner Inc., reports net assets of $480,000 although a building (with a 10-year life) having a book value of $260,000 is now worth $310,000. Plaster Corporation pays $400,000 on that date for a 70 percent ownership in Turner. On December 31, 2005, Turner reports a Building account of $245,000 while Plaster reports a Building account of $510,000. What is the consolidated balance of the Building account?
   a. $779,500
   b. $783,500
   c. $790,000
   d. $805,000
5. On January 1, 2004, Hygille, Inc., reports net assets of $880,000 although a building (with a 10-year life) having a book value of $330,000 is now worth $400,000. Nuyt Corporation pays $840,000 on that date for an 80 percent ownership in Hygille. On December 31, 2006, Hygille reports total expenses of $621,000 while Nuyt reports expenses of $714,000. What is the consolidated total expense balance?
   a. $1,335,000
   b. $1,339,000
   c. $1,345,300
   d. $1,340,600
6. On January 1, 2003, Chamberlain Corporation pays $388,000 for a 60 percent ownership in Neville. Annual excess amortization of $8,800 results from the purchase. On December 31, 2005, Neville reports revenues of $400,000 and expenses of $300,000 while Chamberlain reports revenues of $700,000 and expenses of $400,000. The parent figures contain no income from the subsidiary. What is consolidated net income?
   a. $349,600
   b. $351,200
   c. $360,000
   d. $391,200
7. What is a basic premise of the economic unit concept?
   a. Consolidated financial statements should be primarily for the benefit of the stockholders of the parent company.
   b. Consolidated financial statements should be produced only if both the parent and the subsidiary are in the same basic industry.
   c. A subsidiary is an indivisible part of a business combination and should be included in whole regardless of the degree of ownership.
   d. Consolidated financial statements should not report a noncontrolling interest balance since these outside owners do not hold stock in the parent company.
8. A preacquisition income account
   a. Is an adjustment to Retained Earnings when a pooling of interests is created.
   b. Is a reduction in Consolidated Net Income that allows a subsidiary's revenues and expenses to be reported for the entire year even though acquisition took place during the current year.
   c. Is an income figure that requires the parent to pay an additional amount to create a business combination.
   d. Is the balance in a subsidiary's Retained Earnings account on the date that a business combination is created.
9. Ames, Inc., had a book value of $400,000 on January 1, 2002, and $550,000 on January 1, 2004. On both dates, the book value of the company's assets and liabilities were the same as fair market value. Hitchcock Corporation acquired 30 percent of Ames on January 1, 2002, for $160,000 in cash. Hitchcock purchased an additional 40 percent of Ames on January 1, 2004, for $240,000. On a consolidated balance sheet as of December 31, 2004, what amount of goodwill is reported?
   a. $60,000
   b. $54,000
   c. $53,000
   d. $52,000
10. A parent buys 32 percent of a subsidiary in 2002 and then buys an additional 40 percent in 2004. In a step acquisition of this type, how does the economic unit concept differ from the parent company concept?
    a. In using the economic unit concept, all subsequent purchases are valued based on the implied value at the time of the first acquisition.

b. In using the economic unit concept, the two purchases are recorded as separate acquisitions with their own allocations and goodwill.
c. In using the economic unit concept, the first purchase is adjusted to its implied value based on the acquisition price of the second transaction with a resulting gain or loss being recorded.
d. The economic unit concept views each company as a whole and, thus, cannot be applied unless 100 percent of the subsidiary's stock is held.

11. On April 1, 2004, Guns, Inc., purchases 70 percent of the outstanding stock of Roses Corporation for $430,000. The subsidiary's book value on that date was $500,000. Any excess cost was attributable to goodwill. During 2004, Roses generates revenues of $600,000 and expenses of $360,000. Both figures occur evenly throughout the year. On a December 31, 2004 consolidated income statement, what should be reported as the noncontrolling interest in the subsidiary's net income and as preacquisition income?
    a. $72,000 and $42,000
    b. $70,800 and $60,000
    c. $70,800 and $41,000
    d. $72,000 and $41,300

**Use the following information for Problems 12 through 14:**
David Company acquired 60 percent of Mark Company for $300,000 when Mark's book value was $400,000. On that date, Mark had equipment (with a 10-year life) that was undervalued in the financial records by $60,000. Also, buildings (with a 20-year life) were undervalued by $40,000. Two years later, the following figures are reported by these two companies (stockholders' equity accounts have been omitted).

|  | David Company Book Value | Mark Company Book Value | Mark Company Fair Market Value |
|---|---|---|---|
| Current assets | $ 620,000 | $ 300,000 | $ 320,000 |
| Equipment | 260,000 | 200,000 | 280,000 |
| Buildings | 410,000 | 150,000 | 150,000 |
| Liabilities | (390,000) | (120,000) | (120,000) |
| Revenues | (900,000) | (400,000) |  |
| Expenses | 500,000 | 300,000 |  |
| Investment income | not given |  |  |

12. What is consolidated net income prior to the reduction for the noncontrolling interest's share of the subsidiary's income?
    a. $455,200
    b. $494,000
    c. $497,000
    d. $495,200

13. What is the noncontrolling interest's share of the subsidiary's income and what is the ending balance of the noncontrolling interest in the subsidiary?
    a. $42,000 and $252,000
    b. $40,000 and $212,000
    c. $38,080 and $208,160
    d. $35,200 and $207,200

14. What is the consolidated balance of the Equipment account?
    a. $488,800
    b. $498,400
    c. $500,800
    d. $508,000

**Use the following information for Problems 15 through 19:**
On January 1, 2004, Polk Corporation and Strass Corporation had condensed balance sheets as follows:

|  | Polk | Strass |
|---|---|---|
| Current assets | $ 70,000 | $20,000 |
| Noncurrent assets | 90,000 | 40,000 |
| Total assets | $160,000 | $60,000 |
| Current liabilities | $ 30,000 | $10,000 |
| Long-term debt | 50,000 | — |
| Stockholders' equity | 80,000 | 50,000 |
| Total liabilities and equities | $160,000 | $60,000 |

On January 2, 2004, Polk borrowed $60,000 and used the proceeds to purchase 90 percent of the outstanding common shares of Strass. This debt is payable in 10 equal annual principal payments, plus interest, beginning December 31, 2004. The excess cost of the investment over the underlying book value of the acquired net assets is allocated to inventory (60 percent) and to goodwill (40 percent). On a consolidated balance sheet as of January 2, 2004,

15. Current assets should be:
    a. $99,000
    b. $96,000
    c. $90,000
    d. $79,000
16. Noncurrent assets
    a. $130,000
    b. $134,000
    c. $136,000
    d. $140,000
17. Current liabilities
    a. $50,000
    b. $46,000
    c. $40,000
    d. $30,000
18. Noncurrent liabilities, including noncontrolling interest
    a. $115,000
    b. $109,000
    c. $104,000
    d. $55,000
19. Stockholders' equity
    a. $80,000
    b. $85,000
    c. $90,000
    d. $130,000
    (AICPA adapted)
20. On January 1, 2004, Harrison, Inc., purchased 90 percent of Starr Company. Annual amortization of $8,000 resulted from this transaction. Starr Company reported a Common Stock account of $100,000 and Retained Earnings of $200,000 at that date. The subsidiary earned $70,000 in 2004 and $90,000 in 2005 with dividend payments of $30,000 each year. Without regard for this investment, Harrison had income of $220,000 in 2004 and $260,000 in 2005.
    a. What is consolidated net income in each of these two years?
    b. What is the ending noncontrolling interest balance as of December 31, 2005?
21. Pistol, Inc., purchases 70 percent of Bytvl Company for $406,000. On that date, Bytvl had the following accounts:

|  | Book Value | Fair Market Value |
|---|---|---|
| Current assets | $210,000 | $210,000 |
| Land | 170,000 | 180,000 |
| Buildings | 300,000 | 330,000 |
| Liabilities | 280,000 | 280,000 |

The buildings have a 10-year life. In addition, Bytvl holds a patent worth $140,000 that has a five-year life but is not recorded on its financial records.

a. Assume that the purchase took place on January 1, 2004. At the end of 2004, the two companies report the following balances:

|  | Pistol | Bytvl |
|---|---|---|
| Revenues | $900,000 | $600,000 |
| Expenses | 600,000 | 400,000 |

What figures would appear in a consolidated income statement for this year?

b. Assume that the purchase took place on April 1, 2004. At the end of 2004, the two companies report the following balances:

|  | Pistol | Bytvl |
|---|---|---|
| Revenues | $760,000 | $590,000 |
| Expenses | 540,000 | 380,000 |

What figures would appear in a consolidated income statement for this year?

22. On January 1, Beckman, Inc., purchases 60 percent of the outstanding stock of Calvin for $36,000. Calvin Co. has one recorded asset, a specialized production machine with a book value of $10,000. The fair market value of the machine is $50,000, and the remaining useful life is estimated to be 10 years. Any remaining excess cost is attributable to an unrecorded process trade secret with an estimated future life of 4 years.

At the end of the year, Calvin reports the following in its financial statements:

| Revenues | $50,000 | Machine | $ 9,000 | Common stock | $10,000 |
|---|---|---|---|---|---|
| Expenses | 20,000 | Other assets | 26,000 | Retained earnings | 25,000 |
| Net income | $30,000 | Total assets | $35,000 | Total equity | $35,000 |
| Dividends paid | $ 5,000 | | | | |

For each of the following noncontrolling interest concepts, what amounts should Beckman report in its consolidated financial statements for noncontrolling interest in subsidiary income, end-of-year total noncontrolling interest, Calvin's machine (net of accumulated depreciation), and the process trade secret.

a. Parent company concept.
b. Proportionate consolidation concept.
c. Economic unit concept.

23. Mabry, Inc., purchases 60 percent of Thompson Corporation on August 1, 2003, and an additional 30 percent on October 1, 2004. Annual amortization of $6,000 relates to the first acquisition and $10,000 to the second. Thompson reports the following figures for 2004:

| Revenues | $600,000 |
|---|---|
| Expenses | 420,000 |
| Retained earnings, 1/1/04 | 540,000 |
| Dividends paid | 70,000 |
| Common stock | 310,000 |

Without regard for this investment, Mabry earns $360,000 in net income during 2004.

a. What is consolidated net income for 2004?
b. What is the noncontrolling interest as of December 31, 2004?

24. Clark Corporation acquired 50 percent of Lamp, Inc., several years ago and an additional 30 percent on April 1 of the current year. An excess cost allocation to equipment of $60,000 was computed in connection with the first acquisition, and that amount is being amortized over a 20-year life. No ex-

cess amortizations resulted from the second acquisition. The following figures are reported by these two companies for the current year. Investment income is not included within the balances for Clark shown here. Income is assumed to have been earned evenly throughout the year, and no dividends were paid.

|  | Clark Corporation | Lamp, Inc. |
|---|---|---|
| Revenues | $600,000 | $500,000 |
| Expenses | 380,000 | 300,000 |

    *a.* What is the noncontrolling interest's share of the subsidiary's net income?
    *b.* What is the amount of preacquisition income?
    *c.* What is the consolidated net income for these two companies?

25. Wilson Company acquired 7,000 of the 10,000 outstanding shares of Green Company on January 1, 2000, for $800,000. The subsidiary's book value on that date was $1,000,000. Any cost of this purchase in excess of Green's book value was assigned to a patent with a 10-year life. On January 1, 2004, Wilson reported a $1,085,000 balance in the Investment in Green Company account based on application of the partial equity method. On October 1, 2004, Wilson sells 1,000 shares of the investment for $191,000. During 2004, Green reported net income of $120,000 and paid dividends of $40,000. These amounts are assumed to have been incurred evenly throughout the year.
    *a.* How are the 1,000 shares reported for the period from January 1, 2004, until October 1, 2004?
    *b.* What is the effect on net income of this sale of 1,000 shares?
    *c.* What accounting is now made of the 6,000 shares that Wilson continues to hold?

26. Robert Palmer and Anita Blackwood are the sole owners of Quinn Corporation. Palmer holds 70 percent of the stock while Blackwood owns the remaining 30 percent. On January 1, 2004, Quinn reports $10,000 in common stock and $90,000 in retained earnings. During each month of 2004, the company earns $15,000 in net income. Dividends of $5,000 are paid every month. At the end of the year, Quinn's net income is $180,000 (revenues of $400,000 less $220,000 in expenses), while $60,000 in dividends have been paid.

    The book value of Quinn Corporation on December 1, 2004, is $210,000 ($100,000 beginning balance plus $10,000 growth for 11 months). On that date, Brown, Inc., buys all of Palmer's interest. Blackwood retains her 30 percent share of the company's stock. Brown pays exactly book value for these shares ($147,000, or 70 percent of $210,000). The individual fair market values of Quinn's assets and liabilities are equal to their book values.

    Brown, Inc., is currently preparing consolidated financial statements for the year ending December 31, 2004.
    *a.* What amount of Quinn's revenues would be included in the consolidated income statement?
    *b.* What balance should be reported as the noncontrolling interest in Quinn's net income? Who is the noncontrolling interest?
    *c.* For consolidation purposes, what happens to the $3,500 per month in dividends that Palmer received for the first 11 months of the year?
    *d.* What amount of preacquisition income should be reported for consolidation purposes? Where is this figure disclosed? To whom does this income accrue?
    *e.* Prepare the worksheet entry to eliminate the subsidiary's stockholders' equity. Assume Brown uses the cost method to account for its investment in Quinn.

27. Narcissus acquired 80 percent of the outstanding stock of Goldmund for $156,000. Just prior to this purchase, the following information is gathered from the two companies:

|  | Narcissus Book Value | Goldmund Book Value | Goldmund Fair Market Value |
|---|---|---|---|
| Current assets | $500,000 | $150,000 | $150,000 |
| Land | 100,000 | 30,000 | 40,000 |
| Buildings and equipment (net) | 600,000 | 160,000 | 180,000 |
| Liabilities | 300,000 | 200,000 | 200,000 |
| Common stock | 400,000 | 40,000 |  |
| Retained earnings | 500,000 | 100,000 |  |

The buildings and equipment have a 10-year remaining life; any goodwill is assumed to have an indefinite life.

Subsequently, on December 31, 2004, the two companies report the following account balances. Fair market values are presented where applicable.

|  | Narcissus Book Value | Goldmund Book Value | Goldmund Fair Market Value |
|---|---|---|---|
| Current assets | $300,000 | $ 90,000 | $ 90,000 |
| Investment in Goldmund | 156,000 | –0– | –0– |
| Land | 150,000 | 60,000 | 74,000 |
| Buildings and equipment (net) | 570,000 | 180,000 | 216,000 |
| Liabilities | 246,000 | 185,000 | 185,000 |
| Common stock | 400,000 | 40,000 |  |
| Retained earnings, 1/1/04 | 470,000 | 95,000 |  |
| Revenues | 300,000 | 100,000 |  |
| Expenses | 200,000 | 90,000 |  |
| Dividends paid | 40,000 | –0– |  |

  *a.* On consolidated financial statements as of the date of acquisition, what balances are reported for the Buildings and Equipment account and the Goodwill account?

  *b.* Assume that the purchase was made on January 1, 2000. What would be the consolidated Buildings and Equipment balance on December 31, 2004?

  *c.* Assume that the purchase was made during 2003. What is the consolidated net income for 2004 before subtracting the noncontrolling interest's share of the subsidiary's income?

  *d.* Assume that the purchase was made during 2002. What is the noncontrolling interest's share of the subsidiary's income for the year ending December 31, 2004?

  *e.* Assume that the purchase was made on July 1, 2004. Prepare a consolidated income statement for the year ending December 31, 2004.

  *f.* Assume that the purchase was made on January 1, 2003. On October 1, 2004, Narcissus sells one-fourth of these shares for $82,000 in cash. What income effects appear on the consolidated income statement for 2004?

28. On January 1, 2002, Thacker purchases 70 percent of Barker for $410,000 cash. The new subsidiary reported common stock on that date of $300,000, with retained earnings of $180,000. A building was undervalued in the company's financial records by $20,000. This building had a 10-year remaining life. Goodwill of $60,000 was recognized.

Barker earns income and pays cash dividends as follows:

| Year | Net Income | Dividends Paid |
|---|---|---|
| 2002 | $ 75,000 | $39,000 |
| 2003 | 96,000 | 44,000 |
| 2004 | 110,000 | 60,000 |

On December 31, 2004, Thacker owes $22,000 to Barker.

  *a.* If the equity method has been applied by Thacker, what are the consolidation entries needed as of December 31, 2004?

  *b.* If the cost method has been applied by Thacker, what Entry *C is needed for a 2004 consolidation?

  *c.* If the partial equity method has been applied by Thacker, what Entry *C is needed for a 2004 consolidation?

  *d.* What noncontrolling interest balances will appear in consolidated financial statements for 2004?

29. The Hearts Company acquired an 80 percent interest in Dylan Company as of January 1, 2002. Hearts paid $620,000 to the owners of Dylan to purchase these shares. In addition, Hearts paid several lawyers and merger analysts $44,000 for assisting in the acquisition.

On January 1, 2002, Dylan reported a book value of $600,000 (Common Stock—$300,000; Additional Paid-In Capital—$90,000; Retained Earnings—$210,000). Several of Dylan's buildings were undervalued by a total of $80,000. These buildings had a remaining life of 20 years. Any goodwill resulting from the takeover was assumed to have an indefinite life.

During the 2002–04 time period, Dylan reported the following figures:

| Year | Net Income | Dividends Paid |
|------|-----------|----------------|
| 2002 | $ 70,000  | $10,000 |
| 2003 | 90,000    | 15,000 |
| 2004 | 100,000   | 20,000 |

Determine the appropriate answers for each of the following questions:
a. What amount of amortization expense would be recognized in the consolidated financial statements for the initial years following this purchase?
b. If a consolidated balance sheet is prepared as of January 1, 2002, what amount of goodwill would be recognized?
c. If a consolidation worksheet is prepared as of January 1, 2002, what Entry **S** should be included?
d. On the separate financial records of the parent company, what amount of investment income would be reported for 2002 under each of the following accounting methods:
   (1) The equity method.
   (2) The partial equity method.
   (3) The cost method.
e. On the separate financial records of the parent company, what would be the December 31, 2004, balance for the Investment in Dylan Company account under each of the following accounting methods:
   (1) The equity method.
   (2) The partial equity method.
   (3) The cost method.
f. As of December 31, 2003, Hearts' Buildings account on its separate records has a balance of $800,000 while Dylan has a similar account with a $300,000 balance. What would be the consolidated balance for the Buildings account? What would be the balance if the economic unit concept is used?
g. What would be the balance of consolidated goodwill as of December 31, 2004?
h. Assume that the parent company has been applying the equity method to this investment. On December 31, 2004, the separate financial statements for the two companies present the following information:

|  | Hearts Company | Dylan Company |
|---|---|---|
| Common stock | $500,000 | $300,000 |
| Additional paid-in capital | 280,000 | 90,000 |
| Retained earnings, 12/31/04 | 620,000 | 425,000 |

What will be the consolidated balance of each of these accounts?

30. Following are several of the account balances taken from the records of Bigston and Lytle as of December 31, 2004. A few asset accounts have been omitted here. All revenues, expenses, and dividends occurred evenly throughout the year. Annual tests have indicated no goodwill impairment.

|  | Bigston | Lytle |
|---|---|---|
| Sales | $ 800,000 | $500,000 |
| Cost of goods sold | 400,000 | 280,000 |
| Expenses | 200,000 | 100,000 |
| Investment income | not given | –0– |
| Retained earnings, 1/1/04 | 1,400,000 | 700,000 |
| Dividends | 80,000 | 20,000 |
| Land | 600,000 | 200,000 |
| Buildings (net) | 700,000 | 300,000 |
| Equipment (net) | 400,000 | 400,000 |
| Liabilities | 500,000 | 200,000 |
| Common stock ($10 par value) | 400,000 | 100,000 |
| Additional paid-in capital | 500,000 | 600,000 |

On July 1, 2004, Bigston purchased 80 percent of Lytle for $1,300,000 in cash. In addition, Bigston paid $30,000 in direct consolidation costs. At that time, Lytle's buildings (with a 10-year life) were undervalued on its books by $100,000. On a consolidation prepared at the end of 2004, what balances would be reported for the following:

| | |
|---|---|
| Preacquisition Income | Net Income |
| Sales | Retained Earnings, 1/1/04 |
| Expenses | Buildings (net) |
| Noncontrolling Interest in | Land |
| Subsidiary's Net Income | Goodwill |

31. Monroe, Inc., acquires 60 percent of Sunrise Corporation for $414,000 cash on January 1, 2001. On that date, Sunrise had the following accounts:

| | Book Value | Fair Market Value |
|---|---|---|
| Current assets | $150,000 | $150,000 |
| Land | 200,000 | 200,000 |
| Buildings (net) (6-year life) | 300,000 | 360,000 |
| Equipment (net) (4-year life) | 300,000 | 280,000 |
| Patent (10-year life) | -0- | 100,000 |
| Liabilities | 400,000 | 400,000 |

The companies' financial statements for the year ending December 31, 2004, follow.

| | Monroe | Sunrise |
|---|---|---|
| Revenues | $ 600,000 | $ 300,000 |
| Operating expenses | 410,000 | 210,000 |
| Investment income | 42,000 | -0- |
| Net income | $ 232,000 | $ 90,000 |
| Retained earnings, 1/1/04 | $ 700,000 | $ 300,000 |
| Net income | 232,000 | 90,000 |
| Dividends paid | 92,000 | 70,000 |
| Retained earnings, 12/31/04 | $ 840,000 | $ 320,000 |
| Current assets | $ 330,000 | $ 100,000 |
| Land | 220,000 | 200,000 |
| Buildings (net) | 700,000 | 200,000 |
| Equipment (net) | 400,000 | 500,000 |
| Investment in Sunrise | 414,000 | -0- |
| Total assets | $2,064,000 | $1,000,000 |
| Liabilities | $ 500,000 | $ 200,000 |
| Common stock | 724,000 | 480,000 |
| Retained earnings, 12/31/04 | 840,000 | 320,000 |
| Total liabilities and equities | $2,064,000 | $1,000,000 |

Answer the following questions:
a. How can the accountant determine that the cost method has been applied by the parent?
b. What is the annual excess amortization initially recognized in connection with this purchase?
c. If the partial equity method had been applied, what investment income would have been recorded by the parent in 2004? What if the equity method had been applied?
d. What is the consolidated balance for the Retained Earnings account as of January 1, 2004?
e. What is the Noncontrolling Interest in the Subsidiary's 2004 income?
f. What is consolidated net income for 2004?
g. Within consolidated statements at January 1, 2001, what balance is included for the subsidiary's Buildings account?
h. What is the consolidated Buildings account as of December 31, 2004?

32. Father, Inc., buys 80 percent of the outstanding common stock of Sam Corporation on January 1, 2004, for $680,000 cash. Total book value of Sam on that date was only $600,000. However, Sam possessed several accounts that had fair market values differing from their book values:

| | Book Value | Fair Market Value |
|---|---|---|
| Land | $ 60,000 | $225,000 |
| Buildings and equipment (10-year remaining life) | 275,000 | 250,000 |
| Copyright (20-year life) | 100,000 | 200,000 |
| Notes payable (due in 8 years) | 130,000 | 120,000 |

For internal reporting purposes, Father, Inc., employs the equity method to account for this investment.

The following account balances are for the year ending December 31, 2004, for both companies. Determine consolidated balances for this business combination (either through individual computations or the use of a worksheet).

| | Father | Sam |
|---|---|---|
| Revenues | $(1,360,000) | $(540,000) |
| Cost of goods sold | 700,000 | 385,000 |
| Depreciation expense | 260,000 | 10,000 |
| Amortization expense | –0– | 5,000 |
| Interest expense | 44,000 | 5,000 |
| Equity in income of Sam | (105,000) | –0– |
| Net income | $ (461,000) | $(135,000) |
| Retained earnings, 1/1/04 | $(1,265,000) | $(440,000) |
| Net income (above) | (461,000) | (135,000) |
| Dividends paid | 260,000 | 65,000 |
| Retained earnings, 12/31/04 | $(1,466,000) | $(510,000) |
| Current assets | $ 965,000 | $ 528,000 |
| Investment in Sam | 733,000 | –0– |
| Land | 292,000 | 60,000 |
| Buildings and equipment (net) | 877,000 | 265,000 |
| Copyright | –0– | 95,000 |
| Total assets | $ 2,867,000 | $ 948,000 |
| Accounts payable | $ (191,000) | $(148,000) |
| Notes payable | (460,000) | (130,000) |
| Common stock | (300,000) | (100,000) |
| Additional paid-in capital | (450,000) | (60,000) |
| Retained earnings (above) | (1,466,000) | (510,000) |
| Total liabilities and equities | $(2,867,000) | $(948,000) |

Note: Credits are indicated by parentheses.

33. Answer problem 32 again, this time using the economic unit concept.
34. Burke Corporation purchased 90 percent of the outstanding voting shares of Drexel, Inc., on December 31, 2002. Burke paid a total of $602,000 in cash for these shares. As of that date, Drexel had the following account balances:

| | Book Value | Fair Market Value |
|---|---|---|
| Current assets | $160,000 | $160,000 |
| Land | 120,000 | 150,000 |
| Buildings (10-year life) | 220,000 | 200,000 |
| Equipment (5-year life) | 160,000 | 200,000 |

*(continued)*

|  | Book Value | Fair Market Value |
| --- | --- | --- |
| Patents (10-year life) | –0– | 50,000 |
| Liabilities (5-year life) | 200,000 | 180,000 |
| Common stock | 180,000 | |
| Retained earnings, 12/31/02 | 280,000 | |

December 31, 2004, adjusted trial balances for the two companies follow:

|  | Burke Corporation | Drexel, Inc. |
| --- | --- | --- |
| *Debits* | | |
| Current assets | $ 611,000 | $ 250,000 |
| Land | 380,000 | 150,000 |
| Buildings | 490,000 | 250,000 |
| Equipment | 873,000 | 150,000 |
| Investment in Drexel, Inc. | 701,000 | –0– |
| Cost of goods sold | 500,000 | 100,000 |
| Depreciation expense | 100,000 | 55,000 |
| Interest expense | 20,000 | 5,000 |
| Dividends paid | 110,000 | 70,000 |
| Total debits | $3,785,000 | $1,030,000 |
| *Credits* | | |
| Liabilities | $ 860,000 | $ 230,000 |
| Common stock | 510,000 | 180,000 |
| Retained earnings, 1/1/04 | 1,367,000 | 340,000 |
| Revenues | 940,000 | 280,000 |
| Investment income | 108,000 | –0– |
| Total credits | $3,785,000 | $1,030,000 |

a. Without using a worksheet or consolidation entries, determine the balances to be reported as of December 31, 2004, for this business combination. Any goodwill is not amortized.

b. To verify the figures determined in requirement (*a*), prepare a consolidation worksheet for Burke Corporation and Drexel, Inc., as of December 31, 2004.

35. Using the information presented in problem 34, produce a worksheet to consolidate the financial statements of Burke and Drexel incorporating the economic unit concept rather than the parent company concept.

36. Following are the individual financial statements for Up and Down for the year ending December 31, 2004:

|  | Up | Down |
| --- | --- | --- |
| Sales | $ 600,000 | $ 300,000 |
| Cost of goods sold | 300,000 | 140,000 |
| Operating expenses | 174,000 | 60,000 |
| Dividend income | 24,000 | –0– |
| Net income | $ 150,000 | $ 100,000 |
| Retained earnings, 1/1/04 | $ 700,000 | $ 400,000 |
| Net income | 150,000 | 100,000 |
| Dividends paid | 80,000 | 40,000 |
| Retained earnings, 12/31/04 | $ 770,000 | $ 460,000 |

*(continued)*

|  | Up | Down |
| --- | --- | --- |
| Cash and receivables | $ 250,000 | $ 100,000 |
| Inventory | 500,000 | 190,000 |
| Investment in Down | 526,000 | –0– |
| Buildings (net) | 524,000 | 600,000 |
| Equipment (net) | 400,000 | 400,000 |
| Total assets | $2,200,000 | $1,290,000 |
| Liabilities | 800,000 | 490,000 |
| Common stock | 630,000 | 340,000 |
| Retained earnings, 12/31/04 | 770,000 | 460,000 |
| Total liabilities and stockholders' equity | $2,200,000 | $1,290,000 |

Up acquired 60 percent of Down on April 1, 2004, for $526,000. On that date, equipment (with a six-year life) was overvalued by $30,000. Income is earned by Down evenly during the year but the dividend was paid entirely on November 1, 2004.

a. Prepare a consolidated income statement for the year ending December 31, 2004.
b. Determine the consolidated balance for each of the following accounts as of December 31, 2004:

    Goodwill                    Buildings (net)
    Equipment (net)        Dividends Paid
    Common Stock

37. Bon Air, Inc., acquired 70 percent (2,800 shares) of the outstanding voting stock of Creedmoor Corporation on January 1, 2002, for $250,000 cash. Creedmoor's net assets on that date totaled $230,000, but this balance included three accounts having actual values that differed from their book values:

|  | Book Value | Fair Market Value |
| --- | --- | --- |
| Land | $30,000 | $ 40,000 |
| Equipment (14-year life) | 50,000 | 118,000 |
| Liabilities (10-year life) | 70,000 | 50,000 |

As of December 31, 2005, the two companies report the following balances:

|  | Bon Air | Creedmoor |
| --- | --- | --- |
| Revenues | $ 694,800 | $250,000 |
| Operating expenses | (630,000) | (180,000) |
| Investment income | 44,200 | –0– |
| Net income | $ 109,000 | $ 70,000 |
| Retained earnings, 1/1/05 | $ 760,000 | $260,000 |
| Net income | 109,000 | 70,000 |
| Dividends paid | (68,000) | (10,000) |
| Retained earnings, 12/31/05 | $ 801,000 | $320,000 |
| Current assets | $ 72,000 | $120,000 |
| Investment in Creedmoor Corp. | 321,800 | –0– |
| Land | 241,000 | 50,000 |
| Buildings (net) | 289,000 | 200,000 |
| Equipment (net) | 165,200 | 40,000 |
| Total assets | $1,089,000 | $410,000 |

*(continued)*

|  | Bon Air | Creedmoor |
|---|---|---|
| Liabilities | $ 180,000 | $ 50,000 |
| Common stock | 50,000 | 40,000 |
| Additional paid-in capital | 58,000 | -0- |
| Retained earnings, 12/31/05 | 801,000 | 320,000 |
| Total liabilities and equities | $1,089,000 | $410,000 |

(Each of the following is an independent question.)

a. Consolidated financial statements are being prepared on December 31, 2005. What balance should be reported for each of the following figures?

> Operating expenses
> Noncontrolling interest in Creedmoor's net income
> Revenues
> Retained earnings, 1/1/05
> Net income
> Dividends paid
> Land
> Equipment
> Liabilities
> Common stock
> Retained earnings, 12/31/05
> Noncontrolling interest in Creedmoor, 12/31/05

b. If Bon Air sells 400 shares of this stock on December 31, 2005, for $60,000 cash, what journal entry is recorded?

38. The Seals Corporation purchased 80 percent of the outstanding stock of Croft, Inc., for $384,000. An appraisal of Croft made on that date determined that all book values appropriately reflected the actual worth of the underlying accounts except that a building with a 10-year life was undervalued by $20,000 and a fully amortized trademark with an estimated 20-year remaining life had an $80,000 fair value.

Following are the separate financial statements for the year ending December 31, 2004. Croft's income is assumed to have been earned evenly throughout the year. In addition, the subsidiary's dividend payments have been made as four equal quarterly payments. Seals has inappropriately included the receipt of dividends in its Sales account rather than the separate Dividend Income account.

|  | Seals Corporation | Croft, Inc. |
|---|---|---|
| Sales | $ 600,000 | $210,000 |
| Cost of goods sold | (200,000) | (80,000) |
| Operating expenses | (246,000) | (70,000) |
| Dividend income | -0- | -0- |
| Net income | $ 154,000 | $ 60,000 |
| Retained earnings, 1/1/04 | $ 700,000 | $280,000 |
| Net income (above) | 154,000 | 60,000 |
| Dividends paid | (70,000) | (20,000) |
| Retained earnings, 12/31/04 | $ 784,000 | $320,000 |
| Current assets | $ 400,000 | $220,000 |
| Investment in Croft, Inc. | 384,000 | -0- |
| Buildings (net) | 320,000 | 180,000 |
| Equipment (net) | 360,000 | 210,000 |
| Total assets | $1,464,000 | $610,000 |

*(continued)*

## Consolidated Financial Statements and Outside Ownership

|  | Seals Corporation | Croft, Inc. |
|---|---|---|
| Liabilities | $ 470,000 | $190,000 |
| Common stock | 210,000 | 100,000 |
| Retained earnings, 12/31/04 (above) | 784,000 | 320,000 |
| Total liabilities and equities | $1,464,000 | $610,000 |

a. Prepare a worksheet to consolidate these two companies on the assumption that the purchase was made on January 1, 2004.

b. Without using a worksheet, determine consolidated totals for these two companies on the assumption that the purchase was made on October 1, 2004, for $408,000.

39. Watson, Inc., acquires 60 percent of Houston, Inc., on January 1, 2002, for $400,000 in cash. On that date, assets and liabilities of the subsidiary had the following values:

|  | Book Value | Fair Market Value |
|---|---|---|
| Current assets | $320,000 | $320,000 |
| Equipment (net)(10-year life) | 410,000 | 380,000 |
| Buildings (net)(15-year life) | 300,000 | 455,000 |
| Current liabilities | 190,000 | 190,000 |
| Bonds payable (due in 10 years) | 370,000 | 350,000 |

On December 31, 2005, these two companies report the following figures:

|  | Watson | Houston |
|---|---|---|
| Revenues | $ 640,000 | $ 280,000 |
| Operating expenses | (480,000) | (210,000) |
| Equity in subsidiary earnings | 36,400 | –0– |
| Net income | $ 196,400 | $ 70,000 |
| Retained earnings, 1/1/05 | $ 683,400 | $ 380,000 |
| Net income | 196,400 | 70,000 |
| Dividends paid | (60,200) | (40,000) |
| Retained earnings, 12/31/05 | $ 819,600 | $ 410,000 |
| Current assets | $ 215,000 | $ 260,000 |
| Investment in Houston | 491,600 | –0– |
| Equipment (net) | 500,000 | 420,000 |
| Buildings (net) | 413,000 | 520,000 |
| Total assets | $1,619,600 | $1,200,000 |
| Current liabilities | $ 390,000 | $ 170,000 |
| Bonds payable | 100,000 | 370,000 |
| Common stock | 310,000 | 250,000 |
| Retained earnings, 12/31/05 | 819,600 | 410,000 |
| Total liabilities and equities | $1,619,600 | $1,200,000 |

*Answer each of the following questions:*

a. The parent is recognizing a $36,400 balance as its Equity in Subsidiary Earnings. How was this balance calculated?

b. Is an adjustment needed to the parent's Retained Earnings as of January 1, 2005? Why or why not?

c. How much total amortization expense should be recognized for consolidation purposes in 2005?

d. What is the noncontrolling interest in the subsidiary's net income?

e. Prepare a consolidated income statement.

f. What allocations were made as a result of the purchase price? What amount of each allocation remains at the end of 2005?

g. What is the December 31, 2005, amount in Noncontrolling Interest in the Subsidiary? What three components make up this total?
h. Prepare a consolidated balance sheet as of December 31, 2005.

40. Good Corporation acquired 80 percent of the outstanding stock of Morning, Inc., on January 1, 2002, for $1,400,000 in cash, debt, and stock. One of Morning's buildings, with a 10-year remaining life, was undervalued on the company's accounting records by $80,000. Also, Morning's newly developed unpatented technology, with an estimated 10-year life, was assessed to have a fair value of $550,000.

During subsequent years, Morning reports the following:

|      | Net Income | Dividends Paid |
|------|------------|----------------|
| 2002 | $180,000   | $100,000       |
| 2003 | 200,000    | 100,000        |
| 2004 | 300,000    | 100,000        |
| 2005 | 400,000    | 120,000        |

The following trial balances are for these two companies as of December 31, 2005. Morning owes Good $100,000 as of this date.

|                              | Good        | Morning     |
|------------------------------|-------------|-------------|
| **Debits**                   |             |             |
| Cash                         | $ 300,000   | $ 200,000   |
| Receivables                  | 700,000     | 400,000     |
| Inventory                    | 400,000     | 500,000     |
| Investment in Morning        | 1,400,000   | –0–         |
| Land                         | 700,000     | 600,000     |
| Buildings (net)              | 300,000     | 700,000     |
| Operating expenses           | 400,000     | 100,000     |
| Dividends paid               | 380,000     | 120,000     |
| Total debits                 | $4,580,000  | $2,620,000  |
| **Credits**                  |             |             |
| Liabilities                  | $ 200,000   | $ 620,000   |
| Common stock                 | 1,000,000   | 460,000     |
| Additional paid-in capital   | 600,000     | 40,000      |
| Retained earnings, 1/1/05    | 1,800,000   | 1,000,000   |
| Revenues                     | 884,000     | 500,000     |
| Dividend income              | 96,000      | –0–         |
| Total credits                | $4,580,000  | $2,620,000  |

Prepare consolidated financial statements for this business combination for 2005.

41. On January 1, 2002, Turner Company bought a 30 percent interest in Atlanta Company. The acquisition price was $257,000 and was negotiated under the assumption that all of Atlanta's accounts were fairly valued within the company's accounting records. Any remaining excess cost was assumed to be attributable to goodwill with an indefinite life.

During 2002, Atlanta reported net income of $90,000 and paid cash dividends of $60,000. Turner felt that the ability to significantly influence the operations of Atlanta had been achieved and, therefore, accounted for this investment by means of the equity method.

On April 1, 2003, Turner acquired an additional 30 percent interest in Atlanta for $309,000 in cash. As of this date, the parent believed that a patent developed by Atlanta was worth $100,000, even though it was not recorded within the financial records of the subsidiary. This patent is anticipated to have a remaining life of six years. Although the financial statements now have to be consolidated, Turner elects to continue applying the equity method to this investment for internal reporting purposes.

The following financial information is for these two companies for 2003. In addition, all of the subsidiary's operations as well as dividend payments are considered to have occurred evenly throughout the year.

|  | Turner Company | Atlanta Company |
|---|---|---|
| Revenues | $ 660,000 | $ 400,000 |
| Operating expenses | (398,000) | (280,000) |
| Income of subsidiary | 59,250 | -0- |
| Net income | $ 321,250 | $ 120,000 |
| Retained earnings, 1/1/03 | $ 823,000 | $ 500,000 |
| Net income (above) | 321,250 | 120,000 |
| Cash dividends paid to stockholders | (148,000) | (80,000) |
| Retained earnings, ending balance | $ 996,250 | $ 540,000 |
| Current assets | $ 481,000 | $ 410,000 |
| Investment in subsidiary | 592,250 | -0- |
| Land | 388,000 | 200,000 |
| Buildings | 700,900 | 630,000 |
| Total assets | $2,162,150 | $1,240,000 |
| Liabilities | $ 660,900 | $ 380,000 |
| Common stock | 95,000 | 300,000 |
| Additional paid-in capital | 410,000 | 20,000 |
| Retained earnings, 12/31/03 | 996,250 | 540,000 |
| Total liabilities and equities | $2,162,150 | $1,240,000 |

*Answer each of the following questions:*

a. What allocation would Turner have made of the initial $257,000 acquisition price?
b. What is the book value of the Investment in Atlanta account at the end of 2002?
c. What allocation would Turner have made of the second $309,000 acquisition price?
d. On Turner's separate income statement for 2003, the Income of Subsidiary account has a balance of $59,250. How was this amount derived?
e. On Turner's separate balance sheet as of December 31, 2003, the Investment in Subsidiary account reports a balance of $592,250. How was this balance derived?
f. What is the consolidated Retained Earnings balance as of January 1, 2003? How is this amount determined?
g. Prepare a worksheet to consolidate the financial statements of these two companies as of December 31, 2003.

42. On January 1, 2003, Ace, Incorporated, acquired 60 percent of the outstanding shares of Holt Company for $566,000 in cash. At the time of this purchase, Holt held a building (six-year remaining life) that was undervalued in the accounting records by $70,000. During 2003, Holt reported net income of $150,000 and paid cash dividends of $80,000. On May 1, 2004, Ace bought an additional 30 percent interest in Holt for $366,000. Ace reappraised Holt's assets and liabilities on this date and estimated that the company's buildings were currently undervalued by $260,000. At the time of this second purchase, these buildings had a five-year remaining life. Any goodwill was not to be amortized.

The following financial information is for these two companies for 2004. Holt issued no additional capital stock during either 2003 or 2004. Income and dividends can be assumed as having been earned and paid evenly throughout each of the years.

|  | Ace, Incorporated | Holt Company |
|---|---|---|
| Revenues | $ 400,000 | $ 300,000 |
| Operating expenses | (200,000) | (120,000) |
| Investment income (partial equity method) | 144,000 | -0- |
| Net income | $ 344,000 | $ 180,000 |

*(continued)*

|  | Ace, Incorporated | Holt Company |
|---|---|---|
| Retained earnings, 1/1/04 | $ 800,000 | $ 500,000 |
| Net income (above) | 344,000 | 180,000 |
| Dividends paid | (144,000) | (60,000) |
| Retained earnings, 12/31/04 | $1,000,000 | $ 620,000 |
| Current assets | $ 200,000 | $ 190,000 |
| Investment in Holt Company | 1,070,000 | –0– |
| Land | 100,000 | 600,000 |
| Buildings (net) | 210,000 | 300,000 |
| Equipment (net) | 380,000 | 110,000 |
| Total assets | $1,960,000 | $1,200,000 |
| Liabilities | $ 500,000 | $ 200,000 |
| Common stock | 400,000 | 300,000 |
| Additional paid-in capital | 60,000 | 80,000 |
| Retained earnings, 12/31/04 | 1,000,000 | 620,000 |
| Total liabilities and equities | $1,960,000 | $1,200,000 |

Determine the appropriate balances for consolidated financial statements for Ace, Incorporated, and Holt Company for December 31, 2004, and the year then ended. Show supporting computations in good form.

43. On January 1, 2001, Wilbourne Company acquired 6,000 of the 10,000 outstanding shares of Hampton Corporation. The purchase price included an allocation of $120,000 for a customer base that was not reflected on Hampton's books. All other assets and liabilities of Hampton had fair market values equal to their book values. The customer base was to be amortized over a 20-year life.

On January 1, 2004, Wilbourne bought an additional 2,000 shares of Hampton, increasing ownership to an 80 percent interest. In making this second acquisition, Wilbourne assigned $40,000 of the purchase price to a patent (life of 10 years) held by Hampton. An additional $40,000 was attributed to Hampton's expanding customer base to be amortized at $2,000 per year.

In need of raising cash, Wilbourne sold 1,000 shares of its investment in Hampton on April 1, 2005, for $140,000 in cash. A problem arose in connection with the recording of this sale. Wilbourne's accountants could not agree on the appropriate gain or loss to be recognized so they simply debited cash for $140,000 and credited the Investment account for the same amount. Because of the confusion, Wilbourne prepared no other entries for the investment for the year of 2005, although the equity method had been properly applied through 2004.

The following individual financial records are for these two companies for 2005. Prepare a consolidation worksheet and the resulting financial statements. Assume that an averaging system is used to determine the appropriate book value of the shares that were sold.

|  | Wilbourne Company | Hampton Corporation |
|---|---|---|
| Revenues | $ 920,000 | $ 600,000 |
| Expenses | (650,000) | (440,000) |
| Equity income of Hampton Corporation | –0– | –0– |
| Net income | $ 270,000 | $ 160,000 |
| Retained earnings, 1/1/05 | $1,417,000 | $ 750,000 |
| Net income (above) | 270,000 | 160,000 |
| Dividends paid | (150,000) | –0– |
| Retained earnings, 12/31/05 | $1,537,000 | $ 910,000 |
| Cash | $ 60,000 | $ 98,000 |
| Receivables | 430,000 | 210,000 |

*(continued)*

|  | Wilbourne Company | Hampton Corporation |
|---|---|---|
| Inventories | 677,000 | 620,000 |
| Investment in Hampton Corporation | 870,000 | –0– |
| Buildings and equipment (net) | 620,000 | 514,000 |
| Patents (net) | 40,000 | 90,000 |
| Total assets | $2,697,000 | $1,532,000 |
| Liabilities | $ 690,000 | $ 322,000 |
| Common stock | 470,000 | 300,000 |
| Retained earnings, 12/31/05 | 1,537,000 | 910,000 |
| Total liabilities and equities | $2,697,000 | $1,532,000 |

# Develop Your Skills

## FARS RESEARCH CASE *SFAS 141, SFAS 142*

**Required:**

a. Identify the prescribed method of accounting for the acquisition by a parent company of the noncontrolling interests in its subsidiary.
b. What types of transactions qualify as an acquisition of a noncontrolling interest by a parent?
c. What procedures are appropriate for goodwill impairment testing in the presence of a noncontrolling interest? What complications are introduced by the parent company concept in applying a goodwill impairment test in the presence of a noncontrolling interest?

## EXCEL CASE

Giant Company acquired a controlling interest in Small Company at the beginning of the year. Subsequently, Giant reports net income for the year of $60,000 (without regard for the investment in Small). For the same period, this subsidiary reports earnings of $30,000. In acquiring its interest, Giant paid a total of $224,000, although Small's book value was only $200,000 at the time. A building with a 10-year life was undervalued on Small's accounting records by $10,000. Any other excess cost was attributed to a copyright with a 20-year life.

**Required:**

Using an Excel spreadsheet, compute consolidated net income after reduction is made for the noncontrolling interest claim under each of the following concepts. Formulate your solution to accommodate various controlling interest percentages.
a. Economic unit
b. Proportionate consolidation
c. Parent company

## Computer Project

### A Comparison of Consolidated Financial Statements under the Economic Unit Concept and the Parent Company Concept

The purpose of this project is to assess the sensitivity of alternative concepts of noncontrolling interest valuation on consolidated financial reporting. The project requires the use of a computer and a spreadsheet software package (Microsoft Excel®, Lotus 123®, etc.). The use of these tools allows assessment of the sensitivity of alternative accounting methods on consolidated financial reporting without the necessity of preparing several similar worksheets by hand. Also, by modeling a worksheet process, a better understanding of accounting for combined reporting entities can result.

The project involves preparing two consolidated worksheets for a parent and subsidiary. The first worksheet uses the economic unit concept for the consolidated entity. The second worksheet uses the parent company concept (most prevalent in current practice). Additional analysis is provided to assess the sensitivity of each approach to changes in the percentage of the subsidiary owned by the noncontrolling interest.

### Project Scenario

On January 1, 2004, Pinter purchased a controlling interest in Strong, Inc., for $800,000. At that date Strong's book value was $600,000. Strong's assets and liabilities approximated their market values except for the following items:

|  | Market Value | Book Value |
| --- | --- | --- |
| Land | $ 88,000 | $100,000 |
| Building (six-year remaining life) | 170,000 | 140,000 |
| Equipment (three-year remaining life) | 370,000 | 325,000 |

Pinter accounts for its investment in Strong using the equity method. Strong declared a $25,000 dividend late in 2004. The dividend had not been paid as of December 31, 2004.

Pinter and Strong submit trial balances for consolidation as of December 31, 2004, as indicated in the accompanying worksheet template. Note that the trial balance for Pinter reflects an 80 percent ownership of Strong. However, to provide insights regarding varying levels of outside ownership, the trial balance must be programmed so that this percentage can vary.

### Instructions:

1. Input the information from the **worksheet template** into your spreadsheet as a starting point for two separate consolidation worksheets—one for the economic unit concept and one for the parent company concept. Use either separate worksheets available in Excel or Lotus, or use distinct areas of a single spreadsheet for each consolidation.
2. Designate a single cell as the percentage of Strong acquired by Pinter. Use this cell (e.g., B38 in the worksheet template) as a reference in other cell formulas. **Your worksheets should automatically change when different percentages are entered in this designated cell.**
3. On each worksheet, prepare separate cost allocation schedules using formulas to allow for alternative ownership percentages.
4. To accommodate alternative ownership percentages, the following accounts in Pinter's trial balances require formulas: Equity Income of Strong, Dividend Receivable, Investment in Strong, as well as the carrydown figures (Income and Retained earnings) and the totals. For example, in Excel, cell B17 in Pinter's trial balance can be entered as =C12*B38 so that it will change whenever cell B38 changes. No accounts in Strong's trial balances require formulas.
5. Complete the worksheet adjusting and eliminating entries, the noncontrolling interest amounts, and consolidated balances. Be sure to use formulas to enable the worksheets to automatically change when the percentage acquired is changed.
6. Prepare an accompanying written report that compares and explains the differences between the economic unit concept and parent company concept consolidated figures at 80 percent ownership. Describe the effects on the consolidated balances when 100 percent ownership exists. Indicate which concept you believe should be used in financial reporting and why.

## Worksheet Template

| | A | B | C | D | E | F | G |
|---|---|---|---|---|---|---|---|
| | December 31, 2004 | | | Adjustments & Eliminations | | Noncontrolling | |
| | | Pinter | Strong | Debit | Credit | Interest | Consolidated |
| 3 | Revenues | $(840,000) | $(740,000) | | | | |
| 4 | Operating expenses | 690,000 | 550,000 | | | | |
| 5 | Equity income of Strong | (136,000) | | | | | |
| 6 | Noncontrolling interest in Strong's income | | | | | | |
| 7 | Net income | $(286,000) | $(190,000) | | | | |
| 8 | | | | | | | |
| 9 | Retained earnings—Pinter, 1/1/04 | $(775,000) | | | | | |
| 10 | Retained earnings—Strong, 1/1/04 | | (350,000) | | | | |
| 11 | Net income (above) | (286,000) | (190,000) | | | | |
| 12 | Dividends declared | 115,000 | 25,000 | | | | |
| 13 | Retained earnings, 12/31/04 | $(946,000) | $(515,000) | | | | |
| 14 | | | | | | | |
| 15 | Cash | $102,000 | $32,000 | | | | |
| 16 | Accounts receivable | 96,000 | 140,000 | | | | |
| 17 | Dividends receivable | 20,000 | | | | | |
| 18 | Inventory | 225,000 | 208,000 | | | | |
| 19 | Investment in Strong | 916,000 | | | | | |
| 20 | | | | | | | |
| 21 | | | | | | | |
| 22 | | | | | | | |
| 23 | Land | 200,000 | 100,000 | | | | |
| 24 | Buildings (net) | 550,000 | 120,000 | | | | |
| 25 | Equipment (net) | 350,000 | 310,000 | | | | |
| 26 | Goodwill | | | | | | |
| 27 | Total assets | $2,459,000 | $910,000 | | | | |
| 28 | | | | | | | |
| 29 | Dividends payable | $(25,000) | | | | | |
| 30 | Liabilities | $(513,000) | (120,000) | | | | |
| 31 | Common stock | (1,000,000) | (250,000) | | | | |
| 32 | Noncontrolling interest | | | | | | |
| 33 | | | | | | | |
| 34 | | | | | | | |
| 35 | Retained earnings (above) | (946,000) | (515,000) | | | | |
| 36 | Total liabilities and equity | $(2,459,000) | $(910,000) | | | | |
| 37 | | | | | | | |
| 38 | **Percentage acquired** | 80% | | | | | |

# Chapter Five

# Consolidated Financial Statements—Intercompany Asset Transactions

## Questions to Consider

- How does the intercompany transfer of inventory or other assets between parent and subsidiary affect the consolidation process?

- Gains on intercompany transactions are considered unrealized until the assets are resold to outsiders or consumed. Prior to the realization of these gains, what adjustments are required in producing consolidated financial statements?

- How does the presence of intercompany transactions affect the balances reported for any noncontrolling interest? What impact does the direction of these transfers (upstream versus downstream) have on the reporting of a noncontrolling interest?

- The intercompany sale of land and depreciable assets also can occur between the members of a business combination. What impact does the specific type of property being conveyed have on the consolidation process?

- Why does the transfer of a depreciable asset frequently result in the recording of excess depreciation in subsequent years?

In Chapter 1, the deferral and subsequent recognition of gains created by inventory transfers between two affiliated companies is analyzed in connection with equity method accounting. The central theme of that discussion is that intercompany profits are not considered to be realized until the earning process is culminated by a sale to an unrelated party. This same accounting logic applies to transactions between companies within a business combination. Because a single economic entity is formed, such sales create neither profits nor losses. In reference to this issue, *ARB 51* (par. 7) states:

> As consolidated statements are based on the assumption that they represent the financial position and operating results of a single business enterprise, such statements should not include gain or loss on transactions among the companies in the group. Accordingly, any intercompany profit or loss on assets remaining within the group should be eliminated; the concept usually applied for this purpose is gross profit or loss.

The elimination of the accounting effects created by intercompany transactions is one of the most significant problems encountered in the consolidation process. The volume of transfers within most large enterprises can be large. A recent annual report for the Ford Motor Company, for example, shows the elimination of intersegment revenues amounting to $3.85 billion.

Such transactions are especially common in companies that have been constructed as a vertically integrated chain of organizations. These entities reduce their costs by developing affiliations in which one operation furnishes products to another. As observed by *Mergers & Acquisitions*:

> Downstream acquisitions . . . are aimed at securing critical sources of materials and components, streamlining manufacturing and materials planning, gaining economies of scale, entering new markets, and enhancing overall competitiveness. Manufacturers that combine with suppliers are often able to assert total control over such critical areas as product quality and resource planning.[1]

---

[1] "Acquiring along the Value Chain," *Mergers & Acquisitions,* June–July 1996, p. 8.

Intercompany asset transactions take several forms. In particular, inventory transfers are especially prevalent. However, the sale of land as well as depreciable assets also can occur between the parties within a combination. This chapter examines the consolidation procedures necessitated by each of these different types of intercompany asset transfers.

## INTERCOMPANY INVENTORY TRANSACTIONS

As discussed in previous chapters, companies that make up a business combination frequently retain their legal identities as separate operating centers and maintain their own record-keeping. Thus, any inventory sales between these companies trigger the independent accounting systems of both parties. Revenue is duly recorded by the seller, while the purchase is simultaneously entered into the accounts of the buyer. For internal reporting purposes, recording an inventory transfer as a sale/purchase provides vital data to help measure the operational efficiency of each enterprise.[2]

Despite the informational benefits of accounting for the transaction in this manner, from a consolidated perspective neither a sale nor a purchase has occurred. *An intercompany transfer is merely the internal movement of inventory, an event that creates no net change in the financial position of the business combination taken as a whole.* Thus, in producing consolidated financial statements, the recorded effects of these transfers are eliminated so that consolidated statements reflect only transactions with outside parties. Worksheet entries serve this purpose; they adapt the financial information reported by the separate companies to the perspective of the consolidated enterprise. The entire impact of the intercompany transactions must be identified and then removed. The deleting of the actual transfer is described here first.

### The Sales and Purchases Accounts

To account for related companies as a single economic entity, all intercompany sales/purchases accounts are eliminated. For example, if Arlington Company makes an $80,000 inventory sale to Zirkin Company, an affiliated party within a business combination, both parties record the transfer as a normal sale/purchase. The following worksheet entry is then necessary to remove the resulting balances from the consolidated figures. Cost of Goods Sold is reduced here under the assumption that the Purchases account usually is closed out prior to the consolidation process.

**Consolidation Entry TI** (Transferred Income)
Sales .................................................................. 80,000
    Cost of Goods Sold (purchases component) .................... 80,000
To eliminate effects of intercompany transfer of inventory. (Labeled "TI" in reference to the transferred inventory.)

*In the preparation of consolidated financial statements, the preceding elimination must be made for all intercompany inventory transfers.* The total recorded (intercompany) sales figure is deleted regardless of whether the transaction was downstream (from parent to subsidiary) or upstream (from subsidiary to parent).[3] Furthermore, the elimination is unaffected by any

---

[2] For all intercompany transactions, the two parties involved view the events from different perspectives. Thus, the transfer is both a sale and a purchase, often creating both a receivable and a payable. To indicate the dual nature of such transactions, these accounts are indicated within this text as sales/purchases, receivables/payables, and so on.

[3] Downstream and upstream transactions were introduced in Chapter 1. Although the direction of the transfer did not influence the equity method of accounting (for external reporting), the distinction is significant in the preparation of consolidated statements.

markup included in the transfer price. Because the entire amount of the transfer was between related parties, the total effect must be removed in preparing the consolidated statements.[4]

## Unrealized Gains—Year of Transfer (Year 1)

Removal of the sale/purchase is often just the first in a series of consolidation entries necessitated by inventory transfers. Despite the previous elimination, unrealized gains created by such sales can still exist in the accounting records at year's end. These gains initially result when the merchandise is priced at more than historical cost. Actual transfer prices are established in several ways, including the normal sales price of the inventory, sales price less a specified discount, or at a predetermined markup above cost. In a footnote to its recent financial statements, Ford Motor Company explains that

> Intercompany sales among geographic areas consist primarily of vehicles, parts, and components manufactured by the company and various subsidiaries and sold to different entities within the consolidated group; transfer prices for these transactions are established by agreement between the affected entities.

Regardless of the method used for this pricing decision, intercompany gains that remain unrealized at year-end must be removed in arriving at consolidated figures.

### All Inventory Remains at Year-End

In the preceding illustration, assume that Arlington acquired or produced this inventory at a cost of $50,000 and then sold it to Zirkin, an affiliated party, at the indicated price of $80,000. From a consolidated perspective, the inventory still has a historical cost of only $50,000. However, it is now reported in Zirkin's records as an asset at the $80,000 transfer price. In addition, because of the markup, Arlington has recorded a $30,000 gross profit as a result of this intercompany sale. Because the transaction did not occur with an outside party, recognition of this profit is not appropriate for the combination as a whole.

Thus, although the sale/purchase figures are eliminated by consolidation entry TI shown earlier, the $30,000 inflation created by the transfer price still exists in two areas of the individual statements:

- Ending inventory remains overstated by $30,000.
- Gross profit is artificially overstated by this same amount.

Correction of the ending inventory requires only a reduction in the asset. However, before decreasing gross profit, the accounts affected by the unrealized gain must be identified. The ending inventory total serves as a negative component within the Cost of Goods Sold computation; it represents the portion of acquired inventory that was not sold. Thus, the $30,000 overstatement of the inventory that is still held incorrectly lowers this expense (the inventory that was sold). *Despite Entry TI, the inflated ending inventory figure causes cost of goods sold to be too low and, thus, profits to be too high by $30,000.* For consolidation purposes, the expense must be raised by this amount through a worksheet adjustment that properly removes the unrealized gain from consolidated net income.

Consequently, if all of the transferred inventory is retained by the business combination at the end of the year, the following worksheet entry also has to be included to eliminate the effects of the gain that remains unrealized within ending inventory.

| Consolidation Entry G—Year of Transfer (Year 1) All Inventory Remains | | |
|---|---|---|
| Cost of Goods Sold (ending inventory component) | 30,000 | |
|     Inventory (balance sheet account) | | 30,000 |
| To remove unrealized gain created by intercompany sale. | | |

---

[4] As is shown in the appendix to this chapter, alternative theoretical approaches to consolidation that advocate removing only the parent's portion of intercompany sales/purchases when a noncontrolling interest is present can be identified. In current practice, elimination of all intercompany sales/purchases (as shown here) appears to predominate.

# Discussion Question

**EARNINGS MANAGEMENT**

Enron Corporation's 2001 third quarter 10-Q report disclosed the following transaction with LJM2, a nonconsolidated special purpose entity (SPE) that was formed by Enron:

> In June 2000, LJM2 purchased dark fiber optic cable from Enron for a purchase price of $100 million. LJM2 paid Enron $30 million in cash and the balance in an interest-bearing note for $70 million. Enron recognized $67 million in pre-tax earnings in 2000 related to the asset sale. Pursuant to a marketing agreement with LJM2, Enron was compensated for marketing the fiber to others and providing operation and maintenance services to LJM2 with respect to the fiber. LJM2 sold a portion of the fiber to industry participants for $40 million, which resulted in Enron recognizing agency fee revenue of $20.3 million.

As investigations later discovered, LJM2 was in many ways controlled by Enron.

FASB Interpretation 46 now requires the consolidation of SPEs that are essentially controlled by their sponsor firm.

By selling goods to SPEs that it controlled but did not consolidate, did Enron overstate its earnings? What effect does consolidation have on the financial reporting for transactions between a firm and its controlled entities?

---

This entry (labeled **G** for gain) reduces the consolidated Inventory account to its original $50,000 historical cost. Furthermore, increasing cost of goods sold by $30,000 effectively removes the unrealized gain from gross profit. Thus, both reporting problems created by the transfer price markup are resolved by this worksheet entry.

### *Only a Portion of Inventory Remains*

Obviously, a company does not buy inventory to hold it for an indefinite time. The acquired items are used within the company's operations or resold to unrelated, outside parties. Intercompany gains ultimately are realized by the subsequent consumption or reselling of these goods. Therefore, only the transferred inventory still held at year's end continues to be recorded in the separate statements at a value more than the historical cost. For this reason, *the elimination of unrealized gains (Entry **G**) is not based on total intercompany sales but only on the amount of transferred merchandise retained within the business at the end of the year.*

To illustrate, assume that Arlington transferred inventory costing $50,000 to Zirkin, a related company, for $80,000, thus recording a gross profit of $30,000. Assume further that by year's end Zirkin has resold $60,000 of these goods to unrelated parties but retains the other $20,000 (for resale in the following year). From the viewpoint of the consolidated company, the gain on the $60,000 portion of the intercompany sale has now been earned and no adjustment is required for consolidation purposes.

Conversely, any gain recorded in connection with the $20,000 in merchandise that remains is still a component within Zirkin's Inventory account. Because the markup was 37½ percent ($30,000 gross profit/$80,000 transfer price), this retained inventory is stated at a value $7,500 more than its original cost ($20,000 × 37½%). The required reduction (Entry **G**) is not the entire $30,000 shown previously but only the $7,500 unrealized gain that remains in ending inventory.

| Consolidation Entry G—Year of Transfer (Year 1) 40% of Inventory Remains (replaces previous entry) | | |
|---|---|---|
| Cost of Goods Sold (ending inventory component) | 7,500 | |
|     Inventory | | 7,500 |
| To remove portion of intercompany gain which is unrealized in year of transfer. | | |

## Unrealized Gains—Year Following Transfer (Year 2)

Whenever an unrealized intercompany gain is present in ending inventory, one further consolidation entry is eventually required. Although Entry **G** removes the gain from the *consolidated* inventory balances in the year of transfer, the $7,500 overstatement remains within the separate financial records of the buyer and seller. The effects of this gain are carried into their beginning balances in the subsequent year. Hence, another worksheet elimination is necessary in the period following the transfer. For consolidation purposes, the unrealized portion of the intercompany gain must be adjusted in two successive years (from ending inventory in the year of transfer and from beginning inventory of the next period).

Referring again to Arlington's sale of inventory to Zirkin, the $7,500 unrealized gain is still in Zirkin's Inventory account at the start of the subsequent year. Once again, the overstatement is removed within the consolidation process but this time from the beginning inventory balance (which appears in the financial statements only as a positive component of cost of goods sold). This elimination is termed *Entry \*G*. The asterisk indicates that the intercompany gain was created by a transfer made in a previous year.

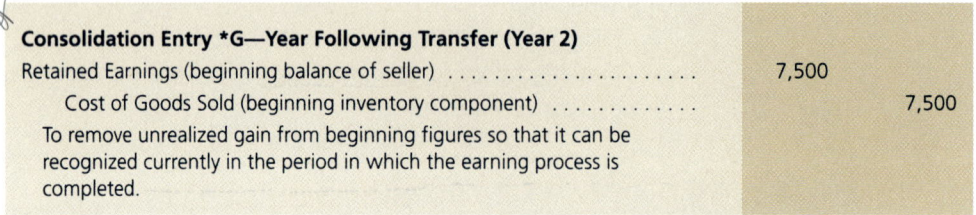

**Consolidation Entry *G—Year Following Transfer (Year 2)**
Retained Earnings (beginning balance of seller) .................... 7,500
    Cost of Goods Sold (beginning inventory component) ............ 7,500
To remove unrealized gain from beginning figures so that it can be recognized currently in the period in which the earning process is completed.

By reducing Cost of Goods Sold (beginning inventory) through this worksheet entry, the gross profit reported for this second year is increased. For consolidation purposes, the gain on the transfer is recognized in the period in which the items are actually sold to outside parties. As shown in the following diagram, Entry **G** initially deferred the $7,500 gain because this amount was unrealized in the year of transfer. Entry **\*G** now increases consolidated net income (by decreasing cost of goods sold) to reflect the earning process in the current year.

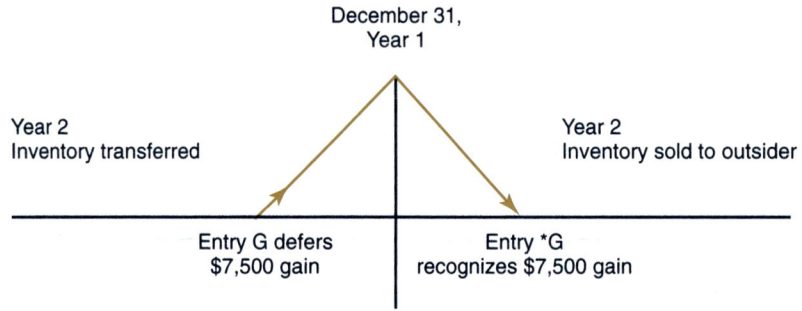

In Entry **\*G**, removal of the $7,500 from beginning inventory (within Cost of Goods Sold) appropriately increases current income and should not pose a significant conceptual problem. However, the rationale for decreasing the seller's beginning Retained Earnings deserves further explanation. This reduction removes the unrealized gain (recognized by the seller in the year of transfer) so that the profit is reported in the period when it is earned. Despite the consolidation entries in Year 1, the $7,500 gain remained on this company's separate books and was closed to Retained Earnings at the end of the period. Recall that consolidation entries are never posted to the individual affiliate's books. Therefore, from a consolidated view, the buyer's Inventory and the seller's Retained Earnings accounts as of the beginning of Year 2 contain the unrealized profit and must both be reduced in Entry **\*G**.

### *Intercompany Beginning Inventory Gain Adjustment—Downstream Sales When Parent Uses Equity Method*

The worksheet elimination of the sales/purchases balances (Entry **TI**) and the entry to remove the unrealized gain from ending Inventory in Year 1 (Entry **G**) are both standard, regardless of the circumstances of the consolidation. Conversely, in one specific situation, the procedure used to eliminate the intercompany gain from Year 2's beginning accounts differs from the Entry *G just presented. If (1) the original transfer is downstream (made by the parent) and (2) the equity method has been applied for internal accounting purposes, the Equity in Subsidiary Earnings account replaces beginning Retained Earnings in Entry *G.

When using the equity method, the parent maintains appropriate income balances within its own individual financial records. Thus, the parent defers any unrealized gain at the end of Year 1 through an equity method adjustment that also decreases the Investment in Subsidiary account. With the gain deferred, the Retained Earnings of the parent/seller at the beginning of the following year is correctly stated. The parent's Retained Earnings does not contain the unrealized gain and needs no adjustment.[5]

At the end of Year 2, both the Equity in Subsidiary Earnings and the Investment accounts are increased in recognition of the previously deferred intercompany gain. The Investment account—having been decreased in Year 1 and increased in Year 2 for the intercompany gain—thus no longer reflects any effects from the original deferral. For consolidation purposes, Entry *G simply transfers the income effect of the realized gain from the Equity in Subsidiary Earnings account to Cost of Goods Sold, appropriately increasing current consolidated income. The remaining balance in the Equity in Subsidiary Earnings account now reflects the same activity represented in the Investment account and is subsequently eliminated against the Investment account.

**Consolidation Entry *G—Year Following Transfer (Year 2)**
**(replaces previous Entry *G when transfers have been downstream and the equity method is in use)[6]**

| | | |
|---|---|---|
| Equity in Subsidiary Earnings | 7,500 | |
|     Cost of Goods Sold (beginning inventory component) | | 7,500 |

To recognize the previously deferred unrealized downstream inventory gain as part of current year income. The Equity in Subsidiary Earnings account replaces the Retained Earnings account (used for upstream profit adjustments) when adjusting for downstream sales. The parent's Retained Earnings account has already been corrected by application of the equity method.

Finally, various markup percentages are employed to determine the dollar values for intercompany profit deferrals. Exhibit 5–1 shows formulas for both the gross profit rate and markup on cost and the relation between the two.

## Unrealized Gains—Effect on Noncontrolling Interest Valuation

The effects of intercompany inventory transfers on business combinations are appropriately accounted for by the worksheet entries just described. However, one question remains: What impact do these procedures have on the valuation of a noncontrolling interest? In regard to this issue, paragraph 13 of *ARB 51* states:

> The amount of intercompany profit or loss to be eliminated in accordance with paragraph 7 is not affected by the existence of a minority interest. The complete elimination of the intercompany profit or loss is consistent with the underlying assumption that consolidated statements

---

[5] For upstream intercompany gains in beginning inventory, the subsidiary's retained earnings remain overstated and must be adjusted through Entry *G.

[6] A widely accepted alternative to recognizing realized intercompany inventory profits in the subsidiary's beginning inventory (downstream sale) when the parent uses the equity method (*G) is as follows:

| | | |
|---|---|---|
| Investment in Subsidiary | 7,500 | |
|     Cost of Goods Sold | | 7,500 |

In this case, the full amount of the Equity in Subsidiary Earnings is eliminated against the Investment in Subsidiaries account in Consolidation Adjustment I. In either alternative adjustment for recognizing realized intercompany inventory profits, the final consolidated balances remain exactly the same: Equity in Subsidiary Earnings = 0, Investment in Subsidiary = 0, and Cost of Goods Sold is reduced by $7,500.

## EXHIBIT 5–1
**Relationship between Gross Profit Rate and Markup on Cost**

In determining appropriate amounts of intercompany profits for deferral and subsequent recognition in consolidated financial reports, two alternative—but mathematically related—profit percentages are often seen. Recalling that Gross Profit = Sales − Cost of Goods Sold, then

$$\text{Gross profit rate (GPR)} = \frac{\text{Gross profit}}{\text{Sales}} = \frac{MC}{1 + MC}$$

$$\text{Markup on cost (MC)} = \frac{\text{Gross profit}}{\text{Cost of goods sold}} = \frac{GPR}{1 - GPR}$$

*Example:*
| | |
|---|---:|
| Sales (transfer price) | $1,000 |
| Cost of goods sold | 800 |
| Gross profit | $ 200 |

Here the GPR = (200/1,000) = 20% and the MC = (200/800) = 25%. In most intercompany purchases and sales, the sales (transfer) price is known and therefore the GPR is the simplest percentage to use to determine the amount of intercompany profit.

$$\text{Intercompany profit} = \text{Transfer price} \times \text{GPR}$$

Instead, if the markup on cost is available, it readily converts to a GPR by the above formula. In this case (0.25/1.25) = 20%.

---

represent the financial position and operating results of a single business enterprise. The elimination of the intercompany profit or loss *may be allocated proportionately* between the majority and minority interests [emphasis added].

The last sentence indicates that alternative approaches are available in computing the noncontrolling interest's share of a subsidiary's net income. According to this pronouncement, recognition of outside ownership *may or may not be* affected by unrealized gains resulting from intercompany transfers. Because consolidated net income is reduced by the amount attributed to a noncontrolling interest, the handling of this issue can affect the reported profitability of a business combination.

To illustrate, assume that Large Company owns 70 percent of the voting stock of Small Company. To avoid extraneous complications, assume that no amortization expense resulted from this purchase. Assume further that Large reports current net income (from separate operations) of $500,000 while Small earns $100,000. During the current period, intercompany transfers of $200,000 occur with a total markup of $90,000. At the end of the year, an unrealized intercompany gain of $40,000 remains within the inventory accounts.

Clearly, the consolidated net income prior to the reduction for the 30 percent noncontrolling interest is $560,000, the two income balances less the unrealized gain. The problem facing the accountant is the computation of the noncontrolling interest's share of Small's income. Because of the flexibility allowed by *ARB 51*, this figure may be reported as either $30,000 (30 percent of the $100,000 earnings of the subsidiary) or $18,000 (30 percent of reported income after that figure is reduced by the $40,000 unrealized gain).

To determine an appropriate valuation for this noncontrolling interest allocation, the relationship between an intercompany transaction and the outside owners must be analyzed. If a transfer is downstream (the parent sells inventory to the subsidiary), a logical view would seem to be that the unrealized gain is that of the parent company. The parent made the original sale; therefore, the gross profit is included in its financial records. Because the subsidiary's income is unaffected, little justification exists for adjusting the noncontrolling interest to reflect the deferral of the unrealized gain. Consequently, in the example of Large and Small, if the transfers were downstream, the 30 percent noncontrolling interest would be $30,000 based on Small's reported income of $100,000.

In contrast, if inventory is sold by the subsidiary to the parent (an upstream transfer), the gross profit would be recognized in the subsidiary's financial records, even though part of this income remains unrealized from a consolidation perspective. Because the outside owners possess their interest in the subsidiary, a reasonable conclusion would be that valuation of the noncontrolling interest is calculated on the income actually earned by this company. The 1995 FASB Exposure Draft, *Consolidated Financial Statements: Policy and Procedures,* supports allocating a proportionate amount of the intercompany profit adjustments (from upstream sales) to the noncontrolling interest:

> The effects on equity of eliminating intercompany profit and losses on assets that remain within the group shall be allocated between the controlling interest and the noncontrolling interest on the basis of their proportionate interest in the selling affiliate.

In this textbook, the noncontrolling interest's share of consolidated net income is computed based on *the reported income of the subsidiary after adjustment for any unrealized upstream gains.* Returning to Large Company and Small Company, if the $40,000 unrealized gain was the result of an upstream sale from subsidiary to parent, only $60,000 of Small's $100,000 reported income actually has been earned by the end of the year. The allocation to the noncontrolling interest is, therefore, reported as $18,000, or 30 percent of this realized income figure.

### *Alternative Concepts of a Noncontrolling Interest*

Although the noncontrolling interest figure is based here on the subsidiary's reported income adjusted for the effects of upstream intercompany transfers, *ARB 51,* as quoted earlier, does not require this treatment. Giving effect to upstream transfers in this calculation but not to downstream transfers is no more than an attempt to select the most logical approach from among acceptable alternatives. Over the years a number of possible methods of consolidating the results of intercompany transfers have been considered. Several of these alternatives are discussed in the appendix at the end of this chapter.

## Intercompany Inventory Transfers Summarized

To assist in overcoming the complications created by intercompany transfers, the consolidation process is demonstrated in three different ways:

- Before proceeding to a numerical example, the impact of intercompany transfers on consolidated figures is reviewed. Ultimately, the accountant must understand how the balances to be reported by a business combination are derived when unrealized gains result from either upstream or downstream sales.
- Next, two different consolidation worksheets are produced: one for downstream transfers and the other for upstream. The various consolidation procedures used in these worksheets are explained and analyzed.
- Finally, several of the worksheet entries used in developing a consolidation worksheet are shown side by side so that the differences created by the direction of the transfers can be better understood.

### *The Development of Consolidated Totals*

The following summary discusses only the accounts impacted by intercompany transactions:

*Revenues.* The parent's balance is added to the subsidiary's balance, but all intercompany transfers are then removed.

*Cost of Goods Sold.* This expense is one of the most difficult figures computed within the consolidation process. The parent's balance is added to the subsidiary's balance but all intercompany transfers are removed. The resulting total is decreased by any beginning unrealized gain (thus, raising net income) and increased by any ending unrealized gain (to reduce net income).

*Expenses.* The parent's balance is added to the subsidiary's balance plus any amortization expense for the year recognized on the purchase price allocations.[7]

---

[7] As discussed later in this chapter, consolidated expenses also have to be reduced to remove excess depreciation recognized whenever a depreciable asset is transferred between the companies within a business combination at a price more than the book value.

*Noncontrolling Interest in Subsidiary's Net Income.* The subsidiary's reported net income is adjusted for the effects of unrealized gains on upstream transfers (but not downstream transfers) and then multiplied by the percentage of outside ownership.

*Retained Earnings at the Beginning of the Year.* As in previous chapters, if the equity method has been applied, the parent's balance mirrors the consolidated total. When any other method is used, the parent's beginning Retained Earnings must be converted to the equity method by Entry *C. Accruals for this purpose are based on the income actually earned by the subsidiary in previous years (reported income adjusted for any unrealized upstream gains).

*Inventory.* The parent's balance is added to the subsidiary's balance. Any unrealized gain remaining at the end of the current year is removed to lower the reported balance to historical cost.

*Land, Buildings, and Equipment.* The parent's balance is added to the subsidiary's balance. This total is adjusted for any purchase price allocations and subsequent amortization.[8]

*Noncontrolling Interest in Subsidiary at End of Year.* The final total begins with the noncontrolling interest at the beginning of the year. This figure is based on the subsidiary's book value on that date after removing any unrealized gains on upstream sales. The beginning balance is updated by adding the portion of the subsidiary's income assigned to these outside owners (computed above) and subtracting the noncontrolling interest's share of the subsidiary's dividend payments.

## Intercompany Inventory Transfers Illustrated

To examine the various consolidation procedures relative to intercompany inventory transfers, assume that Top Company purchases 80 percent of the voting stock of Bottom Company on January 1, 2003. The parent pays a total of $400,000, a price that includes all directly related consolidation costs. Allocation of $40,000 is made to a database, a figure amortized at the rate of $2,000 per year for 20 years.

The subsidiary reports net income of $30,000 in 2003 and $70,000 in 2004, the current year. Dividend payments are $20,000 in the first year and $50,000 in the second. Top applies the cost method so that dividend income of $16,000 ($20,000 × 80 percent) and $40,000 ($50,000 × 80 percent) is recorded by the parent during these two years. Using the cost method in this initial example avoids the problem of computing the parent's investment account balances. However, this illustration is extended to demonstrate the changes necessary if the parent applies the equity method.

After the takeover, intercompany inventory sales occurred between the two companies as shown in Exhibit 5–2. A $10,000 intercompany debt also exists as of December 31, 2004.

The 2004 consolidation of Top and Bottom is presented twice. First, the transfers are assumed to be downstream from parent to subsidiary. Second, consolidated figures are recomputed with the transfers being viewed as upstream. This distinction is only significant because of a noncontrolling interest.

### *Downstream Sales*

In the first example, all inventory transfers are assumed to have been *downstream* from Top to Bottom. Based on that perspective, the worksheet to consolidate these two companies for the year ending December 31, 2004, is in Exhibit 5–3.

Most of the worksheet entries found in Exhibit 5–3 are described and analyzed in previous chapters of this textbook. Thus, only four of these entries are examined in detail along with the computation of the noncontrolling interests in the subsidiary's income.

**Entry *G**  Entry *G removes the unrealized gains carried over from the previous period. Because $16,000 in transferred merchandise was retained by Bottom at the first of the current

---

[8] As discussed later in this chapter, if land, buildings, or equipment have been transferred between parent and subsidiary, the separately reported balances must be returned to historical cost figures in deriving consolidated totals.

**EXHIBIT 5–2**
Intercompany Transfers

|  | 2003 | 2004 |
|---|---|---|
| Transfer prices | $80,000 | $100,000 |
| Historical cost | 60,000 | 70,000 |
| Gross profit | $20,000 | $ 30,000 |
| Inventory remaining at year's end (at transfer price) | $16,000 | $ 20,000 |

year, any related gain is unearned and must be deferred. The 2003 gross profit rate on these items was 25 percent ($20,000 gross profit/$80,000 transfer price), indicating an unrealized gain of $4,000 (25 percent of the remaining $16,000 in inventory). Thus, Entry *G reduces cost of goods sold (or the beginning inventory component of that expense) by that amount as well as the January 1, 2004, Retained Earnings of Top (the seller of the goods).

Two effects are created by Entry *G: First, last year's profits, as reflected by the seller's beginning Retained Earnings, are reduced because the $4,000 gain was not earned at that time. Second, through the reduction in Cost of Goods Sold, an increase in current year income is created. From a consolidation perspective, the gain is being correctly recognized in 2004 when the inventory is sold to an outside party.

*Entry *C* Entry *C is introduced in Chapter 3 as an initial consolidation adjustment required whenever the equity method is not applied by the parent company. Entry *C converts the parent's beginning Retained Earnings to a consolidated total. In the current illustration, Top did not accrue its portion of the 2003 increase in Bottom's book value [($30,000 income less $20,000 paid in dividends) × 80%, or $8,000] or record the $2,000 amortization expense for this same period. Because neither number has been recognized within the parent's individual records, both must be brought into the consolidation process through a $6,000 adjustment (Entry *C). The intercompany transfers did not affect this entry because they were downstream; the gains had no impact on the income recognized in connection with the subsidiary.

*Entry TI* The intercompany sales/purchases for 2004 are eliminated by Entry TI. The entire $100,000 transfer recorded by the two parties during the current period is removed to arrive at consolidated figures for the business combination.

*Entry G* Entry G defers the unrealized gain remaining at the end of 2004. The $20,000 in transferred merchandise retained by Bottom has a markup of 30 percent ($30,000 gross profit/$100,000 transfer price); thus, the unrealized gain amounts to $6,000. On the worksheet, Entry G eliminates this overstatement in the Inventory asset balance as well as the ending inventory (negative) component of Cost of Goods Sold. Because the gain remains unrealized, the increase in this expense account has the appropriate effect of lowering consolidated income.

### Noncontrolling Interest's Share of the Subsidiary's Income

In this first illustration, the intercompany transfers are downstream. Thus, the unrealized gains are considered to relate solely to the parent company, creating no effect on the subsidiary or the outside ownership. For this reason, the noncontrolling interest's share of consolidated income is recorded as a columnar entry of $14,000, 20 percent of the $70,000 net income reported by Bottom.

By including these entries along with the other routine worksheet eliminations and adjustments, the accounting information generated by Top and Bottom can be brought together into a single set of consolidated financial statements. However, this process does more than simply delete intercompany transactions; it also affects reported income. A $4,000 gain is being removed on the worksheet from 2003 figures so that it can be recognized in 2004 (Entry *G). A $6,000 gain is deferred in a similar fashion from 2004 (Entry G) and subsequently recognized in 2005. However, these changes do not affect the noncontrolling interest since the transfers were downstream.

**EXHIBIT 5–3** Downstream Inventory Transfers

*Consolidation: Purchase Method*
*Investment: Cost Method*

### TOP COMPANY AND BOTTOM COMPANY
### Consolidation Worksheet
### For Year Ending December 31, 2004

Ownership: 80%

| Accounts | Top Company | Bottom Company | Consolidation Totals Debit | Consolidation Totals Credit | Noncontrolling Interest | Consolidated Totals |
|---|---|---|---|---|---|---|
| **Income Statement** | | | | | | |
| Sales | (600,000) | (300,000) | (TI) 100,000 | | | (800,000) |
| Cost of goods sold | 320,000 | 180,000 | (G) 6,000 | (*G) 4,000 (TI) 100,000 | | 402,000 |
| Expenses | 170,000 | 50,000 | (E) 2,000 | | | 222,000 |
| Dividend income | (40,000) | –0– | (I) 40,000 | | | –0– |
| Noncontrolling interest in Bottom Company's income | –0– | –0– | | | (14,000) ‡ | 14,000 |
| Net income | (150,000) | (70,000) | | | | (162,000) |
| **Statement of Retained Earnings** | | | | | | |
| Retained earnings, 1/1/04: | | | | | | |
| Top Company | (650,000) | | (*G) 4,000 | (*C) 6,000 | | (652,000) |
| Bottom Company | | (310,000) | (S) 310,000 † | | | –0– |
| Net income (above) | (150,000) | (70,000) | | | | (162,000) |
| Dividends paid | 70,000 | 50,000 | | (I) 40,000 | 10,000 | 70,000 |
| Retained earnings, 12/31/04 | (730,000) | (330,000) | | | | (744,000) |

*continued from page 214*

**Balance Sheet**

| | | | | |
|---|---:|---:|---:|---:|
| Cash and receivables | 280,000 | 120,000 | | 390,000 |
| Inventory | 220,000 | 160,000 | (*C) 6,000 | 374,000 |
| Investment in Bottom Company | 400,000 | –0– | (P) 10,000 | –0– |
| | | | (G) 6,000 | |
| | | | (S) 368,000 | |
| | | | (A) 38,000 | |
| Land | 410,000 | 200,000 | | 610,000 |
| Plant assets (net) | 190,000 | 170,000 | | 360,000 |
| Database | –0– | –0– | (A) 38,000 | 36,000 |
| | | | (E) 2,000 | |
| Total assets | 1,500,000 | 650,000 | | 1,770,000 |
| Liabilities | (340,000) | (170,000) | (P) 10,000 | (500,000) |
| Noncontrolling interest in Bottom Company, 1/1/04 | –0– | –0– | (S) 92,000 | (92,000) |
| Noncontrolling interest in Bottom Company, 12/31/04 | | | | (96,000) |
| Common stock | (430,000) | (150,000) | (S) 150,000 | (430,000) |
| Retained earnings, 12/31/04 (above) | (730,000) | (330,000) | | (744,000) |
| Total liabilities and equities | (1,500,000) | (650,000) | | (1,770,000) |

Note: Parentheses indicate a credit balance.

†Boxed items highlight differences with upstream transfers examined in Exhibit 5–4.

‡Because intercompany sales are made downstream (by the parent), the subsidiary's earned income is the $70,000 reported figure with the 20% noncontrolling interest being allocated ($14,000).

Consolidation entries:

(*G) Removal of unrealized gain from beginning figures so that it can be recognized in current period. Downstream sales attributed to parent.
(*C) Recognition of increase in book value and amortization relating to ownership of subsidiary for year prior to 2004.
(S) Elimination of subsidiary's stockholders' equity accounts along with recognition of January 1, 2004, noncontrolling interest.
(A) Allocation of parent's cost in excess of subsidiary's book value, unamortized balance as of January 1, 2004.
(I) Elimination of intercompany dividends recorded by parent as income.
(E) Recognition of amortization expense for current year on database.
(P) Elimination of intercompany receivable/payable balances.
(TI) Elimination of intercompany sales/purchases balances.
(G) Removal of unrealized gain from ending figures so that it can be recognized in subsequent period.

### Upstream Sales

A different set of consolidation procedures is necessary if the intercompany transfers are upstream from Bottom to Top. As previously discussed, upstream gains are attributed to the subsidiary rather than to the parent company. Therefore, had these transfers been upstream, the $4,000 gain moved from 2003 into the current year (Entry *G) as well as the $6,000 unrealized gain deferred from 2004 into the future (Entry G) are both considered adjustments to Bottom's reported totals.

Tying upstream gains to Bottom's income can be a logical perspective, but such treatment complicates the consolidation process in several ways:

- Deferring the $4,000 gain from 2003 into 2004 dictates that the beginning Retained Earnings balance of the subsidiary (as the seller of the goods) should be adjusted to $306,000 rather than $310,000 found in the company's separate records on the worksheet.
- Because $4,000 of the income reported for 2003 was unearned at that time, Bottom's book value did not increase by $10,000 during the previous period (income less dividends as stated in the introduction) but only by an earned amount of $6,000.
- Bottom's earned income for the year 2004 is $68,000 rather than the $70,000 found within the company's separate financial statements. This $68,000 figure is based on adjusting the timing of the reported income to reflect the deferral and recognition of the intercompany gains.

| Earned Income of Subsidiary—Upstream Transfers | | | |
|---|---|---|---|
| Income Reported by Bottom Company, 2004 | Add: Gain from Previous Period Realized in 2004 | Less: Gain Reported in 2004 to Be Realized in Later Period | 2004 Income of Bottom Company from Consolidated Perspective |
| $70,000 | $4,000 | $(6,000) | $68,000 |

Determining Bottom's beginning Retained Earnings (realized) to be $306,000 and its 2004 income as $68,000 are preliminary calculations made in anticipation of the consolidation process. These newly computed totals are significant because they serve as the basis for several of the worksheet entries. However, the financial records of the subsidiary remain unaffected. In addition, because the cost method has been applied, no change is required in any of the parent's accounts on the worksheet.

To illustrate the effects of upstream inventory transfers, in Exhibit 5–4 we consolidate the financial statements of Top and Bottom once again. *The individual records of the two companies are unchanged from Exhibit 5–3: The only difference in this second worksheet is that the intercompany transfers are assumed to have been made upstream from Bottom to Top.* This single change creates several important differences between Exhibits 5–3 and 5–4:

1. Because the intercompany sales are made upstream, the $4,000 deferral of the beginning unrealized gain (Entry *G) is no longer a reduction in the retained earnings of the parent company. Bottom was the seller of the merchandise; thus, the elimination made in Exhibit 5–4 reduces that company's January 1, 2004, equity balance. Following this entry, Bottom's beginning Retained Earnings on the worksheet is $306,000 which is, as discussed earlier, the appropriate total from a consolidated perspective.

2. Because $4,000 of Bottom's 2003 income is being deferred into 2004, the increase in the subsidiary's book value in the previous year is only $6,000 rather than $10,000 as reported. Consequently, conversion to the equity method (Entry *C) requires an increase of just $2,800:

| | |
|---|---|
| $6,000 earned increase in subsidiary's book value during 2003 × 80% | $4,800 |
| 2003 amortization expense | (2,000) |
| Increase in parent's beginning retained earnings (Entry *C) | $2,800 |

3. Within Entry **S**, the valuation of the initial noncontrolling interest as well as the portion of the parent's investment account to be eliminated differ from the previous example. This worksheet entry removes the stockholders' equity accounts of the subsidiary as of the beginning of the current year. Thus, the $4,000 reduction made to Bottom's Retained Earnings to remove the 2003 unrealized gain must be taken into account in developing Entry **S**. After posting Entry ***G**, only $456,000 remains as the subsidiary's January 1, 2004, book value (the total of Common Stock and beginning Retained Earnings accounts after adjustment for Entry ***G**). This figure forms the basis for the 20 percent noncontrolling interest ($91,200) and the elimination of the 80 percent parent company investment ($364,800).

4. Finally, to complete the consolidation, the noncontrolling interest's share of the subsidiary's net income is recorded on the worksheet as $13,600. This balance represents a 20 percent allocation of the $68,000 earned income figure attributed to Bottom. Upstream transfers affect this computation although the downstream sales in the previous example did not. Thus, the noncontrolling interest balance reported previously in the income statement in Exhibit 5–3 differs from the allocation in Exhibit 5–4.

### *Consolidations—Downstream versus Upstream Transfers*

To help clarify the effect of downstream and upstream transfers, the worksheet entries that differ can be examined in greater detail.

| **Downstream Transfers** | | **Upstream Transfers** | |
|---|---|---|---|
| (Exhibit 5–3) | | (Exhibit 5–4) | |
| **Entry *G** | | **Entry *G** | |
| Retained Earnings, 1/1/04—Top .............. | 4,000 | Retained Earnings, 1/1/04—Bottom .......... | 4,000 |
| Cost of Goods Sold ..... | 4,000 | Cost of Goods Sold ..... | 4,000 |
| To remove 2003 unrealized gain from beginning balances of the seller. | | To remove 2003 unrealized gain from beginning balances of the seller. | |
| **Entry *C** | | **Entry *C** | |
| Investment in Bottom ....... | 6,000 | Investment in Bottom ....... | 2,800 |
| Retained Earnings, 1/1/04—Top ......... | 6,000 | Retained Earnings, 1/1/04—Bottom ...... | 2,800 |
| To convert 1/1/04 cost figures to the equity method. Income accrual is 80% of $10,000 increase in book value less $2,000 amortization. | | To convert 1/1/04 cost figures to the equity method. Income accrual is 80% of $6,000 increase in book value (after removal of unrealized gain) less $2,000 amortization. | |
| **Entry S** | | **Entry S** | |
| Common stock—Bottom .................. | 150,000 | Common stock—Bottom ................ | 150,000 |
| Retained Earnings, 1/1/04—Bottom .......... | 310,000 | Retaining Earnings, 1/1/04—Bottom (as adjusted) ............. | 306,000 |
| Investment in Bottom (80%) ......... | 368,000 | Investment in Bottom (80%) ......... | 364,800 |
| Noncontrolling interest—1/1/04 (20%) ............... | 92,000 | Noncontrolling interest—1/1/04 (20%) .............. | 91,200 |
| To remove subsidiary's stockholders' equity accounts and portion of investment balance. Book value at beginning of year is appropriate. | | To remove subsidiary's stockholders' equity accounts (as adjusted in Entry ***G**) and portion of investment balance. Adjusted book value at beginning of year is appropriate. | |
| **Noncontrolling Interest in Subsidiary's Income** = $14,000. 20% of Bottom's reported income. | | **Noncontrolling Interest in Subsidiary's Income** = $13,600. 20% of Bottom's earned income (reported income after adjustment for unrealized gains). | |

**EXHIBIT 5–4** Upstream Inventory Transfers

## TOP COMPANY AND BOTTOM COMPANY
### Consolidation Worksheet
### For Year Ending December 31, 2004

*Consolidation: Purchase Method*
*Investment: Cost Method*

*Ownership: 80%*

| Accounts | Top Company | Bottom Company | Consolidation Entries Debit | Consolidation Entries Credit | Noncontrolling Interest | Consolidated Totals |
|---|---|---|---|---|---|---|
| **Income Statement** | | | | | | |
| Sales | (600,000) | (300,000) | (TI) 100,000 | | | (800,000) |
| Cost of goods sold | 320,000 | 180,000 | (G) 6,000 | (*G) 4,000 (TI) 100,000 | | 402,000 |
| Expenses | 170,000 | 50,000 | | | | 222,000 |
| Dividend income | (40,000) | –0– | (E) 2,000 (I) 40,000 | | | –0– |
| Noncontrolling interest in Bottom Company's income | –0– | –0– | | | (13,600) ‡ | 13,600 |
| Net income | (150,000) | (70,000) | | | | (162,400) |
| **Statement of Retained Earnings** | | | | | | |
| Retained earnings, 1/1/04: | | | | | | |
|   Top Company | (650,000) | | (*G) 4,000 (S) 306,000 † | (*C) 2,800 | | (652,800) |
|   Bottom Company | | (310,000) | | | | –0– |
| Net income (above) | (150,000) | (70,000) | | | | (162,400) |
| Dividends paid | 70,000 | 50,000 | | (I) 40,000 | 10,000 | 70,000 |
| Retained earnings, 12/31/04 | (730,000) | (330,000) | | | | (745,200) |

*continued from page 218*

**Balance Sheet**

| | | | | | |
|---|---|---|---|---|---|
| Cash and receivables | 280,000 | 120,000 | | | 390,000 |
| Inventory | 220,000 | 160,000 | (*C) 2,800 | | 374,000 |
| Investment in Bottom Company | 400,000 | –0– | | (P) 10,000 | –0– |
| | | | | (G) 6,000 | |
| | | | | (S) 364,800 | |
| | | | | (A) 38,000 | |
| Land | 410,000 | 200,000 | | | 610,000 |
| Plant assets (net) | 190,000 | 170,000 | | | 360,000 |
| Database | –0– | –0– | (A) 38,000 | (E) 2,000 | 36,000 |
| Total assets | 1,500,000 | 650,000 | | | 1,770,000 |
| Liabilities | (340,000) | (170,000) | (P) 10,000 | | (500,000) |
| Noncontrolling interest in Bottom Company, 1/1/04 | –0– | –0– | | (S) 91,200 | |
| Noncontrolling interest in Bottom Company, 12/31/04 | | | | (94,800) | (94,800) |
| Common stock | (430,000) | (150,000) | (S) 150,000 | | (430,000) |
| Retained earnings, 12/31/04 (above) | (730,000) | (330,000) | | | (745,200) |
| Total liabilities and equities | (1,500,000) | (650,000) | | | (1,770,000) |

Note: Parentheses indicate a credit balance.

†Boxed items highlight differences with downstream transfers examined in Exhibit 5–3.

‡Because intercompany sales are made upstream (by the subsidiary), the subsidiary's realized income is the $68,000 ($70,000 reported balance plus $4,000 gain deferred from previous year less $6,000 deferred into next year) with the 20% noncontrolling interest being allocated $13,600.

Consolidation entries:

(*G) Removal of unrealized gain from beginning figures so that it can be recognized in current period. Upstream sales attributed to subsidiary.
(*C) Recognition of earned increase in book value and amortization relating to ownership of subsidiary for year prior to 2004.
(S) Elimination of adjusted stockholders' equity accounts along with recognition of January 1, 2004, noncontrolling interest.
(A) Allocation of parent's cost in excess of subsidiary's book value, unamortized balance as of January 1, 2004.
(I) Elimination of intercompany dividends recorded by parent as income.
(E) Recognition of amortization expense for current year on cost allocated to value of database.
(P) Elimination of intercompany receivable/payable balances.
(TI) Elimination of intercompany sales/purchases balances.
(G) Removal of unrealized gain from ending figures so that it can be recognized in subsequent period.

# Discussion Question

**WHAT PRICE SHOULD WE CHARGE OURSELVES?**

Slagle Corporation is a large manufacturing organization. Over the past several years, Slagle has obtained an important component used in its production process exclusively from Harrison, Inc., a relatively small company in Topeka, Kansas. Harrison charges $90 per unit for this part:

| | |
|---|---:|
| Variable cost per unit | $40 |
| Fixed cost assigned per unit | 30 |
| Markup | 20 |
| Total price | $90 |

In hopes of reducing manufacturing costs, Slagle purchases all of the outstanding common stock of Harrison. This new subsidiary continues to sell merchandise to a number of outside customers as well as to Slagle. Thus, for internal reporting purposes, Harrison is being viewed as a separate profit center.

A controversy has now arisen among company officials about the amount that Harrison should charge Slagle for each component. The administrator in charge of the subsidiary wants to continue with a price of $90 as in the past. He believes this figure best reflects the profitability of the division: "If we are to be judged by our profits, why should we be punished for selling to our own parent company? If that occurs, my figures will look better if I forget Slagle as a customer and try to market my goods solely to outsiders."

In contrast, the vice president in charge of Slagle's production wants the price set at variable cost, total cost, or some derivative of these numbers. "We bought Harrison to bring our costs down. It only makes sense to reduce the transfer price, otherwise the benefits of acquiring this subsidiary are not apparent. I pushed the company to buy Harrison; if our operating results are not improved, I will get the blame."

Will the decision about the transfer price affect consolidated net income? Which method would be easiest for the company's accountant to administer? As the company's accountant, what advice would you give to these officials?

## Effects on Consolidation of Alternative Investment Methods

In Exhibits 5–3 and 5–4, the cost method was utilized. However, when using either the equity method or the partial equity method, consolidation procedures normally continue to follow the same patterns analyzed in the previous chapters of this textbook. As described earlier, though, a variation in Entry *G is required when the equity method is applied and downstream transfers have occurred. The equity in subsidiary earnings account is decreased rather than recording a reduction in the beginning retained earnings of the parent/seller with the remaining amount in equity in subsidiary earnings eliminated in Entry **I**. Otherwise, the specific accounting method in use creates no unique impact on the consolidation process for intercompany transactions.

The major complication when the parent uses the equity method is not always related to a consolidation procedure. Frequently, the composition of the investment balances appearing on the parent's separate financial records proves to be the most complex element of the entire process. Under the equity method, the investment accounts are subjected to (1) income accrual, (2) amortization, (3) dividends, and (4) adjustments required by unrealized intercompany gains. Thus, if Top Company applies the equity method and the transfers are downstream, the Investment in Bottom Company account would grow from $400,000 to $414,000 by the end of 2004. For that year, the Equity Income—Bottom Company account registers a $52,000 balance. Both of these totals result from the accounting shown in Exhibit 5–5.

**EXHIBIT 5–5**
Investment Balances—
Equity Method—
Downstream Sales

### Investment in Bottom Company Analysis, 1/1/03 to 12/31/04

| | | |
|---|---:|---:|
| Cost 1/1/03 . . . . . . . . . . . . . . . . . . . . . . . . . . . . . . . . . . . . . . . . . . . . . | | $400,000 |
|   Top's share of Bottom Co. reported income for 2003 (80%) . . . | $24,000 | |
|   Database amortization . . . . . . . . . . . . . . . . . . . . . . . . . . . . . . . | (2,000) | |
|   Deferred profit from Top's 2003 unrealized gain . . . . . . . . . . . | (4,000) | |
| *Equity in earnings of Bottom Company, 2003* . . . . . . . . . . . . . . . | | 18,000 |
| Top's share of Bottom Co. dividends, 2003 (80%) . . . . . . . . . . . . | | (16,000) |
| Balance 12/31/03 . . . . . . . . . . . . . . . . . . . . . . . . . . . . . . . . . . . . . . | | $402,000 |
|   Top's share of Bottom Co. income for 2004 (80%) . . . . . . . . . | $56,000 | |
|   Database amortization . . . . . . . . . . . . . . . . . . . . . . . . . . . . . . . | (2,000) | |
|   Recognized profit from Top's 2003 unrealized gain . . . . . . . . . | 4,000 | |
|   Deferred profit from Top's 2004 unrealized gain . . . . . . . . . . . | (6,000) | |
| *Equity in earnings of Bottom Company, 2004* . . . . . . . . . . . . . . . | | $ 52,000 |
| Top's share of Bottom Co. dividends, 2004 (80%) . . . . . . . . . . . . | | (40,000) |
| Balance 12/31/04 . . . . . . . . . . . . . . . . . . . . . . . . . . . . . . . . . . . . . . | | $414,000 |

**EXHIBIT 5–6**
Investment Balances—
Equity Method—
Upstream Sales

### Investment in Bottom Company Analysis, 1/1/03 to 12/31/04

| | | |
|---|---:|---:|
| Cost 1/1/03 . . . . . . . . . . . . . . . . . . . . . . . . . . . . . . . . . . . . . . . . . . . . . | | $400,000 |
|   Bottom Co. reported income for 2003 . . . . . . . . . . . . . . . . . . . | $30,000 | |
|   Deferred profit from Bottom's 2003 unrealized gain . . . . . . . . . | (4,000) | |
|   Bottom Company adjusted earnings . . . . . . . . . . . . . . . . . . . . . | 26,000 | |
|   Top Company ownership . . . . . . . . . . . . . . . . . . . . . . . . . . . . . | 80% | |
|   Top's share of Bottom's 2003 earnings . . . . . . . . . . . . . . . . . . . | $20,800 | |
|   Database amortization . . . . . . . . . . . . . . . . . . . . . . . . . . . . . . . | (2,000) | |
| *Equity in earnings of Bottom Company, 2003* . . . . . . . . . . . . . . . | | 18,800 |
| Top's share of Bottom Co. dividends, 2003 (80%) . . . . . . . . . . . . | | (16,000) |
| Balance 12/31/03 . . . . . . . . . . . . . . . . . . . . . . . . . . . . . . . . . . . . . . | | $402,800 |
|   Bottom Co. reported income for 2004 . . . . . . . . . . . . . . . . . . . | $70,000 | |
|   Recognized profit from Bottom's 2003 unrealized gain . . . . . . . | 4,000 | |
|   Deferred profit from Bottom's 2004 unrealized gain . . . . . . . . . | (6,000) | |
|   Bottom Company adjusted earnings . . . . . . . . . . . . . . . . . . . . . | 68,000 | |
|   Top Company ownership . . . . . . . . . . . . . . . . . . . . . . . . . . . . . | 80% | |
|   Top's share of Bottom's 2004 earnings . . . . . . . . . . . . . . . . . . . | $54,400 | |
|   Database amortization . . . . . . . . . . . . . . . . . . . . . . . . . . . . . . . | (2,000) | |
| *Equity in earnings of Bottom Company, 2004* . . . . . . . . . . . . . . . | | $ 52,400 |
| Top's share of Bottom Co. dividends, 2004 (80%) . . . . . . . . . . . . | | (40,000) |
| Balance 12/31/04 . . . . . . . . . . . . . . . . . . . . . . . . . . . . . . . . . . . . . . | | $415,200 |

If transfers are upstream, the individual investment accounts reported by the parent can be determined in the same manner as in Exhibit 5–5. Because of the change in direction, the gains are now attributed to the subsidiary. Thus, both investment accounts hold balances that vary from the totals computed earlier. The Investment in Bottom Company balance becomes $415,200, whereas the Equity Income—Bottom Company account for the year is $52,400. The differences are the result of having upstream rather than downstream transactions. The components of these accounts are identified in Exhibit 5–6. Consolidated worksheets for downstream and upstream inventory transfers when Top uses the equity method are shown in Exhibit 5–7 and Exhibit 5–8.

**EXHIBIT 5–7** Downstream Inventory Transfers

### TOP COMPANY AND BOTTOM COMPANY
### Consolidation Worksheet
### For Year Ending December 31, 2004

*Consolidation: Purchase Method*
*Investment: Equity Method*

| Accounts | Top | Bottom | Adjustments & Eliminations | | NCI | Consolidated Totals |
|---|---|---|---|---|---|---|
| **Income Statement** | | | | | | |
| Sales | (600,000) | (300,000) | (TI) 100,000 | | | (800,000) |
| Cost of goods sold | 320,000 | 180,000 | (G) 6,000 | (*G) 4,000 | | 402,000 |
| | | | | (TI) 100,000 | | |
| Operating expenses | 170,000 | 50,000 | (E) 2,000 | | | 222,000 |
| Noncontrolling interest in Bottom Company's income | | | | | (14,000) ‡ | 14,000 |
| Equity in earnings of Bottom | (52,000) | | (I) 48,000 | | | –0– |
| | | | (*G) 4,000 † | | | |
| Net income | (162,000) | (70,000) | | | | (162,000) |
| **Statement of Retained Earnings** | | | | | | |
| Retained earnings, 1/1/04 | | | | | | |
| Top Company | (652,000) | | (S) 310,000 | | | (652,000) |
| Bottom Company | | (310,000) | | | | |
| Net income | (162,000) | (70,000) | | | | (162,000) |
| Dividends paid | 70,000 | 50,000 | | (D) 40,000 | 10,000 | 70,000 |
| Retained earnings, 12/31/04 | (744,000) | (330,000) | | | | (744,000) |

222

*continued from page 222*

**Balance Sheet**

| | | | | |
|---|---:|---:|---:|---:|
| Cash and receivables | 280,000 | 120,000 | | 390,000 |
| Inventory | 220,000 | 160,000 | | 374,000 |
| Investment in Bottom Company | 414,000 | | (D) 40,000 (P) 10,000<br>(G) 6,000<br>(I) 48,000<br>(S) 368,000<br>(A) 38,000 | –0– |
| Land | 410,000 | 200,000 | | 610,000 |
| Plant assets (net) | 190,000 | 170,000 | (A) 38,000 | 360,000 |
| Database | | | (E) 2,000 | 36,000 |
| Total assets | 1,514,000 | 650,000 | | 1,770,000 |
| Liabilities | (340,000) | (170,000) | (P) 10,000 | (500,000) |
| Noncontrolling interest in Bottom Company, 1/1/04 | | | (S) 92,000 | (92,000) |
| Noncontrolling interest in Bottom Company, 12/31/04 | | | | (96,000) |
| Common stock | (430,000) | (150,000) | (S) 150,000 | (430,000) |
| Retained earnings, 12/31/04 | (744,000) | (330,000) | | (744,000) |
| Total liabilities and equities | (1,514,000) | (650,000) | | (1,770,000) |

Note: Parentheses indicate a credit balance.

†Boxed items highlight differences with upstream transfers examined in Exhibit 5–8.

‡Because intercompany sales are made downstream (by the parent), the subsidiary's earned income is the $70,000 reported figure with the 20% noncontrolling interest being allocated ($14,000).

Consolidation entries:

(*G) Removal of unrealized gain from beginning figures so that it can be recognized in current period. Downstream sales attributed to parent.
(S) Elimination of subsidiary's stockholders' equity accounts along with recognition of January 1, 2004, noncontrolling interest.
(A) Allocation of parent's cost in excess of subsidiary's book value, unamortized balance as of January 1, 2004.
(I) Elimination of intercompany income remaining after *G elimination.
(D) Elimination of intercompany dividend.
(E) Recognition of amortization expense for current year on cost allocated to database.
(P) Elimination of intercompany receivable/payable balances.
(TI) Elimination of intercompany sales/purchases balances.
(G) Removal of unrealized gain from ending figures so that it can be recognized in subsequent period.

**EXHIBIT 5–8** Upstream Inventory Transfers

## TOP COMPANY AND BOTTOM COMPANY
### Consolidation Worksheet
### For Year Ending December 31, 2004

*Consolidation: Purchase Method*
*Investment: Equity Method*

| Accounts | Top | Bottom | Adjustments & Eliminations | | NCI | Consolidated Totals |
|---|---|---|---|---|---|---|
| **Income Statement** | | | | | | |
| Sales | (600,000) | (300,000) | (TI) 100,000 | | | (800,000) |
| Cost of goods sold | 320,000 | 180,000 | (G) 6,000 | (*G) 4,000 | | 402,000 |
| | | | | (TI) 100,000 | | |
| Operating expenses | 170,000 | 50,000 | (E) 2,000 | | | 222,000 |
| Noncontrolling interest in Bottom Company's income | | | | | 13,600 | 13,600 |
| Equity in earnings of Bottom | (52,400) | | (I) 52,400 † | | | |
| Net income | (162,400) | (70,000) | | | | (162,400) |
| **Statement of Retained Earnings** | | | | | | |
| Retained earnings, 1/1/04 | | | | | | |
| Top Company | (652,800) | | | | | (652,800) |
| Bottom Company | | (310,000) | (*G) 4,000 | | | |
| | | | (S) 306,000 | | | |
| Net income | (162,400) | (70,000) | | | | (162,400) |
| Dividends paid | 70,000 | 50,000 | | (D) 40,000 | 10,000 | 70,000 |
| Retained earnings, 12/31/04 | (745,200) | (330,000) | | | | (745,200) |

NCI column: (13,600) ‡

*continued from page 224*

**Balance Sheet**

| | | | | |
|---|---:|---:|---:|---:|
| Cash and receivables | 280,000 | 120,000 | | 390,000 |
| Inventory | 220,000 | 160,000 | | 374,000 |
| Investment in Bottom Company | 415,200 | | (D) 40,000 | -0- |
| | | | (P) 10,000 | |
| | | | (G) 6,000 | |
| | | | (I) 52,400 | |
| | | | (S) 364,800 | |
| | | | (A) 38,000 | |
| Land | 410,000 | 200,000 | | 610,000 |
| Plant assets (net) | 190,000 | 170,000 | | 360,000 |
| Database | | | (A) 38,000 (E) 2,000 | 36,000 |
| Total assets | 1,515,200 | 650,000 | | 1,770,000 |
| Liabilities | (340,000) | (170,000) | (P) 10,000 | (500,000) |
| Noncontrolling interest in Bottom Company, 1/1/04 | | | (S) 91,200 | (91,200) |
| Noncontrolling interest in Bottom Company, 12/31/04 | | | | (94,800) (94,800) |
| Common stock | (430,000) | (150,000) | (S) 150,000 | (430,000) |
| Retained earnings, 12/31/04 | (745,200) | (330,000) | | (745,200) |
| Total liabilities and equities | (1,515,200) | (650,000) | | (1,770,000) |

Note: Parentheses indicate a credit balance.

†Boxed items highlight differences with downstream transfers examined in Exhibit 5–7.

‡Because intercompany sales are made upstream (by the subsidiary), the subsidiary's realized income is the $68,000 ($70,000 reported balance plus $4,000 gain deferred from previous year less $6,000 deferred into next year) with the 20% noncontrolling interest being allocated $13,600.

Consolidation entries:

(*G) Removal of unrealized gain from beginning figures so that it can be recognized in current period. Upstream sales attributed to subsidiary.
(S) Elimination of adjusted stockholders' equity accounts along with recognition of January 1, 2004, noncontrolling interest.
(A) Allocation of parent's cost in excess of subsidiary's book value, unamortized balance as of January 1, 2004.
(I) Elimination of intercompany income.
(D) Elimination of intercompany dividends.
(E) Recognition of amortization expense for current year on database.
(P) Elimination of intercompany receivable/payable balances.
(TI) Elimination of intercompany sales/purchases balances.
(G) Removal of unrealized gain from ending figures so that it can be recognized in subsequent period.

# INTERCOMPANY LAND TRANSFERS

Although not as prevalent as inventory transactions, intercompany sales of other assets occur occasionally. The final two sections of this chapter examine the worksheet procedures necessitated by noninventory transfers. Land transactions are analyzed followed by a discussion of the effects created by the intercompany sale of depreciable assets such as buildings and equipment.

## Accounting for Land Transactions

The consolidation procedures necessitated by intercompany land transfers partially parallel those for intercompany inventory. As with inventory, the sale of land creates a series of effects on the individual records of the two companies. The worksheet process must then adjust the account balances to present all transactions from the perspective of a single economic entity.

By reviewing the sequence of events occurring in an intercompany land sale, the similarities to inventory transfers can be ascertained as well as the unique features of this transaction.

1. A gain (losses are rare in intercompany asset transfers) is reported by the original seller of the land, even though the transaction occurred between related parties. At the same time, the acquiring company capitalizes the inflated transfer price rather than the land's historical cost to the business combination.
2. The unrealized gain recorded by the seller is closed into Retained Earnings at the end of the year. From a consolidated perspective, this account has been artificially increased. Thus, both the Land account of the buyer and the Retained Earnings account of the seller continue to contain the unrealized profit.
3. Only when the land is subsequently disposed of to an outside party is the gain on the original transfer actually earned. Therefore, appropriate consolidation techniques must be designed to eliminate the intercompany gain each period until the time of resale.

Clearly, two characteristics encountered in inventory transfers also are present in intercompany land transactions: inflated book values and unrealized gains subsequently culminated through sales to outside parties. Despite these similarities, significant differences exist. Because of the nature of the transaction, no sales/purchases balances are recorded by the individual companies when land is transferred. Instead, a separate gain account is established by the seller. Because this gain is unearned, the balance has to be eliminated when preparing consolidated statements.

In addition, the subsequent resale of land to an outside party does not always occur in the year immediately following the transfer. Although inventory is normally disposed of within a relatively short time, land is often held by the buyer for years if not permanently. Thus, the overvalued Land account can remain on the books of the acquiring company indefinitely. As long as the land is retained, elimination of the effects of the unrealized gain (the equivalent of Entry *G in inventory transfers) must be made for each subsequent consolidation. By repeating this worksheet entry every year, both the Land and the Retained Earnings accounts are properly stated in the consolidated financial statements.

## Eliminating Unrealized Gains—Land Transfers

To illustrate these worksheet procedures, assume that Hastings Company and Patrick Company are related parties. On July 1, 2003, land that originally cost $60,000 is sold by Hastings to Patrick at a $100,000 transfer price. The seller reports a $40,000 gain; the buyer records the land at the $100,000 acquisition price. At the end of this fiscal period, the intercompany effect of this transaction must be eliminated for consolidation purposes:

**Consolidation Entry TL (year of transfer)**

| | | |
|---|---|---|
| Gain on Sale of Land | 40,000 | |
|     Land | | 40,000 |
| To eliminate effects of intercompany transfer of land. (Labeled "TL" in reference to the transferred land.) | | |

This worksheet entry eliminates the unrealized gain from the consolidated statements of 2003. However, as with the transfer of inventory, the effects created by the original transaction remain in the financial records of the individual companies for as long as the property is held. The gain recorded by Hastings carries through to Retained Earnings while Patrick's Land account retains the inflated transfer price. *Therefore, for every subsequent consolidation until the land is eventually sold, the elimination process must be repeated.* By including the following entry on each subsequent worksheet, the unrealized gain is removed from the asset and from the earnings reported by the combination.

**Consolidation Entry *GL (every year following transfer)**
| | | |
|---|---|---|
| Retained Earnings (beginning balance of seller) | 40,000 | |
|     Land | | 40,000 |

To eliminate effects of intercompany transfer of land made in a previous year. (Labeled as "*GL" in reference to the gain on a land transfer occurring in a prior year.)

Note that the reduction in Retained Earnings is changed to an increase in the investment account whenever the original sale is downstream and the equity method has been applied by the parent. In that specific situation, equity method adjustments have already corrected the timing of the parent's unrealized gain. Removing the gain has created a reduction in the investment account that is appropriately allocated to the subsidiary's Land account on the worksheet. Conversely, if sales were upstream, the Retained Earnings of the seller (the subsidiary) continue to be overstated even if the parent applies the equity method.

One final consolidation concern exists in accounting for intercompany transfers of land. If the property is ever sold to an outside party, the company making the sale records a gain or loss based on its recorded book value. However, this cost figure is actually the internal transfer price. The gain or loss being recognized is incorrect for consolidation purposes; it has not been computed by comparison to the land's historical cost. Once again, the separate financial records fail to reflect the transaction from the perspective of the single economic entity.

Therefore, if the land is eventually sold, the gain deferred at the time of the original transfer must be recognized. This profit finally has been earned by the sale of the property to outsiders. On the worksheet, the gain is removed one last time from beginning Retained Earnings (or the investment account, if applicable). In this instance, though, the entry is completed by reclassifying the amount as a realized gain. The timing of income recognition has been switched from the year of transfer into the fiscal period in which the land is sold to the unrelated party.

Returning to the previous illustration, land was acquired by Hastings for $60,000 and sold to Patrick, a related party, for $100,000. Consequently, the $40,000 unrealized gain was eliminated on the consolidation worksheet in the year of transfer as well as in each succeeding period. However, if this land is subsequently sold to an outside party for $115,000, Patrick would recognize only a $15,000 gain. From the viewpoint of the business combination, the land (having been bought for $60,000) was actually sold at a $55,000 gain. To correct the reporting, the following consolidation entry must be made in the year that the property is sold to the unrelated party. This adjustment increases the $15,000 gain recorded by Patrick to the consolidated balance of $55,000.

**Consolidation Entry *GL (year of sale to outside party)**
| | | |
|---|---|---|
| Retained Earnings (Hastings) | 40,000 | |
|     Gain on Sale of Land | | 40,000 |

To remove intercompany gain from year of transfer so that total profit can be recognized in the current period when land is sold to an outside party.

As in the accounting for inventory transfers, the entire consolidation process demonstrated here accomplishes two major objectives:

1. Historical cost is reported for the transferred land for as long as it remains within the business combination.
2. Income recognition is deferred until the land is sold to outside parties.

### Effect on Noncontrolling Interest Valuation—Land Transfers

The preceding discussion of intercompany land transfers has ignored the possible presence of a noncontrolling interest. In constructing financial statements for an economic entity that includes outside ownership, the guidelines already established for inventory transfers remain applicable.

If the original sale was a *downstream* transaction, neither the annual deferral nor the eventual recognition of the unrealized gain has any effect on the noncontrolling interest. The rationale for this treatment, as previously indicated, is that profits from downstream transfers relate solely to the parent company.

Conversely, if the transfer is made *upstream,* deferral and recognition of gains are attributed to the subsidiary and, hence, to the valuation of the noncontrolling interest. As with inventory, all noncontrolling interest balances are to be computed on the reported earnings of the subsidiary after adjustment for any upstream transfers.

To reiterate, the accounting consequences stemming from land transfers are:

1. In the year of transfer, any unrealized gain is deferred and the Land account is reduced to historical cost. When the gain is created by an upstream sale, the amount also is excluded in calculating the noncontrolling interest's share of the subsidiary's net income for that year.
2. Each year thereafter, the unrealized gain will be removed from the beginning Retained Earnings of the seller. If the transfer was upstream, eliminating this earlier gain directly affects the balances recorded within both Entry *C (if conversion to the equity method is required) and Entry S. The additional equity accrual (Entry *C, if needed) as well as the elimination of beginning Stockholders' Equity (Entry S) must be based on the newly adjusted balance in the subsidiary's Retained Earnings. This deferral process also has an impact on the noncontrolling interest's share of the subsidiary's income but only in the year of transfer and the eventual year of sale.
3. In the event that the land is ever sold to an outside party, the original gain is earned and must be reported by the consolidated entity.

## INTERCOMPANY TRANSFER OF DEPRECIABLE ASSETS

Just as land can be transferred between related parties, the intercompany sale of a host of other assets is possible. Equipment, patents, franchises, buildings, and other long-lived assets can be involved. Accounting for these transactions resembles that demonstrated for land sales. However, the subsequent calculation of depreciation or amortization provides an added challenge in the development of consolidated statements.[9]

### The Deferral of Unrealized Gains

When faced with intercompany sales of depreciable assets, the accountant's basic objective remains unchanged: *the deferral of unrealized gains to establish both historical cost balances and appropriate income recognition within the consolidated statements.* More specifically, gains created by these transfers are deferred until such time as the subsequent use or resale of the asset consummates the original transaction. For inventory sales, the culminating disposal normally occurs currently or in the year following the transfer. In contrast, transferred land is

---

[9] To avoid redundancy within this analysis, all further references are made to depreciation expense alone, although this discussion is equally applicable to the amortization of intangible assets or the depletion of wasting assets.

quite often never resold, thus permanently deferring the recognition of the intercompany profit.

For depreciable asset transfers, the ultimate realization of the gain normally occurs in a different manner; the property's use within the buyer's operations is reflected through depreciation. Recognition of this expense reduces the asset's book value every year and, hence, the overvaluation within that balance.

The depreciation systematically eliminates the unrealized gain not only from the asset account but also from Retained Earnings. For the buyer, excess expense results each year because the computation is based on the inflated transfer cost. This depreciation is then closed annually into Retained Earnings. *From a consolidated perspective, the extra expense gradually offsets the unrealized gain within this equity account. In fact, over the life of the asset, the depreciation process eliminates all effects of the transfer from both the asset balance and the Retained Earnings account.*

## Depreciable Asset Transfers Illustrated

To examine the consolidation procedures required by the intercompany transfer of a depreciable asset, assume that Able Company sells equipment to Baker Company at the current market value of $90,000. The equipment originally had been acquired by Able for $100,000 several years ago; since that time, $40,000 in accumulated depreciation has been recorded. The transfer is made on January 1, 2003, when the equipment has a 10-year remaining life.

### *Year of Transfer*

The 2003 effects on the separate financial accounts of the two companies can be quickly enumerated:

1. Baker, as the buyer, enters the equipment into its records at the $90,000 transfer price. However, from a consolidated view, the $60,000 book value ($100,000 cost less $40,000 accumulated depreciation) is still appropriate.

2. Able, as the seller, reports a profit of $30,000, although nothing has yet been earned by the combination. This gain is then closed into the company's Retained Earnings account at the end of 2003.

3. Assuming application of the straight-line method of depreciation with no salvage value, Baker records expense of $9,000 at the end of 2003 ($90,000 transfer price/10 years). The buyer recognizes this amount rather than the $6,000 depreciation figure applicable to the consolidated entity ($60,000 book value/10 years).

To report these events as seen by the business combination, both the $30,000 unrealized gain and the $3,000 inflation in depreciation expense must be eliminated on the worksheet. For clarification purposes, two separate consolidation entries are shown here for 2003. However, they can be combined into a single adjustment.

**Consolidation Entry TA (year of transfer)**

| | | |
|---|---:|---:|
| Gain on Sale of Equipment | 30,000 | |
| Equipment | 10,000 | |
|     Accumulated Depreciation | | 40,000 |

To remove unrealized gain and return equipment accounts to balances based on original historical cost. (Labeled "TA" in reference to transferred asset.)

**Consolidation Entry ED (year of transfer)**

| | | |
|---|---:|---:|
| Accumulated Depreciation | 3,000 | |
|     Depreciation Expense | | 3,000 |

To eliminate overstatement of depreciation expense caused by inflated transfer price. (Labeled "ED" in reference to excess depreciation.) *Entry must be repeated for all 10 years of the equipment's life.*

From the viewpoint of a single entity, these entries accomplish several objectives.

- The asset's historical cost of $100,000 is reinstated.
- By recording accumulated depreciation of $40,000, the January 1, 2003, book value is returned to the appropriate $60,000 figure.
- The $30,000 unrealized gain recorded by Able is eliminated so that this intercompany profit does not appear in the consolidated income statement.
- Depreciation for the year is reduced from $9,000 to $6,000, the appropriate expense based on historical cost.

In the year of the intercompany depreciable asset transfer, the preceding consolidation entries **TA** and **ED** are applicable regardless of whether the transfer was upstream or downstream. They are likewise applicable regardless of whether the parent applies the equity method, cost method, or partial equity method of accounting for its investment. As discussed subsequently, however, in the years following the intercompany transfer, a slight modification must be made to the Consolidation Entry *TA when the equity method is applied and the transfer was downstream.

### Years Following Transfer

Once again, the preceding worksheet entries do not actually remove the effects of the intercompany transfer from the individual records of these two organizations. Both the unrealized gain and the excess depreciation expense remain on the separate books and are closed into Retained Earnings of the respective companies at year's end. Similarly, the Equipment account along with the related accumulated depreciation continue to hold balances based on the transfer price, not historical cost. *Thus, for every subsequent period, the separately reported figures must be adjusted on the worksheet to present the consolidated totals from the perspective of a single entity.*

To derive worksheet entries at any future point, the balances in the accounts of the individual companies must be ascertained and compared to the figures appropriate for the business combination. As an illustration, the separate records of Able and Baker two years after the transfer (December 31, 2004) follow. Consolidated totals are calculated based on the original historical cost of $100,000 and accumulated depreciation of $40,000.

| Account | Individual Records | Consolidated Perspective | Worksheet Adjustments |
|---|---|---|---|
| Equipment 12/31/04 | $90,000 | $100,000 | $10,000 |
| Accumulated Depreciation 12/31/04 | (18,000) | (52,000)* | (34,000) |
| Depreciation Expense 12/31/04 | 9,000 | 6,000 | (3,000) |
| 1/1/04 Retained Earnings effect | (21,000)† | 6,000 | 27,000 |

*Accumulated depreciation before transfer $(40,000) plus 2 years × $(6,000).
†Intercompany transfer gain $(30,000) less one year's depreciation of $9,000.
*Note:* Parentheses indicate a credit.

Because effects of the transfer continue to exist in the separate financial records, the various accounts have to be corrected in each succeeding consolidation. However, the amounts involved must be updated every period because of the continual impact that depreciation has on these balances. As an example, to adjust the individual figures to the consolidated totals derived earlier, the 2004 worksheet must include the following entries:

**Consolidation Entry *TA (year following transfer)**
| | | |
|---|---|---|
| Equipment . . . . . . . . . . . . . . . . . . . . . . . . . . . . . . . . . . . . . . . . . . . . . . . . . . | 10,000 | |
| Retained Earnings, 1/1/04 (Able) . . . . . . . . . . . . . . . . . . . . . . . . . . . . . . . | 27,000 | |
|     Accumulated Depreciation . . . . . . . . . . . . . . . . . . . . . . . . . . . . . . . . | | 37,000 |

To return the Equipment account to original historical cost and correct the 1/1/04 balances of Retained Earnings and Accumulated Depreciation.

| Consolidation Entry ED (year following transfer) | | |
|---|---|---|
| Accumulated Depreciation | 3,000 | |
|     Depreciation Expense | | 3,000 |
| To remove excess depreciation expense on the intercompany transfer price and adjust Accumulated Depreciation to its correct 12/31/04 balance. | | |
| Note that the $34,000 increase in 12/31/04 consolidated Accumulated Depreciation is accomplished by a $37,000 credit in Entry *TA and a $3,000 debit in Entry ED. | | |

Although adjustments of the asset and depreciation expense remain constant, the change in beginning Retained Earnings and Accumulated Depreciation vary with each succeeding consolidation. At December 31, 2003, the individual companies closed out both the unrealized gain of $30,000 and the initial $3,000 overstatement of depreciation expense. Therefore, as reflected in Entry *TA, the beginning Retained Earnings account for 2004 is overvalued by a net amount of only $27,000 rather than $30,000. *Over the life of the asset, the unrealized gain in retained earnings will be systematically reduced to zero as excess depreciation expense ($3,000) is closed out each year.* Hence, on subsequent consolidation worksheets, the beginning Retained Earnings account is decreased by $27,000 in 2004, by $24,000 in 2005, and $21,000 in the following period. This reduction continues until the effect of the unrealized gain no longer exists at the end of 10 years.

If this equipment is ever resold to an outside party, the remaining portion of the gain would be consummated. As in the previous discussion of land, the intercompany profit that exists at that date must be recognized on the consolidated income statement to arrive at the appropriate amount of gain or loss on the sale.

## Depreciable Intercompany Asset Transfers—Downstream Transfers When the Parent Uses the Equity Method

A slight modification to Consolidation Entry *TA is required when the intercompany depreciable asset transfer is downstream and the parent uses the equity method. In applying the equity method, the parent adjusts its book income for both the original transfer gain and periodic depreciation expense adjustments. Thus, in downstream intercompany transfers when the equity method is used, from a consolidated view the book value of the parent's Retained Earnings balance has been already reduced for the gain. Therefore, continuing with the previous example, the following worksheet consolidation entries would be made for a downstream sale assuming that (1) Able is the parent and (2) Able has applied the equity method to account for its investment in Baker.

| Consolidation Entry *TA (year following transfer) | | |
|---|---|---|
| Equipment | 10,000 | |
| Investment in Baker | 27,000 | |
|     Accumulated Depreciation | | 37,000 |

| Consolidation Entry ED (year following transfer) | | |
|---|---|---|
| Accumulated Depreciation | 3,000 | |
|     Depreciation Expense | | 3,000 |

In Entry *TA, note that the Investment in Baker account replaces the parent's Retained Earnings. The debit to the investment account effectively allocates the write-down necessitated by the intercompany transfer to the appropriate subsidiary equipment and accumulated depreciation accounts.

### Effect on Noncontrolling Interest Valuation—Depreciable Asset Transfers

Because of the lack of official guidance, no easy answer exists about the assignment of any income effects created within the consolidation process. Consistent with the previous sections of this chapter, all income is assigned here to the original seller. In Entry *TA, for example, the beginning Retained Earnings account of Able (the seller) is reduced. Both the unrealized gain on the transfer and the excess depreciation expense subsequently recognized are assigned to that party.

Thus, once again, downstream sales are assumed to have no effect on any noncontrolling interest values. The parent rather than the subsidiary made the sale. Conversely, the impact on income created by upstream sales must be taken into account in computing the balances attributed to these outside owners. Currently, this approach is one of many acceptable alternatives. However, in its future deliberations on consolidation policies and procedures, the FASB could mandate a specific allocation pattern.

## Summary

1. The transfer of assets, especially inventory, between the members of a business combination is a common practice. In producing consolidated financial statements, any effects on the separate accounting records created by such transfers must be removed because the transactions did not occur with an outside, unrelated party.
2. Inventory transfers are the most prevalent form of intercompany asset transaction. Despite being only a transfer, one company records a sale while the other reports a purchase. These balances are reciprocals that have to be offset on the worksheet in the process of producing consolidated figures.
3. Additional accounting problems result if inventory is transferred at a markup. Any portion of the merchandise still held at year-end would be valued at more than historical cost because of the inflation in price. Furthermore, the gross profit reported by the seller on these goods is unrealized from a consolidation perspective. Thus, this gain must be removed from the ending Inventory account, a figure that appears as an asset on the balance sheet and as a negative component within cost of goods sold.
4. Unrealized inventory gains also create a consolidation problem in the year following the transfer. Within the separate accounting systems, the seller closes the gross profit to Retained Earnings. The buyer's ending Inventory balance becomes the beginning balance (within Cost of Goods Sold) of the next period. Therefore, the inflation must be removed again but this time in the subsequent year. Beginning Retained Earnings of the seller is decreased to eliminate the unrealized gain while Cost of Goods Sold is reduced to remove the overstatement from the beginning inventory component. Through this process, the intercompany profit is deferred from the year of transfer so that recognition can be made at the point of disposal or consumption.
5. The deferral and subsequent realization of intercompany gains raises a question concerning the valuation of noncontrolling interest balances: Does the change in the period of recognition alter these calculations? Although the issue is currently under debate, no formal answer to this question is yet found in official accounting pronouncements. In this textbook, the deferral of gains from upstream transfers (from subsidiary to parent) is assumed to affect the noncontrolling interest whereas downstream transactions (from parent to subsidiary) do not. When upstream transfers are involved, noncontrolling interest values are based on the earned figures remaining after adjustment for any unrealized gains.
6. Inventory is not the only asset that can be sold between the members of a business combination. For example, transfers of land sometimes occur. Once again, if the price exceeds original cost, the asset is stated on the buyer's records at an inflated value while an unrealized gain is recognized by the seller. As with inventory, the consolidation process must return the asset's recorded balance to cost while deferring the gain. Repetition of this procedure is necessary in every consolidation for as long as the land remains within the business combination.
7. The consolidation process required by the intercompany transfer of depreciable assets differs somewhat from that demonstrated for inventory and land. Unrealized gain created by the transaction must still be eliminated along with the overstatement of the asset. However, because of subsequent depreciation, these adjustments systematically change from period to period. Following the transfer, depreciation is computed by the buyer based on the new inflated transfer price. Thus, expense is recorded that reduces the carrying value of the asset at a rate in excess of appropriate depreciation; the book value moves closer to the historical cost figure each time that depreciation is recorded. Additionally, because the excess depreciation is closed annually to Retained Earnings, the overstatement of the equity account resulting from the unrealized gain is constantly reduced. To produce consoli-

dated figures at any point in time, the remaining inflation in these figures (as well as in the current depreciation expense) must be determined and removed.

## Comprehensive Illustration
### PROBLEM

*(Estimated Time: 45 to 65 Minutes)* On January 1, 1999, Daisy Company purchased 80 percent of Rose Company for $594,000 in cash. The total book value of Rose on that date was $610,000. The newly acquired subsidiary possessed equipment (10-year remaining life) that was undervalued by $75,000 in the company's accounting records and land that was undervalued by $15,000. Any excess intangibles within the purchase will be amortized over 10 years.

Daisy decided to acquire Rose so that the subsidiary could furnish component parts for the parent's production process. During the ensuing years, Rose sold inventory to Daisy as follows:

| Year | Cost to Rose Company | Transfer Price | Markup on Transfer Price | Transferred Inventory Being Held at End of Year (at transfer price) |
|---|---|---|---|---|
| 1999 | $ 60,000 | $ 90,000 | 33.3% | $10,000 |
| 2000 | 80,000 | 100,000 | 20.0 | 15,000 |
| 2001 | 90,000 | 120,000 | 25.0 | 10,000 |
| 2002 | 100,000 | 140,000 | 28.6 | 20,000 |
| 2003 | 100,000 | 150,000 | 33.3 | 30,000 |
| 2004 | 96,000 | 160,000 | 40.0 | 40,000 |

Any transferred merchandise retained by Daisy at the end of a year was always put into production during the following period.

On January 1, 2002, Daisy sold several pieces of equipment to Rose. These assets had a 10-year remaining life and were being depreciated on the straight-line method with no salvage value. This equipment was transferred at an $80,000 price, although it had an original cost to Daisy of $100,000 and a book value at the date of exchange of $44,000.

On January 1, 2004, Daisy sold land to Rose for $60,000, the fair market value at that date. The original cost had been only $40,000. By the end of 2004, no payment had yet been made by Rose.

The following separate financial statements are for Daisy and Rose as of December 31, 2004. Daisy has applied the equity method to account for this investment.

|  | Daisy Company | Rose Company |
|---|---|---|
| Sales | $ 900,000 | $ 500,000 |
| Cost of goods sold | (600,000) | (300,000) |
| Operating expenses | (210,000) | (80,000) |
| Gain on sale of land | 20,000 | –0– |
| Income of Rose Company | 65,400 | –0– |
| Net income | $ 175,400 | $ 120,000 |
| Retained earnings, 1/1/04 | $ 620,000 | $ 430,000 |
| Net income | 175,400 | 120,000 |
| Dividends paid | (55,400) | (50,000) |
| Retained earnings, 12/31/04 | $ 740,000 | $ 500,000 |
| Cash and accounts receivable | $ 380,000 | $ 410,000 |
| Inventory | 421,600 | 190,000 |
| Investment in Rose Company | 711,600 | –0– |
| Land | 452,800 | 280,000 |
| Equipment | 270,000 | 190,000 |
| Accumulated depreciation | (180,000) | (50,000) |
| Total assets | $2,056,000 | $1,020,000 |
| Liabilities | 716,000 | 120,000 |
| Common stock | 600,000 | 400,000 |
| Retained earnings, 12/31/04 | 740,000 | 500,000 |
| Total liabilities and equities | $2,056,000 | $1,020,000 |

### Required:

Answer the following questions:
a. By how much did Rose's book value increase during the period from January 1, 1999, through December 31, 2003?
b. During the initial years after the takeover, what annual amortization expense was recognized in connection with the parent's purchase price?
c. What amount of unrealized gain exists within the parent's inventory figures at the beginning and at the end of 2004?
d. Equipment has been transferred between the companies. What amount of excess depreciation is recognized in 2004 because of this transfer?
e. The parent reports Income of Rose Company for 2004 of $65,400. How was this figure calculated?
f. Without using a worksheet, determine consolidated totals.
g. Prepare the worksheet entries required at December 31, 2004, by the transfer of inventory, land, and equipment.

## SOLUTION

a. The subsidiary's book value on the date of purchase was given as $610,000. At the beginning of 2004, the company's common stock and retained earnings total is $830,000 ($400,000 and $430,000, respectively). In the previous years, Rose's book value has apparently grown by $220,000 ($830,000 − $610,000).

b. To determine amortization, an allocation of the purchase price must first be made. The following allocations to equipment ($60,000) and intangibles (residual $34,000) lead to additional annual expenses of $9,400 for the initial years of the combination. The $12,000 assigned to land is not subject to amortization.

### Cost Allocation and Excess Amortization Schedule

Purchase price ......... $ 594,000
Book value of
  Rose Company
  ($610,000 × 80%) ... (488,000)
Excess cost over
  book value .......... 106,000

|  | Life (years) | Annual Excess Amortizations | Excess Amortizations 1999–2004 | Unamortized Value, 12/31/04 |
|---|---|---|---|---|
| Equipment undervaluation ($75,000 × 80%) .. 60,000 | 10 | $6,000 | $36,000 | $24,000 |
| Land undervaluation ($15,000 × 80%) .. 12,000 | | | | |
| Intangibles ......... $34,000 | 10 | 3,400 | 20,400 | 13,600 |
| | | $9,400 | | |

c. Of the inventory transferred to Daisy during 2003, $30,000 is still held at the beginning of 2004. This merchandise contains an unrealized gain of $10,000 ($30,000 × 33.3% [rounded] markup for that year). At year's end, $16,000 ($40,000 remaining inventory × 40% markup) is viewed as an unrealized gain.

d. Excess depreciation for 2004 is $3,600. Equipment with a book value of $44,000 was transferred at a price of $80,000. The addition of $36,000 to this asset's account balance would be written off over 10 years for an extra $3,600 per year.

e. According to the separate statements given, the subsidiary reports net income of $120,000. However, in determining the income allocation between the parent and the noncontrolling interest, this reported figure must be adjusted for the effects of any *upstream* transfers. Because the inventory was sold upstream from Rose to Daisy, the $10,000 gain deferred in requirement (*c*) from 2003 into the current period is attributed to the subsidiary (as the seller). Likewise, the $16,000 unrealized gain at year's end is viewed as a reduction in Rose's income.

All other transfers are downstream and not considered to have an effect on the subsidiary. Therefore, the Income of Rose Company balance can be verified as follows:

| | |
|---|---:|
| Rose Company's reported income—2004 | $120,000 |
| Recognition of 2003 unrealized gain | +10,000 |
| Deferral of 2004 unrealized gain | (16,000) |
| Earned income of subsidiary from consolidated perspective | 114,000 |
| Parent's ownership percentage | 80% |
| Equity income accrual | $ 91,200 |
| Adjustments attributed to parent's ownership: | |
|    Excess amortization expense—2004 (see requirement *b*) | (9,400) |
|    Deferral of unrealized gain—land | (20,000) |
|    Removal of excess depreciation (see requirement *d*) | +3,600 |
| Income of Rose Company—2004 | $ 65,400 |

*f.* Each of the 2004 consolidated totals for this business combination can be determined as follows:

*Sales* = $1,240,000. The parent's balance is added to the subsidiary's balance less the $160,000 in intercompany transfers for the period.

*Cost of Goods Sold* = $746,000. The computation begins by adding the parent's balance to the subsidiary's balance less the $160,000 in intercompany transfers for the period. The $10,000 unrealized gain from the previous year is deducted to recognize this income currently. Next, the $16,000 ending unrealized gain is added to cost of goods sold to defer the income until a later year when the goods are sold to an outside party.

*Operating Expenses* = $295,800. The parent's balance is added to the subsidiary's balance. Annual amortization of $9,400 on the purchase price allocations (see requirement *b*) must also be included. Excess depreciation of $3,600 resulting from the transfer of equipment (see requirement *e*) is removed.

*Gain on Sale of Land* = –0–. This amount is eliminated for consolidation purposes because the transaction was intercompany.

*Income of Rose Company* = 0. The equity income figure is removed so that the actual revenues and expenses of the subsidiary can be included in the financial statements without double-counting.

*Noncontrolling Interest in Subsidiary's Income* = $22,800. In requirement (*e*), the earned income of the subsidiary was computed as $114,000 after adjustments were made for unrealized upstream gains. Because outsiders hold 20 percent of the subsidiary, an allocation of $22,800 ($114,000 × 0.20) is necessary.

*Net Income* = $175,400. This total is derived from the previous consolidated balances. Because the equity method has been applied, consolidated net income is also equal to the balance reported by the parent.

*Retained Earnings, 1/1/04* = $620,000. The equity method has been applied; therefore, the parent's balance is equal to the consolidated total.

*Dividends Paid* = $55,400. Only the amount the parent paid is shown in the consolidated statements. Distributions made by the subsidiary to the parent are eliminated as intercompany transfers. Any payment to the noncontrolling interest reduces the ending balance attributed to these outside owners.

*Cash and Accounts Receivable* = $730,000. The two balances are added after removal of the $60,000 intercompany receivable created by the transfer of land.

*Inventory* = $595,600. The two balances are added after removal of the $16,000 ending unrealized gain (see requirement *c*).

*Investment in Rose Company* = –0–. The investment balance is eliminated so that the actual assets and liabilities of the subsidiary can be included.

*Land* = $724,800. The two balances are added. The $20,000 unrealized gain created by the transfer is removed. The $12,000 allocation from the purchase price is added.

*Equipment* = $540,000. The two balances are added. Because of the intercompany transfer, $20,000 must also be included to adjust the $80,000 transfer price to the original $100,000 cost of the asset. A $60,000 allocation within the purchase price must also be recognized.

*Accumulated Depreciation* = $311,200. The balances are added together along with the $36,000 that has been written off in connection with the purchase price allocation to equipment ($6,000 per year for six years). The $56,000 in accumulated depreciation on the equipment (before its transfer) must also be reinstated. A reduction of $10,800 is made to remove the excess depreciation subsequently recorded on this same equipment ($3,600 per year for three years).

*Intangibles* = $13,600. The $34,000 allocation is recognized less six years of amortization ($20,400, or $3,400 per year for six years).

*Total Assets* = $2,292,800. This figure is a summation of the preceding consolidated assets.

*Liabilities* = $776,000. The two balances are added after removal of the $60,000 intercompany payable created by the transfer of land.

*Noncontrolling Interest in Subsidiary, 12/31/04* = $176,800. This figure is composed of several different balances:

| | |
|---|---:|
| Book value of subsidiary, 1/1/04 (common stock and beginning retained earnings) | $830,000 |
| Unrealized gain on upstream transfer as of beginning of year | (10,000) |
| Earned book value of subsidiary, 1/1/04 | $820,000 |
| Noncontrolling interest | 20% |
| Noncontrolling interest, 1/1/04 | $164,000 |
| Noncontrolling interest in subsidiary's income (see above) | 22,800 |
| Less: Dividends paid to noncontrolling interest ($50,000 × 0.20) | (10,000) |
| Noncontrolling interest, 12/31/04 | $176,800 |

*Common Stock* = $600,000. The parent company balance only is reported within the consolidated statements.

*Retained Earnings, 12/31/04* = $740,000. The retained earnings amount is found by adding consolidated net income to the beginning Retained Earnings balance and then subtracting the dividends paid. All of these figures have been computed previously.

*Total Liabilities and Equities* = $2,292,800. This figure is the summation of all consolidated liabilities and equities.

---

**Consolidation Worksheet Entries—
Intercompany Transactions
December 31, 2004**

---

## Inventory

### Entry *G

| | | |
|---|---:|---:|
| Retained Earnings, 1/1/04—Subsidiary | 10,000 | |
|     Cost of Goods Sold | | 10,000 |

To remove 2003 unrealized gain from beginning balances of the current year. Because transfers were upstream, retained earnings of the subsidiary (as the original seller) are being reduced. Balance is computed in requirement (c).

### Entry TI

| | | |
|---|---:|---:|
| Sales | 160,000 | |
|     Cost of Goods Sold | | 160,000 |

To eliminate current year intercompany transfer of inventory.

### Entry G

| | | |
|---|---:|---:|
| Cost of Goods Sold | 16,000 | |
|     Inventory | | 16,000 |

To remove 2004 unrealized gain from ending accounts of the current year. Balance is computed in requirement (c).

## Land

### Entry TL

| | | |
|---|---|---|
| Gain on Sale of Land ....................................... | 20,000 | |
|     Land ................................................ | | 20,000 |

To eliminate gain created on first day of current year by an intercompany transfer of land.

## Equipment

### Entry *TA

| | | |
|---|---|---|
| Equipment .............................................. | 20,000 | |
| Investment in Rose Company ............................... | 28,800 | |
|     Accumulated Depreciation ................................ | | 48,800 |

To remove unrealized gain (as of January 1, 2004) created by intercompany transfer of equipment and to adjust equipment and accumulated depreciation to historical cost figures.

Equipment is increased from the $80,000 transfer price to $100,000 cost.

Accumulated depreciation of $56,000 was eliminated at time of transfer. Excess depreciation of $3,600 per year has been recorded for the two prior years ($7,200); thus, the accumulated depreciation is now only $48,800 less than cost-based figure.

The unrealized gain on the transfer was $36,000 ($80,000 less $44,000). That figure has now been reduced by two years of excess depreciation ($7,200). Because the parent used the equity method and this transfer was downstream, the adjustment here is to the investment account rather than the parent's beginning Retained Earnings.

### Entry ED

| | | |
|---|---|---|
| Accumulated Depreciation ................................... | 3,600 | |
|     Operating Expenses (depreciation) ........................ | | 3,600 |

To eliminate the current year overstatement of depreciation created by inflated transfer price.

# Appendix

## Transfers—Alternative Approaches

In this chapter, we use one method in consolidating the effects of intercompany transfers and unrealized gains when a noncontrolling interest is present. This approach was chosen because it is consistent with the guidelines put forth in *ARB 51*. Over the years, several other possibilities have been devised and considered. The FASB's discussion memorandum, *An Analysis of Issues Related to Consolidation Policy and Procedures,* describes eight methods of consolidating intercompany transactions (three for downstream transfers and five for upstream). The following table indicates the range of potential effects on consolidated totals by demonstrating six of these approaches (two for downstream and four for upstream). All methods except for proportionate consolidation have been included.

The figures used in this illustration are the same as in the Large Company and Small Company example in the first section of this chapter.

Large owns 70 percent of the outstanding stock of Small.
Intercompany inventory transfers during the year amount to $200,000.
The remaining unrealized gain at the end of the year is $40,000.
Subsidiary reported income is $100,000.

## DOWNSTREAM TRANSFERS (FROM PARENT TO SUBSIDIARY)

|  | ARB 51*<br>Economic Unit Concept<br>One Variation of Parent<br>Company Concept<br>(method used in this textbook) | Another Variation of<br>Parent Company Concept |
|---|---|---|
| Sales | Eliminate all $200,000 transfers | Eliminate $140,000 (70%) of the transfers |
| Purchases | Eliminate all $200,000 transfers | Eliminate $140,000 (70%) of the transfers |
| Unrealized gain | Eliminate all $40,000 | Eliminate $28,000 (70%) |
| Income assigned to noncontrolling interests | 30% of $100,000 reported income, or $30,000 | 30% of $100,000 reported income, or $30,000 |

*Titles indicate authority for each approach.

## UPSTREAM TRANSFERS (FROM SUBSIDIARY TO PARENT)

|  | ARB 51<br>Economic<br>Unit Concept<br>(method used in<br>this textbook) | One Variation<br>of Parent<br>Company<br>Concept | Another<br>Approach<br>Based<br>on ARB 51 | Another<br>Variation<br>of Parent<br>Company<br>Concept |
|---|---|---|---|---|
| Sales | Eliminate all $200,000 transfers | Eliminate $140,000 (70%) of the transfers | Eliminate all $200,000 transfers | Eliminate all $200,000 transfers |
| Purchases | Eliminate all $200,000 transfers | Eliminate $140,000 (70%) of the transfers | Eliminate all $200,000 transfers | Eliminate all $200,000 transfers |
| Unrealized gain | Eliminate all $40,000 | Eliminate $28,000 (70%) | Eliminate all $40,000 | Eliminate $28,000 (70%) |
| Income assigned to noncontrolling interests | 30% of $100,000 realized income less $40,000 unrealized gain, or $18,000 | 30% of $100,000 reported income, or $30,000 | 30% of $100,000 reported income, or $30,000 | 30% of $100,000 reported income, or $30,000 |

## Questions

1. Intercompany transfers between the component companies of a business combination are quite common. Why do these intercompany transactions occur so frequently?
2. Barker Company owns 80 percent of the outstanding voting stock of Walden Company. During the current year, intercompany sales amount to $100,000. These transactions were made with a markup equal to 40 percent of the transfer price. In consolidating the two companies, what amount of these sales would be eliminated?

3. Padlock Corp. owns 90 percent of Safeco, Inc. During the year, Padlock sold 3,000 locking mechanisms to Safeco for $900,000. By the end of the year, Safeco had sold all but 500 of the locking mechanisms to outside parties. Padlock marks up the cost of its locking mechanisms by 60 percent in computing its sales price to affiliated and nonaffiliated customers. How much intercompany profit remains in Safeco's inventory at year-end?

4. How are unrealized inventory gains created, and what consolidation entries are necessitated by the presence of these gains?

5. James, Inc., sells inventory to Matthews Company, a related party. The inventory was sold at James's standard markup. At the end of the current fiscal year, some portion of this inventory is still being held by Matthews. If consolidated financial statements are to be prepared, why are worksheet entries required in two different fiscal periods?

6. When intercompany gains are present in any year, how are the noncontrolling interest calculations affected?

7. A worksheet is being developed to consolidate Williams, Incorporated, and Brown Company. Considerable intercompany transactions have been made between these two organizations. How would the consolidation process be affected if these transfers were downstream? How would the consolidation process be affected if these transfers were upstream?

8. King Company owns a 90 percent interest in the outstanding voting shares of Pawn Company. Pawn reports a net income of $110,000 for the current year. Intercompany sales are made at regular intervals between the two companies. Unrealized gains of $30,000 were present in the beginning inventory balances, whereas $60,000 in similar gains were recorded at the end of the year. What is the noncontrolling interest's share of the subsidiary's net income?

9. When a subsidiary sells inventory to a parent, the intercompany profit is removed from the subsidiary's income and reduces the income allocation to the noncontrolling interest. Is the profit permanently eliminated from the noncontrolling interest, or is it merely shifted from one period to the next? Explain.

10. The consolidation process that is applicable when intercompany land transfers have occurred is somewhat different from that used for intercompany inventory sales. What differences should be noted?

11. A subsidiary sells land to the parent company at a significant gain. The parent holds the land for two years and then sells it to an outside party, also for a gain. How are these events accounted for by the business combination?

12. Why does an intercompany sale of a depreciable asset (such as equipment or a building) require subsequent adjustments to depreciation expense within the consolidation process?

13. If an intercompany sale of a depreciable asset has been made at a price above book value, the beginning Retained Earnings of the seller is reduced when preparing each subsequent consolidation. Why does the amount of the adjustment change from year to year?

## Problems

1. What is the impact on consolidated financial statements of upstream and downstream transfers?
    a. No difference exists in consolidated financial statements between upstream and downstream transfers.
    b. Downstream transfers affect the computation of the noncontrolling interest's share of the subsidiary's income but upstream transfers do not.
    c. Upstream transfers affect the computation of the noncontrolling interest's share of the subsidiary's income but downstream transfers do not.
    d. Downstream transfers can be ignored since they are made by the parent company.

2. King Corporation owns 80 percent of Lee Corporation's common stock. During October 2004, Lee sold merchandise to King for $100,000. At December 31, 2004, 50 percent of this merchandise remains in King's inventory. For 2004, gross profit percentages were 30 percent for King and 40 percent for Lee. The amount of unrealized intercompany profit in ending inventory at December 31, 2004, that should be eliminated in the consolidation process is:
    a. $40,000
    b. $20,000
    c. $16,000
    d. $15,000
    (AICPA adapted)

3. When intercompany transfers occur, how is the noncontrolling interest's share of the subsidiary's income computed?

a. The subsidiary's reported income is adjusted for the impact of upstream transfers prior to computing the noncontrolling interest's allocation.
b. The subsidiary's reported income is adjusted for the impact of all transfers prior to computing the noncontrolling interest's allocation.
c. The subsidiary's reported income is not adjusted for the impact of transfers prior to computing the noncontrolling interest's allocation.
d. The subsidiary's reported income is adjusted for the impact of downstream transfers prior to computing the noncontrolling interest's allocation.

4. Bellgrade, Inc., acquired a 60 percent interest in the Hansen Company several years ago. During 2002, Hansen sold inventory costing $75,000 to Bellgrade for $100,000. A total of 16 percent of this inventory was not sold to outsiders until 2003. During 2003, Hansen sold inventory costing $96,000 to Bellgrade for $120,000. A total of 35 percent of this inventory was not sold to outsiders until 2004. In 2003, Bellgrade reported cost of goods sold of $380,000 while Hansen reported $210,000. What is consolidated cost of goods sold?
  a. $465,600
  b. $473,440
  c. $474,400
  d. $522,400

5. Top Company holds 90 percent of the common stock of Bottom Company. In the current year, Top reports sales of $800,000 and cost of goods sold of $600,000. For this same period, Bottom has sales of $300,000 and cost of goods sold of $180,000. During the current year, Top sold merchandise to Bottom for $100,000. The subsidiary still possesses 40 percent of this inventory at the end of the current year. Top had established the transfer price based on its normal markup. What are consolidated sales and cost of goods sold?
  a. $1,000,000 and $690,000
  b. $1,000,000 and $705,000
  c. $1,000,000 and $740,000
  d. $970,000 and $696,000

6. Use the same information as in problem 5 except assume that the transfers were from Bottom Company to Top Company. What are the consolidated sales and cost of goods sold?
  a. $1,000,000 and $720,000
  b. $1,000,000 and $755,000
  c. $1,000,000 and $696,000
  d. $970,000 and $712,000

7. Hardwood, Inc., holds a 90 percent interest in Pittstoni Company. During 2003, Pittstoni sold inventory costing $77,000 to Hardwood for $110,000. A total of $40,000 of this inventory was not sold to outsiders until 2004. During 2004, Pittstoni sold inventory costing $72,000 to Hardwood for $120,000. A total of $50,000 of this inventory was not sold to outsiders until 2005. In 2004, Hardwood reported net income of $150,000 while Pittstoni reported $90,000. What is the noncontrolling interest in the 2004 income of the subsidiary?
  a. $8,000
  b. $8,200
  c. $9,000
  d. $9,800

8. Dunn Corporation owns 100 percent of Grey Corporation's common stock. On January 2, 2003, Dunn sold to Grey, for $40,000, machinery with a carrying amount of $30,000. Grey is depreciating the acquired machinery over a five-year life by the straight-line method. The net adjustments to compute 2003 and 2004 consolidated net income would be an increase (decrease) of

|  | 2003 | 2004 |
| --- | --- | --- |
| a. | $(8,000) | $2,000 |
| b. | $(8,000) | –0– |
| c. | $(10,000) | $2,000 |
| d. | $(10,000) | –0– |

(AICPA adapted)

9. Wallton Corporation owns 70 percent of the outstanding stock of Hastings, Incorporated. On January 1, 2002, Wallton acquired a building with a 10-year life for $300,000. No salvage value was anticipated, and the building was to be depreciated on the straight-line method. On January 1, 2004, Wallton sold this building to Hastings for $280,000. At that time, the building had a remaining life

of eight years but still no expected salvage value. In preparing financial statements for 2004, how does this transfer affect the computation of consolidated net income?
a. Income must be reduced by $32,000.
b. Income must be reduced by $35,000.
c. Income must be reduced by $36,000.
d. Income must be reduced by $40,000.

**Use the following data for problems 10–15:**

On January 1, 2004, Jarel bought 80 percent of the outstanding voting stock of Suarez for $260,000. Of this payment, $20,000 was allocated to equipment (with a five-year life) that had been undervalued on Suarez's books by $25,000. Any excess purchase price was allocated to secret formulas and amortized over a 20-year life.

As of December 31, 2004, the financial statements appeared as follows:

|  | Jarel | Suarez |
|---|---|---|
| Revenues | $ 300,000 | $200,000 |
| Cost of goods sold | 140,000 | 80,000 |
| Expenses | 20,000 | 10,000 |
| Net income | $ 140,000 | $110,000 |
| Retained earnings, 1/1/04 | $ 300,000 | $150,000 |
| Net income | 140,000 | 110,000 |
| Dividends paid | –0– | –0– |
| Retained earnings, 12/31/04 | $ 440,000 | $260,000 |
| Cash and receivables | $ 210,000 | $ 90,000 |
| Inventory | 150,000 | 110,000 |
| Investment in Jarel | 260,000 | –0– |
| Equipment (net) | 440,000 | 300,000 |
| Total assets | $1,060,000 | $500,000 |
| Liabilities | $ 420,000 | $140,000 |
| Common stock | 200,000 | 100,000 |
| Retained earnings, 12/31/04 | 440,000 | 260,000 |
| Total liabilities and equities | $1,060,000 | $500,000 |

During 2004, Jarel bought inventory for $80,000 and sold it to Suarez for $100,000. Only half of this purchase has been paid for by Suarez by the end of the year. Of these goods, 60 percent is still in the company's possession on December 31.

10. What is the total of consolidated revenues?
    a. $500,000
    b. $460,000
    c. $420,000
    d. $400,000
11. What is the total of consolidated expenses?
    a. $30,000
    b. $36,000
    c. $33,000
    d. $39,000
12. What is the total of consolidated cost of goods sold?
    a. $140,000
    b. $152,000
    c. $132,000
    d. $145,000
13. What is the consolidated total of noncontrolling interest appearing on the balance sheet?
    a. $72,000
    b. $69,600

c. $67,000
d. $70,600

14. What is the consolidated total for equipment (net) at December 31?
    a. $680,000
    b. $756,000
    c. $764,000
    d. $848,000

15. What is the consolidated total for inventory at December 31?
    a. $240,000
    b. $248,000
    c. $250,000
    d. $260,000

16. Following are several figures reported for Pop and Sam as of December 31, 2004:

|  | Pop | Sam |
|---|---|---|
| Inventory | $300,000 | $100,000 |
| Sales | 700,000 | 500,000 |
| Investment income | not given |  |
| Cost of goods sold | 300,000 | 200,000 |
| Operating expenses | 200,000 | 200,000 |

Pop acquired 80 percent of Sam on January 1, 1997. An excess $180,000 is allocated to an intangible asset and amortized over a 20-year life. During 2004, Sam sells inventory costing $100,000 to Pop for $150,000. Of this inventory, 10 percent remains at year's end. On a 2004 consolidation, determine the totals that would be reported for the following accounts:

Inventory
Sales
Cost of Goods Sold
Operating Expenses
Noncontrolling Interest in the Subsidiary's Net Income

17. On January 1, 2003, Corgan Company purchased 80 percent of the outstanding voting stock of Smashing, Inc., for $980,000 in cash and other consideration. At the purchase date, Smashing had common stock of $700,000 and retained earnings of $250,000. Corgan attributed the excess of cost over Smashing's book value to various covenants with a 20-year life. Corgan uses the equity method to account for its investment in Smashing.

During the next two years Smashing reported the following:

|  | Net Income | Dividends | Inventory Purchases from Corgan |
|---|---|---|---|
| 2003 | $150,000 | $35,000 | $100,000 |
| 2004 | 130,000 | 45,000 | 120,000 |

Corgan sells inventory to Smashing using a 60 percent markup on cost. At the end of 2003 and 2004, 40 percent of the current year purchases remain in Smashing's inventory.

a. Compute the equity method balance in Corgan's Investment in Smashing, Inc., account as of January 31, 2004.
b. Prepare the worksheet adjustments for the January 31, 2004, consolidation of Corgan and Smashing.

18. Smith Corporation acquired 80 percent of the outstanding voting stock of Kane, Inc., on January 1, 1997, when Kane had a net book value of $400,000. Any unexplained excess purchase price was assigned to intangible assets and amortized at a rate of $5,000 per year.

Smith reported net income for 2004 of $300,000 while Kane reported $110,000. Smith distributed $100,000 in dividends during this period; Kane paid $40,000. At the end of the year, selected figures from the two companies' balance sheets were as follows:

|  | Smith Corporation | Kane, Inc. |
|---|---|---|
| Inventory | $140,000 | $ 90,000 |
| Land | 600,000 | 200,000 |
| Equipment (net) | 400,000 | 300,000 |
| Common stock | 400,000 | 200,000 |
| Retained earnings, 12/31/04 | 600,000 | 400,000 |

During 2003, intercompany sales of $90,000 (original cost of $54,000) were made. Only 20 percent of this inventory was still being held at the end of 2003. In 2004, $120,000 in intercompany sales were made with an original cost of $66,000. Of this merchandise, 30 percent had not been resold to outside parties by the end of the year.

*Each of the following questions should be considered as an independent situation.*

a. If the intercompany sales were upstream, what would be the noncontrolling interest's share of the subsidiary's 2004 net income?
b. What is the consolidated balance in the ending Inventory account?
c. If the intercompany sales were downstream, what would be the noncontrolling interest's share of the subsidiary's 2004 net income?
d. If the intercompany sales were downstream, what would be the consolidated net income prior to the reduction for the noncontrolling interest's share of the subsidiary's income? Assume that Smith uses the cost method to account for this investment.
e. If the intercompany sales were downstream, what would be the consolidated balance of the Retained Earnings account as of the end of 2004? Assume that Smith uses the partial equity method to account for this investment.
f. If the intercompany sales were upstream, what would be the consolidated balance for Retained Earnings as of the end of 2004? Assume that Smith uses the partial equity method to account for this investment.
g. Assume that no intercompany inventory sales occurred between Smith and Kane. Instead, in 2001, Kane sold land costing $30,000 to Smith for $50,000. On the 2004 consolidated balance sheet, what value should be reported for land?
h. Assume that no intercompany inventory or land sales occurred between Smith and Kane. Instead, on January 1, 2003, Kane sold equipment (that originally cost $100,000 but had a $60,000 book value on that date) to Smith for $80,000. At the time of sale, the equipment had a remaining useful life of five years. What worksheet entries are made for a December 31, 2004, consolidation of these two companies to eliminate the impact of the intercompany transfer? For 2004, what is the noncontrolling interest's share of Kane's net income?

19. Rockney owns 60 percent of the outstanding stock of Dabney. Dabney reports net income for 2003 of $120,000. Since being acquired, the subsidiary has regularly supplied inventory to Rockney at 20 percent more than cost. Sales to Rockney amounted to $252,000 in 2002 and $288,000 in 2003. Approximately one-tenth of the inventory purchased during any one year is not used until the following period.

a. What is the noncontrolling interest's share of Dabney's income in 2003?
b. Prepare the 2003 consolidation entries that would be required by the preceding intercompany inventory transfers.

20. Several years ago Penguin, Inc., purchased an 80 percent interest in Snow Company. The book values of Snow's asset and liability accounts at that time were considered to be equal to their fair market values. Penguin paid an amount corresponding to the underlying book value of Snow so that no allocations or goodwill resulted from the purchase price.

The following selected account balances are from the individual financial records of these two companies as of December 31, 2004:

|  | Penguin | Snow |
|---|---|---|
| Sales | $640,000 | $360,000 |
| Cost of goods sold | 290,000 | 197,000 |
| Operating expenses | 150,000 | 105,000 |

*(continued)*

|  | Penguin | Snow |
|---|---|---|
| Retained earnings, 1/1/04 | 740,000 | 180,000 |
| Inventory | 346,000 | 110,000 |
| Buildings (net) | 358,000 | 157,000 |
| Investment income | not given | –0– |

*Each of the following problems is an independent situation:*

a. Assume that Penguin sells inventory to Snow at a markup equal to 40 percent of cost. Intercompany transfers were $90,000 in 2003 and $110,000 in 2004. Of this inventory, $28,000 of the 2003 transfers were retained and then sold by Snow in 2004 while $42,000 of the 2004 transfers were held until 2005.

On consolidated financial statements for 2004, determine the balances that would appear for the following accounts:

Cost of Goods Sold
Inventory
Noncontrolling Interest in Subsidiary's Net Income

b. Assume that Snow sells inventory to Penguin at a markup equal to 40 percent of cost. Intercompany transfers were $50,000 in 2003 and $80,000 in 2004. Of this inventory, $21,000 of the 2003 transfers were retained and then sold by Penguin in 2004, whereas $35,000 of the 2004 transfers were held until 2005.

On consolidated financial statements for 2004, determine the balances that would appear for the following accounts:

Cost of Goods Sold
Inventory
Noncontrolling Interest in Subsidiary's Net Income

c. Penguin sells a building to Snow on January 1, 2003, for $80,000, although the book value of this asset was only $50,000 on this date. The building had a five-year remaining life and was to be depreciated using the straight-line method with no salvage value.

On consolidated financial statements for 2004, determine the balances that would appear for the following accounts:

Buildings (net)
Expenses
Noncontrolling Interest in Subsidiary's Net Income

21. Allen, Inc., owns all of the outstanding stock of Bowen Corporation. Amortization expense of $9,000 per year resulted from the original purchase. For 2004, the companies had the following account balances:

|  | Allen | Bowen |
|---|---|---|
| Sales | $900,000 | $500,000 |
| Cost of goods sold | 400,000 | 300,000 |
| Operating expenses | 300,000 | 120,000 |
| Investment income | not given | –0– |
| Dividends paid | 60,000 | 40,000 |

Intercompany sales of $200,000 occurred during 2003 and again in 2004. This merchandise cost $140,000 each year. Of the total transfers, $60,000 was still held on December 31, 2003, with $45,000 unsold on December 31, 2004.

a. For consolidation purposes, does the direction of the transfers (upstream or downstream) affect the balances to be reported here?
b. Prepare a consolidated income statement for the year ending December 31, 2004.

22. On January 1, 2003, PortFast Company purchased 90 percent of the outstanding voting stock of SpeedNet, Inc., for $1,400,000 in cash and stock options. At the purchase date, SpeedNet had Common Stock of $900,000 and Retained Earnings of $300,000. PortFast attributed the excess of cost over SpeedNet's book value to a database with a five-year life. PortFast uses the equity method to account for its investment in SpeedNet.

During the next two years, SpeedNet reported the following:

|  | Income | Dividends |
|---|---|---|
| 2003 | $ 80,000 | $5,000 |
| 2004 | 115,000 | 8,000 |

On July 1, 2003, PortFast sold communication equipment to SpeedNet for $42,000. The equipment originally cost $48,000 and had accumulated depreciation of $9,000 and an estimated remaining life of three years at the date of the intercompany transfer.

a. Compute the equity method balance in PortFast's Investment in SpeedNet, Inc., account as of 12/31/04.
b. Prepare the worksheet adjustments for the 12/31/04 consolidation of PortFast and SpeedNet.

23. Plimpton holds 100 percent of the outstanding shares of Stanger. On January 1, 2002, Plimpton transferred equipment to Stanger for $70,000. The equipment had cost $110,000 originally but had a $40,000 book value and five-year remaining life at the date of transfer. Depreciation expense is computed according to the straight-line method with no salvage value.

Consolidated financial statements for 2004 currently are being prepared. What worksheet entries are needed in connection with the consolidation of this asset? Assume that the parent applies the partial equity method.

24. On January 1, 2004, Slaughter sold equipment to Bennett (a wholly owned subsidiary) for $120,000 in cash. The equipment had originally cost $100,000 but had a book value of only $70,000 when transferred. On that date, the equipment had a five-year remaining life. Depreciation expense is computed using the straight-line method.

Slaughter earned $220,000 in net income in 2004 (not including any investment income) while Bennett reported $90,000.

a. What is the consolidated net income for 2004?
b. What is the consolidated net income for 2004 if Slaughter owns only 90 percent of Bennett?
c. What is the consolidated net income for 2004 if Slaughter owns only 90 percent of Bennett and the equipment transfer was upstream?
d. What is the consolidated net income for 2005 if Slaughter reports $240,000 (does not include investment income) and Bennett $100,000 in income? Assume that Bennett is a wholly owned subsidiary and the equipment transfer was downstream.

25. Anchovy purchased 90 percent of Yelton on January 1, 2002. Of the original price paid by the parent, $60,000 was allocated to undervalued equipment (with a 10-year life) and $80,000 was attributed to franchises (to be written off over a 20-year period).

Since the takeover, Yelton has transferred inventory to its parent as follows:

| Year | Cost | Transfer Price | Remaining at Year-End |
|---|---|---|---|
| 2002 | $20,000 | $ 50,000 | $20,000 (at transfer price) |
| 2003 | 49,000 | 70,000 | 30,000 (at transfer price) |
| 2004 | 50,000 | 100,000 | 40,000 (at transfer price) |

On January 1, 2003, Anchovy sold a building to Yelton for $50,000. The building had originally cost $70,000 but had a book value at the date of transfer of only $30,000. The building is estimated to have a five-year remaining life (straight-line depreciation is used with no salvage value).

Selected figures from the December 31, 2004, trial balances of these two companies are as follows:

|  | Anchovy | Yelton |
|---|---|---|
| Sales | $600,000 | $500,000 |
| Cost of Goods Sold | 400,000 | 260,000 |
| Operating Expenses | 120,000 | 80,000 |
| Investment Income | not given | –0– |
| Inventory | 220,000 | 80,000 |
| Equipment (net) | 140,000 | 110,000 |
| Buildings (net) | 350,000 | 190,000 |

Determine consolidated totals for each of these account balances.

26. On January 1, 2004, Sledge has common stock of $120,000 and retained earnings of $260,000. During that year, Sledge reported sales of $130,000, cost of goods sold of $70,000, and operating expenses of $40,000.

    On January 1, 1999, 80 percent of Sledge's outstanding voting stock was acquired by Percy, Inc. At that date, $60,000 of the purchase price was assigned to contracts (with a 20-year life) and $20,000 to an undervalued building (with a 10-year life).

    In 2003, Sledge sold inventory costing $9,000 to Percy for $15,000. Of this merchandise, Percy continued to hold $5,000 at the end of that period. During 2004, inventory costing $11,000 was transferred to Percy for $20,000. Half of these items are still being held at year's end.

    On January 1, 2003, Percy sold equipment to Sledge for $12,000. This asset originally cost $16,000 but had a January 1, 2003, book value of $9,000. At the time of transfer, the equipment's remaining life was estimated to be five years.

    Percy has properly applied the equity method to the investment in Sledge.

    a. Prepare worksheet entries to consolidate these two companies as of December 31, 2004.
    b. Compute the noncontrolling interest in the subsidiary's income for 2004.

27. Big purchased 90 percent of the outstanding shares of Little on January 1, 2002, for $345,000 in cash. The subsidiary's stockholders' equity accounts totaled $330,000 on that day. However, a building held by Little (with a nine-year remaining life) was undervalued in the accounting records by $20,000. Any excess purchase price is assigned to patented technology to be amortized over a 10-year period.

    Little reported net income of $60,000 in 2002 and $80,000 in 2003. The company followed a policy of paying dividends each year equal to 30 percent of income.

    Little sells inventory to Big as follows:

| Year | Cost to Little | Transfer Price to Big | Inventory Remaining at Year's End (at transfer price) |
|---|---|---|---|
| 2002 | $69,000 | $115,000 | $25,000 |
| 2003 | 81,000 | 135,000 | 37,500 |
| 2004 | 92,800 | 160,000 | 50,000 |

At December 31, 2004, Big owes Little $16,000 for inventory acquired during the current period.

The following separate account balances are for these two companies for December 31, 2004, and the year then ended. Credits are indicated by parentheses.

|  | Big | Little |
|---|---|---|
| Sales revenues | $ (862,000) | $(366,000) |
| Cost of goods sold | 515,000 | 209,000 |
| Expenses | 186,600 | 67,000 |
| Investment income—Little | (70,600) | — |
| Net income | $ (231,000) | $ (90,000) |

*(continued)*

|  | Big | Little |
|---|---|---|
| Retained earnings, 1/1/04 | $ (488,000) | $(278,000) |
| Net income (above) | (231,000) | (90,000) |
| Dividends paid | 136,000 | 27,000 |
| Retained earnings, 12/31/04 | $ (583,000) | $(341,000) |
| Cash and receivables | $ 146,000 | $ 98,000 |
| Inventory | 255,000 | 136,000 |
| Investment in Little | 456,000 | — |
| Land, buildings, and equipment (net) | 959,000 | 328,000 |
| Total assets | $1,816,000 | $ 562,000 |
| Liabilities | $ (718,000) | $ (71,000) |
| Common stock | (515,000) | (150,000) |
| Retained earnings, 12/31/04 | (583,000) | (341,000) |
| Total liabilities and equities | $(1,816,000) | $(562,000) |

Answer each of the following questions:
 a. How much did the book value of the subsidiary increase during the previous two years of ownership (2002 and 2003)?
 b. What was the annual amortization resulting from the purchase price allocations?
 c. Were the intercompany transfers upstream or downstream?
 d. What unrealized gain existed as of January 1, 2004?
 e. What was the subsidiary's realized retained earnings as of January 1, 2004?
 f. What unrealized gain existed as of December 31, 2004?
 g. What was the subsidiary's realized net income for 2004?
 h. What amounts make up the $70,600 Investment Income—Little account balance for 2004?
 i. What was the noncontrolling interest's share of the subsidiary's net income for 2004?
 j. What amounts make up the $456,000 Investment in Little account balance as of December 31, 2004?
 k. What Entry **S** is required in producing a 2004 consolidation worksheet?
 l. Without preparing a worksheet or consolidation entries, determine the consolidation balances for these two companies.

28. Asphalt acquired 70 percent of Broadway on June 11, 1993. Based on the purchase price, an intangible of $300,000 was recognized and is being amortized at the rate of $10,000 per year. The 2004 financial statements are as follows:

|  | Asphalt | Broadway |
|---|---|---|
| Sales | $ 800,000 | $ 600,000 |
| Cost of goods sold | (535,000) | (400,000) |
| Operating expenses | (100,000) | (100,000) |
| Dividend income | 35,000 | –0– |
| Net income | $ 200,000 | $ 100,000 |
| Retained earnings, 1/1/04 | $1,300,000 | $ 850,000 |
| Net income | 200,000 | 100,000 |
| Dividends paid | (100,000) | (50,000) |
| Retained earnings, 12/31/04 | $1,400,000 | $ 900,000 |
| Cash and receivables | $ 400,000 | $ 300,000 |
| Inventory | 298,000 | 700,000 |
| Investment in Broadway | 902,000 | –0– |
| Fixed assets | 1,000,000 | 600,000 |
| Accumulated depreciation | (300,000) | (200,000) |
| Totals | $2,300,000 | $1,400,000 |

*(continued)*

|  | Asphalt | Broadway |
|---|---|---|
| Liabilities | $ 600,000 | $ 400,000 |
| Common stock | 300,000 | 100,000 |
| Retained earnings | 1,400,000 | 900,000 |
| Totals | $2,300,000 | $1,400,000 |

Asphalt sells inventory costing $72,000 to Broadway during 2003 for $120,000. At year's end, 30 percent is left. Asphalt sells inventory costing $200,000 to Broadway during 2004 for $250,000. At year's end, 20 percent is left. Under these circumstances, determine the consolidated balances for the following accounts:

Sales
Cost of Goods Sold
Operating Expenses
Dividend Income
Noncontrolling Interest in Consolidated Income
Inventory
Noncontrolling Interest in Subsidiary, 12/31/04

29. Compute the balances in problem 28 again, assuming that the intercompany transfers were all made from Broadway to Asphalt.
30. Following are financial statements for Topper Company and Kirby Company for 2004:

|  | Topper | Kirby |
|---|---|---|
| Sales and other income | $ 800,000 | $ 600,000 |
| Cost of goods sold | 500,000 | 400,000 |
| Operating and interest expense | 100,000 | 160,000 |
| Net income | $ 200,000 | $ 40,000 |
| Retained earnings, 1/1/04 | $ 990,000 | $ 500,000 |
| Net income | 200,000 | 40,000 |
| Dividends paid | 130,000 | –0– |
| Retained earnings, 12/31/04 | $1,060,000 | $ 540,000 |
| Cash and receivables | $ 220,000 | $ 170,000 |
| Inventory | 224,000 | 160,000 |
| Investment in Kirby | 654,000 | –0– |
| Equipment (net) | 600,000 | 400,000 |
| Buildings | 1,000,000 | 800,000 |
| Accumulated depreciation—buildings | (100,000) | (200,000) |
| Other assets | 200,000 | 100,000 |
| Total assets | $2,798,000 | $1,430,000 |
| Liabilities | $1,138,000 | $ 590,000 |
| Common stock | 600,000 | 300,000 |
| Retained earnings, 12/31/04 | 1,060,000 | 540,000 |
| Total liabilities and equity | $2,798,000 | $1,430,000 |

- Topper purchased 90 percent of Kirby on January 1, 1993, for $654,000 in cash. On the date of acquisition, Kirby held equipment (five-year life) that was undervalued on the financial records by $50,000 and liabilities (20-year life) that were overvalued by $30,000. Any excess price was assigned to brand names and amortized over a 40-year life.
- Between January 1, 1993, and December 31, 2003, Kirby earned a net income of $600,000 and paid dividends of $340,000.
- Kirby sells inventory each year to Topper with a markup equal to 20 percent of the transfer price. Intercompany sales were $145,000 in 2003 and $160,000 in 2004. On January 1, 2004,

30 percent of the 2003 transfers were still on hand and, on December 31, 2004, 40 percent of the 2004 transfers remained in inventory. Topper still owes $20,000 on the final shipment.
- Topper sold a building to Kirby on January 1, 2003. It had cost Topper $100,000 but had $90,000 in accumulated depreciation at the time of this transfer. The price was $25,000 in cash. At that time, the building had a five-year remaining life.

Determine all consolidated balances either computationally or by the use of a worksheet.

31. Atkins, Inc., and Smith, Inc., formed a business combination on January 1, 1998, when Atkins acquired a 60 percent interest in the common stock of Smith for $372,000. The book value of Smith on that day was $350,000. Patents held by the subsidiary (with a 12-year remaining life) were undervalued within the company's accounting records by $120,000. Any excess purchase price is assigned to a customer list to be amortized over 10 years.

Intercompany inventory sales between the two companies have been made as follows:

| Year | Cost to Atkins | Transfer Price to Smith | Ending Balance (at transfer price) |
|---|---|---|---|
| 1998 | $ 60,000 | $ 72,000 | $15,000 |
| 1999 | 70,000 | 84,000 | 25,000 |
| 2000 | 80,000 | 100,000 | 20,000 |
| 2001 | 100,000 | 125,000 | 40,000 |
| 2002 | 90,000 | 120,000 | 30,000 |
| 2003 | 120,000 | 150,000 | 50,000 |
| 2004 | 112,000 | 160,000 | 40,000 |

Smith sold a building to Atkins on January 1, 2002, for $80,000. The building had a net book value of $30,000 on that date and a five-year life. No salvage value was expected for this asset, which was being depreciated by the straight-line method.

The individual financial statements for these two companies as of December 31, 2004, and the year then ended follow:

|  | Atkins, Inc. | Smith, Inc. |
|---|---|---|
| Sales | $ 700,000 | $ 300,000 |
| Cost of goods sold | (460,000) | (205,000) |
| Operating expenses | (170,000) | (70,000) |
| Income of Smith | 15,000 | –0– |
| Net income | $ 85,000 | $ 25,000 |
| Retained earnings, 1/1/04 | $ 690,000 | $ 400,000 |
| Net income (above) | 85,000 | 25,000 |
| Dividends paid | (45,000) | (5,000) |
| Retained earnings, 12/31/04 | $ 730,000 | $ 420,000 |
| Cash and receivables | $ 185,000 | $ 142,000 |
| Inventory | 233,000 | 229,000 |
| Investment in Smith | 474,000 | –0– |
| Buildings (net) | 308,000 | 202,000 |
| Equipment (net) | 220,000 | 86,000 |
| Patents (net) | –0– | 20,000 |
| Total assets | $1,420,000 | $ 679,000 |
| Liabilities | $ 390,000 | $ 159,000 |
| Common stock | 300,000 | 100,000 |
| Retained earnings, 12/31/04 | 730,000 | 420,000 |
| Total liabilities and equities | $1,420,000 | $ 679,000 |

For each of the following accounts, determine the 2004 consolidated balance:
a. Cost of Goods Sold
b. Operating Expenses

c. Net Income
d. Retained Earnings, 1/1/04
e. Inventory
f. Buildings (net)
g. Patents (net)
h. Common Stock
i. Noncontrolling Interest in Smith, 12/31/04

32. Tall Company purchased 60 percent of the outstanding stock of Short, Inc., on January 1, 2002. A $70,000 portion of the purchase price was allocated to equipment with a 10-year remaining life, and $40,000 was attributed to a building having a 20-year life. A huge database was assigned $60,000 and has been amortized over a 30-year period.

Short sells inventory to Tall at a markup equal to 25 percent of the transfer price. Sales have been as follows:

| Year | Transfer Price to Tall | Inventory Remaining at Year's End (at transfer price) |
|---|---|---|
| 2002 | $ 90,000 | $30,000 |
| 2003 | 120,000 | 20,000 |
| 2004 | 140,000 | 40,000 |

Tall still owes $30,000 to Short for the last inventory shipment.

Following are the account balances at December 31, 2004, for both companies. Credit balances are indicated with parentheses.

|  | Tall | Short |
|---|---|---|
| Revenues | $ (984,000) | $(438,000) |
| Cost of goods sold | 551,000 | 286,000 |
| Operating expenses | 198,000 | 112,000 |
| Equity earnings of Short | (10,000) | –0– |
| Net income | $ (245,000) | $ (40,000) |
| Retained earnings, 1/1/04 | $ (871,000) | $(350,000) |
| Net income (above) | (245,000) | (40,000) |
| Dividends paid | 110,000 | 25,000 |
| Retained earnings, 12/31/04 | $(1,006,000) | $(365,000) |
| Cash and receivables | $ 239,000 | $57,000 |
| Inventory | 454,000 | 95,000 |
| Investment in Short | 440,000 | –0– |
| Land and buildings (net) | 722,000 | 394,000 |
| Equipment (net) | 328,000 | 257,000 |
| Total assets | $ 2,183,000 | $ 803,000 |
| Liabilities | $ (686,000) | $(288,000) |
| Common stock | (320,000) | (90,000) |
| Additional paid-in capital | (171,000) | (60,000) |
| Retained earnings | (1,006,000) | (365,000) |
| Total liabilities and stockholders' equity | $(2,183,000) | $(803,000) |

a. How was the $10,000 balance in the Equity Earnings of Short account determined?
b. Construct a worksheet to arrive at consolidated figures to be used for external reporting purposes.

33. On December 31, 2001, Silvey Company acquired 70 percent of the outstanding common stock of Young Company for $665,000. The stockholders' equity accounts reported by Young on that date were as follows:

| | |
|---|---|
| Common stock—$10 par value | $300,000 |
| Additional paid-in capital | 90,000 |
| Retained earnings | 410,000 |

In establishing the purchase price, Silvey appraised the assets of Young and ascertained that a building (with a five-year life) was undervalued within the accounting records by $50,000. Any excess purchase price is allocated to a franchise agreement to be amortized over 10 years.

During the subsequent years, Young sold inventory to Silvey at a 30 percent markup on the transfer price. Silvey consistently resold this merchandise in the year of acquisition or in the period immediately following. Transfers for the three years after this business combination was created amounted to the following:

| Year | Transfer Price | Inventory Remaining at Year's End (at transfer price) |
|---|---|---|
| 2002 | $60,000 | $10,000 |
| 2003 | 80,000 | 12,000 |
| 2004 | 90,000 | 18,000 |

In addition, Silvey sold several pieces of fully depreciated equipment to Young on January 1, 2003, for $20,000. The equipment had originally cost Silvey $50,000. Young plans to depreciate the cost of these assets over a five-year period.

In 2004, Young earns a net income of $160,000 while distributing $50,000 in cash dividends. These figures increase the subsidiary's Retained Earnings to a $740,000 balance at the end of 2004. During this same year, Silvey reported dividend income of $35,000 and an investment account containing the original cost balance of $665,000.

Prepare the 2004 consolidation worksheet entries for Silvey and Young. In addition, compute the noncontrolling interest's share of the subsidiary's net income for 2004.

34. Assume the same basic information as presented in problem 33 except that Silvey has employed the equity method of accounting. Hence, investment income is being reported for 2004 as $100,740 with an investment account balance of $838,220. Under these circumstances, prepare the worksheet entries required for the consolidation of Silvey Company and Young Company.

35. The individual financial statements for Bumpus Company and Keller Company for the year ending December 31, 2004, follow. Bumpus acquired a 60 percent interest in Keller on January 1, 1999. An internally developed customer list was assigned $100,000 within the original purchase price. This intangible asset is being amortized over 20 years.

Bumpus sold land with a book value of $60,000 to Keller on January 1, 2001, for $100,000. Keller still holds this land at the end of the current year.

Keller annually transfers inventory to Bumpus. In 2003, inventory costing $100,000 was shipped to Bumpus at a price of $150,000. During 2004, intercompany shipments totaled $200,000, although the original cost to Keller was only $140,000. In each of these years, 20 percent of the merchandise was not resold to outside parties until the period following the transfer. Bumpus owes Keller $40,000 at the end of 2004.

| | Bumpus Company | Keller Company |
|---|---|---|
| Sales | $ 800,000 | $ 500,000 |
| Cost of goods sold | (500,000) | (300,000) |
| Operating expenses | (100,000) | (60,000) |
| Income of Keller Company | 84,000 | –0– |
| Net income | $ 284,000 | $ 140,000 |
| Retained earnings, 1/1/04 | $1,116,000 | $ 620,000 |
| Net income (above) | 284,000 | 140,000 |
| Dividends paid | (115,000) | (60,000) |
| Retained earnings, 12/31/04 | $1,285,000 | $ 700,000 |

(continued)

|  | Bumpus Company | Keller Company |
|---|---|---|
| Cash | $ 177,000 | $ 90,000 |
| Accounts receivable | 316,000 | 410,000 |
| Inventory | 440,000 | 320,000 |
| Investment in Keller Company | 766,000 | –0– |
| Land | 180,000 | 390,000 |
| Buildings and equipment (net) | 496,000 | 300,000 |
| Total assets | $2,375,000 | $1,510,000 |
| Liabilities | $ 480,000 | $ 400,000 |
| Common stock | 610,000 | 320,000 |
| Additional paid-in capital | –0– | 90,000 |
| Retained earnings, 12/31/04 | 1,285,000 | 700,000 |
| Total liabilities and equities | $2,375,000 | $1,510,000 |

a. Prepare a worksheet to consolidate the separate 2004 financial statements produced by Bumpus and Keller.

b. How would the consolidation entries in requirement (a) have differed if Bumpus had sold a building with a $60,000 book value (cost of $140,000) to Keller for $100,000 instead of land, as the problem reports? Assume that the building had a 10-year remaining life at the date of transfer.

36. Greene, Inc., obtained 100 percent of Meadow Corporation on January 1, 2000. Meadow reported total stockholders' equity on this date of $300,000 although the stock issued by Greene in the transaction had a $170,000 par value but a fair market value of $450,000. On January 1, 2000, Meadow held land that was undervalued in the company's accounting records by $30,000. Any excess purchase price is assigned to a franchise contract that is to be amortized over a 40-year life.

Inventory has been regularly transferred by Meadow to Greene. In 2003, merchandise costing $60,000 was sold to Greene for $100,000. Of this total, 30 percent was not resold to unrelated parties until the following year. In 2004, $75,000 in inventory was shipped to Greene for $150,000 with $20,000 (transfer price) still held at the end of the period.

On June 19, 2004, Greene sold land costing $12,000 to Meadow for $17,000. This money has not yet been paid.

The following account balances are for both companies as of December 31, 2004, and the year then ended. The parent has used the equity method to record this investment. Produce a worksheet to arrive at consolidated financial statements for this business combination. Credit balances are indicated by parentheses.

|  | Greene | Meadow |
|---|---|---|
| Revenues | $ (477,000) | $(358,000) |
| Cost of goods sold | 289,000 | 195,000 |
| General and administrative expenses | 170,000 | 75,000 |
| Gain on sale of land | (5,000) | –0– |
| Investment income | (82,000) | –0– |
| Net income | $ (105,000) | $ (88,000) |
| Retained earnings, 1/1/04 | $ (365,000) | $(292,000) |
| Net income | (105,000) | (88,000) |
| Dividends distributed | 70,000 | 20,000 |
| Retained earnings, 12/31/04 | $ (400,000) | $(360,000) |
| Cash and receivables | $ 169,000 | $ 210,000 |
| Inventory | 281,000 | 232,000 |
| Investment in Meadow | 630,000 | –0– |
| Land, buildings, and equipment (net) | 487,000 | 284,000 |
| Total assets | $ 1,567,000 | $ 726,000 |

*(continued)*

|  | Greene | Meadow |
|---|---|---|
| Liabilities | $ (466,000) | $(216,000) |
| Common stock | (410,000) | (120,000) |
| Additional paid-in capital | (291,000) | (30,000) |
| Retained earnings, 12/31/04 | (400,000) | (360,000) |
| Total liabilities and stockholders' equity | $(1,567,000) | $(726,000) |

# Develop Your Skills

## EXCEL CASE

On January 1, 2003, Patrick Company purchased 100 percent of the outstanding voting stock of Shawn, Inc., for $1,000,000 in cash and other consideration. At the purchase date, Shawn had Common Stock of $500,000 and Retained Earnings of $185,000. Patrick attributed the excess of cost over Shawn's book value to a trade name with a 25-year life. Patrick uses the equity method to account for its investment in Shawn.

During the next two years, Shawn reported the following:

|  | Income | Dividends | Inventory Transfers to Patrick at Transfer Price |
|---|---|---|---|
| 2003 | $78,000 | $25,000 | $190,000 |
| 2004 | 85,000 | 27,000 | 210,000 |

Shawn sells inventory to Patrick after a markup based on a gross profit rate. At the end of 2003 and 2004, 30 percent of the current year purchases remain in Patrick's inventory.

### Required:

Create an Excel spreadsheet that computes the following:
a. Equity method balance in Patrick's Investment in Shawn, Inc., account as of December 31, 2004.
b. Worksheet adjustments for the December 31, 2004, consolidation of Patrick and Shawn.
Formulate your solution so that Shawn's gross profit rate on sales to Patrick is treated as a variable.

## ANALYSIS AND RESEARCH CASE: ACCOUNTING INFORMATION AND SALARY NEGOTIATIONS

Granger Eagles Players' Association and Mr. Doublecount, the CEO of the Granger Eagles Baseball Company, ask your help in resolving a salary dispute. Mr. Doublecount presents the following income statement to the player representatives.

| GRANGER EAGLES BASEBALL COMPANY INCOME STATEMENT | | |
|---|---|---|
| Ticket revenues |  | $2,000,000 |
| Stadium rent expense | $1,400,000 |  |
| Ticket expense | 25,000 |  |
| Promotion | 35,000 |  |
| Player salaries | 400,000 |  |
| Staff salaries and misc. | 200,000 | 2,060,000 |
| Net income (loss) |  | $ (60,000) |

Mr. Doublecount argues that the Granger Eagles really lose money and, until things turn around, a salary increase is out of the question.

As a result of your inquiry, you discover that the Granger Eagles Baseball Company owns 91 percent of the voting stock in Eagle Stadium, Inc. This venue is specifically designed for baseball and is where the Eagles play their entire home game schedule. However, Mr. Doublecount does not wish to consider the profits of Eagle Stadium in the negotiations with the players. He claims that "the stadium is really a separate business entity that was purchased separately from the team" and therefore does not concern the players. The Eagles Stadium income statement appears as follows:

### EAGLES STADIUM, INC.
### INCOME STATEMENT

| | | |
|---|---:|---:|
| Stadium rent revenue | $1,400,000 | |
| Concession revenue | 800,000 | |
| Parking revenue | 100,000 | $2,300,000 |
| Cost of goods sold | 250,000 | |
| Depreciation | 80,000 | |
| Staff salaries and misc. | 150,000 | 480,000 |
| Net income (loss) | | $1,820,000 |

## Required:

a. What advice would you provide the negotiating parties regarding the issue of considering the Eagles Stadium income statement in their discussions? What authoritative literature could you cite in supporting your advice?

b. What other pertinent information would you need to provide a specific recommendation regarding players' salaries?

# Chapter Six

# Variable Interest Entities, Intercompany Debt, Consolidated Cash Flows, and Other Issues

The consolidation of financial information can be a highly complex process often encompassing a number of practical challenges. This chapter examines the procedures required by several additional issues:

- Variable interest entities.
- Intercompany debt.
- Subsidiary preferred stock.
- The consolidated statement of cash flows.
- Computation of consolidated earnings per share.
- Subsidiary stock transactions.

Each of these can create potential difficulties for an accountant attempting to produce fairly presented financial statements for a business combination.

## FIN 46—CONSOLIDATION OF VARIABLE INTEREST ENTITIES

Starting in the late 1970s, many firms began establishing separate business structures to help finance their operations at favorable rates. These structures became commonly known as special purpose entities, special purpose vehicles, or off-balance sheet structures. In this text, we will

### Questions to Consider

- What is a variable interest entity and when must such an entity be consolidated? How are consolidated values determined for variable interest entities?
- When an affiliate's debt instrument is bought from an outside party, the reciprocal balances (investment and debt, interest revenue and expense, etc.) usually do not agree. How is the consolidation process affected in the year of acquisition as well as in succeeding periods?
- Some preferred stocks are viewed as equity interests but others are considered to be equivalent to debts. What impact does the nature of a subsidiary's preferred stock have on the consolidation process?
- What effect does a business combination have on the consolidated statement of cash flows?
- How are basic and diluted earnings per share computed for business combinations?
- Why would a subsidiary buy or sell more shares of its own stock after coming under the control of a parent company? What effect do such transactions have on consolidated financial statements?

refer to all such entities collectively as special purpose entities or SPEs. Many firms have routinely included their SPEs in their consolidated financial reports. However, others have sought to avoid consolidation. As discussed below, FASB *Interpretation 46* "Consolidation of Variable Interest Entities," January 2003 (*FIN 46*) addresses financial reporting for enterprises involved with SPEs.

## What is an SPE?

An SPE can take the form of a trust, partnership, joint venture, or corporation although typically it has neither independent management nor employees. Most are established for valid business purposes and transactions involving SPEs have become widespread. Common examples of SPE activities include transfers of financial assets, leasing, hedging financial instruments, research and development, and other transactions. An enterprise will often sponsor an SPE to accomplish a well-defined and limited business activity and to provide low-cost financing.

For example, business enterprises (or their financial institutions) often create SPEs to help the business convert large amounts of credit card receivables more quickly into cash. The SPE first buys a block of receivables from an enterprise in exchange for a short-term note payable. The SPE then issues debt securities for cash, which it transfers back to the enterprise. Interest and principle payments on the debt are then paid as the SPE collects the receivables. As long as the SPE is independent, the sponsoring firm effectively transfers the risk of collecting the receivables to the owners of the SPE who, in exchange, obtain a discount on the value of the receivables.

Low-cost financing of asset purchases is another main benefit available through SPEs. Rather than engaging in the transaction directly, the business may sponsor an SPE to purchase and finance an asset acquisition. The SPE then leases the asset to the sponsor. This strategy saves the business money because the SPE is often eligible for a lower interest rate. This advantage is achieved for several reasons. First, the SPE typically operates with a very limited set of assets—in many cases just one asset. By isolating an asset in an SPE, the risk of the asset is isolated from the overall risk of the sponsoring firm. Thus the SPE creditors remain protected by the specific collateral in the asset. Second, the business activities of an SPE can be strictly limited by its governing documents. These limits further protect lenders by preventing the SPE from engaging in any activities not specified in its agreements. As noted by a major public accounting firm

> The borrower/transferor gains access to a source of funds less expensive than would otherwise be available. This advantage derives from isolating the assets in an entity prohibited from undertaking any other business activity or taking on any additional debt, thereby creating a better security interest in the assets for the lender/investor.[1]

Because governing agreements limit activities and decision making in most SPEs, there is often little need for voting stock. In fact, a sponsoring enterprise may own very little, if any of its SPE's voting stock. Prior to FIN 46, because these businesses were technically not majority owners of their SPEs, they often left such entities unconsolidated in their financial reports. In utilizing the SPE as a conduit to provide financing, the related assets and debt were effectively removed from the enterprise's balance sheet.

### *The SPE as a Variable Interest Entity*

Like all business entities, SPEs generally have assets, liabilities, and investors with equity interests. Unlike most businesses, because an SPE's activities are strictly limited, the role of the equity investors can be fairly minor. The SPE may have been created specifically to benefit its sponsoring firm with low-cost financing. Thus the equity investors may serve simply as a

---

[1] KPMG, "Defining Issues: New Accounting for SPEs," March 1, 2002

**EXHIBIT 6–1**

FIN 46 Examples of Variable Interests

> Variable interests in a variable interest entity are contractual, ownership, or other pecuniary interests in an entity that change with changes in the entity's net asset value. Variable interests will absorb portions of a variable interest entity's expected losses if they occur or receive portions of the entity's expected residual returns if they occur.
>
> Expected losses and expected residual returns include
>
> - the expected variability in the entity's net income or loss,
> - the expected variability in the fair value of the entity's assets
>
> The following are some examples of variable interests and the related potential losses or returns:
>
> | Variable interests | Potential losses or returns |
> |---|---|
> | Guarantees of debt | If SPE cannot repay liabilities, honoring a debt guarantee will produce a loss |
> | Subordinated debt instruments | If an SPE's cash flow is insufficient to repay all senior debt, subordinated debt may be required to absorb the loss |
> | Lease residual value guarantees | If leased asset declines below the residual value, honoring the guarantee will produce a loss |
> | Participation rights | Entitles holder to residual profits |
> | Asset purchase options | Entitles holder to benefit from increases in asset fair values |

technical requirement to allow the SPE to function as a legal entity. Because they bear relatively low economic risk, equity investors are typically provided only a small rate of return.

The small equity investments normally are insufficient to induce lenders to provide a low-risk interest rate for the SPE. As a result, another party (often the sponsoring firm that benefits from the SPE's activities) must contribute substantial resources—often loans and/or guarantees—to enable the SPE to secure additional financing needed to accomplish its purpose. For example, the sponsoring firm may guarantee the SPE's debt thus assuming risk of default. Other contractual arrangements may limit returns to equity holders while participation rights provide increased profit potential and risks to the sponsoring firm. Risks and rewards such as these cause the sponsor's economic interest to vary depending on the success of the created entity—hence the term *variable interest entity*. In contrast to a traditional entity, an SPE's risks and rewards are not distributed according to stock ownership, but according to other variable interests. Exhibit 6–1 describes variable interests further and provides several examples presented in FIN 46.

A firm with variable interests in an SPE increases its risk with the level (or potential level in the case of a guarantee) of resources provided. With increased risks come increased incentives to exert greater influence over the decision making of the SPE. In fact, a firm with variable interests will regularly limit the decision making power of the equity investors through the governance documents that establish the SPE. As noted in FIN 46

> If the total equity investment at risk is not sufficient to permit the entity to finance its activities, the parties providing the necessary additional subordinated financial support will not permit an equity investor to make decisions that may be counter to their interests (paragraph C20).

Although technically the equity investors are the owners of the SPE, in reality they may retain little of the traditional responsibilities, risks, and benefits of ownership. In fact, the equity investors often cede financial control of the SPE to those with variable interest in exchange for a guaranteed rate of return.

SPEs can help accomplish legitimate business purposes. Nonetheless, their use was widely criticized in the aftermath of the 2001 collapse of Enron Corporation. Because many firms used SPEs for off-balance sheet financing, such entities were often characterized as vehicles to hide debt and mislead investors. Other critics observed that firms with variable interests recorded questionable profits on sales to their SPEs that were not arm's length transactions.[2]

## Consolidation of SPEs as Variable Interest Entities

Prior to FASB *Interpretation No. 46* "Consolidation of Variable Interest Entities," January 2003 (FIN 46), the assets, liabilities, and results of operations for SPEs frequently were not consolidated with those of the firm that controlled the SPE through variable interests. These firms invoked ARB 51's reliance on voting interests, as opposed to variable interests, to indicate a lack of a controlling financial interest in their SPEs. As FIN 46 observes

> ARB 51 requires that an enterprise's consolidated financial statements include subsidiaries in which the enterprise has a controlling financial interest. That requirement usually has been applied to subsidiaries in which an enterprise has a majority voting interest, but in many circumstances, the enterprise's consolidated financial statements do not include variable interest entities with which it has similar relationships. The voting interest approach is not effective in identifying controlling financial interests in entities that are not controllable through voting interests or in which the equity investors do not bear residual economic risk. (Summary, page 2)

FIN 46 first describes how to identify a variable interest entity (VIE) that is not subject to control through voting ownership interests, but is nonetheless controlled by another enterprise and therefore subject to consolidation. Each enterprise involved with a VIE must determine whether the financial support provided by that enterprise makes it the primary beneficiary of the VIE's activities. The primary beneficiary of the VIE is then required to include the assets, liabilities, and results of the activities of the VIE in its consolidated financial statements.[3]

According to FIN 46, an entity qualifies as a VIE if either of the following conditions exists:

- The total equity at risk is not sufficient to permit the entity to finance its activities without additional subordinated financial support from other parties. In most cases, if equity at risk is less that 10% of total assets, the risk is deemed insufficient.[4]
- The equity investors in the VIE lack any one of the following three characteristics of a controlling financial interest:
  1. The direct or indirect ability to make decisions about an entity's activities through voting rights or similar rights.
  2. The obligation to absorb the expected losses of the entity if they occur (e.g., another firm may guarantee a return to the equity investors)
  3. The right to receive the expected residual returns of the entity (e.g., the investors' return may be capped by the entity's governing documents or other arrangements with variable interest holders).

In assessing whether an enterprise should consolidate the assets, liabilities, revenues, and expenses of a VIE, FIN 46 next relies on an expanded notion of a controlling financial interest. The following characteristics are indicative of an enterprise qualifying as a primary beneficiary with a controlling financial interest in a VIE:

- The direct or indirect ability to make decisions about the entity's activities
- The obligation to absorb the expected losses of the entity if they occur, or
- The right to receive the expected residual returns of the entity if they occur

---

[2] In its 2001 fourth quarter 10-Q Enron recorded earnings restatements of over $400 million related to its failure to properly consolidate several of its SPEs (e.g., Chewco and LMJ1). Enron also admitted an improper omission of $700 million of its SPE's debt. Within a month of the restatements, Enron filed for bankruptcy.

[3] An exception to consolidation requirements is made for firms that employ "qualifying special-purpose entities" that fall under FASB 140, *Accounting for Transfers and Servicing of Financial Assets and Extinguishments of Liabilities*. An enterprise must still report its rights and obligations related to the qualifying SPE.

[4] Alternatively, a 10% or greater equity interest may also be insufficient. According to FIN 46, "some entities may require an equity investment greater than 10 percent of their assets to finance their activities, especially if they engage in high-risk activities, hold high-risk assets, or have exposure to risks that are not reflected in the reported amounts of the entities' assets or liabilities." (paragraph 10).

Note that these characteristics mirror those that the equity investors lack in a VIE. Instead, the primary beneficiary is subject to the majority of risks of losses or entitled to receive a majority of the entity's residual returns or both. The fact that the primary beneficiary may own no voting shares whatsoever becomes inconsequential because such shares do not effectively allow the equity investors to exercise control. Thus, in assessing control, a careful examination of the VIE's governing documents and the contractual arrangements among the parties involved is necessary to determine who bears the majority risk.

The magnitude of the effect of consolidating an enterprise's SPEs can be large. For example, General Motors (GM) in 2003 disclosed that it employed several sets of SPEs with assets in the billions of dollars that it may need to consolidate. In its annual report filed with the Securities and Exchange Commission, GM noted that FIN 46

> makes it "reasonably possible" that it will be obligated to consolidate special-purpose entities—which it referred to as variable interest entities—with total assets of about $18.6 billion . . . One set of entities, with assets estimated at $17.5 billion, facilitates activities of GM's financing and insurance operations through General Motors Acceptance Corp., including securitization of loans, mortgage funding, and other investing activities . . . Another set of entities, with assets estimated at $1.1 billion, was created to facilitate GM's leasing activities related to its "automotive, communications services, and other operations."[5]

FIN 46 emphasizes that its objective is to improve financial reporting by companies involved with VIEs, not to restrict the use of VIEs. FIN 46 reasons that if a "business enterprise has a controlling financial interest in a variable interest entity, assets, liabilities, and results of the activities of the variable interest entity should be included with those of the business enterprise."

### *Example of a Primary Beneficiary and Consolidated Variable Interest Entity*

Assume that Twin Peaks Power Company seeks to acquire from Ace Electric Company a generating plant for a negotiated price of $400 million. Twin Peaks wishes to expand its market share and expects to be able to sell the electricity generated by the plant acquisition at a profit to its owners.

In reviewing financing alternatives, Twin Peaks observed that its general credit rating allowed for a 4% annual interest rate on a debt issue. Twin Peaks also explored the establishment of a separate legal entity whose sole purpose would be to own the electric generating plant and lease it back to Twin Peaks. Because the separate entity would isolate the electric generating plant from Twin Peaks' other risky assets and liabilities, and provide specific collateral, an interest rate of 3% on the debt is available producing before tax savings of $4 million per year. To obtain the lower interest rate, however, Twin Peaks must guarantee the separate entity's debt. Twin Peaks must also maintain certain of its own predefined financial ratios and restrict the amount of additional debt it can assume.

To take advantage of the lower interest rate, on January 1, 2004 Twin Peaks establishes Power Finance Co., a special purpose entity (SPE) designed solely to own, finance, and lease the electric generating plant to Twin Peaks.[6] The documents governing the SPE specify the following:

- The sole purpose of Power Finance is to purchase the Ace Electric generating plant, provide equity and debt financing, and lease the plant to Twin Peaks.
- An outside investor will provide $16 million in exchange for a 100% nonvoting equity interest in Power Finance.
- Power Finance will issue debt in exchange for $384 million. Because the $16 million equity investment by itself is insufficient to attract low-interest rate debt financing, the debt will be guaranteed by Twin Peaks.

---

[5] Dow Jones Newswires, "General Motors Files Annual Report With SEC," March 13, 2003

[6] This arrangement is similar to a "synthetic lease" commonly used in utility companies. Synthetic leases also can have tax advantages because they are accounted for tax purposes by the sponsoring firm as capital leases.

- Twin Peaks will lease the electric generating plant from Power Finance in exchange for payments of $12 million per year based on a 3% fixed interest rate for both the debt and equity investors for an initial lease term of 5 years.
- At the end of the 5-year lease term (or any extension) Twin Peaks must do one of the following:
  - Renew the lease for 5 years subject to the approval of the equity investor
  - Purchase the electric generating plant for $400 million
  - Sell the electric generating plant to an independent third party. If the proceeds of the sale are insufficient to repay the equity investor, Twin Peaks is required to make a payment of $16 million to the equity investor.

Once the purchase of the electric generating plant is complete and the equity and debt are issued, Power Finance Company reports the following balance sheet:

**POWER FINANCE COMPANY**
**Balance Sheet**
**January 1, 2004**

| | | | |
|---|---|---|---|
| Electric Generating Plant | $400M | Long-Term Debt | $384M |
| | | Owner's Equity | 16M |
| Total Assets | $400M | Total Liabilities and OE | $400M |

Exhibit 6–2 shows the relationships between Twin Peaks, Power Finance, the electric generating plant, and the parties financing the asset purchase.

In evaluating whether Twin Peaks Electric Company must consolidate Power Finance Company, two conditions must be met. First, Power Finance must qualify as a VIE by either (a) an inability to secure financing without additional subordinated support or (b) a lack of either the risk of losses or entitlement to residual returns (or both). Second, Twin Peaks must qualify as the primary beneficiary of Power Finance.

In assessing the first condition, several factors point to VIE status for Power Finance. Its owner's equity comprises only 4% of total assets, far short of the 10% benchmark provided by FIN 46. Moreover, Twin Peaks guarantees the Power Finance's debt suggesting insufficient equity to finance its operations without additional support. Finally, the equity investor appears to bear almost no risk with respect to the operations of the Ace electric plant. These characteristics indicate that the Power Finance SPE qualifies as a VIE.

In evaluating the second condition for consolidation, an assessment is made to determine if Twin Peaks qualifies as the primary beneficiary of Power Finance. According to FIN 46, an enterprise must consolidate a VIE if that enterprise has a variable interest that will absorb a majority of the entity's expected losses if they occur, receive a majority of the entity's expected residual returns if they occur, or both. But what possible losses or returns would accrue to Twin Peaks? What are Twin Peaks' variable interests that rise and fall with the fortunes of Power Finance?

As stated in the SPE agreement, Twin Peaks will pay a fixed fee to lease the electric generating plant. It will then operate the plant and sell the electric power in its markets. If the business plan is successful, Twin Peaks will enjoy residual profits from operating while the equity investors of Power Finance receive the fixed fee. On the other hand, if prices for electricity fall, Twin Peaks may generate revenues insufficient to cover its lease payments while Power Finance's equity investors are protected from this risk. Moreover, if the plant's market value increases significantly, Twin Peaks can exercise its option to purchase the plant at a fixed price and either resell it or keep it for its own future use. Alternatively, if Twin Peaks were to sell the plant at a loss, it must pay the equity investors all of their initial investment, furthering the loss to Twin Peaks. Each of these elements points to Twin Peaks as the primary beneficiary of its SPE through variable interests. As the primary beneficiary, Twin Peaks must consolidate the assets, liabilities, and results of operations of Power Finance with its own.

**EXHIBIT 6–2**  Special Purpose Entity to Facilitate Financing

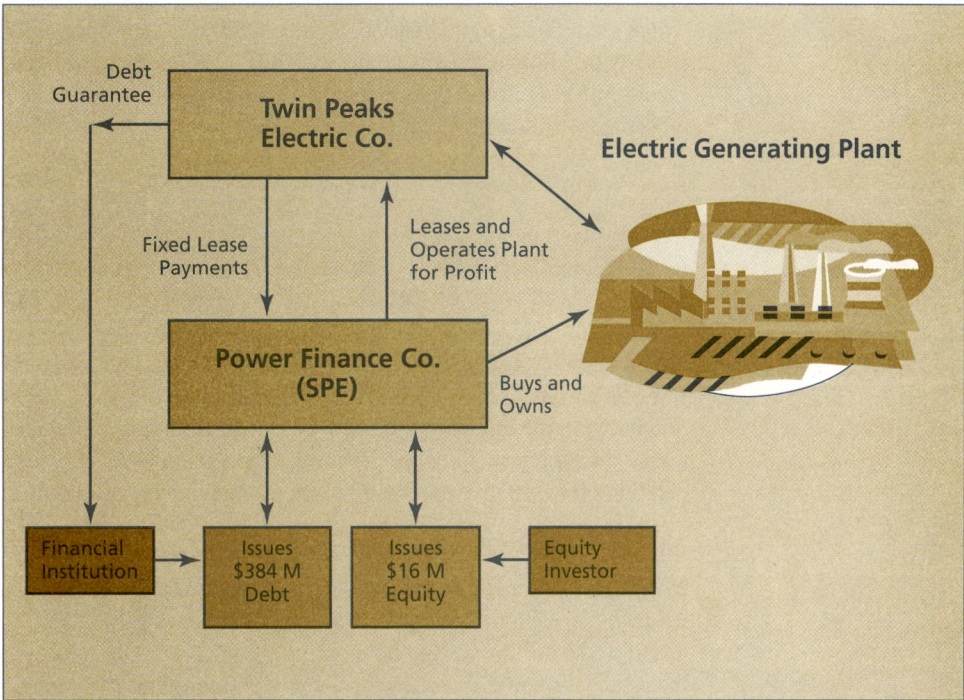

## Procedures to Consolidate Variable Interest Entities

As exemplified by the balance sheet of Power Finance, VIEs typically possess few assets and liabilities. Also, their business activities usually are strictly limited. Thus, the actual procedures to consolidate VIEs are relatively uncomplicated. However, the close nature of the relationship between the primary beneficiary and the VIE presents several measurement issues.

### Initial Measurement Issues

The financial reporting principles for consolidating variable interest entities require asset, liability, and noncontrolling interest valuations. These valuations initially are based on fair market values with two notable exceptions. First, if any of the SPE's assets have been transferred from the primary beneficiary, these assets will continue to be measured as if they had not been transferred. Second, the asset valuation procedures in FIN 46 also rely in part on the allocation principles described in SFAS 141, *Business Combinations*. Recall that SFAS 141 requires an allocation of the cost of an acquisition based on the underlying fair values of its assets and liabilities. However, unlike a voting interest acquisition, in a VIE control is not obtained by incurring a cost, but through governance agreements and contractual arrangements. Therefore, an *implied value* substitutes for the acquisition cost in determining the valuation of a VIE.

In determining the total amount to consolidate for a variable interest entity, the implied value of the entity is considered as the sum of:

- Consideration paid by the primary beneficiary (plus the reported values of any previously held interests), and
- The fair value of the newly consolidated liabilities and noncontrolling interests.

If the assessed fair values of the assets exceed the implied value of the VIE, then the assets are proportionately reduced as specified in SFAS 141.[7] On the other hand, if the implied fair value of the VIE exceeds the assessed fair values of the assets, the difference is reported as an

---

[7] Excluded from the proportionate reduction are financial assets other than equity method investments, assets to be disposed of by sale, deferred tax assets, and prepaid assets related to pension or other post-retirement plans.

extraordinary loss in the period in which the enterprise becomes the primary beneficiary. Consequently, there is no goodwill created in the consolidation of a VIE.

For example, assume that Vax Company invests $5 million in TLH Properties, a variable interest entity. In agreements completed July 1, 2004, Vax establishes itself as the primary beneficiary of TLH Property. Previously, Vax had no interest in TLH. After Vax's investment, TLH presents the following financial information at assessed fair values:

| | |
|---|---|
| Cash | $ 5 million |
| Land | 20 million |
| Production facility | 60 million |
| Long-term debt | 65 million |
| Vax equity investment | 5 million |
| Noncontrolling interest | (see below for alternative valuations) |

The allocations to be used in the consolidation of Vax and TLH Property depend on the relation between the implied value of the VIE and the assessed values of its assets. To demonstrate these valuation principles we use three brief examples, each with a different implied value depending on alternative assessed values of the noncontrolling interest.

### *Implied value of VIE equals assessed values of assets*

In this case, assume that the noncontrolling interest fair value equals $15 million. The implied value is then $85 million ($5 million consideration paid + $65 million fair values for liabilities and $15 million for the noncontrolling interest). Because the implied value is identical to the total assessed fair values for the assets (including cash), the land and production facility are consolidated at their individual fair values of $20 million and $60 million, respectively.

### *Implied value of VIE less than assessed asset values*

Alternatively, assume that the value of the noncontrolling interest was assessed at only $11 million. In this case the implied value of TLH Property would be calculated at $81 million ($5 million consideration paid + $65 million fair values for liabilities and $11 million for the noncontrolling interest). The $81 million implied value compared to the $85 assessed fair value of TLH Property's assets (including cash) produces an excess fair value of $4 million. In this case the fair values of the VIE's long-term assets is reduced proportionately below their fair values by the $4 million excess. The Land account, with an assessed fair value of $20 million (¼ of the $80 million total asset assessed value) will be reduced to a $19 million valuation. Similarly, the Production facility account, with an assessed fair value of $60 million (¾ of the $80 million total asset assessed value) will be reduced to a $57 million valuation. As noted in FIN 46, "this provision is intended to prevent intentional creation of a gain by arranging to become the primary beneficiary of a carefully structured entity, especially if the entity's assets are difficult to measure."

### *Implied value of VIE greater than assessed asset values*

Finally, assume that the value of the noncontrolling interest is assessed at $20 million. In this case the implied value of TLH Property would be calculated at $90 million ($5 million consideration paid + $65 million fair values for liabilities and $20 million for the noncontrolling interest). The $90 million implied value compared to the $85 assessed fair value of TLH Property's assets produces an excess implied value of $5 million. According to FIN 46, the excess $5 million implied value is recorded as an extraordinary loss by Vax Company in the year it became the primary beneficiary.

This treatment of the excess implied value as an extraordinary loss stands in marked contrast to the treatment of an excess cost in a voting interest entity. Under SFAS 141, an excess of an acquisition cost over fair values of underlying net assets is capitalized as goodwill. In FIN 46 however, the FASB notes the following for consolidation of VIEs.

> One exception is that goodwill is not recognized. The difference, if any, between the reported amounts of the variable interest entity's assets and the reported amounts of its liabilities and

noncontrolling interests is recognized in consolidated net income if that difference results in a loss.

Thus the FASB affords differential treatment to regular business combinations accomplished through voting stock acquisition (i.e., goodwill recognized) and those that result from acquiring variable interests (i.e., extraordinary loss for excess implied over assessed value).

### Consolidation of VIEs Subsequent to Initial Measurement

After the initial measurement, consolidations of VIEs with their primary beneficiaries should follow the same process as if the entity were consolidated based on voting interests. Importantly, all intercompany transactions between the primary beneficiary and the VIE including fees, other sources of income or loss, and intercompany inventory purchases) must be eliminated in consolidation. Finally, the income of the VIE must be allocated among the parties involved (i.e., equity holders and the primary beneficiary). For a VIE, contractual arrangements, as opposed to ownership percentages, typically specify the distribution of its income. Therefore, a close examination of these contractual arrangements is needed to determine the appropriate allocation of VIE income to its equity owners and those holding variable interests.

## Other FIN 46 Disclosure Requirements

Primary beneficiaries of VIEs, in addition to consolidated financial statements, must also provide the following in footnotes to the financial statements:

- The nature, purpose, size, and activities of the VIE
- The carrying amount and classification of consolidated assets that are collateral for the VIE's obligations
- Lack of recourse if creditors (or beneficial interest holders) of a consolidated VIE have no recourse to the general credit of the primary beneficiary.

Enterprises that hold a significant variable interest in a VIE but are not the primary beneficiary must disclose the following in footnotes to the financial statements:

- The nature of its involvement with the VIE and when that involvement began
- The nature, purpose, size, and activities of the VIE
- The enterprise's maximum exposure to loss as a result of its involvement with the VIE.

Clearly the FASB wishes to enhance disclosures for all SPEs. Given that in the past SPEs were often created in part to keep debt off a sponsoring firm's balance sheet, these enhanced disclosures are a significant improvement in financial reporting transparency.

## INTERCOMPANY DEBT TRANSACTIONS

The previous chapter explored the consolidation procedures required by the intercompany transfer of inventory, land, and depreciable assets. In consolidating these transactions, all resulting gains were deferred until earned through either the use of the asset or its resale to outside parties. Deferral was necessary because these gains, although legitimately recognized by the individual companies, were unearned from the perspective of the consolidated entity. The separate financial information of each company was adjusted on the worksheet to be consistent with the view that the related companies actually composed a single economic concern.

This same objective applies in consolidating all intercompany transactions: The financial statements must represent the business combination as one enterprise rather than as a group of independent organizations. Consequently, in designing consolidation procedures for intercompany transactions, the effects recorded by the individual companies first must be isolated. After the impact of each action is analyzed, the worksheet entries necessary to recast these events from the vantage point of the business combination are developed. Although this process involves a number of nuances and complexities, the desire for reporting financial information solely from the perspective of the consolidated entity remains constant.

The intercompany sales of inventory, land, and depreciable assets were introduced together (in Chapter 5) because these transfers result in similar consolidation procedures. In each case, one of the affiliated companies recognizes a gain prior to its actually being earned by the consolidated entity. The worksheet entries required by these transactions simply realign the separate financial information to agree with the viewpoint of the business combination. The gain is removed and the inflated asset value is reduced to historical cost.

The next section of this chapter examines the intercompany acquisition of bonds and notes. Although accounting for the related companies as a single economic entity continues to be the central goal, the consolidation procedures applied to intercompany debt transactions are in diametric contrast to the process utilized in Chapter 5 for asset transfers.

Before delving into this topic, note that *direct* loans used to transfer funds between affiliated companies create no unique consolidation problems. Regardless of whether such amounts are generated by bonds or notes, the resulting receivable/payable balances are necessarily identical. Because no money is owed to or from an outside party, these reciprocal accounts must be eliminated in each subsequent consolidation. A worksheet entry simply offsets the two corresponding balances. Furthermore, the interest revenue/expense accounts associated with direct loans also agree and are removed in the same fashion.

## Acquisition of Affiliate's Debt from an Outside Party

*The difficulties encountered in consolidating intercompany liabilities relate to a specific type of transaction: the purchase from an outside third party of an affiliate's debt instrument.* A parent company, for example, could acquire a bond previously issued by a subsidiary on the open market. Despite the intercompany nature of this transaction, the debt remains an outstanding obligation of the original issuer while being recorded as an investment by the acquiring company. Thereafter, even though related parties are involved, interest payments pass periodically between the two organizations.

Although the individual companies continue to report both the debt and the investment, from a consolidation viewpoint this liability is retired as of the date of acquisition. From that time forward, the debt is no longer owed to a party outside of the business combination. Subsequent interest payments are simply intercompany cash transfers. To create consolidated statements, worksheet entries must be developed that adjust the various balances to report the effective retirement of the debt.

Acquiring an affiliate's bond or note from an unrelated party poses no significant consolidation problems if the purchase price equals the corresponding book value of the liability. Reciprocal balances within the individual records would always be identical in value and easily offset in each subsequent consolidation.

Realistically, though, such reciprocity is rare when a debt is purchased from a third party. A variety of economic factors typically produces a difference between the price paid for the investment and the carrying amount of the obligation. The debt is originally sold under market conditions at a particular time. Any premium or discount associated with this issuance is then amortized over the life of the bond, creating a continuous adjustment to book value. The acquisition of this instrument at a later date is made at a price influenced by current economic conditions, prevailing interest rates, and myriad other financial and market factors.

Therefore, the cost paid to purchase the debt could be either more or less than the book value of the liability currently found within the financial records of the issuing company. *To the business combination, this difference is a gain or loss because the acquisition effectively retires the bond; the debt is no longer owed to an outside party.* For external reporting purposes, this gain or loss must be recognized immediately by the consolidated entity as required by *APB Opinion 26,* "Early Extinguishment of Debt," October 1972.

## Accounting for Intercompany Debt Transactions—Individual Financial Records

The accounting problems encountered in consolidating intercompany debt transactions are fourfold:

1. Both the investment and debt accounts have to be eliminated now and for each future consolidation despite containing differing balances.
2. Subsequent interest revenue/expense (as well as any interest receivable/payable accounts) must be removed although these balances also fail to agree in amount.
3. Changes in all of the preceding accounts occur constantly because of the amortization process.
4. The gain or loss on retirement of the debt must be recognized by the business combination, even though this balance does not appear within the financial records of either company.

To illustrate, assume that Alpha Company possesses an 80 percent interest in the outstanding voting stock of Omega Company. On January 1, 2002, Omega issues $1 million in 10-year term bonds paying cash interest annually of 9 percent. Because of market conditions prevailing on that date, the debt is sold for $938,555 to yield an effective interest rate of 10 percent per year. Shortly thereafter, the prime interest rate begins to fall, and by January 1, 2004, the decision is made to retire this debt prematurely and refinance it at the currently lower rates. To carry out this plan, Alpha purchases all of these bonds in the open market on January 1, 2004, for $1,057,466. This price was based on an effective yield of 8 percent, which is assumed to be in line with the interest rates at the time.

Many reasons could exist for having Alpha, rather than Omega, reacquire this debt. For example, company cash levels at that date could necessitate Alpha's role as the purchasing agent. Also, contractual limitations can prohibit Omega from repurchasing its own bonds.

In accounting for this business combination, an early extinguishment of the debt has occurred. Thus, the difference between the $1,057,466 payment and the January 1, 2004, book value of the liability must be recognized in the consolidated statements as a gain or loss. The exact account balance reported for the debt on that date depends on the amortization process. Although the issue was recorded initially at the $938,555 exchange price, after two years the carrying value has increased to $946,651, calculated as follows:[8]

***Bonds Payable—Book Value—January 1, 2004***

| Year | Book Value | Effective Interest (10 percent rate) | Cash Interest | Amortization | Year-End Book Value |
|---|---|---|---|---|---|
| 2002 | $938,555 | $93,855 | $90,000 | $3,855 | $942,410 |
| 2003 | 942,410 | 94,241 | 90,000 | 4,241 | 946,651 |

Because Alpha paid $110,815 in excess of the recorded liability ($1,057,466 − $946,651), a loss of this amount must be recognized by the consolidated concern. After the loss has been acknowledged, the bond is considered to be retired and no further reporting would be necessary by the *business combination* after January 1, 2004.

Despite the simplicity of this approach, neither company accounts for the event in this manner. Omega retains the $1 million debt balance within its separate financial records while amortizing the remaining discount each year. Annual cash interest payments of $90,000 (9 percent) continue to be made. At the same time, the investment is recorded by Alpha at the historical cost of $1,057,466, an amount that also requires periodic amortization. Furthermore, as the owner of these bonds, Alpha receives the $90,000 interest payments made by Omega.

To organize the accountant's approach to this consolidation, a complete analysis of the subsequent financial recording made by each of these companies should be produced. Only two journal entries would be recorded by Omega during 2004 if the assumption is made that interest is paid each December 31.

---

[8] The effective rate method of amortization is demonstrated here because this approach is theoretically preferable. However, the straight-line method can be applied if the resulting balances are not materially different than the figures computed using the effective rate method.

| | | | |
|---|---|---|---|
| | **Omega Company's Financial Records** | | |
| 12/31/04 | Interest Expense .................................... | 90,000 | |
| | Cash ........................................ | | 90,000 |
| | To record payment of annual cash interest on $1 million, 9 percent bonds payable. | | |
| 12/31/04 | Interest Expense .................................... | 4,665 | |
| | Bonds Payable (or Discount on Bonds Payable) ......... | | 4,665 |
| | To adjust interest expense to effective rate based on original yield rate of 10 percent ($946,651 book value for 2004 × 10% = $94,665). Book value increases to $951,316. | | |

Concurrently, Alpha journalizes entries to record its ownership of this investment:

| | | | |
|---|---|---|---|
| | **Alpha Company's Financial Record** | | |
| 1/1/04 | Investment in Omega Company Bonds ................. | 1,057,466 | |
| | Cash ........................................ | | 1,057,466 |
| | To record acquisition of $1,000,000 in Omega Company bonds paying 9 percent cash interest, acquired to yield an effective rate of 8 percent. | | |
| 12/31/04 | Cash ............................................ | 90,000 | |
| | Interest Income ............................... | | 90,000 |
| | To record receipt of cash interest from Omega Company bonds ($1,000,000 × 9%). | | |
| 12/31/04 | Interest Income .................................... | 5,403 | |
| | Investment in Omega Company Bonds ............... | | 5,403 |
| | To reduce $90,000 interest income to effective rate based on original yield rate of 8 percent ($1,057,466 book value for 2004 × 8% = $84,597). Book value decreases to $1,052,063. | | |

Even a brief review of these entries indicates that the reciprocal accounts to be eliminated within the consolidation process do not agree in amount. You can see the dollar amounts appearing in each set of financial records in Exhibit 6–3. Despite the presence of these recorded balances, none of the four intercompany accounts (the liability, investment, interest expense, and interest revenue) appears in the consolidated financial statements. *The only figure to be reported by the business combination is the $110,815 loss created by the extinguishment of this debt.*

**EXHIBIT 6–3**

**ALPHA COMPANY AND OMEGA COMPANY**
**Effects of Intercompany Debt Transaction**
**2004**

| | Omega Company Reported Debt | Alpha Company Investment |
|---|---|---|
| 2004 interest expense* | $ 94,665 | $ –0– |
| 2004 interest income† | –0– | 84,597 |
| Bonds payable* | (951,316) | –0– |
| Investment in bonds, 12/31/04† | –0– | 1,052,063 |
| Loss on retirement | –0– | –0– |

Note: Parentheses indicate credit balances.
*Company total is adjusted for 2004 amortization of $4,665 (see journal entry).
†Adjusted for 2004 amortization of $5,403 (see journal entry).

## Effects on Consolidation Process

As indicated in previous discussions, consolidation procedures serve to convert information generated by the individual accounting systems to the perspective of a single economic entity. A worksheet entry is, therefore, required on December 31, 2004, to eliminate the intercompany balances shown in Exhibit 6–3 and to recognize the loss resulting from the repurchase. Mechanically, the differences in the liability and investment balances as well as the interest expense and interest income accounts stem from the $110,815 deviation between the purchase price of the investment and the book value of the liability. Recognition of this loss, in effect, bridges the gap between the divergent figures.

**Consolidation Entry B (December 31, 2004)**

| | | |
|---|---:|---:|
| Bonds Payable | 951,316 | |
| Interest Income | 84,597 | |
| Loss on Retirement of Bond | 110,815 | |
|     Investment in Omega Company Bonds | | 1,052,063 |
|     Interest Expense | | 94,665 |

To remove intercompany bonds and related interest accounts and record loss on the early extinguishment of this debt. (Labeled "B" in reference to bonds.)

The preceding entry successfully transforms the separate financial reporting of Alpha and Omega to that appropriate for the business combination. The objective of the consolidation process has been met: The statements present the bonds as having been retired on January 1, 2004. The debt and the corresponding investment are eliminated along with both interest accounts. Only the loss now appears on the worksheet to be reported within the consolidated financial statements.

## Assignment of Retirement Gain or Loss

Perhaps the most intriguing issue to be addressed in accounting for intercompany debt transactions concerns the assignment of any gains and losses created by the retirement. Should the $110,815 loss just reported be attributed to Alpha or to Omega? From a practical perspective, this assignment is important only in the calculation and reporting of noncontrolling interest figures. However, at least four different possible allocations can be identified, each of which demonstrates theoretical merit.

First, a strong argument can be made that the liability being extinguished is that of the issuing company and, thus, any resulting income relates solely to that party. This approach assumes that only the debtor is affected by the retirement of any obligation. Proponents of this position hold that the acquiring company is merely serving as a purchasing agent for the original issuer of the bonds. Accordingly, in the previous illustration, the benefits derived from paying off the liability should accrue to Omega because that company's interest rate has been reduced through refinancing. The loss was incurred solely to obtain these lower rates. Therefore, under this assumption, the entire $110,815 is assigned to Omega, the issuer of the debt. This assignment is usually considered to be consistent with the economic unit concept and was recommended in the FASB Exposure Draft, *Consolidated Financial Statements: Policy and Procedures.*

Second, other accountants argue that the loss should be assigned solely to the investor (Alpha). According to proponents of this approach, the income effect is created by the acquisition of the bonds and the price negotiated by the buyer.

A third hypothesis is that the resulting gain or loss should be split in some manner between the two companies. This approach is consistent with both the parent company concept and proportionate consolidation. Since both parties are involved with the debt, this proposition

# Discussion Question

**WHO LOST THIS $300,000?**

Several years ago, the Penston Company purchased 90 percent of the outstanding shares of Swansan Corporation. The acquisition was made because Swansan produced a vital component used in Penston's manufacturing process. Penston wanted to ensure an adequate supply of this item at a reasonable price. The remaining 10 percent of Swansan's stock was retained by the former owner, James Swansan, who agreed to continue managing this organization. He was given responsibility over the subsidiary's daily manufacturing operations but not for any of the financial decisions.

The takeover of Swansan has proven to be a successful undertaking for Penston. The subsidiary has managed to supply all of the parent's inventory needs as well as distribute a variety of items to outside customers.

At a recent meeting, the president of Penston and the company's chief financial officer began discussing Swansan's debt position. The subsidiary had a debt-to-equity ratio that seemed unreasonably high considering the significant amount of cash flows being generated by both companies. Payment of the interest expense, especially on the subsidiary's outstanding bonds, was a major cost, one that the corporate officials hoped to reduce. However, the bond indenture specified that Swansan could retire this debt prior to maturity only by paying 107 percent of face value.

This premium was considered prohibitive. Thus, to avoid contractual problems, Penston acquired a large portion of Swansan's liability on the open market for 101 percent of face value. Penston's purchase created an effective loss on the debt of $300,000: the excess of the price over the book value of the debt as reported on Swansan's books.

Company accountants currently are computing the noncontrolling interest's share of consolidated net income to be reported for the current year. They are unsure about the impact of this $300,000 loss. The subsidiary's debt was retired, but the decision was made by officials of the parent company. Who lost this $300,000?

---

contends that assigning income to only one company is arbitrary and misleading. Normally, such a division is based on the original face value of the debt. Hence, $57,466 of the loss would be allocated to Alpha with the remaining $53,349 assigned to Omega:

| Alpha | | Omega | |
|---|---|---|---|
| Purchase price | $1,057,466 | Book value | $ 946,651 |
| Face value | 1,000,000 | Face value | 1,000,000 |
| Loss—Alpha | $   57,466 | Loss—Omega | $   53,349 |

Allocating the loss in this manner is an enticing solution; the subsequent accounting process creates an identical division within the individual financial records. Because both Alpha's premium and Omega's discount must be amortized, the loss figures eventually affect the reported earnings of the respective companies. Over the life of the bond, the $57,466 is recorded by Alpha as an interest income reduction while Omega increases its own interest expense by $53,349 because of the amortization of the discount.

A fourth perspective takes a more practical view of intercompany debt transactions: All repurchases are ultimately orchestrated by the parent company. As the controlling party in a business combination, the ultimate responsibility for retiring any obligation lies with the parent. The gain or loss resulting from the decision should, thus, be assigned solely to the parent regardless of the specific identity of the debt issuer or the acquiring company. In the current example, Alpha maintains control over Omega. Therefore, according to this theory, the financial consequences of reacquiring these bonds rest with Alpha so that the entire $110,815 loss must be attributed to that party.

Each of these arguments does have conceptual merit, and if the FASB eventually sets an official standard, any one approach (or possibly a hybrid) could be required. Unless otherwise stated, however, all income effects in this textbook relating to intercompany debt transactions are assigned solely to the parent company, as discussed in the final approach. Consequently, the results of extinguishing debt always are attributed to the party most likely to have been responsible for the action.

## Intercompany Debt Transactions—Subsequent to Year of Acquisition

Even though the preceding Entry **B** correctly eliminates Omega's bonds in the year of retirement, the debt remains within the financial accounts of both companies until maturity. Therefore, in each succeeding time period, all balances must again be consolidated so that the liability is always reported as having been extinguished on January 1, 2004. Unfortunately, a simple repetition of Entry **B** is not possible. Developing the appropriate worksheet entry is complicated by the amortization process that produces continual change in the various account balances. Thus, as a preliminary step in each subsequent consolidation, current book values, as reported by the two parties, must be identified.

To illustrate, the 2005 journal entries for Alpha and Omega follow. Exhibit 6–4 (on the following page) shows the resulting account balances as of the end of that year.

**Omega Company's Financial Records—December 31, 2005**

| | | |
|---|---|---|
| Interest Expense . . . . . . . . . . . . . . . . . . . . . . . . . . . . . . . . . . . . . . . . . . . . . . . . . | 90,000 | |
|    Cash . . . . . . . . . . . . . . . . . . . . . . . . . . . . . . . . . . . . . . . . . . . . . . . . . . | | 90,000 |
| To record payment of annual cash interest on $1 million, 9 percent bonds payable. | | |
| Interest Expense . . . . . . . . . . . . . . . . . . . . . . . . . . . . . . . . . . . . . . . . . . . . . . . . . | 5,132 | |
|    Bonds Payable (or Discount on Bonds Payable) . . . . . . . . . . . . . . . . . . . | | 5,132 |
| To adjust interest expense to effective rate based on an original yield rate of 10 percent ($951,316 book value for 2005 × 10% = $95,132). Book value increases to $956,448. | | |

**Alpha Company's Financial Records—December 31, 2005**

| | | |
|---|---|---|
| Cash . . . . . . . . . . . . . . . . . . . . . . . . . . . . . . . . . . . . . . . . . . . . . . . . . . . . . . . . | 90,000 | |
|    Interest Income . . . . . . . . . . . . . . . . . . . . . . . . . . . . . . . . . . . . . . . . . . | | 90,000 |
| To record receipt of cash interest from Omega Company bonds. | | |
| Interest Income . . . . . . . . . . . . . . . . . . . . . . . . . . . . . . . . . . . . . . . . . . . . . . . . | 5,835 | |
|    Investment in Omega Company Bonds . . . . . . . . . . . . . . . . . . . . . . . . . | | 5,835 |
| To reduce $90,000 interest income to effective rate based on an original yield rate of 8 percent ($1,052,063 book value for 2005 × 8% = $84,165). Book value decreases to $1,046,228. | | |

After the information in Exhibit 6–4 has been assembled, the necessary consolidation entry as of December 31, 2005, can be produced. This entry removes the balances reported at that date for the intercompany bonds, along with both of the interest accounts, to reflect the extinguishment of the debt on January 1, 2004. Since retirement took place in a prior period, the adjustment on the worksheet must also create a $110,815 reduction in Retained Earnings to represent the original loss.

## EXHIBIT 6–4

**ALPHA COMPANY AND OMEGA COMPANY**
**Effects of Intercompany Debt Transactions**
**2005**

|  | Omega Company Reported Debt | Alpha Company Investment |
|---|---:|---:|
| 2005 interest expense* | $95,132 | –0– |
| 2005 interest income† | –0– | $(84,165) |
| Bonds payable* | (956,448) | –0– |
| Investment in bonds, 12/31/05† | –0– | 1,046,228 |
| Income effect within retained earnings, 1/1/05‡ | 94,665 | (84,597) |

Note: Parentheses indicate credit balances.
*Company total is adjusted for 2005 amortization of $5,132 (see journal entry).
†Adjusted for 2005 amortization of $5,835 (see journal entry).
‡The balance shown for the Retained Earnings account of each company represents the 2004 reported interest figures.

| Consolidation Entry *B (December 31, 2005) | | |
|---|---:|---:|
| Bonds Payable | 956,448 | |
| Interest Income | 84,165 | |
| Retained Earnings, 1/1/05 (Alpha) | 100,747 | |
|     Investment in Omega Company Bonds | | 1,046,228 |
|     Interest Expense | | 95,132 |
| To eliminate intercompany bond and related interest accounts and to adjust Retained Earnings from $10,068 (currently recorded net debit balance) to $110,815. (Labeled as "*B" in reference to prior year bond transaction.) | | |

In analyzing this latest consolidation entry, several important factors should be emphasized:

1. The individual account balances change during the present fiscal period so that the current consolidation entry differs from Entry **B**. These alterations are a result of the amortization process. To ensure the accuracy of the worksheet entry, the adjusted balances are isolated in Exhibit 6–4.

2. As indicated previously, all income effects arising from intercompany debt transactions are assigned to the parent company. For this reason, the adjustment to beginning Retained Earnings in Entry *B is attributed to Alpha as is the $10,967 increase in current income ($95,132 interest expense elimination less the $84,165 interest revenue elimination).[9] Consequently, the noncontrolling interest balances are not altered by Entry *B.

3. The 2005 reduction to beginning Retained Earnings in Entry *B ($100,747) does not agree with the original $110,815 retirement loss. A net deficit balance of $10,068 (the amount by which previous interest expense exceeds interest revenue) has already been recorded by the individual companies at the start of 2005. To achieve the proper consolidated total, an adjustment of only $100,747 is required ($110,815 − $10,068).

| | | |
|---|---:|---:|
| Retained earnings balance—consolidation perspective (loss on retirement of debt) | | $110,815 |
| Individual retained earnings balances, 1/1/05: | | |
|     Omega Company (interest expense—2004) | $94,665 | |
|     Alpha Company (interest income—2004) | (84,597) | 10,068 |
| Adjustment to consolidated retained earnings, 1/1/05 | | $100,747 |

Parentheses indicate a credit balance.

---

[9] Had the effects of the retirement been attributed solely to the original issuer of the bonds, the $10,967 addition to current income would have been assigned to Omega (the subsidiary), thus creating a change in the noncontrolling interest computations.

The periodic amortization of both the bond payable discount and the premium on the investment impacts the interest expense and revenue recorded by the two companies. As shown in this schedule, these two interest accounts do not offset exactly; a $10,068 net residual amount remains in Retained Earnings after the first year. Because this balance continues to grow each year, the subsequent consolidation adjustments to record the loss decrease to $100,747 in 2005 and constantly get smaller thereafter. *Over the life of the bond, the amortization process gradually brings the totals in the individual Retained Earnings accounts into agreement with the consolidated balance.*

4. Entry **\*B** as shown is appropriate for consolidations in which the parent has applied either the cost or the partial equity method. However, a deviation is required if the parent uses the equity method for internal reporting purposes. As discussed in Chapter 5, proper application of the equity method ensures that the parent's income and, hence, its retained earnings are correctly stated prior to consolidation. Alpha would have already recognized the loss in accounting for this investment. Consequently, no adjustment to Retained Earnings would be needed. In this one case, the $100,747 debit in Entry **\*B** is made to the Investment in Omega Company because the loss has become a component of that account.

## SUBSIDIARY PREFERRED STOCK

When Kohlberg Kravis Roberts & Company purchased the outstanding common stock of Owens-Illinois, Inc., for $60.50 per share, the company also acquired all of the preferred stock of Owens-Illinois for $363 per share or a total of $25.8 million. Although preferred shares are routinely issued by both small and large corporations, their presence within the equity structure of a subsidiary adds a new dimension to the consolidation process. What accounting should be made of a subsidiary's preferred stock and the parent's payments, such as this $25.8 million, that are made to acquire these shares?

The consolidation measures required to report the preferred stock of a subsidiary depend on the specific nature of the shares. Controversy has long existed as to whether such issues are more akin to equity or debt, a distinction that depends on the specified rights granted to the holders. The characteristics of many preferred shares resemble those attributed to long-term liabilities rather than to equity securities. For example, a stock with a call value and no rights except for a set, cumulative dividend is in substance almost identical to a bond payable. Conversely, preferred shares that offer voting and/or participation rights clearly demonstrate essential characteristics associated with an ownership interest.

However, not all preferred stocks lend themselves to easy classification: The legal rights given to shareholders often vary significantly from issue to issue. For example, Ford Motor Company in a recent annual report shows both Series A and Series B preferred stock outstanding, each with specific rights as to dividends, convertibility to common stock, and redemption prices. Such attributes can make the distinction between debt and equity quite nebulous. Because of this identification problem, the FASB has plans to study the issue within its financial instruments project. However, until a guideline is established, as is utilized in earnings per share computations, determining the true nature of many types of preferred stock still requires considerable individual judgment.

In consolidating subsidiary preferred stock, the accountant must evaluate whether the shares are more similar to debt or to equity. If the stock resembles a debt, any shares acquired by the parent are recorded as if retired. Conversely, if a preferred stock is truly an equity instrument, the combination accounts for the purchased shares in the same manner as common stock: Allocations are made to specific assets and liabilities with any residual payment assigned to goodwill.

### Preferred Stock Viewed as a Debt Instrument

If a subsidiary's preferred stock has characteristics that primarily resemble a liability, consolidation techniques should parallel the process previously demonstrated for intercompany debt. To illustrate, assume that on January 1, 2004, High Corporation acquires control over Low Company by purchasing 80 percent of its outstanding common stock as well as 60 percent of its nonvoting, cumulative, preferred stock. Low owns land that is undervalued in its records by $100,000.

The purchase price paid by High was $1 million for the common shares and $62,400 for the preferred. On the date of acquisition, Low reported the following stockholders' equity balances. Note that the 1,000 shares of preferred stock outstanding have a $100 par value but can be called (retired) by Low for $110 per share.

| | |
|---|---:|
| Common stock, $20 par value (20,000 shares outstanding) | $ 400,000 |
| Preferred stock, 6% cumulative with a par value of $100 and a $110 call value (1,000 shares outstanding) | 100,000 |
| Additional paid-in capital | 200,000 |
| Retained earnings | 516,400 |
| Total stockholders' equity (book value) | $1,216,400 |

Low's preferred stock carries no rights other than its cumulative dividend; thus, this issue is considered a debt instrument in nature. The $62,400 price paid by High is handled in a manner consistent with that of an intercompany bond. The payment made for these shares has no influence on the valuation of specific subsidiary accounts (such as the undervalued land) or the recognition of goodwill. Instead, the preferred stock acquired by the parent is eliminated on each subsequent worksheet as if the shares had been retired.

Although this handling parallels that of a long-term liability, one important distinction must be drawn. Preferred stock is legally an equity; thus, its retirement cannot result in the reporting of a gain or loss to the consolidated entity. Instead, the difference between the stock's par value and the acquisition price paid by the parent must be recorded as an adjustment to Additional Paid-In Capital (or to Retained Earnings if a reduction is required and the Additional Paid-In Capital account is not of sufficient size).

The consolidation entry to account for this preferred stock acquisition follows. *Because the stock is viewed as the equivalent of debt, these shares (60 percent of the 1,000 outstanding) are simply eliminated as if retired.*

| | | |
|---|---:|---:|
| Preferred Stock (the 60% owned by High) | 60,000 | |
| Additional Paid-In Capital | 2,400 | |
|     Investment in Low Company's Preferred Stock | | 62,400 |
| To eliminate preferred stock of Low Company acquired by the parent company. | | |

This entry assumes that no part of the cumulative dividend is in arrears at the date of purchase. If a dividend had been owed on the preferred stock, a reduction in the subsidiary's Retained Earnings equal to that amount would have been included here rather than assigning the entire $2,400 difference to Additional Paid-In Capital. This alteration presumes that a portion of the purchase price is paid to reimburse the former owners for the missed dividends.

Although the preceding worksheet entry removes the effects of High's acquisition, it ignores the residual 40 percent noncontrolling interest in the preferred stock. In recording an allocation to these outside owners, the appropriate amount to be recognized must be determined. When preferred stock is viewed as a debt, the call value (if present) is considered to be more relevant to the consolidated entity than par value. Thus, the outside owners are assigned a balance equal to the call value of the securities (plus any dividends in arrears). In the current illustration, the $110 figure reflects the cost required to retire each of the remaining 400 shares (40% of 1,000). Thus, the worksheet entry to recognize this noncontrolling interest is as follows:

| | | |
|---|---:|---:|
| Preferred Stock (40% owned by outsiders) | 40,000 | |
| Additional Paid-In Capital | 4,000 | |
|     Noncontrolling Interest in Low Company (call value) | | 44,000 |
| To recognize the outside ownership of 40 percent of Low Company's preferred stock. | | |

These entries have been presented separately to clarify the difference in consolidating parent-owned and outside-owned shares. In practice, these figures are combined to eliminate all of the subsidiary's preferred stock. Thus, a single consolidation entry actually should be incorporated in this illustration:

**Consolidation Entry PS**

| | | |
|---|---|---|
| Preferred Stock | 100,000 | |
| Additional Paid-In Capital | 6,400 | |
|     Investment in Low Company's Preferred Stock | | 62,400 |
|     Noncontrolling Interest in Low Company | | 44,000 |

To eliminate preferred stock of subsidiary (viewed as a debt) and record noncontrolling interest. (Labeled as "PS" in reference to preferred stock.)

Having accounted for Low's preferred stock, now the elimination of the company's remaining stockholders' equity accounts can be made. As with any purchase combination, a preliminary allocation of the purchase price paid for the common stock is essential. Because of the amounts attributed to preferred stock, only $1,110,000 of Low's total book value is assigned to the common stock at the date of acquisition:

| | | |
|---|---:|---:|
| Total book value of Low Company, 1/1/04 | | $1,216,400 |
| Allocated to preferred stock ownership: | | |
|     Acquisition price of High Company's interest | $62,400 | |
|     Call value of noncontrolling interest | 44,000 | (106,400) |
| Book value allocated to common stock | | $1,110,000 |

Based on this book value, the $1 million paid by High for 80 percent of Low's common stock is allocated as shown in Exhibit 6–5. As indicated previously, land owned by Low is assumed here to be undervalued on the subsidiary's records by $100,000.

By utilizing the information from Exhibit 6–5, basic worksheet entries can be constructed as of January 1, 2004 (the date of purchase). After Entry **PS** removes the preferred shares and recognizes the noncontrolling interest in that stock, the remainder of Low's stockholders' equity accounts are eliminated by Entry **S**. In addition, a 20 percent noncontrolling interest in Low's common stock is established as $222,000 (20 percent of the $1,110,000 book value). The allocations made to the undervalued land and to goodwill then are recognized in Entry **A**. No other consolidation entries are needed because no time has passed since the acquisition took place.

**Consolidation Entry S**

| | | |
|---|---:|---:|
| Common Stock (Low Company) | 400,000 | |
| Additional Paid-In Capital (Low Company) | 193,600 | |
| Retained Earnings (Low Company) | 516,400 | |
|     Investment in Low Company's Common Stock (80%) | | 888,000 |
|     Noncontrolling Interest in Low Company (20%) | | 222,000 |

To eliminate remaining stockholders' equity accounts after removal of preferred stock and to recognize noncontrolling interest in common stock.

**Consolidation Entry A**

| | | |
|---|---:|---:|
| Land | 80,000 | |
| Goodwill | 32,000 | |
|     Investment in Low Company's Common Stock | | 112,000 |

To allocate excess cost paid for Low's common stock to specific account based on fair market value and to goodwill (see Exhibit 6–5).

## EXHIBIT 6–5

**HIGH COMPANY AND LOW COMPANY**
**Allocation of Common Stock Purchase Price**
**January 1, 2004**

| | |
|---|---:|
| Purchase price paid for common stock | $1,000,000 |
| Common stock book value equivalent to High's ownership ($1,110,000 × 80%) | (888,000) |
| Cost in excess of book value | 112,000 |
| Allocation to specific accounts based on fair market value: | |
| Land ($100,000 × 80%) | 80,000 |
| Excess cost not identified with specific accounts—goodwill | $ 32,000 |

In working with this illustration, note the structure that is followed in consolidating a subsidiary's preferred stock. First, a determination is made of the nature of the stock. Identifying Low Company's issue as a debt-type instrument significantly influenced the development of the consolidation process. Second, the subsidiary's book value is divided between the preferred and common stock interests. Assigning $106,400 of Low's book value to the preferred stock (the price of the purchased shares plus the call value of remainder) and the residual $1,110,000 to common stock led directly to the valuations and eliminations incorporated in this consolidation. As is subsequently demonstrated, this allocation of book value can vary considerably, depending on the specific rights granted to the preferred shareholders.

### *Allocation of Subsidiary Income*

The final factor influencing a consolidation that includes subsidiary preferred shares is the allocation of the company's income between the two types of stock. A division must be made for every period subsequent to the takeover (1) to compute the noncontrolling interest's share and (2) for the parent's own recognition purposes. For a cumulative, nonparticipating preferred stock such as the one presently being examined, only the specified annual dividend is attributed to the preferred stock with all remaining income assigned to common stock. Consequently, if the assumption is made that Low reports earnings of $100,000 in 2004 while paying the annual $6,000 dividend on its preferred stock, income is allocated for consolidation purposes as follows:

| | Income |
|---|---:|
| Subsidiary total | $100,000 |
| Preferred stock (6% dividend × $100,000 par value of the stock) | $ 6,000 |
| Common stock (residual amount) | 94,000 |

During 2004, High Company, as the parent, would be entitled to $3,600 in dividends from Low's preferred stock because of its 60 percent ownership. In addition, High holds 80 percent of Low's common stock so that another $75,200 of the income ($94,000 × 0.80) is attributed to the parent. The noncontrolling interest in the subsidiary's income can be calculated in a similar fashion:

| | | Percent Outside Ownership | Noncontrolling Interest |
|---|---:|---:|---:|
| Preferred stock dividend | $ 6,000 | 40% | $ 2,400 |
| Income attributed to common stock | 94,000 | 20 | 18,800 |
| Noncontrolling interest in subsidiary's income | | | $21,200 |

## Preferred Stock Viewed as an Equity Interest

Having established basic principles for a consolidation that includes subsidiary preferred stock that resembles debt, a second example in which the stock is considered an equity can be utilized. Continuing to employ High's acquisition of Low, assume now that the dividends of the subsidiary's preferred stock are fully participating as well as cumulative. Furthermore, the stock is not callable. Because the preferred shares convey additional rights, the relative values of the two classes of stock differ from that of the previous example. Therefore, High is assumed to have paid only $894,496 for an 80 percent interest in Low's common stock but $149,968 for 60 percent of the preferred.

The ability to participate in the earnings of Low Company provides the preferred shareholders an ownership interest that is akin to that of common stock. Thus, altering the rights of this issue has changed its essential nature to that of an equity interest rather than a debt. When subsidiary preferred stock is viewed as an equity, the consolidation process differs significantly from that examined in the previous illustration. *The preferred stock is handled in the same manner as common stock: Any purchase price in excess of underlying book value is allocated to specific accounts as well as to goodwill. Income is accrued by the owners based on subsidiary earnings rather than on dividends.*

The cumulative participation rights entitle the holders of Low's preferred shares to a portion of the subsidiary's earnings each year. The specific division of income would be stipulated on the preferred stock certificate. That percentage is often based on the ratio of the total par values of the two classes of equity. Thus, 20 percent ($100,000 par value of the preferred stock divided by $500,000 total par value) of Low's annual income is assigned to the preferred shares. Additionally, because of the cumulative right, 20 percent of the subsidiary's retained earnings should also be attributed to the preferred stock (assuming that both classes of stock were originally issued on the same date). With these particular rights in force, allocation of the January 1, 2004, book value of Low Company is as follows:

| | | |
|---|---:|---:|
| Total book value of Low Company, 1/1/04 | | $1,216,400 |
| Allocated to preferred stock ownership: | | |
|   Par value of preferred stock (no call value) | $100,000 | |
|   20% of total retained earnings ($516,400) based on cumulative, participation rights | 103,280 | (203,280) |
| Book value allocated to common stock (residual) | | $1,013,120 |

Once the division of the subsidiary's book value has been established, High must allocate each of the acquisition payments. In this manner, the preferred stock is being accounted for as a true equity interest. Exhibit 6–6 analyzes both purchases: The $149,968 price paid for the preferred stock is shown first followed by the $894,496 amount invested in common stock. To complete this allocation, one theoretical question must be addressed: How is the undervaluation of the subsidiary's land to be treated? Since both stocks are considered equity interests, the $100,000 undervaluation is assumed to be reflected in each purchase price. Because of the participation feature of the preferred shares, the logical approach is to divide this $100,000 unrealized gain between the two stocks according to the par value ratio (20:80) or $20,000 to preferred stock and $80,000 to common.

From the information produced in Exhibit 6–6, the following consolidation entries for January 1, 2004 (the date of purchase) can be developed. Note that Entry **A** has been split into **A1** and **A2** to identify the allocations resulting from the preferred stock and common stock, respectively. This segregation is made merely to clarify the process; these two worksheet entries could easily be combined.

| **Consolidation Entry PS** | | |
|---|---:|---:|
| Preferred Stock (Low Company) | 100,000 | |
| Retained Earnings (Low Company) (20%) | 103,280 | |
| | | *(continued)* |

|  |  |  |
|---|---:|---:|
| Investment in Low Company Preferred Stock (60% ownership) | | 121,968 |
| Noncontrolling Interest in Low Company (40%) | | 81,312 |

To eliminate subsidiary's preferred stockholders' equity accounts ($203,280) and recognize noncontrolling interest in preferred stock. Retained earnings is based on par value assignment.

**Consolidation Entry S**

|  |  |  |
|---|---:|---:|
| Common Stock (Low Company) | 400,000 | |
| Additional Paid-In Capital (Low Company) | 200,000 | |
| Retained Earnings (Low Company) (80%) | 413,120 | |
| Investment in Low Company Common Stock (80% ownership) | | 810,496 |
| Noncontrolling Interest in Low Company (20%) | | 202,624 |

To eliminate subsidiary's remaining stockholders' equity accounts ($1,013,120) and recognize noncontrolling interest in common stock. Retained earnings reflects Entry PS.

**Consolidation Entry A1**

|  |  |  |
|---|---:|---:|
| Land | 12,000 | |
| Goodwill | 16,000 | |
| Investment in Low Company Preferred Stock | | 28,000 |

To allocate cost paid for preferred stock in excess of book value. (See Exhibit 6–6.)

**Consolidation Entry A2**

|  |  |  |
|---|---:|---:|
| Land | 64,000 | |
| Goodwill | 20,000 | |
| Investment in Low Company Common Stock | | 84,000 |

To allocate cost paid for common stock in excess of book value. (See Exhibit 6–6.)

**EXHIBIT 6–6**

### HIGH COMPANY AND LOW COMPANY
**Allocation of Preferred and Common Stock Purchase Prices**
**January 1, 2004**

**Preferred Stock**

| | |
|---|---:|
| Purchase price paid for preferred stock | $ 149,968 |
| Preferred stock book value equivalent to High's ownership ($203,280 × 60%) | (121,968) |
| Cost in excess of book value | $ 28,000 |
| Allocation to specific accounts: | |
|    Land ($20,000 × 60%) | 12,000 |
| Excess cost not identified with specific accounts—goodwill | $ 16,000 |

**Common Stock**

| | |
|---|---:|
| Purchase price paid for common stock | $ 894,496 |
| Common stock book value equivalent to High's ownership ($1,013,120 × 80%) | (810,496) |
| Cost in excess of book value | $ 84,000 |
| Allocation to specific accounts: | |
|    Land ($80,000 × 80%) | 64,000 |
| Excess cost not identified with specific accounts—goodwill | $ 20,000 |

## Allocation of Subsidiary Income

The specific rights granted to the owners of the preferred stock also affect the subsequent allocation of the subsidiary's income each year. If the assumption is again made that Low reports net income for 2004 of $100,000, this amount must be divided between the two ownership interests based on the cumulative, participating rights of the preferred stock. These shares constitute 20 percent of the subsidiary's total par value with the remaining 80 percent coming from the holders of the common stock. Thus, net income is prorated according to this same ratio.

|  | Income |
|---|---|
| Subsidiary total | $100,000 |
| Preferred stock—possesses rights to 20% of total (based on relative par values) | $ 20,000 |
| Common stock—residual 80% interest | 80,000 |

Based on this allocation of the subsidiary's income for 2004, the noncontrolling interest's share of consolidated income can be determined:

|  |  | Percent Outside Ownership | Noncontrolling Interest |
|---|---|---|---|
| Income attributed to preferred stock | $20,000 | 40% | $8,000 |
| Income attributed to common stock | 80,000 | 20 | 16,000 |
| Noncontrolling interest in subsidiary's income |  |  | $24,000 |

# CONSOLIDATED STATEMENT OF CASH FLOWS

In November of 1987, the Financial Accounting Standards Board issued *Statement No. 95,* "Statement of Cash Flows," mandating that companies include a statement of cash flows among its financial statements. Because of this pronouncement, details of an organization's cash flows must be reported for each period in which an income statement is presented.

It is important that the consolidated statement of cash flows is not prepared from the individual cash flows of the separate companies. Instead, the income statements and balance sheets are first brought together on the worksheet. The cash flows statement is based then on the resulting consolidated figures. *Thus, this statement is not actually produced by consolidation but is created from numbers generated by that process.*

However, preparing a statement of cash flows for a business combination does introduce several accounting issues. In preparing this statement, noncontrolling interest balances, amortization, and intercompany transactions must all be properly handled.

### Noncontrolling Interest

On the consolidated income statement, the outside ownership of a noncontrolling interest is reflected as a decrease in net income. This reduction represents the earnings accrual assigned to these other owners. However, the only cash actually distributed to the noncontrolling interest is the portion of dividends paid to them by the subsidiary. Although the income statement presents the accrual rather than the dividend, the opposite is true of the cash flow statement: Only cash transactions are included. *Thus, for this statement, two adjustments are made. First, the noncontrolling interest's share of the subsidiary's net income must be eliminated; second, the dividends paid to the outside owners are included.*

The noncontrolling interest's income accrual can be removed from the statement of cash flows in either of two ways. If the business combination is using the direct approach to disclose cash generated by operations, the specific cash inflows and outflows are identified. For example, the cash collected from customers is disclosed along with the cash paid for inventory and expenses. Because the noncontrolling interest's share of consolidated income is a noncash item, this balance is simply omitted from the statement.

The business combination could instead determine the cash from operations by applying the indirect approach. Under this alternative, noncash as well as nonoperational items are removed from net income, which leaves a residual figure representing the increase or decrease in cash resulting from operations. If the indirect approach is used, the noncontrolling interest's share of consolidated income must be eliminated from net income since this reduction in earnings is a noncash amount. The noncontrolling interest balance does not represent an actual cash payment or collection. Because the earnings assigned to these outside owners is a decrease (or negative) within consolidated income, the amount is eliminated by adding the number to net income.

Regardless of which approach is used, the noncontrolling interest income accrual is removed in computing the cash derived from operations. However, any dividend paid to the other owners during the period is an actual cash outflow incurred by the combination and must be included on the statement. Because this distribution is made to an owner, the amount is listed separately under the Cash Flows from Financing Activities section of the statement of cash flows.

### *Amortizations*

The amortizations of allocations made to specific accounts are recorded in the consolidation process by means of a worksheet adjustment (Entry **E**). These expenses do not appear on either set of individual records but are reported in the income statement of the business combination. As a noncash decrease in income, this expense impacts the statement of cash flows in the same manner as the noncontrolling interest's share of consolidated income. If the direct approach is used by the business combination, the balance is omitted because this expense does not affect the amount of cash. In contrast, if the indirect approach is applied, the amortization expense is removed by adding the balance to net income.

### *Intercompany Transactions*

As discussed previously in this text, a significant volume of transfers often occur between the related companies composing a business combination. The resulting effects of this intercompany activity must be eliminated on the worksheet so that the consolidated income statement and balance sheet reflect only transactions with outside parties. Likewise, the consolidated statement of cash flows should not include the impact of these transfers. Although the cash flows can be large, intercompany sales and purchases do not change the amount of cash being held by the business combination when viewed as a whole.

Because the statement of cash flows is derived from the consolidated balance sheet and income statement, the impact of all transfers has been removed prior to producing this last statement. Therefore, no special adjustments are needed to arrive at a proper presentation of cash flows. The elimination entries made on the worksheet have the added effect of providing correct data for the consolidated statement of cash flows.

### *Acquisition Year Cash Flow Adjustments*

In the year of a business acquisition, several additional considerations arise that must be properly reflected in the consolidated cash flow statement. For many business combinations, the following issues frequently are present:

- Cash purchases of businesses must be accounted for as an investing activity. Importantly, the *net cash outflow* (cash paid less subsidiary cash acquired) is reported as the amount paid in a business acquisition.

- For intraperiod purchase acquisitions, *SFAS No. 95* requires that any adjustments from changes in operating balance sheet accounts (Accounts Receivable, Inventory, Accounts Payable, etc.) reflect the amounts acquired in the combination. Therefore, any changes in operating assets and liabilities are reported net of effects of acquired businesses in computing the necessary adjustments to convert consolidated net income to operating cash flows. Under the direct approach of presenting operating cash flows, the separate computations of cash collected from customers and cash paid for inventory are also reported net of effects of any acquired businesses.

- Any adjustments arising from the subsidiary's revenues or expenses (e.g., depreciation, amortization) must reflect only postacquisition amounts. Closing the subsidiary's books at the date of acquisition facilitates the determination of the appropriate postacquisition subsidiary effects on the consolidated entity's cash flows.

- Acquired in-process research and development can represent an allocation of the purchase price that is expensed in the consolidated income statement in the acquisition year. Such in-process research and development costs are considered cash outflows from investing activities.[10] Therefore, under the indirect method, the expense is added back to consolidated net income in determining cash flows from operating activities.

### Consolidated Statement of Cash Flows Illustration

Assume that on July 1, 2004, Pinto Company purchases 90 percent of the outstanding stock of Salida Company for $775,000 in cash. At the date of acquisition, Pinto prepares the following cost allocation schedule based on the fair market values of Salida's assets and liabilities:

| | | |
|---|---:|---:|
| Acquisition cost, July 1, 2004 . . . . . . . . . . . . . . . . . . | | $775,000 |
| Cash . . . . . . . . . . . . . . . . . . . . . . . . . . . . . . . . . . . | $ 35,000 | |
| Accounts receivable . . . . . . . . . . . . . . . . . . . . . . . | 145,000 | |
| Inventory . . . . . . . . . . . . . . . . . . . . . . . . . . . . . . . | 90,000 | |
| Land . . . . . . . . . . . . . . . . . . . . . . . . . . . . . . . . . . . | 100,000 | |
| Buildings . . . . . . . . . . . . . . . . . . . . . . . . . . . . . . . | 136,000 | |
| Equipment . . . . . . . . . . . . . . . . . . . . . . . . . . . . . . | 259,000 | |
| Accounts payable . . . . . . . . . . . . . . . . . . . . . . . . | (15,000) | |
| Net book value . . . . . . . . . . . . . . . . . . . . . . . . . . | $750,000 | |
| Percent acquired . . . . . . . . . . . . . . . . . . . . . . . . . | × 90% | 675,000 |
| | | 100,000 |
| Excess cost over book value allocation | | |
| Equipment (four-year life) . . . . . . . . . . . . . . . . . . | $ 40,000 | |
| In-process research and development . . . . . . . . . . | 22,000 | |
| Database (four-year life) . . . . . . . . . . . . . . . . . . . | 38,000 | 100,000 |
| | | –0– |

At the end of 2004, the following comparative balance sheets and consolidated income statement are available.

#### Pinto Company and Subsidiary Salida Company
#### Comparative Balance Sheets

| | Pinto Co. January 1, 2004 | Consolidated December 31, 2004 |
|---|---:|---:|
| Cash . . . . . . . . . . . . . . . . . . . . . . . . . . . . . . . . . . . | $ 170,000 | $ 449,500 |
| Accounts receivable (net) . . . . . . . . . . . . . . . . . . . | 118,000 | 319,000 |
| Inventory . . . . . . . . . . . . . . . . . . . . . . . . . . . . . . . | 310,000 | 395,000 |
| Land . . . . . . . . . . . . . . . . . . . . . . . . . . . . . . . . . . . | 250,000 | 350,000 |
| Buildings (net) . . . . . . . . . . . . . . . . . . . . . . . . . . . | 350,000 | 426,000 |
| Equipment (net) . . . . . . . . . . . . . . . . . . . . . . . . . | 1,145,000 | 1,379,000 |
| Database . . . . . . . . . . . . . . . . . . . . . . . . . . . . . . . | | 33,250 |
| Total assets . . . . . . . . . . . . . . . . . . . . . . . . . . . . | $2,343,000 | $3,351,750 |

*(continued)*

---

[10] See Compaq's acquisition of Digital or several of DuPont's acquisitions in the late 1990s for examples of acquired in-process research and development classified as an investing activity.

|  | Pinto Co.<br>January 1, 2004 | Consolidated<br>December 31, 2004 |
|---|---:|---:|
| Accounts payable | $ 50,000 | $ 45,000 |
| Long-term liabilities | 18,000 | 519,500 |
| Common stock | 1,500,000 | 1,500,000 |
| Noncontrolling interest |  | 87,500 |
| Retained earnings | 775,000 | 1,199,750 |
| Total liabilities and equities | $2,343,000 | $3,351,750 |

**Pinto Company and Subsidiary Salida Company**
**Consolidated Income Statement**
**For the Year Ended December 31, 2004**

| | | |
|---|---:|---:|
| Revenues | | $1,255,000 |
| Cost of goods sold | $600,000 | |
| Depreciation | 125,000 | |
| Database amortization | 4,750 | |
| In-process research and development | 22,000 | |
| Interest and other expenses | 13,500 | |
| Noncontrolling interest in Salida's income | 15,000 | 780,250 |
| Net income | | $ 474,750 |

*Additional Information*

- At the date of acquisition, Salida Company closed its books. Consequently, the consolidated income statement totals include Salida's postacquisition revenues and expenses.
- During 2004, Pinto paid $50,000 in dividends. On August 1, 2004, Salida paid a $25,000 dividend.
- During 2004, Pinto issued $501,500 in long-term debt at par value.
- No other asset purchases or dispositions occurred during 2004 other than the purchase of Salida.
- The acquired in-process research and development was judged not to have reached technological feasibility and to have no alternative future uses.

In preparing the consolidated statement of cash flows, note that each adjustment derives from the consolidated income statement or changes from Pinto's January 1, 2004, balance sheet to the consolidated balance sheet at December 31, 2004.

***Depreciation and Amortization*** These expenses do not represent current operating cash outflows and thus are added back to convert accrual basis income to cash provided by operating activities.

***Increase in Accounts Receivable, Inventory, and Accounts Payable (net of acquisition)***
SFAS No. 95 requires that changes in balance sheet accounts affecting operating cash flows reflect amounts acquired in business acquisitions. In this case, note that the changes in Accounts Receivable, Inventory, and Accounts Payable are computed as follows:

| | Accounts<br>Receivable | Inventory | Accounts<br>Payable |
|---|---:|---:|---:|
| Pinto's balance 1/1/04 | $118,000 | $310,000 | $50,000 |
| Increase from Salida acquisition | 145,000 | 90,000 | 15,000 |
| Adjusted beginning balance | 263,000 | 400,000 | 65,000 |
| Consolidated balance 12/31/04 | 319,000 | 395,000 | 45,000 |
| Operating cash flow adjustment | $ 56,000 | $ 5,000 | $20,000 |

***Acquired In-Process Research and Development*** The purchase price for Salida Company includes $22,000 for in-process research and development, which is expensed by the combined entity immediately upon acquisition. The $22,000 is added back to net income and included as part of cash outflows from investing activities.

***Noncontrolling Interest*** The noncontrolling interest's share of the combined entity's net income represents neither a distribution nor a collection of cash and therefore is added back to consolidated net income. Ownership divisions between the noncontrolling and controlling interests do not affect reporting for the entity's operating cash flows.

***Purchase of Salida Company*** The Investing Activities section of the cash flow statement shows increases and decreases in assets purchased or sold involving cash. The cash outflow from the purchase of Salida Company's assets is determined as follows:

| | |
|---|---:|
| Purchase price for 90 percent interest in Salida | $775,000 |
| Cash acquired | (35,000) |
| Net cash paid for Salida investment | $740,000 |

Note here that although Pinto acquires only 90 percent of Salida, 100 percent of Salida's cash is offset against the purchase price in determining the investing cash outflow. Ownership divisions between the noncontrolling and controlling interests do not affect reporting for the entity's investing cash flows.

***Issue of Long-Term Debt*** Pinto Company's issuance of long-term debt represents a cash inflow from financing activities.

***Dividends*** The dividends paid to Pinto Company owners ($50,000) combined with the dividends paid to the noncontrolling interest ($2,500) represent cash outflows from financing activities.

Based on the consolidated totals from the comparative balance sheets and the consolidated income statement, the following consolidated statement of cash flows is then prepared. Pinto chooses to use the indirect method of reporting cash flows from operating activities.

**Pinto Company and Subsidiary Salida Company**
**Consolidated Statement of Cash Flows**
**For the Year Ended December 31, 2004**

| | | |
|---|---:|---:|
| Consolidated net income | | $474,750 |
| Depreciation expense | $125,000 | |
| Amortization expense | 4,750 | |
| Increase in accounts receivable (net of acquisition effects) | (56,000) | |
| Decrease in inventory (net of acquisition effects) | 5,000 | |
| Decrease in accounts payable (net of acquisition effects) | (20,000) | |
| Acquired in-process research and development | 22,000 | |
| Noncontrolling interest in income | 15,000 | 95,750 |
| Net cash provided by operations | | 570,500 |
| Purchase of Salida Company (net of cash acquired) | | |
| Net cash used in investing activities | (740,000) | (740,000) |
| Issue long-term debt | 501,500 | |
| Dividends | (52,500) | |
| Net cash provided by financing activities | | 449,000 |
| **Increase in Cash 1/1/04 to 12/31/04** | | **$279,500** |

## CONSOLIDATED EARNINGS PER SHARE

One other intermediate accounting topic, the computation of earnings per share (EPS), is affected by the consolidation process. As required by *Statement of Financial Accounting Standards No. 128* (March 1997), "Earnings per Share," publicly held companies must disclose EPS each period.

Such figures are calculated using the following steps:

- Basic earnings per share is determined by dividing net income (after reduction for preferred stock dividends) by the weighted average number of common stock shares outstanding for the period. If the reporting entity has no dilutive options, warrants, or other convertible items, only basic EPS is presented on the face of the income statement. However, diluted earnings per share also must be presented if any dilutive convertibles are present.
- Diluted earnings per share is computed by combining the effects of *any dilutive securities* with basic earnings per share. Stock options, stock warrants, convertible debt, and convertible preferred stock often qualify as dilutive securities.[11]

In most instances, the computation of earnings per share for a business combination follows the same general pattern. Consolidated net income along with the number of outstanding parent shares provides the basis for calculating basic EPS. Any convertibles, warrants, or options for the parent's stock that can possibly dilute the reported figure must be included as described earlier in determining diluted EPS.

However, a problem arises if warrants, options, or convertibles that can dilute the subsidiary's earnings are outstanding. Although the parent company is not directly affected, the potential impact of these items on consolidated net income must be given weight in computing diluted earnings per share for the business combination as a whole. Because of possible conversion, the subsidiary earnings figure included in consolidated net income is not necessarily applicable to the diluted earnings per share computation. *Thus, the accountant must make a separate determination of the amount of subsidiary income that should be used in deriving diluted earnings per share for the business combination.*

### Earnings per Share Illustration

Assume that Big Corporation has 100,000 shares of its common stock outstanding during the current year. The company also has issued 20,000 shares of nonvoting preferred stock, paying an annual cumulative dividend of $5 per share ($100,000 total). Each of these preferred shares is convertible into two shares of Big's common stock.

Assume further that Big owns 90 percent of Little's common stock and 60 percent of its preferred stock (which pays $12,000 in dividends per year). Annual amortization is $24,000 attributable to various intangibles. EPS computations currently are being made for 2004. During the year, Big reported separate income of $600,000 while Little earned $100,000. A simplified consolidation of the figures for the year indicates net income for the business combination of $662,400:

| | | |
|---|---:|---:|
| Big's separate income for 2004 | | $600,000 |
| Amortization expense resulting from original purchase price | | (24,000) |
| Little's separate income for 2004 | $100,000 | |
| Noncontrolling interest in Little—common stock (10% of income after $12,000 in preferred stock dividends) | (8,800) | |

*(continued)*

---

[11] Complete coverage of the earnings per share computation can be found in virtually any intermediate accounting textbook. To achieve an adequate understanding of this process, a number of complex procedures must be mastered, including these:
- Calculation of the weighted average number of common shares outstanding.
- Understanding the method of including stock rights, convertible debt, and convertible preferred stock within the computation of diluted earnings per share.

| | | |
|---|---:|---:|
| Noncontrolling interest in Little—preferred stock (40% of dividends) | (4,800) | 86,400 |
| Consolidated net income | | $662,400 |

Little has 20,000 shares of common stock and 4,000 shares of preferred stock outstanding. The preferred shares pay a $3 per year dividend, and each can be converted into two shares of common stock (or 8,000 shares in total). Since Big owns only 60 percent of Little's preferred stock, a $4,800 dividend is distributed each year to the outside owners (40 percent of $12,000 total payment).

Assume finally that the subsidiary also has $200,000 in convertible bonds outstanding that were originally issued at face value. This debt has a cash and an effective interest rate of 10 percent ($20,000 per year) and can be converted by the owners into 9,000 shares of Little's common stock. None of these bonds is owned by Big. The tax rate applicable to Little is 30 percent.

To better visualize these factors, the convertible items are scheduled as follows:

| Company | Item | Interest or Dividend | Conversion | Big Owns |
|---|---|---|---|---|
| Big | Preferred stock | $100,000/year | 40,000 shares | Not applicable |
| Little | Preferred stock | 12,000/year | 8,000 shares | 60% |
| Little | Bonds | 14,000/year* | 9,000 shares | –0– |

*Interest on the bonds is shown net of the 30 percent tax effect ($20,000 interest less $6,000 tax savings). No tax is computed for the preferred shares because distributed dividends do not create a tax impact.

Because the subsidiary has convertible items that can affect the company's outstanding shares and net income, Little's diluted earnings per share must be derived *before* consolidated diluted EPS can be determined. As shown in Exhibit 6–7, Little's diluted earnings per share are $3.08. Two aspects of this schedule should be noted:

- The individual impact of the convertibles ($1.50 for the preferred stock and $1.56 for the bonds) did not raise the earnings per share figures. Thus, neither the preferred stock nor the bonds are antidilutive, and both are properly included in these computations.
- Determining diluted earnings per share of the subsidiary is necessary only because of the possible dilutive impact. Without the subsidiary's convertible bonds and preferred stock, consolidated net income would form the basis for computing EPS for the business combination, and only basic EPS would be reported.

According to Exhibit 6–7, Little's income is $114,000 for diluted EPS. The issue for the accountant is how much of this amount should be included in computing consolidated diluted earnings per share. This allocation is based on the percentage of shares controlled by the parent. Note that if the subsidiary's preferred stock and bonds are converted into common shares, Big's ownership falls from 90 to 62 percent. For diluted EPS, 37,000 shares are appropriate. Big's 62 percent ownership (22,800/37,000) is the basis for allocating the subsidiary's $114,000 income to the parent.

### Supporting Calculations for Diluted Earnings per Share

| | Little Company Shares | Big's Percentage | Big's Ownership |
|---|---|---|---|
| Common stock | 20,000 | 90% | 18,000 |
| Possible new shares—preferred stock | 8,000 | 60 | 4,800 |
| Possible new shares—bonds | 9,000 | –0– | –0– |
| Total | 37,000 | | 22,800 |

Big's ownership (diluted): 22,800/37,000 = 62% (rounded)
Income assigned to Big (diluted earnings per share computation):
  $114,000 × 62% = $70,680

**EXHIBIT 6–7**
Subsidiary's Diluted Earnings per Share

### LITTLE COMPANY
### Diluted Earnings per Common Share
### For Year Ending December 31, 2004

|  | Earnings |  | Shares |  |
|---|---|---|---|---|
| As reported | $100,000 |  | 20,000 |  |
| Preferred stock dividends | (12,000) |  |  |  |
| Effect of possible preferred stock conversion: |  |  |  |  |
| Dividends saved | 12,000 | New shares | 8,000 | $1.50 Impact (12,000/8,000) |
| Effect of possible bond conversion: |  |  |  |  |
| Interest saved (net of taxes) | 14,000 |  | 9,000 | $1.56 Impact (14,000/9,000) |
| Diluted EPS | $114,000 |  | 37,000 | $3.08 (rounded) |

Consolidated earnings per share now can be determined. Only $70,680 of subsidiary income is appropriate for the diluted EPS computation. Because two different income figures are utilized, basic and diluted calculations are made separately as shown in Exhibit 6–8. Consequently, as determined in these schedules, this business combination should report basic earnings per share of $5.62, with diluted earnings per share of $4.62.

# SUBSIDIARY STOCK TRANSACTIONS

A footnote to the financial statements of the Gerber Products Company disclosed a transaction carried out by one of the organization's subsidiaries: "The Company's wholly owned Mexican subsidiary sold previously unissued shares of common stock to Grupo Coral, S.A., a Mexican food company, at a price in excess of the shares' net book value." The footnote went on to state that Gerber had increased consolidated Additional Paid-In Capital by $432,000 as a result of this stock sale.

As this illustration shows, subsidiary stock transactions can alter the level of parent ownership. A subsidiary, for example, can decide to sell previously unissued stock to raise needed capital. Although the parent company can acquire a portion or even all of these new shares, such issues frequently are marketed entirely to outsiders. A subsidiary could also be legally forced to sell additional shares of its stock. As an example, companies holding control over foreign subsidiaries occasionally encounter this problem because of laws in the individual localities. Issuance of new shares can be mandated if regulations require a certain percentage of local ownership as a prerequisite for operating within a country. Of course, changes in the level of parent ownership do not result solely from stock sales: A subsidiary also can repurchase its own stock. The acquisition, as well as the possible retirement, of such treasury shares serves as a means of reducing the percentage of outside ownership.

## Changes in Subsidiary Book Value—Stock Transactions

When a subsidiary subsequently buys or sells its own stock, a nonoperational increase or decrease occurs in the company's book value. Because the transaction need not involve the parent, the effect of this change is not automatically reflected in the parent's investment account. *Thus, a separate adjustment must be recorded to maintain reciprocity between the subsidiary's stockholders' equity accounts and the parent's investment balance.* The accountant measures the impact that the stock transaction has on the parent to ensure that this effect is appropriately recorded within the consolidation process.

An example demonstrates the mechanics of this issue. Assume that on January 1, 2004, Small Company's book value is $700,000 as follows:

**EXHIBIT 6–8**

### BIG COMPANY AND CONSOLIDATED SUBSIDIARY
#### Consolidated Basic Earnings per Common Share
#### For Year Ending December 31, 2004

|  | Earnings | Shares |  |
|---|---|---|---|
| Consolidated net income | $662,400 | | |
| Big's shares outstanding | | 100,000 | |
| Preferred stock dividends (Big) | (100,000) | | |
| Basic EPS | $562,400 | 100,000 | $5.62 |

#### Consolidated Diluted Earnings per Common Share
#### For Year Ending December 31, 2004

|  | Earnings | Shares |  |
|---|---|---|---|
| Computed below | $646,680* | | |
| Big's shares outstanding | | 100,000 | |
| Preferred stock dividends (Big) | (100,000) | | |
| Effect of possible preferred stock (Big) conversion: | | | |
| Dividends saved | 100,000  New shares | 40,000 | $2.50 impact (100,000/40,000) |
| Diluted EPS | $646,680 | 140,000 | $4.62 (rounded) |

*Net income computation:

| | |
|---|---|
| Big's separate income for 2004 | $600,000 |
| Amortization expense resulting from original purchase price | (24,000) |
| Portion of Little's income assigned to diluted earnings per share calculation | 70,680 (computed previously) |
| Earnings of the business combination applicable to diluted earnings per share | $646,680 |

| | |
|---|---|
| Common stock ($1.00 par value with 70,000 shares issued and outstanding) | $ 70,000 |
| Retained earnings | 630,000 |
| Total stockholders' equity | $700,000 |

Based on the 70,000 outstanding shares, Small's book value at this time is $10 per common share ($700,000/70,000 shares).

On this same date, Giant Company acquired in the open market an 80 percent interest in Small Company (56,000 of the outstanding shares). To avoid unnecessary complications, the price of this stock is assumed to be $560,000, or $10 per share, exactly equivalent to the book value of the purchased shares. The assumption that no goodwill or other revaluations are indicated by this acquisition also is made.

Under these conditions, the consolidation process is uncomplicated. On the purchase date, only a single worksheet entry is required. The investment account is eliminated and the 20 percent noncontrolling interest recognized through the following routine entry:

**Consolidation Entry S (January 1, 2004)**

| | | |
|---|---|---|
| Common Stock (Small Company) | 70,000 | |
| Retained Earnings (Small Company) | 630,000 | |
|     Investment in Small Company (80%) | | 560,000 |
|     Noncontrolling Interest in Small Company (20%) | | 140,000 |
| To eliminate subsidiary's stockholders' equity accounts and record noncontrolling interest balance on this date. | | |

A subsidiary stock transaction is now introduced to demonstrate the effect created on the consolidation process. Assume that on January 2, 2004, Small sells 10,000 previously unissued shares of its common stock to outside parties for $16 per share.[12] Because of this transaction, Giant no longer possesses an 80 percent interest in a subsidiary having a $700,000 net book value. Instead, the parent now holds 70 percent (56,000 shares of a total of 80,000) of a company with a book value of $860,000 ($700,000 previous book value plus $160,000 capital generated by the sale of additional shares). *Independent of any action by the parent company, the book value equivalency of this investment has risen from $560,000 to $602,000 (70% of $860,000).* This increase has been created by Small's ability to sell shares of stock at $6.00 more than the book value.

Small's new stock issuance has increased the underlying book value component of Giant's investment by $42,000 ($602,000 − $560,000). Thus, even with the rise in outside ownership, the business combination has grown in size by this amount, a change that must be reflected within the consolidated financial figures. As indicated by the Gerber example, this adjustment is frequently recorded to Additional Paid-In Capital. Because the subsidiary's stockholders' equity is eliminated on the worksheet, any equity increase accruing to the business combination must be recognized by the parent. Therefore, the $42,000 increment is entered into Giant's financial records as an adjustment in both the investment account (since the underlying book value of the subsidiary has increased) and Additional Paid-In Capital.

| **Giant Company's Financial Records—January 2, 2004** | | |
|---|---|---|
| Investment in Small Company | 42,000 | |
|     Additional Paid-In Capital (Giant Company) | | 42,000 |
| To recognize change in equity of business combination created by issuance of 10,000 additional shares of common stock by Small Company, the subsidiary, at above book value. | | |

Once the change in the parent's records has been made, the consolidation process can be carried out in a normal fashion. If, for example, the financial statements are brought together immediately following the sale of these additional shares, the following worksheet Entry **S** can be constructed. *Although the investment and subsidiary equity accounts are removed here, the change recorded earlier in Giant's Additional Paid-In Capital remains within the consolidated figures.* Thus, the subsidiary's issuance of stock at more than the book value has increased the reported equity of the business combination.

| **Consolidation Entry S—January 2, 2004—After Subsidiary's Stock Issuance** | | |
|---|---|---|
| Common Stock (Small Company) | 80,000 | |
| Additional Paid-In Capital (Small Company) | 150,000 | |
| Retained Earnings (Small Company) | 630,000 | |
|     Investment in Small Company (70%) | | 602,000 |
|     Noncontrolling Interest in Small Company (30%) | | 258,000 |
| To eliminate subsidiary's stockholders' equity accounts and record noncontrolling interest balance on this date. Small's capital accounts have been updated to reflect the issuance of 10,000 shares of $1 par value common stock at $16 per share. The investment balance has also been adjusted for the $42,000 increment recorded earlier by the parent. | | |

In 1983, because of a lack of formal guidance, the staff of the SEC decided that an adjustment necessitated by subsidiary stock transactions could be made to either Additional Paid-In

---

[12] This example has been created solely for demonstration purposes. Obviously, having the parent acquire stock at book value on one day with an outsider paying $6 per share more than book value on the following day is an unlikely situation. Normally, the prices would be similar or more time would transpire between the two acquisitions. In either case, the consolidation process is fundamentally unchanged.

Capital or to a gain or loss account. For example, Atlantic Richfield Company disclosed that a previously wholly owned subsidiary had "completed an initial public offering of 19,550,000 shares of its common stock, thereby decreasing ARCO's percentage ownership to 80.4 percent. The Company recognized an after-tax gain of $185 million from this transaction."

In its October 2000 Exposure Draft, *Accounting for Financial Instruments with Characteristics of Liabilities, Equity, or Both*, however, the FASB reiterated its support for the view that the effects on a parent of a subsidiary's transactions in its own stock should be reported as adjustments to Additional Paid-In Capital, not gains and losses. As stated in the Exposure Draft (para. 234):

> Having reached a decision that the noncontrolling interest in a subsidiary constitutes part of the equity of a consolidated group, the Board concluded that sales of shares of that subsidiary are sales of the consolidated entity's equity and, therefore, should not result in gain or loss recognition as long as the subsidiary remains consolidated.
>
> The Board believes that [sales of] the stock of a subsidiary by any of the affiliates, whether . . . by the parent or another subsidiary . . . are transactions in the equity of the reporting entity. The stock of the subsidiary is neither an asset nor a liability of the reporting entity comprising a parent and its subsidiaries. Rather, it is part of the residual interest remaining after subtracting consolidated liabilities from consolidated assets. Therefore, no gains or losses should be recognized on those transactions.

Consistent with the recommendation in the Exposure Draft, this textbook treats the effects from subsidiary stock transactions on the consolidated entity as adjustments to Additional Paid-In Capital.

## Subsidiary Stock Transactions—Illustrated

No single example can demonstrate the many possible variations that could be created by different types of subsidiary stock transactions. To provide a working knowledge of this process, several additional cases are analyzed briefly. The original balances presented for Small (the 80 percent–owned subsidiary) and Giant (the parent) as of January 1, 2004, serve as the basis for these illustrations:

| | |
|---|---|
| Small Company (subsidiary): | |
|    Shares outstanding | 70,000 |
|    Book value of company | $700,000 |
|    Book value per share | $ 10.00 |
| Giant Company (parent): | |
|    Shares owned of Small Company | 56,000 |
|    Book value of investment | $560,000 (80%) |

Each of the following cases should be viewed as an independent situation. Also, all adjustments are made here to Additional Paid-In Capital although, as discussed, recognition of a gain or loss remains a possible alternative.

### *Case 1*

Assume that Small Company sells 10,000 shares of previously unissued common stock to outside parties for $8 per share.

Small is issuing its stock here at a price below the company's current book value of $10 per share. Selling shares to outsiders at a discount necessitates a drop in the recorded value of consolidated Additional Paid-In Capital. The parent's ownership interest is being diluted, thus creating a decrease in the underlying book value of the parent's investment. This reduction can be measured as follows:

| | |
|---|---|
| Adjusted book value of subsidiary ($700,000 + $80,000) | $780,000 |
| Current parent ownership (56,000 shares/80,000 shares) | 70% |
|   Book value equivalency of ownership | 546,000 |
| Current book value of investment account | 560,000 |
| Required *reduction* | $ 14,000 |

In the original illustration, new shares were sold by the subsidiary at $6 more than book value, thus increasing consolidated equity. Here, the opposite transpires; the shares are issued at a price less than book value, creating a decrease.

**Giant Company's Financial Records**

| | | |
|---|---:|---:|
| Additional Paid-In Capital (or Retained Earnings) (Giant Company) | 14,000 | |
|     Investment in Small Company | | 14,000 |
| To recognize change in equity of business combination created by issuance of 10,000 additional shares of Small's common stock at less than book value. | | |

### Case 2

Assume that Small issues 10,000 new shares of common stock for $16 per share. Of this total, Giant acquires 8,000 shares to maintain its 80 percent level of ownership. Giant pays a total of $128,000 (8,000 × $16) for this additional stock. The remaining shares are bought by outside parties.

Under these circumstances, both the parent's investment account and the book value of the subsidiary are altered by the stock transaction. Thus, both figures must be updated prior to determining the necessity of an equity revaluation:

| | |
|---|---:|
| Adjusted book value of subsidiary ($700,000 + $160,000) | $860,000 |
| Current parent ownership (64,000 shares/80,000 shares) | 80% |
|   Book value equivalency of ownership | 688,000 |
| Current book value of investment (after including additional $128,000 acquisition) | 688,000 |
| Required change | $ –0– |

No adjustment is required in this case because Giant's underlying interest remains properly aligned with the subsidiary's book value. Any time that new stock is sold to the parent in the same ratio as previous ownership, consolidated Additional Paid-In Capital is unaffected. No proportionate increase or decrease is created by the transaction.

### Case 3

Assume that Small issues 10,000 additional shares of common stock solely to Giant for $16 per share.

A different type of situation is faced here. As shown in the following computational schedule, this issuance causes the parent's investment account to again be in excess of the subsidiary's underlying book value (as in Case 1). However, in this latest example, the $10,500 difference is created by a parent company purchase rather than by the subsidiary's sale of common stock to outside parties. Thus, the reporting of this impact has to be altered to reflect Giant's acquisition of these new shares.

| | |
|---|---:|
| Adjusted book value of subsidiary ($700,000 + $160,000) | $860,000 |
| Current parent ownership (66,000 shares/80,000 shares) | 82.5% |
|   Book value equivalency of ownership | 709,500 |
| Current book value of investment (after including additional $160,000 acquisition) | 720,000 |
| Differences in subsidiary book value and investment book value after second purchase | $ 10,500 |

The $14,000 reduction in Case 1 was caused by the subsidiary's sale of stock to outsiders at a price less than book value, a transaction that mathematically diluted the value of the parent's investment. Because this action realigned the ownership interests to the apparent detriment of the business combination, Additional Paid-In Capital was reduced. This result was achieved for consolidation purposes through a decrease in the parent's equity account as well as in the Investment in Small Company.

Conversely, in Case 3, the $10,500 difference has been created solely by an expenditure made by the parent. Since the price paid was more than the corresponding book value of the subsidiary, the excess is attributed to goodwill (unless the amount can be traced to specific asset or liability accounts). As in any purchase combination, Giant records the entire $160,000 payment as an investment and then utilizes Entry **A** on the consolidation worksheet to report the allocation. Because the parent made the acquisition, the transaction is handled differently than a subsidiary's sale of stock to outsiders at less than book value.

## Case 4

Assume that instead of issuing new stock, Small reacquires 10,000 shares from outside owners. The price paid for this treasury stock is $16 per share.

This illustration is designed to present another type of subsidiary stock transaction: the acquisition of treasury stock. Although the subsidiary's actions have changed, the basic accounting procedures are unaffected.

| | |
|---|---:|
| Adjusted book value of subsidiary ($700,000 − $160,000) | $540,000 |
| Current parent ownership (56,000 shares/60,000 shares) | 93⅓% |
| Book value equivalency of ownership | 504,000 |
| Current book value of investment | 560,000 |
| Required *reduction* | $ 56,000 |

The subsidiary paid an amount in excess of the treasury stock's $10 per share book value. Consequently, the parent's interest is once again being diluted. This effect is created by a transaction between the subsidiary and the noncontrolling interest; the reduction is not the result of a purchase made by the parent. As in Case 1, the change must be reported as an adjustment in the parent's Additional Paid-In Capital accompanied by a corresponding decrease in the investment account (to $504,000 in this case). Again, for reporting purposes, this transaction results in lowering consolidated Additional Paid-In Capital.

**Giant Company's Financial Records**

| | | |
|---|---:|---:|
| Additional Paid-In Capital (Giant Company) | 56,000 | |
| Investment in Small Company | | 56,000 |
| To recognize change in equity of business combination created by acquisition of 10,000 treasury shares by Small at above book value. | | |

This fourth illustration represents a different subsidiary stock transaction, the purchase of treasury stock. Therefore, display of consolidation Entry **S** should also be presented. This entry demonstrates the worksheet elimination required when the subsidiary holds treasury shares.

**Consolidation Entry S**

| | | |
|---|---:|---:|
| Common Stock (Small Company) | 70,000 | |
| Retained Earnings (Small Company) | 630,000 | |
| Treasury Stock (Small Company) (at cost) | | 160,000 |
| Investment in Small Company (93⅓%—subsequent to adjustment) | | 504,000 |
| Noncontrolling Interest (6⅔% of net book value) | | 36,000 |
| To eliminate equity accounts of Small Company and recognize appropriate noncontrolling interest. Book value of Small is now $540,000. | | |

## Case 5

Assume that Small issues a 10 percent stock dividend (7,000 new shares) to its owners when the fair market value of the stock is $16 per share.

This final case illustrates that not all subsidiary stock transactions produce discernible effects on the consolidation process. A stock dividend, whether large or small, serves to capitalize a portion of the issuing company's retained earnings and, thus, does not alter book value. Shareholders recognize the receipt of a stock dividend only as a change in the recorded cost of each share rather than as any type of adjustment in the investment balance. Because no net effect is perceived by either party, the consolidation process proceeds in a routine fashion. Therefore, a subsidiary stock dividend requires no special treatment prior to development of a worksheet.

| | |
|---|---:|
| Book value of subsidiary (no adjustment required) | $700,000 |
| Current parent ownership (adjusted for 10% stock dividend—61,600 shares/77,000 shares) | 80% |
| Book value equivalency of ownership | 560,000 |
| Current book value of investment | 560,000 |
| Adjustment required by stock dividend | $ –0– |

The consolidation Entry **S** that would be made just after the issuance of this stock dividend follows. The $560,000 component of the investment account continues to be offset against the stockholders' equity of the subsidiary. Although the parent's investment was not affected by the dividend, the equity accounts of the subsidiary have been realigned in recognition of the $112,000 stock dividend (7,000 shares of $1 par value stock valued at $16 per share).

**Consolidation Entry S**

| | | |
|---|---:|---:|
| Common Stock (Small Company) | 77,000 | |
| Additional Paid-In Capital (Small Company) | 105,000 | |
| Retained Earnings (Small Company) | 518,000 | |
|     Investment in Small Company (80%) | | 560,000 |
|     Noncontrolling interest (20%) | | 140,000 |

To eliminate stockholders' equity accounts of subsidiary and recognize noncontrolling interest following issuance of stock dividend.

## Summary

1. If one member of a business combination acquires an affiliate's debt instrument (a bond or note, for example) from an outside party, the purchase price usually differs from the book value of the liability. Thus, a gain or loss has been incurred from the perspective of the business combination. However, both the debt and investment remain in the individual financial accounts of the two companies while the gain or loss goes unrecorded. In the consolidation process, all balances must be adjusted to reflect the effective retirement of the debt.
2. Following the acquisition of one company's debt by a related party, Interest Income and Expense are recognized. Because these accounts result from intercompany transactions, they also must be removed in every subsequent consolidation along with the debt and investment figures. Retained Earnings also requires adjustment in each year after the purchase to record the impact of the gain or loss.
3. Amortization of intercompany debt/investment balances often is necessary because of discounts and/or premiums. Consequently, the interest income and interest expense figures reported by the two parties will not agree. The closing of these two accounts into Retained Earnings each year gradually reduces the consolidation adjustment that must be made to this equity account.
4. When acquired, many subsidiaries have preferred stock outstanding as well as common stock. The method of handling any subsidiary preferred shares within the consolidation process is dependent on the nature of the stock. Preferred issues that have a call value, no voting rights, and a set cumulative dividend are not easily distinguished from a debt. Conversely, preferred shares with a voting or participation right are clearly an ownership interest resembling common stock.
5. If a subsidiary's preferred stock is viewed as a debt-type instrument, any shares acquired by the parent are eliminated on the worksheet as if the stock had been retired. Because a gain or loss cannot be recognized in connection with a company's own stock transactions, the difference between par value and the parent's cost is adjusted through Additional Paid-In Capital or Retained Earnings. Any shares still held by outside parties are reported as a noncontrolling interest based on the call value of the stock.

6. A subsidiary preferred stock that is perceived as an equity interest is accounted for in the same manner as a common stock purchase. Any excess acquisition price paid for the preferred stock is assigned to specific accounts based on fair market value with any residual reported as goodwill. As a prerequisite to this process, the book value of the subsidiary must be divided between the two equity interests. This calculation is based on the rights specified for the preferred shareholders.
7. A statement of cash flows is required of every business combination. This statement is not created by consolidating the individual cash flows of the separate companies. Instead, both a consolidated income statement and balance sheet are produced, and the cash flows statement is developed from these figures. Within this statement, the noncontrolling interest's share of the subsidiary's income is not included because no cash flows result. However, the dividends paid to these outside owners must be listed as a financing activity.
8. For most business combinations, the determination of consolidated earnings per share follows the normal pattern presented in intermediate accounting textbooks. However, if the subsidiary has potentially dilutive items outstanding (stock warrants, convertible preferred stock, convertible bonds, etc.), a different process must be followed. The subsidiary's own diluted earnings per share are computed as a preliminary procedure. The earnings used in each of these calculations are then allocated between the parent and the outside owners based on the ownership levels of the subsidiary's shares and the dilutive items. The portion of income assigned to the parent is included in determining the diluted earnings per share figures to be reported for the business combination.
9. After the combination is created, a subsidiary may enter into stock transactions such as the issuance of additional shares or the acquisition of treasury stock. Such actions normally create a proportional increase or decrease in the subsidiary's equity when compared with the parent's investment. The change is measured and then reflected in the consolidated statements through the Additional Paid-In Capital account. Recognition of a gain or loss is also a possibility. To achieve the appropriate accounting, the parent adjusts the Investment in Subsidiary account as well as its own Additional Paid-In Capital. Since this equity balance is not eliminated on the worksheet, the required increase or decrease is created in the consolidated figures.

# Comprehensive Illustration

## PROBLEM: CONSOLIDATED STATEMENT OF CASH FLOWS AND EARNINGS PER SHARE

*(Estimated Time: 35 to 45 Minutes)* Pop, Inc., acquires 90 percent of the 20,000 shares of Son Company's outstanding common stock on December 31, 2003. Of the purchase price, $80,000 was allocated to covenants, a figure amortized at the rate of $2,000 per year. Comparative consolidated balance sheets for 2004 and 2003 are as follows:

|  | 2004 | 2003 |
|---|---|---|
| Cash | $ 210,000 | $ 130,000 |
| Accounts receivable | 350,000 | 220,000 |
| Inventory | 320,000 | 278,000 |
| Land, buildings, and equipment (net) | 1,090,000 | 1,120,000 |
| Covenants | 78,000 | 80,000 |
| Total assets | $2,048,000 | $1,828,000 |
| Accounts payable | $ 290,000 | $ 296,000 |
| Long-term liabilities | 650,000 | 550,000 |
| Noncontrolling interest | 38,000 | 34,000 |
| Preferred stock (2,000 shares outstanding) | 100,000 | 100,000 |
| Common stock (26,000 shares outstanding) | 520,000 | 520,000 |
| Retained earnings, 12/31 | 450,000 | 328,000 |
| Total liabilities and stockholders' equity | $2,048,000 | $1,828,000 |

*Additional information:*

- Consolidated net income for 2004 (after adjustments for all intercompany items) was $172,000.
- Consolidated depreciation and amortization for 2004 equaled $52,000.
- On April 10, 2004, Son sold a building with a $40,000 book value receiving cash of $50,000. Later that month, Pop borrowed $100,000 from a local bank and purchased equipment for $60,000. These transactions were all with outside parties.
- During 2004 Pop paid $50,000 dividends on its common stock, $10,000 on its preferred stock, and Son paid a $20,000 dividend on its common stock.
- Son has long-term convertible debt of $180,000 outstanding included in consolidated liabilities. Interest expense of $16,000 (net of taxes) was recognized on this debt in 2004. This debt can be exchanged for 10,000 shares of the subsidiary's common stock. Pop owns none of this debt.
- Son recorded $60,000 net income from its own operations in 2004. Noncontrolling interest in Son's income was $6,000.
- Pop recorded $4,000 in profits on sales of goods to Son. These goods remain in Son's warehouse at December 31, 2004.
- Pop applies the equity method to account for its Investment in Son. On its own books, Pop recognized $48,000 equity in earnings from Son (90% × $60,000 less $2,000 amortization and $4,000 unrealized intercompany profit on its sales to Son).

### Required:

a. Prepare a consolidated statement of cash flows for Pop, Inc., and Son Company for the year ending December 31, 2004. Use the indirect approach for determining the amount of cash generated by normal operations.[13]

b. Compute basic earnings per share and diluted earnings per share for this business combination.

## SOLUTION

a. *Consolidated Statement of Cash Flows*

The problem specifies that the indirect approach should be used in preparing the consolidated statement of cash flows. Therefore, all items that do not represent cash flows from operations must be removed from the $172,000 consolidated net income. For example, the depreciation and amortization both are eliminated (noncash items) as well as the gain on the sale of the building (a nonoperational item). As discussed in the chapter, the noncontrolling interest's share of Son's net income is another noncash reduction that also is removed. In addition, each of the changes in consolidated Accounts Receivable, Inventory, and Accounts Payable produces a noncash impact on net income. The increase in accounts receivable, for example, indicates that the sales figure for the period was larger than the amount of cash collected so that adjustment is required in producing this statement.

From the information given, only five nonoperational changes in cash can be determined: the bank loan, the acquisition of equipment, the sale of a building, the dividend paid by Son to the minority interest, and the dividend paid by the parent. Each of these transactions is included in the consolidated statement of cash flows shown on the next page in Exhibit 6–9, which explains the $80,000 increase in cash experienced by the entity during 2004.

b. *Consolidated Earnings per Share*

The subsidiary's convertible debt has a potentially dilutive effect on earnings per share. Therefore, diluted EPS cannot be determined for the business combination directly from consolidated net income. First, the diluted EPS figure must be calculated for the subsidiary. This information then is used in the computations made by the consolidated entity.

Diluted earnings per share of $2.53 for the subsidiary is determined as follows:

**Son Company—Diluted Earnings per Share**

|  | Earnings |  | Shares |  |
|---|---|---|---|---|
| As reported | $60,000 |  | 20,000 | $3.00 |
| Effect of possible debt conversion: |  |  |  |  |
| Interest saved (net of taxes) | 16,000 | New shares | 10,000 | $1.60 impact |
|  |  |  |  | (16,000/10,000) |
| Diluted EPS | $76,000 |  | 30,000 | $2.53 (rounded) |

[13] Prior to attempting this problem, a review of an intermediate accounting textbook might be useful to obtain a complete overview of the production of a statement of cash flows.

## EXHIBIT 6-9

**POP, INC., AND SON COMPANY**
**Consolidated Statement of Cash Flows**
**Year Ending December 31, 2004**

| | | |
|---|---:|---:|
| Cash flows from operating activities | | |
| Net income | | $ 172,000 |
| Adjustments to reconcile net income to net cash provided by operating activities: | | |
| Depreciation and amortization | $ 52,000 | |
| Gain on sale of building | (10,000) | |
| Noncontrolling interest in Son's income | 6,000 | |
| Increase in accounts receivable | (130,000) | |
| Increase in inventory | (42,000) | |
| Decrease in accounts payable | (6,000) | (130,000) |
| Net cash provided by operations | | 42,000 |
| Cash flows from investing activities | | |
| Purchase of equipment | (60,000) | |
| Sale of building | 50,000 | |
| Net cash used in investing activities | | (10,000) |
| Cash flows from financing activities | | |
| Payment of cash dividend—Pop | (50,000) | |
| Payment of cash dividend to noncontrolling owners of Son | (2,000) | |
| Borrowed from bank | 100,000 | |
| Net cash provided by financing activities | | 48,000 |
| Net increase in cash | | 80,000 |
| Cash, January 1, 2004 | | 130,000 |
| Cash, December 31, 2004 | | $ 210,000 |

## EXHIBIT 6-10

**POP, INC., AND SON COMPANY**
**Consolidated Earnings per Share**
**Year Ending December 31, 2004**

| | Earnings | Shares | |
|---|---:|---:|---|
| | **Basic Earnings per Share** | | |
| Basic EPS | $172,000 | 26,000 | $6.62 (rounded) |
| | **Diluted Earnings per Share** | | |
| Pop's reported income | $172,000 | | |
| Remove equity income | (48,000) | | |
| Remove unrealized gain | (4,000) | | |
| Recognize amortization expense | (2,000) | | |
| Preferred stock dividend | (10,000) | | |
| Common shares outstanding (Pop, Inc.) | | | |
| Common stock income—Pop (for EPS computations) | $108,000 | 26,000 | |
| Income of Son (above—for diluted EPS) | 45,600 | | |
| | $153,600 | 26,000 | $5.91 (rounded) |
| Effect of possible preferred stock conversion: | | | |
| Dividends saved | 10,000   New shares | 6,000 | $1.67 impact (10,000/6,000) |
| Diluted EPS | $163,600 | 32,000 | $5.11 |

The parent owns none of the convertible debt included in computing diluted earnings per share. Pop holds only 18,000 (90 percent of the outstanding common stock) of the 30,000 shares used in this EPS calculation. Consequently, in determining diluted EPS for the entire business combination, just $45,600 of the subsidiary's income is applicable:

$$\$76,000 \times 18,000/30,000 = \$45,600$$

Exhibit 6–10 reveals consolidated basic earnings per share of $6.62 and diluted EPS of $5.11. Because the subsidiary's earnings figure is included separately in the computation of diluted EPS, the individual income of the parent must be identified in the same manner. Thus, the effect of the equity income, intercompany (downstream) transactions, and amortization are taken into account in arriving at the parent's earnings alone.

## Questions

1. What is a special purpose entity (SPE)?
2. What are variable interests in an entity and how might they provide financial control over an SPE?
3. When is a sponsoring firm required to consolidate the financial statements of its SPE with its own financial statements?
4. A parent company acquires from a third party bonds that had been issued originally by one of its subsidiaries. What accounting problems are created by this purchase?
5. In question 4, why is the consolidation process simpler if the bonds had been acquired directly from the subsidiary than from a third party?
6. When one company's debt instruments are acquired by an affiliated company from a third party, how is the gain or loss on extinguishment of the debt calculated? When should this balance be recognized?
7. Several years ago, Bennett, Inc., bought a portion of the outstanding bonds of Smith Corporation, a subsidiary organization. The acquisition was made from an outside party. In the current year, how should these intercompany bonds be accounted for within the consolidation process?
8. One company purchases the outstanding debt instruments of an affiliated company on the open market. This transaction creates a gain that is appropriately recognized in the consolidated financial statements of that year. Thereafter, a worksheet adjustment is required to correct the beginning balance of the consolidated Retained Earnings. Why is the amount of this adjustment reduced from year to year?
9. A parent acquires the outstanding bonds of a subsidiary company directly from an outside third party. For consolidation purposes, this transaction creates a gain of $45,000. Should this gain be allocated to the parent or the subsidiary? Why?
10. Some preferred stocks possess characteristics that resemble an equity or ownership interest. Others, however, demonstrate traits similar to a debt instrument. How is the distinction drawn as to whether the preferred stock is actually an equity or a debt?
11. Perkins Company acquires 90 percent of the outstanding common stock of the Butterfly Corporation as well as 55 percent of its preferred stock. Because of the rights being conveyed, the preferred stock is considered to be a debt-type instrument. How should these preferred shares be accounted for within the consolidation process? How should the book value of Butterfly be allocated between the common and the preferred stock?
12. Assume the same information as in question 11 except that the preferred stock is viewed as an equity interest. How is the preferred stock now accounted for within the consolidation process? How should the book value of Butterfly be allocated between the common and the preferred stock?
13. The income statement and the balance sheet are produced using a worksheet, but a consolidated statement of cash flows is not. What process is followed in preparing a consolidated statement of cash flows?
14. How do noncontrolling interest balances affect the consolidated statement of cash flows?
15. In many cases, consolidated earnings per share is computed based on consolidated net income and parent company shares and convertibles. However, a different process must be used for some business combinations. When is this alternative approach required?
16. A subsidiary has (1) a convertible preferred stock and (2) a convertible bond. How are these items factored into the computation of earnings per share for the business combination?
17. Why might a subsidiary decide to issue new shares of common stock to parties outside of the business combination?
18. Washburn Company owns 75 percent of the outstanding common stock of Metcalf Company. During the current year, Metcalf issues additional shares to outside parties at a price more than book value. How does this transaction affect the business combination? How is this impact recorded within the consolidated statements?

19. Assume the same information as in question 18 except that the new shares are issued primarily to Washburn. How does this transaction affect the business combination?
20. Assume the same information as in question 18 except that Metcalf issues a 10 percent stock dividend instead of selling new shares of stock. How does this transaction affect the business combination?
21. If a parent must increase its investment because a subsidiary issues additional shares of stock, in what two ways can the adjustment be recorded?

## Problems

1. A subsidiary has a debt outstanding that was originally issued at a discount. At the beginning of the current year, the debt was acquired at a slight premium from outside parties by the parent company. Which of the following statements is true?
   a. Whether the balances agree or not, both the subsequent interest income and interest expense should be reported in a consolidated income statement.
   b. The interest income and interest expense will agree in amount and should be offset for consolidation purposes.
   c. In computing any noncontrolling interest allocation, the interest income should be included but not the interest expense.
   d. Although subsequent interest income and interest expense will not agree in amount, both balances should be eliminated for consolidation purposes.
2. A bond that had been issued by a parent company at a discount was acquired several years ago by its subsidiary from an outside party at a premium. Which of the following statements is true?
   a. The bond has no impact on a current consolidation because the acquisition was made in the past.
   b. The original loss would be reported in the current year's consolidated income statement.
   c. For consolidation purposes, retained earnings must be reduced at the beginning of the current year but by an amount smaller than the original loss.
   d. The various interest balances exactly offset so that no adjustment to retained earnings or to income is necessary.
3. A parent company acquires all of a subsidiary's common stock but only 70 percent of its preferred shares. This preferred stock is callable and pays a 7 percent annual cumulative dividend. No dividends are in arrears at the current time. How is the noncontrolling interest's share of the subsidiary's income computed?
   a. As 30 percent of the subsidiary's preferred dividend.
   b. No allocation is made since the dividends have been paid.
   c. As 30 percent of the subsidiary's income after all dividends have been subtracted.
   d. Income is assigned to the preferred stock based on total par value and 30 percent of that amount is allocated to the noncontrolling interest.
4. Aceton Corporation owns 80 percent of the outstanding stock of Voctax, Inc. During the current year, Voctax made $140,000 in sales to Aceton. How does this transfer affect the consolidated statement of cash flows?
   a. The transaction should be included if payment has been made.
   b. Only 80 percent of the transfers should be included because the sales were made by the subsidiary.
   c. Because the transfers were from a subsidiary organization, the cash flows are reported as investing activities.
   d. Because of the intercompany nature of the transfers, the amount is not reported in the consolidated cash flow statement.
5. Warrenton, Inc., owns 80 percent of Aminable Corporation. On a consolidated income statement, the Noncontrolling Interest in the Subsidiary's Income is reported as $37,000. Aminable paid a total cash dividend of $100,000 for the year. How is the consolidated statement of cash flows impacted?
   a. The dividends paid to the outside owners are reported as a financing activity, but the noncontrolling interest figure is not viewed as a cash flow.
   b. The noncontrolling interest figure is reported as an investing activity, but the dividends amount paid to the outside owners is omitted entirely.
   c. Neither figure is reported on the statement of cash flows.
   d. Both dividends paid and the noncontrolling interest are viewed as financing activities.

**Questions 6 and 7 are based on the following information:**
Comparative consolidated balance sheet data for Iverson, Inc., and its 80 percent–owned subsidiary Oakley Co. follow:

|  | 2004 | 2003 |
|---|---|---|
| Cash | $ 7,000 | $ 20,000 |
| Accounts receivable (net) | 55,000 | 38,000 |
| Merchandise inventory | 85,000 | 45,000 |
| Buildings and equipment (net) | 95,000 | 105,000 |
| Trademark | 85,000 | 100,000 |
| Totals | $327,000 | $308,000 |
| Accounts payable | $ 75,000 | $ 63,000 |
| Notes payable, long-term | –0– | 25,000 |
| Noncontrolling interest | 39,000 | 35,000 |
| Common stock, $10 par | 200,000 | 200,000 |
| Retained earnings (deficit) | 13,000 | (15,000) |
| Totals | $327,000 | $308,000 |

*Additional Information for Fiscal Year 2004*

- Iverson and Oakley's consolidated net income was $40,000.
- Oakley paid $5,000 in dividends during the year.
- Oakley sold $11,000 worth of merchandise to Iverson during the year.
- There were no purchases or sales of long-term assets during the year.

In the 2004 consolidated statement of cash flows for Iverson Company:

6. Net cash flows from operating activities were
   a. $12,000
   b. $20,000
   c. $24,000
   d. $25,000
7. Net cash flows from financing activities were
   a. $(25,000)
   b. $(37,000)
   c. $(38,000)
   d. $(42,000)
8. Thuoy Corporation is computing consolidated earnings per share. One of its subsidiaries has stock warrants outstanding. How do these convertible items affect the consolidated earnings per share computation?
   a. No effect is created since the stock warrants were for the shares of the subsidiary company.
   b. The stock warrants are not included in the computation unless they are antidilutive.
   c. The effect of the stock warrants must be computed in deriving the amount of subsidiary income that is to be included in making the consolidated diluted earnings per share calculation.
   d. The stock warrants are included only in basic earnings per share but never in diluted earnings per share.
9. A parent company owns a controlling interest in a subsidiary whose stock has a book value of $31 per share. At the end of the current year, the subsidiary issues new shares entirely to outside parties at $45 per share. The parent still holds control over this subsidiary. Which of the following statements is true?
   a. Since the shares were all sold to outside parties, the parent's investment account is not affected.
   b. Since the parent now owns a smaller percentage of the subsidiary, the parent's investment account must be reduced.
   c. Since the shares were sold for more than book value, the parent's investment account must be increased.
   d. Since the sale was made at the end of the year, the parent's investment account is not affected.
10. Rodgers, Inc., owns Ferdinal Corporation. For 2004, Rodgers reports net income (without consideration of its investment in Ferdinal) of $200,000 while the subsidiary reports $80,000. The parent had a bond payable outstanding on January 1, 2004, with a book value of $212,000. The subsidiary acquired the bond on that date for $199,000. During 2004, Rodgers reported interest income of $22,000 while Ferdinal reported interest expense of $21,000. What is consolidated net income?
    a. $266,000
    b. $268,000

c. $292,000
d. $294,000

11. Thompkins, Inc., owns Pastimer Company. The subsidiary had a bond payable outstanding on January 1, 2003, with a book value of $189,000. The parent acquired the bond on that date for $206,000. Subsequently, Pastimer reported interest income of $18,000 in 2003 while Thompkins reported interest expense of $21,000. Consolidated financial statements are being prepared for 2004. What adjustment is needed for the Retained Earnings balance as of January 1, 2004?
    a. Reduction of $20,000.
    b. Reduction of $14,000.
    c. Reduction of $3,000.
    d. Reduction of $22,000.

12. Ace Company reports current earnings of $400,000 while paying $40,000 in cash dividends. Byrd Company earns $100,000 in net income and distributes $10,000 in dividends. Ace has held a 70 percent interest in Byrd for several years, an investment that it originally purchased at a price equal to the book value of the underlying net assets. Ace uses the cost method to account for these shares.

    On January 1 of the current year, Byrd acquired in the open market $50,000 of Ace's 8 percent bonds. The bonds had originally been issued several years ago for 92, reflecting a 10 percent effective interest rate. On the date of purchase, the book value of the bonds payable was $48,300. Byrd paid $46,600 based on a 12 percent effective interest rate over the remaining life of the bonds.

    What is consolidated net income for this year prior to reduction for the noncontrolling interest's share of the subsidiary's net income?
    a. $492,160
    b. $493,938
    c. $499,160
    d. $500,258

13. Using the same information presented in problem 12, what is the noncontrolling interest's share of the subsidiary's net income?
    a. $27,000
    b. $28,290
    c. $28,620
    d. $30,000

14. Able Company possesses 80 percent of the outstanding voting stock of Baker Company. Able uses the partial equity method to account for this investment. On January 1, 2000, Able sold 9 percent bonds payable with a $10 million face value (maturing in 20 years) on the open market at a premium of $600,000. On January 1, 2003, Baker acquired 40 percent of these same bonds from an outside party at 96.6 of face value. Both companies use the straight-line method of amortization. For a 2004 consolidation, what adjustment should be made to Able's beginning Retained Earnings as a result of this bond acquisition?
    a. $320,000 increase
    b. $326,000 increase
    c. $331,000 increase
    d. $340,000 increase

15. Top Company spent a total of $4,384,000 to acquire control over Bottom Company. This price was based on paying $424,000 for 20 percent of Bottom's preferred stock and $3,960,000 for 90 percent of its outstanding common stock. As of the date of purchase, Bottom's stockholders' equity accounts were as follows:

| | |
|---|---|
| Preferred stock—9%, $100 par value, cumulative and participating; 10,000 shares outstanding | $1,000,000 |
| Common stock—$50 par value; 40,000 shares outstanding | 2,000,000 |
| Retained earnings | 3,000,000 |
| Total stockholders' equity | $6,000,000 |

The owners of the preferred stock vote on any issues considered by the owners of the common stock.
    Top believes that all of Bottom's accounts are correctly valued within the company's financial statements. What amount of consolidated goodwill should be recognized?
    a. $300,000
    b. $316,000

c. $364,000
d. $384,000

16. On January 1, 2004, Mitchell Company has a net book value of $1,500,000 as follows:

| | |
|---|---:|
| 1,000 shares of preferred stock; par value $100 per share; cumulative, nonparticipating, nonvoting; call value $108 per share | $ 100,000 |
| 20,000 shares of common stock; par value $40 per share | 800,000 |
| Retained earnings | 600,000 |
| Total | $1,500,000 |

Andrews Company acquires all of the outstanding preferred shares for $106,000 and 60 percent of the common stock for $916,400. Andrews believed that one of Mitchell's buildings, with a 12-year life, was undervalued on the company's financial records by $50,000.

What amount of consolidated goodwill would be recognized from this purchase?

a. $50,000
b. $51,200
c. $52,400
d. $56,000

17. Aedion Company owns control over Breedlove, Inc. Aedion reports sales of $300,000 during 2004 while Breedlove reports $200,000. Inventory costing $20,000 was transferred from Breedlove to Aedion (upstream) during the year for $40,000. Of this amount, 25 percent is still in ending inventory at year's end. Total receivables on the consolidated balance sheet were $80,000 at the first of the year and $110,000 at year-end. No intercompany debt existed at the beginning or ending of the year. Using the direct approach, what is the consolidated amount of cash collected by the business combination from its customers?

a. $430,000
b. $460,000
c. $490,000
d. $510,000

18. Ames owns 100 percent of Nestlum, Inc. Although the Investment in Nestlum account has a balance of $596,000, the subsidiary's 12,000 shares have an underlying book value of only $40 per share. On January 1, 2004, Nestlum issues 3,000 new shares to the public for $50 per share. How does this transaction affect the Investment in Nestlum account?

a. It is not affected since the shares were sold to outside parties.
b. It should be increased by $24,000.
c. It should be decreased by $119,200.
d. It should be increased by $30,000.

19. The following describes a set of arrangements between TecPC Company and a special purpose entity as of December 31, 2004:

TecPC Company has entered into agreements with a special purpose entity (SPE) to develop, construct, finance, and lease a computer chip research and development (R&D) facility. The SPE will own the R&D facility and lease it to TecPC Company after construction is completed. Payments under the operating lease are expected to commence in the first quarter of 2006.

The SPE has an aggregate financing commitment from equity and debt participants (Investors) of $4 million and $42 million, respectively. TecPC Company, in its role as construction agent for the SPE, is responsible for completing construction by December 31, 2005. In the event the project is terminated before completion of construction, TecPC Company has the option to either purchase the project for 100% of project costs or terminate the project and make a payment to the SPE for 89.9% of project costs. Total project cost is estimated at $48 million.

The term of the operating lease between the SPE and the TecPC Company is five years with multiple extension options. The lease is a variable rate obligation indexed to a three-month market rate. Consequently as market interest rates increase, the payments under this operating lease will also increase.

If all extension options are exercised, the total term of the lease would be 35 years. TecPC's lease payments to the SPE are sufficient to provide a return to the Investors. TecPC Company has guaranteed a portion of the obligations of the SPE during the construction and post-construction periods.

At the end of the first five-year lease term or any extension, TecPC Company may

- renew the lease at fair market value subject to Investor approval;
- purchase the facility at its original construction cost; or
- sell the facility, on behalf of the SPE, to an independent third party. If the project is sold and the proceeds from the sale are insufficient to repay the Investors, TecPC Company may be required to make a payment to the SPE of up to 85% of the project's cost.

a. What is the purpose of a parent company consolidating its financial statements with a subsidiary?
b. When should an SPE be consolidated into a parent company's financial statements?
c. Identify the risks of the construction project that TecPC has effectively shifted to the owners of the SPE and those risks that remain with TecPC.
d. According to FIN 46 what characteristics of a primary beneficiary does TecPC possess?

20. On December 31, 2004 WideBand Company invests $20,000 in FinCo, a variable interest entity. In contractual agreements completed on that date, WideBand established itself as the primary beneficiary of FinCo. Previously, WideBand had no interest in FinCo. Immediately after WideBand's investment, FinCo presents the following balance sheet:

| | | | |
|---|---|---|---|
| Cash | $ 20,000 | Long-term debt | $120,000 |
| Marketing software | 140,000 | Noncontrolling interest | 60,000 |
| Computer equipment | 40,000 | WideBand equity interest | 20,000 |
| Total assets | $200,000 | Total liabilities and equity | $200,000 |

Each of the above amounts represents an assessed fair market value at December 31, 2004 except for the marketing software.

a. If the marketing software was undervalued by $20,000, what reported amounts for FinCo's financial statement items would appear in WideBand's December 31, 2004 consolidated balance sheet and income statement?
b. If the marketing software was overvalued by $20,000, what reported amounts for FinCo's financial statement items would appear in WideBand's December 31, 2004 consolidated balance sheet and income statement?

**Problems 21 through 23 are based on the following information:**

Chapman Company purchases 80 percent of the common stock of Russell Company on January 1, 1998, when Russell has the following stockholders' equity accounts:

| | |
|---|---|
| Common stock—40,000 shares outstanding | $100,000 |
| Additional paid-in capital | 75,000 |
| Retained earnings | 340,000 |
| Total stockholders' equity | $515,000 |

To acquire this interest in Russell, Chapman pays a total of $487,000 with any excess cost being allocated to goodwill.

On January 1, 2004, Russell reports a net book value of $795,000. Chapman has accrued the increase in Russell's book value through application of the equity method.

The following problems should be viewed as independent situations.

21. On January 1, 2004, Russell issues 10,000 additional shares of common stock for $25 per share. Chapman acquires 8,000 of these shares. How will this transaction affect the Additional Paid-In Capital account of the parent company?
a. Has no effect on it.
b. Increases it by $20,500.

c. Increases it by $36,400.
d. Increases it by $82,300.

22. On January 1, 2004, Russell issues 10,000 additional shares of common stock for $15 per share. Chapman does not acquire any of this newly issued stock. How would this transaction affect the Additional Paid-In Capital account of the parent company?
   a. Has no effect on it.
   b. Increases it by $16,600.
   c. Decreases it by $31,200.
   d. Decreases it by $48,750.

23. On January 1, 2004, Russell reacquires 8,000 of the outstanding shares of its own common stock for $24 per share. None of these shares belonged to Chapman. How would this transaction affect the Additional Paid-In Capital account of the parent company?
   a. Has no effect on it.
   b. Decreases it by $22,000.
   c. Decreases it by $30,500.
   d. Decreases it by $33,000.

24. Darges owns 51 percent of the voting stock of Walrus, Inc. The parent's interest was acquired several years ago on the date that the subsidiary was formed. Consequently, no goodwill or other allocation was recorded in connection with the purchase price.

   On January 1, 2002, Walrus sold $1,000,000 in 10-year bonds to the public at 105. The bonds had a cash interest rate of 9 percent payable every December 31. Darges acquired 40 percent of these bonds on January 1, 2004, for 96 percent of face value. Both companies utilize the straight-line method of amortization.
   a. What consolidation entry would be recorded in connection with these intercompany bonds on December 31, 2004?
   b. What consolidation entry would be recorded in connection with these intercompany bonds on December 31, 2005?
   c. What consolidation entry would be recorded in connection with these intercompany bonds on December 31, 2006?

25. Highlight, Inc., owns all of the outstanding stock of Kiort Corporation. The two companies report the following balances for the year ending December 31, 2004:

| | Highlight | Kiort |
|---|---|---|
| Revenues and interest income | $670,000 | $390,000 |
| Operating and interest expense | (540,000) | (221,000) |
| Other gains and losses | 120,000 | 32,000 |
| Net income | $250,000 | $201,000 |

   On January 1, 2004, Highlight acquired bonds on the open market for $108,000 originally issued by Kiort. This investment had an effective rate of 8 percent. The bonds had a face value of $100,000 and a cash interest rate of 9 percent. At the date of acquisition, these bonds were shown as liabilities by Kiort with a book value of $84,000 (based on an effective rate of 11 percent). Determine the balances that should appear on a consolidated income statement for 2004.

26. Several years ago Absalom, Inc., sold $800,000 in bonds to the public. Annual cash interest of 8 percent ($64,000) was to be paid on this debt. The bonds were issued at a discount to yield 10 percent. At the beginning of 2004, McDowell Corporation (a wholly owned subsidiary of Absalom) purchased $100,000 of these bonds on the open market for $121,655, a price that was based on an effective interest rate of 6 percent. The bond liability had a book value on that date of $668,778.
   a. What consolidation entry would be required for these bonds on December 31, 2004?
   b. What consolidation entry would be required for these bonds on December 31, 2006?

27. Opus, Incorporated, owns 90 percent of Bloom Company. On December 31, 2004, Opus acquires half of Bloom's $500,000 in outstanding bonds. These bonds had been sold on the open market on January 1, 2002, at a 12 percent effective rate. The bonds pay a cash interest rate of 10 percent every December 31 and are scheduled to come due on December 31, 2012. Bloom issued this debt originally for $435,763. Opus paid $283,550 for this investment indicating an 8 percent effective yield.

a. Assuming that both parties use the effective rate method, what gain or loss should be reported on the consolidated income statement for 2004 from the retirement of this debt?
b. Assuming that both parties use the effective rate method, what balances should appear in the Investment in Bloom Bonds account on Opus's records and the Bonds Payable account of Bloom as of December 31, 2005?
c. Assuming that both parties use the straight-line method, what consolidation entry would be required on December 31, 2005, because of these bonds? Assume that the parent is not applying the equity method.

28. Hapinst Corporation has the following stockholders' equity accounts:

| | |
|---|---|
| Preferred stock (6% cumulative dividend) | $500,000 |
| Common stock | 750,000 |
| Additional paid-in capital | 300,000 |
| Retained earnings | 950,000 |

The preferred stock is participating and, therefore, is considered an equity instrument. Westyln Corporation buys 90 percent of this common stock for $1,600,000 and 70 percent of the preferred stock for $800,000. All of the subsidiary's assets and liabilities are viewed as having market values equal to their book values. What amount is attributed to goodwill on the date of acquisition?

29. Mace, Inc., acquires 90 percent of the outstanding common stock of Blade Company from the company's president for $2,520,000 and 40 percent of the preferred stock for $250,000. On the date of purchase, Blade had the following stockholders' equity accounts:

| | |
|---|---|
| Common stock | $ 800,000 |
| Preferred stock | 200,000 |
| Retained earnings | 2,000,000 |
| Total | $3,000,000 |

a. Assume that the preferred stock is both cumulative and fully participating and is, therefore, considered an equity interest. What is the total amount of goodwill to be recognized within consolidated financial statements?
b. Assume that the preferred stock is callable at 120 percent of par value and is, therefore, considered a debt instrument. What is the total amount of goodwill to be recognized within consolidated financial statements?
c. Assume that the preferred stock is callable at 120 percent of par value and is, therefore, considered a debt instrument. What is the total value assigned to the noncontrolling interest on the date of acquisition?

30. Smith, Inc., has the following stockholders' equity accounts as of January 1, 2004:

| | |
|---|---|
| Preferred stock—$100 par, nonvoting and nonparticipating, 8 percent cumulative dividend | $ 2,000,000 |
| Common stock—$20 par value | 4,000,000 |
| Retained earnings | 10,000,000 |

Haried Company purchases all of the common stock of Smith on January 1, 2004, for $14,040,000. The preferred stock (which is callable at 108) remains in the hands of outside parties. Any excess purchase price will be assigned to franchise contracts with a 40-year life.

During 2004, Smith reports earning $450,000 in net income and pays $360,000 in cash dividends. Haried applies the equity method to this investment.
a. What is the noncontrolling interest's share of consolidated net income for this period?
b. What is the balance in the Investment in Smith account as of December 31, 2004?
c. What consolidation entries would be needed for 2004?

31. Through the payment of $10,468,000 in cash, Drexel Company acquires voting control over Young Company. This price was paid for 60 percent of the subsidiary's 100,000 outstanding common shares ($40 par value) as well as all 10,000 shares of 8 percent, cumulative, $100 par value preferred stock. Of the total payment, $3.1 million was attributed to the fully participating and fully voting preferred stock with the remainder paid for the common. This purchase is carried out on January 1, 2004, when Young reports retained earnings of $10 million and a total book value of $15 million. On this same date, a building owned by Young (with a 5-year remaining life) is undervalued in the financial records by $200,000, while equipment with a 10-year life is overvalued by $100,000. Any excess payment is assigned to a brand name with a 20-year life.

    During 2004, Young reports net income of $900,000 while paying $400,000 in cash dividends. Drexel has used the cost method to account for both of these investments.

    Prepare consolidation entries that would be appropriate for the year of 2004.

32. The following information has been taken from the consolidation worksheet of Peak and its 90 percent–owned subsidiary, Valley:
    - Peak reports a $12,000 gain on the sale of a building. The building had a book value of $32,000 but was sold for $44,000 cash.
    - The noncontrolling interest in Valley's income is reported as $23,000.
    - Intercompany inventory transfers of $129,000 occurred during the current period.
    - A $30,000 dividend was paid by Valley during the year with $27,000 of this amount going to Peak.
    - Amortization of an intangible asset recognized by Peak's purchase was $16,000 for the current period.
    - Consolidated accounts payable decreased by $11,000 during the year.

    Indicate how each of these events is reflected on a consolidated statement of cash flows.

33. Ames Company and its 80 percent–owned subsidiary, Wallace, have the following income statements for 2004:

    |  | Ames | Wallace |
    | --- | --- | --- |
    | Revenues | $500,000 | $230,000 |
    | Cost of goods sold | (300,000) | (140,000) |
    | Depreciation and amortization | (40,000) | (10,000) |
    | Other expenses | (20,000) | (20,000) |
    | Gain on sale of equipment | 30,000 | –0– |
    | Equity in earnings of Wallace | 48,000 | –0– |
    | Net income | $218,000 | $ 60,000 |

    *Additional Information*
    - Intercompany transfers during 2004 amounted to $90,000 and were downstream from Ames to Wallace.
    - Unrealized inventory gains at January 1, 2004, were $6,000, but at December 31, 2004, unrealized gains are $9,000.
    - Annual amortization expense resulting from the purchase price is $11,000.
    - Wallace paid dividends totaling $20,000.
    - The noncontrolling interest's share of the subsidiary's income is $12,000.
    - During 2004, consolidated inventory rose by $11,000 while accounts receivable and accounts payable declined by $8,000 and $6,000, respectively.

    Using either the direct or the indirect approach, determine the amount of cash generated from operations during the period by this business combination.

34. Parent Corporation owns all 30,000 shares of the common stock of Subsid, Inc. Parent has 60,000 shares of its own common stock outstanding. In 2004, Parent earns income (without any consideration of its investment in Subsid) of $150,000 while Subsid reports $130,000. Annual amortization of $10,000 is recognized each year on the consolidation worksheet based on allocations within the original purchase price. Both companies have convertible bonds outstanding. During 2004, interest expense (net of taxes) is $32,000 for Parent and $24,000 for Subsid. Parent's bonds can be converted into 10,000 shares of common stock; Subsid's bonds can be converted into 12,000 shares. Parent

owns 20 percent of Subsid's bonds. For consolidation purposes, what are basic and diluted earnings per share for this business combination?

35. Primus, Inc., owns all of the outstanding stock of Sonston, Inc. For 2004, Primus reports income (exclusive of any investment income) of $600,000. Primus has 100,000 shares of common stock outstanding. Sonston reports net income of $200,000 for the period with 40,000 shares of common stock outstanding. Sonston also has 10,000 stock warrants outstanding that allow the holder to acquire shares at $10 per share. The value of this stock was $20 per share throughout the year. Primus owns 2,000 of these warrants. What is the consolidated diluted earnings per share?

36. Garfun, Inc., owns all of the stock of Simon, Inc. For 2004, Garfun reports income (exclusive of any investment income) of $480,000. Garfun has 80,000 shares of common stock outstanding. Garfun also has 5,000 shares of preferred stock outstanding that pay a dividend of $15,000 per year. Simon reports net income of $290,000 for the period with 80,000 shares of common stock outstanding. Simon also has a liability for 10,000 $100 bonds that pay annual interest of $8 per bond. Each of these bonds can be converted into three shares of common stock. Garfun owns none of these bonds. Assume a tax rate of 30 percent. What is the consolidated diluted earnings per share?

37. The following separate income statements are for Mason and its 80 percent–owned subsidiary, Dixon:

|  | Mason | Dixon |
|---|---|---|
| Revenues | $ 400,000 | $ 300,000 |
| Expenses | (290,000) | (225,000) |
| Gain on sale of equipment | –0– | 15,000 |
| Equity earnings of subsidiary | 72,000 | –0– |
| Net income | $ 182,000 | $ 90,000 |
| Outstanding common shares | 50,000 | 30,000 |

*Additional Information*
- Amortization expense resulting from the purchase price paid by Mason is $20,000 per year.
- Mason has convertible preferred stock outstanding. Each of these 5,000 shares is paid a dividend of $4.00 per year. Each share can be converted into four shares of common stock.
- Stock warrants to buy 10,000 shares of Dixon are also outstanding. For $20, each warrant can be converted into a share of Dixon's common stock. The fair market value of this stock is $25 throughout the year. Mason owns none of these warrants.
- Dixon has convertible bonds payable that paid interest of $30,000 (after taxes) during the year. These bonds can be exchanged for 20,000 shares of common stock. Mason holds 15 percent of these bonds.

Compute basic and diluted earnings per share for this business combination.

38. Alice, Inc., owns 100 percent of Rughty, Inc. On Alice's books, the Investment in Rughty account currently is shown as $731,000 although the subsidiary's 40,000 shares have an underlying book value of only $12 per share.

Rughty issues 10,000 new shares to the public for $15.75 per share. How does this transaction affect the Investment in Rughty account that appears on Alice's financial records?

39. Davis, Incorporated, acquired 16,000 shares of Maxwell Company several years ago. At the present time, Maxwell is reporting $800,000 as total stockholders' equity, which is broken down as follows:

| | |
|---|---|
| Common stock ($10 par value) | $200,000 |
| Additional paid-in capital | 230,000 |
| Retained earnings | 370,000 |
| Total | $800,000 |

The following cases should be viewed as independent situations:

a. Maxwell issues 5,000 shares of previously unissued common stock to the public for $50 per share. None of this stock is purchased by Davis. What journal entry should Davis make to recognize the impact of this stock transaction?

b. Maxwell issues 4,000 shares of previously unissued common stock to the public for $25 per share. None of this stock is purchased by Davis. What journal entry should Davis make to recognize the impact of this stock transaction?

c. Maxwell issues 5,000 shares of previously unissued common stock for $42 per share. All of these shares are purchased by Davis. How would this transaction affect a consolidation prepared immediately thereafter?

40. On January 1, 2002, Abraham Company purchased 90 percent of the outstanding shares of Sparks Company. Sparks had a net book value on that date of $480,000: common stock ($10 par value) of $200,000 and retained earnings of $280,000. Sparks also possessed a tract of land that was undervalued by $80,000 on its financial statements.

Abraham paid $584,000 for this investment. Any excess payment is assigned to copyrights, which are to be amortized over a 20-year period. Subsequent to the purchase, Abraham applied the cost method to its investment accounts.

In the 2002–2003 period, the subsidiary's book value rose by $100,000. During 2004, Sparks earned income of $80,000 while paying $20,000 in dividends. Also, at the beginning of the year, Sparks issued 4,000 new shares of common stock for $36 per share to finance the expansion of its corporate facilities. None of these additional shares was sold to Abraham and, hence, no entry was recorded by the parent company.

a. Prepare the consolidation entries that would be appropriate for these two companies for the year of 2004.

b. Assume that Sparks actually issued 5,000 new shares of stock (rather than 4,000 shares) at the beginning of 2004 for $25 per share. Abraham purchased 4,500 of these shares and recorded the acquisition at cost. Under these altered circumstances, prepare consolidation entries for 2004.

41. Giant purchases all of the outstanding shares of Little on January 1, 2001, for $460,000 in cash. Of this price, $30,000 was attributed to equipment with a 10-year remaining life and $40,000 was assigned to trademarks that will be expensed over a 20-year period. Giant applies the partial equity method so that income is accrued each period based solely on the earnings reported by the subsidiary.

On January 1, 2004, Giant reports $200,000 in bonds outstanding with a book value of $188,000. Little purchases half of these bonds on the open market for $97,000.

During 2004, Giant begins to sell merchandise to Little. During that year, inventory costing $80,000 was transferred at a price of $100,000. All but $10,000 (at sales price) of these goods were resold to outside parties by year's end. Little still owes $36,000 for inventory shipped from Giant during December.

The following financial figures are for the two companies for the year ending December 31, 2004. Prepare a worksheet to produce consolidated balances. (Credits are indicated by parentheses.)

|  | Giant | Little |
|---|---|---|
| Revenues | $ (639,000) | $ (466,000) |
| Cost of goods sold | 345,000 | 198,000 |
| Expenses | 134,000 | 161,000 |
| Interest expense—bonds | 24,000 | –0– |
| Interest income—bond investment | –0– | (11,000) |
| Equity in income of Little | (118,000) | –0– |
| Net income | $ (254,000) | $ (118,000) |
| Retained earnings, 1/1/04 | $ (345,000) | |
| Retained earnings, 1/1/04 | | $ (361,000) |
| Net income (above) | (254,000) | (118,000) |
| Dividends paid | 155,000 | 61,000 |
| Retained earnings, 12/31/04 | $ (444,000) | $ (418,000) |

*(continued)*

|  | Giant | Little |
|---|---|---|
| Cash and receivables | $ 133,000 | $ 78,000 |
| Inventory | 171,000 | 87,000 |
| Investment in Little | 608,000 | -0- |
| Investment in Giant bonds | -0- | 98,000 |
| Land, buildings, and equipment (net) | 249,000 | 541,000 |
| Total assets | $ 1,161,000 | $ 804,000 |
| Accounts payable | $ (225,000) | $ (166,000) |
| Bonds payable | (200,000) | (100,000) |
| Discount on bonds | 8,000 | -0- |
| Common stock | (300,000) | (120,000) |
| Retained earnings (above) | (444,000) | (418,000) |
| Total liabilities and stockholders' equity | $(1,161,000) | $ (804,000) |

42. Fred, Inc., and Bub Corporation formed a business combination on January 1, 2000, when Fred purchased a 60 percent interest in the common stock of Bub for $310,000 in cash. The book value of Bub's assets and liabilities on that day totaled $300,000. Patents being held by Bub (with a 12-year remaining life) were undervalued by $100,000 within the company's financial records. Any excess indicated by this acquisition is assigned to a customer list to be amortized over a 10-year period.

Intercompany inventory transfers have been made between the two companies on a regular basis. Merchandise that is carried over from one year to the next is always sold in the subsequent period.

| Year | Original Cost to Bub | Transfer Price to Fred | Ending Balance at Transfer Price |
|---|---|---|---|
| 2000 | $ 60,000 | $ 72,000 | $15,000 |
| 2001 | 70,000 | 84,000 | 25,000 |
| 2002 | 80,000 | 100,000 | 20,000 |
| 2003 | 100,000 | 125,000 | 40,000 |
| 2004 | 90,000 | 120,000 | 30,000 |

Half of the 2004 inventory transfers have not been paid for by Fred by the end of the year.

On January 1, 2001, Fred sold $15,000 in land to Bub for $22,000. Bub is still holding this land.

On January 1, 2004, Bub acquired $20,000 (face value) of Fred's bonds on the open market. These bonds had an 8 percent cash interest rate. On the date of repurchase, the liability was shown within Fred's records at $21,386, indicating an effective yield of 6 percent. Bub's acquisition price was $18,732 based on an effective interest rate of 10 percent.

Bub indicated earning a net income of $15,000 within its 2004 financial statements. The subsidiary also reported a beginning Retained Earnings balance of $300,000, dividends paid of $5,000, and common stock of $100,000. Bub has not issued any additional common stock since its takeover. The parent company has applied the equity method to record its investment in Bub.

a. Prepare consolidation worksheet adjustments for 2004.
b. Calculate the 2004 balance for the noncontrolling interest's share of consolidated net income. In addition, determine the ending 2004 balance for noncontrolling interest in the consolidated balance sheet.
c. Determine the consolidation worksheet adjustments needed in 2005 in connection with the intercompany bonds.

43. On January 1, 2004, Mona, Inc., purchased 80 percent of Lisa Company's common stock as well as 60 percent of its preferred shares. Mona paid $65,000 in cash for the preferred stock, which is considered a debt-type instrument (because no voting rights were granted and the stock has a call value of 110 percent of the $50 per share par value). Mona also paid $552,800 for the common stock, a price that recognized franchise contracts of $40,000. This intangible asset is being amortized over a 40-year period. Lisa pays all preferred stock dividends (a total of $8,000 per year) on an annual basis. During 2004, Lisa's book value increased by $50,000.

On January 2, 2004, Mona acquired one-half of Lisa's outstanding bonds payable to reduce the debt position of the business combination. Lisa's bonds had a face value of $100,000 and paid cash interest of 10 percent per year. These bonds had been issued to the public to yield 14 percent. Interest is paid each December 31. On January 2, 2004, these bonds payable had a total book value of $88,350. Mona paid $53,310, an amount indicating an effective interest rate of 8 percent.

On January 3, 2004, Mona sold fixed assets to Lisa. These assets had originally cost $100,000 but had accumulated depreciation of $60,000 when transferred. The transfer was made at a price of $120,000. These assets were estimated to have a remaining useful life of 10 years.

The individual financial statements for these two companies for the year ending December 31, 2005, are as follows:

|  | Mona, Inc. | Lisa Company |
|---|---|---|
| Sales and other revenues | $ 500,000 | $ 200,000 |
| Expenses | (220,000) | (120,000) |
| Dividend income—Lisa common stock | 8,000 | –0– |
| Dividend income—Lisa preferred stock | 4,800 | –0– |
| Net income | $ 292,800 | $ 80,000 |
| Retained earnings, 1/1/05 | $ 700,000 | $ 500,000 |
| Net income (above) | 292,800 | 80,000 |
| Dividends paid—common stock | (92,800) | (10,000) |
| Dividends paid—preferred stock | –0– | (8,000) |
| Retained earnings, 12/31/05 | $ 900,000 | $ 562,000 |
| Current assets | $ 130,419 | $ 500,000 |
| Investment in Lisa—common stock | 552,800 | –0– |
| Investment in Lisa—preferred stock | 65,000 | –0– |
| Investment in Lisa—bonds | 51,781 | –0– |
| Fixed assets | 1,100,000 | 800,000 |
| Accumulated depreciation | (300,000) | (200,000) |
| Total assets | $1,600,000 | $1,100,000 |
| Accounts payable | $ 400,000 | $ 144,580 |
| Bonds payable | –0– | 100,000 |
| Discount on bonds payable | –0– | (6,580) |
| Common stock | 300,000 | 200,000 |
| Preferred stock | –0– | 100,000 |
| Retained earnings, 12/31/05 | 900,000 | 562,000 |
| Total liabilities and equities | $1,600,000 | $1,100,000 |

a. What consolidation worksheet adjustments would have been required as of January 1, 2004, to eliminate the subsidiary's common and preferred stocks?

b. What consolidation worksheet adjustments would have been required as of December 31, 2004, to account for Mona's purchase of Lisa's bonds?

c. What consolidation worksheet adjustments would have been required as of December 31, 2004, to account for the intercompany sale of fixed assets?

d. Assume that consolidated financial statements are being prepared for the year ending December 31, 2005. Calculate the consolidated balance for each of the following accounts:

Franchises
Fixed Assets
Accumulated Depreciation
Expenses

44. Rogers Company holds 80 percent of the common stock of Andrews, Inc., and 40 percent of this subsidiary's convertible bonds. The following consolidated financial statements are for 2004 and 2005:

### Rogers Company and Consolidated Subsidiary

|  | 2004 | 2005 |
|---|---:|---:|
| Revenues | $ 760,000 | $ 880,000 |
| Cost of goods sold | (510,000) | (540,000) |
| Depreciation and amortization | (90,000) | (100,000) |
| Gain on sale of building | –0– | 20,000 |
| Interest expense | (30,000) | (30,000) |
| Noncontrolling interest | (9,000) | (11,000) |
| Net income | $ 121,000 | $ 219,000 |
| Retained earnings, 1/1 | $ 300,000 | $ 371,000 |
| Net income | 121,000 | 219,000 |
| Dividends paid | (50,000) | (100,000) |
| Retained earnings, 12/31 | $ 371,000 | $ 490,000 |
| Cash | $ 80,000 | $ 140,000 |
| Accounts receivable | 150,000 | 140,000 |
| Inventory | 200,000 | 340,000 |
| Buildings and equipment (net) | 640,000 | 690,000 |
| Databases | 150,000 | 145,000 |
| Total assets | $1,220,000 | $1,455,000 |
| Accounts payable | $ 140,000 | $ 100,000 |
| Bonds payable | 400,000 | 500,000 |
| Noncontrolling interest in Andrews | 32,000 | 41,000 |
| Common stock | 100,000 | 120,000 |
| Additional paid-in capital | 177,000 | 204,000 |
| Retained earnings | 371,000 | 490,000 |
| Total liabilities and equities | $1,220,000 | $1,455,000 |

*Additional Information*
- Bonds were issued during 2005 by the parent for cash.
- Amortization of databases amounts to $5,000 per year.
- A building with a cost of $60,000 but a $30,000 book value was sold by the parent for cash on May 11, 2005.
- Equipment was purchased by the subsidiary on July 23, 2005, using cash.
- Late in November of 2005, the parent issued stock for cash.
- During 2005, the subsidiary paid dividends of $10,000.

Prepare a consolidated statement of cash flows for this business combination for the year ending December 31, 2005. Either the direct or the indirect approach may be used.

45. Following are separate income statements for Alexander, Inc., and Raleigh Corporation as well as a consolidated statement for the business combination as a whole.

|  | Alexander | Raleigh | Consolidated |
|---|---:|---:|---:|
| Revenues | $ 700,000 | $ 500,000 | $1,000,000 |
| Cost of goods sold | (400,000) | (300,000) | (495,000) |
| Operating expenses | (100,000) | (70,000) | (190,000) |
| Equity in earnings of Raleigh | 104,000 | –0– | –0– |
| Noncontrolling interest in Raleigh's income | –0– | –0– | (26,000) |
| Net income | $ 304,000 | $ 130,000 | $ 289,000 |

*Additional Information*
- Intercompany inventory transfers are all downstream.
- The parent applies the partial equity method to this investment.
- Alexander has 50,000 shares of common stock and 10,000 shares of preferred stock outstanding. Owners of the preferred are paid an annual dividend of $40,000, and each share can be exchanged for two shares of common stock.
- Raleigh has 30,000 shares of common stock outstanding. The company also has 5,000 stock warrants outstanding. For $10, each warrant can be converted into a share of Raleigh's common stock. Alexander holds half of these warrants. The price of Raleigh's common stock was $20 per share throughout the year.
- Raleigh also has convertible bonds, none of which is owned by Alexander. During the current year, total interest expense (net of taxes) was $22,000. These bonds can be exchanged for 10,000 shares of the subsidiary's common stock.

Determine basic and diluted earnings per share for this business combination.

46. On January 1, 2004, Paisley, Inc., paid $560,000 for all of the outstanding stock of Skyler Corporation. This cash payment was based on a price of $180 per share for Skyler's $100 par value preferred stock and $38 per share for the company's $20 par value common stock. The preferred shares are voting, cumulative, and fully participating; they have no set call value. At the date of purchase, the book values of Skyler's accounts equaled their market values. Any excess payment is assigned to an intangible asset and will be amortized over a 10-year period.

During 2004, Skyler sold inventory costing $60,000 to Paisley for $90,000. All but $18,000 (measured at transfer price) of this merchandise has been resold to outsiders by the end of the year. At the end of 2004, Paisley continues to owe Skyler for the last shipment of inventory priced at $28,000.

Also, on January 2, 2004, Paisley sold equipment to Skyler for $20,000 although it had a book value of only $12,000 (original cost of $30,000). Both companies depreciate such property according to the straight-line method with no salvage value. The remaining life at this date was four years.

The following financial statements are for each company for the year ending December 31, 2004. Determine consolidated financial totals for this business combination.

|  | Paisley, Inc. | Skyler Corporation |
|---|---|---|
| Sales | $ (800,000) | $(400,000) |
| Costs of goods sold | 528,000 | 260,000 |
| Expenses | 180,000 | 130,000 |
| Gain on sale of equipment | (8,000) | –0– |
| Net income | $ (100,000) | $ (10,000) |
| Retained earnings, 1/1/04 | $ (400,000) | $(150,000) |
| Net income | (100,000) | (10,000) |
| Dividends paid | 60,000 | –0– |
| Retained earnings, 12/31/04 | $ (440,000) | $(160,000) |
| Cash | $ 30,000 | $ 40,000 |
| Accounts receivable | 300,000 | 100,000 |
| Inventory | 260,000 | 180,000 |
| Investment in Skyler Corporation | 560,000 | –0– |
| Land, buildings, and equipment | 680,000 | 500,000 |
| Accumulated depreciation | (180,000) | (90,000) |
| Total assets | $ 1,650,000 | $ 730,000 |
| Accounts payable | $ (140,000) | $ (90,000) |
| Long-term liabilities | (240,000) | (180,000) |
| Preferred stock | –0– | (100,000) |
| Common stock | (620,000) | (200,000) |

*(continued)*

|  | Paisley, Inc. | Skyler Corporation |
|---|---|---|
| Additional paid-in capital | (210,000) | –0– |
| Retained earnings, 12/31/04 | (440,000) | (160,000) |
| Total liabilities and equity | $(1,650,000) | $(730,000) |

Note: Parentheses indicate a credit balance.

47. On June 30, 2004, Plaster, Inc., paid $916,000 for 80 percent of the outstanding stock of Stucco Company. At the date of acquisition, Stucco Company closed its books and reported the following assets and liabilities:

| | |
|---|---|
| Cash | $ 60,000 |
| Accounts receivable | 127,000 |
| Inventory | 203,000 |
| Land | 65,000 |
| Buildings | 175,000 |
| Equipment | 300,000 |
| Accounts payable | (35,000) |

On June 30, Plaster allocated the excess of cost of book value of Stucco's net assets as follows:

| | |
|---|---|
| Equipment (three-year life) | $ 75,000 |
| Database (10-year life) | 125,000 |

At the end of 2004, the following comparative (2003 and 2004) balance sheets and consolidated income statement were available:

| | Plaster, Inc. December 31, 2003 | Consolidated December 31, 2004 |
|---|---|---|
| Cash | $ 43,000 | $ 242,850 |
| Accounts receivable (net) | 362,000 | 485,400 |
| Inventory | 415,000 | 720,000 |
| Land | 300,000 | 365,000 |
| Buildings (net) | 245,000 | 370,000 |
| Equipment (net) | 1,800,000 | 2,037,500 |
| Database | –0– | 118,750 |
| Total assets | $3,165,000 | $4,339,500 |
| Accounts payable | $ 80,000 | $ 107,000 |
| Long-term liabilities | 400,000 | 1,200,000 |
| Common stock | 1,800,000 | 1,800,000 |
| Noncontrolling interest | –0– | 209,750 |
| Retained earnings | 885,000 | 1,022,750 |
| Total liabilities and equities | $3,165,000 | $4,339,500 |

(continued)

#### PLASTER, INC. AND SUBSIDIARY STUCCO COMPANY
#### Consolidated Income Statement
#### For the Year Ended December 31, 2004

| | | |
|---|---:|---:|
| Revenues | | $1,217,500 |
| Cost of goods sold | $737,500 | |
| Depreciation | 187,500 | |
| Database amortization | 6,250 | |
| Interest and other expenses | 9,750 | |
| Noncontrolling interest in Stucco's income | 38,750 | 979,750 |
| Net income | | $ 237,750 |

*Additional Information*
- On December 1, 2004, Stucco paid a $40,000 dividend. During 2004, Plaster paid $100,000 in dividends.
- During 2004, Plaster issued $800,000 in long-term debt at par.
- Plaster reported no other asset purchases or dispositions during 2004 other than the acquisition of Stucco.

Prepare a 2004 consolidated statement of cash flows for Plaster and Stucco. Use the indirect method of reporting cash flows from operating activities.

# Develop Your Skills

## EXCEL CASE: INTERCOMPANY BONDS

Place Company owns a majority voting interest in Sassano, Inc. On January 1, 2002, Place issued $1,000,000 of 11 percent ten-year bonds at $943,497.77 to yield 12 percent. On January 1, 2004, Sassano purchased all of these bonds in the open market at a price of $904,024.59 with an effective yield of 13 percent.

### Required:

Using an Excel spreadsheet, do the following:
a. Prepare amortization schedules for the Place Company bonds payable and the Investment in Place Bonds for Sassano, Inc.
b. Using the values from the amortization schedules, compute the worksheet adjustment for a December 31, 2004 consolidation of Place and Sassano to reflect the effective retirement of the Place bonds. Formulate your solution to be able to accommodate various yield rates (and therefore prices) on the repurchase of the bonds.

### Hints:

Present value of $1 = 1/(1 + r)^n$
Present value of an annuity of $1 = (1 - 1/(1 + r)^n)/r$
Where $r$ = effective yield and $n$ = years remaining to maturity

## RESEARCH CASE

1. Find a recent annual report for a firm with business acquisitions (e.g., Compaq, GE, etc.) accounted for under the purchase method. Locate the firm's consolidated statement of cash flows and answer the following:
   - Does the firm employ the direct or indirect method of accounting for operating cash flows?
   - How does the firm account for the balances in balance sheet operating accounts (e.g., accounts receivable, inventory, accounts payable) in determining operating cash flows?

- Describe the accounting for cash paid for business acquisitions in the statement of cash flows.
- Describe the accounting for any noncontrolling subsidiary interest, acquired in-process research and development costs, and any other business combination—related items in the consolidated statement of cash flows.

## FARS RESEARCH AND ANALYSIS CASE

*Financial Interpretation No. 46*, "Consolidation of Variable Interest Entities," references several of the FASB Concepts Statements in motivating the need to identify and consolidate variable interest entities. FIN 46 also expands the traditional definition of control as provided in *Accounting Research Bulletin 51*, "Consolidated Financial Statements." Review the Summary to FIN 46 and explain the following:

- Why the concepts of relevance and reliability are important to the conclusions of FIN 46.
- How the definitions of assets and liabilities relate to the consolidation of a variable interest entity by its primary beneficiary.
- Why a majority voting interest is insufficient evidence of a controlling finanical interest in a variable interest entity.

# Chapter Seven

# Foreign Currency Transactions and Hedging Foreign Exchange Risk

### Questions to Consider

- How does a company that has transactions in a foreign currency determine the amounts to be reported in the financial statements?

- Does a change in the value of a foreign currency asset or liability held by a company represent a gain or loss that should be reported in income?

- What is foreign exchange risk? How does a company become exposed to foreign exchange risk?

- How are foreign currency derivatives such as forward contracts and options used to hedge foreign exchange risk?

- What is hedge accounting? What are the conditions that must be met for hedge accounting to be applied?

- What is the difference in accounting for a cash flow hedge and a fair value hedge?

- How do hedges of foreign currency denominated assets and liabilities, hedges of foreign currency firm commitments, and hedges of forecasted foreign currency transactions differ? How does the accounting for these different types of hedges differ?

Today, international business transactions are a regular occurrence. In its 2001 annual report, Lockheed Martin Corporation reported export sales of $4.1 billion, representing 17 percent of total sales. Even small businesses are significantly involved in transactions occurring throughout the world as evidenced by this excerpt from Cirrus Logic, Inc.'s 2001 annual report: "Export sales to customers located in the Pacific Rim (excluding Japan) were 36 percent, 47 percent, and 40 percent of net sales in fiscal 2001, 2000, and 1999, respectively." Collections from export sales or payments for imported items may not be made in U.S. dollars but in pesos, pounds, yen, and the like depending on the negotiated terms of the transaction. As the foreign currency exchange rate fluctuates, so does the U.S. dollar value of these export sales and import purchases. Companies often find it necessary to engage in some form of hedging activity to reduce losses arising from fluctuating exchange rates. At the end of fiscal year 2001 as part of its foreign currency hedging activities, Corning Incorporated reported outstanding foreign currency forward contracts in the amount of $379 million and foreign currency options totaling $140 million.

This chapter covers accounting issues related to foreign currency transactions and foreign currency hedging activities. To provide background for subsequent discussions of the accounting issues, the chapter begins with a description of foreign exchange markets. The accounting for import and export transactions is then discussed, followed by coverage of various hedging techniques. Because they are most popular, the discussion concentrates on forward contracts and options. Understanding how to account for these items is important for any company engaged in international transactions.

## FOREIGN EXCHANGE MARKETS

Each country uses its own currency as the unit of value for the purchase and sale of goods and services. The currency used in the United States is the U.S. dollar, the currency used in Mexico is the Mexican peso, and so on. If a U.S. citizen travels to Mexico and wishes to purchase local goods, Mexican merchants require payment to be made in Mexican pesos. To make a purchase, a U.S. citizen has to purchase pesos using U.S. dollars. The price at which the foreign currency can be acquired is known as the *foreign exchange rate*. A variety of factors determines the exchange rate between two currencies; unfortunately for those engaged in international business, the exchange rate can fluctuate over time.[1]

## Exchange Rate Mechanisms

Exchange rates have not always fluctuated. During the period 1945–1973, countries fixed the par value of their currency in terms of the U.S. dollar, and the value of the U.S. dollar was fixed in terms of gold. Countries agreed to maintain the value of their currency within 1 percent of the par value. If the exchange rate for a particular currency began to move outside of this 1 percent range, the country's central bank was required to intervene by buying or selling its currency in the foreign exchange market. Due to the law of supply and demand, the purchase of currency by a central bank would cause the price of the currency to stop falling, and the sale of currency would cause the price to stop rising.

The integrity of the system hinged on the U.S. dollar maintaining its value in gold and the ability of foreign countries to convert their U.S. dollar holdings into gold at the fixed rate of $35 per ounce. As the United States began to incur balance of payment deficits in the 1960s, a glut of U.S. dollars arose worldwide and foreign countries began converting their U.S. dollars into gold. This resulted in a decline in the U.S. government's gold reserve from a high of $24.6 billion in 1949 to a low of $10.2 billion in 1971. In that year, the United States suspended the convertibility of the U.S. dollar into gold, signaling the beginning of the end for the fixed exchange rate system. In March 1973, most currencies were allowed to float in value.

Today, several different currency arrangements exist. Some of the more important ones and the countries affected follow:

1. Independent float—the value of the currency is allowed to fluctuate freely according to market forces with little or no intervention from the central bank (Canada, Japan, Sweden, Switzerland, United States).
2. Pegged to another currency—the value of the currency is fixed (pegged) in terms of a particular foreign currency and the central bank intervenes as necessary to maintain the fixed value. For example, 25 countries peg their currency to the U.S. dollar (including the Bahamas and Syria).
3. European Monetary System (euro)—in 1998, the countries comprising the European Monetary System adopted a common currency called the *euro* and a European Central Bank was established.[2] Until 2002, local currencies such as the German mark and French franc continued to exist but were fixed in value in terms of the euro. On January 1, 2002, local currencies disappeared, and the euro became the currency in 12 European countries. The value of the euro floats against other currencies such as the U.S. dollar.

## Foreign Exchange Rates

Exchange rates between the U.S. dollar and most foreign currencies are published on a daily basis in *The Wall Street Journal* and major U.S. newspapers. To better illustrate exchange rates and the foreign currency market, next we examine the exchange rates published in *The Wall Street Journal* for Monday, July 29, 2002, as shown in Exhibit 7–1.

These exchange rates were quoted in New York at 4:00 P.M. Eastern time. The U.S. dollar price for one Argentinian peso on Monday, July 29 at 4:00 P.M. in New York was 0.2740. The U.S. dollar price for a peso at 4:01 P.M. Eastern time in New York was probably something different, as was the U.S. dollar price for a peso in Buenos Aires at 4:00 P.M. Eastern time. These

---

[1] Several theories attempt to explain exchange rate fluctuations but with little success, at least in the short term. An understanding of the causes of exchange rate changes is not necessary to comprehend the concepts underlying the accounting for changes in exchange rates.

[2] Most members of the European Union (EU) are "euro zone" countries. The major exception is the United Kingdom, which elected not to participate. Switzerland is another important European country not part of the euro zone because it is not a member of the EU.

## EXHIBIT 7–1  The *Wall Street Journal* Foreign Exchange Quotes, Monday, July 29, 2002

Source: Reuters

### Exchange Rates

The New York foreign exchange mid-range rates below apply to trading among banks in amounts of $1 million and more, as quoted at 4 p.m. Eastern time by Reuters and other sources. Retail transactions provide fewer units of foreign currency per dollar.

| Country | U.S. $ equivalent Mon. | U.S. $ equivalent Fri. | Currency per U.S. $ Mon. | Currency per U.S. $ Fri. |
|---|---|---|---|---|
| Argentina (Peso)-y | .2740 | .2740 | 3.6500 | 3.6500 |
| Australia (Dollar) | .5412 | .5348 | 1.8476 | 1.8697 |
| Bahrain (Dinar) | 2.6525 | 2.6525 | .3770 | .3770 |
| Brazil (Real) | .3063 | .3331 | 3.2650 | 3.0025 |
| Britain (Pound) | 1.5622 | 1.5655 | .6401 | .6388 |
| 1-month forward | 1.5595 | 1.5628 | .6412 | .6399 |
| 3-months forward | 1.5539 | 1.5572 | .6435 | .6422 |
| 6-months forward | 1.5455 | 1.5485 | .6470 | .6458 |
| Canada (Dollar) | .6363 | .6295 | 1.5717 | 1.5885 |
| 1-month forward | .6357 | .6290 | 1.5730 | 1.5898 |
| 3-months forward | .6345 | .6278 | 1.5761 | 1.5928 |
| 6-months forward | 6327 | .6260 | 1.5806 | 1.5974 |
| Chile (Peso) | .001431 | .001433 | 699.05 | 697.75 |
| China (Renminbi) | .1208 | .1208 | 8.2767 | 8.2768 |
| Colombia (Peso) | .0003836 | .0003842 | 2606.75 | 2602.70 |
| Czech. Rep. (Koruna) | | | | |
| Commercial rate | .03229 | .03233 | 30.970 | 30.930 |
| Denmark (Krone) | .1318 | .1329 | 7.5880 | 7.5262 |
| Ecuador (US Dollar) | 1.0000 | 1.0000 | 1.0000 | 1.0000 |
| Hong Kong (Dollar) | .1282 | .1282 | 7.8000 | 7.8000 |
| Hungary (Forint) | .004014 | .004034 | 249.10 | 247.90 |
| India (Rupee) | .02053 | .02055 | 48.710 | 48.660 |
| Indonesia (Rupiah) | .0001081 | .0001093 | 9250 | 9150 |
| Israel (Shekel) | .2116 | .2107 | 4.7250 | 4.7450 |
| Japan (Yen) | .008350 | .008412 | 119.76 | 118.88 |
| 1-month forward | .008363 | .008425 | 119.58 | 118.70 |
| 3-months forward | .008389 | .008450 | 119.21 | 118.35 |
| 6-months forward | .008429 | .008487 | 118.65 | 117.83 |
| Jordan (Dinar) | 1.4184 | 1.4184 | .7050 | .7050 |
| Kuwait (Dinar) | 3.3156 | 3.3212 | .3016 | .3011 |
| Lebanon (Pound) | .0006609 | .0006609 | 1513.13 | 1513.00 |
| Malaysia (Ringgit)-b | .2632 | .2632 | 3.8000 | 3.8000 |
| Malta (Lira) | 2.3759 | 2.3861 | .4209 | .4191 |
| Mexico (Peso) | | | | |
| Floating rate | .1031 | .1028 | 9.7015 | 9.7240 |
| New Zealand (Dollar) | .4690 | .4630 | 2.1322 | 2.1598 |
| Norway (Krone) | .1299 | .1300 | 7.6982 | 7.6894 |
| Pakistan (Rupee) | .01680 | .01680 | 59.525 | 59.525 |
| Peru (new Sol) | .2835 | .2831 | 3.5275 | 3.5320 |
| Phillippines (Peso) | .01942 | .01948 | 51.495 | 51.325 |
| Poland (Zloty) | .2414 | .2430 | 4.1425 | 4.1150 |
| Russia (Ruble)-a | .03175 | .03173 | 31.500 | 31.520 |
| Saudi Arabia (Riyal) | .2666 | .2666 | 3.7504 | 3.7504 |
| Singapore (Dollar) | .5657 | .5674 | 1.7677 | 1.7625 |
| Slovak Rep. (Koruna) | .02204 | .02217 | 45.371 | 45.097 |
| South Africa (Rand) | .0989 | .0972 | 10.1110 | 10.2855 |
| South Korea (Won) | .0008403 | .0008472 | 1190.00 | 1180.40 |
| Sweden (Krona) | .1056 | .1059 | 9.4670 | 9.4390 |
| Switzerland (Franc) | .6723 | .6825 | 1.4874 | 1.4653 |
| 1-month forward | .6729 | .6831 | 1.4862 | 1.4640 |
| 3-months forward | .6740 | .6840 | 1.4837 | 1.4620 |
| 6-months forward | .6755 | .6855 | 1.4804 | 1.4588 |
| Taiwan (Dollar) | .02968 | .02986 | 33.690 | 33.490 |
| Thailand (Baht) | .02355 | .02384 | 42.455 | 41.955 |
| Turkey (Lira) | .00000059 | .00000059 | 1691000 | 1690000 |
| United Arab (Dirham) | .2723 | .2723 | 3.6729 | 3.6729 |
| Uruguay (Peso) Financial | .04061 | .04082 | 24.625 | 24.500 |
| Venezuela (Bolivar) | .000752 | .000754 | 1330.50 | 1325.50 |
| SDR | 1.3382 | 1.3378 | .7473 | .7475 |
| Euro | .9801 | .9873 | 1.0203 | 1.0129 |

Special Drawing Rights (SDR) are based on exchange rates for the U.S., British, and Japanese currencies. Source: International Monetary Fund.
a-Russian Central Bank rate. b-Government rate. y-Floating rate.

Source: *The Wall Street Journal*, July 30, 2002, page C–14. Republished with permission of Dow Jones, from *The Wall Street Journal*, July 30, 2002, page C–14; permission conveyed through Copyright Clearance Center, Inc.

exchange rates are for trades between banks in amounts of $1 million or more; that is, these are interbank or wholesale prices. Prices charged to retail customers, such as companies engaged in international business, are higher. These are selling rates, the rates at which banks in New York will sell currency to one another. The prices banks are willing to pay to buy foreign currency (buying rates) are somewhat less than the selling rates. The difference between the buying and selling rates is the spread through which the banks earn a profit on foreign exchange trades.

There are two columns of information for each day exchange rates are published. The first column, U.S. $ equivalent, indicates the number of U.S. dollars needed to purchase one unit of foreign currency. These are known as *direct quotes*. The direct quote for the Swedish krona on July 29 was $0.1056; in other words, one krona could be purchased with $0.1056. The second column, Currency per U.S. $, indicates the number of foreign currency units that could be purchased with one U.S. dollar. These are called *indirect quotes*. Indirect quotes are simply the inverse of direct quotes. If one krona can be purchased with $0.1056, then 9.4670 kroner can be purchased with $1.00. (The arithmetic does not work out perfectly because the direct quotes for the Swedish krona published in *The Wall Street Journal* are carried out to only four decimal points.) To avoid confusion, direct quotes are used exclusively in this chapter.

For each currency, comparative exchange rates for two days are presented. In most cases, there has been a change in the exchange rate from Friday, July 26, 2002, to Monday, July 29, 2002. Some currencies, such as the Canadian dollar, increased in value or appreciated against the U.S. dollar (to $0.6363 from $0.6295). Other currencies, such as the Brazilian real, decreased in value or depreciated against the U.S. dollar (to $0.3063 from $0.3331).

## Spot and Forward Rates

Foreign currency trades can be executed on a spot or forward basis. The *spot rate* is the price at which a foreign currency can be purchased or sold today. In contrast, the *forward rate* is the price today at which foreign currency can be purchased or sold sometime in the future. Because many international business transactions take some time to be completed, the ability to lock in a price today at which foreign currency can be purchased or sold at some future date has definite advantages.

Most of the quotes published in *The Wall Street Journal* are spot rates. In addition, it publishes forward rates quoted by New York banks for the major currencies (British pound, Canadian dollar, Japanese yen, and Swiss franc) on a daily basis. This is only a partial listing of possible forward contracts. A firm and its bank can tailor forward contracts in other currencies and for other time periods to meet the needs of the firm. There is no up-front cost to enter into a forward contract.

The forward rate can exceed the spot rate on a given date, in which case the foreign currency is said to be selling at a *premium* in the forward market, or the forward rate can be less than the spot rate, in which case it is selling at a *discount*. Currencies sell at a premium or a discount because of differences in interest rates between two countries. When the interest rate in the foreign country exceeds the interest rate domestically, the foreign currency sells at a discount in the forward market. Conversely, if the foreign interest rate is less than the domestic rate, the foreign currency sells at a premium.[3] Forward rates are said to be unbiased predictors of the future spot rate.

The spot rate for British pounds on July 29, 2002, indicates that 1 pound could have been purchased on that date for $1.5622. On the same day, the one-month forward rate was $1.5595. By entering into a forward contract on July 29, it was possible to guarantee that pounds could be purchased on August 29 at a price of $1.5595, regardless of what the spot rate turned out to be on August 29. Entering into the forward contract to purchase pounds would have been beneficial if the spot rate on August 29 were more than $1.5595. On the other hand, such a forward contract would have been detrimental if the spot rate were less than $1.5595. In either case, the forward contract must be honored and pounds must be purchased on August 29 at $1.5595.

## Option Contracts

To provide companies more flexibility than exists with a forward contract, a market for *foreign currency options* has developed. A foreign currency option gives the holder of the option *the right but not the obligation* to trade foreign currency in the future. A *put* option is for the sale of foreign currency by the holder of the option; a *call* is for the purchase of foreign currency by the holder of the option. The *strike price* is the exchange rate at which the option will be executed if the holder of the option decides to exercise the option. The strike price is similar to a forward rate. There are generally several strike prices to choose from at any particular time. Foreign currency options can be purchased either on the Philadelphia Stock Exchange or directly from a bank in the so-called over-the-counter market.

---

[3] This relationship is based on the theory of interest rate parity that indicates the difference in national interest rates should be equal to, but opposite in sign to, the forward rate discount or premium. This topic is covered in detail in international financial textbooks.

Unlike a forward contract, for which banks earn their profit through the spread between buying and selling rates, options must actually be purchased by paying an *option premium*. The option premium is a function of two components: intrinsic value and time value. The *intrinsic value* of an option is equal to the gain that could be realized by exercising the option immediately. For example, if a spot rate for a foreign currency is $1.00, a *call* option (to purchase foreign currency) with a strike price of $0.97 has an intrinsic value of $0.03, whereas a *put* option with a strike price of $0.97 has an intrinsic value of zero. An option with a positive intrinsic value is said to be "in the money." The *time value* of an option relates to the fact that the spot rate can change over time and cause the option to become in the money. Even though a 90-day call option with a strike price of $1.00 has zero intrinsic value when the spot rate is $1.00, it will still have a positive time value if there is a chance that the spot rate could increase over the next 90 days and bring the option into the money.

The value of a foreign currency option can be determined by applying an adaptation of the Black-Scholes option pricing formula. This formula is discussed in detail in international finance books. In very general terms, the value of an option is a function of the difference between the current spot rate and strike price, the difference between domestic and foreign interest rates, the length of time to expiration, and the potential volatility of changes in the spot rate. For purposes of this book, the premium originally paid for a foreign currency option and its subsequent fair value up to the date of expiration derived from applying the pricing formula will be given.

Option quotes reported in *The Wall Street Journal* on July 29, 2002, indicated that an August call option in euros with a strike price of $0.99 could have been purchased by paying a premium of $0.0038 per euro. Thus, the right to purchase 10,000 euros in August 2002, at a price of $0.99 per euro could have been acquired by paying $38 ($0.0038 $\times$ 10,000 euros). If the spot rate for euros in August is more than $0.99, the option would have been exercised and euros purchased at the strike price of $0.99. If, on the other hand, the August spot rate is less than $0.99, the option would not be exercised; instead, euros would be purchased at the lower spot rate. The option contract establishes the maximum amount that would have to be paid for euros but does not lock in a disadvantageous price should the spot rate fall below the option strike price.

## FOREIGN CURRENCY TRANSACTIONS

Export sales and import purchases are international transactions; they are components of what is called *trade*. When two parties from different countries enter into a transaction, they must decide which of the two countries' currencies to use to settle the transaction. For example, if a U.S. computer manufacturer sells to a customer in Japan, the parties must decide whether the transaction will be denominated (payment will be made) in U.S. dollars or Japanese yen.

Assume that a U.S. exporter (Amerco) sells goods to a German importer with payment to be made in euros (€). In this situation, Amerco has entered into a foreign currency transaction. It must restate the euro amount that actually will be received into U.S. dollars to account for this transaction. This happens because Amerco keeps its books and prepares financial statements in U.S. dollars. Although the German importer has entered into an international transaction, it does not have a foreign currency transaction (payment will be made in its currency) and no restatement is necessary.

Assume that, as is customary in its industry, Amerco does not require immediate payment and allows its German customer 30 days to pay for its purchases. By doing this, Amerco runs the risk that the euro might depreciate against the U.S. dollar between the sale date and the date of payment. Then, fewer U.S. dollars are generated from the sale than had the euro not decreased in value and the sale is less profitable because it was made on a credit basis. In this situation Amerco is said to have an *exposure to foreign exchange risk*. Specifically, Amerco has a transaction exposure that can be summarized as follows:

- *Export Sale*—a transaction exposure exists when the exporter allows the buyer to pay in a foreign currency and allows the buyer to pay sometime after the sale has been made. The exporter is exposed to the risk that the foreign currency might depreciate (decrease in value) between the date of sale and the date of payment, thereby decreasing the U.S. dollars ultimately collected.
- *Import Purchase*—a transaction exposure exists when the importer is required to pay in foreign currency and is allowed to pay sometime after the purchase has been made. The importer is exposed to the risk that the foreign currency might appreciate (increase in price) between the date of purchase and the date of payment, thereby increasing the U.S. dollars that have to be paid for the imported goods.

## Accounting Issue

The major issue in accounting for foreign currency transactions is how to deal with the change in U.S. dollar value of the sales revenue and account receivable resulting from the export when the foreign currency changes in value. (The corollary issue is how to deal with the change in the U.S. dollar value of the account payable and goods being acquired in an import purchase.) For example, assume that Amerco, a U.S. company, sells goods to a German customer at a price of 1 million euros when the spot exchange rate is $0.92 per euro. If payment were received at the date of sale, Amerco could have converted 1 million euros into $920,000; this amount clearly would be the amount at which the sales revenue would be recognized. Instead, Amerco allows the German customer 30 days to pay for its purchase. At the end of 30 days, the euro has depreciated to $0.90 and Amerco is able to convert the 1 million euros received on that date into only $900,000. How should Amerco account for this $20,000 decrease in value?

## Accounting Alternatives

Conceptually, the two methods of accounting for changes in the value of a foreign currency transaction are the one-transaction perspective and the two-transaction perspective. The *one-transaction perspective* assumes that an export sale is not complete until the foreign currency receivable has been collected and converted into U.S. dollars. Any change in the U.S. dollar value of the foreign currency is accounted for as an adjustment to Accounts Receivable and to Sales. Under this perspective, Amerco would ultimately report Sales at $900,000 and an increase in the Cash account of the same amount. This approach can be criticized because it hides the fact that the company could have received $920,000 if the German customer had been required to pay at the date of sale. The company incurs a $20,000 loss because of the depreciation in the euro, but that loss is buried in an adjustment to Sales. This approach is not acceptable under U.S. GAAP.

Instead, FASB *Statement No. 52* requires companies to use a *two-transaction perspective* in accounting for foreign currency transactions.[4] This perspective treats the export sale and the subsequent collection of cash as two separate transactions. Because management has made two decisions—(1) to make the export sale and (2) to extend credit in foreign currency to the customer—the income effect from each of these decisions should be reported separately. The U.S. dollar value of the sale is recorded at the date the sale occurs. At that point the sale has been completed; there are no subsequent adjustments to the Sales account. Any difference between the number of U.S. dollars that could have been received at the date of sale and the number of U.S. dollars actually received at the date of payment due to fluctuations in the exchange rate is a result of the decision to extend foreign currency credit to the customer. This difference is treated as a foreign exchange gain or loss that is reported separately from Sales in the income statement. Using the two-transaction perspective to account for its export sale to Germany, Amerco would make the following journal entries:

---

[4] FASB, *Statement of Financial Accounting Standards No. 52*, "Foreign Currency Translation" (Stamford, CT: FASB, December 1981).

| | | | |
|---|---|---|---|
| Date of Sale: | Accounts Receivable (€) . . . . . . . . . . . . . . . . . . . . . . . . . | 920,000 | |
| | Sales . . . . . . . . . . . . . . . . . . . . . . . . . . . . . . . . . . . . . . . . | | 920,000 |
| | To record the sale and euro receivable at the spot rate of $0.92. | | |
| Date of Payment: | Foreign Exchange Loss . . . . . . . . . . . . . . . . . . . . . . . . . | 20,000 | |
| | Accounts Receivable (€) . . . . . . . . . . . . . . . . . . . . . . . . . | | 20,000 |
| | To adjust the value of the euro receivable to the new spot rate of $0.90 and record a foreign exchange loss resulting from the depreciation in the euro. | | |
| | Cash . . . . . . . . . . . . . . . . . . . . . . . . . . . . . . . . . . . . . . . . | 900,000 | |
| | Accounts Receivable (€) . . . . . . . . . . . . . . . . . . . . . . . . . | | 900,000 |
| | To record the receipt of 1 million euros and conversion at the spot rate of $0.90. | | |

Sales are reported in income at the amount that would have been received if the customer had not been given 30 days to pay the 1 million euros, that is, $920,000. A separate Foreign Exchange Loss of $20,000 is reported in income to indicate that because of the decision to extend foreign currency credit to the German customer and because the euro decreased in value, fewer U.S. dollars are actually received.[5]

Note that Amerco keeps its Account Receivable (€) account separate from its U.S. dollar receivables. Companies engaged in international trade need to keep separate payable and receivable accounts in each of the currencies in which they have transactions. Each foreign currency receivable and payable should have a separate account number in the company's chart of accounts.

We can summarize the relationship between fluctuations in exchange rates and foreign exchange gains and losses as follows:

| | | Foreign Currency (FC) | |
|---|---|---|---|
| Transaction | Type of Exposure | Appreciates | Depreciates |
| Export sale | Asset | Gain | Loss |
| Import purchase | Liability | Loss | Gain |

A foreign currency receivable arising from an export sale creates an *asset exposure* to foreign exchange risk. If the foreign currency appreciates, the foreign currency asset increases in U.S. dollar value and a foreign exchange gain arises; depreciation of the foreign currency causes a foreign exchange loss. A foreign currency payable arising from an import purchase creates a *liability exposure* to foreign exchange risk. If the foreign currency appreciates, the foreign currency liability increases in U.S. dollar value and a foreign exchange loss results; depreciation of the currency results in a foreign exchange gain.

## Balance Sheet Date before Date of Payment

The question arises as to what accounting should be done if a balance sheet date falls between the date of sale and the date of payment. For example, assume that Amerco shipped goods to its German customer on December 1, 2004, with payment to be received on March 1, 2005. Assume that at December 1, the spot rate for the euro is $0.92, but by December 31, the euro has appreciated to $0.93. Is any adjustment needed at December 31, 2004, when the books are closed to account for the fact that the foreign currency receivable has changed in U.S. dollar value since December 1?

---

[5] Note that the foreign exchange loss results because the customer is allowed to pay in euros and is given 30 days to pay. If the transaction were denominated in U.S. dollars, no loss would result. Nor would there be a loss if the euros had been received at the date the sale was made.

The general consensus worldwide is that a foreign currency receivable or foreign currency payable should be revalued at the balance sheet date to account for the change in exchange rates. Under the two-transaction perspective, this means that a foreign exchange gain or loss arises at the balance sheet date. The next question then is what should be done with these foreign exchange gains and losses that have not yet been realized in cash. Should they be included in net income?

The two approaches to accounting for unrealized foreign exchange gains and losses are the deferral approach and the accrual approach. Under the *deferral approach,* unrealized foreign exchange gains and losses are deferred on the balance sheet until cash is actually paid or received. When cash is paid or received, a *realized* foreign exchange gain or loss would be included in income. This approach is not acceptable under U.S. GAAP.

*SFAS 52* requires U.S. companies to use the *accrual approach* to account for unrealized foreign exchange gains and losses. Under this approach, a firm reports unrealized foreign exchange gains and losses in net income in the period in which the exchange rate changes. *SFAS 52* says: "This is consistent with accrual accounting; it results in reporting the effect of a rate change that will have cash flow effects when the event causing the effect takes place."[6] Thus, any change in the exchange rate from the date of sale to the balance sheet date would result in a foreign exchange gain or loss to be reported in income in that period. Any change in the exchange rate from the balance sheet date to the date of payment would result in a second foreign exchange gain or loss that would be reported in the second accounting period. Amerco would make the following journal entries under the accrual approach:

| Date | Account | Debit | Credit |
|---|---|---|---|
| 12/1/04 | Accounts Receivable (€) | 920,000 | |
| | Sales | | 920,000 |
| | To record the sale and euro receivable at the spot rate of $0.92. | | |
| 12/31/04 | Accounts Receivable (€) | 10,000 | |
| | Foreign Exchange Gain | | 10,000 |
| | To adjust the value of the euro receivable to the new spot rate of $0.93 and record a foreign exchange gain resulting from the appreciation in the euro since December 1. | | |
| 3/1/05 | Foreign Exchange Loss | 30,000 | |
| | Accounts Receivable (€) | | 30,000 |
| | To adjust the value of the euro receivable to the new spot rate of $0.90 and record a foreign exchange loss resulting from the depreciation in the euro since December 31. | | |
| | Cash | 900,000 | |
| | Accounts Receivable (€) | | 900,000 |
| | To record the receipt of 1 million euros and conversion at the spot rate of $0.90. | | |

The net impacts on income in 2004 are a sale of $920,000 and a foreign exchange gain of $10,000; in 2005, a foreign exchange loss of $30,000 is recorded. This results in a net increase in Retained Earnings of $900,000 that is balanced by an equal increase in Cash.

One criticism of the accrual approach is that it leads to a violation of conservatism when an unrealized foreign exchange gain arises at the balance sheet date. In fact, this is one of only two situations in U.S. GAAP in which it is acceptable to recognize an unrealized gain in income. (The other situation relates to trading marketable securities reported at market value.) Germany, Austria, and several other countries more strictly adhere to the concept of conservatism than does the United States. In those countries, if at the balance sheet date the exchange rate has changed so that an unrealized gain arises, the change in exchange rate is ignored, and

---

[6] *SFAS 52,* para. 124.

the foreign currency account receivable or payable continues to be carried on the balance sheet at the exchange rate that existed at the date of the transaction. On the other hand, if the exchange rate had changed to cause a foreign exchange loss, the accounting receivable would be revalued, and an unrealized loss would have been recorded and reported in income. This is a classic application of conservatism.

*SFAS 52* requires restatement at the balance sheet date of all foreign currency assets and liabilities carried on a company's books. In addition to foreign currency payables and receivables arising from import and export transactions, companies might have dividends receivable from foreign subsidiaries, loans payable to foreign lenders, or lease payments receivable from foreign customers that are denominated in a foreign currency and therefore must be restated at the balance sheet date. Each of these foreign currency denominated assets and liabilities is exposed to foreign exchange risk; therefore, fluctuation in the exchange rate results in foreign exchange gains and losses.

Many U.S. companies report foreign exchange gains and losses on the income statement in a line item often titled Other Income (Expense). Other incidental gains and losses such as gains and losses on sales of assets would be included in this line item as well. *SFAS 52* requires companies to disclose the magnitude of foreign exchange gains and losses if material. For example, in the Notes to Financial Statements in its 2001 annual report, Merck indicated that the income statement item Other (Income) Expense, Net included exchange gains of $3.5 million, $34.4 million, and $27.2 million in 2001, 2000, and 1999, respectively.

## HEDGING FOREIGN EXCHANGE RISK

In the preceding example, Amerco has an asset exposure in euros when it sells goods to the German customer and allows the customer three months to pay for its purchase. If the euro depreciates over the next three months, Amerco will incur a foreign exchange loss. For many companies, the uncertainty of not knowing exactly how many U.S. dollars will be received on an export sale is of great concern. To avoid this uncertainty, companies often use foreign currency derivatives to hedge against the effect of unfavorable changes in the value of foreign currencies. The two most common derivatives used to hedge foreign exchange risk are *foreign currency forward contracts* and *foreign currency options*. Through a forward contract, Amerco can lock in the price at which it will sell the euros it receives in three months. An option establishes a price at which Amerco will be able, but is not required, to sell the euros it receives in three months. If Amerco enters into a forward contract or purchases an option on the date the sale is made, the derivative is being used as a *hedge of a recognized foreign currency denominated asset* (the euro account receivable).

Companies engaged in foreign currency activities often enter into hedging arrangements as soon as a noncancelable sales order is received or a noncancelable purchase order is placed. A noncancelable order that specifies the foreign currency price and date of delivery is known as a *foreign currency firm commitment*. Assume that, on June 1, Amerco accepts an order to sell parts to a customer in Korea at a price of 5 million Korean won. The parts will be delivered and payment will be received on August 15. On June 1, before the sale has been made, Amerco enters into a forward contract to sell 5 million Korean won on August 15. In this case, Amerco is using a foreign currency derivative as a *hedge of an unrecognized foreign currency firm commitment*.

Some companies have foreign currency transactions that occur on a regular basis and can be reliably forecasted. For example, Amerco regularly purchases materials from a supplier in Hong Kong for which it pays in Hong Kong dollars. Even if Amerco has no contract to make future purchases, it has an exposure to foreign currency risk if it plans to continue making purchases from the Hong Kong supplier. Assume that, on October 1, Amerco forecasts that it will make a purchase from the Hong Kong supplier in one month. To hedge against a possible increase in the price of the Hong Kong dollar, Amerco acquires a call option on October 1 to purchase Hong Kong dollars in one month. The foreign currency option represents a *hedge of a forecasted foreign currency denominated transaction*.

# ACCOUNTING FOR DERIVATIVES

*SFAS 133*, "Accounting for Derivative Instruments and Hedging Activities," which went into effect in 2001, governs the accounting for all derivatives, including those used to hedge foreign exchange risk. In response to concerns expressed by many companies, *SFAS 138*, "Accounting for Certain Derivative Instruments and Certain Hedging Activities," amends *SFAS 133* with respect to the accounting for hedges of recognized foreign currency denominated assets and liabilities.

*SFAS 133* (as amended by *SFAS 138*) provides guidance for hedges of the following sources of foreign exchange risk:

1. Recognized foreign currency denominated assets and liabilities.
2. Unrecognized foreign currency firm commitments.
3. Forecasted foreign currency denominated transactions.
4. Net investments in foreign operations.

Different accounting applies to each different type of foreign currency hedge. This chapter demonstrates the accounting for the first three types of hedge. Hedges of net investments in foreign operations are covered in Chapter 8.

## Fundamental Requirement of Derivatives Accounting

The fundamental requirement of *SFAS 133* (and *SFAS 138*) is that all derivatives be carried on the balance sheet at their fair value. Derivatives are reported on the balance sheet as assets when they have a positive fair value and as liabilities when they have a negative fair value. The first issue in accounting for derivatives is the determination of fair value.

The fair value of derivatives can change over time, causing adjustments to be made to the carrying values of the assets and liabilities. The second issue in accounting for derivatives is the treatment of the gains and losses that arise from these adjustments.

## Determining the Fair Value of Derivatives

The *fair value of a foreign currency forward contract* is determined by reference to changes in the forward rate over the life of the contract, discounted to the present value. Three pieces of information are needed to determine the fair value of a forward contract at any point in time:

1. The forward rate when the forward contract was entered into.
2. The current forward rate for a contract that matures on the same date as the forward contract entered into.
3. A discount rate, typically, the company's incremental borrowing rate.

Assume that Exim Company enters into a forward contract on December 1 to sell 1 million Mexican pesos on March 1 at a forward rate of $0.085 per peso, or a total of $85,000. There is no cost to Exim Company to enter into the forward contract, which has no value on December 1. On December 31, when Exim closes its books to prepare financial statements, the forward rate to sell Mexican pesos on March 31 has changed to $0.082. On that date, a forward contract for the delivery of 1 million pesos could be negotiated that would result in a cash inflow on March 1 of only $82,000. This represents a favorable change in the value of Exim Company's forward contract of $3,000 ($85,000 − $82,000). The fair value of the forward contract on December 31 is $3,000, discounted to its present value. Assuming that the company's incremental borrowing rate is 12 percent per annum, the fair value of the forward contract must be discounted at the rate of 1 percent per month for two months (from the current date of December 31 to the settlement date of March 1). The fair value of the forward contract at January 31 is $2,940.90 ($3,000 × 0.9803).[7]

The manner in which the *fair value of a foreign currency option* is determined depends on whether the option is traded on an exchange or has been acquired in the over-the-counter

---

[7] The present value factor for two months at 1 percent per month is calculated as $1/1.01^2$, or 0.9803.

market. The fair value of an exchange-traded foreign currency option is its current market price quoted on the exchange. For over-the-counter options, fair value can be determined by obtaining a price quote from an option dealer (such as a bank). If dealer price quotes are unavailable, the company can estimate the value of an option using the modified Black-Scholes option pricing model (briefly mentioned earlier). Regardless of who does the calculation, principles similar to those of the Black-Scholes pricing model will be used in determining the fair value of the option.

### Accounting for Changes in the Fair Value of Derivatives

Changes in the fair value of derivatives must be included in *comprehensive income*. The FASB introduced the reporting of comprehensive income in 1997.[8] *Comprehensive income* is defined as all changes in equity from nonowner sources and consists of two components: *net income* and *other comprehensive income*. Other comprehensive income consists of income items that previous FASB statements required to be deferred in stockholders' equity such as gains and losses on available-for-sale marketable securities. Other comprehensive income is accumulated and reported as a separate line in the stockholders' equity section of the balance sheet. The account title *Accumulated Other Comprehensive Income* is used in this book to describe this stockholders' equity line item.

In accordance with *SFAS 133* (as amended by *SFAS 138*), gains and losses arising from changes in the fair value of derivatives are recognized initially either (1) on the income statement as a part of net income or (2) on the balance sheet as a component of other comprehensive income. Recognition treatment depends partly on whether the derivative is used for hedging purposes or for speculation.[9] For speculative derivatives, the change in the fair value of the derivative (the gain or loss) is recognized immediately in net income. The accounting for changes in the fair value of derivatives used for hedging depends on the nature of the foreign exchange risk being hedged and on whether the derivative qualifies for *hedge accounting*.

## HEDGE ACCOUNTING

Companies enter into hedging relationships to minimize the adverse effect that changes in exchange rates have on cash flows and net income. As such, companies would like to account for hedges in such a way that the gain or loss from the hedge is recognized in net income in the same period as the loss or gain on the risk being hedged. This approach is known as *hedge accounting*. *SFAS 133* and *SFAS 138* allow hedge accounting for foreign currency derivatives only if three conditions are satisfied:

1. The derivative is used to hedge either a fair value exposure or cash flow exposure to foreign exchange risk.
2. The derivative is highly effective in offsetting changes in the fair value or cash flows related to the hedged item.
3. The derivative is properly documented as a hedge.

Each of these conditions is discussed in turn.

### Nature of the Hedged Risk

A *fair value exposure* exists if changes in exchange rates can affect the fair value of an asset or liability reported on the balance sheet. To qualify for hedge accounting, the fair value risk must

---

[8] FASB *SFAS 130*, "Reporting Comprehensive Income," issued in June 1997.

[9] Companies can acquire derivative financial instruments as investments for speculative purposes. For example, assume that the three-month forward rate for British pounds is $1.50, and a speculator believes the British pound spot rate in three months will be $1.47. In that case, the speculator would enter into a three-month forward contract to sell British pounds. At the future date, the speculator purchases pounds at the spot rate of $1.47 and sells them at the contracted forward rate of $1.50, reaping a gain of $0.03 per pound. Of course, such an investment might just as easily generate a loss if the spot rate does not move as expected.

have the potential to affect net income if it is not hedged. For example, a fair value risk is associated with a foreign currency account receivable. If the foreign currency depreciates, the receivable must be written down with an offsetting loss recognized in net income. The FASB has determined that a fair value exposure also exists for foreign currency firm commitments.

A *cash flow exposure* exists if changes in exchange rates can affect the amount of cash flow to be realized from a transaction with changes in cash flow reflected in net income. A cash flow exposure exists for (1) recognized foreign currency assets and liabilities, (2) foreign currency firm commitments, and (3) forecasted foreign currency transactions.

Derivatives for which companies wish to use hedge accounting must be designated as either a *fair value hedge* or a *cash flow hedge*. For hedges of recognized foreign currency assets and liabilities and hedges of foreign currency firm commitments, companies must choose between the two types of designation. Hedges of forecasted foreign currency transactions can qualify only as cash flow hedges. Accounting procedures differ for the two types of hedges. In general, gains and losses on fair value hedges are recognized immediately in net income, and gains and losses on cash flow hedges are included in other comprehensive income.

## Hedge Effectiveness

For hedge accounting to be used initially, the hedge must be expected to be highly effective in generating gains and losses that offset losses and gains on the item being hedged. The hedge actually must be effective in generating offsetting gains and losses for hedge accounting to continue to be applied.

At inception, a foreign currency derivative can be considered an effective hedge if the critical terms of the hedging instrument match those of the hedged item. Critical terms include the currency type, currency amount, and settlement date. For example, a forward contract to purchase 100,000 Canadian dollars in 30 days would be an effective hedge of a 100,000 Canadian dollar liability that is payable in 30 days. Assessing hedge effectiveness on an ongoing basis can be accomplished using a cumulative dollar offset method.

## Hedge Documentation

For hedge accounting to be applied, *SFAS 133* requires formal documentation of the hedging relationship at the inception of the hedge (i.e., on the date a foreign currency forward contract is entered into or a foreign currency option is acquired). The hedging company must prepare a document that identifies the hedged item, the hedging instrument, the nature of the risk being hedged, how the hedging instrument's effectiveness will be assessed, and the risk management objective and strategy for undertaking the hedge.

# HEDGES OF FOREIGN CURRENCY DENOMINATED ASSETS AND LIABILITIES

Hedges of foreign currency denominated assets and liabilities, such as accounts receivable and accounts payable, can qualify as either *cash flow hedges* or *fair value hedges*. To qualify as a cash flow hedge, the hedging instrument must completely offset the variability in the cash flows associated with the foreign currency receivable or payable. If the hedging instrument does not qualify as a cash flow hedge or if the company elects not to designate the hedging instrument as a cash flow hedge, the hedge is designated as a fair value hedge. The following summarizes the basic accounting for the two types of hedges now.

## Cash Flow Hedge

At each balance sheet date, the following are required:

1. The hedged asset or liability is adjusted to fair value based on changes in the spot exchange rate, and a foreign exchange gain or loss is recognized in net income.
2. The derivative hedging instrument is adjusted to fair value (resulting in an asset or liability reported on the balance sheet) with the counterpart recognized as a change in Accumulated Other Comprehensive Income (AOCI).

3. An amount equal to the foreign exchange gain or loss on the hedged asset or liability is then transferred from AOCI to net income; the net effect is to offset any gain or loss on the hedged asset or liability.
4. An additional amount is removed from AOCI and recognized in net income to reflect (a) the current period's amortization of the original discount or premium on the forward contract (if a forward contract is the hedging instrument) or (b) the change in the *time value* of the option (if an option is the hedging instrument).

### Fair Value Hedge

At each balance sheet date, the following are required:

1. The hedged asset or liability is adjusted to fair value based on changes in the spot exchange rate, and a foreign exchange gain or loss is recognized in net income.
2. The derivative hedging instrument is adjusted to fair value (resulting in an asset or liability reported on the balance sheet), with the counterpart recognized as a gain or loss in net income.

## FORWARD CONTRACT USED TO HEDGE A FOREIGN CURRENCY DENOMINATED ASSET

We now return to the Amerco example in which the company has a foreign currency account receivable to demonstrate the accounting for a recognized foreign currency denominated asset.[10] In the preceding example, Amerco has an asset exposure in euros when it sells goods to the German customer and allows the customer three months to pay for its purchase. To hedge its exposure to a decline in the U.S. dollar value of the euro, Amerco decides to enter into a forward contract.

Assume that on December 1, 2004, the three-month forward rate for euros is $0.905 and Amerco signs a contract with New Manhattan Bank to deliver 1 million euros in three months in exchange for $905,000. No cash changes hands on December 1, 2004. Because the spot rate on December 1 is $0.92, the euro (€) is selling at a discount in the three-month forward market (the forward rate is less than the spot rate). Because the euro is selling at a discount of $0.015 per euro, Amerco receives $15,000 less than it would had payment been received at the date the goods are delivered ($905,000 vs. $920,000). This $15,000 reduction in cash flow can be considered as an expense; it is the cost of extending foreign currency credit to the foreign customer.[11] Conceptually, this expense is similar to the transaction loss that arises on the export sale. It exists only because the transaction is denominated in a foreign currency. The major difference is that Amerco knows the exact amount of the discount expense at the date of sale, whereas, when it is left unhedged, Amerco does not know the size of the transaction loss until three months pass. (In fact, it is possible that the unhedged receivable could result in a transaction gain rather than a transaction loss.)

Because the future spot rate turns out to be only $0.90, selling euros at a forward rate of $0.905 is obviously better than leaving the euro receivable unhedged: Amerco will receive $5,000 more as a result of the hedge. This can be viewed as a gain resulting from the use of the forward contract. Unlike the discount expense, the exact size of this gain is not known until three months pass. (In fact, it is possible that use of the forward contract could result in an additional loss. This would occur if the spot rate on March 1, 2005, is more than the forward rate of $0.905.)

---

[10] The comprehensive illustration at the end of this chapter demonstrates the accounting for the hedge of a foreign currency denominated liability.

[11] This should not be confused with the cost associated with normal credit risk; that is, the risk that the customer will not pay for its purchase. That is a separate issue unrelated to the currency in which the transaction is denominated.

**EXHIBIT 7–2**
Hedge of a Foreign Currency Account Receivable with a Forward Contract

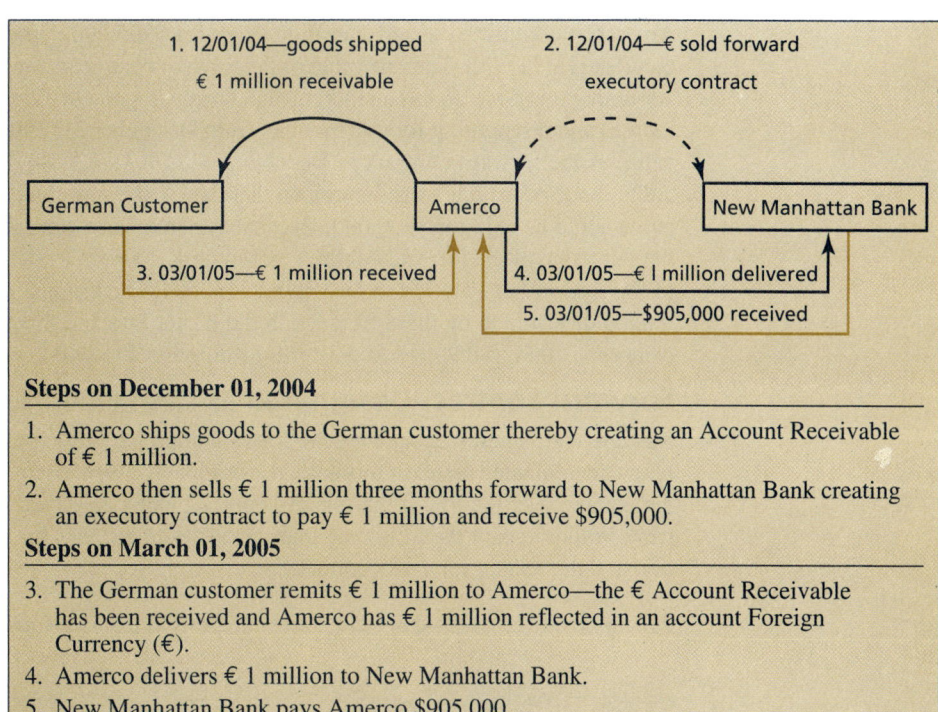

**Steps on December 01, 2004**

1. Amerco ships goods to the German customer thereby creating an Account Receivable of € 1 million.
2. Amerco then sells € 1 million three months forward to New Manhattan Bank creating an executory contract to pay € 1 million and receive $905,000.

**Steps on March 01, 2005**

3. The German customer remits € 1 million to Amerco—the € Account Receivable has been received and Amerco has € 1 million reflected in an account Foreign Currency (€).
4. Amerco delivers € 1 million to New Manhattan Bank.
5. New Manhattan Bank pays Amerco $905,000.

Amerco must account for its foreign currency transaction and the related forward contract simultaneously but separately. The process can be better understood by referring to the steps involving the three parties—Amerco, the German customer, and New Manhattan Bank—shown in Exhibit 7–2.

Because the settlement date, currency type, and currency amount of the forward contract match the corresponding terms of the account receivable, the hedge is expected to be highly effective. If Amerco properly designates the forward contract as a hedge of its euro account receivable position, hedge accounting may be applied. Because it completely offsets the variability in the cash flows related to the account receivable, the forward contract may be designated as a cash flow hedge. Alternatively, Amerco may elect to account for this forward contract as a fair value hedge.

In either case, Amerco determines the fair value of the forward contract by referring to the change in the forward rate for a contract maturing on March 1, 2005. The relevant exchange rates, U.S. dollar value of the € receivable, and fair value of the forward contract are determined as follows:

| | | Account Receivable (€) | | Forward Rate to 3/1/05 | Forward Contract | |
|---|---|---|---|---|---|---|
| Date | Spot Rate | U.S. Dollar Value | Change in U.S. Dollar Value | | Fair Value | Change in Fair Value |
| 12/1/04 | $0.92 | $920,000 | — | $0.905 | –0– | — |
| 12/31/04 | 0.93 | 930,000 | +$10,000 | 0.916 | $(10,783)* | –$10,783 |
| 3/1/05 | 0.90 | 900,000 | –$30,000 | 0.90 | 5,000† | + 15,783 |

*$905,000 − $916,000 = $(11,000) × 0.9803 = $(10,783), where 0.9803 is the present value factor for two months at an annual interest rate of 12 percent (1 percent per month) calculated as $1/1.01^2$.

†$905,000 − $900,000 = $5,000.

Amerco pays nothing to enter into the forward contract at December 1, 2004, and the forward contract has a fair value of zero on that date. At December 31, 2004, the forward rate for a contract to deliver euros on March 1, 2005, is $0.916. A forward contract could be entered into on December 31, 2004, to sell 1 million euros for $916,000 on March 1, 2005. Because

Amerco is committed to sell 1 million euros for $905,000, the nominal value of the forward contract is $(11,000). The fair value of the forward contract is the present value of this amount. Assuming that Amerco has an incremental borrowing rate of 12 percent per year (1 percent per month) and discounting for two months (from December 31, 2004, to March 1, 2005), the fair value of the forward contract at December 31, 2004, is $(10,783), a liability. On March 1, 2005, the forward rate to sell euros on that date is the spot rate, $0.90. At that rate, 1 million euros could be sold for $900,000. Because Amerco has a contract to sell euros for $905,000, the fair value of the forward contract on March 1, 2005, is $5,000. This represents an increase of $15,783 in fair value from December 31, 2004. The original discount on the forward contract is determined by the difference in the € spot rate and three-month forward rate on December 1, 2004: ($0.905 − $0.92) × € 1 million = $15,000.

## Forward Contract Designated as Cash Flow Hedge

Assume that Amerco designates the forward contract as a *cash flow hedge* of a foreign currency denominated asset. In this case, the original forward discount or premium is allocated to net income over the life of the forward contract using an effective interest method. The company would prepare the following journal entries to account for the foreign currency transaction and the related forward contract:

*2004 Journal Entries—Forward Contract Designated as a Cash Flow Hedge*

| 12/1/04 | Accounts Receivable (€) ............................. | 920,000 | |
|---|---|---|---|
| | Sales ......................................... | | 920,000 |
| | To record the sale and € 1 million account receivable at the spot rate of $.920 (Step 1 in Exhibit 7–2). | | |

No formal entry is made for the forward contract because it is an executory contract (no cash changes hands) and has a fair value of zero (Step 2 in Exhibit 7–2).

A memorandum would be prepared designating the forward contract as a hedge of the risk of changes in the cash flow to be received on the foreign currency account receivable resulting from changes in the U.S. dollar–Euro exchange rate.

| 12/31/04 | Accounts Receivable (€) ............................. | 10,000 | |
|---|---|---|---|
| | Foreign Exchange Gain ........................... | | 10,000 |
| | To adjust the value of the € receivable to the new spot rate of $0.93 and record a foreign exchange gain resulting from the appreciation of the € since December 1. | | |
| | Loss on Forward Contract ............................ | 10,000 | |
| | Accumulated Other Comprehensive Income (AOCI) .... | | 10,000 |
| | To record a loss on forward contract to offset the foreign exchange gain on account receivable with a corresponding credit to AOCI. | | |
| | Accumulated Other Comprehensive Income (AOCI) ......... | 10,783 | |
| | Forward Contract ................................ | | 10,783 |
| | To record the forward contract as a liability at its fair value of $10,783 with a corresponding debit to AOCI. | | |
| | Discount Expense .................................... | 5,028 | |
| | Accumulated Other Comprehensive Income (AOCI) .... | | 5,028 |
| | To allocate the forward contract discount to net income over the life of the contract using the effective interest method with a corresponding credit to AOCI. | | |

The implicit interest rate associated with the forward contract is calculated by considering the fact that the forward contract will generate cash flow of $905,000 from a foreign currency asset with an initial value of $920,000. Because the discount of $15,000 accrues over a three-month period, the effective interest rate is calculated as $[1 - \sqrt[3]{\$905{,}000/\$920{,}000}] = .0054647$. The amount of discount to be allocated to net income for the month of December 2004 is $920,000 × 0.0054647 = $5,028.

The impact on net income for the year 2004 follows:

| | | |
|---|---:|---:|
| Sales | | $920,000 |
| Foreign exchange gain | $ 10,000 | |
| Loss on forward contract | (10,000) | |
| Net gain (loss) | | –0– |
| Discount expense | | (5,028) |
| Impact on net income | | $914,972 |

The effect on the December 31, 2004, balance sheet is as follows:

| Assets | | Liabilities and Stockholders' Equity | |
|---|---:|---|---:|
| Accounts receivable (€) | $930,000 | Forward contract | $ 10,783 |
| | | Retained earnings | 914,972 |
| | | AOCI | 4,245 |
| | | | $930,000 |

### 2005 Journal Entries—Forward Contract Designated as Cash Flow Hedge

| 3/1/05 | Foreign Exchange Loss | 30,000 | |
|---|---|---:|---:|
| |     Accounts Receivable (€) | | 30,000 |
| | To adjust the value of the € receivable to the new spot rate of $0.90 and record a foreign exchange loss resulting from the depreciation of the € since December 31. | | |
| | Accumulated Other Comprehensive Income (AOCI) | 30,000 | |
| |     Gain on Forward Contract | | 30,000 |
| | To record a gain on forward contract to offset the foreign exchange loss on account receivable with a corresponding debit to AOCI. | | |
| | Forward Contract | 15,783 | |
| |     Accumulated Other Comprehensive Income (AOCI) | | 15,783 |
| | To adjust the carrying value of the forward contract to its current fair value of $5,000 with a corresponding credit to AOCI. | | |
| | Discount Expense | 9,972 | |
| |     Accumulated Other Comprehensive Income (AOCI) | | 9,972 |
| | To allocate the remaining forward contract discount to net income ($15,000 − 5,028 = $9,972) with a corresponding credit to AOCI. | | |

(As a result of these entries, the balance in AOCI is zero: $4,245 + $15,783 − $30,000 + $9,972 = $0.)

| | Foreign Currency (€) | 900,000 | |
|---|---|---:|---:|
| |     Accounts Receivable (€) | | 900,000 |
| | To record receipt of € 1 million from the German customer as an asset (Foreign Currency) at the spot rate of $0.90 (Step 3 in Exhibit 7–2). | | |

| | | |
|---|---|---|
| Cash | 905,000 | |
|     Foreign Currency (€) | | 900,000 |
|     Forward Contract | | 5,000 |
| To record settlement of the forward contract (i.e., record receipt of $905,000 in exchange for delivery of € 1 million) and remove the forward contract from the accounts (Steps 4 and 5 in Exhibit 7–2). | | |

The impact on net income for the year 2005 follows:

| | | |
|---|---|---|
| Foreign exchange loss | $(30,000) | |
| Gain on forward contract | 30,000 | |
| Net gain (loss) | | –0– |
| Discount expense | | $(9,972) |
| Impact on net income | | $(9,972) |

The net effect on the balance sheet over the two years is an increase in cash of $905,000 with a corresponding increase in Retained Earnings of $905,000 ($914,972 − $9,972). The cumulative amount in the Discount Expense account of $15,000 reflects the cost of extending credit to the German customer.

The net benefit from having entered into the forward contract is $5,000. This "gain" is reflected in net income as the difference between the net gain on the forward contract and the cumulative amount of discount expense ($20,000 − $15,000 = $5,000) recognized over the two periods.

### *Effective Interest vs. Straight-Line Methods*

Use of the effective interest method results in allocation of the forward contract discount of $5,028 at the end of the first month and $9,972 at the end of the next two months. Straight-line allocation on a monthly basis of the $15,000 discount would result in a reasonable approximation of these amounts:

| | |
|---|---|
| 12/31/04 | $15,000 × ⅓ = $5,000 |
| 3/1/05 | $15,000 × ⅔ = $10,000 |

Determining the effective interest rate is complex and provides no conceptual insights. For the remainder of this chapter, we use straight-line allocation of forward contract discounts and premiums, as is allowed by the FASB's Derivatives Implementation Group. The important thing to keep in mind in this example is that with a cash flow hedge, an expense equal to the original forward contract discount is recognized in net income over the life of the contract.

What if the forward rate on December 1, 2004, had been $0.926 (i.e., the euro was selling at a premium in the forward market)? In that case, Amerco would receive $6,000 more through the forward sale of euros ($926,000) than had it received the euros at the date of sale ($920,000). The forward contract premium would be allocated as an increase in net income at the rate of $2,000 per month: $2,000 at December 31, 2004, and $4,000 at March 1, 2005.

## Forward Contract Designated as Fair Value Hedge

Assume that Amerco decides not to designate the forward contract as a cash flow hedge but as a fair value hedge. In that case, the gain or loss on the forward contract is taken directly to net income, and there is no separate amortization of the original discount on the forward contract.

### *2004 Journal Entries—Forward Contract Designated as a Fair Value Hedge*

| | | | |
|---|---|---|---|
| 12/1/04 | Accounts Receivable (€) | 920,000 | |
| |     Sales | | 920,000 |
| | To record the sale and € 1 million account receivable at the spot rate of $0.920. | | |

The forward contract requires no formal entry. A memorandum is prepared to designate the forward contract as a hedge of the risk of changes in the fair value of the foreign currency account receivable resulting from changes in the U.S. dollar–euro exchange rate.

| 12/31/04 | Accounts Receivable (€) | 10,000 | |
|---|---|---|---|
| |     Foreign Exchange Gain | | 10,000 |
| | To adjust the value of the € receivable to the new spot rate of $0.93 and record a foreign exchange gain resulting from the appreciation of the € since December 1. | | |
| | Loss on Forward Contract | 10,783 | |
| |     Forward Contract | | 10,783 |
| | To record the forward contract as a liability at its fair value of $10,783 and record a forward contract loss for the change in the fair value of the forward contract since December 1. | | |

The impact on net income for the year 2004 is as follows:

| | | |
|---|---:|---:|
| Sales | | $920,000 |
| Foreign exchange gain | $10,000 | |
| Loss on forward contract | (10,783) | |
| Net gain (loss) | | (783) |
| Impact on net income | | $919,217 |

The effect on the December 31, 2004, balance sheet follows:

| Assets | | Liabilities and Stockholders' Equity | |
|---|---:|---|---:|
| Accounts receivable (€) | $930,000 | Forward contract | $ 10,783 |
| | | Retained earnings | 919,217 |
| | | | $930,000 |

### 2005 Journal Entries—Forward Contract Designated as a Fair Value Hedge

| 3/1/05 | Foreign Exchange Loss | 30,000 | |
|---|---|---|---|
| |     Accounts Receivable (€) | | 30,000 |
| | To adjust the value of the € receivable to the new spot rate of $0.90 and record a foreign exchange loss resulting from the depreciation of the € since December 31. | | |
| | Forward Contract | 15,783 | |
| |     Gain on Forward Contract | | 15,783 |
| | To adjust the carrying value of the forward contract to its current fair value of $5,000 and record a forward contract gain for the change in the fair value since December 31. | | |
| | Foreign Currency (€) | 900,000 | |
| |     Accounts Receivable (€) | | 900,000 |
| | To record receipt of € 1 million from the German customer as an asset at the spot rate of $0.90. | | |
| | Cash | 905,000 | |
| |     Foreign Currency (€) | | 900,000 |
| |     Forward Contract | | 5,000 |
| | To record settlement of the forward contract (i.e., record receipt of $905,000 in exchange for delivery of € 1 million) and remove the forward contract from the accounts. | | |

# Discussion Question

**DO WE HAVE A GAIN OR WHAT?**

Ahnuld Corporation, a health juice producer, recently has been expanding its sales through exports to foreign markets. Earlier this year, the company negotiated the sale of several thousand cases of turnip juice to a retailer in the country of Tcheckia. The customer is unwilling to assume the risk of having to make payment in U.S. dollars. Desperate to enter the Tcheckian market, the vice president for international sales agrees to denominate the sale in tchecks, the national currency of Tcheckia. The current exchange rate for tchecks is $2.00. In addition, the customer indicates that he cannot make payment until all of the juice has been sold. Payment is scheduled for six months from the date of sale.

Fearful that the tcheck might depreciate in value over the next six months, the head of the risk management department at Ahnuld Corporation enters into a forward contract to sell tchecks in six months at a forward rate of $1.80. The forward contract is designated as a fair value hedge of the tcheck receivable. Six months later, when payment is received from the Tcheckian customer, the exchange rate for the tcheck is $1.70. The corporate treasurer calls the head of the risk management department into her office.

**Treasurer:** I see that your decision to hedge our foreign currency position on that sale to Tcheckia was a bad one.

**Department Head:** What do you mean? We have a gain on that forward contract. We're $10,000 better off from having entered into that hedge.

**Treasurer:** That's not what the books say. The accountants have recorded a net loss of $20,000 on that particular deal. I'm afraid I'm not going to be able to pay you a bonus this year. Another bad deal like this one and I'm going to have to demote you back to the interest rate swap department.

**Department Head:** Those bean counters have messed up again. I told those guys in international sales that selling to customers in Tcheckia was risky, but at least by hedging our exposure, we managed to receive a reasonable amount of cash on that deal. In fact, we ended up with a gain of $10,000 on the hedge. Tell the accountants to check their debits and credits again. I'm sure they just put a debit in the wrong place or some accounting thing like that.

Have the accountants made a mistake? Does the company have a loss, a gain, or both from this forward contract?

---

The impact on net income for the year 2005 follows:

| | |
|---|---:|
| Foreign exchange loss | $(30,000) |
| Gain on forward contract | 15,783 |
| Impact on net income | $(14,217) |

The net effect on the balance sheet for the two periods is an increase in Cash of $905,000 with a corresponding increase in Retained Earnings of $905,000 ($919,217 − $14,217).

Under fair value hedge accounting, the original forward contract discount is not amortized systematically over the life of the contract. Instead, it is recognized in income as the difference between the foreign exchange Gain (Loss) on the account receivable and the Gain (Loss) on the forward contract, that is, $(783) in 2004 and $(14,217) in 2005. The net impact on net income over the two years is $(15,000), which reflects the cost of extending credit to the German customer. The net gain on the forward contract of $5,000 ($10,783 loss in 2004 and

$15,783 gain in 2005) reflects the net benefit (i.e., increase in cash inflow from Amerco's decision to hedge the euro receivable).

The accounting for a fair value hedge of a foreign currency denominated asset or liability is the same as if the forward contract has been considered a speculative derivative; changes in the fair value of the forward contract are immediately recognized in net income. The only advantage to designating the forward contract as a fair value hedge relates to the disclosures that are made in the notes to the financial statements. If designated as a fair value hedge, the forward contract would be included in the discussion of Amerco's hedging activities. Otherwise, it would be disclosed as a speculative derivative position.

## FOREIGN CURRENCY OPTION USED TO HEDGE A FOREIGN CURRENCY DENOMINATED ASSET

As an alternative to a forward contract, Amerco could hedge its exposure to foreign exchange risk arising from the euro account receivable by purchasing a foreign currency put option. A put option would give Amerco the right but not the obligation to sell 1 million euros on March 1, 2005, at a predetermined strike price. Assume that on December 1, 2004, Amerco purchases an over-the-counter option from its bank with a strike price of $0.92 when the spot rate is $0.92 and pays a premium of $0.009 per euro.[12] Thus, the purchase price for the option is $9,000 (€ 1 million × $0.009).

Because the strike price and spot rate are the same, no intrinsic value is associated with this option. The premium is based solely on time value; that is, it is possible that the euro will depreciate and the spot rate on March 1, 2005, will be less than $0.92, in which case the option will be "in the money." If the spot rate for euros on March 1, 2005, is less than the strike price of $0.92, Amerco will exercise its option and sell its 1 million euros at the strike price of $0.92. If the spot rate for euros in three months is more than the strike price of $0.92, Amerco will not exercise its option but will sell euros at the higher spot rate. By purchasing this option, Amerco is guaranteed a minimum cash flow from the export sale of $911,000 ($920,000 from exercising the option less the $9,000 cost of the option). There is no limit to the maximum number of U.S. dollars that could be received.

As is true for other derivative financial instruments, *SFAS 133* requires foreign currency options to be reported on the balance sheet at fair value. The fair value of a foreign currency option at the balance sheet date is determined by reference to the premium quoted by banks on that date for an option with a similar expiration date. Banks (and other sellers of options) determine the current premium by incorporating relevant variables at the balance sheet date into the modified Black-Scholes option pricing model. Changes in value for the euro account receivable and the foreign currency option are summarized as follows:

| Date | Spot Rate | Account Receivable (€) U.S. Dollar Value | Account Receivable (€) Change in U.S. Dollar Value | Option Premium for 3/1/05 | Foreign Currency Option Fair Value | Foreign Currency Option Change in Fair Value |
|---|---|---|---|---|---|---|
| 12/1/04 | $0.92 | $920,000 | — | $0.009 | $9,000 | — |
| 12/31/04 | 0.93 | 930,000 | + $10,000 | 0.006 | 6,000 | − $ 3,000 |
| 3/1/05 | 0.90 | 900,000 | − 30,000 | 0.020 | 20,000 | + 14,000 |

The fair value of the foreign currency option can be decomposed into its intrinsic value and time value components as follows:

---

[12] The price of the option (the premium) was determined by the seller of the option through the use of a variation of the Black-Scholes option pricing formula.

| Date | Fair Value | Intrinsic Value | Time Value | Change in Time Value |
|---|---|---|---|---|
| 12/1/04 | $ 9,000 | –0– | $9,000 | — |
| 12/31/04 | 6,000 | –0– | 6,000 | – $3,000 |
| 3/1/05 | 20,000 | $20,000 | –0– | – 6,000 |

Because the option strike price is less than or equal to the spot rate at both December 1 and December 31, the option has no intrinsic value at those dates. The entire fair value is attributable to time value only. On March 1, the date of expiration, no time value is remaining, and the entire amount of fair value is attributable to intrinsic value.

### Option Designated as Cash Flow Hedge

Assume that Amerco designates the foreign currency option as a *cash flow hedge* of a foreign currency denominated asset. In this case, the change in the option's time value is recognized immediately in net income. The company prepares the following journal entries to account for the foreign currency transaction and the related foreign currency option.

*2004 Journal Entries—Option Designated as a Cash Flow Hedge*

| 12/1/04 | Accounts Receivable (€) . . . . . . . . . . . . . . . . . . . . . . . . . . . | 920,000 | |
|---|---|---|---|
| |     Sales . . . . . . . . . . . . . . . . . . . . . . . . . . . . . . . . . . . . . . . | | 920,000 |
| | To record the sale and € 1 million account receivable at the spot rate of $0.92. | | |
| | Foreign Currency Option . . . . . . . . . . . . . . . . . . . . . . . . . . . | 9,000 | |
| |     Cash . . . . . . . . . . . . . . . . . . . . . . . . . . . . . . . . . . . . . . . . | | 9,000 |
| | To record the purchase of the foreign currency option as an asset at its fair value of $9,000. | | |
| 12/31/04 | Accounts Receivable (€) . . . . . . . . . . . . . . . . . . . . . . . . . . . | 10,000 | |
| |     Foreign Exchange Gain . . . . . . . . . . . . . . . . . . . . . . . . . . . | | 10,000 |
| | To adjust the value of the € receivable to the new spot rate of $0.93 and record a foreign exchange gain resulting from the appreciation of the € since December 1. | | |
| | Loss on Foreign Currency Option . . . . . . . . . . . . . . . . . . . . . | 10,000 | |
| |     Accumulated Other Comprehensive Income (AOCI) . . . . | | 10,000 |
| | To record a loss on foreign currency option to offset the foreign exchange gain on the € account receivable with a corresponding credit to AOCI. | | |
| | Accumulated Other Comprehensive Income (AOCI) . . . . . . . . . | 3,000 | |
| |     Foreign Currency Option . . . . . . . . . . . . . . . . . . . . . . . . . . | | 3,000 |
| | To adjust the fair value of the option from $9,000 to $6,000 with a corresponding debit to AOCI. | | |
| | Option Expense . . . . . . . . . . . . . . . . . . . . . . . . . . . . . . . . . . | 3,000 | |
| |     Accumulated Other Comprehensive Income (AOCI) . . . . | | 3,000 |
| | To recognize the change in the time value of the option as a decrease in net income with a corresponding credit to AOCI. | | |

The impact on net income for the year 2004 follows:

| | | |
|---|---|---|
| Sales . . . . . . . . . . . . . . . . . . . . . . . . . | | $920,000 |
| Foreign exchange gain . . . . . . . . . . . . | $ 10,000 | |
| Loss on foreign currency option . . . . . | (10,000) | |
| Net gain (loss) . . . . . . . . . . . . . . . . . . | | 0 |
| Option expense . . . . . . . . . . . . . . . . . | | (3,000) |
| Impact on net income . . . . . . . . . . . . | | $917,000 |

The effect on the December 31, 2004, balance sheet is as follows:

| Assets | | Liabilities and Stockholders' Equity | |
|---|---|---|---|
| Cash | $ (9,000) | Retained earnings | $917,000 |
| Accounts receivable (€) | 930,000 | AOCI | 10,000 |
| Foreign currency option | 6,000 | | $927,000 |
| | $927,000 | | |

At March 1, 2005, the option has increased in fair value by $14,000—time value decreases by $6,000 and intrinsic value increases by $20,000. The accounting entries made in 2005 are presented next.

### 2005 Journal Entries—Option Designated as a Cash Flow Hedge

| 3/1/05 | Foreign Exchange Loss | 30,000 | |
|---|---|---|---|
| |     Accounts Receivable (€) | | 30,000 |
| | To adjust the value of the € receivable to the new spot rate of $0.90 and record a foreign exchange loss resulting from the depreciation of the € since December 31. | | |
| | Accumulated Other Comprehensive Income (AOCI) | 30,000 | |
| |     Gain on Foreign Currency Option | | 30,000 |
| | To record a gain on foreign currency option to offset the foreign exchange gain on account receivable with a corresponding debit to AOCI. | | |
| | Foreign Currency Option | 14,000 | |
| |     Accumulated Other Comprehensive Income (AOCI) | | 14,000 |
| | To adjust the fair value of the option from $6,000 to $20,000 with a corresponding credit to AOCI. | | |
| | Option Expense | 6,000 | |
| |     Accumulated Other Comprehensive Income (AOCI) | | 6,000 |
| | To recognize the change in the time value of the option as a decrease in net income with a corresponding credit to AOCI. | | |
| | Foreign Currency (€) | 900,000 | |
| |     Accounts Receivable (€) | | 900,000 |
| | To record receipt of € 1 million from the German customer as an asset at the spot rate of $.90. | | |
| | Cash | 920,000 | |
| |     Foreign Currency (€) | | 900,000 |
| |     Foreign Currency Option | | 20,000 |
| | To record exercise of the option (i.e., record receipt of $920,000 in exchange for delivery of € 1 million), and remove the foreign currency option from the accounts. | | |

The impact on net income for the year 2005 follows:

| | | |
|---|---|---|
| Foreign exchange loss | $(30,000) | |
| Gain on foreign currency option | 30,000 | |
| Net gain (loss) | | –0– |
| Option expense | | (6,000) |
| Impact on net income | | $(6,000) |

Over the two accounting periods, Amerco would report Sales of $920,000 and a cumulative Option Expense of $9,000. The net effect on the balance sheet is an increase in the Cash account of $911,000 ($920,000 − $9,000) with a corresponding increase in the Retained Earnings account of $911,000 ($917,000 − $6,000).

The net benefit from having acquired the option is $11,000. This "gain" is reflected in net income as the net Gain on Foreign Currency Option less the cumulative Option Expense ($20,000 − $9,000 = $11,000) recognized over the two accounting periods.

## Option Designated as Fair Value Hedge

Assume that Amerco decides not to designate the foreign currency option as a cash flow hedge but to treat it as a fair value hedge. In that case, the gain or loss on the option is taken directly to net income, and there is no separate recognition of the change in the time value of the option.

*2004 Journal Entries—Option Designated as a Fair Value Hedge*

| | | | |
|---|---|---:|---:|
| 12/1/04 | Accounts Receivable (€) | 920,000 | |
| | Sales | | 920,000 |
| | To record the sale and € 1 million account receivable at the spot rate of $.92. | | |
| | Foreign Currency Option | 9,000 | |
| | Cash | | 9,000 |
| | To record the purchase of the foreign currency option as an asset at its fair value of $9,000. | | |
| 12/31/04 | Accounts Receivable (€) | 10,000 | |
| | Foreign Exchange Gain | | 10,000 |
| | To adjust the value of the € receivable to the new spot rate of $0.93 and record a foreign exchange gain resulting from the appreciation of the € since December 1. | | |
| | Loss on Foreign Currency Option | 3,000 | |
| | Foreign Currency Option | | 3,000 |
| | To adjust the fair value of the option from $9,000 to $6,000 and record a loss on foreign currency option for the change in the fair value of the option since December 1. | | |

The impact on net income for the year 2004 follows:

| | | |
|---|---:|---:|
| Sales | | $920,000 |
| Foreign exchange gain | $10,000 | |
| Loss on foreign currency option | (3,000) | |
| Net gain (loss) | | 7,000 |
| Impact on net income | | $927,000 |

*2005 Journal Entries—Option Designated as a Fair Value Hedge*

| | | | |
|---|---|---:|---:|
| 3/1/05 | Foreign Exchange Loss | 30,000 | |
| | Accounts Receivable (€) | | 30,000 |
| | To adjust the value of the € receivable to the new spot rate of $0.90 and record a foreign exchange loss resulting from the depreciation of the € since December 31. | | |
| | Foreign Currency Option | 14,000 | |
| | Gain on Foreign Currency Option | | 14,000 |
| | To adjust the fair value of the option from $6,000 to $20,000 and record a gain on foreign currency option for the change in fair value since December 31. | | |

| | | | |
|---|---|---|---|
| | Foreign Currency (€) .................................. | 900,000 | |
| |     Accounts Receivable (€) ........................... | | 900,000 |
| | To record receipt of € 1 million from the German customer as an asset at the spot rate of $0.90. | | |
| | Cash ................................................. | 920,000 | |
| |     Foreign Currency (€) ............................. | | 900,000 |
| |     Foreign Currency Option .......................... | | 20,000 |
| | To record exercise of the option (i.e., record receipt of $920,000 in exchange for delivery of € 1 million) and remove the foreign currency option from the accounts. | | |

The impact on net income for the year 2005 follows:

| | |
|---|---|
| Foreign exchange loss ............. | $(30,000) |
| Gain on foreign currency option ..... | 14,000 |
| Impact on net income ............. | $(16,000) |

Over the two accounting periods, Amerco reports Sales of $920,000 and a cumulative net loss of $9,000 ($7,000 net gain in 2004 and $16,000 net loss in 2005). The net effect on the balance sheet is an increase in Cash of $911,000 ($920,000 − $9,000) with a corresponding increase in Retained Earnings of $911,000 ($927,000 − $16,000). The net benefit from having acquired the option is $11,000. This is reflected in net income through the net Gain on Foreign Currency Option ($3,000 loss in 2004 and $14,000 gain in 2005) recognized over the two accounting periods.

The accounting for an option used as a fair value hedge of a foreign currency denominated asset or liability is the same as had the option been considered a speculative derivative. The only advantage to designating the option as a fair value hedge relates to the disclosures made in the notes to the financial statements.

## Spot Rate Exceeds Strike Price

If the spot rate at March 1, 2005, had been more than the strike price of $0.92, Amerco would allow its option to expire unexercised. Instead it would sell its foreign currency (€) at the spot rate. The fair value of the foreign currency option on March 1, 2005, would be zero. The journal entries for 2004 to reflect this scenario would be the same as the preceding ones. The option would be reported as an asset on the December 31, 2004, balance sheet at $6,000 and the € receivable would have a carrying value of $930,000. The entries on March 1, 2005, assuming a spot rate on that date of $0.925 (rather than $0.90), would be as follows:

| | | | |
|---|---|---|---|
| 3/1/05 | Foreign Exchange Loss ............................... | 5,000 | |
| |     Accounts Receivable (€) ........................... | | 5,000 |
| | To adjust the value of the € receivable to the new spot rate of $0.925 and record a foreign exchange loss resulting from the depreciation of the € since December 31. | | |
| | Loss on Foreign Currency Option ...................... | 6,000 | |
| |     Foreign Currency Option .......................... | | 6,000 |
| | To adjust the fair value of the option from $6,000 to $0 and record a loss on foreign currency option for the change in fair value since December 31. | | |
| | Foreign Currency (€) ................................. | 925,000 | |
| |     Accounts Receivable (€) ........................... | | 925,000 |
| | To record receipt of € 1 million from the German customer as an asset at the spot rate of $0.925. | | |

| | | |
|---|---|---|
| Cash | 925,000 | |
|     Foreign Currency (€) | | 925,000 |
| To record the sale of € 1 million at the spot rate of $0.925. | | |

The overall impact on net income for the year 2005 is the same as when the spot rate was less than the strike price of the option:

| | |
|---|---:|
| Foreign exchange loss | $ (5,000) |
| Loss on foreign currency option | (6,000) |
| Impact on net income | $(11,000) |

# HEDGES OF UNRECOGNIZED FOREIGN CURRENCY FIRM COMMITMENTS

In the examples thus far, Amerco does not enter into a hedge of its export sale until the sale is actually made. Assume now that on December 1, 2004, Amerco receives and accepts an order from a German customer to deliver goods on March 1, 2005, at a price of 1 million euros. Assume further that under the terms of the sales agreement, Amerco will ship the goods to the German customer on March 1, 2005, and will receive immediate payment on delivery. In other words, Amerco will not allow the German customer time to pay. Although Amerco will not make the sale until March 1, 2005, it has a firm commitment to make the sale and receive 1 million euros in three months. This creates a euro asset exposure to foreign exchange risk as of December 1, 2004. On that date, Amerco wants to hedge against an adverse change in the value of the euro over the next three months. This is known as a *hedge of a foreign currency firm commitment.* Although *SFAS 133* indicated that only fair value hedge accounting was appropriate for hedges of foreign currency firm commitments, the FASB's Derivatives Implementation Group subsequently concluded that cash flow hedge accounting also could be used. However, because the results of fair value hedge accounting are intuitively more appealing, we do not cover cash flow hedge accounting for firm commitments.

Under fair value hedge accounting, (1) the gain or loss on the hedging instrument is recognized currently in net income and (2) the gain or loss (that is, the change in fair value) on the firm commitment attributable to the hedged risk is also recognized currently in net income. This accounting treatment requires (1) measuring of the fair value of the firm commitment, (2) recognizing the change in fair value in net income, and (3) reporting the firm commitment on the balance sheet as an asset or liability. This raises the conceptual question of how to measure the fair value of the firm commitment. Two possibilities are (1) through reference to changes in the spot exchange rate or (2) through reference to changes in the forward rate. These two approaches are demonstrated in the examples that follow.

## Forward Contract Used as Fair Value Hedge of a Firm Commitment

To hedge its firm commitment exposure to a decline in the U.S. dollar value of the euro, Amerco decides to enter into a forward contract on December 1, 2004. Assume that on that date, the three-month forward rate for euros is $0.905 and Amerco signs a contract with New Manhattan Bank to deliver 1 million euros in three months in exchange for $905,000. No cash changes hands on December 1, 2004. Amerco elects to measure the fair value of the firm commitment through changes in the forward rate. Because the fair value of the forward contract is also measured using changes in the forward rate, the gains and losses on the firm commitment and forward contract exactly offset. The fair value of the forward contract and firm commitment are determined as follows:

| Date | Forward Rate to 3/1/05 | Forward Contract | | Firm Commitment | |
|---|---|---|---|---|---|
| | | Fair Value | Change in Fair Value | Fair Value | Change in Fair Value |
| 12/1/04 | $0.905 | –0– | — | –0– | — |
| 12/31/04 | 0.916 | $(10,783)* | – $10,783 | $10,783* | + $10,783 |
| 3/1/05 | 0.90 (spot) | 5,000† | + 15,783 | (5,000)† | – 15,783 |

*($905,000 − $916,000) = $(11,000) × 0.9803 = $(10,783); where 0.9803 is the present value factor for two months at an annual interest rate of 12 percent (1 percent per month) calculated as $1/1.01^2$.

†($905,000 − $900,000) = $5,000.

Amerco pays nothing to enter into the forward contract at December 1, 2004. Both the forward contract and the firm commitment have a fair value of zero on that date. At December 31, 2004, the forward rate for a contract to deliver euros on March 1, 2005, is $0.916. A forward contract could be entered into on December 31, 2004, to sell 1 million euros for $916,000 on March 1, 2005. Because Amerco is committed to sell 1 million euros for $905,000, the value of the forward contract is $(11,000); present value is $(10,783), a liability. The fair value of the firm commitment is also measured through reference to changes in the forward rate. As a result, the fair value of the firm commitment is equal in amount but of opposite sign to the fair value of the forward contract. At December 31, 2004, the firm commitment is an asset of $10,783.

On March 1, 2005, the forward rate to sell euros on that date is the spot rate, $0.90. At that rate, 1 million euros could be sold for $900,000. Because Amerco has a contract to sell euros for $905,000, the fair value of the forward contract on March 1, 2005, is $5,000 (an asset). The firm commitment has a value of $(5,000), a liability. The journal entries to account for the forward contract fair value hedge of a foreign currency firm commitment are as follows:

*2004 Journal Entries—Forward Contract Fair Value Hedge of Firm Commitment*

| 12/1/04 | No entry records either the sales agreement or the forward contract because both are executory contracts. A memorandum would be prepared to designate the forward contract as a hedge of the risk of changes in the fair value of the firm commitment resulting from changes in the U.S. dollar–euro forward exchange rate. | | |
|---|---|---|---|
| 12/31/04 | Loss on Forward Contract . . . . . . . . . . . . . . . . . . . . . . . . . . . . . . . | 10,783 | |
| |     Forward Contract . . . . . . . . . . . . . . . . . . . . . . . . . . . . . . . . . | | 10,783 |
| | To record the forward contract as a liability at its fair value of $(10,783) and record a forward contract loss for the change in the fair value of the forward contract since December 1. | | |
| | Firm Commitment . . . . . . . . . . . . . . . . . . . . . . . . . . . . . . . . . . . | 10,783 | |
| |     Gain on Firm Commitment . . . . . . . . . . . . . . . . . . . . . . . . . . | | 10,783 |
| | To record the firm commitment as an asset at its fair value of $10,783 and record a firm commitment gain for the change in the fair value of the firm commitment since December 1. | | |

Consistent with the objective of hedge accounting, the gain on the firm commitment offsets the loss on the forward contract, and the impact on 2004 net income is zero. The forward contract is reported as a liability, and the firm commitment is reported as an asset on the December 31, 2004, balance sheet. This achieves the FASB's objective of making sure that derivatives are reported on the balance sheet and ensures that there is no impact on net income.

*2005 Journal Entries—Forward Contract Fair Value Hedge of Firm Commitment*

| 3/1/05 | Forward Contract ................................. | 15,783 | |
|---|---|---|---|
| |     Gain on Forward Contract ..................... | | 15,783 |
| | To adjust the fair value of the forward contract from $(10,783) to $5,000 and record a forward contract gain for the change in fair value since December 31. | | |
| | Loss on Firm Commitment ......................... | 15,783 | |
| |     Firm Commitment ............................. | | 15,783 |
| | To adjust the fair value of the firm commitment from $10,783 to $(5,000) and record a firm commitment loss for the change in fair value since December 31. | | |
| | Foreign Currency (€) ............................. | 900,000 | |
| |     Sales ...................................... | | 900,000 |
| | To record the sale and the receipt of € 1 million as an asset at the spot rate of $0.90. | | |
| | Cash .......................................... | 905,000 | |
| |     Foreign Currency (€) ......................... | | 900,000 |
| |     Forward Contract ............................ | | 5,000 |
| | To record settlement of the forward contract (receipt of $905,000 in exchange for delivery of € 1 million) and remove the forward contract from the accounts. | | |
| | Firm Commitment ................................ | 5,000 | |
| |     Adjustment to Net Income ..................... | | 5,000 |
| | To close the firm commitment as an adjustment to net income. | | |

Once again, the gain on forward contract and the loss on firm commitment offset. As a result of the last entry, the export sale increases 2005 net income by $905,000 ($900,000 in sales plus a $5,000 adjustment to net income). This exactly equals the amount of cash received. In practice, companies might use a variety of account titles for the adjustment to net income that results from closing the firm commitment account.

The net gain on forward contract of $5,000 ($10,783 loss in 2004 plus $15,783 gain in 2005) measures the net benefit to the company from hedging its firm commitment. Without the forward contract, Amerco would have sold the 1 million euros received on March 1, 2005, at the spot rate of $0.90 generating cash flow of $900,000. Through the forward contract, Amerco is able to sell the euros for $905,000, a net gain of $5,000.

## Option Used as Fair Value Hedge of Firm Commitment

Now assume that to hedge its exposure to a decline in the U.S. dollar value of the euro, Amerco purchases a put option to sell 1 million euros on March 1, 2005, at a strike price of $0.92. The premium for such an option on December 1, 2004, is $0.009 per euro. With this option, Amerco is guaranteed a minimum cash flow from the export sale of $911,000 ($920,000 from option exercise less $9,000 cost of the option).

Amerco elects to measure the fair value of the firm commitment through reference to changes in the U.S. dollar–euro spot rate. In this case, the fair value of the firm commitment must be discounted to its present value. The fair value and changes in fair value for the firm commitment and foreign currency option are summarized here:

| Date | Option Premium for 3/1/05 | Foreign Currency Option | | Spot Rate | Firm Commitment | |
|---|---|---|---|---|---|---|
| | | Fair Value | Change in Fair Value | | Fair Value | Change in Fair Value |
| 12/1/04 | $0.009 | $9,000 | — | $0.92 | — | — |
| 12/31/04 | 0.006 | 6,000 | − $3,000 | 0.93 | $9,803* | + $9,803 |
| 3/1/05 | 0.020 | 20,000 | + 14,000 | 0.90 | (20,000)† | − 29,803 |

*$930,000 − $920,000 = $10,000 × 0.9803 = $9,803, where 0.9803 is the present value factor for two months at an annual interest rate of 12 percent (1 percent per month) calculated as $1/1.01^2$.

†$900,000 − $920,000 = $(20,000).

At December 1, 2004, given the spot rate of $0.92, the firm commitment to receive 1 million euros in three months would generate a cash flow of $920,000. At December 31, 2004, the cash flow that could be generated from the firm commitment increases by $10,000 to $930,000. The fair value of the firm commitment at December 31, 2004, is the present value of $10,000 discounted at 1 percent per month for two months. The fair value of the firm commitment on March 1, 2005, is determined through reference to the change in the spot rate from December 1, 2004, to March 1, 2005. Because the spot rate declines by $0.02 over that period, the firm commitment to receive 1 million euros has a fair value of $(20,000) on March 1, 2005. The journal entries to account for the foreign currency option and related foreign currency firm commitment are discussed next.

### 2004 Journal Entries—Option Fair Value Hedge of Firm Commitment

| 12/1/04 | Foreign Currency Option | 9,000 | |
|---|---|---|---|
| | Cash | | 9,000 |
| | To record the purchase of the foreign currency option as an asset. | | |

No entry records the sales agreement because it is an executory contract. A memorandum is prepared to designate the option as a hedge of the risk of changes in the fair value of the firm commitment resulting from changes in the spot exchange rate.

| 12/31/04 | Firm Commitment | 9,803 | |
|---|---|---|---|
| | Gain on Firm Commitment | | 9,803 |
| | To record the firm commitment as an asset at its fair value of $9,803 and record a firm commitment gain for the change in the fair value of the firm commitment since December 1. | | |
| | Loss on Foreign Currency Option | 3,000 | |
| | Foreign Currency Option | | 3,000 |
| | To adjust the fair value of the option from $9,000 to $6,000 and record the change in the value of the option as a loss. | | |

The impact on net income for the year 2004 is as follows:

| | |
|---|---|
| Gain on firm commitment | $ 9,803 |
| Loss on foreign currency option | (3,000) |
| Impact on net income | $ 6,803 |

The effect on the December 31, 2004, balance sheet follows:

|  Assets | | Liabilities and Stockholders' Equity | |
|---|---|---|---|
| Cash | $(9,000) | Retained earnings | $6,803 |
| Foreign currency option | 6,000 | | |
| Firm commitment | 9,803 | | |
| | $ 6,803 | | |

### 2005 Journal Entries—Option Fair Value Hedge of Firm Commitment

| 3/1/05 | Loss on Firm Commitment | 29,803 | |
|---|---|---|---|
| |     Firm Commitment | | 29,803 |
| | To adjust the fair value of the firm commitment from $9,803 to $(20,000) and record a firm commitment loss for the change in fair value since December 31. | | |
| | Foreign Currency Option | 14,000 | |
| |     Gain on Foreign Currency Option | | 14,000 |
| | To adjust the fair value of the foreign currency option from $6,000 to $20,000 and record a gain on foreign currency option for the change in fair value since December 31. | | |
| | Foreign Currency (€) | 900,000 | |
| |     Sales | | 900,000 |
| | To record the sale and the receipt of € 1 million as an asset at the spot rate of $.90. | | |
| | Cash | 920,000 | |
| |     Foreign Currency (€) | | 900,000 |
| |     Foreign Currency Option | | 20,000 |
| | To record exercise of the foreign currency option (receipt of $920,000 in exchange for delivery of € 1 million) and remove the foreign currency option from the accounts. | | |
| | Firm Commitment | 20,000 | |
| |     Adjustment to Net Income | | 20,000 |
| | To close the firm commitment as an adjustment to net income. | | |

The following is the impact on net income for the year 2005:

| | |
|---|---|
| Sales | $900,000 |
| Loss on firm commitment | (29,803) |
| Gain on foreign currency option | 14,000 |
| Adjustment to net income | 20,000 |
| Impact on net income | $904,197 |

The net increase in net income over the two accounting periods is $911,000 ($6,803 in 2004 plus $904,197 in 2005), which is exactly equal to the net cash flow realized on the export sale ($920,000 from exercising the option less $9,000 to purchase the option). The net gain on the option of $11,000 (loss of $3,000 in 2004 plus gain of $14,000 in 2005) reflects the net benefit from having entered into the hedge. Without the option, Amerco would have sold the 1 million euros received on March 1, 2005, at the spot rate of $0.90 for $900,000.

# HEDGE OF FORECASTED FOREIGN CURRENCY DENOMINATED TRANSACTION

*SFAS 133* also allows the use of cash flow hedge accounting for foreign currency derivatives used to hedge the cash flow risk associated with a forecasted foreign currency transaction. For hedge accounting to apply, the forecasted transaction must be probable (likely to occur), the hedge must be highly effective in offsetting fluctuations in the cash flow associated with the foreign currency risk, and the hedging relationship must be properly documented.

The accounting for a hedge of a forecasted transaction differs from the accounting for a hedge of a foreign currency firm commitment in two ways:

1. Unlike the accounting for a firm commitment, there is no recognition of the forecasted transaction or gains and losses on the forecasted transaction.
2. The hedging instrument (forward contract or option) is reported at fair value, but because there is no gain or loss on the forecasted transaction to offset against, changes in the fair value of the hedging instrument are not reported as gains and losses in net income. Instead, they are reported in other comprehensive income. On the projected date of the forecasted transaction, the cumulative change in the fair value of the hedging instrument is transferred from other comprehensive income (balance sheet) to net income (income statement).

## Forward Contract Cash Flow Hedge of a Forecasted Transaction

To demonstrate the accounting for a hedge of a forecasted foreign currency transaction, assume that Amerco has a long-term relationship with its German customer and can reliably forecast that the customer will require delivery of goods costing 1 million euros in March 2005. Confident that it will receive 1 million euros on March 1, 2005, Amerco enters into a forward contract on December 1, 2004, to sell 1 million euros on March 1, 2005, at a rate of $0.905. The facts are essentially the same as those for the hedge of a firm commitment except that Amerco does not receive a sales order from the German customer until late February 2005. Relevant exchange rates and the fair value of the forward contract are as follows:

| Date | Forward Rate to 3/31/05 | Forward Contract Fair Value | Change in Fair Value |
|---|---|---|---|
| 12/1/04 | $0.905 | –0– | — |
| 12/31/04 | 0.916 | $(10,783)* | – $10,783 |
| 3/1/05 | 0.90 (spot) | 5,000 | + $15,783 |

*($905,000 − $916,000) = $(11,000) × 0.9803 = $(10,783), where 0.9803 is the present value factor for two months at an annual interest rate of 12 percent (1 percent per month) calculated as $1/1.01^2$. The original discount on the forward contract is determined by the difference in the € spot rate and the three-month forward rate on December 31, 2004: ($.905 − $.92) × € 1 million = $15,000.

### 2004 Journal Entries—Forward Contract Hedge of a Forecasted Transaction

| 12/1/04 | No entry records either the forecasted sale or the forward contract. A memorandum is prepared to designate the forward contract as a hedge of the risk of changes in the cash flows related to the forecasted sale resulting from changes in the spot rate. | | |
|---|---|---|---|
| 12/31/04 | Accumulated Other Comprehensive Income | 10,783 | |
| |     Forward Contract | | 10,783 |
| | To record the forward contract as a liability at its fair value of $10,783 with a corresponding debit to AOCI. | | |
| | Discount Expense | 5,000 | |
| |     Accumulated Other Comprehensive Income | | 5,000 |
| | To record straight-line allocation of the forward contract discount; $15,000 × ⅓ = $5,000. | | |

Discount expense reduces 2004 net income by $5,000. The impact on the December 31, 2004, balance sheet is as follows:

|                | Assets | Liabilities and Stockholders' Equity | |
|---|---|---|---|
| No effect | | Forward contract | $10,783 |
| | | Retained earnings | (5,000) |
| | | AOCI | (5,783) |
| | | | $ 0 |

*2005 Journal Entries—Forward Contract Hedge of a Forecasted Transaction*

| 3/1/05 | Forward Contract | 15,783 | |
|---|---|---|---|
| | Accumulated Other Comprehensive Income | | 15,783 |
| | To adjust the carrying value of the forward contract to its current fair value of $5,000 with a corresponding credit to AOCI. | | |
| | Discount Expense | 10,000 | |
| | Accumulated Other Comprehensive Income | | 10,000 |
| | To record straight-line allocation of the forward contract discount: $15,000 × 2/3 = $10,000. | | |
| | Foreign Currency (€) | 900,000 | |
| | Sales | | 900,000 |
| | To record the sale and the receipt of € 1 million as an asset at the spot rate of $0.90. | | |
| | Cash | 905,000 | |
| | Foreign Currency (€) | | 900,000 |
| | Forward Contract | | 5,000 |
| | To record settlement of the forward contract (receipt of $905,000 in exchange for delivery of € 1 million) and remove the forward contract from the accounts. | | |
| | Accumulated Other Comprehensive Income | 20,000 | |
| | Adjustment to Net Income | | 20,000 |
| | To close AOCI as an adjustment to net income. | | |

The impact on net income for the year 2005 follows:

| | |
|---|---|
| Sales | $900,000 |
| Discount expense | (10,000) |
| Adjustment to net income | 20,000 |
| Impact on net income | $910,000 |

Over the two accounting periods, the net impact on net income is $905,000, which equals the amount of net cash inflow realized from the sale.

## Option Designated as a Cash Flow Hedge of a Forecasted Transaction

Now assume that Amerco hedges its forecasted foreign currency transaction by purchasing a 1 million euro put option on December 1, 2004. The option, which expires on March 1, 2005, has a strike price of $0.92 and a premium of $0.009 per euro. The fair value of the option at relevant dates is as follows:

| Date | Option Premium for 3/1/05 | Foreign Currency Option ||||| 
| | | Fair Value | Change in Fair Value | Intrinsic Value | Time Value | Change in Time Value |
| --- | --- | --- | --- | --- | --- | --- |
| 12/1/04 | $0.009 | $ 9,000 | — | –0– | $9,000 | — |
| 12/31/04 | 0.006 | 6,000 | – $ 3,000 | –0– | 6,000 | – $3,000 |
| 3/1/05 | 0.020 | 20,000 | + 14,000 | $20,000 | –0– | – 6,000 |

### 2004 Journal Entries—Option Hedge of a Forecasted Transaction

| 12/1/04 | Foreign Currency Option .................................. | 9,000 | |
| --- | --- | --- | --- |
| | Cash ........................................................ | | 9,000 |
| | To record the purchase of the foreign currency option as an asset. | | |

No entry records the forecasted sale. A memorandum is prepared to designate the foreign currency option as a hedge of the risk of changes in the cash flows related to the forecasted sale.

| 12/31/04 | Option Expense ........................................... | 3,000 | |
| --- | --- | --- | --- |
| | Foreign Currency Option ............................. | | 3,000 |
| | To adjust the carrying value of the option to its fair value and recognize the change in the time value of the option as an expense. | | |

The impact on net income for the year 2004 follows:

| Option expense ..................... | $(3,000) |
| --- | --- |
| Impact on net income ................. | $(3,000) |

A Foreign Currency Option of $6,000 is reported as an asset on the December 31, 2004, balance sheet. Cash decreases by $9,000, and Retained Earnings decreases by $3,000.

### 2005 Journal Entries—Option Hedge of a Forecasted Transaction

| 3/1/05 | Foreign Currency Option ............................. | 14,000 | |
| --- | --- | --- | --- |
| | Option Expense ......................................... | 6,000 | |
| |     Accumulated Other Comprehensive Income (AOCI) .... | | 20,000 |
| | To adjust the carrying value of the option to its fair value and recognize the change in the time value of the option as an expense with a corresponding credit to AOCI. | | |
| | Foreign Currency (€) ..................................... | 900,000 | |
| |     Sales ....................................................... | | 900,000 |
| | To record the sale and the receipt of € 1 million as an asset at the spot rate of $0.90. | | |
| | Cash ........................................................ | 920,000 | |
| |     Foreign Currency (€) ............................... | | 900,000 |
| |     Foreign Currency Option ........................ | | 20,000 |
| | To record the exercise of the foreign currency option (receipt of $920,000 in exchange for delivery of € 1 million) and remove the foreign currency option from the accounts. | | |

*(continued)*

| | | |
|---|---|---|
| Accumulated Other Comprehensive Income (AOCI) . . . . . . . . . | 20,000 | |
| Adjustment to Net Income . . . . . . . . . . . . . . . . . . . . . . . | | 20,000 |
| To close AOCI as an adjustment to net income. | | |

The following is the impact on net income for the year 2005:

| | |
|---|---|
| Sales . . . . . . . . . . . . . . . . . . . . . . . . . . . . | $900,000 |
| Option expense . . . . . . . . . . . . . . . . . . . . | (6,000) |
| Adjustment to net income . . . . . . . . . . . . | 20,000 |
| Impact on net income . . . . . . . . . . . . . . . | $914,000 |

Over two periods, net income increases by $911,000, equal to the net cash inflow realized from the export sale (Sales of $920,000 − option purchase price of $9,000).

## USE OF HEDGING INSTRUMENTS

There are probably as many different corporate strategies regarding hedging foreign exchange risk as there are companies exposed to that risk. Some companies simply require hedges of all foreign currency transactions. Others require the use of a forward contract hedge when the forward rate results in a larger cash inflow or smaller cash outflow than with the spot rate. Still other companies have proportional hedging policies that require hedging on some predetermined percentage (e.g., 50 percent, 60 percent, or 70 percent) of transaction exposure.

The notes to financial statements of multinational companies indicate the magnitude of foreign exchange risk and the importance of hedging contracts. The following has been extracted from Coca-Cola Company's 2001 annual report.

| Foreign Currency Management (in millions) | |
|---|---|
| Forward contracts | |
|     Assets . . . . . . . . . . . . . . . . . . . . . . . . . . . . . | $1,812 |
| Swap agreements | |
|     Assets . . . . . . . . . . . . . . . . . . . . . . . . . . . . . | 48 |
|     Liabilities . . . . . . . . . . . . . . . . . . . . . . . . . . . | 359 |
| Purchased options | |
|     Assets . . . . . . . . . . . . . . . . . . . . . . . . . . . . . | 706 |
| Other assets . . . . . . . . . . . . . . . . . . . . . . . . . . | 87 |
| | $3,012 |

Coca-Cola had $3 billion in foreign currency hedging instruments outstanding at December 31, 2001. To better appreciate the significance of this amount, consider that Coca-Cola had total sales of $22 billion and net income of $4 billion in 2001.

Coca-Cola uses a combination of foreign currency forward contracts, swaps, and options in its hedging strategy. In its 2001 annual report, Abbott Laboratories reported using forward contracts only in its management of foreign exchange risk. At December 31, 2001, Abbott had $3.1 billion in foreign currency forward contracts. Dell Computer Company uses purchased options and forward contracts to reduce its exposure related to anticipated foreign currency transactions. The company also uses forward contracts to hedge foreign currency denominated assets and liabilities.

As the Coca-Cola illustration indicates, a third popular means of hedging foreign exchange risk is through a *foreign currency swap*. It is a mechanism for converting a foreign currency receivable (or payable) into the domestic currency (U.S. dollar) prior to actual settlement. A discussion of the mechanics of foreign currency swaps is beyond the scope of this book. As is true for any derivative financial instrument, *SFAS 133* is applied in accounting for foreign currency swaps.

### The Euro

The introduction of the euro as a common currency throughout much of Europe reduces the need for hedging in that region of the world. For example, a German company purchasing goods from a Spanish supplier no longer has an exposure to foreign exchange risk because both countries use a common currency. This is also true for German subsidiaries of U.S. parent companies. However, any euro-denominated transactions between the U.S. parent and its German (or other euro zone) subsidiary continues to be exposed to foreign exchange risk.

One advantage of the euro for U.S. companies is that a euro account receivable from sales to a customer in, say, the Netherlands, acts as a natural hedge of a euro account payable on purchases from, say, a supplier in Italy. Assuming that similar amounts and time periods are involved, any foreign exchange loss (gain) arising from the euro payable is offset by a foreign exchange gain (loss) on the euro receivable. There is no need to hedge the euro account payable with a hedging instrument such as a foreign currency option.

## FOREIGN CURRENCY BORROWING

In addition to the receivables and payables that arise from import and export activities, companies often must account for foreign currency borrowings, another type of foreign currency transaction. Companies borrow foreign currency from foreign lenders either to finance foreign operations or perhaps to take advantage of more favorable interest rates. Accounting for a foreign currency borrowing is complicated by the facts that both the principal and interest are denominated in foreign currency, and both create an exposure to foreign exchange risk.

To demonstrate the accounting for foreign currency debt, assume that on July 1, 2004, Multicorp International borrowed 1 billion Japanese yen (¥) on a one-year note at a per annum interest rate of 5 percent. Interest is payable and the note comes due on July 1, 2005. The following exchange rates apply:

| Date | U.S. Dollars per Japanese Yen Spot Rate |
|---|---|
| July 1, 2004 | $0.00921 |
| December 31, 2004 | 0.00932 |
| July 1, 2005 | 0.00937 |

On July 1, 2004, Multicorp borrows ¥ 1 billion and converts it into $9,210,000 in the spot market. Over the life of the note, Multicorp must record accrued interest expense at year-end and interest payments on the anniversary date of July 1. In addition, the firm must revalue the Japanese yen note payable at year-end, with foreign exchange gains and losses reported in income. These journal entries account for this foreign currency borrowing:

| | | | |
|---|---|---|---|
| 7/1/04 | Cash | 9,210,000 | |
| |     Note Payable (¥) | | 9,210,000 |
| | To record the ¥ note payable at the spot rate of $0.00921 and the conversion of ¥ 1 billion into U.S. dollars. | | |
| 12/31/04 | Interest Expense | 233,000 | |
| |     Accrued Interest Payable (¥) | | 233,000 |
| | To accrue interest for the period July 1–December 31, 2004: ¥ 1 billion × 5% × ½ year = ¥ 25 million × $0.00932 = $233,000. | | |
| | Foreign Exchange Loss | 110,000 | |
| |     Note Payable (¥) | | 110,000 |
| | To revalue the ¥ note payable at the spot rate of $0.00932 and record a foreign exchange loss of $110,000 [¥ 1 billion × ($0.00932 − $0.00921)]. | | |

| 7/1/05 | Interest Expense | 234,250 | |
| | Accrued Interest Payable (¥) | 233,000 | |
| | Foreign Exchange Loss | 1,250 | |
| |     Cash | | 468,500 |
| | To record the interest payment of ¥ 50 million acquired at the spot rate of $0.00937 for $468,500; interest expense for the period of January 1–July 1, 2005: ¥ 25 million × $0.00937; and a foreign exchange loss on the ¥ accrued interest payable: ¥ 25 million × ($0.00937 − $0.00932). | | |
| | Foreign Exchange Loss | 50,000 | |
| |     Note Payable (¥) | | 50,000 |
| | To revalue the ¥ note payable at the spot rate of $0.00937 and record a foreign exchange loss of $50,000 [¥ 1 billion × ($0.00937 − $0.00932)]. | | |
| | Note Payable (¥) | 9,370,000 | |
| |     Cash | | 9,370,000 |
| | To record repayment of the ¥ 1 billion note through purchase of ¥ at the spot rate of $.00937. | | |

### Foreign Currency Loan

At times companies lend foreign currency to related parties, creating the opposite situation as with a foreign currency borrowing. The accounting involves keeping track of a note receivable and interest receivable, both of which are denominated in foreign currency. Fluctuations in the U.S. dollar value of the principal and interest generally give rise to foreign exchange gains and losses that would be included in income. Under *SFAS 52,* an exception arises when the foreign currency loan is being made on a long-term basis to a foreign branch, subsidiary, or equity method affiliate. Foreign exchange gains and losses on "intercompany foreign currency transactions that are of a long-term investment nature (that is, settlement is not planned or anticipated in the foreseeable future)" are deferred in other comprehensive income until the loan is repaid.[13] Only the foreign exchange gains and losses related to the interest receivable are recorded currently in net income.

## Summary

1. Several exchange rate mechanisms are used around the world. Most national currencies fluctuate in value against other currencies over time.
2. Exposure to foreign exchange risk exists when a payment to be made or to be received is denominated (stated) in terms of a foreign currency. Appreciation in a foreign currency results in a foreign exchange gain when the foreign currency is to be received and a foreign exchange loss when the foreign currency is to be paid. Conversely, a decrease in the value of a foreign currency results in a foreign exchange loss when the foreign currency is to be received and a foreign exchange gain when the foreign currency is to be paid.
3. Under *SFAS 52,* foreign exchange gains and losses on foreign currency balances are recorded in income in the period in which an exchange rate change occurs; this is a two-transaction perspective, accrual approach. Foreign currency balances must be revalued to their current U.S. dollar equivalent using current exchange rates whenever financial statements are prepared. This approach violates the conservatism principle when unrealized foreign exchange gains are recognized as income.
4. Exposure to foreign exchange risk can be eliminated through hedging. Hedging involves establishing a price today at which a foreign currency to be received in the future can be sold in the future or at which a foreign currency to be paid in the future can be purchased in the future.
5. The two most popular instruments for hedging foreign exchange risk are foreign currency forward contracts and foreign currency options. A *forward contract* is a binding agreement to exchange currencies at a predetermined rate. An *option* gives the buyer the right, but not the obligation, to exchange currencies at a predetermined rate.

---

[13] *SFAS 52,* para. 20(b).

6. *SFAS 133* (as amended by *SFAS 138*) governs the accounting for derivative instruments used in hedging foreign exchange risk. Hedge accounting is appropriate if the derivative is used to hedge either a fair value exposure or cash flow exposure to foreign exchange risk, the derivative is highly effective in offsetting changes in the fair value or cash flows related to the hedged item, and the derivative is properly documented as a hedge. Under hedge accounting, gains and losses on the hedging instrument are reported in net income in the same period as gains and loss on the item being hedged.
7. All derivatives, including forward contracts and options, must be reported on the balance sheet at their fair value. Changes in fair value are included in other comprehensive income if the derivative is designated as a cash flow hedge and in net income if it is designated as a fair value hedge.
8. *SFAS 133* (as amended by *SFAS 138*) provides guidance for hedges of (a) recognized foreign currency denominated assets and liabilities, (b) unrecognized foreign currency firm commitments, and (c) forecasted foreign currency denominated transactions. Cash flow hedge accounting can be used for all three types of hedge; fair value hedge accounting can be used only for (a) and (b).
9. If a foreign currency firm commitment is being hedged (fair value hedge), gains and losses on the hedging instrument as well as on the underlying firm commitment should be recognized in net income. The firm commitment account created to offset the gain or loss on firm commitment is treated as an adjustment to the underlying transaction when it takes place.
10. If a forecasted transaction is being hedged (cash flow hedge), changes in the fair value of the hedging instrument are reported in other comprehensive income. The cumulative change in fair value reported in other comprehensive income is included in net income in the period in which the forecasted transaction was originally anticipated to take place.

## Comprehensive Illustration

### PROBLEM

(*Estimated Time: 60 to 75 minutes*) Zelm Company is a U.S. company that produces electronic switches for the telecommunications industry. Zelm regularly imports component parts from a supplier located in Guadalajara, Mexico, and makes payments in Mexican pesos. The following spot exchange rates, forward exchange rates, and call option premia for Mexican pesos exist during the period August to October.

| | U.S. Dollar per Mexican Peso | | |
|---|---|---|---|
| Date | Spot Rate | Forward Rate to October 31 | Call Option Premium for October 31 (strike price $0.080) |
| August 1 | $0.080 | $0.085 | $0.0052 |
| September 30 | 0.086 | 0.088 | 0.0095 |
| October 31 | 0.091 | 0.091 | 0.0110 |

*Part A*

On August 1, Zelm imports parts from its Mexican supplier at a price of 1 million Mexican pesos. The parts are received on August 1 but are not paid for until October 31. In addition, on August 1, Zelm enters into a forward contract to purchase 1 million pesos on October 31. The forward contract is appropriately designated as a *cash flow hedge* of the Mexican peso liability exposure. Zelm's incremental borrowing rate is 12 percent per annum (1 percent per month), and the company uses a straight-line method on a monthly basis for allocating forward discounts and premia.

*Part B*

The facts are the same as in Part A, with the exception that Zelm designates the forward contract as a *fair value hedge* of the Mexican peso liability exposure.

*Part C*

On August 1, Zelm imports parts from its Mexican supplier at a price of 1 million Mexican pesos. It receives the parts on August 1 but does not pay for them until October 31. In addition, on August 1, Zelm purchases a three-month call option on 1 million Mexican pesos with a strike price of $0.080. The option is appropriately designated as a *cash flow hedge* of the Mexican peso liability exposure.

### Part D

On August 1, Zelm orders parts from its Mexican supplier at a price of 1 million Mexican pesos. It receives the parts and pays for them on October 31. On August 1, Zelm enters into a forward contract to purchase 1 million Mexican pesos on October 31. The forward contract is designated as a *fair value hedge* of the Mexican peso firm commitment. The fair value of the firm commitment is determined through reference to changes in the forward exchange rate.

### Part E

On August 1, Zelm orders parts from its Mexican supplier at a price of 1 million Mexican pesos. The parts are received and paid for on October 31. On August 1, Zelm purchases a three-month call option on 1 million Mexican pesos with a strike price of $0.080. The option is appropriately designated as a *fair value hedge* of the Mexican peso firm commitment. The fair value of the firm commitment is determined through reference to changes in the spot exchange rate.

### Part F

Zelm anticipates that it will import component parts from its Mexican supplier in the near future. On August 1, Zelm purchases a three-month call option on 1 million Mexican pesos with a strike price of $0.080. The option is appropriately designated as a *cash flow hedge* of a forecasted Mexican peso transaction. Parts costing 1 million Mexican pesos are received and paid for on October 31.

## Required

Prepare journal entries for each of these independent situations in accordance with *SFAS 52*, *SFAS 133*, and *SFAS 138*, and determine the impact each situation has on the September 30 and October 31 trial balances.

## SOLUTION

**Part A. Forward Contract Cash Flow Hedge of a Recognized Foreign Currency Liability**

| Date | Account | Debit | Credit |
|---|---|---|---|
| 8/1 | Parts Inventory | 80,000 | |
|  |     Accounts Payable (Mexican pesos) | | 80,000 |
|  | To record the purchase of parts and a Mexican peso account payable at the spot rate of $0.080. | | |

The forward contract requires no formal entry. A memorandum is prepared to designate the forward contract as a hedge of the risk of changes in the cash flow to be paid on the foreign currency payable resulting from changes in the U.S. dollar–Mexican peso exchange rate.

| Date | Account | Debit | Credit |
|---|---|---|---|
| 9/30 | Foreign Exchange Loss | 6,000 | |
|  |     Accounts Payable (Mexican pesos) | | 6,000 |
|  | To adjust the value of the Mexican peso payable to the new spot rate of $0.086 and record a foreign exchange loss resulting from the appreciation of the peso since August 1. | | |
|  | Accumulated Other Comprehensive Income (AOCI) | 6,000 | |
|  |     Gain on Forward Contract | | 6,000 |
|  | To record a gain on forward contract to offset the foreign exchange loss on account payable with a corresponding debit to AOCI. | | |
|  | Forward Contract | 2,970 | |
|  |     Accumulated Other Comprehensive Income (AOCI) | | 2,970 |
|  | To record the forward contract as an asset at its fair value of $2,970 with a corresponding credit to AOCI. | | |

The fair value of the forward contract is determined by reference to the change in the forward rate for a contract that settles on October 31: [$0.088 − $0.085] × 1 million pesos = $3,000. The present value of $3,000 discounted for one month [from October 31 to September 30] at an interest rate of 12 percent per year [1 percent per month] is calculated as follows: $3,000 × 0.9901 = $2,970.)

| | | |
|---|---|---|
| Premium Expense | 3,333 | |
|     Accumulated Other Comprehensive Income (AOCI) | | 3,333 |
| To allocate the forward contract premium to income over the life of the contract using a straight-line method on a monthly basis ($5,000 × ⅔ = $3,333). | | |

The original premium on the forward contract is determined by the difference in the peso spot rate and three-month forward rate on August 1: ($0.085 − $0.080) × 1 million pesos = $5,000.

| Trial Balance—September 30 | Debit | Credit |
|---|---|---|
| Parts Inventory | $80,000 | |
| Accounts Payable (Mexican pesos) | | $86,000 |
| Forward Contract (asset) | 2,970 | |
| AOCI | | 303 |
| Foreign Exchange Loss | 6,000 | |
| Gain on Forward Contract | | 6,000 |
| Premium Expense | 3,333 | |
| | $92,303 | $92,303 |

| | | | |
|---|---|---|---|
| 10/31 | Foreign Exchange Loss | 5,000 | |
| |     Accounts Payable (Mexican pesos) | | 5,000 |
| | To adjust the value of the Mexican peso payable to the new spot rate of $0.091 and record a foreign exchange loss resulting from the appreciation of the peso since September 30. | | |
| | Accumulated Other Comprehensive Income (AOCI) | 5,000 | |
| |     Gain on Forward Contract | | 5,000 |
| | To record a gain on forward contract to offset the foreign exchange loss on account payable with a corresponding debit to AOCI. | | |
| | Forward Contract | 3,030 | |
| |     Accumulated Other Comprehensive Income (AOCI) | | 3,030 |
| | To adjust the carrying value of the forward contract to its current fair value of $6,000 with a corresponding credit to AOCI. | | |

The current fair value of the forward contract is determined by reference to the difference in the spot rate on October 31 and the original forward rate: ($0.091 − $0.085) × 1 million pesos = $6,000. The forward contract adjustment on October 31 is calculated as the difference in the current fair value and the carrying value at September 30: $6,000 − $2,970 = $3,030.

| | | |
|---|---|---|
| Premium Expense | 1,667 | |
|     Accumulated Other Comprehensive Income (AOCI) | | 1,667 |
| To allocate the forward contract premium to income over the life of the contract using a straight-line method on a monthly basis ($5,000 × ⅓ = $1,667). | | |

350 Chapter 7

|                                                                 | Debit  | Credit |
|-----------------------------------------------------------------|--------|--------|
| Foreign Currency (Mexican pesos) .......................        | 91,000 |        |
|     Cash ....................................               |        | 85,000 |
|     Forward Contract ...............................        |        | 6,000  |

To record settlement of the forward contract; record payment of $85,000 in exchange for 1 million pesos, record the receipt of 1 million pesos as an asset at the spot rate of $0.091, and remove the forward contract from the accounts.

|                                                                 | Debit  | Credit |
|-----------------------------------------------------------------|--------|--------|
| Accounts Payable (pesos) .................................     | 91,000 |        |
|     Foreign Currency (pesos) ......................        |        | 91,000 |

To record remittance of 1 million pesos to the Mexican supplier.

| Trial Balance—October 31 | Debit | Credit |
|---|---|---|
| Cash . . . . . . . . . . . . . . . . . . . . . . . . . . . . . . . . . . . . . |  | $85,000 |
| Parts Inventory . . . . . . . . . . . . . . . . . . . . . . . . . . . | $80,000 |  |
| Retained Earnings, 9/30 . . . . . . . . . . . . . . . . . . . . | 3,333 |  |
| Foreign Exchange Loss . . . . . . . . . . . . . . . . . . . . . . | 5,000 |  |
| Gain on Forward Contract . . . . . . . . . . . . . . . . . . |  | 5,000 |
| Premium Expense . . . . . . . . . . . . . . . . . . . . . . . . | 1,667 |  |
|  | $90,000 | $90,000 |

### Part B. Forward Contract Fair Value Hedge of a Recognized Foreign Currency Liability

| 8/1 | | Debit | Credit |
|---|---|---|---|
|  | Parts Inventory . . . . . . . . . . . . . . . . . . . . . . . . . . . . . . . . . | 80,000 |  |
|  |     Accounts Payable (Mexican pesos) . . . . . . . . . . . . . . . . . |  | 80,000 |

To record the purchase of parts and a peso account payable at the spot rate of $0.080.

The forward contract requires no formal entry. A memorandum is prepared to designate the forward contract as a hedge of the risk of changes in the cash flow to be paid on the foreign currency payable resulting from changes in the U.S. dollar–peso exchange rate.

| 9/30 | | Debit | Credit |
|---|---|---|---|
|  | Foreign Exchange Loss . . . . . . . . . . . . . . . . . . . . . . . . . . . | 6,000 |  |
|  |     Accounts Payable (Mexican pesos) . . . . . . . . . . . . . . . . . |  | 6,000 |

To adjust the value of the peso payable to the new spot rate of $0.086 and record a foreign exchange loss resulting from the appreciation of the peso since August 1.

|  |  | Debit | Credit |
|---|---|---|---|
|  | Forward Contract . . . . . . . . . . . . . . . . . . . . . . . . . . . . . . . | 2,970 |  |
|  |     Gain on Forward Contract . . . . . . . . . . . . . . . . . . . . . . |  | 2,970 |

To record the forward contract as an asset at its fair value of $2,970 and record a forward contract gain for the change in the fair value of the forward contract since August 1.

| Trial Balance—September 30 | Debit | Credit |
|---|---|---|
| Parts Inventory . . . . . . . . . . . . . . . . . . . . . . . . . . . | $80,000 |  |
| Accounts Payable (Mexican pesos) . . . . . . . . . . . |  | $86,000 |
| Forward Contract (asset) . . . . . . . . . . . . . . . . . . | 2,970 |  |
| Foreign Exchange Loss . . . . . . . . . . . . . . . . . . . . . . | 6,000 |  |
| Gain on Forward Contract . . . . . . . . . . . . . . . . . |  | 2,970 |
|  | $88,970 | $88,970 |

| 10/31 | Foreign Exchange Loss ............................... | 5,000 | |
|---|---|---|---|
| | Accounts Payable (Mexican pesos) ................ | | 5,000 |

To adjust the value of the peso payable to the new spot rate of $0.091 and record a foreign exchange loss resulting from the appreciation of the peso since September 30.

| | Forward Contract ...................................... | 3,030 | |
|---|---|---|---|
| | Gain on Forward Contract ........................ | | 3,030 |

To adjust the carrying value of the forward contract to its current fair value of $6,000 and record a forward contract gain for the change in fair value since September 30.

| | Foreign Currency (Mexican pesos) ..................... | 91,000 | |
|---|---|---|---|
| | Cash .................................................. | | 85,000 |
| | Forward Contract ................................. | | 6,000 |

To record settlement of the forward contract: record payment of $85,000 in exchange for 1 million pesos, record the receipt of 1 million pesos as an asset at the spot rate of $0.091, and remove the forward contract from the accounts.

| | Accounts Payable (pesos) ............................. | 91,000 | |
|---|---|---|---|
| | Foreign Currency (pesos) ......................... | | 91,000 |

To record remittance of 1 million pesos to the Mexican supplier.

| Trial Balance—October 31 | Debit | Credit |
|---|---|---|
| Cash ......................................... | | $85,000 |
| Parts Inventory ........................... | $80,000 | |
| Retained Earnings, 9/30 ................ | 3,030 | |
| Foreign Exchange Loss .................. | 5,000 | |
| Gain on Forward Contract ............. | | 3,030 |
| | $88,030 | $88,030 |

### Part C. Option Cash Flow Hedge of a Recognized Foreign Currency Liability

The following schedule summarizes the changes in the components of the fair value of the peso call option with a strike price of $0.080:

| Date | Spot Rate | Option Premium | Fair Value | Change in Fair Value | Intrinsic Value | Time Value | Change in Time Value |
|---|---|---|---|---|---|---|---|
| 8/1 | $0.080 | $0.0052 | $ 5,200 | — | –0– | $5,200* | — |
| 9/30 | 0.086 | 0.0095 | 9,500 | + $4,300 | $ 6,000† | 3,500† | – $1,700 |
| 10/31 | 0.091 | 0.0110 | 11,000 | + 1,500 | 11,000 | –0–‡ | – 3,500 |

*Because the strike price and spot rate are the same, the option has no intrinsic value. Fair value is attributable solely to the time value of the option.
†With a spot rate of $0.086 and a strike price of $0.08, the option has an intrinsic value of $6,000. The remaining $3,500 of fair value is attributable to time value.
‡The time value of the option at maturity is zero.

| 8/1 | Parts Inventory ........................................ | 80,000 | |
|---|---|---|---|
| | Accounts Payable (Mexican pesos) ................ | | 80,000 |

To record the purchase of parts and a peso account payable at the spot rate of $0.080.

| | Foreign Currency Option ............................. | 5,200 | |
|---|---|---|---|
| | Cash .................................................. | | 5,200 |

To record the purchase of a foreign currency option as an asset.

| | | | |
|---|---|---:|---:|
| 9/30 | Foreign Exchange Loss | 6,000 | |
| |     Accounts Payable (pesos) | | 6,000 |
| | To adjust the value of the peso payable to the new spot rate of $0.086 and record a foreign exchange loss resulting from the appreciation of the peso since August 1. | | |
| | Accumulated Other Comprehensive Income (AOCI) | 6,000 | |
| |     Gain on Foreign Currency Option | | 6,000 |
| | To record a gain on forward currency option to offset the foreign exchange loss on account payable with a corresponding debit to AOCI. | | |
| | Foreign Currency Option | 4,300 | |
| |     Accumulated Other Comprehensive Income (AOCI) | | 4,300 |
| | To adjust the fair value of the option from $5,200 to $9,500 with a corresponding credit to AOCI. | | |
| | Option Expense | 1,700 | |
| |     Accumulated Other Comprehensive Income (AOCI) | | 1,700 |
| | To recognize the change in the time value of the foreign currency option as an expense with a corresponding credit to AOCI. | | |

| Trial Balance—September 30 | Debit | Credit |
|---|---:|---:|
| Cash | | $ 5,200 |
| Parts Inventory | $80,000 | |
| Foreign Currency Option (asset) | 9,500 | |
| Accounts Payable (Mexican pesos) | | 86,000 |
| Foreign Exchange Loss | 6,000 | |
| Gain on Foreign Currency Option | | 6,000 |
| Option Expense | 1,700 | |
| | $97,200 | $97,200 |

| | | | |
|---|---|---:|---:|
| 10/31 | Foreign Exchange Loss | 5,000 | |
| |     Accounts Payable (Mexican pesos) | | 5,000 |
| | To adjust the value of the peso payable to the new spot rate of $0.091 and record a foreign exchange loss resulting from the appreciation of the peso since September 30. | | |
| | Accumulated Other Comprehensive Income (AOCI) | 5,000 | |
| |     Gain on Foreign Currency Option | | 5,000 |
| | To record a gain on foreign currency option to offset the foreign exchange loss on account payable with a corresponding debit to AOCI. | | |
| | Foreign Currency Option | 1,500 | |
| |     Accumulated Other Comprehensive Income (AOCI) | | 1,500 |
| | To adjust the carrying value of the foreign currency option to its current fair value of $11,000 with a corresponding credit to AOCI. | | |
| | Option Expense | 3,500 | |
| |     Accumulated Other Comprehensive Income (AOCI) | | 3,500 |
| | To recognize the change in the time value of the foreign currency option as an expense with a corresponding credit to AOCI. | | |

| | | |
|---|---|---|
| Foreign Currency (Mexican pesos) .................... | 91,000 | |
|     Cash ........................................... | | 80,000 |
|     Foreign Currency Option ........................ | | 11,000 |
| To record exercise of the foreign currency option: Record payment of $80,000 in exchange for 1 million pesos, record the receipt of 1 million pesos as an asset at the spot rate of $0.091, and remove the option from the accounts. | | |
| Accounts Payable (pesos) ............................. | 91,000 | |
|     Foreign Currency (pesos) ....................... | | 91,000 |
| To record remittance of 1 million pesos to the Mexican supplier. | | |

| Trial Balance—October 31 | Debit | Credit |
|---|---|---|
| Cash ($5,200 credit balance + $80,000 credit) ... | | $85,200 |
| Parts Inventory ............................. | $80,000 | |
| Retained Earnings, 9/30 ..................... | 1,700 | |
| Foreign Exchange Loss ....................... | 5,000 | |
| Gain on Foreign Currency Option ............. | | 5,000 |
| Option Expense ............................. | 3,500 | |
| | $90,200 | $90,200 |

### Part D. Forward Contract Fair Value Hedge of a Foreign Currency Firm Commitment

| | | | |
|---|---|---|---|
| 8/1 | The forward contract or the purchase order requires no formal entry. A memorandum would be prepared designating the forward contract as a fair value hedge of the foreign currency firm commitment. | | |
| 9/30 | Forward Contract ............................ | 2,970 | |
| |     Gain on Forward Contract ................ | | 2,970 |
| | To record the forward contract as an asset at its fair value of $2,970 and record a forward contract gain for the change in the fair value of the forward contract since August 1. | | |
| | Loss on Firm Commitment .................... | 2,970 | |
| |     Firm Commitment ........................ | | 2,970 |
| | To record the firm commitment as a liability at its fair value of $2,970 based on changes in the forward rate and record a firm commitment loss for the change in fair value since August 1. | | |

| Trial Balance—September 30 | Debit | Credit |
|---|---|---|
| Forward Contract (asset) ................... | $2,970 | |
| Firm Commitment (liability) ................ | | $2,970 |
| Gain on Forward Contract .................. | | 2,970 |
| Loss on Firm Commitment .................. | 2,970 | |
| | $5,940 | $5,940 |

| 10/31 | Forward Contract .................................. | 3,030 | |
|---|---|---|---|
| |     Gain on Forward Contract ................... | | 3,030 |

To adjust the carrying value of the forward contract to its current fair value of $6,000 and record a forward contract gain for the change in fair value since September 30.

| | Loss on Firm Commitment ............................ | 3,030 | |
|---|---|---|---|
| |     Firm Commitment ............................ | | 3,030 |

To adjust the value of the firm commitment to $6,000 based on changes in the forward rate and record a firm commitment loss for the change in fair value since September 30.

| | Foreign Currency (Mexican pesos) .................... | 91,000 | |
|---|---|---|---|
| |     Cash ........................................ | | 85,000 |
| |     Forward Contract ............................ | | 6,000 |

To record settlement of the forward contract: Record payment of $85,000 in exchange for 1 million pesos, record the receipt of 1 million pesos as an asset at the spot rate of $0.091, and remove the forward contract from the accounts.

| | Parts Inventory ...................................... | 91,000 | |
|---|---|---|---|
| |     Foreign Currency (Mexican pesos) ............. | | 91,000 |

To record the purchase of parts through the payment of 1 million pesos to the Mexican supplier.

| | Firm Commitment .................................... | 6,000 | |
|---|---|---|---|
| |     Adjustment to Net Income ..................... | | 6,000 |

To close the firm commitment account as an adjustment to net income.

(*Note:* The final entry to close the Firm Commitment account to Adjustment to Net Income will be made only in the period in which Parts Inventory affects net income through Cost of Goods Sold. The Firm Commitment account remains on the books as a liability until that point in time.)

| Trial Balance—October 31 | Debit | Credit |
|---|---|---|
| Cash ......................................... | | $85,000 |
| Parts Inventory (Cost of Goods Sold) ......... | $91,000 | |
| Gain on Forward Contract .................... | | 3,030 |
| Loss on Firm Commitment ................... | 3,030 | |
| Adjustment to Net Income ................... | | 6,000 |
| | $94,030 | $94,030 |

*Part E. Option Fair Value Hedge of a Foreign Currency Firm Commitment*

| 8/1 | Foreign Currency Option ............................. | 5,200 | |
|---|---|---|---|
| |     Cash ........................................ | | 5,200 |

To record the purchase of a foreign currency option as an asset.

| 9/30 | Foreign Currency Option ............................. | 4,300 | |
|---|---|---|---|
| |     Gain on Foreign Currency Option ............. | | 4,300 |

To adjust the fair value of the option from $5,200 to $9,500 and record an option gain for the change in fair value since August 1.

| | Loss on Firm Commitment ............................ | 5,940 | |
|---|---|---|---|
| |     Firm Commitment ............................ | | 5,940 |

To record the firm commitment as a liability at its fair value of $5,940 based on changes in the spot rate and record a firm commitment loss for the change in fair value since August 1.

The fair value of the firm commitment is determined through reference to changes in the spot rate from August 1 to September 30: ($0.080 − $0.086) × 1 million pesos = $(6,000). This amount must be discounted for one month at 12 percent per annum (1 percent per month): $(6,000) × 0.9901 = $(5,940).

| Trial Balance—September 30 | Debit | Credit |
|---|---|---|
| Cash | | $ 5,200 |
| Foreign Currency Option (asset) | $ 9,500 | |
| Firm Commitment (liability) | | 5,940 |
| Gain on Foreign Currency Option | | 4,300 |
| Loss on Firm Commitment | 5,940 | |
| | $15,440 | $15,440 |

| | | Debit | Credit |
|---|---|---|---|
| 10/31 | Foreign Currency Option | 1,500 | |
| |     Gain on Foreign Currency Option | | 1,500 |
| | To adjust fair value of the option from $9,500 to $11,000 and record an option gain for the change in fair value since September 30. | | |
| | Loss on Firm Commitment | 5,060 | |
| |     Firm Commitment | | 5,060 |
| | To adjust the fair value of the firm commitment from $5,940 to $11,000 and record a firm commitment loss for the change in fair value since September 30. | | |

The fair value of the firm commitment is determined through reference to changes in the spot rate from August 1 to October 31: ($0.080 − $0.091) × 1 million pesos = $(11,000).

| | Debit | Credit |
|---|---|---|
| Foreign Currency (Mexican pesos) | 91,000 | |
|     Cash | | 80,000 |
|     Foreign Currency Option | | 11,000 |
| To record exercise of the foreign currency option: Record payment of $80,000 in exchange for 1 million pesos, record the receipt of 1 million pesos as an asset at the spot rate of $0.091, and remove the option from the accounts. | | |
| Parts Inventory | 91,000 | |
|     Foreign Currency (pesos) | | 91,000 |
| To record the purchase of parts through the payment of 1 million pesos to the Mexican supplier. | | |
| Firm Commitment | 11,000 | |
|     Adjustment to Net Income | | 11,000 |
| To close Firm Commitment account to Adjustment to Net Income. | | |

(*Note:* The final entry to close the Firm Commitment to Adjustment to Net Income will be made only in the period in which Parts Inventory affects net income through Cost of Goods Sold. The Firm Commitment account remains on the books as a liability until that point in time.)

| Trial Balance—October 31 | Debit | Credit |
|---|---|---|
| Cash ($5,200 credit balance + $80,000 credit) | | $85,200 |
| Parts Inventory (Cost of Goods Sold) | $91,000 | |
| Retained Earnings, 9/30 | 1,640 | |
| Gain on Foreign Currency Option | | 1,500 |
| Loss on Firm Commitment | 5,060 | |
| Adjustment to Net Income | | 11,000 |
| | $97,700 | $97,700 |

## Part F. Option Cash Flow Hedge of a Forecasted Foreign Currency Transaction

| 8/1 | Foreign Currency Option | 5,200 | |
| --- | --- | --- | --- |
| |     Cash | | 5,200 |
| | To record the purchase of a foreign currency option as an asset. | | |
| 9/30 | Foreign Currency Option | 4,300 | |
| |     Accumulated Other Comprehensive Income (AOCI) | | 4,300 |
| | To adjust the fair value of the option from $5,200 to $9,500 with a corresponding adjustment to AOCI. | | |
| | Option Expense | 1,700 | |
| |     Accumulated Other Comprehensive Income (AOCI) | | 1,700 |
| | To recognize the change in the time value of the foreign currency option as an expense with a corresponding credit to AOCI. | | |

| Trial Balance—September 30 | Debit | Credit |
| --- | --- | --- |
| Cash | | $ 5,200 |
| Foreign Currency Option (asset) | $ 9,500 | |
| Accumulated Other Comprehensive Income | | 6,000 |
| Option Expense | 1,700 | |
| | $11,200 | $11,200 |

| 10/31 | Foreign Currency Option | 1,500 | |
| --- | --- | --- | --- |
| |     Accumulated Other Comprehensive Income (AOCI) | | 1,500 |
| | To adjust the fair value of the option from $9,500 to $11,000 with a corresponding adjustment to AOCI. | | |
| | Option Expense | 3,500 | |
| |     Accumulated Other Comprehensive Income (AOCI) | | 3,500 |
| | To recognize the change in the time value of the foreign currency option as an expense with a corresponding credit to AOCI. | | |
| | Foreign Currency (Mexican pesos) | 91,000 | |
| |     Cash | | 80,000 |
| |     Foreign Currency Option | | 11,000 |
| | To record exercise of the foreign currency option: Record payment of $80,000 in exchange for 1 million pesos, record the receipt of 1 million pesos as an asset at the spot rate of $0.091, and remove the option from the accounts. | | |
| | Parts Inventory | 91,000 | |
| |     Foreign Currency (Mexican pesos) | | 91,000 |
| | To record the purchase of parts through the payment of 1 million pesos to the Mexican supplier. | | |
| | Accumulated Other Comprehensive Income (AOCI) | 11,000 | |
| |     Adjustment to Net Income | | 11,000 |
| | To close AOCI as an adjustment to net income. | | |

(*Note:* The final entry to close AOCI to Adjustment to Net Income is made at the date that the forecasted transaction was expected to occur, regardless of when the parts inventory affects net income.)

| Trial Balance—October 31 | Debit | Credit |
|---|---|---|
| Cash ($5,200 credit balance + $80,000 credit)... |  | $85,200 |
| Parts Inventory (Cost of Goods Sold)............ | $91,000 |  |
| Retained Earnings, 9/30 ..................... | 1,700 |  |
| Foreign Currency Option expense.............. | 3,500 |  |
| Adjustment to Net Income .................... |  | 11,000 |
|  | $96,200 | $96,200 |

## Questions

1. What is the concept underlying the two-transaction perspective to accounting for foreign currency transactions?
2. A company makes an export sale denominated in a foreign currency and allows the customer one month to pay. Under the two-transaction perspective, accrual approach, how does the company account for fluctuations in the exchange rate for the foreign currency?
3. What factors create a foreign exchange gain on a foreign currency transaction? What factors create a foreign exchange loss?
4. What does the term *hedging* mean? Why do companies elect to follow this strategy?
5. How does a foreign currency option differ from a foreign currency forward contract?
6. How does the timing of hedges of (a) foreign currency denominated assets and liabilities, (b) foreign currency firm commitments, and (c) forecasted foreign currency transactions differ?
7. Why would a company prefer a foreign currency option over a forward contract in hedging a foreign currency firm commitment? Why would a company prefer a forward contract over an option in hedging a foreign currency asset or liability?
8. How are foreign currency derivatives, such as forward contracts and options, reported on the balance sheet?
9. How is the fair value of a foreign currency forward contract determined? How is the fair value of an option determined?
10. What is hedge accounting?
11. Under what conditions can hedge accounting be used to account for a foreign currency option used to hedge a forecasted foreign currency transaction?
12. What are the differences in accounting for a forward contract used as (a) a cash flow hedge and (b) a fair value hedge of a foreign currency denominated asset or liability?
13. What are the differences in accounting for a forward contract used as a fair value hedge of (a) a foreign currency denominated asset or liability and (b) a foreign currency firm commitment?
14. What are the differences in accounting for a forward contract used as a cash flow hedge of (a) a foreign currency denominated asset or liability and (b) a forecasted foreign currency transaction?
15. How are changes in the fair value of an option accounted for in a cash flow hedge? In a fair value hedge?
16. In what way is the accounting for a foreign currency borrowing more complicated than the accounting for a foreign currency account payable?

## Problems

1. Which of the following combinations correctly describes the relationship between foreign currency transactions, exchange rate changes, and foreign exchange gains and losses?

| Type of Transaction | Foreign Currency | Foreign Exchange Gain or Loss |
|---|---|---|
| a. Export sale | Appreciates | Loss |
| b. Import purchase | Appreciates | Gain |
| c. Import purchase | Depreciates | Gain |
| d. Export sale | Depreciates | Gain |

2. In accounting for foreign currency transactions, which of the following approaches is used in the United States?
   a. One-transaction perspective; accrue foreign exchange gains and losses.
   b. One-transaction perspective; defer foreign exchange gains and losses.

c. Two-transaction perspective; defer foreign exchange gains and losses.
d. Two-transaction perspective; accrue foreign exchange gains and losses.

3. On October 1, 2004, Mud Co., a U.S. company, purchased parts from Terra, a Portuguese company, with payment due on December 1, 2004. If Mud's 2004 operating income included no foreign exchange gain or loss, the transaction could have
   a. Resulted in an extraordinary gain.
   b. Been denominated in U.S. dollars.
   c. Generated a foreign exchange gain to be reported as a deferred charge on the balance sheet.
   d. Generated a foreign exchange loss to be reported as a separate component of stockholders' equity.

4. Post, Inc., had a receivable from a foreign customer that is payable in the customer's local currency. On December 31, 2004, this receivable for 200,000 local currency units (LCU) was correctly included in Post's balance sheet at $110,000. When the receivable was collected on February 15, 2005, the U.S. dollar equivalent was $95,000. In Post's 2005 consolidated income statement, how much should be reported as a foreign exchange loss?
   a. $0
   b. $10,000
   c. $15,000
   d. $25,000

5. On July 1, 2004, Houghton Company borrowed 200,000 euros from a foreign lender evidenced by an interest-bearing note due on July 1, 2005. The note is denominated in euros. The U.S. dollar equivalent of the note principal is as follows:

| Date | Amount |
|---|---|
| July 1, 2004 (date borrowed) | $195,000 |
| December 31, 2004 (Haywood's year-end) | 220,000 |
| July 1, 2005 (date repaid) | 230,000 |

In its 2005 income statement, what amount should Houghton include as a foreign exchange gain or loss on the note?
   a. $35,000 gain.
   b. $35,000 loss.
   c. $10,000 gain.
   d. $10,000 loss.

6. Slick Co. had a Swiss franc receivable resulting from exports to Switzerland and a Mexican peso payable resulting from imports from Mexico. Slick recorded foreign exchange gains related to both its franc receivable and peso payable. Did the foreign currencies increase or decrease in dollar value from the date of the transaction to the settlement date?

| | Franc | Peso |
|---|---|---|
| a. | Increase | Increase |
| b. | Decrease | Decrease |
| c. | Decrease | Increase |
| d. | Increase | Decrease |

7. Grete Corp. had the following foreign currency transactions during 2004:
   - Purchased merchandise from a foreign supplier on January 20, 2004, for the U.S. dollar equivalent of $60,000 and paid the invoice on April 20, 2004, at the U.S. dollar equivalent of $68,000.
   - On September 1, 2004, borrowed the U.S. dollar equivalent of $300,000 evidenced by a note that was payable in the lender's local currency on September 1, 2005. On December 31, 2004, the U.S. dollar equivalents of the principal amount and accrued interest were $320,000 and $12,000, respectively. Interest on the note is 10 percent per annum.

In Grete's 2004 income statement, what amount should be included as a foreign exchange loss?
   a. $4,000
   b. $20,000
   c. $22,000
   d. $30,000

8. A U.S. exporter has a Thai baht account receivable resulting from an export sale on April 1 to a customer in Thailand. The exporter signed a forward contract on April 1 to sell Thai baht and designated

it as a cash flow hedge of a recognized Thai baht receivable. The spot rate was $0.022 on that date, and the forward rate was $0.023. Which of the following did the U.S. exporter report in net income?
   a. Discount expense.
   b. Discount revenue.
   c. Premium expense.
   d. Premium revenue.
9. Lawrence Company ordered parts costing FC100,000 from a foreign supplier on May 12 when the spot rate was $0.20 per FC. A one-month forward contract was signed on that date to purchase FC100,000 at a forward rate of $0.21. The forward contract is properly designated as a fair value hedge of the FC100,000 firm commitment. On June 12, when the parts are received, the spot rate is $0.23. At what amount should the parts inventory be carried on Lawrence Company's books?
   a. $20,000
   b. $21,000
   c. $22,000
   d. $23,000
10. On December 1, 2004, Barnum Company (a U.S.-based company) entered into a three-month forward contract to purchase 1,000,000 ringgits on March 1, 2005. The following U.S. dollar per ringgit exchange rates apply:

| Date | Spot Rate | Forward Rate (to March 1, 2005) |
| --- | --- | --- |
| December 1, 2004 | $0.044 | $0.042 |
| December 31, 2004 | 0.040 | 0.037 |
| March 1, 2005 | 0.038 | N/A |

Barnum's incremental borrowing rate is 12 percent. The present value factor for two months at an annual interest rate of 12 percent (1 percent per month) is 0.9803.

Which of the following correctly describes the manner in which Barnum Company will report the forward contract on its December 31, 2004, balance sheet?
   a. As an asset in the amount of $1,960.60.
   b. As an asset in the amount of $3,921.20.
   c. As a liability in the amount of $6,862.10.
   d. As a liability in the amount of $4,901.50.

**Use the following information for problems 11 and 12.**
MNC Corp. (a U.S.-based company) sold parts to a Korean customer on December 1, 2004, with payment of 10 million Korean won to be received on March 31, 2005. The following exchange rates apply:

| Date | Spot Rate | Forward Rate (to March 31, 2005) |
| --- | --- | --- |
| December 1, 2004 | $0.0035 | $0.0034 |
| December 31, 2004 | 0.0033 | 0.0032 |
| March 31, 2005 | 0.0038 | N/A |

MNC's incremental borrowing rate is 12 percent. The present value factor for three months at an annual interest rate of 12 percent (1 percent per month) is 0.9706.

11. Assuming that no forward contract was entered into, how much foreign exchange gain or loss should MNC report on its 2004 income statement with regard to this transaction?
   a. $5,000 gain.
   b. $3,000 gain.
   c. $2,000 loss.
   d. $1,000 loss.
12. Assuming that a forward contract to sell 10 million Korean won was entered into on December 1, 2004, as a fair value hedge of a foreign currency receivable, what is the net impact on net income in 2004 resulting from a fluctuation in the value of the won?

a. No impact on net income.
b. $58.80 decrease in net income.
c. $2,000 decrease in net income.
d. $1,941.20 increase in net income.

13. On March 1, Pimlico Corporation (a U.S.-based company) expects to order merchandise inventory from a supplier in Sweden in three months. On March 1, when the spot rate is $0.10 per Swedish krona, Pimlico enters into a forward contract to purchase 500,000 Swedish kroner at a three-month forward rate of $0.12. At the end of three months, when the spot rate is $0.115 per Swedish krona, Pimlico orders and receives the merchandise, paying 500,000 kroner. What is the amount that Pimlico reports in net income as a result of this cash flow hedge of a forecasted transaction?
    a. $10,000 Premium Expense plus a $7,500 positive Adjustment to Net Income when the merchandise is sold.
    b. $10,000 Discount Expense plus a $5,000 positive Adjustment to Net Income when the merchandise is sold.
    c. $2,500 Premium Expense plus a $5,000 negative Adjustment to Net Income when the merchandise is sold.
    d. $2,500 Premium Expense plus a $2,500 positive Adjustment to Net Income when the merchandise is sold.

14. Palmer Corporation operates as a U.S. corporation. Palmer expects to order goods from a foreign supplier at a price of 200,000 pounds, with delivery and payment to be made on April 15. On January 15, Palmer purchased a three-month call option on 200,000 pounds and designated this option as a cash flow hedge of a forecasted foreign currency transaction. The option has a strike price of $0.25 per pound and costs $2,000. The spot rate for pounds is $0.25 on January 15 and $0.22 on April 15. What amount will Palmer Corporation report as an option expense in net income during the period January 15 to April 15?
    a. $600
    b. $1,000
    c. $2,000
    d. $4,400

**Use the following information for problems 15 through 17.**
On September 1, 2004, Jensen Company received an order to sell a machine to a customer in Canada at a price of 100,000 Canadian dollars. The machine was shipped and payment was received on March 1, 2005. On September 1, 2004, Jensen Company purchased a put option giving it the right to sell 100,000 Canadian dollars on March 1, 2005, at a price of $80,000. Jensen Company properly designates the option as a fair value hedge of the Canadian dollar firm commitment. The option cost $2,000 and had a fair value of $2,300 on December 31, 2004. The fair value of the firm commitment is measured through reference to changes in the spot rate. The following spot exchange rates apply:

| Date | US Dollar per Canadian Dollar |
| --- | --- |
| September 1, 2004 | $0.80 |
| December 31, 2004 | 0.79 |
| March 1, 2005 | 0.77 |

Jensen Company's incremental borrowing rate is 12 percent. The present value factor for two months at an annual interest rate of 12 percent (1 percent per month) is 0.9803.

15. What was the net impact on Jensen Company's 2004 income as a result of this fair value hedge of a firm commitment?
    a. –0–.
    b. $680.30 decrease in income.
    c. $300 increase in income.
    d. $980.30 increase in income.

16. What was the net impact on Jensen Company's 2005 income as a result of this fair value hedge of a firm commitment?
    a. –0–.
    b. $1,319.70 decrease in income.
    c. $77,980.30 increase in income.
    d. $78,680.30 increase in income.

17. What was the net increase or decrease in cash flow from having purchased the foreign currency option to hedge this exposure to foreign exchange risk?
   a. –0–.
   b. $1,000 increase in cash flow.
   c. $1,500 decrease in cash flow.
   d. $3,000 increase in cash flow.

**Use the following information for problems 18 through 20.**
On March 1, 2004, Werner Corp. received an order for parts from a Mexican customer at a price of 500,000 Mexican pesos with a delivery date of April 30, 2004. On March 1, when the U.S. dollar–Mexican peso spot rate is $0.115, Werner Corp. entered into a two-month forward contract to sell 500,000 pesos at a forward rate of $0.12 per peso. The forward contract is designated as a fair value hedge of the firm commitment to receive pesos, and the fair value of the firm commitment is measured through reference to changes in the peso forward rate. The parts are delivered and payment is received on April 30, 2004, when the peso spot rate is $0.118. On March 31, 2004, the Mexican peso spot rate is $0.123, and the forward contract has a fair value of $1,250.

18. What is the net impact on Werner's net income for the quarter ended March 31, 2004, as a result of this forward contract hedge of a firm commitment?
   a. –0–.
   b. $1,250 increase in net income.
   c. $1,500 decrease in net income.
   d. $1,500 increase in net income.

19. What is the net impact on Werner's net income for the quarter ended June 30, 2004, as a result of this forward contract hedge of a firm commitment?
   a. –0–.
   b. $59,000 increase in net income.
   c. $60,000 increase in net income.
   d. $61,500 increase in net income.

20. What was the net increase or decrease in cash flow from having entered into this forward contract hedge?
   a. –0–.
   b. $1,000 increase in cash flow.
   c. $1,500 decrease in cash flow.
   d. $2,500 increase in cash flow.

**Use the following information for problems 21 and 22.**
On November 1, 2004, Dos Santos Company forecasts the purchase of raw materials from a Brazilian supplier on February 1, 2005, at a price of 200,000 Brazilian reais. On November 1, 2004, Dos Santos pays $1,500 for a three-month call option on 200,000 reais with a strike price of $0.40 per real. The option is properly designated as a cash flow hedge of a forecasted foreign currency transaction. On December 31, 2004, the option has a fair value of $1,100. The following spot exchange rates apply:

| Date | U.S. Dollar per Brazilian Real |
| --- | --- |
| November 1, 2004 | $0.40 |
| December 31, 2004 | 0.38 |
| February 1, 2005 | 0.41 |

21. What is the net impact on Dos Santos Company's 2004 net income as a result of this hedge of a forecasted foreign currency purchase?
   a. –0–.
   b. $400 decrease in net income.
   c. $1,000 decrease in net income.
   d. $1,400 decrease in net income.

22. What is the net impact on Dos Santos Company's 2005 net income as a result of this hedge of a forecasted foreign currency purchase? Assume that the raw materials are consumed and become a part of the cost of goods sold in 2005.
   a. $80,000 decrease in net income.
   b. $80,600 decease in net income.

c. $81,100 decrease in net income.
d. $83,100 decrease in net income.

23. Rabato Corporation acquired merchandise on account from a foreign supplier on November 1, 2004, for 60,000 LCU (local currency units). The foreign currency account payable was paid on January 15, 2005. The following currency rates for 1 LCU are known:

| | |
|---|---|
| November 1, 2004 | $0.345 |
| December 31, 2004 | 0.333 |
| January 15, 2005 | 0.359 |

   a. How is Rabato's 2004 income statement affected by the fluctuation in currency values?
   b. How is Rabato's 2005 income statement affected by the fluctuation in currency values?

24. On December 20, 2004, Butanta Company (a U.S. company headquartered in Miami, Florida) sold parts to a foreign customer at a price of 50,000 ostras. Payment is received on January 10, 2005. Currency exchange rates for 1 ostra are as follows:

| | |
|---|---|
| December 20, 2004 | $1.05 |
| December 31, 2004 | 1.02 |
| January 10, 2005 | 0.98 |

   a. How is Butanta's 2004 income statement affected by the fluctuation in currency values?
   b. How is Butanta's 2005 income statement affected by the fluctuation in currency values?

25. New Colony Corporation (a U.S. company) made a sale to a foreign customer on September 15, 2004, for 100,000 foreign currency units (FCU). Payment was received on October 15, 2004. The following exchange rates for 1 FCU apply:

| | |
|---|---|
| September 15, 2004 | $0.40 |
| September 30, 2004 | 0.42 |
| October 15, 2004 | 0.37 |

Prepare all journal entries for New Colony in connection with this sale, assuming that the company closes its books on September 30 to prepare interim financial statements.

26. On December 1, 2004, Dresden Company (a U.S. company located in Albany, New York) purchases inventory from a foreign supplier for 60,000 local currency units (LCU). Payment will be made in 90 days after Dresden sells this merchandise. Sales are made rather quickly, and Dresden pays this entire obligation on January 28, 2005. Currency exchange rates for 1 LCU are as follows:

| | |
|---|---|
| December 1, 2004 | $0.88 |
| December 31, 2004 | 0.82 |
| January 28, 2005 | 0.90 |

Prepare all journal entries for Dresden Company in connection with the purchase and payment.

27. Acme Corporation (a U.S. company located in Sarasota, Florida) has the following import/export transactions in 2004:

| | |
|---|---|
| March 1 | Bought inventory costing 50,000 pesos on credit. |
| May 1 | Sold 60 percent of the inventory for 45,000 pesos on credit. |
| August 1 | Collected 40,000 pesos from customers. |
| September 1 | Paid 30,000 pesos to creditors. |

Currency exchange rates for 1 peso for 2004 are as follows:

|  |  |
|---|---|
| March 1 | $0.17 |
| May 1 | 0.18 |
| August 1 | 0.19 |
| September 1 | 0.20 |
| December 31 | 0.21 |

For each of the following accounts, what will Acme report on its 2004 financial statements?
 a. Inventory
 b. Cost of Goods Sold
 c. Sales
 d. Accounts Receivable
 e. Accounts Payable
 f. Cash

28. Bartlett Company, which has its headquarters in Cincinnati, Ohio, has occasional transactions with companies in a foreign country whose currency is the lira. Prepare journal entries for the following transactions in U.S. dollars. Also prepare any necessary adjusting entries at December 31 caused by fluctuations in the value of the foreign currencies. Assume that the company uses a perpetual inventory system.

**Transactions in 2004**

| | |
|---|---|
| February 1 | Bought equipment for 40,000 lire on credit. |
| April 1 | Paid for the equipment purchased February 1. |
| June 1 | Bought inventory for 30,000 lire on credit. |
| August 1 | Sold 70 percent of inventory purchased June 1 for 40,000 lire on credit. |
| October 1 | Collected 30,000 lire from the sales made on August 1, 2004. |
| November 1 | Paid 20,000 lire on the debts incurred on June 1, 2004. |

**Transactions in 2005**

| | |
|---|---|
| February 1 | Collected remaining 10,000 lire from August 1, 2004, sales. |
| March 1 | Paid remaining 10,000 lire on the debts incurred on June 1, 2004. |

**Currency exchange rates for 1 lira for 2004**

| | |
|---|---|
| February 1 | $0.44 |
| April 1 | 0.45 |
| June 1 | 0.47 |
| August 1 | 0.48 |
| October 1 | 0.49 |
| November 1 | 0.50 |
| December 31 | 0.52 |

**Currency exchange rates for 1 lira for 2005**

| | |
|---|---|
| February 1 | $0.54 |
| March 1 | 0.55 |

29. Benjamin, Inc., operates an export/import business. The company, located in Mobile, Alabama, has considerable dealings with companies in the country of Camerrand. All transactions with these companies are denominated in alaries (AL), the Camerrand currency. During 2004, Benjamin acquires 20,000 widgets at a price of 8 alaries per widget with payment to be made when the items are sold. Currency exchange rates for 1 AL are as follows:

| | |
|---|---|
| September 1, 2004 | $0.46 |
| December 1, 2004 | 0.44 |
| December 31, 2004 | 0.48 |
| March 1, 2005 | 0.45 |

a. Assume that Benjamin's acquisition took place on December 1, 2004, with payment being made on March 1, 2005. What is the effect of the exchange rate fluctuations on reported income in 2004 and in 2005?
b. Assume that Benjamin's acquisition took place on September 1, 2004, with payment being made on December 1, 2004. What is the effect of the exchange rate fluctuations on reported income in 2004?
c. Assume that Benjamin's acquisition took place on September 1, 2004, with payment being made on March 1, 2005. What is the effect of the exchange rate fluctuations on reported income in 2004 and in 2005?

30. On September 30, 2004, Ericson Company negotiated a two-year, 1,000,000 dudek loan from a foreign bank at an interest rate of 2 percent per year. Interest payments are made annually on September 30, and the principal will be repaid on September 30, 2006. Ericson prepares U.S.-dollar financial statements and has a December 31 year-end. Prepare all journal entries related to this foreign currency borrowing assuming the following exchange rates for 1 dudek:

| | |
|---|---|
| September 30, 2004 | $0.100 |
| December 31, 2004 | 0.105 |
| September 30, 2005 | 0.120 |
| December 31, 2005 | 0.125 |
| September 30, 2006 | 0.150 |

Determine the effective cost of borrowing in dollars in each of the three years 2004, 2005, and 2006.

31. Brandlin Company of Anaheim, California, sells parts to a foreign customer on December 1, 2004, with payment of 20,000 korunas to be received on March 1, 2005. Brandlin enters into a forward contract on December 1, 2004, to sell 20,000 korunas on March 1, 2005. Relevant exchange rates for the koruna on various dates are as follows:

| Date | Spot Rate | Forward Rate (to March 1, 2005) |
|---|---|---|
| December 1, 2004 | $2.00 | $2.075 |
| December 31, 2004 | 2.10 | 2.200 |
| March 1, 2005 | 2.25 | N/A |

Brandlin's incremental borrowing rate is 12 percent. The present value factor for two months at an annual interest rate of 12 percent (1 percent per month) is 0.9803. Brandlin must close its books and prepare financial statements at December 31.

a. Assuming that Brandlin designates the forward contract as a cash flow hedge of a foreign currency receivable, prepare journal entries for these transactions in U.S. dollars. What is the impact on 2004 net income? What is the impact on 2005 net income? What is the impact on net income over the two accounting periods?
b. Assuming that Brandlin designates the forward contract as a fair value hedge of a foreign currency receivable, prepare journal entries for these transactions in U.S. dollars. What is the impact on 2004 net income? What is the impact on 2005 net income? What is the impact on net income over the two accounting periods?

32. Use the same facts as in problem 31 except that Brandlin Company purchases parts from a foreign supplier on December 1, 2004, with payment of 20,000 korunas to be made on March 1, 2005. On December 1, 2004, Brandlin enters into a forward contract to purchase 20,000 korunas on March 1, 2005.

a. Assuming that Brandlin designates the forward contract as a cash flow hedge of a foreign currency payable, prepare journal entries for these transactions in U.S. dollars. What is the impact on 2004 net income? What is the impact on 2005 net income? What is the impact on net income over the two accounting periods?
b. Assuming that Brandlin designates the forward contract as a fair value hedge of a foreign currency payable, prepare journal entries for these transactions in U.S. dollars. What is the impact on 2004 net income? What is the impact on 2005 net income? What is the impact on net income over the two accounting periods?

33. On June 1, Alexander Corporation sold goods to a foreign customer at a price of 1,000,000 pesos. Payment will be received in three months on September 1. On June 1, Alexander acquired an option to sell 1,000,000 pesos in three months at a strike price of $0.045. Relevant exchange rates and option premia for the peso are as follows:

| Date | Spot Rate | Call Option Premium for September 1 (strike price $0.045) |
|---|---|---|
| June 1 | $0.045 | $0.0020 |
| June 30 | 0.048 | 0.0018 |
| September 1 | 0.044 | N/A |

Alexander Corporation must close its books and prepare its second-quarter financial statements on June 30.
  a. Assuming that Alexander designates the foreign currency option as a cash flow hedge of a foreign currency receivable, prepare journal entries for these transactions in U.S. dollars. What is the impact on net income over the two accounting periods?
  b. Assuming that Alexander designates the foreign currency option as a fair value hedge of a foreign currency receivable, prepare journal entries for these transactions in U.S. dollars. What is the impact on net income over the two accounting periods?

34. On June 1, Hamilton Corporation purchased goods from a foreign supplier at a price of 1,000,000 markkas. Payment will be made in three months on September 1. On June 1, Hamilton acquired an option to purchase 1,000,000 markkas in three months at a strike price of $0.085. Relevant exchange rates and option premia for the markka are as follows:

| Date | Spot Rate | Call Option Premium for September 1 (strike price $0.085) |
|---|---|---|
| June 1 | $0.085 | $0.002 |
| June 30 | 0.088 | 0.004 |
| September 1 | 0.090 | N/A |

Hamilton Corporation must close its books and prepare its second-quarter financial statements on June 30.
  a. Assuming that Hamilton designates the foreign currency option as a cash flow hedge of a foreign currency payable, prepare journal entries for these transactions in U.S. dollars. What is the impact on net income over the two accounting periods?
  b. Assuming that Hamilton designates the foreign currency option as a fair value hedge of a foreign currency payable, prepare journal entries for these transactions in U.S. dollars. What is the impact on net income over the two accounting periods?

35. On November 1, 2004, Ambrose Company sold merchandise to a foreign customer for 100,000 FCUs with payment to be received on April 30, 2005. At the date of sale, Ambrose entered into a six-month forward contract to sell 100,000 LCUs. The forward contract is properly designated as a cash flow hedge of a foreign currency receivable. The following exchange rates apply:

| Date | Spot Rate | Forward Rate (to April 30, 2005) |
|---|---|---|
| November 1, 2004 | $0.53 | $0.52 |
| December 31, 2004 | 0.50 | 0.48 |
| April 30, 2005 | 0.49 | N/A |

Ambrose Company's incremental borrowing rate is 12 percent. The present value factor for four months at an annual interest rate of 12 percent (1 percent per month) is 0.9610.

a. Prepare all journal entries, including December 31 adjusting entries, to record the sale and forward contract.
b. What is the impact on net income in 2004?
c. What is the impact on net income in 2005?

36. Eximco Corporation (based in Champaign, Illinois) has a number of transactions with companies in the country of Mongagua, where the currency is the mong. On November 30, 2004, Eximco sold equipment at a price of 500,000 mongs to a Mongaguan customer with payment to be received on January 31, 2005. In addition, on November 30, 2004, Eximco purchased raw materials from a Mongaguan supplier at a price of 300,000 mongs; payment will be made on January 31, 2005. To hedge its net exposure in mongs, Eximco entered into a two-month forward contract on November 30, 2004, to deliver 200,000 mongs to the foreign currency broker in exchange for $104,000. Eximco properly designates its forward contract as a fair value hedge of a foreign currency receivable. The following rates for the mong apply:

| Date | Spot Rate | Forward Rate (to January 31, 2005) |
|---|---|---|
| November 30, 2004 | $0.53 | $0.52 |
| December 31, 2004 | 0.50 | 0.48 |
| January 31, 2005 | 0.49 | N/A |

Eximco Corporation's incremental borrowing rate is 12 percent. The present value factor for one month at an annual interest rate of 12 percent (1 percent per month) is 0.9901.
a. Prepare all journal entries, including December 31 adjusting entries, to record these transactions and forward contract.
b. What is the impact on net income in 2004?
c. What is the impact on net income in 2005?

37. On October 1, 2004, Hanks Company entered into a forward contract to sell 100,000 LCUs in four months (on January 31, 2005) and receive $65,000 in U.S. dollars. Exchange rates for the LCU are as follows:

| Date | Spot Rate | Forward Rate (to January 31, 2005) |
|---|---|---|
| October 1, 2004 | $0.69 | $0.65 |
| December 31, 2004 | 0.71 | 0.74 |
| January 31, 2005 | 0.72 | N/A |

Hanks Company's incremental borrowing rate is 12 percent. The present value factor for one month at an annual interest rate of 12 percent (1 percent per month) is 0.9901. Hanks must close its books and prepare financial statements on December 31.
a. Prepare journal entries, assuming that the forward contract was entered into as a fair value hedge of a 100,000 LCU receivable arising from a sale made on October 1, 2004. Include entries for both the sale and the forward contract.
b. Prepare journal entries, assuming that the forward contract was entered into as a fair value hedge of a firm commitment related to a 100,000 LCU sale that will be made on January 31, 2005. Include entries for both the firm commitment and the forward contract. The fair value of the firm commitment is measured through reference to changes in the forward rate.

38. On August 1, Jackson Corporation (a U.S.-based importer) placed an order to purchase merchandise from a foreign supplier at a price of 200,000 rupees. The merchandise will be received and paid for in three months on October 31. On August 1, Jackson entered into a forward contract to purchase 200,000 rupees in three months at a forward rate of $0.30. The forward contract is properly designated as a fair value hedge of a foreign currency firm commitment. The fair value of the firm commitment is measured through reference to changes in the forward rate. Relevant exchange rates for the rupee are as follows:

| Date | Spot Rate | Forward Rate (to October 31) |
|---|---|---|
| August 1 | $0.300 | $0.300 |
| September 30 | 0.305 | 0.325 |
| October 31 | 0.320 | N/A |

Jackson's incremental borrowing rate is 12 percent. The present value factor for one month at an annual interest rate of 12 percent (1 percent per month) is 0.9901. Jackson Corporation must close its books and prepare its third-quarter financial statements on September 30.

a. Prepare journal entries for the forward contract and firm commitment.
b. What is the impact on net income over the two accounting periods?
c. What is the net cash outflow resulting from the purchase of merchandise from the foreign customer?

39. On June 1, Vandervelde Corporation (a U.S.-based manufacturing firm) received an order to sell goods to a foreign customer at a price of 500,000 leks. The goods will be shipped and payment will be received in three months on September 1. On June 1, Vandervelde purchased an option to sell 500,000 leks in three months at a strike price of $1.00. The option is properly designated as a fair value hedge of a foreign currency firm commitment. The fair value of the firm commitment is measured through reference to changes in the spot rate. Relevant exchange rates and option premia for the lek are as follows:

| Date | Spot Rate | Call Option Premium for September 1 (strike price $1.00) |
|---|---|---|
| June 1 | $1.00 | $0.010 |
| June 30 | 0.99 | 0.016 |
| September 1 | 0.97 | N/A |

Vandervelde's incremental borrowing rate is 12 percent. The present value factor for two months at an annual interest rate of 12 percent (1 percent per month) is 0.9803. Vandervelde Corporation must close its books and prepare its second-quarter financial statements on June 30.

a. Prepare journal entries for the foreign currency option and firm commitment.
b. What is the impact on net income over the two accounting periods?
c. What is the net cash inflow resulting from the sale of goods to the foreign customer?

40. Big Arber Company ordered parts from a foreign supplier on November 20 at a price of 50,000 pijios when the spot rate was $0.20 per pijio. Delivery and payment were scheduled for December 20. On November 20, Big Arber acquired a call option on 50,000 pijios at a strike price of $0.20, paying a premium of $0.008 per pijio. The option is designated as a fair value hedge of a foreign currency firm commitment. The fair value of the firm commitment is measured through reference to changes in the spot rate. The parts are delivered and paid for according to schedule. Big Arber does not close its books until December 31.

a. Assuming a spot rate of $0.21 per pijio on December 20, prepare all journal entries to account for the option and firm commitment.
b. Assuming a spot rate of $0.18 per pijio on December 20, prepare all journal entries to account for the option and firm commitment.

41. Based on past experience, Leickner Company expects that it will need to purchase raw materials from a foreign supplier at a cost of 1,000,000 marks on March 15, 2005. To hedge this forecasted transaction, a three-month call option to purchase 1,000,000 marks is acquired on December 15, 2004. Leickner selects a strike price of $0.58 per mark, paying a premium of $0.005 per unit, when the spot rate is $0.58. The spot rate increases to $0.584 at December 31, 2004, causing the fair value of the option to increase to $8,000. By March 15, 2005, when the raw materials are purchased, the spot rate has climbed to $0.59, resulting in a fair value for the option of $10,000.

a. Prepare all journal entries for the option hedge of a forecasted transaction and for the purchase of raw materials, assuming that December 31 is Leickner's year-end and that the raw materials are included in the cost of goods sold in 2005.
b. What is the overall impact on net income over the two accounting periods?
c. What is the net cash outflow to acquire the raw materials?

42. Vino Veritas Company, a U.S.-based importer of wines and spirits, placed an order with a French supplier for 1,000 cases of wine at a price of 200 euros per case. The total purchase price is 200,000 euros. Relevant exchange rates for the euro are as follows:

| Date | Spot Rate | Forward Rate to October 31, 2004 | Call Option Premium for October 31, 2004 (strike price $1.00) |
|---|---|---|---|
| September 15, 2004 | $1.00 | $1.06 | $0.035 |
| September 30, 2004 | 1.05 | 1.09 | 0.070 |
| October 31, 2004 | 1.10 | 1.10 | 0.100 |

Vino Veritas Company has an incremental borrowing rate of 12 percent (1 percent per month) and closes the books and prepares financial statements at September 30.

a. Assume that the wine was received on September 15, 2004, and payment was made on October 31, 2004. There was no attempt to hedge the exposure to foreign exchange risk. Prepare journal entries to account for this import purchase.

b. Assume that the wine was received on September 15, 2004, and payment was made on October 31, 2004. On September 15, Vino Veritas Corporation entered into a 45-day forward contract to purchase 200,000 euros. The forward contract is properly designated as a fair value hedge of a foreign currency payable. Prepare journal entries to account for the import purchase and foreign currency forward contract.

c. The wine was ordered on September 15, 2004. It was received and paid for on October 31, 2004. On September 15, Vino Veritas Corporation entered into a 45-day forward contract to purchase 200,000 euros. The forward contract is properly designated as a fair value hedge of a foreign currency firm commitment. The fair value of the firm commitment is measured through reference to changes in the forward rate. Prepare journal entries to account for the foreign currency forward contract, firm commitment, and import purchase.

d. The wine was received on September 15, 2004, and payment was made on October 31, 2004. On September 15, Vino Veritas Corporation purchased a 45-day call option for 200,000 euros. The option was properly designated as a cash flow hedge of a foreign currency payable. Prepare journal entries to account for the import purchase and foreign currency option.

e. The wine was ordered on September 15, 2004. It was received and paid for on October 31, 2004. On September 15, Vino Veritas Corporation purchased a 45-day call option for 200,000 euros. The option was properly designated as a fair value hedge of a foreign currency firm commitment. The fair value of the firm commitment is measured in reference to changes in the spot rate. Prepare journal entries to account for the foreign currency option, firm commitment, and import purchase.

# Develop Your Skills

## RESEARCH CASE 1—INTERNATIONAL FLAVORS AND FRAGRANCES

Many companies make annual reports available on their corporate internet homepage. Annual reports also can be accessed through the SEC's EDGAR system at www.sec.gov (under Forms, search for ARS or 10-K), or in your school's library. Access the most recent annual report for International Flavors and Fragrances (IFF).

### Required:

a. Identify the location(s) in the annual report where IFF provides disclosures related to its management of foreign exchange risk.
b. Determine the types of hedging instruments the company uses and the types of hedges in which it engages.
c. Determine the manner in which the company discloses the fact that its foreign exchange hedges are effective in offsetting gains and losses on the underlying items being hedged.

# RESEARCH CASE 2—DISCLOSURE OF HEDGING ACTIVITIES

Many companies make annual reports available on their corporate internet homepage. Annual reports also can be accessed through the SEC's EDGAR system at www.sec.gov (under Forms, search for ARS or 10-K), or in your school's library. Access the most recent annual report for the following U.S.-based multinational corporations:
- Federal-Mogul Corporation.
- Ford Motor Company.
- General Motors Corporation.

### Required:

a. Identify the location(s) in the annual report that provides disclosures related to foreign exchange risk management (hedging).
b. Determine the types of hedging instrument each company uses and the types of hedges in which it engages.
c. Identify whether the company reports a concentration of foreign exchange exposure in any particular currency or currencies.
d. Determine whether each company discloses the aggregate amount of foreign exchange gains/loses included in income, and if so, whether this amount is reported as a separate line item in the income statement.

# FARS CASE 1—HEDGE OF FORECASTED FOREIGN CURRENCY TRANSACTION

The French subsidiary of a U.S. parent corporation forecasts that it will purchase parts from a Swiss supplier in six months. The U.S. parent is contemplating the purchase of a Swiss franc call option to hedge this foreign exchange risk. Whether it is acceptable for the U.S. parent corporation to use hedge accounting for the hedge of a forecasted foreign currency transaction of its French subsidiary is in question. Search the FASB's *Original Pronouncements* using either hard copy or the Financial Accounting Research System (FARS) database.

### Required:

a. Identify the authoritative pronouncement and paragraph(s) within it that provide an answer to the issue in question.
b. Summarize the FASB's response with respect to the question that has arisen.

# FARS CASE 2—FOREIGN CURRENCY-DENOMINATED DEBT

Many companies issue fixed-rate foreign currency-denominated debt in which the principal and interest payments are made in a foreign currency. There is some question as to whether a foreign currency-denominated interest payment should be considered (a) an unrecognized firm commitment that could be designated as a hedged item in a foreign currency fair value hedge or (b) a forecasted transaction that could be designated as the hedged item in a foreign currency cash flow hedge. The FASB's Derivatives Implementation Group (DIG) has addressed many implementation issues including this question. Search the Derivative Instruments and Hedging Activities database in the FASB's Financial Accounting Research System (FARS).

### Required:

a. Identify the number of the *Statement 133* Implementation Issue that provides an answer to this issue.
b. Summarize the DIG's response with respect to the issue.

# EXCEL CASE—DETERMINE FOREIGN EXCHANGE GAINS AND LOSSES

Import/Export Company made a number of import purchases and export sales denominated in foreign currency in 2001. Information related to these transactions is summarized in the following table. Each purchase or sale was made on the date in the Transaction Date column, and payment in foreign currency was made or received on the date in the Settlement Date column.

| Foreign Currency | Type of Transaction | Amount in Foreign Currency | Transaction Date | Settlement Date |
|---|---|---|---|---|
| Brazilian real (BRL) | Import purchase | $ (99,150) | 2/1/2001 | 8/1/2001 |
| Swiss franc (CHF) | Import purchase | (82,800) | 3/1/2001 | 5/1/2001 |
| Belgian franc (BEF) | Export sale | 2,286,000 | 4/2/2001 | 7/2/2001 |
| South African rand (ZAR) | Export sale | 401,200 | 5/1/2001 | 11/1/2001 |
| Chinese yuan (CNY) | Export sale | 413,900 | 6/1/2001 | 8/31/2001 |
| Thai baht (THB) | Import purchase | (2,267,000) | 7/2/2001 | 10/1/2001 |
| British pound (GBP) | Import purchase | (34,900) | 8/1/2001 | 11/1/2001 |
| South Korean won (KRW) | Import purchase | (64,200,500) | 8/31/2001 | 11/30/2001 |

**Required:**

a. Create an electronic spreadsheet with the information from the preceding table. Label columns as follows:

> Foreign Currency
> Type of Transaction
> Amount in Foreign Currency
> Transaction Date
> Exchange Rate at Transaction Date
> $ Value at Transaction Date
> Settlement Date
> Exchange Rate at Settlement Date
> $ Value at Settlement Date
> Foreign Exchange Gain (Loss)

b. Use historical exchange rate information available on the internet at www.x-rates.com, Historic Lookup, to find the 2001 exchange rates between the American dollar and each foreign currency on the relevant transaction and settlement dates.

c. Complete the electronic spreadsheet to determine the foreign exchange gain (loss) on each transaction. Determine the total net foreign exchange gain (loss) reported in Import/Export Company's 2001 income statement.

# ANALYSIS CASE—CASH FLOW HEDGE

On February 1, 2004, Linber Company forecasted the purchase of component parts on May 1, 2004, at a price of 100,000 euros. On that date, Linber Company entered into a forward contract to purchase 100,000 euros on May 1, 2004. The forward contract is designated as a cash flow hedge of the forecasted transaction. The spot rate for euros on February 1, 2004, is $1 per euro. On May 1, 2004, the forward contract was settled, and the component parts were received and paid for. The parts were consumed in the second quarter 2004.

The following amounts were reported on Linber Company's financial statements related to this cash flow hedge (credit balances in parentheses).

| Income Statement | First Quarter 2004 | Second Quarter 2004 |
|---|---|---|
| Premium expense | $4,000 | $ 2,000 |
| Cost of goods sold | — | 103,000 |
| Adjustment to net income | — | 3,000 |

| Balance Sheet | 3/31/04 | 5/1/04 |
|---|---|---|
| Forward contract (liability) | $(1,980)* | — |
| AOCI (credit) | (2,020) | — |
| Change in cash | N/A | $(106,000) |

*$2,000 × 0.9901 = $1,980, where 0.9901 is the present value factor for one month at an annual interest rate of 12 percent calculated as 1/1.01.

### Required:

a. On January 15, 2004, what was the U.S. dollar per euro forward rate to May 1, 2004?
b. On March 31, 2004, what was the U.S. dollar per euro forward rate to May 1, 2004?
c. Was Linber Company better off or worse off as a result of having entered into this cash flow hedge of a forecasted transaction? By what amount?
d. What does the total premium expense of $6,000 reflect?

## INTERNET CASE—HISTORICAL EXCHANGE RATES

The Pier Ten Company made credit sales to three customers in Asia on December 17, 2001, with payment received on January 17, 2002. Information related to these sales is as follows:

| Customer | Location | Invoice Price |
| --- | --- | --- |
| Hang Fung Trading Ltd. | Hong Kong, China | 400,000 Hong Kong dollars |
| Daeron Industrial Company | Seoul, South Korea | 66,350,000 Korean won |
| Siam Commercial Ltd. | Bangkok, Thailand | 2,250,000 Thai baht |

The Pier Ten Company's fiscal year ends December 31.

### Required:

a. Use historical exchange rate information available on the internet at www.x-rates.com, Historic Lookup, to find the 2001 exchange rates between the American dollar and each foreign currency for December 17, 2001, December 31, 2001, and January 17, 2002.
b. Determine the foreign exchange gains and losses that Pier Ten would have recognized in net income in 2001 and 2002, and the overall foreign exchange gain or loss for each transaction. Determine for which transaction it would have been most important for Pier Ten to hedge its foreign exchange risk.
c. Pier Ten could have acquired a one-month put option on December 17, 2001, to hedge the foreign exchange risk associated with each of the three export sales. In each case, the put option would have cost $100. Determine for which hedges, if any, Pier Ten would have recognized a net gain on the foreign currency option.

## COMMUNICATION CASE—FORWARD CONTRACTS AND OPTIONS

Palmetto Bug Extermination Corporation (PBEC) regularly purchases chemicals from a supplier in Switzerland with the invoice price denominated in Swiss francs. PBEC has experienced several foreign exchange losses in the past year due to increases in the U.S. dollar price of the Swiss currency. As a result, Dewey Nukem, PBEC's CEO, has asked you to investigate the possibility of using derivative financial instruments, specifically foreign currency forward contracts and foreign currency options, to hedge the company's exposure to foreign exchange risk.

### Required:

Draft a memo to CEO Nukem comparing the advantages and disadvantages of using forward contracts and options to hedge foreign exchange risk. Recommend the type of hedging instrument you believe the company should employ and justify this recommendation.

# Chapter Eight

# Translation of Foreign Currency Financial Statements

## Questions to Consider

- What is a translation adjustment? How is it computed? Where should it be reported in a set of consolidated financial statements?
- What is balance sheet exposure and how does it compare with transaction exposure to foreign exchange risk?
- What are the different concepts underlying the temporal and current rate methods of translation? How does balance sheet exposure differ under these two methods of translation?
- What is a company's functional currency? How is this functional currency identified?
- When is remeasurement appropriate rather than translation of foreign currency balances?
- How does a remeasurement differ from a translation?
- Why would a company hedge a balance sheet exposure and how is this accounted for?

- Johnson & Johnson agreed to buy closely held Belgian drug maker Tibotec-Virco for about $320 million in cash and debt, adding experimental HIV and hepatitis drugs to a product line ranging from baby shampoo to artificial hips.[1]
- The H.J. Heinz Company said yesterday that it would take a 4.9 percent stake in Japan's largest ketchup maker, the Kagome Company, giving Heinz a platform to expand more aggressively in Asia.[2]
- General Motors concluded two years of negotiation for Daewoo Motors today, saying that it would sign an agreement on Tuesday to take over Daewoo for an initial payment of $400 million.[3]
- Vivendi Universal SA's $1.7 billion bid to acquire Houghton Mifflin Co. continues the trend of international media conglomerates taking over U.S. educational publishers; four of five largest U.S. textbook publishers are foreign companies, the exception being McGraw-Hill Cos.[4]

Recent announcements such as these have become more the norm than the exception in today's global economy. Companies establish operations in foreign countries for a variety of reasons including the development of new markets for their products, taking advantage of lower production costs, or gaining access to raw materials. Some multinational companies have reached a stage in their development in which domestic operations are no longer considered to be of higher priority than international operations. For example, U.S.-based International Flavors and Fragrances, Inc., has operations in 45 countries and has 60 percent of its segment assets outside North America. Coca-Cola Company generates more than 60 percent of its sales and 75 percent of its operating profit from foreign operations.

For the parent company, foreign operations create numerous managerial problems that do not exist for domestic operations. Some of these problems arise from cultural differences between the home and foreign countries. Other problems exist because foreign operations generally are required to comply with the laws and regulations of the foreign

---

[1] *Los Angeles Times*, March 23, 2002, part 3, p. 2.
[2] *The New York Times*, July 27, 2001, section C, p. 4.
[3] *The New York Times*, April 30, 2002, section W, p. 1.
[4] *Wall Street Journal*, June 4, 2001, section A, p. 14.

country. For example, in most countries, companies are required to prepare financial statements in the local currency using local accounting rules.

To prepare worldwide consolidated financial statements, a U.S. parent company must (1) convert the foreign GAAP financial statements of its foreign operations into U.S. GAAP and (2) translate the financial statements from the foreign currency into U.S. dollars. This conversion and translation process must be carried out regardless of whether the foreign operation is a branch, joint venture, majority-owned subsidiary, or affiliate accounted for under the equity method. This chapter deals with the issue of translating foreign currency financial statements into the parent's reporting currency.

Two major theoretical issues are related to the translation process: (1) which **translation method** should be used and (2) where the resulting **translation adjustment** should be reported in the consolidated financial statements. In this chapter, these two issues are examined first from a conceptual perspective and second by the manner in which these issues have been resolved by the FASB in the United States.

## EXCHANGE RATES USED IN TRANSLATION

Two types of exchange rates are used in translating financial statements:

1. **Historical exchange rate**—the exchange rate that exists when a transaction occurs.
2. **Current exchange rate**—the exchange rate that exists at the balance sheet date.

Translation methods differ as to which balance sheet and income statement accounts are translated at historical exchange rates and which are translated at current exchange rates.

Assume that the company described in the discussion question on the next page began operations in Gualos on December 31, 2004, when the exchange rate was $0.20 per vilsek. When Southwestern Corporation prepares its consolidated balance sheet at December 31, 2004, it had no choice about the exchange rate it uses to translate the Land account into U.S. dollars. The Land account carried on the foreign subsidiary's books at 150,000 vilseks is translated at an exchange rate of $0.20; $0.20 was both the *historical* and *current* exchange rate for the Land account at December 31, 2004.

| Consolidated Balance Sheet: 12/31/04 | |
|---|---|
| Land (150,000 vilseks × $0.20) . . . . . . . . . . . . . | $30,000 |

During the first quarter of 2005, the vilsek appreciates relative to the U.S. dollar by 15 percent; the exchange rate at March 31, 2005, is $0.23 per vilsek. In preparing its balance sheet at the end of the first quarter of 2005, Southwestern now must decide whether the Land account carried on the subsidiary's balance sheet at 150,000 vilseks should be translated into dollars using the *historical exchange rate* of $0.20 or the *current exchange rate* of $0.23.

If the historical exchange rate is used at March 31, 2005, Land continues to be carried on the consolidated balance sheet at $30,000 with no change from December 31, 2004.

| Historical Rate—Consolidated Balance Sheet: 3/31/05 | |
|---|---|
| Land (150,000 vilseks × $0.20) . . . . . . . . . . . . . | $30,000 |

If the current exchange rate is used, Land is carried on the consolidated balance sheet at $34,500, an increase of $4,500 from December 31, 2004.

# Discussion Question

**HOW DO WE REPORT THIS?**

The Southwestern Corporation operates throughout Texas buying and selling widgets. In hopes of expanding into more profitable markets, the company recently decided to open a small subsidiary in the nearby country of Gualos. The currency in Gualos is the vilsek. For some time, the government of that country held the exchange rate constant: 1 vilsek equaled $0.20 (or 5 vilseks equaled $1.00). Initially, Southwestern invested cash in this new operation; its $90,000 was converted into 450,000 vilseks ($90,000 × 5). One-third of this money (150,000 vilseks, or $30,000) was used to purchase land to be held for the possible construction of a plant, one-third was invested in short-term marketable securities, and one-third was spent in acquiring inventory for future resale.

Shortly thereafter, the Gualos government officially revalued the currency so that 1 vilsek was worth $0.23. Because of the strength of the local economy, the vilsek gained buying power in relation to the U.S. dollar. Now the vilsek was considered more valuable than in the past. The accountants for Southwestern realized that a change had occurred; each of the assets was now worth more in U.S. dollars than the original $30,000 investment: 150,000 vilseks × $0.23 = $34,500. Two of the company's top officers met to determine the appropriate method for reporting this change in currency values.

**Controller:** Nothing has changed. Our cost is still $30,000 for each item. That's what we spent. Accounting uses historical cost wherever possible. Thus, we should do nothing.

**Finance director:** Yes, but the old rates are meaningless now. We would be foolish to report figures based on a rate that no longer exists. The cost is still 150,000 vilseks for each item. You are right, the cost has not changed. However, the vilsek is now worth $0.23, so our reported value must change.

**Controller:** The new rate affects us only if we take money out of the country. We don't plan to do that for many years. The rate will probably change 20 more times before we remove money from Gualos. We've got to stick to our $30,000 historical cost. That's our cost and that's good, basic accounting.

**Finance director:** You mean that for the next 20 years we will be translating balances for external reporting purposes using an exchange rate that has not existed for years? That doesn't make sense. I have a real problem using an antiquated rate for the investments and inventory. They will be sold for cash when the new rate is in effect. These balances have no remaining relation to the original exchange rate.

**Controller:** You misunderstand the impact of an exchange rate fluctuation. Within Gualos, no impact occurs. One vilsek is still one vilsek. The effect is realized only when an actual conversion takes place into U.S. dollars at a new rate. At that point, we will properly measure and report the gain or loss. That is when realization takes place. Until then our cost has not changed.

**Finance director:** I simply see no value at all in producing financial information based entirely on an exchange rate that does not exist. I don't care when realization takes place.

**Controller:** You've got to stick with historical cost, believe me. The exchange rate today isn't important unless we actually convert vilseks to dollars.

How should Southwestern report each of these three assets on its current balance sheet? Does the company have a gain because the value of the vilsek has increased relative to the U.S. dollar?

---

**Current Rate—Consolidated Balance Sheet: 3/31/05**

Land (150,000 vilseks × $0.23) . . . . . . . . . . . . . $34,500

## Translation Adjustments

To keep the accounting equation (A = L + OE) in balance, the increase of $4,500 on the asset (A) side of the consolidated balance sheet when the current exchange rate is used must be offset by an equal $4,500 *increase* in owners' equity (OE) on the other side of the balance sheet. The increase in owners' equity is called a **positive translation adjustment.** It has a *credit* balance.

The increase in dollar value of the Land due to appreciation of the vilsek creates a positive translation adjustment. This is true for any asset on the Gualos subsidiary's balance sheet that is translated at the *current* exchange rate. *Assets translated at the current exchange rate when the foreign currency has appreciated generate a positive (credit) translation adjustment.*

Liabilities on the Gualos subsidiary's balance sheet that are translated at the current exchange rate also increase in dollar value when the vilsek appreciates. For example, Notes Payable of 10,000 vilseks would be reported at $2,000 on the December 31, 2004, balance sheet and at $2,300 on the March 31, 2005, balance sheet. To keep the accounting equation in balance, the increase in liabilities (L) must be offset by a *decrease* in owners' equity (OE), giving rise to a **negative translation adjustment.** This has a *debit* balance. *Liabilities translated at the current exchange rate when the foreign currency has appreciated generate a negative (debit) translation adjustment.*

## Balance Sheet Exposure

Balance sheet items (assets and liabilities) translated at the *current* exchange rate change in dollar value from balance sheet to balance sheet as a result of the change in exchange rate. These items are *exposed* to translation adjustment. Balance sheet items translated at *historical* exchange rates do not change in dollar value from one balance sheet to the next. These items are *not* exposed to translation adjustment. Exposure to translation adjustment is referred to as *balance sheet, translation,* or *accounting exposure.* **Balance sheet exposure** can be contrasted with the **transaction exposure** discussed in Chapter 7 that arises when a company has foreign currency receivables and payables in the following way: *Transaction exposure gives rise to foreign exchange gains and losses that are ultimately realized in cash; translation adjustments arising from balance sheet exposure do not directly result in cash inflows or outflows.*

Each item translated at the current exchange rate is exposed to translation adjustment. In effect, a separate translation adjustment exists for each of these exposed items. However, positive translation adjustments on assets when the foreign currency appreciates are offset by negative translation adjustments on liabilities. If total exposed assets are equal to total exposed liabilities throughout the year, the translation adjustments (although perhaps significant on an individual basis) net to a zero balance. The *net* translation adjustment needed to keep the consolidated balance sheet in balance is based solely on the *net asset* or *net liability* exposure.

A foreign operation has a **net asset balance sheet exposure** when assets translated at the current exchange rate are larger in amount than liabilities translated at the current exchange rate. A **net liability balance sheet exposure** exists when liabilities translated at the current exchange rate are larger than assets translated at the current exchange rate. The relationship between exchange rate fluctuations, balance sheet exposure, and translation adjustments is summarized as follows:

| Balance Sheet | Foreign Currency (FC) | |
| --- | --- | --- |
| Exposure | Appreciates | Depreciates |
| Net Asset | Positive translation adjustment | Negative translation adjustment |
| Net Liability | Negative translation adjustment | Positive translation adjustment |

Exactly how the translation adjustment should be handled in the consolidated financial statements is a matter of some debate. The major issue is whether the translation adjustment should be treated as a *translation gain or loss reported in net income* or whether the translation adjustment should be treated as a *direct adjustment to owners' equity without affecting net income.* We consider this issue in more detail later after examining methods of translation.

# TRANSLATION METHODS

Two major methods of translation are currently used: (1) the current rate (or closing rate) method and (2) the temporal method. We discuss these methods from the perspective of a U.S.-based multinational company translating foreign currency financial statements into U.S. dollars.

## Current Rate Method

The basic assumption underlying the **current rate method** is that a company's *net investment in a foreign operation is exposed* to foreign exchange risk. In other words, a foreign operation represents a foreign currency net asset and if the foreign currency *decreases* in value against the U.S. dollar, there is a *decrease in the U.S. dollar value of the foreign currency net asset.* This decrease in U.S. dollar value of the net investment will be reflected by reporting a *negative* (debit balance) translation adjustment in the consolidated financial statements. If the foreign currency *increases* in value, there is an *increase in the U.S. dollar value of the net asset,* which will be reflected through a *positive* (credit balance) translation adjustment.

To measure the net investment's exposure to foreign exchange risk, *all assets and all liabilities* of the foreign operation are translated at the *current* exchange rate. Stockholders' equity items are translated at historical rates. *The balance sheet exposure under the current rate method is equal to the foreign operation's net asset (total assets minus total liabilities) position.*[5]

Total assets > Total liabilities → Net asset exposure

A positive translation adjustment arises when the foreign currency appreciates and a negative translation adjustment arises when the foreign currency depreciates.

As mentioned earlier, the major difference between the translation adjustment and a foreign exchange gain or loss is that the translation adjustment is not necessarily realized through inflows and outflows of cash. The translation adjustment arising when the current rate method is used is unrealized. It can become a realized gain or loss only if the foreign operation is sold (for its book value) and the foreign currency proceeds from the sale are converted into U.S. dollars.

Under the current rate method, all income statement items are translated at the exchange rate in effect at the date of accounting recognition. In most cases, an assumption can be made that the revenue or expense is incurred evenly throughout the accounting period and a weighted average-for-the-period exchange rate can be used for translation. However, when an income account, such as a gain or loss, occurs at a specific point in time, the exchange rate at that date should be used for translation.[6]

## Temporal Method

The basic objective underlying the **temporal method** of translation is to produce a set of U.S. dollar translated financial statements as if the foreign subsidiary had actually used U.S. dollars in conducting its operations. Continuing with the Gualos subsidiary example presented earlier, the Land account should be reported on the consolidated balance sheet at the amount of U.S. dollars that would have been spent if the U.S. parent had sent dollars to the subsidiary to purchase land. Since the land had a cost of 150,000 vilseks at a time when one vilsek could be acquired with $0.20, the parent would have sent $30,000 to the subsidiary to acquire the land; this is the land's historical cost *in U.S. dollar terms.* Consistent with the temporal method's underlying objective is the following rule:

1. Assets and liabilities carried on the foreign operation's balance sheet at *historical cost* are translated at *historical* exchange rates to yield an equivalent historical cost in U.S. dollars.

---

[5] In rare cases, a foreign subsidiary could have liabilities greater than assets (negative stockholders' equity). In those cases, a net liability exposure exists under the current rate method.

[6] Alternatively, all income statement items may be translated at the current exchange rate. Later we demonstrate that translation at the current rate has a slight advantage over translation at the average-for-the-period rate.

2. Conversely, assets and liabilities carried at a *current or future value* are translated at the *current* exchange rate to yield an equivalent current value in U.S. dollars.

Application of this rule maintains the underlying valuation method (current value or historical cost) used by the foreign subsidiary in accounting for its assets and liabilities. In addition, stockholders' equity accounts are translated at historical exchange rates.

Cash, marketable securities, receivables, and most liabilities are carried at current or future value and translated at the *current* exchange rate under the temporal method.[7] The temporal method generates either a net asset or a net liability balance sheet exposure, depending on whether cash plus marketable securities plus receivables are more than or less than liabilities.

$$\text{Cash} + \text{Marketable securities} + \text{Receivables} > \text{Liabilities} \rightarrow \text{Net asset exposure}$$

$$\text{Cash} + \text{Marketable securities} + \text{Receivables} < \text{Liabilities} \rightarrow \text{Net liability exposure}$$

Because liabilities (current plus long-term) usually are more than assets translated at the current exchange rate, *a net liability exposure generally exists when the temporal method is used.*

One way to understand the concept of exposure underlying the temporal method is to pretend that the foreign operation's cash, marketable securities, receivables, and payables are actually carried on the parent's balance sheet. For example, consider the Japanese subsidiary of a U.S. parent company. The Japanese yen receivables of the Japanese subsidiary that result from sales in Japan may be thought of as Japanese yen receivables of the U.S. parent that result from export sales to Japan. If the U.S. parent had yen receivables on its balance sheet, a decrease in the value of the yen would result in a *foreign exchange* loss. There also would be a foreign exchange loss on the Japanese yen held in cash by the U.S. parent and on the Japanese yen denominated marketable securities. These foreign exchange losses would be offset by a foreign exchange gain on the parent's Japanese yen payables resulting from foreign purchases. Whether a net gain or a net loss exists depends on the relative size of yen cash, marketable securities, and receivables versus yen payables. Under the temporal method, the translation adjustment measures the "net foreign exchange gain or loss" on the foreign operation's cash, marketable securities, receivables, and payables, *as if those items were actually carried on the books of the parent.*

Again, the major difference between the translation adjustment resulting from use of the temporal method and a foreign exchange gain or loss is that the translation adjustment is not necessarily realized through inflows or outflows of cash. The U.S. dollar translation adjustment in this case *could be realized* only if (1) the parent sends U.S. dollars to the Japanese subsidiary to pay off all its yen liabilities and (2) the Japanese subsidiary converts its yen receivables and marketable securities into yen cash and then sends this amount plus the amount in its yen cash account to the parent in the U.S. where it is converted into U.S. dollars.

Under the temporal method, income statement items are translated at exchange rates that exist when the revenue is generated or the expense is incurred. For most items, an assumption can be made that the revenue or expense is incurred evenly throughout the accounting period and an average-for-the-period exchange rate can be used for translation. However, some expenses are related to assets carried at historical cost; for example, cost of goods sold, depreciation of fixed assets, and amortization of intangibles. Since the related assets are translated at historical exchange rates, these expenses must be translated at historical rates as well.

The current rate method and temporal method are the two methods currently used in the United States. They are also the predominant methods used worldwide. A summary of the appropriate exchange rate for selected financial statement items under these two methods is presented in Exhibit 8–1.

---

[7] Under *SFAS 105,* all marketable equity securities and marketable debt securities that are classified as "trading" or "available for sale" are carried at current market value. Marketable debt securities classified as "hold to maturity" are carried at cost. Throughout the remainder of this chapter, it will be assumed that all marketable securities are reported at current value.

**EXHIBIT 8–1**
Exchange Rates for Selected Financial Statement Items

|  | Temporal Method Exchange Rate | Current Rate Method Exchange Rate |
|---|---|---|
| **Balance Sheet** | | |
| **Assets** | | |
| Cash and receivables | Current | Current |
| Marketable securities | Current* | Current |
| Inventory at market | Current | Current |
| Inventory at cost | Historical | Current |
| Prepaid expenses | Historical | Current |
| Property, plant, and equipment | Historical | Current |
| Intangible assets | Historical | Current |
| **Liabilities** | | |
| Current liabilities | Current | Current |
| Deferred income | Historical | Current |
| Long-term debt | Current | Current |
| **Stockholders' equity** | | |
| Capital stock | Historical | Historical |
| Additional paid-in capital | Historical | Historical |
| Retained earnings | Composite | Composite |
| Dividends | Historical | Historical |
| **Income Statement** | | |
| Revenues | Average | Average |
| Most expenses | Average | Average |
| Cost of goods sold | Historical | Average |
| Depreciation of property, plant, and equipment | Historical | Average |
| Amortization of intangibles | Historical | Average |

*Marketable debt securities classified as hold to maturity are carried at cost and translated at the historical exchange rate under the temporal method.

## Translation of Retained Earnings

Stockholders' equity items are translated at historical exchange rates under both the temporal and current rate methods. This creates somewhat of a problem in translating retained earnings. This figure is actually a composite of many previous transactions: all revenues, expenses, gains, losses, and declared dividends occurring over the life of the company. At the end of the first year of operations, foreign currency (FC) retained earnings is translated as follows:

| | | |
|---|---|---|
| Net income in FC | [translated per method used to translate income statement items] | = Net income in $ |
| − Dividends in FC | × historical exchange rate when declared | = − Dividends in $ |
| Ending R/E in FC | | Ending R/E in $ |

The ending dollar amount of retained earnings in year 1 becomes the beginning dollar retained earnings for year 2 and the translated retained earnings in year 2 (and subsequent years) is then determined as follows:

| | | |
|---|---|---|
| Beginning R/E in FC | (from last year's translation) | = Beginning R/E in $ |
| + Net income in FC | [translated per method used to translate income statement items] | = + Net income in $ |
| − Dividends in FC | × historical exchange rate when declared | = − Dividends in $ |
| Ending R/E in FC | | Ending R/E in $ |

The same approach translates retained earnings under both the current rate and the temporal methods. The only difference is that translation of the current period's net income is calculated differently under the two methods.

# COMPLICATING ASPECTS OF THE TEMPORAL METHOD

Under the temporal method, it is necessary to keep a record of the exchange rates when inventory, prepaid expenses, fixed assets, and intangible assets are acquired because these assets, carried at historical cost, are translated at historical exchange rates. Keeping track of the historical rates for these assets is not necessary under the current rate method. Translating these assets at historical rates makes application of the temporal method more complicated than the current rate method.

## Calculation of Cost of Goods Sold (COGS)

Under the *current rate method,* the account COGS in Foreign Currency (FC) is simply translated using the average-for-the-period exchange rate (ER):

$$\text{COGS in FC} \times \text{Average ER} = \text{COGS in \$}$$

Under the *temporal method,* COGS must be decomposed into beginning inventory, purchases, and ending inventory, and each component of COGS must then be translated at its appropriate historical rate. For example, if beginning inventory (FIFO basis) in the year 2004 was acquired evenly throughout the fourth quarter of 2003, then the average exchange rate in the fourth quarter of 2003 is used to translate beginning inventory. Likewise, the fourth quarter (4thQ) 2004 exchange rate is used to translate ending inventory. When purchases can be assumed to have been made evenly throughout 2004, then the average 2004 exchange rate is used to translate purchases:

```
Beginning inventory in FC   ×   Historical ER (4thQ 2003)   =   Beginning inventory in $
+ Purchases in FC           ×   Average ER (2004)           =   + Purchases in $
− Ending inventory in FC    ×   Historical ER (4thQ 2004)   =   − Ending inventory in $
COGS in FC                                                      COGS in $
```

No single exchange rate can be used to directly translate COGS in FC into COGS in $.

## Application of the Lower-of-Cost-or-Market Rule

Under the *current rate method,* the ending inventory reported on the foreign currency balance sheet is translated at the current exchange rate regardless of whether it is carried at cost or a lower market value. Application of the *temporal method* requires the foreign currency cost and foreign currency market value of the inventory to be translated into U.S. dollars at appropriate exchange rates, and the *lower of the dollar cost and dollar market value* is reported on the consolidated balance sheet. As a result of this procedure, it is possible for inventory to be carried at cost on the foreign currency balance sheet and at market value on the U.S. dollar consolidated balance sheet, and vice versa.

## Fixed Assets, Depreciation, Accumulated Depreciation

Under the *temporal method,* fixed assets acquired at different times must be translated at different (historical) exchange rates. The same is true for depreciation of fixed assets and accumulated depreciation related to fixed assets.

For example, assume that a company purchases a piece of equipment on January 1, 2004, for FC 1,000 when the exchange rate is $1.00 per FC. Another item of equipment is purchased on January 1, 2005, for FC 5,000 when the exchange rate is $1.20 per FC. Both pieces of equipment have a five-year useful life. Under the temporal method, the amount at which the equipment would be reported on the consolidated balance sheet on December 31, 2006, when the exchange rate is $1.50 per FC, is as follows:

```
FC  1,000 × $1.00 = $1,000
    5,000 ×  1.20 =  6,000
FC  6,000          $7,000
```

Depreciation expense for 2006 under the temporal method is calculated as shown here:

$$\begin{array}{rl} \text{FC} & 200 \times \$1.00 = \$\ \ 200 \\ & \underline{1{,}000} \times \ \ 1.20 = \underline{1{,}200} \\ \text{FC} & \underline{\underline{1{,}200}} \qquad\qquad \underline{\underline{\$1{,}400}} \end{array}$$

Accumulated depreciation under the temporal method is calculated as shown:

$$\begin{array}{rl} \text{FC} & \ \ 600 \times \$1.00 = \$\ \ 600 \\ & \underline{2{,}000} \times \ \ 1.20 = \underline{2{,}400} \\ \text{FC} & \underline{\underline{2{,}600}} \qquad\qquad \underline{\underline{\$3{,}000}} \end{array}$$

Similar procedures apply for intangible assets as well.

Under the *current rate method,* equipment would be reported on the December 31, 2006, balance sheet at FC 6,000 × $1.50 = $9,000. Depreciation expense would be translated at the average exchange rate of $1.40, FC 1,200 × $1.40 = $1,680, and accumulated depreciation would be FC 2,600 × $1.50 = $3,900.

In this example, the foreign subsidiary has only two fixed assets requiring translation. For subsidiaries that own hundreds and thousands of fixed assets, the temporal method can require substantial additional work as compared to the current rate method.

### Gain or Loss on the Sale of an Asset

Assume that a foreign subsidiary sells land that cost FC 1,000 at a selling price of FC 1,200. A gain on the sale of land of FC 200 is reported in the subsidiary's income statement. The land was acquired when the exchange rate was $1.00 per FC; the sale was made when the exchange rate was $1.20 per FC; and the exchange rate at the balance sheet date is $1.50 per FC.

Under the *current rate method,* the gain on sale of land is translated at the exchange rate in effect at the date of sale:

$$\text{FC } 200 \times \$1.20 = \$240$$

Under the *temporal method*, the gain on the sale of land cannot be translated directly. Instead, the cash received and the cost of the land sold are translated into U.S. dollars separately, with the difference being the U.S. dollar value of the gain. In accordance with the rules of the temporal method, the Cash account is translated at the exchange rate on the date of sale, and the Land account is translated at the historical rate:

$$\begin{array}{lrl} \text{Cash} & \text{FC } 1{,}200 \times \$1.20 = & \$1{,}440 \\ \text{Land} & \underline{1{,}000} \times \ \ 1.00 = & \underline{1{,}000} \\ \text{Gain} & \text{FC } \underline{\underline{\ \ \ 200}} & \underline{\underline{\$\ \ \ 440}} \end{array}$$

## DISPOSITION OF TRANSLATION ADJUSTMENT

The first issue related to the translation of foreign currency financial statements is selecting the appropriate method. The *second issue* in financial statement translation relates to deciding *where the resulting translation adjustment should be reported in the consolidated financial statements*. There are two prevailing schools of thought with regard to this issue:

1. **Translation gain or loss**—Under this treatment, the translation adjustment is considered to be a gain or loss analogous to the gains and losses arising from foreign currency transactions and should be reported in net income in the period in which the fluctuation in the exchange rate occurs.

The first of two conceptual problems with treating translation adjustments as gains or losses in income is the gain or loss is unrealized; that is, there is no accompanying cash inflow or outflow. The second problem is the gain or loss could not be consistent with economic reality. For example, the depreciation of a foreign currency can have a *positive* impact on the foreign operation's export sales and income, but the particular translation method used gives rise to a translation *loss*.

2. **Cumulative translation adjustment in other comprehensive income**—The alternative to reporting the translation adjustment as a gain or loss in net income is to include it in Other Comprehensive Income. In effect, this treatment defers the gain or loss in stockholders' equity until realized in some way. As a balance sheet account, the cumulative translation adjustment is not closed at the end of an accounting period and will fluctuate in amount over time.

The two major translation methods and the two possible treatments for the translation adjustment give rise to these four possible combinations:

| Combination | Translation Method | Treatment of Translation Adjustment |
|---|---|---|
| A | Temporal | Gain or loss in Net Income |
| B | Temporal | Deferred in Other Comprehensive Income |
| C | Current rate | Gain or loss in Net Income |
| D | Current rate | Deferred in Other Comprehensive Income |

# U.S. RULES

Prior to 1975 the United States had no authoritative rules about which translation method to use or where the translation adjustment had to be reported in the consolidated financial statements. Different combinations were used by different companies. As an indication of the importance of this particular accounting issue, the first official pronouncement issued by the newly created FASB in 1974 was *SFAS 1,* "Disclosure of Foreign Currency Translation Information." *SFAS 1* did not express a preference for any particular combination but simply required disclosure of the method used and the treatment of the translation adjustment.

The use of different combinations by different companies created a lack of comparability across companies. To eliminate this noncomparability, in 1975 the FASB issued *SFAS 8,* "Accounting for the Translation of Foreign Currency Transactions and Foreign Currency Financial Statements." *SFAS 8* mandated use of the *temporal method* with *translation gains or losses* reported in net income by all companies for all foreign operations (Combination A).

U.S. multinational companies (MNCs) were strongly opposed to *SFAS 8*. Specifically, they considered reporting translation gains and losses in income to be inappropriate given that they are unrealized. Moreover, as currency fluctuations often reversed themselves in subsequent quarters, artificial volatility in quarterly earnings resulted.

After releasing two exposure drafts proposing new translation rules, the FASB finally issued *SFAS 52,* "Foreign Currency Translation," in 1981. This resulted in a complete overhaul of U.S. GAAP with regard to foreign currency translation. *SFAS 52* was approved by a narrow four-to-three vote of the Board, indicating how contentious the issue of foreign currency translation has been.

## SFAS 52

Implicit in the **temporal method** is the assumption that foreign subsidiaries of U.S. MNCs have very close ties to their parent companies and would actually carry out their day-to-day operations and keep their books in the U.S. dollar if they could. To reflect the integrated nature of the foreign subsidiary with its U.S. parent, the translation process should create a set of U.S. dollar translated financial statements as if the dollar had actually been used by the foreign subsidiary. This is the **U.S. dollar perspective** to translation that was adopted in *SFAS* 8.

In *SFAS 52,* the FASB recognized two types of foreign entities. First, some foreign entities are so closely integrated with their parents that they do conduct much of their business in U.S. dollars. *Second, other foreign entities are relatively self-contained and integrated with the local economy; primarily, they use a foreign currency in their daily operations.* For the first type of entity, the FASB determined that the U.S. dollar perspective still applies and, therefore, *SFAS 8* rules are still relevant.

For the second relatively independent type of entity, a **local currency perspective** to translation is applicable. For this type of entity, the FASB determined that a different translation methodology, namely the *current rate method,* should be used for translation and that translation adjustments should be reported as a *separate component in other comprehensive income* (Combination D on page 381). In addition, the FASB requires using the *average-for-the-period* exchange rate in translating income when the current rate method is used.

In rationalizing the placement of the translation adjustment in stockholders' equity rather than net income, *SFAS 52* (paras. 113, 114) offered two contrasting positions on the conceptual nature of the translation adjustment. One view is that the "change in the dollar equivalent of the net investment is an unrealized enhancement or reduction, having no effect on the functional currency net cash flow generated by the foreign entity which may be currently reinvested or distributed to the parent." Philosophically, this position holds that even though gains and losses are created by changes in the exchange rate, they are unrealized in nature and should, therefore, not be included within net income.

The alternative perspective put forth by the FASB "regards the translation adjustment as merely a mechanical by-product of the translation process." This second contention argues that no meaningful effect is created by exchange rate fluctuation; the resulting translation adjustment merely serves to keep the balance sheet in equilibrium.

*Interestingly enough, the FASB chose not to express preference for either of these theoretical views.* The Board felt no need to offer a hint of guidance as to the essential nature of the translation adjustment because both explanations point to its exclusion from net income. Thus, a balance sheet figure that can amount to millions of dollars is basically undefined.

### *Functional Currency*

To determine whether a specific foreign operation is integrated with its parent or self-contained and integrated with the local economy, *SFAS 52* created the concept of the **functional currency.** The functional currency is the primary currency of the foreign entity's operating environment. It can be either the parent's currency (U.S.$) or a foreign currency (generally the local currency). *SFAS 52's* functional currency orientation results in the following rule:

| Functional Currency | Translation Method | Translation Adjustment |
|---|---|---|
| U.S. dollar | Temporal method | Gain (loss) in Net Income |
| Foreign currency | Current rate method | Separate component of Other Comprehensive Income (Stockholders' Equity) |

In addition to introducing the concept of the *functional currency, SFAS 52* introduced some new terminology. The **reporting currency** is the currency in which the entity prepares its financial statements. For U.S.-based corporations, this is the U.S. dollar. If a foreign operation's functional currency is the U.S. dollar, foreign currency balances must be **remeasured** into U.S. dollars using the temporal method with translation adjustments reported as **remeasurement gains and losses** in income. When a foreign currency is the functional currency, foreign currency balances are **translated** using the current rate method and a **translation adjustment** is reported on the balance sheet.

The functional currency is essentially a matter of fact. However, *SFAS 52* (para. 8) states that for many cases, "management's judgment will be required to determine the functional currency in which financial results and relationships are measured with the greatest degree of relevance and reliability." *SFAS 52* provides a list of indicators to guide parent company management in its determination of a foreign entity's functional currency (see Exhibit 8–2). *SFAS 52* provides no guidance as to how these indicators are to be weighted in determining the functional currency. Leaving the decision about identifying the functional currency up to management allows some leeway in this process. Different companies approach this selection in different ways:

**EXHIBIT 8–2**
SFAS 52 Indicators for Determining the Functional Currency

|  | Indication that Functional Currency Is the | |
|---|---|---|
| **Indicator** | **Foreign Currency** | **Parent's Currency** |
| Cash flow | Primarily in FC and do not affect parent's cash flows | Directly impact parent's cash flows on a current basis |
| Sales price | Not affected on short-term basis by changes in exchange rate | Affected on short-term basis by changes in exchange rate |
| Sales market | Active local sales market | Sales market mostly in parent's country or sales denominated in parent's currency |
| Expenses | Primarily local costs | Primarily costs for components obtained from parent's country |
| Financing | Primarily denominated in foreign currency and FC cash flows adequate to service obligations | Primarily from parent or denominated in parent currency or FC cash flows not adequate to service obligations |
| Intercompany transactions | Low volume of intercompany transactions, not extensive interrelationship with parent's operations | High volume of intercompany transactions and extensive interrelationship with parent's operations |

"For us it was intuitively obvious," versus "It was quite a process. We took the six criteria and developed a matrix. We then considered the dollar amount and the related percentages in developing a point scheme. Each of the separate criteria was given equal weight (in the analytical methods applied)."[8]

Research has shown that the weighting schemes used by U.S. multinationals for determining the functional currency might be biased toward selection of the *foreign currency* as the functional currency.[9] This would be rational behavior for multinationals given that, when the foreign currency is the functional currency, the translation adjustment is reported in stockholders' equity and does not affect net income.

## Highly Inflationary Economies

For those foreign entities located in a **highly inflationary economy,** it is not necessary to determine the functional currency; *SFAS 52* mandates use of the *temporal method* with *remeasurement gains or losses reported in income.*

A country is defined has having a *highly inflationary economy* when its cumulative three-year inflation exceeds 100 percent. With compounding, this equates to an average of approximately 26 percent per year for three years in a row. Countries that have met this definition at some time since *SFAS 52* was implemented include Argentina, Brazil, Israel, Mexico, and Turkey. In any given year, a country may or may not be classified as highly inflationary, depending on its most recent three-year experience with inflation.

One reason for this rule is to avoid a "disappearing plant problem" caused by using the current rate method in a country with high inflation. Remember that under the current rate method, all assets (including fixed assets) are translated at the current exchange rate. To see the problem this creates in a highly inflationary economy, consider the following hypothetical example.

The Brazilian subsidiary of a U.S. parent purchased land at the end of 1984 for 10,000,000 cruzeiros (Cr$) when the exchange rate was $0.001 per Cr$. Under the *current rate method,* the land would be reported in the parent's consolidated balance sheet at $10,000.

---

[8] Jerry L. Arnold and William W. Holder, *Impact of Statement 52 on Decisions, Financial Reports and Attitudes* (Morristown, N.J.: Financial Executives Research Foundation, 1986), p. 89.

[9] Timothy S. Doupnik and Thomas G. Evans, "Functional Currency as a Strategy to Smooth Income," *Advances in International Accounting,* 1988.

|      | Historical Cost |   | Current ER |   | Consolidated B.S. |
|------|-----------------|---|------------|---|-------------------|
| 1984 | Cr$ 10,000,000  | × | $0.001     | = | $10,000           |

In 1985, Brazil experienced roughly 200 percent inflation. Accordingly, with the forces of purchasing power parity at work, the cruzeiro plummeted against the U.S. dollar to a value of $0.00025 at the end of 1985. Under the current rate method, land now would be reported in the parent's consolidated balance sheet at $2,500, and a negative translation adjustment of $7,500 would result.

|      | Historical Cost |   | Current ER |   | Consolidated B.S. |
|------|-----------------|---|------------|---|-------------------|
| 1985 | Cr$ 10,000,000  | × | $0.00025   | = | $2,500            |

Using the current rate method, the land has lost 75 percent of its U.S. dollar value in one year—and land is not even a depreciable asset!

High rates of inflation continued in Brazil with the high point of roughly 1,800 percent reached in 1993. As a result of applying the current rate method, the land originally reported on the 1984 consolidated balance sheet at $10,000 was carried on the 1993 balance sheet at less than $1.00.

In the exposure draft leading to *SFAS 52,* the FASB proposed requiring companies with operations in highly inflationary countries to first **restate** the historical costs for inflation and then **translate** using the current rate method. For example, with 200 percent inflation in 1985, the Land account would have been written up to Cr$ 40,000,000 and then translated at the current exchange rate of $0.00025. This would have produced a translated amount of $10,000, the same as in 1984.

Companies objected to making inflation adjustments, however, because of a lack of reliable inflation indices in many countries. The FASB backed off from requiring the **restate/translate** approach; instead *SFAS 52* requires using the temporal method in high inflationary countries. In the previous example, under the *temporal method,* a firm would use the historical rate of $0.001 to translate the land value year after year. Land would be carried on the consolidated balance sheet at $10,000 each year, thereby avoiding the disappearing plant problem.

## THE PROCESS ILLUSTRATED

To provide a basis for demonstrating the translation and remeasurement procedures prescribed by *SFAS 52,* assume that USCO (a U.S.-based company) forms a wholly owned subsidiary in Switzerland (SWISSCO) on December 31, 2003. On that date, USCO invested $300,000 in exchange for all of the subsidiary's common stock. Given the exchange rate of $0.60 per Swiss franc (CHF), the initial capital investment was CHF 500,000, of which CHF 150,000 was immediately invested in inventory and the remainder held in cash. Thus, SWISSCO began operations on January 1, 2004, with stockholders' equity (net assets) of CHF 500,000 and net monetary assets of CHF 350,000.

**SWISSCO**
**Opening Balance Sheet**
**January 1, 2004**

| Assets    | CHF         | Liabilities and Equity     | CHF         |
|-----------|-------------|----------------------------|-------------|
| Cash      | CHF 350,000 | Common stock               | CHF 100,000 |
| Inventory | 150,000     | Additional paid-in capital | 400,000     |
|           | CHF 500,000 |                            | CHF 500,000 |

During 2004, SWISSCO purchased property and equipment, acquired a patent, and made additional purchases of inventory, primarily on account. A five-year loan was negotiated to help finance the purchase of equipment. Sales were made, primarily on account, and expenses were incurred. Income after taxes of CHF 470,000 was generated, with dividends of CHF 150,000 declared on October 1, 2004.

As a company incorporated in Switzerland, SWISSCO must account for its activities using Swiss accounting rules, which differ from U.S. GAAP in many respects. As noted in the introduction to this chapter, to prepare consolidated financial statements, USCO must first convert SWISSCO's financial statements to a U.S. GAAP basis. SWISSCO's U.S. GAAP financial statements for the year 2004 in Swiss francs appear in Exhibit 8–3.

To properly translate the Swiss franc financial statements into U.S. dollars, USCO must gather exchange rates between the Swiss franc and U.S. dollar at various points in time. Relevant exchange rates are as follows:

| | |
|---|---|
| January 1, 2004 | $0.60 |
| Rate when property and equipment were acquired and long-term debt was incurred, March 15, 2004 | $0.61 |
| Rate when patent was acquired, April 10, 2004 | $0.62 |
| Average 2004 | $0.65 |
| Rate when dividends were declared, October 1, 2004 | $0.67 |
| Average fourth quarter 2004 | $0.68 |
| December 31, 2004 | $0.70 |

As you can see, the Swiss franc steadily appreciated against the dollar during the year.

# TRANSLATION OF FINANCIAL STATEMENTS—CURRENT RATE METHOD

The first step in translating foreign currency financial statements is determining the functional currency. Assuming that the Swiss franc is the functional currency, the income statement and statement of retained earnings would be translated into U.S. dollars using the current rate method as shown in Exhibit 8–4.

All revenues and expenses are translated at the exchange rate in effect at the date of accounting recognition. The weighted average exchange rate for 2004 is utilized here because each revenue and expense in this illustration would have been recognized evenly throughout the year. However, when an income account, such as a gain or loss, occurs at a specific point in time, the exchange rate as of that date is applied. Depreciation and amortization expense also are translated at the average rate for the year. These expenses accrue evenly throughout the year even though the journal entry could have been delayed until year-end for convenience.

The translated amount of net income for 2004 is brought down from the income statement into the statement of retained earnings. Dividends are translated at the exchange rate on the date of declaration.

## Translation of the Balance Sheet

Looking at SWISSCO's translated balance sheet in Exhibit 8–5, note that all assets and liabilities are translated at the current exchange rate. Common stock and additional paid-in capital are translated at the exchange rate on the day the common stock was originally sold. Retained earnings at December 31, 2004, is brought down from the statement of retained earnings. Application of these procedures results in total assets of $1,169,000, and total liabilities and equities of $1,100,000. The balance sheet is brought back into balance by creating a positive translation adjustment of $69,000 that is treated as an increase in Stockholders' Equity.

Note that the translation adjustment for 2004 is a *positive* $69,000 (credit balance). The sign of the translation adjustment (positive or negative) is a function of two factors: (1) the nature of the balance sheet exposure (asset or liability) and (2) the change in the exchange rate (appreciation or depreciation). In this illustration, SWISSCO has a *net asset exposure* (total assets translated at the current exchange rate are more than total liabilities at the current exchange rate), and the Swiss franc has *appreciated,* creating a *positive translation adjustment.*

**EXHIBIT 8–3**
**Foreign Currency Financial Statements**

## SWISSCO
### Income Statement
### For Year Ending December 31, 2004

|  | CHF |
|---|---|
| Sales | 4,000,000 |
| Cost of goods sold | 3,000,000 |
| Gross profit | 1,000,000 |
| Depreciation expense | 100,000 |
| Amortization expense | 10,000 |
| Other expenses | 220,000 |
| Income before income taxes | 670,000 |
| Income taxes | 200,000 |
| Net income | 470,000 |

### Statement of Retained Earnings
### For Year Ending December 31, 2004

|  | CHF |
|---|---|
| Retained earnings, 1/1/04 | –0– |
| Net income, 2004 | 470,000 |
| Less: Dividends, 10/1/04 | 150,000 |
| Retained earnings, 12/31/04 | 320,000 |

### Balance Sheet
### December 31, 2004

| Assets | CHF | Liabilities and Equity | CHF |
|---|---|---|---|
| Cash | 130,000 | Accounts payable | 600,000 |
| Accounts receivable | 200,000 | Total current liabilities | 600,000 |
| Inventory* | 400,000 | Long-term debt | 250,000 |
| Total current assets | 730,000 | Total liabilities | 850,000 |
| Property and equipment | 1,000,000 | Common stock | 100,000 |
| Accumulated depreciation | (100,000) | Additional paid-in capital | 400,000 |
| Patents, net | 40,000 | Retained earnings | 320,000 |
| Total assets | 1,670,000 | Total equity | 820,000 |
|  |  | Total liabilities and equity | 1,670,000 |

*Inventory is valued at FIFO cost under the lower-of-cost-or-market-value rule; ending inventory was acquired evenly throughout the fourth quarter.

### Statement of Cash Flows
### For Year Ending December 31, 2004

|  | CHF |
|---|---|
| Operating activities: |  |
| Net income | 470,000 |
| Add: Depreciation expense | 100,000 |
| Amortization expense | 10,000 |
| Increase in accounts receivable | (200,000) |
| Increase in inventory | (250,000) |
| Increase in accounts payable | 600,000 |
| Net cash from operations | 730,000 |
| Investing activities: |  |
| Purchase of property and equipment | (1,000,000) |
| Acquisition of patent | (50,000) |
| Net cash from investing activities | (1,050,000) |
| Financing activities: |  |
| Proceeds from long-term debt | 250,000 |
| Payment of dividends | (150,000) |
| Net cash from financing activities | 100,000 |
| Decrease in cash | (220,000) |
| Cash at 12/31/03 | 350,000 |
| Cash at 12/31/04 | 130,000 |

**EXHIBIT 8–4**
Translation of Income Statement and Statement of Retained Earnings—Current Rate Method

**Income Statement**
**For Year Ending December 31, 2004**

| | CHF | Translation Rate* | US$ |
|---|---|---|---|
| Sales | CHF 4,000,000 | 0.65 A | $ 2,600,000 |
| Cost of goods sold | (3,000,000) | 0.65 A | (1,950,000) |
| Gross profit | 1,000,000 | | 650,000 |
| Depreciation expense | (100,000) | 0.65 A | (65,000) |
| Amortization expense | (10,000) | 0.65 A | (6,500) |
| Other expenses | (220,000) | 0.65 A | (143,000) |
| Income before income taxes | 670,000 | | 435,500 |
| Income taxes | (200,000) | 0.65 A | (130,000) |
| Net income | CHF 470,000 | | $ 305,500 |

**Statement of Retained Earnings**
**For Year Ending December 31, 2004**

| | CHF | Translation Rate* | US$ |
|---|---|---|---|
| Retained earnings, 1/1/04 | CHF –0– | | $ –0– |
| Net income, 2004 | 470,000 | above | 305,500 |
| Dividends, 10/1/04 | (150,000) | 0.67 H | (100,500) |
| Retained earnings, 12/31/04 | CHF 320,000 | | $ 205,000 |

*Indicates the exchange rate used and whether the rate is the current (C), average (A), or a historical (H) rate.

**EXHIBIT 8–5**
Translation of Balance Sheet—Current Rate Method

**Balance Sheet**
**December 31, 2004**

| | CHF | Translation Rate | US$ |
|---|---|---|---|
| **Assets** | | | |
| Cash | CHF 130,000 | 0.70 C | $ 91,000 |
| Accounts receivable | 200,000 | 0.70 C | 140,000 |
| Inventory | 400,000 | 0.70 C | 280,000 |
| Total current assets | 730,000 | | 511,000 |
| Property and equipment | 1,000,000 | 0.70 C | 700,000 |
| Less: Accumulated depreciation | (100,000) | 0.70 C | (70,000) |
| Patents, net | 40,000 | 0.70 C | 28,000 |
| Total assets | CHF 1,670,000 | | $1,169,000 |
| **Liabilities and Equities** | | | |
| Accounts payable | CHF 600,000 | 0.70 C | $ 420,000 |
| Total current liabilities | 600,000 | | 420,000 |
| Long-term debt | 250,000 | 0.70 C | 175,000 |
| Total liabilities | 850,000 | | 595,000 |
| Common stock | 100,000 | 0.60 H | 60,000 |
| Additional paid-in capital | 400,000 | 0.60 H | 240,000 |
| Retained earnings | 320,000 | above | 205,000 |
| **Cumulative translation adjustment** | | to balance | 69,000 |
| Total equity | 820,000 | | 574,000 |
| Total liabilities and equity | CHF 1,670,000 | | $1,169,000 |

The translation adjustment can be derived as the amount needed to bring the balance sheet back into balance. The translation adjustment also can be calculated by considering the impact of exchange rate changes on the beginning balance and subsequent changes in the net asset position:

1. The net asset balance of the subsidiary at the beginning of the year is translated at the exchange rate in effect on that date.
2. Individual increases and decreases in the net asset balance during the year are translated at the rates in effect when those increases and decreases occurred. Only a few events, such as net income, dividends, stock issuance, and the acquisition of treasury stock, actually change net assets. Transactions such as the acquisition of equipment or the payment of a liability have no effect on total net assets.
3. The translated beginning net asset balance (*a*) and the translated value of the individual changes (*b*) are then combined to arrive at the relative value of the net assets being held prior to the impact of any exchange rate fluctuations.
4. The ending net asset balance is translated then at the current exchange rate to determine the reported value after all exchange rate changes have occurred.
5. The translated value of the net assets prior to any rate changes (*c*) is compared with the ending translated value (*d*). The difference is the result of exchange rate changes during the period. If (*c*) is greater than (*d*), then a negative (debit) translation adjustment arises. If (*d*) is greater than (*c*), a positive (credit) translation adjustment results.

### *Computation of Translation Adjustment*

Based on the process just described, the translation adjustment for SWISSCO in this example is calculated as follows:

| | | | | |
|---|---:|---:|---:|---:|
| Net asset balance, 1/1/04 | CHF 500,000 | × 0.60 | = | $300,000 |
| Change in net assets: | | | | |
|   Net income, 2004 | 470,000 | × 0.65 | = | 305,500 |
|   Dividends declared, 10/1/04 | (150,000) | × 0.67 | = | (100,500) |
| Net asset balance, 12/31/04 | CHF 820,000 | | | $505,000 |
| Net asset balance, 12/31/04 at current exchange rate | CHF 820,000 | × 0.70 | = | (574,000) |
| Translation adjustment, 2004 (positive) | | | | $(69,000) |

Since this subsidiary began operations at the beginning of the current year, the $69,000 translation adjustment is the only amount applicable for reporting purposes. If a balance already had been created by translations in previous years, that beginning balance would have been combined with the $69,000 to arrive at an appropriate year-end total to be presented as other comprehensive income within stockholders' equity.

The translation adjustment is reported in other comprehensive income only until the foreign operation is sold or liquidated. *SFAS 52* (para. 14) stipulates that, *in the period in which sale or liquidation occurs, the cumulative translation adjustment related to the particular entity must be removed from other comprehensive income and reported as part of the gain or loss on the sale of the investment.* In effect, the accumulated unrealized foreign exchange gain or loss that has been deferred in other comprehensive income becomes realized when the entity is disposed of.

## Translation of the Statement of Cash Flows

Under the current rate method, all operating items in the statement of cash flows are translated at the average-for-the-period exchange rate (see Exhibit 8–6). This is the same rate used for translating income statement items. Although the ending balance in Accounts Receivable, Inventory, and Accounts Payable on the balance sheet are translated at the current exchange rate, the average rate is used for the *changes* in these accounts because those changes are caused by operating activities (such as sales and purchases) that are translated at the average rate.

**EXHIBIT 8–6**
Translated Statement of Cash Flows—Current Rate Method

**Statement of Cash Flows**
**For Year Ending December 31, 2004**

|  | CHF | Translation Rate | US$ |
|---|---|---|---|
| Operating activities: |  |  |  |
| Net income | CHF 470,000 | 0.65 A | $ 305,500 |
| Add: Depreciation | 100,000 | 0.65 A | 65,000 |
| Amortization | 10,000 | 0.65 A | 6,500 |
| Increase in accounts receivable | (200,000) | 0.65 A | (130,000) |
| Increase in inventory | (250,000) | 0.65 A | (162,500) |
| Increase in accounts payable | 600,000 | 0.65 A | 390,000 |
| Net cash from operations | 730,000 |  | 474,500 |
| Investing activities: |  |  |  |
| Purchase of property and equipment | (1,000,000) | 0.61 H | (610,000) |
| Acquisition of patent | (50,000) | 0.62 H | (31,000) |
| Net cash from investing activities | (1,050,000) |  | (641,000) |
| Financing activities: |  |  |  |
| Proceeds from long-term debt | 250,000 | 0.61 H | 152,500 |
| Payment of dividends | (150,000) | 0.67 H | (100,500) |
| Net cash from financing activities | 100,000 |  | 52,000 |
| Decrease in cash | (220,000) |  | (114,500) |
| Effect of exchange rate change on cash |  | to balance | (4,500) |
| Cash at December 31, 2003 | CHF 350,000 | 0.60 H | 210,000 |
| Cash at December 31, 2004 | CHF 130,000 | 0.70 C | $ 91,000 |

Investing and financing activities are translated at the exchange rate on the day the activity took place. Although long-term debt is translated in the balance sheet at the current rate, in the statement of cash flows it is translated at the historical rate when the debt was incurred.

The $(4,500) "effect of exchange rate change on cash" is a part of the overall translation adjustment of $69,000. It represents that part of the translation adjustment attributable to a decrease in Cash and is derived as a plug figure.

## REMEASUREMENT OF FINANCIAL STATEMENTS—TEMPORAL METHOD

Now assume that a careful examination of the functional currency indicators outlined in *SFAS 52* leads USCO's management to conclude that SWISSCO's functional currency is the U.S. dollar. In that case, the Swiss franc financial statements must be remeasured into U.S. dollars using the temporal method and the remeasurement gain or loss reported in income. To ensure that the remeasurement gain or loss is reported in income, it is easiest to remeasure the balance sheet first (as shown in Exhibit 8–7).

According to the procedures outlined in Exhibit 8–1, under the temporal method, cash, receivables, and liabilities are remeasured into U.S. dollars using the current exchange rate of $0.70. Inventory (carried at FIFO cost), property and equipment, patents, and the contributed capital accounts (Common Stock and Additional Paid-In Capital) are remeasured at historical rates. These procedures result in total assets of $1,076,800, and liabilities and contributed capital of $895,000. To balance the balance sheet, Retained Earnings must total $181,800. The accuracy of this amount is verified later.

**EXHIBIT 8–7**
Remeasurement of Balance Sheet—Temporal Method

**Balance Sheet**
**December 31, 2004**

|  | CHF | Remeasurement Rate | US$ |
|---|---|---|---|
| **Assets** | | | |
| Cash | CHF 130,000 | 0.70 C | $ 91,000 |
| Accounts receivable | 200,000 | 0.70 C | 140,000 |
| Inventory | 400,000 | 0.68 H | 272,000 |
| Total current assets | 730,000 | | 503,000 |
| Property and equipment | 1,000,000 | 0.61 H | 610,000 |
| Less: Accumulated depreciation | (100,000) | 0.61 H | (61,000) |
| Patents, net | 40,000 | 0.62 H | 24,800 |
| Total assets | CHF 1,670,000 | | $1,076,800 |
| **Liabilities and Equities** | | | |
| Accounts payable | CHF 600,000 | 0.70 C | $ 420,000 |
| Total current liabilities | 600,000 | | 420,000 |
| Long-term debt | 250,000 | 0.70 C | 175,000 |
| Total liabilities | 850,000 | | 595,000 |
| Common stock | 100,000 | 0.60 H | 60,000 |
| Additional paid-in capital | 400,000 | 0.60 H | 240,000 |
| Retained earnings | 320,000 | to balance | 181,800 |
| Total equity | 820,000 | | 481,800 |
| Total liabilities and equity | CHF 1,670,000 | | $1,076,800 |

## Remeasurement of the Income Statement

The remeasurement of SWISSCO's income statement and statement of retained earnings is demonstrated in Exhibit 8–8. Revenues and expenses incurred evenly throughout the year (sales, other expenses, and income taxes) are remeasured at the average exchange rate. Expenses related to assets remeasured at historical exchange rates (depreciation expense and amortization expense) are themselves remeasured at relevant historical rates.

Cost of goods sold is remeasured at historical exchange rates using the following procedure. Beginning inventory acquired on January 1 is remeasured at the exchange rate from that date ($0.60). Purchases made evenly throughout the year are remeasured at the average rate for the year ($0.65). Ending inventory (at FIFO cost) purchased evenly throughout the fourth quarter of 2004 and the average exchange rate for the quarter ($0.68) are used to remeasure that component of cost of goods sold. These procedures result in Cost of Goods Sold of $1,930,500, calculated as follows:

| | | | | |
|---|---|---|---|---|
| Beginning inventory, 1/1/04 | CHF 150,000 | × 0.60 | = | $ 90,000 |
| Plus: Purchases, 2004 | 3,250,000 | × 0.65 | = | 2,112,500 |
| Less: Ending inventory, 12/31/04 | (400,000) | × 0.68 | = | (272,000) |
| Cost of goods sold, 2004 | CHF 3,000,000 | | | $1,930,500 |

The ending balances in Retained Earnings on the balance sheet and on the statement of retained earnings must reconcile with one another. Given that dividends are remeasured into a U.S. dollar equivalent of $100,500 and the ending balance in Retained Earnings on the balance sheet is $181,800, net income must be $282,300.

To reconcile the amount of income reported in the statement of retained earnings and in the income statement, a remeasurement loss of $47,000 is required in the calculation of income. Without this remeasurement loss, the income statement, statement of retained earnings, and balance sheet are not consistent with one another.

**EXHIBIT 8–8**
Remeasurement of Income Statement and Statement of Retained Earnings—Temporal Method

**Income Statement**
**For Year Ending December 31, 2004**

| | CHF | Remeasurement Rate | US$ |
|---|---|---|---|
| Sales | CHF 4,000,000 | 0.65 A | $ 2,600,000 |
| Cost of goods sold | (3,000,000) | calculation | (1,930,500) |
| Gross profit | 1,000,000 | | 669,500 |
| Depreciation expense | (100,000) | 0.61 H | (61,000) |
| Amortization expense | (10,000) | 0.62 H | (6,200) |
| Other expenses | (220,000) | 0.65 A | (143,000) |
| Income before income taxes | 670,000 | | 459,300 |
| Income taxes | (200,000) | 0.65 A | (130,000) |
| Remeasurement Loss | | to balance | (47,000) |
| Net income | CHF 470,000 | | $ 282,300 |

**Statement of Retained Earnings**
**For Year Ending December 31, 2004**

| | CHF | Remeasurement Rate | US$ |
|---|---|---|---|
| Retained earnings, 1/1/04 | CHF –0– | | $ –0– |
| Net income, 2004 | 470,000 | above | 282,300 |
| Dividends | (150,000) | 0.67 H | (100,500) |
| Retained earnings, 12/31/04 | CHF 320,000 | to balance | $ 181,800 |

The remeasurement loss can be calculated by considering the impact of exchange rate changes on the subsidiary's balance sheet exposure. Under the temporal method, SWISSCO's balance sheet exposure is defined by its net monetary asset or net monetary liability position. SWISSCO began 2004 with net monetary assets (cash) of CHF 350,000. During the year, however, expenditures of cash and the incurrence of liabilities caused monetary liabilities (accounts payable + long-term debt = CHF 850,000) to exceed monetary assets (cash + accounts receivable = CHF 330,000). A net monetary liability position of CHF 520,000 exists at December 31, 2004. The remeasurement loss is computed by translating the beginning net monetary asset position and subsequent changes in monetary items at appropriate exchange rates and then comparing this with the dollar value of net monetary liabilities at year-end based on the current exchange rate.

**Computation of Remeasurement Loss**

| | | | |
|---|---|---|---|
| Net monetary assets, 1/1/04 | CHF 350,000 × 0.60 = | $ 210,000 |
| Increase in monetary items: | | |
|   Sales, 2004 | 4,000,000 × 0.65 = | 2,600,000 |
| Decreases in monetary items: | | |
|   Purchases, 2004 | (3,250,000) × 0.65 = | (2,112,500) |
|   Other expenses, 2004 | (220,000) × 0.65 = | (143,000) |
|   Income taxes, 2004 | (200,000) × 0.65 = | (130,000) |
|   Purchase of property and equipment, 3/15/04 | (1,000,000) × 0.61 = | (610,000) |
|   Acquisition of patent, 4/10/04 | (50,000) × 0.62 = | (31,000) |
|   Dividends, 10/1/04 | (150,000) × 0.67 = | (100,500) |
| Net monetary liabilities, 12/31/04 | CHF (520,000) | $ (317,000) |
| Net monetary liabilities, 12/31/04 at the current exchange rate | CHF (520,000) × 0.70 = | (364,000) |
| Remeasurement loss | | $ 47,000 |

If SWISSCO had maintained its net monetary asset position (cash) of CHF 350,000 for the entire year, a remeasurement gain of $35,000 would have resulted. The CHF held in cash was worth $210,000 (CHF 350,000 × $0.60) at the beginning of the year and $245,000 (CHF 350,000 × $0.70) at year-end. However, the net monetary asset position is not maintained. Indeed, a net monetary liability position arises. The *appreciation* of the foreign currency coupled with an increase in *net monetary liabilities* generates a *remeasurement loss* for the year.

### Remeasurement of the Statement of Cash Flows

In remeasuring the statement of cash flows (shown in Exhibit 8–9), the U.S. dollar value for net income is taken directly from the remeasured income statement (I/S). Depreciation and amortization are remeasured at the rates used in the income statement, and the remeasurement loss is added back to net income because it is a noncash item. The increases in accounts receivable and accounts payable relate to sales and purchases and are therefore remeasured at the average rate. The U.S. dollar value for the increase in inventory is determined by referring to the remeasurement of the cost of goods sold.

The resulting U.S. dollar amount of "net cash from operations" ($474,500) is exactly the same as when the current rate method was used in translation. In addition, the investing and financing activities are translated in the same manner under both methods. This makes sense; the amount of cash inflows and outflows is a matter of fact and is not affected by the particular translation methodology employed.

### Nonlocal Currency Balances

One additional issue related to the translation of foreign currency financial statements needs to be considered. If any of the accounts of the Swiss subsidiary are denominated in a currency other than the Swiss franc, those balances would first have to be restated into francs in accordance with the rules discussed in Chapter 7. Both the foreign currency balance and any related foreign exchange gain or loss would then be translated (or remeasured) into U.S. dollars. For example, a note payable of 10,000 British pounds first would be remeasured into Swiss francs before the translation process could commence.

## COMPARISON OF THE RESULTS FROM APPLYING THE TWO DIFFERENT METHODS

The determination of the foreign subsidiary's functional currency (and the use of different translation methods) can have a significant impact on consolidated financial statements. The following chart shows differences for SWISSCO in several key items under the two different translation methods:

| | Translation Method | | |
|---|---|---|---|
| Item | Current Rate | Temporal | Difference |
| Net income . . . . . . . . . . . . . . . . | $ 305,500 | $ 282,300 | + 8.2% |
| Total assets . . . . . . . . . . . . . . . . | 1,169,000 | 1,076,800 | + 8.6 |
| Total equity . . . . . . . . . . . . . . . | 574,000 | 481,800 | +19.1 |
| Return on equity . . . . . . . . . . . | 53.2% | 58.6% | − 9.2 |

In this illustration if the Swiss franc is determined to be SWISSCO's functional currency (and the current rate method is applied), net income reported in the consolidated income statement would be 8.2 percent larger than if the U.S. dollar is the functional currency (and the temporal method is applied). In addition, total assets would be 8.6 percent larger and total equity would be 19.1 percent larger using the current rate method. Because of the larger amount of equity, return on equity using the current rate method is 9.2 percent smaller.

Note that the current rate method does not always result in larger net income and a larger amount of equity than the temporal method. For example, if SWISSCO had maintained its net

**EXHIBIT 8–9**
Remeasurement of Statement of Cash Flows—Temporal Method

### Statement of Cash Flows
### For Year Ending December 31, 2004

| | CHF | Remeasurement Rate | US$ |
|---|---|---|---|
| **Operating activities:** | | | |
| Net income . . . . . . . . . . . . . . . . . . . . CHF | 470,000 | from I/S | $ 282,300 |
| Add: Depreciation expense . . . . . . . . . | 100,000 | 0.61 H | 61,000 |
| Amortization expense . . . . . . . . | 10,000 | 0.62 H | 6,200 |
| **Remeasurement loss** . . . . . . . . | | from I/S | 47,000 |
| Increase in accounts receivable . . . . . . | (200,000) | 0.65 A | (130,000) |
| Increase in inventory . . . . . . . . . . . . . | (250,000) | * | (182,000) |
| Increase in accounts payable . . . . . . . | 600,000 | 0.65 A | 390,000 |
| Net cash from operations . . . . . . . . | 730,000 | | 474,500 |
| **Investing activities:** | | | |
| Purchase of property and equipment . . . | (1,000,000) | 0.61 H | (610,000) |
| Acquisition of patent . . . . . . . . . . . . . | (50,000) | 0.62 H | (31,000) |
| Net cash from investing activities . . | (1,050,000) | | (641,000) |
| **Financing activities:** | | | |
| Proceeds from long-term debt . . . . . . | 250,000 | 0.61 H | 152,500 |
| Payment of dividends . . . . . . . . . . . . . | (150,000) | 0.67 H | (100,500) |
| Net cash from financing activities . . | 100,000 | | 52,000 |
| Decrease in cash . . . . . . . . . . . . . . . . . | (220,000) | | (114,500) |
| Effect of exchange rate changes on cash | | to balance | (4,500) |
| Cash at December 31, 2003 . . . . . . . . . CHF | 350,000 | 0.6 H | $ 210,000 |
| Cash at December 31, 2004 . . . . . . . . . CHF | 130,000 | 0.7 C | $ 91,000 |

*In remeasuring cost of goods sold earlier, beginning inventory was remeasured as $90,000 and ending inventory was remeasured as $272,000; an increase of $182,000.

monetary asset position, a remeasurement gain would have been computed under the temporal method leading to larger income than under the current rate method. Moreover, if the Swiss franc had depreciated during 2004, the temporal method would have resulted in larger net income.

The important point is that the determination of the functional currency and resulting translation method can have a significant impact on the amounts reported by a parent company in its consolidated financial statements. The appropriate determination of the functional currency is an important issue.

> "Within rather broad parameters," says Peat, Marwick, Mitchell partner James Weir, choosing the functional currency is basically a management call. So much so, in fact, that Texaco, Occidental, and Unocal settled on the dollar as the functional currency for most of their foreign operations, whereas competitors Exxon, Mobil, and Amoco chose primarily the local currencies as the functional currencies for their foreign businesses.[10]

Different functional currencies selected by different companies in the same industry could have a significant impact on the comparability of financial statements within that industry. Indeed, one of the concerns raised by those FASB members dissenting on *SFAS 52* was that the functional currency rules might not result in similar accounting for similar situations.

In addition to differences in amounts reported in the consolidated financial statements, the results of the SWISSCO illustration demonstrate several conceptual differences between the two translation methods.

---

[10] John Heins, "Plenty of Opportunity to Fool Around," *Forbes,* June 2, 1986, p. 139.

### Underlying Valuation Method

Using the temporal method, SWISSCO's property and equipment were remeasured as follows:

$$\text{Property and equipment CHF } 1{,}000{,}000 \times \$0.61 \text{ H} = \$610{,}000$$

By multiplying the historical cost in Swiss francs by the historical exchange rate, $610,000 represents the U.S. dollar equivalent historical cost of this asset. It is the amount of U.S. dollars that the parent company would have had to pay to acquire assets having a cost of CHF 1,000,000 when the exchange rate was $0.61 per Swiss franc.

Property and equipment were translated under the current rate method as follows:

$$\text{Property and equipment CHF } 1{,}000{,}000 \times \$0.70 \text{ C} = \$700{,}000$$

The $700,000 amount is not readily interpretable. It does not represent the U.S. dollar equivalent historical cost of the asset; that amount is $610,000. It also does not represent the U.S. dollar equivalent current cost of the asset because CHF 1,000,000 is not the current cost of the asset in Switzerland. The $700,000 amount is simply the product of multiplying two numbers together!

### Underlying Relationships

The following table reports the values for selected financial ratios calculated from the original foreign currency financial statements and from the U.S. dollar translated statements using the two different translation methods:

| Ratio | CHF | US$ Temporal | US$ Current Rate |
|---|---|---|---|
| Current ratio (current assets/current liabilities) | 1.22 | 1.20 | 1.22 |
| Debt/equity ratio (total liabilities/total equities) | 1.04 | 1.23 | 1.04 |
| Gross profit ratio (gross profit/sales) | 25% | 25.8% | 25% |
| Return on equity (net income/total equity) | 57.3% | 58.6% | 53.2% |

The temporal method distorts all of the ratios as measured in the foreign currency. The subsidiary appears to be less liquid, more highly leveraged, and more profitable than it does in Swiss franc terms.

The current rate method maintains the first three ratios, but return on equity is distorted. The distortion occurs because income was translated at the average-for-the-period exchange rate whereas total equity was translated at the current exchange rate. In fact, any ratio combining balance sheet and income statement figures, such as turnover ratios, is distorted by the use of the average rate for income and the current rate for assets and liabilities.

Conceptually, when the current rate method is employed, income statement items can be translated at either the average or the current exchange rate. *SFAS 52* requires using the average exchange rate. In this illustration, if revenues and expenses had been translated at the current exchange rate, net income would have been $329,000 (CHF 470,000 × $0.70), and the return on equity would have been 57.3 percent ($329,000/$574,000), exactly the amount reflected in the Swiss franc financial statements. In several countries in which the current rate method is used, companies are allowed to choose between the average exchange rate and the current exchange rate in translating income. This is true, for example, in France and the United Kingdom.

## HEDGING BALANCE SHEET EXPOSURE

When the U.S. dollar is the functional currency or when a foreign operation is located in a highly inflationary economy, remeasurement gains and losses are reported in the consolidated income statement. Management of U.S. multinational companies could wish to avoid reporting remeasurement losses in net income because of the perceived negative impact this has on the company's stock price. Likewise, when the foreign currency is the functional currency, management could wish to avoid negative translation adjustments because of the adverse impact on the debt to equity ratio.

> More and more corporations are hedging their translation exposure—the recorded value of international assets such as plant, equipment and inventory—to prevent gyrations in their quarterly accounts. Though technically only paper gains or losses, translation adjustments can play havoc with balance-sheet ratios and can spook analysts and creditors alike.[11]

Translation adjustments and remeasurement gains or losses are a function of two factors: (1) changes in the exchange rate and (2) balance sheet exposure. Although there is little if anything a company can do to influence exchange rates, parent companies can use several techniques to hedge the balance sheet exposures of their foreign operations.

Balance sheet exposure can be hedged through the use of a derivative financial instrument such as a forward contract or foreign currency option, or through the use of a nonderivative hedging instrument such as a foreign currency borrowing. To illustrate, assume that SWISSCO's functional currency is the Swiss franc; this creates a net asset balance sheet exposure. USCO believes that the Swiss franc will depreciate, thereby generating a negative translation adjustment that will reduce consolidated stockholders' equity. USCO could hedge this balance sheet exposure by borrowing Swiss francs for a period of time, thus creating an offsetting Swiss franc liability exposure. As the Swiss franc depreciates, a foreign exchange gain will arise on the Swiss franc liability that offsets the negative translation adjustment arising from the translation of SWISSCO's financial statements. As an alternative to the Swiss franc borrowing, USCO might have acquired a Swiss franc call option to hedge its balance sheet exposure. As the Swiss franc depreciates, the fair value of the call option should increase, resulting in a gain. *SFAS 133* provides that the gain or loss on a hedging instrument that is designated and effective as a *hedge of the net investment in a foreign operation* should be reported in the same manner as the translation adjustment being hedged. Thus, the foreign exchange gain on the Swiss franc borrowing or the gain on the foreign currency option would be included in other comprehensive income along with the negative translation adjustment arising from the translation of SWISSCO's financial statements. In the event that the gain on the hedging instrument is larger than the translation adjustment being hedged, the excess is taken to net income.

The paradox of hedging a balance sheet exposure is that in the process of avoiding an unrealized translation adjustment, realized foreign exchange gains and losses can result. Consider USCO's foreign currency borrowing to hedge a Swiss franc exposure. At initiation of the loan, USCO will convert the borrowed Swiss francs into U.S. dollars at the spot exchange rate. When the liability matures, USCO will purchase Swiss francs at the spot rate prevailing at that date to repay the loan. The change in exchange rate over the life of the loan will generate a realized gain or loss. If the Swiss franc depreciates as expected, a realized foreign exchange gain that will offset the negative translation adjustment in other comprehensive income will result. Although the net effect on other comprehensive income is zero, there is a net increase in cash as a result of the hedge. If the Swiss franc unexpectedly appreciates, a realized foreign exchange loss will occur. This will be offset by a positive translation adjustment in Other Comprehensive Income, but a net decrease in cash will exist. While a hedge of a net investment in a foreign operation eliminates the possibility of reporting a negative translation adjustment in Other Comprehensive Income, gains and losses realized in cash can result.

## DISCLOSURES RELATED TO TRANSLATION

*SFAS 52* (para. 31) requires firms to present an analysis of the change in the cumulative translation adjustment account in the financial statements or notes thereto. Many companies comply with this requirement by including an other comprehensive income column in their statement of stockholders' equity. Other companies provide separate disclosure in the notes; see Exhibit 8–10 for an example of this disclosure for the Gillette Company.

---

[11] Ida Picker, "Indecent Exposure," *Institutional Investor,* September 1991, p. 82.

**EXHIBIT 8–10**
The Gillette Company and Subsidiary Companies 2001 Annual Report

**Accumulated Other Comprehensive Loss**

Net exchange gains or losses resulting from the translation of assets and liabilities of foreign subsidiaries, except those in highly inflationary economies, are accumulated in a separate section of stockholders' equity. Also included are the effects of exchange rate changes on intercompany transactions of a long-term investment nature and transactions designated as hedges of net foreign investments. The changes in accumulated foreign currency translation adjustments in 2001 were losses of $93 million, primarily from currency devaluation in Argentina and Brazil. Losses in 2000 were $249 million, with the United Kingdom accounting for $115 million. Losses in 1999 were $205 million, with Brazil accounting for approximately half of the losses.

An analysis of accumulated other comprehensive loss follows:

| (millions) | Foreign Currency Translation | Pension Adjustment | Cash Flow Hedges | Accumulated Other Comprehensive Loss |
|---|---|---|---|---|
| Balance at December 31, 1998 | $ (826) | $(47) | $ — | $ (873) |
| Change in period | (79) | 17 | — | (62) |
| Income tax expense | (126) | — | — | (126) |
| Balance at December 31, 1999 | (1,031) | (30) | — | (1,061) |
| Change in period | (216) | (4) | — | (220) |
| Income tax expense | (33) | — | — | (33) |
| Balance at December 31, 2000 | (1,280) | (34) | — | (1,314) |
| Change in period | (48) | (53) | (13) | (114) |
| Income tax benefit (expense) | (45) | 31 | 5 | (9) |
| Balance at December 31, 2001 | $(1,373) | $(56) | $ (8) | $(1,437) |

Included in other charges in the consolidated statement of income are a net exchange loss of $13 million in 2001, a net exchange gain of $8 million in 2000, and a net exchange loss of $35 million in 1999.

An analysis of the Foreign Currency Translation column indicates negative translation adjustments in each year 1999–2001. From the sign of these adjustments, one can infer that, in aggregate, the foreign currencies in which Gillette has operations depreciated against the U.S. dollar in each of those years. On the whole, Gillette's management is probably pleased that the translation adjustment is not reflected in income. Before-tax income would have been 4 percent smaller in 2001 and 7 percent smaller in 2000 if translation adjustments had been included in net income.

Note that Gillette's Cumulative Translation Adjustment account includes not only "net exchange gains or losses resulting from the translation of assets and liabilities of foreign subsidiaries" but also gains and losses on "intercompany transactions of a long-term investment nature" (as mentioned in Chapter 7) and on "transactions designated as hedges of net foreign investments." Gillette reports its remeasurement gains and losses in a line item titled "Other charges—net" on the income statement.

Although there is no specific requirement to do so, many companies include a description of their translation procedures in their "summary of significant accounting policies" in the notes to the financial statements. The following excerpt from International Business Machines Corporation's 2001 annual report illustrates this type of disclosure:

**Translation of Non-U.S. Currency Amounts**—Assets and liabilities of non-U.S. subsidiaries that operate in a local currency environment are translated to U.S. dollars at year-end exchange rates. Income and expense items are translated at weighted average rates of exchange prevailing during the year. Translation adjustments are recorded in Accumulated gains and losses not affecting retained earnings within stockholders' equity.

Inventories, plant, rental machines and other properties–net, and other nonmonetary assets and liabilities of non-U.S. subsidiaries and branches that operate in U.S. dollars or whose economic environment is highly inflationary, are translated at approximate exchange rates prevailing when the company acquired the assets or liabilities. All other assets and liabilities are translated at year-end exchange rates. Cost of sales and depreciation are translated at historical exchange rates. All other income and expense items are translated at the weighted average rates of exchange prevailing during the year. Gains and loses that result from translation are included in net income.

## CONSOLIDATION OF A FOREIGN SUBSIDIARY

The final section of this chapter demonstrates the procedures used to consolidate the financial statements of a foreign subsidiary with those of its parent. Special attention should be paid to the treatment of the excess of cost over book value. As an item denominated in foreign currency, translation of the excess gives rise to a translation adjustment recorded on the consolidation worksheet.

On January 1, 2003, Altman, Inc., a U.S.-based manufacturing firm, purchased 100 percent of Bradford Ltd. in Great Britain. Altman paid £25,000,000 for its purchase. On January 1, 2003, Bradford had the following balance sheet:

| | | | | |
|---|---:|---|---:|---|
| Cash | £ 925,000 | Accounts payable | £ 675,000 |
| Accounts receivable | 1,400,000 | Long-term debt | 4,000,000 |
| Inventory | 6,050,000 | Common stock | 20,000,000 |
| Plant and equipment (net) | 19,000,000 | Retained earnings | 2,700,000 |
| Total | £27,375,000 | Total | £27,375,000 |

The excess of cost over book value of £2,300,000 was due to undervalued land (part of plant and equipment) and therefore is not subject to amortization. Altman uses the equity method to account for its investment in Bradford.

On December 31, 2004, two years after the date of acquisition, Bradford submitted the following trial balance for consolidation (credit balances are in parentheses):

| | |
|---|---:|
| Cash | £ 600,000 |
| Accounts Receivable | 2,700,000 |
| Inventory | 9,000,000 |
| Plant and Equipment (net) | 17,200,000 |
| Accounts Payable | (500,000) |
| Long-Term Debt | (2,000,000) |
| Common Stock | (20,000,000) |
| Retained Earnings, 1/1/04 | (3,800,000) |
| Sales | (13,900,000) |
| Cost of Goods Sold | 8,100,000 |
| Depreciation Expense | 900,000 |
| Other Expenses | 950,000 |
| Dividends Declared, 6/30/04 | 750,000 |
| | £ –0– |

Although Bradford generated net income of £1,100,000 in 2003, no dividends were declared or paid that year. Other than the payment of dividends in 2004, there were no intercompany transactions between the two affiliates. Altman has determined the British pound to be Bradford's functional currency.

Relevant exchange rates for the British pound were as follows:

| | January 1 | June 30 | December 31 | Average |
|---|---|---|---|---|
| 2003 | $1.51 | — | $1.56 | $1.54 |
| 2004 | 1.56 | $1.58 | 1.53 | 1.55 |

## Translation of Foreign Subsidiary Trial Balance

The initial step in consolidating the foreign subsidiary is to translate its trial balance from British pounds into U.S. dollars. Because the British pound has been determined to be the functional currency, this is carried out using the current rate method. The historical exchange rate for translating Bradford's common stock and January 1, 2003, retained earnings is the exchange rate that existed at the date of acquisition—$1.51.

|  | British Pounds | Rate | U.S. Dollars |
|---|---:|---|---:|
| Cash | £ 600,000 | 1.53 C | $ 918,000 |
| Accounts Receivable | 2,700,000 | 1.53 C | 4,131,000 |
| Inventory | 9,000,000 | 1.53 C | 13,770,000 |
| Plant and Equipment (net) | 17,200,000 | 1.53 C | 26,316,000 |
| Accounts Payable | (500,000) | 1.53 C | (765,000) |
| Long-Term Debt | (2,000,000) | 1.53 C | (3,060,000) |
| Common Stock | (20,000,000) | 1.51 H | (30,200,000) |
| Retained Earnings, 1/1/04 | (3,800,000) | * | (5,771,000) |
| Sales | (13,900,000) | 1.55 A | (21,545,000) |
| Cost of Goods Sold | 8,100,000 | 1.55 A | 12,555,000 |
| Depreciation Expense | 900,000 | 1.55 A | 1,395,000 |
| Other Expenses | 950,000 | 1.55 A | 1,472,500 |
| Dividends Declared, 6/30/04 | 750,000 | 1.58 H | 1,185,000 |
| **Cumulative translation adjustment** |  |  | (401,500) |
|  | £ –0– |  | $ –0– |
| *Retained Earnings, 1/1/03 | £2,700,000 | 1.51 H | $4,077,000 |
| Net Income, 2003 | 1,100,000 | 1.54 A | 1,694,000 |
| Retained Earnings, 12/31/03 | £3,800,000 |  | $5,771,000 |

A positive (credit balance) cumulative translation adjustment is required to make the trial balance actually balance. The cumulative translation adjustment is calculated as follows:

| | | | | |
|---|---:|---|---:|---:|
| Net assets, 1/1/03 | £22,700,000 | 1.51 H | $34,277,000 | |
| Change in net assets, 2003 | | | | |
|   Net income, 2003 | 1,100,000 | 1.54 A | 1,694,000 | |
| Net assets, 12/31/03 | £23,800,000 | | $35,971,000 | |
| Net assets, 12/31/03 at current exchange rate | £23,800,000 | 1.56 C | 37,128,000 | |
| **Translation adjustment, 2003** (positive) | | | | $(1,157,000) |
| Net assets, 1/1/04 | £23,800,000 | 1.56 H | $37,128,000 | |
| Change in net assets, 2004 | | | | |
|   Net income, 2004 | 3,950,000 | 1.55 A | 6,122,500 | |
|   Dividends 6/30/04 | (750,000) | 1.58 H | (1,185,000) | |
| Net assets, 12/31/04 | £27,000,000 | | $42,065,500 | |
| Net assets, 12/31/04 at current exchange rate | £27,000,000 | 1.53 C | 41,310,000 | |
| **Translation adjustment, 2004** (negative) | | | | 755,500 |
| **Cumulative translation adjustment, 12/31/04** (positive) | | | | $ (401,500) |

The translation adjustment in 2003 is positive because the British pound appreciated that year; the translation adjustment in 2004 is negative because of a depreciation in the British pound.

## Determination of Balance in Investment Account—Equity Method

The original cost of the investment in Bradford, the net income earned by Bradford, and the dividends paid by Bradford are all denominated in British pounds. Relevant amounts must be translated from pounds into U.S. dollars so Altman can account for its investment in Bradford under the equity method. In addition, the translation adjustment calculated each year is included in the Investment in Bradford account to update the foreign currency investment to its U.S. dollar equivalent. The counterpart is recorded as a translation adjustment on Altman's books:

| | | | | |
|---|---|---|---|---|
| 12/31/03 | Investment in Bradford | | $1,157,000 | |
| | Cumulative Translation Adjustment | | | $1,157,000 |
| | To record the positive translation adjustment related to the investment in a British subsidiary when the British pound appreciated. | | | |
| 12/31/04 | Cumulative Translation Adjustment | | $ 755,500 | |
| | Investment in Bradford | | | $ 755,500 |
| | To record the negative translation adjustment related to the investment in a British subsidiary when the British pound depreciated. | | | |

The carrying value of the investment account in U.S. dollar terms at December 31, 2004, is determined as follows:

| Investment in Bradford | British Pounds | Exchange Rate | U.S. Dollars |
|---|---|---|---|
| Original cost | £25,000,000 | 1.51 H | $37,750,000 |
| Bradford net income, 2003 | 1,100,000 | 1.54 A | 1,694,000 |
| Translation adjustment, 2003 | | | 1,157,000 |
| Balance, 12/31/03 | £26,100,000 | | $40,601,000 |
| Bradford net income, 2004 | 3,950,000 | 1.55 A | 6,122,500 |
| Bradford dividends, 6/30/04 | (750,000) | 1.58 H | (1,185,000) |
| Translation adjustment, 2004 | | | (755,500) |
| Balance, 12/31/04 | £29,300,000 | | $44,783,000 |

In addition to the investment in Bradford of $44,783,000, Altman also has equity income on its December 31, 2004, trial balance in the amount of $6,122,500.

## Consolidation Worksheet

Once the subsidiary's trial balance has been translated into dollars and the carrying value of the investment is known, the consolidation worksheet at December 31, 2004, can be prepared. As is true in the consolidation of domestic subsidiaries, the investment account, the subsidiary's equity accounts, and the effects of intercompany transactions must be eliminated. The excess of cost over book value at the date of acquisition also must be allocated to the appropriate accounts (in this example, plant and equipment).

Unique to the consolidation of foreign subsidiaries is the fact that the excess of cost over book value, which is denominated in foreign currency, also must be translated into the parent's reporting currency. When the foreign currency is the functional currency, the excess is translated at the current exchange rate with a resulting translation adjustment. The excess is not carried on either the parent or the subsidiary's books but is recorded only in the consolidation worksheet. *The translation adjustment related to the excess has not yet been recognized by either the parent or the subsidiary and must be recorded in the consolidation worksheet.* Exhibit 8–11 presents the consolidation worksheet of Altman and Bradford at December 31, 2004.

**EXHIBIT 8–11** Consolidation Worksheet—Parent and Foreign Subsidiary

## ALTMAN, INC., AND BRADFORD LTD.
### Consolidation Worksheet
### For Year Ending December 31, 2004

| Accounts | Altman | Bradford | Consolidated Entries Debits | Consolidated Entries Credits | Consolidated Totals |
|---|---|---|---|---|---|
| **Income Statement** | | | | | |
| Sales | $ (32,489,000) | $(21,545,000) | | | $ (54,034,000) |
| Cost of goods sold | 16,000,000 | 12,555,000 | | | 28,555,000 |
| Depreciation expense | 9,700,000 | 1,395,000 | | | 11,095,000 |
| Other expenses | 2,900,000 | 1,472,500 | | | 4,372,500 |
| Equity income | (6,122,500) | | (I) 6,122,500 | | –0– |
| Net income | $ (10,011,500) | $ (6,122,500) | | | $ (10,011,500) |
| **Statement of Retained Earnings** | | | | | |
| Retained earnings, 1/1/04 | $ (25,194,000) | $ (5,771,000) | (S) 5,771,000 | | $ (25,194,000) |
| Net income (above) | (10,011,500) | (6,122,500) | | | (10,011,500) |
| Dividends paid | 1,500,000 | 1,185,000 | | (D) 1,185,000 | 1,500,000 |
| Retained earnings, 12/31/04 | $ (33,705,500) | $(10,708,500) | | | $ (33,705,500) |
| **Balance Sheet** | | | | | |
| Cash | $ 3,649,800 | $ 918,000 | | | $ 4,567,800 |
| Accounts receivable | 3,100,000 | 4,131,000 | | | 7,231,000 |
| Inventory | 11,410,000 | 13,770,000 | | | 25,180,000 |
| Investment in Bradford | 44,783,000 | | | (S) 35,971,000 | –0– |
| | | | | (A) 3,473,000 | |
| | | | (D) 1,185,000 | (I) 6,122,500 | |
| | | | | (T) 401,500 | |
| Plant and equipment (net) | 39,500,000 | 26,316,000 | (A) 3,473,000 | | |
| | | | (E) 46,000 | | 69,335,000 |
| Total assets | $ 102,442,800 | $ 45,135,000 | | | $ 106,313,800 |
| Accounts payable | $ (2,500,000) | $ (765,000) | | | $ (3,265,000) |
| Long-term debt | (22,728,800) | (3,060,000) | | | (25,788,800) |
| Common stock | (43,107,000) | (30,200,000) | (S) 30,200,000 | | (43,107,000) |
| Retained earnings, 12/31/04 (above) | (33,705,500) | (10,708,500) | | | (33,705,500) |
| Cumulative translation adjustment | (401,500) | (401,500) | (T) 401,500 | (E) 46,000 | (447,500) |
| Total liabilities and equities | $(102,422,800) | $(45,135,000) | $47,199,000 | $(47,199,000) | $(106,313,800) |

### Explanation of consolidation entries:

S—Eliminates the subsidiary's stockholders' equity accounts as of the beginning of the current year along with the equivalent book value component within the parent's purchase price in the Investment in Bradford account.

A—Allocates the excess of cost over book value at the date of acquisition to land (plant and equipment) and eliminates that amount within the parent's purchase price from the Investment account.

I—Eliminates the amount of equity income recognized by the parent in the current year and included in the Investment in Bradford account under the equity method.

D—Eliminates the subsidiary's dividend payment that was a reduction in the Investment in Bradford account under the equity method.

T—Eliminates the cumulative translation adjustment included in the Investment in Bradford account under the equity method and eliminates the cumulative translation adjustment carried on the parent's books.

E—Revalues the excess of cost over book value for the change in exchange rate since the date of acquisition with the counterpart recognized as an increase in the consolidated cumulative translation adjustment. The revaluation is calculated as follows:

**Excess of Cost over Book Value**

| | | | |
|---|---|---|---|
| U.S. dollar equivalent at 12/31/04 | £2,300,000 × $1.53 | = | $3,519,000 |
| U.S. dollar equivalent at 1/1/03 | 2,300,000 × $1.51 | = | 3,473,000 |
| Cumulative translation adjustment related to excess, 12/31/04 | | | $ 46,000 |

## Summary

1. Because many companies have significant financial involvement in foreign countries, the process by which foreign currency financial statements are translated into U.S. dollars is of special accounting importance. The two major issues related to the translation process are (1) which method to use and (2) where the resulting translation adjustment should be reported in the consolidated financial statements.

2. Translation methods differ on the basis of which accounts are translated at the current exchange rate and which are translated at historical rates. Accounts translated at the current exchange rate are exposed to translation adjustment. Different translation methods give rise to different concepts of balance sheet exposure and translation adjustments of differing signs and magnitude.

3. Under the temporal method, assets carried at current value (cash, marketable securities, receivables) and liabilities are translated at the current exchange rate. Assets carried at historical cost and stockholders' equity are translated at historical exchange rates. When liabilities are more than the sum of cash, marketable securities, and receivables, a net liability balance sheet exposure exists. Appreciation in the foreign currency results in a negative translation adjustment (remeasurement loss). Depreciation in the foreign currency results in a positive translation adjustment (remeasurement gain). By translating assets carried at historical cost at historical exchange rates, the temporal method maintains the underlying valuation method used by the foreign operation, but relationships in the foreign currency financial statements are distorted.

4. Under the current rate method, all assets and liabilities are translated at the current exchange rate, giving rise to a net asset balance sheet exposure. Appreciation in the foreign currency results in a positive translation adjustment. Depreciation in the foreign currency results in a negative translation adjustment. By translating assets carried at historical cost at the current exchange rate, the current rate method maintains relationships in the foreign currency financial statements but the underlying valuation method used by the foreign operation is distorted.

5. From 1975 through 1981, the temporal method—as prescribed by *SFAS 8* of the Financial Accounting Standards Board—was used to translate the financial statements of foreign operations. Translation adjustments were reported as gains and losses in income. Because this approach came under increasing attack from the business community as well as from many accountants, the FASB eventually replaced it with *SFAS 52*.

6. *SFAS 52* creates two separate procedures for translating foreign currency financial statements into the parent's reporting currency. *Translation* through use of the current rate method is appropriate when the foreign operation's functional currency is a foreign currency. In this case, the translation adjustment is reported in Other Comprehensive Income and reflected on the balance sheet as a separate component of stockholders' equity. *Remeasurement* through use of the temporal method is appropriate when the operation's functional currency is the U.S. dollar. Remeasurement also is applied when the operation is in a country with a highly inflationary economy. In these situations, the translation adjustment is treated as a remeasurement gain or loss in net income.

7. Some companies hedge their balance sheet exposures to avoid reporting remeasurement losses in net income and/or negative translation adjustments to Other Comprehensive Income. Gains and losses on derivative or nonderivative instruments used to hedge net investments in foreign operations are reported in the same manner as the translation adjustment being hedged.

## Comprehensive Illustration
### PROBLEM

*(Estimated Time: 55 to 65 Minutes)* Arlington Company is a U.S.-based organization with numerous foreign subsidiaries. As a preliminary step in preparing consolidated financial statements for 2004, the financial information from each of these foreign operations must be translated into the parent's reporting currency, the U.S. dollar.

Arlington owns a subsidiary in Sweden that has been in business for several years. On December 31, 2003, this entity's balance sheet was translated from Swedish kronor (SKr) (its functional currency) into U.S. dollars as prescribed by *SFAS 52*. Equity accounts at that date were as follows (all credit balances):

| | | | |
|---|---|---|---|
| Common stock | SKr 110,000 | = | $21,000 |
| Retained earnings | 194,800 | = | 36,100 |
| Cumulative translation adjustment | | | 3,860 |

At the end of 2004, the Swedish subsidiary produced the trial balance that follows. These figures include all of the entity's transactions for the year except for the results of several transactions related to sales made to a Chinese customer. A separate ledger has been maintained for these transactions denominated in Chinese renminbi (RMB). This ledger follows the company's trial balance.

### Trial Balance—Swedish Subsidiary
### December 31, 2004

| | Debit | Credit |
|---|---|---|
| Cash | SKr 41,000 | |
| Accounts Receivable | 126,000 | |
| Inventory | 128,000 | |
| Land | 160,000 | |
| Fixed Assets | 228,000 | |
| Accumulated Depreciation | | SKr 98,100 |
| Accounts Payable | | 39,000 |
| Notes Payable | | 56,000 |
| Bonds Payable | | 125,000 |
| Common Stock | | 110,000 |
| Retained Earnings, 1/1/04 | | 194,800 |
| Sales | | 350,000 |
| Cost of Goods Sold | 165,000 | |
| Depreciation Expense | 10,900 | |
| Salary Expense | 36,000 | |
| Rent Expense | 12,000 | |
| Other Expenses | 41,000 | |
| Dividends Paid, 7/1/04 | 25,000 | |
| Totals | SKr 972,900 | SKr 972,900 |

### Ledger—Transactions in Chinese Renminbi
### December 31, 2004

| | Debit | Credit |
|---|---|---|
| Cash | RMB 10,000 | |
| Accounts Receivable | 28,000 | |
| Fixed Assets | 20,000 | |
| Accumulated Depreciation | | RMB 4,000 |
| Notes Payable | | 15,000 |
| Sales | | 44,000 |
| Depreciation Expense | 4,000 | |
| Interest Expense | 1,000 | |
| Totals | RMB 63,000 | RMB 63,000 |

**Additional Information:**

- The Swedish subsidiary began selling to the Chinese customer at the beginning of the current year. At that time, 20,000 RMB were borrowed to acquire a truck for delivery purposes. One-fourth of that debt was paid before the end of the year. Sales to China were made evenly during the period.
- The U.S. dollar exchange rates for 1 SKr are as follows:

  | | |
  |---|---|
  | January 1, 2004 | $0.200 = 1.00 SKr |
  | Weighted-average rate for 2004 | 0.192 = 1.00 |
  | July 1, 2004 | 0.190 = 1.00 |
  | December 31, 2004 | 0.182 = 1.00 |

- The exchange rates applicable for the remeasurement of 1 RMB into Swedish kronor are as follows:

  | | |
  |---|---|
  | January 1, 2004 | 1.25 SKr = 1.00 RMB |
  | Weighted-average rate for 2004 | 1.16 = 1.00 |
  | December 1, 2004 | 1.10 = 1.00 |
  | December 31, 2004 | 1.04 = 1.00 |

- The Swedish subsidiary expended SKr 10,000 during the year for research and development. In accordance with Swedish accounting rules, this cost has been capitalized within the Fixed Assets account. This expenditure had no effect on the depreciation recognized for the year.

### Required

Prepare financial statements for the year ending December 31, 2004, for the Swedish subsidiary. Translate these statements according to *SFAS 52* into U.S. dollars to facilitate the preparation of consolidated statements. The Swedish krona is the subsidiary's functional currency.

## SOLUTION

*Remeasurement of Foreign Currency Balances.*

A portion of the Swedish subsidiary's operating results are presently stated in Chinese renminbi. These balances must be remeasured into the functional currency, the Swedish krona, before the translation process can begin. In remeasuring these accounts using the temporal method, the krona value of the monetary assets and liabilities is determined by using the current (C) exchange rate (1.04 SKr per RMB) whereas all other accounts are remeasured at historical (H) or average (A) rates.

### Remeasurement of Foreign Currency Balances

| | Renminbi | | Rate | | Kronor |
|---|---|---|---|---|---|
| Sales | RMB 44,000 | × | 1.16 A | = | SKr 51,040 |
| Interest Expense | (1,000) | × | 1.16 A | = | (1,160) |
| Depreciation Expense | (4,000) | × | 1.25 H | = | (5,000) |
| Income from renminbi transactions | 39,000 | | | | 44,880 |
| Cash | 10,000 | × | 1.04 C | = | 10,400 |
| Accounts Receivable | 28,000 | × | 1.04 C | = | 29,120 |
| Fixed Assets | 20,000 | × | 1.25 H | = | 25,000 |
| Accumulated Depreciation | (4,000) | × | 1.25 H | = | (5,000) |
| Total assets | 54,000 | | | | 59,520 |
| Notes Payable | 15,000 | × | 1.04 C | = | 15,600 |
| Income from renminbi transactions | 39,000 | | from above | | 44,880 |
| | 54,000 | | | | 60,480 |
| Remeasurement Loss | | | | | (960) |
| Total | | | | | 59,520 |

*(continued)*

**Remeasurement Loss for 2004**

|  | Renminbi | | Rate | | Kronor |
|---|---|---|---|---|---|
| Net monetary asset balance, 1/1/04 | –0– | | | | –0– |
| Increases in net monetary items: | | | | | |
|    Operations (sales less interest expense) | RMB 43,000 | × | 1.16 | = | SKr 49,880 |
| Decreases in net monetary items: | | | | | |
|    Purchased truck, 1/1/04 | (20,000) | × | 1.25 | = | (25,000) |
| Net monetary assets, 12/31/04 | RMB 23,000 | | | | SKr 24,880 |
| Net monetary assets, 12/31/04 at current exchange rate | RMB 23,000 | × | 1.04 | = | SKr 23,920 |
| Remeasurement loss (gain) | | | | | SKr 960 |

The net monetary asset exposure (cash and accounts receivable > notes payable) and depreciation of the Chinese renminbi create a remeasurement loss of SKr 960.

The remeasured figures from the Chinese operation must be combined in some manner with the subsidiary's trial balance denominated in Swedish kronor. For example, the accounts can simply be added together on a worksheet. As an alternative, a year-end adjustment can be recorded in the accounting system of the Swedish subsidiary to add the remeasured balances for financial reporting purposes.

| 12/31/04 Adjustment | Debit | Credit |
|---|---|---|
| Cash | 10,400 | |
| Accounts receivable | 29,120 | |
| Fixed assets | 25,000 | |
| Depreciation expense | 5,000 | |
| Interest expense | 1,160 | |
| Remeasurement loss | 960 | |
|    Accumulated depreciation | | 5,000 |
|    Notes Payable | | 15,600 |
|    Sales | | 51,040 |
| To record in Swedish kronor the foreign currency transactions originally denominated in renminbi. | | |

One more adjustment is necessary before the Swedish krona financial statements of the subsidiary can be translated into the parent's reporting currency. The research and development costs incurred by the Swedish entity should be reclassified as an expense as required by *SFAS 2*, "Accounting for Research and Development Costs," December 1974. After this adjustment, the Swedish subsidiary's statements are in conformity with U.S. generally accepted accounting principles.

| 12/31/04 Adjustment | Debit | Credit |
|---|---|---|
| Other expenses | 10,000 | |
|    Fixed assets | | 10,000 |
| To adjust fixed assets and expenses in Swedish kronor to be in compliance with U.S. GAAP. | | |

By combining all remeasured and adjusted balances with the Swedish subsidiary's trial balance, totals can be derived. For example, total sales for the subsidiary are SKr 401,040 (350,000 + 51,040) while cash is SKr 51,400 (41,000 + 10,400), and so on. Having established all account balances in the functional currency (Swedish krona), the subsidiary's statements now can be translated into U.S. dollars. Under the current rate method, the dollar values to be reported for income statement items are based on the average exchange rate for the current year. All assets and liabilities are based on the current exchange rate at the balance sheet date, and equity accounts are based on historical rates in effect at the date of accounting recognition.

## SWEDISH SUBSIDIARY

### Income Statement
### For Year Ending December 31, 2004

| | | | |
|---|---:|---|---:|
| Sales | SKr 401,040 | × 0.192 A = | $ 76,999.68 |
| Cost of goods sold | (165,000) | × 0.192 A = | (31,680.00) |
| Gross profit | 236,040 | | 45,319.68 |
| Depreciation expense | (15,900) | × 0.192 A = | (3,052.80) |
| Salary expense | (36,000) | × 0.192 A = | (6,912.00) |
| Rent expense | (12,000) | × 0.192 A = | (2,304.00) |
| Other expenses | (51,000) | × 0.192 A = | (9,792.00) |
| Interest expense | (1,160) | × 0.192 A = | (222.72) |
| Remeasurement loss | (960) | × 0.192 A = | (184.32) |
| Net income | SKr 119,020 | | $ 22,851.84 |

### Statement of Retained Earnings
### For Year Ending December 31, 2004

| | | | |
|---|---:|---|---:|
| Retained earnings, 1/1/04 | SKr 194,800 | given | $ 36,100.00 |
| Net income, 2004 | 119,020 | above | 22,851.84 |
| Dividends paid, 7/1/04 | (25,000) | × 0.190 H = | (4,750.00) |
| Retained earnings, 12/31/04 | SKr 288,820 | | $ 54,201.84 |

### Balance Sheet
### December 31, 2004

| | | | |
|---|---:|---|---:|
| Cash | SKr 51,400 | × 0.182 C = | $ 9,354.80 |
| Accounts receivable | 155,120 | × 0.182 C = | 28,231.84 |
| Inventory | 128,000 | × 0.182 C = | 23,296.00 |
| Land | 160,000 | × 0.182 C = | 29,120.00 |
| Fixed assets | 243,000 | × 0.182 C = | 44,226.00 |
| Accumulated depreciation | (103,100) | × 0.182 C = | (18,764.20) |
| Total | SKr 634,420 | | $115,464.44 |
| Accounts payable | SKr 39,000 | × 0.182 C = | $ 7,098.00 |
| Notes payable | 71,600 | × 0.182 C = | 13,031.20 |
| Bonds payable | 125,000 | × 0.182 C = | 22,750.00 |
| Common stock | 110,000 | given | 21,000.00 |
| Retained earnings | 288,820 | above | 54,201.84 |
| Cumulative translation adjustment | | | (2,616.60) |
| Total | SKr 634,420 | | $115,464.44 |

The cumulative translation adjustment at 12/31/04 comprises the beginning balance (given) plus the translation adjustment for the current year.

### Cumulative Translation Adjustment

| | |
|---|---:|
| Balance, 1/1/04 | $ 3,860.00 |
| Translation adjustment for 2004 | (6,476.60) |
| Balance, 12/31/04 | $(2,616.60) |

The negative translation adjustment for 2004 of $6,477 is calculated by considering the effect of exchange rate changes on net assets:

**Translation Adjustment for 2004**

| | | | | | |
|---|---|---|---|---|---|
| Net assets, 1/1/04 . . . . . . . . . . . . . . . . . . . | SKr 304,800* | × | 0.200 | = | $60,960.00 |
| Increase in net assets: | | | | | |
| Net income, 2004 . . . . . . . . . . . . . . . . . . | 119,020 | × | 0.192 | = | 22,851.84 |
| Decrease in net assets: | | | | | |
| Dividends, 7/1/04 . . . . . . . . . . . . . . . . . . | (25,000) | × | 0.190 | = | (4,750.00) |
| Net assets, 12/31/04 . . . . . . . . . . . . . . . . | SKr 398,820† | | | | $79,061.84 |
| Net assets, 12/31/04 at current exchange rate . . . . . . . . . . . . . . . | SKr 398,820 | × | 0.182 | = | 72,585.24 |
| Translation adjustment, 2004—negative . . . . . . . . . . . . . . . . . . . | | | | | $ 6,476.60 |

*Indicated by January 1, 2004, stockholders' equity balances—Common Stock, SKr 110,000; Retained Earnings, SKr 194,800.
†Indicated by December 31, 2004, stockholders' equity balances—Common Stock, SKr 110,000; Retained Earnings, SKr 288,820.

## Questions

1. What are the two major issues related to the translation of foreign currency financial statements?
2. What causes balance sheet (or translation) exposure to foreign exchange risk? How does balance sheet exposure compare with transaction exposure?
3. Why might a company want to hedge its balance sheet exposure? What is the paradox associated with hedging balance sheet exposure?
4. Under *SFAS 133*, how are gains and losses on financial instruments used to hedge the net investment in a foreign operation reported in the consolidated financial statements?
5. What is the concept underlying the temporal method of translation? What is the concept underlying the current rate method of translation? How does balance sheet exposure differ under these two methods?
6. In translating the financial statements of a foreign subsidiary, why is the value assigned to retained earnings especially difficult to determine? How is this problem normally resolved?
7. What are the major procedural differences in applying the current rate and temporal methods of translation?
8. Clarke Company has a subsidiary operating in a foreign country. In relation to this subsidiary, what is meant by the term *functional currency?* How is the functional currency determined?
9. A translation adjustment must be calculated and disclosed whenever financial statements of a foreign subsidiary are translated into the parent's reporting currency. How is this figure computed, and where is the amount reported in the financial statements?
10. The FASB put forth two theories about the underlying nature of a translation adjustment. What are these theories, and which one was considered correct by the FASB?
11. When is remeasurement rather than translation appropriate? How does remeasurement differ from translation?
12. Which translation method does FASB *SFAS 52* require for operations in highly inflationary countries? What is the rationale for mandating use of this method?

## Problems

1. What is a subsidiary's functional currency?
    a. The parent's reporting currency.
    b. The currency in which transactions are denominated.
    c. The currency in which the entity primarily generates and expends cash.
    d. Always the currency of the country in which the company has its headquarters.
2. The translation process and the remeasurement process are being compared. Which of the following statements is true?
    a. The reported balance of inventory is normally the same under both methods.
    b. The reported balance of equipment is normally the same under both methods.
    c. The reported balance of sales is normally the same under both methods.
    d. The reported balance of depreciation expense is normally the same under both methods.
3. Which of the following statements is true for the translation process (as opposed to remeasurement)?
    a. A translation adjustment can affect consolidated net income.
    b. Equipment is translated at the historical exchange rate in effect at the date of its purchase.
    c. A translation adjustment is created by the change in the relative value of a subsidiary's net assets caused by currency rate fluctuations.

d. A translation adjustment is created by the change in the relative value of a subsidiary's monetary assets and monetary liabilities caused by currency rate fluctuations.

4. A subsidiary of Byner Corporation has one asset (inventory) and no liabilities. The functional currency for this subsidiary is the peso. The inventory was acquired for 100,000 pesos when the exchange rate was $0.16 = 1$ peso. Consolidated statements are to be produced, and the current exchange rate is $0.19 = 1$ peso. Which of the following statements is true for the consolidated financial statements?
   a. A remeasurement gain must be reported.
   b. A positive translation adjustment must be reported.
   c. A negative translation adjustment must be reported.
   d. A remeasurement loss must be reported.

5. At what rates should the following balance sheet accounts in foreign statements be translated (rather than remeasured) into U.S. dollars?

|    | Accumulated Depreciation—Equipment | Equipment |
|----|------------------------------------|-----------|
| a. | Current                            | Current   |
| b. | Current                            | Average for year |
| c. | Historical                         | Current   |
| d. | Historical                         | Historical |

**Questions 6 and 7 are based on the following information.**
Certain balance sheet accounts of a foreign subsidiary of the Rose Company have been stated in U.S. dollars as follows:

|                                  | Stated at |  |
|----------------------------------|-----------|-----------------|
|                                  | Current Rates | Historical Rates |
| Accounts receivable, current     | $200,000  | $220,000 |
| Accounts receivable, long term   | 100,000   | 110,000 |
| Prepaid insurance                | 50,000    | 55,000 |
| Goodwill                         | 80,000    | 85,000 |
|                                  | $430,000  | $470,000 |

6. A foreign currency is the functional currency of this subsidiary. What total should be included in Rose's balance sheet for the preceding items?
   a. $430,000
   b. $435,000
   c. $440,000
   d. $450,000

7. The U.S. dollar is the functional currency of this subsidiary. What total should be included in Rose's balance sheet for the above items?
   a. $430,000
   b. $435,000
   c. $440,000
   d. $450,000

**Questions 8 and 9 are based on the following information.**
A subsidiary of Salisbury, Inc., is located in a foreign country. The functional currency of this subsidiary is the schweikart (SWK). The subsidiary acquires inventory on credit on November 1, 2003, for SWK 100,000 that is sold on January 17, 2004, for SWK 130,000. The subsidiary pays for the inventory on January 31, 2004. Currency exchange rates for 1 SWK are as follows:

| November 1, 2003  | $0.16 = 1$ SWK |
| December 31, 2003 | $0.17 = 1$ |
| January 17, 2004  | $0.18 = 1$ |
| January 31, 2004  | $0.19 = 1$ |
| Average for 2004  | $0.20 = 1$ |

8. What amount is reported for this inventory on Salisbury's consolidated balance sheet at December 31, 2003?
   a. $16,000
   b. $17,000
   c. $18,000
   d. $19,000
9. What amount is reported for cost of goods sold on Salisbury's consolidated income statement for the year ending December 31, 2004?
   a. $16,000
   b. $17,000
   c. $18,000
   d. $19,000

**Questions 10 and 11 are based on the following information.**

A subsidiary of Clarke Corporation buys marketable equity securities and inventory on April 1, 2004, for 100,000 pesos each. Both of these items are paid for on June 1, 2004 and are still on hand at year's end. Inventory is carried at cost under the lower-of-cost-or-market rule. Currency exchange rates for 1 peso are as follows:

| | |
|---|---|
| January 1, 2004 | $0.15 = 1 peso |
| April 1, 2004 | 0.16 = 1 |
| June 1, 2004 | 0.17 = 1 |
| December 31, 2004 | 0.19 = 1 |

10. Assume that the peso is the subsidiary's functional currency. On a consolidated balance sheet as of December 31, 2004, what balances are reported?
    a. Marketable equity securities = $16,000 and Inventory = $16,000.
    b. Marketable equity securities = $17,000 and Inventory = $17,000.
    c. Marketable equity securities = $19,000 and Inventory = $16,000.
    d. Marketable equity securities = $19,000 and Inventory = $19,000.
11. Assume that the U.S. dollar is the subsidiary's functional currency. On a consolidated balance sheet as of December 31, 2004, what balances are reported?
    a. Marketable equity securities = $16,000 and Inventory = $16,000.
    b. Marketable equity securities = $17,000 and Inventory = $17,000.
    c. Marketable equity securities = $19,000 and Inventory = $16,000.
    d. Marketable equity securities = $19,000 and Inventory = $19,000.
12. A U.S. company's foreign subsidiary had the following amounts in foreign currency units (FCU) in 2004:

| | |
|---|---|
| Cost of goods sold | FCU 10,000,000 |
| Ending inventory | 500,000 |
| Beginning inventory | 200,000 |

The average exchange rate during 2004 was $0.80 = FCU 1. The beginning inventory was acquired when the exchange rate was $1.00 = FCU 1. Ending inventory was acquired when the exchange rate was $0.75 = FCU 1. The exchange rate at December 31, 2004, was $0.70 = FCU 1. Assuming that the foreign country is highly inflationary, at what amount should the foreign subsidiary's cost of goods sold be reflected in the U.S. dollar income statement?
   a. $7,815,000
   b. $8,040,000
   c. $8,065,000
   d. $8,090,000
13. Ace Corporation starts a subsidiary in a foreign country; the subsidiary has the peso as its functional currency. On January 1, 2004, Ace buys all of the subsidiary's common stock for 20,000 pesos. On April 1, 2004, the subsidiary purchases inventory for 20,000 pesos with payment made on May 1, 2004. This inventory is sold on August 1, 2004, for 30,000 pesos, which is collected on October 1, 2004. Currency exchange rates for 1 peso are as follows:

| | |
|---|---|
| January 1, 2004 | $0.15 = 1 peso |
| April 1, 2004 | 0.17 = 1 |
| May 1, 2004 | 0.18 = 1 |
| August 1, 2004 | 0.19 = 1 |
| October 1, 2004 | 0.20 = 1 |
| December 31, 2004 | 0.21 = 1 |

In preparing consolidated financial statements, what translation adjustment will be reported at the end of 2004?
a. $400 positive (credit).
b. $600 positive (credit).
c. $1,400 positive (credit).
d. $1,800 positive (credit).

14. In the translated financial statements, which method of translation maintains the underlying valuation methods used in the foreign currency financial statements?
    a. Current rate method; income statement translated at average exchange rate for the year.
    b. Current rate method; income statement translated at exchange rate at the balance sheet date.
    c. Temporal method.
    d. Monetary/nonmonetary method.

15. Houston Corporation operates a branch operation in a foreign country. Although this branch deals in pesos, the U.S. dollar is viewed as its functional currency. Thus, a remeasurement is necessary to produce financial information for external reporting purposes. The branch began the year with 100,000 pesos in cash and no other assets or liabilities. However, the branch immediately used 60,000 pesos to acquire equipment. On May 1, inventory costing 30,000 pesos was purchased for cash. This merchandise was sold on July 1 for 50,000 pesos cash. The branch transferred 10,000 pesos to the parent on October 1 and recorded depreciation on the equipment of 6,000 pesos for the year. Currency exchange rates for 1 peso follow:

| | |
|---|---|
| January 1 | $0.16 = 1 peso |
| May 1 | 0.18 = 1 |
| July 1 | 0.20 = 1 |
| October 1 | 0.21 = 1 |
| December 31 | 0.22 = 1 |
| Average for the year | 0.19 = 1 |

What is the remeasurement gain to be recognized in the consolidated income statement?
a. $2,100
b. $2,400
c. $2,700
d. $3,000

16. Which of the following items is *not* remeasured using historical exchange rates under the temporal method?
    a. Accumulated depreciation on equipment.
    b. Cost of goods sold.
    c. Marketable equity securities.
    d. Retained earnings.

17. In accordance with U.S. generally accepted accounting principles, which translation combination would be appropriate for a foreign operation whose functional currency is the U.S. dollar?

| | Method | Treatment of Translation Adjustment |
|---|---|---|
| a. | Temporal | Other comprehensive income |
| b. | Temporal | Gain or loss in net income |
| c. | Current rate | Other comprehensive income |
| d. | Current rate | Gain or loss in net income |

18. A foreign subsidiary's functional currency is its local currency, which has not experienced significant inflation. The weighted average exchange rate for the current year is the appropriate exchange rate for translating:

|     | Wages Expense | Wages Payable |
| --- | --- | --- |
| a.  | Yes | Yes |
| b.  | Yes | No |
| c.  | No  | Yes |
| d.  | No  | No |

19. The functional currency of DeZoort, Inc.'s British subsidiary is the British pound. DeZoort borrowed British pounds as a partial hedge of its investment in the subsidiary. In preparing consolidated financial statements, DeZoort's negative translation adjustment on its investment in the subsidiary exceeded its foreign exchange gain on the borrowing. How should the effects of the negative translation adjustment and foreign exchange gain be reported in DeZoort's consolidated financial statements?
    a. The translation adjustment is reported in Other Comprehensive Income on the balance sheet, and the foreign exchange gain is reported in the income statement.
    b. The translation adjustment is reported in the income statement, and the foreign exchange gain is deferred in Other Comprehensive Income on the balance sheet.
    c. The translation adjustment less the foreign exchange gain is reported in Other Comprehensive Income on the balance sheet.
    d. The translation adjustment less the foreign exchange gain is reported in the income statement.
20. Gains from remeasuring a foreign subsidiary's financial statements from the local currency, which is not the functional currency, into the parent's currency should be reported as a(n)
    a. Deferred foreign exchange gain.
    b. Translation adjustment in Other Comprehensive Income.
    c. Extraordinary item, net of income taxes.
    d. Part of continuing operations.
21. The foreign currency is the functional currency for a foreign subsidiary. At what exchange rate should each of the following accounts be translated:
    a. Rent Expense
    b. Dividends Paid
    c. Equipment
    d. Notes Payable
    e. Sales
    f. Depreciation Expense
    g. Cash
    h. Accumulated Depreciation
    i. Common Stock
22. On January 1, 2004, Dandu Corporation started a subsidiary in a foreign country. On April 1, 2004, the subsidiary purchased inventory at a cost of 120,000 local currency units (LCU). One-fourth of this inventory remained unsold at the end of 2004 while 40 percent of the liability from the purchase had not yet been paid. The exchange rates for $1 were as follows:

| | |
| --- | --- |
| January 1, 2004 | $1 = LCU 2.5 |
| April 1, 2004 | 1 = 2.8 |
| Average for 2004 | 1 = 2.7 |
| December 31, 2004 | 1 = 3.0 |

    What should be the December 31, 2004, Inventory and Accounts Payable balances for this foreign subsidiary as translated into U.S. dollars using the current rate method?
23. The following accounts are denominated as of December 31, 2004, in pesos. For reporting purposes, these amounts need to be stated in U.S. dollars. For each balance, indicate the exchange rate that would be used if a translation is made. Then, again for each account, provide the exchange rate that would be necessary if a remeasurement is being made. The company was started in 1980. The buildings were acquired in 1982 and the patents in 1983.

| | Translation | Remeasurement |
| --- | --- | --- |
| Accounts payable | | |
| Accounts receivable | | |

*(continued)*

|  | Translation | Remeasurement |
|---|---|---|
| Accumulated depreciation | | |
| Advertising expense | | |
| Amortization expense (patents) | | |
| Buildings | | |
| Cash | | |
| Common stock | | |
| Depreciation expense | | |
| Dividends paid (10/1/04) | | |
| Notes payable—due in 2006 | | |
| Patents (net) | | |
| Salary expense | | |
| Sales | | |

Exchange rates for 1 peso are as follows:

| 1980 | 1 peso = $0.28 |
|---|---|
| 1982 | 1 = 0.26 |
| 1983 | 1 = 0.25 |
| January 1, 2004 | 1 = 0.24 |
| April 1, 2004 | 1 = 0.23 |
| July 1, 2004 | 1 = 0.22 |
| October 1, 2004 | 1 = 0.20 |
| December 31, 2004 | 1 = 0.16 |
| Average for 2004 | 1 = 0.19 |

24. On December 18, 2004, Stephanie Corporation acquired 100 percent of a Swiss company for CHF 3.7 million Swiss francs (CHF). At the date of acquisition, the exchange rate was $0.70 = CHF 1. The acquisition price is attributable to the following assets and liabilities:

| Cash | CHF | 500,000 |
|---|---|---|
| Inventory | | 1,000,000 |
| Fixed assets | | 3,000,000 |
| Notes payable | | (800,000) |

Stephanie Corporation prepares consolidated financial statements on December 31, 2004. By that date, the Swiss franc has appreciated to $0.75 = CHF 1. Because of the year-end holidays, no transactions took place prior to consolidation.

   a. Determine the translation adjustment to be reported on Stephanie's December 31, 2004, consolidated balance sheet, assuming that the Swiss franc is the Swiss subsidiary's functional currency. What is the economic relevance of this translation adjustment?
   b. Determine the remeasurement gain or loss to be reported in Stephanie's 2004 consolidated net income, assuming that the U.S. dollar is the functional currency. What is the economic relevance of this remeasurement gain or loss?

25. Fenwicke Company began operating a subsidiary in a foreign country on January 1, 2004, by acquiring all of the common stock for LCU 40,000. This subsidiary immediately borrowed LCU 100,000 on a five-year note with 10 percent interest payable annually beginning on January 1, 2005. A building was then purchased for LCU 140,000. This property had a 10-year anticipated life and no salvage value and is to be depreciated using the straight-line method. The building is rented for three years to a group of local doctors for LCU 5,000 per month. By year-end, payments totaling LCU 50,000 had been made. On October 1, LCU 4,000 was paid for a repair made on that date. A cash dividend of LCU 5,000 was transferred back to Fenwicke on December 31, 2004. The functional currency for the subsidiary is the LCU. Currency exchange rates for 1 LCU are as follows:

| | | |
|---|---|---|
| January 1, 2004 | $2.00 = | LCU 1 |
| October 1, 2004 | 1.85 = | 1 |
| Average for 2004 | 1.90 = | 1 |
| December 31, 2004 | 1.80 = | 1 |

Prepare an income statement, statement of retained earnings, and balance sheet for this subsidiary in LCU and then translate these amounts into U.S. dollars.

26. Refer to the information provided in problem 25. Prepare a statement of cash flows in LCU for Fenwicke's foreign subsidiary and then translate these amounts into U.S. dollars.

27. Watson Company has a subsidiary in the country of Alonza where the local currency unit is the kamel (KM). On December 31, 2003, the subsidiary has the following balance sheet:

| | | | | |
|---|---|---|---|---|
| Cash | KM 16,000 | Notes payable (due 2005) | KM | 19,000 |
| Inventory | 10,000 | Common stock | | 20,000 |
| Land | 4,000 | Retained earnings | | 10,000 |
| Building | 40,000 | | | |
| Accumulated depreciation | (21,000) | | | |
| | KM 49,000 | | KM | 49,000 |

This inventory was acquired on August 1, 2003; the land and buildings were acquired in 1984. The common stock was issued in 1978. During 2004, the following transactions took place:

**2004**
| | |
|---|---|
| Feb. 1 | Paid 5,000 KM on the note payable. |
| May 1 | Sold entire inventory for 15,000 KM on account. |
| June 1 | Sold land for 5,000 KM cash. |
| Aug. 1 | Collected all accounts receivable. |
| Sept. 1 | Signed long-term note to receive 6,000 KM cash. |
| Oct. 1 | Bought inventory for 12,000 KM cash. |
| Nov. 1 | Bought land for 4,000 KM on account. |
| Dec. 1 | Paid 3,000 KM cash dividend to parent. |
| Dec. 31 | Recorded depreciation for the entire year of 2,000 KM. |

The exchange rates for 1 KM are as follows:

| | | |
|---|---|---|
| 1978 | 1 KM = | $0.24 |
| 1984 | 1 = | 0.21 |
| August 1, 2003 | 1 = | 0.31 |
| December 31, 2003 | 1 = | 0.32 |
| February 1, 2004 | 1 = | 0.33 |
| May 1, 2004 | 1 = | 0.34 |
| June 1, 2004 | 1 = | 0.35 |
| August 1, 2004 | 1 = | 0.37 |
| September 1, 2004 | 1 = | 0.38 |
| October 1, 2004 | 1 = | 0.39 |
| November 1, 2004 | 1 = | 0.40 |
| December 1, 2004 | 1 = | 0.41 |
| December 31, 2004 | 1 = | 0.42 |
| Average for 2004 | 1 = | 0.37 |

a. If this is a translation, what is the translation adjustment determined solely for 2004?
b. If this is a remeasurement, what is the remeasurement gain or loss determined solely for 2004?

28. Aerkion Company starts the year of 2004 with two assets: cash of 22,000 LCU (local currency units) and land that originally cost 60,000 LCU when acquired on April 4, 1994. On May 1, 2004, the company rendered services to a customer for 30,000 LCU, an amount immediately paid in cash. On October 1, 2004, the company incurred an operating expense of 18,000 LCU that was immediately paid. No other transactions occurred during the year. Currency exchange rates for 1 LCU were as follows:

| | |
|---|---|
| April 4, 1994 | 1 LCU = $0.23 |
| January 1, 2004 | 1 = 0.24 |
| May 1, 2004 | 1 = 0.25 |
| October 1, 2004 | 1 = 0.26 |
| Average for 2004 | 1 = 0.27 |
| December 31, 2004 | 1 = 0.29 |

    *a.* Assume that Aerkion is a foreign subsidiary of a U.S. multinational company that uses the U.S. dollar as its reporting currency. Assume also that the LCU is the functional currency of the subsidiary. What is the translation adjustment for this subsidiary for the year 2004?

    *b.* Assume that Aerkion is a foreign subsidiary of a U.S. multinational company that uses the U.S. dollar as its reporting currency. Assume also that the U.S. dollar is the functional currency of the subsidiary. What is the remeasurement gain or loss for 2004?

    *c.* Assume that Aerkion is a foreign subsidiary of a U.S. multinational company. On the December 31, 2004, balance sheet, what is the translated value of the Land account? On the December 31, 2004, balance sheet, what is the remeasured value of the Land account?

29. Lancer, Inc., starts a subsidiary in a foreign country on January 1, 2003. The following account balances are for the year ending December 31, 2004, and are stated in kanquo (KQ), the local currency.

| | |
|---|---|
| Sales | KQ 200,000 |
| Inventory (bought on 3/1/04) | 100,000 |
| Equipment (bought on 1/1/03) | 80,000 |
| Rent expense | 10,000 |
| Dividends (paid on 10/1/04) | 20,000 |
| Notes receivable (to be collected in 2007) | 30,000 |
| Accumulated depreciation—equipment | 24,000 |
| Salary payable | 5,000 |
| Depreciation expense | 8,000 |

The following exchange rates for $1 are applicable:

| | |
|---|---|
| January 1, 2003 | 13 KQ |
| January 1, 2004 | 18 |
| March 1, 2004 | 19 |
| October 1, 2004 | 21 |
| December 31, 2004 | 22 |
| Average for 2003 | 14 |
| Average for 2004 | 20 |

Lancer is preparing account balances to produce consolidated financial statements.

    *a.* Assuming that the kanquo is the functional currency, what exchange rate would be used to report each of these accounts in U.S. dollar consolidated financial statements?

    *b.* Assuming that the U.S. dollar is the functional currency, what exchange rate would be used to report each of these accounts in U.S. dollar consolidated financial statements?

30. Board Company has a foreign subsidiary that began operations at the start of 2004 with assets of 132,000 kites (the local currency unit) and liabilities of 54,000 kites. During this initial year of operation, the subsidiary reported a profit of 26,000 kites. Two dividends were distributed; each was for 5,000 kites with one dividend paid on March 1 and the other on October 1. Applicable exchange rates for 1 kite are as follows:

| | |
|---|---|
| January 1, 2004 (start of business) | $0.80 |
| March 1, 2004 | 0.78 |
| Weighted-average rate for 2004 | 0.77 |
| October 1, 2004 | 0.76 |
| December 31, 2004 | 0.75 |

a. Assume that the kite is the functional currency for this subsidiary. What translation adjustment would be reported by Board for the year 2004?
b. Assume that on October 1, 2004, Board entered into a forward exchange contract to hedge the net investment in this subsidiary. On that date, Board agreed to sell 200,000 kites in three months at a forward exchange rate of $0.76/1 kite. Prepare the journal entries required by this forward contract.
c. Compute the net translation adjustment to be reported in Other Comprehensive Income by Board for the year 2004 under this second set of circumstances.

31. Kingsfield starts a subsidiary operation in a foreign country on January 1, 2004. The currency in this country is the kumquat (KQ). To get this business started, Kingsfield invests 10,000 kumquats. Of this amount, 3,000 kumquats is expended immediately to acquire equipment. Later, on April 1, 2004, land also is purchased. All operational activities of the subsidiary occur at an even rate throughout the year. The currency exchange rates for the kumquat for this year are as follows:

| | |
|---|---|
| January 1, 2004 | $1.71 |
| April 1, 2004 | 1.59 |
| June 1, 2004 | 1.66 |
| Weighted average—2004 | 1.64 |
| December 31, 2004 | 1.62 |

As of December 31, 2004, the subsidiary reports the following trial balance:

| | Debits | Credits |
|---|---|---|
| Cash | KQ 8,000 | |
| Accounts Receivable | 9,000 | |
| Equipment | 3,000 | |
| Accumulated Depreciation | | KQ 600 |
| Land | 5,000 | |
| Accounts Payable | | 3,000 |
| Notes Payable (due 2006) | | 5,000 |
| Common Stock | | 10,000 |
| Dividends Paid (6/1/04) | 4,000 | |
| Sales | | 25,000 |
| Salary Expense | 5,000 | |
| Depreciation Expense | 600 | |
| Miscellaneous Expenses | 9,000 | |
| Totals | KQ 43,600 | KQ 43,600 |

Kingsfield is a corporation based in East Lansing, Michigan and, therefore, uses the U.S. dollar as its reporting currency.
a. Assume that the functional currency of the subsidiary is the kumquat. Prepare a trial balance for the subsidiary in U.S. dollars so that consolidated financial statements can be prepared.
b. Assume that the subsidiary's functional currency is the U.S. dollar. Prepare a trial balance for the subsidiary in U.S. dollars so that consolidated financial statements can be prepared.

32. Livingston Company is a wholly owned subsidiary of Rose Corporation. Livingston operates in a foreign country with financial statements recorded in goghs (GH), the company's functional currency. Financial statements for the year of 2004 are as follows:

## Income Statement
### For Year Ending December 31, 2004

| | |
|---|---:|
| Sales | GH 270,000 |
| Cost of goods sold | (155,000) |
| Gross profit | 115,000 |
| Less: Operating expenses | (54,000) |
| Gain on sale of equipment | 10,000 |
| Net income | GH 71,000 |

## Statement of Retained Earnings
### For Year Ending December 31, 2004

| | |
|---|---:|
| Retained earnings, 1/1/04 | GH 216,000 |
| Net income | 71,000 |
| Less: Dividends paid | (26,000) |
| Retained earnings, 12/31/04 | GH 261,000 |

## Balance Sheet
### December 31, 2004

**Assets**

| | |
|---|---:|
| Cash | GH 44,000 |
| Receivables | 116,000 |
| Inventory | 58,000 |
| Fixed assets (net) | 339,000 |
| Total assets | GH 557,000 |

**Liabilities and Equities**

| | |
|---|---:|
| Liabilities | GH 176,000 |
| Common stock | 120,000 |
| Retained earnings, 12/31/04 | 261,000 |
| Total liabilities and equities | GH 557,000 |

**Additional Information:**

- The common stock was issued in 1989 when the exchange rate was $1.00 = 0.48 GH; fixed assets were acquired in 1990 when the rate was $1.00 = 0.50 GH.
- As of January 1, 2004, the Retained Earnings balance was translated as $395,000.
- The currency exchange rates for $1 for the current year are as follows:

| | |
|---|---|
| January 1, 2004 | 0.60 goghs |
| April 1, 2004 | 0.62 |
| September 1, 2004 | 0.58 |
| December 31, 2004 | 0.65 |
| Weighted-average rate for 2004 | 0.63 |

- Inventory was acquired evenly throughout the year.
- A translation adjustment was reported on the December 31, 2003, balance sheet with a debit balance of $85,000.
- Dividends were paid on April 1, 2004, and a piece of equipment was sold on September 1, 2004.

Translate the foreign currency statements into the parent's reporting currency, the U.S. dollar.

33. The following account balances are for the Agee Company as of January 1, 2004, and again as of December 31, 2004. All figures are denominated in the kroner (Kr).

|  | January 1, 2004 | December 31, 2004 |
|---|---|---|
| Accounts payable | (18,000) | (24,000) |
| Accounts receivable | 35,000 | 79,000 |
| Accumulated depreciation—buildings | (20,000) | (25,000) |
| Accumulated depreciation—equipment | -0- | (5,000) |
| Bonds payable—due 2009 | (50,000) | (50,000) |
| Buildings | 118,000 | 97,000 |
| Cash | 35,000 | 8,000 |
| Common stock | (70,000) | (80,000) |
| Depreciation expense | -0- | 15,000 |
| Dividends (10/1/04) | -0- | 32,000 |
| Equipment | -0- | 30,000 |
| Gain on sale of building | -0- | (6,000) |
| Rent expense | -0- | 14,000 |
| Retained earnings | (30,000) | (30,000) |
| Salary expense | -0- | 20,000 |
| Sales | -0- | (80,000) |
| Utilities expense | -0- | 5,000 |

**Additional Information:**

- Additional shares of common stock were issued during the year on April 1, 2004. Common stock at January 1, 2004, also was sold at the start of operations in 1980.
- Buildings were purchased in 1982. One building with a book value of Kr 16,000 was sold on July 1 of the current year.
- Equipment was acquired on April 1, 2004.
- Retained earnings as of January 1, 2004, was reported as $62,319.

Relevant exchange rates for 1 Kr were as follows:

| | |
|---|---|
| 1980 | $2.40 |
| 1982 | 2.20 |
| January 1, 2004 | 2.50 |
| April 1, 2004 | 2.60 |
| July 1, 2004 | 2.80 |
| October 1, 2004 | 2.90 |
| December 31, 2004 | 3.00 |
| Average for 2004 | 2.70 |

    *a.* If a remeasurement is being carried out, what would be the remeasurement gain or loss for 2004?
    *b.* If a translation is being carried out, what would be the translation adjustment for 2004?

34. Sendelbach Corporation is a U.S.-based organization with operations throughout the world. One of the company's subsidiaries is headquartered in Toronto. Although this wholly owned company operates primarily in Canada, some transactions are carried out through a branch in Mexico. Therefore, the subsidiary maintains a ledger denominated in Mexican pesos (Ps) as well as a general ledger in Canadian dollars (C$). As of December 31, 2004, the Canadian subsidiary is preparing financial statements in anticipation of consolidation with the U.S. parent corporation. Both ledgers for the subsidiary are as follows:

**Main Operation—Canada**

| | Debit | Credit |
|---|---|---|
| Accounts payable | | C$ 35,000 |
| Accumulated depreciation | | 27,000 |
| Buildings and equipment | C$167,000 | |

*(continued)*

### Main Operation—Canada (continued)

|  | Debit | Credit |
|---|---|---|
| Cash | 26,000 | |
| Common stock | | 50,000 |
| Cost of goods sold | 203,000 | |
| Depreciation expense | 8,000 | |
| Dividends paid, 4/1/04 | 28,000 | |
| Gain on sale of equipment, 6/1/04 | | 5,000 |
| Inventory | 98,000 | |
| Notes payable—due in 2006 | | 76,000 |
| Receivables | 68,000 | |
| Retained earnings, 1/1/04 | | 135,530 |
| Salary expense | 26,000 | |
| Sales | | 312,000 |
| Utility expense | 9,000 | |
| Branch operation | 7,530 | |
| Totals | C$640,530 | C$640,530 |

### Branch Operation—Mexico

|  | Debit | Credit |
|---|---|---|
| Accounts payable | | Ps 49,000 |
| Accumulated depreciation | | 19,000 |
| Building and equipment | Ps 40,000 | |
| Cash | 59,000 | |
| Depreciation expense | 2,000 | |
| Inventory (beginning—income statement) | 23,000 | |
| Inventory (ending—income statement) | | 28,000 |
| Inventory (ending—balance sheet) | 28,000 | |
| Purchases | 68,000 | |
| Receivables | 21,000 | |
| Salary expense | 9,000 | |
| Sales | | 124,000 |
| Main office | | 30,000 |
| Totals | Ps 250,000 | Ps 250,000 |

**Additional Information:**

- The functional currency for the Canadian subsidiary is the Canadian dollar, and the reporting currency for Sendelbach is the U.S. dollar. The Canadian and Mexican operations are not viewed as separate accounting entities.
- The building and equipment used in the Mexican operation were acquired in 1983 when the currency exchange rate was C$0.25 = Ps 1.
- Purchases should be assumed as having been made evenly throughout the fiscal year.
- Beginning inventory was acquired evenly throughout 2003; ending inventory was acquired evenly throughout 2004.
- The Main Office account found on the Mexican records should be considered an equity account. This balance was remeasured into C$ 7,530 on December 31, 2003, and no further transactions have occurred.
- Currency exchange rates for 1 Ps applicable to the Mexican operation are as follows:

| | |
|---|---|
| Weighted average, 2003 | C$0.30 |
| January 1, 2004 | 0.32 |
| Weighted average rate for 2004 | 0.34 |
| December 31, 2004 | 0.35 |

- On the December 31, 2003, consolidated balance sheet, a cumulative translation adjustment was reported with a $36,950 credit (positive) balance.
- The subsidiary's common stock was issued in 1976 when the exchange rate was $0.45 = C$ 1.
- The December 31, 2003, Retained Earnings balance for this subsidiary was C$ 135,530, a figure that has been translated into US$70,421.
- The applicable currency exchange rates for 1 C$ for translation purposes are as follows:

| | |
|---|---|
| January 1, 2004 | US$ $0.70 |
| April 1, 2004 | 0.69 |
| June 1, 2004 | 0.68 |
| Weighted-average rate for 2004 | 0.67 |
| December 31, 2004 | 0.65 |

a. Remeasure the Mexican peso operation's figures into Canadian dollars (Hint: Back into the beginning net monetary asset or liability position.)
b. Prepare financial statements (income statement, statement of retained earnings, and balance sheet) for the Canadian subsidiary in its functional currency.
c. Translate the Canadian dollar functional currency financial statements into U.S. dollars so that Sendelbach can prepare consolidated financial statements.

35. On January 1, 2004, Cayce Corporation purchased 100 percent of Simbel Company at a cost of $126,000. Cayce is a U.S.-based company headquartered in Buffalo, New York, and Simbel is in Cairo, Egypt. Cayce accounts for its investment in Simbel under the cost method. Any excess of purchase price over book value is attributable to undervalued land on Simbel's books. Simbel had no retained earnings at the date of acquisition. Following are the 2005 financial statements for the two operations. Cayce's information is stated in U.S. dollars ($), and Simbel's statements are reported in Egyptian pounds (£E).

| | Cayce Corporation | Simbel Company |
|---|---|---|
| Sales | $200,000 | £E 800,000 |
| Cost of goods sold | (93,800) | (420,000) |
| Salary expense | (19,000) | (74,000) |
| Rent expense | (7,000) | (46,000) |
| Other expenses | (21,000) | (59,000) |
| Dividend income—from Simbel | 13,750 | –0– |
| Gain on sale of fixed asset, 10/1/05 | –0– | 30,000 |
| Net income | $ 72,950 | £E 231,000 |
| Retained earnings, 1/1/05 | $318,000 | £E 133,000 |
| Net income | 72,950 | 231,000 |
| Dividends paid | (24,000) | (50,000) |
| Retained earnings, 12/31/05 | $366,950 | £E 314,000 |
| Cash and receivables | $110,750 | £E 146,000 |
| Inventory | 98,000 | 297,000 |
| Prepaid expenses | 30,000 | –0– |
| Investment in Simbel (cost) | 126,000 | –0– |
| Fixed assets (net) | 398,000 | 455,000 |
| Total assets | $762,750 | £E 898,000 |
| Accounts payable | $ 60,800 | £E 54,000 |
| Notes payable—due in 2008 | 132,000 | 140,000 |
| Common stock | 120,000 | 240,000 |
| Additional paid-in capital | 83,000 | 150,000 |
| Retained earnings, 12/31/05 | 366,950 | 314,000 |
| Total liabilities and equities | $762,750 | £E 898,000 |

**Additional Information:**

- During 2004, the first year of joint operation, Simbel reported income of £E 163,000 earned evenly throughout the year. A dividend of £E 30,000 was paid to Cayce on June 1 of that year. The 2005 dividend paid by Simbel also was made on June 1.
- On December 9, 2005, Simbel classified a £E 10,000 expenditure as a rent expense, although this payment related to prepayment of rent for the first few months of 2006.
- The exchange rates for 1 £E are as follows:

| | |
|---|---|
| January 1, 2004 | $0.300 |
| June 1, 2004 | 0.290 |
| Weighted-average rate for 2004 | 0.288 |
| December 31, 2004 | 0.280 |
| June 1, 2005 | 0.275 |
| October 1, 2005 | 0.273 |
| Weighted average rate for 2005 | 0.274 |
| December 31, 2005 | 0.270 |

Prepare a consolidation worksheet for Cayce Corporation and its Egyptian subsidiary. Assume that the U.S. dollar is the reporting currency of the parent company and the Egyptian pound is the subsidiary's functional currency.

36. Diekmann Company, a U.S.-based company, acquired a 100 percent interest in Rakona A.S. in the Czech Republic on January 1, 2004, when the exchange rate for the Czech koruna (Kčs) was $0.05. The financial statements of Rakona as of December 31, 2005, two years later, are as follows:

**Balance Sheet**
**December 31, 2005**

**Assets**

| | | |
|---|---|---|
| Cash | Kčs | 2,000,000 |
| Accounts receivable (net) | | 3,300,000 |
| Inventory | | 8,500,000 |
| Equipment | | 25,000,000 |
| Less: accumulated depreciation | | (8,500,000) |
| Building | | 72,000,000 |
| Less: accumulated depreciation | | (30,300,000) |
| Land | | 6,000,000 |
| Total assets | Kčs | 78,000,000 |

**Liabilities and Stockholders' Equity**

| | | |
|---|---|---|
| Accounts payable | Kčs | 2,500,000 |
| Long-term debt | | 50,000,000 |
| Common stock | | 5,000,000 |
| Additional paid-in capital | | 15,000,000 |
| Retained earnings | | 5,500,000 |
| Total liabilities and stockholders' equity | Kčs | 78,000,000 |

**Statement of Retained Earnings**
**For Year Ending December 31, 2005**

| | | |
|---|---|---|
| Sales | Kčs | 25,000,000 |
| Cost of goods sold | | (12,000,000) |
| Depreciation expense—equipment | | (2,500,000) |
| Depreciation expense—building | | (1,800,000) |
| Research and development expense | | (1,200,000) |
| Other expenses (including taxes) | | (1,000,000) |
| Net income | Kčs | 6,500,000 |
| Plus: Retained earnings, 1/1/05 | | 500,000 |
| Less: Dividends, 2005 | | (1,500,000) |
| Retained earnings, 12/31/05 | Kčs | 5,500,000 |

**Additional Information:**

- The January 1, 2005, beginning inventory of Kčs 6,000,000 was acquired on December 18, 2004, when the exchange rate was $0.043. Purchases of inventory during 2005 were acquired uniformly throughout the year. The December 31, 2005, ending inventory of Kčs 8,500,000 was acquired in the latter part of 2005 when the exchange rate was $0.032. All fixed assets were on the books when the subsidiary was acquired except for Kčs 5,000,000 of equipment acquired on January 3, 2005, when the exchange rate was $0.036, and Kčs 12,000,000 in buildings acquired on March 5, 2005, when the exchange rate was $0.034. Straight-line depreciation is 10 years for equipment and 40 years for buildings. A full year's depreciation is taken in the year of acquisition.
- Dividends were declared and paid on December 15, 2005, when the exchange rate was $0.031.
- Other exchange rates per 1 Kčs follow:

| | |
|---|---|
| January 1, 2005 | $0.040 |
| Average 2005 | 0.035 |
| December 31, 2005 | 0.030 |

**Part I.** Translate the Czech koruna financial statements into U.S. dollars in accordance with *SFAS 52* at December 31, 2005, in the following three situations:

    *a.* The Czech koruna is the functional currency. The December 31, 2004, U.S. dollar translated balance sheet reported retained earnings of $22,500. The December 31, 2004, cumulative translation adjustment was negative $202,500 (debit balance).

    *b.* The U.S. dollar is the functional currency. The December 31, 2004, Retained Earnings account in U.S. dollars (including a 2004 remeasurement gain) that appeared in Rakona's remeasured financial statements was $353,000.

    *c.* The U.S. dollar is the functional currency, but Rakona has no long-term debt. Instead, Rakona has common stock of Kčs 20,000,000 and additional paid-in capital of Kčs 50,000,000. The December 31, 2004, U.S. dollar translated balance sheet reported a negative balance in retained earnings of $147,000 (including a 2004 remeasurement loss).

**Part II.** Explain the positive or negative sign of the translation adjustment in part I(*a*) and explain why there is a remeasurement gain or loss in parts I(*b*) and I(*c*).

# Develop Your Skills

## RESEARCH CASE 1—FOREIGN CURRENCY TRANSLATION AND HEDGING ACTIVITIES

Many companies make annual reports available on their corporate Internet homepage. Annual reports also can be accessed through the SEC's EDGAR system at www.sec.gov (under Forms, search for ARS or 10-K), or in your school's library.

Access the most recent annual report for a U.S.-based multinational company with which you are familiar.

### Required:

*a.* Identify the location(s) in the annual report that provides disclosures related to the translation of foreign currency financial statements and foreign currency hedging.

*b.* Determine whether the company's foreign operations have a predominant functional currency.

*c.* Determine the amount of remeasurement gain or loss, if any, reported in net income in each of the three most recent years.

*d.* Determine the amount of translation adjustment, if any, reported in other comprehensive income in each of the three most recent years. Explain the sign (positive or negative) of the translation adjustment in each of the three most recent years.

*e.* Determine whether the company hedges net investments in foreign operations. If so, determine the type(s) of hedging instrument used.

# RESEARCH CASE 2—FOREIGN CURRENCY TRANSLATION DISCLOSURES IN THE COMPUTER INDUSTRY

Many companies make annual reports available on their corporate Internet homepage. Annual reports also can be accessed through the SEC's EDGAR system at www.sec.gov (under Forms, search for ARS or 10-K), or in your school's library.

Access the most recent annual report for the following U.S.-based multinational corporations:

Dell Computer Company.
International Business Machines Corporation.

## Required:

a. Identify the location(s) in the annual report that provides disclosures related to foreign currency translation and foreign currency hedging.
b. Determine whether the company's foreign operations have a predominant functional currency. Discuss the implication this has for the comparability of financial statements of the two companies.
c. Determine the amount of translation adjustment, if any, reported in other comprehensive income in each of the three most recent years. Explain the sign (positive or negative) of the translation adjustment in each of the three most recent years. Compare the relative magnitude of these translation adjustments for the two companies.
d. Determine whether each company hedges the net investment in foreign operations. If so, determine the type(s) of hedging instrument used.
e. Prepare a brief report comparing and contrasting the foreign currency translation and foreign currency hedging policies of these two companies.

# RESEARCH CASE 3—FOREIGN CURRENCY TRANSLATION DISCLOSURES IN THE SEMI-CONDUCTOR INDUSTRY

Many companies make annual reports available on their corporate Internet homepage. Annual reports also can be accessed through the SEC's EDGAR system at www.sec.gov (under Forms, search for ARS or 10-K), or in your school's library.

Access the most recent annual report for the following U.S.-based multinational corporations:

Intel Corporation.
Advanced Micro Devices, Inc.

## Required:

a. Identify the location(s) in the annual report that provides disclosures related to foreign currency translation and foreign currency hedging.
b. Determine whether foreign operations have a predominant functional currency. Discuss the implication this has for the comparability of financial statements of the two companies.
c. Determine the amount of translation adjustment, if any, reported in other comprehensive income in each of the three most recent years.

# FARS CASE 1—MORE THAN ONE FUNCTIONAL CURRENCY

A foreign subsidiary of a U.S.-based parent company can have more than one distinct and separable operation. For example, a foreign subsidiary can have one operation that sells products produced by the parent company and another operation that manufactures and sells its own products. The question arises whether a single foreign entity could be considered to have more than one functional currency. Search the FASB's *Original Pronouncements* using either hard copy or the Financial Accounting Research System (FARS) database.

## Required:

a. Identify the authoritative pronouncement and paragraph(s) within that pronouncement that addresses whether a foreign entity can have different functional currencies.
b. Summarize the guidance provided by the FASB with respect to this particular issue.

## FARS CASE 2—CHANGE IN FUNCTIONAL CURRENCY

A U.S.-based parent company must determine the functional currency of each of its foreign entities to determine the appropriate translation method to be used in translating the financial statements of each entity. The question arises whether the functional currency of an entity could be considered to change over time, and if so, how this change should be handled. Search the FASB's *Original Pronouncements* using either hard copy or the Financial Accounting Research System (FARS) database.

### Required:

a. Identify the authoritative pronouncement and paragraph(s) within that pronouncement that addresses whether the determination of functional currency of a foreign entity can change over time.
b. Summarize the guidance provided by the FASB with respect to this particular issue.

## ANALYSIS CASE—BELLSOUTH CORPORATION

BellSouth Corporation invested in two wireless communications operations in Brazil in the mid-1990s that it accounted for under the equity method. The following note is taken from BellSouth Corporation's interim report for the quarter ended March 31, 1999.

> *Note E—Devaluation of Brazilian Currency*
>
> *We hold equity interests in two wireless communications operations in Brazil. During January 1999, the government of Brazil allowed its currency to trade freely against other currencies. As a result, the Brazilian Real experienced a devaluation against the U.S. Dollar. The devaluation resulted in the entities recording exchange losses related to their net U.S. Dollar-denominated liabilities. Our share of the foreign exchange rate losses for the first quarter was $280.*
>
> *These exchange losses are subject to further upward or downward adjustment based on fluctuations in the exchange rates between the U.S. Dollar and the Brazilian Real.*

In a press release announcing first quarter 1999 results, BellSouth Corporation provided the following information (as found on the company's website):

> *BellSouth Corporation (NYSE: BLS) reported a 15-percent increase in first quarter earnings per share (EPS) before special items. EPS was 46 cents before a non-cash expense of 14 cents related to Brazil's currency devaluation.*

### BELLSOUTH CORPORATION
Normalized Earnings Summary ($ in millions, except per share amounts)
(unaudited)

|  | Quarter Ended | | |
|---|---|---|---|
|  | 3/31/99 | 3/31/98 | %Change |
| Reported Net Income | $615 | $892 | (31.1%) |
| Foreign currency loss (a) | 280 | — |  |
| Gain on sale of ITT World Directories (b) | — | (96) |  |
| Normalized Net Income | $895 | $796 | 12.4% |
|  | Quarter Ended | | |
|  | 3/31/99 | 3/31/98 | %Change |
| Reported Diluted Earnings per Share | $0.32 | $0.45 | (28.9%) |
| Foreign currency loss (a) | 0.14 | — |  |
| Gain on sale of ITT World Directories (b) | — | (0.05) |  |
| Normalized Diluted Earnings per Share | $0.46 | $0.40 | 15.0% |

(a) Represents our share of foreign currency losses recorded during first quarter 1999 as a result of the devaluation of the Brazilian Real during January 1999.
(b) Represents the after-tax gain associated with additional proceeds received in first quarter 1998 on the July 1997 sale of ITT World Directories.

### Required:

Based on the disclosure provided by BellSouth Corporation presented here, answer these questions:
a. Why did the company report a foreign currency loss as a result of the devaluation of the Brazilian real?
b. What does the company mean when it states, "These exchange losses are subject to further upward or downward adjustment based on fluctuations in the exchange rates between the U.S. Dollar and the Brazilian Real"?
c. What is the company's objective in reporting Normalized Net Income?
d. Do you agree with the company's assessment that it had a 15 percent increase in first-quarter earnings per share?

## EXCEL CASE—TRANSLATING FOREIGN CURRENCY FINANCIAL STATEMENTS

Charles Edward Company established a subsidiary in a foreign country on January 1, 2005, by investing FC 3,200,000 when the exchange rate was $0.50/FC. Charles Edward negotiated a bank loan of FC 3,000,000 on January 5, 2005, and purchased plant and equipment in the amount of FC 6,000,000 on January 8, 2005. Plant and equipment are depreciated on a straight-line basis over a 10-year useful life. Beginning inventory of FC 1,000,000 was purchased on January 10, 2005. Additional inventory of FC 4,000,000 was acquired at three points in time during the year at an average exchange rate of $0.43/FC. The first-in, first-out (FIFO) method is used to determine cost of goods sold. Additional exchange rates per FC 1 during the year 2005 are as follows:

January 1-31, 2005 . . . . . . . . . . . . . . $0.50
Average 2005 . . . . . . . . . . . . . . . . . .  0.45
December 31, 2005 . . . . . . . . . . . . .  0.38

The foreign subsidiary's income statement for 2005 and balance sheet at December 31, 2005, follow:

**INCOME STATEMENT**
For the Year Ended December 31, 2005
FC (in thousands)

| | |
|---|---:|
| Sales | FC 5,000 |
| Cost of goods sold | 3,000 |
| Gross profit | 2,000 |
| Selling expense | 400 |
| Depreciation expense | 600 |
| Income before tax | 1,000 |
| Income taxes | 300 |
| Net income | 700 |
| Retained earnings, 1/1/05 | 0 |
| Retained earnings, 12/31/05 | FC 700 |

**BALANCE SHEET**
At December 31, 2005
FC (in thousands)

| | |
|---|---:|
| Cash | FC 1,000 |
| Inventory | 2,000 |
| Fixed assets | 6,000 |
| Less: Accumulated depreciation | (600) |
| Total assets | FC 8,400 |

*(continued)*

|   |   |
|---|---|
| Current liabilities . . . . . . . . . . . . . . . . . . . . . . . . . . . . . . . . . . . . . | FC 1,500 |
| Long-term debt . . . . . . . . . . . . . . . . . . . . . . . . . . . . . . . . . . . . . . | 3,000 |
| Contributed capital . . . . . . . . . . . . . . . . . . . . . . . . . . . . . . . . . . . | 3,200 |
| Retained earnings . . . . . . . . . . . . . . . . . . . . . . . . . . . . . . . . . . . | 700 |
| Total liabilities and stockholders' equity . . . . . . . . . . . . . . . . . . | FC 8,400 |

As the controller for Charles Edward Company, you have evaluated the characteristics of the foreign subsidiary to determine that the FC is the subsidiary's functional currency.

### Required:

a. Use an electronic spreadsheet to translate the foreign subsidiary's FC financial statements into U.S. dollars at December 31, 2005, in accordance with *SFAS* 52. Insert a row in the spreadsheet after retained earnings and before total liabilities and stockholders' equity for the cumulative translation adjustment. Calculate the translation adjustment separately to verify the amount obtained as a balancing figure in the translation worksheet.
b. Use an electronic spreadsheet to remeasure the foreign subsidiary's FC financial statements in U.S. dollars at December 31, 2005, assuming that the U.S. dollar is the subsidiary's functional currency. Insert a row in the spreadsheet after depreciation expense and before income before taxes for the remeasurement gain (loss).
c. Prepare a report for James Edward, CEO of Charles Edward Company, summarizing the differences that will be reported in the company's 2005 consolidated financial statements because the FC, rather than the U.S. dollar, is the foreign subsidiary's functional currency. In your report, discuss the relationship between the current ratio, the debt-to-equity ratio, and profit margin calculated from the FC financial statements and from the translated U.S. dollar financial statements. Also, include a discussion of the meaning of the translated U.S. dollar amounts for inventory and for fixed assets.

## EXCEL AND ANALYSIS CASE—PARKER, INC. AND SUFFOLK PLC

On January 1, 2004, Parker, Inc., a U.S.-based firm, purchased 100 percent of Suffolk PLC located in Great Britain. Parker paid 52,000,000 British pounds (£) for its purchase. The excess of cost over book value is attributable to land (part of property, plant, and equipment) and is not subject to depreciation. Parker accounts for its investment in Suffolk at cost. On January 1, 2004, Suffolk reported the following balance sheet:

| | | | | |
|---|---|---|---|---|
| Cash . . . . . . . . . . . . . . . . . . . . | £ 2,000,000 | Accounts payable . . . . . . . . | £ 1,000,000 |
| Accounts receivable . . . . . . . . . | 3,000,000 | Long-term debt . . . . . . . . . . | 8,000,000 |
| Inventory . . . . . . . . . . . . . . . . . | 14,000,000 | Common stock . . . . . . . . . . | 44,000,000 |
| Property, plant & | | | |
| equipment (net) . . . . . . . . . . . | 40,000,000 | Retained earnings . . . . . . . . | 6,000,000 |
| | £ 59,000,000 | | £ 59,000,000 |

Suffolk's 2004 income was recorded at £2,000,000. No dividends were declared or paid by Suffolk in 2004.

On December 31, 2005, two years after the date of acquisition, Suffolk submitted the following trial balance to Parker for consolidation.

| | |
|---|---|
| Cash . . . . . . . . . . . . . . . . . . . . . . . . . . . . . . . . . . . . . . . . . | £ 1,500,000 |
| Accounts Receivable . . . . . . . . . . . . . . . . . . . . . . . . . . . . . | 5,200,000 |
| Inventory . . . . . . . . . . . . . . . . . . . . . . . . . . . . . . . . . . . . . . | 18,000,000 |
| Property, Plant, and Equipment (net) . . . . . . . . | 36,000,000 |
| Accounts Payable . . . . . . . . . . . . . . . . . . . . . . . . . . . | (1,450,000) |
| Long-Term Debt . . . . . . . . . . . . . . . . . . . . . . . . . . . . . . . . . | (5,000,000) |
| Common Stock . . . . . . . . . . . . . . . . . . . . . . . . . . . . . . . . . | (44,000,000) |
| Retained Earnings (1/1/05) . . . . . . . . . . . . . . . . | (8,000,000) |
| Sales . . . . . . . . . . . . . . . . . . . . . . . . . . . . . . . . . . . . . . . . | (28,000,000) |
| Cost of Goods Sold . . . . . . . . . . . . . . . . . . . . . . . . . . . . . | 16,000,000 |

*(continued)*

| | | | | |
|---|---|---|---|---|
| Depreciation | | | | 2,000,000 |
| Other Expenses | | | | 6,000,000 |
| Dividends Paid (1/30/05) | | | | 1,750,000 |
| | | | | –0– |

Other than the payment of dividends, no intercompany transactions occurred between the two companies. Relevant exchange rates for the British pound were as follows:

| | January 1 | January 30 | Average | December 31 |
|---|---|---|---|---|
| 2004 | $1.60 | $1.61 | $1.62 | $1.64 |
| 2005 | 1.64 | 1.65 | 1.66 | 1.68 |

December 31, 2005, financial statements (before consolidation with Suffolk) follow. Dividend income is the U.S. dollar amount of dividends received from Suffolk translated at the $1.65/£ exchange rate at January 30, 2005. The amounts listed for dividend income and all affected accounts (i.e., net income, December 31 retained earnings, and cash) reflect the $1.65/£ exchange rate at January 30, 2005. Credit balances are in parentheses.

| | Parker |
|---|---|
| Sales | $ (70,000,000) |
| Cost of goods sold | 34,000,000 |
| Depreciation | 20,000,000 |
| Other expenses | 6,000,000 |
| Dividend income | (2,887,500) |
| Net income | $ (12,887,500) |
| Retained earnings, 1/1/05 | $ (48,000,000) |
| Net income, 2005 | (12,887,500) |
| Dividends, 1/30/05 | 4,500,000 |
| Retained earnings, 12/31/05 | $ (56,387,500) |
| Cash | $ 3,687,500 |
| Accounts receivable | 10,000,000 |
| Inventory | 30,000,000 |
| Investment in Suffolk | 83,200,000 |
| Plant and equipment (net) | 105,000,000 |
| Accounts payable | (25,500,000) |
| Long-term debt | (50,000,000) |
| Common stock | (100,000,000) |
| Retained earnings, 12/31/05 | (56,387,500) |
| | –0– |

Parker's chief financial officer (CFO) wishes to determine the effect that a change in the value of the British pound would have on consolidated net income and consolidated stockholders' equity. To help assess the foreign currency exposure associated with the investment in Suffolk, the CFO requests assistance in comparing consolidated results under actual exchange rate fluctuations with results that would have occurred had the dollar value of the pound remained constant or declined during the first two years of Parker's ownership.

## Required:

Use an electronic spreadsheet to complete the following four parts.

*Part I* Given the relevant exchange rates presented:
a. Translate Suffolk's December 31, 2005, trial balance from British pounds to U.S. dollars. The British pound is Suffolk's functional currency.

b. Prepare a schedule that details the change in Suffolk's cumulative translation adjustment (i.e., beginning net assets, income, dividends, etc.) for 2004 and 2005.
c. Prepare the December 31, 2005, consolidation worksheet for Parker and Suffolk.
d. Prepare the 2005 consolidated income statement and the December 31, 2005, consolidated balance sheet.

*Note:* Worksheets should possess the following qualities.
- Each spreadsheet should be programmed so that all relevant amounts adjust appropriately when different values of exchange rates (subsequent to January 1, 2004) are entered into it.
- Be sure to program Parker's dividend income, cash, and retained earnings to reflect the dollar value of alternative January 30, 2005, exchange rates.

*Part II* Repeat tasks (*a*), (*b*), (*c*), and (*d*) from part I to determine consolidated net income and consolidated stockholders' equity if the exchange rate had remained at $1.60/£ over the period 2004 to 2005.

*Part III* Repeat tasks (*a*), (*b*), (*c*), and (*d*) from part I to determine consolidated net income and consolidated stockholders' equity if the following exchange rates had existed:

|      | January 1 | January 30 | Average | December 31 |
|------|-----------|------------|---------|-------------|
| 2004 | $1.60     | $1.59      | $1.58   | $1.56       |
| 2005 | 1.56      | 1.55       | 1.54    | 1.52        |

*Part IV* Prepare a report that provides Parker's CFO with the risk assessments requested. Focus on profitability, cash flow, and the debt-to-equity ratio.

# Chapter Nine

# Partnerships: Formation and Operation

A reader of college accounting textbooks might well come to the conclusion that business activity is carried out exclusively by corporations. Because most large companies are legally incorporated, a vast majority of textbook references and illustrations concern corporate organizations. Contrary to the perception being relayed, partnerships (as well as sole proprietorships) make up a vital element of the business community. Based on the filing of income tax returns, nearly 2.2 million partnerships were in the United States in 2001 (as compared to nearly 5.6 million corporations). One author contributes a very important assessment of the significance of partnerships to the growth of the economy: "One-quarter of all start-ups begin as partnerships."[1]

The partnership form is found in a wide range of business activities, from small local operations to worldwide enterprises. Examples found in the American economy include these:

> **Questions to Consider**
>
> - Why are some businesses legally organized as partnerships rather than as corporations?
> - Why do the equity accounts of a partnership differ from those of a corporation?
> - If a partner brings an intangible attribute (such as a business expertise or an established clientele) to a partnership, how is this contribution valued and recorded?
> - How is the annual net income that is earned by a partnership allocated among the individual capital accounts maintained for each partner?
> - If a partner withdraws from a partnership and receives more cash than the amount recorded in the appropriate capital account, what accounting does the business make of the excess payment?

- Individual proprietors often join together in the formation of a partnership as a means of reducing expenses, expanding services, and adding increased expertise. As will be discussed, partnerships also provide important tax benefits.
- Partnerships are a common means by which friends and relatives can easily create and organize a business endeavor.
- Historically doctors, lawyers, and other professionals have formed partnerships because of legal prohibitions against the incorporation of their practices. Although most states now permit alternative forms for such organizations, operating as a partnership or sole proprietorship is still necessary in many areas.

---

[1] Nick Kochan, "Two Is Company," *Director,* August 1996, p. 42.

Over the years, some partnerships have grown to enormous sizes. Connell Limited Partnership, for example, recycles and manufactures metal products; in 2001 it had revenues of $1 billion while the international accounting firm of PriceWaterhouseCoopers reported revenues of more than $16 billion.[2] In November 2002, Deloitte Touche Tohmatsu indicated operations in 140 countries[3] and KPMG International reported having more than 100,000 employees.[4]

Certainly some of the most successful organizations in business today are partnerships. "Winning teams include Hanson's James Hanson and Gordon White, the Body Shop's Anita and Gordon Roddick, the partners of the U.S. investment bank Goldman Sachs, and in a different way, the partners of the country's largest law and accounting firms."[5]

## PARTNERSHIPS—ADVANTAGES AND DISADVANTAGES

The popularity of the partnership format is based on several advantages inherent to this type of organization. An analysis of these attributes explains why nearly 2.2 million enterprises in the United States are partnerships rather than corporations.

One of the most common motives is the ease of formation. Only an oral agreement is necessary to create a legally binding partnership. In contrast, depending on specific state laws, incorporation requires the filing of a formal application along with the completion of various other forms and documents. Operators of small businesses may find the convenience and reduced cost involved in creating a partnership to be an especially appealing characteristic.

Other justifications for structuring a business as a partnership can be discovered within the tax laws.

> The partnership form of business has become increasingly popular in the United States, and it may account for a significant portion of new business formation in the future. One reason for the burgeoning of partnerships is that this form of business offers many of the risk-sharing opportunities of the corporate form without the burden of corporate income taxation.[6]

> A lawyer and expert on pipeline regulation, Kinder has capitalized on a tax advantage inherent in the partnership structure that Kinder Morgan employs. Similar to a real estate investment trust, a partnership of this sort pays no corporate income tax as long as it distributes virtually all of its earnings as dividends. It avoids the double taxation of dividends that afflicts the ordinary corporation. This means that a partnership's entire pretax earnings go to shareholders, while at an ordinary corporation, federal, state and local governments skim off 40 percent and more of that earnings stream.[7]

Although a detailed investigation of taxation rules and regulations goes beyond the scope of this accounting textbook, a few aspects are quite relevant to the current discussion. One area of the law warrants particular attention: the method by which partnerships are taxed. Although an informational tax return must be filed on an annual basis, *the partnership itself pays no income taxes.* For taxation purposes, the government does not view a partnership as an entity apart from its owners.

Partnership revenue and expense items (as defined by the tax laws) must be assigned directly each year to the individual partners who pay the income taxes. By passing income balances through to the partners in this manner, double taxation of the profits that are earned by a business and then distributed to its owners is avoided. In a corporation, income is taxed

---

[2] "Forbes Largest Private Companies," *Forbes,* November 2002.

[3] www.deloitte.com.

[4] www.kpmg.com.

[5] Kochan, "Two Is Company," p. 42.

[6] Harry Watson, "An Analysis of the Formation and Behavior of Partnerships," *Public Finance Quarterly,* July 1989, p. 281.

[7] Daniel Fisher, "Sweet Consolation," *Forbes,* September 21, 1998, p. 144.

twice: when earned and again when conveyed as a dividend. A partnership's income is taxed only at the time that the business initially earned it.

As an illustration, assume that a business earns $100. After paying any income taxes, the remainder is immediately conveyed to its owners. A tax rate of 30 percent is assumed for both individuals and corporations. As the following table shows, if this business is a partnership rather than a corporation, the owners are left with $21 more expendable income, which is 21 percent of the business income. Although significant in amount, this difference narrows as tax rates are lowered.

|  | Partnership | Corporation |
| --- | --- | --- |
| Income before income taxes | $100 | $100 |
| Income taxes paid by business (30%) | –0– | (30) |
| Income distributed to owners | $100 | $ 70 |
| Income taxes paid by owners (30%) | (30) | (21) |
| Expendable income | $ 70 | $ 49 |

The advantage of single taxation has led some large companies in recent years to convert to the partnership form: The Boston Celtics and Motel 6 are just two corporations that converted to partnerships to maximize after-tax returns to investors.[8]

Historically, a second tax advantage has long been associated with partnerships. Because income is taxable to the partners as the business earns it, any operating losses can be used to reduce their personal taxable income directly. In contrast, a corporation is viewed as legally separate from its owners, so losses cannot be passed through to them. A corporation has the ability to carry back any net operating losses and reduce previously taxed income (usually for the two prior years) and carry forward remaining losses to decrease future taxable income (for up to 20 years). However, if a corporation is newly formed or has not been profitable, operating losses provide no immediate benefit to a corporation or its owners as losses do for a partnership.

The tax advantage of deducting partnership losses has been reduced somewhat in recent years by changes in the tax laws. Because of the chance to pass through losses and reduce personal taxes, partnerships were often structured as tax shelters to report immediate losses (and, hence, create tax deductions) with profits deferred into the future. Now, ownership of a partnership is labeled as a passive activity unless the partner materially participates in the actual business activities. For tax purposes, passive activity losses serve only to offset other passive activity profits. In most cases, these partnership losses can no longer be used to reduce earned income such as salaries. Thus, unless a taxpayer has significant passive activity income (from rents, for example), little or no tax advantage is created by losses reported by a partnership unless the partner materially participates in the actual business activity.

The partnership form of business also has certain significant disadvantages. Perhaps the most severe problem is the unlimited liability automatically incurred by each partner. Partnership law specifies that any partner can be held personally liable for *all* debts of the business. The potential risk is especially significant when coupled with the concept of *mutual agency*. This legal term refers to the right that each partner has to incur liabilities in the name of the partnership. Consequently, partners acting within the normal scope of the business have the power to obligate the company for any amount. If the partnership fails to pay these debts, creditors can seek satisfactory remuneration from any partner that they choose.

> Partners are jointly and severally liable for the firm's obligations. As an example, if a bank had made a $10 million loan to the partnership that it could not pay, and the bank obtained a judgment against the partnership, the bank could attempt to attach the assets of any particular partner

---

[8] Keith Wishon and Robert P. Roche, "Making the Switch: Corporation to Partnership," *Journal of Accountancy,* March 1987, p. 90.

in the firm. The bank could pick and choose the partners it wished to proceed against in order to satisfy the judgment. If a partner ended up paying more than his or her share, he or she would have a right to recover from the other partners.[9]

This problem is more than just a theoretical concern. As noted in *The Wall Street Journal*,

At least 10 partners of Laventhol & Horwath, a major accounting firm that collapsed two years ago, have filed for personal bankruptcy. They are trying to protect their savings and their homes because partners and principals of the now-defunct firm owe creditors $47.3 million.[10]

Such legal concepts as unlimited liability and mutual agency describe partnership characteristics that have been defined and interpreted over a number of years. To provide consistent application across state lines in regard to these terms as well as many other legal aspects of a partnership, the Uniform Partnership Act (UPA) was created. This act, which was first proposed in 1914 (and revised in 1994) now has been adopted by all states in some form. It establishes uniform standards in such areas as the nature of a partnership, the relationship of the partners to outside parties, and the dissolution of the partnership. For example, the most common legal definition of a partnership is provided by Section 6 of the act: "an association of two or more persons to carry on a business as co-owners for profit."

# ALTERNATIVE LEGAL FORMS

Because of the possible liability, partnerships often experience difficulty in attracting large amounts of capital. Potential partners frequently prefer to avoid the risk that is a basic characteristic of a partnership. However, the tax benefits of avoiding double taxation still provide a strong pull toward the partnership form. Hence in recent years, a number of alternative types of organizations have been developed. The availability of these legal forms depends on state laws as well as applicable tax laws. In each case, though, the purpose is to limit the owners' personal liability while providing the tax benefits of a partnership.[11]

### *Subchapter S Corporation*

A Subchapter S Corporation (often referred to as an *S Corporation*) is created as a corporation and, therefore, has all of the legal characteristics of that form.[12] According to the U.S. tax laws, if certain regulations are met, the corporation will be taxed in virtually the same way as a partnership. Thus, the Subchapter S Corporation pays no income taxes although any income (and losses) pass directly through to the taxable income of the individual owners. Double taxation is avoided but the owners do not face unlimited liability. To qualify, the business can have only one class of stock and is limited to 75 stockholders. All owners must be individuals, estates, certain tax-exempt entities, or certain types of trusts. The most significant problem associated with this business form is that its growth potential is limited because of the restriction on the number and type of owners.

### *Limited Partnership (LPs)*

A limited partnership is a type of investment designed primarily for individuals who want the tax benefits of a partnership but who do not wish to work in a partnership or have unlimited liability. In such organizations, a number of limited partners invest money as owners but are not allowed to participate in the management of the company. These partners can still incur a loss on their investment, but the amount is restricted to what has been contributed. To protect

---

[9] An interview with Leslie D. Corwin, Esq., "What's a Partner to Do?" *The CPA Journal,* April 1991, p. 22.

[10] Lee Berton and Joann S. Lublin, "Partnership Structure Is Called in Question as Liability Risk Rises," *The Wall Street Journal,* June 10, 1992, p. A9.

[11] Many factors should be considered in choosing a specific legal form for an organization. The information shown here is merely an overview. For more information, consult a tax guide or a business law textbook.

[12] Unless a corporation qualifies as a Subchapter S Corporation or some other legal variation, it is referred to as a *Subchapter C Corporation.* Therefore, a vast majority of all businesses are C Corporations.

the creditors of a limited partnership, one or more general partners must be designated to assume responsibility for all obligations created in the name of the business.

Buckeye Partners, L.P. (with annual revenues of more than $208 million) is an example of a limited partnership that trades on the New York Stock Exchange. According to Buckeye's December 31, 2000, balance sheet, capital of $2.8 million is reported for the company's general partners whereas the same account shows a total of $346.6 million for its limited partners.

Many limited partnerships were originally formed as tax shelters to create immediate losses (to reduce the taxable income of the partners) with profits spread out into the future. As mentioned earlier, changes in the tax laws to limit the deduction of passive activity losses have significantly reduced the number of limited partnerships being formed.

### *Limited Liability Partnerships (LLPs)*

The limited liability partnership has most of the same characteristics of a general partnership except that the liability of the partners is significantly reduced. Partners may lose their investment in the business and are also responsible for the contractual debts of the business. The advantage here is created in connection with any liability resulting from damages. In such cases, the partners are responsible only for their own acts or omissions plus the acts and omissions of individuals under their supervision. Thus, a partner in the Houston office of a public accounting firm would probably not be held liable for a poor audit performed by that firm's San Francisco office. Not surprisingly, limited liability partnerships have become very popular with professional service organizations that have multiple offices. In 1994, for example, all of the five largest accounting firms became LLPs.

Unfortunately, however, the limited liability partnership concept is relatively new and the degree of protection it provides has not been well established legally.

> Arthur Andersen LLP's 1,700 partners could be held personally liable for major chunks of the firm's debts, Enron Corp. creditors asserted in a bankruptcy-court filing Friday. Enron's official committee of unsecured creditors accused Andersen of trying to protect its partners by paying off the firm's ordinary business debts, for which partners are liable, it said. That practice will leave less money to pay malpractice claims, for which most partners cannot be held personally liable, the committee claimed. Enron's creditors have indicated they intend to press claims against Andersen stemming from its botched audit of Enron. Concern has been rampant among partners about whether they will ultimately face personal liability in connection with Enron. Andersen is incorporated in Illinois as a limited-liability partnership, a structure designed to shield partners from firmwide liabilities. But the protection such structures offer has never been tested in a case as large as Andersen's.[13]

### *Limited Liability Companies (LLCs)*

The limited liability company is a new type of organization in the United States although it has long been used in Europe and other areas of the world. It is classified as a partnership for tax purposes. However, depending on state laws, the owners are risking only their own investments. In contrast to a Subchapter S Corporation, the number of owners is not usually restricted so that growth is easier to accomplish.

## PARTNERSHIP ACCOUNTING—CAPITAL ACCOUNTS

Despite legal distinctions, questions should be raised as to the need for an entirely separate study of partnership accounting.

- Does an association of two or more persons require accounting procedures significantly different from those of a corporation?
- Does proper accounting depend on the legal form of an organization?

---

[13] Mitchell Pacelle, "Creditors Target Andersen's Partners," *The Wall Street Journal*, June 3, 2002, p. A3.

The answer to these questions is both yes and no. Accounting procedures are normally standardized for assets, liabilities, revenues, and expenses regardless of the legal form of a business. *Partnership accounting, though, does exhibit unique aspects that warrant study, but they lie primarily in the handling of the partners' capital accounts.*

The stockholders' equity accounts of a corporation do not correspond directly with the capital balances found in a partnership's financial records. The various equity accounts reported by an incorporated enterprise display a greater range of information. This characteristic reflects the wide variety of equity transactions that can occur in a corporation as well as the influence of state and federal laws. Government regulation has had enormous effect on the accounting for corporate equity transactions in that extensive disclosure is required to protect stockholders and other outside parties such as potential investors.

To provide adequate information as well as to meet legal requirements, corporate accounting must provide details about numerous equity transactions and account balances. For example, the amount of a corporation's paid-in capital is shown separately from earned capital and other comprehensive income; the par value of each class of stock is disclosed; treasury stock, stock options, stock dividends, and other capital transactions are reported based on prescribed accounting principles.

In comparison, partnerships provide only a limited amount of equity disclosure primarily in the form of individual capital accounts that are accumulated for every partner or every class of partners. These balances measure each partner or group's interest in the book value of the net assets of the business. Thus, the equity section of a partnership balance sheet is composed solely of capital accounts that can be affected by many different events: contributions from partners as well as distributions to them, earnings, and any other equity transactions.

However, no differentiation is drawn in the reporting of a partnership between the various sources of ownership capital. Disclosing the composition of the partners' capital balances has not been judged necessary because partnerships have historically tended to be small with equity transactions that were rarely complex. Additionally, absentee ownership is not common, a factor that minimizes both the need for government regulation and outside interest in detailed information about the capital balances.

## Articles of Partnership

Because the demand for information about capital balances is limited, accounting principles specific to partnerships are based primarily on traditional approaches that have evolved over the years rather than on official pronouncements. These procedures attempt to mirror the relationship between the partners and their business especially as defined by the partnership agreement. This legal covenant, which may be either oral or written, is often referred to as the *Articles of Partnership* and forms the central governance for the operation of a partnership. The financial arrangements spelled out in this contract establish guidelines for the various capital transactions. Therefore, the Articles of Partnership, rather than either laws or official rules, provide much of the underlying basis for partnership accounting.

Since the articles of partnership is a negotiated agreement created by the partners, an unlimited number of variations can be encountered in practice. Partners' rights and responsibilities frequently differ from business to business. Consequently, accountants often are hired in an advisory capacity to participate in the creation of this document to ensure the equitable treatment of all parties. Although the articles of partnership may contain a number of provisions, an explicit understanding should always be reached in regard to the following:

- Name and address of each partner.
- Business location.
- Description of the nature of the business.
- Rights and responsibilities of each partner.
- Initial contribution to be made by each partner along with the method to be used for valuation.
- Specific method by which profits and losses are to be allocated.
- Periodic withdrawal of assets by each partner.
- Procedure for admitting new partners.

- Method for arbitrating partnership disputes.
- Life insurance provisions enabling remaining partners to acquire the interest of any deceased partner.
- Method for settling a partner's share in the business upon withdrawal, retirement, or death.[14]

Despite the importance of the articles of partnership, an unusual number of partnerships fail to produce this needed document.

> "You'd be surprised at the number of American law firms that operate without partnership agreements or [use] agreements that are out of date," says Ward Bower of Altman & Weil, a consulting firm that specializes in law-firm management. "Lawyers," he adds, "will sign agreements they'd never let their clients sign."[15]

> But despite 20 years of advice on the value of partnership agreements, the reality is that, in the majority of cases, well-structured agreements are the exception, rather than the rule, in practice units.[16]

## Accounting for Capital Contributions

Several types of capital transactions occur in a partnership: allocation of profits and losses, retirement of a current partner, admission of a new partner, and so on. The initial transaction, however, is the contribution made by the original partners to begin the business. In the simplest situation, the partners invest only cash amounts. For example, assume that Carter and Green form a business to be operated as a partnership. Carter contributes $50,000 in cash and Green invests $20,000. The initial journal entry to record the creation of this partnership is as follows:

| | | |
|---|---:|---:|
| Cash | 70,000 | |
|     Carter, Capital | | 50,000 |
|     Green, Capital | | 20,000 |
| To record cash contributed to start new partnership. | | |

Complications have been avoided in this first illustration by the assumption that only cash was invested. Often, though, one or more of the partners transfers noncash assets such as inventory, land, equipment, or a building to the business. Although fair market value is used to record these assets, a case could be developed for initially valuing any contributed asset at the partner's current book value. According to the concept of unlimited liability (as well as present tax laws), a partnership does not exist as an entity apart from its owners. A logical extension of the idea is that the investment of an asset is not a transaction occurring between two independent parties such as would warrant revaluation. This contention holds that the semblance of an arm's-length transaction is necessary to justify a change in the book value of any account.

Although retaining the recorded value for assets contributed to a partnership may seem reasonable, this method of valuation proves to be inequitable to any partner investing appreciated property. A $50,000 capital balance always results from a cash investment of that amount, but the recording of other assets would depend entirely on the original book value.

For example, should a partner who contributes a building having a recorded value of $18,000 but a fair market value of $50,000 be credited with only an $18,000 interest in the partnership? Since $50,000 in cash and $50,000 in appreciated property are equivalent contributions, a $32,000 difference in the partners' capital balances cannot be justified. To prevent

---

[14] A complete discussion of the provisions to be included in a partnership agreement can be found in "Get It in Writing," *C A Magazine,* August 1996, and "The Importance of Partnership Agreements," *Journal of Accountancy,* January 1994.

[15] Christi Harlan, "Lawyers Find It Difficult to Break Up Partnerships," *The Wall Street Journal,* October 6, 1988, p. B1.

[16] Herman J. Lowe, "Partnership Agreements: Realities into Formalities," *Journal of Accountancy,* September 1986, p. 158.

# Discussion Question

**WHAT KIND OF BUSINESS IS THIS?**

After graduating from college, Shelley Williams held several different jobs but found that she did not enjoy working for other people. Finally, she and Yvonne Hargrove, her college roommate, decided to start a business of their own. They rented a small building and opened a florist shop selling cut flowers such as roses and chrysanthemums that they bought from a local greenhouse.

Williams and Hargrove agreed orally to share profits and losses equally, although they also decided to take no money from the operation for at least four months. No other arrangements were made but the business did reasonably well and, after the first four months had passed, each began to draw out $500 in cash every week.

At year's end, they took their financial records to a local accountant so that they could get their income tax returns completed. He informed them that they had been operating as a partnership and that they should draw up a formal articles of partnership or consider incorporation or some other legal form of organization. They confessed that they had never really considered the issue and asked for his advice on the matter.

What advice should the accountant give to these clients?

---

such inequities, each item transferred to a partnership is initially recorded for external reporting purposes at current value.[17]

Requiring revaluation of contributed assets can, however, be advocated for reasons other than just the fair treatment of all partners. Despite some evidence to the contrary, a partnership can be viewed legitimately as an entity standing apart from its owners. As an example, a partnership maintains legal ownership of its assets and (depending on state law) can instigate lawsuits. For this reason, accounting practice traditionally has held that the contribution of assets (and liabilities) to a partnership is an exchange between two separately identifiable parties that should be recorded based on fair market values.

The determination of an appropriate valuation for each capital balance is more than just an accounting exercise. Over the life of a partnership, these figures serve in a number of important capacities:

1. The totals in the individual capital accounts often influence the assignment of profits and losses to the partners.
2. The capital account balance is usually one factor in determining the final distribution that will be received by a partner at the time of withdrawal or retirement.
3. Ending capital balances indicate the allocation to be made of any assets that remain following the liquidation of a partnership.

To demonstrate, assume that Carter invests $50,000 in cash to begin the previously discussed partnership and Green contributes the following assets:

|  | Book Value to Green | Fair Market Value |
|---|---|---|
| Inventory | $ 9,000 | $10,000 |
| Land | 14,000 | 11,000 |
| Building | 32,000 | 46,000 |
| Totals | $55,000 | $67,000 |

---

[17] For federal income tax purposes, the $18,000 book value is retained as the basis for this building, even after transfer to the partnership. Within the tax laws, no difference is seen between partners and their partnership so that no adjustment to market value is warranted.

As an added factor, Green's building is encumbered by a $23,600 mortgage that the partnership has agreed to assume.

Green's net investment is equal to $43,400 ($67,000 less $23,600). The following journal entry records the formation of the partnership created by these contributions:

| | | |
|---|---:|---:|
| Cash | 50,000 | |
| Inventory | 10,000 | |
| Land | 11,000 | |
| Building | 46,000 | |
|     Mortgage Payable | | 23,600 |
|     Carter, Capital | | 50,000 |
|     Green, Capital | | 43,400 |
| To record properties contributed to start partnership. Assets and liabilities are recorded at fair market value. | | |

One additional point should be made before leaving this illustration. Although Green has contributed inventory, land, and a building, this partner holds no further right to these individual assets; they now belong to the partnership. The $43,400 capital balance represents an ownership interest in the business as a whole but does not constitute a specific claim to any asset. Having transferred title to the partnership, Green has no more right to these assets than does Carter.

### Intangible Contributions

In forming a partnership, the contributions made by one or more of the partners may go beyond assets and liabilities. A doctor, for example, can bring a particular line of expertise to a partnership, and a practicing dentist might have already developed an established clientele. These attributes, as well as many others, are frequently as valuable to a partnership as cash and fixed assets. *Hence, formal accounting recognition of such special contributions may be appropriately included as a provision of any partnership agreement.*

To illustrate, assume that James and Joyce plan to open an advertising agency and decide to organize the endeavor as a partnership. James contributes cash of $70,000, and Joyce invests only $10,000. Joyce, however, is an accomplished graphic artist, a skill that is considered especially valuable to this business. Therefore, in producing the Articles of Partnership, the partners agree to start the business with equal capital balances. Often such decisions result only after long, and sometimes heated, negotiations. Because the value assigned to an intangible contribution such as artistic talent is arbitrary at best, proper reporting depends on the ability of the partners to arrive at an equitable arrangement.

In recording this agreement, James and Joyce have two options available: (1) the bonus method and (2) the goodwill method. Each of these approaches achieves the desired result of establishing equal capital account balances. Recorded figures, however, can vary significantly, depending on the procedure selected. Thus, the partners should reach an understanding prior to beginning business operations as to the method to be used. The accountant can help avoid conflicts by assisting the partners in evaluating the impact created by each of these two alternatives.

**The Bonus Method**  The bonus method assumes that a specialization such as Joyce's artistic abilities does *not* constitute a recordable partnership asset with a measurable cost. Hence, this approach recognizes only the assets that are physically transferred to the business (such as cash, patents, inventory). Although total partnership capital is determined by these contributions, the establishment of specific capital balances is viewed as an independent process based solely on the agreement of the partners. Because the initial equity figures are the result of negotiation, they do not need to correspond directly with the individual investments.

James and Joyce have contributed a total of $80,000 in identifiable assets to their partnership and have decided on equal capital balances. According to the bonus method, this agreement is fulfilled simply by splitting the $80,000 capital evenly between the two partners. The following entry records the formation of this partnership under this assumption:

| | | |
|---|---|---|
| Cash | 80,000 | |
|     James, Capital | | 40,000 |
|     Joyce, Capital | | 40,000 |
| To record cash contributions with bonus to Joyce because of artistic abilities. | | |

Joyce received a capital bonus here of $30,000 (the $40,000 recorded capital balance in excess of the $10,000 cash contribution) from James in recognition of the artistic abilities she brought into the business.

***The Goodwill Method*** The goodwill method is based on the assumption that an implied value can be calculated mathematically and recorded for any intangible contribution made by a partner. In the present illustration, Joyce invested $60,000 less cash than James but receives an equal amount of capital according to the partnership agreement. Proponents of the goodwill method argue that Joyce's artistic talent has an apparent value of $60,000, a figure that should be included as part of this partner's capital investment. If not recorded, Joyce's primary contribution to the business is ignored completely within the accounting records.

| | | |
|---|---|---|
| Cash | 80,000 | |
| Goodwill | 60,000 | |
|     James, Capital | | 70,000 |
|     Joyce, Capital | | 70,000 |
| To record cash contributions with goodwill attributed to Joyce in recognition of artistic abilities. | | |

***Comparison of Methods*** Both of these approaches achieve the intent of the partnership agreement: Equal capital balances are recorded despite a difference in the partners' cash contributions. The bonus method allocates the $80,000 invested capital according to the percentages designated by the partners, whereas the goodwill method capitalizes the implied value of Joyce's intangible contribution.

Although nothing prohibits the use of either technique, the recognition of goodwill poses definite theoretical problems. In previous discussions of both the equity method (Chapter 1) and purchase consolidations (Chapter 2), goodwill was recorded but only as a result of an acquisition made by the reporting entity. Consequently, this asset had a historical cost in the traditional accounting sense. Partnership goodwill has no such cost; the business recognizes an asset even though no funds have been spent.

The partnership of James and Joyce, for example, is able to record $60,000 in goodwill without any expenditure. Furthermore, the value attributed to this asset is based solely on a negotiated agreement between the partners; the $60,000 balance has no objectively verifiable basis. Thus, although partnership goodwill is sometimes encountered in actual practice, this "asset" should be viewed with a strong degree of professional skepticism.

## Additional Capital Contributions and Withdrawals

Subsequent to the formation of a partnership, the owners may choose to contribute additional capital amounts during the life of the business. These investments can be made to stimulate expansion or to assist the business in overcoming working capital shortages or other problems. Regardless of the reason, the contribution is again recorded as an increment in the partner's capital account based on fair market value. For example, in the previous illustration, assume that James decides to invest another $5,000 cash in the partnership to help finance the purchase of new office furnishings. The partner's capital account balance is immediately increased by this amount to reflect the transfer being made to the partnership.

The partners also may reverse this process by withdrawing assets from the business for their own personal use. For example, one partnership, Andersons, reported recently in its financial statements partner withdrawals for the year of $1,759,072 as well as increases in invested capital of $733,675. To protect the interests of the other partners, the amount and timing of such withdrawals should be clearly specified in the articles of partnership.

In many instances, withdrawals are allowed on a regular periodic basis as a reward for ownership or as compensation for work done in the business. Often such distributions are recorded initially in a separate drawing account that is closed into the individual partner's capital account at year's end. Assume, for illustration purposes, that James and Joyce take out $1,200 and $1,500, respectively, from their business. The journal entry to record these payments is as follows:

| | | |
|---|---:|---:|
| James, Drawing | 1,200 | |
| Joyce, Drawing | 1,500 | |
|     Cash | | 2,700 |
| To record withdrawal of cash by partners. | | |

Larger amounts might also be withdrawn from a partnership on occasion. A partner may have a special need for money or just desire to reduce the basic investment that has been made in the business. Such transactions are usually sporadic occurrences and in amounts significantly greater than the partner's periodic drawing. Prior approval by the other partners may be required by the articles of partnership.

## Allocation of Income

At the end of each fiscal period, partnership revenues and expenses are closed out with the resulting net income or loss being reclassified to the partners' capital accounts. Since a separate capital balance is maintained for each partner, a method must be devised for this assignment of annual income. Because of the importance of the process, the procedure established by the partners should always be stipulated in the articles of partnership. If no arrangement has been specified, state partnership law normally holds that all partners receive an equal allocation of any income or loss earned by the business. If an agreement has been set forth specifying only the division of profits, any subsequent losses must be divided in that same manner.

An allocation pattern can be extremely important to the success of an organization because it can help emphasize and reward outstanding performance.

> The goal of a partner compensation plan is to inspire each principal's most profitable performance—and make a firm grow. When a CPA firm's success depends on partner contributions other than accounting expertise—such as bringing in business, developing a specialty or being a good manager—its compensation plan has to encourage those qualities, for both fairness and firm health.[18]

Actual procedures for allocating profits and losses can range from the simple to the elaborate.[19]

> Our system is as follows: a base draw to all partners, which grows over an eight-year period from 0.63x to a maximum of x, to which is added a 7 percent return on our accrual capital and our intangible capital. (Intangible capital is defined as the goodwill of the firm valued at 75 percent of gross revenues.) A separate pool of funds (about 20 percent of our compensation) is reserved for the performance pool. Each partner assesses how his or her goals helped firm goals for the year, reviews the other partners' assessment reports and then prepares an allocation schedule. Bonus pool shares are based on a group vote.[20]

Partnerships can avoid all complications by assigning net income on an equal basis among all partners. Other organizations attempt to devise plans that reward such factors as the expertise of

---

[18] Michael Hayes, "Pay for Performance," *Journal of Accountancy*, June 2002, p. 24.

[19] See, for example, "Profit Allocation in CPA Firm Partnership Agreements," in the *Journal of Accountancy*, March 1986, pp. 91–95; "Paying Partners: A Challenge for the 1990s," June 1989 issue of the *Journal of Accountancy*, pp. 117–22; "Selecting the Best Partner Compensation Method," December 1991 *Journal of Accountancy*, pp. 40–44; or "Pay for Performance," *Journal of Accountancy*, June 2002, pp. 24–28.

[20] Richard Kretz, "You Want to Minimize the Pain," *Journal of Accountancy*, June 2002, p. 28.

# Discussion Question

**HOW WILL THE PROFITS BE SPLIT?**

James J. Dewars has been the sole owner of a small CPA firm for the past 20 years. Now 52 years old, Dewars is concerned about the continuation of his practice after he retires. He would like to begin taking more time off now although he wants to remain active in the firm for at least another 8 to 10 years. He has worked hard over the decades to build up the practice so that he presently makes a profit of $180,000 annually.

Lewis Huffman has been working for Dewars for the past four years. He now earns a salary of $68,000 per year. He is a very dedicated employee who generally works 44–60 hours per week. In the past, Dewars has been in charge of the bigger, more profitable audit clients whereas Huffman, with less experience, worked with the smaller clients. Both Dewars and Huffman do some tax work although that segment of the business has never been emphasized.

Sally Scriba has been employed for the past seven years with another CPA firm as a tax specialist. She has no auditing experience but has a great reputation in tax planning and preparation. She currently earns an annual salary of $80,000.

Dewars, Huffman, and Scriba are negotiating the creation of a new CPA firm as a partnership. Dewars plans to reduce his time in this firm although he will continue to work with many of the clients that he has served for the past two decades. Huffman will begin to take over some of the major audit jobs. Scriba will start to develop an extensive tax practice for the firm.

Because of the changes in the firm, the three potential partners anticipate earning a total net income in the first year of operations of between $130,000 and $260,000. Thereafter, they hope that profits will increase at the rate of 10 to 20 percent annually for the next five years or so.

How should this new partnership allocate its future net income among these partners?

---

the individuals, number of years with the organization, or the amount of time that each works. Some agreements also consider the capital invested in the business as an element that should be recognized within the allocation process.

To serve as an initial illustration, assume that Tinker, Evers, and Chance form a partnership by investing cash of $120,000, $90,000, and $75,000, respectively. The articles of partnership is drawn up to specify that Evers will be allotted 40 percent of all profits and losses because of previous business experience while Tinker and Chance are to divide the remaining 60 percent equally. This agreement also stipulates that each partner is allowed to withdraw $10,000 in cash annually from the business. The amount of this withdrawal does not directly depend on the method utilized for income allocation. *From an accounting perspective, the assignment of income and the setting of withdrawal limits are two separate decisions.*

At the end of the first year of operations, the partnership reports net income of $60,000. To reflect the changes made in the partners' capital balances, the closing process consists of the following two journal entries. The assumption is made here that each partner has taken the allowed amount of drawing during the year. In addition, for convenience, all revenues and expenses already have been closed into the Income Summary account.

| | | |
|---|---|---|
| Tinker, Capital | 10,000 | |
| Evers, Capital | 10,000 | |
| Chance, Capital | 10,000 | |
|     Tinker, Drawing | | 10,000 |
|     Evers, Drawing | | 10,000 |
|     Chance, Drawing | | 10,000 |
| To close out drawing accounts recording payments made to the three partners. | | |

| | | 60,000 | |
|---|---|---|---|
| Income Summary ................................... | | 60,000 | |
|     Tinker, Capital (30%) ............................. | | | 18,000 |
|     Evers, Capital (40%) .............................. | | | 24,000 |
|     Chance, Capital (30%) ........................... | | | 18,000 |
| To allocate net income based on provisions of partnership agreement. | | | |

### Statement of Partners' Capital

Because no Retained Earnings balance is separately disclosed by a partnership, the statement of retained earnings usually reported by a corporation is replaced by a statement of partners' capital. The following financial statement is based on the data presented for the partnership of Tinker, Evers, and Chance. The changes made during the year in the individual capital accounts are outlined along with totals representing the partnership as a whole.

**TINKER, EVERS, AND CHANCE**
**Statement of Partners' Capital**
**For Year Ending December 31, Year 1**

| | Tinker, Capital | Evers, Capital | Chance, Capital | Totals |
|---|---|---|---|---|
| Capital balances beginning of year ............... | $120,000 | $ 90,000 | $ 75,000 | $285,000 |
| Allocation of net income ....................... | 18,000 | 24,000 | 18,000 | 60,000 |
| Drawings ..................................... | (10,000) | (10,000) | (10,000) | (30,000) |
| Capital balances end of year ................... | $128,000 | $104,000 | $ 83,000 | $315,000 |

### Alternative Allocation Techniques—Example 1

Assigning net income based on a ratio may be simple, but this approach is not necessarily equitable to all partners. For example, assume that Tinker does not participate in the operations of the partnership but is the contributor of the largest amount of capital. Evers and Chance both work full time in the business, but Evers has considerably more experience in this line of work.

Under these circumstances, no single ratio is likely to reflect properly the various contributions being made by each of the partners. Indeed, an unlimited number of alternative allocation plans could be devised in hope of achieving fair treatment for all parties. For example, because of the different levels of capital being invested, consideration should be given to the inclusion of interest within the allocation process to reward the contributions. A compensation allowance is also a possibility, usually in an amount corresponding to the number of hours worked or the level of a partner's business expertise.

To demonstrate one possible option, assume that Tinker, Evers, and Chance begin their partnership based on the facts presented originally except that they arrive at a more detailed method of allocating profits and losses. After considerable negotiations, an articles of partnership agreement is drawn up to credit each partner annually for interest in an amount equal to 10 percent of that partner's beginning capital balance for the year. Evers and Chance also will be allotted $15,000 apiece as a compensation allowance in recognition of their participation in daily operations. Any remaining profit or loss will be split 4:3:3, with the largest share going to Evers because of the work experience that this partner brings to the business. As with any appropriate allocation, this pattern is an attempt to provide fair treatment for all three of the partners.

Under this arrangement, the $60,000 net income earned by the partnership in the first year of operation would be prorated as follows. The sequential alignment of the various provisions is irrelevant except that the ratio, which is used to assign the remaining profit or loss, must be calculated last.

|  | Tinker | Evers | Chance | Totals |
|---|---|---|---|---|
| Interest (10% of beginning capital) | $12,000 | $ 9,000 | $ 7,500 | $28,500 |
| Compensation allowance | –0– | 15,000 | 15,000 | 30,000 |
| Remaining income: $60,000 (28,500) (30,000) $ 1,500 | 450 (30%) | 600 (40%) | 450 (30%) | 1,500 |
| Totals | $12,450 | $24,600 | $22,950 | $60,000 |

For the partnership of Tinker, Evers, and Chance, the allocations just calculated led to the following year-end closing entry:

| | | |
|---|---|---|
| Income Summary | 60,000 | |
|     Tinker, Capital | | 12,450 |
|     Evers, Capital | | 24,600 |
|     Chance, Capital | | 22,950 |
| To allocate income for the year to the individual partner's capital accounts based on partnership agreement. | | |

### Alternative Allocation Techniques—Example 2

As indicated by the preceding illustration, the assignment process is no more than a series of mechanical steps reflecting the change in each partner's capital balance resulting from the provisions of the partnership agreement. The number of different allocation procedures that could be employed is limited solely by the imagination of the partners. Although interest, compensation allowances, and various ratios are the predominant factors encountered in practice, other possibilities exist. Therefore, another approach to the allocation process is presented to further illustrate some of the variations that can be utilized. A two-person partnership is used here to simplify the computations.

Assume that Webber and Rice formed a partnership in 1990 to operate a bookstore. Webber contributed the initial capital while Rice managed the business. With the assistance of their accountant, they wrote an articles of partnership agreement that contains the following provisions:

1. Each partner is allowed to draw $1,000 in cash from the business every month. Any withdrawal in excess of that figure will be accounted for as a direct reduction to the partner's capital balance.
2. Partnership profits and losses will be allocated each year according to the following plan:
   a. Interest of 15 percent will be accrued by each partner based on the monthly average capital balance for the year (calculated without regard for normal drawings or current income).
   b. As a reward for operating the business, Rice is to receive credit for a bonus equal to 20 percent of the year's net income. However, no bonus is earned if the partnership reports a net loss.
   c. Any remaining profit or loss will be divided equally between the two partners.

Assume that Webber and Rice subsequently begin the year 2004 with capital balances of $150,000 and $30,000, respectively. On April 1 of that year, Webber invests an additional $8,000 cash in the business, and on July 1, Rice withdraws $6,000 in excess of the specified drawing allowance. Assume further that the partnership reports income of $30,000 for 2004.

Because the interest factor established in this allocation plan is based on a monthly average figure, the specific amount to be credited to each partner has to be determined by means of a preliminary calculation:

*Webber—Interest Allocation*

| | | |
|---|---|---|
| Beginning balance: | $150,000 × 3 months = | $ 450,000 |
| Balance, 4/1/04: | $158,000 × 9 months = | 1,422,000 |
| | | 1,872,000 |
| | | × 1/12 |
| Monthly average capital balance ....... | | 156,000 |
| Interest rate ................... | | × 15% |
| Interest credited to Webber ......... | | $ 23,400 |

*Rice—Interest Allocation*

| | | |
|---|---|---|
| Beginning balance: | $30,000 × 6 months = | $180,000 |
| Balance, 7/1/04: | $24,000 × 6 months = | 144,000 |
| | | 324,000 |
| | | × 1/12 |
| Monthly average capital balance ....... | | 27,000 |
| Interest rate ................... | | × 15% |
| Interest credited to Rice ........... | | $ 4,050 |

Following this initial computation, the actual assignment of income can proceed according to the provisions specified in the partnership agreement. The stipulations drawn up by Webber and Rice must be followed exactly, even though the business's $30,000 profit in 2004 is not sufficient to cover both the interest and the bonus. Income allocation is a mechanical process that should always be carried out as stated in the articles of partnership without regard for the specific level of income or loss.

Based on the plan that was created, Webber's capital increases by $21,675 during 2004 but Rice is assigned only $8,325:

| | Webber | Rice | Totals |
|---|---|---|---|
| Interest (above) .................... | $23,400 | $ 4,050 | $27,450 |
| Bonus (20% × $30,000) ............. | –0– | 6,000 | 6,000 |
| Remaining income (loss): | | | |
| $ 30,000 | | | |
| (27,450) | | | |
| (6,000) | | | |
| $ (3,450) ...................... | (1,725) (50%) | (1,725) (50%) | (3,450) |
| Totals ..................... | $21,675 | $ 8,325 | $30,000 |

## ACCOUNTING FOR PARTNERSHIP DISSOLUTION

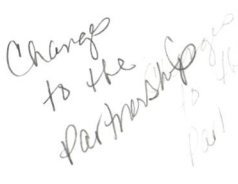

In many partnerships, capital transactions are limited almost exclusively to contributions, drawings, and profit and loss allocations. Normally, though, over any extended period, changes occur in the members who make up a partnership. Employees may be promoted into the partnership or new owners brought in from outside the organization to add capital or expertise to the business. Current partners eventually retire, die, or simply elect to leave the partnership. Large operations may even experience such changes on a routine basis. One international accounting firm has estimated that 50 to 70 partners leave the organization each year for a variety of reasons. That, apparently, is not an isolated situation; "major accounting firms have gotten rid of between 5 percent and 14 percent of their partners over the past 18 months."[21]

---

[21] Berton and Lublin, "Partnership Structure," p. A9.

Regardless of the nature or the frequency of the event, any alteration in the specific individuals composing a partnership automatically leads to legal dissolution. In many instances, the breakup is merely a prerequisite to the formation of a new partnership. For example, if Abernethy and Chapman decide to allow Miller to become a partner in their business, the legally recognized partnership of Abernethy and Chapman has to be dissolved first. The business property as well as the right to future profits can then be conveyed to the newly formed partnership of Abernethy, Chapman, and Miller. The change is a legal change. Actual operations of the business would probably continue unimpeded by this alteration in ownership.

Conversely, should the partners so choose, dissolution can be a preliminary step in the termination and liquidation of the business. The death of a partner, lack of sufficient profits, or internal management differences may lead the partners to the breakup of the partnership business. Under this circumstance, partnership properties are sold, debts paid, and any remaining assets distributed to the individual partners. Thus, in liquidations (which are analyzed in detail in the next chapter), both the partnership and the business cease to exist.

## Dissolution—Admission of a New Partner

One of the most prevalent changes in the makeup of a partnership is the addition of a new partner. An employee may have worked for years to gain this opportunity, or a prospective partner might offer the new investment capital or business experience necessary for future business success. An individual can gain admittance to a partnership in one of two ways: (1) by purchasing an ownership interest from a current partner or (2) by contributing assets directly to the business.

In recording either type of transaction, the accountant has the option, once again, to retain the book value of all partnership assets and liabilities (as exemplified by the bonus method) or revalue these accounts to their present market values (the goodwill method). The decision as to a theoretical preference between the bonus and goodwill methods hinges on one single question: *Should the dissolved partnership and the newly formed partnership be viewed as two separate reporting entities?*

If the new partnership is merely an extension of the old, no basis exists for restatement. The transfer of ownership is a change only in a legal sense and has no direct impact on business assets and liabilities. However, if the continuation of the business represents a legitimate transfer of property from one partnership to another, revaluation of all accounts and recognition of goodwill can be justified.

Because both approaches are encountered in practice, each is presented in this textbook. However, the concerns previously discussed in connection with partnership goodwill still exist: Recognition is not based on historical cost and no objective verification can be made of the amount being capitalized. One alternative revaluation approach that attempts to circumvent the problems involved with partnership goodwill has been devised. This hybrid method revalues all partnership assets and liabilities to fair market value without any corresponding recognition being made of goodwill.

### *Admission through Purchase of a Current Interest*

As mentioned, one method of gaining admittance to a partnership is by the purchase of a current interest. One or more partners may choose to sell their portion of the business to an outside party. This type transaction is most common in operations that rely primarily on monetary capital rather than on the business expertise of the partners.

In making a transfer of ownership, a partner can actually convey only three rights:

1. *The right of co-ownership in the business property.* This right justifies the partner's periodic drawings from the business as well as the distribution settlement paid at liquidation or at the time of a partner's withdrawal.
2. *The right to share in profits and losses as specified in the articles of partnership.*
3. *The right to participate in the management of the business.*

Unless restricted by the articles of partnership, every partner has the power to sell or assign the first two of these rights at any time. Their transfer poses no threat of financial harm to the remaining partners. In contrast, partnership law states that the right to participate in the management of the business can be conveyed only with the consent of all partners. This particular right is considered essential to the future earning power of the enterprise as well as the maintenance of business assets. Therefore, current partners are protected from the intrusion of parties who might be considered detrimental to the management of the company.

As an illustration, assume that Scott, Thompson, and York formed a partnership several years ago. Subsequently, York decides to leave the partnership and offers to sell his interest to Morgan. Although York may transfer the right of property ownership as well as the specified share of future profits and losses, Morgan is not automatically admitted into the partnership. York legally remains a partner until such time as both Scott and Thompson agree to allow Morgan to participate in the management of the business.

To demonstrate the accounting procedures applicable to the transfer of a partnership interest, assume that the following information is available relating to the partnership of Scott, Thompson, and York:

| Partner | Capital Balance | Profit and Loss Ratio |
|---|---|---|
| Scott | $ 50,000 | 20% |
| Thompson | 30,000 | 50 |
| York | 20,000 | 30 |
| Total capital | $100,000 | |

As often happens, the relationship of the capital accounts to one another does not correspond with the partners' profit and loss ratio. Capital balances are historical cost figures. They result from contributions and withdrawals made throughout the life of the business as well as from the allocation of partnership income. Therefore, any correlation between a partner's recorded capital at a particular point in time and the profit and loss percentage would probably be coincidental. Scott, for example, has 50 percent of the current partnership capital ($50,000/$100,000), but is entitled to only a 20 percent allocation of income.

Instead of York selling his interest to Morgan, assume that each of these three partners elects to transfer a 20 percent interest to Morgan for a total payment of $30,000. According to the sales contract, *the money is to be paid directly to the owners.*

One approach to the recording of this transaction is that, since Morgan's purchase is carried out between the individual parties, the acquisition has no impact on the assets and liabilities held by the partnership. Because the business is not involved directly, the transfer of ownership requires a simple capital reclassification without any accompanying revaluation. Book value is retained. This approach is similar to the bonus method; only a legal change in ownership is occurring so that neither revaluation of assets or liabilities nor goodwill is appropriate.

| Book Value Approach | | |
|---|---|---|
| Scott, Capital (20% of capital balance) | 10,000 | |
| Thompson, Capital (20%) | 6,000 | |
| York, Capital (20%) | 4,000 | |
| Morgan, Capital (20% of total) | | 20,000 |
| To reclassify capital to reflect Morgan's acquisition. Money is paid directly to partners. | | |

An alternative for recording this acquisition by Morgan relies on a different perspective of the new partner's admission. Legally, the partnership of Scott, Thompson, and York is transferring all assets and liabilities to the partnership of Scott, Thompson, York, and Morgan. Therefore, according to the logic underlying the goodwill method, a transaction is occurring between two separate reporting entities, an event that necessitates the complete revaluation of all assets and liabilities.

Because Morgan is paying $30,000 for a 20 percent interest in the partnership, the implied value of the business as a whole is $150,000 ($30,000/20%). However, the book value is only

$100,000; thus, a $50,000 upward revaluation is indicated. This adjustment is reflected by restating specific partnership asset and liability accounts to market value with any remaining balance being recorded as goodwill. After the implied value of the partnership is established, the reclassification of ownership can be recorded based on the new capital balances.

| **Goodwill (Revaluation) Approach** | | |
|---|---|---|
| Goodwill (or specific accounts) . . . . . . . . . . . . . . . . . . . . . . . . . . . . . . . . . | 50,000 | |
|     Scott, Capital (20% of goodwill) . . . . . . . . . . . . . . . . . . . . . . . . . . | | 10,000 |
|     Thompson, Capital (50%) . . . . . . . . . . . . . . . . . . . . . . . . . . . . . . | | 25,000 |
|     York, Capital (30%) . . . . . . . . . . . . . . . . . . . . . . . . . . . . . . . . . . | | 15,000 |
| To recognize goodwill and revaluation of assets and liabilities based on value of business implied by size of Morgan's purchase price. | | |
| Scott, Capital (20% of new capital balance) . . . . . . . . . . . . . . . . . . . . . . | 12,000 | |
| Thompson, Capital (20%) . . . . . . . . . . . . . . . . . . . . . . . . . . . . . . . . . . . . | 11,000 | |
| York, Capital (20%) . . . . . . . . . . . . . . . . . . . . . . . . . . . . . . . . . . . . . . . . | 7,000 | |
|     Morgan, Capital (20% of new total) . . . . . . . . . . . . . . . . . . . . . . . . | | 30,000 |
| To reclassify capital to reflect Morgan's acquisition. Money is paid directly to partners. | | |

As this entry indicates, the $50,000 revaluation is credited to the original partners based on the profit and loss ratio rather than on their percentages of capital. Recognition of goodwill (or an increase in the book value of specific accounts) indicates that unrecorded gains have accrued to the business during the previous years of operation. Therefore, the equitable treatment is to allocate this increment among the partners according to their profit and loss percentages.

### Admission by a Contribution Made to the Partnership

Entrance into a partnership is not obtained solely by the purchase of a current partner's interest. An outsider may be admitted to the ownership by contributing cash or other assets directly to the business rather than to the partners. For example, assume that King and Wilson maintain a partnership and presently report capital balances of $80,000 and $20,000, respectively. According to the articles of partnership, King is entitled to 60 percent of all profits and losses with the remaining 40 percent credited each year to Wilson. By agreement of the partners, Simpson is being allowed to enter the partnership for a payment of $20,000 *with this money going into the business.* Based on negotiations that preceded the acquisition, all parties have agreed that Simpson receives an initial 10 percent interest in partnership property.

**Bonus Credited to Original Partners** The bonus (or no revaluation) method maintains the same recorded value for all partnership assets and liabilities despite Simpson's admittance. The capital balance for this new partner is simply set at the appropriate 10 percent level based on the book value of the partnership taken as a whole (after the payment is recorded). Since $20,000 is being invested, total reported capital increases to $120,000. Thus, Simpson's 10 percent interest is computed as $12,000. *The $8,000 difference between the amount contributed and this allotted capital balance is viewed as a bonus.* Because Simpson is willing to accept a capital balance that is less than the investment being made, this bonus is attributed to the original partners (again based on their profit and loss ratio). As a result of the nature of the transaction, no need exists to recognize goodwill or revalue any of the assets or liabilities.

| | | |
|---|---|---|
| Cash . . . . . . . . . . . . . . . . . . . . . . . . . . . . . . . . . . . . . . . . . . . . . . . . . . . . . | 20,000 | |
|     Simpson, Capital (10% of total capital) . . . . . . . . . . . . . . . . . . . . . . | | 12,000 |
|     King, Capital (60% of bonus) . . . . . . . . . . . . . . . . . . . . . . . . . . . . | | 4,800 |
|     Wilson, Capital (40% of bonus) . . . . . . . . . . . . . . . . . . . . . . . . . . | | 3,200 |
| To record Simpson's entrance into partnership with $8,000 extra payment recorded as a bonus to the original partners. | | |

***Goodwill Credited to Original Partners*** The goodwill method views Simpson's payment as evidence that the partnership as a whole possesses an actual value of $200,000 ($20,000/10 percent). Since, even with the new partner's investment, only $120,000 in net assets is being reported, a valuation adjustment of $80,000 is implied.[22] Over the previous years, unrecorded gains have apparently accrued to the business. This $80,000 figure might reflect the need to revalue specific accounts such as inventory or equipment, although the entire amount, or some portion of it, may simply be recorded as goodwill.

| | | |
|---|---:|---:|
| Goodwill (or specific accounts) | 80,000 | |
|     King, Capital (60% of goodwill) | | 48,000 |
|     Wilson, Capital (40%) | | 32,000 |
| To recognize goodwill based on Simpson's purchase price. | | |
| Cash | 20,000 | |
|     Simpson, Capital | | 20,000 |
| To record Simpson's admission into partnership. | | |

***Comparison of Bonus Method and Goodwill Method*** Completely different capital balances as well as asset and liability figures result from these two approaches. In both cases, though, the new partner is credited with the appropriate 10 percent of total partnership capital.

| | Bonus Method | Goodwill Method |
|---|---:|---:|
| Assets less liabilities (as reported) | $100,000 | $100,000 |
| Simpson's contribution | 20,000 | 20,000 |
| Goodwill | –0– | 80,000 |
| Total | $120,000 | $200,000 |
| Simpson's capital | $ 12,000 | $ 20,000 |

Because Simpson contributed an amount more than 10 percent of the resulting book value of the partnership, this business is perceived as being worth more than the recorded accounts presently indicate. Therefore, the bonus in the first instance and the goodwill in the second were both assumed as accruing to the two original partners. Such a presumption is not unusual in an established business, especially if profitable operations have developed over a number of years.

***Hybrid Method of Recording Admission of New Partner*** One other approach to the admission of Simpson can be devised. Assume that the assets and liabilities of the King and Wilson partnership have a book value of $100,000 as stated earlier. Also assume that a piece of land held by the business is actually worth $30,000 more than its currently recorded book value. Thus, the identifiable assets of the partnership are worth $130,000. Simpson pays $20,000 for a 10 percent interest.

In this approach, the identifiable assets (such as land) are revalued but no goodwill is recognized.

| | | |
|---|---:|---:|
| Land | 30,000 | |
|     King, Capital (60% of revaluation) | | 18,000 |
|     Wilson, Capital (40%) | | 12,000 |
| To record current market value of land in preparation for admission of new partner. | | |

---

[22] Because the $20,000 is being put into the business in this example, total capital to be used in the goodwill computation has increased to $120,000. If, as in the previous illustration, payment had been made directly to the partners, the original capital of $100,000 is retained in determining goodwill.

The admission of Simpson and the payment of $20,000 brings the total capital balance to $150,000. Because Simpson is acquiring a 10 percent interest, a capital balance of $15,000 is recorded. The extra $5,000 payment ($20,000 − $15,000) is attributed as a bonus to the original partners. In this way, asset revaluation and a capital bonus are both used to align the accounts.

| | | |
|---|---:|---:|
| Cash | 20,000 | |
|     Simpson, Capital (10% of total capital) | | 15,000 |
|     King, Capital (60% of bonus) | | 3,000 |
|     Wilson, Capital (40% of bonus) | | 2,000 |
| To record entrance of Simpson into partnership and bonus assigned to original partners. | | |

***Bonus or Goodwill Credited to New Partner***   As previously discussed, Simpson also may be contributing some attribute other than tangible assets to this partnership. Therefore, the articles of partnership may be written to credit the new partner rather than the original partners, with either a bonus or goodwill. Because of an excellent professional reputation, valuable business contacts, or myriad other possible factors, Simpson might be able to negotiate a beginning capital balance in excess of the $20,000 cash contribution. This same circumstance may also result if the business is desperate for new capital and is willing to offer favorable terms as an enticement to the potential partner.

To illustrate, assume that Simpson receives a 20 percent interest in the partnership (rather than the originally stated 10 percent) in exchange for the $20,000 cash investment. The specific rationale for the higher ownership percentage need not be identified.

The bonus method sets Simpson's initial capital at $24,000 (20 percent of the $120,000 book value). To achieve this balance, a capital bonus of $4,000 must be credited to Simpson and taken from the present partners:

| | | |
|---|---:|---:|
| Cash | 20,000 | |
| King, Capital (60% of bonus) | 2,400 | |
| Wilson, Capital (40% of bonus) | 1,600 | |
|     Simpson, Capital | | 24,000 |
| To record Simpson's entrance into partnership with reduced payment reported as a bonus from original partners. | | |

If goodwill rather than a bonus is attributed to the *entering partner*, a mathematical problem arises in determining the implicit value of the business as a whole. In the current illustration, Simpson paid $20,000 for a 20 percent interest. Therefore, the value of the company is calculated as only $100,000 ($20,000/20 percent), a figure that is less than the $120,000 in net assets being reported after the new contribution. Negative goodwill appears to exist. One possibility is that individual partnership assets are overvalued and require reduction. As an alternative, the cash contribution might not be an accurate representation of the new partner's investment. Simpson could be bringing an intangible contribution (goodwill) to the business along with the $20,000. This additional amount must be determined algebraically:

$$\text{Simpson's capital} = 20 \text{ percent of partnership capital}$$

Therefore

$$\$20,000 + \text{Goodwill} = 0.20\ (\$100,000 + \$20,000 + \text{Goodwill})$$
$$\$20,000 + \text{Goodwill} = \$20,000 + \$4,000 + 0.20\ \text{Goodwill}$$
$$0.80\ \text{Goodwill} = \$4,000$$
$$\text{Goodwill} = \$5,000$$

If the partners determine that Simpson is, indeed, making an intangible contribution (a particular skill, for example, or a loyal clientele), Simpson should be credited with a $25,000 capital investment: $20,000 cash and $5,000 goodwill. When added to the original $100,000 in net assets reported by the partnership, this contribution raises the total capital for the business to $125,000. As specified by the purchase agreement, Simpson's interest now represents a 20 percent share of the partnership ($25,000/$125,000).

Recognizing $5,000 in goodwill has established the proper relationship between the new partner and the partnership. Therefore, the following journal entry should be recorded to reflect this transaction:

| | | |
|---|---|---|
| Cash | 20,000 | |
| Goodwill | 5,000 | |
|     Simpson, Capital | | 25,000 |
| To record Simpson's entrance into partnership with goodwill attributed to this new partner. | | |

## Dissolution—Withdrawal of a Partner

Admission of a new partner is not the only method by which a partnership can undergo a change in composition. Over the life of the business, partners might leave the organization. Death or retirement can occur, or a partner may simply elect to withdraw from the partnership. The articles of partnership also can allow for the expulsion of a partner under certain conditions. Once again, any change in membership legally dissolves the partnership, although the business's operations usually continue uninterrupted under the ownership of the remaining partners.

Regardless of the reason for dissolution, some method of establishing an equitable settlement of the withdrawing partner's interest in the business is necessary. Often, the partner (or the partner's estate) may simply sell the interest to an outside party, with approval, or to one or more of the remaining partners. As an alternative, cash or other assets can be distributed from the business as a means of settling a partner's right of co-ownership. Consequently, life insurance policies are held by many partnerships solely to provide adequate cash to liquidate a partner's interest upon death.

Whether withdrawal is caused by death or some other reason, a final distribution will not necessarily equal the book value of the partner's capital account. A capital balance is only a recording of historical transactions and rarely represents the true value inherent in a business. Instead, payment is frequently based on the value of the partner's interest as ascertained by either negotiation or appraisal. Since the determination of a settlement can be derived in many ways, the articles of partnership should contain exact provisions regulating this procedure.

The withdrawal of an individual partner and the resulting distribution of partnership property can, as before, be accounted for by either the bonus (no revaluation) method or the goodwill (revaluation) method. Once again, a hybrid option is also available.

As in earlier illustrations, if a bonus is recorded, the amount can be attributed to either of the parties involved: the withdrawing partner or the remaining partners. Conversely, any revaluation of partnership property (as well as the establishment of a goodwill balance) is allocated among all partners in recognition of possible unrecorded gains. The hybrid approach restates assets and liabilities to fair market value but makes no recording of goodwill. In this last alternative, the legal change in ownership is reflected but the theoretical problems associated with partnership goodwill are avoided.

### Accounting for the Withdrawal of a Partner—Illustration

To demonstrate the various approaches that can be taken to account for a partner's withdrawal, assume that the partnership of Duncan, Smith, and Windsor has existed for a number of years. At the present time, the partners have the following capital balances as well as the indicated profit and loss percentages:

| Partner | Capital Balance | Profit and Loss Ratio |
|---|---|---|
| Duncan | $ 70,000 | 50% |
| Smith | 20,000 | 30 |
| Windsor | 10,000 | 20 |
| Total capital | $100,000 | |

Windsor decides to withdraw from the partnership, but Duncan and Smith plan to continue operating the business. As per the original partnership agreement, a final settlement distribution for any withdrawing partner is computed based on the following specified provisions:

1. An appraisal will be made by an independent expert to determine the estimated fair market value of the business.
2. Any individual who leaves the partnership is to receive cash or other assets equal to that partner's current capital balance after including an appropriate share of any adjustment indicated by the previous valuation. The allocation of unrecorded gains and losses is based on the normal profit and loss ratio.

Following Windsor's decision to withdraw from the partnership, an immediate appraisal of the business and its property is made. Total fair market value is estimated at $180,000, a figure $80,000 in excess of book value. According to this valuation, land held by the partnership is currently worth $50,000 more than its original cost. In addition, $30,000 in goodwill is attributed to the partnership based on the value of the business as a going concern. *Therefore, Windsor is paid $26,000 on leaving the partnership: the original $10,000 capital balance plus a 20 percent share of this $80,000 increment.* The amount of payment is not in dispute, but the method of recording the withdrawal is in question.

### Bonus Method Applied

If the bonus method is used by the partnership to record this transaction, the extra $16,000 paid to Windsor is simply assigned as a decrease in the remaining partners' capital accounts. Historically, Duncan and Smith have been credited with 50 percent and 30 percent of all profits and losses, respectively. This same relative ratio is used now to allocate the reduction between these two remaining partners on a 5/8 and 3/8 basis:

**Bonus Method**

| | | |
|---|---|---|
| Windsor, Capital (to remove account balance) | 10,000 | |
| Duncan, Capital (5/8 of excess distribution) | 10,000 | |
| Smith, Capital (3/8 of excess distribution) | 6,000 | |
|     Cash | | 26,000 |
| To record Windsor's withdrawal with $16,000 excess distribution taken from remaining partners. | | |

### Goodwill Method Applied

This same transaction can also be accounted for by means of the goodwill (or revaluation) approach. The appraisal indicates that land is undervalued on the partnership's records by $50,000 and that goodwill of $30,000 has apparently accrued to the business over the years. The first of the following entries recognizes these valuations. This adjustment properly equates Windsor's capital balance with the $26,000 cash amount to be distributed. Windsor's equity balance is merely removed in the second entry at the time of payment.

| Goodwill Method | | |
|---|---|---|
| Land | 50,000 | |
| Goodwill | 30,000 | |
|     Duncan, Capital (50%) | | 40,000 |
|     Smith, Capital (30%) | | 24,000 |
|     Windsor, Capital (20%) | | 16,000 |
| To recognize land value and goodwill as a preliminary step to Windsor's withdrawal. | | |
| Windsor, Capital (to remove account balance) | 26,000 | |
|     Cash | | 26,000 |
| To distribute cash to Windsor in settlement of partnership interest. | | |

*The implied value of a partnership as a whole cannot be determined directly from the amount distributed to a withdrawing partner.* For example, paying Windsor $26,000 did not indicate that total capital should be $130,000 ($26,000/20%). This computation is appropriate only when (1) a new partner is admitted or (2) the percentage of capital is the same as the profit and loss ratio. Here, an outside valuation of the business indicated that the company was worth $80,000 more than book value. As a 20 percent owner, Windsor was entitled to $16,000 of that amount, raising the partner's capital account from $10,000 to $26,000, the amount of the final payment.

### Hybrid Method Applied

As indicated previously, a hybrid approach also can be adopted to record a partner's withdrawal. Asset and liability revaluations are still recognized but goodwill is ignored. A bonus must then be recorded to reconcile the partner's adjusted capital balance with the final distribution.

In the following journal entry, for example, no goodwill is recorded. However, the book value of the land is increased by $50,000 in recognition of present worth. This adjustment increases Windsor's capital balance to $20,000, a figure that is still less than the $26,000 distribution. The $6,000 difference is recorded as a bonus taken from the remaining two partners according to their relative profit and loss ratio.

| Hybrid Method | | |
|---|---|---|
| Land | 50,000 | |
|     Duncan, Capital (50%) | | 25,000 |
|     Smith, Capital (30%) | | 15,000 |
|     Windsor, Capital (20%) | | 10,000 |
| To adjust Land account to fair market value as a preliminary step in Windsor's withdrawal. | | |
| Windsor, Capital (to remove account balances) | 20,000 | |
| Duncan, Capital (⅝ of bonus) | 3,750 | |
| Smith, Capital (⅜ of bonus) | 2,250 | |
|     Cash | | 26,000 |
| To record final distribution to Windsor with $6,000 bonus taken from remaining partners. | | |

## Summary

1. A partnership is defined as "an association of two or more persons to carry on a business as co-owners for profit." This form of business organization exists throughout the U.S. economy ranging in size from small, part-time operations to international enterprises. The partnership format is popular for many reasons, including the ease of creation and the avoidance of the double taxation that is inherent in corporate ownership. However, the unlimited liability incurred by each general partner

normally restricts the growth potential of most partnerships. Thus, although the number of partnerships in the United States is great, the size of each tends to be small.
2. Over the years, a number of different types of organizations have been developed to take advantage of both the single taxation of partnerships and the limited liability afforded to corporate stockholders. Such legal forms include S Corporations, Limited Partnerships, Limited Liability Partnerships, and Limited Liability Companies.
3. The unique elements of partnership accounting are found primarily in the capital accounts that are accumulated for each partner. The basis for recording these balances is the articles of partnership, a document that should be established as a prerequisite to the formation of any partnership. One of the principal provisions of this agreement is the initial investment to be made by each partner. Noncash contributions such as inventory or land are entered into the partnership's accounting records at fair market value.
4. In forming a partnership, the contributions made by the partners need not be limited to tangible assets. A particular line of expertise possessed by a partner or an established clientele are attributes that can have a significant value to a partnership. Two methods of recording this type of investment are found in practice. Under the bonus method, only identifiable assets are recognized. The capital accounts are then aligned to indicate the balances negotiated by the partners. According to the goodwill approach, all contributions (even those of a nebulous nature such as an expertise) are valued and recorded, often as goodwill.
5. Another accounting issue to be resolved in forming a partnership is the allocation of annual net income. In closing out the revenue and expense accounts at the end of each period, some assignment must be made to the individual capital balances. Although an equal division can be used to allocate any profit or loss, partners frequently devise unique plans in an attempt to be equitable. Such factors as time worked, expertise, and invested capital should be considered in creating an allocation procedure.
6. Over time, changes occur in the makeup of a partnership because of death or retirement or because of the admission of new partners. Such changes dissolve the existing partnership, although the business frequently continues uninterrupted through a newly formed partnership. If, for example, a new partner is admitted by the acquisition of a present interest, the capital balances can simply be reclassified to reflect the change in ownership. As an alternative, the purchase price may be viewed as evidence of the underlying value of the organization as a whole. Based on this calculation, asset and liability balances are adjusted to market value, and any residual goodwill is recognized.
7. Admission into an existing partnership also can be achieved by a direct capital contribution to the business. Because of negotiations between the parties, the amount invested will not always agree with the beginning capital balance attributed to the new partner. The bonus method resolves this conflict by simply reclassifying the various capital accounts to align the balances with specified totals and percentages. No revaluation is carried out under this approach. Conversely, according to the goodwill method, all asset and liability accounts are adjusted first to fair market value. The price paid by the new partner is used to compute an implied value for the partnership, and any excess over market value is recorded as goodwill.
8. The composition of a partnership also can undergo changes because of the death or retirement of a partner. Individuals may decide to withdraw. Such changes legally dissolve the partnership, although business operations frequently continue under the ownership of the remaining partners. In compensating the departing partner, the final asset distribution may differ from the ending capital balance. This disparity can, once again, be accounted for by means of the bonus method, which adjusts the remaining capital accounts to absorb the bonus being paid. The goodwill approach by which all assets and liabilities are restated to fair market value with any goodwill being recognized also can be applied. Finally, a hybrid method revalues the assets and liabilities but ignores goodwill. Under this last approach, any amount paid to the departing partner in excess of the newly adjusted capital balance is accounted for by means of the bonus method.

## Comprehensive Illustration
### PROBLEM

*(Estimated Time: 30 to 55 Minutes)* Heyman and Mullins begin a partnership on January 1, 2004. Heyman invests $40,000 cash as well as inventory costing $15,000 but with a current appraised value of only $12,000. Mullins contributes a building with a $40,000 book value and a $48,000 fair market value. The partnership also accepts responsibility for a $10,000 note payable owed in connection with this building.

The partners agree to begin operations with equal capital balances. The Articles of Partnership also provide that at the end of each year, profits and losses are allocated as follows:

1. For managing the business, Heyman is credited with a bonus of 10 percent of partnership income after subtracting the bonus. No bonus is accrued if the partnership records a loss.
2. Both partners are entitled to interest equal to 10 percent of the average monthly capital balance for the year without regard for the income or drawings of that year.
3. Any remaining profit or loss is divided 60 percent to Heyman and 40 percent to Mullins.
4. Each partner is allowed to withdraw $800 per month in cash from the business.

On October 1, 2004, Heyman invests an additional $12,000 cash in the business. For 2004, the partnership reports income of $33,000.

Lewis, an employee, is allowed to join the partnership on January 1, 2005. The new partner invests $66,000 directly into the business for a one-third interest in the partnership property. The revised partnership agreement still allows for both the bonus to Heyman and the 10 percent interest, but all remaining profits and losses are now split 40 percent each to Heyman and Lewis with the remaining 20 percent to Mullins. Lewis is also entitled to $800 per month in drawings.

Mullins chooses to withdraw from the partnership a few years later. After negotiations, all parties agree that Mullins should be paid a $90,000 settlement. The capital balances on that date were as follows:

| | |
|---|---:|
| Heyman, capital | $88,000 |
| Mullins, capital | 78,000 |
| Lewis, capital | 72,000 |

## Required

a. Assuming that the bonus method is used exclusively by this partnership, make all necessary journal entries. Entries for the monthly drawings of the partners are not required.
b. Assuming that the goodwill method is used exclusively by this partnership, make all necessary journal entries. Again, entries for the monthly drawings are not required.

## SOLUTION

a. **Bonus Method**

**2004**

Jan. 1   All contributed property is recorded at fair market value. Under the bonus method, total capital is then divided as specified between the partners.

| | | |
|---|---:|---:|
| Cash | 40,000 | |
| Inventory | 12,000 | |
| Building | 48,000 | |
|    Note Payable | | 10,000 |
|    Heyman, Capital (50%) | | 45,000 |
|    Mullins, Capital (50%) | | 45,000 |

To record initial contributions to partnership along with equal capital balances.

Oct. 1

| | | |
|---|---:|---:|
| Cash | 12,000 | |
|    Heyman, Capital | | 12,000 |

To record additional investment by partner.

Dec. 31   Both the bonus assigned to Heyman and the interest accrual must be computed as preliminary steps in the income allocation process. Since the bonus is based on income after subtracting the bonus, the amount must be calculated algebraically:

$$\text{Bonus} = 0.10\,(\$33{,}000 - \text{Bonus})$$
$$\text{Bonus} = \$3{,}300 - 0.10\,\text{Bonus}$$
$$1.10\,\text{Bonus} = \$3{,}300$$
$$\text{Bonus} = \$3{,}000$$

According to the partnership agreement, the interest allocation is based on a monthly average figure. Mullins's capital balance of $45,000 did not change during the year; therefore $4,500 (10 percent) is the appropriate interest accrual for that partner. However, because of the October 1, 2004, contribution, Heyman's interest must be determined as follows:

|  |  |  |
|---|---|---|
| Beginning balance: | $45,000 × 9 months = | $405,000 |
| New balance: | $57,000 × 3 months = | 171,000 |
|  |  | 576,000 |
|  |  | × 1/12 |
| Monthly average—capital balance | | 48,000 |
| Interest rate | | × 10% |
| Interest credited to Heyman | | $ 4,800 |

Following the bonus and interest computations, the $33,000 income earned by the business in 2004 can be allocated according to the previously specified arrangement:

|  | Heyman | Mullins | Totals |
|---|---|---|---|
| Bonus | $ 3,000 | –0– | $ 3,000 |
| Interest | 4,800 | $ 4,500 | 9,300 |
| Remaining income: | | | |
| $33,000 | | | |
| (3,000) | | | |
| (9,300) | | | |
| $20,700 | 12,420 (60%) | 8,280 (40%) | 20,700 |
| Income allocation | $20,220 | $12,780 | $33,000 |

Thus, the partnership's closing entries for the year of 2004 would be recorded as follows:

| | | |
|---|---|---|
| Heyman, Capital | 9,600 | |
| Mullins, Capital | 9,600 | |
|     Heyman, Drawing | | 9,600 |
|     Mullins, Drawing | | 9,600 |
|   To close out $800 per month drawing accounts for the year of 2004. | | |
| Income Summary | 33,000 | |
|     Heyman, Capital | | 20,220 |
|     Mullins, Capital | | 12,780 |
|   To close out profit for year to capital accounts as computed above. | | |

At the end of this initial year of operation, the partners' capital accounts hold the following balances:

|  | Heyman | Mullins | Totals |
|---|---|---|---|
| Beginning balance | $45,000 | $45,000 | $ 90,000 |
| Additional investment | 12,000 | –0– | 12,000 |
| Drawing | (9,600) | (9,600) | (19,200) |
| Net income (above) | 20,220 | 12,780 | 33,000 |
| Total capital | $67,620 | $48,180 | $115,800 |

**2005**
**Jan. 1** Lewis contributed $66,000 to the business for a one-third interest in the partnership property. Combined with the $115,800 balance computed above, the partnership now has total capital of $181,800. Since no revaluation is recorded under the bonus approach, a one-third interest in the partnership equals $60,600 ($181,800 × 1/3). Lewis has invested $5,400 in excess of this amount, a balance viewed as a bonus accruing to the original partners:

| | | |
|---|---|---|
| Cash | 66,000 | |
|     Lewis, Capital | | 60,600 |
|     Heyman, Capital (60% of bonus) | | 3,240 |
|     Mullins, Capital (40% of bonus) | | 2,160 |
|   To record Lewis's entrance into partnership with bonus to original partners. | | |

**Several years later** The final event in this illustration is Mullins's withdrawal from the partnership. Although a capital balance of only $78,000 is reported for this partner, the final distribution is set at $90,000. The extra $12,000 payment represents a bonus assigned to Mullins, an amount that decreases the capital of the remaining two partners. Since Heyman and Lewis have previously accrued equal 40 percent shares of all profits and losses, the reduction is split evenly between the two.

| | | |
|---|---|---|
| Mullins, Capital | 78,000 | |
| Heyman, Capital (½ of bonus payment) | 6,000 | |
| Lewis, Capital (½ of bonus payment) | 6,000 | |
|     Cash | | 90,000 |
| To record withdrawal of Mullins with bonus taken from remaining partners. | | |

### b. Goodwill Method

**2004**

**Jan. 1** The fair market value of Heyman's contribution is $52,000, whereas Mullins is investing only a net $38,000 (the value of the building less the accompanying debt). Because the capital accounts are initially to be equal, Mullins is presumed to be contributing goodwill of $14,000.

| | | |
|---|---|---|
| Cash | 40,000 | |
| Inventory | 12,000 | |
| Building | 48,000 | |
| Goodwill | 14,000 | |
|     Note payable | | 10,000 |
|     Heyman, Capital | | 52,000 |
|     Mullins, Capital | | 52,000 |
| Creation of partnership with goodwill attributed to Mullins. | | |

**Oct. 1**

| | | |
|---|---|---|
| Cash | 12,000 | |
|     Heyman, Capital | | 12,000 |
| To record additional contribution by partner. | | |

**Dec. 31** Although Heyman's bonus is still $3,000 as derived in requirement (a), the interest accruals must be recalculated because the capital balances are different. Mullins's capital for the entire year was $52,000; thus, interest of $5,200 (10 percent) is appropriate. However, Heyman's balance changed during the year so that a monthly average must be determined as a basis for computing interest:

| | | |
|---|---|---|
| Beginning balance: | $52,000 × 9 months = | $468,000 |
| New balance: | $64,000 × 3 months = | 192,000 |
| | | 660,000 |
| | | × 1/12 |
| Monthly average—capital balance | | 55,000 |
| Interest rate | | × 10% |
| Interest credited to Heyman | | $ 5,500 |

Consequently, the $33,000 partnership income reported for 2004 is allocated as follows:

| | Heyman | Mullins | Totals |
|---|---|---|---|
| Bonus (above) | $ 3,000 | –0– | $ 3,000 |
| Interest (above) | 5,500 | $ 5,200 | 10,700 |
| Remaining income: | | | |
| $33,000 | | | |
| (3,000) | | | |
| (10,700) | | | |
| $19,300 | 11,580 (60%) | 7,720 (40%) | 19,300 |
| Income allocation | $20,080 | $12,920 | $33,000 |

The 2004 closing entries made under the goodwill approach would be as follows:

|  | Heyman, Capital | 9,600 |  |
|---|---|---|---|
|  | Mullins, Capital | 9,600 |  |
|  |     Heyman, Drawing |  | 9,600 |
|  |     Mullins, Drawing |  | 9,600 |
|  | To close out drawing accounts for the year. |  |  |
|  | Income Summary | 33,000 |  |
|  |     Heyman, Capital |  | 20,080 |
|  |     Mullins, Capital |  | 12,920 |
|  | To assign 2004 profits per allocation determined above. |  |  |

After the closing process, the capital balances are composed of the following items:

|  | Heyman | Mullins | Totals |
|---|---|---|---|
| Beginning balance | $52,000 | $52,000 | $104,000 |
| Additional investment | 12,000 | –0– | 12,000 |
| Drawing | (9,600) | (9,600) | (19,200) |
| Net income | 20,080 | 12,920 | 33,000 |
| Total capital | $74,480 | $55,320 | $129,800 |

**2005**
**Jan. 1** Lewis's investment of $66,000 for a one-third interest in the partnership property implies that the business as a whole is worth $198,000 ($66,000 divided by ⅓). After adding Lewis's contribution to the present capital balance of $129,800, the business reports total net assets of only $195,800. Thus, a $2,200 increase in value ($198,000 − $195,800) is indicated and will be recognized at this time. Under the assumption that all partnership assets and liabilities are valued appropriately, this entire balance is attributed to goodwill.

|  | Goodwill | 2,200 |  |
|---|---|---|---|
|  |     Heyman, Capital (60%) |  | 1,320 |
|  |     Mullins, Capital (40%) |  | 880 |
|  | To recognize goodwill based on Lewis's acquisition price. |  |  |
|  | Cash | 66,000 |  |
|  |     Lewis, Capital |  | 66,000 |
|  | To admit Lewis to the partnership. |  |  |

**Several years later** To conclude this illustration, Mullins's withdrawal must be recorded. This partner is to receive a distribution that is $12,000 more than the corresponding capital balance of $78,000. Since Mullins is entitled to a 20 percent share of profits and losses, the additional $12,000 payment indicates that the partnership as a whole is undervalued by $60,000 ($12,000/20%). Only in that circumstance would the extra payment to Mullins be justified. Therefore, once again, goodwill is recognized with the final distribution then being made.

|  | Goodwill | 60,000 |  |
|---|---|---|---|
|  |     Heyman, Capital (40%) |  | 24,000 |
|  |     Mullins, Capital (20%) |  | 12,000 |
|  |     Lewis, Capital (40%) |  | 24,000 |
|  | Recognition of goodwill based on withdrawal amount paid to Mullins. |  |  |
|  | Mullins, Capital | 90,000 |  |
|  |     Cash |  | 90,000 |
|  | To distribute money to partner. |  |  |

## Questions

1. What are the advantages of operating a business as a partnership rather than as a corporation? What are the disadvantages?
2. How does partnership accounting differ from corporate accounting?
3. What information is conveyed by the capital accounts found in partnership accounting?
4. Describe the differences between a Subchapter S Corporation and a Subchapter C Corporation.
5. A company is being created and the owners are trying to decide whether to form a general partnership, a limited liability partnership, or a limited liability company. What are the advantages and disadvantages of each of these legal forms?

6. What is an articles of partnership agreement, and what information should this document contain?
7. What valuation should be recorded for noncash assets transferred to a partnership by one of the partners?
8. If a partner is contributing attributes to a partnership such as an established clientele or a particular expertise, what two methods can be applied to record the contribution? Describe each of these methods.
9. What is the purpose of a drawing account in a partnership's financial records?
10. At what point in the accounting process does the allocation of partnership income become significant?
11. What provisions can be used in a partnership agreement to establish an equitable allocation of income among all partners?
12. If no agreement exists in a partnership as to the allocation of income, what method is appropriate?
13. What is a partnership dissolution? Does dissolution automatically necessitate the cessation of business and the liquidation of partnership assets?
14. By what methods can a new partner gain admittance into a partnership?
15. When a partner sells an ownership interest in a partnership, what rights are conveyed to the new owner?
16. A new partner enters a partnership and goodwill is calculated and credited to the original partners. How is the specific amount of goodwill assigned to these partners?
17. Under what circumstance might goodwill be allocated to a new partner entering a partnership?
18. When a partner withdraws from a partnership, why is the final distribution often based on the appraised value of the business rather than on the book value of the capital account balance?

## Problems

1. Which of the following is *not* a reason for the popularity of partnerships as a legal form for businesses?
   a. Partnerships need be formed only by an oral agreement.
   b. Partnerships can more easily generate significant amounts of capital.
   c. Partnerships avoid the double-taxation of income that is found in corporations.
   d. In some cases, losses may be used to offset gains for tax purposes.

2. How does partnership accounting differ from corporate accounting?
   a. The matching principle is not considered appropriate for partnership accounting.
   b. Revenues are recognized at a different time by a partnership than is appropriate for a corporation.
   c. Individual capital accounts replace the contributed capital and retained earnings balances found in corporate accounting.
   d. All assets are reported by partnerships at fair market value as of the latest balance sheet date.

3. Pat, Jean Lou, and Diane are partners with capital balances of $50,000, $30,000, and $20,000, respectively. These three partners share profits and losses equally. For an investment of $50,000 cash (being paid to the business), MaryAnn is to be admitted as a partner with a one-fourth interest in capital and profits. Based on this information, the amount of MaryAnn's investment can best be justified by which of the following?
   a. MaryAnn will receive a bonus from the other partners upon her admission to the partnership.
   b. Assets of the partnership were overvalued immediately prior to MaryAnn's investment.
   c. The book value of the partnership's net assets was less than the fair value immediately prior to MaryAnn's investment.
   d. MaryAnn is apparently bringing goodwill into the partnership, and her capital account will be credited for the appropriate amount.

4. A partnership has the following capital balances:

| | |
|---|---|
| Albert (50% of gains and losses) | $ 80,000 |
| Barrymore (20%) | 60,000 |
| Candroth (30%) | 140,000 |

Danville is going to invest $70,000 into the business to acquire a 30 percent ownership interest. Goodwill is to be recorded. What will be Danville's beginning capital balance?
   a. $70,000
   b. $90,000
   c. $105,000
   d. $120,000

5. A partnership has the following capital balances:

| | |
|---|---|
| Elgin (40% of gains and losses) | $100,000 |
| Jethro (30%) | 200,000 |
| Foy (30%) | 300,000 |

Oscar is going to pay a total of $200,000 to these three partners to acquire a 25 percent ownership interest from each. Goodwill is to be recorded. What will be Jethro's capital balance after the transaction?

a. $150,000
b. $175,000
c. $195,000
d. $200,000

6. The capital balance for Bolcar is $110,000 and for Neary is $40,000. These two partners share profits and losses 70 percent (Bolcar) and 30 percent (Neary). Kansas invests $50,000 in cash into the partnership for a 30 percent ownership. The bonus method will be used. What is Neary's capital balance after Kansas's investment?

a. $35,000
b. $37,000
c. $40,000
d. $43,000

7. Bishop has a capital balance of $120,000 in a local partnership, and Cotton has a $90,000 balance. These two partners share profits and losses by a ratio of 60 percent to Bishop and 40 percent to Cotton. Lovett invests $60,000 in cash in the partnership for a 20 percent ownership. The goodwill method will be used. What is Cotton's capital balance after this new investment?

a. $99,600
b. $102,000
c. $112,000
d. $126,000

8. The capital balance for Messalina is $210,000 and for Romulus is $140,000. These two partners share profits and losses 60 percent (Messalina) and 40 percent (Romulus). Claudius invests $100,000 in cash in the partnership for a 20 percent ownership. The bonus method will be used. What are the capital balances for Messalina, Romulus, and Claudius after this investment is recorded?

a. $216,000, $144,000, $90,000
b. $218,000, $142,000, $88,000
c. $222,000, $148,000, $80,000
d. $240,000, $160,000, $100,000

9. A partnership begins 2004 with the following capital balances:

| | |
|---|---|
| Arthur, Capital | $ 60,000 |
| Baxter, Capital | 80,000 |
| Cartwright, Capital | 100,000 |

The articles of partnership stipulate that profits and losses be assigned in the following manner:
- Each partner is allocated interest equal to 10 percent of the beginning capital balance.
- Baxter is allocated compensation of $20,000 per year.
- Any remaining profits and losses are allocated on a 3:3:4 basis, respectively.
- Each partner is allowed to withdraw up to $5,000 cash per year.

Assuming that the net income for 2004 is $50,000 and that each partner withdraws the maximum amount allowed, what is the balance in Cartwright's capital account at the end of that year?

a. $105,800
b. $106,200
c. $106,900
d. $107,400

10. A partnership begins its first year of operations with the following capital balances:

| | |
|---|---|
| Winston, Capital | $110,000 |
| Durham, Capital | 80,000 |
| Salem, Capital | 110,000 |

According to the articles of partnership, all profits will be assigned as follows:
- Winston will be awarded an annual salary of $20,000 with $10,000 assigned to Salem.
- The partners will be attributed with interest equal to 10 percent of the capital balance as of the first day of the year.
- The remainder will be assigned on a 5:2:3 basis, respectively.
- Each partner is allowed to withdraw up to $10,000 per year.

Assume that the net loss for the first year of operations is $20,000 with net income of $40,000 in the subsequent year. Assume also that each partner withdraws the maximum amount from the business each period. What is the balance in Winston's capital account at the end of the second year?
a. $102,600
b. $104,400
c. $108,600
d. $109,200

11. A partnership has the following capital balances:

| | |
|---|---|
| Allen, Capital | $60,000 |
| Burns, Capital | 30,000 |
| Costello, Capital | 90,000 |

Profits and losses are split as follows: Allen (20%), Burns (30%), and Costello (50%). Costello wants to leave the partnership and is paid $100,000 from the business based on provisions in the articles of partnership. If the partnership uses the bonus method, what is the balance of Burns's capital account after Costello withdraws?
a. $24,000
b. $27,000
c. $33,000
d. $36,000

12. As of December 31, 2004, the Cisco partnership has the following capital balances:

| | |
|---|---|
| Montana, Capital | $130,000 |
| Rice, Capital | 110,000 |
| Craig, Capital | 80,000 |
| Taylor, Capital | 70,000 |

Profits and losses are split on a 3:3:2:2 basis, respectively. Craig decides to leave the partnership and is paid $90,000 from the business based on the original contractual agreement. If the goodwill method is to be applied, what is the balance of Montana's capital account after Craig withdraws?
a. $133,000
b. $137,500
c. $140,000
d. $145,000

**Problems 13 and 14 are *independent* problems based on the following capital account balances:**

| | |
|---|---|
| William (40% of gains and losses) | $220,000 |
| Jennings (40%) | 160,000 |
| Bryan (20%) | 110,000 |

13. Darrow invests $270,000 in cash for a 30 percent ownership interest. The money goes to the original partners. Goodwill is to be recorded. How much goodwill should be recognized, and what is Darrow's beginning capital balance?
a. $410,000 and $270,000
b. $140,000 and $270,000
c. $140,000 and $189,000
d. $410,000 and $189,000

14. Darrow invests $250,000 in cash for a 30 percent ownership interest. The money goes to the business. No goodwill or other revaluation is to be recorded. After the transaction, what is Jennings's capital balance?
    a. $160,000
    b. $168,000
    c. $170,200
    d. $171,200
15. Lear is to become a partner in the WS partnership by paying $80,000 in cash to the business. At present, the capital balance for Hamlet is $70,000 and for MacBeth is $40,000. Hamlet and MacBeth share profits on a 7:3 basis. Lear is acquiring 40 percent of the new partnership.
    a. If the goodwill method is applied, what will the three capital balances be following the payment by Lear?
    b. If the bonus method is applied, what will the three capital balances be following the payment by Lear?
16. The AKS partnership has the following capital balances at the beginning of the current year:

    | | |
    |---|---|
    | Arond (40% of profits and losses) | $80,000 |
    | Kant (40%) | 70,000 |
    | Selvin (20%) | 60,000 |

    a. If Tronsty invests $60,000 in cash in the business for a 20 percent interest, what journal entry is recorded? Assume the bonus method is used.
    b. If Tronsty invests $50,000 in cash in the business for a 20 percent interest, what journal entry is recorded? Assume the bonus method is used.
    c. If Tronsty invests $55,000 in cash in the business for a 20 percent interest, what journal entry is recorded? Assume the goodwill method is used.
17. A partnership has the following account balances: Cash $50,000; Other Assets $600,000; Liabilities $240,000; Nixon, Capital (50% of profits and losses) $200,000; Hoover, Capital (20%) $120,000; and Polk, Capital (30%) $90,000. Each of the following questions should be viewed as an independent situation:
    a. Grant invests $80,000 in the partnership for an 18 percent capital interest. Goodwill is to be recognized. What are the capital accounts thereafter?
    b. Grant invests $100,000 in the partnership to get a 20 percent capital balance. Goodwill is not to be recorded. What are the capital accounts thereafter?
18. The C-P partnership has the following capital account balances on January 1, 2004:

    | | |
    |---|---|
    | Com, Capital | $150,000 |
    | Pack, Capital | 110,000 |

    Com is allocated 60 percent of all profits and losses with the remaining 40 percent assigned to Pack after interest of 10 percent is given to each partner based on beginning capital balances.
    On January 2, 2004, Hal invests $76,000 cash for a 20 percent interest in the partnership. This transaction is recorded by the goodwill method. After this transaction, 10 percent interest is still to go to each partner. Profits and losses will then be split as follows: Com (50%), Pack (30%), and Hal (20%). In 2004, the partnership reports a net income of $36,000.
    a. Prepare the journal entry to record Hal's entrance into the partnership on January 2, 2004.
    b. Determine the allocation of income at the end of 2004.
19. The partnership agreement of Jones, King, and Lane provides for the annual allocation of the business's profit or loss in the following sequence:
    - Jones, the managing partner, receives a bonus equal to 20 percent of the business's profit.
    - Each partner receives 15 percent interest on average capital investment.
    - Any residual profit or loss is divided equally.

    The average capital investments for 2004 were as follows:

    | | |
    |---|---|
    | Jones | $100,000 |
    | King | 200,000 |
    | Lane | 300,000 |

How much of the $90,000 partnership profit for 2004 should be assigned to each partner?

20. Purkerson, Smith, and Traynor have operated a bookstore for a number of years as a partnership. At the beginning of 2004, capital balances were as follows:

| | |
|---|---|
| Purkerson | $60,000 |
| Smith | 40,000 |
| Traynor | 20,000 |

Because of a cash shortage, Purkerson invests an additional $8,000 in the business on April 1, 2004. Each partner is allowed to withdraw $1,000 cash each month.

The partners have used the same method of allocating profits and losses since the business's inception:
- Each partner is given the following compensation allowance for work done in the business: Purkerson, $18,000; Smith, $25,000; and Traynor, $8,000.
- Each partner is credited with interest equal to 10 percent of the average monthly capital balance for the year without regard for normal drawings.
- Any remaining profit or loss is allocated 4:2:4 to Purkerson, Smith, and Traynor, respectively.

The net income for 2004 is $23,600. Each partner withdraws the allotted amount each month. What are the ending capital balances for 2004?

21. On January 1, 2004, the dental partnership of Left, Center, and Right was formed when the partners contributed $20,000, $60,000, and $50,000, respectively. Over the next three years, the business reported net income and (loss) as follows:

| | |
|---|---|
| 2004 | ($30,000) |
| 2005 | $20,000 |
| 2006 | $40,000 |

During this period, each partner withdrew cash of $10,000 per year. Right invested an additional $12,000 in cash on February 9, 2005.

At the time that the partnership was created, the three partners agreed to allocate all profits and losses according to a specified plan written as follows:
- Each partner is entitled to interest computed at the rate of 12 percent per year based on the individual capital balances at the beginning of that year.
- Because of prior work experience, Left is entitled to an annual salary allowance of $12,000, and Center is credited with $8,000 per year.
- Any remaining profit will be split as follows: Left, 20 percent; Center, 40 percent; and Right, 40 percent. If a loss remains, the balance will be allocated: Left, 30 percent; Center, 50 percent; and Right, 20 percent.

Determine the ending capital balance for each partner as of the end of each of these three years.

22. The HELP partnership has the following capital balances as of December 31, 2005:

| | |
|---|---|
| Lennon | $230,000 |
| McCartney | 190,000 |
| Harrison | 160,000 |
| Starr | 140,000 |
| Total capital | $720,000 |

Answer each of the following *independent* questions:
a. Assume that the partners share profits and losses 3:3:2:2, respectively. Harrison retires and is paid $190,000 based on the terms of the original partnership agreement. If the goodwill method is in use, what is the capital balance of the remaining three partners?
b. Assume that the partners share profits and losses 4:3:2:1, respectively. Lennon retires and is paid $280,000 based on the terms of the original partnership agreement. If the bonus method is in use, what is the capital balance of the remaining three partners?

23. In the early part of 2005, the partners of Page, Childers, and Smith went to a local accountant seeking assistance. They had begun a new business in 2004 but had never previously used the services of an accountant.

    Page and Childers began the partnership by contributing $80,000 and $30,000 in cash, respectively. Page was to work occasionally at the business, and Childers was to be employed full-time. They decided that year-end profits and losses should be assigned as follows:
    - Each partner was to be allocated 10 percent interest computed on the beginning capital balances for the period.
    - A compensation allowance of $5,000 was to go to Page with a $20,000 amount assigned to Childers.
    - Any remaining income would be split on a 4:6 basis to Page and Childers, respectively.

    In 2004, revenues totaled $90,000, and expenses were $64,000 (not including the compensation allowance assigned to the partners). Page withdrew cash of $8,000 during the year, and Childers took out $11,000. In addition, $5,000 for repairs made to Page's home was paid by the business and charged to repair expense.

    On January 1, 2005, a 20 percent interest in the partnership was sold to Smith for $43,000 cash. This money was contributed to the business with the bonus method used for accounting purposes.

    Answer the following questions:
    a. Why was the original profit and loss allocation, as just outlined, designed by the partners?
    b. Why did the drawings for 2004 not agree with the compensation allowances provided for in the partnership agreement?
    c. What journal entries should have been recorded by the partnership on December 31, 2004?
    d. What journal entry should have been recorded by the partnership on January 1, 2005?

24. Following is the current balance sheet for a local partnership of doctors:

    | | | | |
    |---|---:|---|---:|
    | Cash and current assets | $ 30,000 | Liabilities | $ 40,000 |
    | Land | 180,000 | A, capital | 20,000 |
    | Building and equipment (net) | 100,000 | B, capital | 40,000 |
    | | | C, capital | 90,000 |
    | | | D, capital | 120,000 |
    | Totals | $310,000 | Totals | $310,000 |

    The following questions represent *independent* situations:
    a. E is going to invest enough money in this partnership to receive a 25 percent interest. No goodwill or bonus is to be recorded. How much should E invest?
    b. E contributes $36,000 in cash to the business to receive a 10 percent interest in the partnership. Goodwill is to be recorded. Profits and losses have previously been split according to the following percentages: A, 30%; B, 10%; C, 40%; and D, 20%. After E makes this investment, what are the individual capital balances?
    c. E contributes $42,000 in cash to the business to receive a 20 percent interest in the partnership. Goodwill is to be recorded. The four original partners share all profits and losses equally. After E makes this investment, what are the individual capital balances?
    d. E contributes $55,000 in cash to the business to receive a 20 percent interest in the partnership. No goodwill or other asset revaluation is to be recorded. Profits and losses have previously been split according to the following percentages: A, 10%; B, 30%; C, 20%; and D, 40%. After E makes this investment, what are the individual capital balances?
    e. C retires from the partnership and, as per the original partnership agreement, is to receive cash equal to 125 percent of her final capital balance. No goodwill or other asset revaluation is to be recognized. All partners share profits and losses equally. After the withdrawal, what are the individual capital balances of the remaining partners?

25. Boswell and Johnson form a partnership on May 1, 2004. Boswell contributes cash of $50,000; Johnson conveys title to the following properties to the partnership:

    | | Book Value | Fair Market Value |
    |---|---:|---:|
    | Land | $15,000 | $28,000 |
    | Building and equipment | 35,000 | 36,000 |

The partners agree to start their partnership with equal capital balances. No goodwill is to be recognized.

According to the articles of partnership written by the partners, profits and losses are allocated based on the following formula:
- Boswell receives a compensation allowance of $1,000 per month.
- All remaining profits and losses are split 60:40 to Johnson and Boswell, respectively.
- Annual cash drawings of $5,000 can be made by each partner beginning in 2005.

Net income of $11,000 is earned by the business during 2004.

Walpole is invited to join the partnership on January 1, 2005. Because of Walpole's business reputation and financial expertise, she is given a 40 percent interest for $54,000 cash. The bonus approach is used to record this investment, made directly to the business. The articles of partnership are amended to give Walpole a $2,000 compensation allowance per month and an annual cash drawing of $10,000. Remaining profits are now allocated:

| | |
|---|---|
| Johnson | 48% |
| Boswell | 12% |
| Walpole | 40% |

All drawings are taken by the partners during 2005. At the end of that year, the partnership reports an earned net income of $28,000.

On January 1, 2006, Pope (previously a partnership employee) is admitted into the partnership. Each partner transfers 10 percent to Pope. Pope makes the following payments directly to the partners:

| | |
|---|---|
| Johnson | $5,672 |
| Boswell | 7,880 |
| Walpole | 8,688 |

Once again, the articles of partnership must be amended to allow for the entrance of the new partner. This change entitles Pope to a compensation allowance of $800 per month and an annual drawing of $4,000. Profits and losses are now assigned.

| | |
|---|---|
| Johnson | 40.5% |
| Boswell | 13.5% |
| Walpole | 36.0% |
| Pope | 10.0% |

For the year of 2006, the partnership earned a profit of $46,000, and each partner withdrew the allowed amount of cash.

Determine the capital balances for the individual partners as of the end of each year: 2004 through 2006.

26. Gray, Stone, and Lawson open an accounting practice on January 1, 2004, in San Diego, California. The business is to be operated as a partnership with Gray and Stone serving as the senior partners because of their years of experience. To establish the business, Gray, Stone, and Lawson contribute cash and other properties valued at $210,000, $180,000, and $90,000, respectively. A partnership agreement is drawn up that carries the following stipulations:
- Personal drawings are allowed annually up to an amount equal to 10 percent of the beginning capital balance for the year.
- Profits and losses are allocated according to the following plan:
    (1) A salary allowance is credited to each partner in an amount equal to $8 per billable hour worked by that individual during the year.
    (2) Interest is credited to the partners' capital accounts at the rate of 12 percent of the average monthly balance for the year (computed without regard for current income or drawings).
    (3) An annual bonus is to be credited to Gray and Stone. Each bonus is to be 10 percent of net income after subtracting the bonus, the salary allowance, and the interest. Also included in the agreement is the provision that the bonus cannot be a negative amount.
    (4) Any remaining partnership profit or loss is to be divided evenly among all partners.

Because of monetary problems encountered in getting the business started, Gray invests an additional $9,100 on May 1, 2004. On January 1, 2005, the partners allow Monet to buy into the partnership. Monet contributes cash directly to the business in an amount equal to a 25 percent interest in the book value of the partnership property subsequent to this contribution. The partnership agreement as to splitting profits and losses is not altered at the time of Monet's entrance into the firm; the general provisions continue to be applicable.

The billable hours for the partners during the first three years of operation are as follows:

|  | 2004 | 2005 | 2006 |
|---|---|---|---|
| Gray | 1,710 | 1,800 | 1,880 |
| Stone | 1,440 | 1,500 | 1,620 |
| Lawson | 1,300 | 1,380 | 1,310 |
| Monet | –0– | 1,190 | 1,580 |

The partnership reports net income for 2004 through 2006 as follows:

| 2004 | $ 65,000 |
|---|---|
| 2005 | (20,400) |
| 2006 | 152,800 |

Each partner withdraws the maximum allowable amount each year.

a. Determine the allocation of income for each of these three years (to the nearest dollar).
b. Prepare in appropriate form a statement of partners' capital for the year ending December 31, 2004.

27. A partnership of attorneys in the St. Louis, Missouri, area has the following balance sheet accounts as of January 1, 2005:

| Assets | $320,000 | Liabilities | $120,000 |
|---|---|---|---|
|  |  | Athos, capital | 80,000 |
|  |  | Porthos, capital | 70,000 |
|  |  | Aramis, capital | 50,000 |

According to the articles of partnership, Athos is to receive an allocation of 50 percent of all partnership profits and losses while Porthos gets 30 percent and Aramis 20 percent. The book value of each asset and liability should be considered an accurate representation of fair market value.

For each of the following *independent* situations, prepare the journal entry or entries to be recorded by the partnership. (Round to nearest dollar.)

a. Porthos, with permission of the other partners, decides to sell half of his partnership interest to D'Artagnan for $50,000 in cash. No asset revaluation or goodwill is to be recorded by the partnership.
b. All three of the present partners agree to sell 10 percent of each partnership interest to D'Artagnan for a total cash payment of $25,000. Each partner receives a negotiated portion of this amount. Goodwill is being recorded as a result of the transaction.
c. D'Artagnan is allowed to become a partner with a 10 percent ownership interest by contributing $30,000 in cash directly into the business. The bonus method is used to record this admission.
d. Use the same facts as in requirement *(c)*, except that the entrance into the partnership is recorded by the goodwill method.
e. D'Artagnan is allowed to become a partner with a 10 percent ownership interest by contributing $12,222 in cash directly to the business. The goodwill method is used to record this transaction.
f. Aramis decides to retire and leave the partnership. An independent appraisal of the business and its assets indicates a current fair market value of $280,000. Goodwill is to be recorded. Aramis will then be given the exact amount of cash that will close out his capital account.

28. Steve Reese is a well-known interior designer in Fort Worth, Texas. He wants to start his own business and convinces Rob O'Donnell, a local merchant, to contribute the capital to form a partnership. On January 1, 2004, O'Donnell invests a building worth $52,000 and equipment valued at $16,000

as well as $12,000 in cash. Although Reese makes no tangible contribution to the partnership, he will operate the business and be an equal partner in the beginning capital balances.

To entice O'Donnell to join this partnership, Reese draws up the following profit and loss agreement:
- O'Donnell will be credited annually with interest equal to 20 percent of the beginning capital balance for the year.
- O'Donnell will also have added to his capital account 15 percent of partnership income each year (without regard for the preceding interest figure) or $4,000, whichever is larger. All remaining income is credited to Reese.
- Neither partner is allowed to withdraw funds from the partnership during 2004. Thereafter, each can draw out $5,000 annually or 20 percent of the beginning capital balance for the year, whichever is larger.

A net loss of $10,000 is reported by the partnership during the first year of its operation. On January 1, 2005, Terri Dunn becomes a third partner in this business by contributing $15,000 cash to the partnership. Dunn receives a 20 percent share of the business's capital. The profit and loss agreement is altered as follows:
- O'Donnell is still entitled to (1) interest on his beginning capital balance as well as (2) the share of partnership income just specified.
- Any remaining profit or loss will be split on a 6:4 basis between Reese and Dunn, respectively.

Partnership income for 2005 is reported as $44,000. Each partner withdraws the full amount that is allowed.

On January 1, 2006, Dunn becomes ill and sells her interest in the partnership (with the consent of the other two partners) to Judy Postner. Postner pays $46,000 directly to Dunn. Net income for 2006 is $61,000 with the partners again taking their full drawing allowance.

On January 1, 2007, Postner elects to withdraw from the business for personal reasons. The articles of partnership contain a provision stating that any partner may leave the partnership at any time and is entitled to receive cash in an amount equal to the recorded capital balance at that time plus 10 percent.

a. Prepare journal entries to record the preceding transactions on the assumption that the bonus (or no revaluation) method is used. Drawings need not be recorded, although the balances should be included in the closing entries.
b. Prepare journal entries to record the previous transactions on the assumption that the goodwill (or revaluation) method is used. Drawings need not be recorded, although the balances should be included in the closing entries.

(Round all amounts off to the nearest dollar)

# Develop Your Skills

## RESEARCH CASE 1

Jim Hammonds is a partner in a regional CPA firm that covers three states in the northwest section of the United States. The firm was organized as a limited liability partnership. A partner in an office in another state performed a client audit well below the level required by professional standards. As a result, stockholders and lenders of the audited company lost a significant amount of money and have filed suit against the CPA firm. Hammonds has never had any interaction with this particular client but he is concerned by the potential loss that could result from this lawsuit.

### Required:

Obtain a copy of the article "Partners at Risk" in the August 2002 issue of the *ABA Journal*. With that article as a basis, write an explanation of the possible liability that Hammonds may face.

## RESEARCH CASE 2

Go to the website www.sec.gov where forms filed with the SEC are available. Look for a section entitled "Filings & Forms (EDGAR)," and click on "Search for Company Filings" within that section. On the

next screen that appears, click on "Search Companies and Filings." On the next screen, enter the following company name: Buckeye Partners. A list of SEC filings made by that company will appear; scroll down to the first 10–K (annual report) filing that is available from Buckeye Partners. Click on that 10–K. This path will provide the latest financial information available for Buckeye Partners. Scroll through the statement information until the actual financial statements, followed by the notes, appear.

### Required:

Look over this set of financial statements as well as the accompanying notes. List information included for this partnership that would typically not appear in financial statements produced for a corporation.

## ANALYSIS CASE 1

Brenda Wilson, Elizabeth Higgins, and Helen Poncelet form a partnership as a first step in creating a business. Wilson invests most of the capital but does not plan to be actively involved in the day-to-day operations. Higgins has had some experience and is expected to do a majority of the daily work. Poncelet has been in this line of business for some time and has many connections. Therefore, she will devote a majority of her time to getting new clients.

### Required:

Read the article "Pay for Performance" in the June 2002 issue of the *Journal of Accountancy*. Write a memo to these three partners suggesting at least two different ways in which the profits of the partnership can be allocated each year in order to be fair to all parties.

## ANALYSIS CASE 2

Read the following as well as any other published materials available describing the choice of a legal structure for a business:

"A New Breed of Company," *Financial Executive*, January–February 1996.
"What Form of Ownership is Best?" *The CPA Journal*, August 1998.
"Should You Convert Your Practice to a Limited Liability Company?" *Law Practice Management*, September 1996.
"Selecting a Form of Business," *The CPA Journal*, April 1997.

Assume that you and two friends are going to open a small restaurant near campus to serve hamburgers, hot dogs, and the like to college students. The business will be open for only three hours each day to serve lunch. Because of the limited hours of operation, the three partners expect to do all of the work and have no employees. They plan to split all profits and losses evenly.

### Required:

List possible legal structures that could be used for this business. Give two advantages and two disadvantages of each alternative.

## COMMUNICATION CASE 1

Heidi Birmingham and James T. Roberts have decided to create a business. They have financing available and have a well-developed business plan. However, they have not yet decided which type of legal business structure would be best for them.

### Required:

Write a report for these two individuals outlining the types of situations in which the corporate form of legal structure would be the best choice.

## COMMUNICATION CASE 2

Use the information in Communication Case 1.

### Required:
Write a report for these two individuals outlining the types of situations in which the partnership form of legal structure would be the best choice.

## EXCEL CASE 1

The Red and Blue partnership has been created to operate a law firm. The partners have been attempting to devise a fair system to allocate profits and losses. Red plans to work more billable hours each year than Blue. However, Blue has more experience and can charge a higher hourly rate. Red expects to invest more money in the business than Blue.

### Required:
Build a spreadsheet that can be used to allocate profits and losses to these two partners each year. The spreadsheet should be constructed so that the following variables can be entered:

Net income for the year.
Number of billable hours for each partner.
Hourly rate for each partner.
Capital investment by each partner.
Interest rate on capital investment.
Profit and loss ratio.

Use this spreadsheet to determine the allocation if partnership net income for 2004 is $200,000, the number of billable hours is 2,000 for Red and 1,500 for Blue, the hourly rate for Red is $20 and for Blue is $30, and investment by Red is $80,000 and by Blue is $50,000. Interest on capital will be accrued each year at 10 percent of the beginning balance. Any remaining income amount will be split 50-50.

Use the spreadsheet a second time but make these changes: Blue reports 1,700 billable hours, Red invests $100,000, and interest will be recognized at a 12 percent annual rate. How do these three changes impact the allocation of the $200,000?

# Chapter Ten

# Partnerships: Termination and Liquidation

### Questions to Consider

- Under what conditions would a partnership be liquidated?
- What information should an accountant report to reflect the liquidation of a partnership?
- In a partnership liquidation, what happens if one or more partners report a deficit capital balance?
- How are any remaining assets distributed if a partnership or one of its partners becomes insolvent?
- What are safe capital balances and how are they determined?
- How does an accountant determine which partners receive cash during a partnership liquidation?

Partnerships can be rather frail organizations. Termination of business activities followed by the liquidation of partnership property can take place for a variety of reasons, both legal and personal.

> I'm spending a great deal of time helping physician clients patch up partnership disputes and pull together. That is until I run up against a group where personalities, philosophies, or work styles are truly irreconcilable. In these cases, the best solution is a split. . . . Once the doctors know they want to split, they can meet to discuss their problems. While these sessions are often stormy, in the end the doctors usually find themselves agreeing for once. Their consensus? They'll each benefit more from going their separate ways than enduring a situation that's not working. Still, there's no denying that severing any partnership is emotionally wrenching.[1]

Although a business organized as a partnership can exist indefinitely through periodic changes within the ownership, the actual cessation of operations is not an uncommon occurrence. The partners may simply be incompatible and choose to cease operations. The same conclusion could result if profit figures fail to reach projected levels. "In the best of times, partnerships are fragile. But in the current recession, the breakup rate has worsened as cost-cutting and other pressures heighten tensions between partners.[2]

The death of a partner is yet another event that dissolves a partnership and frequently leads to the termination of business operations. Rather than continuing under a new partnership arrangement, the remaining owners could discover that liquidation is necessary to settle the claims of the deceased partner's estate. A similar action could be required if one or more partners elect to change careers or retire. Under that circumstance, liquidation is often the most convenient method for winding up the financial affairs of the business.

As a final possibility, a partnership can be legally forced into selling its noncash assets by the bankruptcy of the business or even that of an individual partner. Laventhol & Horwath, the seventh largest public accounting firm in the United States at the time, filed for bankruptcy protection after the firm came under intense financial pressure from numerous lawsuits. "Laventhol said that at least 100 lawsuits are pending in state and federal courts. Bankruptcy court protection 'is absolutely necessary in order to protect the

---

[1] Leif C. Beck, "When a Group Is Better Off Splitting Up," *Medical Economics,* March 5, 1984, p. 183.
[2] Sue Shellenbarger, "Cutting Losses When Partners Face a Breakup," *Wall Street Journal,* May 21, 1991, p. B1.

debtor and its creditors from the devastating results a destructive race for assets will cause' the firm said.[3]

The bankruptcy of Laventhol & Horwath was not an isolated incident.

> Law firms are going out of business at a steady clip, and a few major accounting firms have collapsed in recent years. "At least a dozen [major law] firms have failed in the past three or four years," figures Bradford W. Hildebrandt, chairman of a legal consulting firm in Somerville, N.J. "In the next year or two, there could be another half-dozen.[4]

## TERMINATION AND LIQUIDATION—PROTECTING THE INTERESTS OF ALL PARTIES

Accounting for the termination and liquidation of a business can prove to be a delicate task. Losses are commonly incurred. For example, "Former partners in Keck, Mahin and Cate have pledged to pay slightly over $3 million to general unsecured creditors to settle the bankrupt firm's debts . . . this figure represents about 36 percent of the money owed."[5] Here, both the partners and the debtors suffered heavy losses.

Other partnerships have experienced a similar fate.

> In 1990, prior to the advent of limited-liability partnerships, the accounting firm of Laventhol & Horwath filed for Chapter 11 bankruptcy-court protection, in part due to lawsuits over questionable accounting. The firm's assets were insufficient to cover the claims of creditors and litigants. Under a plan negotiated with the firm's creditors, the 360 partners and former partners who had spent time at the firm since 1984 were required to dig into their own pockets to share a $46 million liability. Under a formula hammered out by partner Jacob Brandzel, now an executive at American Express Co. in Chicago, they were obligated to contribute between about $5,000 and $450,000, depending on factors including seniority. Managers were levied a 5 percent to 10 percent surcharge on top. Everyone was given 10 years to pay.[6]

Consequently, throughout any liquidation, both creditors and owners demand continuous accounting information that enables them to monitor and assess their financial risks. In generating these data for a partnership, the accountant must record the following:

- The conversion of partnership assets into cash.
- The allocation of the resulting gains and losses.
- The payment of liabilities and expenses.
- Any remaining unpaid debts to be settled or the distribution of any remaining assets to the partners based on their final capital balances.

Beyond the goal of merely reporting these transactions, the accountant must work to ensure the equitable treatment of all parties involved in the liquidation. The accounting records, for example, serve as the basis for allocating available assets to creditors as well as to the individual partners. If assets are limited, the accountant also may have to make recommendations as to the appropriate method for distributing any remaining funds. Protecting the interests of partnership creditors is an especially significant duty since the Uniform Partnership Act specifies that they have first priority to the assets held by the business at the time of dissolution. The accountant's desire for an equitable settlement is enhanced, no doubt, in that any party to a liquidation who is not treated fairly can seek legal recovery from the responsible party.

---

[3] Peter Pae, "Laventhol Bankruptcy Filing Indicates Liabilities May Be as Much as $2 Billion," *The Wall Street Journal,* November 23, 1990, p. A4.

[4] Lee Berton and Joann S. Lublin, "Partnership Structure Is Called in Question as Liability Risk Rises," *The Wall Street Journal,* June 10, 1992, p. A9.

[5] *Chicago Daily Law Bulletin*, August 13, 1999, p. 3.

[6] Mitchell Pacelle and Ianthe Jeanne Dugan, "Partners Forever? Within Andersen, Personal Liability May Bring Ruin," *The Wall Street Journal,* April 2, 2002, p. C1.

Not only the creditors but also the partners themselves have a great interest in the financial data produced during the period of liquidation. They must be concerned, as indicated above, by the possibility of incurring substantial monetary losses. The potential for loss is especially significant because of the unlimited liability to which the partners are exposed.

Even the new legal formats that have been developed do not necessarily provide safety. "Because it is unclear how much protection the LLP structure will provide Andersen partners, partnership and bankruptcy lawyers are expected to be following the matter closely. 'As far as I know, there has never been a litigation test of the extent of the LLP shield, and there have been very few LLP cases about liability at all,' said Larry Ribstein, a law professor at George Mason University."[7]

As long as a partnership can meet all of its obligations, a partner's risk is normally no greater than that of a corporate stockholder. However, should the partnership become insolvent, each partner faces the possibility of having to satisfy *all* remaining obligations personally. Although any partner suffering more than a proportionate share of these losses can seek legal retribution from the remaining owners, this process is not always an effective remedy. The other partners may themselves be insolvent, or anticipated legal costs might discourage the damaged party from seeking recovery. Therefore, each partner usually has a keen interest in monitoring the progress of a liquidation as it transpires.

## Termination and Liquidation Procedures Illustrated

The procedures involved in terminating and liquidating a partnership are basically mechanical. Partnership assets are converted into cash that is then used to pay business obligations as well as liquidation expenses. *Any remaining assets are distributed to the individual partners based on their final capital balances.* Because no other ledger accounts exist, the partnership's books are permanently closed. If each partner has a capital balance large enough to absorb all liquidation losses, the accountant should experience little difficulty in recording this series of transactions.

To illustrate the typical process, assume that Morgan and Houseman have been operating an art gallery as a partnership for a number of years. On May 1, 2004, the partners decide to terminate business activities, liquidate all noncash assets, and dissolve their partnership. Although a specific explanation for this action is not given, any number of reasons could exist. The partners, for example, could have come to a disagreement so that they no longer believe they can work together. As an alternative possibility, business profits could have been inadequate to warrant the continuing investment of their time and capital.

Following is a balance sheet for the partnership of Morgan and Houseman as of the termination date. The revenue, expense, and drawing accounts have been closed as a preliminary step in terminating the business. A separate reporting will subsequently be made of the gains and losses that occur during the final winding-down process.

**MORGAN AND HOUSEMAN**
**Balance Sheet**
**May 1, 2004**

| Assets | | Liabilities and Capital | |
|---|---|---|---|
| Cash | $ 45,000 | Liabilities | $ 32,000 |
| Accounts receivable | 12,000 | Morgan, capital | 50,000 |
| Inventory | 22,000 | Houseman, capital | 38,000 |
| Land, building, and equipment (net) | 41,000 | | |
| Total assets | $120,000 | Total liabilities and capital | $120,000 |

The assumption that the liquidation of Morgan and Houseman proceeds in an orderly fashion through the following events is made here:

[7] Ibid.

**2004**

June 1   The inventory is sold at auction for $15,000. Morgan and Houseman allocate all profits and losses on a 6:4 basis, respectively.

July 15   Of the total accounts receivable, $9,000 is collected with the remainder being written off as bad debts.

Aug. 20   The fixed assets are sold for a total of $29,000.

Aug. 25   All partnership liabilities are paid.

Sept. 10   A total of $3,000 in liquidation expenses is paid to cover costs such as accounting and legal fees as well as the commissions incurred in disposing of partnership property.

Oct. 15   All remaining cash is distributed to the owners based on their final capital account balances.

Accordingly, the partnership of Morgan and Houseman incurred a number of losses in liquidating its property. Such losses are almost anticipated because the need for immediate sale is usually held as a high priority in a liquidation. Furthermore, a portion of the assets used by any business, such as its equipment and buildings, could have a utility that is strictly limited to a particular type of operation. If the property is not easily adaptable, disposal at any reasonable price often proves to be a problem.

To record the liquidation of Morgan and Houseman, the following journal entries would be made. Rather than report specific income and expense balances, gains and losses are traditionally recorded directly to the partners' capital accounts. Because operations have ceased, determination of a separate net income figure for this period would provide little informational value. *Instead, a primary concern of the parties involved in any liquidation is the continuing changes in each partner's capital balance.*

| Date | Account | Debit | Credit |
|---|---|---|---|
| 6/1/04 | Cash | 15,000 | |
| | Morgan, Capital (60% of loss) | 4,200 | |
| | Houseman, Capital (40% of loss) | 2,800 | |
| |     Inventory | | 22,000 |
| | To record sale of partnership inventory at a $7,000 loss. | | |
| 7/15/04 | Cash | 9,000 | |
| | Morgan, Capital | 1,800 | |
| | Houseman, Capital | 1,200 | |
| |     Accounts Receivable | | 12,000 |
| | To record collection of accounts receivable with write off of remaining $3,000 in accounts as bad debts. | | |
| 8/20/04 | Cash | 29,000 | |
| | Morgan, Capital | 7,200 | |
| | Houseman, Capital | 4,800 | |
| |     Land, Building, and Equipment (net) | | 41,000 |
| | To record sale of fixed assets and allocation of $12,000 loss. | | |
| 8/25/04 | Liabilities | 32,000 | |
| |     Cash | | 32,000 |
| | To record payment made to settle the liabilities of the partnership. | | |
| 9/10/04 | Morgan, Capital | 1,800 | |
| | Houseman, Capital | 1,200 | |
| |     Cash | | 3,000 |
| | To record payment of liquidation expenses with the amounts recorded as direct reductions to the partners' capital accounts. | | |

After liquidating the partnership assets and paying off all obligations, the cash that remains can be divided between Morgan and Houseman personally. The following schedule is utilized to determine the partners' ending capital account balances and, thus, the appropriate distribution for this final payment.

### Cash and Capital Account Balances*

|  | Cash | Morgan, Capital | Houseman, Capital |
|---|---|---|---|
| Beginning balances | $ 45,000 | $50,000 | $38,000 |
| Sold inventory | 15,000 | (4,200) | (2,800) |
| Collected accounts receivable | 9,000 | (1,800) | (1,200) |
| Sold fixed assets | 29,000 | (7,200) | (4,800) |
| Paid liabilities | (32,000) | –0– | –0– |
| Paid liquidation expenses | (3,000) | (1,800) | (1,200) |
| Final totals | $ 63,000 | $35,000 | $28,000 |

*Because of the presence of other assets as well as liabilities, the Cash and capital accounts will not be in agreement until the end of the liquidation process.

After the ending capital balances have been calculated, the remaining cash can be distributed to the partners to close out the financial records of the partnership:

| | | | | |
|---|---|---|---|---|
| 10/15/04 | Morgan, Capital | | 35,000 | |
| | Houseman, Capital | | 28,000 | |
| | Cash | | | 63,000 |
| | To record distribution of cash to partners in accordance with final capital balances. | | | |

## Schedule of Liquidation

Liquidation may take a considerable length of time to complete. Because the various parties involved seek continually updated financial information, the accountant should produce frequent reports summarizing the transactions as they occur. Consequently, a statement (often referred to as the *schedule of liquidation*) can be prepared at periodic intervals to disclose:

- Transactions to date.
- Property still being held by the partnership.
- Liabilities remaining to be paid.
- Current cash and capital balances.

Although the preceding Morgan and Houseman example has been condensed into a few events occurring during a relatively brief period of time, partnership liquidations usually require numerous transactions that transpire over months and, perhaps, even years. By receiving frequent schedules of liquidation, both the creditors and the partners are able to stay apprised of the results of this lengthy process.

Exhibit 10–1 presents the final schedule of liquidation for the partnership of Morgan and Houseman. Previous statements should have been distributed by the accountant at each important juncture of this liquidation to meet the informational needs of the parties involved. The example produced here demonstrates the stair-step approach incorporated in preparing a schedule of liquidation. The effects of each transaction (or group of transactions) are outlined in a horizontal fashion so that current account balances as well as all prior transactions are evident. This structuring also facilitates the preparation of future statements: A new layer summarizing recent events can simply be added at the bottom each time that a new schedule is to be produced.

## EXHIBIT 10–1

**MORGAN AND HOUSEMAN**
**Schedule of Partnership Liquidation**
**Final Balances**

|  | Cash | Noncash Assets | Liabilities | Morgan, Capital (60%) | Houseman, Capital (40%) |
|---|---|---|---|---|---|
| Beginning balances, 5/1/04 | $ 45,000 | $ 75,000 | $ 32,000 | $ 50,000 | $ 38,000 |
| Sold inventory, 6/1/04 | 15,000 | (22,000) |  | (4,200) | (2,800) |
| Updated balances | 60,000 | 53,000 | 32,000 | 45,800 | 35,200 |
| Collected receivables, 7/15/04 | 9,000 | (12,000) |  | (1,800) | (1,200) |
| Updated balances | 69,000 | 41,000 | 32,000 | 44,000 | 34,000 |
| Sold fixed assets, 8/20/04 | 29,000 | (41,000) |  | (7,200) | (4,800) |
| Updated balances | 98,000 | –0– | 32,000 | 36,800 | 29,200 |
| Paid liabilities, 8/25/04 | (32,000) |  | (32,000) |  |  |
| Updated balances | 66,000 | –0– | –0– | 36,800 | 29,200 |
| Paid liquidation expenses, 9/10/04 | (3,000) |  |  | (1,800) | (1,200) |
| Updated balances | 63,000 | –0– | –0– | 35,000 | 28,000 |
| Distributed remaining cash, 10/15/04 | (63,000) |  |  | (35,000) | (28,000) |
| Closing balances | –0– | –0– | –0– | –0– | –0– |

## Deficit Capital Balance—Contribution Made by Partner

In Exhibit 10–1, the liquidation process ended with all partners continuing to report positive capital balances. Thus, Morgan and Houseman were both able to share in the $63,000 cash that remained. Unfortunately, such an outcome is not always assured. At the end of a liquidation, one or more partners could report a negative capital account, or the partnership could not be able to generate even enough cash to satisfy all of the claims of its creditors. Such deficits are most likely to occur when the partnership is already insolvent at the start of the liquidation or when the disposal of noncash assets results in material losses. Under these circumstances, the accounting procedures to be applied depend on legal regulations as well as the individual actions of the partners.

To illustrate, assume that the partnership of Holland, Dozier, and Ross was dissolved at the beginning of the current year. Business activities were terminated and all noncash assets were subsequently converted into cash. During the liquidation process, the partnership incurred a number of large losses that have been allocated to the partners' capital accounts on a 4:4:2 basis, respectively. A portion of the resulting cash is then used to pay all partnership liabilities and liquidation expenses.

Following these transactions, assume that only the following four account balances remain open within the partnership's records:

| | | | |
|---|---|---|---|
| Cash | $20,000 | Holland, Capital | $(6,000) |
| | | Dozier, Capital | 15,000 |
| | | Ross, Capital | 11,000 |
| | | Total | $20,000 |

Holland is now reporting a negative capital balance of $6,000; the assigned share of partnership losses has exceeded this partner's net contribution. In such cases, the Uniform Partnership Act (Section 18[a]) stipulates that the partner "must contribute toward the losses, whether of capital or otherwise, sustained by the partnership according to his share in the profits." Therefore, Holland legally is required to convey an additional $6,000 to the partnership at this time to eliminate the deficit balance. This contribution raises the cash balance to $26,000 so that a complete distribution can be made to Dozier ($15,000) and Ross ($11,000) in line with their capital accounts. The journal entry for this final payment closes out the partnership records.

| | | |
|---|---:|---:|
| Cash | 6,000 | |
|     Holland, Capital | | 6,000 |
| To record contribution made by Holland to extinguish negative capital balance. | | |
| Dozier, Capital | 15,000 | |
| Ross, Capital | 11,000 | |
|     Cash | | 26,000 |
| To record distribution of remaining cash to partners in accordance with their ending capital balances. | | |

## Deficit Capital Balance—Loss to Remaining Partners

Unfortunately, an alternative scenario can easily be conceived for the previous partnership liquidation. Although Holland's capital account shows a $6,000 deficit balance, this partner could resist any attempt to force an additional investment, especially because the business is in the process of being terminated. The possibility of such recalcitrance is enhanced if the individual is having personal financial difficulties. Thus, the remaining partners may eventually have to resort to formal litigation to gain Holland's contribution. Until that legal action is concluded, the partnership records remain open although inactive.

### Distribution of Safe Payments

While awaiting the final resolution of this matter, no compelling reason exists for the partnership to continue holding $20,000 in cash. These funds will eventually be paid to Dozier and Ross regardless of any action taken by Holland. An immediate transfer should be made to these two partners to allow them the use of their money. However, because Dozier has a $15,000 capital account balance and Ross currently reports $11,000, a complete distribution is not possible. A method must be devised, therefore, to allow for a fair allocation of the available $20,000.

*To ensure the equitable treatment of all parties, this initial distribution is based on the assumption that the $6,000 capital deficit will prove to be a total loss to the partnership.* Holland may, for example, be completely insolvent so that no additional payment will ever be forthcoming. By making this conservative presumption, the accountant is able to calculate the lowest possible amounts (or safe balances) that Dozier and Ross must retain in their capital accounts to be able to absorb all future losses.

Should Holland's $6,000 deficit (or any portion of it) prove uncollectible, the loss will be written off against the capital accounts of Dozier and Ross. Allocation of this amount is based on the relative profit and loss ratio specified in the articles of partnership. According to the information provided, Dozier and Ross are credited with 40 percent and 20 percent of all partnership income, respectively. This 40:20 ratio equates to a 2:1 relationship (or $\frac{2}{3}:\frac{1}{3}$) between the two. Thus, if no part of the $6,000 deficit balance is ever recovered from Holland, $4,000 (two-thirds) of the loss will be assigned to Dozier and $2,000 (one-third) to Ross.

### Allocation of Potential $6,000 Loss

| | |
|---|---|
| Dozier | $\frac{2}{3}$ of $(6,000) = $(4,000) |
| Ross | $\frac{1}{3}$ of $(6,000) = $(2,000) |

These amounts represent the maximum potential reductions that could still be incurred by the two remaining partners. Depending on Holland's actions, Dozier could be forced to absorb an additional loss of $4,000, and Ross's capital account could decrease by as much as $2,000. These balances must therefore remain in the respective capital accounts until the issue is resolved. Hence, Dozier is entitled to receive $11,000 in cash at the present time; this distribution reduces that partner's capital account from $15,000 to the minimum $4,000 level. Likewise, a $9,000 payment to Ross decreases the $11,000 capital balance to the $2,000 limit. These $11,000 and $9,000 amounts represent safe payments that can be distributed to the partners without fear of new deficits being created in the future.

| | | |
|---|---|---|
| Dozier, Capital | 11,000 | |
| Ross, Capital | 9,000 | |
|     Cash | | 20,000 |
| To record distribution of cash to Dozier and Ross based on safe capital balances, using the assumption that Holland will not contribute further to the partnership. | | |

After this $20,000 in cash has been distributed, only a few other events can possibly occur during the remaining life of the partnership. Holland, either voluntarily or through legal persuasion, may contribute the entire $6,000 needed to eradicate the capital deficit. In that situation, the money should be immediately turned over to Dozier ($4,000) and Ross ($2,000) based on their remaining capital balances. The partnership records are effectively closed by this final distribution.

A second possibility is that Dozier and Ross could be unable to recover any part of the deficit from Holland. These two remaining partners must then absorb the $6,000 loss themselves. Because adequate safe capital balances have been maintained, recording a complete default by Holland serves to close out the partnership books.

| | | |
|---|---|---|
| Dozier, Capital (⅔ of loss) | 4,000 | |
| Ross, Capital (⅓ of loss) | 2,000 | |
|     Holland, Capital | | 6,000 |
| To record allocation of deficit capital balance of insolvent partner. | | |

### Deficit Is Partly Collectible

One other ending to this partnership liquidation is conceivable. A portion of the $6,000 could be recovered from Holland although the remainder proves to be uncollectible. This partner could become bankrupt or the other partners could simply give up trying to collect. The partners could also negotiate this settlement to avoid protracted legal actions.

To illustrate, assume that Holland manages to contribute $3,600 to the partnership but subsequently files for relief under the provisions of the bankruptcy laws. In a later legal arrangement, $1,000 additional cash goes to the partnership, but the final $1,400 will never be collected. This series of events creates the following effects within the liquidation process:

1. The $3,600 contribution is distributed to Dozier and Ross based on a new computation of their safe capital balances.
2. The $1,400 default is charged against the two positive capital balances in accordance with the relative profit and loss ratio.
3. The final $1,000 contribution is then paid to Dozier and Ross in amounts equal to their ending capital accounts, a transaction that closes the partnership's financial records.

The distribution of the first $3,600 depends on a recalculation of the minimum capital balances that Dozier and Ross must maintain to absorb all potential losses. Each of these computations is necessary because of a basic realization: Holland's remaining deficit balance

($2,400 at this time) could prove to be a total loss. This approach guarantees that the other two partners will continue to report sufficient capital until the liquidation is ultimately resolved.

|  | Current Capital | Allocation of Potential Loss | Safe Capital Payments |
|---|---|---|---|
| Dozier | $4,000 | ⅔ of $(2,400) = $(1,600) | $2,400 |
| Ross | 2,000 | ⅓ of $(2,400) = $ (800) | 1,200 |

Thus, the $3,600 in cash that is now available is distributed immediately to Dozier and Ross based on their safe balances.

| | | |
|---|---|---|
| Cash .................................................................... | 3,600 | |
|     Holland, Capital ................................................ | | 3,600 |
| Dozier, Capital ..................................................... | 2,400 | |
| Ross, Capital ........................................................ | 1,200 | |
|     Cash ................................................................ | | 3,600 |
| To record capital contribution by Holland and subsequent distribution of funds to Dozier and Ross based on safe capital balances. | | |

After recording this $3,600 contribution from Holland and the subsequent disbursement, the capital accounts for the partnership stay open, registering the following individual balances:

| | |
|---|---|
| Holland, Capital (deficit) ................ | $(2,400) |
| Dozier, Capital (safe balance) ............... | 1,600 |
| Ross, Capital (safe balance) ................ | 800 |

These accounts continue to remain on the partnership books until the final resolution of Holland's obligation.

In this illustration, the $1,000 legal settlement and the remaining $1,400 loss ultimately allow the parties to close out the records:

| | | |
|---|---|---|
| Cash ..................................................................... | 1,000 | |
| Dozier, Capital (⅔ of loss) ..................................... | 933 | |
| Ross, Capital (⅓ of loss) ........................................ | 467 | |
|     Holland, Capital ................................................ | | 2,400 |
| To record final $1,000 cash settlement of Holland's interest and resulting $1,400 loss. | | |
| Dozier, Capital ..................................................... | 667 | |
| Ross, Capital ........................................................ | 333 | |
|     Cash ................................................................ | | 1,000 |
| To record distribution of final cash balance based upon remaining capital account totals. | | |

## Marshaling of Assets

In the previous example, one partner (Holland) became insolvent during the liquidation process. Personal bankruptcy is not uncommon and raises questions as to the legal right that damaged partners have to proceed against an insolvent partner. *More specifically, is a deficit capital balance the legal equivalent of any other personal liability? Do partners who must absorb additional losses have the same rights against their partners as other creditors?*

Addressing this issue, the Uniform Partnership Act (Section 40[i]) stipulates the following:

Where a partner has become bankrupt or his estate is insolvent the claims against his separate property shall rank in the following order:

(I) Those owing to separate creditors,
(II) Those owing to partnership creditors,
(III) Those owing to partners by way of contribution.

This ranking of the claims against an individual is normally referred to as the *marshaling of assets* and allows for an orderly distribution of property in bankruptcy cases. It clearly shows that partners rank last in collecting from a bankrupt partner.

To demonstrate the effects created by this legal doctrine, assume that Stone is a partner in a business that is undergoing final liquidation. The partnership is insolvent: All assets have been expended but liabilities of $15,000 still remain. Stone is also personally insolvent. The assets currently held by this individual cannot satisfy all obligations:

| | |
|---|---:|
| Personal assets | $50,000 |
| Personal liabilities | 40,000 |
| Deficit capital balance—partnership | 19,000 |

Under these circumstances, the ranking established by the Uniform Partnership Act becomes extremely important. Stone does hold $50,000 in assets. However, because these assets are limited, recovery by the various parties depends on the pattern of distribution. According to the marshaling of assets doctrine, Stone's own creditors have first priority. After these claims have been satisfied, the $10,000 in remaining assets should be used to remunerate any partnership creditors who have sought recovery directly from Stone.

As indicated, partnership debts are $15,000, and these creditors can seek to collect from Stone (or any other general partner). Only then, after personal creditors as well as partnership creditors are paid, can the other partners lay claim to the residual portion of Stone's assets. Obviously, because of this individual's financial condition, the chances are not good that these partners will be able to recover all or even a significant portion of the $19,000 deficit capital balance. By ranking last on this priority list, partners are forced to accept whatever assets remain.

To help analyze and understand the possible effects created by the marshaling of assets concept, a variety of other scenarios should be considered. Assume, as an alternative to the previous example, that Stone failed to have sufficient property to satisfy even personal creditors: Stone holds $50,000 in assets but $80,000 in personal liabilities. Because of the volume of these debts, neither the partnership creditors nor the other partners will be able to recoup any money from this partner. All of the personal assets must be used to pay Stone's own obligations. Even with preferential treatment, the personal creditors still face a $30,000 shortfall because of the limited amount of available assets. This potential loss raises another legal question: Can Stone's personal creditors seek recovery of the $30,000 remaining debt directly from the partnership?

In response to this question, the marshaling of assets doctrine specifies that personal creditors can, indeed, claim a partner's share of partnership assets. However, recovery of all, or even a portion, of the $30,000 is possible only if two specific criteria are met:

1. Payment of all partnership debts must be assured.
2. The insolvent partner has to have a positive capital balance.

Even if both of these conditions are met, personal creditors have no right to receive more than the total of that partner's capital balance nor more than the amount of the debt.

This priority ranking of claims provides legal guidance in insolvency cases. For a more complete demonstration of the marshaling of assets principle, three additional examples follow. Each presents the legal and accounting responses to a specific partnership liquidation problem. In the first two illustrations, one or more of the partners is personally insolvent. The third analyzes the marshaling of assets in connection with an insolvent partnership.

### Insolvency—Example 1

The following balance sheet has been produced for the Able, Baker, Cannon, and Duke partnership. Profit and loss allocation percentages are also included.

| | | | | |
|---|---|---|---|---|
| Cash | $ 30,000 | Liabilities | | $ 80,000 |
| Noncash assets | 150,000 | Able, capital (40%) | | 15,000 |
| | | Baker, capital (30%) | | 40,000 |
| | | Cannon, capital (20%) | | 30,000 |
| | | Duke, capital (10%) | | 15,000 |
| Total assets | $180,000 | Total liabilities and capital | | $180,000 |

Baker is insolvent, and personal creditors have filed a $30,000 claim against this partner's share of partnership property. The litigation has forced the partnership to begin liquidation to settle Baker's interest. As shown in the balance sheet, the partnership has $30,000 in cash and Baker has a capital balance of $40,000.

Assume, in this example, that the noncash assets (with a book value of $150,000) are sold for $100,000 and then the partnership's liabilities ($80,000) are paid. These two actions increase the cash balance by $20,000 to a $50,000 figure. No other assets or liabilities exist. The adjusted capital accounts for each partner follow. Other than Baker, all partners are personally solvent.

| | Able, Capital | Baker, Capital | Cannon, Capital | Duke, Capital |
|---|---|---|---|---|
| Beginning balances | $15,000 | $40,000 | $30,000 | $15,000 |
| $50,000 loss on liquidating of assets | (20,000) (40%) | (15,000) (30%) | (10,000) (20%) | (5,000) (10%) |
| Capital balances | $(5,000) | $25,000 | $20,000 | $10,000 |

An additional contribution of $5,000 should be forthcoming from Able to eradicate the single negative capital balance. When made, this investment raises the partnership's cash to $55,000 and permits a final distribution to Cannon ($20,000), Duke ($10,000), and *Baker's creditors* ($25,000). The liquidation losses have reduced Baker's capital account below the $30,000 level; therefore, this partner's personal creditors will be unable to recover the entire amount of their claims. Despite the remaining $5,000 debt, they have no further legal recourse here; no right of recovery exists against the other partners once the capital account has been depleted.

Baker will receive nothing from this liquidation settlement because the personal obligations have not been completely satisfied. In contrast, if the final capital balance had been in excess of $30,000, Baker would have been entitled to any residual amount after all of the personal liabilities were extinguished.

### Insolvency—Example 2

The following balance sheet for the partnership of Morris, Newton, Olsen, and Prince also indicates the applicable profit and loss percentages. Both Morris and Prince are personally insolvent. Morris's creditors have brought an $8,000 claim against the partnership's assets, and Prince's creditors are seeking $15,000. These claims have forced the partnership to terminate operations so that the business property can be liquidated. The question as to which partner is entitled to any cash balance that remains is again raised.

| | | | | |
|---|---|---|---|---|
| Cash | $ 10,000 | Liabilities | | $ 70,000 |
| Noncash assets | 140,000 | Morris, capital (40%) | | 15,000 |
| | | Newton, capital (20%) | | 10,000 |
| | | Olsen, capital (20%) | | 23,000 |
| | | Prince, capital (20%) | | 32,000 |
| Total assets | $150,000 | Total liabilities and capital | | $150,000 |

Assume that the noncash assets are sold for a total of $80,000 creating a $60,000 loss and all liabilities are paid. The partnership's accounting system records these two events as follows:

| | | |
|---|---|---|
| Cash | 80,000 | |
| Morris, Capital (40% of loss) | 24,000 | |
| Newton, Capital (20% of loss) | 12,000 | |
| Olsen, Capital (20% of loss) | 12,000 | |
| Prince, Capital (20% of loss) | 12,000 | |
|     Noncash Assets (or specific accounts) | | 140,000 |
| To record sale of noncash assets and allocation of resulting $60,000 loss. | | |
| Liabilities | 70,000 | |
|     Cash | | 70,000 |
| To record extinguishment of partnership obligations. | | |

Because of these two transactions, the partnership's cash has risen from $10,000 to $20,000.

After the allocation of this loss, the capital accounts for Morris and Newton report deficit balances of $9,000 ($15,000 − $24,000) and $2,000 ($10,000 − $12,000), respectively. Although Newton is solvent and would be expected to compensate the partnership, Morris's personal financial condition does not allow for any further contribution. Morris's $9,000 deficit must, therefore, be absorbed by Newton, Olsen, and Prince. Because these three partners have historically shared profits evenly (20:20:20), they continue to do so in recording this additional capital loss.

| | | |
|---|---|---|
| Newton, Capital (⅓ of loss) | 3,000 | |
| Olsen, Capital (⅓ of loss) | 3,000 | |
| Prince, Capital (⅓ of loss) | 3,000 | |
|     Morris, Capital | | 9,000 |
| To record write-off of deficit capital balance of insolvent partner. | | |

This last allocation increases Newton's deficit to a $5,000 balance ($2,000 + $3,000), an amount which the partner should now contribute in accordance with partnership law.

| | | |
|---|---|---|
| Cash | 5,000 | |
|     Newton, Capital | | 5,000 |
| To record contribution from solvent partner necessitated by negative capital balance. | | |

Following this series of transactions, only the cash balance (now $25,000) as well as the capital accounts of Olsen and Prince remain open within the partnership records:

| | Cash | Morris, Capital | Newton, Capital | Olsen, Capital | Prince, Capital |
|---|---|---|---|---|---|
| Beginning balances | $10,000 | $15,000 | $10,000 | $23,000 | $32,000 |
| Sold assets | 80,000 | (24,000) | (12,000) | (12,000) | (12,000) |
| Paid liabilities | (70,000) | –0– | –0– | –0– | –0– |
| Default by Morris | –0– | 9,000 | (3,000) | (3,000) | (3,000) |
| Contribution by Newton | 5,000 | –0– | 5,000 | –0– | –0– |
| Current balances | $25,000 | –0– | –0– | $ 8,000 | $17,000 |

Although $8,000 of the partnership's remaining cash goes directly to Olsen, the $17,000 attributed to Prince is first subjected to the claims of the partner's personal creditors. Because of their claims, $15,000 of this amount must be used to satisfy these obligations, with only the final $2,000 being paid to Prince.

### Insolvency—Example 3

The two previous illustrations have analyzed liquidations in which one or more of the partners has been personally insolvent. Another possibility is that the partnership itself meets this same fate. In an active partnership, insolvency can occur if losses, partner drawings, or litigation deplete the working capital of the operation. A bankruptcy petition could follow if debts cannot be met as they come due. Liquidation of business assets could be necessary unless additional capital is quickly generated. Even a financially sound partnership can become insolvent if material losses are incurred during a voluntary liquidation.

To serve as a basis for examining the accounting and legal ramifications of an insolvent partnership, assume that the law firm of Keller, Lewis, Monroe, and Norris is in the final stages of liquidation. All noncash assets have been sold, and available cash has been used to pay a portion of the business's liabilities. Following these transactions, the following account balances remain open within the partnership's records. The four partners in this endeavor share profits and losses equally.

| | |
|---|---:|
| Liabilities | $ 20,000 |
| Keller, capital | (30,000) |
| Lewis, capital | (5,000) |
| Monroe, capital | 5,000 |
| Norris, capital | 10,000 |

Note: Parentheses indicate deficit.

This partnership is insolvent; it continues to owe creditors $20,000, even after liquidation and distribution of all assets. However, additional money should be forthcoming from two of the partners. Because of their deficit capital accounts, Keller and Lewis are legally required to contribute an additional $30,000 and $5,000, respectively, to the business. With these newly available funds, the partnership will be able to pay all $20,000 of its remaining liabilities as well as make cash distributions to Monroe ($5,000) and Norris ($10,000) in accordance with their capital account balances. The partnership books would be closed by this final payment.

Once again, the possibility exists that one or more of the partners who are reporting a negative capital balance will not step forward to make any further investment. Assume, for example, that Keller is personally insolvent and cannot contribute, whereas Lewis simply refuses to supply additional funds in hope of avoiding the obligation. *At this point, the remaining creditors can instigate legal recovery proceedings against any or all of the partners regardless of their capital balances.* Any action, however, against the insolvent partner could prove to be a futile effort because of the marshaling of assets principle.

Predicting the exact outcome of litigation is rarely possible. Thus, the assumption is made here that Norris is forced to contribute $20,000 cash to settle the remaining liabilities. The following journal entries would then be required for this partnership:

| | | |
|---|---:|---:|
| Cash | 20,000 | |
|     Norris, Capital | | 20,000 |
| Liabilities | 20,000 | |
|     Cash | | 20,000 |
| To record capital contribution by Norris made to pay remaining partnership creditors. | | |

After all liabilities have been extinguished, the partners who still maintain positive capital accounts can demand remuneration from any partner with a negative balance. Despite this legal obligation, the chances of a significant recovery from the insolvent Keller, especially un-

# Discussion Question

**WHAT HAPPENS IF A PARTNER BECOMES INSOLVENT?**

In 1995, three dentists—Ben Rogers, Judy Wilkinson, and Henry Walker—formed a partnership to open a practice in Toledo, Ohio. The primary purpose of the partnership was to reduce expenses since the partners could share building and equipment costs, supplies, and the services of a clerical staff. Each contributed $70,000 in cash and, with the help of a bank loan, constructed a building and acquired furniture, fixtures, and equipment. Because the partners maintained their own separate clients, annual net income has been allocated as follows: Each partner receives the specific amount of revenues that he or she generated during the period less one-third of all expenses. From the beginning, the partners did not anticipate expansion of the practice; consequently, they could withdraw cash each year up to 90 percent of their share of income for the period.

The partnership had been profitable for a number of years. Over the years, Rogers used much of his income to speculate in real estate in the Toledo area. By 2004, he was spending less time with the dental practice so that he could concentrate on his investments. Unfortunately, a number of these deals proved to be bad decisions and he incurred significant losses. On November 8, 2004, while Rogers was out of town, a $97,000 claim was filed by his personal creditors against the partnership assets. Unbeknownst to Wilkinson and Walker, Rogers had become insolvent.

Wilkinson and Walker hurriedly held a meeting to discuss the problem since Rogers could not be located. Rogers' capital account was currently at $105,000, but the partnership had only $27,000 in cash and liquid assets. The partners knew that Rogers' equipment had been used for a number of years and could be sold for relatively little. In contrast, the building has appreciated in value and the claim could be satisfied by selling the property. However, this action would have a tremendously adverse impact on the dental practice of the remaining two partners.

What alternatives are available to Wilkinson and Walker, and what are the advantages and disadvantages of each?

---

der the marshaling of assets doctrine, is not likely. Thus, the partners could choose to write off this deficit as a step toward closing the partnership's financial records. Legal recovery proceedings can still continue against Keller regardless of the accounting treatment. As equal partners, the $30,000 loss is absorbed evenly by Lewis, Monroe, and Norris.

| | |
|---|---:|
| Lewis, Capital (⅓ of loss) | 10,000 |
| Monroe, Capital (⅓ of loss) | 10,000 |
| Norris, Capital (⅓ of loss) | 10,000 |
|     Keller, Capital | 30,000 |
| To record write-off of deficit capital balance of insolvent partner. | |

The partners' capital accounts now hold the following balances:

| | Keller, Capital | Lewis, Capital | Monroe, Capital | Norris, Capital |
|---|---:|---:|---:|---:|
| Beginning balances | $(30,000) | $ (5,000) | $ 5,000 | $ 10,000 |
| Capital contribution | –0– | –0– | –0– | 20,000 |
| Write off of deficit balance | 30,000 | (10,000) | (10,000) | (10,000) |
| Current balances | –0– | $(15,000) | $(5,000) | $ 20,000 |

Both Lewis and Monroe now have a legal obligation to reimburse the partnership to offset their deficit capital balances. Upon their payment of $15,000 and $5,000, respectively, the entire $20,000 will be distributed to Norris (the only partner with a positive balance), and the partnership's books will be closed. Should either Lewis or Monroe fail to make the appropriate contribution, the additional loss must be allocated between the two remaining partners.

## Preliminary Distribution of Partnership Assets

In all of the illustrations analyzed in this chapter, distributions were made to the partners only after all assets were sold and all liabilities paid. As previously mentioned, a liquidation can take an extended time to complete. During this lengthy process, the partnership need not retain those assets that will eventually be disbursed to the partners. If the business is safely solvent, waiting until all affairs have been settled before transferring property to the owners is not warranted. The partners should be allowed to make use of their own funds at the earliest possible time.

*The objective in making any type of preliminary distribution is to ensure that enough capital is maintained by the partnership to absorb all future losses.* Any capital in excess of this maximum requirement is a safe balance, an amount that can be immediately conveyed to the partner. To determine safe capital balances at any time, the accountant simply assumes that all subsequent events will result in maximum losses: No cash will be received in liquidating remaining noncash assets and each partner is personally insolvent. Any positive capital balance that would remain even after the inclusion of all potential losses can be paid to the partner without delay. Although the assumption that no further funds will be generated could be unrealistic, it does ensure that negative capital balances are not created by premature payments being made to any of the partners.

### *Preliminary Distribution Illustrated*

To demonstrate the computation of safe capital distributions, assume that a liquidating partnership reports the following balance sheet:

| | | | |
|---|---|---|---|
| Cash | $60,000 | Liabilities | $40,000 |
| Noncash assets | 140,000 | Mason, loan | 20,000 |
| | | Mason, capital (50%) | 60,000 |
| | | Lee, capital (30%) | 30,000 |
| | | Dixon, capital (20%) | 50,000 |
| Total assets | $200,000 | Total liabilities and capital | $200,000 |

Assume also that the partners estimate that $6,000 will be the maximum expense incurred in carrying out this liquidation. Consequently, the partnership needs only $46,000 to meet all obligations: $40,000 to satisfy partnership liabilities and $6,000 for these final expenses. Since $60,000 in cash is being held, the partnership can transfer the extra $14,000 to the partners immediately without fear of injuring any of the participants in the liquidation. However, the appropriate allocation of this money is not readily apparent; safe capital balances must be computed to guide the actual distribution.

Before the allocation of this $14,000 is demonstrated, the appropriate handling of a partner's loan balance should be examined. According to the balance sheet, Mason has conveyed $20,000 to the business at some point in the past, an amount that was considered a loan rather than additional capital. Perhaps the partnership was in desperate need of funds and Mason was willing to contribute only if the contribution was structured as a loan. Regardless of the reason, the question as to the status of this account remains: Is the $20,000 to be viewed as a liability to the partner or as a capital balance? The answer becomes especially significant during the liquidation process because available funds often are limited. In this regard, the Uniform Partnership Act (UPA) (Section 40[b]) stipulates that loans to partners rank behind obligations to outside creditors in order of payment but ahead of the partners' capital balances.

Although this legal provision indicates that the debt to Mason must be repaid entirely before any distribution of capital can be made to the other partners, actual accounting practice takes a different view. "In preparing predistribution schedules, accountants typically offset partners' loans with the partners' capital accounts and then distribute funds accordingly."[8] In

[8] Robert E. Whitis and Jeffrey R. Pittman, "Inconsistencies between Accounting Practices and Statutory Law in Partnership Liquidations," *Accounting Educators' Journal*, Fall 1996, p. 99.

other words, the loan is merged in with the partner's capital account balance at the beginning of liquidation. Thus, practice and the UPA seem to differ on the handling of a loan from a partner.

To illustrate the potential problem with this conflict, assume that a partnership has $20,000 in cash left after liquidation. Partner A has a positive capital balance of $20,000 whereas Partner B has a negative capital balance of $20,000. In addition, Partner B has previously loaned the partnership $20,000. If Partner B is insolvent, a distribution problem arises.[9] If the provisions of the UPA are followed literally, the $20,000 cash should be given to Partner B (probably to the creditors of Partner B) to repay the loan. Because Partner B is insolvent, no more assets can be expected from this individual. Thus, Partner A would have to absorb the entire $20,000 deficit capital balance and will get no portion of the $20,000 in cash that is held by the business.

However, despite the UPA, common practice appears to be that the loan from Partner B will be used to offset that partner's negative capital balance. Using that approach, Partner B is left with a zero capital balance so that the entire $20,000 goes to Partner A; neither Partner B nor the creditors of Partner B get anything. Thus, when a loan comes from a partner who later becomes insolvent and reports a negative capital balance, the handling of the loan becomes significant. Unfortunately, further legal guidance does not exist at this time because "no reported state or federal opinion has directly ruled on the right of offset of potential capital deficits."[10]

In this textbook, in order to follow common practice, a loan from a partner will be accounted for in liquidation as if the balance were a component of the partner's capital. By this offset, the accountant can reduce the amount accumulated as a negative capital balance for any insolvent partner. Any such loan can be transferred into the corresponding capital account at the start of the liquidation process. Similarly, any loans due from a partner should be shown as a reduction in the appropriate capital balance.

### *Proposed Schedule of Liquidation*

Returning to the current illustration, the accountant needs to determine an equitable distribution for the $14,000 cash presently available. To structure this computation, a proposed schedule of liquidation is developed *based on the underlying assumption that all future events will result in total losses.* In Exhibit 10–2, this statement is presented for the Mason, Lee, and Dixon partnership. To expedite coverage, the $20,000 loan has already been transferred into Mason's capital account. Thus, regardless of whether this partner arrives at a deficit or a safe capital balance, the loan figure already will have been included.

In producing Exhibit 10–2, complete losses ($140,000) are forecast in connection with the disposition of all noncash assets, and liquidation expenses are anticipated at maximum amounts ($6,000). Following the projected payment of liabilities, any partner reporting a negative capital account is assumed to be personally insolvent. These potential deficit balances are written off with the losses being assigned to the remaining solvent partners based on their relative profit and loss ratio. Lee, with a negative $13,800, is eliminated first. This allocation creates a deficit of $2,857 for Mason, an amount that must be absorbed solely by Dixon. After this series of maximum losses has been simulated, any positive capital balance that still remains is considered safe; a cash distribution of that amount can be made to the specific partners.

Exhibit 10–2 indicates that only Dixon has a large enough capital balance at the present time to absorb all possible future losses. Thus, the entire $14,000 can be distributed to this partner with no fear that the capital account will ever report a deficit. Based on current practice, Mason, despite having made a $20,000 loan to the partnership, is entitled to no part of this initial distribution. The loan is of insufficient size to prevent potential deficits from occurring in Mason's capital account.

---

[9] The same problem should not exist if the partner is solvent. The partner is legally required to contribute enough funds to delete any capital deficit. Thus, in this case, Partner B would be entitled to the $20,000 loan repayment but then has to contribute $20,000 because of the negative capital balance. That cash amount would go to Partner A because of that partner's positive capital balance.

[10] Whitis and Pittman, "Inconsistencies between Accounting Practices," p. 93.

## EXHIBIT 10–2

### MASON, LEE, AND DIXON
### Proposed Schedule of Liquidation—Initial Safe Capital Balances

| | Cash | Noncash Assets | Liabilities | Mason, Capital (50%) | Lee, Capital (30%) | Dixon, Capital (20%) |
|---|---|---|---|---|---|---|
| Beginning balances | $ 60,000 | $140,000 | $40,000 | $80,000 | $ 30,000 | $ 50,000 |
| Maximum loss on noncash assets | –0– | (140,000) | –0– | (70,000) | (42,000) | (28,000) |
| Maximum liquidation expenses | (6,000) | –0– | –0– | (3,000) | (1,800) | (1,200) |
| Payment of liabilities | (40,000) | –0– | (40,000) | –0– | –0– | –0– |
| Potential balances | 14,000 | –0– | –0– | 7,000 | (13,800) | 20,800 |
| Assume Lee to be insolvent | –0– | –0– | –0– | (9,857) (5/7) | 13,800 | (3,943) (2/7) |
| Potential balances | 14,000 | –0– | –0– | (2,857) | –0– | 16,857 |
| Assume Mason to be insolvent | –0– | –0– | –0– | 2,857 | –0– | (2,857) |
| Safe balances | $ 14,000 | –0– | –0– | –0– | –0– | $ 14,000 |

One series of computations found in this proposed schedule of liquidation merits additional attention. The simulated losses initially create a $13,800 negative balance in Lee's capital account while the other two partners continue to report positive figures. Lee's projected deficit must then be absorbed by Mason and Dixon according to their relative profit and loss percentages. Previously, Mason has been allocated 50 percent of net income with 20 percent recorded to Dixon. These figures equate to a 50/70:20/70, or a 5/7:2/7 ratio. Based on this realigned relationship, the $13,800 potential deficit is allocated between Mason (5/7, or $9,857) and Dixon (2/7, or $3,943), reducing Mason's own capital account to a negative balance as shown in Exhibit 10–2.

Continuing with the assumption that maximum losses occur in all cases, Mason's $2,857 deficit is accounted for as if that partner were also personally insolvent. Therefore, the entire negative balance is assigned to Dixon, the only partner still retaining a positive capital account. Since all potential losses have been recognized at this point, the remaining $14,000 capital is a safe balance that should be paid to this partner. Even after the money is distributed, Dixon's capital account will still be large enough to absorb all future losses.

### Liquidation in Installments

In practice, maximum liquidation losses are not likely to occur to any business. Thus, at various points during this process, additional cash amounts can become available as partnership property is sold. If the assets are disposed of in a piecemeal fashion, cash can actually flow into the company on a regular basis for an extended period of time. As needed, updated safe capital schedules have to be developed to dictate the recipients of newly available funds. Because numerous capital distributions could be required, this process is often referred to as a *liquidation made in installments.*

To illustrate, assume that the partnership of Mason, Lee, and Dixon actually undergoes the following events in connection with its liquidation:

- As indicated by the proposed schedule of liquidation in Exhibit 10–2, Dixon receives $14,000 in cash as a preliminary capital distribution.
- Noncash assets with a book value of $50,000 are sold for $20,000.
- All $40,000 in liabilities are settled.
- Liquidation expenses of $2,000 are paid; the partners now believe that only a maximum of $3,000 more will be expended in this manner. The original estimation of $6,000 was apparently too high.

As a result of these transactions, the partnership has an additional $21,000 in cash that is now available for distribution to the partners: $20,000 received from the sale of noncash assets

## EXHIBIT 10–3  Liquidation for Installments

**MASON, LEE, AND DIXON**
**Proposed Schedule of Liquidation—Subsequent Safe Capital Balances**

|  | Cash | Noncash Assets | Liabilities | Mason, Capital (50%) | Lee, Capital (30%) | Dixon, Capital (20%) |
|---|---|---|---|---|---|---|
| Beginning balances | $ 60,000 | $140,000 | $ 40,000 | $ 80,000 | $ 30,000 | $ 50,000 |
| Capital distribution—safe balances | (14,000) | –0– | –0– | –0– | –0– | (14,000) |
| Disposal of noncash assets | 20,000 | (50,000) | –0– | (15,000) | (9,000) | (6,000) |
| Liabilities paid | (40,000) | –0– | (40,000) | –0– | –0– | –0– |
| Liquidation expenses | (2,000) | –0– | –0– | (1,000) | (600) | (400) |
| Current balances | 24,000 | 90,000 | –0– | 64,000 | 20,400 | 29,600 |
| Maximum loss on remaining noncash assets | –0– | (90,000) | –0– | (45,000) | (27,000) | (18,000) |
| Maximum liquidation expenses | (3,000) | –0– | –0– | (1,500) | (900) | (600) |
| Potential balances | 21,000 | –0– | –0– | 17,500 | (7,500) | 11,000 |
| Assume Lee to be insolvent | –0– | –0– | –0– | (5,357) (⅗) | 7,500 | (2,143) (⅖) |
| Safe balances—current | $ 21,000 | –0– | –0– | $ 12,143 | –0– | $ 8,857 |

and another $1,000 because of the reduced estimation of liquidation expenses. Once again, the accountant must assume maximum future losses as a means of determining the appropriate distribution of these funds. A second proposed schedule of liquidation is produced in Exhibit 10–3, indicating that $12,143 of this amount should go to Mason with the remaining $8,857 to Dixon. To facilitate a better visual understanding, actual transactions are recorded first on this schedule, followed by the assumed losses. *A dotted line separates the real from the potential occurrences.*

## Predistribution Plan

The liquidation of a partnership can require numerous transactions occurring over a lengthy time. The continual production of proposed schedules of liquidation could become a burdensome chore. Two separate statements already have been required in the previous illustration, and the partnership still possesses $90,000 in noncash assets awaiting conversion. *Therefore, at the start of a liquidation, most accountants produce a single predistribution plan to serve as a guideline for all future payments.* Thereafter, whenever cash becomes available, this plan indicates the appropriate recipient(s) without the necessity of drawing up ever-changing proposed schedules of liquidation.

A predistribution plan is developed by simulating a series of losses each of which is just large enough to eliminate, one at a time, all of the partners' claims to partnership property. This approach recognizes that the individual capital accounts exhibit differing degrees of sensitivity to losses. Capital accounts possess varying balances and could be charged with losses at different rates. Consequently, a predistribution plan is based on calculating the losses (the "maximum loss allowable") that would eliminate each of these capital balances in a sequential pattern. This series of absorbed losses then forms the basis for the predistribution plan.

To demonstrate the creation of a predistribution plan, assume that the following partnership is to be liquidated:

| | | | |
|---|---|---|---|
| Cash | –0– | Liabilities | $100,000 |
| Noncash assets | $221,000 | Rubens, capital (50%) | 30,000 |
| | | Smith, capital (20%) | 40,000 |
| | | Trice, capital (30%) | 51,000 |
| Total assets | $221,000 | Total liabilities and capital | $221,000 |

The partnership capital reported by this organization totals $121,000. However, the individual balances for the partners range from $30,000 to $51,000, and profits and losses are assigned according to three different percentages. Thus, each partner's current capital balance would be reduced to zero by differing losses. *As a prerequisite to developing a predistribution plan, the sensitivity to losses exhibited by each of these capital accounts must be measured.*

| Partner | Capital Balance/ Loss Allocation | Maximum Loss that Can Be Absorbed |
|---|---|---|
| Rubens | $30,000/50% | $60,000 ✔ |
| Smith | 40,000/20 | 200,000 |
| Trice | 51,000/30 | 170,000 |

According to this initial computation, Rubens is the partner in the most vulnerable position at the present time. Based on a 50 percent share of income, a loss of only $60,000 would reduce this partner's capital account to a zero balance. If the partnership does incur a loss of this amount, Rubens can no longer hope to recover any funds from the liquidation process. Thus, the potential effects of this loss (referred to as a *Step 1 loss*) is simulated through the following schedule:

|  | Rubens, Capital | Smith, Capital | Trice, Capital |
|---|---|---|---|
| Beginning balances | $ 30,000 | $ 40,000 | $ 51,000 |
| Assumed $60,000 loss | (30,000) (50%) | (12,000) (20%) | (18,000) (30%) |
| Step 1 balances | –0– | $ 28,000 | $ 33,000 |

As previously discussed, the predistribution plan is based on describing the series of losses that would eliminate each partner's capital in turn and, thus, all claims to cash. In the previous Step 1 schedule above, the $60,000 loss did reduce Rubens's capital account to zero. Assuming, as a precautionary step, that Rubens is personally insolvent, all further losses would have to be allocated between Smith and Trice. Since these two partners have previously shared partnership profits and losses on a 20 percent and 30 percent basis, a 20/50:30/50 (or 40%:60%) relationship exists between them. Therefore, these realigned percentages must now be utilized in calculating a Step 2 loss, the amount just large enough to exclude another of the remaining partners from sharing in any future cash distributions.

| Partner | Capital Balance/ Loss Allocation | Maximum Loss that Can Be Absorbed |
|---|---|---|
| Smith | $28,000/40% | $70,000 |
| Trice | 33,000/60 | 55,000 ✔ |

Since Rubens' capital balance already has been eliminated, Trice is now in the most vulnerable position: only a $55,000 Step 2 loss is required to reduce this partner's capital account to a zero balance.

|  | Rubens, Capital | Smith, Capital | Trice, Capital |
|---|---|---|---|
| Beginning balances | $ 30,000 | $ 40,000 | $ 51,000 |
| Assumed $60,000 loss | (30,000) (50%) | (12,000) (20%) | (18,000) (30%) |
| Step 1 balances | –0– | $ 28,000 | $ 33,000 |
| Assumed $55,000 loss | –0– | (22,000) (40%) | (33,000) (60%) |
| Step 2 balances | –0– | $6,000 | –0– |

According to this second schedule, a total loss of $115,000 ($60,000 from Step 1 plus $55,000 from Step 2) would leave capital of only $6,000, a balance attributed entirely to Smith. At this final point in the simulation, an additional loss of this amount also ends Smith's right to receive any funds from the liquidation process. Having the sole positive capital account remaining, this partner would have to absorb the entire amount of the final loss.

|  | Rubens, Capital | Smith, Capital | Trice, Capital |
| --- | --- | --- | --- |
| Beginning balances | $ 30,000 | $ 40,000 | $ 51,000 |
| Assumed $60,000 loss | (30,000) (50%) | (12,000) (20%) | (18,000) (30%) |
| Step 1 balances | –0– | $ 28,000 | $ 33,000 |
| Assumed $55,000 loss | –0– | (22,000) (40%) | (33,000) (60%) |
| Step 2 balances | –0– | 6,000 | –0– |
| Assumed $6,000 loss | –0– | (6,000) (100%) | –0– |
| Final balances | –0– | –0– | –0– |

Once each partner's capital account has been reduced to zero through this series of simulated losses, a predistribution plan for the liquidation can be devised. *This procedure requires working backward through the final schedule above, determining the effects that will result if the assumed losses do not occur.* Without these losses, cash becomes available for the partners; therefore, a direct relationship exists between the volume of losses and the distribution pattern. The last $6,000 loss, for example, is to be absorbed entirely by Smith. Should that loss fail to materialize, Smith is left with a positive safe capital balance of this amount. Thus, as cash becomes available, the first $6,000 received (in excess of partnership obligations and anticipated liquidation expenses) should be distributed solely to Smith.

In a similar manner, the preceding $55,000 Step 2 loss was divided between Smith and Trice on a 4:6 basis. Again, if such losses do not occur, these balances need not be retained to protect the partnership against capital deficits. Therefore, after Smith has received the initial $6,000, any further cash that becomes available (up to an additional $55,000) will be split between Smith (40 percent) and Trice (60 percent). For example, if exactly $61,000 in cash is held by the partnership in excess of liabilities and possible liquidation expenses, the following distribution should be made:

|  | Rubens | Smith | Trice |
| --- | --- | --- | --- |
| First $6,000 | –0– | $ 6,000 | –0– |
| Next $55,000 | –0– | 22,000 (40%) | $33,000 (60%) |
| Cash distribution | –0– | $28,000 | $33,000 |

The predistribution plan can be completed by including the Step 1 loss, an amount that was to be absorbed by the partners on a 5:2:3 basis. Thus, all money that becomes available to the partners after the initial $61,000 is to be distributed according to the original profit and loss ratio. At this point in the liquidation, enough cash would have been generated to ensure that each partner has a safe capital balance: No possibility exists that a future deficit can occur. Any further increases in the projected capital balances will be allocated by the 5:2:3 allocation pattern. *For this reason, once all partners begin to receive a portion of the cash disbursements, any remaining funds are divided based on the original profit and loss percentages.*

To inform all parties of the pattern by which available cash will be disbursed, the predistribution plan should be formally prepared in a schedule format prior to beginning liquidation. Following is the predistribution plan for the partnership of Rubens, Smith, and Trice. To complete this illustration, liquidation expenses of $12,000 have been estimated. Because these expenses have the same effect on the capital accounts as losses, they do not change the sequential pattern by which assets eventually will be distributed.

### RUBENS, SMITH, AND TRICE
#### Predistribution Plan

| Available Cash | | Recipient |
|---|---|---|
| First | $112,000 | Creditors ($100,000) and liquidation expenses (estimated at $12,000) |
| Next | 6,000 | Smith |
| Next | 55,000 | Smith (40%) and Trice (60%) |
| All further cash balances | | Rubens (50%), Smith (20%), and Trice (30%) |

## Summary

1. Although a partnership can exist indefinitely through the periodic admission of new partners, termination of business activities and liquidation of property can take place for a number of reasons. A partner's death or retirement as well as the insolvency of a partner or even the partnership itself can trigger this process. Because of the risk that large losses will be incurred during liquidation, all parties usually seek frequent and timely information describing ongoing developments. The accountant is expected to furnish these data while also working to ensure the equitable treatment of all parties.

2. The liquidation process entails (a) converting partnership property into cash, (b) paying off liabilities and liquidation expenses, and (c) conveying any remaining property to the partners based on their final capital balances. As a means of reporting these transactions, a schedule of liquidation should be produced at periodic intervals. This statement discloses all recent transactions, the assets and liabilities still being held, and the current capital balances. Distribution of this schedule on a regular basis allows the various parties involved in the liquidation to monitor the progress being made.

3. During a liquidation, negative capital balances can arise for one or more of the partners, especially if material losses are incurred in disposing of partnership property. In such cases, the specific partner or partners should contribute enough additional assets to eliminate their deficits. If payment is slow in coming, any cash still held by the partnership can be immediately divided among the partners who have safe capital balances. A *safe balance* is the amount of capital that would remain even if maximum future losses occur: Noncash assets are lost in total and all partners with deficits fail to fulfill their legal obligations. In making these computations, negative capital balances are absorbed by the remaining partners based on their relative profit and loss ratio.

4. To enable an orderly and fair distribution during liquidation, the Uniform Partnership Act establishes a priority listing for all claims, a ranking referred to as the *marshaling of assets*. This principle states that partners with positive capital balances can recover losses from a partner reporting a deficit but only after adequate protection has been ensured for that individual's creditors as well as the partnership's creditors. The Act also specifies that a partner's personal creditors can seek recovery of losses from the partnership to the extent of that person's capital balance after protection of partnership creditors is assured.

5. The actual liquidation of a partnership can take an extended period to complete. Oftentimes, cash is generated during the early stages of this process in excess of the amount needed to cover liabilities and liquidation expenses. The accountant should propose a fair and immediate distribution of these available funds. A proposed schedule of liquidation can be created as a guide for such cash distributions. This statement is based on a *simulated* series of transactions: sale of all noncash assets, payment of liquidation expenses, and so on. At every point, maximum losses are assumed: Noncash assets have no resale value, liquidation expenses are set at the maximum level, and all partners are personally insolvent. Any safe capital balance that would remain after incurring such losses represents a distribution that can be made at the present time. Even after this payment, the capital account will still be large enough to absorb all potential losses.

6. The liquidation of a partnership can require numerous transactions occurring over a lengthy time. Thus, the accountant could discover that the continual production of proposed schedules of liquidation becomes a burdensome chore. For this reason, a single predistribution plan is usually produced at the start of the liquidation process. This plan serves as a definitive guideline for all payments to be made to the partners. To create this plan, a series of losses is simulated with each one, in turn, exactly eliminating the capital balance of a partner. After all capital accounts have been reduced to zero through these assumed losses, the predistribution plan is devised by working backward through the series. In effect, the accountant is measuring the cash that will become available if such losses do not occur.

# Comprehensive Illustration PROBLEM

*(Estimated Time: 30 to 40 Minutes)* For the past several years, the partnership of Andrews, Caso, Quinn, and Sheridan has operated a local department store. Based on the provisions of the original articles of partnership, all profits and losses have been allocated on a 4:3:2:1 ratio, respectively. Recently, both Caso and Quinn have undergone personal financial problems, and as a result, these two individuals are now insolvent. Caso's creditors have filed a $20,000 claim against the partnership's assets, and $22,000 is being sought to repay Quinn's personal debts. To satisfy these legal obligations, the partnership property must be liquidated. The partners estimate that they will incur $12,000 in expenses in disposing of all non-cash assets.

At the time that active operations cease and the liquidation is begun, the following balance sheet is produced for this partnership. All measurement accounts have been closed out to arrive at the current capital balances.

| | | | |
|---|---:|---|---:|
| Cash | $ 20,000 | Liabilities | $140,000 |
| Noncash assets | 280,000 | Caso, loan | 10,000 |
| | | Andrews, capital (40%) | 76,000 |
| | | Caso, capital (30%) | 14,000 |
| | | Quinn, capital (20%) | 51,000 |
| | | Sheridan, capital (10%) | 9,000 |
| Total assets | $300,000 | Total liabilities and capital | $300,000 |

During the lengthy liquidation process, the following transactions take place:

- Noncash assets with a book value of $190,000 are sold for $140,000 cash.
- Liquidation expenses of $14,000 are paid. No further expenses are expected.
- Safe capital distributions are made to the partners.
- Payment of all business liabilities is made.
- The remaining noncash assets are sold for $10,000.
- Deficit capital balances for any insolvent partners are deemed to be uncollectible.
- Appropriate cash contributions from any solvent partner who is reporting a negative capital balance are received.
- Final cash distributions are made.

## Required

a. Using the information that is available prior to the start of the liquidation process, develop a predistribution plan for this partnership.
b. Prepare journal entries to record the actual liquidation transactions.

## SOLUTION

a. This partnership begins the liquidation process with capital amounting to $160,000. This total includes the $10,000 loan from Caso since the liability must be retained as a possible offset against any eventual deficit capital balance. Therefore, the predistribution plan is based on the assumption that $160,000 in losses will be incurred, entirely eliminating all partnership capital. As discussed in this chapter, these simulated losses are arranged in a series so that each capital account is sequentially reduced to a zero balance.

At the start of the liquidation, Caso's capital position is the most vulnerable.

| Partner | Capital Balance/ Loss Allocation | Maximum Loss that Can Be Absorbed |
|---|---|---|
| Andrews | $76,000/40% | $190,000 |
| Caso | 24,000/30 | 80,000 ✔ |
| Quinn | 51,000/20 | 255,000 |
| Sheridan | 9,000/10 | 90,000 |

As indicated by this schedule, an $80,000 loss would eradicate both Caso's $14,000 capital balance and the $10,000 loan. Therefore, to start the development of a predistribution plan, this loss is assumed to have occurred.

|  | Andrews, Capital | Caso, Loan and Capital | Quinn, Capital | Sheridan, Capital |
|---|---|---|---|---|
| Beginning balances | $76,000 | $24,000 | $51,000 | $9,000 |
| Assumed $80,000 loss | (32,000) (40%) | (24,000) (30%) | (16,000) (20%) | (8,000) (10%) |
| Step 1 balances | $44,000 | –0– | $35,000 | $1,000 |

With Caso's capital account eliminated, further losses are to be split among the remaining partners in the ratio of 4:2:1 (or $\frac{4}{7}:\frac{2}{7}:\frac{1}{7}$). Because only an additional $7,000 loss (the $1,000 capital above divided by $\frac{1}{7}$) is now needed to reduce Sheridan's account to zero, this partner is in the second most vulnerable position.

|  | Andrews | Caso | Quinn | Sheridan |
|---|---|---|---|---|
| Step 1 balances (above) | $44,000 | –0– | $35,000 | $1,000 |
| Assumed $7,000 loss | (4,000) ($\frac{4}{7}$) | –0– | (2,000) ($\frac{2}{7}$) | (1,000) ($\frac{1}{7}$) |
| Step 2 balances | $40,000 | –0– | $33,000 | –0– |

Following these two simulated losses, only Andrews and Quinn continue to report positive capital balances. Thus, they divide further losses on a 4:2 basis, or 66⅔%:33⅓%. Based on these realigned percentages, Andrews's position has become the more vulnerable. A further loss of $60,000 ($40,000/66⅔%) reduces this partner's remaining capital to zero whereas a $99,000 loss ($33,000/33⅓%) is required to eliminate Quinn's balance.

|  | Andrews | Caso | Quinn | Sheridan |
|---|---|---|---|---|
| Step 2 balances (above) | $40,000 | –0– | $33,000 | –0– |
| Assumed $60,000 loss | (40,000) (66⅔%) | –0– | (20,000) (33⅓%) | –0– |
| Step 3 balances | –0– | –0– | $13,000 | –0– |

The final $13,000 capital balance belongs to Quinn; an additional loss of this amount is necessary to remove the last element of partnership capital.

Based on the results of this series of simulated losses, a predistribution plan can be created. However, the $140,000 in liabilities owed by the partnership still retain first priority to any available cash. Additionally, $12,000 must be held to cover the anticipated liquidation expenses.

### ANDREWS, CASO, QUINN, AND SHERIDAN
### Predistribution Plan

| Available Cash | | Recipient |
|---|---|---|
| First | $152,000 | Creditors and anticipated liquidation expenses |
| Next | 13,000 | Quinn |
| Next | 60,000 | Andrews (66⅔%) and Quinn (33⅓%) |
| Next | 7,000 | Andrews ($\frac{4}{7}$), Quinn ($\frac{2}{7}$), and Sheridan ($\frac{1}{7}$) |
| All further cash | | Andrews (40%), Caso (30%), Quinn (20%), and Sheridan (10%) |

Because of their insolvency, initial payments to Caso ($20,000) and Quinn ($22,000) will actually go to their personal creditors.

b. Journal entries for the liquidation:

| | | |
|---|---:|---:|
| Caso, Loan | 10,000 | |
|     Caso, Capital | | 10,000 |
| To record offset of loan against capital balance in anticipation of liquidation. | | |
| Cash | 140,000 | |
| Andrews, Capital (40% of loss) | 20,000 | |
| Caso, Capital (30% of loss) | 15,000 | |
| Quinn, Capital (20% of loss) | 10,000 | |
| Sheridan, Capital (10% of loss) | 5,000 | |
|     Noncash Assets | | 190,000 |
| To record sale of noncash assets and allocation of $50,000 loss. | | |
| Andrews, Capital (40%) | 5,600 | |
| Caso, Capital (30%) | 4,200 | |
| Quinn, Capital (20%) | 2,800 | |
| Sheridan, Capital (10%) | 1,400 | |
|     Cash | | 14,000 |
| To record payment of liquidation expenses. | | |

- The partnership now holds $146,000 in cash, $6,000 more than is needed to satisfy all liabilities and estimated expenses. According to the predistribution plan drawn up in requirement (a), this entire amount can be safely distributed to Quinn (or to Quinn's creditors).

| | | |
|---|---:|---:|
| Quinn, Capital | 6,000 | |
|     Cash | | 6,000 |
| To record distribution of available cash based on safe capital balance. | | |
| Liabilities | 140,000 | |
|     Cash | | 140,000 |
| To record extinguishment of all partnership debts. | | |
| Cash | 10,000 | |
| Andrews, Capital (40% of loss) | 32,000 | |
| Caso, Capital (30% of loss) | 24,000 | |
| Quinn, Capital (20% of loss) | 16,000 | |
| Sheridan, Capital (10% of loss) | 8,000 | |
|     Noncash Assets | | 90,000 |
| To record sale of remaining noncash assets and allocation of $80,000 loss. | | |

- At this point in the liquidation, only the cash and the capital accounts remain open on the partnership books.

| | Cash | Andrews, Capital | Caso, Capital | Quinn, Capital | Sheridan, Capital |
|---|---:|---:|---:|---:|---:|
| Beginning balances | $ 20,000 | $ 76,000 | $ 14,000 | $ 51,000 | $ 9,000 |
| Loan offset | –0– | –0– | 10,000 | –0– | –0– |
| Sale of noncash assets | 140,000 | (20,000) | (15,000) | (10,000) | (5,000) |
| Liquidation expenses | (14,000) | (5,600) | (4,200) | (2,800) | (1,400) |
| Cash distribution | (6,000) | –0– | –0– | (6,000) | –0– |
| Payment of liabilities | (140,000) | –0– | –0– | –0– | –0– |
| Sale of noncash assets | 10,000 | (32,000) | (24,000) | (16,000) | (8,000) |
| Current balances | $ 10,000 | $ 18,400 | $ (19,200) | $ 16,200 | $(5,400) |

Because Caso is personally insolvent, the $19,200 deficit balance will not be repaid and must be absorbed by the remaining three partners on a 4:2:1 basis.

| | | |
|---|---:|---:|
| Andrews, Capital (4/7 of loss) | 10,971 | |
| Quinn, Capital (2/7 of loss) | 5,486 | |
| Sheridan, Capital (1/7 of loss) | 2,743 | |
|     Caso, Capital | | 19,200 |
| To record write-off of deficit capital balance of insolvent partner. | | |

- This last allocation decreases Sheridan's capital account to an $8,143 negative total. Since this partner is personally solvent, that amount should be contributed to the partnership in accordance with regulations of the Uniform Partnership Act.

| | | |
|---|---:|---:|
| Cash | 8,143 | |
|     Sheridan, Capital | | 8,143 |
| To record contribution made to eliminate deficit capital balance. | | |

- Sheridan's contribution brings the final cash total for the partnership to $18,143. This amount is distributed to the two partners who continue to maintain positive capital balances: Andrews and Quinn (or Quinn's creditors).

| | Andrews, Capital | Quinn, Capital |
|---|---:|---:|
| Balances above | $18,400 | $16,200 |
| Caso deficit | (10,971) | (5,486) |
| Final balances | $ 7,429 | $10,714 |

| | | |
|---|---:|---:|
| Andrews, Capital | 7,429 | |
| Quinn, Capital | 10,714 | |
|     Cash | | 18,143 |
| To record distribution of remaining cash according to final capital balances. | | |

## Questions

1. What is the difference between the dissolution of a partnership and the liquidation of partnership property?
2. Why would the members of a partnership elect to terminate business operations and liquidate all noncash assets?
3. Why are liquidation gains and losses usually recorded as direct adjustments to the partners' capital accounts?
4. After liquidating all property and paying partnership obligations, on what basis is the remaining cash allocated among the partners?
5. What is the purpose of a schedule of liquidation? What information does this statement convey to its readers?
6. According to the Uniform Partnership Act, what events should occur if a partner incurs a negative capital balance during the liquidation process?
7. How are safe capital balances computed when preliminary distributions of cash are to be made during a partnership liquidation?
8. What is the purpose of the marshaling of assets doctrine? What does this doctrine specifically state?
9. A partner is personally insolvent. Can this partner's creditors claim partnership assets?

10. How do loans from partners affect the distribution of assets in a partnership liquidation? What alternatives can affect the handling of such loans?
11. What is the purpose of a proposed schedule of liquidation, and how is it developed?
12. How is a predistribution plan created for a partnership liquidation?

## Problems

1. If a partnership is liquidated, how is the final allocation of business assets made to the partners?
   a. Equally.
   b. According to the profit and loss ratio.
   c. According to the final capital account balances.
   d. According to the initial investment made by each of the partners.
2. Which of the following statements is true concerning the accounting that is made for a partnership going through liquidation?
   a. Gains and losses are reported directly as increases and decreases in the appropriate capital account.
   b. A separate income statement is created to measure only the profit or loss generated during liquidation.
   c. Since gains and losses rarely occur during liquidation, no special accounting treatment is warranted.
   d. Within a liquidation, all gains and losses are divided equally among the partners.
3. During a liquidation, if a partner's capital account balance drops below zero, what *should* happen?
   a. The other partners should file a legal suit against the partner with the deficit balance.
   b. The partner with the highest capital balance should contribute sufficient assets to eliminate the deficit.
   c. The deficit balance should be removed from the accounting records with only the remaining partners sharing in future gains and losses.
   d. The partner with a deficit should contribute enough assets to offset the deficit balance.
4. What is the marshaling of assets?
   a. A list of all partnership assets that is prepared whenever a formal accounting is to be made.
   b. A ranking of claims to be paid when a partner has become insolvent.
   c. The method by which a retiring partner's share of partnership is determined.
   d. The gathering of partnership assets just prior to the commencement of the liquidation process.
5. A local partnership is in the process of liquidating and is currently reporting the following capital balances:

   | | |
   |---|---:|
   | Angela, capital (50% share of all profits and losses) | $ 19,000 |
   | Woodrow, capital (30%) | 18,000 |
   | Cassidy, capital (20%) | (12,000) |

   Cassidy has indicated that the $12,000 deficit will be covered by a forthcoming contribution. However, the two remaining partners have asked to receive the $25,000 in cash that is presently available. How much of this money should each partner be given?
   a. Angela, $13,000; Woodrow, $12,000.
   b. Angela, $11,500; Woodrow, $13,500.
   c. Angela, $12,000; Woodrow, $13,000.
   d. Angela, $12,500; Woodrow, $12,500.
6. A local partnership is considering possible liquidation because one of the partners (Bell) is insolvent. Capital balances at the current time are as follows. Profits and losses are divided on a 4:3:2:1 basis, respectively.

   | | |
   |---|---:|
   | Bell, capital | $50,000 |
   | Hardy, capital | 56,000 |
   | Dennard, capital | 14,000 |
   | Suddath, capital | 80,000 |

Bell's creditors have filed a $21,000 claim against the partnership's assets. The partnership currently holds assets reported at $300,000 and liabilities of $100,000. If the assets can be sold for $190,000, what is the minimum amount that Bell's creditors would receive?
   a. –0–
   b. $2,000
   c. $2,800
   d. $6,000
7. What is a predistribution plan?
   a. A guideline for the cash distributions made to partners during a liquidation.
   b. A list of the procedures to be performed during a liquidation.
   c. A determination of the final cash distribution to be made to the partners on the settlement date.
   d. A detailed list of the transactions that will transpire in the reorganization of a partnership.
8. A partnership has the following balance sheet just before final liquidation is to begin:

| | | | |
|---|---|---|---|
| Cash | $ 26,000 | Liabilities | $ 50,000 |
| Inventory | 31,000 | Art, capital (40% of profits and losses) | 18,000 |
| Other assets | 62,000 | Raymond, capital (30%) | 25,000 |
| | | Darby, capital (30%) | 26,000 |
| Total | $119,000 | Total | $119,000 |

Liquidation expenses are estimated to be $12,000. The other assets are sold for $40,000. What distribution can be made to the partners?
   a. –0– to Art, $1,500 to Raymond, $2,500 to Darby.
   b. $1,333 to Art, $1,333 to Raymond, $1,334 to Darby.
   c. –0– to Art, $1,200 to Raymond, $2,800 to Darby.
   d. $600 to Art, $1,200 to Raymond, $2,200 to Darby.
9. A partnership has the following capital balances: A (20% of profits and losses) = $100,000; B (30% of profits and losses) = $120,000; C (50% of profits and losses) = $180,000. If the partnership is to be liquidated and $30,000 becomes immediately available, who gets that money?
   a. $6,000 to A, $9,000 to B, $15,000 to C.
   b. $22,000 to A, $3,000 to B, $5,000 to C.
   c. $22,000 to A, $8,000 to B, –0– to C.
   d. $24,000 to A, $6,000 to B, –0– to C.
10. A partnership is currently holding $400,000 in assets and $234,000 in liabilities. The partnership is to be liquidated and $20,000 is the best estimation of the expenses that will be incurred during this process. The four partners share profits and losses as shown. Capital balances at the start of the liquidation are as follows:

| | |
|---|---|
| Kevin, capital (40%) | $59,000 |
| Michael, capital (30%) | 39,000 |
| Brendan, capital (10%) | 34,000 |
| Jonathan, capital (20%) | 34,000 |

The partners realize that Brendan will be the first partner to start receiving cash. How much cash will Brendan receive before any of the other partners collect any cash?
   a. $12,250
   b. $14,750
   c. $17,000
   d. $19,500
11. Carney, Pierce, Menton, and Hoehn are partners who share profits and losses on a 4:3:2:1 basis, respectively. They are presently beginning to liquidate the business. At the start of this process, capital balances are as follows:

| | |
|---|---|
| Carney, capital | $60,000 |
| Pierce, capital | 27,000 |
| Menton, capital | 43,000 |
| Hoehn, capital | 20,000 |

Which of the following statements is true?
a. The first available $2,000 will go to Hoehn.
b. Carney will be the last partner to receive any available cash.
c. The first available $3,000 will go to Menton.
d. Carney will collect a portion of any available cash before Hoehn receives money.

12. A partnership has gone through liquidation and now reports the following account balances:

| | |
|---|---|
| Cash | $16,000 |
| Loan from Jones | 3,000 |
| Wayman, capital | (2,000) (deficit) |
| Jones, capital | (5,000) (deficit) |
| Fuller, capital | 13,000 |
| Rogers, capital | 7,000 |

Profits and losses are allocated on the following basis: Wayman, 30 percent; Jones, 20 percent; Fuller, 30 percent; and Rogers, 20 percent. Which of the following events should occur now?
a. Jones should receive $3,000 cash because of the loan balance.
b. Fuller should receive $11,800 and Rogers $4,200.
c. Fuller should receive $10,600 and Rogers $5,400.
d. Jones should receive $3,000, Fuller $8,800, and Rogers $4,200.

13. A partnership has the following account balances: Cash, $70,000; Other Assets, $540,000; Liabilities, $260,000; Nixon (50% of profits and losses), $170,000; Cleveland (30%), $110,000; Pierce (20%), $70,000. The company liquidates, and $8,000 becomes available to the partners. Who gets the $8,000?

14. A local partnership has only two assets (cash of $10,000 and land with a cost of $35,000). All liabilities have been paid and the following capital balances are currently being recorded. The partners share profits and losses as follows. All partners are insolvent.

| | |
|---|---|
| Brown, capital (40%) | $25,000 |
| Fish, capital (30%) | 15,000 |
| Stone, capital (30%) | 5,000 |

a. If the land is sold for $25,000, how much cash does each partner receive in a final settlement?
b. If the land is sold for $15,000, how much cash does each partner receive in a final settlement?
c. If the land is sold for $5,000, how much cash does each partner receive in a final settlement?

15. A local dental partnership has been liquidated and the final capital balances are as follows:

| | |
|---|---|
| Atkinson, capital (40% of all profits and losses) | $ 60,000 |
| Kaporale, capital (30%) | 20,000 |
| Dennsmore, capital (20%) | (30,000) |
| Rasputin, capital (10%) | (50,000) |

If Rasputin contributes additional cash of $20,000 to the partnership, what should happen to that money?

16. A partnership currently holds three assets: cash, $10,000; land, $35,000; and a building, $50,000. The partners anticipate that expenses required to liquidate their partnership will amount to $5,000. Capital balances are as follows:

| | | |
|---|---|---|
| Ace, capital | | $25,000 |
| Ball, capital | | 28,000 |
| Eaton, capital | | 20,000 |
| Lake, capital | | 22,000 |

The partners share profits and losses as follows: Ace (30%), Ball (30%), Eaton (20%), and Lake (20%). If a preliminary distribution of cash is to be made, how much will each of these partners receive?

17. The following condensed balance sheet is for the partnership of Hardwick, Saunders, and Ferris, who share profits and losses in the ratio of 4:3:3, respectively:

| | | | | |
|---|---|---|---|---|
| Cash | $ 90,000 | Accounts payable | | $210,000 |
| Other assets | 820,000 | Ferris, loan | | 40,000 |
| Hardwick, loan | 30,000 | Hardwick, capital | | 300,000 |
| | | Saunders, capital | | 200,000 |
| | | Ferris, capital | | 190,000 |
| Total assets | $940,000 | Total liabilities and capital | | $940,000 |

The partners decide to liquidate the partnership. Forty percent of the other assets are sold for $200,000. Prepare a proposed schedule of liquidation.

18. The following condensed balance sheet is for the partnership of Miller, Tyson, and Watson, who share profits and losses in the ratio of 6:2:2, respectively:

| | | | | |
|---|---|---|---|---|
| Cash | $ 40,000 | Liabilities | | $ 70,000 |
| Other assets | 140,000 | Miller, capital | | 50,000 |
| | | Tyson, capital | | 50,000 |
| | | Watson, capital | | 10,000 |
| Total assets | $180,000 | Total liabilities and capital | | $180,000 |

For how much money must the other assets be sold so that each partner receives some amount of cash in a liquidation?

19. A partnership's balance sheet is as follows:

| | | | | |
|---|---|---|---|---|
| Cash | $ 60,000 | Liabilities | | $ 50,000 |
| Noncash assets | 120,000 | Babb, capital | | 60,000 |
| | | Whitaker, capital | | 20,000 |
| | | Edwards, capital | | 50,000 |
| Total assets | $180,000 | Total liabilities and capital | | $180,000 |

Babb, Whitaker, and Edwards share profits and losses in the ratio of 4:2:4, respectively. This business is to be terminated, and the partners estimate that $8,000 in liquidation expenses will be incurred. How should the $2,000 in safe cash that is presently held be disbursed?

20. A partnership has liquidated all assets but still reports the following account balances:

| | |
|---|---|
| Loan from White | $ 6,000 |
| Black, capital | 3,000 |
| White, capital | (9,000) (deficit) |
| Green, capital | (3,000) (deficit) |
| Brown, capital | 15,000 |
| Blue, capital | (12,000) (deficit) |

The partners split profits and losses as follows: Black, 30 percent; White, 30 percent; Green, 10 percent; Brown, 20 percent; and Blue, 10 percent.

Assuming that all partners are personally insolvent except for Green and Brown, how much cash must Green now contribute to this partnership?

21. The following balance sheet is for a local partnership in which the partners have become very unhappy with each other.

| | | | |
|---|---|---|---|
| Cash | $ 40,000 | Liabilities | $ 30,000 |
| Land | 130,000 | Adams, capital | 80,000 |
| Building | 120,000 | Baker, capital | 30,000 |
| | | Carvil, capital | 60,000 |
| | | Dobbs, capital | 90,000 |
| Total assets | $290,000 | Total liabilities and capital | $290,000 |

To avoid further conflict, they have decided to cease operations and sell all assets. Using this information, answer the following questions. Each question should be viewed as an *independent* situation.

a. The partnership is to be liquidated, and the $10,000 cash that exceeds the partnership liabilities is to be disbursed immediately. If profits and losses are allocated to Adams, Baker, Carvil, and Dobbs on a 2:3:3:2 basis, respectively, how will the $10,000 be divided?

b. The partnership is to be liquidated and the $10,000 cash that exceeds the partnership liabilities is to be disbursed immediately. If profits and losses are allocated on a 2:2:3:3 basis, respectively, how will the $10,000 be divided?

c. The partnership is to be liquidated. The building is immediately sold for $70,000 to give total cash of $110,000. The liabilities are then paid, leaving a cash balance of $80,000. This cash is to be distributed to the partners. How much of this money will each partner get if profits and losses are allocated to Adams, Baker, Carvil, and Dobbs on a 1:3:3:3 basis, respectively?

d. The partnership is to be liquidated. Assume that profits and losses are allocated to Adams, Baker, Carvil, and Dobbs on a 1:3:4:2 basis, respectively. How much money must be received from selling the land and building to ensure that Carvil receives a portion?

22. The partnership of Larson, Norris, Spencer, and Harrison has decided to terminate operations and liquidate all business property. During this process, the partners expect to incur $8,000 in liquidation expenses. All of the partners are currently solvent.

The balance sheet reported by this partnership at the time that the liquidation commenced follows. The percentages indicate the allocation of profits and losses to each of the four partners.

| | | | |
|---|---|---|---|
| Cash | $ 28,250 | Liabilities | $ 47,000 |
| Accounts receivable | 44,000 | Larson, capital (20%) | 15,000 |
| Inventory | 39,000 | Norris, capital (30%) | 60,000 |
| Land and buildings | 23,000 | Spencer, capital (20%) | 75,000 |
| Equipment | 104,000 | Harrison, capital (30%) | 41,250 |
| Total assets | $238,250 | Total liabilities and capital | $238,250 |

Based on the information that has been provided, prepare a predistribution plan for the liquidation of this partnership.

23. The following partnership is being liquidated beginning on July 13, 2004:

| | | | |
|---|---|---|---|
| Cash | $ 36,000 | Liabilities | $50,000 |
| Noncash assets | 174,000 | Able, loan | 10,000 |
| | | Able, capital (20%) | 40,000 |
| | | Moon, capital (30%) | 60,000 |
| | | Yerkl, capital (50%) | 50,000 |

a. Liquidation expenses are estimated to be $12,000. Prepare a predistribution schedule to guide the distribution of cash.
b. Assume that assets costing $28,000 are sold for $40,000. How is the available cash to be divided?

24. A local partnership is to be liquidated. Commissions and other liquidation expenses are expected to total $19,000. The business's balance sheet prior to the commencement of liquidation is as follows:

| | | | |
|---|---|---|---|
| Cash | $ 27,000 | Liabilities | $ 40,000 |
| Noncash assets | 254,000 | Simpson, capital (20%) | 18,000 |
| | | Hart, capital (40%) | 40,000 |
| | | Bobb, capital (20%) | 48,000 |
| | | Reidl, capital (20%) | 135,000 |
| Total assets | $281,000 | Total liabilities and capital | $281,000 |

Prepare a predistribution schedule for this partnership.

25. The following information concerns two different partnerships. These problems should be viewed as independent situations.

**Part A**

The partnership of Ross, Milburn, and Thomas has the following account balances:

| | | | |
|---|---|---|---|
| Cash | $36,000 | Liabilities | $17,000 |
| Noncash assets | 100,000 | Ross, capital | 69,000 |
| | | Milburn, capital | (8,000) (deficit) |
| | | Thomas, capital | 58,000 |

This partnership is in the process of being liquidated. Ross and Milburn are each entitled to 40 percent of all profits and losses with the remaining 20 percent to Thomas.

a. What is the maximum amount that Milburn might have to contribute to this partnership because of the deficit capital balance?
b. How should the $19,000 cash that is presently available in excess of liabilities be distributed?
c. If the noncash assets are sold for a total of $41,000, what is the minimum amount of cash that Thomas could receive?

**Part B**

The partnership of Sampson, Klingon, Carton, and Romulan is being liquidated and currently holds cash of $9,000 but no other assets. Liabilities amount to $24,000. The capital balances are as follows:

| | |
|---|---|
| Sampson | $ 9,000 |
| Klingon | (17,000) |
| Carton | 5,000 |
| Romulan | (12,000) |

Profits and losses are allocated on the following basis: Sampson, 40 percent, Klingon, 20 percent, Carton, 30 percent, and Romulan, 10 percent.

a. If both Klingon and Romulan are personally insolvent, how much money must Carton contribute to this partnership?
b. If only Romulan is personally insolvent, how much money must Klingon contribute? How will these funds be disbursed?
c. If only Klingon is personally insolvent, how much money should Sampson receive from the liquidation?

26. March, April, and May have been in partnership for a number of years. The partners allocate all profits and losses on a 2:3:1 basis, respectively. Recently, the partners have each become personally insolvent and, thus, have decided to liquidate the business in hope of remedying their personal financial problems. As of September 1, 2004, the partnership balance sheet is as follows:

| | | | |
|---|---|---|---|
| Cash | $ 11,000 | Liabilities | $ 61,000 |
| Accounts receivable | 84,000 | March, capital | 25,000 |
| Inventory | 74,000 | April, capital | 75,000 |
| Land, building, and equipment (net) | 38,000 | May, capital | 46,000 |
| Total assets | $207,000 | Total liabilities and capital | $207,000 |

Prepare journal entries for the following transactions:
a. Sold all of the inventory for $56,000 cash.
b. Paid $7,500 in liquidation expenses.
c. Paid $40,000 of the partnership's liabilities.
d. Collected $45,000 of the accounts receivable.
e. Distributed safe cash balances; no further liquidation expenses are anticipated by the partners.
f. Sold remaining accounts receivable for 30 percent of face value.
g. Sold land, building, and equipment for $17,000.
h. Paid all remaining liabilities of the partnership.
i. Distributed cash held by the business to the partners.

27. The partnership of W, X, Y, and Z has the following balance sheet:

| | | | |
|---|---|---|---|
| Cash | $30,000 | Liabilities | $42,000 |
| Other assets | 220,000 | W, capital (50% of profits and losses) | 60,000 |
| | | X, capital (30%) | 78,000 |
| | | Y, capital (10%) | 40,000 |
| | | Z, capital (10%) | 30,000 |

Z is personally insolvent and one of his creditors is considering suing the partnership for the $5,000 that is currently due. The creditor realizes that liquidation could result from this litigation and does not wish to force such an extreme action unless the creditor is reasonably sure of getting the money that is due. If the other assets are sold, how much money must the partnership receive to ensure that $5,000 would become available from Z's portion of the business? Liquidation expenses are expected to be $15,000.

28. On January 1, 2004, the partners of Van, Bakel, and Cox (who share profits and losses in the ratio of 5:3:2, respectively) decide to liquidate their partnership. The trial balance at this date is as follows:

| | Debit | Credit |
|---|---|---|
| Cash | $ 18,000 | |
| Accounts receivable | 66,000 | |
| Inventory | 52,000 | |
| Machinery and equipment, net | 189,000 | |
| Van, loan | 30,000 | |
| Accounts payable | | $ 53,000 |
| Bakel, loan | | 20,000 |
| Van, capital | | 118,000 |
| Bakel, capital | | 90,000 |
| Cox, capital | | 74,000 |
| Totals | $355,000 | $355,000 |

The partners plan a program of piecemeal conversion of the business's assets to minimize liquidation losses. All available cash, less an amount retained to provide for future expenses, is to be distributed to the partners at the end of each month. A summary of the liquidation transactions is as follows:

**2004**

January   Collected $51,000 of the accounts receivable; the balance is deemed uncollectible.

Received $38,000 for the entire inventory.

Paid $2,000 in liquidation expenses.

Paid $50,000 to the outside creditors after offsetting a $3,000 credit memorandum received by the partnership on January 11, 2004.

Retained $10,000 cash in the business at the end of January to cover any unrecorded liabilities and anticipated expenses. The remainder is distributed to the partners.

February   Paid $3,000 in liquidation expenses.

Retained $6,000 cash in the business at the end of the month to cover unrecorded liabilities and anticipated expenses.

March   Received $146,000 on the sale of all machinery and equipment.

Paid $5,000 in final liquidation expenses.

Retained no cash in the business.

Prepare a schedule to compute the safe installment payments made to the partners at the end of each of these three months.

29. Following is a series of *independent cases*. In each situation, indicate the cash distribution to be made at the end of the liquidation process. *Unless otherwise stated, assume that all solvent partners will reimburse the partnership for their deficit capital balances.*

### Part A

The following accounts are presently being reported by the Simon, Haynes, and Jackson partnership: Jackson is personally insolvent and can contribute only an additional $3,000 to the partnership. Simon is also insolvent and has no available funds.

| | |
|---|---:|
| Cash | $ 30,000 |
| Liabilities | 22,000 |
| Haynes, loan | 10,000 |
| Simon, capital (40%) | 16,000 |
| Haynes, capital (20%) | (6,000) |
| Jackson, capital (40%) | (12,000) |

### Part B

Hough, Luck, and Cummings operate a local accounting firm as a partnership. After working together for several years, they have decided to liquidate the partnership's property. The partners have prepared the following balance sheet:

| | | | |
|---|---:|---|---:|
| Cash | $ 20,000 | Liabilities | $ 40,000 |
| Hough, loan | 8,000 | Luck, loan | 10,000 |
| Noncash assets | 162,000 | Hough, capital (50%) | 90,000 |
| | | Luck, capital (40%) | 30,000 |
| | | Cummings, capital (10%) | 20,000 |
| Total assets | $190,000 | Total liabilities and capital | $190,000 |

The noncash assets are sold for $80,000, with $21,000 of this amount being used to pay liquidation expenses. All three of these partners are personally insolvent.

### Part C

Use the same information as in Part B, but assume that the profits and losses are split 2:4:4 to Hough, Luck, and Cummings, respectively, and that liquidation expenses are only $6,000.

### Part D

Following the liquidation of all noncash assets, the partnership of Redmond, Ledbetter, Watson, and Sandridge has the following account balances:

| | |
|---|---|
| Liabilities | $ 28,000 |
| Redmond, loan | 5,000 |
| Redmond, capital (20%) | (21,000) |
| Ledbetter, capital (10%) | (30,000) |
| Watson, capital (30%) | 3,000 |
| Sandridge, capital (40%) | 15,000 |

Redmond is personally insolvent.

30. The partnership of Frick, Wilson, and Clarke has elected to cease all operations and liquidate its business property. A balance sheet drawn up at this time shows the following account balances:

| | | | |
|---|---|---|---|
| Cash | $ 48,000 | Liabilities | $ 35,000 |
| Noncash assets | 177,000 | Frick, capital (60%) | 101,000 |
| | | Wilson, capital (20%) | 28,000 |
| | | Clarke, capital (20%) | 61,000 |
| Total assets | $225,000 | Total liabilities and capital | $225,000 |

The following transactions occur in liquidating this business:
- Distributed safe capital balances immediately to the partners. Liquidation expenses of $9,000 are estimated as a basis for this computation.
- Sold noncash assets with a book value of $80,000 for $48,000.
- Paid all liabilities.
- Distributed safe capital balances again.
- Sold remaining noncash assets for $44,000.
- Paid liquidation expenses of $7,000.
- Distributed remaining cash to the partners and closed the financial records of the business permanently.

Produce a final schedule of liquidation for this partnership.

31. **Part A**

The partnership of Wingler, Norris, Rodgers, and Guthrie was formed several years ago as a local architectural firm. Several of the partners have recently undergone personal financial problems and decided to terminate operations and liquidate the business. The following balance sheet is drawn up as a guideline for this process:

| | | | |
|---|---|---|---|
| Cash | $ 15,000 | Liabilities | $ 74,000 |
| Accounts receivable | 82,000 | Rodgers, loan | 35,000 |
| Inventory | 101,000 | Wingler, capital (30%) | 120,000 |
| Land | 85,000 | Norris, capital (10%) | 88,000 |
| Building and | | Rodgers, capital (20%) | 74,000 |
| equipment (net) | 168,000 | Guthrie, capital (40%) | 60,000 |
| Total assets | $451,000 | Total liabilities and capital | $451,000 |

When the liquidation commenced, expenses of $16,000 were anticipated as being necessary to dispose of all property.

Prepare a predistribution plan for this partnership.

**Part B**

The following transactions transpire during the liquidation of the Wingler, Norris, Rodgers, and Guthrie partnership:
- Collected 80 percent of the total accounts receivable with the rest judged as uncollectible.

- Sold the land, building, and equipment for $150,000.
- Made safe capital distributions.
- Guthrie, who has become personally insolvent, will make no further contributions.
- Paid all liabilities.
- Sold all inventory for $71,000.
- Made safe capital distributions again.
- Paid liquidation expenses of $11,000.
- Made final cash disbursements to the partners based on the assumption that all partners other than Guthrie are personally solvent.

Prepare journal entries to record these liquidation transactions.

# Develop Your Skills

## RESEARCH CASE 1

One of the clients of the CPA firm of Harston and Mendez is a medical practice of seven local doctors. One doctor has been sued for several million dollars as the result of a recent operation. Because of what appears to be very poor judgment by this doctor, a patient died. Although that doctor was solely involved with the patient in question, the lawsuit names the entire practice as a defendant. Originally, four of these doctors formed this business as a general partnership. However, five years ago, the partners converted the business to a limited liability partnership based on the laws of the state in which they operate.

Read the following articles as well as any other published information that is available on partner and partnership liability:

"Partners Forever, Within Andersen, Personal Liability May Bring Ruin," *The Wall Street Journal*, April 2, 2002, p. C1.

"Collapse: Speed of Andersen's Demise Amazing," *Milwaukee Journal Sentinel*, June 16, 2002, p. D1.

### Required:
Based on the facts presented in this case, answer these questions:
a. What liability do the other six partners in this medical practice have in connection with this lawsuit?
b. What factors will be important in determining the exact liability (if any) of these six doctors?

## ANALYSIS CASE 1

Go to the website http://www.napico.com/napico/10q/99q4/NTCI_10K_99.pdf.

At this site, the 1999 financial statements for the partnership National Tax Credit Investors II can be found. Read these financial statements as well as the accompanying notes, especially any that discuss the partnership form of organization.

Assume that an investor is considering making an investment in this partnership and has downloaded these statements for study and analysis.

### Required:
a. What differences are there between these statements and those of an incorporated entity?
b. Assume that this investor is not aware of the potential implications of owning a partnership rather than a corporation. What information is available in these statements to advise this individual of the unique characteristics of this legal business form?

## COMMUNICATION CASE 1

Read the following as well as any other published articles on the bankruptcy of the partnership of Laventhol & Horwath:

> "Laventhol Says It Plans to File for Chapter 11," *The Wall Street Journal*, November 20, 1990, p.A3.
> "Laventhol Partners Face Long Process That Could End in Personal Bankruptcy," *The Wall Street Journal*, November 20, 1990, p. B5.
> "Laventhol Bankruptcy Filing Indicates Liabilities May Be As Much As $2 Billion," *The Wall Street Journal*, November 23, 1990. p. A4.

### Required:

Write a report describing the potential liabilities incurred by the members of a partnership.

## COMMUNICATION CASE 2

Read the following as well as any other published articles on the breakup of a partnership:

> "Partnerships: If There's a Beginning . . . There's an End," *National Public Accountant*, April 1992.
> "Reconcilable Differences," *Inc.*, April 1991.
> "Cutting Losses When Partners Face a Breakup," *The Wall Street Journal*, May 21, 1991, p. B1.

### Required:

Write a report describing various situations that can lead to the dissolution of a partnership.

## EXCEL CASE 1

The partnership of Wilson, Cho, and Arrington has the following account information:

| Partner | Capital Balance | Share of Profits and Losses |
|---|---|---|
| Wilson | $200,000 | 40% |
| Cho | 180,000 | 20 |
| Arrington | 110,000 | 40 |

This partnership will be liquidated, and the partners are scheduled to receive cash equal to any ending positive capital balance. If a negative capital balance results, the partner is expected to contribute that amount.

Assume that losses of $50,000 occur during the liquidation followed later by additional and final losses of $100,000.

### Required:

a. Create a spreadsheet to determine the capital balances that remain for each of the three partners after these two losses are incurred.
b. Modify this spreadsheet so that it can be used for different capital balances, different allocation patterns, and different liquidation gains and losses.

# Chapter Eleven

# Accounting for State and Local Governments (Part 1)

### Questions to Consider

- Why did the GASB believe that radical changes were needed in the reporting of state and local governments?
- How has *GASB Statement No. 34* affected the financial reporting of state and local governments?
- Who are the users of the financial data produced by state and local government units, and why is such a wide variety of informational needs encountered?
- What is fund accounting, and why do state and local governments utilize it?
- Why is budgetary control considered so important in a government? In what ways is budgetary control established in the accounting system?
- How do government-wide financial statements differ from fund-based financial statements and why are two sets of financial statements necessary?
- What measurement focus and basis of accounting are utilized in the various financial statements produced for a state or local government?
- When does a government recognize revenues, expenses, and expenditures?

Probably no pronouncement in the history of accounting has had more impact on an area of financial reporting than *Statement 34* of the Governmental Accounting Standards Board (GASB) entitled "Basic Financial Statements—and Management's Discussion and Analysis—for State and Local Governments." This 400-page document issued in June 1999 affected virtually every area of financial reporting by state and local government units. Major changes were made in the way that these governments had traditionally reported their operations and financial position. More important, an entirely new method of reporting was devised and added to the financial statements being externally distributed.

Consequently, with just this one official statement, fund accounting, which had served as the basis of reporting by state and local governments for decades, was modified significantly and an entirely new group of financial statements was created based on a completely different approach to financial reporting. State and local government units now must produce and report not one but two sets of financial statements with widely differing information. Not surprisingly, reaction to *GASB Statement 34* was quite vocal:

> With *GASB Statement 34,* the board has taken a bold step forward in the evolution and refinement of government financial reporting.[1]

> *GASB 34* changes the notion of accountability, elevating the importance of full cost, giving prominence to long-term debt and assets, assessing year-to-year financial improvements for the government as a whole, and in general, making greater use of business criteria.[2]

> The Governmental Accounting Standards Board (GASB) describes *Statement 34* as "the most comprehensive governmental accounting rule ever developed." Unfortunately, the statement has serious defects, but they can be remedied.[3]

---

[1] Robert J. Freeman and Craig D. Shoulders, "A Bold Step Forward," *The Government Accountants Journal,* Spring 2000, p. 15.

[2] John Sacco, "Part of Changing Political and Global Market Pressures," *The Government Accountants Journal,* Spring 2000, p. 20.

[3] Robert N. Anthony and Susan M. Newberry, "GASB 34 Should Be Revised," *The Government Accountants Journal,* Spring 2000, p. 36.

Because of the magnitude of the changes, the application of *GASB Statement 34* has been phased in over several years. Governments with total annual revenues of $100 million or more had to follow the provisions of this pronouncement starting in fiscal periods beginning after June 15, 2001. If total annual revenues were $10 million or more but less than $100 million, *GASB Statement 34* had to be utilized for financial statements created for periods beginning after June 15, 2002. Smaller governments with less than $10 million in total revenues were not required to apply these new rules until periods beginning after June 15, 2003. Therefore, most large government units adopted these new requirements in their financial statements for the year ending June 30, 2002. Obviously, this is a period of extreme change in government accounting.

After adopting *GASB Statement 34*, governments must still report information through fund-based financial statements that are similar to the traditional method of reporting that has been used for decades. In addition, the same events must be reported in a very different manner through newly created government-wide financial statements. To help understand both approaches, this chapter focuses on the handling of typical transactions. Where necessary, two different methods of accounting are shown. Only in that way can the distinctions between the traditional fund-based accounting and the new government-wide accounting be highlighted. The next chapter demonstrates how all of the resulting information is actually reported within the various financial statements that must be produced.

## INTRODUCTION TO THE ACCOUNTING FOR STATE AND LOCAL GOVERNMENTS

In this country, literally thousands of state and local government reporting entities touch the lives of the citizenry on a daily basis. In 2002, nearly 90,000 local government units existed just in the United States.[4] Income and sales taxes are collected, property taxes are assessed, schools are operated, fire departments are maintained, garbage is collected, and roads are paved. Actions of one or more governments affect every individual.

Accounting for a government is not merely a matching of expenses with revenues so that net income can be determined. The allocation of limited resources between such worthy causes as education, police, welfare, and the environment creates heated debates throughout the nation. To keep the public informed so that proper decisions can be made, government reporting has historically identified the source of financial resources and what use is made of them, which activities are financed and which are not. Indeed, this approach is appropriate for the short-term decisions necessitated by gathering and allocating financial resources. For the longer term, though, information is needed to reflect the overall financial stability of the government, one primary goal of the changes mandated by *GASB Statement 34*.

A slow evolution has transpired in the generally accepted accounting principles used by state and local governments. The American Institute of Certified Public Accountants (AICPA) and the National Council on Governmental Accounting (NCGA) made significant strides during previous decades in establishing sound accounting principles.[5] In June 1984, the Governmental

---

[4] U.S. Department of Commerce, Bureau of the Census, 2002 Census of Governments, GC02-1(P) (Washington, DC: U. S. Government Printing Office), p. 1.

[5] The NCGA was a quasi-independent agency of the Government Finance Officers Association. The NCGA held authority for state and local government accounting from 1973 through 1984. The National Committee on Municipal Accounting had this responsibility from 1934 until 1941, and the National Committee on Governmental Accounting established government accounting principles from 1949 through 1954 and again from 1967 until 1973. During several periods, no group held primary responsibility for the development of governmental accounting. For an overview of the history of governmental accounting standards and the creation of the GASB, see David R. Bean, "The Evolution of Governmental Accounting Standard Setting," *Governmental Finance*, December 1984. Another coverage of the history in this area can be found in Martin Ives, "The Governmental Accounting Standards Board: Factors Influencing Its Operation and Initial Technical Agenda," *The Government Accountants Journal*, Spring 2000.

Accounting Standards Board (GASB) became the public sector counterpart of the Financial Accounting Standards Board. The GASB holds the primary responsibility in the United States for setting authoritative accounting standards for state and local government units.

In the same manner as the Financial Accounting Standards Board, the GASB is an independent body functioning under the oversight of the Financial Accounting Foundation. Thus, a formal mechanism is in place to continue the development of governmental accounting. Since the time of its creation, the GASB has produced a number of governmental accounting standards as well as technical bulletins, interpretations, and a concepts statement. In 1997, the GASB produced a codification of authoritative pronouncements as a guideline for reporting purposes.

## Governmental Accounting—User Needs

The unique aspects of governmental accounting are a direct result of the perceived needs of financial statement users. Identification of these informational requirements is, therefore, a logical first step in the study of the accounting principles applied to state and local governments. Specific procedures utilized in the reporting process can be understood best as an outgrowth of these needs. Often, though, user expectations are complex and even contradictory. The taxpayer, the government employee, the bondholder, and the public official may each be seeking distinctly different types of financial information about a governmental unit.

> My own reflection on the subject leads me to the conviction that appropriate and adequate accounting for state and local governmental units involves a far more complex set of interrelationships, to be reported to a more diverse set of users with a greater variety of interests and needs, than exists in business accounting and reporting.[6]

In its *Concepts Statement No. 1*, "Objectives of Financial Reporting," the GASB recognized this same problem by identifying three groups of primary users of external state and local governmental financial reports: the citizenry, legislative and oversight bodies, and creditors and investors. The needs and interests of each of these groups were then described:

**Citizenry**—Want to evaluate the likelihood of tax or service fee increases, to determine the sources and uses of resources, to forecast revenues in order to influence spending decisions, to ensure that resources were used in accordance with appropriations, to assess financial condition, and to compare budgeted to actual results.
**Legislative and oversight bodies**—Want to assess the overall financial condition when developing budgets and program recommendations, to monitor operating results to assure compliance with mandates, to determine the reasonableness of fees and the need for tax changes, and to ascertain the ability to finance new programs and capital needs.
**Investors and creditors**—Want to know the amount of available and likely future financial resources, to measure the debt position and the ability to service that debt, and to review operating results and cash flow data.[7]

Thus, a significant obstacle is encountered in the quest for fair governmental reporting: User needs are so broad that no one set of financial statements or accounting principles can possibly satisfy all expectations. How can voters, bondholders, city officials, and the other users of the financial statements provided by state and local governments all receive the information that they need for decision-making purposes? The question of satisfying a wide variety of user needs is a constant theme in discussions of state and local government accounting.

Eventually, the desire to produce financial statements that would satisfy such diverse demands for information led the GASB to require the production of two distinct sets of statements.

> **Fund-based financial statements** have been designed "to show restrictions on the planned use of resources or to measure, *in the short term*, the revenues and expenditures arising from certain activities."[8]

---

[6] Robert K. Mautz, "Financial Reporting: Should Government Emulate Business?" *Journal of Accountancy,* August 1981, p. 53.
[7] *GASB Concepts Statement No. 1,* "Objectives of Financial Reporting," May 1987, para. 33–37.
[8] *Governmental Accounting Standards Board Statement No. 34,* "Basic Financial Statements—and Management's Discussion and Analysis—for State and Local Governments," June 1999, preface p. 1.

• **Government-wide financial statements** will have a longer-term focus because they will report "*all* revenues and *all* costs of providing services each year, not just those received or paid in the current year or soon after year-end."[9]

Fund-based financial statements focus on specific activities and the amount of financial resources given to those activities as well as the use made of those resources. For example, these fund-based financial statements should tell the amount spent this year on such services as public safety, education, health and sanitation, and the construction of a new road. The primary measurement focus in these statements is on the flow and amount of current financial resources while the timing of recognition in most cases is a system known as *modified accrual accounting*. Modified accrual accounting recognizes revenues when the current financial resources are measurable and available to be used and expenditures when they cause a reduction in current financial resources.

In contrast, government-wide financial statements report a government's activities and financial position as a whole. This approach helps users make long-term evaluations of the financial decisions and stability of the government by allowing them to:

- Assess the finances of the government in its entirety, including the year's operating results.
- Determine whether the government's overall financial position improved or deteriorated.
- Evaluate whether the government's current-year revenues were sufficient to pay for current-year services.
- See the cost of providing services to its citizenry.
- See how the government finances its programs—through user fees and other program revenues versus general tax revenues.
- Understand the extent to which the government has invested in capital assets, including roads, bridges, and other infrastructure assets.
- Make better comparisons between governments.[10]

To achieve these goals, the government-wide financial statements measurement focus is on all economic resources (not just current financial resources), and it utilizes accrual accounting much like any for-profit entity. All assets and liabilities are reported and all revenues and expenses are recognized in a way comparable to business-type accounting. In announcing the change to *GASB Statement 34*, the city manager of Sacramento, California, explained: "New government-wide financial statements are designed to provide readers with a broad overview of the City in a manner similar to a private-sector business."

## Financial Accountability

Despite the variety of users, one aspect of governmental reporting has remained constant over the years: the goal of making the government accountable to the public. Because of the essential role of democracy within U.S. society, governmental accounting principles have attempted to provide a vehicle for evaluating the actions of the government. Citizens should be aware of the means used by officials to raise money and the allocations made of these scarce resources. Voters must evaluate the wisdom, as well as the honesty, of the members of government. Since most voters are also taxpayers, they naturally exhibit special interest in the results obtained from their involuntary contributions, such as taxes. *Because elected and appointed officials hold authority over the public's money, governmental reporting has traditionally stressed this stewardship responsibility.*

> Accountability is the cornerstone of all financial reporting in government. . . . Accountability requires governments to answer to the citizenry—to justify the raising of public resources and the purposes for which they are used. Governmental accountability is based on the belief that the citizenry has a "right to know," a right to receive openly declared facts that may lead to public debate by the citizens and their elected representatives.[11]

---

[9] Ibid., p. 2.
[10] Ibid., p. 3.
[11] *GASB Concepts Statement No. 1*, para. 56.

For this reason, accounting emphasis has traditionally been directed toward measuring and identifying the resources generated and expended by each of a government's diverse activities. *GASB Statement 34* is not an attempt to overturn this reporting philosophy. Instead, this pronouncement actually seeks to refine the reporting of individual government activities and then go beyond that to provide information about the government as a whole.

Accountability is most associated with the fund-based statements. In general, the fund-based financial statements are used to answer three questions:

- How did the government generate its current financial resources?
- Where did those financial resources go?
- What amount of those financial resources is presently held?

The term *current financial resources* normally encompasses monetary assets that are available to be spent by officials to meet the government's needs. Thus, when measuring current financial resources, a government is primarily monitoring cash, investments, and receivables. To stress and monitor financial accountability, the traditional government accounting system has focused on these financial resources as well as current claims against them. For this reason, little reporting emphasis has been historically placed on accounts such as Buildings, Equipment, and Long-Term Debts that have no direct impact on current financial resources.

Obviously, stressing government accountability in the use of current financial resources is an approach to accounting that by itself is not capable of meeting all user needs; thus, many conventional reporting objectives long have been ignored. Not surprisingly, investors and creditors have frequently been sharp critics of governmental accounting. "When cities get into financial trouble, few citizens know about it until the day the interest can't be met or the teachers paid. . . . Had the books been kept like any decent corporation's that could never have happened."[12]

Although accountability is a central concern, other user needs must be addressed in government reporting. Consequently, the inclusion of government-wide financial statements has now been mandated by *GASB Statement 34* to provide an additional dimension for government reporting. These statements do not focus on current financial resources but seek to report all of the assets at the disposal of government officials as well as all liabilities that must eventually be paid. Likewise, all revenues and expenses are recognized according to accrual accounting to provide a completely different level of financial information.

## Control of Public Funds

Over the decades, the desire to stress accountability has led to a system of procedures that convey information to the public about current financial resources while helping to establish control over these public funds. This process is especially important since public officials often hold authority over sums of money that can be staggering in size. The city of Boston, Massachusetts, for example, reported revenues of nearly $1.5 billion for the year ending June 30, 2001. Such funds are accumulated through charges and taxes. Although laws require the appropriate utilization of such monies, compliance is not always easy for the average citizen to ascertain.

Stressing accountability and the stewardship role played by government officials is in diametric contrast to a profit-oriented business to which stockholders contribute capital voluntarily and then elect a board of directors to monitor operating and financial activities. Board members along with stockholders and other interested parties have access to accounting data, such as net income, earnings per share, and return on investment, which allows an assessment to be made of management's utilization of the resources provided. In a government, though, oversight and computed measures of success are more difficult to achieve. For example, neither net income nor earnings per share can measure the performance of a fire department.

Because of the citizens' desire to monitor elected officials, governmental accounting has developed its own specialized control procedures. Budgets, for example, must be legally adopted by a government's legislative body to indicate anticipated revenues and approved expenditures. To highlight these projections, many of the budget figures are physically entered

---

[12] Richard Greene, "You Can't Fight City Hall—If You Can't Understand It," *Forbes,* March 3, 1980, p. 92.

into the government's accounting records and then presented within required supplemental information attached to the annual financial statements. In this manner, comparisons can be drawn between the expected activity for each specific function and actual revenue and expenditure figures.

Additional control over government spending is achieved by recording purchase commitments (commonly referred to as *encumbrances*). The acquisition of a fax machine, for example, is formally journalized as an encumbrance when the item is ordered rather than when the title transfers. By measuring both expended as well as committed funds, the entity is less likely to overspend available resources. Through the creation of two separate sets of financial statements, the GASB obviously wanted to retain the control features traditionally found in government accounting while adding another layer of information to report the overall finances and activities of the state or locality.

## Reporting Diverse Governmental Activities—Fund Accounting

Financial accountability and the desire to establish control over financial resources have had major impacts on the historical development of government accounting. In addition, the accountant also faces the challenge of reporting the diverse array of activities found within most government units. Because no common profit motive exists to tie all of these functions and services together, consolidated balances have historically been omitted. Combining operating results from the city zoo, the fire department, the motor pool, the water system, and the like would provide figures of questionable utility if accountability and control over the usage of current financial resources is the primary goal.

For this reason, an underlying assumption of government accounting has been that most statement users prefer information segregated by function so that each activity can be assessed individually. Hence, the accounting process has evolved over the years to accumulate separate data to describe the financial affairs of every activity (library, school system, police department, road construction, etc.). Then revenues, expenditures, financial resources, and the like can be reported for each specific function. *GASB Statement 34* continues to retain much of this focus while adding government-wide financial statements to provide a broader view of the government as a whole.

The diversity inherent within most state or local government units mandates that a single set of accounting records simply is not sufficient to monitor all of the various activities. Therefore, financial transactions and adjustments are recorded in quasi-independent bookkeeping systems referred to as *funds*. *Each fund is a self-balancing set of accounts used to record data generated by an identifiable government function.* In other words, a fund is the accounting system for a particular activity.

> The diverse nature of governmental operations and the necessity of assuring legal compliance preclude recording and summarizing all governmental financial transactions and balances in a single accounting entity. Unlike a private business, which is accounted for as a single entity, a governmental unit is accounted for through several separate fund and account group entities, each accounting for designated assets, liabilities, and equity or other balances.[13]

Although a single list of separately reportable functions of a state or local government is not possible, the following frequently are encountered:

| | |
|---|---|
| Public safety | Judicial system |
| Highway maintenance | Debt repayment |
| Sanitation | Bridge construction |
| Health | Water and sewer system |
| Welfare | Municipal swimming pool |
| Culture and recreation | Data processing center |
| Education | Endowment funds |
| Parks | Employee pensions |

---

[13] *Codification of Governmental Accounting and Financial Reporting Standards* (Norwalk, Conn.: Governmental Accounting Standards Board, 1997), sec. 1300.101.

For external control purposes, the actual number of separate funds in use depends on the extent of services being offered by the government and the grouping of related activities. As an example, separate funds may be set up to account for a high school and its athletic programs, or these activities may be combined into a single fund.

> The general rule is to establish the minimum number of separate funds consistent with legal specifications and operational requirements. . . . Using too many funds causes inflexibility and undue complexity . . . and is best avoided in the interest of efficient and economical financial administrations.[14]

If a government had to account for only service activities such as police and fire protection, reporting problems could be minimized. Although establishing separate funds would still be necessary for the individual functions, accounting procedures could be similar in each case if not identical. However, many government operations (such as municipal golf courses, toll roads, convention centers, and airports) attempt to generate revenues rather than simply serve the populace. Because this goal parallels that held by business-type enterprises, traditional government accounting procedures are not appropriate to these functions. In effect, a municipality cannot fully report the activities of a police department and a golf course by using the same accounting principles; the objectives are simply viewed as too diverse.

To add to the accountant's difficulty, a third distinct type of government function (beyond governmental activities and business-type activities) also can be identified. State and local governments frequently serve in a trustee capacity, holding money or other assets for the benefit of an outside party. Employee pension funds, for example, often are maintained by a government so that workers can receive benefits after their retirement.

## Fund Accounting Classifications

Consequently, all funds of a state or local government can be categorized into one of three distinct groups. In reporting under traditional governmental accounting, this classification system allows for a clearer reporting of the government's various activities. Furthermore, having three separate groups of accounts allows for different accounting principles to be applied to different activities. The three groups are as follows:

- *Governmental funds*—account for activities of a government that are carried out primarily to provide services to citizens and that are financed primarily through taxes. A police department should be reported within the governmental funds.
- *Proprietary funds*—account for a government's ongoing organizations and activities that are similar to those operated by for-profit organizations. This fund type normally encompasses operations that assess a user charge so that determining operating income or cost recovery is important. A toll road would be reported within the proprietary funds.
- *Fiduciary funds*—account for monies held by the government in a trustee capacity. Such assets must be held for others and cannot be used by the government for its own programs. Assets held for a pension plan would be reported within the fiduciary funds.

### Governmental Funds

In most state or municipal accounting systems, the governmental funds tend to dominate because a service orientation usually prevails. For internal reporting purposes, individual records are maintained for every distinct function: public safety, libraries, construction of a town hall, and so on. In each of these governmental funds, current financial resources are accumulated and expended to achieve one or more desired public goals.

To provide better reported information and control, the governmental funds are subdivided into five categories: the General Fund, Special Revenue Funds, Capital Projects Funds, Debt Service Fund, and Permanent Funds. This classification system allows specific accounting guidelines to be directed toward each fund type while providing an overall structure for financial reporting purposes.

---

[14] GASB Cod. Sec. 1100.108.

***The General Fund*** The GASB's definition of the General Fund appears to be somewhat understated: "to account for all financial resources except those required to be accounted for in another fund."[15] This description seems to imply that the General Fund records only miscellaneous revenues and expenditures when, in actuality, this fund type accounts for many of a government's most important services. Whereas the other governmental funds report specific events or projects, the General Fund records a broad range of ongoing activities. For example, the 2001 financial statements for the city of Baltimore, Maryland, disclose 11 major areas of current expenditures within its General Fund: general government, public safety and regulations, conservation of health, social services, education, public library, recreation and culture, highways and streets, sanitation and waste removal, public service, and economic development. Expenditures reported for these categories of the General Fund made up more than 60 percent of the total for all of the city's governmental funds for the year ended June 30, 2001.

***Special Revenue Funds*** Special Revenue Funds account for revenues that have been legally restricted as to expenditure. Because of donor restrictions or legislative mandates, these financial resources must be spent in a specified fashion. Saint Paul, Minnesota, for example, reported approximately $84 million of revenues within 34 Special Revenue Funds during the 2001 fiscal year. This money was generated from sources as diverse as cable television franchising fees, rent received from the use of Municipal Stadium, administration fees for charitable gambling, money received from recycling programs, and parking facilities. The Special Revenue Funds category accounts for these monies because *legal restrictions had been attached to the revenue to require that expenditure be limited to specific purposes.* As an example, the city council of Saint Paul had specified that any money collected from the sale of zoo animals had to be spent to acquire new animals. Thus, any financial resources received from this source are monitored within the accounting system by inclusion in the special revenue funds until properly expended.

***Capital Projects Funds*** As the title implies, this fund type accounts for costs incurred in acquiring or constructing major government facilities such as bridges, high schools, roads, or municipal office complexes. Funding for these projects is normally derived from grants or the sale of bonds or is transferred from general revenues. The actual asset being obtained is not recorded here, but the money to finance the purchase or construction is recorded. For example, the Lexington-Fayette Urban County Government in Kentucky reported as of June 30, 2001, that it was holding more than $20 million in financial resources in its Capital Projects Funds to be used in projects such as the renovation of a public swimming pool, the construction of a performing arts and exhibit facility, the construction of a new fire station, and the like.

***Debt Service Funds*** These funds record financial resources accumulated to pay long-term liabilities and interest as they come due.[16] However, this fund type does not account for a government's long-term debt. Rather, Debt Service Funds monitor the monetary balances currently available to satisfy long-term liabilities and make the eventual payment. Thus, on June 30, 2001, the city of Birmingham, Alabama, reported nearly $60 million of cash and investments in its debt service funds, money being held to pay long-term debt and interest. For the year then ended, over $11 million in principal payments had been made from this fund along with another $15 million in interest payments.

***Permanent Funds*** The Permanent Funds category is a new fund type within the governmental funds. It accounts for assets contributed to the government by an external donor with the stipulation that the principal cannot be spent but any income can be used within the

---

[15] GASB Cod. Sec. 1300.104.
[16] Some state and local governments choose to maintain assets for debt service within the General Fund rather than in a separate category. This approach is acceptable, especially if the amounts are relatively small.

government, often for a designated purpose. As an example, the City of Dallas, Texas, reported holding nearly $8 million as of September 30, 2001, that had come entirely from private donations whose income was designated for specific use such as park maintenance. Such gifts are frequently referred to as *endowments*. Prior to *GASB Statement 34*, they were reported as Nonexpendable Trust Funds within the fiduciary funds. However, because the income can be used to support government programs, this new category was placed within the governmental funds.

### *Proprietary Funds*

The proprietary funds account for ongoing activities similar to those found in the business world. To facilitate financial reporting, the proprietary funds are broken down into two major divisions:

***Enterprise Funds*** Any government operation that is financed, at least in part, by outside user charges may be classified as an Enterprise Fund. A municipality, for example, may generate revenues from the use of a public swimming pool, golf course, airport, water and sewage service, and the like. As an illustration, the city of Charlotte, North Carolina, reports the operation of its airport as an Enterprise Fund.

A question arises, though, as to how much revenue an activity must generate before it is viewed as an Enterprise Fund. For example, if a city wants to promote mass transit and charges only a nickel to ride on its bus line, should that activity be viewed as part of an Enterprise Fund (a business-type activity) or within the General Fund (a governmental activity)?

According to *GASB Statement 34,* any activity that charges a user fee to the public can be classified as an Enterprise Fund. However, this designation is required if the activity meets any one of the following criteria so that the revenue is viewed as significant:

- Net revenues generated by the activity provide the sole security for the debts of the activity.
- Laws or regulations require the activity's costs (including depreciation and debt service) to be recovered through fees or charges.
- Fees and charges are set at prices intended to recover costs including depreciation and debt service.

Because customers are assessed direct fees, Enterprise Fund activities resemble businesses. Not surprisingly, even in the fund-based financial statements, the accounting process parallels that found in for-profit reporting. The funds use accrual basis accounting with a focus on economic, not just current financial, resources.

***Internal Service Funds*** This second proprietary fund accounts for any operation that provides services to another department or agency within the government on a cost-reimbursement basis. As with Enterprise Funds, fees are charged, but the service is performed for the primary benefit of the government rather than for outside users. Also, in the same manner as Enterprise Funds, Internal Service Funds are accounted for similarly to that of a for-profit operation in the private sector.

The city of Lincoln, Nebraska, lists seven operations in its 2001 financial statements that are accounted for as separate internal service funds:

*Information services fund*—to account for the cost of operating a central data processing facility.

*Engineering revolving fund*—to account for the cost of operating a central engineering pool.

*Insurance revolving fund*—to account for the cost of providing several types of self-insurance programs.

*Fleet services fund*—to account for the operations of a centralized maintenance facility for city equipment.

*Police garage fund*—to account for the operation of a maintenance facility for police and other government vehicles.

*Communication services fund*—to account for the costs of providing graphic arts and telecommunications services.

*Copy services fund*—to account for the cost of providing copy services.

### Fiduciary Funds

The final classification, the fiduciary funds account for assets that are held in a trustee capacity for external parties so that the money cannot be used to support the government's own programs. Like proprietary funds, all fiduciary funds use the economic resources measurement focus and accrual accounting for the timing of revenues and expenses. Because these assets are not used for the government, fiduciary funds are not included in government-wide financial statements but have separate statements presented within the fund-based financial statements.

Four distinct types of fiduciary funds can exist:

***Investment Trust Funds*** The first fund type accounts for the outside portion of investment pools when the reporting government has accepted funds from other governments to have more money to invest and, it is hoped, earn a higher return for both parties.

***Private-Purpose Trust Funds*** The second fund type accounts for any monies held in a trustee capacity when principal and interest are for the benefit of external parties outside the government such as individuals, private organizations, or other governments.

***Pension Trust Funds*** The third type accounts for an employee retirement system. Because of the need to provide adequate benefits for government workers, this fund type can become quite large. The State of Alaska, as an example, reported assets of more than $9.8 billion in its pension trust fund at the end of 1996.

***Agency Funds*** The fourth type records any resources held by a government as an agent for individuals, private organizations, or other government units. Taxes and tolls, for example, are occasionally collected by one body on behalf of another. To ensure safety and control, this money should be separately maintained in the Agency Fund until transferred to the proper authority.

### Coverage of Fund Accounting Procedures

The formal classification system just described is extremely useful in the financial reporting of a state or local government. However, a basic understanding of appropriate accounting procedures can best be achieved by setting up a matrix:

|  | Fund-Based Financial Statements | Government-Wide Financial Statements |
| --- | --- | --- |
| Governmental funds | Use the current financial resources measurement focus and modified accrual accounting for the timing of revenue and expenditure recognition. | Use the economic resources measurement focus and accrual accounting for the timing of revenue and expense recognition. |
| Proprietary funds | Use the economic resources measurement focus and accrual accounting for the timing of revenue and expense recognition. | Use the economic resources measurement focus and accrual accounting for the timing of revenue and expense recognition. |
| Fiduciary funds | Use the economic resources measurement focus and accrual accounting for the timing of revenue and expense recognition. | Funds are not included. |

The reporting process utilized by the governmental funds is examined in this chapter, both for fund-based financial statements and government-wide financial statements. In the following chapter, accounting by the proprietary funds and the fiduciary funds will be analyzed along with the actual structure of both sets of financial statements.

# OVERVIEW OF STATE AND LOCAL GOVERNMENT FINANCIAL STATEMENTS

Although a complete review of the financial statements of a state or local government is presented in the following chapter, an overview of four basic financial statements is helpful here to illustrate how certain events are reported. These outlines are not complete but simply show the presentation of various accounts.

### Government-Wide Financial Statements

Only two financial statements make up the governmental-wide financial statements: *the statement of net assets* and *the statement of activities*. The statements here separately present the governmental activities (all governmental funds and most Internal Service Funds) and the business-type activities (all Enterprise Funds and any remaining Internal Service Funds).

Exhibit 11–1 shows the basic outline of a statement of net assets. Under the economic resources measurement focus used in the government-wide financial statements, all assets and liabilities are reported. The final section of this statement, the net assets category, indicates (1) the amount of capital assets less related debt, (2) restrictions on any net assets, and (3) the total amount of unrestricted net assets. Note that, as mentioned earlier, in these government-wide financial statements, the assets of any fiduciary funds are not reported but are shown only in a separate fund-based financial statement.

In Exhibit 11–2, the statement of activities provides details about revenues and expenses, once again separated into governmental activities and business-type activities. Direct expenses and program revenues are shown for each function. Program revenues are fines, fees, grants, and the like that are generated by the specific activity. Thus, the net revenues or net expenses are determined horizontally for each function as a way of indicating each financial burden or financial benefit. The total of these amounts is summed vertically to show the total cost of operating the government, an amount that is offset by general revenues such as property taxes and sales taxes.

### Fund-Based Financial Statements

A number of fund-based financial statements are produced by a state or local government. However, at this introductory stage, only the two fundamental statements that parallel the two government-wide statements just produced are presented. First, in Exhibit 11–3, *a balance sheet* is shown for the governmental funds and then, in Exhibit 11–4, *a statement of revenues, expenditures, and changes in fund balances* is produced for the same governmental funds. Note that the figures here will not be the same as those presented for the governmental activities in the government-wide statement of net assets (Exhibit 11–1) and statement of activities (Exhibit 11–2) for three reasons:

1. Internal service funds are not included in these statements but in separate fund-based financial statements for proprietary funds.
2. The current financial resources measurement basis is used in Exhibits 11–3 and 11–4 instead of the economic resources measurement basis.
3. Modified accrual accounting rather than accrual accounting is used to time revenues and expenditures.

Because of these differences, a reconciliation between the governmental totals presented in Exhibits 11–1 and 11–3 and also between Exhibits 11–2 and 11–4 should be reported. Those reconciliations are discussed in the following chapter.

Two accounts should be noted specifically on these statements because they reflect the size of the activity or organization. On the government-wide financial statements, the Net Assets balance is a measure of the assets less the liabilities. Thus, if revenues exceed expenses, the net assets of the government will increase. On the fund-based statements for the governmental funds, a fund balance amount is reported. Once again, this amount reflects the assets minus the liabilities, but these assets are current financial resources, and the liabilities are limited to claims that will be paid from those resources. Each separate fund will report its own fund balance to indicate the amount of resources being held.

**EXHIBIT 11–1**
Statement of Net Assets—Government-Wide Financial Statements

|  | Governmental Activities | Business-Type Activities | Total |
|---|---|---|---|
| **Assets** | | | |
| Cash | $ 100 | $ 130 | $ 230 |
| Investments | 900 | 40 | 940 |
| Receivables | 600 | 400 | 1,000 |
| Internal amounts due | 50 | (50) | –0– |
| Supplies and materials | 30 | 40 | 70 |
| Capital assets (net of depreciation) | 2,950 | 2,750 | 5,700 |
| Total assets | $4,630 | $3,310 | $7,940 |
| **Liabilities** | | | |
| Accounts payable | $ 750 | $ 230 | $ 980 |
| Noncurrent liabilities | | | |
|   Due within one year | 400 | 180 | 580 |
|   Due in more than one year | 1,800 | 700 | 2,500 |
| Total liabilities | $2,950 | $1,110 | $4,060 |
| **Net Assets** | | | |
| Invested in capital assets, net of related debt | $1,410 | $2,110 | $3,520 |
| Restricted for: | | | |
|   Capital projects | 50 | –0– | 50 |
|   Debt service | 140 | 60 | 200 |
| Unrestricted | 80 | 30 | 110 |
| Total net assets | $1,680 | $2,200 | $3,880 |

The final fund-based financial statement to be shown at this time is found in Exhibit 11–4. The statement of revenues, expenditures, and changes in fund balances discloses the inflow and outflow of current financial resources for the governmental funds. Once again, a difference is seen here and in the statement of activities in Exhibit 11–2 because only current financial resources are being measured, the modified accrual method is used to guide the timing of recognition, and no internal service funds are included.

In looking at both of the fund-based financial statements, note that a separate column is required for the General Fund and every other individual fund that qualifies as major. The assumption here is that the Library Fund is the only fund outside the General Fund that is considered to be major. All other funds are grouped together. Identification of a "major" fund becomes quite important here for disclosure purposes. It is defined as follows:

> The reporting government's main operating fund (the general fund or its equivalent) should always be reported as a major fund. Other individual governmental and enterprise funds should be reported in separate columns as major funds based on these criteria:
>
> a. Total assets, liabilities, revenues, or expenditures/expenses of that individual governmental or enterprise fund are at least 10 percent of the corresponding total (assets, liabilities, and so forth) for all funds of that category or type (that is, total governmental or total enterprise funds), *and*
>
> b. Total assets, liabilities, revenues, or expenditures/expenses of the individual governmental fund or enterprise fund are at least 5 percent of the corresponding total for all governmental and enterprise funds combined.
>
> In addition to funds that meet the major fund criteria, any other governmental or enterprise fund that the government's officials believe is particularly important to financial statement users (for example, because of public interest or consistency) may be reported as a major fund.[17]

---

[17] *GASB Statement 34,* para. 76.

**EXHIBIT 11–2** Statement of Activities—Government-Wide Financial Statements

| | | | Net (Expense) Revenue | | |
|---|---|---|---|---|---|
| Function | Expenses | Program Revenues | Governmental Activities | Business-Type Activities | Total |
| Governmental activities | | | | | |
|   General government | $ 3,200 | $ 1,400 | $ (1,800) | n/a | $ (1,800) |
|   Public safety | 9,700 | 880 | (8,820) | n/a | (8,820) |
|   Public works | 2,600 | 600 | (2,000) | n/a | (2,000) |
|   Education | 8,400 | 300 | (8,100) | n/a | (8,100) |
| Total governmental activities | $23,900 | $ 3,180 | $(20,720) | n/a | $(20,720) |
| Business-type activities | | | | | |
|   Water | $ 3,600 | $ 4,030 | n/a | $ 430 | $ 430 |
|   Sewer | 4,920 | 5,610 | n/a | 690 | 690 |
|   Airport | 2,300 | 3,120 | n/a | 820 | 820 |
| Total business-type activities | $10,820 | $12,760 | n/a | $1,940 | $ 1,940 |
| Total government | $34,720 | $15,940 | $(20,720) | $1,940 | $(18,780) |
| General revenues: | | | | | |
|   Property taxes | | | $ 20,400 | –0– | $ 20,400 |
|   Investment earnings | | | 420 | 70 | 490 |
|   Transfers | | | 600 | (600) | –0– |
| Total general revenues and transfers | | | $ 21,420 | $ (530) | $ 20,890 |
| Change in net assets | | | $ 700 | $1,410 | $ 2,110 |
| Beginning net assets | | | 980 | 790 | 1,770 |
|     Ending net assets | | | $ 1,680 | $2,200 | $ 3,880 |

# ACCOUNTING FOR GOVERNMENTAL FUNDS

The remainder of this chapter presents many of the unique aspects of the accounting process utilized within the governmental funds: the General Fund, Special Revenue Funds, Capital Projects Funds, Debt Service Funds, and Permanent Funds. Because of the dual nature of the reporting required by *GASB Statement 34,* much of this accounting must be demonstrated twice. For the traditional fund-based financial statements, the current financial resources measurement focus requires events to be viewed in one particular manner. However, in creating government-wide financial statements that utilize the economic resources measurement focus, most recording procedures are designed to correspond to the financial accounting utilized by for-profit enterprises.

For demonstration purposes, separate journal entries are shown for the fund-based financial statements and the government-wide financial statements as if two sets of books were being kept. That method of creating the dual set of financial statements is possible. More likely, though, the state or local government will continue to maintain its internal records solely using fund accounting. At the end of the year, adjustments will be required to convert each of these fund-based figures to the balance necessary for government-wide financial statements. The authors believe that a better understanding of what is being reported can be achieved by showing and contrasting both sets of actual journal entries rather than presenting one set of fund-based entries along with the mechanical conversion process to arrive at the final government-wide figures. However, students should realize that actually encountering dual entries will probably not be common in the "real" world.

## The Importance of Budgets and the Recording of Budgetary Entries

"Financing is an important part of the governmental environment, particularly for governmental type activities. For those activities, the budget is the primary method of directing and

### EXHIBIT 11–3  Balance Sheet—Governmental Funds
Fund-Based Financial Statements

|  | General Fund | Library Program | Other Governmental Funds | Total Governmental Funds |
|---|---|---|---|---|
| **Assets** | | | | |
| Cash | $ 40 | $ 10 | $ 50 | $ 100 |
| Investments | 580 | 120 | 200 | 900 |
| Receivables | 120 | 200 | 210 | 530 |
| Supplies and materials | 10 | 10 | 10 | 30 |
| Total assets | $750 | $340 | $470 | $1,560 |
| **Liabilities** | | | | |
| Accounts payable | $230 | $170 | $110 | $ 510 |
| Notes payable | 300 | –0– | 100 | 400 |
| Total liabilities | $530 | $170 | $210 | $ 910 |
| **Fund Balances** | | | | |
| Reserved for: | | | | |
| Supplies | $ 10 | $ 10 | $ 10 | $ 30 |
| Encumbrances | 120 | 30 | 40 | 190 |
| Debt service | –0– | –0– | 110 | 110 |
| Unreserved: | | | | |
| General fund | 90 | –0– | –0– | 90 |
| Special revenue fund | –0– | 130 | 20 | 150 |
| Capital projects fund | –0– | –0– | 80 | 80 |
| Total fund balances | $220 | $170 | $260 | $ 650 |
| Total liabilities and fund balances | $750 | $340 | $470 | $1,560 |

controlling the financial process."[18] In a chronological sense, the first significant accounting procedure encountered in a state or locality is the recording of budgetary entries. To enhance accountability, government officials normally are required to adopt an annual budget for each separate activity to anticipate the inflow of financial resources and establish approved expenditure levels.

In its "Objectives of Financial Reporting," the GASB indicates that the budget serves several important purposes:

1. Expresses public policy. If, for example, more money is budgeted for child care and less for the environment, the citizens are made aware of the decision that has been made to allocate limited government resources.
2. Serves as an expression of financial intent for the upcoming fiscal year. The budget presents the financial plan for the government for the period.
3. Provides control because authorized spending limitations are established.
4. Offers a means of evaluating performance by allowing a comparison between actual results and the levels of funding found in the budget.

The GASB even states that "many believe the budget is the most significant financial document produced by a government unit."[19]

*Once a budget has been produced and enacted into law, formal accounting recognition is frequently required as a means of enhancing the benefits just described.* In this way, the

---

[18] *GASB Statement No. 11,* para. 9.
[19] *GASB Concepts Statement No. 1,* para. 19.

# EXHIBIT 11–4 Statement of Revenues, Expenditures, and Changes in Fund Balances—Governmental Funds
Fund-Based Financial Statements

|  | General Fund | Library Program | Other Governmental Funds | Total Governmental Funds |
|---|---|---|---|---|
| **Revenues** | | | | |
| Property taxes | $ 17,200 | $ 900 | $ 2,300 | $20,400 |
| Investment earnings | 100 | 200 | 180 | 480 |
| Program revenues | 500 | 100 | 2,500 | 3,100 |
| Total revenues | $ 17,800 | $1,200 | $ 4,980 | $23,980 |
| **Expenditures** | | | | |
| Current: | | | | |
|   General government | $ 3,400 | –0– | $ 100 | $ 3,500 |
|   Public safety | 5,100 | –0– | 400 | 5,500 |
|   Education | 6,700 | 800 | –0– | 7,500 |
| Debt service: | | | | |
|   Principal | –0– | –0– | 1,000 | 1,000 |
|   Interest | –0– | –0– | 600 | 600 |
| Capital outlay | 1,100 | 300 | 3,300 | 4,700 |
| Total expenditures | $ 16,300 | $1,100 | $ 5,400 | $22,800 |
| Excess (deficiency) of revenues over expenditures | $ 1,500 | $ 100 | $ (420) | $ 1,180 |
| **Other Financing Sources (Uses)** | | | | |
| Bond proceeds | –0– | –0– | $ 1,000 | $ 1,000 |
| Transfers in | –0– | $ 20 | 580 | 600 |
| Transfers out | $ (1,300) | –0– | $ (1,000) | (2,300) |
| Total other financing sources and uses | $ (1,300) | $ 20 | $ 580 | $ (700) |
| Change in fund balances | $ 200 | $ 120 | $ 160 | $ 480 |
| Fund balances—beginning | 20 | 50 | 100 | 170 |
| Fund balances—ending | $ 220 | $ 170 | $ 260 | $ 650 |

public is given the opportunity to learn of the expected amounts to be received and the expenditures to be made with these financial resources. Reporting revenue projections as well as compliance with spending limitations is considered essential for government accountability. Furthermore, many governments must legally have balanced budgets. Therefore, the approved budget figures are entered into the accounting records formally at the start of each fiscal year. Citizens can then draw comparisons between actual and budgeted figures at any interim point during the period.

In recognition of the importance of the information conveyed by budget figures, each government must report comparisons between the original budget, the final budget, and the actual figures for the period as required supplemental information presented after the notes to its financial statements. This budget information must be disclosed for the General Fund and each major fund within the Special Revenue Funds. As an alternative, the information can be shown as a separate statement within the government's fund-based financial statements.

As an illustration of the budgetary process, assume that a city enacts a motel excise tax to promote tourism and conventions. Because the funding is legally restricted for this specified purpose, a separate Special Revenue Fund is established. Assume further that for the 2004 fiscal year the tax is estimated to generate $490,000 in revenues. Based on this projection, the city council authorizes the expenditure of $400,000 (referred to as an *appropriation*) for programs during the current year. Of this amount, $200,000 is designated for salaries, $30,000 for utilities, $80,000 for advertising, and $90,000 for supplies. The $90,000 difference between the anticipated inflow and this appropriation is a budgeted surplus accumulated by the government in case the levy proves to be too small or for future use.

To highlight the council's action, the following journal entry is included in the accounting records of this fund. Because this information falls outside of both the fund-based financial statements and the government-wide financial statements, it is made using the budgetary basis applied by the reporting entity.

| Special Revenue Fund—Tourism and Convention Promotions | | |
|---|---|---|
| Estimated Revenues—Tax Levy | 490,000 | |
|     Appropriations—Salaries | | 200,000 |
|     Appropriations—Utilities | | 30,000 |
|     Appropriations—Advertising | | 80,000 |
|     Appropriations—Supplies | | 90,000 |
|     Fund Balance | | 90,000 |
| To record annual budget for tourism and convention promotions. | | |

This entry indicates the source of the funding (the tax revenue) as well as the approved amount of expenditures. The Fund Balance account indicates the presence of an anticipated surplus (or, in some cases, a shortage) projected for the period. Here, the size of the fund is expected to increase by $90,000 during the year.

Each of these figures will remain within the records of this Special Revenue Fund for the entire year to allow for planning and control. Citizens can see how much is to be spent for each program and the source of this funding.

Use of budgetary entries is also one method by which readers can be made aware of *interperiod equity*. This concept is designed to measure whether spending and revenues are in alignment for a period or whether money must be borrowed to fund current expenditures, debt that will be paid back by future citizens. If revenues are projected as $10 million but expenditures are budgeted at $11 million, the extra million must be paid for in some manner, usually by debt to be repaid in the future. The benefits of the additional expenditures are enjoyed today, but the cost must be borne by the citizens of a later time period. "Financial reporting should help users assess whether current-year revenues are sufficient to pay for services provided that year and whether future taxpayers will be required to assume burdens for services previously provided."[20]

The original budget is not always the final appropriations budget for the year. For example, more or less money may become available than had been anticipated and government officials may vote to change the appropriations. Assume, to illustrate, that officials in charge of tourism for this city make an appeal during the year for an additional $50,000 to create a special advertising campaign. If properly approved, the original budgetary entry must be adjusted:

| Special Revenue Fund—Tourism and Convention Promotions | | |
|---|---|---|
| Fund Balance | 50,000 | |
|     Appropriations—Advertising | | 50,000 |
| To record additional appropriation for advertising. | | |

If this activity meets the criteria for a major fund, budgetary data for the year are included as required supplemental information with the financial statements of this city. Assume that $488,000 was actually received during the year and $437,000 was spent as follows:

| | |
|---|---|
| Salaries | $196,000 |
| Utilities | 29,000 |
| Advertising | 125,000 |
| Supplies | 87,000 |

[20] GASB Concepts Statement No. 1, para. 61.

This information should be disclosed as follows. The Variance column is recommended but not required:

**TOURISM AND CONVENTION PROMOTIONS**
Year ended December 31, 2004
Budget Comparison Schedule

|  | Budgeted Amounts | | Actual Amounts (budgetary basis) | Variance with Final Budget—Positive (negative) |
|---|---|---|---|---|
|  | Original | Final | | |
| **Resources (inflows):** | | | | |
| Tax levy | $490,000 | $490,000 | $488,000 | $ (2,000) |
| **Charges to appropriations (outflows):** | | | | |
| Salaries | $200,000 | $200,000 | $196,000 | $ 4,000 |
| Utilities | 30,000 | 30,000 | 29,000 | 1,000 |
| Advertising | 80,000 | 130,000 | 125,000 | 5,000 |
| Supplies | 90,000 | 90,000 | 87,000 | 3,000 |
| Total charges | $400,000 | $450,000 | $437,000 | $13,000 |
| Change in fund balance | $ 90,000 | $ 40,000 | $ 51,000 | $11,000 |

Because of the numerous activities encompassed by the General Fund (or any other fund), the accounting system is often designed to utilize subsidiary ledgers so that each balance can be identified separately by specific function. For example, the overall budget for the General Fund could include revenue projections and approved spending limitations for scores of diverse activities such as the school system, garbage collection, and the fire department. To facilitate the recording process, control accounts can be maintained in the general ledger with balances that are explained in detail elsewhere in the system using individual subsidiary ledgers.

In some governmental funds, budgets need not be recorded if oversight can be established by alternative means. Formal budgetary entries, for example, are normally omitted from Debt Service Funds. All activities of this particular fund type (accumulation of financial resources and payment of long-term debts and interest) are governed by contractual provision. Budget entries would provide little additional control or other informational value; thus, accounting recognition is not warranted. Likewise, in Permanent Funds, a budget is not normally necessary because spending is legally restricted by the person or organization conveying the funds to the government.

Conversely, the recording of a budget is optional in reporting Capital Projects Funds. This fund type accounts for the construction and acquisition of projects that in some instances consist of no more than a simple contractual arrangement. A city, as an example, might hire an independent contractor to construct a sidewalk. In such cases, a signed contract usually sets the legal level of expenditure; thus, a budgetary entry is not necessary. However, if the government unit is building a major facility (such as a fire station) or if a number of contractors are involved in a single project, the inclusion of budgetary entries may be helpful to accentuate planning and control.

## Encumbrances

One additional budgetary procedure that plays a central role in this system is the recording of financial commitments referred to as *encumbrances*. *In diametric contrast to for-profit accounting, purchase commitments and contracts are recorded in the governmental funds prior to becoming legal liabilities.* Encumbrance accounting is appropriate in any governmental fund. Maintaining a record of these encumbrances provides an additional means of controlling fund spending. At any point during the fiscal year, information on both expended and committed funds is available. "An encumbrance accounting system acts as an early warning device. By controlling expenditure commitments, the government significantly reduces the opportunity to overexpend an appropriation."[21]

To illustrate, assume that a city's police department orders $18,000 in equipment. As an ongoing service activity, the police department is accounted for within the General Fund. Because only an order has been made but no transaction has occurred, a for-profit business would make no entry at this point. However, this amount of the government's financial resources has been committed even though no formal liability will exist until the equipment is received. To control against spending more than has been appropriated, a commitment is physically recorded through the following journal entry any time a purchase order, contract, or other formal commitment is made by one of the governmental funds.

*Fund-Based Financial Statements*

| General Fund—Police Department | | |
|---|---|---|
| Encumbrances Control . . . . . . . . . . . . . . . . . . . . . . . . . . . . . . . . . . . . . . . . . . . | 18,000 | |
|     Fund Balance—Reserved for Encumbrances . . . . . . . . . . . . . . . . . . . . . | | 18,000 |
| To record an order placed for equipment. | | |

The encumbrances account records the commitment that has been incurred while the Fund Balance—Reserved account is an equity-type balance indicating the amount of the city's resources required to fulfill future obligations.

Although this commitment to use the city's current financial resources appears on the fund-based financial statements, it is not included in the government-wide statements. Because no liability has yet been incurred by the government, no entry is made within this second set of financial statements.

When the equipment is received, the commitment is replaced by a legal liability. Hence, the encumbrance is removed from the accounting records and an expenditures account is recognized. Often, because of sales taxes, freight costs, or other price adjustments, the actual invoice total differs from the estimated figure recorded when the order was processed. For this reason, the expenditure does not necessarily agree with the corresponding encumbrance. Assume, for illustration purposes, that the equipment received here is accompanied by an invoice for $18,160.

*Fund-Based Financial Statements*

| General Fund | | |
|---|---|---|
| Fund Balance—Reserved for Encumbrances . . . . . . . . . . . . . . . . . . . . . . . . . . | 18,000 | |
|     Encumbrances Control . . . . . . . . . . . . . . . . . . . . . . . . . . . . . . . . . . . . . . . | | 18,000 |
| To remove encumbrance for equipment that has now been received. | | |
| Expenditures—Equipment . . . . . . . . . . . . . . . . . . . . . . . . . . . . . . . . . . . . . . . . | 18,160 | |
|     Vouchers Payable . . . . . . . . . . . . . . . . . . . . . . . . . . . . . . . . . . . . . . . . . . . . | | 18,160 |
| To record the receipt of equipment and the accompanying liability. | | |

In producing government-wide financial statements, the only entry created by this ordering and receiving of equipment is an increase in the asset and the related liability when legal title is received.

A problem arises for any encumbrances that have not been filled by the end of the year. In such cases, the commitment of current resources simply lapses and the entry creating the encumbrance is reversed off the financial records. However, in many cases, a government

---

[21] Government Finance Officers Association, *Governmental Accounting, Auditing, and Financial Reporting* (Chicago: 1988), p. 17.

chooses to honor these commitments even though the financial resources must come from a subsequent period. From an accounting perspective, a government can reflect this type of commitment in several ways. Assume, for example, that this equipment is not received in the year of order but in the subsequent period. One approach would be to take the following steps:

- At the end of the first year, the encumbrance entry is reversed to remove the commitment from the financial records.
- On the year-end balance sheet, $18,000 of the Ending Fund Balance is presented as "reserved for encumbrances" rather than as "unrestricted." In this manner, the reader can see that this amount of financial resources needs to be held to fulfill a commitment that has been made.
- At the start of the subsequent year, the encumbrance entry is returned to the records to monitor the committed resources.

### Recognition of Expenditures for Operations and Capital Additions

Although budgetary and encumbrance entries are unique, their impact on the accounting process is somewhat limited because they do not directly affect a fund's financial results for the period. Conversely, the method by which a state or locality records the receipt and disbursement of assets can significantly alter the entire meaning of the reported data. For example, because a primary emphasis in the governmental funds is on the measurement of changes in current financial resources, *neither expenses nor capital assets are recorded in the fund-based financial statements.*

Instead, as shown earlier, an expenditures account reflects any outflow or reduction of net financial resources from the acquisition of a good or service (or some other utility). The actual decrease is recorded as an expenditure whether it is for rent, a fire truck, salaries, or a computer. As shown in Exhibit 11–4, this method of recording allows the reader to see the utilization of an activity's current financial resources. Spending $1,000 for electricity for the past three months is an expenditure of a fund's financial resources in exactly the same way that buying a $70,000 ambulance is.

*Fund-Based Financial Statements*

| | | |
|---|---|---|
| Expenditures—Electricity | 1,000 | |
|     Vouchers (or Accounts) Payable | | 1,000 |
| To record charges covering the past three months. | | |
| Expenditures—Ambulance | 70,000 | |
|     Vouchers (or Accounts) Payable | | 70,000 |
| To record acquisition of new ambulance. | | |

Within the governmental funds, the timing of the recognition of expenditures (and revenues) follows the *modified accrual basis* of accounting. For expenditures, modified accrual accounting requires recognition to be made when a claim against current financial resources is created. If a claim is established in one period to be settled in the second period using year-end current financial resources, the expenditure and liability are recorded in the initial year. That length of time—often 60 days into the subsequent period—should be disclosed. Thus, if equipment is received 15 days before the end of the year but payment will not be made until 75 days later, the recording is still made in the first year.

The recording of expenditures rather than expenses and capital assets is one of the most distinctive characteristics of traditional governmental accounting. A for-profit business enterprise that purchases a building or a machine capitalizes all related costs and then recognizes depreciation expense during each year of the asset's useful life. This depreciation is a factor in the computation of the organization's annual net income.

In contrast, a governmental fund records the entire cost of all buildings, machines, and other capital assets as expenditures. The outflow of current financial resources is important and is reflected in the statement of revenues, expenditures, and changes in fund balances (Exhibit 11–4) of the fund-based financial statements. No income figure is calculated for these funds; thus, the computation and recording of subsequent depreciation is not relevant to the reporting process and is omitted entirely.

For the government-wide financial statement, all economic resources are being measured, and accrual accounting is utilized. Consequently, the previous two journal entries would be changed as follows, with the entry recorded as incurred.

### Government-Wide Financial Statements

| | | |
|---|---:|---:|
| Utilities Expense | 1,000 | |
|     Voucher (or Accounts) Payable | | 1,000 |
|     To record electricity charges for the past three months. | | |
| Ambulance | 70,000 | |
|     Voucher (or Accounts) Payable | | 70,000 |
|     To record acquisition of new ambulance. | | |

### Capital Assets and Fund-Based Financial Statements

One interesting result of measuring and reporting only expenditures within the governmental funds is that virtually no assets are reported in their fund-based statements other than current financial resources such as cash, receivables, and investments. All capital assets such as buildings, equipment, vehicles, and the like have been recorded as expenditures at the time of purchase and then closed out at the end of the fiscal period.

With the creation of *GASB Statement 34,* a record of all capital assets can be found in the statement of net assets (see Exhibit 11–1) within the government-wide financial statements. Thus, recording only expenditures in the fund-based financial statements does not leave a gap in the information being presented. Previously, a separate account group had been maintained for such assets (as well as for the long-term liabilities of the governmental funds). These two account groups (the General Fixed Assets Account Group and the General Long-Term Debt Account Group) were no more than a listing of the individual accounts, balances not otherwise recorded or presented by the traditional accounting model. *Statement 34* eliminated the need for these two account groups since fixed assets and long-term liabilities are now reported in the government-wide statements.

In conversion to the production of government-wide financial statements, officials can simply take the cost of fixed assets found in the General Fixed Assets Account Group (or fair market value for donated items) to determine the initial asset balances to be reported. One problem, though, is the initial reporting of "infrastructure" assets. These assets include roads, sidewalks, bridges, and the like that are normally stationary and can be preserved for a significant period of time. A bridge, for example, might last for more than 100 years. Traditionally, the recording of such infrastructure assets within the General Fixed Assets Account Group was optional. To save time and energy, many governments simply did not record these assets after the initial expenditure was recorded. Thus, in creating government-wide financial statements, records could well be unavailable for some or all of the infrastructure assets that have been bought or constructed over the years.

Because of the problem of establishing initial balances for infrastructure assets, the GASB made an exception in the reporting of government-wide financial statements. After adopting *Statement 34,* an entity must capitalize infrastructure assets bought or built. However, an additional four years beyond the date when *Statement 34* became effective is allowed to establish the capitalization of previous infrastructure assets. In this manner, government officials are given extra time to arrive at cost figures for miles of highways, curbing, sidewalks, and the

# Discussion Question

**IS IT AN ASSET OR A LIABILITY?**

In the August 1989 issue of the *Journal of Accountancy*, R.K.Mautz discusses the unique reporting needs of governments and not-for-profit organizations (such as charities) in "Not-For-Profit Financial Reporting: Another View." As an illustration of their accounting problems, Mautz examines the method by which a city should record a newly constructed high school building. Conventional business wisdom would say that such a property represents an asset of the government. Thus, the cost should be capitalized and then depreciated over an estimated useful life. However, in paragraph 26 of FASB *Concepts Statements No. 6*, an essential characteristic of an asset is "a probable future benefit . . . to contribute directly or indirectly to future cash inflows."

Mautz reasons that the school building cannot be considered an asset because it provides no net contribution to cash inflows. In truth, a high school requires the government to make significant cash outflows for maintenance, repairs, utilities, salaries, and the like. Public educational facilities (as well as many of the other properties of a government such as a fire station or municipal building) are acquired with the understanding that net cash outflows will result.

Consequently, Mautz considers whether the construction of a high school is not actually the incurrence of a liability since the government is taking on an obligation that will necessitate future cash payments. This idea also is rejected, once again based on the guidance of *Concepts Statement No. 6* (paragraph 36) because the cash outflow is not required at a "specified or determinable date, on occurrence of a specified event, or on demand."

Is a high school building an asset or is it a liability? If it is neither, how should the cost be recorded? Prior to adoption of *GASB Statement 34*, how would a government have reported a high school building? After adoption of *Statement 34*, how would a government report a high school building? Which of these two approaches provides the best portrayal of the decision to acquire or construct this building? Can a government be accounted for in the same manner as a for-profit enterprise?

---

like. If accurate information is not available within the accounting system, the GASB suggests methods by which these costs may be approximated for reporting purposes. For example, current costs for such projects can be determined and then adjusted for inflation and usage since the assets were originally obtained. However, this type of estimation and reporting is required only for major general infrastructure assets acquired or significantly improved since June 30, 1980. Thus, a cost approximation is not required for a sidewalk built in 1928.

In fund-based financial statements, as mentioned previously, depreciation expense has not been recognized in connection with governmental funds for two reasons:

1. These funds recorded expenditures rather than expenses and the entire cost of the asset was reported as an expenditure at the time of the original claim against current financial resources. Thus, the impact of the acquisition was recorded when obtained so that reporting a depreciation expense account would reflect the impact twice: once when acquired and once when depreciated.
2. These funds traditionally do not record expenses. The reporting of depreciation expense (rather than an expenditure) is not consistent with measuring the change in current financial resources.

However, the government-wide financial statements list assets rather than expenditures so that depreciation is appropriate. Consequently, on these financial statements, depreciation on all long-lived assets other than land should be calculated and reported each period.

### *Supplies and Prepaid Items*

In gathering information for government-wide financial statements, the acquisition of items such as supplies and prepaid costs such as rent or insurance is not particularly complicated. An asset is recorded at the time of acquisition and then subsequently reclassified to an expense account as the utility of the asset is consumed. However, in reporting the governmental funds in the fund-based financial statements, appropriate handling is not so clear. Such assets are neither current financial resources that can be expended nor are they capital assets with long lives to be reported immediately as expenditures. Thus, neither method of recording utilized for these fund-based statements seems to apply exactly.

Traditionally, supplies and prepaid items have been recorded as expenditures at the point in time that a claim to current financial resources is created. No asset is recorded initially because neither supplies nor prepaid items (such as rent or insurance) can be expended. For reporting purposes, though, materials or prepayments that remain at year's end have been entered into the accounting records as assets prior to production of financial statements for disclosure purposes. This adjustment is created by utilizing a balance with a title such as Fund Balance Reserved for Inventory of Supplies (or Prepaid Items). This account indicates that an asset is being reported but it is not available for spending purposes.

This traditional approach, referred to as the *purchases method,* is based on the modified accrual method of accounting. The expenditure is recorded when the claim to current financial resources is first incurred. However, many governments choose to measure supplies expenditures on an alternative method, the *consumption method.*

The consumption method parallels the process applied by a for-profit business. Any supplies or prepayments are recorded as assets when acquired. Subsequently, as the items are consumed by usage or over time, the cost is reclassified into an expenditures account. Therefore, under this approach, the expenditure is matched with the period of specific usage. Because this asset cannot be spent for government programs or other needs, a portion of the Fund Balance account should be reclassified as Reserved for Inventory of Supplies as is shown in Exhibit 11–3.

As an illustration, assume that $20,000 in supplies is purchased by a municipality for various General Fund activities. During the remainder of the period, $18,000 of this amount is used so that only $2,000 remains at year's end. These events could be recorded through either of the following sets of entries:

### *Fund-Based Financial Statements*

**Purchases Method**

| | | |
|---|---|---|
| Expenditures—Supplies | 20,000 | |
|     Vouchers Payable | | 20,000 |
| To record purchase of supplies for various ongoing activities. | | |
| Inventory of Supplies | 2,000 | |
|     Fund Balance—Reserved for Inventory of Supplies | | 2,000 |
| To record supplies remaining at year's end. | | |

**Consumption Method**

| | | |
|---|---|---|
| Inventory of Supplies | 20,000 | |
|     Vouchers Payable | | 20,000 |
| To record purchase of supplies for various ongoing activities. | | |
| Expenditures—Control | 18,000 | |
|     Inventory of Supplies | | 18,000 |
| To record consumption of supplies during period. Because a $2,000 asset that cannot be spent remains, an equal portion of the Fund Balance should be reclassified as Reserved for Inventory of Supplies. | | |

## Recognition of Revenues—Overview

The recognition of revenues has always posed a problem for state and local government units. For most revenues, such as property taxes, income taxes, and grants, no earning process exists in the same manner as is encountered in a for-profit business. Neither property taxes nor income taxes nor many other sources of government fund are "earned." Taxes, fines, and the like are assessed or imposed on the citizens to support the government's operations.

For decades, state and local government units have used a modified accrual system to determine the proper timing of revenue recognition. Under this approach to reporting, such revenues were recognized when they were both measurable and available. The term *measurable* meant subject to a reasonable estimation, and *available* indicated that the resulting financial resources would be received within the fiscal period or soon enough thereafter to pay current claims (often 60 days). In practice, these two criteria meant that revenues were rarely recognized prior to being received because most revenues were either not measurable or available until collected. Consequently, modified accrual accounting frequently resembled a cash accounting system. Property taxes represented one major exception; they were normally accrued when levied based on an estimation of the amounts to be collected using historical data.

In December 1998 the GASB released its *Statement Number 33*, "Accounting and Financial Reporting for Nonexchange Transactions," to provide a comprehensive system for recognizing many of the revenues specifically applicable to state and local government units. This statement did not apply to true revenues such as interest or rents for which an earning process exists. Instead, the GASB concentrated on "nonexchange transactions," a classification that would encompass most taxes, fines, grants, and the like because the government does not have to provide a direct and equal benefit for the amount received.

> In a nonexchange transaction, a government (including the federal government, as a provider) either gives value (benefit) to another party without directly receiving equal value in exchange or receives value (benefit) from another party without directly giving equal value in exchange.[22]

For organizational purposes, the GASB classified all such nonexchange transactions into four distinct classifications, each with its own rules as to proper recognition:

- *Derived tax revenues.* Income taxes and sales taxes are the best example of this type of revenue. In a derived tax revenue transaction, a tax assessment is imposed when an underlying exchange takes place. A sale occurs and a tax is imposed, or income is earned and an income tax is assessed.

- *Imposed nonexchange revenues.* Property taxes and fines and penalties are viewed as imposed nonexchange revenues because the government imposes an assessment but no underlying transaction exists. For example, real estate or other property is owned and a property tax is levied each period. Ownership, not a specific transaction, is being taxed by the government.

- *Government-mandated nonexchange transactions.* This category is used for monies such as grants conveyed from one government to another to help cover the costs of required programs. For example, if a state specifies that a city must create a homeless shelter and then provides a grant of $400,000 to help defray the cost, that money should be recorded using these prescribed rules because the final goal for the money has been mandated by the state. City officials have no choice; the state government has required the shelter to be constructed and provided part or all of the funding.

- *Voluntary nonexchange transactions.* In this final classification, money has been conveyed willingly to the state or local government by an individual, another government, or an organization usually for a particular purpose. For example, assume that a state grants a city $300,000 to help improve reading programs in its schools. Unless the state has mandated an improvement in these reading programs, this grant would be accounted for as a voluntary nonexchange transaction. The decision has been made that use of the money will provide an important benefit but no government requirement that led to the conveyance exists.

---

[22] *GASB Statement 33*, "Accounting and Financial Reporting for Nonexchange Transactions," December 1998, para. 7.

## Derived Tax Revenues Such as Income Taxes and Sales Taxes

Accounting for derived tax revenues is relatively straightforward. According to *GASB Statement 33,* these revenues are normally recognized in government-wide financial statements when the underlying transaction occurs. Thus, when a taxpayer earns income, the government should record the income tax revenue. Likewise, when a sale is made, the government should recognize the resulting sales tax revenue. Obviously, a government cannot make an entry every time that income is earned or a sale made. For convenience, recognition of such revenues is normally made when information becomes available.

Assume, for example, that sales within a government amount to $10 million for 2004 and a sales tax of 4 percent is assessed. In the period in which the sales are made, the following entry is required. The amounts should be reported net of any estimated refunds or uncollectible balances.

### *Government-Wide Financial Statements*

| | | |
|---|---|---|
| Receivable—Sales Taxes | 400,000 | |
|     Revenue—Sales Taxes | | 400,000 |
| To recognize amount of sales tax that will be collected in connection with sales for the current period. | | |

For fund-based financial statements, the above rules are also used except for one additional requirement that the resources must be available before the revenue can be recognized. That is, the amounts must be received during the year or soon enough thereafter to satisfy claims to current financial resources. In that way, the essence of modified accrual accounting is still being utilized at the fund level of reporting.

A separate issue is raised if government officials have specified that a certain use must be made of the resources. For example, in the preceding entry, assume that the city government has stated that 25 percent of this tax must be used for park beautification. Thus, $100,000 must be spent in this designated fashion. Such restrictions are disclosed in the financial statements by reclassifying an appropriate amount of the fund balance to disclose the intended usage. As indicated here, revenue recognition is not altered:

> Purpose restrictions do not affect the timing of recognition for any class of nonexchange transactions. Rather, recipients of resources with purpose restrictions should report resulting net assets (or equity or fund balance, as appropriate) as restricted until the resources are used for the specified purpose or for as long as the provider requires the resources to be maintained intact (for example, endowment principal.)"[23]

Consequently, in the statement of net assets for the government-wide financial statements (as shown in Exhibit 11–1), a $100,000 amount should be reclassified in the net assets section as restricted for park beautification. A similar treatment is proper for the balance sheet created according to the fund-based financial statements (as shown in Exhibit 11–3) except that the amount is shown as a separate fund balance amount reserved for park beautification.

## Imposed Nonexchange Revenues Such as Property Taxes and Fines

Accounting for imposed nonexchange revenues is a bit more complicated than for derived tax revenues because no underlying transaction is present to guide the timing of the revenue recognition. Interestingly, the GASB set up separate rules for recognizing the asset and the related revenue. The asset is to be recorded when the government first has an enforceable legal claim as defined in that particular jurisdiction (or when cash is received if a prepayment is made). For the revenue side of the transaction, recognition should be made in the time period when the resulting resources are to be used or in the first period in which use is permitted.

[23] Ibid, para. 14.

For example, assume that officials of the City of Alban need to generate property tax revenues of at least $500,000 to finance budgeted government spending for Year 2. On October 1, Year 1, property tax assessments for a total of $530,000 are mailed to the citizens. Assume that according to applicable state law, the city has no enforceable claim until January 1, Year 2 (often called the *lien date*). However, to encourage early payment, the city gives a 5 percent discount on any payment received by December 31, Year 1.

No entry is recorded on October 1, Year 1. Although the assessments have been delivered, no enforceable legal claim yet exists, and the proceeds from the tax cannot be used until Year 2. However, assume that $30,000 of the assessments is collected from citizens during the first three months. After reduction for the 5 percent discount, the collection would be $28,500. In either set of financial statements, the city records the following entry:

| Year 1 | | |
|---|---|---|
| Cash | 28,500 | |
|     Deferred Property Tax Revenues | | 28,500 |
| To record collection of property tax prior to the start of the levy year. | | |

Assume that city officials expect to collect 96 percent of the $500,000 remaining assessments, or $480,000. At the beginning of Year 2, both this receivable and the related revenue can be recognized. The receivable is reported because there is an enforceable claim and the revenue is reported because Year 2 is the year in which the money is to be used.

| January 1, Year 2 | | |
|---|---|---|
| Property Tax Receivable | 500,000 | |
|     Allowance for Uncollectible Taxes | | 20,000 |
|     Revenues—Property Taxes | | 480,000 |
| To recognize property tax assessment for Year 2. | | |

In addition, the previously collected amount should be recognized in Year 2 as revenue because this is the period for which use is allowed.

| January 1, Year 2 | | |
|---|---|---|
| Deferred Property Tax Revenues | 28,500 | |
|     Revenues—Property Taxes | | 28,500 |
| To recognize property tax proceeds for Year 2 collected during Year 1. | | |

## Government-Mandated Nonexchange Transactions and Voluntary Nonexchange Transactions

Although these two sources of revenues are identified separately, the timing of accounting recognition is the same so that they are frequently discussed together. The government recognizes these grants and other revenue sources when all eligibility requirements have been met. Until eligibility has been established, the existence of some degree of uncertainty precludes recognition. Thus, revenue recognition occurs at the time of eligibility even if the money was actually received earlier.

*GASB Statement 33* divides all eligibility requirements into the following four general classifications. All applicable requirements must be met before revenues can be recorded for either government-mandated nonexchange transactions or voluntary nonexchange transactions.

1. *Required characteristics of the recipients.* In many programs, the unit receiving funds is provided with standards that must be met in advance. For example, assume that a state grant has been awarded to a city to help teach all kindergarten children in its school system to

read. However, as part of this program, state law has been changed to mandate that all kindergarten teachers must become properly accredited. Consequently, the grant will not be conveyed to the city until all kindergarten teachers have achieved accreditation. The city must conform to state law first. Because of this requirement by the state, revenue recognition should be delayed until all teachers have qualified.

2. *Time requirements.* Programs can specify when money is to be used. To illustrate, assume that in April, a state provides a grant to a city to buy milk for each child during the subsequent school year starting in September. The grant should be recognized as revenue in the period of use or in the period when the use of the funds is first permitted.

3. *Reimbursement.* Many grants and other programs are designed to reimburse a designated government for amounts appropriately spent. These arrangements are often called expenditure-driven programs. For example, assume that a state informs a locality that it will reimburse the city government for money paid to provide milk to school children who could not otherwise afford it. In such cases, no revenue is recognized until the money is spent. Thus, the expense should equal the amount of revenue recognized.

4. *Contingencies.* In voluntary nonexchange transactions (but not in government-mandated nonexchange transactions), revenue may be withheld until a specified action has been taken. A grant might be given to buy park equipment, for example, but only after an appropriate piece of land has been acquired for the park. Until the lot is obtained, a contingency exists, and the revenue should not be recognized.

To aid in understanding the appropriate timing of revenue recognition, page 48 of *GASB Statement 33* provides the chart in Exhibit 11–5 to outline the criteria for each classification of revenue.

## Issuance of Bonds

Although not a revenue, the issuance of bonds serves as a major source of funding for many state and local governments. Proceeds from such sales may be used for many purposes, including general financing and a wide variety of construction projects. As of December 31, 2001, the city of Seattle, Washington, had approximately $780 million of long-term debts outstanding. Of that amount, $701.1 million represented general long-term debts whereas $80.2 million was for various proprietary funds.

Because the proceeds of a bond must be repaid, no revenues are recognized under either method of financial reporting. In the government-wide financial statements, the reporting is quite easy: Both the cash and the debt are increased to reflect the issuance. Conversely, in the fund-based financial statements, recording is not so simple since cash is received but the debt is not a claim on current financial resources. Thus, the inflow is neither a revenue nor a debt to be reported.

Assume, for example, that the town of Ruark sells $5 million in general obligation bonds to finance the construction of a new school building. Because of the intended use of this money, a Capital Projects Fund is designated to receive the cash. To emphasize that this money is not derived from a revenue, a special designation, *Other Financing Sources,* is utilized. Note in Exhibit 11–4 the placement of Other Financing Sources (Uses) at the bottom of statement of revenues, expenditures, and changes in fund balance to identify changes in the amount of financial resources that were created through transactions other than revenues and expenditures.

Thus, the following journal entry is needed to reflect the sale of these bonds:

### *Fund-Based Financial Statements*

| Capital Projects Funds—School Building | | |
|---|---|---|
| Cash | 5,000,000 | |
|     Other Financing Sources—Bond Proceeds | | 5,000,000 |
| To record issuance of bonds to finance construction project. | | |

### EXHIBIT 11–5   Classes and Timing of Recognition of Nonexchange Transactions

| Class | Recognition |
|---|---|
| **Derived tax revenues**<br>Examples: sales taxes, personal and corporate income taxes, motor fuel taxes, and similar taxes on earnings or consumption | **Assets***<br>Period when *underlying exchange has occurred* or when resources are received, whichever is first.<br><br>**Revenues**<br>Period when *underlying exchange has occurred*. (Report advance receipts as deferred revenues.) When modified accrual accounting is used, resources *also* should be "available." |
| **Imposed nonexchange revenues**<br>Examples: property taxes, most fines and forfeitures | **Assets***<br>Period when an *enforceable legal claim has arisen* or when resources are received, whichever is first.<br><br>**Revenues**<br>Period when *resources are required to be used* or first period that use is permitted (for example, for property taxes, the *period for which levied*). When modified accrual accounting is used, resources also should be "available." (For property taxes, apply NCGA Interpretation 3, as amended.) |
| **Government-mandated nonexchange transactions**<br>Examples: federal government mandates on state and local governments<br><br>**Voluntary nonexchange transactions**<br>Examples: certain grants and entitlements, most donations | **Assets* and liabilities**<br>Period when *all eligibility requirements have been met* or (for asset recognition) when resources are received, whichever is first.<br><br>**Revenues and expenses or expenditures**<br>Period when *all eligibility requirements have been met*. (Report advance receipts or payments for use in the following period as deferred revenues or advances, respectively. However, when a provider precludes the sale, disbursement, or consumption of resources for a specified number of years, until a specified event has occurred, or permanently [for example, permanent and term endowments], report revenues and expenses or expenditures when the resources are, respectively, received or paid and report resulting net assets, equity, or fund balance as restricted.) When modified accrual accounting is used for revenue recognition, resources also should be "available." |

*If there are purpose restrictions, report restricted net assets (or equity or fund balance) or, for governmental funds, a reservation of Fund Balance.

Although an inflow of cash into this fund has taken place, no revenue has been generated. However, in the same manner as a revenue, Other Financing Sources is a measurement account that is closed out at the end of the year. As shown in the preceding entry, the $5 million liability is completely omitted from the Capital Projects Funds. In line with fund-based accounting, only the amount of the current financial resource and an explanation of its source are shown. Since the governmental funds stress accountability for the inflows and outflows of financial resources, recognition of long-term debts in these funds has traditionally been considered inappropriate. For example, a look at the balance sheet in Exhibit 11–3 shows no long-term liabilities at all for the governmental funds but only claims to current financial resources.

Government-wide financial statements now provide information about such long-term debts as can be seen in the statement of net assets found in Exhibit 11–1. Prior to the creation of these statements, though, a method had to be devised to report the long-term liabilities incurred by the governmental funds. A separate account group, termed the General Long-Term Debt Account Group, maintained and reported a list of these debts. As with the General Fixed Assets Account Group, this system was devised to report balances that were outside of current financial resources. Because of the change in reporting, both of these account groups will no longer be necessary.

### Payment of Long-Term Liabilities

The payment of long-term liabilities once again demonstrates the huge differences between the government-wide financial statements and the fund-based financial statements. For the government-wide financial statements, payment of principal and interest is the same as by a for-profit organization. Conversely, for the fund-based statements, an expenditure account is recognized for the debt and related interest (usually in the Debt Service Funds) but only when the amounts come due so that they are a claim on the current financial resources. This approach was developed so that the expenditure is reported in the same time period as the appropriation for the expenditure. In that way, the budgeting of financial resources is properly handled.

Assume, as an illustration, that a government has a $500,000 bond payment coming due in October with three months of interest that amounts to $10,000. This example assumes that cash had been set aside previously in the Debt Service Fund to satisfy this payment. The needed entries are as follows:

#### Fund-Based Financial Statements

| **Debt Service Funds** | | |
|---|---|---|
| Expenditure—Bond Principal | 500,000 | |
| Expenditure—Interest | 10,000 | |
|     Cash | | 510,000 |
| To record payment of bond and related interest. | | |

#### Government-Wide Financial Statements

| | | |
|---|---|---|
| Bond Payable | 500,000 | |
| Interest Expense | 10,000 | |
|     Cash | | 510,000 |
| To record payment of bond and related interest. | | |

### Tax Anticipation Notes

One type of formal debt is recorded in the same manner for government-wide and fund-based financial statements. State and local governments often issue short-term debts to provide financing until revenue sources have been collected. For example, if property tax payments are expected at a particular point in time, the government could need to borrow money for operations until that date. These short-term liabilities are often referred to as *tax anticipation notes* because they are being issued until a sufficient amount of taxes can be collected. As short-term liabilities, these debts are a claim on current financial resources. Thus, for the fund-based financial statements, the issuance is not recorded as an other financing source but rather as a liability in the same manner as the government-wide financial statements. Amounts paid for interest, though, would be recorded as an expenditure in producing the fund-based statements and as an expense on the government-wide financial statements.

To illustrate, assume that a city borrows $300,000 on a 60-day note on January 1 and agrees to pay back $305,000 on March 1. The debt will be repaid with receipts from property taxes. For both sets of financial statements, the following entry is made on January 1:

| | | |
|---|---|---|
| Cash | 300,000 | |
|     Tax Anticipation Note Payable | | 300,000 |
| To record issuance of short-term debt to be repaid using money collected from property taxes. | | |

At repayment, though, two different entries are used because the fund-based statement is measuring current financial resources while the government-wide statement measures all economic resources.

### Fund-Based Financial Statement

| | | |
|---|---|---|
| Tax Anticipation Note Payable | 300,000 | |
| Expenditure—Interest | 5,000 | |
|     Cash | | 305,000 |
| To record payment of short-term debt and interest for two months. | | |

### Government-Wide Financial Statements

| | | |
|---|---|---|
| Tax Anticipation Note Payable | 300,000 | |
| Interest Expense | 5,000 | |
|     Cash | | 305,000 |
| To record payment of short-term debt and interest for two months. | | |

## Special Assessments

Governments occasionally provide improvements or services that directly benefit a particular property and assess the costs (in whole or part) to the owner. In many cases, the owners actually petition the government to initiate such projects because of the enhancement of property values. Paving streets, laying water and sewage lines, and the construction of curbing and sidewalks are typical examples. To finance the work being done, the government usually issues debt and places a lien on the property to ensure reimbursement.

The owners often pay in installments, sometimes stretching over several years. In 2001, the city of St. Paul, Minnesota, reported collecting more than $24 million in such special assessments. If public property also is benefited or if the governing body so chooses, a portion of the cost may be absorbed by the state or locality.

In the government-wide financial statements, the debt and subsequent construction are handled as they would be by a for-profit enterprise. The asset is recorded at cost and taxes are assessed and collected. These receipts are then used to settle the debt. For example, assume that a sidewalk is to be added to a neighborhood by a city at a cost of $20,000. A bond of this amount is to be sold to finance the construction with repayment being made using funds collected from the owners of the property benefited. Total interest to be paid is $2,000. Of that amount, $1,300 accrued during construction and is considered a capitalized cost. The assessment to the owners is set at $22,000 to cover all costs.

### Government-Wide Financial Statements

| | | |
|---|---|---|
| Cash | 20,000 | |
|     Bond Payable—Special Assessment | | 20,000 |
| To record debt issued to finance sidewalk construction. | | |
| Infrastructure Asset—Sidewalk | 20,000 | |
|     Cash | | 20,000 |
| To record payment of the cost of building new sidewalk to the contractor. | | |
| Taxes Receivable—Special Assessment | 22,000 | |
|     Revenue—Special Assessment | | 22,000 |
| To record citizens charges for special assessment project. | | |

| | | |
|---|---:|---:|
| Cash | 22,000 | |
|     Taxes Receivable—Special Assessment | | 22,000 |
|         To record collection of money from assessment of citizens for sidewalk construction. | | |
| Bond Payable—Special Assessment | 20,000 | |
| Interest Expense | 700 | |
| Infrastructure Asset—Sidewalk | 1,300 | |
|     Cash | | 22,000 |
|         To record paying off debt on special assessment bond. Interest incurred during construction is capitalized. | | |

In the fund-based financial statements, this same series of transactions has a completely different appearance. Neither the infrastructure nor the long-term debt would be recorded since the current financial resources measurement basis is being used.

### Fund-Based Financial Statements

| **Capital Projects Fund—Special Assessment Project** | | |
|---|---:|---:|
| Cash | 20,000 | |
|     Other Financing Sources—Bond Proceeds | | 20,000 |
|         To record issuance of bonds to finance sidewalk construction with payment to be made from a special assessment levy. | | |
| Expenditures—Special Assessment | 20,000 | |
|     Cash | | 20,000 |
|         To record payment to contractor for the cost of constructing sidewalk. | | |

| **Debt Service Fund—Special Assessment Project** | | |
|---|---:|---:|
| Tax Receivable—Special Assessment | 22,000 | |
|     Revenue—Special Assessment | | 22,000 |
|         To record assessment that will be used to pay bond principal and related interest incurred after construction. | | |
| Cash | 22,000 | |
|     Tax Receivable—Special Assessment | | 22,000 |
|         To record collection of assessment paid by citizens to extinguish bond and interest incurred in construction of sidewalk. | | |
| Expenditure—Special Assessment Bond | 20,000 | |
| Expenditure—Interest | 2,000 | |
|     Cash | | 22,000 |
|         To record payment of bonds payable and interest incurred in construction of sidewalk. | | |

One other aspect of special assessment projects should be mentioned. In some cases, the government may facilitate a project but accept no legal obligation for it. The government's role will be limited to conveying funds from one party to another although assuming no liability (either primary or secondary) for the debt. Normally, the money goes from citizens to the government and then directly to the contractors. If the government has no liability for defaults, overruns, or other problems, the recording of special assessment assets, liabilities, revenues, expenses, other financing sources, and expenditures is not really relevant to the resources of the government. In that situation, all transactions are recorded in an agency fund as increases and decreases in accounts such as cash, amount due from citizens, and amount due to contractors. No reportable impact appears within the government-wide or the fund-based financial statements (except for the Agency Fund).

## Interfund Transactions

Interfund transactions are commonly used within government units as a means of directing sufficient resources to all activities and functions. Monetary transfers made from the General Fund are especially prevalent since general tax revenues are initially accumulated in this fund. For internal reporting, such transfers should be recorded in both funds simultaneously at the time of authorization.

However, within the government-wide financial statements, many such transfers are not reported at all because they occur solely within either the governmental activities or the business-type activities. A transfer from the General Fund to the Debt Service Fund would be reported in both funds on fund-based financial statements but creates no net impact to the governmental activities found in the government-wide financial statements.

Thus, for government-wide financial reporting, the following distinctions are drawn between transfers:

- *Intra-activity transactions* occur between governmental funds (totals reported for governmental activities are not affected), or between enterprise funds (totals reported for business-type activities are not affected). Transfers between governmental funds and most Internal Service Funds are also included in this classification because, as discussed in Chapter 12, Internal Service Funds are usually reported as governmental activities in government-wide statements despite being proprietary funds. Intra-activity transactions are not reported on government-wide financial statements because they create no overall change in either governmental or business-type activities.

- *Interactivity transactions* occur between governmental funds and enterprise funds. In these cases, the totals reported for both governmental activities and business-type activities are impacted. Interactivity transactions are reported on government-wide financial statements. In Exhibit 11–1, for example, within the asset section of the statement of net assets, internal amounts due are reported and then eliminated to arrive at overall government totals. Likewise in Exhibit 11–2, transfers are shown at the very bottom of the general revenues section. Again, individual totals are shown and then offset so that no total figure is reported.

Consequently, in discussing interfund transactions, the reporting for government-wide statements is only appropriate when an interactivity transaction is involved.

### *Interfund Transfers*

The most common interfund transactions are transfers used primarily within the government funds to ensure adequate financing of budgeted expenditures. A county might transfer unrestricted funds, for example, to debt service to ensure that future obligations can be paid. A city council could vote to transfer $800,000 from the General Fund to the Capital Projects Funds to cover a portion of the cost of a new school building. In this second scenario, the following entries are recorded:

### *Fund-Based Financial Statements*

**General Fund**
| | | |
|---|---|---|
| Other Financing Uses—Transfers Out—Capital Projects Fund | 800,000 | |
|     Due to Capital Projects Fund | | 800,000 |
| To record authorization transfer for school construction. | | |

**Capital Projects Funds**
| | | |
|---|---|---|
| Due from General Fund | 800,000 | |
|     Other Financing Sources—Transfers In—General Fund | | 800,000 |
| To record transfer to be received for school construction. | | |

The *Other Financing Uses/Sources* designations are appropriate here; financial resources are being moved into and out of these funds although neither revenues nor expenditures have been earned or incurred. As shown in Exhibit 11–4, these balances are eventually reported by each fund in the statement of revenues, expenditures, and changes in fund balances. Both accounts are then closed out at the end of the current year. The *Due to/Due from* accounts are the equivalent of interfund payable and receivable balances, and each account is reported within the proper fund.

Because they are intra-activity transactions, none of the above entries would be made within the government-wide financial statements. Financial resources are simply being shifted around within the governmental activities.

Not all monetary transfers are for normal operating purposes; nonrecurring or nonroutine transfers may also take place. For example, money might be transferred from the General Fund to create or expand an enterprise fund such as a subway system. Assume that a city sets aside $1 million of unrestricted money to help finance a new subway system that will be open to the public. For convenience here, the transaction is being recorded as if the cash is transferred immediately so that no type of receivable or payable is necessary.

### Fund-Based Financial Statements

**General Fund**
| | | |
|---|---|---|
| Other Financing Uses—Transfers Out—Subway System | 1,000,000 | |
|     Cash | | 1,000,000 |
| To record transfer to help finance subway system. | | |

**Enterprise Fund**
| | | |
|---|---|---|
| Cash | 1,000,000 | |
|     Other Financing Sources—Transfers In—General Fund | | 1,000,000 |
| To record receipt of transfer from unrestricted funds. | | |

Because this transfer is an interactivity transaction, a similar entry will be made for the government-wide financial statements. In this case, the assets of the governmental activities are being reduced while the assets in the business-type activities increase.

### Government-Wide Financial Statements

**Governmental Activities**
| | | |
|---|---|---|
| Transfers Out—Subway System | 1,000,000 | |
|     Cash | | 1,000,000 |
| To record transfer to help finance subway system. | | |

**Business-Type Activities**
| | | |
|---|---|---|
| Cash | 1,000,000 | |
|     Transfers In—General Fund | | 1,000,000 |
| To record receipt of transfer from unrestricted funds. | | |

### Internal Exchange Transactions

Some transfers made within a government actually replace revenues and expenditures. For example, a payment made by a city to its own print shop (or any other Internal Service Fund or Enterprise Fund) for services or materials is treated as the equivalent of a transaction with an outside party. To avoid confusion in reporting, such transfers are recorded as revenues and expenditures or expenses just as if the transaction had occurred with an unrelated party. No differentiation is made; these are not transfers designed to shift resources.

All internal exchange transactions are recorded by the fund-based financial statements. However, because Internal Service Funds are usually reported as governmental activities in the government-wide statements, any such exchanges between governmental funds and an internal service fund has no net impact on overall figures being reported and should be omitted.

To illustrate, assume that a government pays its print shop (an internal service fund) $8,000 for work done for the fire department. In addition, another $1,000 is paid to a toll road operated by the government as an enterprise fund. The payment is made to allow government vehicles to ride on the highway without individual payments having to be made. Both of these transfers are made for services being rendered.

### *Fund-Based Financial Statements*

**General Fund**
| | | |
|---|---|---|
| Expenditures—Printing | 8,000 | |
| Expenditures—Toll Road Privileges | 1,000 | |
|     Cash | | 9,000 |
| To record payment for printing supplies for fire department and for use of toll road. | | |

**Internal Service Fund—Print Shop**
| | | |
|---|---|---|
| Cash | 8,000 | |
|     Revenues | | 8,000 |
| To record collection of money paid by the fire department for printing supplies. | | |

**Enterprise Fund—Toll Road**
| | | |
|---|---|---|
| Cash | 1,000 | |
|     Revenues | | 1,000 |
| To record money collected from government for vehicular use of toll roads. | | |

On government-wide financial statements, the $8,000 transaction with the print shop would not be reflected. An internal service fund is usually reported as a government activity rather than a business-type activity so that this transfer is viewed as an intra-activity transaction. The payment made to the enterprise fund, though, is with a business-type activity and is recorded because it is an interactivity transaction.

### *Government-Wide Financial Statements*

**Governmental Activities**
| | | |
|---|---|---|
| Expenses—Toll Road Privileges | 1,000 | |
|     Cash | | 1,000 |
| To record payment for use of toll road by government's vehicles. | | |

**Business-Type Activities**
| | | |
|---|---|---|
| Cash | 1,000 | |
|     Revenues | | 1,000 |
| To record money collected from government for vehicular use of toll roads. | | |

## Summary

1. Government accounting was radically altered in 1999 when the Governmental Accounting Standards Board issued *Statement 34,* "Basic Financial Statements—and Management's Discussion and Analysis—for State and Local Governments." This pronouncement made numerous changes in traditional government accounting procedures and added a second set of financial statements to reflect government-wide activities.
2. The readers of government financial statements have a wide variety of informational needs. No one set of financial statements seems capable of meeting all user needs, a factor that influenced the actions taken by the GASB in its *Statement 34.* Accountability of government officials and control over public spending have always been essential elements of government accounting. In *Statement 34,* the GASB has attempted to keep those priorities in place while broadening the scope of the financial statements being produced.
3. Fund-based financial statements are produced by a state or local government unit utilizing fund accounting. In this system, activities are classified into three broad categories (governmental, proprietary, and fiduciary). Governmental funds account for service activities; proprietary funds account for activities for which a user charge is assessed; and fiduciary funds account for assets held by the government for an external party.
4. Governmental funds are composed of several fund types: the General Fund, Special Revenue Funds, Capital Projects Funds, Debt Service Funds, and Permanent Funds. Proprietary funds are made up of Enterprise Funds and Internal Service Funds. Fiduciary Funds encompass Pension Trust Funds, Investment Trust Funds, Private-Purpose Trust Funds, and Agency Funds.
5. Government-wide financial statements present a statement of net assets and a statement of activities that are divided between governmental activities (the governmental funds and usually the Internal Service Funds) and business-type activities (enterprise funds and occasionally an internal service fund). These statements measure all economic resources with timing of recognition guided by accrual accounting.
6. Fund-based financial statements include a number of financial statements. This chapter focused on the balance sheet and the statement of revenues, expenditures, and changes in fund balances for the governmental funds. In these statements, the General Fund and any other major fund must be shown separately. These statements measure current financial resources with timing of recognition guided by modified accrual accounting.
7. To aid in control over financial resources, most governmental funds record their approved budgets each year. This initial budget as well as any final amended budget and actual figures for the period are then reported as required supplemental information to the financial statements.
8. Commitments for purchase orders and contracts are actually recorded in the individual governmental funds through the recognition of encumbrances. These balances are recorded when the commitment is made and removed when replaced by an actual claim to current financial resources.
9. The fund-based financial statements recognize expenditures for capital outlay, long-term debt payment, and expense-type costs when a claim to current financial resources comes into existence. Government-wide financial statements capitalize capital outlay, reduce liabilities for debt payments, and record expenses in expense accounts.
10. Revenue recognition by governments is based on a classification system. Recognition depends on whether the revenue is a derived tax revenue, imposed nonexchange revenue, government-mandated nonexchange transaction, or voluntary nonexchange transaction.
11. The issuance of long-term bonds is recorded as an "other financing source" by the governmental funds but as a long-term liability both in the proprietary funds and in the government-wide financial statements.
12. Transfers between funds are normally reported as an "other financing source" and "other financing use" within the fund-based financial statements. Such transactions are not reported in the government-wide statements unless they create an impact in overall governmental activities and business-type activities. For internal exchange transactions where payment is being made for a good or service, a revenue is recognized along with an expenditure in the fund-based statements. The government-wide financial statements normally do not reflect such transfers unless between an enterprise fund and a governmental fund. In that case, a revenue is increased along with an expense.

## Comprehensive Illustration PROBLEM

*(Estimated Time: 50 Minutes).* The Town of Drexel has the following financial transactions. The government has formally adopted *GASB Statement 34.*

1. The town council adopts an annual budget for the General Fund estimating general revenues of $1.7 million, approved expenditures of $1.5 million, and approved transfers out of $120,000.

2. Property taxes of $1.3 million are levied. The town expects to collect all but 3 percent of these taxes during the year.
3. Two new police cars are ordered at an approximate cost of $150,000.
4. A transfer of $50,000 is made from the General Fund to the Debt Service Fund.
5. A bond payable of $40,000 is paid along with $10,000 of interest using money previously set aside.
6. A $2 million bond is issued at face value to acquire a building to be converted into a high school.
7. The two police cars are received with an invoice price of $152,000. The voucher has been approved for this amount but not yet paid.
8. The building for the high school is acquired for $2 million in cash. Renovation is immediately begun.
9. Depreciation on the new police cars is computed as $30,000 for the period.
10. The town borrows $100,000 on a 90-day tax anticipation note.
11. A special assessment curbing project is begun. The government sells $80,000 in bonds at face value to finance this project. If the debt is not paid by the assessments collected, the town has pledged to guarantee the debt.
12. A contractor completes the curbing project and is paid $80,000.
13. Citizens are assessed $85,000 for the curbing project that has been completed.
14. The special assessments of $85,000 are collected in full. The debt is repaid plus $5,000 in interest.
15. The town receives a $10,000 cash grant to beautify a park. The grant must be used to reimburse specific costs incurred by the town.
16. The town spends $4,000 to beautify the above park.

### Required:

a. Prepare journal entries for the town based on the production of fund-based financial statements.
b. Prepare journal entries in anticipation of preparing government-wide financial statements.

## SOLUTION

### a. Fund-Based Financial Statements

**1.** **General Fund**

| | | |
|---|---|---|
| Estimated Revenues Control | 1,700,000 | |
| Appropriations Control | | 1,500,000 |
| Estimated Other Financing Uses Control | | 120,000 |
| Fund Balance | | 80,000 |

**2.** **General Fund**

| | | |
|---|---|---|
| Property Tax Receivable | 1,300,000 | |
| Allowance for Uncollectible Taxes | | 39,000 |
| Revenues—Property Taxes | | 1,261,000 |

**3.** **General Fund**

| | | |
|---|---|---|
| Encumbrances Control | 150,000 | |
| Fund Balance—Reserved for Encumbrances | | 150,000 |

**4.** **General Fund**

| | | |
|---|---|---|
| Other Financing Uses—Transfers Out | 50,000 | |
| Cash | | 50,000 |

**Debt Service Funds**

| | | |
|---|---|---|
| Cash | 50,000 | |
| Other Financing Sources—Transfers In | | 50,000 |

5. **Debt Service Funds**

| | | |
|---|---|---|
| Expenditures—Principal | 40,000 | |
| Expenditures—Interest | 10,000 | |
|     Cash | | 50,000 |

6. **Capital Projects Funds**

| | | |
|---|---|---|
| Cash | 2,000,000 | |
|     Other Financing Sources—Bond Proceeds | | 2,000,000 |

7. **General Fund**

| | | |
|---|---|---|
| Fund Balance—Reserved for Encumbrances | 150,000 | |
|     Encumbrances Control | | 150,000 |
| Expenditures Control | 152,000 | |
|     Vouchers Payable | | 152,000 |

8. **Capital Projects Funds**

| | | |
|---|---|---|
| Expenditures—Building | 2,000,000 | |
|     Cash | | 2,000,000 |

9. No entry is recorded. Expenditures rather than expenses are recorded by the governmental funds.

10. **General Fund**

| | | |
|---|---|---|
| Cash | 100,000 | |
|     Tax Anticipation Note Payable | | 100,000 |

11. **Capital Projects Funds**

| | | |
|---|---|---|
| Cash | 80,000 | |
|     Other Financing Sources—Special Assessments Note | | 80,000 |

12. **Capital Projects Funds**

| | | |
|---|---|---|
| Expenditures—Curbing | 80,000 | |
|     Cash | | 80,000 |

13. **Debt Service Funds**

| | | |
|---|---|---|
| Taxes Receivable—Special Assessment | 85,000 | |
|     Revenues—Special Assessment | | 85,000 |

14. **Debt Service Funds**

| | | |
|---|---|---|
| Cash | 85,000 | |
|     Taxes Receivable—Special Assessment | | 85,000 |
| Expenditures—Principal | 80,000 | |
| Expenditures—Interest | 5,000 | |
|     Cash | | 85,000 |

15. **Special Revenue Funds**

| | | |
|---|---|---|
| Cash | 10,000 | |
|     Deferred Revenues | | 10,000 |

16. **Special Revenue Funds**

| | | |
|---|---|---|
| Expenditures—Park Beautification | 4,000 | |
|     Cash | | 4,000 |
| Deferred Revenues | 4,000 | |
|     Revenues—Grants | | 4,000 |

b. *Government-Wide Financial Statements*

1. Budgetary entries are not reported within the government-wide financial statements. They are recorded in the individual funds and then shown as required supplementary information.

2. **Governmental Activities**

| | | |
|---|---|---|
| Property Tax Receivable | 1,300,000 | |
|     Allowance for Uncollectible Taxes | | 39,000 |
|     Revenues—Property Taxes | | 1,261,000 |

3. Commitments are not reported in the government-wide financial statements.

4. This transfer was within the governmental funds and, therefore, had no net effect on the governmental activities. No journal entry is needed.

5. **Governmental Activities**

| | | |
|---|---|---|
| Bonds Payable | 40,000 | |
| Interest Expense | 10,000 | |
|     Cash | | 50,000 |

6. **Governmental Activities**

| | | |
|---|---|---|
| Cash | 2,000,000 | |
|     Bonds Payable | | 2,000,000 |

7. **Governmental Activities**

| | | |
|---|---|---|
| Police Cars (or Vehicles) | 152,000 | |
|     Vouchers Payable | | 152,000 |

| | | | |
|---|---|---|---|
| 8. | **Governmental Activities** | | |
| Building | | 2,000,000 | |
|     Cash | | | 2,000,000 |
| 9. | **Governmental Activities** | | |
| Depreciation Expense | | 30,000 | |
|     Accumulated Depreciation | | | 30,000 |
| 10. | **Governmental Activities** | | |
| Cash | | 100,000 | |
|     Tax Anticipation Note Payable | | | 100,000 |
| 11. | **Governmental Activities** | | |
| Cash | | 80,000 | |
|     Special Assessment Notes Payable | | | 80,000 |
| 12. | **Governmental Activities** | | |
| Infrastructure Assets—Curbing | | 80,000 | |
|     Cash | | | 80,000 |
| 13. | **Governmental Activities** | | |
| Taxes Receivable—Special Assessment | | 85,000 | |
|     Revenues—Special Assessment | | | 85,000 |
| 14. | **Governmental Activities** | | |
| Cash | | 85,000 | |
|     Taxes Receivable—Special Assessment | | | 85,000 |
| Special Assessment Notes Payable | | 80,000 | |
| Interest Expense | | 5,000 | |
|     Cash | | | 85,000 |
| 15. | **Governmental Activities** | | |
| Cash | | 10,000 | |
|     Deferred Revenues | | | 10,000 |
| 16. | **Governmental Activities** | | |
| Expenses—Park Beautification | | 4,000 | |
|     Cash | | | 4,000 |
| Deferred Revenues | | 4,000 | |
|     Revenues—Grants | | | 4,000 |

## Questions

1. How have users' needs impacted the development of accounting principles for state and local government units?
2. Why have accountability and control been so important in the traditional accounting for state and local government units?
3. In general, how has *GASB Statement 34* impacted the financial reporting of state and local governments?
4. What are the basic financial statements now produced by a state or local government?
5. What measurement basis is used in fund-based financial statements, and what system is applied to determine the timing of revenue and expenditure recognition?
6. What measurement basis is used in government-wide financial statements, and what system is applied to determine the timing of revenue and expense recognition?
7. What accounts are included in current financial resources?
8. In applying the current financial resources measurement basis, when are liabilities recognized?
9. What are the three classifications of funds? What funds are included in each of these three?
10. What are the five fund types within the governmental funds? For each of these five, what types of events are reported?
11. What are the two fund types within the proprietary funds? For each of these two, what types of events are reported?
12. What are the four fund types within the fiduciary funds? For each of these four, what types of events are reported?
13. What are the two major divisions that are reported in government-wide financial statements? What funds are *not* reported in these financial statements?
14. In fund-based financial statements, separate columns are reported for each activity. Which activities are reported in this manner?
15. Why are budgetary entries recorded in the individual funds of a state or local government?
16. How are budget results shown in the financial reporting of a state or local government?
17. When is an encumbrance recorded? What happens to this balance? How are encumbrances reported in government-wide financial statements?
18. An encumbrance is still outstanding at the end of the fiscal year. The government anticipates that it will honor this encumbrance in the next year. What reporting is made of this encumbrance?
19. What costs cause a governmental fund to report an expenditure?
20. At what point in time does a governmental fund report an expenditure?
21. How do governmental funds report capital outlay? How are capital expenditures reported in the government-wide financial statements?
22. What are the two different ways that supplies and prepaid items can be recorded on fund-based financial statements?
23. What are the four classifications of revenues that a state or local government can recognize? In each case, when are revenues normally recognized?
24. When is a receivable recognized for property tax assessments? When is the revenue recognized?
25. How is the issuance of a long-term bond reported on fund-based financial statements? How is the issuance of a long-term bond reported on government-wide financial statements?
26. What is a special assessment project? How are special assessment projects reported?
27. How are interfund transfers reported in fund-based financial statements?
28. What is the difference in government-wide financial statements between an intra-activity transaction and an interactivity transaction? How is each reported?
29. What is an internal exchange transaction, and how is it reported?

## Problems

1. Which of the following is *not* a Governmental Fund?
    a. Special Revenue Fund.
    b. Internal Service Fund.
    c. Capital Projects Fund.
    d. Debt Service Fund.
2. What is the purpose of a Special Revenue Fund?
    a. To account for revenues legally restricted as to expenditure.
    b. To account for ongoing activities.
    c. To account for gifts when only subsequently earned income can be expended.
    d. To account for the cost of long-lived assets bought with designated funds.
3. What is the purpose of Enterprise Funds?

a. To account for operations that provide services to other departments within a government.
   b. To account for asset transfers.
   c. To account for ongoing activities such as the police and fire departments.
   d. To account for operations financed in whole or in part by outside user charges.
4. Which of the following statements is true?
   a. There are three different types of Proprietary Funds.
   b. There are three different types of Fiduciary Funds.
   c. There are five different types of Fiduciary Funds.
   d. There are five different types of Governmental Funds.
5. A government expects to receive revenues of $400,000 but has approved expenditures of $430,000. The anticipated shortage will have an impact on which of the following terms?
   a. Interperiod equity.
   b. Modified accrual accounting.
   c. Consumption accounting.
   d. Account groups.
6. A citizen of the City of Townsend gives it a gift of $22,000 in investments. The citizen requires that the investments be held but any resulting income must be used to help maintain the city's cemetery. In which fund should this asset be maintained?
   a. Special Revenue Funds.
   b. Capital Projects Funds.
   c. Permanent Funds.
   d. General Fund.
7. Which of the following statements is correct for the governmental funds?
   a. Fund-based financial statements measure economic resources.
   b. Government-wide financial statements measure only current financial resources.
   c. Fund-based financial statements measure both economic resources and current financial resources.
   d. Government-wide financial statements measure economic resources.
8. Which of the following statements is correct for the governmental funds?
   a. Fund-based financial statements measure revenues and expenditures based on modified accrual accounting.
   b. Government-wide financial statements measure revenues and expenses based on modified accrual accounting.
   c. Fund-based financial statements measure revenues and expenses based on accrual accounting.
   d. Government-wide financial statements measure revenues and expenditures based on accrual accounting.
9. Which financial statements match up properly with which level of reporting?

   | | Fund-Based Financial Statements | Government-Wide Financial Statements |
   |---|---|---|
   | a. | Statement of net assets | Balance sheet |
   | b. | Statement of net assets | Statement of net assets |
   | c. | Balance sheet | Statement of net assets |
   | d. | Balance sheet | Balance sheet |

10. Which of the following statements is true concerning the recording of a budget?
    a. At the beginning of the year, Appropriations is debited.
    b. A debit to the Budgetary Fund Balance account indicates an expected surplus.
    c. At the beginning of the year, Estimated Revenues is debited.
    d. At the end of the year, Appropriations is credited.
11. Rent for two months is paid by the General Fund. Which of the following is *not* correct?
    a. In the government-wide financial statements, rent expense should be reported.
    b. In the General Fund, rent expense should be reported.
    c. In the fund-based financial statements, an expenditure should be reported.
    d. If one month of rent is in one year with the other month in the next year, either the purchases method or the consumption method can be used in fund-based statements.
12. In the General Fund, a purchase order for $3,000 is recorded for the purchase of a new computer. The computer is received at an actual cost of $3,020. Which of the following is correct?
    a. Machinery is increased in the General Fund by $3,020.
    b. An encumbrance account is reduced by $3,020.
    c. An expenditure is increased by $3,020.
    d. An expenditure is recorded for the additional $20.

13. At the end of the current year, a government reports a fund balance reserved for encumbrances of $9,000. What information is being conveyed?
    a. A donor has given the government $9,000 that must be used in a specified fashion.
    b. The government has made $9,000 in commitments in one year that will be honored in the subsequent year.
    c. Encumbrances exceeded expenditures by $9,000 during the current year.
    d. The government spent $9,000 less than was appropriated.
14. A government buys equipment for its police department at a cost of $54,000. Which of the following is *not* true?
    a. In the government-wide financial statements, equipment will increase by $54,000.
    b. Depreciation in connection with this equipment will be reported in the fund-based financial statements.
    c. In the fund-based financial statements, the equipment will not appear within the reported assets.
    d. In the fund-based financial statements, an expenditure for $54,000 will be reported.
15. A city acquires supplies and is using the consumption method of accounting. Which of the following statements is true for the fund-based statements?
    a. An expenditures account was debited at the time of receipt.
    b. An expense is recorded as the supplies are consumed.
    c. An inventory account is debited at the time of the acquisition.
    d. The supplies are recorded within the General Fixed Assets Account Group.
16. An income tax is an example of which of the following:
    a. Derived tax revenue.
    b. Imposed nonexchange revenue.
    c. Government-mandated nonexchange revenue.
    d. Voluntary nonexchange transaction.
17. The state government passes a law requiring localities to upgrade their water treatment facilities. The state awards a grant of $500,000 to the Town of Midlothian to help pay for this cost. What type of revenue is this grant?
    a. Derived tax revenue.
    b. Imposed nonexchange revenue.
    c. Government-mandated nonexchange revenue.
    d. Voluntary nonexchange transaction.
18. The state awards a grant of $50,000 to the Town of Glenville. The grant money will be paid to the town as a reimbursement for money spent on road repair. At the beginning, $8,000 is paid in advance. During the first year of this program, the town spent $14,000 and applied for reimbursement. What amount of revenue should be recognized?
    a. $0
    b. $8,000
    c. $14,000
    d. $50,000
19. A city issues a 60-day tax anticipation note to fund operations. What recording should be made?
    a. In the government-wide financial statements, the liability should be reported; in the fund-based financial statements, an other financing source should be shown.
    b. In the government-wide financial statements and in the fund-based financial statements, a liability should be reported.
    c. In the government-wide financial statements and in the fund-based financial statements, an other financing source should be shown.
    d. In the government-wide financial statements, an other financing source should be shown; in the fund-based financial statements, a liability is reported.
20. A city issues five-year bonds payable to finance construction of a new school. What recording should be made?
    a. In the government-wide financial statements, the liability should be reported; in the fund based financial statements, an other financing source should be shown.
    b. In the government-wide financial statements and in the fund-based financial statements, a liability should be reported.
    c. In the government-wide financial statements and in the fund-based financial statements, an other financing source should be shown.
    d. In the government-wide financial statements, an other financing source should be shown; in the fund-based financial statements, a liability is reported.

21. A $110,000 payment is made on a long-term liability. Of this amount, $10,000 represents interest. Which of the following is *not* true?
    a. In the government-wide financial statements, liabilities are reduced by $100,000.
    b. In the fund-based financial statements, an expenditure is recorded for $110,000.
    c. In the fund-based financial statements, liabilities are reduced by $100,000.
    d. In the government-wide financial statements, interest expense of $10,000 is recognized.

22. A city constructs a special assessment project (a sidewalk) for which it is secondarily liable. The city issues bonds of $90,000. Another $10,000 is authorized and transferred out of the General Fund. The sidewalk is built for $100,000. The citizens are billed for $90,000. They pay this amount and the debt is paid off. Where is the $100,000 expenditure recorded?
    a. It is not recorded by the city.
    b. It is recorded in the Agency Fund.
    c. It is recorded in the General Fund.
    d. It is recorded in the Capital Projects Fund.

23. A city constructs curbing in a new neighborhood. It is financed as a special assessment. Under what condition should this activity be recorded in the Agency Fund?
    a. Never; the work is reported in the Capital Projects Funds.
    b. Only if the city is secondarily liable for any debt incurred to finance construction costs.
    c. Only if the city is in no way liable for the costs of the construction.
    d. In all cases.

24. Which of the following is an example of an interactivity transaction?
    a. Money is transferred from the General Fund to the Debt Service Fund.
    b. Money is transferred from the Capital Projects Fund to the General Fund.
    c. Money is transferred from the Special Revenue Fund to the Debt Service Fund.
    d. Money is transferred from the General Fund to the Enterprise Fund.

25. Cash of $60,000 is transferred from the General Fund to the Debt Service Fund. On the government-wide financial statements, what is reported?
    a. No reporting is made.
    b. Other Financing Sources increase by $60,000; Other Financing Uses increase by $60,000.
    c. Revenues increase by $60,000; Expenditures increase by $60,000.
    d. Revenues increase by $60,000; Expenses increase by $60,000.

26. Cash of $60,000 is transferred from the General Fund to the Debt Service Fund. On the fund-based financial statements, what is reported?
    a. No reporting is made.
    b. Other Financing Sources increase by $60,000; Other Financing Uses increase by $60,000.
    c. Revenues increase by $60,000; Expenditures increase by $60,000.
    d. Revenues increase by $60,000; Expenses increase by $60,000.

27. Cash of $20,000 is transferred from the General Fund to the Enterprise Fund to pay for work that was done. On the government-wide financial statements, what is reported?
    a. No reporting is made.
    b. Other Financing Sources increase by $20,000; Other Financing Uses increase by $20,000.
    c. Revenues increase by $20,000; Expenditures increase by $20,000.
    d. Revenues increase by $20,000; Expenses increase by $20,000.

28. Cash of $20,000 is transferred from the General Fund to the Enterprise Fund to pay for work that was done. On the fund-based financial statements, what is reported?
    a. No reporting is made.
    b. Other Financing Sources increase by $20,000; Other Financing Uses increase by $20,000.
    c. Revenues increase by $20,000; Expenditures increase by $20,000.
    d. Revenues increase by $20,000; Expenses increase by $20,000.

29. The board of commissioners of the City of Hartmoore adopted a General Fund budget for the year ending June 30, 2004, which included revenues of $1,000,000, bond proceeds of $400,000, appropriations of $900,000, and operating transfers out of $300,000. If this budget is formally integrated into the accounting records, what is the required journal entry at the beginning of the year? What later entry is required?

30. A city orders a new computer at an anticipated cost of $88,000. It is received with an actual cost of $89,400. Payment is subsequently made. Give all required journal entries and identify the type of fund or account group in which each entry is recorded. What information is presented in the government-wide financial statements? What information is presented in the fund-based financial statements?

31. Cash of $90,000 is transferred from a city's General Fund to start construction on a police station. The city issues a bond of $830,000 at face value. The police station is built for $920,000. Prepare all

necessary journal entries for these transactions and identify the type of fund or account group in which each entry is recorded. Assume that the commitment is not recorded by the city. What information is presented in the government-wide financial statements? What information is presented in the fund-based financial statements?

32. A local government incurs the following transactions during the current fiscal period. Prepare journal entries without dollar amounts. Prepare the entries the first time for fund-based financial statements. Then prepare them again for government-wide financial statements.
   a. The budget for the police department, ambulance service, and other ongoing activities is passed. Funding is from property taxes, transfers, and bond proceeds. All monetary outflows will be for expenses and fixed assets. A deficit is projected.
   b. A bond is issued at face value to fund the construction of a new municipal building.
   c. A computer is ordered to be used by the tax department.
   d. The computer is received.
   e. The invoice for the computer is paid.
   f. City council agrees to transfer money from the General Fund as partial payment for a special assessments project. This money has not yet been transferred. The city will be secondarily liable for any money borrowed for this work.
   g. City council creates a motor pool to service all government vehicles. Money is transferred from the General Fund to provide permanent financing for this facility.
   h. Property taxes are levied. Although officials believe that most of these taxes should be collected during the current period, a small percentage is estimated to be uncollectible.
   i. Grant money is collected from the state to be spent as a supplement to the salaries of the police force. No entry has previously been recorded.
   j. A portion of the grant money in (i) is properly spent.

33. Make journal entries for the governmental funds of the City of Pudding to record the following transactions. Prepare the entries the first time for fund-based financial statements. Then prepare them again for government-wide financial statements.
   a. A new truck for the sanitation department was ordered at a cost of $94,000.
   b. The city print shop did $1,200 worth of work for the school system (but has not yet been paid).
   c. A $700,000 bond was issued to build a new road.
   d. Cash of $20,000 is transferred from the General Fund to provide permanent financing for a municipal swimming pool that will be viewed as an Enterprise Fund.
   e. The truck ordered in (a) is received at an actual cost of $96,000. Payment is not made at this time.
   f. Cash of $32,000 is transferred from the General Fund to the Capital Projects Fund.
   g. A state grant of $30,000 is received that must be spent to promote recycling.
   h. The first $5,000 of the state grant received in (g) is appropriately expended.

34. Prepare journal entries for a local government to record the following transactions. Prepare the entries the first time for fund-based financial statements. Then prepare them again for government-wide financial statements.
   a. The government sells $300,000 in bonds at face value to finance construction of a warehouse.
   b. A $400,000 contract is signed for construction of the warehouse.
   c. A $20,000 transfer of unrestricted funds was made for the eventual payment of the debt in (a).
   d. Equipment for the fire department is received with a cost of $12,000. When it was ordered, an anticipated cost of $11,800 had been recorded.
   e. Supplies to be used in the schools are bought for $2,000 cash. The consumption method is being used.
   f. A state grant of $5,000 is awarded to supplement police salaries. The money will be paid to reimburse the government after the supplements have been paid to the police officers.
   g. Property tax assessments are mailed to citizens of the government. The total assessment is $600,000 although officials anticipate that 4 percent will never be collected.

35. The following trial balances are for the governmental funds of the City of Copeland prepared from the current accounting records:

| General Fund | Debit | Credit |
|---|---|---|
| Cash | $ 19,000 | |
| Taxes Receivable | 112,000 | |

*(continued)*

|  | Debit | Credit |
|---|---|---|
| Allowance for Uncollectible Taxes | | $ 2,000 |
| Vouchers Payable | | 24,000 |
| Due to Debt Service Fund | | 10,000 |
| Deferred Revenues | | 16,000 |
| Fund Balance—Reserved for Encumbrances | | 9,000 |
| Fund Balance—Unreserved, Undesignated | | 103,000 |
| Revenues Control | | 176,000 |
| Expenditures Control | 110,000 | |
| Other Financing Uses Control | 90,000 | |
| Encumbrances Control | 9,000 | |
| Estimated Revenues Control | 190,000 | |
| Appropriations Control | | 171,000 |
| Budgetary Fund Balance | | 19,000 |
| Totals | $530,000 | $530,000 |

**Debt Service Fund**

|  | Debit | Credit |
|---|---|---|
| Cash | $ 8,000 | |
| Investments | 51,000 | |
| Taxes Receivable | 11,000 | |
| Due from General Fund | 10,000 | |
| Fund Balance—Designated for Debt Service | | $ 45,000 |
| Revenues Control | | 20,000 |
| Other Financing Sources—Operating Transfers In | | 90,000 |
| Expenditures Control | 75,000 | |
| Totals | $155,000 | $155,000 |

**Capital Projects Fund**

|  | Debit | Credit |
|---|---|---|
| Cash | $ 70,000 | |
| Special Assessments Receivable | 90,000 | |
| Contracts Payable | | $ 50,000 |
| Deferred Revenues | | 90,000 |
| Fund Balance—Reserved for Encumbrances | | 16,000 |
| Fund Balance—Unreserved, Undesignated | | —0— |
| Other Financing Sources | | 150,000 |
| Expenditures Control | 130,000 | |
| Encumbrances | 16,000 | |
| Estimated Other Financing Sources | 150,000 | |
| Appropriations | | 150,000 |
| Totals | $456,000 | $456,000 |

**Special Revenue Fund**

|  | Debit | Credit |
|---|---|---|
| Cash | $ 14,000 | |
| Taxes Receivable | 41,000 | |
| Inventory of Supplies | 4,000 | |
| Vouchers Payable | | $ 25,000 |
| Deferred Revenues | | 3,000 |
| Fund Balance—Reserved for Inventory of Supplies | | 4,000 |
| Fund Balance—Reserved for Encumbrances | | 3,000 |
| Fund Balance—Unreserved, Undesignated | | 19,000 |
| Revenues Control | | 56,000 |
| Expenditures Control | 48,000 | |
| Encumbrances | 3,000 | |
| Estimated Revenues | 75,000 | |
| Appropriations | | 60,000 |
| Budgetary Fund Balance | | 15,000 |
| Totals | $185,000 | $185,000 |

Based on the information presented for each of these governmental funds, answer the following questions:
   a. How much more money can be expended or committed by the General Fund during the remainder of the current year?
   b. Why does the Capital Projects Fund have no construction or capital asset accounts?
   c. What does the $150,000 Appropriations balance found in the Capital Projects Fund represent?
   d. Several of the funds have balances for Encumbrances and Fund Balance—Reserved for Encumbrances. How will these amounts be accounted for at the end of the fiscal year?
   e. Why does the Fund Balance—Unreserved, Undesignated account in the Capital Projects Fund have a zero balance?
   f. What are possible explanations for the $150,000 Other Financing Sources balance found in the Capital Projects Fund?
   g. What does the $75,000 balance in the Expenditures Control account of the Debt Service Fund represent?
   h. What is the purpose of the Special Assessments Receivable found in the Capital Projects Fund?
   i. In the Special Revenue Fund, what is the purpose of the Fund Balance—Reserved for Inventory of Supplies account?
   j. Why does the Debt Service Fund not have budgetary account balances?

36. Following are descriptions of transactions and other financial events for the City of Tetris for the year ending December 2004. Not all transactions have been included here. Only the General Fund formally records a budget. No encumbrances were carried over from 2003.

| | |
|---|---:|
| Paid salary for police officers | $ 21,000 |
| Received government grant to pay ambulance drivers | 40,000 |
| Estimated revenues | 232,000 |
| Received invoices for rent on equipment used by fire department during last four months of the year | 3,000 |
| Paid for newly constructed city hall | 1,044,000 |
| Made commitment to acquire new ambulance | 111,000 |
| Received cash from bonds sold for construction purposes | 300,000 |
| Placed order for new sanitation truck | 69,000 |
| Paid salary to ambulance drivers—money derived from state government grant given for that purpose | 24,000 |
| Paid for supplies for school system | 16,000 |
| Made transfer from General Fund to eventually pay off a long-term debt | 33,000 |
| Received but did not pay for new ambulance | 120,000 |
| Levied property tax receivables. City anticipates that 95 percent will be collected and 5 percent will be bad | 200,000 |
| Acquired and paid for new school bus | 40,000 |
| Received cash from business taxes and parking meters (not previously accrued) | 14,000 |
| Made appropriations | 225,000 |

The following questions are *independent* although each is based on the preceding information. Assume that the government is preparing information for its fund-based financial statements.
   a. What is the balance in the Fund Balance account for the budget for the year? Is it a debit or credit?
   b. Assume that 60 percent of the school supplies are used during the year so that 40 percent remain. If the consumption method is being applied, how is this recorded?
   c. The sanitation truck that was ordered was not received prior to the end of the year. The commitment will be honored in the subsequent year when the truck arrives. What reporting is made at the end of 2004?
   d. Assume that the ambulance was received on December 31, 2004. Provide all necessary journal entries on that date.
   e. Give all journal entries that should have been made when the $33,000 transfer was made to eventually pay off a long-term debt.
   f. What amount of revenue would be recognized for the period? Explain the makeup of this total.

g. What are the total expenditures? Explain the makeup of this total.
h. What journal entry or entries were prepared when the bonds were issued?

37. Chesterfield County incurred the following transactions. Prepare the entries the first time for fund-based financial statements. Then prepare them again for government-wide financial statements.
   a. A budget is passed for all ongoing activities. Revenue is anticipated to be $834,000 with approved spending of $540,000 and operating transfers out of $242,000.
   b. A contract is signed with a construction company to build a new central office building for the government at a cost of $8 million. A budget for this project has previously been recorded.
   c. Bonds are sold for $8 million (face value) to finance construction of the new office building.
   d. The new building is completed. An invoice for $8 million is received and paid.
   e. Previously unrestricted cash of $1 million is set aside to begin paying the bonds issued in (c).
   f. A portion of the bonds comes due and $1 million is paid. Of this total, $100,000 represents interest. The interest had not been previously accrued.
   g. Citizens' property tax levies are assessed. Total billing for this tax is $800,000. On this date, the assessment is a legally enforceable claim according to the laws of this state. The money to be received is designated for the current period. Ninety percent is assumed to be collectible in this period with receipt of an additional 6 percent during subsequent periods but in time to be available to pay current period claims. The remainder is expected to be uncollectible.
   h. Cash of $120,000 is received from a toll road. This money must be spent on highway maintenance.
   i. Investments valued at $300,000 are received by the county as a donation from a grateful citizen. Income from these investments must be used to beautify local parks.

38. The following trial balance is taken from the General Fund of the City of Jennings for the year ending December 31, 2004. Prepare a condensed statement of revenues, expenditures, and changes in fund balance and also prepare a condensed balance sheet.

|  | Debit | Credit |
|---|---|---|
| Accounts Payable |  | $ 90,000 |
| Cash | $ 30,000 |  |
| Contracts Payable |  | 90,000 |
| Deferred Revenues |  | 40,000 |
| Due from Capital Projects Funds | 60,000 |  |
| Due to Debt Service Funds |  | 40,000 |
| Expenditures | 510,000 |  |
| Fund Balance—Unreserved, Undesignated |  | 170,000 |
| Investments | 410,000 |  |
| Revenues |  | 740,000 |
| Other Financing Sources—Bond Proceeds |  | 300,000 |
| Other Financing Sources—Transfers In |  | 50,000 |
| Other Financing Uses—Transfers Out | 470,000 |  |
| Taxes Receivable | 220,000 |  |
| Vouchers Payable |  | 180,000 |
| Totals | $1,700,000 | $1,700,000 |

39. A city has only one activity, its school system. The school system is accounted for within the General Fund. For convenience, assume that, at the start of 2004, the school system and the city have no assets. During the year, the city assessed $400,000 in property taxes. Of this amount, $320,000 was collected during the year, $50,000 was received within a few weeks after the end of the year, and the remainder is expected to be collected about six months later. The city makes the following payments during 2004: salary expense, $100,000; rent expense, $70,000; equipment (received on January 1 with a five-year life and no salvage value), $50,000; land, $30,000; and maintenance expense, $20,000. In addition, on the last day of the year, the city purchased a $200,000 building by signing a long-term liability. The building has a 20-year life and no salvage value, and the liability accrues interest at a 10 percent annual rate. Also, the city buys two computers on the last day of the year for $4,000 each. One will be paid for in 30 days and the other in 90 days. The computers should last for four years and have no salvage value. During the year, the school system charged the students $3,000 for school fees and collected the entire amount. Any depreciation is recorded using the straight-line method.

a. Produce a statement of net assets and a statement of activities for this city's government-wide financial statements.
b. Produce a balance sheet and a statement of revenues, expenditures, and changes in fund balance for the fund-based financial statements. Assume that "available" is defined by the city as anything to be received within 60 days.

40. The following transactions relate to the General Fund of the city of Lost Angel for the year ending December 31, 2004. For this General Fund, prepare a statement of revenues, expenditures, and changes in fund balance for the period to be included in the fund-based financial statements. Assume the fund balance at the beginning of the year was $180,000. Assume also that the purchases method is applied to the supplies and that receipt within 60 days is used as the definition of available resources.
   a. Collected property tax revenue of $400,000. A remaining assessment of $100,000 will be collected in the subsequent period. Half of that amount should be collected within 30 days, and the remainder will be received in about five months after the end of the year.
   b. Spent $100,000 on two new police cars with 10-year lives. A price of $104,000 had been anticipated when the cars were ordered. The city calculates all depreciation using the straight-line method with no salvage value. The half-year convention is used.
   c. Transferred $90,000 to a debt service fund.
   d. Issued a long-term bond for $200,000 on July 1. Interest at a 10 percent annual rate will be paid each year starting on June 30, 2005.
   e. Ordered a new computer with a 5-year life for $40,000.
   f. Paid salaries of $30,000. Another $10,000 will be owed at the end of the year but will not be paid for 30 days.
   g. Received the new computer but at a cost of $41,000, payment to be made in 45 days.
   h. Bought supplies for $10,000.
   i. Used $8,000 of the supplies in (h).

41. Use the transactions in problem 40 but prepare a statement of net assets for the government-wide financial statements. Assume that the General Fund had $180,000 in cash on the first day of the year and no other assets or liabilities.

42. Government officials of the City of Jones expect to receive General Fund revenues of $400,000 in 2004 but approve spending only $380,000. Later in the year, as more information is received, the revenue projection is increased to $420,000 so that the officials approve the spending of an additional $15,000. For each of the following, indicate whether the statement is true or false and, if false, explain why.
   a. In recording this budget, appropriations should be credited initially for $380,000.
   b. The city must disclose this budgetary data within the required supplemental information section reported after the notes to the financial statements.
   c. When reporting budgetary information for the year, three figures should be reported: amended budget, initial budget, and actual figures.
   d. In making the budgetary entry, a debit must be made to some type of Fund Balance account to indicate the projected surplus.
   e. The reporting of the budget is reflected in the government-wide financial statements.

43. On December 1, 2004, a state government awards a city government a grant of $1 million to be used specifically to provide hot lunches for all school children. No money is received until June 1, 2005. For each of the following, indicate whether the statement is true or false and, if false, explain why.
   a. Because no money is received by the government until June 1, 2005, no amount of revenue can be recognized in 2004 on the government-wide financial statements.
   b. If this grant has no eligibility requirements and the money is properly spent in September 2005 for the hot lunches, the revenue should be recognized in September.
   c. Because the money came from the state government and because the government specified the use, this is a government-mandated nonexchange transaction.
   d. If the money had been received by the government on December 1, 2004, but eligibility requirements had not been met yet, a deferred revenue of $1 million would have been recognized on the government-wide financial statements.
   e. The rules for recognition of this revenue were created by *GASB Statement 34*.

44. A government has adopted *GASB Statement 34* and will apply it for the first time in 2004. Citizens of a local neighborhood agreed to pay $100,000 for sidewalks to be built on their street. On January 1, 2004, the government borrowed $100,000 on a two-year bond. The government built the sidewalk immediately at a cost of $100,000 and paid for it with the proceeds of the bond. The citizens are charged $100,000, and they all pay immediately. However, no payment has been made on the debt.

Assume that the government is directly liable on this bond. For each of the following, indicate whether the statement is true or false and, if false, explain why.
  a. Before adopting *GASB Statement 34*, reporting the sidewalk as an asset would have been optional but now is required for the government-wide financial statements.
  b. Within the fund-based financial statements, the government should report both a revenue and an other financing source of $100,000.
  c. If all of the facts are the same as in (*a*) and (*b*) except that the government had no liability on the bond, neither a revenue, an expenditure, nor even an other financing source would be recognized on the government-wide financial statements.
  d. If the sidewalk is capitalized on the government-wide financial statements, it must be depreciated.

45. Fund A transfers $20,000 to Fund B. For each of the following, indicate whether the statement is true or false and, if false, explain why.
  a. If Fund A is the General Fund and Fund B is an enterprise fund, nothing will be shown for this transfer on the statement of activities within the government-wide financial statements.
  b. If Fund A is the General Fund and Fund B is a debt service fund, nothing will be shown for this transfer on the statement of activities within the government-wide financial statements.
  c. If Fund A is the General Fund and Fund B is an enterprise fund, a $20,000 reduction will be reported on the statement of revenues, expenditures, and other changes for the governmental funds within the fund-based financial statements.
  d. If Fund A is the General Fund and Fund B is a special revenue fund (which is not considered a major fund), no changes will be shown on the statement of revenues, expenditures, and other changes within the fund-based financial statements.
  e. If Fund A is the General Fund and Fund B is an internal service fund and this is for work done, the General Fund will report an expense of $20,000 within the fund-based financial statements.

**Use the following information for problems 46–52.**
Assume that the City of Coyote has already produced its financial statements for December 31, 2004, and the year then ended. The city's General Fund was made up of education and parks. Its Capital Projects Funds benefited each of these functions at times. The city also had established an enterprise fund to account for its art museum.

On the government-wide financial statements, the following figures were indicated:

- Education reported net expenses of $600,000.
- Parks reported net expenses of $100,000.
- Art museum reported net revenues of $50,000.
- General government revenues for the year were $800,000 with an overall increase in the city's net assets of $150,000.

On the fund-based financial statements, the following were indicated for the year:

- The General Fund reported an increase in its fund balance of $30,000.
- The Capital Projects Fund reported an increase in its fund balance of $40,000.
- The Enterprise Fund reported an increase in its net assets of $60,000.

The CPA firm of Abernethy and Chapman has been asked to review several transactions that occurred during 2004 and indicate how to correct any erroneous reporting and the impact of each error. Each situation should be viewed as *independent*.

46. During 2004, the City of Coyote contracted to build a sidewalk costing $10,000 as a special assessments project for which it collected $10,000 from affected citizens. The government had no obligation in connection with this project. A $10,000 revenue and a $10,000 expenditure were both recorded in the Capital Projects Funds. In preparing government-wide financial statements, an asset and a general revenue were recorded later.
  a. What was the correct change in the Capital Projects Fund's fund balance during 2004?
  b. What was the correct overall change in the city's net assets on the government-wide financial statements?

47. On December 30, 2004, the City of Coyote borrowed $20,000 for the General Fund on a 60-day note. In that fund, both Cash and Other Financing Sources were recorded. What was the correct change in the General Fund's fund balance for 2004?

48. An art display set up for the community was recorded within the General Fund and generated revenues of $9,000 but had expenditures of $45,000 ($15,000 in expenses and $30,000 to buy land for the display). The CPA firm has determined that this program should have been recorded as an enterprise fund because it was offered in association with the art museum.

a. What was the correct change in the General Fund's fund balance for 2004?
b. What was the correct overall change in the city's net assets on the government-wide financial statements?
c. What was the correct change in the net assets of the Enterprise Funds on the fund-based financial statements?

49. Property tax bills for 2005 were mailed to the citizens of Coyote during August 2004. Payments could be made early to receive a discount. The levy becomes legally enforceable on February 15, 2005. All money received must be spent during 2005 or later. The total assessment is $300,000; 40 percent of that amount less a 10 percent discount is collected in 2004. The city expects to receive all of the remaining money during 2005 with no discount. During 2004, the government increased cash as well as a revenue for the same amount. No change was made in creating the government-wide financial statements.
    a. What was the correct overall change in the city's net assets as shown on the government-wide financial statements?
    b. What was the correct change for 2004 in the fund balance reported in the General Fund?

50. Property tax bills for 2005 were mailed to the citizens of Coyote during August 2004. Payments could be made early to receive a discount. The levy becomes legally enforceable on February 15 2005. All money received must be spent during 2005 or later. The total assessment is $300,000, and 40 percent of that amount is collected in 2004 less a 10 percent discount. The city expects to get all of the rest of the money during 2005 with no discount. During 2004, the government increased cash as well as a revenue for the amount received. In addition, a receivable account and a deferred revenue account for $180,000 were recognized.
    a. What was the correct overall change in the city's net assets as reported on the government-wide financial statements?
    b. What was the correct change during 2004 in the General Fund's fund balance?

51. In 2004, the City of Coyote received a $320,000 cash grant from the state to stop air pollution. Although a special revenue fund could have been set up, assume that the money remained in the General Fund. Cash was received immediately but had to be returned if the city had not lowered air pollution by 25 percent by 2007. On December 31, 2004, $210,000 of this money was spent for a large machine to help begin to reduce pollution. The machine is expected to last for five years and was recorded as an expenditure in the General Fund and as an asset on the government-wide financial statements where it was depreciated based on the straight-line method and the half-year convention. Because the money had been received, all $320,000 was recorded as a revenue on both the fund-based and the government-wide financial statements.
    a. What was the correct change for 2004 in the General Fund's fund balance?
    b. What was the correct overall change in the net assets reported on the government-wide financial statements?

52. During 2004, the City of Coyote's General Fund received $10,000, which was recorded as a general revenue when it was actually a program revenue earned by its park program.
    a. What was the correct overall change for 2004 in the net assets reported on the government-wide financial statements?
    b. What was the correct amount of net expenses reported by the parks?

# Develop Your Skills

## RESEARCH CASE 1

The City of Hampshore is in the process of converting its financial statements to the requirements of *GASB Statement 34*, "Basic Financial Statements—and Management's Discussion and Analysis—for State and Local Governments." The city manager is concerned because the city encountered some unusual transactions during the current fiscal period and is unsure as to their handling.

### Required:

Use a copy of *GASB Statement 34* to answer each of the following questions.
a. For government accounting, what is the definition of *extraordinary item*?

b. For government accounting, what is the definition of *special item*?
  c. On government-wide financial statements, how should extraordinary items and special items be reported?

## RESEARCH CASE 2

The City of Danmark is in the process of converting its financial statements to the requirements of *GASB Statement 34*, "Basic Financial Statements—and Management's Discussion and Analysis—for State and Local Governments." A question has arisen as to the whether a particular revenue should be identified on government-wide statements as a program revenue or a general revenue.

### Required:

Use a copy of *GASB Statement 34* to answer each of the following questions.
  a. How is a program revenue defined?
  b. What are common examples of program revenues?
  c. How is a general revenue defined?
  d. What are common examples of general revenues?

## ANALYSIS CASE 1

Go to the website www.ci.san-ramon.ca.us/admin/financialstmt.html and download the general purpose financial statements for the City of San Ramon, California. Answer each of the following questions.

### Required:

  a. How does the audit opinion given to this city by its independent auditors differ from the opinion rendered on the financial statements for a for-profit business?
  b. Has the City of San Ramon adopted *GASB Statement 34* in these financial statements?
  c. What were the city's largest sources of general revenues?
  d. What was the total amount of expenditures recorded by the General Fund during the period? How were those expenditures classified?
  e. What assets are reported for the General Fund?
  f. Why were no long-term liabilities reported in the General Fund?
  g. Did the size of the General Fund balance increase or decrease during the most recent year and by how much?

## ANALYSIS CASE 2

Go to the website www.gasb.org and click on "What's New?" Scroll down to the topic "Exposure Drafts." Review any exposure drafts currently being considered by the GASB.

### Required:

Identify the major impacts that would be created in government accounting by the proposed changes.

## COMMUNICATION CASE 1

Go to the website www.gasb.org and click on "Site Map." Find the GASB Mission Statement.

### Required:

Write a memo on the changes created by *GASB Statement 34* and how those changes reconcile with the GASB's mission.

## COMMUNICATION CASE 2

Obtain a copy of *GASB Statement 34*. Read paragraphs 239 through 277.

### Required:

Write a report describing alternatives that were considered when *GASB Statement 34* was being created. Indicate the alternative that you would have viewed as most appropriate and describe why the GASB did not choose it.

## EXCEL CASE 1

The City of Bainland has been undergoing financial difficulties because of a decrease in its tax base caused by corporations leaving the area. On January 1, 2004, the city has a fund balance of $400,000 in its governmental funds. In 2003, the city had revenues of $1.4 million and expenditures of $1.48 million. The city's treasurer has forecast that, unless something is done, revenues will decrease at 2 percent per year while expenditures will increase at 3 percent per year.

### Required:

a. Create a spreadsheet to predict what year the government will have a zero fund balance.
b. One proposal is that the city slash its expenditures by laying off government workers. That action will lead to a 3 percent decrease in expenditures each year rather than a 3 percent increase. However, because of the unemployment, the city will receive less tax revenues. Thus, instead of a 2 percent decrease in revenues, the city expects a 5 percent decrease per year. Adapt the spreadsheet created in requirement (*a*) to predict what year the government will have a zero fund balance if this option is taken.
c. Another proposal is to increase spending to draw new businesses to the area. This action will lead to a 7 percent increase in expenditures every year but revenues are expected to rise by 4 percent per year. Adapt the spreadsheet created in requirement (*a*) to predict what year the government will have a zero fund balance under this option.

# Chapter Twelve

# Accounting for State and Local Governments (Part 2)

The previous chapter of this book served as an introduction to the unique aspects of financial reporting applicable to state and local governments. Fund accounting, budgetary entries, encumbrances, expenditures, revenue recognition, and the like were all analyzed in light of traditional government accounting procedures and the massive changes brought by the creation of government-wide financial statements. That initial coverage was designed to present the basic essentials underlying the accounting required of these government entities, especially because of the dual nature of financial reporting that leads to the preparation of both fund-based financial statements and government-wide financial statements.

The current chapter carries this analysis further by delving into more complex financial situations. Obviously, many state and local government units are quite large and have transactions as complicated as any encountered by a for-profit business. In this chapter, issues such as the way to handle solid waste landfills, donated artworks, and the depreciation of infrastructure assets are examined to broaden the scope of understanding of state and local government accounting. Next, the overall financial reporting model is studied. Within this coverage, the actual composition of a government is described. Because of the wide variety of agencies and other activities that can operate in connection with a government, necessary inclusion within the financial statements is not as easy to define as in a for-profit business where ownership of more than 50 percent of the voting stock is the primary criterion.

**Questions to Consider**

- How does the accounting for capital leases utilized for fund-based financial statements differ from the procedures used in producing government-wide financial statements?
- What liability does a government have for closure and cleanup costs of a solid waste landfill and how are these costs reported?
- How does a state or local government record artworks or historical treasures that are bought or obtained through donation?
- What is meant by using the modified approach in connection with the depreciation of infrastructure assets?
- What is included in the management's discussion and analysis (MD&A) and why is it now required of state and local governments?
- What is a component unit and how is it reported by a state or local government?
- How does governmental accounting apply to public colleges and universities?

# CAPITAL LEASES

The notes to the 2001 financial statements of the City of Birmingham, Alabama, describe specific capital leases as follows:

> The City entered into lease agreements as lessee to finance the acquisition of fire equipment and telecommunication equipment. Two leases for the fire pumpers required advance rental payments and transaction fees in the amount of $933,809. The leases are for five years with annual payments in the amount of $884,110.

Likewise, the City of Greensboro, North Carolina, notes in 2001 that "the City has entered into lease-purchase and other financing agreements for certain equipment, land and infrastructure that bear interest rates from 2.6 percent to 6.7 percent and redevelopment projects that bear interest at graduated rates from 7.7 percent to 8.2 percent."

Obviously, state and local governments (in the same manner as a for-profit business) sometimes obtain the use of property by lease rather than by direct purchase. Leasing can provide lower interest rates or reduce the risk of obsolescence and damage. Leasing is simply a way that many organizations (private or governmental) can acquire needed equipment, machinery, buildings, or other assets.

For reporting purposes, such leases must be recorded as either capital leases or operating leases. The initial issue is to separate one type from another. In that regard, the GASB has accepted the method applied in FASB *SFAS 13*, "Accounting for Leases," as the method of differentiation. That pronouncement established the following four criteria; a lease that meets any one of these is held to be a *capital lease:*

1. The lease transfers ownership of the property to the lessee by the end of the lease term.
2. The lease contains an option to purchase the leased property at a bargain price.
3. The lease term is equal to or more than 75 percent of the estimated economic life of the leased property.
4. The present value of rental or other minimum lease payments equals or exceeds 90 percent of the fair value of the leased property less any investment tax credit retained by the lessor.

Thus, for example, assume that a city leases a truck that has a 10-year life and a fair market value of $50,000. In each of these four sample situations, the city is required to account for the property as a capital lease:

- The lease is for six years, but the city automatically receives title to the truck at the end of that term (so that criterion 1 is met).
- The lease is for five years but the city can buy the truck for $3,000 at the end of that time, an amount that is viewed as significantly less than the expected fair value at that point in time (so that criterion 2 is met).
- The lease is for eight years after which the truck will be returned to the lessor (so that criterion 3 is met).
- The lease is for seven years, but the present value of minimum lease payments is more than $45,000 or 90 percent of the fair market value (so that criterion 4 is met). In this last example, the lessee is viewed as paying the equivalent of the purchase price to obtain the use of the asset.

## Government-Wide Financial Statements

In reporting a capital lease, the accounting is the same within the government-wide financial statements as that appropriate for a for-profit enterprise. Both an asset and a liability are reported initially at the present value of the minimum lease payments in the same manner as a debt-financed acquisition. Assume, for example, that a police department signs an 8-year lease for a truck with a 10-year life. Because the third criterion is met, this transaction must be recorded as a capital lease. Assume also that the lease calls for annual payments of $10,000 per year with the first payment made at the signing of the lease and that a 10 percent interest rate is appropriate for the city.

The present value of the minimum lease payments applying a 10 percent interest rate to an annuity due for eight years is $58,680 (rounded). The following entry would be reported within the governmental activities because it relates to the police department. However, the same reporting is appropriate within the business-type activities if an enterprise fund had been involved. As indicated in the previous chapter, no accounting distinction is made for the two types of activities.

*Government-Wide Financial Statements*

| | | |
|---|---|---|
| Truck—Capital Lease | 58,680 | |
|     Cash | | 10,000 |
|     Capital Lease Obligation | | 48,680 |
| To record capital lease and first payment. | | |

Assuming that the straight-line method is being used, depreciation expense of $7,335 should be recognized ($58,680/8 years) at the end of this first year. However, if title to the asset is to transfer to the city or if a bargain purchase option exists, the full 10-year life should be used for depreciation purposes because the lessee will expect to get full use of the asset.

At the end of the first year, when the next payment is made, part of that $10,000 will be attributed to interest with the remainder viewed as a reduction in the liability principal. Because the obligation is reported at $48,680 and the interest rate is 10 percent, the interest recorded for the first year will be $4,868. The remaining $5,132 ($10,000 less $4,868) decreases the debt to $43,548.

*Government-Wide Financial Statements*

| | | |
|---|---|---|
| Interest Expense | 4,868 | |
| Capital Lease Obligation | 5,132 | |
|     Cash | | 10,000 |
| To record payment on capital lease at end of first year. | | |

## Fund-Based Financial Statements

Assume that the same lease is being recorded in the fund-based financial statements. If a proprietary fund is involved, the handling is the same as in the preceding situation. A difference appears only for the governmental funds.

For example, assume the same lease as above is being recorded to produce fund-based financial statements. Using the same eight-year lease in connection with the truck requiring payments of $10,000 per year, an amount with a present value of $58,680, the General Fund (or whichever governmental fund was gaining use of the asset) records the following entry:

*Fund-Based Financial Statements*

| | | |
|---|---|---|
| **General Fund** | | |
| Expenditures—Leased Asset | 58,680 | |
|     Cash | | 10,000 |
|     Other Financing Sources—Capital Lease | | 48,680 |
| To record signing of an eight-year lease for a truck that meets the requirements of a capital lease. | | |

Note that neither the asset nor the long-term liability is reported because it does not fall within the definition of current financial resources. Prior to *GASB Statement 34,* an asset account would have appeared in the General Fixed Assets Account Group with the related liability in the General Long-Term Debt Account Group. Those balances now are reported in the government-wide financial statements so that the account groups are no longer needed for this purpose.

At the end of this initial year, when the next payment is made, $4,868 (10 percent of the obligation after the first payment) is considered interest; the rest reduces the principal.

### Fund-Based Financial Statements

| General Fund | | |
|---|---|---|
| Expenditures—Interest | 4,868 | |
| Expenditures—Principal | 5,132 | |
|     Cash | | 10,000 |
| To record payment at the end of first year on leased truck being recorded as a capital lease. | | |

At first glance, the fund-based journal entries appear to be double counting the expenditures, once when the asset is obtained and later when periodic payments are made. This approach, though, can be justified. The government had an option; it could have either leased the asset or borrowed money and bought the asset. Since the overall result is the same in both cases, the reporting should not create different pictures. The preceding two entries seek to mirror the presentation that would have resulted in fund-based statements if the city had followed an alternative strategy for acquiring the asset: (1) money was borrowed on a long-term liability, (2) the money, along with a down payment, was used to acquire the asset, and (3) the long-term liability was subsequently paid. If this borrow-and-buy approach had been used, the recording would have been as follows in the fund-based statements:

1. To reflect the borrowing, the city would have reported another financing source because the money received did not come from a revenue.
2. At the time of the asset's acquisition, an expenditure would have been shown in keeping with the goal of presenting the changes in current financial resources.
3. For the same reason, the subsequent payment of debt and interest would have led to a second recording of expenditures.

Consequently, if money had been borrowed and the asset bought, one "other financing source" and two separate "expenditures" would have been recorded. The preceding journal entries created for the capital lease are structured to arrive at that same impact.

The radical differences between fund-based financial statements and government-wide financial statements are, once again, quite striking. At the end of this first year, the resulting figures are not comparable in any way. Because the capital lease is being recorded within the governmental funds, the distinctions are quickly apparent:

|  | Fund-Based Financial Statements | Government-Wide Financial Statements |
|---|---|---|
| Asset | Not applicable | $58,680 |
| Accumulated depreciation | Not applicable | 7,335 |
| Liability | Not applicable | 43,548 |
| Expenditures: | | |
|     Asset | $58,680 | Not applicable |
|     Debt principal | 5,132 | Not applicable |
|     Interest | 4,868 | Not applicable |
| Other financing sources | 48,680 | Not applicable |
| Depreciation expense | Not applicable | 7,335 |
| Interest expense | Not applicable | 4,868 |

# SOLID WASTE LANDFILL

The following information is disclosed in the notes to the financial statements of the City of Lincoln, Nebraska, as of August 31, 2000.

> The City of Lincoln currently owns and operates a solid waste disposal area and a construction and demolition disposal area. State and federal laws require the City to close the landfills once capacity is reached and to monitor and maintain the site for thirty subsequent years on the solid waste disposal area and five subsequent years on the construction and demolition disposal area. The City recognizes a portion of the closure and postclosure care costs in each operating period even though actual payouts will not occur until and subsequent to closure of the landfill. The amount recognized each year to date is based on the percentage of the landfill capacity. At August 31, 2000, the City had incurred a liability of $5,116,000 for the solid waste disposal area which represents the amount of costs reported to date based on the approximately 26 percent of landfill capacity used to date. The remaining estimated liability for these costs is approximately $18 million which will be recognized as the remaining capacity is used (estimated to be approximately 24 years).

A great many governments operate solid waste landfills to provide a place for citizens and local companies to dispose of trash and other forms of garbage and refuse. Landfill operations are frequently reported within the enterprise funds because many of these facilities require a user fee. However, some landfills are open to the public for free so that reporting within the General Fund is more appropriate.

Regardless of the type of fund utilized, solid waste landfills can be sources of huge liabilities for governments. The U.S. Environmental Protection Agency has strict rules on closure requirements as well as groundwater monitoring and other postclosure activities. Satisfying such requirements can be quite costly. Thus, the operation of a landfill almost always necessitates large payments to ensure that the facility is properly closed and then monitored and maintained for an extended period. Theoretically, the question has always been how to report closure costs while the landfill is still in operation.

To illustrate, assume that a city opens a landfill in Year 1 that is expected to take 10 years to fill. Currently, the city expects that a total of $1 million in closure costs will be necessary as well as an additional $400,000 in postclosure costs. During Year 1, the city makes an initial $30,000 payment toward the closure costs. At the end of the year, the city estimates that 16 percent of the space has been filled.

## Government-Wide Financial Statements

Regardless of whether this solid waste landfill is reported as a governmental activity (within the General Fund) or as a business-type activity (within an enterprise fund), recognition in the government-wide statements is based on accrual accounting and the economic resources measurement basis. Because the government anticipates total costs of $1.4 million and the landfill is 16 percent filled, $224,000 should be accrued in this first year ($1.4 million × 16%).

*Year 1*

| | | |
|---|---|---|
| Expense—Landfill Closure | 224,000 | |
|     Landfill Closure Liability | | 224,000 |
| To recognize the Year 1 portion of total costs for eventual closure of landfill. | | |

An initial payment was made during the year. This payment simply reduces the liability being reported.

| | | |
|---|---|---|
| Landfill Closure Liability | 30,000 | |
|     Cash | | 30,000 |
| To record first payment of costs necessitated by eventual closure of the landfill. | | |

To extend this example, assume that the landfill is judged to be 27 percent filled at the end of Year 2 and another $30,000 payment has been made. However, because of inflation and newly anticipated changes in technology, the city now believes that closure costs will total $1.1 million and postclosure costs will amount to $500,000.

Using this new and revised information, the city should recognize total costs of $432,000 incurred by the end of Year 2 ($1.6 million × 27%). Because $224,000 has already been recorded in Year 1, an additional $208,000 is accrued for Year 2 ($432,000 less $224,000).

*Government-Wide Financial Statements: Year 2*

| | | |
|---|---:|---:|
| Expense—Landfill Closure | 208,000 | |
|     Landfill Closure Liability | | 208,000 |
| To recognize Year 2 portion of costs for eventual closure of landfill. | | |
| Landfill Closure Liability | 30,000 | |
|     Cash | | 30,000 |
| To record second payment of costs necessitated by eventual closure of the landfill. | | |

Consequently, in the Year 2 government-wide financial statements, the city reports:

| | |
|---|---:|
| Expense—Landfill closure | $208,000 |
| Landfill closure liability ($224,000 + $208,000 − $30,000 − $30,000) | 372,000 |

## Fund-Based Financial Statements

If a solid waste landfill is being recorded as an enterprise fund, the reporting will be the same in the fund-based financial statements as shown above. All economic resources are still being measured based on accrual accounting.

However, if the landfill is recorded in the General Fund, only the change in current financial resources is reported. Despite the huge eventual liability, the change in current financial resources has been limited to the annual payment of $30,000. Thus, the only entry required each year in this example for the fund-based financial statements is as follows.

*Fund-Based Financial Statements: Year 1 and Year 2*

| | | |
|---|---:|---:|
| **General Fund** | | |
| Expenditures—Closure Costs | 30,000 | |
|     Cash | | 30,000 |
| To record annual payment toward the eventual closure costs of the city's solid waste landfill. | | |

As with capital leases, before the adoption of *GASB Statement 34,* the long-term obligation ($372,000 in this case, at the end of Year 2) would be reported to the public through the use of a General Long-Term Debt Account Group. This method of disclosure will no longer be necessary after a government has published government-wide financial statements.

# COMPENSATED ABSENCES

State and local governments have numerous employees: police officers, school teachers, maintenance workers, and the like. As of June 30, 2001, the City of Baltimore, Maryland, reported having 15,871 employees.[1] In the same manner as the employees of a for-profit organization,

---

[1] Statistical information listed at the end of the comprehensive annual financial report provides a wide array of information about the reporting government. For example, in 2001, Baltimore had 2,000 miles of streets, 46 fire stations, 3,100 miles of sanitary sewer lines, 5 golf courses, 26 libraries, and 2 ice rinks.

government employees earn vacation days, sick leave days, and holidays that can amount to a fairly significant amount of money. At the end of the fiscal period, any liability for such compensated absences should be reported. For example, footnotes to the financial statements for the city of Baltimore spell out this issue:

> Employees earn one day of sick leave for each completed month of service; there is no limitation on the number of sick leave days that may be accumulated. At June 30, 2001, the estimated accumulated sick leave for the City was $64,438,000.

Clearly, a city such as Baltimore has a liability for any compensated absences that have been earned by government employees. In many ways, accounting for such liabilities is the same as was demonstrated for capital leases and solid waste landfills. In the government-wide financial statements, the expense is accrued as incurred. Conversely, for the governmental funds producing fund-based financial statements, only actual payments and claims to current financial resources are included. For example, assume that a city reaches the end of Year 1 and owes its General Fund employees $40,000 because of compensated absences to be taken in the future for vacation days, holidays, and sick leave that have been earned but not yet taken. However, $5,000 of these absences is expected early enough in Year 2 to require current financial resources. Perhaps a number of employees are expected to take their vacations in the first month of the subsequent period.

Consequently, a liability of $40,000 exists at the end of Year 1 but only $5,000 of that amount will be a claim on the government's current financial resources:

### *Government-Wide Financial Statements: Year 1*

| | | |
|---|---|---|
| Expenses—Compensated Absences | 40,000 | |
|     Liability—Compensated Absences | | 40,000 |
| To accrue amount owed at the end of Year 1 to employees for vacations, sick leave, and holidays. | | |

In contrast, when reporting the governmental funds in the fund-based financial statements, the changes in current financial resources are reflected. Thus, as shown in the following entry, only the $5,000 that will be paid early in the next year is included. The remainder of the debt is not reported because it is not a claim to current financial resources, although the reader can determine the total amount from the government-wide statements. Once again, though, if the employees work in an area reported as an enterprise fund, the accounting is the same as in the preceding government-wide statements.

### *Fund-Based Financial Statements: Year 1*

| | | |
|---|---|---|
| **General Fund** | | |
| Expenditures—Compensated Absences | 5,000 | |
|     Liability—Compensated Absences | | 5,000 |
| To accrue amount of compensated absences that will be taken early in Year 2 so that it requires the use of Year 1 financial resources. | | |

## WORKS OF ART AND HISTORICAL TREASURES

Private not-for-profit organizations have long debated the proper reporting of artworks and other museum pieces that are bought or given to them. This same issue is faced in governmental accounting. Should works of art, museum artifacts, and other historical treasures be reported and, if so, what is the proper method of inclusion within the financial statements?

Assume, for example, that a city maintains a small museum in the basement of its main office building. The museum was created to display documents, maps, and paintings that depict the history of the city and the surrounding area. Several of these items were bought by the city government, but a number were donated by local citizens. Many of these purchased and donated pieces are quite valuable.

*GASB Statement 34* is quite clear on the handling of the items acquired for this city museum. Paragraph 27 states that, except in certain specified cases, "governments should capitalize works of art, historical treasures, and similar assets at their historical cost or fair value at date of donation." Thus, the government-wide statement of net assets should report an antique map bought for $5,000 as an asset at cost. In the same manner, a similar map received as a gift is also recorded as a $5,000 asset owned by the city.

If the map is bought by the city for cash, the appropriate journal entry is:

*Government-Wide Financial Statements*

| | | |
|---|---|---|
| Museum Piece—Map | 5,000 | |
|     Cash | | 5,000 |
| To record acquisition of map for the city's museum. | | |

Because cash was paid for the map, a decrease occurs in current financial resources so that an entry is also needed in the fund-based financial statements if the museum is accounted for within the General Fund. However, if the museum has a user charge and is reported in an enterprise fund, the preceding entry is replicated in accounting for the proprietary funds.

*Fund-Based Financial Statements*

**General Fund**

| | | |
|---|---|---|
| Expenditure—Museum Piece | 5,000 | |
|     Cash | | 5,000 |
| To record acquisition of map for the city's museum, an activity which is being reported within the General Fund. | | |

Conversely, if this map had been donated to the city, capitalization of the asset for government-wide financial statements should still be reported based on its fair market value at the date of the gift. *GASB Statement 33* classifies such a gift as a voluntary nonexchange transaction so that a revenue is properly recognized when all eligibility requirements have been met. If no eligibility requirements exist, the following entry is appropriate. No parallel entry is made in the fund-based financial statements for the governmental funds because no change is occurring in the amount of available current financial resources.

*Government-Wide Financial Statements*

| | | |
|---|---|---|
| Museum Piece—Map | 5,000 | |
|     Revenue—Donation | | 5,000 |
| To record gift of map for the city's museum. | | |

A theoretical problem arises in the recognition of this asset for government-wide financial reporting regardless of whether it was obtained by purchase or by gift. Unless a user charge is assessed, a map displayed for the public to see does not generate cash flows or any other direct economic benefit. Therefore, does the map actually qualify as an asset to be reported?

In *Statement 34*, the GASB "encouraged" the recognition of all such artworks and historical treasures. However, if the following three criteria are met, recording the item as an asset is optional.

1. Held for public exhibition, education, or research in furtherance of public service, rather than financial gain.
2. Protected, kept unencumbered, cared for, and preserved.
3. Subject to an organizational policy that requires the proceeds from sales of collection items to be used to acquire other items for collections.[2]

If a government chooses not to record a qualifying asset in its government-wide financial statements as demonstrated on the previous page, an expense must be reported in place of the asset regardless of whether the item was obtained by purchase or gift. The GASB's handling of this issue closely parallels rules established previously by the FASB in its *SFAS 116*, "Accounting for Contributions Received and Contributions Made," issued in June 1993 and utilized by private not-for-profit organizations. However, the optional handling does differ.

If a work of art or other historical treasure is capitalized, an additional theoretical question arises, this time about depreciation. Does the map on display in the museum actually depreciate in value over time? In connection with this type of asset, *GASB Statement 34* requires depreciation only if the asset is "exhaustible," in other words, its utility will be used up by display, education, or research. Depreciation is not required, though, if the work of art or historical treasure is viewed as being inexhaustible. For example, a bronze statue could well be viewed as an inexhaustible asset according to these guidelines so that depreciation would be allowed but not required.

## INFRASTRUCTURE ASSETS AND DEPRECIATION

Infrastructure assets are defined in paragraph 19 of *GASB Statement 34* as "long-lived capital assets that normally are stationary in nature and normally can be preserved for a significantly greater number of years than most capital assets." Examples include roads, bridges, tunnels, lighting systems, curbing, and sidewalks. As discussed in the previous chapter, recording of infrastructure items as assets was an optional practice prior to the issuance of *GASB Statement 34*. However, this pronouncement (once adopted by a government) mandates that new infrastructure costs be recorded as assets on the government-wide statement of net assets. In contrast, for the governmental funds these same costs are recorded as expenditures in the fund-based statements because they do not represent current financial resources.

Beyond simply recording new infrastructure items as assets, a state or local government also has to capitalize general infrastructure assets previously acquired. A major road system constructed in 1988, for example, must be shown as an asset in the government-wide statements. Because cost figures on these earlier acquisitions and constructions may not be available, estimations often are necessary. In addition, since approximating the cost of all previously acquired infrastructure items would be virtually impossible, this requirement is limited to major assets that (1) were acquired in fiscal years ending after June 30, 1980, or that (2) had major renovations, restorations, or improvements since that date.

To allow sufficient time for governments to develop these figures, application of the retroactive reporting of these major infrastructure assets is one area of *GASB Statement 34* where required implementation has been delayed.

- For governments with revenues of $100 million or more, this particular reporting is not required until fiscal years beginning after June 15, 2005, (although all other aspects of *Statement 34* are mandated for years beginning after June 15, 2001).
- For governments with revenues of $10 million or more but less than $100 million, retroactive reporting of major infrastructure assets is required for years beginning after June 15, 2006, with other changes necessary in years beginning after June 15, 2002.

---

[2] *Governmental Accounting Standards Board Statement No. 34*, "Basic Financial Statements—and Management's Discussion and Analysis—for State and Local Governments," June 1999, para. 27.

- For governments with revenues of less than $10 million, capitalization of previous infrastructure items is encouraged but not required. All other requirements of *Statement 34* must be in place for years beginning after June 15, 2003.

As has been discussed previously, *GASB Statement 34* requires depreciation of all capital assets appearing in the government-wide financial statements except for land and art works and historical treasures that are deemed to be inexhaustible. A similar issue was debated in connection with infrastructure items: Is depreciation appropriate for this type of asset? For example, construction of the Brooklyn Bridge was finished in 1883 at a cost of about $15 million. That particular piece of infrastructure has been operating for approximately 120 years and, with proper maintenance, might well be able to continue to carry traffic for another 120 years. Much the same can be said of some roads, sidewalks, and the like being built today. With appropriate repair and maintenance care, such assets could have lives that are almost indefinite. What life should New York City use to depreciate the initial cost incurred in constructing a street such as Fifth Avenue?

Consequently, *GASB Statement 34* provides an alternative to depreciating eligible infrastructure assets such as the Brooklyn Bridge or Fifth Avenue. This method, known as the *modified approach,* eliminates the need for depreciation for qualifying infrastructure. If specified guidelines are met, the government can choose to expense all maintenance costs each year in lieu of recording depreciation. Additions and improvements still must be capitalized, but the cost of maintaining the infrastructure in proper working condition is expensed. Thus, the amount spent by New York City on repair and other maintenance of Fifth Avenue can be expensed directly so that depreciation of the street's capitalized cost is not recorded.

Use of the modified approach requires the government to accumulate information about particular infrastructure assets within either a network or a subsystem of a network. For example, all roads could be deemed a network while state roads, rural roads, and interstate highways might make up three subsystems of that network.

- For these eligible assets, the government must establish a minimum acceptable condition level for the network or subsystem of the network and then maintain documentation that this minimum level is being met.
- The government must have an asset management system in place to monitor the particular network or subsystem of a network in question. This system should assess the ongoing condition of the eligible assets to ensure that they are, indeed, able to operate at the predetermined level.

For example, a city could view its entire water system as an infrastructure network. The city could then state that it wants to maintain this network so that water stoppages occur less than two days per year on the average. To achieve this level of performance, the city believes that it will have to spend at least $5 million per year in repair and other maintenance costs. To apply the modified approach, the city must establish an asset management system to (1) keep an up-to-date inventory of the water system, (2) assess the system to determine whether it is operating at (or above) the minimum condition level established, and (3) document the level of operations achieved. As a result, no depreciation is reported in connection with the capitalized cost of the water system. All costs to maintain the water system should be expensed as incurred although additions and actual improvements still must be capitalized. For example, if the water system is extended into a new neighborhood, that is a capitalized cost, not a maintenance expense.

*GASB Statement 34* provides an example of the type of disclosure that is necessary to explain the use of the modified approach:

> The City manages its streets using the XYZ pavement management system. The City's policy is to maintain 85 percent of its streets at a pavement condition index of at least 70 (on a 100-point scale) and no more than 10 percent of its streets at a pavement condition index below 50. The most recent assessment found that the City's streets were within the prescribed parameters with 87 percent having a pavement condition index of 70 or better and only 2 percent of the streets having a pavement condition index below 50.[3]

---

[3] Ibid., p. 181.

## MANAGEMENT'S DISCUSSION AND ANALYSIS

Inclusion of a verbal explanation of a for-profit company's operations and financial position to accompany its financial statements has long been advocated by the Security and Exchange Commission. This memorandum, known generally as the management's discussion and analysis (MD&A), provides a wealth of vital information for the reader of the financial statements. Thus, in evaluating such organizations, outside decision makers are quite used to having a "plain English" explanation of the figures and other critical information disclosed within the statements. For example, the 2001 financial statements of the General Electric Company contained

- 11 pages of explanation entitled "Management's Discussion of Operations."
- 5 pages of explanation entitled "Management's Discussion of Financial Resources and Liquidity."
- 2 pages of explanation entitled "Management's Discussion of Selected Financial Data."
- Nearly 2 pages of explanation entitled "Management's Discussion of Critical Accounting Policy."

Consequently, a stockholder, creditor, potential investor, or other interested party is provided with extensive details to describe and supplement the facts and figures presented within the company's financial statements.

One of the most important changes created by *GASB Statement 34* was the requirement that a similar MD&A be required of state and local governments. This authoritative pronouncement actually divided the general purpose external financial statements of a state or local government into three distinct sections:

1. Management's discussion and analysis.
2. Financial statements:
   *a.* Government-wide financial statements.
   *b.* Fund-based financial statements.
   *c.* Notes to the financial statements.
3. Required supplementary information (other than the MD&A). For example, comparison of budgetary figures to actual figures is now shown in this final section although a separate statement within the financial statements can also be used.

In *Statement 34,* the GASB explains its justification for requiring officials to provide readers of the government's financial statements with an MD&A:

> The basic financial statements should be preceded by MD&A, which is required supplementary information (RSI). MD&A should provide an objective and easily readable analysis of the government's financial activities based on currently known facts, decisions, or conditions. The financial managers of governments are knowledgeable about the transactions, events, and conditions that are reflected in the government's financial report and of the fiscal policies that govern its operations. MD&A provides financial managers with the opportunity to present both a short- and a long-term analysis of the government's activities. MD&A should discuss current-year results in comparison with the prior year, with emphasis on the current year. This fact-based analysis should discuss the positive and negative aspects of the comparison with the prior year. The use of charts, graphs, and tables is encouraged to enhance the understandability of the information.[4]

As further guidance for the government officials who will have to write this MD&A, *GASB Statement 34* provides an extensive sample of the type of information and format that should be included. Reproduction of GASB's complete MD&A illustration is beyond the scope of this textbook. However, the following small sample provided in *Statement 34* facilitates an understanding of the intended purpose of the MD&A. This particular portion of the illustration

---

[4] Ibid., para. 8 and 9.

explains operating changes that occurred during the year in connection with the government's business-type activities:

> Revenues of the City's business-type activities increased by 5.6 percent ($15 million in 2002 compared to $14.2 million in 2001) and expenses decreased by 1.7 percent. The factors driving these results include:
>
> - The City water and sewer system, benefiting from growth in hook-ups by residential customers who are converting from septic systems, saw its operating revenues climb 10 percent to $11.3 million, but operating expenses rose only 4 percent, to $6.9 million. High maintenance costs—caused by the harsh winter months in 2001—did not occur this year.
> - The City parking facilities, however, continue to operate at a deficit (by $1.4 million this year versus $1.3 million in 2001). In both years, this decrease is attributable primarily to the largest of the three City-owned parking garages, located on State Street. This year, the garage had to be closed for two extended periods due to ruptured gas lines beneath nearby streets, which now have been repaired, and the State Street Mall fire. These closings stopped revenues from being generated by the garage for two months, while only slightly reducing expenses.[5]

As can be seen from this one short example, the MD&A is intended to provide a clear description of events to highlight and explain financial results for the period. The MD&A goes well beyond just numerical totals to convey background information so that the causes of the various figures and the changes encountered are more understandable.

*GASB Statement 34* provides requirements for the types of disclosures that must be included in the MD&A. The MD&A presented by a government must have all of the following according to paragraph 11:

1. A brief discussion of the basic financial statements. This discussion should describe the relationship of the statements to each other and the significant differences in information provided. Analysis should also be included to help explain why measurements and results reported in the fund-based statements reinforce or provide additional information to the government-wide financial statements.

2. Condensed financial information derived from government-wide financial statements comparing the current year to the prior year. At a minimum, governments should include:
    a. Total assets, distinguishing between capital and other assets.
    b. Total liabilities, divided between long-term and other liabilities.
    c. Total net assets, distinguishing among amounts invested in capital assets, net of related debt; restricted amounts; and unrestricted amounts.
    d. Program revenues, by major source.
    e. General revenues, by major source.
    f. Total revenues.
    g. Program expenses, at a minimum by function.
    h. Total expenses.
    i. Excess or deficiency before contributions to term and permanent endowments or permanent fund principal, special and extraordinary items, and transfers.
    j. Contributions.
    k. Special and extraordinary items.
    l. Transfers.
    m. Change in net assets.
    n. Ending net assets.

3. An analysis of overall financial position and results of operations to aid assessment of whether financial position has improved or deteriorated as a result of the year's operations.

---

[5] Ibid., p. 191.

4. An analysis of balances and transactions of individual funds explaining the reasons for significant changes in fund balances or net assets as well as any significant restrictions.
5. An analysis of significant variations between original and final budget amounts along with variations between final budget amounts and actual results for the General Fund.
6. A description of significant capital asset and long-term debt activity during the year.
7. If the modified approach is used for some or all infrastructure assets, information should be provided about its application.
8. A description of currently known facts, decisions, or conditions that are expected to have a significant effect on financial position or results of operations.

As can be seen, the MD&A is intended to provide a broad range of information to help decision makers evaluate the operations and financial position of the government unit.

The general purpose external financial statements outlined previously are presented to the public as part of a comprehensive annual financial report (often referred to as a *CAFR*). Even prior to *GASB Statement 34*, the CAFR included extensive information about the reporting government. For example, the 2001 CAFR for the city of Saint Paul, Minnesota, with total revenues of about $348 million was 234 pages long. In comparison, the 2001 annual report for Duke Energy Corporation with $59 billion in revenues was only 92 pages.

*GASB Statement 34* stipulates that the CAFR of a state or local government include three broad sections:

1. *Introductory Section*—includes a letter of transmittal from appropriate government officials, an organization chart, and a list of principal officers.
2. *Financial Section*—presents the general purpose external financial statements. In addition, the auditor's report is reproduced. The government also usually prepares additional supplementary information such as combining statements to present financial information for funds that do not qualify as major.
3. *Statistical Section*—presents a wide range of data about the government. For example, the 2001 CAFR for Dallas, Texas, included the following within its statistical section as well as a considerable amount of other information:

> 10-year recap of general government expenditures.
> 10-year recap of property tax revenues.
> 10-year recap of property tax rates.
> Principal taxpayers for the current year.
> 10-year recap of special assessment collections.
> 70-year look at population changes.
> Number of registered voters.
> Number of building permits issued.

# THE PRIMARY GOVERNMENT AND COMPONENT UNITS

Although gathering and maintaining financial information is a vital step in government accounting, the actual reporting of this data to the public is equally important.

> Governmental accountability is based on the belief that the citizenry has a "right to know," a right to receive openly declared facts that may lead to public debate by the citizens and their elected representatives. Financial reporting plays a major role in fulfilling government's duty to be publicly accountable in a democratic society.[6]

---

[6] *Codification of Governmental Accounting and Financial Reporting Standards* (Norwalk, Conn.: Governmental Accounting Standards Board, 1997), sec. 100.156.

In producing financial statements, a state or locality often encounters a unique problem—determining the specific activities to be included. Except in rare cases, a business enterprise such as IBM or Ford Motor Company simply consolidates all corporations over which control has been achieved. A state or locality, however, can interact with numerous departments, agencies, boards, institutes, commissions, and the like that have various relationships with these governments. Should all of these functions be included as either governmental activities or business-type activities within the CAFR of the government? If not, what reporting is appropriate?

An almost unlimited number of activities create problems for government officials attempting to outline the parameters of the entity being reported. Separate organizations such as turnpike commissions, port authorities, public housing boards, and downtown development commissions have become commonplace in recent years. Many of these are created by the government but remain legally separate from it. Such entities are designed to focus attention on specific issues or problems and can offer better efficiency because of their corporate-style structure.

In the introductory section of its 2001 CAFR, the city of Boston, Massachusetts, discusses various organizations that are related to the government including:

- Boston Redevelopment Authority.
- Boston Housing Authority.
- Boston Public Health Commission.

Likewise, the 2001 CAFR for the City of Greensboro, North Carolina, identifies several legally separate activities that are still reported within the city's financial statements:

- Redevelopment Commission of Greensboro.
- Greensboro Transit Authority.
- Greensboro ABC Board.

Because of the extremely wide variety of possible activities and functions, determining which components actually comprise a state or locality is not always an easy task. According to paragraphs 2 and 8 of *GASB Statement 14,* "The Financial Reporting Entity," the major criterion for inclusion in a government's comprehensive annual financial report is financial accountability:

> Financial reporting based on accountability should enable the financial statement reader to focus on the body of organizations that are related by a common thread of accountability to the constituent citizenry. . . . Elected officials are accountable to those citizens for their public policy decisions, regardless of whether these decisions are carried out directly by the elected officials through the operations of the primary government or *by their designees through the operations of specially created organizations* (emphasis added).

In defining the overall reporting entity, the primary government must be identified. A primary government includes and must report all funds, activities, organizations, agencies, offices, and departments that are not legally separate from it. A primary government is any state government or general purpose local government such as a city or county. However, a special purpose local government such as a school system is also deemed a primary government if it meets three criteria:

1. It has a separately elected governing body.
2. It is legally independent, which can be demonstrated by having corporate powers such as the right to sue and be sued in its own name as well as the right to buy, sell, and lease property in its own name.
3. It is fiscally independent of other state and local governments.

The term *fiscally independent* requires some clarification. Fiscal independence is normally demonstrated by an activity if its leadership can determine its own budget without having to seek approval of an outside party, levy taxes or set rates without having to seek outside approval, and issue bonded debt without having to seek outside approval. The City of Colonial Heights, Virginia, indicates in its 2001 financial statements that its school board is not a primary government when it states, "The elected five-member School Board serves staggered four-year terms of office. The School Board functions independently of the City Council, but is required to prepare and submit an annual budget to the City Council for approval. The School Board may not levy taxes or incur indebtedness under Virginia law, and therefore, funds for school operations are provided in part by appropriation from the City's General Fund."

Based on these criteria, a city is clearly a primary government, but its police department and fire department are not. However, if a school system or other special purpose government is a legally separate entity and has a publicly elected board that sets its own budget, levies its own taxes or fees, and issues its own bonds, it is a primary government and would issue its own CAFR. According to the U.S. Census Bureau, approximately 49,000 special purpose local governments existed at June 30, 2002.

## Component Units

Some activities can be legally separate from a primary government but still be so closely connected that omission from the statements of the primary government cannot be justified. Due to the relationship, the elected officials of the primary government are still financially accountable for these separate organizations known as *component units*.

Despite being legally separate, component units are included within the financial statements of the primary government. Thus, identification of such activities can be quite important. Two sets of criteria have been established for this purpose. If either set of criteria is met, the activity in question is a component unit to be reported within the CAFR of the primary government.

### *Criterion 1*

The separate organization is viewed as a component unit if it fiscally depends on the primary organization regardless of the extent of other relationships. As defined, *fiscal dependency* means that the organization cannot do one or more of the following without approval of the primary government: adopt its own budget, levy taxes or set rates, or issue bonded debt.

### *Criterion 2*

First, the officials of the primary government must appoint a voting majority of the governing board of the separate organization. Second, either the primary government must be able to impose its will on the board of the separate organization or the separate organization must provide a financial benefit or impose a financial burden on the primary government.

For example, a commission to oversee off-track betting might be established legally as a separate entity. However, if the state (the primary government) appoints a voting majority of the board membership and the financial benefits from revenues generated by the commission accrue to the state, the commission will be considered a component unit of the state for reporting purposes.

Several aspects of this second criterion should be explained to allow for proper application.

***Voting Majority of the Governing Board*** The authority to elect a voting majority must be substantive. If, for example, the primary government simply confirms the choices made by other parties, financial accountability is not created. In the same way, financial accountability does not result when the primary government is allowed to select the governing board from only a limited slate of candidates (such as picking three individuals from an approved list of five). Thus, the primary government must have the actual responsibility of appointing a voting majority of the board before the organization qualifies as a component unit.

***Imposition of the Primary Government's Will on the Governing Board*** Such power is indicated if the government can significantly influence the programs, projects, activities, or the level of services provided by the organization. This degree of influence is present if the primary government can remove an appointed board member at will, modify or approve budgets,

# Discussion Question

### IS IT PART OF THE COUNTY?

Harland County is in a financially distressed portion of Missouri. In hope of enticing business to this area, the state legislature appropriated $3 million to start an industrial development commission. The federal government provided an additional $1 million. The state appointed 15 individuals to a board to oversee the operations of this commission, and county officials named 5 members. The commission began operations by raising funds from local citizens and businesses. It received $700,000 in donations and pledges. The county provided clerical assistance and allowed the commission to use one floor of the county office building for its headquarters. The commission's budget must be approved by the county government.

During the current period, the commission spent $2.4 million and produced financial statements. It achieved notable success as several large manufacturing companies have recently begun to explore the possibility of opening plants in the county.

Harland County is presently beginning the process of producing its own comprehensive annual financial report. Should the revenues, expenditures, assets, and liabilities of the industrial development commission be included? Is it part of the county's primary government, a component unit, or a related organization?

Is the industrial development commission a component unit of the state of Missouri? How should its activities be presented in the state's comprehensive annual financial report?

---

override decisions of the board, modify or approve rate or fee changes, and hire or dismiss the individuals responsible for day-to-day operations.

***Financial Benefit or Financial Burden on the Primary Government*** A financial connection exists between the organization and the primary government if the government is entitled to the organization's resources, the government is legally obligated to finance any deficits or provide support, or the government is responsible for the debts of the organization.

Component units normally are reported in one of two ways: Many component units are discretely presented at the far right side of the government-wide statements. For example, the 2001 CAFR for the City of Dallas, Texas, shows that the primary government had total revenues of more than $1.8 billion and its discretely presented component units shown just to the right of the primary government had revenues of $229 million.

As an alternative placement, certain component units can be included by a primary government as if they were part of the government (a process referred to as *blending*). Although the organization is legally separate, it is so intertwined with the primary government that inclusion is necessary for the appropriate presentation of the financial information. In discussing the accounting for the Housing and Redevelopment Authority of the City of Saint Paul, the notes to the 2001 financial statements explain that the "following component unit has been presented as a blended component unit because the component unit's governing body is substantively the same as the governing body of the city."

One other aspect of the reporting process should be noted: the possible existence of related organizations. In such cases, the primary government is accountable because it appoints a voting majority of the governing board. However, financial accountability does not exist. Fiscal dependency as defined earlier is not present, and the primary government cannot impose its will on the board or gather financial benefits or burdens from the relationship. Without financial accountability, the organization does not qualify as a component unit to be included in the government's financial reporting. Instead, the primary government must disclose the nature of the relationship. For example, the 1998 CAFR for the City of Charlotte, North Carolina, indicates "the Charlotte Housing Authority (Housing Authority), which is excluded from the City's financial statements, is considered a related organization. The City Council appoints the Housing Authority's governing board; however, the City is not financially accountable for the Housing Authority."

# GENERAL PURPOSE EXTERNAL FINANCIAL STATEMENTS

As described in the previous chapter, a central element of the reporting requirements created by *GASB Statement 34* was the development of a new set of general purpose external financial statements for governments. The first two of these statements are deemed to be government-wide financial statements because they present all of the governmental funds and the proprietary funds. These statements measure economic resources and utilize accrual accounting to time the recognition of revenues and expenses.

A number of other financial statements also have been designed to present information describing individual funds. These fund-based statements are quite similar to the financial statements traditionally reported by state and local government units. At the fund level, the method of accounting depends on the fund in question. For governmental funds, the current financial resources measurement basis is used along with modified accrual accounting. However, both proprietary funds and fiduciary funds use accrual accounting to measure economic resources.

In the previous chapter, four of these statements were outlined briefly to provide an introduction to the initial coverage. However, now that a deeper understanding of government accounting has been established, these same statements as well as several others can be studied in more detail. Having an appreciation for the end result of the accounting process helps to show how the elements of government accounting fit together into a complete reporting package.

## Statement of Net Assets—Government-Wide Financial Statements

Exhibit 12–1 presents the June 30, 2001, statement of net assets for the City of Sacramento, California. As a government-wide financial statement, it is designed to report the economic resources of the government as a whole (except for the fiduciary funds). Fiduciary funds are not included because those assets must be used for a purpose outside the primary government. Such funds are shown only in the fund-based statements.

Several aspects of the statement of net assets should be noted specifically:

- All assets including capital assets are reported because the measurement basis is the economic resources controlled by the government. Long-term liabilities are presented for the same reason.
- Capital assets are reported net of accumulated depreciation because depreciation is required to be reported on the government-wide statements. Newly acquired infrastructure assets are included within the capital assets. Eventually, the reporting of most of the major infrastructure assets previously obtained will be required.
- The primary government is divided into governmental activities and business-type activities. At the government-wide level, both of these columns are based on accrual accounting. Governmental funds are in the governmental activities whereas enterprise funds comprise most, if not all, of the business-type activities. Even though recorded within the proprietary funds, internal service funds are normally included within the governmental activities because those services are rendered primarily to benefit activities within the governmental funds. However, if a particular internal service fund predominately serves an enterprise fund, that internal service fund should be included here as a business-type activity.
- The internal balances shown in the asset section come from interactivity transactions between the governmental activities and the business-type activities. The internal balances reported on this statement offset each other so that no impact affects the total for the primary government. Intra-activity transactions occur solely within a category and should not be reported here because the liability and receivable cancel out.
- Investments are reported at fair market value rather than historical cost.
- Discretely presented component units are grouped and shown to the far right side of the statement so that the reported amounts do not affect the primary government figures. However, if any blended component units exist, those balances are included, as appropriate,

## EXHIBIT 12–1 Government-Wide Financial Statements

**CITY OF SACRAMENTO**
**Statement of Net Assets**
**June 30, 2001**
**(in thousands)**

|  | Primary Government | | | Component Units |
|---|---|---|---|---|
|  | Governmental Activities | Business-Type Activities | Total |  |
| **Assets** | | | | |
| Cash and investments | $ 415,114 | $ 136,534 | $ 551,648 | $ 3,424 |
| Receivables, net | 229,499 | 32,295 | 261,794 | 129 |
| Internal balances | 17,245 | (17,245) | –0– | –0– |
| Inventories | 1,519 | 1,448 | 2,967 | –0– |
| Prepaid items | 6,710 | 528 | 7,238 | 5 |
| Restricted cash and investments | 24,986 | 231,646 | 256,632 | 38,468 |
| Deferred charges | 256 | 6,827 | 7,083 | 3,237 |
| Capital assets, net | 1,245,028 | 703,485 | 1,948,513 | 79,433 |
| Total assets | 1,940,357 | 1,095,518 | 3,035,875 | 124,696 |
| **Liabilities** | | | | |
| Securities lending obligations | 21,491 | 33,799 | 55,290 | –0– |
| Payables | 124,191 | 23,778 | 147,969 | 9,163 |
| Deferred revenue | 22,780 | 842 | 23,622 | –0– |
| Long-term liabilities: | | | | |
| Due within one year | 32,369 | 6,279 | 38,648 | –0– |
| Due in more than one year | 447,572 | 477,630 | 925,202 | 96,826 |
| Total liabilities | 648,403 | 542,328 | 1,190,731 | 105,989 |
| **Net Assets** | | | | |
| Invested in capital assets, net of related debt | 1,074,793 | 458,699 | 1,533,492 | 10,872 |
| Restricted for: | | | | |
| Capital projects | 79,305 | –0– | 79,305 | –0– |
| Debt service | 13,022 | –0– | 13,022 | –0– |
| Housing and redevelopment | 113,091 | 700 | 113,791 | –0– |
| Other | 17,230 | –0– | 17,230 | 420 |
| Unrestricted | (5,487) | 93,791 | 88,304 | 7,415 |
| Total net assets | $1,291,954 | $553,190 | $1,845,144 | $18,707 |

within either the governmental activities or the business-type activities as if they were individual funds.

- Since this is a statement of net assets, the format is not structured to stress that assets are equal to liabilities plus equities as is found in a typical balance sheet. Rather, the assets ($3.04 billion for the primary government) less liabilities of $1.19 billion leaves net assets of $1.85 billion.

- As seen in the final section, several amounts within the net assets being held have been restricted for capital projects, debt service, and the like. Restrictions are shown in this manner only if assets have been restricted either externally by creditors, grantors, or the like, or because of laws passed through constitutional provisions or enabling legislation.

- Although not restricted, the amount of net assets tied up in capital assets less any related debt is reported as a separate figure within the net assets.

## Statement of Activities—Government-Wide Financial Statements

The statement of activities is one of the most important governmental financial statements because of the wide array of information that it presents. As can be seen in the statement for the City of Sacramento, California, in Exhibit 12–2, the same general classification system of governmental activities, business-type activities, and component units used in Exhibit 12–1 provides the basis for reporting revenues and expenses. However, the format is much more complex and requires close analysis.

- Expenses are not presented according to individual causes such as salaries, rent, depreciation, or insurance. Instead, all expenses are shown by function: general government, police, fire, public works, and the like. As stated in paragraph 41 of *GASB Statement 14,* "as a minimum, governments should report direct expenses for each function. Direct expenses are those that are specifically associated with a service, program, or department and, thus, are clearly identifiable to a particular function." Many indirect expenses are simply assigned to a relatively generic function such as general government; however, as an alternative, indirect expenses can be allocated in some appropriate manner to the various operating functions.

- Interest expense on general long-term debt is normally an indirect expense because it benefits many government operations; because of its size, informational value, and the difficulty of allocation, this expense frequently is shown as in Exhibit 12–2 as a separate "function."

- After expenses have been determined for each function (governmental activities, business-type activities, and component units), related program revenues should be reported. Program revenues are those revenues derived from the program itself or from outsiders seeking to reduce the cost of the function. As can be seen in Exhibit 12–2, program revenues are divided into three columns:

    1. *Charges rendered for services.* For example, a monthly charge is normally assessed for water service; therefore, the first business-type activity shows more than $36.8 million in program revenues.
    2. *Operating grants and contributions.* This column reports revenues from grants and similar sources that were designated for some type of operating purpose. For example, $46.8 million in operating grants and contributions is shown for housing and development.
    3. *Capital grants and contributions.* This column shows revenues from grants and similar sources designated for capital asset additions.

- After expenses have been assigned to each function as well as related program revenues, a net (expense) or revenue figure can be determined for each function. This net figure provides a measure of the cost of the various operations of the government. As explained in paragraph 38 of *GASB Statement 14,* "an objective of using the net (expense) revenue format is to report the relative financial burden of each of the reporting government's functions on its taxpayers." For example, in Exhibit 12–2, the City of Sacramento shows that the police department had more than $88 million in operating expenses but generated program revenues of only $23 million from charges for services and operating grants and contributions. Thus, as disclosed on this statement, the taxpayers of that city had to bear the financial burden for police protection of over $65 million. That cost should be important information to any citizen reading these statements. In contrast, the water system reported operating expenses of $28 million, but its charges and other grants and contributions totaled $49 million. Thus, this business-type activity within the government generated net revenues of $21 million during the year.

- Net expenses and revenues can be determined in total for each category of the government. In this example, all of the governmental activities combined for net expenses of more than $126 million while the business-type activities generated net revenues of approximately $29 million. The two component units reported net revenues of just over $2 million.

- Once again, the internal service funds have been combined with the governmental activities (or with the business-type activities if that is more appropriate). The revenues and

**EXHIBIT 12–2** Government-Wide Financial Statements

### CITY OF SACRAMENTO
### Statement of Activities
### For the Fiscal Year Ended June 30, 2001
### (in thousands)

| Functions/Programs | Operating Expenses | Program Revenues | | | Net (Expense) Revenue and Changes in Net Assets | | | |
| --- | --- | --- | --- | --- | --- | --- | --- | --- |
| | | Charges for Services | Operating Grants and Contributions | Capital Grants and Contributions | Primary Government | | | Component Units |
| | | | | | Governmental Activities | Business-Type Activities | Total | |
| **Primary government:** | | | | | | | | |
| Governmental activities: | | | | | | | | |
| General government | $ 23,839 | $ 4,201 | $ 191 | $ –0– | $ (19,447) | | $ (19,447) | |
| Police | 88,513 | 3,212 | 20,131 | –0– | (65,170) | | (65,170) | |
| Fire | 48,846 | 4,295 | 2,750 | –0– | (41,801) | | (41,801) | |
| Public works | 89,704 | 31,278 | 8,617 | 101,527 | 51,718 | | 51,718 | |
| Economic development | 2,918 | 336 | 647 | –0– | (1,935) | | (1,935) | |
| Convention, culture & leisure | 7,323 | 3,374 | 975 | 972 | (2,002) | | (2,002) | |
| Parks and recreation | 30,980 | 3,356 | 6,294 | 15,370 | (5,960) | | (5,960) | |
| Planning and development | 9,763 | 13,774 | –0– | –0– | 4,011 | | 4,011 | |
| Neighborhood services | 5,346 | 245 | –0– | –0– | (5,101) | | (5,101) | |
| Housing and redevelopment | 112,463 | 7,043 | 46,780 | 38,968 | (19,672) | | (19,672) | |
| Library | 7,392 | –0– | –0– | –0– | (7,392) | | (7,392) | |
| Nondepartmental | 23,336 | 627 | 924 | 32,917 | 11,132 | | 11,132 | |
| Interest on long-term debt | 25,133 | –0– | –0– | –0– | (25,133) | | (25,133) | |
| Total governmental activities | 475,556 | 71,741 | 87,309 | 189,754 | (126,752) | | (126,752) | |
| Business-type activities: | | | | | | | | |
| Water | 28,006 | 36,802 | 122 | 12,273 | | 21,191 | 21,191 | |
| Sewer | 11,436 | 13,098 | –0– | 4,882 | | 6,544 | 6,544 | |
| Storm drainage | 21,061 | 27,636 | –0– | 5,104 | | 11,679 | 11,679 | |
| Solid waste | 31,503 | 30,558 | –0– | –0– | | (945) | (945) | |
| Community center | 18,695 | 5,027 | –0– | –0– | | (13,668) | (13,668) | |
| Parking | 11,368 | 13,703 | –0– | –0– | | 2,335 | 2,335 | |
| Advanced life support | 6,117 | 9,411 | –0– | –0– | | 3,294 | 3,294 | |
| Golf | 5,442 | 4,956 | –0– | –0– | | (486) | (486) | |
| 4th R | 3,811 | 3,559 | 347 | –0– | | 95 | 95 | |

*continued from page 572*

| | | | | | |
|---|---|---|---|---|---|
| Marina | 1,680 | 1,440 | –0– | (240) | (240) |
| Housing and development | 5,161 | 2,665 | 598 | 1,897 | (1) |
| Total business-type activities | 144,280 | 148,855 | 1,067 | 24,156 | 29,798 |
| Total primary government | $619,836 | $220,596 | $88,376 | $213,910 | $(96,954) |

**Component units:**

| | | | | | |
|---|---|---|---|---|---|
| The Natomas Basin Conservancy | $ 741 | $ 114 | $ 753 | $ 1,221 | $1,347 |
| Sacramento Hotel Corporation | 1,024 | 1,802 | –0– | 88 | 866 |
| Total component units | $ 1,765 | $ 1,916 | $ 753 | $ 1,309 | $ 2,213 |

| | | | |
|---|---|---|---|
| Change in net assets: | | | |
| Net (expense) revenue | $ (126,752) | $ 29,798 | $ (96,954) | $ 2,213 |
| General revenues: | | | | |
| Taxes: | | | | |
| Property taxes | 48,837 | –0– | 48,837 | –0– |
| Redevelopment tax increment | 22,537 | –0– | 22,537 | –0– |
| Sales taxes | 58,590 | –0– | 58,590 | –0– |
| Utility user taxes | 49,969 | –0– | 49,969 | –0– |
| Other taxes | 39,420 | 13,187 | 52,607 | –0– |
| Grants and other intergovernmental revenue not restricted to specific programs | 4,391 | –0– | 4,391 | –0– |
| Investment earnings | 37,351 | 15,378 | 52,729 | 231 |
| Miscellaneous | 12,782 | 1,678 | 14,460 | –0– |
| Gain or loss on sale of capital assets | (801) | (434) | (1,235) | –0– |
| Transfers | (10,290) | 10,290 | –0– | –0– |
| Total general revenues and transfers | 262,786 | 40,099 | 302,885 | 231 |
| Change in net assets | 136,034 | 69,897 | 205,931 | 2,444 |
| Net assets, beginning of year | 1,155,920 | 483,293 | 1,639,213 | 16,263 |
| Net assets, end of year | $1,291,954 | $553,190 | $1,845,144 | $18,707 |

expenses should be assigned to the appropriate functions. For example, the cost of work done by an internal service fund for engineering services should be assigned to that function. However, in allocating such amounts, any intra-activity figures must be eliminated to avoid double counting.

- General revenues are reported at the bottom of the statement as additions to either the governmental activities, business-type activities, or component units. All taxes are general revenues because they do not reflect a charge for services; they are obtained from the population as a whole. In addition, such transactions as unrestricted grants and investment income fall under this same category.

- Transfers made between governmental activities and business-type activities are also shown under the general revenues, but they are offset so that no impact is created on the total that is reported for the primary government.

## Balance Sheet—Governmental Funds—Fund-Based Statements

Exhibit 12–3 presents a balance sheet for the governmental funds recorded by the City of Sacramento. This statement measures only current financial resources and uses modified accrual accounting for timing purposes. No proprietary funds, component units, or fiduciary funds are included; the statement reflects just the governmental funds. Several parts of this statement should be noted:

- *GASB Statement 34* requires that a separate column be shown here for the General Fund and any other major fund monitored within the governmental funds. In this example, the Sacramento Housing and Redevelopment Agency's Special Revenue Fund and Capital Projects Fund have both been identified as major. The government can classify any fund as major if officials believe it is particularly important to statement users. However, as mentioned in the previous chapter, a fund is considered major and reported separately if it meets two criteria:

  1. Total assets, liabilities, revenues, or expenses/expenditures of the fund are at least 10 percent of the corresponding total for all such funds.
  2. Total assets, liabilities, revenues, or expenses/expenditures of the fund are at least 5 percent of the corresponding total for all governmental funds and enterprise funds combined.

  All funds that are not considered to be major are combined and reported as "other governmental funds."

- No capital assets or long-term debts are being reported on this balance sheet because only current financial resources are being measured.

- Totals for the governmental funds appear in the final column. However, internal balances such as "due from other funds" (a receivable) and "due to other funds" (a liability) have not been offset. Thus, the governmental totals are just mathematical summations.

- In the Fund Balance section of this balance sheet, both "reserved" and "designated" amounts are shown. The term *reserved* is used to indicate that some of the assets being reported (such as inventory) cannot be spent or have been separated for legal reasons. Designated figures are used to disclose tentative plans that are subject to change in the future.

- The final total fund balances figure for the governmental funds of $368.104 million is significantly different from the $1,291.954 million in total net assets reported for governmental activities as a whole in the statement of net assets (Exhibit 12–1). To help understand that large discrepancy, a reconciliation is included along with the balance sheet. The reconciliation reported by the City of Sacramento has not been included in these examples, but the four largest items that create the link between the governmental activities of the government-wide financial statements and the governmental funds of the fund-based financial statements were:

  1. More than $1.2 billion of capital assets reported by the governmental activities on the government-wide financial statements were omitted on the comparable fund-based financial statement.

**EXHIBIT 12–3** Fund-Based Financial Statements

**CITY OF SACRAMENTO**
Balance Sheet
Governmental Funds
June 30, 2001 (in thousands)

| | General Fund | SHRA Special Revenue Fund | SHRA Capital Projects Fund | Other Governmental Funds | Total Governmental Funds |
|---|---|---|---|---|---|
| **Assets** | | | | | |
| Cash and investments held by City | $ 99,073 | $35,323 | $ 62,950 | $165,326 | $362,672 |
| Cash and investments held by fiscal agent | –0– | –0– | –0– | 3,213 | 3,213 |
| Receivables, net: | | | | | |
|   Taxes | 17,120 | 649 | 4 | 498 | 18,271 |
|   Accounts | 6,752 | 503 | 133 | 1,708 | 9,096 |
|   Loans | 172 | 40,732 | 38,546 | 50 | 79,500 |
|   Intergovernmental | –0– | 1,812 | 2,652 | 27,613 | 32,077 |
|   Interest | 1,075 | –0– | –0– | 1,010 | 2,085 |
| Due from other funds | –0– | 2,329 | 4,720 | 3 | 7,052 |
| Inventories | 214 | 336 | –0– | –0– | 550 |
| Prepaid items | 386 | –0– | –0– | 160 | 546 |
| Restricted assets: | | | | | |
|   Cash and investments held by City | –0– | 1,558 | –0– | 12,019 | 13,577 |
|   Cash and investments held by fiscal agent | –0– | –0– | –0– | 11,285 | 11,285 |
| Advances to other funds | 619 | 8,248 | 1,960 | 7,510 | 18,337 |
| Total assets | $125,411 | $91,490 | $110,965 | $230,395 | $558,261 |
| **Liabilities and Fund Balances** | | | | | |
| Liabilities: | | | | | |
|   Securities lending obligations | $ 9,123 | –0– | –0– | $ 7,318 | $ 16,441 |
|   Accounts payable | 19,176 | 65,472 | 4,485 | 17,477 | 106,610 |
|   Accrued compensated absences | 467 | –0– | –0– | –0– | 467 |
|   Due to other funds | 2 | 1,403 | 756 | 15,056 | 17,217 |
|   Matured bonds and interest payable | –0– | –0– | –0– | 3,142 | 3,142 |
|   Deposits | 653 | 1,493 | 230 | 1,186 | 3,562 |
|   Deferred revenue | 1,167 | 7,105 | 952 | 28,002 | 37,226 |
|   Advances from other funds | –0– | 1,194 | 100 | 4,198 | 5,492 |
|     Total liabilities | 30,588 | 76,667 | 6,523 | 76,379 | 190,157 |
| Fund balances: | | | | | |
|   Reserved: | | | | | |
|     For noncurrent assets | 1,373 | 3,036 | 39,827 | 7,510 | 51,746 |
|     For encumbrances | 9,296 | 895 | 4,842 | 17,804 | 32,837 |
|     For debt service | –0– | 648 | 3 | 17,469 | 18,120 |
|     For housing/redevelopment | –0– | 2,749 | 58,652 | –0– | 61,401 |
|     For trust obligations | –0– | –0– | –0– | 878 | 878 |
|   Unreserved: | | | | | |
|     Designated for economic uncertainty | 17,532 | –0– | –0– | –0– | 17,532 |
|     Designated for federal mandates | 9,000 | –0– | –0– | –0– | 9,000 |
|     Designated for capital projects | 18,199 | –0– | –0– | –0– | 18,199 |
|     Designated for City Hall project | 8,000 | –0– | –0– | –0– | 8,000 |
|     Designated for three year capital improvement program | 5,525 | –0– | –0– | –0– | 5,525 |
|     Designated for energy reserve | 2,500 | –0– | –0– | –0– | 2,500 |
|     Designated for subsequent years' expenditures | 14,500 | –0– | –0– | –0– | 14,500 |
|     Undesignated | 8,898 | –0– | –0– | –0– | 8,898 |
|   Unreserved, reported in: | | | | | |
|     Special revenue funds | –0– | 7,495 | –0– | 64,263 | 71,758 |
|     Debt service funds | –0– | –0– | –0– | 4,035 | 4,035 |
|     Capital projects funds | –0– | –0– | 1,118 | 39,293 | 40,411 |
|     Permanent funds | –0– | –0– | –0– | 2,764 | 2,764 |
|     Total fund balances | 94,823 | 14,823 | 104,442 | 154,016 | 368,104 |
| Total liabilities and fund balances | $125,411 | $91,490 | $110,965 | $230,395 | $558,261 |

2. Long-term notes receivable of almost $75 million were not presented in the fund-based financial statements; they did not represent current financial resources.
3. Long-term liabilities of approximately $434 million were reported only on the government-wide financial statements because they did not represent claims to current financial resources.
4. Internal service funds with net assets of $65 million were included in the governmental activities although, for fund-based financial statements, they would have been judged as proprietary funds.

### Statement of Revenues, Expenditures, and Changes in Fund Balances—Governmental Funds—Fund-Based Statements

As shown in Exhibit 12–4, a statement of revenues, expenditures, and changes in fund balances should be shown for the governmental funds. Once again, the General Fund is detailed in a separate column along with each of the other major funds previously identified in the balance sheet in Exhibit 12–3. All remaining nonmajor funds are then accumulated and shown together.

By examining Exhibit 12–4, each of the following can be noted:

- Revenues are not separately identified as either program revenues or general revenues as was the case in Exhibit 12–2. For that reason, no net revenue or expense figure is determined for each of the functions such as general government or public safety. Therefore, individual burden/benefit amounts are not shown.
- Because the current financial resources measurement basis is being utilized, expenditures rather than expenses are being reported. For example, Capital Outlay is presented here but would not have been appropriate on the statement of activities. In the same way, Debt Service—principal is reported on the statement in Exhibit 12–4 as an expenditure.
- Because the modified accrual method of accounting is being used for timing purposes, reported amounts will be different than reported previously. For example, total expenditures for interest and fiscal charges are listed on Exhibit 12–4 as $24,247,000 whereas interest on long-term debt disclosed in Exhibit 12–2 is $25,133,000. The difference results largely because the first figure measures expenditures during the period using modified accrual accounting but the second figure is the amount of expense recognized according to accrual accounting.
- Other financing sources and uses are presented in this statement to reflect the issuance of long-term debt, the sale of property, and transfers made between the funds. Because the fund-based statements are designed to present fund activities rather than government-wide figures, no elimination of the transfers is made.
- A reconciliation should be shown between the ending change in governmental fund balances (an increase of $58,351,000) in Exhibit 12–4 and the ending change in net assets for governmental activities in Exhibit 12–2 (an increase of $136,034,000). Because of space considerations, that reconciliation is not being presented here although it would need to be included in the general purpose external financial statements. For the City of Sacramento, the major differences shown on this reconciliation involved the acquisition of capital assets, the recording of depreciation, the recording of revenues that did not provide current financial resources, the issuance of long-term debt, and the repayment of long-term debt.

### Statement of Net Assets—Proprietary Funds

The assets and liabilities of the proprietary funds of the City of Sacramento are presented in Exhibit 12–5. Information about five individual enterprise funds is shown separately with a single total column for all other enterprise funds. In addition, a column is presented to provide a total for all of these business-type activities. In this way, specific information is available for the water fund, sewer fund, storm drainage fund, solid waste fund, and community center fund as well as for all enterprise funds in total.

Accounting for State and Local Governments (Part 2) 577

**EXHIBIT 12-4** Fund-Based Financial Statements

**CITY OF SACRAMENTO**
Statement of Revenues, Expenditures, and Changes in Fund Balances
Governmental Funds
For the Fiscal Year Ended June 30, 2001 (in thousands)

| | General Fund | SHRA Special Revenue Fund | SHRA Capital Project Fund | Other Governmental Funds | Total Governmental Funds |
|---|---|---|---|---|---|
| **Revenues:** | | | | | |
| Taxes | $177,789 | $ 4,506 | $ 0 | $ 22,708 | $205,003 |
| Intergovernmental | 36,208 | 77,046 | 9,456 | 99,778 | 222,488 |
| Charges for services | 22,231 | 6,062 | 207 | 7,740 | 36,240 |
| Fines, forfeits and penalties | 4,907 | –0– | –0– | 2,829 | 7,736 |
| Interest, rents, and concessions | 7,169 | 2,562 | 2,559 | 15,085 | 27,375 |
| Community service fees | –0– | –0– | –0– | 23,263 | 23,263 |
| Assessment levies | –0– | –0– | –0– | 13,378 | 13,378 |
| Contributions from property owners | –0– | –0– | –0– | 37,238 | 37,238 |
| Donations | –0– | –0– | –0– | 1,414 | 1,414 |
| Miscellaneous | 1,019 | 10,937 | 332 | 2,049 | 14,337 |
| Total revenues | 249,323 | 101,113 | 12,554 | 225,482 | 588,472 |
| **Expenditures:** | | | | | |
| Current: | | | | | |
| General government | 18,864 | –0– | –0– | 382 | 19,246 |
| Police | 72,669 | –0– | –0– | 14,699 | 87,368 |
| Fire | 48,079 | –0– | –0– | 259 | 48,338 |
| Public works | 10,776 | –0– | –0– | 33,865 | 44,641 |
| Economic development | 2,271 | –0– | –0– | 647 | 2,918 |
| Convention, culture and leisure | 3,144 | –0– | –0– | 2,135 | 5,279 |
| Parks and recreation | 16,524 | –0– | –0– | 12,633 | 29,157 |
| Planning and development | 9,044 | –0– | –0– | 715 | 9,759 |
| Neighborhood services | 5,346 | –0– | –0– | –0– | 5,346 |
| Library | 6,915 | –0– | –0– | –0– | 6,915 |
| Housing and redevelopment | –0– | 77,021 | 5,088 | –0– | 82,109 |
| Nondepartmental | 17,241 | –0– | –0– | 496 | 17,737 |
| Capital outlay | 4,002 | 20,887 | 15,677 | 94,055 | 134,621 |
| Debt service: | | | | | |
| Principal | 1,132 | 1,341 | –0– | 22,311 | 24,784 |
| Interest and fiscal charges | 310 | 1,718 | –0– | 22,219 | 24,247 |
| Total expenditures | 216,317 | 100,967 | 20,765 | 204,416 | 542,465 |
| Excess (deficiency) of revenues over (under) expenditures | 33,006 | 146 | (8,211) | 21,066 | 46,007 |
| **Other financing sources (uses):** | | | | | |
| Transfers in | 15,222 | 4,604 | 6,697 | 19,191 | 45,714 |
| Transfers out | (13,199) | (4,468) | (4,116) | (34,221) | (56,004) |
| Proceeds from long-term debt | –0– | –0– | –0– | 44,359 | 44,359 |
| Proceeds from sale of property | –0– | –0– | 114 | –0– | 114 |
| Payment to refunded bond escrow | –0– | –0– | –0– | (21,839) | (21,839) |
| Total other financing sources (uses) | 2,023 | 136 | 2,695 | 7,490 | 12,344 |
| Net change in fund balances | 35,029 | 282 | (5,516) | 28,556 | 58,351 |
| Fund balances, beginning of year, as originally reported | 63,708 | 12,766 | 111,368 | 127,993 | 315,835 |
| Prior period adjustments | (3,914) | 1,775 | (1,410) | (2,533) | (6,082) |
| Fund balances, beginning of year, as restated | 59,794 | 14,541 | 109,958 | 125,460 | 309,753 |
| Fund balances, end of year | $ 94,823 | $ 14,823 | $104,442 | $154,016 | $368,104 |

**EXHIBIT 12–5** Fund-Based Financial Statements

## CITY OF SACRAMENTO
### Statement of Net Assets
### Proprietary Funds
### June 30, 2001
### (in thousands)

| | Business-Type Activities—Enterprise Funds | | | | | | Governmental Activities—Internal Service Funds |
|---|---|---|---|---|---|---|---|
| | Water Fund | Sewer Fund | Storm Drainage Fund | Solid Waste Fund | Community Center Fund | Other Enterprise Funds | Total | |
| **Assets** | | | | | | | | |
| Current assets: | | | | | | | | |
| Cash and investments held by City | $ 63,498 | $ 8,774 | $ 30,549 | $ 6,218 | $ 4,514 | $ 21,738 | $ 135,291 | $ 49,175 |
| Cash and investments held by fiscal agent | 692 | —0— | 117 | —0— | 179 | 255 | 1,243 | 54 |
| Receivables, net | | | | | | | | |
| Taxes | —0— | —0— | —0— | —0— | 1,881 | —0— | 1,881 | —0— |
| Accounts | 5,554 | 5,098 | 4,886 | 6,451 | 242 | 2,488 | 24,719 | 178 |
| Loans | —0— | —0— | —0— | —0— | 42 | —0— | 42 | 291 |
| Intergovernmental | 345 | 337 | 289 | 464 | —0— | 41 | 1,476 | —0— |
| Interest | 3,065 | 99 | 369 | 215 | 99 | 271 | 4,118 | 595 |
| Due from other funds | —0— | —0— | —0— | —0— | —0— | —0— | —0— | 10,357 |
| Inventories | 1,159 | 115 | 174 | —0— | —0— | —0— | 1,448 | 969 |
| Prepaid items | 525 | —0— | —0— | —0— | 1 | 2 | 528 | 6,164 |
| Total current assets | 74,838 | 14,423 | 36,384 | 13,348 | 6,958 | 24,795 | 170,746 | 67,783 |
| Noncurrent assets: | | | | | | | | |
| Restricted assets: | | | | | | | | |
| Cash and investments held by City | 195,896 | 156 | 469 | 12,106 | —0— | 9,113 | 217,740 | 124 |
| Cash and investments held by fiscal agent | —0— | —0— | 765 | —0— | 10,618 | 2,523 | 13,906 | —0— |
| Advances to other funds | —0— | —0— | —0— | —0— | —0— | 1,000 | 1,000 | 15,318 |
| Loans receivable | —0— | —0— | —0— | —0— | 59 | —0— | 59 | 6,385 |
| Deferred charges | 3,106 | —0— | 83 | 722 | 2,098 | 818 | 6,827 | —0— |
| Capital assets: | | | | | | | | |
| Land | 645 | 1,098 | 702 | 1,133 | 21,739 | 13,728 | 39,045 | 979 |
| Buildings and improvements | 23,278 | 4,198 | 7,772 | 26,417 | 109,586 | 92,969 | 264,220 | 6,230 |
| Machinery and equipment | 2,920 | 1,768 | 3,124 | 5,410 | 2,699 | 2,460 | 18,381 | 3,771 |
| Vehicles | 391 | 584 | 844 | 3,491 | —0— | —0— | 5,310 | 73,062 |
| Transmission and distribution system | 158,185 | 83,104 | 157,974 | —0— | —0— | 3,571 | 402,834 | —0— |
| Construction in progress | 36,897 | 18,700 | 79,223 | 2,256 | 59 | 23,159 | 160,294 | 71 |

*continued from page 578*

| | | | | | | | | |
|---|---:|---:|---:|---:|---:|---:|---:|---:|
| Less: accumulated depreciation | (62,788) | (23,551) | (30,211) | (10,539) | (25,411) | (34,099) | (186,599) | (47,366) |
| Total noncurrent assets | 358,530 | 86,057 | 220,745 | 40,996 | 121,447 | 115,242 | 943,017 | 58,574 |
| Total assets | $433,368 | $100,480 | $257,129 | $54,344 | $128,405 | $140,037 | $1,113,763 | $126,357 |

**Liabilities**

Current liabilities:

| | | | | | | | | |
|---|---:|---:|---:|---:|---:|---:|---:|---:|
| Securities lending obligation | $ 26,001 | $ 840 | $ 3,064 | $ 1,822 | $ 0 | $ 2,072 | $ 33,799 | $ 5,050 |
| Accounts payable and accrued expenses | 4,379 | 3,055 | 1,371 | 2,798 | 482 | 4,878 | 16,963 | 7,548 |
| Accrued compensated absences | 77 | 29 | 46 | 51 | 37 | 49 | 289 | 38 |
| Interest payable | 2,591 | 349 | 1,133 | 127 | 1,568 | 837 | 6,605 | –0– |
| Liability for landfill closure, current portion | –0– | –0– | –0– | 760 | –0– | –0– | 760 | –0– |
| Deposits | –0– | –0– | –0– | –0– | –0– | 210 | 210 | –0– |
| Deferred revenue | –0– | –0– | –0– | 113 | 691 | 38 | 842 | 342 |
| Accrued claims | –0– | –0– | –0– | –0– | –0– | –0– | –0– | 14,226 |
| Revenue bonds, net, current portion | 190 | –0– | 194 | –0– | 2,136 | 1,046 | 3,566 | –0– |
| Certificates of participation, net, current portion | –0– | –0– | –0– | –0– | 1,273 | –0– | 1,273 | –0– |
| Notes payable | –0– | 27 | 80 | –0– | –0– | 284 | 391 | –0– |
| Total current liabilities | 33,238 | 4,300 | 5,888 | 5,671 | 6,187 | 9,414 | 64,698 | 27,204 |

Noncurrent liabilities:

| | | | | | | | | |
|---|---:|---:|---:|---:|---:|---:|---:|---:|
| Accrued compensated absences | 1,839 | 542 | 1,399 | 1,157 | 362 | 740 | 6,039 | 955 |
| Advances from other funds | –0– | –0– | –0– | –0– | 6,373 | 11,872 | 18,245 | 4,859 |
| Accrued claims | –0– | –0– | –0– | –0– | –0– | –0– | –0– | 28,075 |
| Liability for landfill closure | –0– | –0– | –0– | 17,469 | –0– | –0– | 17,469 | –0– |
| Revenue bonds, net | 201,722 | –0– | 8,892 | 27,423 | 87,107 | 55,457 | 380,601 | –0– |
| Certificates of participation, net | –0– | –0– | –0– | –0– | 20,842 | –0– | 20,842 | –0– |
| Notes payable | –0– | 9,690 | 29,071 | –0– | –0– | 13,918 | 52,679 | –0– |
| Total noncurrent liabilities | 203,561 | 10,232 | 39,362 | 46,049 | 114,684 | 81,987 | 495,875 | 33,889 |
| Total liabilities | 236,799 | 14,532 | 45,250 | 51,720 | 120,871 | 91,401 | 560,573 | 61,093 |

**Net Assets**

| | | | | | | | | |
|---|---:|---:|---:|---:|---:|---:|---:|---:|
| Invested in capital assets, net of related debt | 150,892 | 75,991 | 181,292 | 6,361 | 6,364 | 37,799 | 458,699 | 36,625 |
| Restricted for: | | | | | | | | |
| Housing and redevelopment | –0– | –0– | –0– | –0– | –0– | –0– | 700 | –0– |
| Unrestricted | 45,677 | 9,957 | 30,587 | (3,737) | 1,170 | 10,137 | 93,791 | 28,639 |
| Total net assets | $196,569 | $ 85,948 | $211,879 | $ 2,624 | $ 7,534 | $ 48,636 | $ 553,190 | $ 65,264 |

A considerable amount of other significant information should be noted in examining Exhibit 12–5:

- The internal service funds also are combined and exhibited in this statement because they are proprietary funds. However, in the government-wide financial statements, these same internal service funds were reported as part of the governmental activities.
- Assets and liabilities are classified as either current or noncurrent to provide additional information to the users of the statements.
- Because the proprietary funds utilize accrual accounting to measure economic resources, most of the totals for the business-type activities in Exhibit 12–5 will agree with the total figures found in Exhibit 12–1. The amount of detail, though, is more extensive in Exhibit 12–5. For example, seven different figures are reported under Capital Assets rather than just one.
- The Internal Balance amount of $17,245,000, which was reported in Exhibit 12–1 within the assets so that it could be eliminated, is reported in Exhibit 12–5 in the assets within Advances to Other Funds as $1,000,000 and in the liabilities within Advances from Other Funds of $18,245,000, but neither of these balances is eliminated in the Total column. That is the reason that the total assets and the total liabilities reported in Exhibit 12–1 for the business-type activities differ from the reported figures shown in Exhibit 12–5.
- Restricted cash and investments of more than $230 million are listed under noncurrent assets. Use of this money must have been designated in some manner by an external source or by specific laws.

### Statement of Revenues, Expenses, and Changes in Fund Net Assets—Proprietary Funds

Just as the previous statement of net assets provides individual information about specific enterprise funds (as well as the total for the internal service funds), the statement of revenues, expenses, and changes in fund net assets shown in Exhibit 12–6 gives the revenues and expenses for those same funds. In Exhibit 12–2, expenses of the water fund amounted to $28,006,000. That figure is more completely delineated in Exhibit 12–6 within several categories: employee services ($12,272,000), depreciation and amortization ($4,127,000), interest ($1,925,000), and so forth. Because this statement measures all changes in net assets, both capital contributions and transfers are also reported.

### Statement of Cash Flows—Proprietary Funds

One of the most interesting of the fund-based financial statements is the statement of cash flows for the proprietary funds, as demonstrated in Exhibit 12–7. Because the proprietary funds operate in a manner similar to for-profit businesses, information about cash flows is considered vital just as it is for Xerox or Coca-Cola. In addition, this information is not already available within the government-wide financial statements.

As compared to a for-profit business, the statement of cash flows shown here has four sections rather than just three:

1. Cash flows from operating activities.
2. Cash flows from noncapital financing activities.
3. Cash flows from capital and related financing activities.
4. Cash flows from investing activities.

- The presentation of cash flows from operating activities is very similar to that prepared by a for-profit business. However, in *GASB Statement 34,* the direct method of reporting operating activities has been required. In for-profit accounting, the direct method is recommended but not required so that the indirect method often is used when adjustments and eliminations are made to net income to arrive at cash from operating activities.
- Because the direct approach to reporting cash flows from operating activities is required here, the proprietary funds must also provide a reconciliation of operating income to net

cash from operating activities. This reconciliation for the City of Sacramento has not been included.

- Cash flows from noncapital financing activities should include (1) proceeds and payments on debt *not* attributable to the acquisition or construction of capital assets and (2) grants and subsidies *not* restricted for capital purposes or operating activities.
- Cash flows from capital and related financing activities focuses on the amounts spent on capital assets and the source of that funding. Exhibit 12–7 shows typical examples: issuance of proceeds from capital debt, capital contributions (from the governmental funds), acquisition and construction of capital assets, principal payments on capital debt, and the like.
- Cash flows from investing activities discloses amounts paid and received from investments.

## Financial Statements—Fiduciary Funds

Fiduciary funds monitor assets being held for the benefit of an individual, group, or government outside of the reporting entity. The government cannot use these funds for its own programs and obtains no direct benefit from holding the assets. For that reason, information about the fiduciary funds is not included in the government-wide financial statements. Therefore, any financial data about these funds must be obtained by examining their fund-based financial statements or their independently released statements (if those are prepared).

The statement of fiduciary net assets is shown in Exhibit 12–8 and the statement of changes in fiduciary net assets appears in Exhibit 12–9. According to *GASB Statement 34,* these two statements should appear within the general purpose external financial statements produced by a state or locality. As indicated in the previous chapter, a government can have as many as four separate fiduciary fund types:

1. *Pension trust funds as well as other employee benefit trust funds.* These funds are used to report resources that are held for qualified employees within defined benefit pension plans, defined contribution plans, other postemployment benefit plans, or other employee benefit plans. As shown in Exhibit 12–8, such trust funds tend to hold large amounts of investments that are expected to grow and provide anticipated benefits for employees and their families. In Exhibit 12–9, the changes occurring in the pension trust fund are reported. Additions can come from contributions made to the plan by employees or by employers or both and actual investment income such as dividends and interest. Because any investments being held are reported at fair market value, the change in value during the period is also reflected in this statement. Deductions from a pension trust fund include benefits paid to employees and other beneficiaries, contribution refunds, and administrative expenses (professional services).

The City of Lincoln, Nebraska, provides the following information in the notes to its 2000 financial statements: "The employees of the City are covered by several retirement plans. The Police and Fire Department Plan is administered by the City and is included in the Fiduciary Fund type. All other plans are administered by outside trustees and are not included in the City's combined financial statements." The notes go on to say that 891 current and former employees are covered by the Police and Fire Department Plan and the statements show that more than $130 million of net assets is held in the pension trust fund.

2. *Investment trust funds.* This fund category reports the external portion of any investments that are being held by the entity for other governments. Such investment pools may be created in hope of generating higher returns. Exhibit 12–8 shows that the City of Sacramento holds more than $30 million of such assets.

3. *Private-purpose trust funds.* This trust fund category reports assets held for the benefit of outside parties. Governments can be required to hold assets in a fiduciary capacity for a score of reasons. For example, if a person dies without a will and without heirs, the person's property is maintained in this trust fund until properly distributed according to state law. Likewise, cash abandoned in a savings or checking account is often turned over to the government to dispose of based on the proper legal regulations. The City of Sacramento is not reporting a private-purpose trust fund.

**EXHIBIT 12–6  Fund-Based Financial Statements**

## CITY OF SACRAMENTO
### Statement of Revenues, Expenses, and Changes in Fund Net Assets
### Proprietary Funds
### For the Fiscal Year Ended June 30, 2001
### (in thousands)

| | Business-Type Activities—Enterprise Funds | | | | | | Governmental Activities—Internal Service Funds |
|---|---|---|---|---|---|---|---|
| | Water Fund | Sewer Fund | Storm Drainage Fund | Solid Waste Fund | Community Center Fund | Other Enterprise Funds | Total | |
| **Operating revenues:** | | | | | | | | |
| Charges for services: | | | | | | | | |
| User fees and charges | $34,444 | $11,945 | $27,544 | $30,558 | $1,721 | $32,570 | $138,782 | $45,716 |
| Rents and concessions | –0– | –0– | –0– | 335 | 3,040 | 2,439 | 5,814 | –0– |
| Charges to Regional Sanitation District for operating and maintaining treatment plant | –0– | 1,136 | –0– | –0– | –0– | –0– | 1,136 | –0– |
| Miscellaneous | 2,358 | 17 | 92 | 1,043 | 266 | 1,072 | 4,848 | 433 |
| Total operating revenues | 36,802 | 13,098 | 27,636 | 31,936 | 5,027 | 36,081 | 150,580 | 46,149 |
| **Operating expenses:** | | | | | | | | |
| Employee services | 12,272 | 4,808 | 10,222 | 11,212 | 3,641 | 12,739 | 54,894 | 10,356 |
| Services and supplies | 9,682 | 4,084 | 5,760 | 17,766 | 4,599 | 13,433 | 55,324 | 15,234 |
| Depreciation and amortization | 4,127 | 2,334 | 3,807 | 923 | 2,667 | 2,855 | 16,713 | 6,886 |
| Insurance premiums | –0– | –0– | –0– | –0– | –0– | –0– | –0– | 732 |
| Claim settlements | –0– | –0– | –0– | –0– | –0– | –0– | –0– | 16,714 |
| Total operating expenses | 26,081 | 11,226 | 19,789 | 29,901 | 10,907 | 29,027 | 126,931 | 49,922 |
| Operating income (loss) | 10,721 | 1,872 | 7,847 | 2,035 | (5,880) | 7,054 | 23,649 | (3,773) |
| **Nonoperating revenues (expenses):** | | | | | | | | |
| Interest and investment revenue | 5,621 | 912 | 2,975 | 2,340 | 932 | 2,598 | 15,378 | 5,689 |
| Transient occupancy taxes | –0– | –0– | –0– | –0– | 13,187 | –0– | 13,187 | –0– |
| Revenue from other agencies | 122 | –0– | –0– | 300 | –0– | 598 | 1,020 | –0– |
| Interest expense | (1,925) | (210) | (1,272) | (1,602) | (7,788) | (4,552) | (17,349) | –0– |
| Gain (loss) on disposition of fixed assets | (268) | (12) | (10) | (29) | (63) | (52) | (434) | (37) |
| Total nonoperating revenue (expenses) | 3,550 | 690 | 1,693 | 1,009 | 6,268 | (1,408) | 11,802 | 5,652 |

*continued from page 582*

|  |  |  |  |  |  |  |
|---|---:|---:|---:|---:|---:|---:|
| Income before contributions and transfers | 14,271 | 2,562 | 9,540 | 3,044 | 388 | 5,646 | 35,451 | 1,879 |
| Capital contributions | 12,273 | 4,882 | 5,104 | –0– | –0– | 1,897 | 24,156 | 1,664 |
| Transfers in | 1,596 | 2,119 | 18,698 | –0– | 1,315 | 1,949 | 25,677 | –0– |
| Transfers out | (3,677) | (1,308) | (3,001) | (3,333) | (1,482) | (2,586) | (15,387) | –0– |
| Change in net assets | 24,463 | 8,255 | 30,341 | (289) | 221 | 6,906 | 69,897 | 3,543 |
| Net assets, beginning of year, as originally reported | 172,106 | 77,693 | 181,538 | 2,913 | 7,313 | 34,556 | 476,119 | 61,721 |
| Prior period adjustments | –0– | –0– | –0– | –0– | –0– | 7,174 | 7,174 | –0– |
| Total net assets, beginning of year, as restated | 172,106 | 77,693 | 181,538 | 2,913 | 7,313 | 41,730 | 483,293 | 61,721 |
| Total net assets, end of year | $196,569 | $85,948 | $211,879 | $ 2,624 | $ 7,534 | $48,636 | $553,190 | $65,264 |

**EXHIBIT 12–7** Fund-Based Financial Statements

**CITY OF SACRAMENTO**
**Statement of Cash Flows**
**Proprietary Funds**
**For the Fiscal Year Ended June 30, 2001**
*(in thousands)*

|  | Business-Type Activities—Enterprise Funds | | | | | | Governmental Activities—Internal Service Funds |
|---|---|---|---|---|---|---|---|
|  | Water Fund | Sewer Fund | Storm Drainage Fund | Solid Waste Fund | Community Center Fund | Other Enterprise Funds | Total | |
| **Cash flows from operating activities:** | | | | | | | | |
| Receipts from customers and users | $ 36,510 | $12,822 | $ 27,799 | $ 31,372 | $ 5,604 | $ 35,600 | $149,707 | $ 62,913 |
| Payments to suppliers | (8,646) | (3,677) | (6,612) | (17,321) | (4,699) | (10,463) | (51,418) | (38,272) |
| Payments to employees | (11,988) | (4,697) | (9,937) | (11,023) | (3,533) | (12,618) | (53,796) | (10,246) |
| Claims paid | –0– | –0– | –0– | –0– | –0– | –0– | –0– | (13,788) |
| Net cash provided by (used for) operating activities | 15,876 | 4,448 | 11,250 | 3,028 | (2,628) | 12,519 | 44,493 | 607 |
| **Cash flows from noncapital financing activities:** | | | | | | | | |
| Transient occupancy taxes | –0– | –0– | –0– | –0– | 12,992 | –0– | 12,992 | –0– |
| Landfill closure expense | –0– | –0– | –0– | (759) | –0– | –0– | (759) | –0– |
| Operating transfers in from other funds | 1,596 | 2,120 | 18,698 | –0– | 1,315 | 1,949 | 25,678 | –0– |
| Operating transfers out to other funds | (3,677) | (1,308) | (3,001) | (3,333) | (1,482) | (2,587) | (15,388) | –0– |
| Increase in due from other funds | –0– | –0– | –0– | –0– | –0– | 229 | 229 | –0– |
| Decrease in due from other funds | –0– | –0– | –0– | –0– | –0– | –0– | –0– | 11,863 |
| Increase in advances to other funds | –0– | –0– | –0– | –0– | –0– | –0– | –0– | (10,772) |
| Increase in advances from other funds | –0– | –0– | –0– | –0– | 2,007 | –0– | 2,007 | 3,680 |
| Decrease in advances to other funds | –0– | –0– | –0– | –0– | –0– | –0– | –0– | 257 |
| Decrease in advances from other funds | –0– | –0– | –0– | –0– | –0– | (500) | (500) | (5,581) |
| Issuance of notes receivable | –0– | –0– | –0– | –0– | –0– | –0– | –0– | (203) |
| Net cash (used for) provided by noncapital financing activities | (2,081) | 812 | 15,697 | (4,092) | 14,832 | (909) | 24,259 | (756) |

*continued from page 584*

| Cash flows from capital and related financing activities: | | | | | |
|---|---:|---:|---:|---:|---:|
| Proceeds from issuance of capital debt | 200,497 | 1,089 | 3,266 | -0- | 27,132 | 231,984 | -0- |
| Payments for costs of issuance | (1,766) | -0- | -0- | -0- | -0- | (1,766) | -0- |
| Bond issuance costs | -0- | -0- | -0- | -0- | (125) | (125) | -0- |
| Acquisition and construction of capital assets | (22,708) | (8,903) | (33,655) | (11,707) | (67) | (24,331) | (101,371) | (5,196) |
| Proceeds from sale of capital assets | 9 | -0- | -0- | -0- | -0- | 9 | 277 |
| Principal payments on capital debt | (1,335) | (26) | (373) | -0- | (2,854) | (1,783) | (6,371) | -0- |
| Interest payments on capital debt | (66) | (15) | (575) | (1,531) | (6,219) | (4,227) | (12,633) | -0- |
| Revenue from other agencies | 122 | -0- | -0- | 206 | -0- | 599 | 927 | -0- |
| Capital contributions | 5,589 | 463 | -0- | -0- | -0- | 185 | 6,237 | 211 |
| Net cash provided by (used for) capital and related financing activities | 180,342 | (7,392) | (31,337) | (13,032) | (9,140) | (2,550) | 116,891 | (4,708) |
| Cash flows from investing activities: | | | | | | | | |
| Collection of interest | 3,457 | 1,038 | 3,325 | 2,747 | 934 | 2,601 | 14,102 | 6,080 |
| Issuance of loans receivable | -0- | -0- | -0- | -0- | (42) | -0- | (42) | (1,735) |
| Loan repayments | -0- | -0- | -0- | -0- | 63 | -0- | 63 | -0- |
| Net cash provided by investing activities | 3,457 | 1,038 | 3,325 | 2,747 | 955 | 2,601 | 14,123 | 4,345 |
| Net increase (decrease) in cash and cash equivalents | 197,594 | (1,094) | (1,065) | (11,349) | 4,019 | 11,661 | 199,766 | (512) |
| Cash and cash equivalents, beginning of year | 42,782 | 10,755 | 34,861 | 32,191 | 11,292 | 21,614 | 153,495 | 51,514 |
| Cash and cash equivalents, end of year | 240,376 | 9,661 | 33,796 | 20,842 | 15,311 | 33,275 | 353,261 | 51,002 |
| Reconciling item—change in securities lending assets | 19,710 | (731) | (1,896) | (2,518) | -0- | 354 | 14,919 | (1,649) |
| Cash and cash equivalents, end of year | $260,086 | $ 8,930 | $ 31,900 | $ 18,324 | $15,311 | $ 33,629 | $368,180 | $ 49,353 |

**EXHIBIT 12–8**
Fund-Based Financial Statements

**CITY OF SACRAMENTO**
Statement of Fiduciary Net Assets
Fiduciary Funds
June 30, 2001
(in thousands)

|  | Pension Trust Fund | Investment Trust Fund | Agency Funds | Total Fiduciary Funds |
|---|---|---|---|---|
| **Assets** | | | | |
| Cash and investments | $472,882 | $30,086 | $44,694 | $547,662 |
| Receivables, net: | | | | |
|   Accounts | 37 | –0– | 3 | 40 |
|   Intergovernmental | –0– | –0– | 190 | 190 |
|   Interest | 3,119 | –0– | 317 | 3,436 |
|   Total assets | 476,038 | 30,086 | 45,204 | 551,328 |
| **Liabilities** | | | | |
| Securities lending obligations | 40,530 | –0– | 1,867 | 42,397 |
| Accounts payable | 632 | –0– | 598 | 1,230 |
| Due to other funds | –0– | –0– | 193 | 193 |
| Due to bondholders | –0– | –0– | 39,412 | 39,412 |
| Deposits | –0– | –0– | 9 | 9 |
| Advances from other funds | –0– | –0– | 3,125 | 3,125 |
|   Total liabilities | 41,162 | –0– | 45,204 | 86,366 |
| **Net Assets** | | | | |
| Held in trust for pension benefits and other purposes | $434,876 | $30,086 | –0– | $464,962 |

4. *Agency funds.* A government often holds money temporarily that must be transferred to some outside party. A city, for example, might have to share a portion of the collections from a toll road with the local county government. As stated in the notes to the 2001 financial statements of the City of Seattle, Washington, "Agency Funds are custodial in nature (assets equal liabilities) and do not measure the results of operations." Until transferred, these funds should be managed within the agency funds. As can be seen in Exhibit 12–8, only assets and liabilities are reported in the agency funds. An asset is obtained that must be turned over to an external individual, organization, or government; no accounting beyond the asset and related liability is needed.

### Reporting Public Colleges and Universities

During the past 10 to 15 years, public colleges and universities such as The Ohio State University and the University of Kansas have been in a somewhat awkward position in terms of financial accounting. Private schools including Harvard, Duke, and Stanford must follow the pronouncements of the FASB, especially those created for private not-for-profit organizations. FASB statements issued on contributions and the form of financial statements have provided a significant amount of official guidance for the financial information reported by these private institutions. The reporting standards developed for not-for-profit organizations have progressed greatly over the last few years.

In contrast, the GASB has retained primary authority over the reporting of public colleges and universities. Much of the GASB's work, though, has been directed at improving the accounting standards utilized by state and local government units. Consequently, the evolution of financial statements for public schools has lagged behind other types of reporting.

For example, the June 30, 2000, balance sheet of the University of Iowa resembles one for a not-for-profit organization from an earlier period of time. Separate columns are reported for

**EXHIBIT 12–9**
Fund-Based Financial Statements

**CITY OF SACRAMENTO**
Statement of Changes in Fiduciary Net Assets
Fiduciary Funds
For the Fiscal Year Ended June 30, 2001
(in thousands)

|  | Pension Trust Fund | Investment Trust Fund | Total Fiduciary Funds |
|---|---|---|---|
| Additions: |  |  |  |
| Contributions: |  |  |  |
| Employees | $ 989 | –0– | $ 989 |
| Investment income: |  |  |  |
| Net (depreciation) appreciation in fair value of investments | (34,622) | $ 535 | (34,087) |
| Interest | 21,149 | 1,652 | 22,801 |
| Dividends | 1,327 | –0– | 1,327 |
| Real estate operating income, net | (30) | –0– | (30) |
| Total investment (loss) earnings | (12,176) | 2,187 | (9,989) |
| Less investment expenses: |  |  |  |
| Banking and fiscal agent expenses | 71 | 44 | 115 |
| Professional services | 1,611 | –0– | 1,611 |
| Net investment expenses | 1,682 | 44 | 1,726 |
| Net investment (loss) income | (13,858) | 2,143 | (11,715) |
| Deposits by pool participants | –0– | 25,700 | 25,700 |
| Total additions | (12,869) | 27,843 | 14,974 |
| Deductions: |  |  |  |
| Benefits | 24,926 | –0– | 24,926 |
| Refunds of contributions | 161 | –0– | 161 |
| Withdrawals by pool participants | –0– | 60,552 | 60,552 |
| Total deductions | 25,087 | 60,552 | 85,639 |
| Change in net assets | (37,956) | (32,709) | (70,665) |
| Net assets, beginning of the year | 472,832 | 62,795 | 535,627 |
| Net assets, end of the year | $434,876 | $ 30,086 | $464,962 |

two Current Funds, Loan Funds, Endowment and Similar Funds, Agency Funds, and four Plant Funds. In the statement of changes in fund balances, revenues and expenditures (not expenses) are reported along with both mandatory and nonmandatory transfers in eight individual columns. Literally, eight different figures are shown for Total Revenues and Other Additions. Furthermore, these statements indicate that "The University does not depreciate buildings, improvements, or equipment." Clearly, such financial statements do not resemble those shown in the government financial statements outlined earlier in this chapter (Exhibits 12–1 through 12–9).

Generally, the operations of public colleges and universities differ in at least two important ways from private schools: First, the state or local government directly provides a significant amount of funding (at least for qualifying students) so that reliance on tuition charges tends to be reduced. For example, information provided with the 2001 financial statements of Utah State University disclosed that the State of Utah had contributed $121.3 million in current funds during the year and that revenues from tuition and fees totaled only $57.9 million.

Second, because of the ability to generate money each year from the government, the amount of endowment funds raised and accumulated is often smaller than private school endowments. Private schools usually try to build up a large endowment to ensure financial security; this is not always necessary at a public school backed by the state or another government. That is one of the main reasons that at June 30, 2001, Princeton University held investments with a market value of nearly $9 billion, an amount almost beyond the comprehension of officials at most public colleges.

The question of whether such differences warrant unique financial statements for public colleges and universities should be raised. In many ways, public and private schools are very much alike: They both educate students, charge tuition and other fees, conduct scholarly research, maintain libraries and sports teams, operate cafeterias and museums, and the like. What measurement basis should be applied and what should be the form of the financial statements to reflect the financial activity and position of a public college or university? These questions are especially relevant because of the frustration about the utilization of such statements: "The Board has found that few resource providers—especially citizens and legislators—or others with an interest in the financial activities of public colleges and universities read the institutions' external financial reports."[7]

Four alternatives as to the proper construction of the financial statements that should be prepared and distributed by public colleges and universities have been put forth:

1. Simply adopt the requirements of the FASB for private not-for-profit organizations so that all colleges and universities (public and private) would prepare financial statements that are comparable. The private reporting model is now relatively well developed. This suggestion holds some problems, though, because the unique aspects of public schools could be misunderstood by the FASB, a group that has not had to deal with the intricacies found in governmental entities. The unique reporting needs associated with public schools might simply be ignored. In addition, this loss of authority would appear to weaken the GASB somewhat. Politically, reducing the power of this board might not be pleasing to those organizations that provide much of the GASB's support and financing.

2. Leave the financial statements as they are currently, utilizing a fund basis for reporting. However, as indicated earlier, the current statements seem to have few readers so that some change appears to be warranted. Private not-for-profit organizations and governments (at least in part) have abandoned the reporting of individual funds so that continuing to rely on this approach for a public school seems to be outdated.

3. Create an entirely new set of financial statements designed to meet the unique needs of a public college or university. If the pronouncements of the FASB are not going to be followed, then the fundamental differences between the two types of schools must be quite significant. If all of those differences can be identified, new statements could be developed to satisfy the informational needs of users and mirror the events and transactions of these public institutions. Unfortunately, though, creation of a new set of financial statements would require an enormous amount of work by the GASB. Would the benefit gained from tailor-made financial statements outweigh the cost of producing new standards for reporting by public schools?

4. Adopt the same reporting model that has recently been created for states and local governments in *GASB Statement 34*. In many cases, public schools are component units of a primary government or can even be viewed as a special purpose government unit. Because a large amount of funding comes directly from the government based on oversight by the appropriate legislative body, the same financial statements utilized by a city or county could be applied.

In *GASB Statement 35*, "Basic Financial Statements—and Management's Discussion and Analysis—for Public Colleges and Universities," issued in November 1999, this fourth option was officially selected. According to paragraph 25, "the objective of this Statement is to amend Statement 34 to include public colleges and universities in the financial reporting model established by that Statement."

---

[7] *GASB Statement 35,* "Basic Financial Statements—and Management's Discussion and Analysis—for Public Colleges and Universities—An Amendment of GASB Statement 34," (1999), para. 25.

With just these few words, all of the requirements of the previous chapter and the first part of the current chapter have been applied to public colleges and universities:

- A Management's Discussion and Analysis (MD&A) must be written to provide oral explanations for the numerical information being provided.
- A government-wide statement of net assets (Exhibit 12–1) and statement of activities (Exhibit 12–2) must be produced if the school conducts both governmental activities and business-type activities. A slightly different version is produced if the school conducts only governmental or business-type activities.
- For these government-wide statements, the economic resource measurement basis is applied based on using accrual accounting for timing purposes.
- If governmental activities are conducted, statements must also be produced at the fund level for the General Fund and other major governmental funds (Exhibits 12–3 and 12–4).
- Business-type activities such as food services, the bookstore, and external training programs are monitored within proprietary funds and reported at the fund level through various fund-based statements (Exhibits 12–5, 12–6, and 12–7).

*GASB Statement 35* will become effective on the same staggered schedule as *Statement 34*. Thus, over the next several years, public colleges and universities will be adapting their financial statements to meet these new requirements. Consequently, the new financial statements will closely parallel those of state and local governments but will demonstrate a number of distinct differences from the statements prepared and distributed by private colleges and universities. Whether this severe change in the reporting process will improve the use made by potential readers of these financial statements can be determined only over time. However, when this statement was issued, reactions were certainly mixed. "A few schools have said the changes will cost them time and resources for no reason. Some will have to buy new systems for their capital assets so that they can report their depreciation. Those with older systems will have a harder time adjusting. . . . Jeffrey West, associate controller at the University of Arizona, said he expects the new rules to be more beneficial to public schools than harmful."[8]

## Summary

1. As with businesses, state and local governments can obtain assets through lease arrangements. The same criteria used by a for-profit organization for identifying a capital lease are applied in government accounting. For government-wide financial statements, both the resulting asset and liability are reported initially at the present value of the minimum lease payments. This asset is depreciated over the time that the government uses it. Interest expense is recognized on the reported liability each period. For fund-based financial statements, an expenditure and an other financing source are recognized at present value when the contract is initiated. Subsequent payments on the debt and interest also are recognized as expenditures.

2. Solid waste landfills create large potential debts for a government because of closure and postclosure costs. In the government-wide statements, this liability is accrued each period based on the latest estimations and the portion of the property that has been filled. Fund-based financial statements report no expenditures until a claim to current financial resources is made.

3. Government employees often have the right to future compensated absences because of holidays, vacations, sick leave, and the like. Government-wide statements must estimate and report the debt for these days when the employees earn them. Fund-based statements do not recognize a liability until current financial resources are expected to be used.

4. When a state or local government obtains a work of art or historical treasure, it normally must be recorded as a capital asset on the government-wide financial statements. However, if specified guidelines are met, recognition of the asset can be replaced by an expense. If a work of art or historical treasure is received through donation, revenue must be recognized according to the rules established for voluntary nonexchange transactions. In contrast, no capital assets are reported in the fund-based financial statements.

5. Depreciation must be recorded each period for works of art and historical treasures that are capitalized unless they are viewed as inexhaustible.

[8] Sonja Ryst, "Accounting Standards: Public Colleges Must Report Depreciation under GASB Rule," *The Bond Buyer*, December 13, 1999, p. 6.

6. Infrastructure assets must now be capitalized and depreciated on the government-wide financial statements. However, depreciation is not recorded if the modified approach is applied. Under this method, if a system is created to ensure that a network of infrastructure is maintained yearly at a predetermined condition, the cost of this care is expensed in lieu of recording depreciation.
7. A state or local government must now include a Management's Discussion and Analysis (MD&A) as part of its general purpose external financial reporting. This MD&A provides a verbal explanation of the operations and financial position of the government. Extensive requirements have been established by the GASB for the contents of the MD&A.
8. A primary government must produce a comprehensive annual financial report (CAFR). Both state and local governments as well as any special purpose government that meets certain provisions are viewed as primary governments. In addition, a component unit is any function that is legally separate from the primary government but for which financial accountability still exists. Component units can be discretely presented to the right of the primary government or can be blended within the actual funds of the primary government.
9. A statement of net assets and a statement of activities are produced as government-wide financial statements based on the economic resources measurement basis and accrual accounting. These statements separate governmental activities from business-type activities. Internal service funds are usually included within the governmental activities. The statement of activities reports expenses by function along with related program revenues to determine the net expenses or revenues resulting from each function.
10. Fund-based financial statements report the governmental funds by showing separately the General Fund and any other major fund. When reporting the governmental funds, the statements are based on measuring current financial resources using modified accrual accounting. Additional statements are presented for proprietary funds and fiduciary funds.
11. The financial statements to be produced by public colleges and universities must now follow the same guidelines as those created in *GASB Statement 34* for state and local government units. Those statements differ from statements produced by private schools that follow the FASB. Thus, statements of public schools will have a structure that is basically the same as the financial statements for a state or local government.

## Comprehensive Illustration PROBLEM

*(Estimated Time: 40 minutes)* The following is a series of transactions for a city. For each transaction, indicate how the event should be reported on the government-wide financial statements and then on the fund-based financial statements. Assume that this city has adopted the requirements of *GASB Statement 34*.

1. Money is borrowed by issuing a 20-year bond for $3 million, its face value. This money is to be used to construct a highway around the city.
2. Cash of $100,000 is transferred from the General Fund to the debt service funds to make the first payment of principal and interest on the above bonds.
3. The cash in (2) is paid on the bond. Of this total, $70,000 is recorded as interest with the remainder reducing the principal of the bond payable.
4. Construction of the highway is completed and the entire $3 million is paid.
5. The highway is expected to last for 30 years. However, the government qualifies to use the modified approach, which it has adopted for this system. A cost of $35,000 is incurred during the year to maintain the highway at an appropriate, predetermined condition. Of this amount, $29,000 was paid immediately, but the other $6,000 will not be paid until the sixth month of the subsequent year.
6. A local business donates lights for the new highway. The lights are valued at $200,000 and should last for 20 years. The modified approach is not used for this network of infrastructure, but straight-line depreciation is applied.
7. A truck is leased by the city to maintain the new highway. The lease qualifies as a capital lease. The present value of the minimum payments is $70,000. Depreciation for this year is $10,000 and interest is $6,000. A single payment of $11,000 in cash is made.
8. The local subway system takes in cash revenues of $2 million and records salary expense payments of $300,000 to its employees.
9. At the beginning of the year, a solid waste landfill is opened that will take 20 years to fill completely. This year an estimated 4 percent of the capacity is filled. The city anticipates total closure and postclosure costs of $2 million although no costs have been incurred to date.

# SOLUTION

1. *Government-wide financial statements.* On the statement of net assets, under the Governmental Activities column, both Cash and Noncurrent Liabilities will be increased by $3 million.
   *Fund-based financial statements.* The Cash balance will increase on the balance sheet whereas Other Financing Sources will increase on the statement of revenues, expenditures, and changes in fund balances. These amounts will be shown in the column for Other Governmental Funds unless this particular capital projects fund is judged to be major so that a separate column is presented.

2. *Government-wide financial statements.* No recording of this transfer is shown because the amount was an intra-activity transaction entirely carried out within the governmental activities.
   *Fund-based financial statements.* On the balance sheet, the Cash balance for the General Fund will go down while the cash listed for other governmental funds (or debt service fund) will rise. On the statement of revenues, expenditures, and other changes in fund balances, the General Fund will show An Other Financing Use whereas the other governmental funds will report an Other Financing Source. These balances will not be offset.

3. *Government-wide financial statements.* On the statement of net assets, for the governmental activities, Cash will go down by $100,000 while the Noncurrent Liabilities will drop by $30,000 because of the principal payment. The statement of activities should report $70,000 in interest expense as a governmental activity.
   *Fund-based financial statements.* First, Cash will be reduced by $100,000 on the balance sheet under the Other Governmental Funds (or Debt Service Fund) column. Second, on the statement of revenues, expenditures, and changes in fund balances, a $30,000 principal expenditure is reported with a $70,000 interest expenditure. These amounts are shown within the other governmental funds under debt service.

4. *Government-wide financial statements.* Under the governmental activities listed on the statement of net assets, Cash will decrease by the $3 million amount and Capital Assets will go up by the same amount. All new infrastructure costs must be capitalized according to *GASB Statement 34*.
   *Fund-based financial statements.* On the balance sheet, cash reported for other governmental funds will decrease. Once again, though, if this particular capital projects fund qualifies as major, the effects will be shown in a separate column rather than in the Other column. Within the statement of revenues, expenditures, and changes in fund balances, a $3 million expenditure will be reported as a capital outlay.

5. *Government-wide financial statements.* Under governmental activities on the statement of net assets, Cash will decrease by $29,000 and a current liability of $6,000 will be reported. On the statement of activities, the $35,000 expense will be included within an appropriate function such as public works. Since the modified approach is being applied, depreciation expense is not recorded; the maintenance expense is recognized instead.
   *Fund-based financial statements.* Because the $6,000 liability will not require the use of current financial resources, it will not be recorded at this time at the fund level. Thus, only a $29,000 drop in cash is reported in the balance sheet, probably under the General Fund. On the statement of revenues, expenditures, and changes in fund balances, a $29,000 expenditure will be recorded for public works.

6. *Government-wide financial statements.* The lights do not qualify as works of art or historical treasures and must therefore be reported as capital assets on the statement of net assets at the $200,000 market value. Based on a 20-year life, accumulated depreciation of $10,000 must be recognized to reduce the reported net asset to $190,000. For the statement of activities, a revenue of $200,000 is appropriate unless eligibility requirements for the donation have not yet been fulfilled. This revenue should be shown as a program revenue (Capital Grants and Contributions) to offset the expenses reported for public works. Depreciation of $10,000 should also be included as an expense for public works.
   *Fund-based financial statements.* No reporting is required because current financial resources were not affected.

7. *Government-wide financial statements.* On the statement of net assets, under the governmental activities, the leased truck and the lease liability will both be reported at $70,000. The truck will then be reduced by $10,000 in accumulated depreciation while the liability is reduced by $5,000, the amount of the $11,000 payment less $6,000 attributed to interest. Next, on the statement of activities, interest of $6,000 and depreciation of $10,000 are both reported as expenses directly related to the public works function.
   *Fund-based financial statements.* On the balance sheet, probably under the General Fund, an $11,000 reduction in cash is reported. In the statement of revenues, expenditures, and changes in fund balances, a $70,000 expenditure should be recorded as a capital outlay. Also, An Other Financing Source of the same amount is recognized. Finally, another $11,000 in expenditures should be shown: $6,000 as interest and $5,000 for debt reduction.

8. *Government-wide financial statements.* For the statement of net assets, Cash is increased under the business-type activities by $1.7 million. On the statement of activities, expenses for the subway system are reported as $300,000 while the related program revenues for charges for services rendered would go up by $2 million so that the net revenue resulting from this business-type activity is $1.7 million.

   *Fund-based financial statements.* On the statement of net assets for the proprietary funds (see Exhibit 12–5), a separate column for the subway system should be set up assuming that it is a major fund. Cash in this column increases by $1.7 million. Likewise, on the statement of revenues, expenses, and changes in fund net assets for the proprietary funds (see Exhibit 12–6), operating revenues of $2 million are reported for the subway system. In addition, personnel services of $300,000 should be recognized under the list of operating expenses. Both the inflow and outflow of cash are also reported on the statement of cash flows (see Exhibit 12–7) under Cash Flows from Operating Activities.

9. *Government-wide financial statements.* Because the landfill is 4 percent filled, that portion of the overall $2 million ($80,000) cost must be recognized. On the statement of net assets, this amount is shown as a noncurrent liability. The balance could be presented as either a governmental activity or a business-type activity depending on the internal classification of the landfill. Likewise, on the statement of activities, the same $80,000 expense figure is reported.

   *Fund-based financial statements.* This liability does not require the use of current financial resources and would not be reported if the landfill is considered a governmental fund. However, if the landfill is viewed as an enterprise fund, both the $80,000 expense and liability are shown on the separate statements prepared for the proprietary funds (see Exhibits 12–5 and 12–6).

## Questions

1. What criteria are applied by a state or local government to determine whether a lease should be capitalized?
2. On January 1, 2004, a city signs a capital lease for new equipment for the police department. How is this transaction reported on the government-wide financial statements? How is this transaction reported on the fund-based financial statements?
3. On December 31, 2004, the city indicated in question 2 makes its first annual lease payment. How is the payment reported on the government-wide financial statements? How is the payment reported on the fund-based financial statements?
4. Why does the operation of a solid waste landfill create reporting concerns for a local government?
5. A landfill is scheduled to be filled to capacity over a 10-year period. However, at the end of the first year of operations, the landfill is only 7 percent filled. How much liability for closure and postclosure costs should be recognized on the government-wide financial statements? How much liability should be recognized on the fund-based financial statements assuming that the landfill is recorded in an enterprise fund? How much liability should be recognized on the fund-based financial statements assuming that the landfill is recorded in the General Fund?
6. A city operates a solid waste landfill. This facility is 11 percent filled after the first year of operation and 24 percent filled after the second year. For government-wide financial statements, how much expense should be recognized in the second year for closure costs? Assuming the landfill is reported in the General Fund, how much of an expenditure should be recognized in the second year on the fund-based financial statements?
7. A teacher in the City of Lights earns vacation pay of $2,000 during 2004. However, the vacation will not be taken until the end of 2005. In the government-wide financial statements for 2004, how is this compensated absence reported? In the fund-based financial statements for 2004, how is this compensated absence reported?
8. In question 7, assume the teacher takes the vacation late in 2005 and is paid the entire $2,000. What journal entry is reported for each of the two methods of reporting?
9. The City of Salem is given a painting by Picasso to display in its city hall. Under what condition will the city *not* report this painting as a capital asset on its government-wide financial statements? If the painting is reported as a capital asset, must depreciation be reported?
10. In question 9, assume that the painting is not reported on the government-wide financial statements as a capital asset. Must the city report a revenue for the gift?
11. Under what condition is the modified approach applied?
12. What impact does the use of the modified approach have on the reporting within the government-wide financial statements?

13. What is normally included in the Management's Discussion and Analysis (MD&A)? Where is this information presented by a state or local government?
14. What is included in a comprehensive annual financial report (known as the *CAFR*)?
15. How does a reporting entity qualify as a primary government?
16. How does a reporting entity qualify as a component unit?
17. What is the difference between a blended component unit and a discretely presented component unit?
18. What are the two government-wide financial statements? What does each normally present?
19. What are the two fund-based financial statements for governmental funds? What does each normally present?
20. What is the difference in program revenues and general revenues and why is that distinction important?
21. Why does a government determine the net expenses or revenues for each of the functions within its governmental activities?
22. How are internal service funds reported on government-wide financial statements?
23. How are fiduciary funds reported on government-wide financial statements?
24. What are some of the major differences that exist between private colleges and universities and public colleges and universities?
25. What is the appropriate form for the financial statements of public colleges and universities?

## Problems

1. A city government has obtained an asset through a capital lease. For the government-wide financial statements, which of the following is true?
   a. The accounting parallels that used in for-profit accounting.
   b. The city must report an other financing source.
   c. The city must report an expenditure.
   d. Recognition of depreciation is optional.
2. A city government has a six-year capital lease for property being used within the General Fund. Minimum lease payments total $70,000 starting next year but have a current present value of $49,000. For the fund-based financial statements, what is the total amount of expenditures to be recognized over the six-year period?
   a. $0
   b. $49,000
   c. $70,000
   d. $119,000
3. A city government has a six-year capital lease for property being used within the General Fund. Minimum lease payments total $70,000 starting next year but have a current present value of $49,000. For the fund-based financial statements, what is the total amount of other financing sources to be recognized over the six-year period?
   a. $0
   b. $49,000
   c. $70,000
   d. $119,000
4. A city government has a nine-year capital lease for property being used within the General Fund. The lease was signed on January 1, 2004. Minimum lease payments total $90,000 starting at the end of the first year but have a current present value of $69,000. Annual payments are $10,000, and the interest rate being applied is 10 percent. When the first payment is made on December 31, 2004, which of the following recordings is made?

   | Government-wide statements | Fund-based statements |
   | --- | --- |
   | a. Interest Expense $0 | Interest Expense $0 |
   | b. Interest Expense $6,900 | Expenditures $6,900 |
   | c. Expenditures $10,000 | Expenditures $10,000 |
   | d. Interest Expense $6,900 | Expenditures $10,000 |

5. A city government has a nine-year capital lease for property being used within the General Fund. The lease was signed on January 1, 2004. Minimum lease payments total $90,000 starting at the end of the first year but have a current present value of $69,000. Annual payments are $10,000, and the interest rate being applied is 10 percent. On the fund-based financial statements, what liability is reported as of December 31, 2004, after the first payment is made?

a. $0
b. $59,000
c. $65,900
d. $80,000

6. A city creates a solid waste landfill. Every person or company that uses the landfill is assessed a charge based on the amount of materials contributed. The landfill will probably be recorded in which of the following?
   a. General Fund.
   b. Special revenues funds.
   c. Internal service funds.
   d. Enterprise funds.

**Use the following information for problems 7, 8, and 9.**

A city starts a solid waste landfill that it expects to fill to capacity evenly over a 10-year period. At the end of the first year, it is 8 percent filled. At the end of the second year, it is 19 percent filled. Closure and postclosure costs are estimated at $1 million. None of this amount will be paid until the landfill has reached its capacity.

7. On government-wide financial statements, which of the following is true for the Year 2 statements?
   a. Both expense and liability will be zero.
   b. Both expense and liability will be $110,000.
   c. Expense will be $110,000 and liability will be $190,000.
   d. Expense will be $100,000 and liability will be $200,000.

8. If this landfill is judged to be a proprietary fund, what liability will be reported at the end of the second year on fund-based financial statements?
   a. $0
   b. $110,000
   c. $190,000
   d. $200,000

9. If this landfill is judged to be a governmental fund, what liability will be reported at the end of the second year on fund-based financial statements?
   a. $0
   b. $110,000
   c. $190,000
   d. $200,000

**Use the following information for problems 10 and 11.**

The employees of the City of Jones earn vacation time that totals $1,000 per week during the year. Of this amount, $12,000 is actually taken in Year 1 and the remainder is taken in Year 2.

10. On government-wide financial statements, what liability should be reported at the end of Year 1?
    a. It depends on whether the employees work at governmental activities or business-type activities.
    b. $0
    c. $40,000
    d. $52,000

11. On fund-based financial statements, what amount of liability should be recognized at December 31, Year 1? *Assume that all vacations will be taken in July.*
    a. It depends on whether the employees work at governmental activities or business-type activities.
    b. $0
    c. $40,000
    d. $52,000

12. The City of Wilson receives a large piece of sculpture valued at $240,000 as a gift to be placed in front of the municipal building. Which of the following is true for the government-wide financial statements?
    a. A capital asset of $240,000 must be reported.
    b. No capital asset will be reported.
    c. If conditions are met, recording the sculpture as a capital asset is optional.
    d. The sculpture will be recorded but only for the amount paid by the city.

13. In question 12, which of the following statements is true about reporting a revenue?
    a. A revenue should be reported.
    b. Revenue is reported but only if the asset is reported.
    c. If the asset is not capitalized, no revenue should be recognized.
    d. As a gift, no revenue would ever be reported.

14. In question 12, assume that the work is reported as a capital asset. Which of the following is true?
    a. Depreciation is not recorded because the city has no cost.
    b. Depreciation is not required if the asset is held to be inexhaustible.
    c. Depreciation must be recognized because the asset is capitalized.
    d. Because the property was received as a gift, recognition of depreciation is optional.
15. A city builds sidewalks throughout its various neighborhoods at a cost of $200,000. Which of the following is *not* true?
    a. Because the sidewalks qualify as infrastructure, the asset is viewed in the same way as land so that depreciation is not recorded.
    b. Depreciation is required unless the modified approach is utilized.
    c. The modified approach recognizes maintenance expense in lieu of depreciation expense for qualifying infrastructure assets.
    d. The modified approach is allowed only if the city maintains the network of sidewalks at least at a predetermined condition.
16. Which of the following is true about use of the modified approach?
    a. The modified approach can be applied to all capital assets of a state or local government.
    b. The modified approach is used to adjust depreciation expense either up or down based on conditions for the period.
    c. The modified approach is required for infrastructure assets.
    d. For qualified assets, the modified approach eliminates the recording of depreciation.
17. Which of the following is true about the Management's Discussion and Analysis (MD&A)?
    a. It is an optional addition to the comprehensive annual financial report, but the GASB encourages inclusion.
    b. It adds a verbal explanation for the numbers and trends presented in the financial statements.
    c. It appears at the very end of a government's comprehensive annual financial report.
    d. It replaces a portion of the fund-based financial statements traditionally produced by a state or local government.
18. Which of the following is *not* necessary for a special-purpose local government to be viewed as a primary government for reporting purposes?
    a. It must have a separately elected governing body.
    b. It must have specifically defined geographic boundaries.
    c. It must be fiscally independent.
    d. It must have corporate powers to prove that it is legally independent.
19. An accountant is trying to determine whether the school system of the City of Abraham is fiscally independent. Which of the following is *not* a requirement for being deemed fiscally independent?
    a. Holding property in its own name.
    b. Issuing bonded debt without outside approval.
    c. Passing its own budget without outside approval.
    d. Setting taxes or rates without outside approval.
20. An employment agency for the handicapped works closely with the City of Hanover. The employment agency is legally separate from the city but still depends fiscally on it. How should Hanover report the employment agency in its comprehensive annual financial report?
    a. Not at all because the agency is legally separate.
    b. As a part of the General Fund.
    c. As a component unit.
    d. As a related organization.
21. Which of the following statements is reported within the government-wide financial statements?
    a. Statement of net assets and statement of cash flows.
    b. Balance sheet and statement of net assets.
    c. Statement of activities and statement of changes in fund balances.
    d. Statement of net assets and statement of activities.
22. For component units, what is the difference in discrete presentation and blending?
    a. A blended component unit is shown to the left of the statements; a discretely presented component unit is shown to the right.
    b. A blended component unit is shown at the bottom of the statements; a discretely presented component unit is shown within the statements like a fund.
    c. A blended component unit is shown within the statements like a fund; a discretely presented component unit is shown to the right.
    d. A blended component unit is shown to the right of the statements; a discretely presented component unit is shown in completely separate statements.

23. A government reports that its public safety function had expenses of $900,000 last year and program revenues of $200,000 so that its net expenses were $700,000. On which financial statement is this information presented?
    a. Statement of activities.
    b. Statement of cash flows.
    c. Statement of revenues and expenditures.
    d. Statement of net assets.

24. On government-wide financial statements, a difference is made between program revenues and general revenues. How is that difference shown?
    a. Program revenues are offset against the expenses of a specific function; general revenues are assigned to governmental activities and business-type activities in general.
    b. General revenues are shown at the top of the statement of revenues and expenditures; program revenues are shown at the bottom.
    c. General revenues are labeled as operating revenues; program revenues are shown as miscellaneous income.
    d. General revenues are broken down by type; program revenues are reported as a single figure.

25. Which of the following is true about the statement of cash flows for the proprietary funds of a state or local government?
    a. The indirect method of reporting cash flows from operating activities is allowed although the direct method is recommended.
    b. The structure of the statement is virtually identical to that of a for-profit business.
    c. The statement is divided into four separate sections of cash flows.
    d. Amounts spent on capital assets are reported in a separate section from amounts raised to finance those capital assets.

26. Which of the following is true about the financial reporting of a public college or university?
    a. It resembles the financial reporting of private colleges and universities.
    b. It will continue to use its own unique style of financial reporting.
    c. It resembles the financial reporting of state and local governments.
    d. It will soon be reported using a financial statement format unique to the needs of public colleges and universities that the GASB is scheduled to create.

27. On January 1, 2004, a city government leased the following pieces of equipment. Each lease qualifies as a capital lease. Initial payments are on December 31, 2004. An interest rate of 10 percent is viewed as appropriate. No bargain purchase options exist.

| Fund | Annual Payments | Total Payments | Present Value of Total Payments |
|---|---|---|---|
| General | $8,000 | $40,000 | $33,350 |
| Enterprise | 6,000 | 36,000 | 28,750 |

    a. On government-wide financial statements for December 31, 2004, and the year then ended, what balances should be reported?
    b. On fund-based financial statements for December 31, 2004, and the year then ended, what balances should be reported?

28. On January 1, 2004, a city government leased the following pieces of equipment. Each lease qualifies as a capital lease. Initial payments are on December 31, 2004. An interest rate of 12 percent is viewed as appropriate. No bargain purchase options exist.

| Fund | Annual Payments | Total Payments | Present Value of Total Payments |
|---|---|---|---|
| General | $3,000 | $30,000 | $19,000 |
| Enterprise | 9,000 | 36,000 | 30,600 |

    a. Prepare journal entries for the year of 2004 for both of these leases for government-wide financial statements.
    b. Prepare journal entries for the year of 2004 for both of these leases for fund-based financial statements.

29. On January 1, 2004, the City of Verga leased a large truck for five years and made the initial annual payment of $22,000 immediately. The present value of these payments based on an 8 percent interest rate is assumed to be $87,800. The truck has an expected useful life of five years.
    a. Assuming that the truck will be used by the city's fire department, what journal entries should be made for 2004 and 2005 for the government-wide financial statements?
    b. Assuming that the truck will be used by the city's fire department, what journal entries should be made for 2004 and 2005 for the fund-based financial statements?
    c. Assuming that the truck will be used by the airport (an enterprise fund) operated by the city, what journal entries should be made for 2004 and 2005 for the fund-based financial statements?

30. On January 1, 2004, the City of Hastings created a solid waste landfill that it expects to reach capacity gradually over the next 20 years. The city anticipates that closure costs will be $1.2 million and postclosure costs will be an additional $700,000. Of these totals, $50,000 must be paid on December 31 of each year for preliminary closure work. At the end of 2004, the landfill reached 3 percent of capacity. At the end of 2005, the landfill reached 9 percent of capacity. Also, at the end of 2005, a reassessment is made; total closure costs are determined to be $1.4 million rather than $1.2 million.
    a. Assuming that the landfill is viewed as an enterprise fund, what journal entries are made in 2004 and 2005 for the government-wide financial statements?
    b. Assuming that the landfill is viewed as a general fund, what journal entries are made in 2004 and 2005 for the government-wide financial statements?
    c. Assuming that the landfill is viewed as an enterprise fund, what journal entries are made in 2004 and 2005 for fund-based financial statements?
    d. Assuming that the landfill is viewed as a general fund, what journal entries are made in 2004 and 2005 for fund-based financial statements?

31. The City of Lawrence opens a solid waste landfill in 2004 that is at 54 percent of capacity on December 31, 2004. The city had initially anticipated closure costs of $2 million but later that year decided that closure costs should actually be $2.4 million. None of these costs will be incurred until 2011 when the landfill is scheduled to be closed.
    a. What will appear on the government-wide financial statements for this landfill for December 31, 2004, and the year then ended?
    b. Assuming that the landfill is recorded within the General Fund, what will appear on the fund-based financial statements for this landfill for December 31, 2004, and the year then ended?

32. Mary T. Lincoln works for the City of Columbus. She volunteered to work over the 2004 Christmas break so that she could earn a short vacation during the first week of January 2005. She earns three vacation days because of working on the holiday and will be paid $400 per day. She takes her vacation in January and is paid for those days.
    a. For government-wide financial statements, prepare journal entries for 2004 and 2005 because of these events.
    b. Assuming that Lincoln works in an activity reported within the General Fund, prepare journal entries for 2004 and 2005 for the fund-based financial statements because of these events.
    c. Assume that Lincoln works in an activity reported within the General Fund. However, assume that she does not plan to take her three vacation days until near the end of 2005. For the fund-based financial statements, what journal entries should be made in 2004 and 2005?

33. On January 1, 2004, a rich citizen of the Town of Ristoni donates a painting valued at $300,000 to be displayed to the public in a government building. This painting meets the qualifications for not being capitalized. However, town officials choose to record the asset. There are no eligibility requirements for the gift. The asset is judged to be inexhaustible so that depreciation will not be reported.
    a. On government-wide financial statements for December 31, 2004, and the year then ended, what will be reported in connection with this gift?
    b. How does the answer to question (a) change if the government had decided to depreciate this asset over a 10-year period using straight-line depreciation?
    c. How does the answer to question (a) change if the government had decided not to capitalize the asset?

34. On January 1, 2004, a city pays $60,000 for a work of art. The city will put it on display in the local library and will take appropriate measures to protect and preserve the piece. However, if the work is ever sold, the money received will go into unrestricted funds. The work is viewed as inexhaustible, but the city has opted to depreciate the cost over 20 years (using the straight-line method).
    a. How will this work be reported in the government-wide financial statements for December 31, 2004, and the year then ended?
    b. How will this work be reported in the fund-based financial statements for December 31, 2004, and the year then ended?

35. A city government adds street lights within its boundaries at a total cost of $100,000. The lights should burn for at least 10 years but can last significantly longer if maintained properly. The city sets up a system to monitor these lights with the goal that 97 percent will be working at any one time. During the year, the city spends $6,300 to clean and repair the lights so that they are working according to the specified conditions. However, another $9,000 is spent to construct lights for several new streets within the city.

    For government-wide reporting purposes, describe the various ways by which these costs could be reported.

36. The City of Francois, Texas, has begun the process of producing its comprehensive annual financial report (CAFR). Within the city, several organizations operate that are related in some way to the primary government. The city's accountant is attempting to determine how these organizations should be included in the reporting process.
    a. What is the major criterion for inclusion in a government's CAFR?
    b. How is a primary government unit identified?
    c. How is the legal separation of a government unit evaluated?
    d. How is the fiscal independence of a government unit evaluated?
    e. What is a component unit and how is it normally reported on the government-wide financial statements?
    f. How does a primary government prove that it can impose its will on a component unit?
    g. What is meant by the blending of a component unit?
    h. What is a related organization and how does a primary government report it?

37. The County of Maxnell decides to create a sanitation department and offer its services to the public for a fee. As a result, county officials plan to account for this activity with the enterprise funds. Make journal entries for this operation for the following 2004 transactions as well as necessary adjusting entries at the end of the year. Only entries for the sanitation department are required here.

    January 1—Received unrestricted funds of $90,000 as a transfer from the General Fund as permanent financing.
    February 1—Borrowed an additional $130,000 from a local bank at a 12 percent annual interest rate.
    March 1—Ordered a truck at an expected cost of $108,000.
    April 1—Received the truck and made payment. The actual costs amount to $110,000. The truck has a 10-year life and no salvage value. Straight-line depreciation is to be used.
    May 1—Received a cash grant of $20,000 from the state to help supplement the pay of the sanitation workers.
    June 1—Rented a garage for the truck at a cost of $1,000 per month with 12 months of rent being paid in advance.
    July 1—Charged citizens $13,000 for services. Of this amount, $11,000 has been collected.
    August 1—Made a $10,000 cash payment on the 12 percent note of February 1. This payment covers both interest and principal.
    September 1—Paid salaries of $18,000 using the grant received on May 1.
    October 1—Paid truck maintenance costs of $1,000.
    November 1—Paid additional salaries of $10,000 partially using the rest of the grant money received May 1.
    December 31—Sent invoices to customers for services over the past six months that total $19,000. Cash of $3,000 is collected immediately.

38. The following information pertains to the City of Williamson for 2004, its first year of legal existence. For convenience, assume that all transactions are for the General Fund, which carries out three separate functions: general government, public safety, and health and sanitation.

    | Receipts: | |
    |---|---:|
    | Property taxes | $320,000 |
    | Franchise taxes | 42,000 |
    | Charges for general government services | 5,000 |
    | Charges for public safety services | 3,000 |
    | Charges for health and sanitation services | 42,000 |
    | Issued long-term note payable | 200,000 |

    *(continued)*

| | |
|---|---:|
| Receivables at end of year: | |
|    Property taxes (90 percent estimated to be collected) | 90,000 |
| Payments: | |
|    Salary: | |
|       General government | 66,000 |
|       Public safety | 39,000 |
|       Health and sanitation | 22,000 |
|    Rent: | |
|       General government | 11,000 |
|       Public safety | 18,000 |
|       Health and sanitation | 3,000 |
|    Maintenance: | |
|       General government | 21,000 |
|       Public safety | 5,000 |
|       Health and sanitation | 9,000 |
|    Insurance: | |
|       General government | 8,000 |
|       Public safety ($2,000 still prepaid at end of year) | 11,000 |
|       Health and sanitation | 12,000 |
|    Interest on debt | 16,000 |
|    Principal payment on debt | 4,000 |
|    Building | 120,000 |
|    Equipment | 80,000 |
|    Supplies (20 percent still held) (public safety) | 15,000 |
|    Investments | 90,000 |
| Ordered but not received: | |
|    Equipment | 12,000 |
| Due in one month at end of year: | |
|    Salaries: | |
|       General government | 4,000 |
|       Public safety | 7,000 |
|       Health and sanitation | 8,000 |

Compensated absences for general government workers at the end of the year amount to $13,000. These amounts will not be taken until late in the year 2005.

The city received art this year valued at $14,000 that is being used for general government purposes. There are no eligibility requirements. The city chose not to capitalize this property.

The building is used for the general government and is being depreciated over 10 years using the straight-line method with no salvage value. The equipment is used for health and sanitation and is depreciated using the straight-line method over five years with no salvage value.

The investments are valued at $103,000 at the end of the year.

a. Prepare a statement of activities and a statement of net assets for governmental activities for December 31, 2004, and the year then ended.
b. Prepare a statement of revenues, expenditures, and changes in fund balances and a balance sheet for the General Fund as of December 31, 2004, and the year then ended. Assume that the consumption method is being applied.

39. The City of Bernard starts the year of 2004 with the following unrestricted amounts in its General Fund: cash of $20,000 and investments of $70,000. In addition, it holds a building bought on January 1, 2003, for general government purposes for $300,000 and related long-term debt of $240,000. The building is being depreciated on the straight-line method over 10 years. The interest rate is 10 percent. The General Fund carries out four separate functions: general government, public safety, public works, and health and sanitation.

| | |
|---|---:|
| Receipts: | |
|    Property taxes | $510,000 |
|    Sales taxes | 99,000 |

*(continued)*

| | |
|---|---:|
| Dividend income | 20,000 |
| Charges for general government services | 15,000 |
| Charges for public safety services | 8,000 |
| Charges for public works | 4,000 |
| Charges for health and sanitation services | 31,000 |
| Charges for landfill | 8,000 |
| Grant to be used for salaries for health workers (no eligibility requirements) | 25,000 |
| Issued long-term note payable | 200,000 |
| Sold above investments | 84,000 |
| Receivables at end of year: | |
|   Property taxes ($10,000 is expected to be uncollectible) | 130,000 |
| Payments: | |
|   Salary: | |
|     General government | 90,000 |
|     Public safety | 94,000 |
|     Public works | 69,000 |
|     Health and sanitation (all from grant) | 22,000 |
|   Utilities: | |
|     General government | 9,000 |
|     Public safety | 16,000 |
|     Public works | 13,000 |
|     Health and sanitation | 4,000 |
|   Insurance: | |
|     General government | 25,000 |
|     Public safety | 12,000 |
|     Public works (all prepaid as of the end of the year) | 6,000 |
|     Health and sanitation | 4,000 |
|   Miscellaneous: | |
|     General government | 12,000 |
|     Public safety | 10,000 |
|     Public works | 9,000 |
|     Health and sanitation | 7,000 |
|   Interest on previous debt | 24,000 |
|   Principal payment on previous debt | 10,000 |
|   Interest on new debt | 18,000 |
|   Building (public works) | 210,000 |
|   Equipment (public safety) | 90,000 |
|   Public works supplies (30 percent still held) | 20,000 |
|   Investments | 111,000 |
| Ordered but not received: | |
|   Equipment | 24,000 |
|   Supplies | 7,000 |
| Due at end of year: | |
|   Salaries: | |
|     General government | 14,000 |
|     Public safety | 17,000 |
|     Public works | 5,000 |

A truck was leased on the last day of the year. The first payment will be at the end of the next year. Total payments amount to $90,000 but have a present value of $64,000.

The city started a landfill within its General Fund this year. It is included as a public works function. Closure costs are expected to be $260,000 in about nine years. No costs have been incurred to date although the landfill is now 15 percent filled.

The new building is being depreciated over 20 years using the straight-line method and no salvage value whereas the equipment is similar except that the life is only 10 years.

The investments are valued at $116,000 at the end of the year.

a. Prepare a statement of activities and a statement of net assets for governmental activities for December 31, 2004, and the year then ended.
b. Prepare a statement of revenues, expenditures, and changes in fund balances and a balance sheet for the General Fund as of December 31, 2004, and the year then ended. Assume that the purchases method is being applied.

40. The City of Pfeiffer starts the year of 2004 with the General Fund and an enterprise fund. The General Fund has two activities: education and parks/recreation. For convenience, assume that the General Fund holds cash of $123,000 and a new school building costing $1 million. The city utilizes straight-line depreciation. The school has a 20-year life and no salvage value. The enterprise fund has cash of $62,000 and a new $600,000 civic auditorium with a 30-year life and no salvage value. The enterprise fund monitors just one activity: the rental of the civic auditorium for entertainment and other cultural affairs.

The following transactions for the city take place during 2004. Assume that the city's fiscal year ends on December 31.

a. Decides to build a municipal park and transfers $70,000 into a capital projects fund and immediately expends $20,000 for a piece of land.
b. Borrows cash of $110,000 on a long-term bond for use in creating the new municipal park.
c. Assesses property taxes on the first day of the year. The assessment, which is immediately enforceable, totals $600,000. Of this amount $510,000 will be collected during 2004 and another $50,000 is expected in the first month of 2005. The remainder is expected about half way through 2005.
d. Constructs a building on the park in (b) for $80,000 in cash to be used for playing basketball and other sports. It is put into service on July 1 and should last 10 years with no salvage value.
e. Builds a sidewalk around the new park for $10,000 in cash and puts it into service on July 1. It should last for 10 years, but the city plans to keep it up to a predetermined quality level so that it will last almost indefinitely.
f. Opens the park and charges an entrance fee. The fee is only a token amount and is recorded, therefore, in the General Fund. Collections during this first year total $8,000.
g. Buys a new parking deck for $200,000, paying cash of $20,000 and signing a long-term note for the rest. The parking deck, which is to go into operation on July 1, is across the street from the city auditorium and is considered part of that activity. It has a 20-year life and no salvage value.
h. Receives a cash grant of $100,000 for the city school system. The money must be spent for school lunches for the poor. Appropriate spending of these funds is viewed as an eligibility requirement of this grant. During the current year, $37,000 of the amount received was properly spent.
i. Charges students in the school system a total fee of $6,000 for books and the like. Of this amount, 90 percent is collected during 2004 with the remainder expected to be collected in the first few weeks of 2005.
j. Buys school supplies for $22,000 cash and uses $17,000 of them. The purchases method is being used in the General Fund
k. Receives a painting by a local artist to be displayed in the local school. It qualifies as a work of art, and officials have chosen not to capitalize it. The painting has a value of $80,000. It is viewed as inexhaustible.
l. Transfers cash of $20,000 from the General Fund to the Enterprise Fund as a capital contribution.
m. Orders a school bus for $99,000.
n. Receives the school bus and pays an actual cost of $102,000. The bus is put into operation on October 1 and should last for five years with no salvage value.
o. Pays salaries of $240,000 to school teachers. In addition, $30,000 is owed and will be paid during the first two weeks of 2005. Vacations of $23,000 have also been earned but will not be taken until July 2005.
p. Pays salaries of $42,000 to city auditorium workers. In addition, $3,000 is owed and will be paid in the first two weeks of 2005. Vacations of $5,000 have also been earned but will not be taken until July 2005.
q. Has charged customers $130,000 for the rent of the city auditorium. Of this balance, $110,000 was collected in cash, and the remainder will be collected in April 2005.
r. Pays maintenance charges of $9,000 for the building and sidewalk in (d) and (e).
s. Pays $14,000 on the note in (b) on the last day of 2004: $5,000 principal and $9,000 interest.
t. Accrues interest of $13,000 on the note in (g) as of the end of 2004, an amount that will be paid in June 2005.

u. Assumes that a museum that operates within the city is a component unit that will be discretely presented. The museum reports to city officials that it had direct expenses of $42,000 this past year and revenues of $50,000 from charges. The only assets that it had at the end of the year were cash of $24,000, building (net of depreciation) of $300,000, and a long-term liability of $210,000.

Produce the 2004 government-wide financial statements for this city. Assume modified approach is used.

41. Use the information in problem 40 to produce the 2004 fund-based financial statements for the governmental funds and the proprietary funds. A statement of cash flows is not required. Assume "available" is defined as within 60 days and that all funds are major.

42. For each of the following, indicate whether the statement is true or false.
   a. A pension trust fund appears in the government-wide financial statements but not in the fund-based financial statements.
   b. Permanent funds are included as one of the governmental funds.
   c. Orders of $20,000 are placed for equipment by a fire department. The equipment is received at a cost of $20,800. In compliance with requirements for fund-based financial statements, an encumbrance of $20,000 was recorded when the order was placed, and an expenditure of $20,800 was recorded when the order was received.
   d. A landfill is reported in the enterprise fund. At the end of Year 1, the government estimated that the landfill will cost $800,000 to clean up when it is eventually full. Currently, it is 12 percent filled. At the end of Year 2, the estimation was changed to $860,000 when it was 20 percent filled. No payments are due for several years. On fund-based financial statements for Year 2, an expense of $76,000 should be recognized.
   e. A landfill is reported in the General Fund of a city. At the end of Year 1, the government anticipated the landfill to cost $900,000 to clean up when it is full, and reported that it was 11 percent filled. At the end of Year 2, the estimation was changed to $850,000 and 20 percent filled. No payments are due for several years. On government-wide financial statements for Year 2, an expense of $71,000 should be recognized.
   f. A lease for a computer (that has a six-year life) is signed on January 1, Year 1, with six annual payments of $10,000. The computer is to be used by the police department. The first payment is to be made immediately. The present value of the $60,000 in cash flows is $39,000 based on a 10 percent rate. On fund-based financial statements for Year 1, total expenditures of $10,000 should be recognized.
   g. An agency fund has neither revenues nor expenditures but reports expenses.
   h. A lease for a computer (that has a six-year life) is signed on January 1, Year 1, with six annual payments of $10,000. The computer is to be used by the police department. The first payment is to be made immediately. The present value of the $60,000 in cash flows is $39,000 based on a 10 percent rate. On government-wide financial statements for Year 1, expenses of $9,400 should be recognized.

**For problems 43 through 48, use the following introductory information.**

The City of Wolfe has issued its financial statements for Year 4 (assume the city uses a calendar year). The city maintains the General Fund made up of (a) education and (b) parks. The city also utilizes capital projects funds for construction projects and an enterprise fund to account for its art museum. It also has one discretely presented component unit.

On the government-wide financial statements that were issued, the following Year 4 totals were indicated:

Education had net expenses of $710,000.
Parks had net expenses of $130,000.
Art museum had net revenues of $80,000.
General revenues were $900,000; the overall increase in net assets was $140,000.

The fund-based financial statements that were issued for Year 4 indicated the following:

The General Fund had an increase of $30,000 in its fund balance.
The Capital Projects Fund had an increase of $40,000 in its fund balance.
The Enterprise Fund had an increase of $60,000 in its net assets.

Wolfe defines "available" as current financial resources to be paid or collected within 60 days.

43. On the first day of Year 4, the city receives as a gift a piece of art that qualifies as a work of art. It has a 30-year life, is worth $15,000 and is being displayed at one of the parks. It was accidentally

capitalized and depreciated by the accountant although officials had wanted to use the allowed alternative.

Respond to the following.

a. If city officials had used the accounting they had wanted, what would have been the correct change in the fund balance for the General Fund for the year?

b. What should have been the correct net expenses for parks for the year?

c. Assume the same information except that the art was given to the art museum but no recording at all was made. On government-wide financial statements, what should have been the overall change in net assets for Year 4 assuming that officials still preferred the allowed alternatives.

44. On January 1, Year 4, the government leased a police car for five years at $20,000 per year with the first payment being made on December 31, Year 4. This is a capitalized lease. Assume that, at a reasonable interest rate of 10 percent, the present value of a five-year annuity due is $62,000. In the government-wide financial statements, the government recorded an increase in expense for $20,000 and a reduction in cash for $20,000 as its only entry. In the fund-based financial statements, the government increased Expenditures by $20,000 and reduced Cash for $20,000 as its only entry.

a. What was the correct overall change in the net assets in the government-wide financial statements?

b. What was the correct change in the fund balance for the General Fund?

45. Assume that the one component unit had program revenues of $30,000 and expenses of $42,000 and spent $10,000 for land during Year 4. However, it should have been handled as a blended component unit, not as a discretely presented component unit. What was the correct overall change in the net assets in the government-wide financial statements?

46. At the end of Year 4, teachers were owed $60,000 in vacation pay that had never been recorded. The assumption is that these vacations will be taken evenly over the next year.

a. What was the correct change in the fund balance of the General Fund for the year?

b. What was the correct overall change in the net assets in the government-wide financial statements?

47. The city has a landfill that has been recorded within its parks. The landfill generated program revenues of $4,000 in Year 4 and cash expenses of $15,000. It also paid $3,000 cash for a piece of land. These transactions were recorded as would have been anticipated, but no other recording was made. The city assumes that it will have to pay $200,000 to clean up the landfill when it is closed in several years. The landfill was 18 percent filled at the end of Year 3 and is 26 percent filled at the end of Year 4. No payments will be necessary for several more years. For convenience, assume that the entries in all previous years were correctly handled regardless of the situation.

a. The city believes that the landfill was included correctly in all previous years as one of its Enterprise Funds. What is the correct overall change in the net assets in the government-wide financial statements?

b. The city believes that the landfill was included correctly in all previous years in one of the enterprise funds. What is the correct change in the net assets of the enterprise fund in the fund-based financial statements?

c. The city realizes that the landfill was included correctly in all previous years within the General Fund. What is the correct change in the fund balance of the General Fund?

48. The city bought a $20,000 machine with a five-year life and no salvage value for its school system. It was capitalized and no other entries were ever made. The machine was monitored using the modified approach.

a. What was the correct overall change in the net assets in the government-wide financial statements?

b. What was the total of correct net expenses for education in the government-wide statements?

49. A police department leases a car on July 1, Year 1 with five annual payments of $20,000 each. The first payment is made immediately, and the present value of the annuity due is $78,000 based on an assumed rate of 10 percent. The car has a five-year life. Assume that this is a capitalized lease. Indicate whether each of the following statements is true or false.

a. The fund-based financial statements will show a total liability of $3,900 at the end of Year 1.

b. The government-wide financial statements will show a total liability of $58,000 at the end of Year 1.

c. The government-wide financial statements will show total interest expense of $2,900 in Year 1.

d. The fund-based financial statements will show total expenditures of $20,000 in Year 1.

e. The government-wide financial statements will show a net leased asset of $70,200 at the end of Year 1.

*f.* If this were an ordinary annuity so that the first payment was made in Year 2, no expenditure would be reported in the fund-based financial statements in Year 1.
   *g.* If the car had an eight-year life, this contract could not be a capitalized lease.
   *h.* Over the entire life of the car, the amount of expense recognized in the government-wide financial statements will be the same as the amount of expenditures recognized in the fund-based financial statements.

50. A city has a solid waste landfill that was filled 12 percent in Year 1 and 26 percent in Year 2. During those periods, the government expected that total closure costs would be $2 million. As a result, $50,000 was paid to an environmental company on July 1 of each of these two years. Such payments will continue for several years to come. Indicate whether each of the following statements is true or false.
    *a.* The government-wide financial statements will show an expense of $230,000 in Year 2 but only if reported in an enterprise fund.
    *b.* The fund-based financial statements will show a liability of $50,000 in Year 2 if this landfill is reported in the General Fund.
    *c.* The fund-based financial statements will show a liability of $50,000 at the end of Year 2 if this landfill is reported in an enterprise fund.
    *d.* If this landfill is reported in an enterprise fund, the government-wide financial statements and the fund-based financial statements will basically have the same reporting.
    *e.* The government-wide financial statements will show a liability of $420,000 at the end of Year 2.
    *f.* Over the entire life of the landfill, the amount of expense recognized in the government-wide financial statements will be the same as the amount of expenditures recognized in the fund-based financial statements.

51. Use the exact same information as in problem 50 except that, by the end of Year 3, the landfill is 40 percent filled. The city realizes that the total closure costs will be $3 million. Indicate whether each of the following statements is true or false.
    *a.* If the city had known the costs were going to be $3 million from the beginning, the reporting on the fund-based financial statements would have been different than if it had been reported in an enterprise fund.
    *b.* If the landfill is monitored in the General Fund, a liability will be reported for the governmental activities in the government-wide financial statements at the end of Year 3.
    *c.* In the government-wide financial statements, an expense of $680,000 should be recognized in Year 3.
    *d.* Because the closure costs reflect a future flow of cash, any liability reported in the government-wide financial statements must be reported at present value.

52. A city receives a copy of its original charter from the year 1799 as a gift from a citizen. The document will be put under glass and displayed in the city hall for all to see. The fair market value is estimated at $10,000. Indicate whether each of the following statements is true or false.
    *a.* If the city government does not have a policy in place as to the handling of proceeds if the document is ever sold, the city will have to report a $10,000 asset within its government-wide financial statements.
    *b.* Assume that this gift qualifies for optional handling and that the city chooses to report it as an asset. For the government-wide financial statements, depreciation is required.
    *c.* Assume this gift qualifies for optional handling and the document is deemed to be exhaustible. The city must report an immediate expense of $10,000 in the government-wide financial statements.
    *d.* Assume that this gift qualifies for optional handling. The city must make a decision as to whether to recognize a revenue of $10,000 in the government-wide financial statements.
    *e.* Assume that this gift qualifies for optional handling. The city can choose to report the gift in the statement of net activities for the government-wide financial statements in a way so that there is no overall net effect.

53. A city starts a public library that has separate incorporation and gets some of its money from the state and some from private donations. Indicate whether each of the following statements is true or false.
    *a.* If the city appoints 7 of the 10 directors, it must report the library as a component unit.
    *b.* If the library is a component unit and its financial results are shown as part of the governmental activities of the city, it is known as a *blended component unit*.
    *c.* If the library appoints its own board but the city must approve its budget, the library must be reported as a blended component unit.
    *d.* The choice of whether a component unit is blended or reported discretely is up to the discretion of the city.

# Develop Your Skills

## RESEARCH CASE 1

The City of Abernethy has adopted the requirements of *GASB Statement 34*, "Basic Financial Statements—and Management's Discussion and Analysis—for State and Local Governments" in its financial reporting. The individual in charge of accounting for the city has now shifted attention to the reporting of infrastructure items that were acquired or constructed prior to adoption of this pronouncement. The city has three large bridges built in the later part of the 1980s that were not capitalized at the time. The accountant is interested in receiving suggestions as to how to determine a valid amount to report for these bridges.

### Required:

Use a copy of *GASB Statement 34* as the basis for writing a report to this accountant to indicate various ways to make this calculation. Use examples if that will help illustrate the process.

## RESEARCH CASE 2

In the November 2001 issue of *The Journal of Accountancy*, the article "How to Implement *GASB Statement No. 34*," presented financial statements created according to *GASB Statement 34* for the City of Alexandria, Virginia. Obtain a copy of that article and do the following.

### Required:

a. Identify the component units included on these statements.
b. Determine whether these component units are discretely presented or blended?
c. Using a copy of *GASB Statement 34*, discuss the possible reasons that each of these component units was not judged to be part of the primary government.

## ANALYSIS CASE 1

Go to the website www.cityofsacramento.org/cafr/2000.htm. Find the 2000 financial statements for the City of Sacramento that were produced prior to adoption of *GASB Statement 34*. In the current chapter of the textbook, the 2001 financial statements for the same city are presented after implementation of *GASB Statement 34*. Compare the form and informational content of the 2000 statements to those prepared for 2001.

### Required:

Prepare the following two lists with adequate explanation.
a. Three aspects of the 2001 financial statements that seem to be superior to the 2000 financial statements.
b. Three aspects of the 2000 financial statements that seem to be superior to the 2001 financial statements.

## ANALYSIS CASE 2

Go to the website www.village.grafton.wi.us/CAFR/contents.htm and find the 2001 financial statements for the Village of Grafton, Wisconsin. They were produced using *GASB Statement 34*. One of the most important changes created by this statement was the requirement for inclusion of Management's Discussion and Analysis. Read this section of the report.

### Required:

Write a report indicating the types of information found in this government's MD&A that would not have been available previously from the financial statements.

## COMMUNICATION CASE 1

Read the following articles and any other papers that are available on the setting of governmental accounting standards:

"25 Years of State and Local Governmental Financial Reporting—An Accounting Standards Perspective," *The Government Accountants Journal,* Fall 1992.

"The Governmental Accounting Standards Board: Factors Influencing Its Operation and Initial Technical Agenda," *The Government Accountants Journal,* Spring 2000.

### Required:

Write a short paper discussing the changes in governmental accounting that have occurred in the past few decades.

## COMMUNICATION CASE 2

The City of Richardson is in the process of adopting the requirements of *GASB Statement 34.* The city manager is concerned about making certain that the conversion goes smoothly. Read "How to Implement *GASB Statement No. 34*" in the November 2001 issue of the *Journal of Accountancy.*

### Required:

Use that article as the basis to write a report to the city manager describing the procedures that will be necessary to implement this statement. Indicate which parts of this process will probably prove most difficult.

## EXCEL CASE 1

The City of Loveland has adopted *GASB Statement 34.* Now city officials are attempting to determine reported values for major infrastructure assets that were obtained prior to the implementation of the statement. The chief concern is determining a value for the city's hundreds of miles of roads that were built at various times over the past 20 years. Each road is assumed to last for 50 years (depreciation is 2 percent per year).

As of December 31, 2004, city engineers believe that one mile of new road would cost $2.3 million. For convenience, each road is assumed to have been acquired as of January 1 of the year in which it was put into operation. Officials have done some investigation and believe that the cost of a mile of road has increased by 8 percent each year over the past 20 years.

### Required:

Build a spreadsheet to determine what reported value should be shown now for each mile of road depending on the year it was put in operation. For example, what reported value should be disclosed in the government-wide financial statements for 10 miles of roads put into operation on January 1, 1997?

# Index

Note: Page numbers followed by n refer to footnotes.

## A

Abbott Laboratories, 344
Absences, compensated, in governmental accounting, 558–559
Accounting Principles Board (APB)
   *Accounting Interpretations, No. 1,* 20
   Opinions
      No. 16, 59, 60, 65, 66
      No. 18, 3, 4, 8, 9n, 11, 21–22
      No. 26, 264
      No. 30, 10, 176n
   *Accounting Research Bulletin (ARB) 51,* 3, 39–40, 41–42, 57, 171, 174, 204, 209, 210
   *Accounting Research Study*
      *No. 5 (ARS 5),* 65
Accrual accounting
   foreign currency transactions and, 319
   modified, 505, 520
Accumulated depreciation, financial statement translation and, 379–380
Advanced Semiconductor Engineering, Inc. (ASE), 174
Agency Funds, 511
   financial statements for, 586
AICPA. *See* American Institute of Certified Public Accountants (AICPA)
AirTouch Communications Inc., 37
Alliant Food Service, Inc., 92
American Express Co., 467
American Institute of Certified Public Accountants (AICPA), 503
America OnLine, 37
Amoco, 393
Amortizations
   consolidated statement of cash flows and, 278
   in equity method of accounting for investments, 14–17
Anthony, Robert N., 502n
APB. *See* Accounting Principles Board (APB)
*ARB (Accounting Research Bulletin) 51,* 3, 39–40, 41–42, 57, 171, 174, 204, 209, 210
ARCO, 287
Arnold, Jerry L., 383n
*ARS 5 (Accounting Research Study No. 5),* 65
Arthur Andersen LLP, 431, 468
Articles of partnership, 432–433
Art works, in governmental accounting, 559–560
Ascend Communications Inc., 37
ASE (Advanced Semiconductor Engineering, Inc.), 174
Assets
   capital, in governmental financial statements, 521–522
   depreciable, intercompany transfers of. *See* Depreciable assets, intercompany transactions involving
   fixed, financial statement translation and, 379–380
   infrastructure, in governmental accounting, 561–562
   intangible, consolidations subsequent to date of acquisition and, 91
   marshaling of, partnership termination and liquidation and, 474–480
   preliminary distribution of, partnership termination and liquidation and, 480–483
Atlantic Richfield Company, 37, 287
AT&T Broadband, 53
AT&T Corp., 37, 44, 53
Available-for-sale securities, 2, 7

## B

Balance sheet
   in government accounting, 574–576
   hedging balance sheet exposure and, 394–395
   translation of, current rate method for, 385, 387, 388
Balance sheet exposure, 375
BCS Corp., 37
Bean, David R., 503n
Beck, Leif C., 466n
Benston, G., 21n
Berton, Lee, 430n, 441n, 467n
Body Shop, 428
Bond issuance, 527–530
Bonuses
   to new partners, 446–447
   to original partners, admission of new partner and, 444
   withdrawal of partner and, 448
Bonus method, for intangible contributions to partnerships, 435–436
Book value
   of investment, establishing, 176–177
   investment cost exceeding, 13–17
Book value method, 121
Borrowing, foreign currency, 345–346
BP Amoco PLC, 37
Brady, Thomas, 67n
Brandzel, Jacob, 467
British Petroleum-Amoco, 39
Broadcast.com, 37
Buckeye Partners, L.P., 431
Budgets, in governmental accounting, 514–518

Business combinations, 36. *See also* Consolidated financial statements; Consolidations
Business decisions, equity method and, 20–21

## C

Call options, in foreign exchange market, 315, 316
Capital, withdrawal from partnerships, 436–437
Capital assets, in governmental financial statements, 521–522
Capital balance deficits, partnership termination and liquidation and, 471–474
Capital contributions to partnerships, 433–437
Capital leases, in governmental accounting, 554–556
Capital Projects Funds, 509
Cash flow exposures, 323
Cash flow hedges, 323–324
   foreign currency options designated as, 332–334, 342–344
   forward contracts designated as, 326–328, 341–342
Cash flows, consolidated statement of, 277–281
   acquisition year cash flow adjustments and, 278–279
   amortizations and, 278
   intercompany transactions and, 278
   noncontrolling interest and, 277–278
Catlett, George R., 4n
CCE (Coca-Cola Enterprises Inc.), 17, 19
C corporations, 430n
Celeron Corporation, 58, 59
Chesapeake Corporation, 120
Chevron, 39
Cirrus Logic, Inc., 312
Cisco Systems, Inc., 36
Coach, 175–176
Coca-Cola Company, 17, 19, 21, 344, 372
Coca-Cola Enterprises Inc. (CCE), 17, 19
Colleges, public, financial statements for, 586–589
Communication services fund, 511
Compaq, 279n
Compensated absences, in governmental accounting, 558–559
Component units, in governmental accounting, 567–568
Comprehensive income, 322
Computer Horizons Corporation, 117–118
Conglomerates, 38
Connell Limited Partnership, 428
Consolidated earnings per share, 282–284
Consolidated financial statements, 2–3

Consolidated statement of cash flows, 277–281
    acquisition year cash flow adjustments and, 278–279
    amortizations and, 278
    intercompany transactions and, 278
    noncontrolling interest and, 277–278
Consolidations, 36–68
    cost method for, 220–225
        for acquisitions made during current year, 103–106
        for consolidations subsequent to date of acquisition, 91, 92, 107–108
        with noncontrolling interest, 167
    equity method for, 220–225
    of foreign subsidiaries, 397–401
    intercompany transactions and. *See* Debt, intercompany transactions involving; Intercompany transactions
    involving noncontrolling interest, 150–158
        consolidated statement of cash flows and, 277–278
        economic unit concept and, 152–153, 171
        intercompany depreciable asset transactions and, 232
        intercompany inventory transactions and, 213, 217
        intercompany land transactions and, 228
        parent company concept and, 154–158, 168–169, 170
        preacquisition income and, 174–175
        proportionate consolidation concept and, 153–154
        sales of subsidiary stock and, 175–178
        step acquisitions and, 167–171
        subsequent to acquisition, 158–167
    partial equity method for, 220–225
    pooling of interest method for, 58–67
        continuity of ownership and, 58–59
        controversy over, 65–67
        with dissolution, 59–62
        when separate incorporation is maintained, 62–65
    process of, 39–43
    purchase method for, 43–57
        change in ownership and, 43–44
        in-process research and development and, 54–57
        intangibles and, 53–54
    segment reporting and. *See* Segment reporting
    single-line, 92
    statutory, 40
    subsequent to acquisition, 90–123
        contingent consideration and, 117–119
        cost method for, 92, 107–108
        effects created by passage of time and, 90–91
        equity method for, 91, 92–103
        goodwill and intangible assets and, 91
        goodwill impairment and, 114–117

Consolidations—*Cont.*
    subsequent to acquisition—*Cont.*
        intangibles and, 112–113
        investment accounting by acquiring company and, 91–92
        noncontrolling interest and, 158–167
        partial equity method for, 92, 108–111
        pooling of interests method for, 121–123
        purchase method for, 111
        push-down accounting and, 119–121
        subsidiary preferred stock and, 271–277
            as debt instrument, 271–274
            as equity interest, 275–277
    through corporate takeovers, 37–39
    valuation theory overview for, 158, 159
    of variable interest entities, 255–263
        FIN 46 disclosure requirements for, 263
        SPEs and, 256–261
Contingent consideration, consolidations subsequent to date of acquisition and, 117–119
Contributions, of capital to partnership, admission of new partner by, 444–447
Control, consolidations and, 41–42. *See also* Consolidations, involving noncontrolling interest
Copy services fund, 511
Corporate takeovers, 37–39
    reasons for, 37–38
Corwin, Leslie D., 430n
Cost method
    for acquisitions made during current year, 103–106
    for consolidations, 220–225
    for consolidations subsequent to date of acquisition, 91, 92, 107–108
    with noncontrolling interest, 167
Cost of goods sold, financial statement translation and, 379
C&S/Sovran Corporation, 41
Current exchange rate, financial statement translation and, 373
Current rate method, for financial statement translation, 376, 385, 387–389
    temporal method compared with, 392–394

### D

Daewoo Motors, 372
Davidson, Sidney, 66
Davis, Michael, 65n
Debt, intercompany transactions involving, 263–271
    acquisition of affiliate's debt from outside party and, 264
    assignment of retirement gain or loss and, 267–269
    effects on consolidation process, 266–267
    individual financial records and, 264–266, 267
    subsequent to year of acquisition, 269–271
Debt Service Funds, 509

Deferral, of unrealized gains, intercompany depreciable assets transactions and, 228–229
Deferral approach, to foreign currency transactions, 319
Dell Computer Corporation, 13, 344
Deloitte Touche Tohmatsu, 428
Depreciable assets, intercompany transactions involving, 228–232
    deferral of unrealized gains and, 228–229
    equity method for downstream transfers and, 231
    illustration of, 229–231
    noncontrolling interest valuation and, 232
Depreciation
    financial statement translation and, 379–380
    in governmental accounting, 561–562
Derivatives, 321–322
    fair value of
        changes in, 322
        determining, 321–322
        fundamental requirement of accounting for, 321
Digi International, 56
Digital, 279n
Direct quotes, in foreign exchange market, 314
Discounts, in foreign exchange market, 315
Dissolution
    by admission of new partner, 442–447
    of partnerships, 441–449
    pooling of interest method for consolidations and, 59–62
    by withdrawal of partner, 447–449
Doupnik, Timothy S., 383n
Downstream sales, of inventory, 18, 212–215
Downstream transfers
    alternative approaches for, 237–238
    equity method for, intercompany depreciable asset transactions and, 231
Dugan, Ianthe Jeanne, 467n
Duke University, 586
DuPont, 279n

### E

E. I du Pont de Nemours and Company, 279n
Earehart, Allen, 92
Earnings per share (EPS), consolidated, 282–284
Economic unit concept, consolidations involving noncontrolling interest and, 152–153, 171
Edison Electric Institute, 157
Encumbrances, 507, 518–520
Engineering revolving fund, 510
Enron Corporation, 208, 257, 258n
Enterprise Funds, 510
Enterprise Solutions Group, LLC, 117–118
Entity theory, consolidations involving noncontrolling interest and, 152–153, 171
EPS (earnings per share), consolidated, 282–284

Equity investments, sale of, 12
Equity method, 1–22
    for acquisitions made during current year, 92–94
    applying, 3–7
        criteria for using method and, 4–5
        reporting changes to method and, 8–12
        sale of investments and, 12
    for consolidations, 220–225
        depreciable intercompany asset transfers and, 231
    for consolidations subsequent to date of acquisition, 91, 92–103
    for corporate equity security investments, 103
    for downstream transfers, intercompany depreciable asset transactions and, 231
    elimination of unrealized gains in inventory and, 17–22
    excess of investment cost over book value acquired and, 13–17
    with noncontrolling interest, 167
European Union (EU), 313
Euros, 313, 345
Evans, Thomas G., 383n
Exchange rate mechanisms, 313
Exxon Corp., 37, 393
Exxon Mobil, 39

## F

Fair value, of derivatives
    changes in, 322
    determining, 321–322
Fair value exposures, 322–323
Fair value hedges, 323, 324
    foreign currency options designated as, 334–335
    forward contracts designated as, 328–331
    forward contracts used as, 336–340
Fair-value method, 2
FASB. *See* Financial Accounting Standards Board (FASB)
Fiduciary funds, 511
    financial statements for, 581, 586, 587
Financial accountability, governmental reporting and, 505–506
Financial Accounting Standards Board (FASB)
    Emerging Task Force *Issue 96-16* of, 5
    Exposure Drafts
        *Accounting for Financial Instruments with Characteristics of Liabilities, Equity, or Both,* 150n, 156, 287
        *Business Combinations and Intangible Assets,* 54
        *Consolidated Financial Statements: Policy and Procedures,* 211, 267
    *Interpretations*
        *No. 35,* 5
        *No. 46,* 3n, 36–37, 255–263, 256, 258, 262

Financial Accounting Standards Board (FASB)—*Cont.*
    *Statements*
        *No. 6,* 17n
        *No. 13,* 554
        *No. 52,* 317, 319, 320
        *No. 57,* 20
        *No. 94,* 40, 57
        *No. 115,* 2, 3
Financial statements. *See also specific statements*
    consolidation of, 2–3
    fund-based, 511, 512–513, 515, 516, 555–556
    government-wide, 511, 512, 513, 514, 554–555
Financial statement translation, 372–401
    balance sheet exposure and, 375
    consolidation of foreign subsidiaries and, 397–401
    current rate method for, 376, 385, 387–389
        temporal method compared with, 392–394
    disclosures related to, 395–397
    exchange rates used in, 373–375
    hedging balance sheet exposure and, 394–395
    illustration of, 384–385, 386
    retained earnings and, 378
    temporal method for, 376–377, 378, 389–392
        complicating aspects of, 379–380
        current rate method compared with, 392–394
        for income statement remeasurement, 390–392
        for nonlocal currency balances, 392
        for statement of cash flows remeasurement, 392, 393
    translation adjustments and, 375
        disposition of, 380–381
    U.S. rules for, 381–384
        for highly inflationary economies, 383–384
        *SFAS 52,* 381–384
Fioriti, Andrew, 67n
Fisher, Daniel, 428n
Fixed assets, financial statement translation and, 379–380
Fleet services fund, 510
Ford Motor Company, 37, 204, 206, 207, 271
Foreign currency financial statements, translation of. *See* Financial statement translation
Foreign currency options, 315–316
    hedging foreign currency denominated assets using, 331–336
        cash flow hedges and, 332–334, 342–344
        fair value hedges and, 334–335, 338–340
        spot rate exceeding strike price and, 335–336
Foreign currency swaps, 344

Foreign currency transactions, 316–320
    accounting alternatives for, 317–318
    accounting use for, 317
    balance sheet before date of payment and, 318–320
    borrowing, 345–346
    firm commitments and, hedges of, 336–340
    forecasted, hedges of, 340–344
Foreign exchange markets, 312–316
    exchange rate mechanisms and, 313
    exchange rates and, 313–315
    forward rates and, 315
    option contracts and, 315–316
    spot rates and, 315
Foreign exchange rates, 313–315
    exchange rate mechanisms and, 313
    financial statement translation and, 373–375
Foreign exchange risk, hedging, 320
Forward contracts, hedging foreign currency denominated assets using, 324–331
    cash flow hedges and, 326–328, 341–342
    fair value hedges and, 328–331, 336–338
Forward rates, in foreign exchange markets, 315
Freeman, Catherine M., 120n
Freeman, Robert J., 502n
Frito-Lay, 36
Functional currency, 382–383
Fund accounting. *See* Government accounting, fund accounting and
Fund-based financial statements, 511, 512–513, 515, 516, 555–556

## G

Gains
    retirement, assignment of, 267–269
    on sale of assets, financial statement translation and, 380
    translation adjustments and, 380
    unrealized. *See* Unrealized gains
GASB. *See* Governmental Accounting Standards Board (GASB)
General Electric Company (GE), 41, 90, 563
General Fund, 509
General Motors (GM), 57, 259, 372
General Motors Acceptance Corporation (GMAC), 57
Gerber Products Company, 284
Gillette Company, 395–396
GM (General Motors), 57, 259, 372
GMAC (General Motors Acceptance Corporation), 57
Goldman Sachs, 428
Goodwill, 47
    consolidations subsequent to date of acquisition and, 91
    impairment of, 114–117
    credited to new partner, 446–447
    credited to original partners, admission of new partner and, 445

Goodwill—*Cont.*
    impairment of, 114–117
    withdrawal of partner and, 448–449
Goodwill method, for intangible contributions to partnerships, 436
Goodyear Tire & Rubber Company, 58, 59
Government accounting, 502–535, 553–590
    capital leases and, 554–556
    compensated absences and, 558–559
    control of public funds and, 506–507
    financial accountability and, 505–506
    fund accounting and, 507–511, 514–534
        bond issuance and, 527–530
        budgets and recording of budgetary entries and, 514–518
        encumbrances and, 518–520
        interfund transactions and, 532–534
        recognition of expenditures and, 520–523
        recognition of revenues and, 523–527, 528
        special assessments and, 530–531
    fund-based financial statements and, 511, 512–513, 515, 516, 555–556
    general purpose external financial statements and, 569–589
        balance sheet, 574–576
        for fiduciary funds, 581, 586
        for public colleges and universities, 586–589
        statement of activities, 571–574
        statement of cash flows—proprietary funds, 580–581, 584–585
        statement of net assets, 569–570
        statement of net assets—proprietary funds, 576, 578–580
        statement of revenues, expenditures, and changes in fund balances, 576, 577
    government-wide financial statements and, 511, 512, 513, 514, 554–555
    infrastructure assets and depreciation and, 561–562
    management's discussion and analysis and, 563–565
    primary government and component units and, 565–568
    solid waste landfill and, 557–558
    user needs and, 504–505
    works of art and historical treasures and, 559–561
Governmental Accounting Standards Board (GASB), 503–504, 607
    *Concepts Statements, No. 1,* 515n
    *Concept Statement No. 1,* 504
    *Statements*
        *No. 11,* 515n
        *No. 14,* 571
        *No. 33,* 524, 525, 526, 527
        *No. 34,* 502–503, 505, 506, 507, 510, 513n, 514, 521, 522, 555–556, 560–562, 563–565, 569, 574, 580, 588
        *No. 35,* 588–589
Governmental funds, 508–510, 511

Government-wide financial statements, 511, 512, 513, 514, 554–555
Greene, Richard, 506n
Grupo Coral, S.A., 284
GTE Corporation, 157

## H

Halvorson, Newman T., 9n
Hanson, James, 428
Hanson's, 428
Harhan, Timothy M., 120n
Harlan, Christi, 433n
Hartgraves, A., 21n
Harvard University, 586
Hayes, Michael, 437n
Hedge accounting, 322–323
Hedging
    of balance sheet exposure, 394–395
    of foreign exchange risk, 320, 322–345
        cash flow hedges and, 323–324, 326–328, 332–334, 341–344
        documentation of hedge and, 323
        effectiveness of hedge and, 323
        fair value hedges and, 323, 324, 328–331, 334–335
        of forecasted foreign currency denominated transactions, 340–341
        foreign currency options for, 331–336
        forward contracts for, 324–331
        hedging instruments and, 344–345
        nature of risk and, 322–323
        of unrecognized foreign currency firm commitments, 336–340
Heins, John, 393n
Hertz Rental, 37
Hildebrandt, Bradford W., 467
Historical exchange rate, financial statement translation and, 373
Historical treasures, in governmental accounting, 559–560
H.J. Heinz Company, 372
Holder, William W., 383n
Horngren, Charles, 4n, 66
Houghton Mifflin Co., 372
Hybrid method
    for admission of new partner, 445–446
    for withdrawal of partner, 449

## I

IBM (International Business Machines Corporation), 157, 396
Income
    comprehensive, 322
    of partnerships, allocation of, 437–441
    preacquisition, consolidations involving noncontrolling interest and, 174–175
    from sources other than operations, equity method for, 10–11
    subsidiary, allocation of, 274, 276–277

Income statement, translation of, temporal method for, 390–392
Income taxes, for consolidations. *See* Consolidations, income tax accounting for
Incorporation, separate, pooling of interest method for consolidations and, 62–65
Indefinite life, 112
Independent float, 313
Indirect quotes, in foreign exchange market, 314–315
Inflation, financial statement translation and, 383–384
Influence, significant, 4
Information services fund, 510
Infrastructure assets, in governmental accounting, 561–562
In-process research and development (IPR&D), purchase method for consolidations and, 54–57
Insolvency, partnership termination and liquidation and, 471–480
Installments, partnership liquidation in, 482–483
Insurance revolving fund, 510
Intangibles
    consolidations subsequent to date of acquisition and, 91, 112–113
    contribution to partnerships, 435–436
    purchase method for consolidations and, 53–54
Intel Corporation, 115–116
Intercompany transactions, 204–233, 237–238
    depreciable asset, 228–232
        deferral of unrealized gains and, 228–229
        equity method for downstream transfers and, 231
        illustration of, 229–231
        noncontrolling interest valuation and, 232
    inventory, 205–221
        illustration of, 212–225
        noncontrolling interest valuation and, 209–211
        Sales and Purchases accounts and, 205–206
        summary of, 211–212
        unrealized gains and, 206–211
    land, 226–228
        noncontrolling interest valuation and, 228
        unrealized gains and, 226–228
Interest
    current, admission of new partner by purchase of, 442–444
    noncontrolling (minority). *See* Consolidations, involving noncontrolling interest
Interfund transactions, in governmental accounting, 532–534
Internal Service Funds, 510–511
*International Accounting Standard No. 27,* 156

International Business Machines Corporation (IBM), 157, 396
International Flavors and Fragrances, Inc., 372
International Paper Company, 4–5
Interperiod equity, 517
Intrinsic value, of foreign exchange options, 316
Inventory
 downstream sales of, 18
 elimination of unrealized gains in, 17–22
 intercompany transactions involving. See Intercompany transactions, inventory
 upstream sales of, 18–20
Investment account, of foreign subsidiaries, determination of balance in, equity method for, 399
Investment Trust Funds, 511
 financial statements for, 581
IPR&D (in-process research and development), purchase method for consolidations and, 54–57
Ives, Martin, 503n

## J

JB Hunt Transport Services, 1, 3
JDS Uniphase, 114
Johnson, L. Todd, 114n
Johnson & Johnson, 372

## K

Kagome Company, 372
Keck, Mahin and Cate, 467
Kelly, J. Michael, 157
Kochan, Nick, 427n, 428n
Kohlberg Kravis Roberts & Company, 271
Kretz, Richard, 437n

## L

Land, intercompany transactions involving, 226–228
 noncontrolling interest valuation and, 228
 unrealized gains and, 226–228
Lands' End, Inc., 38–39
Laventhol & Horwath, 466–467
Leases, capital, in governmental accounting, 554–556
Liabilities, long-term, payment of, in governmental accounting, 529
Lien date, 526
Life, indefinite, 112
Limited liability partnerships (LLPs), 431
Limited partnerships (LPs), 430–431
Liquidation, of partnerships. See Partnerships, termination and liquidation of
LLPs (limited liability partnerships), 431
Loans, foreign currency, 346
Local governments. See Government accounting

Lockheed Martin Corporation, 312
Long-term liabilities, payment of, in governmental accounting, 529
Losses
 equity method for, 11–12
 retirement, assignment of, 267–269
 on sale of assets, financial statement translation and, 380
 translation adjustments and, 380
Lowe, Herman J., 433n
Lower-of-cost-or-market rule, financial statement translation and, 379
LPs (limited partnerships), 430–431
Lublin, Joann S., 430n, 441n, 467n
Lucent Technologies Inc., 37
Lynch, P. J., 157

## M

McGraw-Hill Companies, 372
Management's Discussion and Analysis (MD&A), in governmental financial statements, 563–565
Marriott International, Inc., 167–168
Martin, Joseph J., 157
Mautz, Robert K., 504n, 522
MCI Worldcom Inc., 37
MD&A (Management's Discussion and Analysis), in governmental financial statements, 563–565
MediaOne Group Inc., 37
Merck & Co., Inc., 149, 150
Mergers. See also Consolidations
 statutory, 40
Mesloh, John J., 157
Microsoft Corporation, 3
Minority interest. See Consolidations, involving noncontrolling interest
Mobil Corp., 37, 393
Modified accrual accounting, 505, 520
MSNBC, 3
Munsingwear, Inc., 118

## N

National Broadcasting Company (NBC), 3, 41, 90
National Council on Governmental Accounting (NCGA), 503
NationsBank Corporation, 41
NBC (National Broadcasting Company), 3, 41, 90
NCGA (National Council on Governmental Accounting), 503
NCNB Corporation, 41
Negative translation adjustments, 375
Net asset/liability balance sheet exposure, 375
Newberry, Susan M., 502n
Noise Cancellation Technologies, Inc., 11–12
Noncontrolling interest, consolidated statement of cash flows and, 277–278
Nonexchange revenues, in governmental accounting, 525–527, 528

Nonlocal currency balances, financial statement translation and, 392
Not-for-profit organizations. See Private not-for-profit organizations

## O

Occidental, 393
Ohio State University, 586
One-transaction perspective, on foreign currency transactions, 317
Operating segments. See Segment reporting
Option contracts, in foreign exchange markets. See Foreign currency options
Option premiums, in foreign exchange market, 316
Other comprehensive income, 2
 translation adjustments and, 381
Owens, David K., 157
Owens-Illinois, Inc., 271
Ownership, continuity of, pooling of interest method for consolidations and, 58–59

## P

Pacelle, Mitchell, 431n, 467n
Pae, Peter, 467n
Parent company concept, consolidations involving noncontrolling interest and, 154–158, 168–169, 170
Partial equity method
 for acquisitions made during current year, 106–107
 for consolidations, 220–225
 for consolidations subsequent to date of acquisition, 92, 108–111
 with noncontrolling interest, 167
Partnerships, 427–450
 advantages and disadvantages of, 428–430
 alternative legal forms and, 430–431
 articles of partnership and, 432–433
 capital contributions to, 433–436
 dissolution of, 441–449
  by admission of new partner, 442–447
  by withdrawal of partner, 447–449
 income of, allocation of, 437–441
 limited, 430–431
 limited liability, 431
 termination and liquidation of, 466–486
  with deficit capital balance, 471–474
  illustration of procedures for, 468–470
  marshaling of assets and, 474–480
  predistribution plan for, 483–486
  preliminary distribution of partnership assets and, 480–483
  schedule of liquidation and, 470–471
 withdrawals from, 436–437
Pension Trust Funds, 511
 financial statements for, 581
PepsiCo, Inc., 3, 36
Pepsi-Cola Company, 36
Permanent Funds, 509–510
Petrone, Kimberly R., 114n

Pfizer, Inc., 37, 39, 157
Pfizer–Warner-Lambert, 58
Picker, Ida, 395n
Pittman, Jeffrey R., 480n, 481n
Police garage fund, 510
Pooling of interest method for consolidations, 58–67
    continuity of ownership and, 58–59
    controversy over, 65–67
    with dissolution, 59–62
    when separate incorporation is maintained, 62–65
Pooling of interests method for consolidations, subsequent to date of acquisition, 121–123
Positive translation adjustments, 375
Preacquisition income, consolidations involving noncontrolling interest and, 174–175
Predistribution plan, for partnership liquidation, 483–486
Preferred stock, of subsidiaries, 271–277
    as debt instrument, 271–274
    as equity interest, 275–277
Premiums
    in foreign exchange market, 315
    option, in foreign exchange market, 316
Prepaid items, in governmental financial statements, 522–523
PriceWaterhouseCoopers, 428
Private-Purpose Trust Funds, 511
    financial statements for, 581
Proportionate consolidation concept, consolidations involving noncontrolling interest and, 153–154
Proprietary funds, 510–511
    financial statements for, 576, 578–581, 582–585
Public colleges and universities, financial statements for, 586–589
Purchase method, for consolidations subsequent to date of acquisition, 111
Purchase method for consolidations, 43–57
    in-process research and development and, 54–57
    intangibles and, 53–54
Purchase price
    equal to fair market value, 45–46
    exceeding fair market value, 46–47
    less than fair market value, 47–49
Purchases account, Intercompany inventory transactions and, 205–206
Push-down accounting, consolidations subsequent to date of acquisition and, 119–121
Put options, in foreign exchange market, 315

## Q

Qwest Communications Inc., 37

## R

Rademacher, Richard G., 157

Reporting units, 46n
    assigning values to, goodwill impairment and, 115–117
Research and development, in-process, purchase method for consolidations and, 54–57
Retained earnings, translation of, 378
Retirement gain/loss, assignment of, 267–269
Revenues, recognition of, in governmental accounting, 523–527, 528
Reynolds Metals Corporation, 92
Ribstein, Larry, 468
Risk, hedged, 322–323
Ritz-Carlton Hotel Company LLC, 167–168
RJR Nabisco, 47
Roche, Robert P., 429n
Roddick, Anita, 428
Roddick, Gordon, 428
Ryst, Sonja, 589n

## S

Sacco, John, 502n
Sales
    downstream, of inventory, 18
    of equity investments, 12
    of subsidiary stock, consolidations involving noncontrolling interest and, 175–178
    upstream, of inventory, 18–20
Sales account, Intercompany inventory transactions and, 205–206
Sara Lee Corporation, 157, 175–176
SBC Communications, 5
Schedule of liquidation, 470, 471
Schools, M. R., Jr., 157
Scitex Corporation, 4–5
S corporations, 430
Sears, Roebuck & Company, 3, 38–39, 157
Securities and Exchange Commission (SEC), on push-down accounting, 120
Segment reporting, *SFAS 131* and, 115
Seidman, J. S., 66
SFACs. *See Statements of Financial Accounting Concepts (SFACs)*
Shellenbarger, Sue, 466n
Shoulders, Craig D., 502n
Significant influence, 4
Single-line consolidation, 92
Solid-waste landfill, 557–558
Special assessments, in governmental accounting, 530–531
Special purpose entities (SPEs), 256–261
    as variable interest entities, 256–261
Special Revenue Funds, 509
SPEs (special purpose entities), 256–261
    as variable interest entities, 256–261
Spot rates
    exceeding strike price, foreign currency options as hedges and, 335–336
    in foreign exchange markets, 315
Sprint Corp., 37
Stanford University, 586
State governments. *See* Government accounting

Statement of activities, in government accounting, 571–574
Statement of cash flows
    consolidated, 277–281
        acquisition year cash flow adjustments and, 278–279
        amortizations and, 278
        intercompany transactions and, 278
        noncontrolling interest and, 277–278
    translation of
        current rate method for, 388–389
        temporal method for, 392, 393
Statement of cash flows—proprietary funds, in government accounting, 580–581, 584–585
Statement of net assets, in government accounting, 569–570
Statement of net assets—proprietary funds, in government accounting, 576, 578–580
Statement of revenues
    expenditures, and changes in fund balances, in government accounting, 576, 577
    expenditures, and changes in fund net assets—proprietary funds, in government accounting, 580, 582–583
*Statements of Financial Accounting Concepts (SFACs)*
    *No. 1*, 381
    *No. 6*, 156
    *No. 8*, 381
    *No. 52*, 381–383, 394, 395
    *No. 95*, 278, 280
    *No. 105*, 377n
    *No. 128*, 282
    *No. 130*, 322n
    *No. 131*, 115
    *No. 133*, 321, 322, 323, 331, 336, 340, 344, 395
    *No. 138*, 322
    *No. 141*, 36, 37, 40, 48n, 49, 53, 57, 58, 59n, 112, 114, 261, 262
    *No. 142*, 3, 15, 36, 91, 114
Statutory consolidations, 40
Statutory mergers, 40
Step acquisitions, consolidations involving noncontrolling interest and, 167–171
Stock
    preferred, of subsidiaries, 271–277
        as debt instrument, 271–274
        as equity interest, 275–277
    subsidiary, 284–290
        changes in book value and, 284–287
        sale of, consolidations involving noncontrolling interest and, 175–178
Strike price, in foreign exchange market, 315
Subchapter C corporations, 430n
Subchapter S corporations, 430
Subsidiaries, 36. *See also* Consolidations
Subsidiary stock, 284–290
    changes in book value and, 284–287
    sale of, consolidations involving noncontrolling interest and, 175–178

## T

Supplies, in governmental financial statements, 522–523

Tax anticipation notes, 529–530
Taxes, income. *See* Consolidations, income tax accounting for
Tax revenues, derived, 525
TCI, 53
Temporal method, for financial statement translation. *See* Financial statement translation, temporal method for
Termination, of partnerships. *See* Partnerships, termination and liquidation of
Texaco, Inc., 39, 157, 393
Tibotec-Virco, 372
Time value, of foreign exchange options, 316
Time Warner, 37
Tomczak, Joe, 92
TPC (Transplace, Inc.), 1
Trading securities, 2
Translation. *See* Financial statement translation
Translation adjustments, disposition of, 380–381
Transplace, Inc. (TPC), 1
Trial balances, of foreign subsidiaries, translation of, 398
Tropicana Products, 36
Turner, Lynn, 56
Two-transaction perspective, in foreign currency transactions, 317

## U

Unisys, 47
U.S. Environmental Protection Agency, 557
Universities, public, financial statements for, 586–589
University of Iowa, 586–587
University of Kansas, 586
Unocal, 393
Unrealized gains
 deferral of, intercompany depreciable assets transactions and, 228–229
 intercompany inventory transactions and, 206–211
 intercompany land transactions and, 226–228
 in inventory, equity method for elimination of, 17–22
Upstream sales, of inventory, 18–20, 216–219
Upstream transfers, alternative approaches for, 237–238
US West, Inc., 37
Utah State University, 587

## V

Valuation theories, for consolidations involving noncontrolling interest, overview of, 158, 159
Variable interest entities (VIEs), 255–263
 *FIN 46* disclosure requirements for, 263
 SPEs as, 256–261
Variable interests, control exercised through, 42
Viacom Inc., 37
VIEs (variable interest entities), 255–263
 *FIN 46* disclosure requirements for, 263
 SPEs as, 256–261
Virginia Power, 157
Vivendi Universal SA, 372
Vodafone Group PLC, 37
Voting interests, control exercised through, 41–42

## W

Warner-Lambert, Inc., 37, 39
Watson, Harry, 428n
Weir, James, 393
White, Gordon, 428
Whitis, Robert E., 480n, 481n
Wishon, Keith, 429n
Withdrawal, of partner, 447–449
Works of art, in governmental accounting, 559–560
Wyatt, Arthur, 65

## Y

Yahoo! Inc., 37